PARTE PRIMERA

ESPAÑOL
INGLÉS

ABBREVIATIONS USED IN THIS DICTIONARY

adj.	adjective
adv.	adverb
Am.	Americanism
conj.	conjunction
contr.	contraction
def. art.	definite article
f.	feminine noun
m.	masculine noun
pl.	plural
p.p.	past participle
prep.	preposition
rel.	relative
rel. pron.	relative pronoun
v.	verb
v. irr.	irregular verb

PRONUNCIATION: The Spanish alphabet consists of twenty-eight letters: a, b, c, ch, d, e, f, g, h, i, j, l, ll, m, n, ñ, o, p, q, r, rr, s, t, u, v, x, y, z, (k and w are used only in words of foreign origin). Generally, they retain the same sound in every case, but there are some exceptions according to their place in the word or syllable. However, there are some general rules, fairly constant, which can be used as a reliable guide in the pronunciation of the Spanish language. Therefore, once these principles are mastered, there is no need to give the pronunciation of each word in this dictionary.

Vowels and diphthongs. The vowels are five in number and are pronounced as follows: *a* as in father (*casa* house, *vaca* cow), *e* as in met (*pelò* hair, *mesa* table), *i* as in police (*mina* mine, *pino* pine), *o* as in notary (*polo* pole, *cola* tail) and *u* as in moon (*nube* cloud, *uno* one).

Vowels may be divided into strong *(a, e, o)* or weak *(i, u)*, on the basis of their sonority. The combination of a strong and a weak vowel or two weak vowels forms a diphthong; but in Spanish do not exist proper diphthongs, as met with in English (oo, ou) or in French (eu, eau), and each vowel of the dipthong should be distinctly pronounced.

Nevertheless, there are slight changes in some vowels when they form a diphthong: *i*, when first member of a diphthong, it is a semiconsonant and is pronounced like the English *y* in yes (*bien* well, *viento* wind); when it is the second member of a diphthong, it is a semivowel and has the English equivalent of *y* in they. (At the end of a word, the *i* becomes *y*: *ley* law, *rey* king). When *u* is the first member of a diphthong, it is a semiconsonant and is pronounced like the English *w* in wet (*bueno* good, *escuela* school); when it is the second member of a diphthong, it is a semivowel and has the English equivalents of *w* in few (*viuda* widow) or like the *ou* in foul (*cauto* cautious). The Spanish dipththong *eu* has no equivalent in English, and in this case the *u* is pronounced distinclty, but shorter and closer than in English. In the syllables *que, qui, gue, gue, gui*, the vowel u is generally silent.

Consonants. They have the following sounds:

b is softer than in English; it is a fricative, not an explosive.

c has two sounds: before *a, o, u*, or before a consonant, it is similar to the English *k*; before *e, i*, it has the sound of *th* in think, but in Spanish America it is pronounced like the *s* in sound.

ch is like the English *ch* in choose.

d is softer than in English, and the sound resembles that of *th* in *though*. At the end of a word, it is almost inaudible.

f is similar to the English *f*.

g, before *a, o, u*, or before a consonant, or after *n*, has the sound of the English *g* in gas; before *e, i*, it is pronounced like the Spanish *j*. In the combinations *gue, gui*, the *u* is silent, being only a sign to indicate the *g* is not to be pronounced like the Spanich *j*, but like *g* in gas.

h is always silent.

j has no equivalent in English. It is the German *ch* in ach; noch; it is a strongly aspirated English *h*.

l is similar to the English *l* in leave.

ll sounds like the English *ll* in brilliant, but in current speach is pronounced as *y*.

m is pronounced as in English.

n sounds as in English.

ñ sound like *ny* in canyon.

p is similar to the English p.

q only occurs in the combinations *que, qui*, being an equivalent of the English *k*. As we have seen, in this case the *u* is silent.

r has two sounds: between two vowels has the sound of English *r* in caramel; when it begins a word or is preceded by *l, n* or *s*, it sounds like the Spanish *rr*.

rr has the same sound that *r*, with a strong trill.

s has the sound of English *ss* in essence.

t is more vigorous than the English *t*.

v is like the Spanish *b*.

x sounds like *ks* between vowels and like *gs* before a consonant. In current speech, it is sometimes pronounced like the *s* in sound.

y sounds as in the English word year.

z is similar to the Spanish *c* before *e* or *i*, but in Spanish America is pronounced as the *s* in sound.

Accentuation. Words ending in a vowel, or in *s* or *n*, stress the next to the last syllable (*padre* father, *dicen* they say, *nombres* names); words ending in a consonant other than *s* or *n* stress the last syllable (*papel* paper, *ciudad* city, *comer* to eat); words stressed in violation of the preceding rules must have the written accent on the stressed syllable (*café* coffee, *capitán* captain, *después* after, *árbol* tree, *lápiz* pencil, *último* last). An accent is also used to distinguish certain words that are written alike but have different meanings (*sí* yes, *si* if; *él* he, *el* the).

THE ARTICLE: The article indicates the gender of nouns. There are two genders: *masculine* and *feminine*.

The masculine definite article is *el* the (plural *los* the); the feminine definite article is *la* the (plural *las* the).

The indefinite article for masculine nouns is *un*; for feminine nouns, *una* (both mean a, an); the plural of this article, *unos, unas*, means several, any, a few, etc. Before feminine nouns beginning with *a* or *ha* and accented on the first syllable, the articles *el* and *un* are used instead of *la* or *una*, respectively. However, if the stress is laid on any other syllable than the first, *la* and *una* are used.

THE NOUN: Nouns are either masculine or feminine. Names of male beings, and those terminating in *e, y, o,* or *u,* as well as the names of the days of the week, months, rivers, oceans, and mountains are masculine (*hombre* man, *muchacho* boy, *rey* king, *lunes* Monday, *enero* January, *Tajo* Tagus, *Atlántico* Atlantic).

Names of female beings, and those terminating in *a, ión, tad, dad* and *umbre,* as well as the names of the letters of the alphabet are feminine (*mujer* woman, *muchacha* girl, *estación* station, *amistad* friendship, *ciudad* city, *muchedumbre* crowd).

Formation of the feminine. Nouns ending in *o,* change *o* into *a* (*hijo*, son, *hija* daugther); those ending in *án, ón,* or *or,* add *a* (*holgazán* lazy man, *holgazana* lazy woman; *patrón* patron) *patrona* patroness; *pastor* shepherd, *pastora* shepherdess). Some nouns express the difference of gender by a different word (*poeta* poet, *poetisa* poetess; *man* hombre, woman *mujer*).

Plural of nouns. Nouns ending in a unaccented vowel form the plural by adding *s* (*libro* book, *libros* books); nouns ending in an accented vowel or in a consonant (includding the letter *y*) form the plural by adding *es* (*rubí* ruby, *rubíes* rubies; *canción* song, *canciones* songs; *rey* king, *reyes* kings). Nouns ending in *es* or *is* do not change in the plural (*lunes* Monday, *lunes* Mondays). Nouns ending in *z* change the z to *c* before the plural ending es (*cruz* cross, *cruces* crosses).

THE ADJECTIVE. The Spanish adjective agrees with the noun it qualifies (*hombre bueno* good man, *mujer buena* good woman; *hombres buenos* good men, *mujeres buenas* good women).

Plural of adjectives. They follow the same rules as nouns.

Formation of the feminine. Adjectives ending in *o* change *o* to *a* (*bueno, buena* good); adjectives ending in other vowels are invariable (*verde* green); adjectives ending in consonant are invariable (*fácil* easy) except those ending in *ón, án, or,* which add an *a.*

Adjectives denoting nationality add *a* to form the feminine (*francés, francesa* French).

Some adjectives (*alguno* someone, *ninguno* no one, *bueno* good, *malo* bad, and *santo* saint, the numerals *uno* a, *primero* first, *tercero* third, *postrero* last, and *ciento* one hundred) undergo a slight variation when used before a masculine noun in the singular, and become *algún, ningún, buen, mal, san, un, primer, tercer, postrer,* and *cien.*

An adjective qualifying two nouns must be plural (*la hermana y la hija están felices* the sister and the daughter are happy); if the nouns are different of genders, the adjective is put in the plural masculine (*el hombre y la mujer están contentos* the man and the woman are satisfied).

Position of adjectives. Adjectives are divided into two classes, limiting and descriptive. Limiting adjectives are the articles, demonstratives, possessives, numerals, and indefinites. They regularly precede the noun they modify (*la casa* the house, *esta casa* this house, *mi casa* my house, *dos casas* two houses, *ninguna casa* no house).

Descriptive adjectives may either precede or follow the noun according to well-defined laws of usage. They precede when they denote an inherent or logical characteristic of the noun they modify (*la blanca nieve* the white snow); they follow when they denote a differentiating characteristic of the noun they modify (*la casa blanca* the white house).

Degrees of comparison. Adjectives form the comparative and superlative by means of the modifying adverb *más* (more). While the comparative and superlative are identical in form, their difference in meaning is made clear by the context of the sentence (*hermoso* beautiful, *más hermoso* more beautiful, *el más hermoso* the most beautiful, or *la más hermosa*, feminine). After superlative expressions, *de* is equivalent to in (*Pedro es el alumno más alto de la clase* Peter is the tallest student in the class). In Spanish there is also an absolute superlative which is formed by the addition of the syllable *ísimo* for the masculine and *ísima* for the feminine to the positive degree of the adjective (*santo* holy, *santísimo* very holy).

Some adjectives have an irregular comparison in addition to the regular one (*bueno* good, *mejor* better, *mejor* best; *malo* bad, *peor* worse, *peor* worst; *grande* large, *mayor* larger, *mayor* largest; *pequeño* small, *menor* smaller, *menor* smallest, etc.).

THE PRONOUN. In Spanish, there are six kinds of pronouns: personal, demonstrative, possessive, interrogative, relative and indefinite.

Personal pronouns. They are as follows:

Singular	Plural
yo I	*nosotros, nosotras* we
me me	*nos, nos* us
me me	*nosotros, nosotras* us
conmigo with me	*con nosotros, con nosotras* with us
tú thou	*vosotros, vosotras* you
te thee	*os, os* you
ti thee	*vosotros, vosotras* you
contigo with thee	*con vosotros, con vosotras* with [you

usted you
a usted, le, la, se you
a usted le, se; a él, sí you

con usted, consigo with you
él he, it
le, se; él, sí him, it
le, se; él, sí him, it
con él, consigo with him, with it
ella she, it
la, se; ella, sí her, it
le, se; ella, sí her, it
con ella, consigo, with her, with it

usted you
a usted, los, las, se you
a ustedes les, se, a ellos, ellas, sí [you
con ustedes o consigo with you
ellos they
los, se; ellos, sí them
les, se; ellos, sí them
con ellos, consigo with them
ellas they
las, se; ellas, sí them
les, se; ellas, sí them
con ellas, consigo with them

Mí, ti, si, are always preceded by prepositions.

me, te, se, le, las, la, las, les, are governed by verbs and never placed after prepositions.

Demostrative pronouns. The following words are pronouns when used instead of a noun:

ésto this, ésta this, esto this, éstos these, éstas these:

ése that, ésa that, eso that, ésos those, ésas those; aquél that, aquélla that, aquéllo that, aquéllos those, aquéllas those.

These same works, when followed by a noun, are demonstrative adjectives, but in this latter case they are used without the written accent.

Possessive pronouns. With the possessive pronouns, the first thing to decide is whether a stress is laid on them or not. It not, the short forms are used (adjectives):

Singular	Plural
mi, mis my	nuestro, nuestra, nuestros, nuestra [our
tu, tus thy	vuestro, vuestra, vuestros, vuestras [your
su, sus (de usted) your	su, sus (de ustedes) your
su, sus (de él) his	su, sus (de ellos) their
su, sus (de ella) her	su, sus (de ellas) their

If a stress is laid on the possessive pronoun, longer and more sonorous forms should be used, which always follow the noun. They are as follows:

XIII

Singular	Plural
mío, mía, míos, mías my	nuestro, nuestra, nuestros, nues-[tras our
tuyo, tuya, tuyos, tuyas thy	vuestro, vuestra, vuestros, vuestras [your
suyo, suya, suyos, suyas (de usted) [your	suyo, suya, suyos, suyas (de uste-[des your
suyo, suya, suyos, suyas (de él) his	suyo, suya, suyos, suyas (de ellos) [their
suyo, suya, suyos, suyas (de ella) [her	suyo, suya, suyos, suyas (de ellas) [their

Conjunctive and personal pronouns. These pronouns, called in Spanish *pronombres complementos,* are used as direct or indirect objects of the verb. They are called "conjunctive" because they are used in conjunction with the verb, and no other word can intervene. They generally precede the verb.

Accusative	Dative
me me	me to me
te thee	te to thee
le, lo you	le to you
le, lo him, it	le to him, to it
la her, it	le to her, to it
nos us	nos to us
os you	os to you
les, los you	les to you
los them	les to them
las them	les to them

Redundant personal pronouns. In view of the fact that the pronouns of the third person, *le, la, los, las, les,* have, respectively, more than one meaning, there is a possible ambiguity when the antecedent is not clearly established by the context. To avoid such ambiguity we use a redundant construction; for this purpose, we retain the ambigous construction intact, and add to it the prepositional form of the pronoun (*le digo* I tell him, I tell her, I tell you: *le digo a él*).

The same thing happens with the possessive adjective *su, sus* (*Juan lee su libro* John reads his book, John reads her book, John reads their book, John reads your book: *Juan lee su libro de ellos*).

Interrogative and relative pronouns. The interrogative pronouns differ only from the relative pronouns in as much as they have the written accent:

Interrogative pronouns	Relative pronouns
quién, quiénes who?	quien, quienes who
cuál, cuáles which?, what?	cual, cuales which, that
qué what?	que that
cúyo, cuya, cuyos, cúyas, whose?	cúyo, cuya, cuyos, cuyas, whose?

With the exception of *quién, quiénes*, the forms of the interrogative pronouns serve also as interrogative adjectives.

Indefinite pronouns. They are: *alguien* (somebody, anybody); *nadie* (nobody), *alguno, alguna, algunos, algunas* (somebody, some); *ninguno, ninguna, ningunos, ningunas* (nobody, none); *algo* (something); *nada* (nothing); *quienquiera, quienesquiera* (whoever).

The following indefinite adjectives may also be used as indefinite pronouns: *uno, una, unos, unas* (one, some); *cada* (each); *cada uno, cada una* (each one); *ambos, ambas* (both); *los demás, las demás* (the rest of); *cualquiera, cualesquiera* (whichever, whatever); *mucho, mucha, muchos, muchas* (much, many); *poco, poca, pocos, pocas* (little, few); *todo, toda, todos, todas* (all); *otro, otra, otros, otras* (another, other); *tanto, tanta, tantos, tantas* (so much, so many); *cuanto, cuanta, cuantos, cuantas* (as many, all that); *tal, tales* (such a, such); *mismo, misma, mismos, mismas* (self, selves).

THE ADVERB. Adverbs modify verbs, adjectives, or other adverbs. They are either proper adverbs, as *bien* well, or formed from adjectives or participles by the addition of the termination *mente* to the feminine singular of adjectives. (The suffix *mente* is simply the feminine noun *mente* mind, intelligence. The feminine gender of this noun accounts for the use of the feminine form of the adjective).

If the adjective ends in *o*, this *o* is changed into *a* before adding *mente (diestro* desterous, *diestramente* dexterously); if the adjective does not end in *o*, *mente* is simply added to the termination *(fácil* easy, *fácilmente* easily). When the adjective has a written accent, this accent is retained in the adverbial compound (*último* last, *últimamente* lastly, recently).

If several adverbs ending in *mente* follow each other, this termination is, for the sake of euphony, added to the last only *(hablo correcta y rápidamente* I speak correctly and rapidly, instead of *correctamente y rápidamente).*

Adverbs form their comparative like adjectives.

THE PREPOSITION. The Spanish prepositions govern no particular case. They are simply placed before the noun. The most frequent are: *a* (at, to, for) *ante, antes* (before) *con* (with) *contra* (against), *de* (of, from), *desde* (from), *en* (in, on, at), *entre* (between, among), *hacia* (towards), *hasta* (until), *para* (for, to), *por* (by, for, through), *según* (according), *sin* (without), *sobre* (on, upon), and *tras, detrás* (behind).

THE CONJUNCTION. Conjunctions are invariable; only *e* is used instead of *y* (and) when the following word begins by *i* or *hi;* *u* is employed instead of *o*, when the following word begins by *o* or *ho*).

THE VERB. By the termination of the infinitive mood we distinguish three different forms of conjugation: The first conjugation, with the infinitive mood ending in *ar* (*amar* to love); the second conjugation, with the infinitive mood ending in *er* (*temer* to fear); and the third conjugation, with the infinitive mood ending in *ir* (*batir* to split).

In the following table we give the endings in the simple tenses of all regular verbs. The numbers in the margin refer to the conjugation, those at the head of the columns, to the person.

INFINITIVE MOOD

Present: *ar, er, ir;* **Present participle:** *ando, iendo, iendo;* **Past participle:** *ado, ada, ido, ida.*

INDICATIVE MOOD

Present

Singular:

	1	2	3
1	o	as	a
2	o	es	e
3	o	es	e

Plural:

	1	2	3
1	amos	áis	an
2	emos	éis	en
3	imos	ís	en

Imperfect

Singular:

	1	2	3
1	aba	abas	aba
2	ía	ías	ía
3	ía	ías	ía

Plural:

	1	2	3
1	ábamos	abais	aban
2	íamos	íais	ían
3	íamos	íais	ían

Perfect

Singular:

	1	2	3
1	é	aste	ó
2	í	iste	ió
3	í	iste	ió

Future

Singular:

	1	2	3
1	aré	arás	ará
2	aré	erás	erá
3	iré	irás	irá

Plural:

	1	2	3
1	amos	asteis	aron
2	imos	isteis	ieron
3	imos	isteis	ieron

Plural:

	1	2	3
1	aremos	aréis	arán
2	eremos	eréis	erán
3	iremos	iréis	irán

IMPERATIVE MOOD

Singular:

	1	2	3
1		a	e
2		e	a
3		e	a

Plural:

	1	2	3
1	emos	ad	en
2	amos	ed	an
3	amos	id	an

SUBJUNTIVE MOOD

Present

Singular:

	1	2	3
1	e	es	e
2	a	as	a
3	a	as	a

Imperfect (First termination)

Singular:

	1	2	3
1	ara	aras	ara
2	iera	ieras	iera
3	iera	ieras	iera

Plural:

	1	2	3
1	emos	éis	en
2	amos	áis	an
3	amos	áis	an

Plural:

	1	2	3
1	áramos	arais	aran
2	iéramos	ierais	ieran
3	iéramos	ierais	ieran

Imperfect (Second Termination)

Singular:

	1	2	3
1	aría	arías	aría
2	ería	erías	ería
3	iría	irías	iría

Imperfect (Third Termination)

Singular:

	1	2	3
1	ase	ases	ase
2	iese	ieses	iese
3	iese	ieses	iese

Plural:

	1	2	3
1	aríamos	aríais	arían
2	eríamos	eríais	erían
3	iríamos	iríais	irían

Plural:

	1	2	3
1	ásemos	aseis	asen
2	iésemos	ieseis	iesen
3	iésemos	ieseis	iesen

Future:

Singular:

	1	2	3
1	are	ares	are
2	iere	ieres	iere
3	iere	ieres	iere

Plural:

	1	2	3
1	áremos	areis	aren
2	iéremos	iereis	ieren
3	iéremos	iereis	ieren

Compound tenses. These are formed by placing after the verb *haber* (to have), the past participle of the verb conjugated *(yo he amado* I have loved, *tú habías amado* you had loved, etc.).

Auxiliary verbs. We give the complete conjugation of verbs *haber* or *tener* (to have) and *ser* or *estar* (to be).

INFINITIVE MOOD

Present: *haber, tener — ser, estar*; Present participle: *habiendo, teniendo — siendo, estando*; Past participle: *habido, tenido — sido, estado*

INDICATIVE MOOD
Present:

he	tengo	soy	estoy	I have (am)
has	tienes	eres	estás	you have (are)
ha	tiene	es	está	he has (is)
hemos	tenemos	somos	estamos	we have (are)
hais	tenéis	sois	estáis	you have (are)
han	tienen	son	están	they have (are)

Imperfect:

había	tenía	era	estaba	I had (was)
habías	tenías	eras	estabas	you had (were)
había	tenía	era	estaba	he had (was)
habíamos	teníamos	éramos	estábamos	we had (were)
habíais	teníais	erais	estabais	you had (were)
habían	tenían	eran	estaban	they had (were)

Perfect:

hube	tuve	fui	estuve	I had (was)
hubiste	tuviste	fuiste	estuviste	you had (were)
hubo	tuvo	fue	estuvo	he had (was)
hubimos	tuvimos	fuimos	estuvimos	we had (were)
hubisteis	tuvisteis	fuisteis	estuvisteis	you had (were)
hubieron	tuvieron	fueron	estuvieron	they had (were)

Future:

habré	tendré	seré	estaré	I shall have (be)
habrás	tendrás	serás	estarás	you will have (be)
habrá	tendrá	será	estará	he will have (be)
habremos	tendremos	seremos	estaremos	we shall have (be)
habréis	tendréis	seréis	estaréis	you will have (be)
habrán	tendrán	serán	estarán	they will have (be)

IMPERATIVE MOOD

	ten	sé	está	have (be)
	tenga	sea	esté	let him have (be)
	tengamos	seamos	estemos	let us have (be)
	tened	sed	estad	have (be)
	tengan	sean	estén	let them have (be)

SUBJUNTIVE MOOD
Present:

haya	tenga	sea	esté	I may have (be)
hayas	tengas	seas	estés	you may have (be)
haya	tenga	sea	esté	he may have (be)
hayamos	tengamos	seamos	estemos	we may have (be)
hayáis	tengáis	seáis	estéis	you may have (be)
hayan	tengan	sean	estén	they may have (be)

Imperfect (First Termination)

hubiera	tuviera	fuera	estuviera	I would have (be)
hubieras	tuvieras	fueras	estuvieras	you would have (be)
hubiera	tuviera	fuera	estuviera	he would have (be)
hubiéramos	tuviéramos	fuéramos	estuviéramos	we would have (be)
hubierais	tuvierais	fuerais	estuvierais	you would have (be)
hubieran	tuvieran	fueran	estuvieran	they would have (be)

Imperfect (Third Termination)

hubiese	tuviese	fuese	estuviese	I should have (be)
hubieses	tuvieses	fueses	estuvieses	you should have (be)
hubiese	tuviese	fuese	estuviese	he should have (be)
hubiésemos	tuviésemos	fuésemos	estuviésemos	they should have (be)
hubiéseis	tuvieseis	fueseis	estuvieseis	you should have (be)
hubiesen	tuviesen	fuesen	estuviesen	they should have (be)

Future

hubiere	tuviere	fuere	estuviere	(if) I shall have (be)
hubieres	tuvieres	fueres	estuvieres	(if) you will have (be)
hubiere	tuviere	fuere	estuviere	(if) he will have (be)
hubiéremos	tuviéremos	fuéremos	estuviéremos	(if) we shall have (be)
hubiéreis	tuviéreis	fuéreis	estuviéreis	(if) you will have (be)
hubieren	tuvieren	fueren	estuvieren	(if) they will have (be)

Imperfect (Second Termination)

habría	tendría	sería	estaría	I would have (be)
habrías	tendrías	serías	estarías	you would have (be)
habría	tendría	sería	estaría	he would have (be)
habríamos	tendríamos	seríamos	estaríamos	we would have (be)
habríais	tendríais	seríais	estaríais	you would have (be)
habrían	tendrían	serían	estarían	they would have (be)

Irregular Verbs. Irregular verbs are such as suffer change either in their radical letters or in the terminations of the conjugations to which they belong, or in both. The total number of such verbs in the Spanish language is about eight hundred and eighty. To learn them, the student must master by heart six models or paradigms, which we can not give here.

A

a prep. to; in, into; according to; on, by.
abacería f. grocery; grocery store.
abacero m. grocer.
abad m. abbot.
abadía f. abbey.
abajarse v. to lower oneself, to humiliate oneself.
abajo adv. under, underneath; downstairs.
abalanzar v. to balance; to hurl, to wave; to rush with impetuosity, to rush (upon), swoop (upon); Am. to rear, balk.
abandonar v. to abandon, to forsake, to give up.
abandono m. neglect, desertion.
abanicar v. to fan.
abanico m. fan; a sprit-sail; **en —** fan-formed.
abaratar v. to cheapen, to abate, to lower the price of.
abarcar v. to embrace, to contain; **quien mucho abarca poco aprieta** grasp all, loose all; Am. to buy up.
abarrotero m. grocer.
abarrotes m. pl. small packages (in hold of a ship); Am. groceries; **tienda de —** Am. grocery store.
abastecer v. irr. to supply, to provide necessaries, to purvey.
abastecimiento m. supply, supplying, victualling, provisions.
abasto m. supply; **no dar — a** to be unable to cope with; adv. copiously.
abatido adj. dejected, mean, depressed, crestfallen, abject, lowered.
abatimiento m. lowness of spirit, depression, heaviness, faintness; **— del rumbo** the leeway of a ship.
abatir v. to throw down, to overthrow, to lower, to knock down; to depress, to humble; **—se** to become discouraged, to be disheartened.
abdicar v. to abdicate, to annul.
abdomen m. abdomen.
abecedario m. the alphabet, a spelling book.
abedul m. birch.
abeja f. bee.
abejera f. beehive, apiary; balmmint.
abejón m. drone, bumblebee.
abejorro m. bumblebee.
aberración f. aberration; mental or moral deviation.
abertura f. aperture, beginning, hole; fissure, gap, slit.
abeto m. fir; the silver tree.
abierto p.p. adj. open; frank, sincere; full blown; **a cielo —** in the open air.
abigarrado adj. motley, variegated, multicolored.
abismado p.p. absorbed; buried in thought; overwhelmed.
abismar v. to overwhelm; to depress; **—se** to be plunged (into); to bury oneself (in thought, grief, etc.).
abismo m. abyss; gulf; hell.
ablandar v. to soften, to mellow.
abnegación f. abnegation, self-denial.
abnegado adj. self-sacrificing.
abnegarse v. to deny oneself; sacrifice oneself.
abobado adj. stultified, stupid, silly.
abochornar v. to overheat, to provoke; **—se** to get overheated; to blush.
abofetear v. to slap, to insult.
abogado m. lawyer, advocate counsellor, barrister, attorney.
abogar v. to advocate, to plead the cause of another.
abolengo m. ancestry, lineage, inheritance, patrimony.
abolición f. abolition.
abolir v. to abolish, to annul.
abolsarse v. to bag (said of trousers, skirts, etc.).
abollado p.p. & adj. puckered, dented, bumped.
abolladura f. dent, bump, inequality.
abollar v. to dent; to crush; to stun and confound.
abominable adj. abominable, detestable.
abominar v. to abominate, to detest, to abhor.
abonado m. a suscriber; p.p. of abonar.
abonar v. to bail, to make a payment; to fertilize; **—se** to suscribe.
abonaré m. I.O.U., a promisory note.
abono m. payment; installment, warrant; dung, fertilizer.
abordar v. to board a ship, to run foul of a ship, to undertake, take up (a matter, a problem, etc.)
aborigen adj. aboriginal, indigenous, native.
aborrecer v. to hate, to abhor, to detest.

aborrecible adj. hateful, detestable, forbidding.
aborrecimiento m. abhorrence, detestation; grudge.
abortar v. to miscarry; to give birth prematurely.
aborto m. abortion, miscarriage; a monster.
abotagarse v. to be swollen, to bloat, to swell.
abotonador m. buttonhook.
abotonar v. to button, button up, to bud; —se to button up.
abovedar v. to vault, to arch; to cover with a vault.
abra f. cove, mountain gap or pass; a bay, a haven; Am. breach; leaf (of a door).
abrasador adj. burning; very hot; m. burner.
abrasar v. to burn; to parch, to fire; to dissipate; to be agitated by any violent passion; to glow.
abrazar v. to hug, to embrace, to caress; to surround; to comprise, to contain.
abrazo m. hug, embrace, accolade.
abrelatas m. can opener.
abrevadero m. drinking trough; a watering place for cattle.
abrevar v. to water cattle.
abreviación f. abbreviation.
abreviar v. to abbreviate, to shorten, to abridge, to cut short, to reduce.
abreviatura f. abbreviation; **en —** briefly.
abrigar v. to shelter, to cover, to protect, to patronize; to wrap up; to harbor (fear), cherish (hope); —se to find shelter, to wrap oneself up.
abrigo m. shelter, aid, cover, protection.
abril m. April; **estar hecho un —** to be gay, florid.
abrillantar v. to polish, to shine; to cut a diamond into angles.
abrir v. to open, to unlock, to begin; to remove obstacles; **— el ojo** to be alert; **— la mano** to accept bribes, to be generous.
abrochar v. to button.
abrogación f. repeal, abrogation.
abrogar v. to abrogate, repeal, annul.
abrumador adj. crushing, overwhelming, oppressive; m. a teaser.
abrumar v. to crush, overwhelm, to cause great pain or trouble; —se to become foggy.

abrupto adj. abrupt, steep.
abrutado adj. brutish.
absceso m. abscess.
absolución f. absolution, acquittal.
absoluto adj. absolute; unconditional.
absolver v. irr. to absolve, to acquit, to free from guilt; to pardon.
absorbente adj. & m. absorbent.
absorber v. to absorb, to imbibe.
absorción f. absorption.
absorto p.p. & adj. amazed, absorbed, engrossed.
abstenerse v. irr. to abstain, to refrain, to forbear.
abstinencia f. abstinence, fasting.
abstracción f. abstraction, reverie.
abstracto adj. abstract.
abstraer v. irr. to abstract, to pass over in silence; to withdraw; —se to be lost in thought; to withdraw the intelect from sensible objects.
abstraído adj. retired; lost in thought, absent-minded; aloof.
absuelto p.p. absolved, acquitted.
absurdo adj. absurd, ridiculous, senseless; m. absurdity.
abuela f. grandmother.
abuelo m. grandfather, ancestor; **—s** grandparents, ancestors.
abulia f. abulia.
abultado adj. bulky, increased.
abultar v. to bulge, to be bulky, to enlarge.
abundancia f. abundance, plenty.
abundante adj. abundant, plentiful.
abundar v. to abound, to be plentiful.
aburrido p.p. & adj. weary, tired, bored, tiresome.
aburrimiento m. weariness, dullness; uneasiness of mind, heaviness.
aburrir v. to vex; to be tedious, to weary.
abusar v. to abuse, mistreat; to misuse; **— de** to take unfair advantage of; to impose upon.
abuso m. misusage, abuse.
acá adv. here, over here, hither, this way, this side; **— y allá** here and there.
acabamiento m. finish, end, completion, death; Am. exhaustion, physical decline.
acabar v. to end, to finish, to complete; to make up, to achieve; to harass; to terminate, to die, to consume, to extinguish; **— de** (and inf.) to have just;

— **por** (and inf.) to end by; — **con** to put an end to; **—se to be over**; Am. to wear oneself out; **to age or decline in health**; **es cosa de nunca —** it is an endless affair.

academia f. academy; a special school; a scientific or literary society.

académico adj. academic; m. academician, academical; a member of an academy.

acaecer v. irr. to happen, to occur, to come to pass.

acaecimiento m. event, happening, incident.

acalorado adj. heated, excited, angry.

acaloramiento m. ardour, ardor, excitement, agitation.

acalorar v. to heat, warm, to inflame; to urge on, to grow warm.

acallar v. to silence, to quiet, to calm.

acampar v. to encamp, to camp.

acanalar v. to groove, to make a channel (for a); to flute.

acantilado adj. sheer, steep (cliff); m. shore with steep sides; bluff, cliff.

acantonar v. to quarter (troops), to canton.

acaparar v. to corner, to monopolize, to gather in (for one's gain or profit).

acariciar v. to caress, pet, cherish (a hope or illusion); to fondle.

acarrear v. to cart, to transport, to carry; to occasion, to cause, to bring about (harm, disaster).

acarreo m. cartage, carriage, transport, haul.

acaso adv. perhaps, chance; **por si —** just in case.

acatamiento m. homage, esteem, respect, veneration, obeissance, reverence.

acatar v. to revere, to respect, to obey; Am. to realize; to notice, pay attention.

acatarrar v. to chill, to catch cold; to bother, to annoy; **—se to get chilled**; Am. to get tipsy.

acaudillar v. to lead, command.

acceso m. access; entrance; admittance; communication; attack, fit (of anger, madness, etc.).

accesorio adj. y m. accessory.

accidentado adj. seized with a fit; in a swoon; rough; uneven (ground).

accidental adj. accidental, casual.

accidentarse v. to have a seizure or fit, to swoon, to faint.

accidente m. accident, mishap, chance; sudden fit; haphazard.

acción f. action, act; feat; battle; stock, share; **— de gracias** thanksgiving.

accionar v. to gesticulate, make gestures; Am. to act; to be active.

accionista m. & f. shareholder, stockholder.

acechanza f. snare; ambush.

acechar v. to lurk, to spy, to waylay, to lay in ambush.

acecho m. ambush; spying; **al (or en) —** waiting in ambush, lying in wait.

acedo adj. rancid, sour; harsh, disagreeable.

aceitar v. to oil, to grease, to rub with oil.

aceite m. oil; **— de comer** olive o sweet oil; **— de linaza** leenseed oil; **— de hígado de bacala** codliver oil; **— de ricino** castor oil.

aceitera f. oil jar; oil cruet (bottle for the table).

aceitoso adj. oily, greasy.

aceituna f. olive.

aceitunado adj. olive green, of an olive color.

aceleración f. acceleration.

acelerador m. accelerator.

acelerar v. to accelerate; to speed up, to quicken, to hurry, to hasten; to expedite.

acémila f. pack mule; a beast of burden.

acendrado adj. pure; without blemish; refined, purified.

acento m. accent, emphasis; **— gramatical** grammatical accent.

acentuar v. to accentuate, to emphasize; **—se to become worse** (as in an illness).

acepción f. acceptation, usual meaning.

acepillar v. to brush; to plane; to polish.

aceptación f. acceptance, approval; acceptance of a bill of exchange.

aceptar v. to accept, to approve. **— una letra** to accept a bill of exchange.

acequia f. canal, drain; irrigation canal or ditch; sewer; Am. small stream.

acera f. sidewalk.

acerado adj. steely, made of steel; steeled; steel-like; sharp.
acerar v. to steel; to impregnate with steel; to strengthen.
acerbo adj. bitter, cruel; rough to the taste.
acerca prep. about, relating to, concerning; — **de** in regard to.
acercamiento m. approach; approaching; rapprochement.
acercar v. to bring near, draw up, —**se** to get near.
acero m. steel; spirit, courage; — **colado** cast steel; — **moldeado** cast steel; — **niquelado** nickel steel.
acérrimo adj. very sour, very tart, very strong; stanch, stalwart.
acertar v. irr. to hit (the mark); to succeed; to conjecture right; to happen unexpectedly; — **a** (and inf.) to happen to.
acertijo m. riddle.
aciago adj. ill-fated, unlucky, unfortunate, fatal.
acicalado p.p. & adj. polished, dressed up; affected, made pretty.
acicalar v. to polish; to adorn; —**se** to dress up, doll up.
acicate m. spur, incentive.
acidez f. acidity, sourness.
ácido m. acid; adj. acid, sour.
acierto m. a good hit; a right guess, good aim, good judgment; **con —** effectively, successfully.
aclamación f. acclamation, applause.
aclamar v. to acclaim, cheer, hail, applaud; to cry up.
aclaración f. explanation, illustration.
aclarar v. to clarify, explain, to make bright; to rinse; to dawn.
aclimatar v. to acclimatize; to accustom to a climate.
acobardar v. to frighten, to intimidate.
acoger v. to receive; to give shelter; to admit one into one's house; —**se** to take refuge.
acogida f. reception; retirement, asylum; welcome, refuge.
acogimiento m. reception, welcome, shield, protection.
acojinar v. to cushion, to quilt.
acolchar v. to quilt.
acólito m. acolyte, altar boy.
acometer v. to attack; to undertake; to assault; to begin, to tempt.
acometida f. attack, assault.

acomodado adj. well-off, wealthy, suitable, fit.
acomodador m. usher (in a theater); box keeper.
acomodar v. to arrange, adjust; to fit, to suit, to lodge, to place; —**se** to make oneself comfortable; to adapt oneself.
acomodo m. occupation, employment, place, situation.
acompañador m. companion, accompanist.
acompañamiento m. accompaniment, attendance, company.
acompañante m. companion; scort, chaperon.
acompañar v. to accompany; to scort; to enclose (in a letter).
acompasado adj. rhythmical; measured; with uniformity; slow.
acondicionado adj. conditioned; comfortable; Am. adequate, suitable; **bien o mal —** of a good or bad disposition.
acondicionar v. to condtion, to prepare, to adapt; —**se** to become conditioned or prepared.
acongojar v. to grieve, to oppress, to afflict; —**se** to be distressed.
aconsejar v. to advise, to counsel, to take advise.
acontecer v. irr. to happen, to occur, to come about.
acontecimiento m. event, happening, incident, occurrence.
acopiar v. to gather, to accumulate, to store up.
acopio m. storing, gathering, accumulation, stock, store, supply.
acoplamiento m. coupling, joint, connection.
acoplar v. to couple, to connect, to adjust, to fit or joint together, to yoke, to pair, to mate.
acorazado m. armored ship, battleship.
acorazar v. to armor.
acordar v. irr. to agree; to decide; to tune; to resolve by common consent; to remind; to deliberate; to remember, to be in accord with, to ponder; Am. to grant.
acorde adj. in harmony, in tune; equal, correspondent; m. consonance, concord.
acordonar v. to tie with a cord, string or rope; to tie a rope around (a place); to mill (a coin).
acornear v. to gore, to wound

— 4 —

acorralar v. to corral, to surround, to shut up cattle; to intimidate.

acortamiento m. shortening, restraint.

acortar v. to shorten, diminish; —se to shrink, to lessen.

acosar v. to pursue, to harass; to pursue close.

acostado adj. reclining, lying down in bed; tilted, stretched.

acostar v. irr. to put in bed, to lay down; —se con to sleep with.

acostumbrado adj. accustomed, used, usual, habitual.

acostumbrar v. to accustom, to train, to be used to, to habituate; —se to get accustomed.

acotación f. marginal note; stage directions (for a play); bounds, limit.

acotar v. to mark off (with boundary marks); to make marginal notes or citations; to put elevation marks (on maps).

acre adj. sour, tart, sharp; rude, harsh; mordant, keen; m. acre.

acrecentamiento m. growth, increase.

acrecentar v. irr. to increase, to advance, to promote.

acreditar v. to credit; to bring fame or credit to; —se to win credit or fame.

acreedor adj. worthy; deserving; m. creditor, a meritorious person.

acribillar v. to riddle; to perforate, to pierce; to molest, to torment.

acróbata m. & f. acrobat; ropedancer.

acta f. minutes (of a meeting); document; record of proceedings; levantar el — to write minutes.

actitud f. attitude; posture, pose, position.

activar v. to activate, make active; to speed up, to hasten.

actividad f. activity, energy.

activo adj. active, lively, diligent, industrious; m. assets.

acto m. act, action, deed, ceremony; — continuo (or seguido) inmediately after; en el — at once, inmediately.

actor m. actor.

actriz f. actress.

actuación f. action; intervention, participation; performance; —es legal proceedings.

actual adj. present (time); of the present month, existing; —mente adv. at present, nowadays.

actualidad f. present time; actuality, reality; —es lastest news, fashions or events; de — up to date.

actuar v. to act, perform a function or act; to set in motion, cause to act.

actuario m. actuary.

acuarela f. aquarelle, water color.

acuario m. aquarium.

acuartelar v. to quarter (troops).

acuático adj. aquatic; deportes —s water sports.

acuchillar v. to knife; to stab; to slash; to give cuts with a sabre; to kill with a knife; to fight with swords.

acudir v. to go or come (in' response to a call); to attend, to be present; to resort or turn to for help; to assist, to support, to run to.

acueducto m. aqueduct, water channel or pipe.

acuerdo m. agreement; decision, resolution; opinion; remembrance; act, mandate or order; result of a deliberation; body of the members of a tribunal; estar de — to be in agreement; ponerse de — to come to an agreement; tomar un — to take a decision.

acumulación f. accumulation, gathering.

acumulador m. storage battery; accumulator.

acumular v. to accumulate, gather, pile up; to heap together, to treasure up, to hoard.

acuñación f. coinage, minting; milling, wedging.

acuñar v. to mint, to coin, to wedge; to make moneys; to hoard up money.

acuoso adj. watery.

acurrucarse v. to cuddle, to nestle, to huddle; to muffle oneself up.

acusación f. accusation, charge.

acusado p.p. & adj. accused; m. defendant.

acusar v. to accuse, denounce, to criminate; to indict; to acknowledge sins to a confessor; to acknowledge (receipt).

acústica f. acoustics.

achacar v. to impute, attribute; to charge.

achacoso adj. sickly, unhealthy.

achaparrado adj. scrub; of shrub size.

achaque m. slight chronic illness; excuse; pretext; infirmity.

achicar v. to shorten; to make small; to bail (water); to humiliate; Am. to kill, to tie, to fasten; —se to get smaller, to shrink.

adagio m. adage, proverb, wise saying; adagio.

adaptar v. to adapt, to fit, to adjust, to apply, to fashion.

adecuado adj. adequate, fit, suitable, competent.

adecuar v. to fit, adapt; to accommodate, adjust.

adefesio m. absurdity, nonsense; ridiculous sight, dress or person; extravagance, folly.

adelantado p.p. & adj. anticipated, advanced; ahead; premature; forehand, precocius, early; por — in advance.

adelantamiento m. advancement, progress, betterment, increase, furtherance, anticipation.

adelantar v. to advance, to move forward, to progress, to better; to accelerate, to pay beforehand; —se to get ahead.

adelante adv. forward, ahead; farther off; higher up; en — from now on.

adelanto m. advance, advancement, progress, betterment.

adelgazar v. to thin out, taper; to attenuate, to lessen; —se to get thin, slender.

ademán m. gesture, gesticulation, attitude; look, manner, movement.

además adv. moreover, besides, further; — de esto or eso in addition to this or that.

adentro adv. within, inside, internally, inwardly; ser muy de — to be intimate in a house; tierra — inland; mar — out to sea; hablar para sus —s to talk to oneself.

aderezamiento m. dressing; adornment, decoration.

aderezar v. to fix up, adorn, beautify; to garnish (food); to prepare; to starch, stiffen.

aderezo m. adornment, garnish, trappings, finery; set of jewels; dressing, seasoning; starch, stiffener.

adeudado adj. indebted; in debt.

adeudar v. to owe; to debit, to charge; to pay duty; to contract debts; —se to run into debt.

adeudo m. debt, indebtedness, duty (on imports), debit, charge

adherencia f. adherence, attachment; adhesion, alliance.

adherir v. irr. to adhere, stick; to be allied to.

adhesión f. adhesion; attachment.

adicto adj. addicted, devoted, m addict, follower; constant, affectionate.

adinerado adj. wealthy, rich.

¡adiós! interj. good bye!; farewell!

aditamento m. addition, annex.

adivinación f. divination, prediction; guess.

adivinanza f. conundrum, riddle.

adivinar v. to guess, to divine, to foretell, to predict, to conjecture.

adivino m. fortuneteller, soothsayer.

adjetivo m. & adj. adjective.

adjudicar v. to adjudge, award, asign; —se to appropriate.

adjunto adj. adjoining, attached, enclosed, joined, annexed.

adminículo m. accesory; gadget, adminicle.

administración f. administration, management; headquarters; Am. extreme unction.

administrador m. administrator, manager.

administrar v. to administer, to manage; —se Am. to receive the extreme unction or last sacrament.

administrativo adj. administrative.

admirable adj. admirable, wonderful; marvelous, astonishing.

admiración f. admiration, wonder; punto de — exclamation point.

admirador m. admirer.

admirar v. to admire, to marvel; to wonder; —se to be seized with admiration.

admisión f. admission; acceptance.

admitir v. to admit; to let in; to accept; to allow, to permit, to concede; — la oferta to accept the offering.

adobar v. to fix, to cook, to prepare (food); to tan (hides); to pickle (meats, fish); to dress or make anything up.

adobe m. adobe, sun-dried mud brick.

adobo m. mending; sauce for seasoning or pickling; mixture

— 6 —

for dressing skins or cloth; rouge; cosmetics.
adoctrinar v. to indoctrinate, teach, instruct.
adolecer v. irr. to suffer (from an illness, deffect, etc.); to labour under disease.
adolescencia f. adolescence.
adolescente adj. adolescent.
adonde rel. adv. where; ¿adónde? int. adv. where to?; where?, whither?
adoptar v. to adopt; to accept (an opinion); to father.
adoptivo adj. adoptive, related by adoption; adopted.
adoración f. adoration, worship.
adorar v. to adore, to worship.
adormecer v. irr. to make sleepy or drowsy; to lull; to calm; —se to get sleepy; to get numb; to fall asleep; to grow torpid.
adormilado adj. drowsy.
adornar v. to adorn, to decorate, to beautify, to embellish.
adorno m. adornment, ornament, garniture.
adquirir v. irr. to acquire, to gain, to win, to obtain, to get.
adquisición f. acquisition, attainment.
adrede adv. on purpose, intentionally; knowingly.
aduana f. customhouse.
aduanero m. customhouse officer; adj. customhouse.
aducir v. irr. to cite, to allege, to offer as proof, to exhibit.
adueñarse v. to take possession.
adulación f. flattery, fawning.
adulador m. flatterer.
adular v. to flatter, to soothe; to fawn.
adulterar v. to adulterate, to corrupt, to make impure; to commit adultery.
adulterio m. adultery.
adúltero m. adulterer.
adulto m. y adj. adult.
adusto adj. stern, severe, austere.
advenedizo m. newcomer, stranger; upstart; foreign.
advenimiento m. advent, arrival, coming.
adverbio m. adverb.
adversario m. adversary, opponent, foe, antagonist.
adversidad f. adversity, calamity, misfortune.
adverso adj. adverse, contrary, unfavorable, calamitous.

advertencia f. notice, warning; advice, admonition.
advertir v. irr. to notice, to warn, to advise, to observe, to mark, to note.
adyacente adj. adjacent, contiguous.
aéreo adj. aerial, airy; correo — air mail.
aeródromo m. airport, aerodrome.
aeronave f. airship, air-balloon.
aeroplano m. airplane.
aeropuerto m. airport.
afabilidad f. friendliness, pleasantness, courtesy.
afable adj. affable, pleasant, courteous.
afamado adj. famous, famed, celebrated, noted.
afán m. eagerness, anxiety, ardor, solicitude, agitation.
afanar v. to urge, to press, to toil, to labor; —se to hurry, to worry, to work eagerly.
afear v. to make ugly; to disfigure; to blame, to censure, to condemn; to deface.
afección f. affection, fondness; inclination; disease.
afectado p.p. & adj. affected; Am. hurt, harmed; estar — del corazón to have heart trouble.
afectar v. to affect, to move, to act upon; Am. to injure, hurt, harm.
afecto m. affection; adj. fond; — a fond of, given to, prone to.
afectuoso adj. affectionate, tender, kind, gracious, loving.
afeitada f. Am. shave, shaving.
afeitar v. to shave; —se to shave oneself; to use paints or rouge.
afeite m. make-up cosmetics, paint, rouge.
afeminado adj. effeminate.
aferrado adj. stubborn, obstinate, headstrong, tenacious.
aferrar v. to seize, to grasp, to grapple, to fasten; —se to take or seize hold of; to cling.
afianzar v. to fasten, to secure, to guarantee; to give bail or bond.
afición f. taste, inclination, fondness, affection; — ciega razón love is blind.
aficionado adj. fond; amateur, fan.
aficionar v. to inspire a liking or fondness; to affect; —se a to become fond of.
afilador m. grinder, sharpener.
afilar v. to sharpen, to grind, to

whet; Am. to make love to, to woo, to flatter; — con to flirt with.

afín adj. kindred, related; **ideas —es** related ideas.

afinador m. finisher, tuning key, piano tuner.

afinar v. to refine, to polish, to tune; — **los metales** to refine metals; — **la voz** to tune the voice.

afinidad f. affinity; similarity, relationship; analogy; attraction.

afirmación f. affirmation, assertion, affirming.

afirmar v. to affirm, to assert; to assure for certain; to secure, to clinch; — **un golpe** Am. to deal a blow.

afirmativo adj. affirmative.

aflicción f. affliction, trouble, pain, grief, mournfulness, heaviness.

afligir v. to afflict, to trouble, to grief, to torment, to morfify; to lament; to languish; Am. to mistreat, harm, beat, strike; —se to worry, to grieve.

aflojar v. to slacken; to loosen, to unfasten, to relax, to relent; Am. to let go of money, to spend easily; — **un golpe** Am. to give a blow.

afluente m. tributary, afluent; adj. abundant.

afluir v. irr. to flow (into).

afortunado adj. fortunate, lucky.

afrenta f. affront, offense, insult, dishonour, reproach; outrage.

afrentar v. to insult, to offend, to dishonor, to affront, to reproach, to outrage; —se to be ashamed of.

afrentoso adj. outrageous, shameful, disgraceful, ignominious.

africano adj. & m. African.

afrontar v. to face, to confront.

afuera adv. out, outside, abroad, outward, outskirts, in public; besides; moreover.

agachar v. to lower, to bend down; —se to stoop, bend down, to squat, to crouch; Am. to give in, yield; —se con algo Am. to make away with or steal something; — **las orejas** to be humble.

agalla f. gill; tonsil; gallnut; —s glands in the throat; windgalls of a horse; beaks of a shuttle; **tener** —s to have guts, have courage; Am. to be unscrupulous and bold in business deals; to be greedy or stingy; to be smart, astute.

agarrar v. to seize, to grasp, to grab; to obtain, to come upon, to clinch, to grapple; —se to cling, hold on.

agarrón m. tight clench, sudden grasp, grab; Am. tug, pull.

agasajar v. to entertain; to receive and treat kindly; to flatter, to regale.

agasajo m. entertainment; kind reception, graceful and affectionate reception; friendliness; deference, benevolence, flattery.

agazapar v. to nab, to seize (a person); —se to crouch, to squat, to hide oneself.

agencia f. agency, ministration, commission, branch; Am. pawnshop.

agenciar v. to negotiate, to procure by negotiation; to promote; to solicit.

agente m. agent, minister, solicitor, attorney; Am. officer, official.

ágil adj. agile, nimble, limber, fast, light.

agilidad f. agility, nimbleness, activity, lightness.

agitación f. agitation, excitement, flutter; stirring; fluctuation, fidget.

agitar v. to agitate, to excite; to stir, to wave; to shake, to ruffle, to fret.

aglomeración f. conglomeration, heap, pile, mass, aglomeration.

aglomerar v. to mass together, to cluster, to aglomerate, to briquet; —se to crowd together, to pile up.

agobiar v. to oppress, to weighdown; to overwhelm; to bend the body down.

agolparse v. to crowd together.

agonía f. agony, affliction, suffering.

agonizante adj. dying; m. dying person.

agonizar v. to be dying, to be in the agony of death.

agorero adj. ominous, of bad omen, prophetic; m. augur, prophet, diviner, fortuneteller.

agostar v. to parch, to dry up, to pasture; to pasture cattle on stubbles in summers; to plow (in August).

agosto m. August; harvest time;

hacer su — to make the best of circumstances, to make hay while the sun shines.

agotado adj. & p.p. exhausted; out-of-print.

agotamiento m. exhaustion, draining.

agotar v. to exhaust, to use up; to drain off; to beat out one's brains; **—se** to be exhausted, used up.

agraciado adj. graceful; m. winner (of a favor, prize, etc.).

agraciar v. to grace, to adorn, to grant a favor, to grant pardons.

agradable adj. agreeable, pleasant; merry, glad; lovely, gracious.

agradar v. to please, to be agreeable (to), to gratify, to like, to be pleased.

agradecer v. irr. to thank for, to be grateful for, to ackowledge a favor, to reward.

agradecido adj. thankful, grateful, acknowledged.

agradecimiento m. gratitude, gratefulness, thankfulness.

agrado m. agreableness; liking, pleasure, comfortableness, affability; **de su —** to his liking.

agrandar v. to enlarge; to aggrandize, to make greater, to increase, to augment.

agravar v. to aggravate, to make worse, to make heavier; to oppress, to aggrieve; to render more intolerable; to oppress with taxes; **—se** to get worse.

agraviar v. to offend, to insult, to affront, to grieve; **—se** to be aggrieved.

agravio m. offense, insult, affront, harm, grievance, injury.

agredir v. to assail, to assault, to attack.

agregado m. attaché; person attached to a staff; aggregate; congregation, collection; an assistant.

agregar v. to add, to join, to attach; to aggregate, to collect.

agresivo adj. aggresive, offensive.

agresor m. aggressor, assailant.

agreste adj. rustic, wild, savage.

agriar v. to sour, to make sour or tart; to make peevish, to irritate; **—se** to sour, turn sour, become sour.

agrícola adj. agricultural.

agricultor m. agriculturist, farmer.

agricultura f. agriculture.

agrietarse v. to crack; to chap (the skin).

agrimensura f. survey, surveying; act of surveying land.

agrio adj. sour, acrid, rough, sharp, rude, unpleasant; **una respuesta agria** a smart reply.

agrupación f. group, bunch; grouping, gathering.

agrupar v. to group, to bunch up, to cluster, to crowd.

agrura f. acidity, acerbity, sourness.

agua f. water, rain; lustre of diamonds; **— de azahar** orange flower water; **— de olor** scented water; **— llovediza** rain water; **— fuerte** aqua fortis; **— regia** aqua regia; **— bendita** holy water; **— viva** running water; **—s muertas** neaptides; **— vivas** spring tides; **entre dos —s** between wind and water, in doubt; **— abajo** under stream; **— arriba** against the stream.

aguacate m. Am. avocado, alligator pear; avocado tree; phlegmatic person.

aguacero m. shower, heavy rain.

aguada f. watering place, supply of drinking water; flood in a mine; wall wash; water on board a ship; **hacer —** to water.

aguado adj. watered, watery, abstemious; Am. soft, unstarched, weak, limp, insipid, uninteresting, dull; **sopa aguada** thin soup.

aguantar v. to endure, to suffer, to maintain; **—se** to be silent, restrain oneself.

aguante m. endurance, fortitude, firmness, resistance, patience.

aguar v. to water, to dilute with water, to mix water with wine or other liquors; to disturb pleasure; **—se** to become diluted, to get watery; **se aguó la fiesta** the party was spoiled.

aguardar v. to wait, to wait for, to expect.

aguardentoso adj. alcoholic, spirituous; hoarse, raucous.

aguardiente m. brandy, hard liquor; **— de caña** rum; **— de cabeza** the first brandy distilled.

aguarrás m. turpentine, oil of turpentine, spirit of turpentine.

agudeza f. sharpness, keenness, wit, repartee, smartness; witty remark or saying.

agudo adj. sharp, keen-edged, sharp-pointed, smart.

agüero m. augury, prognostication, omen, prediction; Am. fortuneteller.

aguijar v. to prick, spur, goad; to incite; to stimulate.

aguijón m. prick, sting, spur; sting of a bee or wasp.

aguijonear v. to goad, to thrust, to stimulate.

águila f. eagle; **es un —** he is a shark.

aguileño adj. aquiline, eaglelike.

aguinaldo m. Christmas or New Year's gift; Christmas box.

aguja f. needle; crochet hook; watch hand; church spire; railroad switch; bodkin; **— de marear** a mariner's compass.

agujerear v. to pierce, to perforate, to bore, to make holes; to riddle.

agujero m. hole, needle, peddler, needle maker, pincushion.

aguzar v. to sharpen, to goad, to stimulate, to excite; **— el ingenio** to sharpen the wit; **— las orejas** to prick up the ears.

ahí adv. there, in that place, in that yonder; **— está la dificultad** there is the trouble; **por —** over there.

ahijado m. godchild; a client.

ahínco m. effort, eagerness, zeal; earnestness; ardor.

ahogar v. to drown, to choke, to strangle, to smother, to throttle, to extinguish; to hang.

ahogo m. suffocation, oppression, grief, anguish, breathlessness, pain, severe affliction.

ahondar v. to deepen; to dig, to penetrate, to sink, to hollow out; to advance in the knowledge of things.

ahora adv. now, at present, just now; **— mismo** this moment, right now; **por —** for the present; **— bien** well; **hasta —** hitherto; **— que** Am. as soon as; **ahorita** instantly, this very minute; **ahoritita** Am. this very second, in a jiffy.

ahorcar v. to hang, to kill by hanging.

ahorrar v. to save, to spare, to enfranchise, to avoid, to economize.

ahorro m. saving, economy; parsimony, **husbandry; caja de —s savings bank.**

ahuecar v. to make hollow, to excavate, to scoop out; **— la voz** to speak in a hollow voice; **¡ahueca!** Am. get out of here!

ahumado adj. smoked, smoky.

ahumar v. to smoke, to fume; to cure in smoke.

ahuyentar v. to drive away, to scare away, to put to flight; Am. to stop frequenting a place.

airar v. to annoy, irritate; **—se** to get angry.

aire m. air; wind; tune, appearance, gracefulness, aspect, countenance; **—s naturales** the native air; **—cito** m. breeze; a little tune.

airear v. to air, ventilate.

airoso adj. windy, airy, graceful; successful; lively, spirited.

aislador m. insulator, isolator; adj. insulating, isolating.

aislamiento m. isolation, insulation.

aislar v. to isloate; place apart; to insulate.

ajar v. to crumple, wither; to spoil, to offend; m. a garlic field.

ajedrez m. chess.

ajeno adj. alien, another's; unaware; foreign, strange; **— a mi voluntad** beyond my control; **— de cuidados** free from cares.

ajetrearse v. to hustle and bustle.

ajetreo m. bustle, hustle, fatigue.

ají m. Am. chili pepper, chili sauce.

ajo m. garlic, garlic clove, garlic sauce; swear word.

ajuar m. furniture set; trousseau, brides outfit; apparel.

ajustado adj. tight, fitting tight, exact, right; agreed upon (as a price); **— a la ley** in accordance with the law.

ajustamiento m. agreement, adjustment.

ajustar v. to adjust; to fit tight, to regulate, to accord, to measure, to concert, to reconcile, to examine accounts, to settle a balance, to press close; to hire (a person); Am. to stint, to scrimp, to save; **— una bofetada** Am. to give a good slap; **hoy ajusta quince años** Am. he is just fifteen years old today.

ajuste m. adjustment, fit, agreement, contract, accommodation, settlement, engagement.

ajusticiar v. to execute, to put to death.
al contraction of a and el: to the.
ala f. wing, aisle, row or file, fort flank, brim of the hat.
alabanza f. praise, commendation, glory.
alabar v. to praise, to exalt, to glorify.
alacena f. cupboard, closet. Am. booth, stall, market stand.
alacrán m. scorpion; stop or hook.
alado adj. winged, feathered.
alambicado p.p. & adj. distilled, over-refined, over-subtle (applied to style).
alambique m. still.
alambrada m. wire fence, entanglement.
alambrado m. wire screening, wiring.
alambre m. wire.
alameda f. poplar grove, park.
álamo m. poplar.
alano m. mastiff.
alarde m. boast, bluff, brag, vanity, ostentation.
alardear v. to boast, to brag.
alargar v. to lengthen; to prolong; to stretch out, to extend; to increase.
alarido m. shout, scream, howl, outcry.
alarma f. alarm.
alarmar v. to alarm.
alazán adj. chestnut-colored; sorrel-colored.
alba f. dawn; alb (white robe worn by priests).
albacea m. executor; testamentary executor.
albañal m. sewer.
albañil m. mason, brickmason.
albañilería f. masonry.
albaricoque m. apricot.
albaricoquero m. apricot tree.
albayalde m. white lead.
albazo m. Am. early morning serenade; bad surprise; surprise attack at dawn.
albear v. to show white, to whiten; Am. to rise at dawn.
albedrío m. free will, freedom of will.
alberca f. a pond or pool; tank, water reservoir.
albergar v. to house, shelter, lodge; to harbour.
albo adj. white; Am. white footed (horse).
albor f. dawn whiteness.

alborada f. dawn, twilight; reveille (morning bugle call).
alborear v. to dawn.
alborotador m. agitator, troublemaker, rioter; alborotator of the peace.
alborotar v. to disturb, upset; Am. to excite, arouse enthusiasm; —se to get upset; to mutiny, to riot.
alboroto m. uproar, tumult, riot.
alborozado adj. elated, excited.
alborozar v. to gladden; —se to rejoice.
alborozo m. joy, delight, merriment, gaiety.
albricias f. pl. good news; reward for good news.
albur m. dace; Am. a sort of game at cards.
alcachofa f. artichoke; Am. sock, blow.
alcahueta f. procuress.
alcahuete m. procurer, pander; gobetween, pimp, bawd.
alcaide m. warden of a fortress or prison, jailer.
alcalde m. mayor; judge who administers justice in a town; — de barrio justice of the peace of a ward; — mayor mayor.
alcance m. reach, scope, talent, capacity; following and overtaking a person; last minute news, newspaper extra; range of firearms; cortos —s meagre intellect; dar — a to catch up with.
alcancía f. money box with slit for coins; savings bank.
alcanfor m. camphor; in Mex. gobetween.
alcanzar v. to reach, to overtake, to follow or pursue; to come up; to befall, to be enough; Am. to hand, to pass, to put within reach.
alcayata f. wall hook; meat hook.
alcázar m. castle, fortress; quarterdeck.
alcoba f. alcove, bedroom.
alcohol m. alcohol; highly rectified spirit of wine.
alcohólico adj. alcoholic.
alcornoque m. cork tree; cork wood; blockhead, dunce.
alcuza f. oil can; cruet; oil bottle.
aldaba f. knocker of a door; crossbar, bolt, latch; handle of a door, chest, etc. tener buenas —s to have "pull", influential connections.

aldabón m. large iron knocker; large handle.
aldabonazo m. knock, knocking.
aldea f. village, a small town.
aldeano m. villager, rustic, countrified; peasant.
aldehuela f. hamlet.
alear v. to flutter; to move the arms quickly; to flap; to alloy, to mix.
aleccionar v. to instruct, to teach, to coach, to train, to drill.
aledaños m. pl. common boundary; border, limit, frontier.
alegar v. to affirm, to quote, to adduce, to assert; Am. to argue, to dispute.
alegato m. assertion, allegation.
alegrar v. to make merry, to gladden, to cheer up, to exhilarate; —se to be glad, to get tipsy; to enliven, to beautify; to congratulate; to grow merry by drinking.
alegre adj. content, gleeful, merry, gay, joyful, cheerful, bright.
alegría f. mirth, merriment, joy, gaiety, pleasure.
alejamiento m. elongation, distance, withdrawal, retirement, aloofness.
alejar v. to remove, to move away from, to separate, to deviate; —se to move away, to be aloof.
alelado adj. stupefied, silly, openmouthed.
alemán adj. & m. German; German language.
alentar v. irr. to respire, to breathe, to animate; to encourage, to cheer up; —se to take heart; Am. to recover.
alergia f. allergy.
alero m. projecting roof; eaves.
alerto adj. vigilant, alert, guarded, watchful; ¡alerta! attention! look out!; estar alerta to be on the alert.
aleta f. fin of a fish; small wing; flap.
aletargado adj. drowsy, sluggish.
aletargarse v. to fall into a state of lethargy; to become drowsy.
aletazo m. stroke of a wing or fin.
aletear v. to flutter, to take short flights.
aleteo m. flapping of the wings.
aleve adj. perfidious, treacherous.
alevosía f. breach of trust, perfidy, treachery;

alevoso adj. false, treacherous.
alfabeto m. alphabet.
alfalfa m. alfalfa, lucern.
alfalfar m. alfalfa field.
alfarería f. pottery.
alfarero m. potter.
alfeñique m. a sugar paste; delicate person.
alférez m. ensign; second lieutenant; — de navío midshipman in the Navy.
alfil m. bishop in the game of chess.
alfiler m. pin; —es de pelo hairpin; —es pin money; ponerse de veinticinco —es to doll up, to dress up.
alfombra f. carpet, floor carpet.
alfombrilla f. small carpet; rug; measles; Am. plant of the vervain family; black smallpox; skin eruption.
alforja f. saddlebag; knapsack, food provisions for a trip; pasarse a la otra — Am. to take undue liberties.
alforza f. tuck, pleat, fold; scar.
algarabía f. jargon, chatter, uproar; the Arabic tongue.
algarrobo m. locust tree, carob tree.
algazara f. clamor; huzza; the shout of a multitude.
álgebra f. algebra; the art of reducing dislocations.
algo pron. something, somewhat.
algodón m. cotton plant, cotton; — en rama raw cotton; — pólvora guncotton.
algodonal m. cotton plantation.
alguacil m. constable, policeman; a peace officer; a bumbailiff, a market clerk; an outrider.
alguien pron. somebody, someone.
algún(o) adj. some, any; pron. someone; — tanto a little, somewhat.
alhaja f. jewel, showy ornament.
alharaca f. angry vociferation, clamor, racket.
aliado adj. allied; m. ally, confederate.
alianza f. alliance, league, union, coalition, confederacy; Am. wedding ring; mixture of liquors.
aliar v. to unite, to ally; —se to form an alliance.
alicaído adj. drooping, crestfallen, downcast, discouraged.
alicates m. pl. pliers, nippers, fine pointed pincers.

aliciente m. inducement, attraction, incitement, incentive.
alienista m. alienist.
aliento m. breath, vigor of mind, spirit, courageousness; smell, scent.
aligerar v. to lighten, to alleviate, to ease, to hasten.
alimentación f. alimentation, food, nourishment, nutrition, feeding.
alimentar v. to feed, to nourish, to nurse, to fatten; to sustain.
alimenticio adj. nutritious, nourishing.
alimento m. food; —s pension, alimony.
alinear v. to line up to lay out by line; to level; to dress; —se to fall in line, to form into a line.
aliño m. dress, ornament, decoration; condiment, dressing, seasoning.
alisar v. to smooth, to plane, to polish.
alistamiento m. enrollment, conscription, levy.
alistar v. to enlist, to enroll, to recruit; to make ready; —se to get ready; Am. to dress up.
aliviar v. to lighten, to alleviate, to relieve; to help; to loose; —se to get better, to recover.
alivio m. alleviation, ease, calm, relieve, remedy, aid, help.
aljibe m. cistern, reservoir, tank; Am. well, artesian well, spring.
alma m. soul, the human being, spirit, ghost.
almacén m. warehouse, store, department store.
almacenaje m. storage, warehouse rent.
almacenar v. to store, to warehouse goods; to store up, to put in storage.
almacenista m. & f. warehouse owner or manager or keeper, department store owner, wholesale merchant.
almanaque m. almanac, calendar.
almeja f. clam.
almendra f. almond.
almendro m. almond tree.
almíbar m. syrup.
almidón m. starch; Am. paste for gluing.
almidonar v. to starch.
almirante m. admiral.
almirez m. metal mortar.
almohada f. pillow, bolster.

almohadón m. large cushion or pillow.
almohaza f. currycomb (for grooming horses).
almoneda f. auction.
almorzar v. irr. to lunch, to eat lunch; to breakfast.
almuerzo m. lunch.
alojamiento m. lodging.
alojar v. to lodge, to let lodgins; to house, to quarter troops; —se to lodge, to room.
alondra f. lark.
alpaca f. alpaca (sheeplike animal of South America); llama; alpaca wool, alpaca cloth.
alpargata f. sandal; a sort of shoe made of hemp or canvas.
alquería f. farmhouse.
alquilar v. to rent, to hire, to let; —se to hire out.
alquiler m. rent, rental; **de —** for rent, for hire.
alquitrán m. tar.
alrededor adv. about, around; **— de** prep. around; **—es** m. pl. environs, outskirts, surroundings.
altanería f. hawking, haughtiness.
altanero adj. haughty proud.
altar m. altar; **— mayor** high altar.
altavoz m. loud-speaker.
alteración f. alteration, mutation, change; strong emotion; tumult, disturbance.
altercado m. controversy, contest, strife, quarrel, wrangle.
alterar v. to alter, change; to disturb.
alternar v. to alternate; to take turns; **— con** to rub elbows with, be friendly with.
alternativa f. alternative, choice.
alternativo adj. alternating, alternative.
alterno adj. alternate.
alteza f. highness, lofty height.
altibajo m. downward thrust; **—s** ups and downs, uneven ground; vicissitudes.
altiplanicie f. upland, high plateau.
altisonante adj. noisy, high sounding.
altitud f. altitude.
altivez f. haughtiness, pride, arrogance.
altivo adj. lofty, lordlike, haughty, proud, arrogant.
alto adj. high, tall, loud, elevated; adv. loud; m. height, story of a building; halt; Am. heap, pile; **—s** Am. upper floors; **hacer —**

ALTOPARLANTE   **AMENAZAR**

to halt, to stop; **pasar por —** to omit, to overlook; ¡-! halt!
altoparlante m. loud-speaker.
altura f. height, altitude.
alud m. avalanche.
aludir v. to allude, to refer indirectly.
alumbrado m. lighting; adj. lit, lighted, tipsy.
alumbramiento m. childbirth; ligthting.
alumbrar v. to light, give birth; —se to get tipsy.
aluminio m. aluminum.
alumno m. student, disciple, pupil.
alusión f. allusion.
alza f. rise, lift.
alzada f. height of a horse.
alzamiento m. rising, lifting, uprising, insurrection.
alzar v. to lift, to rise, to cut (cards); —se to rebel; Am. to puff up with pride; —se con algo to run off with something, steal something.
allá adv. there, over there, in that place, thither, anciently; **más —** farther.
allanar v. to level, even off; to invade, to break into, to raid; **— una dificultad** to smooth out a difficulty.
allegado adj. near, related, allied; m. relative; partisan, follower.
allegar v. to accumulate, heap up; to gather.
allende adv. on the other side, beyond; **— el mar** across the sea, overseas.
allí adv. there, in that place; **por —** there, by there, through that place, around there; **— mismo** in that very place.
ama f. mistress, owner; **— de casa** housekeeper; **— de leche** wetnurse.
amabilidad f. amiability, kindness, courtesy.
amable adj. kind, amiable.
amaestrar v. to teach, to tame, to break in, to couch, to master.
amagar v. to threaten, to be in a threatening attitude; to have some symptoms of disease; to strike at.
amago m. threat; indication, manifestation of the intention to do or say something; symptom of disease.
amalgamar v. to amalgamate, combine, mix, blend; to alloy.
amamantar v. to nurse, suckle.

amanecer v. irr. to dawn; **al —** at the break of the day; **— malo** to wake up ill; m. dawn, sunrise.
amansar v. to tame, to domesticate, to subdue, to pacify.
amante m. lover, loving, sweetheart.
amapola f. poppy.
amar v. to love, to like, to fancy; **quien a feo ama, hermoso le parece** love is blind.
amargar v. to embitter, to make bitter.
amargo m. bitter; Am. mate (Paraguayan tea) without sugar.
amargor m. bitterness.
amargura f. bitterness, grief, sorrow, acerbity.
amarillear v. to turn or make yellow, to incline to yellow.
amarillento adj. yellowish.
amarillo adj. yellow; gold color; m. jaundice.
amarra f. cable, rope, strap.
amarrar v. to tie, fasten; to lash; to rope; to moor (a ship); **amarrárselas** Am. to get tight, drunk.
amasar v. to knead, mix; to mash; Am. to amass, to accumulate (a fortune).
amatista f. amethyst.
ambages m. pl. circumlocutions; **hablar sin —** to go straight to the point, speak plainly; not to beat about the bush.
ámbar m. amber.
ambarino adj. amber, like amber.
ambición f. ambition, aspiration.
ambicionar v. to seek, to aspire after; to pursue with anxious desire; to covet.
ambicioso adj. covetous, ambitious, eager, greedy, grasping.
ambiente m. atmosphere, surrounding enviroment.
ambigüedad f. ambiguity.
ambiguo adj. ambiguous, uncertain, doubtful.
ámbito m. precint, enclosure; circuit, circumference.
ambos adj. & pron. both.
ambulancia f. ambulance; field hospital.
ambulante adj. ambulatory, walking, itinerant, moving, wandering.
amedrentar v. to scare, frighten; to discourage; to fear.
amenaza f. threat, menace, acing.
amenazador adj. threatening, menamenazar v. to threat, to menace.

amenguar v. to lessen, to diminish, to defame, to dishonor.
amenidad f. amenity, agreeableness, pleasantness.
amenizar v. to render pleasant or agreeable; to cheer, brighten.
ameno adj. pleasant, agreeable, delicious; florid, elegant.
americana f. suit coat.
americano adj. & m. American.
ametrallador m. gunner, machine-gunner.
ametralladora f. machine gun.
amigable adj. friendly, affable, pleasant.
amígdala f. tonsil.
amigdalitis f. tonsilitis.
amigo m. friend, comrade; boy friend; lover; — de fond of.
aminorar v. to lessen, to slow.
amistad f. friendship, friendliness.
amistoso adj. friendly.
amo m. master, owner, boss, chief.
amodorrado adj. drowsy, heavy with sleep.
amodorrar v. to make drowsy; —se to become drowsy.
amolador m. grinder, sharpener, whetter; adj. grinding, sharpening.
amolar v. irr. to whet, to hone, to grind, to sharpen, to annoy; Am. to ruin, to harm; —se Am. to go to rack and ruin.
amoldar v. to shape, to mold, to adjust; to cast in a mould, to adapt.
amonestación f. admonition, warning, advice; —es publications of marriage bans.
amoníaco m. ammonia.
amontonamiento m. accumulation, pile, heap.
amontonar v. to heap up, pile up, to gather.
amor m. love, tenderness, affection, fancy; — propio self-esteem.
amoratado adj. livid, bluish, ghastly, purplish.
amordazar v. to gag, to muzzle.
amorío m. love affair; love making.
amoroso adj. loving, tender, affectionate.
amortajar v. to shroud a corpse.
amortiguador m. amortizer, shock absorber; silencer, muffler.
amortiguar v. to muffle, to deaden, to deafen (a sound), to tone down.
amortizar v. to liquidate, to pay on account, to provide a sinking fund.
amoscarse v. to get peeved, annoyed; Am. to blush, to be inhibited or embarrassed.
amostazar v. to exasperate, to anger; —se to get angry or irritated.
amotinar v. to excite to rebellion; —se to mutiny, to riot.
amparar v. to shelter, to defend, to protect; Am. to grant mining rights; —se to seek protection or refuge; to protect oneself.
amparo m. shelter, protection, refuge, habeas corpus (a protection against the law).
ampliación f. enlargement, widening.
ampliar v. to amplify, to enlarge, to distend, to extend.
amplificar v. to amplify, to enlarge, to extend.
amplio adj. ample, extensive, large, roomy.
amplitud f. extent, greatness.
ampolla f. blister; vial, cruet, water bubble.
ampollar v. to blister; —se to blister.
ampolleta f. small vial or cruet.
ampuloso adj. grand, pompous, inflated, wordy, bombastic.
amputar v. to amputate, cut off.
amueblar v. to furnish with furniture.
ánade m. & f. duck.
anales m. pl. historical records; annals.
analfabeto adj. & m. illiterate.
analfabetismo m. illiteracy.
análisis m. analysis.
analizar v. to analyze, to examine.
analogía f. analogy, similitary.
análogo adj. analogous, equal, similar, comparable.
ananá f. pineapple. See piña.
anaquel m. shelf; bookshelf.
anaquelería f. shelves, bookshelves, library stacks.
anaranjado adj. orange-colored; m. orange color.
anarquía f. anarchy.
anatomía f. anatomy.
anca f. haunch, hind quarter, rump; Am. popcorn.
ancianidad f. old age.
anciano adj. old aged; m. old man.
ancla f. anchor.
anclar v. to anchor.
ancho adj. broad, large, wide;

anchoa f. anchovy.
loose, roomy; Am. self-satisfied, conceited; **a sus anchas** at one's ease; comfortable, leisurely; m. width.

anchoa f. anchovy.

anchura f. width, breadth, comfort, ease.

anchuroso adj. vast, extensive, broad.

andada f. Am. walk, stroll; —s track, footprints; **volver a las —s** to fall back into one's ways or habits.

andaderas f. pl. go-carts.

andaluz adj. Andalusian, of or pertaining to Andalusia, Spain; m. Andalusian, native of Andalusia.

andamio m. scaffold, scaffolding.

andanada f. grandstand, broadside (discharge of the guns of one side of a ship); **soltar una —** to discharge a broadside; to reprimand.

andante adj. walking; errant; wandering; andante, moderately slow; **caballero —** knight-errant.

andanzas f. pl. rambles, wanderings.

andar v. irr. to walk; to go; to go about; to run; to come or to move along; to act, to behave, to transact; **— con cuidado** to be careful; **anda en quince años** he is about fifteen years old; **a todo —** at full (walking) speed; **a más —** walking briskly; **¡anda!** move on!, well, never mind, stand out of the way!; **¿qué andas haciendo?** what are you doing?; **— andando** Am. to be walkin around; **¡ándale!** Am: hurry!

andariego adj. restless, of a roving disposition, fond of walking; m. walker.

andas f. pl. portable platform; litter; a bier with shafts.

andén m. railway station, platform.

andino adj. Andean, of or from the Andes.

andrajo m. rag, worn clothes; a despicable person.

andrajoso adj. ragged, in rags.

anécdota f. anecdote, story.

anegar v. to drown; to flood; to inundate, to submerge.

anejo adj. annexed, attached.

anestésico m. & adj. anesthetic.

anexar v. to annex, to join, to unite, to add to.

anexo m. annex; adj. annexed, joined.

anfiteatro m. amphitheater.

anfitrión m. amphitryon, generous host.

ángel m. angel; **— de la guarda** or **custodio** guardian angel.

angélico adj. angelic.

angina f. angina, inflammation of the throat; Am. tonsil; **— del pecho** angina pectoris.

anglosajón adj & m. Anglo-Saxon.

angostar v. to narrow, to contract; **—se** to narrow, to become narrow.

angosto adj. narrow, close.

angostura f. narrowness; narrows (narrow part of a river, valley, strait, etc).

anguila f. eel.

angular f. angular; **piedra —** corner stone.

ángulo m. angle, corner, nook.

angustia f. anguish, sorrow, pang, affliction, heaviness.

angustiar v. to afflict, to grieve, to distress, to worry.

angustioso adj. anguished, worried, grievous; distressing.

anhelante adj. anxious, desirous, longing, panting.

anhelar v. to long for; to breath with difficulty, to pant.

anhelo m. longing.

anheloso adj. anxious, eager.

anidar v. to nest; to nestle, to dwell, to shelter; to cherish.

anillo m. ring, circuit.

ánima f. soul, spirit.

animación f. animation, liveliness, life.

animal m. animal; adj. animal; stupid; beastly.

animar v. to animate, give life to; to comfort, to revive, to inspire, to encourage.

ánimo m. spirit, soul, fortitude, bravery; mind, intention, meaning, will.

animosidad f. daring, courage, boldness, animosity, energy.

animoso adj. brave, spirited, courageous.

aniñado adj. boyish; childish.

aniquilar v. to annihilate, overthrow, to reduce to nothing, to wipe out, to destroy completely.

aniversario m. anniversary, holiday.

anoche adv. last nigt.

anochecer v. irr. to grow dark; to

be or **arrive** at nightfall; m. nightfall.
anonadar v. to annihilate, to humiliate.
anónimo adj. anonymous; nameless; m. anonymous letter or note.
anormal adj. abnormal.
anotación f. annotation, note.
anotar v. to write notes, to comment, to annotate.
anquilosado adj. stiff-jointed; gnarled.
anquilosarse v. to become stiff in the joints; to become mentally stagnant.
ansia f. ardent desire, hankering, anxiety, anguish; longing; Am. nausea; —s anguish.
ansiar v. to hanker, to long for, to desire eagerly.
ansiedad f. anxiety; worry.
ansioso adj. anxious, troubled; eager, greedy.
antagonismo m. antagonism.
antagonista m. & f. antagonist, adversary, opponent.
antaño adv. yesteryear, last year, formely; **días de** — days of old.
ante prep. before, in the presence of; — **todo** above all; m. elk; buckskin.
anteanoche adv. night before last.
anteayer adv. day before yesterday; a short time since.
antebrazo m. forearm.
antecámara f. antechamber, lobby, waiting room, hall.
antecedente m. antecedent; adj. antecedent, preceding.
antecesor m. predecessor, forefather; —es ancestors.
antedicho adj. aforesaid, foresaid.
antelación f. precedence, preference, priority (in time).
antemano: de — beforehand, anticipated.
antena f. antenna (of a radio or wireless); lateen yard (of a ship); —s antennae, feelers.
antenoche See anteanoche.
anteojera f. blinder, spectacle case; eyeflap.
anteojo m. spyglass; small telescope; eyeglass; —s spectacles; —s de larga vista field glasses; —s de puño or teatro opera glasses.
antepasado adj. passed, elapsed; **año** — year before last; m. ancestor.

antepecho m. sill, railing, breastwork, parapet, battlement.
anteponer v. irr. to prefer, to place before.
anterior adj. anterior, former, previous, front, toward the front, earlier; **el día** — the day before.
antes adv. before, formerly, beforehand; — **de** or — **que** (conj) before; first, rather, better, heretofore; **haga usted esto** — do this first; — **morir que pecar** better to die than to sin; — **bien** rather; — **del día** before day or at day break; **cuanto** — as quick as possible, the soonest possible.
antesala f. antechamber, anteroom, waiting room.
antiaéreo adj. antiaircraft.
anticipación f. anticipation, expectation, foretaste; **con** — in advance.
anticipado adj. early, ahead of time, advanced (payment); **por** — in advance.
anticipar v. to anticipate, to forestall, to take up beforehand.
anticipo m. advance, advance payment.
anticlericalismo m. anticlericalism (opposition or antagonism to the clergy).
anticuado adj. antiquated, obsolete, out of use, out-of-date.
antídoto m. antidote, counterpoison.
antigualla f. antique; anything old; antiquity.
antigüedad f. antiquity, ancient times, oldness, seniority; the days of yore; —es antique objects, antiques.
antiguo adj. ancient, old, antique; —s the ancients.
antílope m. antelope.
antiparras f. pl. goggles, spectacles.
antipatía f. antipathy, dislike, mutual antagonism, aversion, repugnance.
antipático adj. disagreeable, unlikeable, unpleasant, repugnant.
antiséptico m. antiseptic.
antojadizo adj. fanciful, whimsical, longing, capricious, humorous, fickle.
antojarse v. : **antojársele a uno** to take a notion or fancy to; to want, to long, to desire.
antojo m. whim, notion, fancy, caprice, a vehement desire, a longing, a hankering.

antorcha f. torch; flambeau; taper; cresset.

antracita f. anthracite, hard coal.

anual adj. annual, yearly.

anuario m. annual, yearbook.

anublar v. to cloud; to dim; to obscure; to overcast; —se to become cloudy; to be blasted.

anudar v. to knot, to unite, to join; **anudársele a uno la garganta** to choke up with emotion.

anulación f. cessation, abrogation, voiding, cancellation, abscission.

anular v. to annul, to void, to cancel, to abolish, to frustrate.

anunciador m. announcer, advertiser; adj. announcing, advertising.

anunciante m. & f. announcer; advertiser.

anunciar v. to announce, to advertise; to forbode, to prophecy.

anuncio m. announcement, advertisement, omen, forerunner, notice.

anzuelo m. fishhook; lure, attraction, allurement, incitement.

añadidura f. addition, access.

añadir v. to add, to increase, to augment, to exaggerate.

añejado adj. aged.

añejo adj. old; stale, musty.

añicos m. pl. bits, shatters, fragments; **hacer(se)** — to shatter, break into pieces.

añil m. indigo, indigo blue.

año m. year; — **bisiesto** leap year; **¿cuántos —s tiene usted?** how old are you?; **el día de** — nuevo new year's day; **por, al, cada** — yearly.

añoranza f. nostalgia, longing.

añorar v. to long for; to make reminiscences.

añoso adj. aged.

apabullar v. to crush, crumple.

apacentar v. irr. to graze; to pasture; to feed (the spirit, desires, passions, etc.); to tend grazing cattle; to teach spiritually; —se to graze, to pasture.

apacibilidad f. affability, mildness of manners; meekness of temper, suavity, gentleness; pleasantness.

apacible adj. pleasant, quiet, gentle.

apaciguamiento m. pacification, appeasement.

apaciguar v. to sooth, to pacify, to compose, to tranquilize, to appease; —se to calm down.

apachurrar v. Am. to crush. See **despachurrar**.

apadrinar v. to support, to patronize, to protect, to sponsor, to act as a godfather; to act as a second in a duel.

apagar v. to quench, to put out, to extinguish; — **la cal** to slake lime.

apalabrar v. to speak for; to appoint a meeting for consultation, to engage, to reserve; —se con to make a verbal agreement with.

apalear v. to beat up; to cane; to thrash, to thresh.

aparador m. sideboard; cupboard; showcase; show window, workshop.

aparato m. apparatus, preparation; disposition, pomp, ostentation, show.

aparatoso adj. pompous, ostentatious.

aparcero m. partner in a farm; co-owner, co-proprietor; Am. pal; comrade.

aparear v. to mate, to match, to pair, to suit one thing to another; —se to mate; to be coupled in pairs.

aparecer v. irr to appear; to show up.

aparecido m. ghost, specter, phantom.

aparejar v. to get ready; to prepare, to harness; to rig, to equip; to furnish.

aparejo m. preparation, disposition, harness; packsaddle; rigging (of a ship); fishing tackle; —s tools, equipment.

aparentar v. to make a false show; to seem; to appear; to pretend; to feign; to affect.

aparente adj. apparent, feigned, simulated.

aparición f. apparition, ghost, vision.

apariencia f. appearance; outside; face; likeness; resemblance.

apartado m. compartment; — postal post office box.

apartamento m. apartment.

apartamiento m. separation; retirement; aloofness; retreat; refuge; Am. apartment, flat.

apartar v. to set apart; to separate; to remove; to part; to divide; — **las reses** Am. to sport out cattle; —se to withdraw; to step aside; to go away.

— 18 —

APARTE   **APLICACION**

aparte adj. apart; aside; separately; **punto y —** new paragraph; **dejar —** to lay aside.

apasionado adj. passionate; very fond of; emotional; devoted; admirer.

apasionar v. to inspire a passion; to arouse passion; **—se** to become impassioned; to fall ardently in love.

apatía f. apathy, indolence, indifference.

apático adj. apathetic, indifferent.

apear v. to dismount; to alight from a horse; to lower, to take down; to shackle (a horse); to fell (a tree); to scotch a wheel; to prop; Am. to fire, dismiss from a position; **— el tratamiento** to omit the title in addressing a person; **—se** to get off, to alight; **—se por la cola** (or **por las orejas**) Am. to give some absurd answer.

apechugar v. to push with the breast, to push ahead; to undertake with spirit; **— con** to accept reluctantly, to go through with (something) courageously; Am. to snatch; to take possession of.

apedrear v. to stone; to kill with stones.

apegado adj. devoted; attached.

apegarse v. to become attached (to); to be much taken with a thing.

apego m. attachment, fondness.

apelotonar v. to form or roll into a ball; to pile up, to bunch together.

apellidar v. to call, to name; **—se** to be named; to have the surname of.

apenar v. to grieve, to afflict; **—se** to be grieved, to be sorry; Am. to feel embarrassed, to feel ashamed.

apenas adv. scarcely, hardly; conj. as soon as; no sooner than.

apéndice m. appendix, supplement.

apercibir v. to prepare beforehand; to supply; to warn, to advice, to admonish; **—se a la pelea** to get ready to fight; **—se de** to notice.

apergaminado adj. parchment-like; dried up.

aperitivo m. aperitif, appetizer; cocktail.

apero m. the implementes used in a farm; the tools necessary for a trade; Am. saddle and trappings.

apertura f. opening, beginning.

apestar v. to infect; to corrupt; to sicken; to stink; **—se** to turn putrid; to become corrupted; Am. to catch cold.

apestoso adj. putrid; foul-smelling; stinky.

apetecer v. irr. to desire, to crave, to long for, to hanker, to wish.

apetecible adj. desirable, appetizing; worthy of being wished for.

apetencia f. hunger, appetite.

apetito m. appetite, hunger.

apetitoso adj. appetizing; gluttonous; savory.

apiadarse v. to pity; to commiserate; **— de** to pity, take pity on.

ápice m. apex, top, summit; the upper part of a thing.

apilar v. to pile up, to stack, to heap.

apiñado p.p. & adj. shaped like a pine cone; crowded, jammed; cone-shaped; pyramidal.

apiñamiento m. crowd, jam (of people or animals); crowding together.

apiñar v. to cram together; to crowd, to join, to group; **—se** to pile up; crowd together.

apio m. celery.

apisonar v. to pack down; to flatten by pounding; to ram with a rammer.

aplacar v. to appease, to pacify, to soothe; to mitigate.

aplanar v. to level, to flatten; **— las calles** Am. to tramp the streets; **—se** to be flattened out; to lose one's strength; Am. to give in.

aplastar v. to squash, to crush, to flatten, to cake; Am. to tire out, to break a horse; **—se** Am. to overstay a call (remaining seated).

aplaudir v. to clap, to applaud, to approve, to praise.

aplauso m. applause; praise; approval.

aplazamiento m. postponement, adjournment; convocation, citation.

aplazar v. to postpone, to adjourn, to summon.

aplicable adj. applicable, suitable, fitting.

aplicación f. application; effort; diligence; **—es** appliqué.

— 19 —

aplicado adj. studious, industrious; diligent.

aplicar v. to apply; to put on, lay on; —se to apply oneself, work hard; — el oído to listen attentively.

aplomado adj. gray, lead-colored; to be perpendicular.

aplomar v. to plumb (a well); to make vertical; —se Am. to become ashamed or embarrassed; to be slow.

aplomo m. assurance, confidence, serenity, self-possession; estar — to be plumb, vertical.

apocado adj. cowardly, timid.

apocamiento m. timidity, bashfulness; belittling, pusillanimity; abjectness of mind, meanness of spirit.

apocar v. to lessen; to belittle; to shorten; to give little importance to; —se to humble oneself.

apodar v. to nickname; to ridicule.

apoderado m. attorney; proxy; substitute.

apoderar v. to empower, to give power of atorney; —se de to take possession of, seize.

apodo m. nickname.

apogeo m. apogee.

apolillado adj. moth-eaten; worm-eaten.

apología f. apology.

apoplejía f. apoplexy, stroke.

aporrear v. to beat; to maul, to knock; Am. to defeat.

aportación f. contribution.

aportar v. to bring; to contribute; to arrive at port; to reach an unexpected place.

aporte m. contribution.

aposento m. room; lodging.

apostar v. irr. to bet; to post; to station.

apóstol m. apostle; religious leader.

apostólico adj. apostolic.

apostura f. gentleness, neatness, agreeable behavior.

apoyar v. to lean, to rest; to back, to support; to aid, to favor, to confirm; —se to lean (on).

apoyo m. support, favor, protection.

apreciable adj. appreciable, noticeable, estimable, esteemed; valuable, appraisable.

apreciación f. appreciation; valuation, estimation.

apreciar v. to appreciate, to appraise, to estimate, to value; to fix the price of.

aprecio m. esteem, high regard, appraisal, valuation, estimate; hacer — Am. to notice, to pay attention.

aprehender v. to apprehend, seize, to arrest.

aprehensión f. apprehension; fear, dread; seizure, arrest; Am. prejudice.

aprehensor m. captor.

apremiante adj. pressing, urgent.

apremiar v. to press, to urge onward, to hurry, to compel, to oblige.

apremio m. pressure, urgency, force, constriction.

aprender v. to learn.

aprendiz m. apprentice, learner.

aprendizaje m. apprenticeship.

aprensión f. See aprehensión.

apresar v. to seize, to grab, to capture, to imprison.

aprestar v. to prepare, to make ready, to dispose, to arrange; —se to get ready.

apresto m. preparation; readiness; arrangement.

apresurado adj. hasty; quick.

apresurar v. to hurry, hasten; to accelerate; —se to hurry, hasten.

apretado adj. tight, compact, close; stingy, miserly; difficult.

apretar v. irr. to press, squeeze, tighten; to urge on; Am. to increase in strength or intensity (as rain, wind, etc.); to redouble one's effort; — a correr to start to run; —se Am. to gorge, to overeat.

apretón m. sudden pressure or squeeze; dash, short run; — de manos handshake.

apretura f. jam, crush; tight squeeze; narrow place; difficulty, predicament, dire poverty.

aprieto m. tight spot, difficulty, danger.

aprisa adv. quickly, fast, speedily.

aprisco m. sheepfold.

aprisionar v. to imprison; to tie; to fasten.

aprobación f. approbation, approval, consent; pass, passing grade; praise, applause, consent.

aprobar v. irr. to approve, to pass (in an examination).

aprontar v. to prepare hastily; to make ready; to expedite; to hand over without delay; Am. to pay in advance.

apropiación f. appropriation; confiscation.
apropiado adj. appropriate, proper, fitting, suitable.
aprovechable adj. available; usable; fit to use.
aprovechado adj. diligent, industrious.
aprovechamiento m. use, utility, profit, benefit, progress, advantage.
aprovechar v. to profit, be profitable; to progress, get ahead; to utilize; —se de to take advantage of; ¡que aproveche! may you enjoy it!; — la ocasión to profit by the occasion.
aproximado adj. approximate; near, close; nearly correct.
aproximar v. to place or bring near, to approximate; —se to get near.
aproximativo adj. approximate.
aptitud f. aptitude, capacity, ability; expediency.
apto adj. apt; competent.
apuesta f. bet, wager.
apuesto adj. smart, stylish; good-looking.
apuntalar v. to prop; to shore up.
apuntar v. to point; to aim; to write, to mark, to indicate; to prompt (an actor); to sharpen; to stitch, mend; to begin to show; — el día to begin to dawn; —se Am. to sprout (said of wheat, corn, etc.).
apunte m. note, memorandum.
apuñalar v. to stab.
apuración f. worry; trouble.
apurado adj. worried, needy; difficult; dangerous; in a hurry.
apurar v. to drain to the last drop; to exhaust; to press; to hurry; to worry; to annoy; —se to be or get worried; to hurry up.
apuro m. need, worry, predicament, want, exigency; anguish, affliction; Am. rush, hurry.
aquejar v. to grieve, to afflict.
aquel, aquella dem. adj. that (at a distance); **aquellos, aquellas** those; **aquél, aquélla** m. f. dem. pron. that thing; **aquéllos, aquéllas** m. f. pl. those, the former.
aquí adv. here; por — this way, through here, around here.
ara f. altar.
árabe adj. & m. Arab, Arabic.
arado m. plow; Am. plowed land, piece of cultivated land.

aragonés adj. Aragonese, of or from Aragón, Spain; m. Aragonese.
arancel m. tariff; the fixed rate of duties, fees, taxes, etc.; — de aduanas customs, duties.
araña f. spider; chandelier.
araño m. scratch.
arar v. to plow.
arbitrador m. arbitrator, referee, umpire.
arbitraje m. arbitration.
arbitrar v. to arbitrate, to umpire.
arbitrario adj. arbitrary.
arbitrio m. free will; scheme, means, compromise; arbitration; sentence (of a judge); judgment.
árbitro m. arbitrator, sole judge, umpire, referee.
árbol m. tree; mast.
arbolado adj. wooded; m. grove of trees.
arboleda f. grove; plantation of trees, wooded ground.
arbusto m. shrub.
arca f. ark; chest, coffer.
arcada f. arcade; archway; violent motion of the stomach, which excites vomiting, nausea.
arcaico adj. archaic.
arcano adj. hidden, secret, recondite; reserved; m. secret, mystery.
arce m. maple, maple tree.
arcilla f. clay, argil, alumina.
arco m. arc; arch; bow; violin bow; — iris rainbow.
archipiélago m. archipelago.
archisabido adj. very well known.
archivo m. archives; file; public records; Am. office, business office.
arder v. to burn, to blaze, to glow; to be consumed (with fever or passion); Am. to smart, sting.
ardid m. trick, scheme, stratagem, artifice.
ardiente adj. ardent, burning, fervent, passionate; fiery.
ardilla f. squirrel; **andar como —** to fly about from place to place.
ardite m. ancient coin of small value; bit; trifle; **no valer un —** not to be worth a penny.
ardor m. ardor; heat; fervor, eagerness, hotness.
ardoroso adj. ardent, fiery, restless.
arduo adj. arduous, hard, difficult.
área f. area.
arena f. sand; arena; —s kidney stones.

arenal m. sand pit.
arenga f. address, speech, oration, harangue.
arenoso adj. sandy, gritty.
arenque m. herring; — **ahumado** red herring.
arete m. earring.
argamasa f. mortar.
argentar v. to plate or cover with silver; to polish.
argentino adj. silvery; Argentine; m. Argentine; Argentine gold coin worth 5 pesos.
argolla f. large iron ring, staple; Am. plain finger ring; engagement ring; **tener —** Am. to be lucky.
argucia f. cunning, subtlety; astuteness, scheme.
argüir v. irr. to argue, to deduce, to infer, to dispute, to oppose.
argumentación f. argumentation, argument, reasoning.
argumento m. argument, reasoning, subject matter, resumé, plot.
aridez f. barrenness; dryness; drought.
árido adj. arid, dry, barren, insipid, monotonous, uninteresting; **—s** grains and dry vegetables; **medida para —s** dry measure.
ariete m. ram, battering ram; **— hidráulico** hydraulic ram.
arisco adj. gruff, harsh, unsociable, fierce, wild; Am. shy, distrustful.
arista f. sharp edge; ridge.
aristocracia f. aristocracy.
aristócrata m. & f. aristocrat.
aristocrático adj. aristocratic.
aritmética f. arithmetic.
arma f. arm, weapon, branch (of the Army); **—s** armed forces; **— arrojadiza** missile weapon; **— blanca** sword; **de —s tomar** ready for any emergency; ready to fight.
armada f. armada; fleet.
armador m. shipbuilder; assembler.
armadura f. armor; armature (of a generator or dynamo); framework, mounting.
armamento m. armament, equipment, warlike preparation.
armar v. to arm; to set up; to assemble; to ring up; to set a snare; **— una pendencia** to start a quarrel; **— un trique** Am. to lay a snare, to set a trap; **—se** to prepare oneself to war; **—se** Am. to balk, to be stubborn; **—se con alguna cosa** Am. to refuse to return something.

armario m. wardrobe, clothes closet; cabinet, cupboard.
armatoste m. unwieldly machine; hulk; clumsy thing; heavy, clumsy fellow.
armazón m. framework, skeleton; hulk of a ship; Am. shelf, set of shelves.
armella f. staple; screw eye.
armiño m. ermine.
armisticio m. armistice.
armonía f. harmony, harmoniousness; number, concord; metrical cadence.
armónico adj. harmonic, harmonious, harmonical.
armonioso adj. harmonious, musical; sonorous.
armonizar v. to harmonize.
arnés m. harness; coat of mail; armour; **—es** harness and trappings; equipment; outfit; **— de caballo** gear.
aro m. hoop, ring of wood, iron, or other metals; iron staple, hoop-poles; rim (of a wheel); Am. finger ring; earring.
aroma m. aroma, scent, perfume; f. flower of the aromatic myrrh tree.
aromático adj. aromatic, fragant, spicy, aromatical; **sales aromáticas** smelling salts.
arpa f. harp, lyre.
arpía f. shrew; harpy.
arpón m. harpoon, spear, harping iron.
arqueado adj. arched.
arquear v. to arch; **— las cejas** to frown.
arquitecto m. architect.
arquitectónico adj. architectural, architectonic.
arrabal m. outlying district, suburb; **—es** outskirts, suburbs.
arracada f. earring.
arraigar v. to root, to take root; to give security; **—se** to become rooted, attached.
arrancar v. to uproot; to pull up by the roots; to start, start out; Am. to flee, run away; **— de raíz** to extirpate.
arranque m. start, pull; uprooting; automobile starter; **— de ira** fit or outburst of anger; **punto de —** starting point.
arrasar v. to level, to make even; to tear down, to raze; to fill to the brim; **—se** to clear up (the sky); **—se de lágrimas** to fill up with tears.
arrastrado adj. poor, destitute,

arrastrar

vile, mean; dragged; wretched; rascally; **llevar una vida arrastrada** to lead a dog's life.

arrastrar v. to drag, to haul, to creep, to crawl; Am. to harrow (land); **—se** to crawl along, to drag.

arrayán m. myrtle.

¡arre! interj. gee!; get up there!

arrear v. to drive (mules, cattle); Am. to rustle, steal cattle; **—le a uno una bofetada** Am. to give a person a slap.

arrebatar v. to snatch away, to carry off; to attract attention, notice, etc.; **—se de cólera** to have a fit of anger; to be led away by passion.

arrebatiña f. grab, snatch; scramble.

arrebato m. rage; rapture, ecstasy; fit, surprise, paroxysm, start.

arrebol m. red color of the sky; rouge; **—es** red clouds.

arreciar v. to increase in intensity, to get stronger.

arrecife m. reef.

arredrar v. to frighten, to intimidate; to terrify, to cause dread; **—se** to be or get scared.

arreglar v. to arrange, to put in order, to regulate, to guide; to compound; to frame; to adjust; to fix; to settle; Am. to pay (a debt); to correct, to punish; **—se** to doll up, fix oneself up; to settle differences; to come to an agreement.

arreglo m. arrangement; adjustment; rule; order; settlement; conformity, **con — a** according to.

arrellanarse v. to sprawl, to lounge; to be self-satisfied; to seat at ease.

arremangado adj & p.p. turned up; **nariz arremangada** turned up nose.

arremangar v. to tuck up, to turn up, to roll up (the sleeves, trousers, etc.); **—se** to roll up one's sleeves; **—se los pantalones** to roll up one's trousers.

arremeter v. to attack, to assail, to assault.

arremetida f. thrust, push, attack.

arremolinarse v. to whirl, to swirl, to eddy; to mill around.

arrendamiento m. renting, lease, hiring, rental, rent.

arrendar v. irr. to rent, to lease, to let, to hire; to tie (a horse); to bridle; Am. to head for.

arrodillarse

arrendatario m. renter, tenant.

arreo m. raiment, dress, ornament, decoration; Am. driving of horses or mules; drove of horses or mules; **—s** trappings; equipment; finery; adv. uninterruptedly, without interruption.

arrepentido adj. repentant.

arrepentimiento m. repentance, regret, penitence.

arrepentirse v. irr. to repent, to regret.

arrestado adj. daring, rash.

arrestar v. to arrest; Am. to return, to strike back (a ball); to reprimand; **—se** to dare, to venture.

arresto m. arrest, imprisonment; detention; spirit, boldness in undertaking an enterprise; a rash act.

arriar v. to haul down, lower (the flag); to lower (the sails); to slacken (a rope).

arriba adv. above, over, up, high, on, overhead; **de — abajo** from top to bottom; up and down; **río — ** up stream; **¡—!** hurrah!

arribada f. arrival of a vessel in a port; Am. back talk, impudent answer.

arribar v. to arrive; to put into port; Am. to prosper, to better one's lot.

arribo m. arrival.

arriero m. muleteer.

arriesgado adj. risky, daring, perilous, dangerous, hazardous, adventurous, exposed, arduous.

arriesgar v. to risk; **—se** to dare, to run a risk.

arrimar v. to bring or to place near; to lay aside, to approach; to strike (a blow); **—se** to lean (on); to get near; to seek shelter.

arrinconar v. to corner, to put in a corner, to lay aside, to reject; to retire from the world; **—se** to retire; to live a secluded life.

arriscado adj. bold; daring; brisk; spirited (horse); craggy, rugged.

arriscar v. to risk, to venture; Am. to roll up, curl up, tuck up, fold back; **—se** to get angry; Am. to dress up; to doll up.

arroba f. weight of 25 pounds.

arrobamiento m. trance, rapture, amazement.

arrobarse v. to be entranced, to be in a trance; to be enraptured.

arrodillarse v. to kneel.

arrogancia f. arrogance, pride, haughtiness, loftiness.

arrogante adj. arrogant, lofty, proud, haughty.

arrogarse v. to appropriate, to usurp, to assume (power or rights).

arrojadizo adj. missile; **arma arrojadiza** missile weapon.

arrojado adj. daring, rash, fearless, bold, intrepid, resolute.

arrojar v. to throw, to hurl, to cast, to dart or fling anything, to expel; Am. to throw up, to vomit; — **un saldo de** to show a balance of; —**se a** to hurl oneself upon or at; to dare to.

arrojo m. boldness, daring, intrepidity, fearlessness.

arrollador adj. sweeping, overwhelming, violent, roller, winding (that serves to wind or roll up).

arrollar v. to roll up; to sweep away, to trample upon; to destroy, to subjugate.

arropar v. to wrap, to cover; Am. to snap up, accept on the spot (a deal); —**se** to wrap up, to cover up.

arrostrar v. to face, to defy; —**se** to dare to fight face to face.

arroyo m. brook, small stream; the water course of a street; rivulet, gutter.

arroz m. rice.

arrozal m. rice field.

arruga f. wrinkle.

arrugar v. to wrinkle; Am. to bother, to annoy; —**se** to get wrinkled; Am. to crouch with fear, to be afraid.

arruinar v. to ruin, to destroy, to throw down, to demolish; —**se to** become ruined; Am. to go "broke", to lose all one's fortune.

arrullar v. to lull; to coo.

arrullo m. lullaby; cooing.

arrumbar v. to lay aside as useless; to put away in a corner, to discard, to dismiss; to remove (from office or a position or trust); to take bearings; — **a su adversario** to corner one's opponent, to overpower him.

arsenal m. navy yard, dockyard.

arsénico m. arsenic.

arte m. & f. art, skill, ability, cunning, craft; **usar de** — to be astute, cunning, or artful; **por** — **de** by way or means of; **bellas** —**s** fine arts; —**s mecánicas** mechanical arts, occupations or handicrafts.

artefacto m. piece of workmanship, manufacture, contraption, handiwork, contrivance.

arteria f. artery.

artero adj. crafty, astute, dexterous, cunning.

artesa f. trough.

artesanía f. arts and crafts; workmanship, craftsmanship.

artesano m. artisan, artist, mechanic manufacturer.

artesonado m. ceiling decorated with carved panels; shaped in the form of a trough.

ártico adj. arctic.

articulación f. articulation, joint; pronunciation.

articular v. to articulate, to join, to unite; to pronounce distinctly; adj. articular.

artículo m. article; section; — **de fondo** editorial.

artífice m. artisan, craftsman, artificer, inventor, contriver.

artificial adj. artificial; **fuegos** —**es** fireworks.

artificio m. artifice, clever device, trick, finesse, craft, fraud, skill, cunning, deceit.

artificioso adj. cunning, astute, deceitful, skilful, artful.

artillería f. artillery, gunnery; — **de plaza** (or **de sitio**) heavy artillery, siege guns; — **de montaña** light mountain artillery.

artillero m. artilleryman, gunner.

artimaña f. trick, stratagem.

artista m. & f. artist, artisan, tradesman, craftmaster.

arzobispo m. archbishop.

arzón m. saddletree.

as m. ace.

asa f. handle.

asado m. roast; p.p. & adj. roasted.

asador m. spit.

asaltador m. assailant, higway robber, assaulter.

asaltar v. to assault, to attack, to assail; —**le a uno una idea** to be struck by an idea; — **la casa de un amigo** Am. to give a surprise party.

asalto m. assault, attack; Am. surprise party.

asamblea f. assembly, legislature, meeting.

asar v. to roast; —**se** to roast; **to** feel hot.

asaz adv. enough, very, abundantly.

ascendencia f. ancestry; origin.

ascendente adj. ascendent, ascending, upward, rising.

— 24 —

ascender v. irr. to ascend, to climb, to promote, to amount to.
ascendiente m. ancestor; influence.
ascensión f. ascension; ascent; feast of the Ascension of Christ.
ascenso m. ascent, rise, promotion.
ascensor m. elevator.
asco m. disgust, loathing; nausea; **me da —** it makes me sick; it disgusts me; **poner a uno del — Am.** to call a person all kinds of bad names; to soil; **es un —** it is a mean thing; **hacer —s** to turn the stomach.
ascua f. ember.
aseado adj. clean, neat.
asear v. to adorn, to make neat, to wash; **—se** to clean oneself up.
asechanza See **acechanza**.
asediar v. to besiege, to attack, to blockade.
asedio m. siege, blockade.
asegurar v. to assure, to secure, to affirm; to insure; **—se** to make sure.
asemejar v. to liken, to compare, to assimilate, to resemble; **—se a** to resemble.
asentaderas f. pl. buttocks.
asentador m. razor strop.
asentar v. irr. to set, to put down in writing; to assert; to seat; to stop at; to iron out; to hone; to strop; to establish; **—se** to settle.
asentimiento m. assent, acquiescence, agreement.
asentir v. irr. to assent, to affirm, to agree; to coincide in opinion with another.
aseo m. neatness, cleanliness.
asequible adj. obtainable, available, attainable.
aserción f. assertion, affirmation.
aserradero m. sawmill.
aserrar v. irr. to saw.
aserrín m. sawdust.
aserto m. assertion.
asesinar v. assassination, murder.
asesino m. assassin, murderer; adj. murderous.
asestar v. to point, to aim, to direct, to level; **— un golpe** to deal a blow; **— un tiro** to fire a shot.
aseveración f. assertion, affirmation, contention, asseveration.
aseverar v. to assert, to affirm, to asseverate.
asfalto m. asphalt.
asfixia f. suffocation, asphyxia.
asfixiar v. to suffocate, to smother.

así adv. so, thus, like this, in this manner, in this way, in this form; therefore; so that, also, equally; **— — so-so; — que so that; — que (or como) conj.** as soon as; **— no más Am.** so-so, just so; **— que asá** or **asado** let it be as it will.
asiático m. & adj. Asiatic.
asidero m. handle; hold; occasion, pretext.
asiduo adj. assiduous, diligent, persevering.
asiento m. seat; site; location; bottom; entry; sediment; treaty, contract; judgment; **—s** dregs.
asignación f. assignment; allowance, assignation.
asignar v. to assign; to allot; to attribute; to appoint; to make out, to ascribe.
asilado m. inmate (of an asylum).
asilar v. to house, to shelter; to put in an asylum.
asilo m. asylum, refuge, shelter, sanctuary, harbourage.
asimilar v. to assimilate, to digest, to absorb; to liken; to compare; **—se** to be assimilated.
asimismo adv. likewise, also, exactly so, identically; precisely.
asir v. irr. to seize, to take hold of, to grab, to grasp.
asistencia f. presence, attendance; assistance, help, aid; **Am.** sitting room; **—s** allowance; **casa de — Am.** boarding house.
asistente m. assistant, helper; helpmate; military orderly; **Am.** servant; **los —s** those present.
asistir v. to attend, to be present, to help; to assist; **Am.** to board; to serve meals.
asno m. ass, donkey; a dull, stupid, heavy fellow.
asociación f. association; fellowship, co-partnership.
asociado m. associate.
asociar v. to associate, to conjoin, to consociate; **—se** to join, to associate.
asolamiento m. devastation, ravage, havoc, destruction, depopulation.
asolar v. irr. to destroy, to pillage, to devastate; to lay waste, to parch; **—se** to dry up, to become parched; to settle (as wine).
asolear v. to sun, to expose to the sun; **—se** to bask in the sun; to get sunburnt.
asomar v. to show, to appear, to become visible; **— la cabeza** to

asombrar

stick one's head out; —se to look out (of a window); to peep out (or into); Am. to draw near, to approach.

asombrar v. to astonish, to amaze, to frighten, to terrify; to cast a shadow; to darken; —se to be astonished, to be amazed.

asombro m. astonishment, amazement; dread, fear, consternation.

asombroso adj. astonishing, amazing; wonderful, marvelous, admirable.

asomo m. sign, indication, mark, token, suspicion; **ni por —** by no means.

aspa f. wing of a windmill; blade.

aspecto m. aspect, look, sight, countenance.

aspereza f. roughness, ruggedness; harshness, acerbity, acrimony.

áspero adj. rough, uneven, harsh.

aspiración f. aspiration, ambition, longing, inspiration, inhalation, breathing in.

aspirante m. & f. applicant, candidate.

aspirar v. to aspire, to inspire the air; to covet, to long for, to seek; to inhale, to breath in; to aspirate.

asquear v. to disgust, to nauseate, to sicken.

asqueroso adj. loathsome, disgusting, sickening, filthy.

asta f. horn, antler, handle of a pencil; brush, mast pole, staff, flagstaff, lance; **a media —** at half mast.

asterisco m. asterisk.

astilla f. chip, splinter, splint; **sacar —** to make profit or benefit out of anything.

astillar v. to chip; to splinter; —se to break into splints, to splinter.

astillero m. dry dock; shipyard; lumber yard; rack on which lances, spears, etc., are placed.

astro m. star, planet; heavenly body; illustrious person.

astronomía f. astronomy.

astrónomo m. astronomer.

astucia f. shrewdness, cunning trick, craft, finesse, astuicity.

asturiano adj. Asturian, of or from Asturias, Spain; m. Asturian.

astuto adj. astute, shrewd; wily, crafty.

asueto m. recess, vacation; **día de —** holiday.

asumir v. to assume.

asunto m. topic, subject matter, business affair.

asustadizo adj. shy, scary, easily frightened, jumpy; excessively timid.

asustar v. to frigten, to scare.

atacante m. attacker; adj. attacking.

atacar v. to attack; to tighten, to fasten, to ram, to plug; to assault.

atadura f. tie, knot, fastening.

atajar v. to intercept, to stop, to obstruct, to cut off, to take a short cut; to cross out.

atajo m. short cut; interception, cut by which a road or path is shortened; Am. drove. See **hatajo**.

atalaya f. lookout, watchtower; m. lookout, watchman, guard.

atañer v. to concern, to belong, to appertain.

ataque m. attack, fit, onset.

atar v. to tie, to fasten, to bind, to knit; —se to get tied up; **loco de —** a fool or a madman that should wear a strait-waistcoat.

atareado adj. busy, over-worked.

atarear v. to overwork, load with work; to task; —se to toil, to work hard; to be very busy.

atascadero m. muddy place, obstruction, impediment.

atascar v. to stop up, to jam, to obstruct; to throw an obstacle in the way of an undertaking; —se to get stuck, to stick, to jam, to get obstructed; to stall.

ataúd m. coffin.

ataviar v. to attire, to adorn, to deck, to dress out, to trim, to embellish, to doll up.

atavío m. attire, costume, ornaments, finery, gear.

atemorizar v. to frighten, to scare, to terrify, to strike with terror.

atención f. attention, care, thought, courtesy, civility, kindness; **—es** business, affairs; **en —** having in mind, considering.

atender v. irr. to heed, to pay attention, to attend to, to take care of, to hearken, to wait on, to take into account or consideration.

atendido adj. Am. attentive, courteous.

atenerse v. irr. to relay (on), to accept, to abide (by).

atenido adj. Am. habitually dependent on another.

atentado m. offense, violation; crime; violence; excess; transgression.

atentar v. irr. to attempt, to try; — **contra la vida de alguien** to attempt the life of someone.

atento adj. attentive, courteous, polite, civil.

atenuar v. to attenuate, to lessen, to tone down, to diminish, to dim, to macerate, to mince, to make thin or slender.

ateo m. atheist; adj. atheistic.

aterciopelado adj. velvety, velvetlike.

aterido adj. stiff with cold, numb with cold.

aterirse v. irr. to become numb with cold, to grow stiff with cold.

aterrador adj. appalling, terrifying, horrible.

aterrar v. to terrify, to frighten, to destroy, to pull or strike down.

aterrizaje m. landing (of a plane); **pista de —** landing strip.

aterrizar v. to land (said of a plane).

aterrorizar v. to terrify, to appall, to frighten.

atesorar v. to treasure, to hoard, to lay up, to accumulate.

atestado adj. crowded, jammed, stuffed; attested, witnessed.

atestar v. to attest, to testify, to witness; to cram, to stuff, to overstock, to crowd.

atestiguar v. to testify, to witness, to attest, to depose.

atiborrar v. to stuff, to cram with victuals; **—se** to cram oneself.

atiesar v. to stiffen, to make hard or stiff.

atildado adj. spruce, trim, painstaking in dress or style.

atinar v. to hit the mark, to guess right, to touch the mark, to hit upon.

atisbar v. to spy, to look cautiously, to scrutinize, to watch, to pry, to examine closely, to catch a glimpse of, to peek.

atisbo m. glimpse; insight, peek, spying.

atizar v. to poke, to stir (the fire), to kindle, to rouse; to trim (a wick); to stir the fire with a poker; to stir up or rouse and incite the passions; **— un bofetón** to give a wallop.

atlántico adj. Atlantic; **el océano —** Atlantic Ocean.

atlas m. atlas.

atleta m. & f. athlete.

atlético adj. athletic.

atletismo m. athletics.

atmósfera f. atmosphere, air.

atmosférico adj. atmospheric, atmospherical.

atolondrado p.p. & adj. confused, muddled; stunned; heedless; harebrained; thoughtless.

atolondramiento m. thoughtlessness; recklessness; confusion; perplexity, stupefaction.

atolondrar v. to confuse, to muddle, to perplex; to stun, to stupefy; **—se** to get muddled, to get confused, to grow stupid, to get stunned.

átomo m. atom; small particle, tiny bit; iota, jot.

atónito adj. astonished, amazed.

atontado adj. stupefied, stupid, stunned, mopish, foolish.

atontar v. to stupefy, to stun; to confuse; **—se** to stupefy, to get stuck (in the mud), to be stupid, to get clogged, to get jammed; to choke (with food).

atormentar v. to torment, to worry, to afflict; to tease, to bother, to vex, to cause affliction, to be agitated.

atornillar v. to screw; Am. to bother, to torment, to tease.

atorrante m. Am. vagabond, tramp

atrabancar v. to rush awkwardly, to run over; **—se** Am. to get involved in difficulties; to rush into things.

atrabiliario adj. melancholy, bad-tempered, bilious.

atracar v. to cram; to stuff; to moor; to approach land; to hold up, to assault; to overtake another ship; to cram with food and drink; to berth; Am. to seize; to pursue, harass; to treat severely; to thrash, to beat; **— al muelle** to dock, to moor to the wharf; Am. to have a fist fight; to falter, stutter; **—se a** to come alongside of (a ship).

atracción f. attraction.

atraco m. holdup, assault.

atracón m. stuffing, gorging, overeating, gluttony; Am. violent quarrel; **darse un — de comida** Am. to stuff oneself, to gorge.

atractivo adj. attractive; engaging, enchanting; m. attractiveness, charm.

atraer v. irr. to attract, to lead, to allure.

ATRAGANTARSE   **AUSCULTAR**

atragantarse v. to gobble up; to choke (with food); to stick in the throat; to be cut short in conversation.

atrancar v. to bolt, to fasten with a bolt, to bar a door; —se to get crammed, obstructed; Am. to be stubborn, to stick to one's opinion; to stuff oneself; to choke (with food).

atrapar v. to trap, ensnare; to seize, to overtake, to nab, to grab.

atrás adv. back, behind, backward, towards the back; echarse — (or para —) to back out; to go back on one's word; quedarse — to remain behind.

atrasado adj. late, behind time, backward; ignorant; behind (in one's word, payments, etc.); slow (said of a clock).

atrasar v. to delay; to be slow or be delayed or behind time; to lose time; Am. to suffer a setback (in one's health or fortune); — los pagos to suspend or delay payments.

atraso m. backwardness; delay; setback; —s arrears.

atravesar v. irr. to cross, to walk across; to go through; to pierce, to cross over, to pass over; Am. to overpass; Am. to buy wholesale.

atreverse v. to dare, to risk, to be insolent, saucy; to be too forward; to venture, to run a risk.

atrevido adj. bold, daring, insolent, audacious.

atrevimiento m. boldness, daring, insolence, audaciousness, confidence.

atribuir v. irr. to attribute, to ascribe, to impute, to count, to charge, to assume.

atribular v. to grieve, to distress, to vex, to afflict, to annoy, to worry, to torment; —se to be distressed.

atributo m. attribute, quality.

atril m. lectern, reading desk; book stand, music stand.

atrincherar v. to intrench, to fortify with trenches, to cover oneself from the enemy by means of trenches; —se to intrench oneself.

atrio m. court, patio in front of a church; entrance hall; porch.

atrocidad f. atrocity; atrociousness; excess.

atronador adj. thunderous, deafening, thunderer.

atronar v. irr. to deafen, to stun, to make a great noise.

atropellar v. to run over, to run down; to knock down, to trample down, to overcome with violence; to tread under foot; — las leyes to act in defiance of the law; — por to knock down; —se to rush.

atropello m. violent act; insult; outrage; trampling; upset, abuse.

atroz adj. atrocious, awful, inhuman, enormous.

atún m. tunny fish, tuna fish.

aturdido adj. & p.p. stupid, awkward, harebrained, mad-brain, stunned, bewildered.

aturdimiento m. daze, bewilderment, confusion, perturbation of mind, giddiness.

aturdir v. to stun, to deafen, to bewilder, to perturbe, to confuse, to stupefy.

audacia f. daring, boldness, audacity, insolence.

audaz adj. daring, bold, brave.

audiencia f. audience, hearing, court of justice.

auditor m. judge, advocate.

auditorio m. audience, auditorium, auditory.

auge m. boom (in the market); boost (in prices); topmost height; apogee; estar (or ir) en — to be on the increase.

augurar v. to foretell, to predict; to vaticinate.

augusto adj. venerable, majestic, august.

aula f. schoolroom, classroom, lecture hall.

aullar v. to howl; to shriek; to bawl.

aullido m. howl.

aumentar v. to augment, to increase.

aumento m. increase, rise, promotion, advancement.

aun (aún) adv. even, still, yet, nevertheless, notwithstanding.

aunque conj. though, although.

aura f. breeze; favor, applause; Am. bird of prey, buzzard, vulture.

áureo adj. golden, golden number, the lunar cycle.

aureola f. aureole, halo.

aurora f. dawn, beginning; daybreak; — boreal aurora borealis, northern lights.

auscultar v. to sound, to examine

— 28 —

AUSENCIA

by listening to (the chest, lungs, heart, etc.); to auscultate.
ausencia f. absence.
ausentarse v. to absent oneself; to be absent, to leave.
ausente adj. absent.
auspicios m. pl. auspices, patronage; omens; prediction.
austeridad f. austerity, severity, sternness, harshness, rigour.
austero adj. austere, stern, strict, harsh, severe.
austral adj. austral, southern.
austriaco adj. & m. Austrian.
austro m. auster, south wind.
auténtico adj. authentic, true, genuine, original.
auto m. auto, automobile; oneact play; order; a judicial decree or sentence, writ, warrant; an edict, ordinance; — **de fe** the sentence given by the inquisition; — **interlocutorio** an interlocutory sentence; — **definitivo** definitive act; —**s pleadings and proceedings in a law-suit; estar en** —**s** to know a thing profoundly; — **sacramental** religious play.
autobús m. bus, autobus.
autóctono adj. indigenous, native, autochthonous, aboriginal.
automático adj. automatic, automatical.
automotriz adj. automotive, self-moving, self-acting.
automovilista m. & f. motorist.
autonomía f. autonomy.
autor m. author, maker, composer, writer; plaintiff or claimant.
autoridad f. authority.
autoritario adj. authoritative; authoritarian, domineering; bossy, despotic.
autorización f. authorization, sanction.
autorizar v. to authorize, to give power (to), to attest, to legalize, to confirm.
auxiliar v. to aid, to help, to assist, to attend; adj. auxiliary, helping, assisting, auxiliatory; m. assistant.
auxilio m. aid, help, assistance.
avaluar v. to value, to appraise.
avalúo m. valuation, appraisal.
avance m. advance, progress, headway, attack, assault; advanced payment.
avanzada f. advance guard; outpost; advanced unit, reconnoitring body.

AVERIAR

avanzar v. to advance, to attack, to come on, to go forward.
avaricia f. avarice, greed, cupidity.
avariento adj. avaricious, miserly; covetous, niggard, miserable; m. miser.
avaro adj. miserly, greedy; m. miser.
avasallar v. to subject, to dominate, to subdue, to slave, to reduce to vassalage.
ave f. bird, fowl; — **de corral** domestic fowl; — **de rapiña** bird of prey.
avecindarse v. to settle, to locate, to establish oneself, to take up residence.
avellana f. hazelnut; filbert.
avellano m. hazelnut tree.
avellanado adj. hazel, light brown.
avena f. oats.
avenencia f. harmony, agreement, compromise.
avenida f. avenue, flood, inundation.
avenir v. irr. to adjust; to reconcile; to join, to unite; to settle differences on friendly terms; —**se a** to adapt oneself; —**se con alguien** to get along with someone.
aventador m. fan (for fanning a fire), ventilator, winnower (machine for separating wheat from chaff); a wooden fork with three or four prongs, used for winnowing corn.
aventajar v. to exceed, to excel; to be ahead (of); to acquire advantages; to meliorate, to surpass; —**se a** to get ahead of.
aventar v. irr. to fan, to winnow, to blow chaff from grain; to throw out, to expel, to drive away; Am. to dry sugar (in the open); to rouse (game); —**se** to be full of wind; Am. to attack, to hurt oneself.
aventura f. adventure; risk, danger, chance; event, incident.
aventurado adj. adventurous, risky, bold, daring.
aventurar v. to venture, to risk, to hazard; —**se** to run the risk of, to dare.
aventurero adj. adventurous; m. adventurer.
avergonzar v. irr. to shame, to confound; —**se** to feel ashamed.
avería f. damage; aviary, birdhouse; Am. misfortune; mischief.
averiar v. to damage, to spoil, to

— 29 —

hurt, —se to become damaged; to spoil.

averiguar v. to find out, to investigate, to inquire; — **secretos ajenos** to pry into other people's secrets.

aversión f. aversion, dislike, reluctance, antipathy.

avestruz m. ostrich; an ignoramus.

avezado p.p. & adj. accustomed, trained.

aviación f. aviation.

aviador m. aviator, flyer; purveyor, provider; Am. moneylender or promoter.

aviar v. to equip, to supply, to prepare, to make ready; Am. to lend money or equipment; **estar aviado** to be surrounded by difficulties; to be in a fix.

ávido adj. eager, greedy, avid.

avinagrado adj. sour; acid; cross; crabbed; peeved; morose.

avío m. provision, supply, preparation; Am. loan of money or equipment; —**s** equipment; —**s de pescar** fishing tackle.

avión m. airplane; martin.

avisar v. to inform, to give notice; to advise, to announce; to warn; to admonish.

aviso m. notice, advice, announcement, warning, advertisement.

avispa f. wasp.

avispado adj. lively, keen, clever, wideawake, brisk, vigorous; Am. frightened, scared.

avispar v. to spur, to incite; to hurry, to stimulate; —**se** to be on the alert, to be uneasy; Am. to become frightened, scared.

avispero m. wasp's nest.

avispón m. hornet.

avistar v. to glimpse, to catch sight of: —**se** to see each other, to meet.

avivar v. to enliven, to give life to, to animate, to revive, to bright, to quicken.

avizor adj. alert, watchful.

avizorar v. to watch with attention.

aya f. child's nurse, governess, instructress.

ayer adv. yesterday; lately; not long ago; **de** — **acá** from yesterday to this moment.

ayo m. tutor, guardian.

ayuda f. aid, help, assistance, succour.

ayudante m. assistant; aid-de-camp; adjutant.

ayudar v. to aid, to help, to assist.

ayunar v. to fast.

ayunas: en — fasting; **en** — **de** totally ignorant of.

ayuno m. fast, abstinence.

ayuntamiento m. municipal government; town hall.

azabache m. jet; titmouse; —**s** ornaments.

azada f. spade; hoe.

azadón m. hoe.

azafrán m. saffron.

azahar m. orange or lemon blossom; **agua de** — orange-flower water.

azar m. hazard, chance; accident.

azogue m. quicksilver.

azolvar v. to clog, to obstruct water conducts.

azorar v. to disturbe, to startle; to bewilder, to terrify, to confound; —**se** to be startled, perplexed; to be uneasy.

azotaina f. flogging, lashing, beating.

azotar v. to whip, to lash, to beat, to flagellate; Am. to thresh (rice); — **las calles** to "beat the pavement", walk the streets.

azote m. whip; lash with a whip; calamity; scourge, affliction.

azotea f. flat roof.

azteca m. & f. Aztec (ancient inhabitant of Mexico), coin of gold worth 20 pesos.

azúcar m. sugar; — **de pilón** loaf sugar; — **mascabado** brown sugar.

azucarar v. to sugar, to sweeten; to soften; to ice with sugar, to coat with sugar; —**se** Am. to crystallize, to turn sugar.

azucarera f. sugar bowl; sugar mill.

azucena f. white lily.

azufre m. sulphur.

azul adj. blue; — **celeste** sky blue; — **marino** navy blue; **tiempos** —**es** Am. hard times.

azulado adj. bluish, azure, azured.

azular v. to dye or color blue, to turn blue.

azulejo m. glazed tile; Am. bluebird; adj. bluish.

azuzar v. to urge, to egg on; to incite; to halloo, to set on dogs; to irritate.

B

baba f. drivel, slaver, saliva; slime, slimy secretion, spittle; Am. small alligator.
babear v. to drivel; to slobber; to slaver.
babero m. baby's bib, chin cloth.
babor m. port, port side.
babosear v. to slaver, to drivel, to keep one's mouth open; to act like a fool.
baboso adj. driveling; slobbering, slimy, silly; foolishly sentimental; Am. silly, idiotic, foolish.
babucha f. slipper; a — Am. pickaback, on the back or shoulders.
bacalao m. codfish.
bacilo m. bacillus.
bacín m. pot, chamber pot.
bacinica f. chamber pot.
bacteria f. bacterium; —s bacteria.
bacteriología f. bacteriology.
bacteriológico adj. bacteriological, pertaining to bacteriology.
báculo m. staff, cane; aid, support; walking stick; — pastoral bishop's crosier.
bache m. rut, hole in the road.
bachiller m. bachelor (one who holds degree); talkative person, babbler, prater.
bachillerato m. bachelor's degree; studies for the bachelor's degree.
badajo m. clapper of a bell; foolish talker.
badana f. sheepskin.
bagaje m. baggage, army pack mule.
bagatela f. trifle, bagatelle.
bagazo m. the remains of sugar cane, grapes, olives, palms, etc., which have been pressed; residue.
bahía f. bay, harbor.
bailador m. dancer; adj. dancing.
bailar v. to dance, to spin around.
bailarín m. dancer.
baile m. dance; ball; ballet.
bailotear v. to jig, jiggle; to dance poorly; to dance around; to dance without spirit.
baja f. fall (of prices), war casualty; places vacant in a company or regiment; dar de — to discharge, to muster out.
bajada f. descent; slope, dip (on a road); de — on the way down; subidas y —s ups and downs.
bajar v. to go down; to descend; to come down; to drop (as price or value); to lower; to take or carry down; to humble; —se to get down or off; to alight; Am. to stop at a hotel.
bajel m. boat, ship, vessel.
bajeza f. vile act or remark, meanness, fawning, abjectness, lowliness, baseness, degradation.
bajío m. shoal, sand bank, shallow; Am. low land.
bajo adj. low, short; soft; bass; shallow, subdued, humble; abject, despicable, vile, infamous, degraded; piso — ground floor, first floor; prep. under, underneath; por lo — on the sly.
bala f. bullet, shot, ball; bale.
balada f. ballad.
baladí adj. trivial, flimsy; despicable, worthless.
balance m. balance, equilibrium, fluctuation, vibration; balance sheet; rocking, rolling.
balancear v. to balance; to rock, to roll; to swing, to sway, to waver.
balanceo m. rocking, rolling, swinging, balancing; wavering; wabbling, oscillation.
balanza f. balance, scale.
balar v. to bleat.
balaustrada f. balustrade, banisters, railing.
balaustre v. banister.
balazo m. shot, bullet wound; adj. Am. clever, cunning.
balbucear v. to stammer, to stutter, to babble.
balbuceo m. babble, babbling.
balcón m. balcony.
baldado m. cripple; adj. & p.p. crippled.
baldar v. to cripple; to trump (a card)
balde m. pail; bucket; de — free of charge; en — in vain, es en — it is time lost.
baldío adj. barren; fallow; uncultivated, untilled; m. fallow land, wasteland.
baldón m. infamy, insult, opprobium, censure.
baldosa f. floor tile; paving stone.
balido m. bleat, bleating.
balneario m. bathing resort; adj. pertaining to bathing resorts or medicinal springs.
balompié m. football.
balota f. ballot.
balsa f. pond, pool; raft; Am. marsh
bálsamo m. balsam, balm.
baluarte m. bulwark.
ballena f. whale; whalebone.

— 31 —

bambolear v. to sway, to swing, to rock, to reel, to stagger, to totter; to vacilate.
bambú m. bamboo.
banana f. banana.
banano m. banana tree.
banasta f. large basket.
banca f. bench; banking, banking house.
bancario adj. bank, pertaining to a bank.
bancarrota f. bankruptcy, failure, collapse.
banco m. bank, bench, stool; school (of fish); Am. pile of grain; small hill on a plain.
banda f. band; ribbon; sash; gang; group; party; flock; side; edge, border.
bandada f. flock of birds; Am. gang.
bandeja f. tray, a kind of metallic waiter; Am. bowl.
bandera f. banner, standard, flag, ensign; **parar uno —** Am. to take the lead, to be a gangleader.
banderilla f. dart with a small flag used for baiting bulls; **clavar a uno una —** to goad or taunt someone; **pegar una —** Am. to touch for a loan.
banderillero m. bullfighter who sticks the **banderillas** into the bull.
banderín m. banneret, small flag.
banderola f. streamer, small banner or flag; pennant.
bandidaje m. banditry, highway robbery; bandits.
bandido m. highwayman, bandit, robber; gangster.
bandurria f. bandore.
banquero m. banker.
banqueta f. bench without a back, tripod; a stool with three legs; Am. sidewalk.
banquete m. banquet.
banquetear v. to banquet, to feast.
banquillo m. bench, stool.
bañada f. shower, spray, dip, bath.
bañar v. to bathe, to wash, to dip; **—se** to take a bath.
bañera f. bathtub.
bañista m. & f. bather, bathkeeper.
baño m. bath, bathtub, bathing, bathing place, balneary; cover, coating; **— de María** double boiler; **— ruso** Am. steam bath; **— de asiento** hip bath.
baqueta f. rod, ramrod, gunstick, **—s** drumsticks; **tratar a la —** to treat scornfully, despotically.
baquiano m. Am. native guide through the wilderness, pampas etc.; adj. having an instinctive sense of direction.
bar m. bar, taproom, tavern.
baraja f. pack of cards.
barajar v. to shuffle the cards, to mix, to jumble together; to scuffle, to wrangle; Am. to hinder, to obstruct.
baranda f. railing; **echar de —** to exaggerate.
barandal m. banister, railing.
barandilla f. balustrade, railing.
barata f. barter, exchange; **Am.** bargain sale.
baratear v. to sell cheap; to cheapen; to cut the price of; to sell under price.
baratija f. trinket, trifle, toy.
barato adj. cheap, bought or sold at a low price; m. bargain sale.
baratura f. cheapness.
baraúnda f. noise, hurly-burly, confusion, fluttering, clamor, uproar.
barba f. chin, beard; **—s** whiskers; **—s de ballena** whalebone.
barbacoa f. barbecue, barbecued meat.
barbado adj. bearded, barbed, barbated.
barbaridad f. barbarism, barbarity, cruelty; rudeness; **una — de** a lot of; **¡qué —!** what nonsense!; what an atrocity!
barbarie f. barbarity, cruelty; barbarousness, savagery, lack of culture, ignorance; brutality.
bárbaro adj. barbarous, barbarian, fierce, cruel, savage, crude, coarse.
barbechar v. to plow, to plough; to fallow.
barbecho m. first plowing of the land; plowed land; fallow ground ploughed in order to be sown.
barbería f. barbershop; trade of a barber.
barbero m. barber; Am. flatterer.
barbilla f. point of the chin.
barbón adj. bearded.
barca f. boat, bark, launch, barge.
barco m. boat, ship.
bardo m. bard, minstrel, poet.
barniz m. varnish; glaze; printer's ink.
barnizar v. to varnish, to glaze.
barómetro m. barometer.
barquero m. boatman, bargeman, waterman, ferryman.
barquillo m. rolled wafer.
barra f. bar; rod; railing; sand bar; **— de jabón** bar of soap.

— 32 —

barrabasada f. mischief; mean prank; rash, hasty act; trick, plot, intrigue.

barraca f. hut, cabin, cottage, shack; Am. large shed, warehouse.

barranca f. ravine, gorge; Am. cliff.

barreminas m. mine-sweeper.

barrena f. auger, drill; gimlet (small tool for boring holes); spinning dive (of a plane).

barrenar v. to drill, to bore; to scuttle (a ship); to blast (a rock).

barrendero m. sweeper.

barrer v. to sweep; to sweep away; to scour; Am. to defeat; al — Am. altogether, as a whole.

barrera f. barrier, obstacle, barricade, parapet.

barreta f. small iron bar; lining of a shoe; Am. pick, pickaxe.

barrica f. cask, keg.

barrida f. Am. sweep, sweeping.

barrido m. sweep, sweeping, sweepings.

barriga f. belly, bulge; abdomen.

barrigón adj. big-bellied.

barril m. barrel, keg.

barrio m. district, neighborhood; suburb; —s bajos slums.

barro m. mud, clay, pimple; earthenware; hacer (or cometer) un — Am. to commit a blunder.

barroso adj. muddy; pimply; reddish; camino — muddy road.

barrote m. iron bar; brace; rung.

barruntar v. to foresee, to calculate, to conjecture by signs, to have a presentiment.

barrunto m. foreboding, conjecture, mark, sign, guess, indication, hint.

bártulos m. pl. household goods, implements, tools.

barullo m. hubbub, racket, disorder, confusion.

basar v. to base, to place, to fix, to establish.

basca f. nausea, sickness to one's stomach, squeamishness; tener —s to be nauseated, to be sick to one's stomach.

báscula f. scale; platform scale; lever, pole, staff.

base f. base, basis, foundation, ground, foot, footing.

básico adj. basic.

basquetbol m. basketball.

bastante adj. enough, sufficient; adv. enough.

basta adv. stop.

bastar v. to be enough; to suffice.

bastardilla f. italic type, italics.

bastardo adj. bastard, spurious, illegitimate.

bastidor m. wing; frame; embroidery frame; window sash; easel; entre —es behind the scene, off stage.

bastilla f. hem, the edge of a cloth doubled and sewed; the Bastille.

bastimento m. supply, provisions; vessel, ship.

basto adj. coarse; m. pack saddle for beasts of burden; club (in cards).

bastón m. walking stick, cane; military command; empuñar el — to take the command.

basura f. rubbish, scraps, garbage, refuse, sweepings, filth swept away; dung, manure, ordure.

basurero m. garbage or rubbish dump; manure pile; garbage man, rubbish man; street cleaner; dust man.

bata f. morning or night gown, lounging robe; housecoat, wrapper, dressing gown, smock.

batahola f. hubbub, racket, uproar.

batalla f. battle, struggle, fight, combat.

batallar v. to battle, to struggle, to fight, to combat.

batallón m. battalion.

batata f. sweet potato, Spanish potato.

bate m. Am. baseball bat.

batea f. tray, trough; bowl; barge; Am. washtub.

bateador m. Am. batter (in baseball).

batería f. battery (military, naval or electric); — de cocina set of kitchen utensils; dar — Am. to rise a rumpus; to plod, work hard.

batidor m. beater; scout; one of the lifeguards who rides before a royal coach.

batintín m. gong.

batir v. to beat, to whip, to defeat; to reconnoiter, to explore; to flap; Am. to rinse (clothes); to denounce; —se to fight; — palmas to clap, to applaud.

baturrillo m. meddley, mixture, hodgepodge, mash, salmagundi.

batuta f. orchestra conductor's baton or wand; llevar la — to lead, to be the leader.

baúl m. trunk, chest; — mundo large trunk; llenar el — to fill the paunch, the belly.

bautismo m. baptism, christening; **nombre de —** Christian name; **romper a uno el —** to give one a blow on the head.
bautista m. & f. Baptist; baptizer.
bautizar v. to baptize, to christen; **— el vino** to mix water with wine.
bautizo m. christening, baptism.
baya f. berry.
bayetón m. thick wool cloth.
bayo adj. bay, reddish brown.
baza f. trick (cards played in one round); **meter —** to meddle, to butt into a conversation; **no dejar meter —** not to let a person put a word in edgewise.
bazar m. bazaar; department store.
bazo m. spleen.
bazofia f. scraps, refuse, garbage, offal, hogwash, dregs.
beatitud f. bliss, blessedness, beatitude.
beato adj. blessed, beatified; devout; overpious; hypocritical.
bebé m. baby.
bebedero m. drinking trough; spout.
bebedor m. drinker; drunkard; tippler; toper.
beber v. to drink, to drink in, to absorb.
bebida f. drink, beverage; **dado a la —** given to drink.
beca f. scholarship, fellowship, pension; sash worn over the academic gown.
becerro m. young bull; calf; calfskin.
becuadro m. natural sign (in music).
befa f. scoff, jeer, derision, mock.
befar v. to scoff, to jeer at, to mock.
bejuco m. cane; **silla de —** cane chair.
beldad f. beauty.
belga adj. m. & f. Belgian.
bélico adj. warlike, martial, military.
beligerante adj. m. & f. belligerent.
bellaco adj. sly, deceitful, villain; swindler, rascal, wicked.
bellaquear v. to cheat, to play tricks; to play knavish tricks, to swindle.
bellaquería f. cunning, trickery, knavery; sly act or remark.
belleza f. beauty, fairness, handsomeness, flourish.
bello adj. beautiful, handsome, fair, fine, perfect; **el — sexo** the fair sex.

bellota f. acorn.
bendecir v. irr. to bless, to consecrate.
bendición f. benediction, blessing; **echarle la — a una cosa** Am. to give something up for lost.
bendito adj. blessed; sainted, saintly; **es un —** he is a saint, he is a simple soul.
benefactor m. benefactor, patron.
beneficencia f. beneficence, charity, kindness.
beneficiar v. to benefit, to do good; to cultivate (land); to exploit (a mine); to treat (metals); Am. to slaugter (cattle) for marketing.
beneficio m. benefit, profit, favour, kindness, benefaction; exploitation of a mine; land cultivation; Am. fertilizer; slaughtering (of cattle).
benemérito m. worthy, notable, meritorious; adj. worthy.
benevolencia f. benevolence, kindness.
benévolo adj. benevolent, good, kindly.
benigno adj. benign, gentle, mild, kind; merciful, pious.
beodo adj. drunk; m. drunkard.
berenjena f. eggplant; Am. kind of squash.
bergantín m. brig, brigantine.
bermejo adj. crimson, of a bright reddish color.
berrear v. to bellow, to bleat like a calf, to low; to sing off key; to scream.
berrido m. bellow, bellowing, scream.
berrinche m. fit of anger, passion; tantrum.
berza f. cabbage.
besar v. to kiss; to touch closely.
beso m. kiss.
bestia f. beast; dunce, idiot.
bestialidad f. bestiality, brutality, filthiness.
besugo m. sea bream.
besuquear v. to kiss repeatedly.
betabel f. Am. beet.
betún m. bitumen; black pitch, shoeblacking.
Biblia f. Bible.
bíblico adj. Biblical.
biblioteca f. library, set of volumes, bookcase.
bibliotecario m. librarian.
bicicleta f. bicycle.
biciclista m. & f. bicyclist, bicycle rider.

BICHO   **BOCA**

bicho m. insect, bug; any small animal; an insignificant person.
bien adv. well; — que although; ahora — now then; más — rather; si — although; m. supreme goodness; object of esteem or love; good, utility, benefit; —es raíces real estate; —es property; —es inmuebles real estate.
bienaventurado adj. blessed, happy; fortunate.
bienaventuranza f. blessedness; beatitude; bliss; prosperity, human felicity.
bienestar m. well-being, comfort, welfare; peace of mind, calm, felicity.
bienhechor m. benefactor.
bienvenida f. welcome.
bienvenido adj. welcome.
biftec, bistec, bisté m., beefsteak.
bifurcación f. fork, forking, bifurcation, branching out; railway junction; branch railroad.
bifurcarse v. to fork, branch off; to divide in two branches; to bifurcate.
bigamia f. bigamy.
bigote m. mustache.
bilis f. bile.
billar m. billiards; billiard room.
billete m. ticket, note, bill, banknote.
billón m. billion, a million of millions.
bimestre m. two month period; bimonthly salary, rent, etc; adj. bimonthly.
bimestral adj. bimonthly.
biografía f. biography.
biología f. biology.
biombo m. folding screen.
birlar v. to snatch away, to steal; to dispossess; to kill or knock down with one blow.
bisabuela f. great-grandmother.
bisabuelo m. great-grandfather.
bisagra f. hinge.
bisiesto adj. leap (year).
bisojo m. squint-eyed.
bisturí m. bistoury.
bitoque m. barrel plug, stopper; bung; Am. faucet; injection point.
bizarría f. gallantry, bravery; generosity, fortitude, liberality.
bizarro adj. gallant, brave, high-spirited, generous.
bizco adj. cross-eyed.
bizcocho m. hardtack, hard biscuit; cooky; whiting; — borracho cake dipped in wine.
biznieta f. great-granddaughter.

biznieto m. great-grandson.
blanco adj. white; blank, hoar, hoary, fair; m. white man; blank sheet; aim, target, goal; — del ojo white of the eye; dar en el — to hit the mark; tela or ropa blanca linen; de punta en — point blank; tirar al — to shoot at the target.
blancura f. whiteness.
blancuzco adj. whitish.
blandir v. to brandish, to flourish, to swing, to hurtle, to whirl around; to quiver tremulously.
blando adj. bland, smooth, soft; pliant; milky, flabby; liquid; mild; moderate; effeminate, delicate; tractable; good-natured.
blanducho adj. flabby; soft.
blandura f. softness; mildness, gentleness, daintiness, delicay.
blanquear v. to whiten, to bleach; to whitewash; to show white; to begin to turn white.
blanqueo m. whitening, bleach, bleaching, whitewash.
blanquillo adj. whitish; m. Am. egg; white peach.
blasfemar v. to blaspheme; to curse, to swear.
blasfemia f. blasphemy.
blasón m. coat of arms, heraldry, blazonry; armorial.
blasonar v. to boast; to blazon.
blindaje m. armor, armor plating; blind.
block m. Am. tablet, pad of paper.
blondo adj. blond.
bloque m. block; Am. pad of paper, tablet; political block.
bloquear v. to blockade.
bloqueo m. blockade.
blusa f. blouse.
boato m. pomp, ostentation, pompous show.
bobada f. foolishness, folly; a silly speech.
bobalicón adj. foolish, silly; m. simpleton, blockhead, dunce.
bobear v. to act or talk in a stupid or foolish manner; to fool around; to stare foolishly.
bobería f. foolishness, folly, nonsense; foolish remark; foolery.
bobina f. bobbin; electric coil.
bobo adj. simple, foolish, stupid; dunce, dolt; easily cheated, booby.
boca f. mouth, entrance, opening, hole; muzzle; chops; taste, flavour; — abajo face downward; — arriba face upward; a — de jarro at close range; andar de

— 35 —

— en — to be the talk of the town; **andar con la — abierta** to go gaping about; **torcer la —** to pout or frown.
bocacalle f. street intersection.
bocado m. mouthful, morsel; gobbet; small portion; bite.
bocanada f. mouthful; a puff of smoke; **— de viento** a sudden blast of wind.
boceto m. sketch; outline; skit.
bocina f. horn; trumpet; a bugle horn; speaking trumpet; megaphone.
bochorno m. sultry weather; suffocating heat; blush; flush; embarrassment; shame.
bochornoso adj. sultry, embarrassing; shameful.
boda f. marriage, wedding, nuptials; **— de negros** a noisy party; **—s de Camacho** lavish feast, banquet.
bodega f. cellar; wine cellar; storeroom; warehouse; magazine; grocery; Am. grocery store.
bodeguero m. keeper of a wine cellar, liquor dealer; storekeeper; Am. dealer.
bofe m. lungs; Am. snap, easy job; **echar uno los —s** to throw oneself into a job; to work hard; **ser un —** Am. to be a bore; to be repulsive.
bofetada f. slap; **dar una —** to treat with the utmost contempt.
bofetón m. a cuff or violent blow with the fist upon the face; a big slap, blow, hard sock, wallop.
boga f. vogue, fashion; **estar en —** to be fashionable; rowing; m. rower.
bogar v. to row.
bohemio adj. & m. Bohemian.
bohío m. Am. cabin, shack, hut.
boina f. cap.
bola f. ball; game of bowling; fib, lie; shoe polish; Am. brawl, riot, disturbance, revolution; **no dar pie con —** not to do things right, not to hit the mark; to make mistakes; **darle a la —** Am. to hit the mark.
boleada f. Am. lassoing with boleadoras; hunting expedition (with boleadoras); shoeshine.
boleadoras f. pl. Am. lasso with balls at the ends.
bolear v. to play billiards; to bowl; to lie, to fib; Am. to lasso with boleadoras; to entangle; to polish (shoes).
boleta f. ticket; ticket or warrant for receiving money; certificate, pass; Am. ballot; first draft of a deed.
boletín m. bulletin.
boletería f. ticket office.
boleto m. Am. ticket.
boliche m. bowl; bowling alley; Am. cheap tavern; gambling joint; cheap store or shop, notions' store, variety store.
bolita f. small ball; Am. ballot (small ball used in voting); marble.
bolo m. one of the ninepins (used in bowling); dunce, stupid fellow; Am. a present given by the godfather; **jugar a los —s** to bowl.
bolsa f. bag, purse, pouch; Am. pocket; exchange.
bolsillo m. pocket, pocketbook.
bolsista m. stockbroker, market operator.
bollo m. bun, muffin; bump; lump; Am. loaf of bread; **—s** Am. difficulties, troubles.
bomba f. bomb, pump; lamp globe; Am. false news; firecracker, skyrocket; **estar a prueba de —** to be bomb-proof; **— para incendios** fire engine; **estar con una —** to be drunk; **— de achique** bilge pump.
bombachas f. pl. Am. loose fitting breeches.
bombacho adj. loose fitting (trousers or breeches).
bombardear v. to bomb, to bombard.
bombardeo m.; bombardment, bombing; **avión de —** bomber, bombing plane.
bombardero m. bombardier, bomber.
bombear v. to bomb; to pump; to praise, to extol; Am. to pump; to puff hard on a cigar or cigarette.
bombero m. fireman; pumper.
bombilla f. electric-light bulb; Am. kerosene lamp tube; small tube for drinking mate.
bombo m. large drum, bass drum; player on a bass drum; Am. pomp, ostentation; buttocks, rump; **dar —** to praise; to extol; **darse —** Am. to put on airs; **irse uno al —** Am. to fail; adj. stunned; Am. lukewarm; slightly rotten; stupid, silly, simple; **fruta bomba** Am. papaya.
bombón m. bombon, candy, chocolate; **— de altea** marshmallow.

bonachón adj. good-natured; native; simple.
bonanza f. fair weather; prosperity; rich vein of ore.
bondad f. goodness, kindness.
bondadoso adj. good, kind.
bonito adj. pretty; affecting elegance and neatness; m. striped tunny.
bono m. certificate, bond, share.
boñiga f. dung, manure; cowdung.
boqueada f. gape, gasp; the last gasp.
boquear v. to open one's mouth, to gape, to gasp; to breathe one's last, to expire.
boquete m. breach, gap, hole, opening, narrow entrance.
boquiabierto adj. openmouthed; having the mouth open.
boquilla f. little mouth; small opening; cigarette or cigar holder; opening in a canal for irrigating lands.
borbollón m. spurt; spurting; big bubble; bubbling up; flash.
borbotar v. to gush out; to flash; to bubble up; to spurt; to boil over.
bordado m. embroidery.
bordadura f. embroidery.
bordar v. to embroider.
borde m. border, edge; margin, verge, fringe; brim of a vessel.
bordear v. to skirt, to go along the edge of; Am. to trim with a border.
bordo m. board; side of a ship; tack; Am. ridge; **hacer un —** Am. to make a small, temporary dam; **a — on** board.
borla f. tassel; tuft, lock, flaunt; doctor's cap, doctor's degree; powder puff; **tomar uno la —** to get a doctor's degree.
borlarse v. Am. to get a doctor's degree.
borrachera f. drunkenness; madness; great folly; drunken spree.
borrachín m. toper.
borracho adj. drunk; m. drunkard, intoxicated.
borrador m. rough draft, rough copy; Am. rubber, eraser.
borrar v. to blot out; to erase; to rub off.
borrasca f. storm, tempest; danger.
borrascoso adj. stormy.
borrego m. lamb from one to two years old; simpleton; Am. false news.
borrico m. donkey, ass, jument; fool; sawhorse.

borrón m. blotch; blur, blot.
borronear v. to blotch, to blot; to scribble; to blur, to make a rough sketch.
boruca f. racket, noise.
boscaje m. grove, thicket, woods, landscape; boscage, clump or cluster of trees.
bosque m. forest, woods, grove.
bosquejar v. to sketch, to plan, to outline, to design, to project.
bosquejo m. sketch, plan, outline; **en —** in an unfinished state.
bostezar v. to yawn; to gape.
bostezo m. yawn.
bota f. small leather wine bag; boot; butt or pipe; adj. Am. stupid, clumsy; drunk.
botar v. to launch; to cast; to throw; to fling; to bounce; Am. to waste, to squander; to fire, to dismiss; **—se** Am. to lie down.
botarate m. fool; braggart; madcap; Am. spendthrift.
bote m. small jar; boat; bounce; blow; jump; gallipot; Am. liquor bottle; jail; **estar de — en —** to be crowded.
botella f. bottle.
botica f. drugstore; apothecary's shop.
boticario m. druggist, apothecary.
botija f. earthen jug; fat person; Am. buried treasure; belly; **poner a uno como — verde** Am. to dress down, to scold, to insult a person.
botín m. booty, plunder; high shoe; Am. sock.
botiquín m. medicine cabinet; medicine kit, medicine chest; Am. liquor store, wine shop.
botón m. button, bud; knob, handle; **—es** bellboy.
bóveda f. arch or vault, arched roof, underground cellar; burial place.
boxear v. to box; to fight with the fists.
boxeo m. boxing.
boya f. buoy; float net; Am. crease, dent; **estar en la buena —** Am. to be in good humor.
bozal m. muzzle; a temporary headstall for a horse; bells on a harness; beginner, novice; adj. unexperienced, wild, green, untamed, stupid.
bozo m. down (on the upper lip) which precedes the beard; mustache; outside part of the mouth.
bracear v. to move or to swing the

arms; to struggle; to crawl, swim with a crawl.
bracero m. one who walks arm in arm with another; day-labourer; de — arm in arm; servir de — a una señora to serve as an escort, to give a lady one's arm.
bramante m. pack thread, hemp cord, hemp string; Brabant linen; adj. roaring, bellowing.
bramido m. cry, roar, bellow, howl, clamour, tempestuos roaring.
brasa f. live coal; red-hot coal; burning wood.
brasero m. brazier; fire pan, grate, hearth; Am. brick cooking stove.
bravata f. bravado, brag, boastfulness, defiance.
bravear v. to bully, to hector, bluster.
bravío adj. savage, ferocious, wild, rustic, untamed, coarse.
bravo adj. brave, valiant, wild, ferocious, hectoring, bullying; Am. angry; hot, highly seasoned.
bravura f. ferocity, fierceness; courage, bravado; show of boldness.
braza f. fathom.
brazada f. armful; movement of the arms; a una — at arm's length.
brazalete m. armlet, bracelet.
brazo m. arm; branch, bough of a tree; valour; —s day laborers; del — Am. arm in arm; luchar a — partido to wrestle; to fight hand to hand.
brea f. tar, pitch; artificial bitumen; coarse canvas; Am. money.
brecha f. breach, gap, opening.
bregar v. to struggle; to fight; to contend.
breve adj. brief; en — shortly.
brevedad f. brevity, briefness, shortness conciseness.
bribón m. vagrant, impostor, a knave; adj. rascal; idle, indolent.
brida f. bridle of a horse; rein.
brigada f. brigade.
brillante adj. brilliant, bright, shining, sparkling, radiant.
brillantez f. brilliance, dazzle.
brillar v. to shine, to sparkle, to glitter, to gleam.
brillo m. brilliancy, luster, sparkle, shine.
brincar v. to jump, to leap, to frisk, to skip, to hop, to bounce.
brinco m. jump, leap, frisk, skip, hop, jerk, bounce.
brindar v. to toast, to drink to the health of; to offer cheerfully; to invite.
brío m. vigor, liveliness; valor; courage; strength, force.
brioso adj. lively, brave, vigourous, spirited.
brisa f. breeze.
británico adj. British, Britannic.
brizna f. particle, chip, fragment, splinter, morsel; blade of grass.
brocal m. curb, curbstone (of a well); metal rim of the scabbard of a sword.
brocha f. painter's brush; loaded dice; **cuadro de — gorda** badly done painting; **pintor de — gorda** house painter.
brochada f. stroke of the brush; stroke.
brochazo m. blow with a brush; brush stroke.
broche m. brooch, clasp, clip, fastener; hooks and eyes, locket.
broma f. jest, joke; fun, merriment; rubbish mixed with mortar; gruel made of oatmeal; clatter; Am. disappointment, irrigation; de — in jest; fuera de — all joking aside.
bromear v. to joke, to jest, to droll.
bronca f. quarrel, dispute, wrangle; armar una — to cause a disturbance; to raise a rumpus.
bronce m. bronze; trumpet.
bronceado adj. bronzed; bronze-colored; act and effect of bronzing.
bronco adj. hoarse; raspy, harsh; coarse, rough, unpolished, crusty, morose; rude; untamed; uncouth, wild.
broquel m. buckler, support, protection, shield.
brotar v. to shoot forth; to bud; to break out on the skin; to gush; to flow; to spring forth; to germinate.
broza f. brushwood, underbrush; remains of leaves; thicket, rubbish, refuse, trash; coarse, hard brush.
bruces: de — face downward, mouth downward.
bruja f. witch; hag; sorceress; a mischievous woman.
brujo m. sorcerer, conjurer, magician, wizard.
brújula f. compass; magnetic needle; peephole, gun sight.
bruma f. mist, fog, haze.
brumoso adj. haziness, foggy, misty.

bruñir v. irr. to burnish, to polish; to put on make up; to cut diamonds.
brusco adj. blunt, rude, abrupt.
brutal adj. brutal, brutish, bestial, savage.
brutalidad f. brutality, brutishness.
bruto adj. brutal, stupid, coarse; **peso —** gross weight; **diamante en —** rough diamond; m. brute, beast.
bucal adj. oral, buccal.
bucear v. to dive; to dive into, to plunge into; to explore thoroughly a subject; to go under water in search of anything.
bucle m. curl, ringlet; buckle.
buche m. crop; mouthful; maw or stomach; wrinkle; Am. goiter.
budín m. pudding.
buen(o) adj. good, kind, useful, well, simple, fair, plain; in good health; **de buenas a primeras** all of a sudden; **por la(s) buena(s) o por la(s) mala(s)** willingly or unwillingly.
buey m. ox, bullock.
búfalo m. buffalo.
bufanda f. muffler, scarf.
bufar v. to snort; to puff and blow with anger; to swell with indignation or pride; to grumble; —**se** Am. to swell, to bulge.
bufete m. desk, writing table; lawyer's office.
bufido m. snort, bellow.
bufón m. buffoon, harlequin, merry andrew, scoffer, jester, clown, humorist; adj. comical, funny; jocose.
bufonada f. buffoonery, drollery, jesting raillery; wisecrack.
bufonear v. to clown, to jest.
buhardilla f. small garret, attic, skylight.
búho m. owl.
buhonero m. peddler, hawker.
buitre m. vulture.
bujía f. candle, candle power, waxcandle, candlestick; spark plug.
bula f. bull (papal document); papal seal.
bulevar m. boulevard.
bulto m. bulk, volume; lump, swelling, body, bundle, protuberance, tumor; Am. briefcase; **a —** indistinctly, confusedly, by guess; **escurrir el —** to dodge; **imagen de —** statue, sculpture; **una verdad de —** an evident true.
bulla f. shouting, uproar; noisy crowd.

bullicio m. noise, uproar.
bullicioso adj. boisterous, noisy; gay; lively; turbulent, stormy.
bullir v. irr. to boil; to buzz about; to bustle; to move; Am. to deride.
buñuelo m. fritter; botch; poor piece of work.
buque m. ship, boat, vessel.
burbuja f. bubble.
burdo adj. coarse.
burgués adj. bourgeois, burgher, middle-class citizen.
burla f. jest, mockery, scoff; **de —** in jest.
burlador m. practical joker; jester, scoffer; seducer; mocker, jeerer.
burlar v. to mock, to ridicule, to deceive, to scoff, to laugh, to hoax, jibe; to make fun of; to jest, to fleer, to dally; —**se de** to scoff at, to laugh at.
burlón m. jester, teaser, great wag or scoffer.
burro m. ass, donkey, jument; a stupid, ignorant being; Am. stepladder; adj. stupid.
busca f. search; hunting party; pursuit, terrier; —**s** profit on the side; graft.
buscar v. to seek, to search, to look for; to look after, to hunt, to pursuit; **ir a —** to go for; Am. to provoke.
búsqueda f. search, research, inquiry.
busto m. bust (upper part of the body).
butaca f. armchair; orchestra seat; lounging chair.
buzo m. diver.
buzón m. mailbox, letter drop; conduit, canal.

C

cabal adj. complete, entire; exact; just, perfect, accomplished, faultless, consummate; **estar uno en sus —es** to be in one's right mind.
cabalgar v. to ride, to mount (a horse), to ride horseback, to parade on horseback, to horse, to get on horseback; to cover a mare.
caballada f. herd of horses; a number of horses; Am. nonsense, stupidity, blunder.
caballejo m. nag, poor horse.
caballeresco adj. gentlemanly; knightly; chivalrous, gallant.

caballería f. cavalry; horsemanship; mount, horse, knighthood, chivalry, riding beast.

caballeriza f. stable, horses of a stable; number of horses, etc.; stud of horses.

caballerizo m. groom, stableman; head groom of a stable.

caballero m. gentleman; knight, cavalier, nobleman; rider; adj. gentlemanly.

caballerosidad f. chivalry, gentlemanly conduct; nobleness.

caballeroso adj. chivalrous, gentlemanly, nobleness, generous.

caballete m. small horse, sawhorse; easel; ridge of a roof; bridge of the nose; Am. knife and fork rest.

caballo m. horse, knight (chess); Am. stupid or brutal person; a — on horseback; — **padre** stallion; — **castrado** or **capado** gelding.

cabaña f. hut, cabin, cottage, cot; Am. cattle ranch.

cabecear v. to nod, to shake the head, lower the head, to incline to one side; to hang over; to pitch; Am. to begin to rise or fall (a river).

cabeceo m. nodding, pitching, nod of the head.

cabecera f. upper end of; seat; chief city.

cabecilla f. small head; m. leader.

cabellera f. head of hair, long hair, wig, false hair; tail of a comet.

cabello m. hair of the head; fibres of plants; traer algo por los —s to bring in a far fetched fact or quotation; tomar la ocasión por los —s to seize time by the forelock; —s de ángel preserve of fruit cut into small threads.

cabelludo adj. hairy; cuero — scalp.

caber v. irr. to fit into, to go into; to have enough room for; to befall; **no cabe duda** there is no doubt; no cabe más there is no room for more; no — uno en sí to be puffed up with pride; no cabe en lo posible it is absolutely impossible.

cabestrillo m. sling (for an arm).

cabestro m. halter; leading ox; Am. rope cord; advance payment.

cabeza f. head; chief; leader, upper part; capital (city); Am. source (of a river); — **de playa** beachhead; — **de puente** bridgehead.

cabezada f. butt (with the head); bump on the head; nod; shake of the head; pitching (of a ship); headgear (of a harness).

cabezazo m. butt (with the head); bump on the head.

cabezudo adj. big-headed; hardheaded, pig-headed, stubborn, headstrong, chub, chub-bed; obstinate, morose.

cabezón adj. big-headed, pig-headed, stubborn; m. large head; Am. rapids or whirpool in a river.

cabida f. space, room, capacity; tener — con alguien to have influence with some one.

cabildo m. cathedral chapter; municipal council; council room, town hall.

cabina f. cabin (of an airplane).

cabizbajo adj. crestfallen, downcast, pensive.

cable m. cable.

cablegrafiar v. to cable.

cablegrama f. cablegram.

cabo m. end, tip, handle; piece of rope, extreme, extremity; cape, headland; corporal; al — finally; al fin y al — anyway; de — a rabo from beginning to end; estar al — de to be well informed about; llevar a — to carry out; to finish.

cabra f. goat; engine formely used to throw stones; Am. fraud, trick; loaded dice; light two-wheeled carriage; red marks on the legs caused by fire.

cabrillas f. pl. whitecaps (small waves with white crests); Pleiades (constellation); game of skipping stones on the water.

cabrío adj. goatish; macho — he-goat; m. heard of goats.

cabriola f. caper, movement made in dancing; leap, hop, skip, somersault; hacer —s to cut capers, to prance.

cabriolar v. to prance; to caper, to romp, to frolic, to frisk, to jump, to curvet.

cabrito m. kid, kidling, cheveril; kidskin.

cabrón m. he-goat; cuckold (man whose wife is unfaithful).

cacahuate m. peanut.

cacao m. cocoa.

cacarear v. to cackle; to boast, to crow, to brag; Am. to run away from a fight.

cacareo m. cackle; crowing of a cock.

cacería f. hunt, hunting; hunting or fowling party.
cacerola f. saucepan, stewpan.
cacique m. chieftain, chief, political boss; Am. tyrant; one who leads an easy life.
caciquismo m. political bossism.
cacto m. cactus.
cacumen m. acumen, keen insight, understanding, capacity.
cacharro m. earthen pot or vase; broken piece of a pot; crude utensil; Am. cheap trinket.
cachaza f. inactivity, tardiness; slowness, calm, rum.
cachazudo adj. slow, easy going, cool, calm, tranquil.
cachetada f. Am. slap on the face.
cachete m. cheek; slap on the cheek.
cachivache m. piece of junk; broken crockery; worthless fellow; Am. trinket.
cachorro m. cub, small pistol, grown whelp or puppy; Am. rude, ill-bred person.
cachucha f. cap, rowboat; well known Spanish dance; Am. slap.
cada adj. each, every; — uno each one; — y cuando que whenever; a — nada every second.
cadalso m. gallows; sacaffold raised for the excecution of malefactors; platform.
cadáver m. corpse, cadaver.
cadavérico adj. deadly, ghastly, pale, like a corpse; cadaverous.
cadena f. chain, net.
cadencia f. cadence, rhythm.
cadencioso adj. rhythmical.
cadera f. hip.
cadete m. cadet.
caducar v. to dote, to be in one's dotage; to lapse, to expire, to end; to finish; to become extinct, to fall into disuse.
caduco adj. decrepit, very old, feeble; perishable; broken, exhausted.
caer v. irr. to fall, to fall down, to fall off; to decrease, to decline, to die; to tumble; — a to face, overlook; — bien to fit; be becoming; — en cama to fall ill; — en la cuenta to catch on, to get the point; — en gracia, to please; —se de sueño to fall asleep; — de la gracia de alguno to lose one's favour; al — de la noche at nightfall; dejar — to drop.
café m. coffee; café; Am. annoyance, bad time.
cafeína f. caffein.
cafetal m. coffee plantation.
cafetera f. coffeepot; woman cafe owner; coffee service; cofee vendor or merchant; coffee-bean picker.
cafetero m. coffe-house keeper; coffee grower; coffee merchant; owner of a café or coffee-house; Am. coffee drinker.
cafeto m. coffee tree.
caída f. fall, drop, descent, tumble; a la — del sol (or de la tarde) at sunset.
caimán m. cayman, alligator.
caja f. box or case; coffin; chest; drum; — de ahorros savings bank; — fuerte safe; echar a uno con —s destempladas to give someone the gate.
cajero m. cashier; box maker.
cajetilla f. small box; package of cigarettes.
cajón m. large box; chest; coffin; drawer; vendor's booth or stand; Am. narrow canyon; — de muerto coffin; — de ropa clothing store; ser de — or una cosa de — to be a matter of course or a common thing.
cal f. lime; — viva quick or unslaked lime; — muerta slaked lime; apagar la — to slake lime.
calabaza f. pumpkin, squash; gourd; an ignorant person; dar —s to jilt, to turn down (a suitor); to flunk, fall.
calabozo m. dungeon; prison cell; pruning-hook.
calado m. drawn work; open work in metal, wood or linen; draught, the depth of water. Am. wet.
calamar m. squid, cuttlefish.
calambre m. cramp; spasm.
calamidad f. calamity, misfortune.
calandria f. lark, skylark; bunting, calendar lark; mangle.
calar v. to penetrate, to pierce, to plug; to soak through; to make openwork (in cloth, metal or wood); to cut out a sample of; to taste; —se el sombrero to put on one's hat.
calavera f. skull; Am. tail light; m. madcap, wild, hot-brained; reckless fellow.
calcar v. to trace, to copy, to imitate, to counter-draw; to trample on.
calceta f. hose, stocking; hacer — to knit.
calcetería f. hosiery shop; hosiery (business of making hose).

— 41 —

calcetín m. sock.
calcinar v. to burn, to char, to heat.
calcio m. calcium.
calco m. tracing, tracing copy; exact copy; imitation; counter-drawing.
calcular v. to calculate, to figure, to estimate; to reckon.
cálculo m. calculation; estimate, computation; calculus; gravel (in the gall blader, kidney, etc.).
caldear v. to heat; to weld iron and render it to be forged; to warm; Am. —se to become overheated, excited; to get "lit up", to get drunk.
caldera f. cauldron, boiler, kettle.
calderilla f. copper coin.
caldo m. broth; gravy; —s wines.
calefacción f. heat, heating.
calendario m. calendar, almanac; datebook.
caléndula f. marygold.
calentador m. heater; warmer; warmerpan.
calentar v. irr. to warm, to heat, to calefy, to spank; Am. to annoy, to bother; —se to warm oneself; to become heated, excited; to be in heat; to become angry.
calentura f. fever; Am. fit of temper; — tóxica yellow fever; — de pollo feigned illness.
calenturiento adj. feverish; feversick; Am. tubercular.
caletre m. judgment, understanding, discernment, acumen, keenness.
calibrar v. to gauge, to measure the caliber of a ball or a fire arm.
calibre m. caliber, diameter; bore; gauge.
calicanto m. stone masonry.
calicó m. calico, cotton cloth.
calidad f. quality, condition, character.
cálido adj. warm, hot; piquant, calid.
caliente adj. warm, hot, calid, scalding, heated; fiery; Am. angry; bold, brave; brandy in hot water.
calificación f. qualification, grade; judgement.
calificar v. to qualify; to rate; to consider; to judge; to grade; to authorize, to empower; to attest, to certify; Am. to compute (election returns); —se Am. to qualify or register (as a voter).
caligrafía f. penmanship, calligraphy.
cáliz m. chalice, communion cup; goolet; calyx (of a flower).
calma f. quiet, calm, calmness, tranquility.
calmante adj. soothing; mitigating; m. mitigant; sedative; narcotic.
calmar v. to calm, to quiet, to soothe, to alleviate; to pacify.
calmo adj. calm, quiet, slow.
calmoso adj. calm, soothing; slow; phlegmatic; tranquil.
calor m. heat, warmth, ardor, hotness.
calorífero m. heater, radiator; caloriferous; calorifer.
calosfrío m. chill.
calumnia f. slander, calumny.
calumniar v. to slander, to calumniate.
caluroso adj. hot, warm; heated; heating.
calva f. bald head; bald spot; barren spot; game among country people.
calvario m. calvary, place of the Cross; suffering, tribulation.
calvo adj. bald, barren.
calza f. wedge; shoehorn; Am. gold inlay, tooth filling; —s long, loose breeches.
calzada f. paved road; highway; causeway; Am. wide avenue.
calzado m. footwear.
calzador m. shoehorn.
calzar v. to put on (shoes, gloves, spurs); to put a wedge under a wheel; Am. to fill (a tooth).
calzón m. (or **calzones**) breeches, short trousers; Am. drawers; white cotton trousers.
calzoncillos m. pl. drawers, men's shorts.
callado adj. silent, quiet, noisless, discreet.
callar v. to be silent; to hush; to omit speaking of a thing, to pass it over in silence; to conceal; —se to be or keep silent.
calle f. street, paved way; lane; — de árboles alley or walk in a garden.
calleja f. small street, alley lane.
callejear v. to walk the streets, to loiter about the streets, to ramble.
callejero m. street-rambler, street-stroller, street-loiterer; gadder; adj. fond of walking the streets; rambling.

callejón m. alley, lane, narrow pass; — **sin salida** blind alley.
callo m. callous, corn; —**s** tripe (food).
calloso adj. callous, hard, corny, corneous.
cama f. bed, couch, cot, litter; **caer en —** to fall ill; **guardar —** to be confined to bed; **tenderle uno la — a otro** to help one in his love affairs, to set a trap for someone.
camada f. litter, brood.
cámara f. chamber, hall, parlor; house (of a legislative body); cabin, stateroom; chamber (of a gun); **— de aire** inner tube; **— alta** or **de los Pares** the House of Lords **— baja o de los Comunes** the house of Commons; **ayuda de —** valet; **— fotográfica** camera.
camarada m. comrade, partner, fellow, companion.
camaradería f. comradeship, companionship.
camarera f. waitress; chambermaid, stewardess.
camarero m. waiter; chamberlain; steward, valet.
camarilla f. political lobby; a clique of secret counsellors; small group of politicians; "kitchen cabinet"; small room.
camarón m. shrimp.
camarote m. cabin; stateroom, room on board a ship, berth.
cambalache m. swap, barter, exchange.
cambalachear v. to swap, to barter, to exchange.
cambiador m. barterer; money changer; Am. switchman.
cambiante adj. changing; exchanging; bartering; —**s** m. pl. iridiscent colors.
cambiar v. to change, to exchange; to shift, to barter, to commute, to alter; **— de marcha** to shift gears.
cambiavía m. Am. railway switchman. See **guardagujas** and **cambiador.**
cambio m. change; exchange; barter; commutation, railway switch; **libre —** free trade; **en — de** on the other hand; in exchange; **letra de —** bill of exchange.
cambista m. exchange broker, banker; trader in money, cambist; Am. railway switchman.
camello m. camel; engine for setting ships afloat in shoal water.

camilla f. stretcher; small bed, cot, pallet.
camillero m. stretcher berarer.
caminante m. & f. walker, traveler.
caminar v. to walk, to go, to march, to travel; Am. to progress, to prosper.
caminata f. long walk, excursion; hike, jaunt.
camino m. road; course; journey; Am. table runner; **— de hierro** railroad; **— real** highway; **todos los —s llevan a Roma** there are more ways than one to heaven; **de —** on the way.
camión m. truck; wagon; Am. bus.
camionero m. truck driver.
camioneta f. small truck; Am. bus.
camisa. f. shirt; chemise; shift; **— de fuerza** strait jacket; **meterse en — de once varas** to attempt more than one can manage; bite off more than one can chew; **tomar la mujer en —** to marry a woman without money.
camiseta f. undershirt.
camisón m. long shirt; Am. nightgown; gown, dress.
camote m. Am. a variety of sweet potato.
campamento m. encampment; camp; quarters.
campana f. bell; Am. spy, lookout (for thieves); **— de chimenea** mantel, the funnel of a chimney.
campanada f. stroke of a bell; Am. **por — de vacante** once in a blue moon, very seldom.
campanario m. bell tower; belfry.
campanilla f. small bell; bubble; uvula; tassel; bellflower; handbell.
campanillazo m. violent ringing of a bell.
campanilleo m. ringing, tinkling.
campaña f. campaign; level, open country; campaign of an army; period of active service.
campear v. to pasture; to be in the field; to be eminent; Am. to search the plains for lost cattle; to act the bully.
campechano adj. frank, open, gay; ready for amusement.
campeón m. champion, defender; combatant.
campeonato m. championship.
campesino adj. rural, rustic, campestral; m. peasant, countryman, farmer.
campiña f. large field, open country; flat tract of arable land.

campo m. country, field, camp; a — raso in the open; a — traviesa cross-country.

camposanto m. cemetery; burial-ground: churchyard.

camuflaje m. camouflage.

can m. dog; trigger (of a gun); quien quiere a Beltrán, quiere a su — love me, love my dog.

cana f. white hair, gray hair; Am. kind of palm; echar una — al aire to go out for a good time; to go out on a fling; peinar —s to grow old; tener —s to be old.

canadiense adj. m. & f. Canadian.

canal m. canal, channel; strait; duct; gutter on the street; drinking trough for cattle.

canalla f. rabble, mob; m. mean fellow.

canana f. cartridge belt.

canapé m. couch, lounge, sofa, settee.

canario m. canary bird; native of the Canary Islands; interj. great Scott!

canasta f. basket; crate; hamper.

cancelación f. cancellation.

cancelar v. to cancel.

canciller m. chancellor.

canción f. song, verses set to music; poem of one or more stanzas; volver a la misma — to repeat, harp on the same thing.

cancha f. court (for tennis, etc.); sports ground or field; cockpit, enclosure for cockfights; Am. ¡abran —! gangway!; make room!

candado m. padlock; Am. goatee.

candela f. candle, fire; forest fire, light.

candelero m. candlestick; lamp; fishing torch.

candente adj. incandescent, white-hot, red-hot; hierro — red-hot iron.

candidato m. candidate.

candidatura f. candidacy; candidateship.

candidez f. candor, simplicity; whiteness.

candil m. lamp; Am. chandelier.

candileja f. small oil lamp; oil receptacle (of a lamp); —s footlights (of a stage).

candor m. candor, simplicity, innocence, frankness, sincerity; purity of mind.

canela f. cinnamon; an exquisite thing.

cangrejo m. crab.

canguro m. kangaroo.

caníbal m. cannibal.

canica f. marble (small glass or marble ball).

canilla f. long bone (of the arm or leg); cock (of a barrel); faucet; spool (for a sewing machine); Am. slender leg; calf (of the leg); tener — Am. to have physical strength.

canino adj. canine; tener un hambre canina to be ravenous; to be hungry as a dog.

canje m. interchange, exchange; barter.

canjear v. to interchange, to exchange, to barter.

cano adj. gray-headed; gray-haired.

canoa f. canoe.

canon m. canon; precept, rule, principle; catalogue of the books which compose the Holy Scriptures.

canónigo m. canon (churchman).

canonizar v. to canonize, to saint.

canoso adj. gray, gray-haired.

cansado adj. tired, tiresome, weary, boring.

cansancio m. fatigue, weariness.

cansar v. to tire, to fatigue, to weary; —se to get tired.

cantar v. to sing; to squeal, to confess; to recite in poetical manner; — alto Am. to ask a high price; — claro or — a las claras to speak with brutal frankness; m. song, epic poem.

cántaro m. pitcher, jug; llover a —s to rain by bucketfuls.

cantatriz f. singer.

cantera f. quarry; Am. stone block.

cántico m. canticle, religious song.

cantidad f. quantity, amount, measure.

cantilena f. song, ballad; monotonous repetition.

cantimplora f. canteen; metal vessel for cooling water; Am. flask for carrying gunpowder.

cantina f. mess hall; canteen; wine cellar; wine shop; Am. barroom, tavern; Am. saddlebag.

cantinela See cantilena.

cantinero m. bartender; tavernkeeper; canteen-keeper.

canto m. song; singing; canto (division of a long poem); stone; edge; Am. lap; piece.

cantón m. canton, region, corner, district; Am. cotton cloth.

cantor m. singer; song bird.

canturrear or **canturriar** v. to hum, to sing softly; to trill.

canturreo m. hum, humming.
caña f. cane, reed; tall, thin glass; stem; Am. sugar cane brandy; a kind of dance; bluff, boast.
cañada f. narrow canyon, dale, dell, gully, ravine; Am. brook.
cáñamo m. hemp; hemp cloth; Am. hemp cord, rope.
cañamazo m. canvas.
cañaveral m. cane field, reed field, sugar cane plantation.
cañería f. conduit, pipe line, tubing, piping; gas or water main.
caño m. pipe, tube; spout; sewer, narrow channel; Am. branch of a river; stream.
cañón m. cannon, gun; cylindrical tube or pipe; ravine; gorge; canyon; barrel (gun); pinfeather; quill (feather); chimney shaft.
cañonazo m. cannon shot.
cañonear v. to cannonade, to bombard.
cañoneo m. cannonade; bombardment.
cañonero m. gunboat; gunner; **lancha cañonera** gunboat.
caoba f. mahogany.
caos m. chaos, confusion.
capa f. cloak; mantle; layer; stratum, lamina; covering; coating; scum; **so — de** under de guise of, under pretense of; **defender una cosa a — y espada**, to defend a thing with all one's might.
capacidad f. capacity, ability; extent; opportunity; talent.
capacitar v. to enable, to prepare; to fit; to qualify; Am. to empower, to authorize.
capataz m. boss, foreman, overseer; superintendent; conductor.
capaz adj. capable, able, competent; serious; capacious, ample, spacious; roomy.
capellán m. chaplain, clergyman, priest, father.
caperuza f. pointed hood; large hood.
capilla f. chapel; hood; **— ardiente** place with tapers burning around a coffin; **estar en —** to prepare for death.
capirote m. hood; **tonto de —** blockhead; ignorant; fool.
capital m. capital, funds, fortune; f. capital, capital city; adj. capital.
capitalismo m. capitalism.
capitalista m. & f. capitalist; adj. capitalistic.
capitalizar v. to capitalize.

capitán m. captain.
capitanear v. to command, to lead; to head a troop of people.
capitolio m. capitol.
capitular v. to surrender; to capitulate; m. capitular.
capítulo m. chapter.
caporal m. boss, leader, chief; Am. foreman in a cattle ranch.
capote m. cloak (with sleeves); bullfighter's cloak; Am. thrashing; beating; **decir para su —** to say to oneself; **a mi —** in my opinion.
capricho m. caprice, whim, fancy.
caprichoso adj. capricious, whimsical, obstinate, fanciful.
caprichudo adj. obstinate, stubborn, capricious; wilful.
cápsula f. capsule; percussion cap; cartridge shell; metal cap (on bottles).
captar v. to captivate, to win by endearing words; to attract; Am. to get; to tune in on (a radio wave).
captura f. capture, arrest.
capturar v. to capture, to arrest.
capucha f. hood.
capullo m. pod of a silk worm; germ or bud of flowers; cup of an acorn.
cara f. face, visage, countenance; surface of a thing, front; **de —** opposite; **echar (or dar) en —** to reproach, to blame; **sacar la — por alguien** to take someone's part, to defend him.
caracol m. snail; winding stairs; Am. embroidered blouse; curl.
caracolear v. to caper, to prance around (said of horses); to caracole; Am. to muddle, to entangle; to sidestep an obligation.
caracoleo m. the act of caracoling, prancing around, winding.
carácter m. character, temper.
característica f. characteristic, trait.
característico adj. characteristic.
caracterizar v. to characterize.
¡caramba! interj. great guns!; great Scott!
carámbano m. icicle.
caramelo m. caramel, burnt sugar.
caramillo m. reed pipe; flageolet, a small flute; deceit, fraudulent thing; **armar un —** to raise a rumpus.
carancho m. Am. hawk, buzzard.
carátula f. mask of pasteboard; Am. title page of a book; dial, face of a watch.

caravana f. caravan.
carbólico adj. carbolic.
carbón m. carbon, coal, charcoal; cinder; — **de la leña** charcoal; — **de piedra** coal, pitcoal.
carbonera f. coal bin, coal cellar, woman coal or charcoal vendor; charcoal burners; coal house; coal-hole; Am. coal mine.
carbonero m. coal dealer, charcoal vendor; adj. coal, relating to coal or charcoal.
carbono m. carbon.
carburador m. carburetor.
carcajada f. loud laughter, horse-laugh; peal of laughter.
cárcel f. jail, prison.
carcelero m. jailer, warden; adj. relating to a jail.
carcomido adj. worm-eaten, consumed, decayed.
cardar v. to card or comb wool; to raise the nap on cloth with a teasel.
cardenal m. cardinal; Virginian nightingale; bruise; lividity.
cardo m. thistle; a kind of cactus.
carear v. to confront criminals, to bring face to face; to compare; —**se** to meet face to face.
carecer v. irr. to lack, to be in need of, to want.
carencia f. lack, want, deprivation.
carente adj. lacking.
carero adj. overcharging; profiteering; selling things dear; m. profiteer.
carestía f. dearth, scarcity; want; famine; high price.
careta f. mask.
carga f. load, burden; freight; cargo, charge of gunpowder; loading; impost, duty, tax; **volver a la** — to insist again and again.
cargado p.p. & adj. loaded; strong (as tea or cofee); cloudy, sultry; full; fraught; — **de espaldas** round or stoop-shouldered.
cargador m. freighter, loader, stevedore; rammer; ramrod; Am. carrier, errand boy, mover.
cargamento m. cargo.
cargar v. to load, to burden, to freight; to charge, to attack; to ship goods; to bother, to annoy; Am. to carry, to lug; to punish; — **con** to carry away; to assume (resposibility); — **con el muerto** to get the blame (unjustly).
cargo m. burden, loading; total amount; employment, dignity, office; ministry; charge, keeping, care; obligation; **hacerse** — **de** to take charge of; — **de conciencia** remorse, sense of guilt.
carguero adj. freight-carrying; load-carrying; Am. beast of burden; skilled loader of pack animals; patient, long-suffering person.
caribe adj. Caribbean; m. Carib, Caribbean Indian; cannibal; savage.
caricatura f. caricature; cartoon.
caricia f. caress.
caridad f. charity, charitableness; alms.
caries f. decay (of a bone); tooth decay.
cariño m. affection, love; Am. gift.
cariñoso adj. affectionate, loving.
caritativo adj. charitable.
carmesí m. crimson.
carnal adj. carnal, sensual; fleshy.
carnaval m. carnival.
carne f. meat, flesh; — **de gallina** "goose flesh", "goose pimples"; **echar —s** to put on weight, to get fat; — **de res** Am. beef; **ser uña y** — to be hand and glove, to be intimate or familiar.
carnear v. to slaugter; Am. to kill.
carnero m. ram; male sheep; mutton; Am. a weak-willed person; waste basket; — **de la tierra** Am. llama (or any fleece-bearing animal); **cantar uno el** — Am. to die.
carnicería f. meat market; butchery; slaughter; Am. slaughterhouse.
carnicero m. butcher; adj. carnivorous; flesh-eating; bloodthirsty; cruel.
carnosidad f. carnosity; fatness; abundance of flesh and blood; fleshiness.
carnoso adj. fleshy, meaty; carnous; pulpy; pulpous (fruit).
caro adj. expensive, dear, high priced; costly; beloved, affectionate.
carpa f. carp (fresh-water fish); Am. canvas tent; circus tent; — **dorada** gold fish.
carpeta f. table cover; desk pad; portfolio; letter case or file; Am. office desk; bookkeeping department.
carpetazo: dar — to table (a motion); to set aside, pigeonhole or dismiss.
carpintería f. carpentry, carpenter's shop.

carpintero m. carpenter; joiner; pájaro — woodpecker.
carraspear v. to cough, to clear one's throat; to be hoarse.
carraspera f. hoarseness.
carrera f. career; running; course; race; run, sprint; stocking run; highroad; alley; avenue; profession.
carreta f. long, narrow wagon; cart; Am. wheelbarrow.
carretaje m. cartage (transporting by cart, truck, etc.); price paid for cartage.
carrete m. spool; reel; fishing-pulley.
carretel m. reel, spool, bobbin; fishing reel; log reel (of a boat).
carretera f. highway.
carretero m. carter, teamster, cart maker; cartwright; **camino —** highway.
carretilla f. wheelbarrow; small cart; go-cart; squib, cracker; small wheel; Am. wagon; jaw; string, series (of lies, blunders, etc); firecracker; **— de** by custom.
carretón m. truck, wagon, cart.
carril m. rail; rut; furrow.
carrillo m. cheek; pulley; small cart; **comer a dos —s** to eat on both sides.
carro m. cart; cartload; Am. car; auto; streetcar, coach; .pararle a uno el **—** Am. to restrain someone; pasarle a uno el **—** Am. to suffer an injury or misfortune.
carroña f. carrion, putrid flesh; decaying carcass.
carroza f. large and luxurious carriage; chariot.
carruaje m. carriage, vehicle.
carta f. letter; royal ordinance; playing card; map, charter; **— blanca** full authority, freedom to act; **— de naturaleza** nationalization papers; **— de venta** bill of sale; **retirar —** Am. to repent, to back down; **ser la última — de la baraja** Am. to be the worst or most insignificant person or thing.
cartearse v. to correspond, to write to each other.
cartel m. poster; placard; edict; handbill; cartel; written agreement.
cartelera f. billboard.
cartelón m. large poster.
cartera f. portfolio; wallet; briefcase; desk pad; letter case; pocket flap of a coat.

cartero m. mailman, letter carrier, postman.
cartilla f. primer; note; short letter; horn-book; **leerle a uno la —** to scold, to lecture someone concerning his duties.
cartografiar v. to chart, to make charts.
cartón m. cardboard, pasteboard.
cartuchera f. cartridge belt; cartridge box.
cartucho m. cartridge; roll of coins; paper cone or bag.
cartulina f. fine pasteboard.
casa f. house, home; edifice; household; business firm; square of a chessboard; Am. bet; wager; **— de empeños** pawnshop; **— de moneda** mint; **— de huéspedes** boarding house; **echar la — por la ventana** to spend recklessly, to squander everything; **poner —** to set up housekeeping; **ser muy de —** to be on familiar terms; **— del Señor** church.
casabe or **cazabe** m. Am. cassava; cassava bread.
casaca f. long military coat; **volver —** to be a turncoat, change sides or parties.
casamiento m. wedding; marriage; matrimony, match.
casar v. to marry, to couple, to match; to come together; **—se to** get married.
cascabel m. jingle bell, tinkle bell; hawksbell; rattlesnake.
cascada f. cascade, waterfall.
cascajo m. coarse gravel; crushed stone; gravel; rubbish.
cascanueces m. nutcracker.
cascar v. to crack, to break; to burst; to crunch; to lick; to beat; **—se** to crack or break open.
cáscara f. rind; peel; hull; husk; bark of a tree; **dar a uno — de novillo** Am. to give someone a whipping.
cascarrabias m. & f. crab, grouch, ill-tempered person; adj. grouchy, cranky, irritable.
casco m. helmet; hoof; skull; crown of a hat; Am. compound, main buildings of a farm; **caliente de —s** hot-headed; **ligero de —s** lightheaded, frivolous; **romperse los —s** to rack one's brain.
casera f. landlady, housekeeper.
caserío m. hamlet, village or very small town; small settlement.
casero adj. domestic, homely;

— 47 —

homemade; homebred; m. landlord, janitor, caretaker, steward; Am. customer; delivery boy.
caseta f. small house, cottage, booth, stall.
casi adv. almost, nearly, somewhat, more or less, just.
casilla f. stall, booth; square (of a checkerboard); pigeonhole; post-office box; **sacarle a uno de sus —s** to change someone's ways or habits, to irritate, to annoy, to try someone's patience; **salirse de sus —s** to lose one's temper; to do something out of the way.
casino m. club, society; clubhouse; recreation hall.
caso m. case; point; matter; event; occurrence, contingency; hap, casualty; accident; occasion; opportunity; **— que** (or **en — de que**) in case that; **dado —** supposing; **hacer — omiso de** to omit; **no viene al —** that is not to the point.
casorio m. wedding, marriage.
caspa f. dandruff, scurf.
casta f. caste, race, generation, breed, distinct class, quality; kind.
castaña f. chestnut; bottle, jug; jar; Am. small barrel; trunk, large suitcase.
castañear v. to rattle the castanets; to chatter (said of the teeth); to crackle (said of the knees or joints); **— con los dedos** to snap one's fingers.
castañeteo m. clacking, rattle or sound of castanets; chatter, chattering (of the teeth).
castaño m. chestnut (tree and wood); adj. chestnut-colored.
castañuela f. castanet.
castellano adj. & m. Castilian.
castidad f. chastity, continence.
castigar v. to chastise, to punish; to castigate, to afflict.
castigo m. punishment, correction, penalty.
castillo m. castle.
castizo adj. pure, correct (language); pure-blooded; noble.
casto adj. chaste, pure.
castor m. beaver; beaver cloth.
casual adj. casual, accidental.
casualidad f. chance, accident, hazard.
casucha f. hut, cottage, crib.
catadura f. aspect, appearance, face, countenance.
catalán adj. Catalan, Catalonian, of or from Cataluña, Spain; m. Catalan.
catalogar v. to catalogue.
catálogo m. catalogue, roll, file.
catar v. to look at, to examine, to taste, to sample, to view, to inspect, to inquire.
catarata f. cataract, waterfall, cascade.
catarro m. catarrh, cold.
catástrofe f. catastrophe, mishap.
catear v. to explore, to look around; to investigate; Am. to search or raid (a home); to explore for ore; to test, to try.
catecismo m. catechism.
cátedra f. class; subject; chair; seat; professorship.
catedral f. cathedral.
catedrático m. professor.
categoría f. category, rank; kind, class, character.
categórico adj. categorical, positive, categoric.
catequizar v. to catechize, to persuade; to give religious instruction (to); to induce.
católico adj. Catholic; general; universal; m. Catholic.
catolicismo m. Catholicism.
catre m. small bedstead, cot; Am. raft; float; camp stool; folding stool; **— de tijera** folding cot.
catrín m. Am. dandy; adj. Am. overelegant, dressy.
cauce m. riverbed, drain for conveying water.
cauchero m. Am. rubber gatherer; rubber producer; adj. rubber, pertaining to rubber.
caucho m. caoutchouc, India-rubber; Am. rubber raincoat or cloak.
caudal m. wealth; river current; volume of water.
caudaloso adj. wealthy, abundant.
caudillaje m. military leadership; Am. political bossism; tyrany.
caudillo m. commander, chief, leader, boss, director; Am. political boss.
causa f. cause; case, lawsuit; occasion; consideration; Am. light lunch, snack.
causar v. to cause.
cautela f. caution, cunning, craftiness, trick, deception.
cauteloso adj. cautious, heedful, prudent.
cautivar v. to capture, to imprison; to captivate, to charm.
cautiverio m. captivity.

cautivo m. captive; war prisoner; one charmed by beauty.
cauto adj. cautious, wary; cunning.
cavar v. to dig, to excavate; to penetrate.
caverna f. cavern, cave; hollow.
cavernoso adj. cavernous; like a cavern; hollow; **voz cavernosa** deep, hollow voice.
cavidad f. cavity.
cayado m. shepherd's crook or hook.
cayo m. key, island reef, shoal, islet.
caza f. hunt, hunting; wild game; fowling, field sports; **dar —** to pursue, to track down.
cazador adj. hunter, chaser.
cazar v. to chase, to hunt, to track down.
cazatorpedero m. destroyer, torpedo-boat.
cazo m. dipper, pot, pan; ladle; large kettle or boiler.
cazuela f. stewing pan; earthen pan; topmost theater gallery; Am. stewed hen; candied sweet potaoes with spices.
cebada f. barley; Am. brewing of mate.
cebar v. to feed; to fatten (animals); to encourage, to nourish (a passion); to prime (a gun, pump, etc.); to bait (a fish hook); Am. to brew and serve mate or tea; **—se** to vent one's fury.
cebo m. food given to animals; fodder; bait; incentive.
cebolla f. onion.
cecear v. to lisp.
ceceo m. lisp, lisping.
cecina f. dried beef; jerked beef.
cedazo m. sieve.
ceder v. to cede, to transfer; to yield; to surrender, to deliver up; to submit; to diminish, to abate.
cedro m. cedar.
cédula f. slip of paper; certificate; **— de vecindad** or **—** personal official identification card.
céfiro m. zephyr, soft breeze; Am. fine muslin.
cegar v. irr. to blind; to become blind; to confuse; to fill up, stop up (a hole).
ceguera f. blindness.
ceiba f. Am. ceiba, silk-cotton tree.
ceja f. eyebrow; brow of a hill.
cejar v. to go backward; to back; to backdown, give in, yield; to slacken.
cejijunto adj. frowning; knitted eyebrows.
celada f. ambush, lurch, trap.
celaje m. colored clouds; skylight; presage, portent; Am. shadow, ghost; **como un —** Am. like lightning.
celar v. to guard, to watch; to watch over jealously; to conceal.
celda f. cell.
celebración f. celebration.
celebrar v. to celebrate; to praise, ` honor; to be glad.
célebre adj. famous; funny, witty; Am. graceful, pretty woman.
celebridad f. fame, renown; celebration.
celeridad f. swiftness, speed.
celeste adj. celestial, heavenly.
celestial adj. celestial, heavenly, divine.
célibe adj. unmarried; m. & f. unmarried person.
celo m. zeal, ardor; envy; heat (sexual excitement in animals); **—s** jealousy, suspicion; **tener —s** to be jealous.
celosía f. window lattice; Venetian blind.
celoso adj. jealous; zealous, eager; suspicious.
célula f. cell; cellule.
celuloide m. celluloid.
cellisca f. squall; sleet; rain and snow.
cementar v. to cement.
cementerio m. cemetery.
cemento m. cement; **— armado** reinforced concrete.
cena f. supper.
cenegal m. quagmire, muddy ground, swamp.
cenagoso adj. muddy, miry.
cenar v. to eat supper; to sup.
cencerrear v. to jingle continually; to make a racket with cowbells, tin cans, etc.
cencerro m. cowbell.
cendal m. light thin stuff; crape; gauze; thin veil.
cenicero m. ash tray; ash hole; ash pit; ash pan.
ceniciento adj. cenerous; ashen, ash-colored.
cenit m. zenith.
ceniza f. ashes, cinders; **miércoles de —** Ash-Wednesday.
cenizo adj. ash-colored; ashy.
censo m. census.
censor m. censor; proctor; critic.

censura f. censure, blame, reproach, reprimand, reprehension, criticism, disapproval; censorship.
censurador m. censurer, censor, critic; critical person; adj. critical.
censurar v. to censure; to blame; to accuse; to condemn; to criticize; to reprove; to censor.
centavo m. cent; hundredth.
centella f. lightning, flash, spark.
centelleante adj. sparkling; flashing.
centellear v. to twinkle; to spark; to glitter; to flash.
centelleo m. spark; scintillation, glitter.
centenar m. one hundred; field sown with rye.
centenario m. centennial, centenary; one hundredth aniversary; adj. centennial; old, ancient.
centeno m. rye.
centésimo adj. & m. hundredth, centesimal.
centímetro m. centimeter, centimetre (one hundredth part of a meter).
céntimo m. centime, one hundredth part of a peseta.
centinela m. sentry, sentinel; guard.
central adj. central; centric; f. main office; headquarters; Am. main sugar mill or refinery.
centrar v. to center.
céntrico adj. central, centric.
centro m. center, middle.
ceñidor m. girdle, belt, sash.
ceñir v. to irr. to gird, to girdle, to surround; to environ; to tighten; to encircle; to limit; diminish; —se to limit oneself to.
ceño m. frown; scowl; a supercilious look; fruncir el — to frown, to scowl.
cepa f. stump, stub, stock of a tree or plant; vinestock; origin, stock (of a family); Am. mass of plants growing from a common root; excavation (for a building); hole, pit (for planting trees); de buena — of good stock.
cepillo m. brush; plane, carpenter's tool; poor-box, alms-box; Am. flatterer; — de dientes toothbrush.
cera f. wax.
cerámica f. ceramics, pottery.
cerca adv. near, near by, at hand, not far off, close by; m. enclosure, wall, hedge, fence; — de prep. near, nearly.
cercado m. a garden or field inclosed by a fence; inclosure; Am. Peruvian political division.
cercanía f. proximity; neighbourhood, vicinity; —s surroundings, vicinity.
cercano adj. near; neighboring, close by.
cercar v. to fence, to enclose; to surround; to besiege; to environ; to hem.
cercenar v. to clip off; to pare; to retrench; to lop off the ends or extremities; to curtail; to diminish; to reduce.
cerciorar v. to assure; to ascertain; to affirm; —se to find out.
cerco m. fence, enclosure; siege; circle; Am. small farm or orchard.
cerda f. bristle; strong hair in the horse's hair or mane; Am. ir en —s to go halves or share in a deal.
cerdo m. hog, pig, pork, swine.
cerdoso adj. bristly.
cereal m. cereal, grain.
cerebro m. brain.
ceremonia f. ceremony.
ceremonial adj. & m. ceremonial.
ceremonioso adj. ceremonious.
cereza f. cherry.
cerezo m. cherry tree; cherry wood.
cerilla f. wax taper, wax match; earwax.
cerillo m. Am. match.
cerner v. irr. to sift, to drizzle; to bolt; Am. to strain through a sieve; —se to hover (as a bird or plane).
cero m. zero; nothing; ser un — to be a nothing.
cerquita adv. quite near, nice and near.
cerrado adj. closed, reserved, dissembling; secreted, concealed; obstinate; Am. stubborn.
cerradura f. locking, closing, lock; — de golpe spring lock.
cerrajería f. locksmith's shop; locksmith's trade.
cerrajero m. locksmith.
cerrar v. irr. to close, to shut, to lock, to occlude, to foreclose, to obstruct; to terminate or finish a thing; — la carta to fold the letter; — los ojos to die; to sleep; —se to close; —se el cielo to become overcast or cloudy.

— 50 —

cerrazón f. cloudiness, darkness; dark and cloudy weather.
cerro m. hill.
cerrojo m. latch, bolt.
certamen m. contest, controversy, literary contest or controversy; debate, competition.
certero adj. accurate, exact; well-aimed; sharpshooter; **tirador —** good shot.
certeza f. certainty.
certidumbre f. certainty.
certificado adj. certified, registered; m. certificate.
certificar v. to assure, to affirm, to certify; to register (a letter).
cervato m. fawn, young deer.
cervecería f. beer tavern, brewery.
cerveza f. beer, ale, malt liquor.
cesante adj. unemployed.
cesar v. to cease, to give over, to forbear, to stop, to quit; to leave, to leave off, to desist.
cesta f. basket; a kind of racket for playing jai alai (Basque ball game).
cesto m. large basket, hamper.
cetrino adj. greenish-yellow, lemon-colored; citronlike; melancholy, gloomy.
cetro f. scepter, staff.
cicatero adj. miserly, stingy; niggardly, sordid.
cicatriz f. scar, cicatrice, cicatrix; gash, mark of a wound.
cicatrizar v. to heal, to close a wound, to cicatrize.
ciclo m. cycle; period of time; school term.
ciclón m. cyclone.
ciego adj. blind; choked or shut up; m. blindman; **a ciegas** blindly.
cielo m. sky, heaven; paradise; climate; **— de la boca** palate; **poner el grito en el —** to "hit the ceiling".
ciemplés m. centipede.
ciénaga f. swamp, bog, quagmire, marsh, moor.
ciencia f. science; learning; knowledge, certainty; **a (or de) —** **cierta** with certainty.
cieno m. mud, mire.
científico adj. scientific; m. scientist.
cierre m. clasp, fastener; closing, fastening, locking; method of closing.
cierto adj. certain, evident, true, sure; **por —** or **de —** certainly, surely, in truth; **ciertas hierbas** Am. so-and-so (person not named).
ciervo m. deer; **cierva** f. doe, hind, female deer.
cierzo m. North wind; cold wind.
cifra f. cipher, number, abridgment, summary, code; monogram, emblem.
cifrar v. to write in code; to cipher or write in cipher; to summarize; **— la esperanza en** to place one's hope in.
cigarra f. balm-cricket; cicada, locust.
cigarrera f. cigar or cigarette case; woman cigar maker or vendor.
cigarrillo m. cigarette.
cigarro m. cigar, cigarette.
cigüeña f. stork; crank; handle; winch.
cilíndrico adj. cylindrical, cylindric.
cilindro m. cylinder, roller; Am. hand organ.
cima f. peak, summit, top; **dar —** to complete, to carry out.
cimarrón adj. Am. wild, untamed.
cimarronear v. Am. to drink mate without sugar.
cimbrar, cimbrear v. to brandish a rod or wand; to flourish, to swing; to shake; to bend; Am. to swing around, change suddenly one's direction; **— a uno de un golpe** to knock a person down with a blow; **—se** to swing, sway; to vibrate, to shake.
cimiento m. foundation, base; basis, origin; source; root; **abrir los —s** to break ground for a building.
cinc m. zinc.
cincel m. chisel.
cincelar v. to chisel; to engrave, to emboss, to chase.
cincha f. cinch, girth, cingle; Am. blows with the flat of a sword; Am. **a revienta —s** unwillingly; hurriedly; at break-neck speed.
cinchar v. to cinch, to tighten the saddle girth; to bind with a girth; Am. to hit with the flat of a sword.
cine m. cinema, motion picture, movie.
cinematógrafo m. cinematrograph, motion picture.
cíngulo m. girdle, cord, belt, band.
cínico adj. cynical, cynic, sarcastic, sneering. m. cynic.
cinta f. ribbon, band; tape, string; movie film; coarse fishing net; Am. tin can; **— entintada** type-

writer ribbon; **estar en —** to be pregnant.
cintarada f. beating, flogging.
cintarazo m. blow with the flat of a sword, punishment of a horse with the stirrup leather.
cintilar v. to sparkle, to twinkle; to glimmer; to glitter.
cinto m. belt; girdle.
cintura f. waist; narrow part of a chimney; **meter en —** to subdue, to subject.
cinturón m. belt; **— de seguridad** safety belt.
ciprés m. cypress.
circo m. circus.
circuito m. circuit.
circulación f. circulation, traffic; currency.
circular v. to circulate; to circle; adj. circular, circulatory; f. circular letter, notice.
círculo m. circle; group; club; clubhouse.
circundante adj. surrounding.
circundar v. to surround, to circle, to compass.
circunferencia f. circumference.
circunspección f. circumspection, decorum, prudence, restraint.
circunspecto adj. circumspect, prudent, cautious.
circunstancia f. circumstance; incident, event.
circunstante adj. surrounding, present, circumstant; **—s** bystanders, onlookers, audience, presents.
circunvecino adj. neighboring, surrounding.
cirio m. wax candle.
ciruela f. plum; prune; **— pasa** prune, dried prune.
ciruelo m. plum tree.
cirugía f. surgery.
cirujano m. surgeon.
cisne m. swan; Am. powder puff.
cisterna f. cistern, reservoir.
cita f. date, appointment; citation; summons; quotation; assignation.
citación f. citation, quotation, summons, judicial notice.
citar v. to cite, to convoke, to make a date or appointment with; to quote, to summon; to incite; to provoke (a bull).
ciudad f. city, town; civic body.
ciudadanía f. citizenship.
ciudadano m. citizen, resident of a city; adj. of or pertaining to a city.
ciudadela f. citadel.

cívico adj. civic.
civil adj. civil; polite, courteous.
civilidad f. civility; courtesy.
civilización f. civilization.
civilizador adj. civilizing; m. civilizer.
civilizar v. to civilize.
cizaña f. weed, darnel; vice; discord; disagreement.
clamar v. to clamor, to shout, to call; to cry out in a mournful tone.
clamor m. clamor, shout; scream, knell; outcry, shriek.
clamoreo m. clamoring, shouting, knell.
clandestino adj. clandestine, secret, private.
clara f. clear spot, bald spot; **— de huevo** white of egg; **a las —s** clearly, openly.
claraboya f. skylight.
clarear v. to dawn, to grow light, to clarify, to make clear; to clear up; Am. to pierce through and through; **—se** to become transparent, to reveal oneself.
claridad f. clarity, brightness, light, clearness, distinctness; blunt remark.
claridoso adj. Am. blunt, outspoken.
clarificar v. to clarify, to make clear; to purify, to refine.
clarín m. bugle; bugler; clarion; trumpet; organ stop; Am. song bird.
clarinete m. clarinet, clarinet player.
clarividencia f. clairvoyance; perspicacity.
claro adj. clear, bright, transparent; pellucid, limpid; thin, rare; light, not deeply tinged; open, frank, ingenuous; m. skylight; space, gap; **pasar la noche de — en —** not to sleep a wink; **en —** Am. without eating or sleeping; **poner en —** Am. to copy.
clase f. class; classroom; quality; kind; sort.
clásico adj. classic, classical.
clasificación f. classification.
clasificar v. to classify, to class.
claustro m. cloister; corridor around the court of a convent; assembly or meeting of a convent; assembly or meeting of the principal members of a university; womb; **— de profesores** university faculty.

— 52 —

cláusula f. clause; period; condition.
clavar v. to nail; to fix; to deceive; to fasten with nails; to force in; to stick; to prick.
clave f. key, code; keystone; clef; tune.
clavel m. carnation, pink.
clavetear v. to nail; to garnish with nails.
clavija f. peg, pin, stopple; electric plug; **apretar a uno las —s** to push home an argument.
clavijero m. hat or clothes rack.
clavo m. nail; corn, a hard and painful excrescence on the feet; spot in the eye; lint for wounds or sores; clove (spice); rudder of a ship; severe pain or grief; Am. mineral vein; worry; surprise; **dar en el —** to hit the nail on the head; **meter a uno en un —** Am. to put a person in a predicament; **ser un —** Am. to be punctual.
clemencia f. mercy, clemency.
clemente adj. merciful.
clerical adj. clerical.
clérigo m. clergyman.
clero m. clergy.
cliente m. & f. client, customer.
clientela f. clientele, customers, patronage.
clima f. climate, clime.
clímax m. climax.
clínica f. clinic.
clíper m. clipper.
cloaca f. sewer.
cloquear v. to cluck.
cloqueo m. cluck, clucking.
cloro m. chlorine.
club m. club, clubhouse.
clueca f. brooding hen.
coacción f. compulsion, force, coaction.
coagular v. to coagulate, to condense, to clot; to curd; to curdle; **—se** to clot, to coagulate, to curd, to curdle.
coágulo m. coagulation, clot.
coartar v. to restrain, to limit.
coba f. flattery, **dar —** to flatter.
cobarde adj. cowardly; timid; fearful, weak; m. coward.
cobardía f. cowardice; dastardy, dastardice.
cobertizo m. shed; hovel, a covered passage.
cobertor m. bedcover, coverlet.
cobija f. cover; shelter; blanket; **—s** Am. bedclothes.
cobijar v. to cover, to shelter.
cobrador m. collector; receiver.

cobranza f. collection.
cobrar v. to collect, to recover; to fetch game that is killed; to charge, to cash; to regain; to gain, to acquire; Am. to demand payment; **— cariño a** to take a liking to; **por —** charge on delivery (C.O.D.).
cobre m. copper; kitchen furniture; Am. copper coin; **—s** brass instruments of an orchestra; **batir el —** to hustle, work with energy; **mostrar el —** Am. to show one's worse side.
cobrizo adj. coppery, copper-colored; cupreous.
cobro m. collection; place of safety; **poner en —** to put in a safe place; **ponerse en —** to take refuge.
coca f. Am. coca, cocaine; fruit skin or rind; **de —** Am. gratis; in vain.
cocaína f. cocaine.
cocear v. to kick; to repugn; to resist.
cocer v. irr. to cook, to boil, to bake, to dress victuals; to bake bricks, tiles or earthenware; to ferment.
cocido m. Spanish stew.
cociente m. quotient.
cocimiento m. cooking, baking, coction, concoction, decoction.
cocina f. kitchen; cuisine, cooking.
cocinar v. to cook.
cocinero m. cook.
coco m. coconut; coconut tree; cotton gin; goblin; Am. derby hat; head; blow on the head; **hacer —s a** to make eyes at; **pelar a —** Am. to crop the hair.
cocodrilo m. crocodile; **lágrimas de —** false crying.
coche m. coach, car, automobile.
cochero m. coachman, cabman, taximan.
cochinada f. herd of swine; filth; filthiness; filthy act; dirty trick; mean action.
cochino adj. dirty, nasty, filthy; **— de monte** wild boar; adj. Am. miserly, stingy; m. hog, pig.
codazo m. blow with the elbow; nudge.
codear v. to elbow; to nudge; **—se con alguien** to be in good terms with someone.
codicia f. greed; covetousness, cupidity.
codiciar v. to covet.

codicioso adj. covetous, greedy, avaricious.
código m. code of laws.
codo m. elbow, bend; **dar de — to** elbow; **alzar** (or **empinar**) **el —** to drink too much; **hablar hasta por los —s** to talk too much; **meterse** (or **estar metido**) **hasta los —s** to be up to the elbows.
codorniz f. partridge.
coetáneo adj. contemporary.
cofrade m. & f. fellow member of a brotherhood; cofriar.
cofradía f. brotherhood, sisterhood; guild; confraternity.
cofre m. trunk (for clothes); coffer, jewel box; chest.
coger v. to seize, to catch, to get, to grasp, to gather; **—se una cosa** Am. to steal something.
cogote m. nape, occiput.
cohechar v. to bribe.
coheredero m. joint heir; coheir.
coherente adj. coherent; connected.
cohete m. skyrocket; rocket; **al —** Am. in vain.
cohibido p.p. & adj. inhibited, embarrassed, restrained.
cohibir v. to restrain, to repress; to inhibit.
coincidencia f. coincidence.
coincidir v. to coincide.
cojear v. to limp, to halt, to hobble; to deviate from virtue; **cojeamos del mismo pie** we both have the same weakness.
cojera f. limp, lameness.
cojín m. cushion, pad.
cojo adj. lame; crippled; one-legged.
col f. cabbage; **— de Bruselas** Brussels sprouts.
cola f. tail; line of people; cue; train; glue; **hacer — to** stand in line; **comer —** Am. to be the last one in a contest.
colaboración f. collaboration, mutual help; contribution.
colaborar v. to collaborate, to work together.
coladera f. colander, strainer, sieve; Am. drain.
colar v. irr. to strain, to filter; to drain; to collate; to pass counterfeit money; to pass through a narrow place; to drink wine; to steal into a place; **—se a fondo** to founder.
colcha f. quilt; bedspread, coverlet; **—s** Am. saddle and trappings; gaucho clothing.
colchón m. mattress.

colear v. to wag; to grab a bull by the tail and overturn him; to wriggle or move in a ridiculous maner in walking; Am. to flunk (a student); to trail, tag behind a person; to smoke a cigarette arter another.
colección f. collection; set; gathering.
coleccionista m. & f. collector (of stamps, coins, etc.).
coleccionar v. to collect, to form a collection.
colecta f. collection of voluntary offerings; assessment; collect, a prayer of the mass.
colectivo adj. collective; Am. small bus.
colector m. collector; water conduit; gatherer; tax or rent gatherer.
colega m. & f. colleague, fellow worker.
colegiatura f. college fellowship; Am. tuition in a college.
colegio m. college, school, seminary; boarding school; academy; body of dignitaries, etc.
colegir v. to gather, to conclude, to infer, to collect.
cólera f. anger, rage, fury, passion; bile; cholera; cholera morbus; **montar en —** to be angry, to be in a passion; **— negra** black bile.
colérico adj. irritable, angry; passionate, irascible.
coleto m. leather jacket; one's inner self; Am. impudence, shamelessness; **decir para su — to** say to oneself; **echarse al —** to eat or drink.
colgadero m. hanger; hook, peg; hat or clothes rack.
colgadura f. drape, drapery, tapestry, bunting.
colgante adj. hanging, dangling, pending; **puente —** suspension bride.
colgar v. irr. to hang, to suspend; to flow, to hover, to dangle; to impute, to attribute; to kill by hanging; Am. to flunk, to fail (a student); **—se** Am. to fall behind.
colibrí m. hummingbird.
coliflor f. cauliflower.
coligarse v. to colligate; to band together; to confederate.
colilla f. small tail; butt, stub (of a cigar).
colina f. hill, hillock; hummock; seed of cabbage.

colindante adj. contiguous, adjacent; neighboring.
colindar v. to border (on); to be adjoining.
colisión m. collision; clash; crush.
colmar v. to fill to the brim; to heap up; to fulfil; to make up; to confer great favours; — **de** to fill with; to give in plenty; —**le a uno el plato** to exhaust one's patience.
colmena f. beehive.
colmillo m. eyetooth, canine tooth; tusk, fang; **mostrar los** —**s** to show spirit and resolution.
colmo m. overfullness; limit; overmeasure; height; — **de la locura** height of folly; **¡eso es el** —**!** that's the limit! adj. overfull.
colocación f. place; arrangement; position; job, employment, situation.
colocar v. to place; to arrange; to put in due place or order; to collocate; to give employment to; —**se** to be placed.
colombiano adj. Colombian, of or pertaining to Colombia, South America.
colon m. colon.
colonia f. colony; silk ribbon two fingers wide; Am. city district; plantation.
colonización f. colonization.
colonizador m. colonizer; adj. colonizing.
colonizar v. to colonize, settle.
colono m. colonist, settler, tenant, farmer, planter; Am. owner of a plantation; Am. bootlicker, flatterer.
coloquio m. conversation, colloquy, talk, literary dialogue; Am. street comedy, farce.
color m. color; coloring; paint; rouge; hue, appearance; pretext; **so** — under pretext.
coloración f. coloring.
colorado adj. red, reddish; colored; **ponerse** — to blush.
colorante adj. y m. coloring.
colorar v. to color, to stain, to dye.
colorear v. to color; to redden; to grow red; to give color to.
colorete m. rouge.
colorido m. coloring, color; pretext, pretense; adj. colored, colorful.
colosal adj. colossal, gigantic, huge.
columbrar v. to see faintly, to glimpse; to discern at a distance.
columna f. column.

columpiar v. to swing; to fly forward or backward on a rope; —**se** to swing, to sway.
columpio m. swing.
collado m. hillock, knoll, fell.
collar m. necklace; dog collar; Am. collar (of a draft horse).
collera f. horse collar.
coma f. comma; m. coma, stupor, insensibility, unconsciousness.
comadre f. gossip; woman friend; midwife; name used to express kinship between mother and godmother; **riñen las** —**s y se dicen las verdades** when gossips fall out, they tell bitter truths.
comadreja f. weasel.
comadrona f. midwife.
comandancia f. command; position and office of a commander; — **militar** military command.
comandante m. commander, major.
comandar v. to command, to govern.
comandita f. silent partnership; jointstock company; **sociedad en** — limited company.
comando m. command.
comarca f. district, region, territory.
comba f. bulge, warp; curvature, convexity.
combar v. to warp, to bend, to twist, to curve; —**se** to warp; to bulge; to jut, to sag.
combate m. combat, battle, fight.
combatiente m. combatant, fighter, combative.
combatir v. to combat; to fight; to contest; to attack; to struggle.
combinación f. combination; association.
combinar v. to combine, to unite, to join.
combustible adj. combustible; inflammable; m. fuel.
combustión f. combustion; burning.
comedero m. feeding trough; dining room; adj. eatable, edible.
comedia f. comedy; farce.
comediante m. actor, comedian, player.
comedido adj. obliging, civil, polite, gentle, courteous; moderate.
comedirse v. irr. to be civil, polite, obliging; Am. to meddle; — **a hacer algo** Am. to volunteer to do something.
comedor m. dining room; eater; feeder.

comelón m. Am. big eater.
comendador m. commander (of a military order).
comensal m. & f. table companion; dinner guest; commensal.
comentador m. commentator.
comentar v. to comment.
comentario m. commentary, explanation.
comentarista m. & f. commentator.
comenzar v. irr. to begin, to commence.
comer v. to eat, to feed, to dine, to take (in chess or checkers); to have an itching all over the body; to corrode, to consume; **dar de —** to feed; **ganar de —** to earn a living; —**se to eat**; to eat up; to skip (a letter, syllable, word, etc.); —**se uno a otro** Am. to deceive each other; — **pan con corteza** to be independent; —**se de risa** to refrain from laughing.
comercial adj. commercial, trading.
comerciante m. merchant; storekeeper; trader.
comerciar v. to trade; to traffic; to have intercourse (with).
comercio m. commerce, trade, traffic, intercourse, interchange.
comestible adj. edible, eatable; —s m. pl. food, groceries.
cometa m. comet; kite.
cometer v. to commit; to intrust; to charge, to undertake; to attempt.
cometido m. commission; assignment, charge, task, duty.
comezón f. itch, itching.
comicios m. pl. primaries, elections.
cómico adj. comic, comical; funny, amusing; ludicrous; m. comedian, actor, player.
comida f. meal; dinner; food.
comidilla f. small meal; gossip; **la — de la vecindad** the talk of the town.
comienzo m. beginning; origin; initiation.
comilitona f. spread, big feast.
comilón m. big eater.
comillas f. pl. quotation marks.
comisario m. commissary, delegate; manager; Am. police inspector.
comisión f. commision; trust.
comisionado adj. commissioned, charged, delegated; m. commissioner, Am. constable.
comisionar v. to commission, to depute, to empower.
comistrajo m. mess, strange food,
concoction, mixture; hodgepodge.
comité m. committee, commission.
comitiva f. retinue; followers.
como adv. & conj. as, like, such as, if, provided that, since, when, how, in what manner, in what degree; Am. about, approximately; ¿**cómo**? interr. adv. how? what?; **¡cómo!** Am. yes, of course! — **quiera que sea** however; — **quiera que** notwithstanding that, although.
cómoda f. bureau, chest of drawers.
comodidad f. comfort; convenience, accommodation; ease; leisure.
cómodo adj. comfortable; convenient; m. Am. bedpan.
compacto adj. compact, close, dense.
compadecer v. irr. to pity, sympathize with; —**se con** to be in harmony with; —**se** to pity, to be compassionate; —**se de** to take pity on.
compadrazgo m. compaternity; friendship; realtionship; clique, group of friends.
compadre m. co-sponsor; protector; benefactor, crony, pal, comrade, chum, compeer, friend.
compañerismo m. companionship.
compañero m. companion, partner; mate; colleague, fellow member; condisciple, compeer.
compañía f. company; society; assembly, meeting; — **del ahorcado** Am. silent companion, poor company.
comparación f. comparison.
comparar v. to compare.
comparativo adj. comparative.
comparecer v. irr. to appear (before a judge, etc.).
compartimiento m. compartment.
compartir v. to share; to divide into equal parts.
compás m. compass, measure; beat; **llevar el —** to beat time; **a —** in right musical time.
compasión f. compassion, pity.
compasivo adj. compassionate, sympathetic; merciful.
compatible adj. compatible, in harmony.
compatriota m. & f. compatriot, fellow countryman (or countrywoman).
compeler v. to compel, to force, to constrain; to extort.

COMPENDIAR   **COMUNICACION**

compendiar v. to abstract, to summarize, to condense, to epitomize, to shorten, to abridge.
compendio m. summary, condensation, compendium, abridgment.
compensación f. compensation, recompense, reward.
compensar v. to balance; to counterbalance; to make equal, to make amends, to make up, to compensate, to recompense.
competencia f. competition, rivalry; competence, ability.
competente adj. competent, sufficient; adequate, capable, apt.
competidor m. competitor, rival; opponent; adj. competing.
competir v. irr. to compete; to contest, to contend, to cope.
compilar v. to compile.
compinche m. chum, pal, comrade; bossom friend.
complacencia f. complacency, satisfaction, contentment, pleasure, gratification.
complacer v. irr. to please, to humor; to comply; to render oneself agreeable, to content; —se to take pleasure or satisfaction (in).
complaciente adj. obliging, agreeable, willing to please, pleasing.
complejidad f. complexity.
complejo adj. & m. complex, complicated.
complemento m. complement; object (of a verb).
completamiento m. completion.
completar v. to complete; to finish, to perfect.
completo adj. complete, full, perfect, finished, absolute.
complicar v. to complicate; to jumble together.
cómplice m. & f. accomplice; cooperator, associate.
complot m. plot, conspiracy, intrigue.
componenda f. adjustment; compromise.
componente adj. component, constituent; m. component.
componer v. irr. to fix, to repair; to fix up; to adorn, to compose; to set up (type); to settle (a dispute); to compound; to construct; to sum up; to mend; to heal, to restore.
comportamiento m. conduct, behavior; manners.
composición f. composition; settlement; composure; adjustment.
compositor m. composer.

compostura f. repair; composure, dignity; neatness; composition; settlement; mending; modesty, circumspection.
compota f. fruit preserves; stewed fruit; — de manzana applesauce.
compra f. purchase, buying; ir de —s to go shopping.
comprador m. buyer, purchaser.
comprar v. to buy, to purchase; to shop.
comprender v. to understand, to grasp; to comprehend; to comprise, to embrace, to contain; to conceive.
comprensible adj. comprehensible; understandable.
comprensión f. understanding; comprehension; keenness.
comprensivo adj. comprehensive; understanding.
compresión f. compression.
comprimir v. to compress; to repress, to condense; to restrain.
comprobación f. confirmation, check, proof, test; attestation, verification.
comprobante adj. proving, verifying; m. proof; evidence; certificate; voucher; warrant.
comprobar v. irr. to verify; to check; to prove; to comprobate; to compare.
comprometer v. to compromise; to endanger; to bind; to engage; to expose; —se to promise; to bind oneself, to become engaged; to compromise oneself.
compromiso m. compromise; engagement; appointment; predicament; trouble; arbitration; bond.
compuerta f. sluice; floodgate.
compuesto p.p. & adj. repaired; fixed; adorned; composed; composite; compound; made up; m. composite, compound.
compungirse v. to feel compunction or remorse.
computar v. to compute, to calculate.
comulgar v. to commune, to take communion; to communicate.
común adj. common; usual, general, customary, ordinary, familiar; por lo — generally; m. toilet; el — de las gentes the man in the street; the average person.
comunero adj. common, popular. m. commoner; Am. member of an Indian community.
comunicación f. communication.

— 57 —

comunicar v. to communicate; to notify, to impart; to discover or make known; —se to correspond; to connect; to be in mutual communication.

comunicativo adj. communicative; talkative, unreserved.

comunidad f. community; commonwealth; the common people; commonness; guild, corporation; society.

comunión f. communion; political party.

comunismo m. communism.

comunista m. & f. communist; adj. communistic, communist.

con prep. with; — **tal que** so that, provided that; — **que** then, therefore; — **todo** or — **todo eso** nevertheless, notwithstanding; — **ser** in spite of being.

concavidad f. hollow, cavity; hollowness.

cóncavo adj. concave, hollow.

concebible adj. conceivable.

concebir v. irr. to conceive; to imagine; to understand; to grasp; to become pregnant.

conceder v. to concede, to grant, to admit, to allow.

concejal m. councilman, alderman.

concentración f. concentration.

concentrar v. to concentrate.

concepción f. conception.

concepto m. concept, idea, thought; opinion.

concernir v. irr. to concern, to regard, to belong to.

concertar v. irr. to arrange, to plan; to settle; to conclude (an arrangement); to harmonize; to agree; to concert; to regulate; to accord.

concesión f. concession, grant, granting; acknowledgment.

conciencia f. conscience.

concienzudo adj. conscientious.

concierto m. concert; harmony; concerto; **de** — by agreement.

conciliar v. to conciliate, to reconcile, to win over; — **el sueño** to induce sleep.

concilio m. council.

concisión f. conciseness, brevity.

conciso adj. concise, brief.

conciudadano m. fellow citizen, fellow countryman.

concluir v. irr. to conclude, to finish, to infer.

conclusión f. conclusion.

concordancia f. concord, agreement, harmony; concordance.

concordar v. irr. to accord, to regulate, to make agree.

concordia f. concord, conformity; union, harmony; agreement.

concretar v. to summarize, to condense; to limit; —**se a** to confine oneself to.

concreto adj. concrete, real, specific; **en** — concretely; m. Am. concrete.

concupiscente adj. sensual; concupiscent.

concurrencia f. gathering, audience; coincidence.

concurrido adj. well-patronized; frequented.

concurrir v. to concur; to contribute; to coincide.

concurso m. contest; competition.

concha f. shell, shellfish; prompter's box; **tener** — Am. to be indifferent, tough.

conchabar v. to unite, to plot, to conspire; to mix inferior wool with superior; Am. to hire (labor); —**se** to join, to gang together; Am. to hire oneself out; to get a job.

conde m. count.

condecoración f. badge, decoration, medal.

condecorar v. to decorate.

condena f. term in prison, sentence, penalty.

condenación f. condemnation; damnation.

condenar v. to condemn; to sentence; —**se** to be damned; to go to hell.

condensar v. to condense.

condesa f. countess.

condescendencia f. condescension, compliance.

condescender v. irr. to condescend; to comply; to yield.

condición f. condition.

condimentar v. to season; to dress victuals.

condimento m. condiment, seasoning.

condolerse v. irr. to condole (with); to sympathize (with); to be sorry (for).

cóndor m. Am. condor, vulture; gold coin of Ecuador, Chile and Colombia.

conducir v. irr. to conduct, to lead; to drive (an auto); —**se** to behave, to act.

conducta f. conduct, behavior; convoy; escort; management.

conducto m. conduit, pipe, channel; **por** — **de** through.

conductor adj. conducting; m. leader; guide; conductor (electrical); Am. conductor, tickets collector (on trains, buses, streetcars); teamster, driver.
conectar v. to connect.
condiscípulo m. schoolmate, classmate.
conejo m. rabbit; **conejillo de Indias** guinea pig.
conexión f. connection.
conexo adj. connected, coherent.
confección f. making, confection; fabrication, manufacture.
confeccionar v. to make, to manufacture; to mix, to put up (prescriptions).
confederación f. confederation, alliance, league.
confederar v. to confederate; —se to confederate, to form into a confederacy.
conferencia f. lecture, conference, meeting.
conferenciante m. & f. lecturer.
conferencista m. & f. lecturer.
conferir v. irr. to confer, to give; to bestow.
confesar v. irr. to confess.
confesión f. confession.
confesionario m. confessional, confessional box.
confesor m. confessor.
confiado adj. confident, secure; presumptuous; arrogant.
confianza f. confidence, trust; presumptuousness; familiarity; informality; **reunión de —** informal gathering.
confianzudo adj. over-friendly, over-familiar; Am. meddlesome.
confiar v. to confide, to trust in, to entrust; to credit; to hope.
confidencia f. confidence; trust; secret; confidential remark.
confidencial adj. confidential.
confidente m. confident, intimate, counsellor; sofa for two people; adj. faithful; trustworthy.
confín m. limit, border, boundary; adj. bordering, limiting.
confinar v. to confine; to banish, to exile; to imprison; to border upon.
confirmación f. confirmation.
confirmar v. to confirm.
confiscar v. to confiscate.
confite m. candy, bonbon.
confitería f. confectionery; candy shop.
confitura f. cofection.
conflicto m. conflict.
confluencia f. confluence.

conformar v. to adapt, to adjust; —se to conform; to agree; to yield; —se con la voluntad de Dios to be resigned to the will of God.
conforme adj. in agreement; alike; similar; **— a** in accordance with.
conformidad f. conformity, agreement; **en — con** in compliance with; **estar de — con** to be in accordance or agreement with.
confortar v. to comfort, to console.
confraternidad f. brotherhood.
confrontar v. to confront; to compare.
confundir v. to confound, to confuse, to bewilder, to shame.
confusión f. confusion.
confuso adj. confused, bewildered, blurred; vague.
congelado p.p. & adj. frozen, icy.
congelar v. to congeal, to freeze.
congeniar v. to be congenial; to sympathize.
congoja f. anguish, grief, anxiety.
congratular v. to congratulate.
congregación f. congregation, brotherhood; fraternity.
congregar v. to congregate, to assemble, to meet.
congresista m. congressman; f. congresswoman.
congreso m. congress, assembly; **— de los diputados** House of Representatives.
conjetura f. conjecture, guess, surmise.
conjeturar v. to conjecture, to guess, to surmise.
conjugación f. conjugation; coupling.
conjugar v. to conjugate.
conjunción f. conjunction; union; association; combination.
conjunto m. total; whole; **en —** as a whole.
conjuración f. conspiracy, conjuration, complot.
conjurado m. conspirator.
conjurar v. to conjure, to conspire, to plot, to exorcise, to summon in a sacred name, to entreat, to implore; to ward off.
conmemorar v. to commemorate.
conmemorativo adj. commemorative; memorial.
conmigo pers. pron. with me, with myself.
conminación f. commination, threat.
conminatorio adj. threatening, comminatory.

conmoción f. commotion, concitation; stirring up; concussion.
conmovedor adj. moving, touching; stirring; disturbing.
conmover v. irr. to disturb, to affect; to move; to touch; to stir up.
conmutador m. electric switch; cuadro — switchboard.
connatural adj. connatural, inborn.
cono m. cone; pine cone.
conocedor adj. connoisseur; judge; critic; knowing, aware, expert; ser — de to be familiar with.
conocer v. irr. to know, to be acquainted with; to comprehend; to experience; to observe, to conjecture; to recognize; to meet; **se conoce que** it is clear or evident that.
conocido p.p. & adj. acquaintance; known; well known.
conocimiento m. knowledge; understanding, skill; cleverness; cognition; comprehension; acquaintance; bill of lading; **poner en —** to inform.
conque conj. so then, well then, so.
conquista f. conquest; subjection.
conquistador m. conqueror; adj. conquering, victorious.
conquistar v. to conquer, to overcome, to subdue; to dominate; to defeat, to win.
consabido adj. already known; before-mentioned, aforesaid.
consagración f. consecration.
consagrar v. to consecrate, to hallow, to make sacred; to devote; to dedicate.
consciente adj. conscious.
consecuencia f. consequence, inference, result; **a — de** as a result of; **por (or en) —** therefore; consequently.
consecuente adj. consequent, logical; consistent.
consecutivo adj. consecutive; successive.
conseguir v. irr. to attain; to get.
conseja f. story, fable.
consejero m. adviser, counsellor.
consejo m. counsel, advice, council, court; **— de ministros** cabinet.
consentimiento m. consent, connivance, acknowledgement.
consentir v. irr. to consent; to agree; to comply; to acquiesce; to permit, to pamper, to spoil.
conserje m. janitor, caretaker; keeper or warden of a royal palace or castle.
conserva f. conserve, preserve; pickles; Am. filling (for tarts or candy).
conservación f. conservation.
conservador m. conservator, preserver; conservative; adj. conservative.
conservar v. to conserve, to maintain; to preserve, to guard, to keep; to candy.
considerable adj. considerable.
consideración f. consideration; regard, notice, sake, account, reflection, contemplation, meditation; **ser de —** to be of great importance.
considerado adj. prudent, considerate; circumspect, thoughtful.
considerar v. to consider; to treat with consideration.
consigna f. watchword, password; Am. checkroom.
consignar v. to consign, to lay by, to deposit, to deliver, to assign, to check.
consigo pers. pron. with oneself; with himself (herself, yourself, themselves, yourselves); **— mismo** by oneself.
consiguiente m. consequence, result, adj. consequent, consecutive; **de (or por) —** adv. consequently.
consistente adj. consistent, firm, solid, substantial.
consistir v. to consist, to subsist, to be comprised; to be based on.
consocio m. associate, partner, fellow.
consolación f. consolation, comfort.
consolar v. irr. to console, to comfort, to reanimate, to cheer.
consolidar v. to consolidate, to compact, to harden; to make solid, to unite, to combine.
consonante m. perfect rythm; consonant; adj. consistent, agreeable.
consorte m. & f. consort, companion, partner, mate.
conspicuo adj. conspicuous, obvious, eminent.
conspiración f. conspiracy, plot.
conspirador m. conspirator, plotter.
conspirar v. to conspire, to plot.
constancia f. constancy, steadiness, perseverance; evidence, certainty; Am. documentary proof, record.
constante adj. constant, firm, per-

constar severing, loyal, continual, faithful.
constar v. to be clear, to be evident, to be certain, to be composed of, to consist in; to be on record.
constatación f. Am. proof, evidence.
constelación f. constellation.
constipado adj. suffering from cold; m. cold in the head.
constipar v. to cause a cold; —se to catch a cold.
constitución f. constitution.
constitucional adj. constitutional, constitutionalist.
constituir v. irr. to constitute, to erect, to establish; to make, to create, to appoint, to depute; —se en to set oneself up as.
constituyente adj. constituent.
constreñir v. irr. to constrain, to compel, to force.
construcción f. construction, building; structure.
construir v. irr. to form, to build, to construct; to translate literally.
consuelo m. consolation, comfort; joy, merriment; relief; cheer.
consuetudinario adj. customary, habitual; **derecho —** common law.
cónsul m. consul.
consulado m. consulate, consulship.
consulta f. consultation, consult, conference; question proposed.
consultar v. to consult, to deliberate.
consultorio m. office for consultation; doctor's office or clinic.
consumado p.p. & adj. consummate, complete, perfect, accomplished; m. jellybroth.
consumar v. to consummate, to finish; to complete.
consumidor m. consumer; adj. consuming.
consumir v. to consume, to destroy; to waste; —se to be consumed; to burn out; to be exhausted; to waste away.
consumo m. consumption.
consunción f. consumption.
contabilidad f. accounting, bookkeeping.
contacto m. contact, touch, union.
contado: al — cash; **de —** immediately; **por de —** of course; **—s** adj. few, scarce, rare.
contador m. computer, accountant, numberer, numerator, counter; desk; auditor; purser; meter.

contaduría f. auditor's or accountant's office; auditorship; box office; cashier's office; accounting.
contagiar v. to infect, to communicate a disease, to corrupt.
contagio m. contagion; infection; corruption of morals.
contagioso adj. contagious, malign; infectious.
contar v. irr. to count, to reckon, to number, to compute, to relate, to class, to consider; to depend, rely; to tell; **— con** to count on, rely on; **a — desde** starting from, beginning with.
contemplación f. contemplation, meditation.
contemplar v. to contemplate, to study, to meditate, to muse; to gaze at; to examine.
contemporáneo adj. contemporaneous, contemporary.
contender v. irr. to contend, to contest, to conflict, to debate, to litigate, to argue, to fight.
contener v. irr. to contain, to comprise, to refrain, to curb, to restrain, to repress, to check; —se to refrain, to restrain oneself.
contenido adj. moderate, temperate, modest m. contents.
contentamiento m. contentment, joy.
contentar v. to content, to satisfy; to please; to indorse; to give pleasure, to make happy; —se to be satisfied; Am. to make up, to renew friendship.
contento adj. glad, pleased, contented, satisfied, content; m. contentment, gladness.
contera f. shoe (of a cane, umbrella, etc.); tip, end, refrain of a song; **por —** as a finish.
contertulio m. fellow-member.
contestación f. answer, reply, contestation; debate, strife, altercation, argument.
contestar v. to answer, to reply.
contextura f. contexture, context, texture, composition.
contienda f. contest, dispute, debate, conflict.
contigo pers. pron. with thee, with you.
contiguo adj. contiguous, close, adjacent.
continental adj. continental.
continente m. continent; countenance; adj. continent, abstinent; moderate, sober.

— 61 —

contingencia f. contingence, contingency, possibility, risk.
contingente adj. contingent, accidental; m. contingent; share.
continuación f. continuation, continuity, continuance; **a —** below, as follows.
continuar v. to continue, to hold, to last, to endure, to pursue.
continuidad f. continuity.
continuo adj. continuous, continual, constant, lasting.
contonearse v. to walk with an affected air or manner; to strut; to swagger; to waddle.
contoneo m. waddling, strut.
contorno m. environs, vicinity, contour, outline, surrounding.
contra prep. against, in opposition to, counter, contrary to, opposite to; **el pro y el —** the pro and con; **ni a favor ni en —** neither pro nor con; **—s** Am. play off, final game (to determine the winner); **llevar a uno la —** to contradict a person, to take the opposite view.
contraalmirante m. rear admiral.
contrabandear v. to smuggle.
contrabandista m. smuggler.
contrabando m. contraband trade, smuggled goods; smuggling.
contracción f. contraction, shrinking, constriction; corrugation; abbreviation; abridgment.
contradecir v. irr. to contradict; **espíritu de —** contradictory temper.
contradictorio adj. contradictory; contrary, opposing.
contraer v. irr. to contract, to knit, to join, to unite; to shrink up; to crumple; **— deudas** to run in debt; **— enfermedad** to contract a disease; **— matrimonio** to get married; **—se** to shrink, to contract.
contrafuerte m. buttress; spur; **—s** secondary chain of mountains.
contrahecho p.p. & adj. counterfeit, forged; deformed; hump-backed.
contralor m. comptroller, inspector. See **controlador**.
contraorden f. countermand.
contrapelo: a — against the grain.
contrapesar v. to counterbalance, balance; to offset; to counterpoise.
contrariar v. to oppose, to contradict; to irritate, to vex; to counteract.

contrariedad f. opposition; contradiction; bother, irritation; disappointment; contrariety.
contrario adj. contrary, repugnant, opposite, contradictory; adverse; **al —** or **por el —** on the contrary; m. opponent, antagonist; competitor, rival; contrary, hurtful.
contrarrestar v. to resist, to oppose; to counterbalance; to counteract; to strike back (a ball).
contraseña f. countersign, countermark; password, wartchword; **— de salida** theater check (to readmit one who goes out).
contrastar v. to contrast, to oppose; to resist, to contradict; to test (weights, measures, etc.); to assay (metals).
contraste m. assayer of the mint, assayer's office; assayer of weights and measures; counterview; contrast; opposition and strife; dissimilitude.
contrata f. contract; **— de arriendo** lease; **— de fletamiento** charterparty.
contratar v. to contract for; to trade, to engage, to hire (men); **—se** to come to, or make an agreement.
contratiempo m. disappointment, misfortune, mishap, accident.
contratista m. & f. contractor.
contrato m. contract.
contribución f. contribution, tax.
contribuir v. irr. to contribute; to concur; to promote.
contribuyente m. contributor, taxpayer; adj. contributing.
control m. Am. control.
controlador m. Am. comptroller.
controlar v. Am. to control.
controversia f. controversy.
contumacia f. stubborness, obstinacy, perverseness; contempt to court, failure to appear in court; contumacy.
contumaz adj. obstinate, stubborn, contumacious.
contusión f. bruise, contusion.
convalecer v. irr. to convalesce; to recover from an illness; to recover lost property, etc.
convecino adj. near, neighboring; m. neighbor.
convencer v. to convince.
convencimiento m. conviction, belief; convincing.
convención f. convention, contract, pact, assembly, agreement; Am. political convention.

CONVENCIONAL   **CORNADA**

convencional adj. conventional.
convenido adj. agreed, O. K., all right.
conveniencia f. convenience, comfort; utility, profit.
conveniente adj. convenient, useful, profitable; accordant, conformable; fit, suitable, agreeable; expedient, opportune; commodious; timely.
convenio m. convention, contract; agreement, pact; plot.
convenir v. irr. to agree, to coincide; to cohere; to fit, to harmonize; to correspond, to belong; to assemble, to convene; —se to agree, to suit.
conventillo m. Am. tenement house; small convent.
convento m. convent.
convergente adj. convergent, converging.
converger v. to converge.
conversación f. conversation.
conversar v. to converse.
conversión f. conversion.
convertir v. irr. to convert.
convicción f. conviction.
convicto p.p. convicted, guilty.
convidado m. guest; — y con ollita Am. guest who abuses hospitality.
convidar v. to invite, to bid, to treat; to allure, to persuade; —se to offer one's services; to invite oneself.
convincente adj. convincing.
convite m. invitation, treat.
convocación f. convocation.
convocar v. to convoke, to convene, to call together.
convoyar v. to convoy, to escort.
convulsión f. convulsion.
convulsivo adj. convulsive; tos convulsiva whooping cough.
conyugal adj. conjugal; vida — married life.
cónyuge m. husband f. wife.
cooperación f. cooperation.
cooperador adj. cooperating, cooperative; m. cooperator.
cooperar v. to cooperate.
cooperativa f. cooperative; cooperative society.
coordinación f. coordination.
coordinar v. to coordinate.
copa f. cup, goblet, wineglass; treetop; crown of a hat; brazier, fire pan; **empinar la —, tomar la —** to drink, to get drunk; **invitar la —** to buy a drink.

copartícipe adj. participant; m. & f. joint partner.
copete m. tuft, crest; top, summit; crownwork of furniture; **de —** of high rank, important; proud; **estar uno hasta el —** to be stuffed; to be fed up; **tener mucho —** to be arrogant, haughty.
copia f. copy, imitation; abundance.
copiar v. to copy.
copioso adj. copious, abundant.
copita f. little glass, little drink.
copla f. couplet; popular song.
copo m. snowflake; wad; tuft (of wool, cotton, hemp, etc.).
coqueta f. coquette, flirt.
coquetear v. to flirt.
coquetería f. coquetry, flirting.
coraje m. courage, valor, anger; bravery, passion.
coral m. coral; Am. a poisonous snake; **—es** coral beads; adj. coral, belonging to a choir.
coralino adj. coral, like coral.
coraza f. cuirass, armor; armor plate or plating; carapace (of a turtle).
corazón m. heart, core, middle.
corazonada f. presentiment, foreboding; hunch.
corbata f. necktie; cravat.
corcel m. charger, steed; steady horse.
corcova f. hump, hunch.
corcovado adj. hunchbacked; m. hunchback.
corcovear v. to prance about, to leap; Am. to kick, to protest.
corcho m. cork, beehive; adj. corklike, spongy.
cordel m. cord, rope.
cordero m. lamb; lambskin.
cordial adj. cordial, friendly; **dedo —** middle finger; a comforting medicine or drink.
cordialidad f. cordiality, friendliness. warmth.
cordillera f. mountain range.
cordobés adj. Cordovan, of or pertaining to Cordova; m. native of Cordova.
cordón m. cord; braid; cordon; **— de la acera;** Am. curb.
cordoncillo m. small cord; drawstring, lace, lacing; braid; mill (ridged edge a coin); ridge, rib.
cordura f. prudence, practical wisdom, judgment, good sense.
cornada f. goring; butt with the horns; **dar —s** to gore, to horn, to butt with the horns.

corneta f. cornet; bugle; horn; m. bugler.
cornisa f. cornice.
coro m. choir; chorus.
corona f. crown, wreath.
coronar v. to crown; to top.
coronel m. colonel.
coronilla f. small crown; crown of the head; **estar uno hasta la —** to be fed up, to be satiated.
corpachón m. large body or carcass.
corpiño m. bodice.
corporación f. corporation.
corporal adj. corporal, bodily; m. corporal (small piece of cloth used in mass).
corpóreo adj. corporeal, corporeous; bodily; tangible, material.
corpulento adj. corpulent, fat, stout; fleshy.
corral m. yard, corral, cattle yard.
correa f. leather strap; leash; resistance carrier; **tener muchas —s** Am. to be phlegmatic, calm.
corrección f. correction, correctness.
correcto adj. correct, proper.
corredizo adj. sliding; sliping; **nudo —** runnig knot.
corredor m. runner; racer; race horse; corridor, gallery, covert way; forerunner; broker; Am. covered porch; beater of wild game; **— de cambios** exchange broker; adj. unning, speedy.
corregidor m. corrector; Spanish magistrate.
corregir v. irr. to correct, to reprove, to amend, to mend, to reprehend, to admonish; to mitigate; **—se** to mend, to reform.
correligionario adj. of the same religion or political party; m. correligionist.
correo m. post, poster, express, courier; letter-carrier; post office; mail; mail service; bag of mail; **— aéreo** air mail.
correoso adj. leathery, tough; ductile, flexible, easily bent.
correr v. to run; to blow; to flow, to stream; to pass away, to elapse; to race, to chase; Am. to dismiss, to throw out; **—se** to slip through; to slide; to be confused.
correría f. foray, raid; excursion, short trip; **—s** raids, escapades, wanderings.
correspondencia f. correspondence; commerce, intercourse; friendship; proportion, symmetry, congruity; consent, agreement; letters, mail.
corresponder v. to reciprocate; to return a favor; to correspond, to answer; to fit, to suit; to agree; to belong, to concern; **—se** to keep up intercourse by mail; to respect or esteem each other.
correspondiente adj. corresponding, agreeing; respective; m. correspondent.
corresponsal m. correspondent, agent, newspaper reporter.
corretear v. to run around; to roam; to rove; to walk the streets; to ramble, to flirt; Am. to pursue, to chase.
corrida f. race; course; career; Am. row, file; night spree; beating up of game; **— del tiempo** swiftness of time; **— de toros** bullfight; **de —** without stopping.
corrido adj. embarrased, ashamed; wordly-wise; flowing, fluent; **de —** without stopping; Am. popular romance in words and music.
corriente adj. running, flowing, fluent; usual, common, ordinary; Am. frank, open; **¡—!** all right! O.K.!; **el cuatro del —** the fourth of the present month; **estar al —** to be up-to-date; to be well informed; **poner a uno al —** to keep someone well informed; f. current, stream, course; **hay que llevarle la —** Am. you must humor him.
corrillo m. group of gossipers or loungers.
corro m. group of talkers or spectators.
corroer v. irr. to corrode.
corromper v. to corrupt; to seduce; to bribe; **—se** to rot; to become corrupted.
corrompido adj. corrupt, rotten; spoiled; degenerate.
corrupción f. corruption.
corrupto adj. corrupt, rotten.
corsé m. corset.
cortada f. Am. cut, slash.
cortador m. cutter; Am. tailor.
cortadura f. cut, gash, slash.
cortaplumas m. penknife.
cortar v. to cut, to cut off, to cut out, to curtail; to disjoin, to separate, to hew, to chop; to interrupt; Am. to harvest; to pick; to gossip, to speak ill of someone; **—se** to be embarrassed; to be ashamed; to sour, to cur-

corte — **dle;** Am. to become separated, cut off; to leave in a hurry; to die.

corte m. cut; cutting; cutting edge; style; Am. cut (in cards); f. royal court; retinue; Am. court of justice; —s Spanish parliament; **hacer la —** to court, to woo; **darse uno —** to put on airs.

cortedad f. smallness; timidity; bashfulness, shyness.

cortejar v. to court, to woo, to make love.

cortejo m. cortege, procession; retinue; courtship; suitor.

cortés adj. courteous, gentle, complaisant, genteel, polite.

cortesana f. courtesan, prostitute.

cortesano adj. courtlike, gentle, courteous, courtly; polite, astute; m. courtier.

cortesía f. courtesy, compliment; gift; present; gratification; days of grace; mercy; favor.

corteza f. bark, peel, skin, rind, crust; rusticity; want of politeness.

cortijo m. farmhouse.

cortina f. curtain; covering.

corto adj. short, scanty, narrow, curt; small, little; bashful; dull; stupid; imperfect, defective; **— de vista** shortsighted; **— de oído** hard of hearing; **a la corta o a la larga** sooner or later.

corveta f. buck, leap, bound; **hacer —s** to prance.

corvo adj. See curvo.

cosa f. thing, substance; **— de** approximately, about; **no es gran —** it is but a trifle; **otra —** something else; **como si tal —** serene, as if nothing had happened; **ni por una de estas nueve —s** Am. absolutely not, not for anything in the world; **— de ver** a thing worth seeing; **¿ qué —?** what is the matter?

cosecha f. crop, harvest.

cosechar v. to reap, to harvest.

coser v. to sew, to stitch.

cosmético m. & adj. cosmetic.

cosquillas f. pl. ticklishness, tickling; **hacer —** to tickle, to excite; **tener —** to be ticklish.

cosquillear v. to tickle, to excite.

costa f. coast; cost, expense, price; **a toda —** at any price, by all means.

costado m. side, flank.

costal m. sack; large bag; rammer; **esa es harina de otro —** that is a quite different thing; **estar hecho un — de huesos** to be nothing but skin and bones, to be very thin.

costanero adj. coastal; belonging to a coast; sloping.

costar v. irr. to cost; **— trabajo** to be difficult.

costarricense adj., m. & f. Costa Rican.

coste m. cost, expense.

costear v. to pay cost; to pay, to be profitable; to navigate along the coast; to go along the edge of; **no costea** it does not pay.

costero adj. coastal; **navegación costera** coastal navigation.

costilla f. rib, chop, cutlet; Am. wife.

costo m. See coste.

costoso adj. costly, expensive.

costra f. crust, scab.

costroso adj. crusty, scaby.

costumbre f. custom, habit; periodical indisposition of women; **—s populares** folklore.

costura f. sewing; stitching; seam.

costurera f. seamstress.

costurero m. sewing room; sewing cabinet, sewing box.

costurón m. coarse stitching; large seam; patch, mend; big scar.

cotejar v. to confront, to compare.

cotejo m. comparison.

cotense m. Am. burlap.

cotidiano adj. daily.

cotizable adj. quotable.

cotización f. quotation; current price.

cotizar v. to quote; Am. to contribute one's share or quota; to distribute proportionally.

coto m. inclosure; landmark, limitation, limit, boundary; **poner — a** to set a limit to; to put an end to.

cotorra f. small parrot; magpie; talkative person, chatterbox.

cotorrear v. to chatter, to gossip.

covacha f. small cave; grotto; Am. hut, shanty; cubbyhole; small dark room.

coyote m. Am. coyote, prairie wolf; shyster, tricky lawyer; agent, broker (illegal).

coyuntura f. joint, articulation; occasion; opportunity.

coz f. kick; recoil of a gun; butt of a fire arm; **dar (or tirar) coces** to kick.

cráneo m. cranium, skull; **tener seco el —** to be stupid.

craso adj. fat, thick, coarse,

gross; **ignorancia crasa** gross ignorance.
cráter m. crater.
creación f. creation.
creador m. creator; adj. creating, creative.
crear v. to create.
crecer v. irr. to grow, to increase; to augment; —**se** to swell.
creciente adj. growing, increasing; f. river flood; m. crescent.
crecimiento m. growth, increase.
credenciales f. pl. credentials.
crédito m. credit, belief; fame, reputation; **carta de —** letter of credit; **dar —** a to loan on credit; to belive.
credo m. creed; **en un —** in a trice; in a minute.
crédulo adj. credulous.
creencia f. belief, faith.
creer v. to believe; to think, to suppose; to feel; **¡ya lo creo!** yes, of course!
creíble adj. credible, believable.
crema f. cream; custard; cold cream.
crepitar v. to crackle, to snap, to creak, to rattle.
crepuscular adj. twilight.
crepúsculo m. twilight.
crespo adj. curly.
crespón m. crepe.
cresta f. crest, top, summit; tuft, comb (of a bird).
cretona f. cretone.
creyente m. & f. believer; adj. believing.
creyón m. Am. crayon.
cría f. brood; suckling, breeding.
criadero m. nursery; breeding place, hotbed; rich mine.
criada f. maid; servant.
criado m. servant, menial, groom; adj. educated, instructed, bred; **mal —** ill-bred.
criador m. breeder, raiser, rearer; creator; adj. creating, creative; breeding, nourishing.
crianza f. breeding, nursing, manners.
criar v. to breed; to bring up, to rear, to educate, to nurse; to suckle, to foster; to fatten; **— molleja** to grow lazy.
criatura f. creature; baby; child.
criba f. sieve.
cribar v. to sift.
crimen m. crime; offense, guilt.
criminal adj., m. & f. criminal.
crin f. mane.
crinudo adj. Am. with a long or thick mane.

criollo m. Am. creole; adj. Am. national, domestic.
crisantema m. & f. chrysanthemum.
crisis f. crisis.
crisol m. crucible, melting pot; hearth of a furnace.
crispar v. to shrivel; to contract; to clench; to twitch.
cristal m. crystal; glass; mirror; lens.
cristalería f. glassware shop or factory; glasware.
cristalino adj. crystalline, transparent, clear; m. crystalline of the eye.
cristalizar v. to crystallize.
cristiandad f. Christianity; Christendom.
cristianismo m. Christianity; Christianism.
cristiano m. Christian; person; **hablar en —** to speak clearly; adj. Christian.
criterio m. criterion, rule, standard; judgment.
crítica f. criticism; censure, gossip.
criticador adj. critical; m. critic, judge; Am. faultfinder; adj. critical, over-critical, faulfindering.
croar v. to croak.
crónica f. chronicle, history.
crónico adj. cronic.
cronómetro m. chronometer; timepiece.
croquis m. rough sketch.
cruce m. crossing, crossroads.
crucero m. cross-bearer; crossing, crossingroads; cruiser; transept; crossbeam; Cross (constellation).
crucificar v. to crucify.
crucifijo m. crucifix.
crucigrama m. crossword puzzle.
cruda f. Am. hang-over.
crudo adj. raw, uncooked; unripe; harsh; rude, cruel, pitiless, grievous; **agua cruda** hard water; **petróleo —** crude oil; **estar —** to have a hang-over.
cruel adj. cruel, hard, severe.
crueldad f. cruelty.
crujido m. creak, crack, creaking; rustle.
crujir v. to creak, to crackle; to rustle; to crunch.
cruz f. cross.
cruzada f. crusade; holy war.
cruzado m. crusader; adj. crossed, cross, crosswise, transverse.
cruzamiento m. crossing, crossroads.
cruzar v. to cross; **—se con** to meet.

cuaco m. Am. horse.

cuaderno m. notebook, memorandum book; Am. pamphlet.

cuadra f. hall, large room; stable; hospital or prison ward; Am. city block; reception room.

cuadrado adj. square; m. square; square ruler; die, metal block or plate.

cuadrante m. dial, face of a clock or watch; sundial; quadrant.

cuadrar v. to square; to fit, to suit, to adjust; to please; Am. to be becoming (said of clothes); to be ready; to contribute a great sum; Am. to come out well, to succeed; —se to stand at attention.

cuadricular v. to square off, to divide into squares.

cuadrilla f. group, troupe, gang; armed band; quadrille, square dance.

cuadro m. square, picture, scene; frame; flower bed; Am. blackboard; Am. slaughterhouse.

cuajada f. curd.

cuajado p.p. & adj. coagulated, curdled; filled, covered; — de full of, covered with.

cuajar v. to coagulate, to thicken, to curd, to curdle; to turn out well; to please, to like; Am. to chatter, to prattle; —se to coagulate, to curd; to be filled, to become crowded; **la cosa no cuajó** the thing did not work.

cuajarón m. clot.

cual rel. pron. which; **cada —** each one; **— más, — menos** some people more, other less; **el —, la —, lo —, las —es, los —es** which; who; adv. as, like; **— más — menos todos hacen lo mismo** more or less they all do the same.

cualidad f. quality, trait.

cualquier(a) indef. adj. & pron. any, anyone; whichever; **un hombre —** any man whatever.

cuando rel. adv. & conj. when; **aun —** even though.

cuantía f. quantity, rank, importance.

cuantioso adj. plentiful, abundant; numerous.

cuanto rel. adj. & pron. as much as, as many as; all that; **— antes** as soon as possible, immediately; **en —** conj. as soon as; **en — a** as for, with regard to; **unos —s** a few.

cuarentena f. quarantine; forty units; period of forty days, months, or years.

cuarentón m. man in his forties.

cuarentona f. woman in her forties.

cuaresma f. lent.

cuarta f. fourth, fourth part; span of a hand; Am. horse whip; **echar —** Am. to beat, to flog.

cuartear v. to quarter, to divide into four parts; to bid a fourth more on at public sales; to make a fourth person at a game; Am. to whip; —se to crack, to split; Am. to go back on one's word.

cuartel m. quarter, one fourth; quarters, barracks; district; quarter, mercy; **no dar —** to give no quarter.

cuartelada f. military coup d'état, uprising, insurrection.

cuartelazo m. Am. military coup d'état, insurrection.

cuarterón m. quarter, fourth part; fourth of a pound; adj. & m. quadroon.

cuarteto m. quartet.

cuartilla f. sheet of paper; fourth of an arroba; Am. three cents worth; **no valer uno una —** Am. not to be worth a penny.

cuartillo m. fourth of a peck; about a pint; fourth of a real.

cuarto m. room; quarter; one fourth; **tener —s** to have money; adj. fourth.

cuarzo m. quartz.

cuate adj., m. & f. Am. twin.

cuatrero m. horse thief, cattle thief.

cuba f. cask, barrel; tub, vat; bigbellied person; toper, drunkard.

cubano adj. & m. Cuban.

cubeta f. small barrel or keg; bucket, pail.

cúbico adj. cubic.

cubierta f. cover; covering; envelope; deck (of a ship).

cubo m. cube; bucket, pail;; hub of a wheel; mill pond; Am. finger bowl.

cubremesa f. table cover.

cubrir v. irr. to cover, to lay, to spread over; to screen, to palliate; to disguise, to cloak; to roof; to settle or pay a bill; —se to cover oneself; to put on one's hat.

cucaracha f. cockroach.

cuclillas: en — in a squatting position; **sentarse en —** to squat.

cuclillo m. cuckoo.

cuco adj. dainty, cute; sly, shrewd:

CUCURUCHO

cucurucho m. cuckoo; a kind or caterpillar; card game; Am. peach. **hacer** — Am. to make fun of; to fool.
cucurucho m. paper cone; Am. peak, summit; cowl, cloak with a hood worn by penitents in Holy Week processions.
cuchara f. spoon; scoop; mason's trowel; **media** — mediocre person; Am. mason's helper; **hacer** — Am. to pout; **meter uno su** — Am. to butt into a conversation; to meddle.
cucharada f. spoonful; scoop.
cucharón m. large spoon; ladle; dipper, scoop.
cuchichear v. to whisper.
cuchicheo m. whispering, whisper.
cuchilla f. large knife, cleaver; blade; Am. penknife; mountain ridge.
cuchillada f. slash with a knife, stab, cut, gash.
cuchillería f. cutlery, cutlery shop.
cuchillo m. knife, gore (in a garment); — **de monte** hunting knife.
cueca f. Am. Chilean dance.
cuello m. neck, collar.
cuenca f. river basin; deep valley; wooden bowl; socket of the eye.
cuenco m. earthen bowl.
cuenta f. computation, calculation; account, count, reckoning; narrative; bead of a rosary; reason, satisfaction; **a fin de** —s in the final analysis; **caer en la** — to see, to get the point; **darse** — to realize; **de toda** — Am. anyway; **eso corre de mi** — that is my responsibility; I'll take charge of that; **eso no tiene** — that is not profitable or advantageous; **en resumidas** —s in short; **hacerle** — **una cosa a uno** Am. to be useful or profitable for one; **tomar en** — to take into account; **tomar una cosa por su** — to take charge of something, to take the responsibility for it; **vamos a** —s let's understand or settle this.
cuentagotas m. dropper (for counting drops).
cuento m. story, tale; — **de nunca acabar** never-ending tale; **déjese de** —s come to the point; **no viene al** — it is not pertinent or to the point.
cuerda f. cord, string, rope; chord; watch spring; **dar** — **a** to wind up (a watch).
cuerdo adj. sane, wise, sensible.

CULPABILIDAD

cuereada f. Am. flogging, whipping.
cuerear v. Am. to flog, to whip; to harm, to dishonor; to beat in a game.
cuerno m. horn; antenna, feeler; **poner** —s a to be unfaithful to, to deceive (a husband); **mandar al** — Am. to send to the devil.
cuero m. hide, skin; leather; wineskin; Am. whip; **en** —s naked.
cuerpo m. body, trunk; corpse, dead body; matter; corporation; volume, book; bulk; corps; **en** — without hat or cloak; **luchar** — **a** — to fight in single combat; **sacar el** — Am. to dodge, to escape, to avoid doing something.
cuervo m. crow, raven; buzzard; Am. dishonest priest; **hacer uno la del** — Am. to leave abruptly and not return.
cuesta f. slope; **a** —s on one's shoulders or back; to one's care; — **abajo** down hill; — **arriba** up hill.
cuestión f. question; controversy, dispute; problem; matter.
cuestionario m. questionary.
cueva f. cave, cavern; cellar.
cuico m. Am. cop, policeman; gossiper, half breed; short, chubby person.
cuidado m. care, attention; worry, misgiving; **al** — **de** in care of; **tener** — to be careful; ¡ — ! look out!; be careful!
cuidadoso adj. careful; attentive; anxious.
cuidar v. to take care of, look after; to keep; to make or to do carefully; to mind.
cuita f. grief, care, anxiety; Am. bird dung.
cuitado adj. unfortunate; timid; shy.
culata f. haunch, buttock; rear; butt of a firearm.
culatazo m. blow with the butt of a firearm, recoil of a gun.
culebra f. snake; coil; Am. money belt.
culebrear v. to zigzag; to twist, to wriggle.
culminación f. culmination, climax.
culminar v. to culminate; to come to a climax.
culpa f. fault; guilt; blame; **echar la** — **a** to blame; **tener la** — to be to blame.
culpabilidad f. guilt.

— 68 —

culpable adj. guilty.
culpar v. to blame; to condemn.
cultivador m. cultivator.
cultivar v. to cultivate.
cultivo m. cultivation, culture.
culto adj. cultured; m. cult, worship; religious sect; **rendir —** to pay homage; to worship.
cultura f. culture, cultivation.
cumbre f. summit, top.
cumpleaños m. birthday.
cumplido adj. complete, full; polished, polite, civil; large, plentiful, high; p.p. fulfilled; due; **tiene tres años —s** he is just over three years old; m. courtesy; attention; compliment.
cumplimentar v. to compliment; to congratulate; to carry out.
cumplimiento m. fulfilment; courtesy; completion; compliment; **de —** formal.
cumplir v. to fulfill; to comply; to carry out; to fall due; **— años** to have a birthday; to be (so many) years old.
cúmulo m. pile, heap, accumulation; cumulus (clouds).
cuna f. cradle; origin; Am. coffin for the poor; dive, den.
cundir v. to spread (as news, liquids); to propagate, to extend, to multiply.
cuña f. wedge; splinter; Am. influential person.
cuñada f. sister-in-law.
cuñado m. brother-in-law.
cuota f. quota, share, fee; **— de entrada** admission fee.
cuotidiano adj. everyday, daily.
cupé m. coupé, landau, cab.
cupón m. coupon, dividend.
cúpula f. dome, cupola.
cura f. cure, healing; parsonage; m. curate, priest, rector, parson, clergyman.
curandero m. medicaster; quack.
curar v. to cure, to heal, to restore to health; to administer medicines to a patient; to treat; to salt or cure; to tan; Am. to load (dice); to fix (cards); **— de** to take care of; **—se** to cure oneself; to get well; Am. to get drunk.
curiosear v. to snoop; to peek, to peer, to pry; to observe with curiosity.
curiosidad f. curiosity; neatness, daintiness.
curioso adj. curious; neat, dainty; **libros raros y —s** rare books.

curro adj. showy, gawdy, flashy; m. dandy.
currutaco m. fop, dandy; adj. affected; dudish.
cursi adj. common; in bad taste; cheap, ridiculous.
cursilería f. bad taste, cheapness; false elegance.
curso m. course, direction, course of study.
curtidor m. tanner.
curtiduría f. tannery.
curtir v. to tan; to harden, to accustom to hardships; Am. to dirty, to soil; **—se** to get tanned or sunburned; to become accustomed to hardships.
curva f. curve.
curvo adj. curved; bent, crooked; arched.
cúspide f. summit, peak, top; spire, steeple.
custodia f. custody; guard, guardian; monstrance.
custodiar v. to guard, to watch; to keep in custody.
custodio m. guardian, keeper.
cutícula f. cuticle.
cutis m. skin; complexion.
cuyo rel. poss. adj. whose, of whom, of which.

CH

chabacano adj. crude, unpolished; cheap, in bad taste; m. Am. a variety of apricot.
chacota f. fun, jest; **echar a —** to take as a joke; **hacer — de** to make fun of.
chacotear v. to frolic, to joke, to make merry.
chacra f. Am. small farm; cultivated field.
chal m. shawl.
chalán m. horse trader; Am. horse breaker.
chaleco m. waistcoat, vest.
chalupa f. sloop, sailboat; launch; Am. canoe; raft; Am. Mexican tortilla with sauce.
chamaco m. Am. boy.
chamarra f. coarse wool jacket or sweater; Am. sheepskin jacket, leather jacket; heavy wool blanket.
chamarreta f. short loose jacket; Am. square poncho.
chambón adj. clumsy, awkward.
champaña f. champagne.
champú m. shampoo.
champurrado m. Am. a mixed drink

— 69 —

of chocolate and **atole**; a mixed alcoholic beverage.
chamuscada f. Am. singe, scorch.
chamuscar v. to scorch; to singe; to sear; Am. to sell at a low cost; —**se** to get scorched or seared; Am. to get peeved, offended.
chamusquina f. singe, scorch.
chancear v. to fool, to joke, to jest.
chancero m. jester, joker; adj. jolly.
chancla f. slipper; old shoe.
chancleta f. slipper; m. Am. good-for-nothing.
chanclo m. galosh, overshoe; clog; rubber overshoe.
changador m. Am. carrier, porter; handy man.
chantaje m. blackmail, black-mailing.
chanza f. joke, jest.
chapa f. metal plate; veneer; rosy spot on the cheeks; Am. lock; —**s** game of tossing up coins; **hombre de** — serious, reliable man.
chapado adj. veneered; — **a la antigua** old-fashioned.
chapalear See **chapotear**.
chaparro m. shrub oak; short, shubby person; Am. a kind of tropical shrub with rough leaves; short whip; adj. short, squatty.
chaparrón m. downpour, heavy shower.
chapitel m. spire, steeple; capital of a column.
chapotear v. to splash, paddle in the water.
chapoteo m. splash.
chapucear v. to fumble; to bungle, to do or make clumsily; Am. to deceive, to trick.
chapulín m. Am. grasshoper.
chapurrar v. to speak brokenly; to mix (liquors).
chapuz m. dive, duck, ducking.
chapuza f. botch, clumsy piece of work; Am. foul trick, fraud.
chapuzar v. to duck; to dive.
chaqueta f. jacket.
chaquetón m. long jacket, coat.
charamusca f. Am. twisted candy; brushwood, firewood; hubbub, uproar.
charamusquero m. Am. vendor or maker of twisted candy.
charca f. pond.
charco m. puddle, pool; **pasar el** — to cross the big pond (the ocean).
charla f. chat, chatter, prattle.

charlar v. to chat, chatter, to prate.
charlatán m. chatterer, prater; gossiper; quack.
charol m. varnish; patent leather.
charola f. Am. tray.
charolar v. to varnish, to polish.
chascarrillo m. joke, funny story.
chasco m. joke, prank; surprise; disappointment; **llevarse** — to be disappointed; adj. Am. thick, curly; ruffled.
chasquear v. to play a trick on; to disappoint; to crack (a whip); to smack (the lips); Am. to chatter (the teeth); Am. to munch (food); —**se** to be disappointed or disillusioned; to be tricked or fooled.
chasqui m. Am. courier, messenger.
chasquido m. crack of a whip; smack (of the lips); click (of the tongue).
chata f. bedpan; barge, flat-bottomed boat; Am. platform, wagon, platform car, flat car.
chatita f. Am. "honey", "cutie", "funny face".
chato adj. snub-nosed, flat-nosed; flat; flattened; squatty; **quedarse uno** — Am. to be left flat or in the lurch; to be disappointed.
che Am. word used in Argentina as a familiar form of address; ¡ — ! interj. Am. say! listen!
cheque m. check, bank check.
chica f. little girl; girl; maid, servant.
chicle m. Am. chicle; chewing gum.
chico adj. small, little; m. child, boy.
chicote m. cigar; piece of rope; Am. whip; cigar butt.
chicotear v. to lash, to whip, to flog; Am. to fight, to quarrel; to kill.
chicoteo m. Am. whipping; shooting, killing; Am. quarreling.
chicha f. Am. **chicha** (a popular fermented beverage); thick-soled shoe; **no ser ni** — **ni limonada** to be worth nothing, to be neither fish nor fowl.
chícharo m. pea; Am. bad cigar; apprentice.
chicharra f. cicada, locust; talkative person; Am. person with a shrill voice; rickety, squeaky car.
chicharrón m. creaking, crisp piece of fried porkskin; sunburnt person; Am. dried-up, wringled person; bootlicker, flatterer.

chichón m. bump, lump; Am. joker, jester.
chichona adj. Am. large-breasted.
chiflado adj. crazy.
chifladura f. craziness, mania; mockery, jest.
chiflar v. to whistle; to hiss; to mock, to jest; to tipple; —se to lose one's head; to become unbalanced, crazy.
chiflido m. whistle; hiss; Am. en un — in a jiffy, in a second.
chile m. chili, red pepper.
chileno adj. & m. Chilean.
chillante adj. flashy, bright, showy, loud; shrieking.
chillar v. to scream, to shriek, to crackle, to creak; to hiss; Am. to shout, to protest, to moan; to "squeal", to turn informer; no — Am. not to say a word.
chillido m. squeak, shriek, scream.
chillón adj. shrieking, screaming; shrill; loud, gaudy; Am. whining, discontented; touchy.
chimenea f. chimney; fireplace; the head.
china f. Chinese woman; pebble; porcelain; China silk or cotton; Am. girl, young woman; servant girl; sweet orange; spinning top.
chinche f. bedbug; thumb tack; tiresome person, bore; tener la sangre de — to be excessively unfortunate.
chino adj. Chinese; Am. curly; m. Chinese, Chinaman; Am. pig; half-breed; house servant; coarse, rough, ugly person; curl.
chiquero m. hog-sty, pigpen; hut for goats and kids; Am. place where bulls are shut up in bullfights.
chiquilín m. Am. tot, little boy.
chiquilina f. Am. little girl.
chiquito adj. tiny, very small; hacerse — to affect to be modest.
chiripa f. stroke of good luck; fortunate chance.
chiripá m. Am. loose riding trousers.
chirona f. "jug", jail.
chirriar v. to squeak, to creak; to sizzle; to crepitate; to go on a spree.
chirrido m. creak, squeak; chirp; squeaking, creaking, chirping.
chisguete m. squirt; small draft of wine.
chisme m. gossip, piece of gossip; trifle, trinket, knickknack, gadget.
chismear v. to gossip; to tattle.

chismoso adj. gossiping; m. gossip; talebearer, tattletale.
chispa f. spark; flake; very small diamond; wit, penetration, acumen; Am. false rumor, lie; two-wheeled cart; brazen, shameless woman; da — Am. it clicks, works, functions; ponerse — Am. to get drunk.
chispeante adj. sparkling.
chispear v. to spark, to sparkle; to twinkle; to drizzle.
chisporrotear v. to sputter.
chiste m. joke, jest, fun; dar en el — to guess right.
chistera f. top hat; hand basket for fish.
chistoso adj. funny, amusing, gay, lively, humorous, facetious.
¡chito! or **¡chitón!** interj. hush!
chiva f. female goat; Am. goateé.
chivo m. he-goat; Am. fit of anger; insulting remark; estar hecho un — Am. to be very angry; adj. Am. angry.
chocante adj. provoking, irritating, offensive, shocking, disgusting; Am. tiresome, annoying, impertinent.
chocar v. to bump, to collide, to clash; to strike, to knock; to hustle; to meet, to fight; me choca ese hombre I loathe that man.
chocarrear v. to tell coarse jokes; to clown; to jest.
chocarrería f. coarse jest.
chocarrero adj. coarse, vulgar, clownish.
choclo m. overshoe; clog; galosh; Am. low shoe or slipper; ear of corn; corn stew; spike, ear of wheat.
chocolate m. chocolate.
chochear v. to dote.
chochera f. senility, dotage.
chocho adj. doting; m. childish old man.
chofer m. chauffeur, driver.
cholo m. Am. half-breed; half civilized Indian; adj. Am. coarse, rude; dark-skinned.
chopo m. Am. black poplar; adj. Am. stupid.
choque m. collision, bump, shock, slash, dash, conflict, dispute.
chorizo m. sausage; Am. string of things; fool.
chorrear v. to drip, to spout.
chorro m. spurt, jet; stream, flow; — de voz a sonorous, rich voice; a —s abundantly, copiously.
choteador m. Am. joker, jester.

chotear v. Am. to make fun of, to jeer, to jest, to mock, to kid.

choteo m. Am. joking, jeering, kidding.

choza f. hut, cottage, cabin.

chubasco m. squall, sudden shower; **aguantar el —** to weather the storm.

chuchería f. trifle, trinket, tidbit, gewgaw.

chueco adj. crooked, bent; Am. crook-legged, bow-legged; knock-kneed, **comerciar en —** Am. to trade in stolen goods.

chuleta f. cutlet, chop; blow, slap; **— empanizada** cutlet dressed with bread crumbs.

chulo m. dandy; effeminate man; clownish fellow; bullfighter's assistant; good-looking, pretty.

chupada f. sucking; suction; suck, sip; Am. puff from a cigarette; big swallow of liquor.

chupador m. sucker; teething ring; Am. toper, heavy drinker, smoker.

chupaflor or **chuparrosa** m. Am. hummingbird.

chupar v. to suck; to sip, to absorb, to imbibe; to take in; Am. to smoke; to drink, to get drunk; **—se** to shrivel up.

churrasco m. Am. roasted meat; barbecued meat; large piece of meat for barbecuing.

churrasquear v. Am. to barbecue, to roast over coals; to prepare meat for barbecuing; to eat barbecued meat.

churrasquito m. Am. small piece of roast.

churrigueresco adj. baroque, ornate; overloaded.

chuscada f. jest, joke, pleasantry, drollery, buffoonery.

chusco adj. funny; witty; ridiculous; **perro —** Am. mongrel dog.

chusma f. rabble, mob.

D

dable adj. feasible, possible, easy.

daca word formed by **da** and **acá**, give me.

dádiva f. gift, present, grant, gratification, keepsake.

dadivoso adj. liberal, generous; magnificent.

dado m. die, **—s** dice; **— falso** (or **cargado**) cogged die; **a una vuelta de los —s** at the cast of the dice.

dador m. giver, donor.

daga f. dagger.

dama f. lady; dame; mistress or concubine; queen in the game of draughts; actress who performs the principal part in a play; **jugar a las —s** to play checkers.

damisela f. damsel, girl; gentlewoman; courtesan.

danza f. dance, ball.

danzante m. & f. dancer.

danzar v. to dance.

danzarina f. dancer.

dañar v. to harm, to hurt, to damage, to mar, to spoil, to rot; **—se** to get hurt, to get damaged.

dañino adj. harmful; destructive; hurtful.

daño m. damage, harm, loss, injury.

dar v. irr. to give, to bestow; to supply; to afford; to minister; to deliver; to confer; to hit, to strike, to beat, to knock; to allow, to grant; to appoint; to emit; to give off; **— contra alguna cosa** to hit against; **— crédito** to believe; **— cuenta de** to account; **— de comer** to feed; **— en el blanco** to hit the mark; **— en el rostro** to reproach; **— fiado** to give in credit; **— que hacer** to give trouble; **— prestado** to lend, to borrow; **— a bulto** to give by the lump or bulk; **— gana** to excite a desire, to have a mind to; **— al traste** to destroy; **— a luz** to give birth; to publish; **— con** to encounter, to find; **— de sí** to give, to stretch; **— en** to hit upon; to persist in; **— largas a un asunto** to prolong or postpone an affair; **— cuero** (**guasca, puños**) Am. to beat; to thrash, to lash; **lo mismo da** it makes no difference; **—se** to give up; **—selas de** to boast of.

dardo m. dart, arrow; **— de pescador** fishing harpoon.

dares y tomares m. pl. give and take; disputes, dealings.

dársena f. dock, wharf.

datar v. to date; **— de** to date from.

dátil m. date.

dato m. datum.

de prep. of, from, about, concerning; in; with, by, on, some, for, to; **— no llegar** if he does not come; **el — la nariz roja** the one

with the red nose; más — lo que cree more than he thinks.
debajo adv. under, underneath, below; — de prep. under.
debate m. debate; dispute, quarrel, altercation, discussion.
debatir v. to debate, to argue, to discuss; to fight; to combat; —se to struggle.
debe m. debit; debtor side, debit side.
debelar v. to subdue, to defeat; to debellate.
deber v. to owe; to have to; **debe de ser** it must be, probably is; ¡me la debes! I have an account to settle with you.
deber m. duty, obligation; debt; debit, debit side (in bookkeeping); **cumplir con su —** to fulfil one's duty.
debido adj. due, owing, just, appropiate.
débil adj. weak, feeble; extenuated, debilitated.
debilidad f. weakness, feebleness.
debilitación f. weakening; weakness.
debilitar v. to debilitate, to weaken.
débito m. debt; conjugal duty.
debutar v. to make one's debut, to make a first public appearance.
década f. decade, ten.
decadencia f. decadence, decline; decay.
decaer v. irr. to decay, to decline, to wither, to fade; to fall to leeward, to languish, to fail.
decaimiento m. decline, decay; dejection; weakness.
decano m. dean; oldest member of a group.
decantado p.p. & adj. much talked about; overrated, boasted.
decapitar v. to behead, to decapitate.
decencia f. decency.
decenio m. decade, space of ten years.
decente adj. decent; respectable; fair.
decepción f. disillusion, disappointment.
decepcionante adj. disappointing.
decepcionar v. to disillusion, to disappoint.
decidir v. to decide, to resolve; to determine; —se a to make up one's mind to; to decide to, to be determined.
décima f. tenth; ten-line stanza.
décimo adj. tenth.

decir v. irr. to say; to tell; to speak; to assure; to persuade; to declare; **es —** that is; **querer —** to mean, to signify; **¿qué se dice?** what is cooking?
decisión f. decision.
decisivo adj. decisive, final, conclusive.
declamar v. to declaim, to recite, to harangue.
declaración f. declaration; statement; deposition, testimony; manifestation.
declarar v. to declare, to state, to affirm; to testify; to manifest; to expound; —se to propose, to declare one's love; to give one's views or oppinion.
declinar v. to decline; to go down; to lose vigor, to decay; to bend down.
declive m. declivity, slope, inclination; **en —** downwards.
decoración f. decoration, ornament; stage setting.
decorar v. to decorate, to adorn; to ornament, to dress up; to doll up
decorativo adj. decorative, ornamental.
decoro m. decorum, propriety; dignity; honor.
decoroso adj. decorous, becoming, proper, decent; honourable.
decrépito adj. decrepit, old, feeble; very old.
decretar v. to decree.
decreto m. decree; decision, order, resolution.
dechado m. model, pattern, example; sample.
dedal m. thimble.
dedicar v. to dedicate; to devote; to consecrate; —se to devote oneself.
dedicatoria f. dedication, inscription.
dedillo m. small finger; **saber al —** to know perfectly, to know by heart.
dedo m. finger; toe; **— del corazón** middle finger; **— meñique** little finger; **— pulgar** thumb; **no mamarse el —** not to be easily fooled.
deducción f. deduction; inference, consequence.
deducir v. irr. to deduce, to conclude; to deduct; to infer.
defecto m. defect, fault, failing; **a —** default.
defectuoso adj. defective, faulty.

defender v. irr. to defend, to protect.
defensa f. defense; bumper of a car; shelter.
defensiva f. defense.
defensivo adj. defensive; defensory; m. defense, safeguard.
defensor m. defender, counsellor; protector.
deficiencia f. deficiency.
deficiente adj. deficient, defective, faulty.
déficit m. deficit, shortage; deficiency.
definición f. definition.
definido adj. definite.
definir v. to define, to explain; to determine, to describe.
definitivo adj. definitive; conclusive; final; **en definitiva** in short, in conclusion; definitely.
deformación f. deformation, deformity.
deformar v. to deform; to disfigure; —**se** to become deformed; to lose its shape or form.
deforme adj. deformed; ugly; disfigured.
deformidad f. deformity.
defraudar v. to defraud, to cheat; to rob of; to trick.
defunción f. death, decease.
degenerado adj. & m. degenerate.
degenerar v. to degenerate.
deglución f. swallowing.
deglutir v. to swallow.
degollar v. irr. to behead; to slash the throat, to decapitate; to destroy.
degradar v. to degrade, to debase.
degüello m. beheading, throat-slashing.
dehesa f. pasture ground.
deidad f. deity.
dejadez f. lassitude, languor, listlessness; neglect, slovenliness.
dejado adj. indolent, listless; slovenly, lazy, idle, low-spirited.
dejar v. to leave; to quit; to let go; to omit, to let; to permit; to abandon; to go from; to allow; to desert; to yield; — **de** to stop, cease; — **caer** to drop; **no** —**se** Am. not to be an easy mark, not to let others pick on one; — **en cueros** to strip one of his property; — **fresco a alguno** to frustrate, to baffle.
dejo m. aftertaste; slight accent; peculiar inflection; negligence, carelessness.
del contraction of **de** and **el**.
delantal m. apron.

delante adv. before, in front; — **de** in front of.
delantera f. lead, forepart, front.
delantero adj. front, foremost, first.
delatar v. to denounce, to accuse, to inform against.
delator m. accuser, informer; denouncer.
delegación f. delegation.
delegado m. delegate.
delegar v. to delegate.
deleitable adj. delightful, enjoyable.
deleitar v. to delight, to please.
deleite m. delight, joy, pleasure, gratification.
deleitoso adj. delightful, agreeable, pleasing.
deletrear v. to spell.
deleznable adj. perishable; brittle; fragile.
delgadez f. thinness, slenderness; fineness.
delgado adj. thin, slender, slim; delicate.
deliberado adj. deliberate.
deliberar v. to deliberate, to consider, to ponder.
delicadeza f. fineness, delicacy, softness, exquisiteness; tenderness.
delicado adj. delicate; weak; frail; exquisite; dainty; tender.
delicia f. delight.
delicioso adj. delicious, delightful.
delincuente adj., m. & f. delinquent, offender.
delineación f. delineation, design, outline, drawing, portrayal, sketch, draft.
delinear v. to delineate, to sketch, to outline.
delirante adj. delirious.
delirar v. to be delirious; to rave; to talk nonsense.
delirio m. delirium, temporary madness; wild excitement; nonsense.
delito m. crime; misdemeanor; transgression.
demacrado adj. scrawny, emaciated, thin.
demanda f. demand, petition, question; claim; complaint.
demandado m. defendant.
demandante m. & f. plaintiff.
demandar v. to demand; to sue; to indict; to claim, to covet.
demás indef. adj. & pron. **los** — the rest; the others; **las** — **personas** the other people; **lo** — the rest; **por** — useless, uselessly;

por lo — as to the rest; moreover.
demasía f. excess; boldness, insolence; offense, outrage; **en —** excessively.
demasiado adv. too much, excessively; too; adj. too much, excessive.
demente adj. demented, insane, crazy.
democracia f. democracy.
demócrata m. & f. democrat.
democrático adj. democratic.
demoler v. irr. to demolish, to tear down.
demonio m. demon, devil; evil spirit.
demontre m. devil; ¡—! the deuce!
demora f. delay.
demorar v. to delay; to retard; **—se** to linger; to be delayed.
demostración f. demonstration; proof, explanation.
demostrar v. irr. to demonstrate, to show, to prove, to explain.
demostrativo adj. demonstrative.
demudar v. to change, to alter; to disguise; **—se** to change color of one's facial expression; to turn pale.
dengue m. fastidiousness; prudery; primness; coyness, affectation; dengue, breakbone fever; Am. marigold; zigzag; Am. a wagger; **hacer —s** to act coy, to make grimaces.
denigrar v. to denigrate, to defame, to revile, to insult, to calumniate.
denodado adj. dauntless, daring, bold.
denominación f. denomination; name, title, designation.
denominar v. to name, to call, to entitle, to denominate.
denostar v. irr. to insult, to abuse, to outrage, to revile.
densidad f. density.
denso adj. dense, compact; thick.
dentado adj. toothed, notched, denticulated.
dentadura f. set of teeth.
dentar v. irr. to tooth, to furnish with teeth; to indent; to cut teeth.
dentellada f. bite; tooth mark; nip; **a —s** with the teeth.
dentición f. teething.
dentífrico m. dentifrice, tooth cleanser; **pasta dentífrica** toothpaste; **polvos dentífricos** toothpowder.
dentista m. dentist.

dentro adv. inside, within; **— de** prep. inside of; **por —** on the inside.
denuedo m. spirit, courage, daring, boldness.
denuesto m. affront, insult.
denuncia f. denunciation, condemnation, accusation; denouncement.
denunciar v. to denounce, to accuse; to proclaim, to advise, to give notice.
deparar v. to furnish, to offer, to present, to supply.
departamento m. department; compartment; apartment, division.
departir v. to talk, to converse; to speak.
dependencia f. dependence, dependency; branch office.
depender v. to depend, to rely(on).
dependiente m. clerk; dependent; subordinate, retainer; adj. dependent.
deplorar v. to deplore, to lament, to regret, to bewail.
deponer v. irr. to set aside; to depose; to remove from office; to testify, to declare; to affirm; to depose, to divest; to evacuate the bowels; Am. to vomit.
deportar v. to deport, to banish; to exile.
deporte m. sport; recreation, amusement.
deportista m. sportman; f. sportwoman.
deportivo adj. sport, sporting; **copa deportiva** loving cup.
deposición f. declaration, assertion; testimony; dismissal, removal; bowel movement.
depositar v. to deposit; to deliver, to intrust; to commit; to give, to bestow; to inclose.
depositario m. receiver, trustee.
depósito m. deposit, trust; depository; storage; warehouse; **— de agua** reservoir.
depravado adj. depraved; corrupt; degenerate; bad, lewd.
depravar v. to corrupt, to pervert, to contaminate, to vitiate.
depreciar v. to depreciate, to reduce the value of.
depresión f. depression; dip; abasement.
deprimente adj. depressing.
deprimir v. to depress; to press down; to humiliate; to belittle; to sink.

depurar v. to purify.
derecha f. right hand; right side; right wing (in politics); **a la —** to the right.
derecho adj. even, straight; perfect, complete, true.
derechura f. straightness.
deriva f. drift; **irse** (or **andar**) **a la —** to drift, be drifting.
derivar v. to derive; to come (from); to deduce.
derogar v. to revoke; to repeal; to abolish; to derogate.
derramamiento m. spill, spilling, shedding, overflow; scattering; **— de sangre** bloodshed.
derramar v. to spill; to spread; to scatter, to shed; to pour; to leak.
derrame m. spill, spilling, shedding; overflow; discharge; slope.
derredor m. circuit; contour; circumference; **al —** around; **en —** around.
derrengado p.p. & adj. lame, crippled, dislocated.
derrengar v. irr. to dislocate, to sprain; to cripple; to bend.
derretimiento m. thaw, thawing, melting.
derretir v. irr. to melt, to dissolve; to liquefy; **—se** to thaw; to melt.
derribar v. to demolish, to knock down; to overthrow; to depose; **—se** to tumble down; to throw oneself down.
derrocamiento m. overthrow.
derrocar v. to fling down; to overthrow; to pull down.
derrochador m. squanderer, spendthrift; adj. wasteful, extravagant.
derrochar v. to waste; to squander, to dissipate.
derroche m. waste; dissipation; lavish spending.
derrota f. rout, defeat; ship's course; road, path.
derrotar v. to defeat; to destroy, to ruin; to lose or shift its course; to drift.
derrotero m. course, direction; ship's course; book of seacharts.
derrumbadero m. precipice.
derrumbamiento m. landslide; collapse.
derrumbar v. to fling down; to precipitate; Am. to knock down; to go down in a hurry; **—se** to crumble away; to topple over; Am. to dwindle.
derrumbe m. landslide, collapse.

desabotonar v. to unbutton.
desabrido adj. tasteless, insipid; harsh; sour, peevish.
desabrigar v. to uncover; **—se** to uncover oneself.
desabrimiento m. tastelessness; sourness, insipidity.
desabrochar v. to unfasten, to unbutton, to unclasp; to burst open; **—se** to unbutton oneself, to unfasten one's clothes.
desacato m. irreverence, disrespect, profanation.
desacierto m. mistake, error, blunder.
desacostumbrado adj. unaccustomed; unusual; unfamiliar.
desacostumbrar v. to disaccustom; to rid of a habit, to disuse; **—se** to become unaccustomed; to lose a custom.
desacreditar v. to discredit; to disgrace.
desacuerdo m. disagreement; blunder; forgetfulness.
desafiar v. to challenge; to compete, to defy; to dare.
desafinado adj. out of tune, untuned.
desafinar v. to be discordant; to be out of tune; to be inharmonious.
desafío m. challenge, defiance, duel; contest; struggle.
desafortunado adj. unfortunate, unlucky.
desafuero m. violation; outrage; abuse, excess; open violence.
desagradable adj. disagreeable, unpleasant.
desagradar v. to displease, to offend.
desagradecido adj. ungrateful.
desagrado m. displeasure; discontent, asperity.
desagraviar v. to make amends; to compensate for a damage or injury; to right a wrong, to apologize; to vindicate; to give satisfaction.
desagravio m. reparation; compensation for damages; vindication; apology, relief.
desaguadero m. drain, drain pipe, water outlet; channel.
desaguar v. to drain, to draw off, to flow (into); to empty or flow into the sea; Am. to extract the juice from; to urinate; **—se** to drain.
desagüe m. drainage; drain; outlet; channel.

desaguisado m. outrage, violence, wrong.

desahogado p.p. & adj. relieved; roomy, spacious, free; **estar —** to be in easy or comfortable circumstances.

desahogar v. to relief from pain or trouble; to ease pain, to alleviate distress; **—se** to find relief or release; to unbosom oneself, disclose one's feelings.

desahogo m. relief from pain or trouble; release; ease; comfort; relaxation; freedom.

desairar v. to slight, to snub, to disdain; to rebuff; to disappoint; to neglect; to disregard.

desaire m. rebuff, snub, slight, disdain; disregard.

desalentar v. irr. to put out of breath; to discourage; to dismay; **—se** to get discouraged.

desaliento m. discouragement; dismay; faintness; depression.

desaliñado adj. disheveled, slovenly, unkempt, untidy.

desaliño m. slovenliness, untidiness; neglect, carelessness; disorder.

desalmado adj. soulless, cruel, inhuman, merciless, impious.

desalojar v. to dislodge; to evict; to displace.

desamarrar v. to untie, to unfasten; to unmoor; to unbend a rope.

desamparar v. to abandon, to forsake, to quit.

desamparo m. desertion, abandonment, dereliction.

desamueblado adj. unfurnished.

desangrar v. to bleed, to draw blood from; to drain; to make poor; **—se** to bleed, to lose blood.

desanimado adj. discouraged; lifeless; dull.

desanimar v. to dishearten, to discourage.

desaparecer v. irr. to disappear; to hide; **—se** to disappear, to vanish

desaparición f. disappearance.

desapasionado adj. dispassionate; calm; impartial.

desapego m. aloofness; indifference, detachment, coolness.

desapercibido adj. unprepared, unprovided.

desaprobación f. disapproval, censure.

desaprobar v. irr. to disapprove.

desarmar v. to disarm, to dismount; to take apart; to undo.

desarme m. disarmament.

desarraigar v. to root out, to uproot.

desarreglado p.p. & adj. disordered; disorderly; slovenly, untidy.

desarreglar v. to disarrange, to disorder, to disturb, to upset; to derange.

desarreglo m. disorder, confusion.

desarrollar v. to unroll, to unfold; to develop, to explain; **—se** to develop; to unfold.

desarrollo m. development.

desaseado adj. unkempt, untidy.

desaseo m. slovenliness, untidiness.

desasir v. irr. to loosen, to unfasten, to disentangle; **—se** to get loose (from); to let go (of).

desasosiego m. unrest, uneasiness, restlessness.

desastrado adj. unfortunate, unhappy; dirty, untidy; miserable.

desastre m. disaster.

desastroso adj. disastrous, unfortunate.

desatar v. to untie, to loosen, to dissolve; to unfold; **—se** to let loose, let go; to break loose; **—se en** to let out.

desatención f. inattention, disrespect.

desatento adj. inattentive; discourteous.

desatinado adj. senseless; reckless.

desatinar v. to act or talk foolishly; to blunder; to rave; to lose one's bearings.

desatino m. blunder, error; folly; nonsense; madness.

desatracar v. to push off (from shore of from another ship); to cast off, to unmoor; to sheer off, to bear away.

desavenencia f. disagreement, discord; dispute; misunderstanding.

desayunarse v. to breakfast; to have the first intelligence of anything; **— con la noticia** to hear a piece of news for the first time.

desayuno m. breakfast.

desazón f. uneasiness, anxiety; insipidity, flatness, displeasure; disquietness.

desbandarse v. to disband, to scatter, to disperse.

desbaratar v. to destroy, to ruin; to upset, to disturb; to disperse; talk nonsense; **—se** to be upset; to be in disorder; to fall to pieces.

desbocado adj. runaway (horse);

foul-mouthed, abusive; broken-mouthed.

desbordamiento m. overflow; flood.

desbordante adj. overflowing; Am. frantic.

desbordar v. to overflow, to flood; —se to spill over; to get over-excited.

descabezado p.p. beheaded; adj. headless; harebrained, thoughtless.

descabezar v. to behead, to chop off the head or tip of; to decapitate; — el sueño to take a nap; —se to break one's head; to rack one's brain.

descaecido adj. feeble, weak; — de ánimo depressed, dejected.

descaecimiento m. languor, weakness; depression, dejection.

descalabradura f. blow or wound on the head; scar on the head.

descalabrar v. to wound in the head; to hurt, to injure, to damage; —se to suffer a head wound or skull fracture.

descalabro m. loss, misfortune.

descalzar v. to take off (someone's) shoes or (and) stockings; to remove an impediment; —se to take off one's shoes or (and) stockings.

descalzo adj. barefoot; shoeless.

descaminar v. to mislead, lead astray; —se to go astray.

descamisado adj. shirtless; in rags; m. ragamuffin, ragged fellow.

descansar v. to rest.

descanso m. rest; staircase landing.

descarado adj. shameless, impudent, brazen.

descarga f. discharge; unloading.

descargar v. to discharge; to unload.

descargo m. discharge; unloading; relief.

descargue m. unloading; discharge.

descarnado adj. fleshless, scrawny.

descarnar v. to excarnate; to corrode, to eat away; —se to become thin, emaciated.

descaro m. effrontery, shamelessness, impudence, audacity.

descarriar v. to mislead, to lead astray; to separate (cattle) from the herd; —se to stray, to go astray.

descarrilar v. to derail; —se to run off the track; to go astray.

descartar v. to discard, to put aside.

descascarado p.p. & adj. peeled off; chipped off.

descascarar v. to shell, to hull, to husk; to peel; to chip off; to decorticate; —se to chip off, to peel off.

descendencia f. descent, lineage; descendants, offspring.

descendente adj. descending, downward.

descender v. irr. to descend, to go or get down; to come (from), originate; to decline in esteem.

descendiente m. & f. descendant; adj. descending .

descendimiento m. descent.

descenso m. descent; fall.

descifrar v. to decipher, puzzle out, figure out; to unravel, to unfold.

descolgar v. irr. to unhang, to take down; to let down; —se to climb down; to drop in.

descolorar v. to discolor, to fade; —se to fade, to lose its color; to discolor.

descolorido adj. pale.

descollar v. irr. to excel; to stand out, to tower.

descomedido adj. rude, discourteous, impolite; inobliging; lofty, haughty.

descompletar v. to make incomplete..

descomponer v. irr. to upset, to disturb; to put out of order; to decompose; to be out of temper; to be indisposed; —se to decompose; to rot; to become upset, ill; to get out of order; Am. se me descompuso el brazo I dislocated my arm, my arm got out of joint.

descomposición f. decomposition; decay, corruption; disorder; confusion.

descompuesto p.p. adj. out of order; insolent; brazen; immodest; audacious, impudent.

descomunal adj. colossal, enormous, monstruous, uncommon.

desconcertante adj. disconcerting, disturbing, confusing, baffling, embarrassing.

desconcertar v. irr. to disconcert, to bewilder, to confuse, to disturb, to confound; to displace; to discard; —se to be confused, to be perplexed.

desconcierto m. disorder; confusion; disagreement.

desconchadura f. chip, chipping off, peeling off.

desconchar v. to scrap off (plaster, or stucco); —se to peel off, chip off.

desconectar v. to disconnect.
desconfiado adj. distrustful, suspicious.
desconfianza f. mistrust, distrust.
desconfiar v. to distrust; to have no confidence.
desconocer v. irr. to fail to recognize or remember; to disown; to disregard.
desconocido adj. unknown, unrecognizable; m. foreign, stranger.
desconocimiento m. disregard; ignorance.
desconsolado p.p. & adj. disconsolate, forlorn; disheartened, grieved.
desconsolador adj. disheartening, saddening.
desconsolar v. irr. to sadden, to grieve; to discourage; to afflict; —se to become disheartened, grieved.
desconsuelo m. dejection, sadness.
descontar v. irr. to discount; to deduct; to allow; to abate, to diminish.
descontentadizo adj. discontented, fretful, hard to please.
descontentar v. to displease, to discontent.
descontento adj. discontent, displeased; m. discontent, displeasure.
descorazonado adj. disheartened, discouraged, depressed.
descorchar v. to uncork.
descortés adj. discourteous, rude, unpolite.
descortesía f. discourtesy, rudeness, impoliteness.
descortezar v. to bark; to strip the bark; to remove the crust or shell; to peel; to civilize.
descoser v. to rip, unsew, unstitch; —se to rip, come unstitched.
descosido m. rip; adj. too talkative, indiscreet; disorderly.
descostrar v. to flake, to scale off; to remove the crust from; —se to flake, to scale off.
descoyuntado p.p. de & adj. dislocated, out of joint.
descoyuntar v. to dislocate, to put out of joint; —se to get out of joint.
descrédito m. discredit.
descreído adj. incredulous, unbelieving; m. unbeliever.
descreimiento m. unbelief, lack of faith.
describir v. to describe.
descripción f. description.

descriptivo adj. descriptive.
descuartizar v. to quarter.
descubierto p.p. & adj. discovered, uncovered; hatless; m. deficit, shortage; al — openly; in the open; en — uncovered; unpaid.
descubridor m. discoverer.
descubrimiento m. discovery; find; invention.
descubrir v. to discover; to uncover; —se to uncover; to take off one's hat.
descuento m. discount; deduction.
descuidado adj. careless, negligent; untidy; slovenly; unaware; tautless.
descuidar v. to neglect; to overlook; —se to be careless or negligent.
descuido m. carelessness; neglect; oversight, disregard; inattention; slip, error.
desde prep. from; since; after; thereupon; — luego immediately; of course; — que conj. since; ever since.
desdecir v. irr. to differ; to detract (from); —se to retract, to recant.
desdén m. disdain, scorn.
desdentado adj. toothless.
desdeñar v. to disdain, to scorn.
desdeñoso adj. disdainful, scornful.
desdicha f. misfortune; misery; poverty.
desdichado adj. unfortunate; unhappy, wretched; miserable; m. wretch.
desdoblamiento m. unfolding.
desdoblar v. to unfold; to spread out.
desdorar v. to remove the gilt from; to tarnish; to dishonor.
desdoro m. tarnish, blemish, dishonor.
deseable adj. desirable.
desear v. to wish, to desire, to want.
desecación f. drying, drainage, desiccation.
desecar v. to dry; to dry up; to drain; to desiccate.
desechar v. to discard; to reject; to refuse, to decline; to undervalue; Am. to cut across, to take a short cut.
desecho m. remainder, residue; waste material; refuse, offal; derelict; piece of junk; discard; —s refuse, scraps, junk; **hierro**

DESEMBALAR   **DESESPERANZAR**

de — scrap iron; **papel de —** wastepaper, scraps of paper.
desembalar v. to unpack.
desembarazar v. to rid, to free, to clear; to disembarras; to disengage; Am. to give birth; —se to get rid of.
desembarazo m. ease, naturalness, freedom, disembarrassment.
desembarcadero m. dock, wharf, pier, quay.
desembarcar v. to land, to unload; to go ashore; to unship.
desembarco m. landing, unloading, unshipment.
desembocadura f. mouth (of a river, canal, etc.); outlet.
desembocar v. to flow (into); to lead (to); to disembogue.
desembolsar v. to disburse, to pay out; to empty a purse; to expend.
desembolso m. disbursement, outlay; expediture.
desembragar v. to throw out the clutch; to disconnect.
desemejante adj. unlike.
desemparar v. to unpack.
desempeñar v. to recover, to redeem, to take out of pawn; to clear from debt; — un cargo to perform the duties of a position; — un papel to play a part; —se to get out of debt.
desempeño m. fulfilment, carrying out; discharge; performance; acting; redeeming.
desempleado adj. unemployed.
desempleo m. unemployment.
desempolvar v. to dust, to remove the dust from.
desencadenar v. to unchain, to free from chains; to loosen, to set free; to break the chain; —se to free oneself; to break loose.
desencajado p.p. & adj. disjointed; disfigured; sunken; emaciated; luxated.
desencantar v. to disillusion, to disappoint; to disenchant.
desencanto m. disillusion, disappointment, disenchantment.
desenfado m. ease, freedom; calmness; facility, relaxation.
desenfrenado p.p. & adj. unbridled; wanton, reckless, unruled, licentious, loose, immoral.
desenganchar v. to unhitch; to unhook; to unfasten.
desengañador adj. disappointing, disillusioning.
desengañar v. to undeceive, to disillusion, to disappoint.

desengaño m. disillusion, disappointment; censure; warning.
desengranar v. to throw out of gear.
desenmarañar v. to untangle; to unravel; to extricate; to explain.
desenmascarar v. to unmask.
desenredar v. to disentangle, to unravel; to outwind; to extricate.
desenrollar v. to unroll.
desensartar v. to unstring; to unthread, to unfasten.
desensillar v. to unsaddle.
desentenderse v. irr. to neglect, to ignore; to feign not to understand; to pay no attention.
desentendido adj. unmindful, heedless; **hacerse el —** to pretend not to notice.
desenterrar v. irr. to unearth, to dig up, to disinter, to unbury.
desentonado adj. inharmonious, out of tune.
desentonar v. to be out of tune; to be out of harmony; to humble, to wound the pride of; to be rude; to raise the voice in disrespect.
desenvoltura f. sprightliness; impudence, effrontery; freedom, ease, abandon, boldness.
desenvolver v. irr. to unfold, to unroll; to discover, to unravel; to unwrap, to develop; —se to be forward.
desenvolvimiento m. development, unfolding.
desenvuelto adj. forward, impudent; quick, expeditious; free, easy, bold, shameless, brazen.
deseo m. desire, wish, mind, liking, lust; **a la medida del —** according to one's wishes.
deseoso adj. desirous, eager; longing.
desequilibrado adj. unbalanced, fool, senseless.
desequilibrar v. to unbalance, to derange.
desequilibrio m. lack of balance, derangement, mental disorder.
deserción f. desertion.
desertar v. to desert; to abandon; —se de to desert.
desertor m. deserter; quitter; forsaker.
desesperación f. despair; desperation; despondency; fury, anger.
desesperado adj. desperate; despairing; hopeless.
desesperanzado p.p. & adj. desperate, discouraged.
desesperanzar v. to discourage,

deprive of hope; —**se** to be discouraged; to despair, lose hope.

desesperar v. to despair, to lose hope, to make (someone) despair; to fret, to be grievously vexed; to be desperate; —**se** to despair; to be furious.

desfachatez f. shamelessness, effrontery, impudence.

desfalcar v. to embezzle; to cut off, to peculate, to remove a part of.

desfalco m. embezzlement; defalcation; diminution; decrease; peculation; diminishing.

desfallecer v. irr. to grow weak; to faint; to swoon, to pine; to fall away; to debilitate.

desfallecimiento m. faintness; weakness; languor; swoon, faint; decline.

desfavorable adj. unfavorable.

desfigurar v. to disfigure; to distort; to deform; to misform; to disguise, to cloud.

desfiladero m. narrow passage, narrow gorge; road on the side of a precipice, defile.

desfilar v. to march, parade, pass by; to defile; to march off by files, to file off.

desgana f. lack of appetite; repugnance, reluctance; disgust.

desgarrado p.p. torn; adj. shameless; impudent; licentious; dissolute.

desgarradura f. tear.

desgarrar v. to tear; to rend; to claw; —**se** to tear; to separate oneself (from).

desgastar v. to waste; to consume, wear away; to corrode; to gnaw; —**se** to waste away, lose one's strength or vigor; to wear off.

desgaste m. waste; wear and tear.

desgracia f. misfortune, mishap; disgrace; adversity; misadventure; enmity; caer en — to be disgraced or lose favour.

desgranar v. to thrash; to remove the grain from; to shell (as peas) out the grain.

desgreñado adj. disheveled.

deshabitado adj. uninhabited; empty, vacant; deserted.

deshacer v. irr. to undo; to dissolve; to destroy; to untie; to consume; to efface; to melt; to liquefy; —**se** to dissolve; to melt; —**se de** to get rid of.

desharrapado adj. ragged; shabby; tattered.

deshecha f. simulation; pretense; evation; shift; polite farewell; **hacer la —** to feign, pretend.

deshecho p.p. & adj. undone; destroyed; wasted; fatigued; in pieces; melted.

deshelar v. irr. to melt; to thaw; —**se** to melt; to thaw.

desherbar v. irr. to weed, to pluck; to extirpate herbs.

deshielo m. thaw.

deshilachar v. to ravel; to fray.

deshilar v. to unravel; to distract bees; —**se** to unravel; to fray.

deshojar v. to strip off the leaves, petals or pages; to display rhetorical elegance; —**se** to lose its leaves (a plant or book); to lose petals.

deshollejar v. to husk, to hull; to peel, to pare; to skin; to shell (as beans).

deshonesto adj. inmmodest; unchaste, lewd; dishonest; unreasonable.

deshonra f. dishonor; disgrace; injury; insult, discredit.

deshonrar v. to dishonor, to disgrace; to insult; to offend, to seduce; to affront, to difame; to seduce an honest woman.

deshonroso adj. dishonorable; indecent; shameful.

deshora f. inopportune time; an unseasonable or inconvenient time; **a —** untimely, unseasonable; extemporary; **comer a —** to eat between meals.

deshuesar v. to stone; to take the bones; to remove the pits or stones from; to bone; to remove the bones from (an animal).

desidia f. indolence, laziness; idleness.

desidioso adj. lazy, idle, negligent, indolent; listless.

desierto adj. deserted, uninhabited; alone; lonesome, solitary, lonely; m. desert, wilderness; **predicar en el —** to preach in the wilderness.

designación f. designation; appointment.

designar v. to designate, to design; to appoint, to express; to name; to select; to intented; to plan.

designio m. design, purpose, intention; mind.

desigual adj. unequal; unlike; uneven; broken; arduous; variable; abrupt; changeable.

desigualdad f. inequality, dissimilitude; variableness; inconstancy;

unevenness; cragginess; roughness.
desilusión f. disillusion, disappointment.
desilusionar v. to disillusion, to disappoint; —se to become disillusioned; to lose an illusion.
desinencia f. termination, ending, desinence.
desinfectante adj. disinfecting; m. disinfectant.
desinfectar v. to disinfect.
desinflado adj. deflated, not inflated, flat.
desinterés m. disinterestedness.
desinteresado adj. disinterested, impartial, unselfish, fair.
desistir v. to desist, to leave; to abandon; to stop; to cease.
deslavado p.p. & adj. impudent, barefaced; faded; pale.
deslavar v. to wash away; to wet; to wash out; to fade.
desleal adj. disloyal, faithless.
desleír v. irr. to dilute, to dissolve; —se to become dilute.
deslindar v. to mark the limits; to clear up a thing.
desliz m. slip, slipping; false step; error.
deslizador m. slider; glider.
deslizamiento m. slip, slipping, glide, sliding, skidding.
deslizar v. to slip, to slide, to speak or act carelessly; to skid; —se to slip; to glide.
deslucido p.p. & adj. unadorned, ungraceful; useless; fruitless; dull; shabby; awkward.
deslucir v. irr. to tarnish; to dull the lustre of; to discredit.
deslumbrador adj. dazzling, glaring.
deslumbramiento m. glare; dazzling; confusion of sight or mind; hallucination; dazzle, daze.
deslumbrar v. to dazzle, to glare; to puzzle.
deslustrado adj. & p.p. tarnished; dim, dull, opaque.
deslustrar v. to tarnish; to obscure; to soil; to stain (one's honor or reputation).
deslustre m. spot, stain; disgrace, stigma, tarnish.
desmadejado p.p & adj. enervated, exhausted; depressed.
desmadejar v. to enervate, to produce languor; to weaken.
desmán m. misfortune, disaster; misbehaviour, slip, misconduct, abuse, insult.

desmantelar v. to dismantle; to abandon, to forsake; to unmast.
desmañado adj. lazy, idle; unskilful, awkward, clumsy.
desmayar v. to faint, swoon; to dismay; to lose courage; —se to faint.
desmayo m. swoon, fainting fit; lowering of strenght or vigour; faint, dismay; discouragement.
desmazalado adj. weak, dejected, spiritless; depressed.
desmejorar v. to impair; to debase; to make worse; to decline; —se to grow worse; to decay; to waste away; to lose one's health.
desmentir v. irr. to give the lie; to counterfeit; to excel, to surpass; to retract; to contradict; —se to retract; to take back one's word.
desmenuzar v. to crumble; to crumb; to chip, to tritter; to break into bits; to mince; to shred; —se to crumble, to fall to small pieces.
desmerecer v. irr. to become unworthy of; to deteriorate, to lose merit or value; to demerit; to be inferior to.
desmigajar v. to crumble; to comminute; —se to crumble.
desmochar v. to cut off, to mutilate; to lop off; to chop off (the top or tip); to unhorn.
desmolado adj. toothless, without molars.
desmontar v. to dismount, to alight; to fell wood; to remove (dirt); to clear (a forest); to dismantle; to take apart; to tear down; —se to dismount, to alight, to get off.
desmoronar v. to crumble; —se to crumble, to fall.
desnatar v. to skim, to take the cream from.
desnaturalizado adj. unnatural, cruel; **alcohol** — denatured alcohol.
desnudar v. to undress, to uncover; —se to undress.
desnudez f. nudity, nakedness.
desnudo adj. nude, naked, bare, uncovered.
desobedecer v. irr. to disobey.
desobediencia f. disobedience.
desobediente adj. disobedient.
desocupación f. unemployment; idleness; vacationing; leisure; want of business.
desocupado adj. unoccupied; unemployed, vacant.

desocupar v. to empty, to vacate, to evacuate, to quit; —se de un negocio to get rid of, or not pay attention to, a business.

desoír v. irr. to refuse (a petition); to pretend not to hear.

desolación f. desolation; ruin; loneliness; affliction, grief; havoc, extermination.

desolado adj. desolate.

desolar v. irr. to lay waste, to ruin, to desolate; to harass; —se to be in aguish; to grieve.

desollar v. irr. to skin; to flay; to fleece; to extort money from.

desorbitado adj. out of its orbit; out of place or proportion; Am. popeyed, with bulging eyes; crazy, eccentric.

desorden m. disorder, confusion.

desordenado adj. disorderly; lawless; unsettled; irregular; disordered.

desordenar v. to disturb, to confuse, to upset, to confound; to disorder; —se to exceed; to lust; to be out of order.

desorientar v. to cause to lose one's bearings; to misdirect; to mislead; to confuse; to turn from the right direction; —se to lose one's bearings; to go astray, to get lost.

despabilado adj. wakeful, wide-awake; bright; lively, watchful, vilígant; active.

despabilar v. to snuff, to trim; to enliven; to sharpen; to cut off a superfluity, to dispatch expeditiously; —se to wake up, to rouse oneself.

despacio adv. slowly, leisurely; continually; softly.

despacioso adj. slow.

despachar v. to despatch; to send; to facilitate; to ship; to dispatch; to expedite; to pack.

despacho m. despatch; office, bureau; message; official communication; sending, shipment; Am. country store.

despachurrar v. to crush, to squash; to make a speech.

desparejo adj. unequal, uneven.

desparpajar v. to upset, to disarrange, to rant; to prattle at random; Am. to disperse, to scatter.

desparpajo m. ease, freedom of manner; freshness; pertness of speech or action; Am. dispersion; scattering; disorder, jumble.

desparramar v. to scatter, to spread; to spill; to squander; to disseminate.

desparramo m. Am. scattering, spreading, spilling; disorder; commotion.

despatarrarse v. to sprawl; to fall sprawling to the ground.

despecho m. spite; grudge; despair; displeasure; wrath; a — de in spite of.

despedazar v. irr. to break; to cut, to tear into pieces, to limb; to claw; to lacerate; to mangle.

despedida f. farewell; departure; dismissal; leave-taking.

despedir v. irr. to discharge, to emit, to dismiss; to throw off, to give off; to see (a person) off (on a journey); to deny, to refuse; to dart; —se to take leave; say good bye.

despegar v. irr. to detach; to unglue; to unfasten; to take off; to separate; to disjoin; — los labios to speak; no — los labios not to say a word; not to open one's mouth; —se to grow apart; to come loose or detached.

despego See **desapego**.

despegue m. take-off.

despejado adj. clear; cloudless; smart, brigth; vivacious; sagacious; sprightly, dexterous.

despejar v. to clear; to remove obstacles from; to remove impediments; to surmount obstacles; —se to clear up; to clear one's mind.

despellejar v. to skin, to flay.

despensa f. pantry; storeroom; larder; store of provisions; steward's room; food provisions.

despensero m. butler; steward.

despeñadero m. steep cliff; precipice; crag.

despeñar v. to fling down a precipice; to precipitate.

despepitar v. to seed; to remove the seeds from; —se to talk or shout vehemently; rave; to talk wildly; —se por una cosa to long for something; to be dying about something.

desperdiciado adj. wasteful; destroyed; squandered.

desperdiciar v. to squander; to waste; to misspend.

desperdicio m. waste; prodigality; refuse; remains; —s leftovers; garbage; residue; rubbish.

desperdigar v. to disperse; to scat-

desperezarse v. to stretch oneself.
desperfecto m. damage, flaw; defect.
despertador m. alarm clock; awakener.
despertar v. irr. to awaken; to wake up; to awake; to excite; to enliven; —se to wake up.
despiadado adj. pitiless, heartless, cruel.
despierto adj. awake; vigilant, watchful, diligent; strong; brisk; sprightly; lively.
despilfarrado adj. wasteful; ragged, in tatters.
despilfarrar v. to squander; to waste.
despilfarro m. extravagance; squandering; waste; slovenliness.
despistar v. to throw off the trail.
desplante m. arrogance; impudent remark or act; an oblique posture in fencing.
desplazar v. to displace.
desplegar v. irr. to unfold; to unfurl; to show; to manifest; to display; to extend; to explain; to elucidate.
desplomar v. to cause to lean; bulge out; —se to slump; to topple over, to tumble down; to collapse.
desplome m. collapse; toppling over; landslide.
desplumar v. to pick, to pluck; to deplume; to despoil; to fleece; to skin; to rob; to strip; —se to moult.
despoblado adj. uninhabited, desolate; desert; m. open country; uninhabited place; wilderness.
despojar v. to despoil; to rob; to strip; to deprive; to abridge; —se to undress; to deprivate oneself.
despojo m. plundering, robbery; spoil, booty; leftover, scrap; despoliation; —s remains.
desportilladura f. chip; nick.
desportillar v. to chip, **to nick**; to break the neck of a bottle, pot, etc.
desposar v. to marry; to betroth; to match; —se to become formally engaged; to get married.
déspota m. & f. despot, tyrant.
despótico adj. despotic, tyrannical, despotical.
despotismo m. despotism, tyranny.
despreciable adj. contemptible; despicable or despisable; worthless; insignificant; negligible.

despreciar v. to despise; to scorn.
desprecio m. disregard, scorn, dispraise, contempt.
desprender v. to unfasten, to loose; to detach, to disjoin; to separate; — se to get loose; to come unfastened; to climb down; to get rid (of); to be inferred; to be deduced.
desprendimiento m. detachment; generosity; disinterestedness; unfastening; landslide.
despreocupado p.p. & adj. unbiased; liberal, broadminded; unconventional; carefree; Am. careless, slovenly; indifferent to criticism.
desprestigiar v. to discredit, harm the reputation of; —se to lose one's reputation.
desprestigio m. discredit, loss of prestige.
desprevenido adj. unprepared; unaware; unprovided; improvident.
despropósito m. absurdity; oddity, nonsense.
después adv. after, afterward, then, next, later; — **de** after; — **de que** conj. after.
despuntado adj. blunt, dull.
despuntar v. to blunt; to cut off, to nip; to be clever; to be witty; to excel; — **el alba** to dawn.
desquitar v. to retrieve, to restore (a loss); —se to get even; to take revenge; to win back one's money.
desquite m. retaliation, revenge, compensation; getting even; recovery of a loss; return game or match.
desrazonable adj. unreasonable.
destacado adj. outstanding.
destacamento m. military detachment; station or military post.
destacar v. to detach; to make stand out; to stand out; **hacer** — to emphasize; to make stand out; —se to stand out.
destapar v. to uncover, to uncork; Am. to start running; —se to uncover, to get uncovered; to get uncorked; Am. to burst out talking.
destartalado adj. in disorder; in rack and ruin; dismantled, stripped of furniture; juddled, incompact.
destechado adj. roofless.
destellar v. to flash; to sparkle; to twinkle; to gleam.

destello m. flash, sparkle, scintillation, gleam.
destemplado adj. inharmonious; out of tune; immoderate; incongruous; **sentirse** — not to feel well; to feel feverish.
desteñir v. irr. to discolor, to fade, to bleach; —**se** to become discolored; to fade.
desternillarse v. — **de risa** to split one's sides with laughter.
desterrado m. exile; outcast; p.p. and adj. exiled; banished.
desterrar v. irr. to exile; to banish; to expel.
destetar v. to wean.
destierro m. exile; banishment.
destilación f. distillation; flow of humours; extillation.
destiladera f. still, alembic; filter.
destilar v. to distil; to drop, to trickle, to filter; to fall in drops.
destilería f. distillery.
destinación f. destination.
destinar v. to destine, to employ; to destinate; to designate.
destinatario m. addressee.
destino m. destiny, fate, destination; profession; employment, job.
destituido adj. destitute.
destituir v. irr. to deprive, to make destitute; to dismiss from office.
destornillador m. screwdriver; unscrewer.
destrabar v. to unlock, to unfasten; to untie; to separate; to unfetter.
destreza f. dexterity, skill, ability, expertness; cunning.
destronar v. to dethrone, to depose; to overthrow.
destrozar v. to shatter; to rout; to massacre; to destroy; to defeat.
destrozo m. destruction; ruin, havoc, defeat, massacre.
destrucción f. destruction.
destructivo adj. destructive.
destructor adj. destroyer.
destruir v. irr. to destroy, to ruin, to waste, to harass; to moulder.
desunir v. to divide, to separate, to disunite.
desusado adj. unusual, unaccustomed, obsolete; out of use.
desuso m. disuse; obsoleteness.
desvaído adj. lanky; tall and awkward; gaunt; dull; faded.
desvainar v. to shell, to husk.
desvalido adj. abandoned; destitute; helpless; unprotected.

desvalijar v. to ransack the contents of a valise; to rob; to strip.
desván m. garret; attic; loft.
desvanecer v. irr. to fade, to dissolve; to swell with pride; —**se** to evaporate; to vanish; to fade out, disappear; swoon.
desvanecido adj. dizzy, faint; proud, haughty.
desvanecimiento m. dizziness, faintness; pride, loftiness; vanity.
desvariar v. to rave, to dote; to rant, talk excitedly; to talk nonsense.
desvario m. raving, delirium, madness; inconstancy.
desvelado adj. sleepless, watchful, awake, vigilant, careful.
desvelar v. to keep awake; to be watchful or vigilant; to have insomnia; to lose sleep; to be worried, anxious.
desvelo m. lack of sleep; restlessness; vigilance, watchfulness; worry, anxiety.
desvencijado adj. tottering, rickety, shaky, falling apart.
desventaja f. disadvantage, damage.
desventura f. misfortune, unhappiness, calamity; misery.
desventurado adj. unfortunate, unhappy, miserable, wretched, unlucky.
desvergonzado adj. shameless; impudent, brazen.
desvergüenza f. shamelessness, disgrace, effrontery, assurance, shame; insolence.
desvestir v. irr. to undress; —**se** to undress.
desviación f. deviation, shift, detour.
desviar v. to deviate, to lead off; to swerve; to dissuade; to avert; —**se** to shift direction; to branch off, to turn off.
desvío m. deviation; indifference, coldness; side track; aversion.
desvirtuar v. to impair, to lessen the value or quality of; to pall.
desvivirse v. to love excessively; —**se por** to long for; to be excessively fond of; to be crazy about.
desyerbar See **desherbar**.
detallar v. to detail, to report in detail; to retail.
detalle m. detail, retail; ¡ahí está el —! that's the point.
detallista m. & f. retailer, detailer.

DETECTIVE   **DIENTE**

detective m. detective.
detención f. detention, arrest; stop, halt; delay.
detener v. irr. to detain, to stop; to arrest; to fix; to keep; —se to halt; to stay.
detenimiento m. detention; delay; care; deliberation.
deteriorar v. to deteriorate, to damage; —se to deteriorate; to wear out.
deterioro m. deterioration, impairment.
determinación f. determination; firmness; resolution, decision.
determinar v. to determine; to decide; to resolve, to distinguish, to discern; to assign; —se to resolve, to decide.
detestable adj. detestable, hateful.
detestar v. to detest, to hate; to abhor.
detonación f. detonation, report; noise.
detonar v. to detonate, to flash, to explode; to pop.
detrás adv. behind; — **de** prep. behind; **por** — **from the rear**; by the rear; — **de la puerta** behind the door; in the absence.
deuda f. debt; fault, offense; indebtedness.
deudo m. parent, relative, kinsman.
deudor m. debtor; adj. indebted, obligated.
devanar v. to spool; —se los sesos to rack one's brains.
devaneo m. delirium; frenzy; dissipation; wandering; idle pursuit; heedlness.
devastar v. to desolate, to devastate; to lay waste, to destroy.
devenir v. irr. to befall; to become; to be tranformed into.
devoción f. devotion, piety, attachment; godliness; prayer; ardent love; devoutness.
devocionario m. prayer book.
devolución f. return, devolution, restitution; replacement.
devolver v. irr. to return, to restore, to pay back.
devorador adj. devouring, absorbing, ravenous; m. devourer.
devorar v. to devour, to swallow up; to gobble up, to consume.
devoto adj. devout, pious, religious; very fond (of).
día m. day; al otro — on the next day; —s caniculares dog days; **hoy** — nowadays; — **de años** or **cumpleaños** birthday; **un** — **sí y otro no** every other day.
diablo m. devil, demon, Satan.
diablura f. deviltry, mischief; wild prank.
diabólico adj. diabolic, devilish, fiendish.
diácono m. deacon.
diadema f. diadem, crown.
diáfano adj. transparent, clear, sheer.
diagnosticar v. to diagnose.
diagrama m. diagram, graph.
dialecto m. dialect.
dialogar v. to dialogue, to dialogize.
diálogo m. dialogue.
diamante m. diamond.
diámetro m. diameter.
diantre m. devil.
diapasón m. pitch; tuning-fork; diapason; octave.
diario adj. daily; m. journal, diary; daily newspaper; daily expense.
diarrea f. diarrhea.
dibujante m. & f. draftsman.
dibujar v. to draw, to design, to sketch, to delineate; to depict, to portrait, to describe; —se to appear, to show.
dibujo m. drawing, delineation, design, portrayal, sketch, picture; — **natural** drawing from live model.
dicción f. diction, style, language, expression; word; choice of words.
diccionario m. dictionary, lexicon.
diciembre m. December.
dictado m. dictation; title; dictate; **escribir al** — to take dictation.
dictador m. dictator.
dictadura f. dictatorship.
dictamen m. opinion, judgment; sentiments, notion, suggestion.
dictaminar v. to express an opinion or judgment.
dictar v. to dictate. [tune
dicha f. happiness, felicity, fortune.
dicharachero adj. fond of making wisecracks; witty.
dicharacho m. a vulgar, low, or slang expression; wisecrack, smart remark; malicious remark.
dicho m. saying; p.p. — **y hecho** no sooner said than done.
dichoso adj. happy, fortunate, prosperous, lucky.
diente m. tooth, tusk; — **de león** dandelion; pelar el — to smile

diestra affectedly; **de —s afuera**, insincerely.

diestra f. right hand; favour, support, protection.

diestro adj. skilful, right; sagacious, prudent; m. matador; skilful fencer.

dieta f. diet; assembly; salary, fee.

diezmo m. tithe, tenth part; duty of ten per cent.

difamación f. libel, slander.

difamador m. defamer, libeller, slanderer.

difamar v. to defame, to discredit; to libel, to malign; to slander.

difamatorio adj. scandalous, slandering, defamatory, libellous.

diferencia f. difference; dissimilitude.

diferenciar v. to differentiate, to differ, to change; to disagree; to distinguish; **—se** to distinguish oneself, to become different.

diferente adj. different, dissimilar, unlike.

diferir v. irr. to defer, to delay, to differ, to disagree; to be different.

difícil adj. difficult, arduous, hard.

dificultad f. difficulty, embarrassment, hardness; objection.

dificultar v. to make difficult; to render difficult; **— el paso** to impede or obstruct the passage, **—se** to become difficult.

dificultoso adj. difficult, hard, laborious, painful; deformed; ugly.

difteria f. diphtheria.

difundir v. to diffuse, to extend, to outspread; to divulge; to scatter; to broadcast.

difunto adj. defunct, dead; deceased; m. corpse.

difusión f. diffusion, spreading, scattering; worthiness, broadcasting.

difuso adj. diffuse, diffusive, diffused, widespread.

digerible adj. digestible.

digerir v. irr. to digest.

dignarse v. to deign, to condescend.

dignatario m. dignitary.

dignidad f. dignity, rank; grandeur, nobleness.

digno adj. worth; dignified, meritorious, worthy, deserving; condign; suitable; **— de alabanza** worthy to be praised.

digresión f. digression.

dije m. trinket; any small piece of jewelry; woman of fine qualities.

dilación f. delay, dilation, procrastination.

dilatado adj. vast, spacious, extensive.

dilatar v. to dilate, to expand, to defer, to retard, to protract; to lengthen, to extend, to spread out, to comfort, to cheer up; **—se** to expand; to be diffuse, worthy; Am. to delay oneself, to take long.

diligencia f. diligence, assiduity; haste, speed, activity, care, industry; stage coach; business, affair; return of a writ, judicial proceeding; errand.

diligente adj. diligent, assiduous. laborious; quick; speedy; swift; ready.

diluir v. irr. to dilute.

diluvio m. flood, deluge, overflow; inundation; vast abundance.

dimensión f. dimension, extent, capacity, bulk.

dimes: **— y diretes** quibbling, arguing; **andar en — y diretes** to quibble, to argue.

diminución f. diminution, decrease; losing, exhaustion.

diminutivo adj. diminutive, tiny; diminishing; m. diminutive.

diminuto adj. tiny, little.

dimisión f. resignation (from an office).

dimitir v. to give up, to relinquish; to resign, to give up (a position, office, etc.).

dinámica f. dynamics.

dinamismo m. dynamism; vigor, forcefulness.

dinamita f. dynamite.

dínamo m. dynamo.

dineral m. large sum of money.

dinero m. coin, money, gold, coinage, currency; Am. Peruvian silver coin; **— contante y sonante** ready money, cash.

dios m. god; **Dios God**; **a la buena de —** without malice; **vaya usted con —** farewell, God be with you; **por — for** God's sake.

diosa f. goddess.

diplomacia f. diplomacy; tact.

diplomático adj. diplomatic; tactful; m. diplomat.

diputación f. deputation; committee.

diputado m. deputy, representative.

diputar v. to depute, to delegate; to commission.

dique m. dike, barrier; **— de carena** dry dock.
dirección f. direction, course; advise, guidance; management, board of directors; office of the board of directors, address.
directivo adj. directive, directing, guiding; **mesa directiva** board of directors.
directo adj. direct, straight.
director m. director, manager; adj. directing.
directorio adj. directory, directive, directing; m. directory, book of instructions; directorate, board of directors.
dirigente adj. directing, leading; m. leader, director.
dirigir v. to direct, to manage, to govern; to guide, to address; to dedicate; **—se a** to address; to go to or toward.
discernimiento m. discernment, keen judgment; insight; discrimination.
discernir v. irr. to discern; to distinguish; to discriminate.
disciplina f. discipline, training; rule of conduct; order; any art or science; scourge; whip.
disciplinar v. to discipline, to train; to drill; **—se** to discipline oneself; to scourge oneself.
discípulo m. pupil, disciple.
disco m. discus, disk; phonograph record.
díscolo adj. unruly, disobedient; unfriendly.
discordancia f. discord, disagreement.
discordia f. discord.
discreción f. discretion, keenness; wit; **darse (or rendirse) a —** to surrender unconditionally.
discrecional adj. optional.
discrepancia f. discrepancy.
discreto adj. discreet, prudent; clever.
disculpa f. excuse, apology.
disculpable adj. excusable.
disculpar v. to excuse, to exculpate; **—se** to apologize.
discurrir v. to ramble about; to reason, to think over; to invent; to think out.
discursear v. to make a speech.
discutible adj. debatable, questionable.
discutir v. to discuss.
disecar v. to dissect, to stuff (dead animals).
diseminación f. dissemination, spread, scattering.

diseminar v. to disseminate, to scatter, to spread.
disensión f. dissension, disent, disagreement.
disentería f. dysentery.
disentir v. irr. to dissent, to differ, to disagree.
diseñador m. designer.
diseñar v. to design; to sketch; to outline.
diseño m. design; sketch; outline.
disertar v. to discourse, to discuss.
disforme adj. deformed; ugly, hideous.
disfraz m. disguise, mask; masquerade costume.
disfrazar v. to disguise, to conceal; **—se** to disguise oneself, to masquerade.
disfrutar v. to enjoy; to benefit by; to make use of.
disfrute m. enjoyment, benefit, use.
disgustar v. to disgust, to displease; **—se** to get angry.
disgusto m. displeasure; unpleasantness; annoyance; quarrel, grief; disgust.
disimulado adj. underhanded, sly, cunning.
disimular v. to feign, to hide, to mask; to overlook, to excuse.
disimulo m. dissimulation, feigning, pretense; slyness; reserve.
disipación f. dissipation; waste; extravagance.
disipar v. to dissipate, scatter, squander; **—se** to vanish.
dislocar v. to dislocate, to put out of joint; **—se** to become dislocated; to get out of joint.
disminución See **diminución**.
disminuir v. irr. to diminish, to decrease, to lessen.
disociación f. dissociation, separation.
disociar v. to dissociate, to separate.
disolución f. dissolution; dissoluteness, lewdness.
disoluto adj. dissolute; loose; immoral, dissipated.
disolver v. irr. to dissolve; to melt.
disonancia f. discord.
disparada f. Am. rush, run.
disparar v. to shoot, to fire, to discharge, to throw; **—se** to run away, to dart out.
disparatado adj. absurd, foolish; senseless.
disparatar v. to talk nonsense; to blunder; to act absurdly.

disparate m. nonsense, blunder.
disparidad f. inequality.
disparo m. shooting, discharge, explosion; shoot; sudden dash, run.
dispensa f. dispensation, exemption.
dispensar v. to excuse, to absolve, to pardon, to grant, to give.
dispensario m. dispensary, pharmaceutical laboratory.
dispersar v. to disperse, to scatter.
dispersión f. dispersion, dispersal.
displicencia f. displeasure, discontent, dislike.
displicente adj. unpleasant, disagreeable.
disponer v. irr. to dispose; to arrange, to put in order; to prepare; to order, to command; —se to get ready; to make one's will and testament.
disponible adj. spare, available; on hand.
disposición f. disposition; arrangement; order, command; attitude; disposal.
dispuesto p.p. & adj. disposed; ready; fit; smart, clever.
disputa f. dispute.
disputar v. to dispute.
distancia f. distance.
distante adj. distant.
distar v. to be distant.
distender v. irr. to distend, to stretch; to inflate; —se to distend, to expand.
distinción f. distinction.
distinguido adj. & p.p. distinguished.
distinguir v. to distinguish; —se to distinguish oneself; to excel; to differ, to be different.
distintivo adj. distinctive, distinguishing; m. distinguishing characteristic; mark, sign; badge.
distinto adj. distinct, plain, clear, different.
distracción f. distraction; diversion; amusement; heedlessness.
distraer v. irr. to distract, to divert, to amuse; —se to have a good time; to be absent-minded; to be unattentive.
distraído adj. distracted; inattentive, absent-minded; Am. slovenly, untidy.
distribución f. distribution, apportionment, division; separation; collocation; **caja de —, tablero de —** switch board.
distribuidor m. distributor, divider, adj. distributing.

distribuir v. irr. to distribute, to sort, to classify, to divide, to dispose, to range; to allot.
distrito m. district; region, country, territory.
disturbio m. disturbance.
divagación f. rambling; digression.
divagar v. irr. to ramble; to digress.
diván m. divan, sofa.
divergencia f. divergence; difference.
divergir v. to diverge; to differ.
diversidad f. diversity; variety; dissimilitude.
diversión f. amusement; diversion, sport.
diverso adj. diverse; different; various; multiform; —s several.
divertido adj. amusing; funny, merry, diverted; festive; absent.
divertir v. irr. to amuse, to sport; to divert; to entertain; to turn aside; —se to have a good time, amuse oneself.
dividendo m. dividend, share.
dividir v. to divide, to split, to cut, to disjoin; to disunite; to distribute.
divinidad f. divinity; deity; godhead; the Supreme Being; ¡que —! what a beauty!
divino adj. divine; heavenly; heaven-born; godlike; excelent.
divisa f. device; emblem; motto; badge.
divisar v. to sight; to make out; to distinguish; to descry at distance.
división f. division; partition; distribution; disunion.
divorciar v. to divorce; to separate; —se to be divorced.
divorcio m. divorce; rupture.
divulgar v. to divulge; to spread; to make public; to give out; to publish; to go abroad.
diz See **dice**; **dizque** they say that.
dobladillar v. to hem.
dobladillo m. hem; adj. squat and broad, short and thick; **— de ojo** hemstitch.
doblar v. to bend, to fold; to double; to toll; to knell; to coil; Am. to knock down; **— la esquina** to turn the corner; **—se** to stoop; to bend down; to give in.
doble adj. double, twofold; double-faced, hypocritical; strong, robust; artful; Am. broke, poor; m. fold, toll, tolling of bells, knell.
doblegar v. to bend; to fold; to

inflect; —**se** to bend over; to stoop, to submit, to yield.

doblez m. fold; crease; f. duplicity; doubleness; hypocrisy.

docena f. dozen.

docente adj. teaching; educational.

dócil adj. docile; obedient; manageable; meek; flexible.

docilidad f. obedience, meekness, gentleness; flexibility.

docto adj. learned; expert.

doctor m. doctor.

doctorar v. to grant a doctor's degree to; to doctorate; —**se** to get a doctor's degree.

doctrina f. doctrine.

documentar v. to document.

documento m. document.

dogal m. halter; noose.

dogma m. dogma.

dogmático adj. dogmatic, pertaining to dogma; positive.

dolencia f. ailment; ache; aching; disease, affliction.

doler v. irr. to ache, to hurt; to cause grief; to be unwilling to act; —**se de** to feel pity for; feel sorry for; to repent from.

doliente adj. sorrowful; suffering; aching; m. sick person; patient, pallbearer; mourner.

dolor m. pain; ache; sorrow; grief; — **de cabeza**, headache; — **de muelas** toothache; **estar con** — to be in labour.

dolorido adj. aching; sore; afflicted; repentant; d o l e f u l; m. mourner.

doloroso adj. painful; sorrowful; afflicted; dolorous.

doma f. breaking of horses.

domador m horsebreaker, broncobuster; tamer, subduer.

domar v. to tame, to subdue; to break in; to conquer.

domeñar v. to tame; to subdue; to dominate; to make tractable.

domesticar v. to domesticate; to tame.

doméstico adj. domestic; domesticai; domesticant; m. house servant; domestic; menial.

domiciliar v. to house; to lodge; Am; to adress (a letter); —**se** to take up residence; to settle down; to dwell, reside.

domicilio m. home; dwelling; habitation; abode; domicile.

dominación f. domination, rule, authority.

dominador adj. dominant; dominating; domineering; bossy; m. dominator; ruler; boss.

dominante adj. dominant; domineering; tyrannical, prevailing; predominant, dictatory; excelling; imperious.

dominar v. to dominate; to rule; to master; to command; to lead; to stand out; to tower above.

dómine m. teacher; pedagogue; pedant.

domingo m. Sunday; — **de Ramos** Palm Sunday; — **de Resurrección** Easter Sunday; — **de Cuasimodo** Low Sunday.

dominio m. domain; dominion; power; region, territory.

dominó m. domino.

don m. gift; ability; knack; **Don** (title used only before Christian names of men).

donación f. donation; grant; gift; cession of property.

donador m. donor, giver, bestower.

donaire m. grace, elegance; wit; gentility; humour; witty remark; witty saying.

donairoso adj. elegant; graceful; pleasant; witty.

donar v. to donate; to make gifts; to bestow.

doncella f. virgin, maiden; maid servant; lass; waiting maid.

donde rel. adv. where, in which; **a** — (adonde) where, to which; Am. to the house of; **de** — from where, from which; **en** — where, in which; **por** — where, through which; wherefore; — no otherwise; if not; ¿**dónde?** interr. adv. where?; ¿**por** —? which way?

dondequiera adv. wherever; anywhere.

donoso adj. witty, gay; pleasant; graceful.

doña f. Doña (title used only before Christian names of women); lady, mistress.

dorado p.p. & adj. gilded; gilt; golden; m. gilding; Am. a kind of hummingbird.

dorar v. to gild, as with gold; to palliate; to excuse.

dormir v. irr. to sleep; —**se** to go to sleep; fall asleep; to become numb; — **la siesta** to take a nap after dinner.

dormitar v. to doze; to nap; to mope.

dormitorio m. dormitory; bedroom.

dorso m. back; reverse; the back part of anything.

dosel m. canopy.

dosis f. dose.

dotación f. endowment; endowing;

dotation; donation; foundation; dowry.
dotar v. to endow, to provide with a dowry; to give a portion; to endow with a fortune; to portion.
dote m. & f. dowry; f. natural gift, dower; dowery; talent; quality; blessings; endowments.
draga f. dredge, dredging machine.
dragado m. dredging.
dragaminas m. mine sweeper.
dragar v. to dredge.
dragón m. dragon; a fabulous monster; weather fish; dragoon; white spots in the eyes; draco; — marino sea dragon.
drama m. drama.
dramático adj. dramatical; dramatic; m. dramatic actor; playwright, dramatist.
dramatizar v. to dramatize.
dramaturgo m. playwright, dramatist.
drástico adj. drastic.
drenaje m. Am. drainage.
drenar v. Am. to drain.
dril m. drill.
droga f. drug, medicine; lie; fib; trick; bother; nuisance; stratagem; artifice, deceit; Am. bad debt; drug on the market; unsaleable article.
droguería f. drug store; drug business.
droguero m. druggist; cheat; Am. debt evader.
droguista m. & f. druggist; cheat; crook; impostor.
ducha f. shower bath; list; a strip of cloth, douche.
ducho adj. expert, skilful, dexterous, accustomed.
duda f. doubt; suspense; fluctuation, hesitation; irresolution, doubtfulness; sin — doubtlessly, without doubt.
dudable adj. dubitable; doubtful.
dudar v. to doubt; to hesitate.
dudoso adj. doubtful; dubious; uncertain.
duela f. stave; Am. long, narrow floor board.
duelo m. grief; sorrow; mourning; duel, mourners; challenge; affliction; condolement; estar de — to be in mourning, to mourn; sin — abundantly.
duende m. goblin; elf; fairy; ghost.
dueña f. owner; landlady; duenna, chaperon or governess; proprietress; a married lady.
dueño m. owner; proprietor; master or mistress; master with respect to a servant.
dueto m. duet.
dulce adj. sweet; pleasant; agreeable, fresh (water); soft (metal); mild; gentle; comfortable; ductile; m. sweetmeat; candy; confiture; confection; candied or dried fruits; Am. sugar, honey.
dulcería f. candy shop.
dulcificar v. to sweeten; to soften; to dulcify.
dulzón adj. over-sweet; sickeningly sweet.
dulzura f. sweetness; meekness, gentleness; pleasure; comfortableness.
duplicado adj. & m. duplicate; doubled; por — in duplicate.
duplicar v. to duplicate; to double; to repeat.
duplicidad f. duplicity; deceit; falseness; deceitfulness.
duque m. duke.
duquesa f. duchess; species of couch.
durabilidad f. durability; durable quality; wear.
durable adj. durable; lasting.
duración f. duration; continuance; durability.
duradero adj. durable; lasting.
durante prep. during, for; in the meantime.
durar v. to last; to endure; to wear well; to continue.
duraznero m. peach tree.
durazno m. peach, peach tree.
dureza f. hardness; harshness; solidity; firmness.
durmiente adj. sleeping; sleeper; dormant; m. in buildings, dormant or dormer crossbeam; Am. railroad tie.
duro adj. hard; firm; solid; strong; untiring; stubborn; obstinate harsh; rigid, cruel; miserable avaricious; rude; rough; a duras penas with difficulty; — y parejo Am. eagerly, tenaciously; hacer — Am. to resist stubbornly; m. duro (Spanish dollar).

E

e conj. and (before words beginning with i or hi).
ébano m. ebony; a hard black wood.
ebrio adj. drunk; inebriated, tipsy, intoxicated.
ebullición f. boiling, bubbling up, ebullition.

eclesiástico adj. ecclesiastical; m. ecclesiastic, priest, clergyman.

eclipsar v. to eclipse; to outshine, to surpass.

eco m. echo; **hacer —** to accord, to agree.

economía f. economy; prudent management; moderation; scantiness; **— política** economics; political economy.

economizar v. to economize, to save.

ecuación f. equation.

ecuador m. equator.

echar v. to throw, to cast; to expel; to jet; to turn, to reject; to shoot; to bud, to issue; to give off; to put; to apply; to eat; **—se a perder** to spoil; **— a correr** to run away; **— carnes** to get fat; **— de menos** to miss.

edad f. age; ages; **menor —** minority, infancy.

edén m. Eden; paradise.

edición f. edition; publication.

edificación f. edification; construction.

edificar v. to construct, to build, to edify; to uplift; to instruct.

edificio m. edifice, building; structure.

editar v. to publish.

editor m. publisher; adj. publishing.

editorial adj. publishing, editorial; m. editorial; f. publishing house.

edredón m. down quilt, comforter; eiderdown; quilted blanket.

educación f. education; training; breeding; manners, instruction.

educador m. educator; adj. educating.

educando m. pupil.

educar v. to educate; to teach, to train, to raise, to bring up; to instruct.

educativo adj. educational.

efectivo adj. effective; real; active; m. cash; **en —** in hard money; in coin.

efecto m. effect; result; end, purpose, operation; **en —** in fact; actually; **llevar a —** to carry out; **surtir —** to come out as expected; to give good results.

efectuar v. to effect; to bring about.

eficacia f. efficiency; effectiveness; activity.

eficiencia f. efficiency.

eficiente adj. efficient.

efímero adj. ephemeral, short-lived, brief, ephemerous.

efluvio m. emanation, exhalation, vapors.

efusión f. effusion, unrestrained expression of feeling; gushy manner; efflux; **— de sangre** bloodshed.

efusivo adj. effusive, too demonstrative; over-emotional.

egipcio adj. & m. Egyptian.

égloga f. eclogue.

egocéntrico adj. egocentric; self-centered.

egoísmo m. selfishness, self-love; egoism.

egoísta adj. selfish; m. & f. selfish person.

egolatría f. self-worship.

eje m. axis, axle; center.

ejecución f. execution; carrying out; performance; law; a judicial writ, distraint; seizure.

ejecutar v. to execute; to carry out, to perform, to make, to do, to act.

ejecutivo adj. executive; active; m. executive.

ejecutor m. executor; **— de la justicia** executioner, executer.

ejemplar adj. exemplary, m. model; precedent, example; copy, specimen.

ejemplo m. example, model, pattern.

ejercer v. to practice; to exert; to exercise.

ejercicio m. exercise; practice; military drill; excercise (of authority); task, employment, office, ministry; **hacer —** to take exercise.

ejercitar v. to practice, to exercise, to drill, to train; **—se** to train oneself; to practice; **— la paciencia de alguno** to try the patience of someone.

ejército m. army.

ejido m. public land, common.

ejote m. Am. string bean.

el def. art. m. the; **— de** the one with; that one with; **— que** rel. pron. he who, the one that; **él** pers. pron. he; him, it (after a prep).

elaborar v. to elaborate, to finish with care.

elasticidad f. elasticity.

elástico adj. elastic; flexible; m. elastic; elastic tape; wire spring; **—s** Am. suspenders.

elección f. election; choice.

electo adj. elect, chosen; m. elect; person chosen.

elector m. elector; voter; adj. electoral, electing.
electoral adj. electoral.
electricidad f. electricity.
electricista m. electrician; electrical engineer.
eléctrico adj. electric, electrical.
electrizar v. to electrify; to thrill, to excite; Am. to anger, to irritate.
elefante m. elephant.
elegancia f. elegance, grace, distinguished manner.
elegante adj. elegant, graceful, stylish, poslihed, gallant, fine, nice.
elegir v. irr. to elect, to chose.
elemental adj. elementary; elemental; fundamental, essential; constitutive.
elemento m. element; rudiment; —s elements, fundamentals; ser (or estar) hecho un — Am. to be an idiot, a fool.
elevación f. elevation; height; rise; rapture; highness; loftiness; ecstasy; dignity; altitude.
elevador m. Am. elevator, hoist.
elevar v. to elevate, to raise, to lift; —se to go up, to soar.
eliminación f. elimination, removal.
eliminar v. to eliminate.
elocuencia f. eloquence.
elogiar v. to praise, to extol, to laud, to eulogize.
elogio m. praise.
elote m. Am. ear of corn, corn on the cob.
elucidación f. elucidation, explanation.
elucidar v. to elucidate; to explain, to illustrate.
eludir v. to elude, to avoid; to dodge.
ella pers. pron. she, her; it (after a prep).
ello pron. it; — es que the fact is that.
emanación f. emanation, flow, fumes, odor, vapor; manifestation.
emanar v. to emanate, to spring, to issue.
emancipación f. emancipation.
emancipar v. to emancipate, to set free; —se to become free.
embajada f. embassy; errand, mission.
embajador m. ambassador.
embalador m. packer.
embalaje m. packing.
embalar v. to pack; to bale; to crate; to embale.

embaldosar v. to pave with flagstones or tiles.
embalsamar v. to embalm; to scent; to perfume.
embarazar v. to embarras, to hinder; to obstruct; to make pregnant; —se to become pregnant; to become embarrassed.
embarazo m. impediment, obstacle; pregnancy; embarrassment; bashfulness; awkwardness.
embarazoso adj. embarrassing; cumbersome, unwieldy.
embarcación f. ship, boat; embarkation.
embarcar v. to embark, to ship; Am. to ship by train or any vehicle; —se to embark, to sail, to engage (in); Am. to board, get on a train.
embarco m. embarkation.
embargar v. to impede; to restrain; to attach; to confiscate; to lay an embargo on; estar embargado de emoción to be overcome with emotion.
embargo m. embargo, restriction on commerce; attachment, confiscation; sin — nevertheless.
embarque m. shipment.
embarrado p.p. & adj. smeared; plastered; muddy.
embarrar v. to smear, to daub.
embaucador m. cheat, impostor, sharper, abuser.
embaucar v. to fool, to trick, to swindle, to deceive.
embebecido p.p. & adj. amazed; absorbed.
embeber v. to imbibe, to absorb, to soak; to shrink; —se to be fascinated; to be absorbed.
embelesar v. to enrapture; to delight, to astonish, to charm.
embeleso m. deligth, ecstasy.
embellecer v. irr. to embellish; to beautify; to adorn.
embestida f. sudden attack, onset; assault.
embestir v. irr. to attack, to assail.
embetunar v. to cover with pitch; to black; to cover with bitumen.
emblanquecer v. irr. to whiten; to bleach; to become white; —se to whiten, become white.
emblema m. emblem.
embobar v. to fool; to amuse; to amaze, to fascinate; to entertain the mind; —se to be amazed, to be fascinated.
embocadura f. mouth (of a river); entrance (through a narrow pas-

sage); mouthpiece (of a wind instrument); bit (of a bridle); taste; flavor (said of wines).

embolado m. bull whose horns have been tipped with balls; impotent, ineffectual person.

embolar v. to tip a bull's horns with balls; to black; to polish; —se Am. to get drunk.

émbolo m. piston; plunger (of a pump); embolus (clot in a blood vessel).

embolsar v. to put into a pocket or purse; —se to pocket, put into one's pocket.

emborrachar v. to intoxicate; —se to get drunk.

emborronar v. to blot; to scribble.

emboscada f. ambush, ambuscade.

emboscar v. to ambush; to emboss, to conceal; —se to lie in ambush; to go into a forest.

embotado adj. dull, blunt.

embotamiento m. dullness, bluntness, dulling, blunting.

embotar v. to dull; to blunt; to enervate; to weaken.

embotellar v. to bottle, to bottle up; Am. to jail.

embozado adj. cloaked; muffled; covered up to the face.

embozar v. to muffle; to cloak, to conceal; to disguise; to muzzle, to dissemble; —se to muffle oneself, wrap oneself.

embragar v. to engage or throw in the clutch.

embrague m. clutch (of a machine); coupling.

embriagar v. to intoxicate; to inebriate; to enrapture; —se to get drunk; to get intoxicated.

embriaguez f. intoxication; drunkenness.

embrollar v. to involve; to ensnare; to entangle; to confuse.

embrollo m. confusion; tangle; trickery, lie, deception.

embromar v. to chaff; to make fun of; "kid"; Am. to bother, to molest; to delay unneccessarily; to ruin, harm; —se Am. to be bothered, disgusted; to get delayed.

embrujar v. to bewitch; to enchant.

embrujo m. charm; enchantment; glamour.

embrutecer v. irr. to stupefy, to render brutish; to dull the mind, to make insensible.

embudo m. funnel; trick.

embuste m. lie, fraud; trinket.

embustero m. liar; adj. deceitful, tricky.

embutido m. sausage; inlaid work; Am. insertion of embroidery or lace.

embutir v. to insert, to inlay; to stuff.

emerger v. to emerge; to come out.

emigración f. emigration.

emigrante m. & f. emigrant.

emigrar v. to emigrate; to migrate.

eminencia f. eminence; height.

eminente adj. eminent; high; lofty.

emisión f. issue (of bonds, money, etc); radio broadcast; emission.

emisor adj. emitting; broadcasting; m. radio transmitter.

emisora f. broadcasting station.

emitir v. to emit; to give off; to utter; to send forth; to issue; to broadcast.

emoción f. emotion.

emocional adj. emotional.

emocionante adj. moving; touching, thrilling.

emocionar v. to cause emotion; to touch; to move; —se to be touched, moved, stirred.

emotivo adj. emotional.

empacador m. packer.

empacar v. to pack up, to wrap up; to bale, to crate; Am. to goad, irritate (an animal); —se to be stubborn; to get angry; Am. to balk; to put on airs.

empachado p.p. & adj. clogged; stuffed; upset from indigestion; bashful; embarrassed.

empachar v. to stuff; to cram; to cause indigestion; —se to get upset; to get clogged; to be stuffed; to suffer indigestion; to get embarrassed.

empacho m. indigestion; bashfulness; **no tener — en** to have no objection to; to feel free to.

empalagar v. to cloy; to pall; to become distasteful; to disgust.

empalagoso adj. cloying; sickeningly sweet; boring; wearisome.

empalizada f. stockade, palisade; fort.

empalmar v. to splice; to join; to scarf; to dovetail; **— con** to join.

empalme m. junction; joint; splice, connection.

empanada f. pie; meat pie, swindle; fraud.

empanizar v. Am. to bread.

empañar v. to blur; to dim; to tarnish; to swaddle.

empapar v. to soak; to drench; to saturate.
empapelador m. paper hanger.
empapelar v. to paper; to wrap in paper.
empaque m. packing; looks; appearance, air; importance; Am. impudence.
empaquetar v. to pack, to pack in; to make a package; to clap together; —se to dress up, doll up.
emparedado adj. shut up; confined; recluse; m. sandwich; prisoner confined in a narrow cell.
emparejar v. to even up, level off; to match; to pair off; to overtake; catch up with.
emparentado adj. & p.p. related by marriage.
emparentar v. to become related by marriage.
emparrado m. vine arbor.
empastar v. to paste; to fill (a tooth); to bind (books); —se Am. to get lost in the pasture; to become overgrown with grass.
empaste m. tooth filling; binding (of a book).
empatar v. to tie (as in voting), to have an equal score; to hinder, to obstruct; Am. to tie, join.
empate m. tie, draw, equal score, equal number of votes; obstruction; hindrance; Am. joint, junction.
empecinado adj. Am. stubborn.
empedernido adj. hardened, hardhearted.
empedernir v. to harden; to toughen; —se to become hardened.
empedrado m. stone pavement; p.p. & adj. paved with stones.
empedrar v. irr. to pave with stones.
empeine m. instep; groin.
empellón m. push; shove; a —es by pushing rudely.
empeñar v. to pawn; to oblige, to compel; —se to persist, to insist; to apply oneself; to go into debt; —se por to mediate; intercede for.
empeño m. pledge, pawn; persistence, insistence; perseverance; eagerness; Am. pawnshop; tener — en to be eager to.
empeorar v. to impair; to make worse; —se to grow worse.
empequeñecer v. irr. to diminish; to make smaller; to belittle.
emperador m. emperor.
emperatriz f. empress.

emperifollar v. to decorate; to adorn; —se to dress up, deck up, doll up.
empero conj. however, nevertheless.
empezar v. irr. to begin.
empiezo m. beginning.
empinado adj. steep, lofty.
empinar v. to raise, to lift; to incline, to bend; — el codo to drink; —se to stand on tiptoes; to rise high; Am. to overeat.
empiojado adj. lousy, full of lice.
emplasto m. plaster, poultice.
empleado m. employee.
emplear v. to employ; to occupy; to invest; to spend; —se to be employed in.
empleo m. employment, position, job, business, occupation; aim; investment.
emplumar v. to feather; to adorn with feathers; to tar and feather; Am. to deceive; to send away to a house of correction or prison; — con algo Am. to run away with something, to steal it; —las (or emplumárselas) Am. to take to one's heels, to flee, to escape.
empobrecer v. irr. to impoverish; —se to become poor.
empobrecimiento m. impoverishment.
empolvado adj. dusty, covered with dust or powder.
empolvar v. to sprinkle powder; to cover with dust; to powder; to dust; —se to get dusty; to powder one's face.
empollar v. to hatch, to brood.
emponzoñar v. to poison.
emprendedor adj. enterprising; undertaking.
emprender v. to undertake; to attempt.
empreñar v. to impregnate, to make pregnant; to beget.
empresa f. enterprise, undertaking; symbol, motto; company, management.
empresario m. manager; impresario; promoter.
empréstito m. loan.
empujar v. to push; to shove; to press forward.
empujón m. shove, push.
empuñar v. to grasp, to grab; to clutch, to seize, to clinch; to hold with the fist.
en prep. in, on, upon; estar — México to be in Mexico; — el otro lado on the other side; — domingo upon Sunday.

enaguas f. pl. underskirt, petticoat; short skirt; — **blancas** the inner skirt.
enajenamiento m. trance, alienation, absence of mind; transfer of property; — **mental** mental derangement; — **de los sentidos** loss of consciousness.
enajenar v. to dispossess, to transfer property; to enrapture; to alienate; to transport; to charm; — **el afecto de** to alienate the affection of; —**se** to be enraptured, to be in trance.
enaltecer v. to extol, to exalt.
enamorado adj. in love; enamored; lovesick; m. lover.
enamorar v. to make love, to woo, to court, to enamore; to inspire love; —**se** to fall in love.
enano m. dwarf; adj. dwarfish, tiny, low, small, little.
enarbolar v. to hoist, to lift; to hang out; to brandish (a sword, club, etc.); —**se** to rear, to balk.
enarcar v. to arch; to hoop (barrels); — **las cejas** to arch one's eyebrows, to frown.
enardecer v. irr. to excite, to kindle; to fire with passion, to inflame; —**se** to become excited; to become passionate; to get angry.
enardecimiento m. ardor, passion; unbridled enthusiasm.
encabezado m. headline; heading; adj. headed.
encabezamiento m. heading; headline; tax roll; census; registration of taxpayers.
encabezar v. to put a heading or title to; to head; to lead; to make up a list or tax roll; to strenghten (wine).
encabritarse v. to rear, to balk, to rise on the hind legs.
encadenar v. to chain; to link together.
encajar v. to thrust in, to fit into, to insert, to drive in, to inclose; — **bien** to be opportune; —**se** to squeeze into; to intrude; to meddle.
encaje m. lace; fitting together; socket, groove; hole, inlaid work.
encajonar v. to box, to put or pack in a box.
encallar v. to strand, to run aground; to get stuck; to fail.
encamado p.p. confined in bed.
encaminar v. to direct, to guide, to put on the right road, to show the way; —**se** to betake oneself, to go (toward); to be on the way.
encanecer v. irr. to get grey-haired, to grow old.
encanijado adj. emaciated, thin, sickly.
encanijar v. to weaken; —**se** to get thin, to get emaciated; to pine.
encantado p.p. & adj. delighted, charmed; enchanted.
encantador adj. charming; m. charmer, sorcerer.
encantamiento m. enchantment.
encantar v. to charm, to enchant.
encanto m. charm, enchantment, delight; spell; fascination.
encapillar v. Am. to confine in the death cell.
encapotado p.p. & adj. cloaked, overcast, cloudy; in bad humor.
encapotarse v. to become overcast, cloudy; to cover up; to put on a cloak or raincoat; to frown.
encapricharse v. to indulge in whims; to get stubborn.
encaramar v. to raise, to elevate; to extol; to climb; —**se** to climb, to climb upon, to get upon, to perch upon; Am. to be ashamed; to go to one's head (wine).
encarar v. to face; to confront; to address, to accost; to aim; —**se con** to face; to confront.
encarcelación f. imprisonment.
encarcelamiento See encarcelación.
encarcelar v. to imprison, to jail.
encarecer v. irr. to raise the value, to overrate, to overvalue; to make dear, to raise the price of; to exaggerate; to extol; to recommend highly; to enhance.
encarecidamente adj. earnestly.
encargar v. to recommend, to commission; to put in charge; to entrust, to advise; to order; to beg; —**se de** to take charge of.
encargo m. recommendation, advise, command, request; charge; order; errand.
encariñado adj. & p.p. attached, fond, enamored.
encariñamiento m. affection, fondness, attachment.
encariñar v. to inspire affection, fondness or love; —**se** to become passionately fond of; to become attached to.
encarnado adj. flesh-colored; red.
encarnar v. to incarnate, to incarn, to breed flesh; to embody; to bait (a fishhook).

encarnizado adj. bloody; hard-fought; irate, furious; fierce.

encarnizar v. to infuriate, to enrage; to flesh; to satiate with flesh; —se to get furious, enraged, to fight with fury.

encasillar v. to put in a pigeonhole or compartment, to put in a stall; to classify; to sort out.

encender v. irr. to light, to kindle; to set on fire; —se to take fire, to be on fire; to get red.

encendido adj. red, high-colored; ignition (of an internal combustion engine).

encerado m. like wax, wax-colored; blackboard; oilcloth; wax coating.

encerramiento m. enclosure, confinement; locking up.

encerrar v. irr. to lock, to close; to shut up, to confine; to contain, to include, to comprenhend; —se to live in seclusion; to be locked up.

encía f. gum (of the mouth).

encima adv. over, above, overhead; on the top, besides; on; — de on the top of; por — de over; de — Am. besides, in addition; echárselo todo — Am. to spend everything on clothes.

encina f. live oak.

encinta adj. pregnant.

encintado m. curb (of a side walk).

enclaustrar v. to cloister.

enclavar v. to nail; to fix with nails; to fasten; to prick horses in shoeing; — la artillería v. to spike guns.

enclenque adj. sickly, weak, feeble.

encoger v. to shrink, to shrivel, to shorten, to contract, to shrug; to discourage; —se to be low spirited; — se de hombros to shrug the shoulders.

encogido p.p. & adj. shrunk, shrivelled; bashful; timid; fearful, shy.

encogimiento m. shrinking; timidity; contraction, contracting; constriction, corrugation; — de hombros shrug.

encolerizar v. to anger; —se to be angry.

encomendar v. irr. to charge, to advise; to recommend, to commit; to praise; to entrust; —se to put oneself in the hands of; to send regards; to pray to.

encomiar v. to extol, to praise.

encomienda f. charge, commission, recommendation; message; royal land grant (including Indian inhabitants); Am. warehouse for agricultural products; parcel post package.

encomio m. encomium, high praise, eulogy.

enconado p.p. & adj. inflamed, infected; sore; angry.

enconar v. to inflame; to infect; to irritate; to provoke; to increase the inflammation in a wound; —se to become inflamed, infected, irritated; to get irritated.

encono m. rancor, animosity, ill will; malevolence; Am. inflammation, swelling.

encontrado adj. opposite; opposing; contrary.

encontrar v. irr. to encounter, to meet, to find, to clash; —se to meet, to coincide; to be found; to be situated; to collide; to conflict; —se con to come across; to meet up with.

encontrón m. bump; collision; darse un — to collide with, to bump into.

encordelar v. to string; to tie with strings; to bind with cords.

encorvar v. to curve, to bend, to crook; —se to bend down, to stoop; to get crooked.

encrespar v. to curl; to ruffle; to irritate; to frizzle, to crimp; —se to curl; to get ruffled; to become rough (the sea).

encrucijada f. crossroads, street intersection; ambush; crossway.

encuadernación f. binding (of books).

encuadrar v. to enclose in a frame; to encompass, to fit into; Am. to suit; to summarize briefly; to give a synthesis of.

encubrir v. to cover, to hide; to cloak, to mask.

encuentro m. encounter, meeting; find, finding; conflict, clash; collision; salir al — de to go to meet; to make a stand against; to oppose; llevarse de — Am. to run over; to knock down, to drag along.

encuerado adj. naked, ragged.

encuerar v. Am. to strip of clothes; to skin; to fleece; to strip of money; —se to strip, to get undressed.

encuesta f. search, inquiry, investigation.

encumbrado p.p. & adj. elevated; exalted; high; lofty.

— 97 —

encumbramiento m. elevation; exaltation; height; eminence; raising.

encumbrar v. tó elevate, to raise, to extol; to ascend; —se to be elevated, to be proud; to soar.

encurtido m. pickle.

encurtir v. to pickle.

enchilada f. Am. rolled tortilla served with chili.

enchuecar v. to bend, to twist; —se Am. to get bent or twisted.

enchufar v. to plug in, to telescope; to fit (a tube) into another.

enchufe m. socket, plug; electric oulet.

ende : por — hence, therefore.

endeble adj. weak, feeble, forceless; flimsy.

endemoniado adj. possessed with the devil; fiendish; devilish; mischievous.

endentar v. irr. to indent, to form notches in; to furnish with teeth; to mesh.

enderezar v. to straighten; to right; to correct; to rectify; to address, to dedicate; —se to go straight (to); to straighten up.

endeudado p.p. & adj. indebted; in debt.

endeudarse v. to get into debt; to become indebted, to contract debts.

endiablado adj. devilish; possessed by the devil; diabolical; diabolic; ugly; deformed; mean; wicked; Am. dangerous, risky.

endomingado p.p. & adj. dressed up in one's Sunday, or best, clothes.

endosante m. indorser.

endosar v. to indorse (a check, etc.).

endose m. indorsement.

endulzar v. to sweeten, to soften.

endurecer v. irr. to harden, to indurate; to inure; —se to get hardened; to get cruel.

enemigo m. enemy, antagonist, foe; adj. hostile; unfriendly; inimical; contrary; adverse; ser de — una cosa to dislike a thing.

enemistad f. enmity, hatred.

enemistar v. to cause enmity between; —se con to become an enemy of.

energía f. energy, power, vigour, force.

energético adj. energetic.

enero m. January.

enervar v. to enervate, to weaken, to enerve, to deprive of force.

enfadar v. to anger, to vex, to molest, to fret; —se to get angry; to fret.

enfado m. anger, disgust; trouble; vexation.

enfadoso adj. annoying, troublesome; vexatious.

enfardar v. to bale, to pack; to embale.

énfasis m. emphasis.

enfático adj. emphatic, emphatical.

enfermar v. to become ill; to make ill; to fall sick; —se to become ill.

enfermedad f. sickness, illness.

enfermera f. nurse (for the sick).

enfermería f. infirmary.

enfermero m. male nurse.

enfermizo adj. sickly, unhealthy, infirm, healthless.

enfermo adj. sick, feeble, ill, weak; m. patient.

enflaquecer v. irr. to become lean; to make thin; to weaken.

enfocar v. to focus.

enfrenar v. to bridle; to brake, to put the brake on; to check; to curb.

enfrentar v. to put face to face; —se con to confront, to face; to meet face to face.

enfrente adv. over, against, opposite, in front.

enfriamiento m. cooling; chill; refrigeration.

enfriar v. to cool; Am. to kill; —se to cool, to cool off; Am. to die.

enfurecer v. irr. to infuriate, to enrage, to irritate, to make furious; —se to enrage; to become furious; to get rough, stormy.

enfurruñarse v. to get angry; to grumble.

engalanar v. to adorn, to decorate, to deck; —se to dress up, primp.

enganchamiento See **enganche**.

enganchar v. to hitch; to hook; to draft; to accroach; to entrap; to recruit; —se to engage; to interlock, to get hooked; to enlist in the army.

enganche m. hooking; coupling; draft (into the army).

engañador adj. deceitful, deceiving; m. cheat, impostor, deceiver.

engañar v. to deceive; to cheat; to delude, to trick; to fool; to hoax; to abuse; to gull; —se to deceive oneself; to be mistaken.

engaño m. deceit, trick, fraud;

mistake; misunderstanding; mistaking; hoax.

engañoso adj. deceitful, tricky; misleading; artful.

engastar v. to mount, to set (jewels); to enchase.

engaste m. setting (for a stone).

engatusar v. to coax; to entice; to fool; to rob.

engendrar v. to engender, to beget; to produce, to cause.

engolfarse v. to get deep into; to become absorbed; to go deeply into.

engomar v. to gum; to glue.

engordar v. to fatten; to get fat; to become rich; to lard; —se to fat; to grow rich.

engorroso adj. cumbersome; tiresome; bothersome.

engranaje m. gear, gears, gearing.

engranar v. to gear, to throw in gear; to interlock.

engrandecer v. irr. to aggrandize, to augment, to make greater; to exaggerate, to magnify.

engrane m. engagement (of gears); gear.

engrasar v. to lubricate, to grease, to oil, to fat; to stain with grease; to fertilize; to manure; to dress (cloth).

engreído adj. & p.p. conceited, vain; Am. attached, fond.

engreír v. irr. to make vain, conceited; —se to get conceited; Am. to become fond of; to become attached to.

engrosar v. irr. to enlarge; to thicken; to fatten; to get fat.

engrudo m. paste (for gluing).

engullir v. to gobble, to devour; to gorge; to glut.

enhebrar v. to thread; to string.

enhiesto adj. straight, upright, erect.

enhorabuena f. congratulation; felicitation; adv. safely; well and good; all right.

enigma m. enigma, riddle, puzzle.

enjabonar v. to soap; to flatter.

enjaezar v. to harness.

enjalbegar v. to whitewash; to make white; —se to paint (one's face).

enjambre m. swarm; crowd.

enjaular v. to cage; to imprison; to jail.

enjuagar v. to rinse, to rinse out.

enjuague m. mouth wash; rinse; rinsing; scheme; plot.

enjugar v. to dry; to wipe; —se to dry oneself.

enjuiciar v. to indict; to prosecute; to prepare a lawsuit for judgement; to try (a case); to judge.

enjundia f. substance, essence; fat; force, strength.

enjuto adj. dried; thin; skinny.

enlace m. link; tie; bond; marriage, connection.

enladrillado m. brick pavement or floor.

enladrillar v. to pave with brick.

enlatar v. to can; Am. to roof with tin.

enlazar v. to join, to bind, to tie, to rope; to unite; to connect; to marry; Am. to lasso; —se to join, to marry; to become joined in marriage.

enlodar v. to bemire, to bedaub, to cover with mud; to smear; to soil; to dirty; —se to get in the mud; to get muddy.

enloquecer v. irr. to make crazy; to madden; to enrage; to lose one's mind; —se to madden, to become mad; to go crazy.

enlosado m. tile pavement.

enlosar v. to pave with flags.

enmantecado m. Am. ice cream. See mantecado.

enmantecar v. to butter; to grease with lard or butter.

enmarañar v. to entangle; to snarl; to confuse; to mix up; to perplex; to puzzle.

enmascarar v. to mask; to cloak; to go on disguise; —se to put on a mask; to masquerade.

enmendar v. irr. to amend, to correct; to repair; to indemnify; to compensate; —se to reform; to mend; to grow better; to lead a new life.

enmienda f. correction; amendment; reform, indemnity; compensation; emendation; amendment.

enmohecer v. to rut; to mold; to mildew; —se to grow moldy or rusty.

enmudecer v. irr. to silence; to remain silent; to lose one's voice; to become dumb; to be still.

ennegrecer v. irr. to blacken; to darken; —se to become dark; to get cloudy.

ennoblecer v. irr. to ennoble; to dignify; to illustrate; to embellish.

enojadizo adj. irritable; ill-tempered; fretful; peevish.

enojado adj. angry.

enojar v. to make angry, to vex, to annoy, to irritate; to tease, to molest; —se to grow angry.

enojo m. anger; annoyance; fretfulness; peevishness; choler; passion.

enojoso adj. bothersome; annoying.

enorgullecer v. irr. to fill with pride; —se to swell with pride; to get proud.

enorme adj. enormous, exorbitant.

enramada f. arbor, bower; shady grove.

enrarecer v. irr. to rarefy, to thin; —se to become rarefied; to become scarce.

enrarecimiento m. rarity; rarefaction.

enredadera f. climbing vine.

enredar v. to entangle, snare; to snarl; to mix up; to raise a rumpus; to confound, to perplex, to involve in difficulties; —se to get tangled up, mixed up; to get trapped; —se con to have an affair with.

enredista m. Am. liar; talebearer.

enredo m. tangle; confusion; lie; plot; entangling; ensnaring.

enredoso adj. tangled up; Am. tattler.

enrejado m. trellis; grating; lattice.

enrevesado adj. intricate, complicated; unruly.

enriquecer v. irr. to enrich; to aggrandize; to adorn; —se to become rich.

enrojecer v. irr. to redden; —se to get red; to blush.

enrollar v. to roll, to roll up; to coil.

enronquecer v. irr. to make hoarse; to become hoarse; —se to become hoarse.

enroscar v. to coil, to twist, to twine; —se to coil; to curl up.

ensalada f. salad; hodgepodge, mixture, medley.

ensalzar v. to exalt, to praise, to extol, to aggrandize.

ensanchar v. to widen, to enlarge, to extend; —se to expand; to puff up.

ensanche m. widening, expansion, extension; augment, dilatation; widening.

ensangrentado adj. gory, bloody.

ensangrentar v. to imbrue, to stain with blood; —se to be covered with blood; to get red with anger.

ensartar v. to string; to thread; to link, to rattle off; Am. to tie to a ring; to swindle; to trick; —se Am. to fall into a trap.

ensayar v. to try; to attempt.

ensayo m. rehearsal; test, experiment; practice; essay.

ensenada f. small bay; creek, cove.

enseñanza f. teaching, education, training; knowledge; instruction; doctrine.

enseñar v. to show, to teach; to train; to instruct; to educate; to point out.

enseres m. pl. household goods; utensils, implements; equipment; furniture; fixtures.

ensillar v. to saddle; Am. to abuse; to mistreat, to domineer; — el picazo Am. to get angry.

ensimismarse v. to become absorbed in thought; Am. to become conceited or vain.

ensoberbecer v. irr. to make proud or haughty, to puff up; —se to become haughty; to get rough, to get choppy (said of the elements).

ensordecer v. irr. to deafen; to become deaf; to become silent.

ensortijar v. to curl, to ring, to encircle; to ring the nose of an animal; —se to curl.

ensuciar v. to dirty, to soil, to stain; —se to dirt one's bed, clothes, etc.; to be dishonest.

ensueño m. illusion, dream.

entablar v. to board up; to plank; to splint; to open negotiations; — una conversación to start a conversation; — un pleito to bring a lawsuit.

entablillar v. to splint; to bind up a broken bone; Am. to cut (chocolate) into tablets or squares.

entallar v. to fit closely a dress; to carve, to engrave, to sculpture.

entapizar v. to cover with tapestry.

entarimar v. to floor with boards.

ente m. entity, being; queer man; ridiculous fellow.

enteco adj. sickly, skinny, infirm, weak, languid.

entender v. irr. to understand; to comprehend, to believe, to hear; to remark; to reason, to judge; a mi modo (or manera) de — in my opinion; — de to know, to be an expert in; —se en to take care of; to deal with; —se con to have dealings or relations

entendido with; to have an understanding with.
entendido adj. wise, learned, prudent, knowing; able, skillful; **no darse por —** to pretend not to hear or understand; to ignore.
entendimiento m. understanding; intellect, mind, judgment; conceiving.
enterado p.p. & adj. informed, aware; acquainted, instructed.
enterar v. to inform, to acquaint; to instruct; **—se** to know, to learn, to find out; to understand, to get the idea.
entereza f. entirety; integrity; fortitude; rectitude; firmness; serenity; haughtiness; perfection.
enternecedor adj. touching, moving, pitiful.
enternecer v. irr. to soften, to touch, to stir, to move; to melt; to affect; to pity; **—se** to become tender; to be moved to compassion.
entero adj. entire, undiminished; perfect, complete, whole; just, right, firm; m. Am. payment, reimbursement; balance of an account; **caballo —** stallion.
enterramiento m. burial.
enterrar v. irr. to bury, to inter; Am. to sink, stick into; **—se** to live alone.
entibiar v. to make lukewarm; to cool; **—se** to become lukewarm.
entidad f. entity, unit; group, organization; **de —** of value or importance.
entierro m. burial, funeral, interment; grave, tomb; Am. hidden treasure.
entintar v. to ink; to stain with ink; to dye.
entoldar v. to cover with an awning; **—se** to dress pompously; to swell with pride; to become overcast, cloudy.
entonación f. intonation.
entonar v. to tune, to intonate; to sing in tune; to start a song; to harmonize; **—se** to put on airs.
entonces adv. then, at that time; **pues —** well then; **hasta —** until then.
entornado adj. half-open; half-closed; ajar.
entornar v. to turn; to set ajar.
entorpecer v. irr. to stupefy; to benumb; to paralyze; to delay; to obstruct; to thwart, to frustrate.

entorpecimiento m. numbness; dullness; torpor; stupidity; delay; obstruction.
entrada f. entrance, entry; gate; avenue, access; ingress; Am. attack, assault, goring; beating; **—s** cash receipts.
entrambos adj. & pron. both.
entrampar v. to trap, to ensnare; to trick; to burden with debts; **—se** to get trapped or entangled: to run into debt.
entrante adj. entering; coming; **el año —** next year.
entraña f. entrail, bowel; the inmost parts of anything; heart; disposition, temper; **—s** entrails, insides; **hijo de mis —s** child of my heart; **no tener —s** to be cruel.
entrar v. to enter, to go in, to come in; to begin; **ahora entro yo** now I begin; **me entró miedo** I became afraid; **—se** to slip in, to sneak in, to enter.
entre prep. between; among; **dijo — sí** he said to himself; **— tanto** meanwhile; **— más habla menos dice** Am. the more he talks the less he says.
entreabierto p.p. & adj. ajar, partially open.
entreabrir v. to half-open; to leave ajar.
entreacto m. intermission; interval, interlude; small cigar.
entrecano adj. greyish; between black and gray.
entrecejo m. space between the eyebrows; **fruncir el —** to frown.
entrecortado adj. hesitating, faltering; breathless, choking; p.p. interrupted.
entrecortar v. to cut in the middle dividing; to interrupt at intervals.
entrecruzar v. to intercross, to interlace; **—se** to cross.
entredicho m. prohibition, injunction.
entrega f. delivery, surrender; instalment; **novela por —s** serial novel.
entregar v. to deliver, to give, to give up; to hand over; **—se** to surrender, to submit, to give up; to devote oneself to; to abandon oneself to.
entrelazar v. to interlace, to intermix; to weave together.
entremés m. side dish; interlude; farce; interval.
entremeter v. to insert; to place

**between; to intermeddle; —se to meddle, to intrude.
entremetido** adj. meddlesome; meddling, intermeddling; officious; m. meddler, busybody, intruder.
entremetimiento m. intrusion, meddling.
entremezclar v. to intermix, to intermingle, to interweave.
entrenador m. Am. trainer.
entrenamiento m. Am. training, drill.
entrenar v. Am. to train, to drill, —se Am. to train.
entresacar v. to pick out, to select.
entresuelo m. mezzanine, second floor.
entretanto adv. meanwhile.
entretejer v. to interweave; to insert; to weave together; to intertwine.
entretener v. irr. to delay, to detain, to amuse, to entertain; to put off, to trifle with; —se to amuse oneself; to delay oneself; — el tiempo to while away the time.
entretenido adj. amusing; entertaining.
entretenimiento m. entertainment; pastime; amusement; delay.
entrever v. to glimpse; to catch a glimpse of; to half see; to see imperfectly.
entreverar v. to intermingle, to intermix; to insert.
entrevista f. interview; date; appointment; meeting, conference.
entrevistar v. to interview; —se con to have an interview with.
entristecer v. irr. to sadden, to make sad; to grieve, to afflict; —se to become sad.
entrometer See **entremeter**.
entrometido See **entremetido**.
entumecer v. irr. to benumb, to make torpid; —se to get numb; to surge; to swell.
entumido adj. numb, stiff; Am. timid, shy, awkward.
entumirse v. to get numb.
enturbiar v. to make muddy; to muddle; to disturbe; to obscure; —se to get muddy; to get muddled; to derange a thing.
entusiasmar v. to excite, to fill with enthusiasm; —se to get enthusiastic, excited.
entusiasmo m. enthusiasm.
entusiasta m. & f. enthusiast; visionary.

entusiástico adj. enthusiastic, enthusiastical.
enumeración f. counting, enumeration.
enumerar v. to enumerate.
enunciar v. to express, to state, to declare, to enunciate.
envainar v. to sheathe.
envalentonar v. to make bold or haughty; to encourage; to inspirit; —se to get bold; to brag, swagger.
envanecer v. irr. to make vain; —se to become vain, proud.
envasar v. to pack, to put into any container; to bottle; to can; to barrel.
envase m. packing; container; jar, bottle, can.
envejecer v. irr. to make old; to grow old; —se to grow old, to get old; to be of an old fashion.
envenenamiento m. poisoning.
envenenar v. to poison; to infect.
envergadura f. span (of an airplane); spread (of a bird's wings); breath (of sails).
envés m. back or wrong side.
enviado m. envoy.
enviar v. to send, to convey, to transmit; — a uno a paseo to give someone his walking ticket.
enviciar v. to vitiate, to corrupt; —se to become addicted to; to be immoderately addicted to.
envidar v. to stake (in cards); to bet; —el resto to stake all that one has left.
envidia f. envy.
envidiable adj. enviable, desirable.
envidiar v. to envy, to feel envy; to grudge.
envidioso adj. envious.
envilecer v. irr. to revile, to malign, to degrade; to debase; —se to degrade oneself.
envilecimiento m. degradation, humiliation, shame, debasement.
envío m. remittance, sending, shipment; consignment.
envite m. bid, stake (in cards); invitation, polite offer; push.
envoltorio m. bundle, package.
envoltura f. wrapping, cover, wrapper.
envolver v. irr. to involve, to entangle; to convolve; to surround; —se to be implicated; to be involved, entangled; to wrap up.
enyesar v. to plaster, to chalk; to whitewash.
enzolvar v. Am. to clog, to ob-

struct; —se Am. to clog, to get clogged.
¡epa! interj. Am. hey! listen! stop! look out!
épico adj. epic.
epidemia f. epidemic.
episodio m. episode.
epístola f. epistle, letter.
epitafio m. epitaph.
época f. epoch.
epopeya f. epic poem, epopee.
equidad f. equity, justice, fairness.
equidistante adj. equidistant, equally distant, halfway, midway.
equilibrar v. to balance, to poise.
equilibrio m. equilibrium, balance, poise, counterpoise.
equipaje m. baggage, luggage; equipment, outfit, crew.
equipar v. to equip, to fit out; to man.
equipo m. equipment, equipping; outfit, fitting out; work crew; port team; — de novia trousseau.
equitación f. horsemanship; horseback riding; equitation.
equitativo adj. fair, just; equitable.
equivalente adj. equivalent.
equivaler v. irr. to be equivalent.
equivocación f. error, mistake.
equivocado p.p. & adj. mistaken.
equivocar v. to mistake; —se to be mistaken; to make a mistake.
equívoco adj. equivocal, ambiguous, vague; Am. mistaken; m. pun, play on words; Am. mistake, error.
era f. era, age; thrashing floor; bed in a garden.
erario m. public treasury, exchequer.
erguido adj. erect.
erguir v. irr. to erect, to raise up straight; to lift; —se to sit or stand erect; to swell with pride; to become proud and haughty.
erial m. uncultivated land; adj. unplowed; untilled.
erizado adj. bristly, prickly; — de bristling with.
erizar v. to set on end, to make bristle; to stand on end (hair).
erizo m. hedgehog, porcupine, urchin; thistle; — de mar sea urchin; ser un — to be irritable, harsh.
ermitaño m. hermit.
erosión f. erosion.

errabundo adj. wandering.
errado adj. mistaken, erroneous, wrong, on error.
errante adj. errant, roving, wandering, erring.
errar v. irr. to err, to make mistakes; to miss; to rove; to wander; to misjudge; — el camino to miss the right way; — el golpe to miss a blow.
errata f. misprint, printer's error; erratum.
erróneo adj. erroneous; mistaken; wrong, incorrect.
error m. error, fault, mistake; mispersuasion, deceit, falsity; misguidance; deficiency.
eructar v. to belch, to eructate.
eructo m. belch, eructation.
erudición f. erudition, learning; knowledge.
erudito adj. erudite, scholarly; learned; lettered; m. scholar.
erupción f. eruption; outburst; outbreak, bursting forth; rash.
esbelto adj. slender, tall, genteel and well shaped.
esbozar v. to sketch, to outline.
esbozo m. sketch, outline; a rough draught.
escabechar v. to pickle, to souse.
escabeche m. pickled fish; souse, pickle.
escabel m. stool; footstool.
escabrosidad f. roughness, harshness; unevenness; improper word or phrase; inequality; asperity; cragginess.
escabroso adj. rough; rugged; rather indecent; cragged, crabbed, rude, unpolished.
escabullirse v. irr. to sneak away, to slip through; to scamper; to scurry; to evade; to escape.
escala f. ladder; scale, port of call; stopover; any port, bay; hacer — en to stop at.
escalafón m. army register.
escalar v. to scale; to climb.
escaldar v. to scald, to make red-hot; to burn.
escalera f. stairs, staircase; ladder.
escalfar v. to poach (eggs).
escalinata f. flight of stairs.
escalofriarse v. to become chilled.
escalofrío m. chill; —s chills and fever.
escalón m. step (of a ladder or staircase); stepping stone; degree; —es Am. tribe of quichua Indians.
escalonar v. to form in echelon; to terrace; —se to rise in terraces.

escama f. scale, fish scale; flake.
escamoso adj. scaly; squamous.
escamotear v. to whisk out of sight; to rob or snatch away with cunning; to conceal by a trick or sleight of hand.
escandalizar v. irr. to scandalize, to shock; —se to be shocked.
escandaloso adj. scandalous, shocking; Am. showy, loud.
escapada f. escape, flight.
escapar v. to escape, to flee, to avoid; to get out of danger, to make off; —se to run away, escape.
escaparate m. show window; glass case, glass cabinet or cupboard; press, case.
escapatoria f. escape, loophole, excuse; flying; flight; subterfuge.
escape m. escape; vent; outlet; exhaust; a — rapidly, at full speed.
escarabajo m. black beetle.
escaramuza f. skirmish; quarrel; slight engagement.
escarbar v. to scrape; to scratch; to dig out; to pry into, to investigate.
escarcear v. Am. to prance.
escarcha f. frost, frosting; white frost.
escarchar v. to frost; to be frozen.
escardar v. to weed; to part good from bad; to root out vice.
escarlata f. scarlet; scarlet fever; scarlet cloth.
escarlatina f. scarlet fever.
escarmentar v. irr. to punish (as an example or warning); to profit by one's misfortunes, punishment, etc; — **en cabeza ajena** to profit by anothe's mistake or misfortune.
escarmiento m. lesson, example, warning; punishement; fine; chastisement.
escarnecer v. irr. to jeer, to insult, to mock; to scoff; to ridicule.
escarnio m. scoff, jeer; gibe.
escarpa f. steep slope, bluff, cliff; declivity.
escarpado adj. steep; rugged, sloped; craggy.
escarpia f. hook (for hanging); tenterhook.
escasear v. to be scarce; to grow less, to become scarce; to give sparingly; to decrease.
escasez f. scarcity, lack, scantiness, niggardliness.
escaso adj. scarce, limited; scant; scanty; stingy; small; short; hard; churlish.
escatimar v. to stint, to skimp; to curtail.
escena f. scene; scenery; theatre, stage.
escenario m. stage.
escenificación f. dramatization, stage adaptation.
escepticismo m. skepticism; doubt; unbelief.
escéptico m. & adj. skeptic, skeptical.
esclarecer v. irr. to lighten; to illuminate; to elucidate; to illustrate; to make clear; to explain.
esclavitud f. slavery.
esclavizar v. to enslave.
esclavo m. slave, captive.
esclusa f. lock; flood gate, milldam.
escoba f. broom.
escobazo m. blow with a broom.
escobilla f. whisk broom, brush; sweepings of gold or silver.
escocer v. irr. to sting; to smart; to cause a sharp pain.
escocés adj. Scotch; m. Scotch; Scotchman.
escoger v. to choose, to select; to elect; to pick out.
escolar adj. scholastic, scholastical; m. scholar, student, clerk, learner.
escolástico adj. & m. scholastic; scholastical.
escolta f. escort; convoy, guard.
escoltar v. to escort, to convoy; to guard.
escollo m. reef, danger, obstacle; embarrassment; difficulty.
escombro m. débris, rubbish, fragments; mackerel.
esconder v. to hide; to conceal, to skulk; to disguise; —se to hide, go into hiding.
escondidas: a — on the sly; under cover; privately; in a secret manner; **jugar a las** — Am. to play hide-and-seek.
escondite m. concealment; lurking place, hiding place; **jugar al** — to play hide-and-seek.
escondrijo m. hiding place.
escopeta f. shotgun.
escopetazo m. gunshot; gunshot wound; sudden bad news; Am. offensive or ironic remark.
escoplo m. chisel.
escoria f. slag; scum; derelict.
escorial f. dump, dumping place; pile of slag.
escorpión m. scorpion.

— 104 —

escote m. low neck; sloping of a jacket or other garment; tucker.
escotilla f. hatchway.
escotillón m. hatch, hatchway; trap door; trap in a stage.
escozor m. smarting sensation; sting; a lively sensation.
escribano m. court clerk; lawyer's clerk; notary public; penman.
escribiente m. clerk, office clerk; amanuensis.
escribir v. to write.
escrito p.p. written; m. writing, manuscript.
escritor m. writer.
escritorio m. desk, office.
escritura f. writing; hand writing; deed, contract; **Sagrada Escritura** Holy Scripture, Holy Bible.
escrúpulo m; scruple, doubt.
escrupuloso adj. scrupulous; particular, exact.
escrutador adj. scrutinizing, examining; peering; m. scrutinizer; inspector for election returns.
escrutar v. to scrutinize.
escrutinio m. scrutiny, inspection.
escuadra f. squadron, square; socket; squad; fleet.
escuadrón m. squadron.
escualidez f. squalor.
escuálido adj. squalid, filthy, poor, miserable; thin, emaciated.
escuchar f. to listen, to hear, to give ear, to pay attention.
escudar v. to shield.
escudero m. squire.
escudo m. shield, escutcheon; coat of arms; patronage; protection; crown (an ancient coin); Chilean gold coin.
escudriñar v. to scrutinize; to search; to pry into; to consult.
escuela f. school.
escueto adj. plain; disengaged, free from encumbrances; unadorned, bare.
esculcar v. Am. to search; to frisk (a person's pockets).
esculpir v. to sculpture; to engrave.
escultor m. sculptor.
escultura f. sculpture.
escupir v. to spit.
escurrir v. to drip; to drain off; to drop, to fall in drops; —se to ooze out, to trickle; to slip out, to sneak out.
ese, esa dem. adj. that; **esos, esas** those; **ésa, ése** m. f. pron. that one; **ésos, ésas** m. f. pl. those.
esencia f. essence.

esencial adj. essential.
esfera f. sphere, clock dial.
esférico adj. spherical.
esforzado adj. strong; valiant; courageous; vigorous.
esforzar v. irr. to strengthen; to invigorate; to enforce; to encourage; —se to make an effort; to strive; to try hard.
esfuerzo m. effort, courage, vigour, stress.
esfumar v. to shade, to tone down; —se to vanish, to disappear.
esgrima f. fencing.
esgrimir v. to fence; to brandish; to wield.
eslabón m. link of a chain; steel knife sharpener; black scorpion; Am. a kind of lizard.
eslabonar v. to link; to join; to connect; to add, to unite.
esmaltar v. to enamel; to adorn; to embellish.
esmalte m. enamel; enamel work; smalt.
esmerado adj. painstaking, careful, conscientious.
esmerar v. to polish, to brighten; to clean.
esmero m. care, precision.
esmoquin m. tuxedo; dinner coat.
eso dem. pron. that, that thing; that fact; — **es** that is; **a — de** at about (referring to time); Am. ¡**eso!** that's right.
espaciar v. to space; to spread; to expand; —se to enlarge; to relax; to cheer up; to grow gay.
espacio m. space, interval; slowness, delay; procrastination; adv. Am. slowly.
espacioso adj. spacious, capacious; slow, deliberate.
espada f. sword; swordman; matador (bullfighter who kills the bull).
espalda f. back, shoulders; aid, protection; —**s** back, back part; **a —s** behind one's back; **de —** on one's back; **dar la —** to turn one's back on.
espaldar m. back (of a seat); trellis (for plants); backplate of a cuirass.
espaldilla f. shoulder blade.
espantadizo adj. timid, easily frightened; scary, shy, timid.
espantajo m. scarecrow.
espantapájaros m. scarecrow.
espantar v. to frighten, to terrify; to scare; to drive away; Am. to haunt; —se to be scared; to be surpised or astonished; —**selas**

Am. to be wide-awake; to catch on quickly.
espanto m. fright, consternation; menace, threat; surprise, horror; **Am.** ghost.
espantoso adj. frightful; dreadful; horrid; terrifying; fearful.
español adj. Spanish; m. Spaniard; Spanish language.
esparadrapo m. cerecloth; court plaster, adhesive tape.
esparcir v. to scatter; to disseminate; to spread; to divulge; —**se** to relax, to make merry.
espárrago m. asparagus.
esparto m. feather-grass; Spanish grass hemp; esparto grass.
espasmo m. spasm, horror.
especia f. spice.
especial adj. special, particular; **en —** in particular.
especialidad f. specialty, particularity.
especialista m. & f. specialist.
especializar v. to specialize; —**se en** to specialize in.
especie f. species; kind, sort; pretext; idea.
especificar v. to specify, to name.
específico adj. specific; m. specific.
espécimen m. specimen, sample.
espectacular adj. spectacular.
espectáculo m. spectacle.
espectador m. spectator.
espectro m. spectre, phantom, ghost; **—** solar solar spectrum.
especulación f. speculation.
especulador m. speculator.
especular v. to speculate.
especulativo adj. speculative.
espejismo m. mirage, illusion.
espejo m. mirror, looking-glass; model; **— de cuerpo entero** full length mirror.
espeluznante adj. hair-raising, terrifying.
espeluznarse v. to be terrified; to have the hair set on end with fear; to bristle with fear.
espera f. expectation, expectance; wait; stay (granted by judge), delay; extension of time (for payment); **sala de —** waiting room; **estar en — de** to be waiting for, to be expecting.
esperanza f. hope; expectation.
esperanzado adj. hopeful.
esperanzar v. to give hope to.
esperar v. to wait, to hope; to expect; to trust; to await; to wait for; **— en alguien** to place hope or confidence in someone.

esperezarse See **desperezarse**.
esperpento m. ugly thing; nonsense.
espesar v. to thicken, to make dense; —**se** to thicken; to become thick or dense.
espeso adj. thick, dense; compact; slovenly; **Am.** bothersome, boring.
espesor m. thickness.
espesura f. density, thickness; thicket; thickest part (forest).
espetar v. to spring on; to surprise with; to spit; to put upon a spit; to tell, to relate; to pop (a question); to pierce; —**se** to be stiff, pompous.
espía m. & f. spy.
espiar v. to spy, to lurk; —**se Am.** to bruise the hoofs, to get lame
espiga f. ear of wheat; peg; spike.
espigar v. to glean; to grow spikes; —**se** to grow tall and slender.
espina f. thorn; splinter; fishbone; spine; fear; suspicion; scruple, doubt; **dar mala —** to arouse suspicion.
espinaca f. spinach.
espinazo m. backbone, spine.
espinilla f. shin bone; blackhead.
espino m. hawthorn; shrub; thorny branch.
espinoso adj. thorny; difficult; dangerous.
espionaje m. espionage, spying.
espiral adj. & f. spiral.
espirar v. to exhale; to emit; to give off; to die. See **expirar**.
espíritu m. spirit; soul; courage; vigor; essence; ghost.
espiritual adj. spiritual.
espita f. spigot, faucet, tap; topper; drunkard.
esplendidez f. splendor.
espléndido adj. splendid.
esplendor m. splendor.
esplendoroso adj. splendorous, resplendent; shining.
espliego m. lavender.
espolear v. to spur; to incite; to urge forward.
espolón m. spur; ram; buttress.
espolvorear v. to powder, to sprinkle with powder.
esponja f. sponge, sponger, parasite; **Am.** souse, habitual drunkard.
esponjado adj. spongy, fluffy, puffed up.
esponjar v. to fluff; to make spongy or porous; —**se** to fluff up, to become spongy or porous; to swell, puff up.

ESPONJOSO

esponjoso adj. spongy.
esponsales m. pl. betrothal.
espontaneidad f. spontaneity; spontaneousness; ease, naturalness.
espontáneo adj. spontaneous.
esposa f. wife; —s handcuffs.
esposo m. husband.
espuela f. spur.
espulgar v. to remove lice or fleas from; to scrutinize.
espuma f. foam, froth; scum; — de jabón suds.
espumar v. to skim; to froth; to foam.
espumarajo m. froth, foam (from the mouth); echar —s to froth at the mouth, to be very angry.
espumoso adj. foamy.
esputo m. sputum, spit, saliva.
esquela f. note, letter; announcement.
esqueleto m. skeleton, carcass; framework; Am. blank for filling out; outline.
esquema f. scheme, outline.
esquí m. ski.
esquiar v. to ski.
esquila f. small bell; cow bell; sheepshearing.
esquilar v. to shear, to clip; to crop.
esquina f. corner, angle.
esquinazo m. corner; Am. serenade; dar — to avoid meeting someone.
esquivar v. to avoid, to dodge; to shun; —se to withdraw, to shy away.
esquivez f. shyness; aloofness; disdain, scorn, asperity, coolness.
esquivo adj. reserved, unsociable; shy; disdainful, aloof, scornful; stubborn, fastidious.
estabilidad f. stability.
estable adj. stable, firm, steady; durable, permanent.
establecer v. irr. to establish; to found; to decree; to ordain; to settle down.
establecimiento m. establishment; foundation; settlement; footing; statute, law.
establero m. groom.
establo m. stable.
estaca f. stake, club, stick; picket.
estacada f. stockade; palisade; picket fence; Am. predicament.
estacar v. to stake; to stake off, mark off with stakes; Am. to fasten down with stakes; —se to remain stiff or rigid.
estación f. station, season; railway station.

ESTANQUILLO

estacionar v. to station; to place; to park (a car); —se to remain stationary; to park.
estacionario adj. stationary; motionless.
estada f. sojourn, stay.
estadía f. detention, stay; Am. sojourn, stay.
estadio m. stadium.
estadista m. statesman.
estadística f. statistics.
estado m. state, condition; station, rank, estate; footing; account, statement, report; — mayor army staff; hombre de — statesman; en — interesante Am. pregnant.
estadounidense adj. from the United States.
estafa f. swindle, fraud, trick, deceit.
estafador m. swindler, crook.
estafar v. to swindle, to defraud, to cheat.
estallar v. to explode, to burst, to creak, to crackle.
estallido m. explosion, outburst, crash; creaking; crack (of a gun), report (of a gun).
estambre m. woolen yarn; stamen; woolen thread.
estampa f. image; print; stamp; cut, picture; footprint.
estampado m. print, printed fabric; printing.
estampar v. to stamp, to print.
estampida f. crack; sharp sound; Am. stampede.
estampido m. crak, sharp sound; report (of a gun).
estampilla f. stamp, seal; Am. postage stamp.
estancar v. to stem; to stanch; to stop the flow of, to corner; —se to stagnate, to become stagnant.
estancia f. stay; hall; room; mansion; Am. farm, cattle ranch; main building of a farm or ranch.
estanciero m. Am. rancher, ranch owner; cattle raiser; adj. pertaining to an estancia.
estanco m. monopoly; tank, reservoir; Am. liquor store.
estándar m. Am. standard, norm.
estandardizar v. Am. to standardize.
estandarte m. standard, flag, banner.
estanque m. pond, pool, reservoir.
estanquillo m. tobacco store; Am.

small store; small liquor store, tavern.

estante m. shelf; bookshelf; Am. prop, support.

estantería f. shelves; bookcases.

estaño m. tin.

estaquilla f. peg; spike.

estar v. irr. to be; —**le bien a uno** to be becoming to one; —**de prisa** to be in a hurry; **¿a cuántos estamos?** what day of the month is it today?; —**se** to keep, remain.

estática f. statics; radio static.

estático adj. static.

estatua f. statue.

estatura f. stature, height.

estatuto m. statute.

este, esta dem. adj. this; **estos, estas** these; **éste, ésta** m. f. dem. pron. this one, this thing; the latter; **esto** this, this thing; **éstos, éstas** m., f. pl. these; the latter.

este m. East; East wind.

estela f. wake of a ship.

estenógrafo m. stenographer.

estentóreo adj. loud, stentorian.

estepa f. steppe, treeless plain.

estera f. matting; matt.

estercolar v. to manure, to fertilize with manure.

estercolero m. manure pile, manure dump; manure collector.

estéril adj. sterile, barren.

esterilidad f. sterility, barrenness.

esterilizar v. to sterilize.

esterlina adj. sterling; **libra —** pound sterling.

estero m. estuary.

estertor m. death-rattle; snort.

estética f. aesthetics.

estético adj. aesthetic.

estetoscopio m. stethoscope.

estibador m. stevedore; longshoreman.

estibar v. to stow; to pack down, to compress.

estiércol m. manure; fertilizer.

estigma m. stigma; brand; mark of disgrace; birthmark.

estilar v. to use, to be accustomed to using; —**se** to be in stlye (said of clothes).

estilete m. stiletto, narrow-blade dagger; long, narrow sword.

estilo m. style, fashion.

estima f. esteem.

estimación f. esteem, regard, valuation.

estimar v. to esteem, to regard; to estimate, to appraise; to judge; to think.

estimulante adj. stimulant; stimulating; m. stimulant.

estimular v. to stimulate; to incite, to encourage; to goad.

estímulo m. stimulation, incitement; stimulus.

estío m. summer.

estipulación f. stipulation, specification, provision, proviso.

estipular v. to stipulate, to specify.

estirado p.p. & adj. stretched; extended, drawn; stuck up; conceited.

estirar v. to stretch, to extend; **— la pata** to die; —**se** to stretch out; Am. to die.

estirón m. hard pull, tug, stretch.

estirpe f. lineage, family, race.

estival adj. summer, relating to the summer.

estocada f. thrust, stab, stab wound.

estofa f. stuff, cloth; class, quality; **gente de baja —** low class people, rabble.

estofado m. stew, stewed meat.

estofar v. to quilt; to stew.

estoico adj. & m. stoic.

estómago m. stomach.

estopa f. burlap, oakum.

estoque m. long, narrow sword.

estorbar v. to hinder; to obstruct.

estorbo m. hindrance; nuisance; bother.

estornudar v. to sneeze.

estornudo m. sneeze.

estrado m. dais (for a throne, etc.); main part of a parlor or drawing room.

estragado p.p. & adj. corrupted; spoiled; ruined; tired, worn out.

estragar v. to corrupt, to contaminate, to spoil; to ruin.

estrago m. havoc, ruin, massacre.

estrangulador m. strangler, choke (of an automobile); adj. strangling.

estrangular v. to strangle; to choke, to throttle.

estratagema f. stratagem, scheme.

estrategia f. strategy.

estratégico adj. strategic; m. strategist.

estrato m. stratum, layer; stratus.

estratosfera f. stratosphere.

estrechar v. to tighten; to narrow; to embrace, to hug; **— la mano** to squeeze, grasp another's hand; to shake hands.

estrechez f. narrowness; tightness; austerity; strait; poverty; closeness.

ESTRECHO — **EXACTITUD**

estrecho adj. narrow; tight; m. strait, narrow passage.
estrella f. star; **— de mar** starfish.
estrellado adj. starry; spangled with stars; **huevos —s** fried eggs.
estrellar v. to shatter; to dash to pieces; to star, spangle with stars; **—se** to shatter, to break into pieces; to fail.
estremecer v. irr. to shake; **—se** to shiver, to shudder, to vibrate.
estremecimiento m. shiver, shudder, vibration, shaking.
estrenar v. to use or wear for the first time; to perform (a play) for the first time; to inaugurate; to begin.
estreno m. début, inauguration.
estreñimiento m. constipation.
estreñir v. irr. to constipate; **—se** to become constipated.
estrépito m. racket, noise, crash.
estrepitoso adj. noisy; boisterous.
estriado p.p. & adj. fluted, grooved; streaked.
estriar v. to groove, to flute.
estribación f. spur (of a mountain), counterfort.
estribar v. to rest (upon); **eso estriba en que...** the basis or reason for it is that...
estribillo m. refrain.
estribo m. stirrup, footboard, running board; support; brace; spur (of a mountain); **perder los —s** to lose one's head; to lose control of oneself.
estribor m. starboard.
estricto adj. strict.
estrofa f. strophe, stanza.
estropajo m. mop; dishcloth; **tratar a uno como un —** to treat someone scornfully.
estropear v. to spoil, to ruin, to damage; to mutilate, to maim; to cripple.
estructura f. structure.
estructural adj. structural.
estruendo m. clatter; confusion, bustle; din, racket.
estruendoso adj. thunderous; uproaring, deafening, noisy; clamorous.
estrujamiento m. crushing, squeezing.
estrujar v. to squeeze, to press; to crush.
estrujón m. squeeze, crush, smashing; the last pressing of grapes.
estuario m. estuary.
estuco m. stucco.
estuche m. jewel box; instrument case; kit; small casket; sheath.

estudiante m. & f. student, scholar.
estudiar v. to study.
estudio m. study; studio.
estudioso adj. studious; m. learner.
estufa f. heater, stove; hothouse; steam room; steam cabinet; small brasier.
estupefacto adj. stunned; speechless, petrified.
estupendo adj. stupendous, marvelous, wonderful.
estupidez f. stupidity.
estúpido adj. stupid.
etapa f. stage, lap (of a journey or race); halting place; army food rations; epoch, period.
éter m. ether.
etéreo adj. ethereal; heavenly.
eterno adj. eternal, everlasting, endless.
ética f. ethics.
ético adj. ethical, moral.
etiqueta f. etiquette, ceremony, formality; tag; **de —** formal, ceremonious.
eucalipto m. eucalyptus.
europeo adj. & m. European.
evacuación f. evacuation; bowel movement.
evacuar v. to evacuate, to empty; to vacate.
evadir v. to evade, to elude, to escape; **—se** to slip away; to make one's escape.
evaluar v. to evaluate, to appraise; to value.
evangelio m. gospel.
evaporar v. to evaporate; to disperse; **—se** to vanish, to disappear, to evaporate.
evasión f. evasion, dodge, escape; subterfuge.
evasiva f. evasion, dodge, escape; subterfuge.
evasivo adj. evasive.
evasor m. evader, dodger.
evento m. event, accident, issue.
evidencia f. evidence, proof.
evidenciar v. to prove, to show, to make evident.
evidente adj. evident.
evitable adj. avoidable.
evitar v. to avoid, to shun.
evocar v. to evoke, to call forth.
evolución f. evolution.
evolucionar v. to evolve; to perform manoeuvers; to go through changes.
exacerbar v. to exasperate, to irritate; to aggravate, to make worse.
exactitud f. exactness, precision, punctulality, accuracy.

exacto adj. exact, precise, accurate, punctual.
exagerar v. to exaggerate.
exaltación f. exaltation, excitement.
exaltado adj. elated; excited; hotheaded.
exaltar v. to exalt, to elevate, to glorify, to praise, to lift; —se to get excited; to become irritated.
examen m. examination; inspection; examen.
examinar v. to examine; to inspect; to investigate.
exánime adj. lifeless, motionless; weak.
exasperar v. to exasperate, to irritate, to annoy, to offend.
excavar v. to excavate, to dig, to dig out, to hollow.
excedente m. surplus; adj. exceeding, extra; excessive.
exceder v. to exceed, to surpass; to overdo, to excel; —se to go too far; to overgo; to misbehave.
excelencia f. excellence, superiority; excellency (title).
excelente adj. excellent.
excelso adj. sublime, lofty; el Excelso the Most High.
excéntrico adj. eccentrinc, queer, odd.
excepción f. exception, exclusion.
excepcional adj. exceptional, unusual.
excepto adv. except that, besides that, with the exception of.
exceptuar v. to except, to exclude.
excesivo adj. excessive.
exceso m. excess, superfluity; excessiveness; crime; — de equipaje express baggage; en — in excess, excessively.
excitante adj. exciting; stimulating.
excitar v. to excite, to stir, to stimulate; to rouse, to animate; —se to get excited.
exclamación f. exclamation.
exclamar v. to exclaim.
excluir v. irr. to exclude.
exclusivo adj. exclusive.
excomunicar v. to excommunicate.
excomunión f. excommunication.
excrecencia f. excrescence.
excursión f. excursion, tour, trip.
excusa f. excuse.
excusado p.p. & adj. excused; exempt, superfluous; reserved; m. toilet.
excusar v. to excuse, to avoid, to shun, to exempt; —se to excuse oneself, to apologize, to decline.

exención f. exemption.
exentar v. to exempt. See eximir.
exento adj. exempt, freed, free; unobstructed.
exequias f. pl. obsequies, funeral rites, exequies.
exhalar v. to exhale; to emit, to give off; to breathe forth; —se to evaporate; — el espíritu to die.
exhibición f. exhibition; exposition; Am. payment of an installment.
exhibir v. to exhibit; to expose; to lay; Am. to pay for in installments; —se to exhibit oneself, show off.
exhortar v. to exhort, to admonish.
exigencia f. demand; urgent want; pressing necessity; emergency.
exigente adj. demanding, exacting, urgent.
exigir v. to require, to demand, to exact.
exiguo adj. scanty, meager.
eximio adj. eximious, famous, very eminent.
eximir v. to exempt, to except, to excuse; —se de to avoid, to shun.
existencia f. existence; —s stock on hand, goods; en — in stock, on hand.
existente adj. existent, existing; in stock.
existir v. to exist.
éxito m. outcome, result; success; tener buen (mal) — to be successful (unsuccessful).
éxodo m. exodus, emigration.
exonerar v. to exonerate, to free from blame; to relieve of a burden or position; to dismiss; to unload; to acquit.
exorbitante adj. exorbitant, excessive; extravagant.
exótico adj. exotic, foreign, strange, quaint, extraneous.
expansión f. expansion; relaxation; recreation; extension
expansivo adj. expansive; demonstrative, effusive.
expatriar v. to expatriate, to exile; —se to expatriate oneself; to emigrate.
expectación f. expectation.
expectativa f. expectation; hope, prospect; estar en — de algo to be expecting something.
expectorar v. to expectorate.
expedición f. expedition; speed, activity; brevet or bull dispatched by the See of Rome.
expedicionario adj. expeditionary;

m. member of an expedition; explorer.
expediente m. certificate; file of papers pertaining to a business matter; expedient; means; dispatch; promptness.
expedir v. irr. to dispatch, to issue officially; to remit, to send.
expeler v. to expel, to eject.
experiencia f. experience; experiment.
experimentado adj. & p.p. experienced.
experimental adj. experimental.
experimentar v. to experiment, to try, to test; to experience, to feel.
experimento m. experiment, trial.
experto adj. expert, skilful; m. expert.
expiación f. expiation, atonement.
expiar v. to atone for; to make amends for; to purify.
expirar v. to die; to expire.
explayar v. to extend, to enlarge; —se to become extended; to relax in the open air; to dwell upon a subject; —se con un amigo to unbosom oneself, to speak with the utmost frankness with a friend.
explicable adj. explainable.
explicación m. explanation.
explicar v. to explain, to elucidate, to comment; — una cátedra to teach a course; —se to explain oneself; to account for one's conduct.
explicativo adj. explanatory, explaining.
explícito adj. explicit, express, clear, definite, manifest.
exploración f. exploration.
explorador m. explorer, scout; adj. exploring.
explorar v. to explore.
explosión f. explosion.
explosivo adj. & m. explosive.
explotación m. exploitation; working of a mine; development of a business plant.
explotar v. to exploit, to operate, to develop; to carry on, to improve; to make unfair use of; Am. to explode.
exponer v. irr. to expose, to reveal; to show; to exhibit; to explain; to lay open, to leave unprotected; to expound; —se a to expose oneself; to run the risk of; to hazard, to adventure, to try the chance.
exportación f. exportation.

exportar v. to export.
exposición f. exposition; exhibition; explanation; exposure.
exprés m. Am. express; express company.
expresar v. to express; —se to express oneself, to speak.
expresión f. expression; utterance; present, gift; —es regards.
expresivo adj. expressive; affectionate.
expreso adj. expressed; express, clear, exact, fast; m. express train.
exprimir v. to squeeze, to extract (juice); to wring out; to express, to utter; to press out.
expuesto p.p. & adj. exposed; expressed; displayed; liable; obnoxious; risky, dangerous; lo — what has been said.
expulsar v. to expel, to eject.
expulsión f. expulsion, expelling.
exquisitez f. exquisiteness.
exquisito adj. exquisite.
extasiado adj. rapt, in ecstasy.
extasiar v. to delight; —se to be in ecstasy; to be enraptured.
éxtasis m. ecstasy.
extender v. irr. to spread, to extend; to stretch out; to unfold to enlarge, to widen; —se to extend, to spread; to be too wordy.
extensión f. extension; extent; expanse; expansion.
extensivo adj. extensive.
extenso p.p. extended; adj. extensive, vast, spacious; por — extensively, in detail.
extenuado adj. wasted, weak, emaciated.
exterior adj. exterior, outer; external; m. exterior; outside; outward appearance.
exterminar v. to exterminate; to banish, to root out.
exterminio m. extermination, destruction; expulsion; banishment.
externo adj. external, outward; visible, foreign.
extinguir v. to extinguish, to put out; to destroy; to suppress.
extinto adj. extinct; deceased.
extirpar v. to eradicate, to pull out by the roots, to root out, to remove completely, to destroy completely.
extorsión f. extortion.
extorsionar v. Am. to extort, to extract money; to blackmail.
extorsionista m. Am. extortioner, racketeer.

— 111 —

extracto m. extract; abstract; summary.
extraer v. irr. to extract.
extranjero adj. foreign; m. foreigner.
extrañamiento m. wonder, surprise, amazement.
extrañar v. to miss, to wonder at; to banish; Am. to miss (a person or thing); —se to marvel, to be astonished.
extrañeza f. strangeness; surprise; astonishment; oddity, odd thing.
extraño adj. strange, rare; odd; m. stranger.
extraordinario adj. extraordinary.
extravagancia f. extravagance, filly.
extravagante adj. extravagant, fantastic; queer, odd.
extraviar v. to lead astray; to strand; to misplace; —se to lose one's way; to get stranded; to get lost; to miss the road.
extravío m. deviation, straying; error; misconduct; damage.
extremado adj. extreme; extremely good or extremely bad.
extremar v. to carry to an extreme; —se to take great pains, to exert great effort.
extremidad f. extremity; extreme degree; remotest part; —es extremities, hands and feet.
extremo adj. extreme, last; farthest; excessive; utmost; m. extreme, highest degree or point; end, extremity; extreme care; con (en or por) — very much, extremely.
exuberante adj. exuberant, luxuriant, overabundant.

F

fábrica f. manufacture; factory, mill; structure; frame, building, edifice.
fabricación f. manufacture; fabrication, make.
fabricante m. manufacturer, maker; builder, architect; fabricator; artificer.
fabril adj. manufacturing; fabrile.
fábula f. fable, tale; falsehood; a fiction, a lie; rumour, report, common talk.
fabuloso adj. fabulous; false; imaginary; feigned; fictitious.
facción f. faction, band; party; battle; military exploit; action, engagement; —es features; estar de — to be on duty.

faceto adj. Am. cute, funny; affected.
fácil adj. easy; docile, yielding, manageable; likely; flexible; easily persuaded; frail; easy of access; probable.
facilidad f. facility; ease: ready compliance; opportunity.
facilitar v. to facilitate, to make easy; to furnish, to give; to expedite; — todos los datos to furnish all the data.
facón m. Am. dagger, large knife
faconazo m. Am. stab.
factible adj. feasible, practicable.
factor m. factor; element, joint cause; commercial agent; baggage man; performer.
factura f. invoice, itemized bill; make; workmanship, form; Am. roll, biscuit, muffin; — simulada temporary invoice, memorandum.
facturar v. to invoice; to bill; to check (baggage).
facultad f. faculty; ability; aptitude; power, right; permission; branch of learning; privilege, authority; science, art; license.
facultativo m. doctor; physician; master of science or art.
facundia f. eloquence, fluency, facility in speaking; facundity.
facha f. appearance, figure, aspect; looks; mien; face; — a — adv. face to face; en — backed.
fachada f. facade, front (building); title page; frontispiece.
fachenda f. ostentation, vanity; m. busybody.
fachendoso adj. vain, boastful, ostentatious.
faena f. task, job, duty; Am. extra job; work crew; labor gang.
faja f. sash, girdle; band; Am. belt, waist band.
fajar v. to girdle; to bind; to wrap with a strip of cloth; Am. to beat; to strike, to thrash; — un latigazo a uno Am. to whip, thrash someone; —se to put on a sash or belt; to tighten one's sash or belt; —se con Am. to have a fight with, come to blows with.
fajo m. bundle; sheaf.
falaz adj. illusive, illusory; deceitful; deceiving; fraudulent.
falda f. skirt; lap; hat brim; flap; foothill, slope.
faldear v. to skirt (a hill).
faldón m. coattail; shirttail.
falsario m. crook, forger, liar.
falsear v. to falsify, to misrepre-

falsedad f. falsehood, lie, untruth, fib; deceit, dissimulation.
falsificación f. falsification, forgery, counterfeit.
falsificar v. to falsify, to make false, to counterfeit; to forge.
falso adj. false, untrue, unreal, deceitful; counterfeit, sham, supposed; Am. cowardly; m. inside facing of a dress; lining; Am. false testimony, slander; en — upon a false foundation; without proper security; coger a uno en — Am. to catch one lying.
falta f. lack, fault, defect, want, absence, deficiency, mistake, misdemeanor, offense; por — de for want of; hacer — to be necessary; to be missing; me hace — I need it; sin — without fail.
faltar v. to be deficient, to be lacking, to be wanting; to fail, to be in fault; not to fulfil (a promise or duty); to die; Am. to insult; — poco para las cinco to be almost five o'clock; ¡no faltaba más! that's the last straw!; why, the very idea!
falto adj. lacking, wanting, deficient; defective, short; Am. foolish; stupid.
faltriquera f. pocket.
falla f. fault, defect, failure; dislocation of terrestrial strata; Am. baby's bonnet.
fallar v. to give sentence, to judge; to fail, to be deficient; to default; to miss, to fail to hit; to give way, to break; to trump.
fallecer v. irr. to die.
fallecimiento m. decease, death.
fallido adj. frustrated; bankrupt; deceived; disappointed.
fallo m. judgment, sentence, decision, verdict; adj. lacking (a card, or suit, in card games); Am. silly, foolish.
fama f. fame, reputation, report, glory, name; Am. bull's eye, center of a target.
famélico adj. ravenous, hungry, starved.
familia f. family.
familiar adj. familiar, domestic, homelike, common, well-known; friendly, informal; colloquial; m. intimate friend, member of a household; domestic servant; demon, **familiar spirit**; Am. relative.
familiaridad f. familiarity, acquaintance, informality.
familiarizar v. to familiarize; to acquaint; —se to acquaint oneself, to become familiar.
famoso adj. famed, famous, excellent.
fanal f. beacon m. beacon, lighthouse, lantern.
fanático adj. & m. fanatic, fanatical.
fanatismo m. fanaticism.
fanega f. Spanish bushel; — **de tierra** land measure (variable according to region).
fanfarrón m. braggart, boaster; inflated.
fanfarronada f. boast, brag, swagger, bluff.
fanfarronear v. to bluff, to brag; to swagger.
fango m. mud, mire.
fangoso adj. muddy, miry.
fantasear v. to fancy, to imagine.
fantasía f. fantasy, imagination, fancy, whim; —s string of pearls; tocar por — Am. to play by ear.
fantasma m. phantom, image; vision; ghost; spirit; f. scarecrow.
fantasmagórico adj. fantastic, unreal, illusory.
fantástico adj. fantastic.
fardel m. knapsack; bag; bundle.
fardo m. bundle, bale, parcel, pack, package; pasar el — Am. to shift the resposibility to someone else
farmaceútico m. pharmacist, druggist; adj. pharmaceutical.
farmacia f. pharmacy; drugstore.
faro m. lighthouse; beacon; lantern; Am. headlight.
farol m. lantern; street lamp; conceit, self-importance; Am. balcony; presumptuous man; bluff; darse — to show off, to put on airs.
farolero adj. vain, ostentatious; m. lamp maker or vendor; lamplighter.
farra f. Am. spree, revelry, wild party, noisy merrymaking; ir de — Am. to go on a spree.
farsa f. farce; company of actors; sham, fraud.
farsante m. charlatan, bluffer; quack; comedian; wag.
fascinación f. fascination; glamour.
fascinador adj. fascinating, glamorous, charming.
fascinar v. to fascinate, to bewitch, to charm, to allure.

fase f. phase, aspect.
fastidiar v. to annoy, to bother, to bore; Am. to hurt, to harm, to ruin.
fastidio m. boredom; disgust; nuisance, annoyance.
fastidioso adj. fastidious, annoying, bothersome; boring, tiresome.
fatal adj. fatal; mortal; deadly; unfortunate.
fatalidad f. fatality, destiny; calamity, misfortune.
fatiga f. fatigue, weariness; toil; —s hardships.
fatigar v. to fatigue, to weary; to bother.
fatigoso adj. fatiguing, tiring.
fatuo adj. foolish, stupid; vain; **fuego —** will-o'-the-wisp.
favor m. favor; kindness; help, aid; protection; Am. ribbon bow; **a — de** in favor of; **hágame el —** please.
favorable adj. favorable.
favorecer v. irr. to favor, to help, to protect.
favoritismo m. favoritism.
favorito m. favorite, beloved, darling.
faz f. face.
fe f. faith; **— de bautismo** baptismal certificate.
fealdad f. ugliness; homeliness; foulness; foul or immoral action; deformity.
febrero m. February.
febril adj. feverish, febrile.
fécula f. starch.
fecundar v. to fertilize.
fecundo adj. fruitful, fertile, productive.
fecha f. date.
fechar v. to date.
fechoría f. misdeed, misdemeanor.
federación f. federation, union.
federal adj. federal.
felicidad f. happiness, felicity; **¡—es!** congratulations!
felicitar v. to congratulate.
feligrés m. parishioner.
feliz adj. happy, lucky, fortunate.
felpudo adj. plushy; like plush; m. small plushlike mat; door mat.
femenil adj. womanly, feminine; womanish.
femenino adj. feminine.
fementido adj. false; treacherous; unfaithful.
fenecer v. irr. to die; to finish, to end, to conclude; to decline.

fénix m. phoenix; unique, exquisite.
fenómeno m. phenomenon.
feo adj. ugly, homely, deformed, hideous; Am. bad (referring to taste or odor).
féretro m. bier, coffin, hearse.
feria f. fair; market; rest, repose; Am. change (money); tip; **—s** present given to the poor or servants during holidays.
feriante m. & f. trader at fairs; trader, peddler.
fermentar v. to ferment, to heat.
fermento m. ferment; yeast, leaven.
ferocidad f. ferocity, fierness; wildness.
feroz adj. ferocious, wild, fierce, cruel, savage.
férreo adj. ferrous, ironlike; harsh; stern; severe; **vía férrea** railroad.
ferretería f. hardware shop; hardware; iron works, forge.
ferrocarril m. railroad.
ferroviario adj. railway, railroad (used as adjective); railroad man; railroad employee.
fértil adj. fertile, fruitful, productive.
fertilidad f. fertility, fruitfulness.
fertilizar v. to fertilize; to fructify.
ferviente adj fervent, ardent.
fervor m. fervor, zeal, devotion, warmth.
fervoroso adj. fervent, ardent; pious, devout; zealous, active, officious.
festejar v. to feast, to entertain, to celebrate; to woo; to court; Am. to thrash, to beat.
festejo m. entertainment, festival, celebration; courtship; obsequiousness; Am. revelry.
festín m. feast, banquet; entertainment.
festividad f. festival; holiday; festivity; gaiety, rejoicing.
festivo adj. festive, gay; festival, festal; **día —** holiday.
fétido adj. foul, fetid, stinking.
fiado: al — on credit.
fiador m. guarantor, backer, bondsman; Am. chin strap, hat guard.
fiambre m. cold meat; cold or late news; Am. cold meat salad; flop, failure (a party); corpse.
fianza f. bond, security, bail, surety, guarantee, caution.
fiar v. to trust; to guarantee, to back; to bail, to give credit; Am.

— 114 —

to borrow on credit; **—se de to place confidence in.**
fibra f. fiber; Am. strength.
fibroso adj. fibrous.
ficción f. fiction; novel.
ficticio adj. fictitious.
ficha f. chip; token; domino; file card; Am. rascal, scamp.
fichero m. file, card index, filing cabinet.
fidedigno adj. trustworthy, reliable.
fidelidad f. fidelity, faithfulness.
fideo m. vermicelli, thin noodle; thin person.
fiebre f. fever; excitement; agitation; Am. astute person.
fiel adj. faithful; true; accurate; m. public inspector; pointer of a balance or scale; pin of the scissors; **los —es** the worshipers; the congregation.
fieltro m. felt; felt hat; felt rug.
fiera f. wild beast; Am. go-getter, hustle; **ser una — para el trabajo** to be a demon for work.
fiereza f. ferocity, fierceness; cruelty, ugliness, hardness; loftiness.
fiero adj. fierce, ferocious, wild; cruel; ugly; horrible; huge; fiery; rough, rude; m. threat; **echar (or hacer) —s** to threaten, to boast.
fierro m. Am. iron; iron bar; cattle brand; **—s** Am. tools, implements; money. See **hierro.**
fiesta f. feast, festivity, celebration, entertainment; holiday; **estar de —** to be in a holiday mood; **hacer —s a uno** to fawn on a person.
fiestero adj. fond of parties, fond of entertainment; gay, festive; playful; m. merrymaker.
figón m. cheap eating house, "joint".
figura f. figure; shape; form; countenance; face card.
figurado adj. figurative.
figurar v. to figure; to form; to represent; to symbolize; **—se to** imagine; **se me figura** I think, guess, or imagine.
figurín m. fashion plate, dandy.
fijar v. to fix, to fasten; to establish; **—se** to settle; **—se en to** notice, pay attention to.
fijeza f. firmness, solidity, steadiness.
fijo adj. fixed; firm; secure.
fila f. row, tier; rank.
filamento m. filament.

filete m. edge, rim; fillet, tenderloin; hem; screw thread.
filial adj. filial.
filmar v. to film, to screen.
filo m. cutting edge; Am. hunger; **por —** exactly; **de — Am.** resolutely.
filón m. seam, vein.
filoso adj. Am. sharp, sharp edged.
filosofía f. philosophy.
filosófico adj. philosophic, philosophical.
filósofo m. philosopher.
filtrar v. to filter; **—se** to leak through, to leak out; to filter.
filtro m. filter.
filudo adj. Am. sharp-edged.
fin m. end, ending; purpose; **al —** at last; **al — y al cabo** at last, anyway; **in the end; a — de que** so that; **a —es de mes** toward the end of the month; **en —** in conclusion; well, in short.
final adj. final; m. end.
finalizar v. to finish; to end.
financiamiento m. Am. financing.
financiar v. Am. to finance.
financiero adj. financial; m. financier.
finanza f. Am. finance; **—s** Am. public treasury; government funds.
finca f. real estate; property; country house; Am. ranch, farm.
fincar v. to build real estate; Am. to rest (on), to be based (on); to build a farm house or country house.
fineza f. fineness; nicety, courtesy; favor, kindness; present.
fingimiento m. pretense, sham.
fingir v. to feign, to pretend; to fake; to imagine.
finiquito m. settlement of an account; quittance, final receipt; **dar —** to finish up.
fino adj. fine; nice; delicate; sharp; subtle; refined.
finura f. fineness; nicety; subtlety; courtesy; good manners.
firma f. signature; firm, firm name; concern.
firmamento m. firmament, sky, heaven.
firmante m. & f. signer, subscriber.
firmar v. to sign, to subscribe.
firme adj. firm; solid; hard, stable, fast; **de —** hard, steadily.
firmeza f. firmness, stability.
fiscal m. public prosecutor, district attorney; censurer; adj. fiscal.
fisgar v. to pry; to snoop; to spy.

fisgón m. snoop, snooper; adj. snooping; curious.
fisgonear v. to pry; to snoop.
física f. physics.
físico adj. physical; Am. vain, prudish, affected; real; m. physicist.
fisiología f. physiology.
fisiológico adj. physiological.
fisonomía f. face, features.
flaco adj. lean, skinny; frail; weak; **su lado —** his weak side, his weakness.
flacura f. thinness.
flama f. flame.
flamante adj. bright, shiny; brand-new.
flameante adj. flaming, flashing.
flamear v. to flame; to flap, to flutter (in the wind).
flamenco adj. Flemish; Am. skinny; m. Flemish, Flemish language; flamingo.
flan m. custard.
flanco m. flank, side.
flanquear v. to flank.
flaquear v. to weaken, to flag.
flaqueza f. thinness, leanness; weakness, frailty.
flauta f. flute.
flautista m. & f. flute player.
fleco m. fringe; bangs, fringe of hair.
flecha f. arrow, dart.
flechar v. to dart, to shoot an arrow; to strike, wound or kill with an arrow; to cast an amorous or ardent glance; Am. to prick; to sting; to burn (said of the sun).
fletamento m. charter, charter party (of a ship).
fletar v. to charter (a ship, plane, etc.); to freight; Am. to hire (pack animals); to let loose (strong words); scatter (false rumors); **—se** Am. to run away; to slip away; to slip in uninvited; **salir fletado** Am. to leave on the run.
flete m. freight, freightage, cargo; load; Am. fine horse, race horse; bother, nuisance; **salir sin —** Am. to leave in a hurry.
flexibilidad f. flexibility.
flexible adj. flexible.
flexión f. bending, bend, sag.
flojear v. to slacken; to weaken; to idle; to be lazy.
flojedad f. laxity, looseness; slackness; laziness; slack.
flojera See **flojedad**.

flojo adj. lax; loose; slack; lazy; weak; Am. timid.
flor f. flower, blossom; compliment; **— de la edad** prime; **— de lis** iris (flower); **— y nata** the best, the cream, the chosen few; **a — de** flush with; **echar —es** to throw a bouquet; to compliment, flatter.
floreado p.p. & adj. flowered; made of the finest wheat.
florear v. to decorate with flowers; to brandish, to flourish; to make a flourish on the guitar; to flatter, compliment; to bolt, to sift out (the finest flour); Am. to flower, to bloom; to choose the best; **—se** Am. to shine, to excel; to burst open like a flower.
florecer v. irr. to flower, to bloom; to flourish, to thrive.
floreciente adj. flourishing, thriving, prosperous.
florecimiento m. flourishing, flowering, bloom.
floreo m. flourish; idle talk; flattery; compliment.
florería f. flower shop; florist's shop.
florero m. florist, flower vase; flatterer; adj. flattering.
floresta f. wooded place, grove, arbor.
florete m. fencing foil.
florido adj. flowery.
flota f. fleet; **echar —s** Am. to brag, to boast.
flotador m. floater; float; pontoon (of a hydroplane); adj. floating.
flotante adj. floating; m. Am. braggart, bluffer.
flotar v. to float.
flote: a — afloat.
fluctuación f. fluctuation; wavering; hesitation.
fluctuar v. to fluctuate, to wave; to hesitate.
fluente adj. fluent, flowing.
flujo m. flux; flow; flood, tide.
flux m. flush (cards); Am. suit of clothes; **hacer —** to spend one's funds; to lose every time; Am. **tener uno —** to be lucky.
foca f. seal, sea lion.
foco m. focus, center; Am. electric light bulb.
fofo adj. spongy, porous; light (weight); soft.
fogata f. fire, blaze, bonfire.
fogón m. heat, fireplace; cooking grill; vent of a gun; Am. fire, bonfire.
fogonazo m. flash (of gun powder).

follaje m. foliage.
folletín m. small pamphlet; serial story.
folleto m. pamphlet.
fomentar v. to foment, to encourage; to promote, to foster.
fomento m. promotion, encouragement; development; aid.
fonda f. inn; restaurant.
fondear v. to cast anchor; to sound, to make soundings; to search (a ship); —se Am. to save up for the future.
fondero m. Am. innkeeper.
fondillos m. pl. seat of trousers.
fondista m. & f. innkeeper.
fondo m. bottom, depth; background; back, rear end; nature; gear, inner self; fund; thickness of a diamond; Am. underskirt; —s funds; a — thoroughly; echar a — to sink.
fonducho m. cheap eating place.
fonética f. phonetics.
fonógrafo m. phonograph.
forajido m. outlaw, fugitive; highwayman, bandit, robber.
foráneo adj. foreign; m. outsider, stranger.
forastero m. stranger; foreigner; outsider; adj. foreign.
forcejear v. to struggle, to strive, to contest, to contend, to oppose, to resist.
forja f. forge; forging; blacksmith's shop; mortar (cement).
forjador m. forger; smith, blacksmith; inventor (of lies, stories, etc.).
forjar v. to forge; to form, to shape; to blacksmith; to invent; to feign; to fake.
forma f. form, shape; figure; manner; format; host for communion.
formación f. formation.
formal adj. formal; serious; trustworthy; punctual; reliable.
formalidad f. formality; seriousness; reliability, gravity, dignity; punctuality, red tape.
formalizar v. to give proper form to; to legalize; to make official; —se to settle down, to become serious.
formar v. to form, to shape, to mould; —se to get into line; to be molded, educated; to take form; to fashion; to frame; to make up.
formidable adj. formidable; fearful; terrific.
formón m. chisel.
fórmula f. formula.

formular v. to formulate, to word.
fornido adj. stout, strong, sturdy, robust, corpulent.
foro m. stage; back, rear (of a stage); forum, court, bar (law).
forraje m. forage, green grass, fodder, feed; foraging.
forrajear v. to forage, to gather forage.
forrar v. to line, to cover.
forro m. lining, sheathing, casing; covering; book cover.
fortalecer v. irr. to fortify; to strengthen.
fortaleza f. fortress; fortitude; strength; vigor; Am. stench, stink.
fortificación f. fortification; fort.
fortificar v. to fortify.
fortuito adj. fortuitous; accidental; unexpected.
fortuna f. fortune, fate, chance; wealth; good luck; por — fortunately.
forzar v. irr. to force; to compel; to rape; — la entrada en to break into.
forzoso adj. compulsory, necessary.
fosa f. grave; cavity.
fosco adj. dark, cross, irritable; frowning; browbeaten.
fosfato m. phosphate.
fosforecer v. to glow.
fósforo m. phosphorus; match.
fósil adj. & m. fossil.
foso m. hole, pit, stage pit; ditch; moat.
fotografía f. photograph; photography; picture.
fotografiar v. to photograph.
fotógrafo m. photographer.
fracasado adj. failed; m. failure.
fracasar v. to fail; to come to ruin; to crumble, to break in pieces.
fracaso m. failure, ruin, calamity; crash; downfall; destruction.
fracción f. fraction.
fractura f. fracture, break, crack; breach; separation.
fracturar v. to fracture; to break; to rupture.
fragancia f. fragance, sweetness of smell, scent, perfume.
fragante adj. fragrant; en — in the act.
fragata f. frigate.
frágil adj. fragile, breakable; frail, weak; brittle; frangible.
fragmento m. fragment.
fragor m. clang, din, crash, noise.

fragoroso adj. deafening; thunderous.

fragoso adj. rugged, craggy, rough; uneven; full of brambles; noisy.

fragua f. forge; blacksmith's shop.

fraguar v. to forge; to scheme; to plan; to contrive.

fraile m. friar; priest; brother.

frambuesa f. raspberry.

frambueso m. raspberry bush.

francés adj. French; m. Frenchman; French language.

franco adj. frank, open, candid, sincere, liberal; free; exempt; m. franc.

franela f. flannel.

franja f. fringe, girdle, stripe; braid; border.

franquear v. to exempt; to free; to dispatch, to send; to make grants; to enfranchise; — el paso to permit the passage; —se to unbosom oneself, to disclose one's innermost thoughts and feelings.

franqueo m. postage; franking; enfranchisement.

franqueza f. frankness; openheartedness; freedom; freeness; liberality of sentiment.

franquicia f. franchise, grant, privilege; exemption from taxes; immunity.

frasco m. flask, vial, small bottle; powder horn.

frase f. phrase, sentence; gastar —s to affect eloquence.

fraternal adj. fraternal, brotherly.

fraternidad f. fraternity, brotherhood.

fraude m. fraud, deceit.

fraudulento adj. fraudulent; deceitful.

fray m. (contraction of fraile) friar; brother.

frazada f. blanket.

frecuencia f. frequency; con — frequently.

frecuentar v. to frequent.

frecuente adj. frequent.

fregadero m. sink.

fregado m. scrub, scrubbing. adj. Am. bothersome, annoying; stubborn; brazen.

fregar v. irr. to scour, to scrub, to rub; to cleanse; to wash; Am. to molest, to annoy.

fregona f. scrub woman; kitchen maid, kitchen wench.

freir v. irr. to fry, to tease; to bother.

frenesí m. frenzy, madness.

frenético adj. frantic; furious, in a frenzy.

freno m. bridle; brake; control; bit (for horses).

frente f. forehead; countenance; m. front; en — de in front of; — a in front of, facing; hacer — to face.

fresa f. strawberry.

fresca f. fresh air; fresh remark.

fresco adj. fresh; cool; calm, serene; forward, bold; m. coolness; cool air; fresco (painting); Am. refreshment; al — in the open air; pintura al — painting in fresco.

frescor m. freshness, coolness.

frescura f. freshness, coolness, calm; freedom, ease; boldness, impudence; impudent remark.

fresno m. ash, ash tree.

fresquecillo adj. nice and cool; m. cool air, fresh breeze.

frialdad f. coolness; coldness, indifference.

fricción f. friction, rub, rubbing.

friccionar v. to rub; to massage.

friega f. rub, rubbing; Am. bother, nuisance, irritation; flogging, beating.

frigorífico adj. freezing; m. refrigerator, ice-box; Am. meat-packing house.

frijol m. bean; kidney bean, navy bean.

frío adj. cold; frigid; cool; indifferent; m. cold; —s Am. chills and fever; malaria.

friolento adj. cold-blooded, sensitive to cold; chilly.

friolera f. trifle.

fritada f. dish of fried food.

frito p.p. fried; m. fry, dish of fried food.

fritura f. fry, dish of fried food; fritter.

frivolidad f. frivolity.

frívolo adj. frivolous.

fronda f. leaf, fern leaf, frond, foliage.

frondoso adj. leafy, frondose.

frontera f. frontier, border; limit, confine.

fronterizo adj. frontier, opposite, facing.

frontero adj. facing, opposite; in front; frontlet.

frontis m. facade, front, frontispiece.

frontispicio m. front, facade; frontispiece; front page.

frontón m. main wall of a hand-

ball court; wall for playing at fives.
frotación f. friction, rubbing.
frotar v. to rub; to scour; to stroke gently.
frote m. rubbing; friction.
fructificar v. to fruit; to bear or produce fruit; to give profit; to benefit.
fructuoso adj. fruitful, fructuous.
frugal adj. frugal, parsimonious, sparing, economical.
frugalidad f. frugality, thrift, parsimony.
fruncir v. to wrinkle; to gather in pleats; to contract; to shrivel; to plait; to knit; — **las cejas** to knit the eyebrows; to frown; — **los labios** to purse the lips, to curl the lips.
fruslería f. trifle, trinket; frivolity.
frustración f. frustration, failure.
frustrar v. to frustrate, to thwart, to foil; to defeat; **—se** to miscarry; to be defeated.
fruta f. fruit, fruitage.
frutería f. fruitery; fruit store.
frutero m. fruit vendor; fruit dish; adj. fruit; **barco —** fruit boat; **plato —** fruit dish.
fruto m. fruit, any organic product of the earth; benefice, profit; result.
¡fuche! interj. Am. phew! ugh! pew! phooey!
fuego m. fire, eruption or breaking out of humours in the skin; Am. cold sore; **—s artificiales** fireworks; **hacer —** to shoot, to fire; **estar hecho un —** to be very angry; **romper —** to begin to fire, to start shooting.
fuelle m. bellows; pucker, wrinkle, fold; tattletale; talebearer, windbag, gossiper.
fuente f. fountain; jet, a spout of water; source, origin; spring; platter, serving dish.
fuera adv. outside, out; **— de** prep. outside of; in addition to.
fuereño m. outsider, stranger.
fuero m. law, statute; power, jurisdiction, code of laws; exemption, privilege.
fuerte adj. strong, firm, compact; fortification, fort; grave, serious, excessive; Am. stinking; m. fort, strong point; Am. alcohol, liquor; adv. strongly; excessively; loud; hard.
fuerza f. force, power, strength, vigor; fortitude, courage, manliness, constancy; virtue, efficacy; **a — de** by dint of; **a la — (por —, por la —, de por —, de —)** Am. by force, forcibly; necessarily; **ser —** to be necessary.
fuetazo m. Am. lash.
fuete m. Am. whip.
fuga f. flight, escape, elopement; leak, leakage; fugue (music).
fugarse v. to flee, to escape; to fly.
fugaz adj. fleeing; fleeting, passing, brief; fugacious, volatile, fugitive.
fugitivo adj. fugitive; fleeting, passing; perishable; m. fugitive.
fulano m. so-and-so; such a one.
fulgor m. radiance, brilliance; fulgency, resplendence.
fulgurar v. to gleam, to flash, to shine, to fulgurate.
fulminar v. to thunder, to thunder forth; to utter; to fulminate.
fullero m. cardsharp; crooked gambler; cheat.
fumada f. puff, whiff (of smoke).
fumadero m. smoking room.
fumador m. smoker, habitual smoker.
fumar v. to smoke (tobacco); **—se a uno** Am. to swindle or cheat someone.
fumigar v. to fumigate.
función f. function, profession or office; show, performance; religious festival.
funcionamiento m. functioning, action, working, operation.
funcionar v. to function; to work; to act, to perform.
funcionario m. public employee, officer, official; functionary.
funda f. cover, case, sheath; Am. skirt; **— de almohada** pillowcase.
fundación f. foundation, groundwork; basis, rise, origin.
fundir v. to smelt, to fuse, to melt, to liquate; to cast, to mold; Am. to ruin; **—se** to fuse, to melt together; to unite; Am. to be ruined.
fundo m. farm, country estate; property, land.
fúnebre adj. funeral; mournful, sad.
funeral adj. & m. funeral.
funeraria f. funeral parlor.
funesto adj. ill-fated; doleful; sad, unlucky, unfortunate.
fungosidad f. fungus, fungous growth.
furgón m. freight car, boxcar.
furgonada f. carload.
furia f. fury, rage; speed.
furibundo adj. furious.

furioso adj. furious, mad, frantic.
furor m. fury, rage, anger, frenzy.
furtivo adj. furtive, sly, secret.
fuselaje m. fuselage (airplane).
fusible adj. fusible; m. electric fuse.
fusil m. gun, rifle; small musket.
fusilar v. to shoot, to execute.
fustigar v. to lash, to whip, to censure severly, to scold sharply.
fútil adj. futile, useless, trivial.
futilidad f. futility, uselessness.
futuro adj. future; future tense; m. fiancé, future husband; future.

G

gabacho adj. applied to the natives of some places at the foot of the Pyrenees; used also in derision to the French; Am. me salió — it turned out wrong; m. Frenchman (used depreciatively).
gabán m. overcoat.
gabinete m. cabinet (of a government); studio; study, library room; sitting room; private room; dentist's office; laboratory.
gaceta f. gazette, official newspaper; professional periodical; Am. any newspaper.
gacetilla f. short newspaper article; column of short news items; gossip column; m. & f. newsmonger; tattletale.
gacetillero m. newspaper reporter; newsmonger.
gacha f. watery mash or mush; Am. china or earthenwere bowl; —s porridge, mush; caresses; —s de avena oatmeal.
gacho adj. drooping; bent downward; turned down; stooping, slouching; with horns curved downward; curvated; sombrero — slouch hat; a gachas on all fours; con las orejas gachas with drooping ears; crestfallen, discouraged.
gafas f. pl. spectacles; grappling hooks, can hooks.
gaita f. flageolet; bagpipe; cornemuse; hand-organ; Am. good-for-nothing, lazy bum; — **gallega** bagpipe; sacar la — to stick out one's neck.
gaitero m. piper, bagpipe player.
gaje m. fee; —s wages, salary, pay, fees; perquisites.
gala f. elegance; full dress or uniform; ostentation; Am. award, prize; —s finery, regalia, best clothes; —s de novia trousseau; hacer — de to boast of; día de — courtday; holiday.
galán m. gallant, lover; leading man (theatre).
galante adj. gallant; attentive to ladies; polite; brave, generous; liberal; elegant.
galanteador m. gallant; lady's man; flatterer; wooer; lover.
galantear v. to court; to woo; to make love.
galanteo m. wooing; courtship; gallantry, compliment, attention to ladies; courtesy; gracefulness; generosity; elegance.
galardón m. recompense; reward; guerdon.
galeote m. galley slave.
galera f. galley; large wagon; women's jail; printer's galley; Am. jail; tall hat.
galerada f. galley, galley proof; wagon load, van load.
galería f. gallery; corridor.
galgo m. greyhound; adj. Am. gluttonous, always hungry.
galillo m. uvula.
galón m. galloon; braid; trimming; gallon.
galoneado adj. gallooned, trimmed with braid.
galopada f. gallop; pegar una — to break into a gallop.
galopar v. to gallop.
galope m. gallop; haste, speed; a (al or de) — at gallop; speedily.
galopear See galopar.
galpón m. Am. large open shed.
gallardete m. streamer; pendant.
gallardía f. elegance; gracefulness; bravery.
gallardo adj. elegant, graceful, brave.
gallego adj. Galician, from or of Galicia, Spain; m. Galician; Am. Spaniard (used as a nickname).
galleta f. cracker; hardtack, hard biscuit; hard cookie; blow, slap; small pot; Am. bread of coarse meal or bran; **colgarle la —** a uno Am. to fire, dismiss someone; tener — Am. to have strength, muscle.
gallina f. hen; m. & f. chicken-hearted person.
gallinero m. chicken coop, house or yard; flock of chickens; basket for carrying chickens; poultryman; noisy gathering; top gallery of a theatre.
gallo m. cock, rooster; aggresive

**bossy person; cork float; false note (singing); Am. secondhand clothing; fire wagon; serenade.

gamo m. buck, male deer.

gamuza f. chamois, chamois skin.

gana f. desire, appetite; hunger; inclination, mind; **de buena (mala) —** willingly (unwillingly); **tener —** (or **—s**) to feel like, want to; **no me da la —** I don't want to.

ganadero m. cattleman; cattle dealer; adj. cattle, pertaining to cattle; grazier.

ganado m. cattle; herd; livestock; **— mayor** cattle; horses; mules; **— menor** sheep; **— de cerda** swine.

ganador m. winner; adj. winning.

ganancia f. profit, gain; advantage; Am. something to boot; something extra.

ganancioso adj. winning; profitable; m. winner.

ganar v. to win; to profit; to gain; to conciliate; to attain; to acquire, to conquer; to get ahead of; **— la vida** to earn a living; **— terreno** to gain ground.

gancho m. hook; hooked staff; Am. hairpin; bait, lure, trick; **aguja de —** crochet hook; **echar a uno el —** to hook someone; **tener —** to be attractive, alluring.

gandul m. bum, loafer.

ganga f. bargain; snap, easy job; kind of prairie hen.

gangoso adj. twangy, nasal.

gangrena f. gangrene.

gangrenar v. to gangrene, to cause gangrene; **—se** to gangrene.

ganoso adj. desirous; Am. lively; spirited.

ganso m. goose, gander; dunce; lazy, slovenly peson.

garabato m. hook; scrawl, scribble; a graceful gait and deportment; **hacer —s** to scribble, write poorly.

garaje m. garage.

garantía f. guaranty; security; bail, bond, warranty.

garantizar v. to guarantee, to vouch for.

garañón m. jackass, male ass; male camel (for breeding); Am. stallion.

garapiñar v. to candy; to ice; to turn to ice, to cover with ice.

garbanzo m. chickpea.

garbo m. elegance, graceful air; good carriage; gentility; frankness; disinterestedness; generosity.

garboso adj. graceful; elegant; sprightly; genteel; liberal; generous.

garfio m. hook; draghook; gaff.

garganta f. throat, neck; gorge; ravine; gullet; the instep.

gargantilla f. necklace.

gárgara f. gargling; **—s** Am. gargle, gargling solution; **hacer —s** to gargle.

gargarear m. gargling; gargle, gargling solution.

gargarizar v. to gargle, to gargarize.

garita f. sentry box; watchman's booth; a porter's lodge; water closet.

garito m. gambling house, gambling joint; gambler's winnings; gaming house.

garra f. claw; paw; hook; Am. skinny person or animal; margin of profit in a business deal; **echar la —** to arrest; to grab; **hacer —s** Am. to tear to pieces.

garrafa f. decanter; vessel for cooling liquors.

garrafón m. large decanter.

garrapata f. cattle tick; a short little person.

garrapatear v. to scribble, to scrawl, to write poorly.

garrocha f. pole; Am. goad stick.

garrotazo m. blow with a club; huge stick.

garrote m. club; cudgel; heavy stick; Am. brake; **dar —** to strangle; Am. to brake; set the brakes.

garrotero m. Am. brakeman; beater (with a club); adj. Am. stingy.

garrucha f. pulley.

garúa f. Am. drizzle.

garza f. heron.

garzo adj. blue, bluish; blue-eyed; agaric.

gas m. gas, vapor; Am. gasoline.

gasa f. gauze; **— labrada** embroidered muslin.

gaseosa f. soda water; soda pop; mineral water.

gaseoso adj. gaseous.

gasolina f. gasoline.

gastador adj. lavish, extravagant; wasteful; spendthrift, prodigal; m. lavish spender.

gastar v. to spend; to wear; to use; to waste; to expend; **—se** to wear out; to get old.

gasto m. expense, expenditure; wear; cost; consumption.
gatas: a — on all fours; **andar a** — to creep, crawl; **salir a** — to crawl out of a difficulty.
gateado adj. catlike; veined, streaked; m. Am. light-colored horse with black streaks.
gatear v. to creep, to crawl; to walk on all fours; to claw, to scratch; to steal; to climb up; to clamber.
gatillo m. kitten; trigger; dentist's forceps; petty thief.
gato m. cat; moneybag; jack (for lifting weights); sneak thief; sly fellow; Am. trigger; outdoor market; hot-water bottle; a gaucho song and tap dance (by extension, the dancer); bundler.
gatuperio m. fraud, intrigue; an intricate affair.
gauchada f. Am. gaucho deed or exploit.
gauchaje m. Am. band of Gauchos, Gaucho folk.
gauchesco adj. Am. relating to Gauchos.
gaucho m. Gaucho, Argentine and Uruguay cowboy; Am. good horseman; adj. Am. relating to Gauchos, gaucho-like; sly, crafty.
gaveta f. drawer, locker.
gavilla f. sheaf; gang, band.
gaviota f. sea gull.
gaza f. loop; Am. noose of a lasso.
gazmoñería f. prudery, affected modesty.
gazmoño adj. prudish; affected; coy; hypocritical, dissembling.
gaznate m. windpipe; a kind of fritter; Am. a sweetmeat made of pineapple or coconut; gorge.
gelatina f. gelatin; jelly.
gema f. gem, jewel, bud.
gemelo m. twin; —s twins, binoculars, opera glasses, field glasses; cuff links.
gemido m. moan; wail; cry, lamentation, groan.
gemir v. irr. to moan, to wail, to cry, to howl; to groan; to roar.
gendarme m. Am. policeman.
generación f. generation.
general adj. & m. general; **por lo —** generally.
generalizar v. to generalize; **—se** to spread, become general.
género m. kind, sort, class, gender; goods, material, cloth; **— humano** human race.
generosidad f. generosity; magnanimity, liberality; openheartedness; valour and fortitude.
generoso adj. generous; choice (wine); noble, magnanimous; liberal; frank; munificent; strong, vigorous, excellent.
genial adj. genial, jovial, pleasant.
genio m. genious; temperament, spirit, disposition; character.
gente f. people; crowd, race, nation, folks, clan; **— bien** Am. upper-class or important person; **ser —** Am. to be a somebody; to be cultured; be socially important.
gentil adj. graceful; genteel, courteous; m. pagan; gentile.
gentileza f. grace, courtesy; favour; nobility; gentility; elegance; easiness, freedom.
gentío m. crowd, throng; multitude.
gentuza f. rabble, mob.
genuino adj. genuine; pure, real, natural.
geografía f. geography.
geográfico adj. geographical.
geología f. geology.
geológico adj. geological.
geometría f. geometry.
geométrico adj. geometric.
geranio m. geranium; crane's bill.
gerencia f. management, administration.
gerente m. manager; director.
germen m. germ; origin; source.
germinar v. to germinate, to bud.
gerundio m. gerund; present participle.
gesticular v. to gesticulate; to make gestures.
gestión f. action, step, manoeuvre; intervention; **—es** negotiations; conduct, exertion; effort.
gestionar v. to manage; to take steps; to negotiate or carry out.
gesto m. face, expression; grimace; gesture; visage; **estar de buen (or mal) —** to be in a good (or bad) humor; **hacer — a** to make faces at.
giba f. hump; hunch, crooked back; gibbosity.
gigante adj. gigantic; m. giant.
gigantesco adj. gigantic.
gimnasia f. gymnastics.
gimnasio m. gymnasium.
gimotear v. to whimper, to whine.
gimoteo m. whimper, whining; crying very frequently.
ginebra f. gin (liquor).
gira f. excursion, tour; outing; picnic.

girador m. drawer (of a check or draft).

girar v. to revolve, to rotate, to whirl, to send; to issue or draw (checks, drafts, etc.); to manage (a business).

girasol m. sunflower.

giratorio adj. rotary, revolving; giratory.

giro m. rotation; trend, bend, direction, turn; turn of phrase; line of business; draft; circumference; — **postal** money order; adj. yellowish, (rooster); Am. black and white (rooster); cocky.

gitano adj. gypsy; gypsylike; sly, clever; m. gypsy.

gitomate Am. See jitomate.

glacial adj. glacial, icy, very cold, resembling ice.

glaciar m. glacier.

glándula f. gland.

glasear v. to glaze (paper, fruits, etc.), to make glossy.

globo m. globe, sphere, world, balloon; en — summarily.

gloria f. glory, gloria.

gloriarse v. to glory (in), delight (in); to be proud (of); to boast (of); to take delight in anything.

glorieta f. arbor, bower; secluded nook in a park (with benches).

glorificar v. to glorify; —**se** to glory (in), take great pride (in).

glorioso adj. glorious.

glosar v. to gloss, to comment upon, to explain (a text).

glosario m. glossary.

glotón adj. gluttonous; m. glutton.

glotonería f. gluttony.

gobernador adj. governing; m. governor, ruler, master.

gobernante adj. governing, ruling; m. governor, ruler.

gobernar v. irr. to govern, to rule, to lead, to direct; to steer, helm.

gobierno m. government; management, control; helm; rudder; administration of public affairs, executive power; **ama de** — housekeeper; — **de casa** household.

goce m. enjoyment, joy, fruition, possession.

goleta f. schooner.

golfo m. gulf; open sea; faro (gambling game); vagabond, bum; ragamuffin.

golondrina f. swallow; swallow fish.

golosina f. sweet, dainty, tidbit.

goloso adj. sweet-toothed, fond of sweets; gluttonous.

golpazo m. bang, whack, heavy blow, hard knock.

golpe m. blow, hit, stroke, knock; beat; dash, hunch; Am. facing (of a garment); sledge hammer; — **de fortuna** stroke of good luck; — **de gente** crowd, throng; — **de gracia** death blow; finishing stroke; **de** — suddenly; **de un** — all at once; **pestillo de** — spring latch; **al** — Am. instantly, at once; **al** — **de vista** Am. at one glance; **de** — **y zumbido** unexpectedly, unaware; — **de mar** surge, a heavy sea; — **de remo** stroke in rowing.

golpear v. to strike, to hit, to knock, to beat; Am. to knock at a door.

golpetear v. to tap, to knock or pound continuously; to flap; to rattle.

golpeteo m. tapping, pounding, knocking; flapping; rattling.

gollería f. dainty; delicacy, superfluous thing.

goma f. gum; rubber, elastic; eraser; tire; — **de repuesto** spare tire; **estar de** — Am. to have a hangover (after excessive drinking).

gomero adj. rubber, pertaining to rubber; m. Am. gum or rubber tree; rubber producer; rubber-plantation worker; glue container or bottle.

gomoso adj. gummy, sticky; m. dandy.

gordiflón adj. fat, chubby.

gorda f. Am. thick **tortilla** or cornmeal cake; **se armó la** — hell broke loose; there was a big rumpus.

gordo adj. fat, plump, corpulent, obese; greasy, oily; m. suet, fat; **tocino** — fat pork; **lienzo** — coarse linen; **hablar** — to speak thick.

gordura f. fatness, stoutness; fat, grease, corpulence.

gorgojo m. weevil, puny person; Am. wood borer, wood louse.

gorgojoso adj. infested with weevils.

gorila m. gorilla.

gorjeador m. warbler; adj. warbling; **pájaro** — warbler.

gorjear v. to warble; to chirp.

gorjeo m. warble; warbling.

gorra f. cap; bonnet; **de** — at

another's expense; **vivir de —** to sponge, live at another's expense; m. parasite, sponger.

gorrión m. sparrow.

gorro m. cap; bonnet.

gorrón m. sponge, parasite, bum; spindle, pivot; lazy, unhealty silkworm; a round smooth pebble.

gota f. drop, gout; **sudar la — gorda** to sweat profusely; toil, work hard.

gotear v. to drip; to leak; to dribble, to trickle; to sprinkle, begin to rain; —se to leak.

goteo m. trickle, drip.

gotera f. leak hole; —s Am. surroundings, outskirts.

gotero m. Am. dropper (for counting drops).

gótico adj. Gothic, m. Goth; Gothic language.

gozar v. to enjoy, to possess, have; —se to rejoice.

gozne m. hinge.

gozo m. pleasure, joy, satisfaction.

gozoso adj. joyful, glad, merry.

gozque m. cur dog.

grabado adj. engraved; m. engraving, woodcut, print; **al agua fuerte** etching.

grabar v. to engrave, to carve, to fix, impress; **— al agua fuerte** to etch.

gracejada f. Am. clownish act or expression.

gracejo m. grace, cuteness; humor, wit.

gracia f. grace; favor; pardon; joke, witty remark; **caer en —** to please; **hacer —** to amuse, make (someone) laugh; ¡—s! thanks! **dar —s** to thank.

gracioso adj. graceful, attractive; witty, amusing, gracious; pleasing; benevolent; m. & f. comedian, clown, mime.

grada f. step of a staircase; harrow; —s steps; seats of an amphitheatre.

gradación f. gradation.

gradería f. series of steps; rows of seats (in an amphitheater or stadium); **— cubierta** grandstand; —s bleachers.

grado m. degree; step; **de buen —** willingly, with pleasure; **de mal —** unwillingly; **de — en —** by degrees, gradually; **mal de su —** unwillingly.

graduación f. graduation; rank; measuring; condition or quality of a person.

gradual adj. gradual; m. response sung at mass.

graduar v. to graduate; to give a diploma; to gauge; to classify, to grade; —se to graduate, take a degree.

gráfica f. graph, diagram, chart.

gráfico adj. graphic; vivid, lifelike.

grafito m. graphite.

grajo m. jay.

grama f. grama grass.

gramática f. grammar.

gramático adj. grammatical; m. grammarian.

gramo m. gram.

gran contr. of **grande**.

grana f. cochineal, kermes; scarlet color; scarlet cloth; any small seed.

granada f. pomegranate; grenade, shell, small bomb; **— de mano** hand grenade.

granado m. pomegranate tree; adj. notable; principal, chief; select; illustrious.

grande adj. large, big; great; grand; **mamá (papá) —** Am. grandmother (grandfather); m. grandee; **en —** on a large scale.

grandeza f. greatness, grandeur, splendor; bigness; size; body of grandees; grandeeship; grandness.

grandiosidad f. grandeur, grandness; greatness.

grandioso adj. grandiose, great, grand, magnificent.

granero m. granary, grain bin; country or region rich in grain.

granito m. granite; small grain; small pimple.

granizada f. hailstorm, shower; volley.

granizar v. to hail.

granizo m. hail; hailstorm; web or film in the eye; adj. Am. spotted (horse).

granja f. grange, farm; country house, farmhouse.

granjear v. to earn; to gain; to acquire; to obtain; Am. to steal; —se to win for oneself (favor, goodwill, esteem, etc.).

granjería f. farming; business; profit.

granjero m. farmer, husbandman.

grano m. grain, seed; pimple; corn; grain (unit of measure); **ir al —** to come to the point.

granuja m. ragamuffin, urchin; scamp, ripe grape; grapestone.

granular v. to granulate; —se to

become granulated; to break out with pimples.
grapa f. clamp.
grasa f. grease; fat; tallow; Am. shoe polish; dar — Am. to polish (shoes).
grasiento adj. greasy, oily.
grasoso adj. greasy, oily.
gratificación f. gratuity, bonus, tip, recompense; reward.
gratis adv. gratis, for nothing, free.
gratitud f. gratitude.
grato adj. pleasing, pleasant; gratuitous; su grata your favor, your letter.
gratuito adj. gratuitous, free; unfounded.
grava f. gravel.
gravamen m. burden; mortgage.
grave adj. grave; serious; weighty, heavy; grievous; deep, low.
gravedad f. gravity; seriousness; depth (of a sound).
gravoso adj. burdensome; serle a uno — to be burdensome; to weigh on one's conscience.
graznar v. to caw, to croak, to squawk; to cackle; to quack.
graznido m. caw, croak, squawk, quack, cackle.
greda f. clay; chalk.
gremio m. guild, society, brotherhood, trade union.
greña f. shock of hair, tangled mop of hair (usually —s).
grey f. flock; congregation of the faithful.
griego adj. Greek, Grecian; m. Greek.
grieta f. crieve; crack, fissure.
grifo m. faucet; Am. cheap tavern; gas station; colored person; drug addict; drunkard; adj. curly, wooly (hair); Am. vain, conceited; letra grifa script; ponerse — to bristle, stand on end (hair).
grillo m. cricket, sprout, shoot; —s fetters.
grima f. uneasiness; displeasure; disgust; Am. sadness; compassion, pity; bit, small particle; dar — to disgust; to make uneasy; Am. to make sad, inspire pity.
gringo adj. Am. foreigner (not Spanish); Yankee or English-speaking person.
gripe f. grippe, flu, influenza.
gris adj. grey.
grisáceo adj. greyish.
grita f. shouting, clamor, uproar.
gritar v. to shout, to cry.

gritería f. shouting, clamor, uproar, outcry, shout, exclamation.
grito m. shout; cry; poner el — en el cielo to complain loudly; to cry to heaven.
grosella f. currant; — blanca gooseberry.
grosellero m. currant bush.
grosería f. rudeness; coarseness; crudeness; insult, churlishness.
grosero adj. rough, coarse; rude; impolite; not elegant, not fine.
grotesco adj. grotesque, fantastic; absurd.
grúa f. crane, derrick.
gruesa f. gross, twelve dozen.
grueso adj. fat, stout, thick; coarse; bulky, big, heavy, gross, dense; m. thickness; bulk; density, main part; en — in gross, in bulk, by wholesale.
grulla f. crane (bird).
gruñido m. growl, grumble, grunt.
gruñir v. irr. to grunt, to growl, to snarl, to grumble.
gruñón adj. growling, grunting; grumbly; m. growler; grumbler.
grupa f. rump; volver —s to turn around (usually in horseback).
grupo m. group, set, cluster.
gruta f. grotto, cavern, cave.
guacal m. Am. crate (for fruits, vegetables, etc). Also huacal.
guacamayo m. Am. macaw; Am. flashily dressed person.
guacho m. birdling, chick; young animal; Am. orphan; foundling, abandoned child; adj. Am. odd, not paired; forlorn, alone, abandoned.
guadal m. Am. small dune, sand hill; Am. quagmire, bog, swamp; growth of bamboo grass.
guadaña f. scythe.
guagua f. Am. bus; trifle, insignificant thing; m. & f. baby; de — Am. for nothing, gratis, free.
guaje m. Am. a species of gourd; vessel or bowl made of a gourd; simpleton, fool; trifle, trinket, piece of junk; adj. Am. foolish; hacerse uno — Am. to play the fool; hacer a uno — Am. to fool, to deceive someone.
guajiro m. Indian of the Guajira Peninsula (in Venezuela and Colombia); Am. rustic, peasant.
guajolote m. Am. turkey; fool.
guanaco m. Am. guanaco (a kind of llama); tall, lanky, gawky person; fool, simpleton.
guano m. Am. palm tree; palm

guantada f. wallop, blow, slap.
guante m. glove; Am. scourge, whip; —s de cabritilla kid gloves; **echar el** — a uno to seize or grab a person.
guantelete m. gauntlet.
guapo adj. handsome, good-looking; spruce, neat, elegant; daring, brave, corageous; Am. harsh, severe; angry; m. brawler, quarreler, bully.
guarache m. Am. Mexican leather sandal; tire patch. Also **huarache**.
guaraní adj. pertaining to the Guaraní Indians of Paraguay; m. & f. Guaraní Indian.
guarapo m. Am. juice of the sugar cane; sugar cane liquor; low grade brandy.
guarda m. & f. guard, keeper; Am. ticket collector on a streetcar; f. custody, care, keeping; observance of a law; —s outside ribs of a fan; fly leaves.
guardabarros m. fender.
guardabosques m. forest ranger, forester, forest keeper.
guardabrisa f. windshield.
guardafrenos m. brakeman.
guardagujas m. switchman.
guardapapeles m. file, filing cabinet or box.
guardapelo m. locket.
guardar v. to keep, to watch over; to observe; to protect; to store; to conserve; to fulfil; —se to avoid, to abstain from; —se de to guard against, to keep from, to avoid.
guardarropa m. wardrobe; cloakroom.
guardia f. guard, body of guards; defense, protection; m. guard, guardman.
guardiamarina f. midshipman.
guardián m. guardian, keeper; superior of a Franciscan monastery.
guarecer v. irr. to protect, to shelter; to preserve, to cure; —se to take shelter.
guarnición f. garrison; garniture, ornament, adornment; trimming; setting; guard of a sword; —es trappings, harness.
guasca f. Am. leather tong; rope, cord; whip; **dar** — Am. to whip, to beat, to thrash.
guaso m. Am. stag, male deer; peasant; half-breed; lasso; adj. Am. rustic, peasantlike.
guasón adj. funny, comical; m. joker, jester.
guata f. padding; Am. fib; a species of potato; paunch, belly; **echar** — Am. to get fat.
guatemalteco m. & adj. Guatemalan.
guayaba f. guava fruit.
guayabo m. guava tree; Am. lie, fraud; trick.
gubernativo adj. governmental, administrative.
guedeja f. forelock, lock of hair, lion's mane.
güero adj. Am. blond; m. Am. cassava liquor. See **huero**.
guerra f. war; — a muerte war to the finish; **dar** — to bother, to trouble.
guerrear v. to war; Am. to do mischief or to bother (said of children).
guerrero adj. warlike, martial; m. warrior, soldier.
guerrilla f. guerrilla; small war; squirmish; body of soldiers; band of fighters.
guerrillero m. guerrilla fighter.
guía m. & f. guide, leader; f. guide book, directory; sign post; shoot, sprout; Am. garland of flowers.
guiar v. to guide; to drive (a car).
guija f. pebble.
guijarro m. pebble.
guijo m. gravel.
guinda f. a kind of cherry.
guiñada f. wink.
guiñapo m. tag, tatter, rag; ragamuffin, ragged person.
guiñar v. to wink.
guiño m. wink.
guión m. hyphen; repeat sign (music); Cross (carried before a prelate in procession); guide, leader (among birds and animals); leader in a dance; standard, royal standard; master of ceremonies.
guirnalda f. garland, wreath.
guisa f. way, manner; **a** — **de** like, in the manner of.
guisado m. stew; made dish, ragout, fricassee.
guisante m. pea; — **de olor** sweet pea.
guisar v. to cook, to prepare, to arrange, to adjust.
guiso m. dish, dish of food; sauce of meat, condiment.
guitarra f. guitar.

gula f. gluttony.

gusano f. worm, caterpillar; **— de la conciencia** remorse; **— de luz** glowworm; **matar el — Am.** to satisfy need or desire.

gustar v. to taste, to like, to love; **—le a uno una cosa** to like something; **— de** to have a liking for, to be fond of.

gusto m. taste; pleasure, delight; liking, mind; **dar —** to please; **tomar — a un cosa** to become fond of something.

gustoso adj. tasty, pleasant; dainty; glad, merry, willing; adv. willingly.

H

haba f. large bean, Lima bean.

haber v. irr. to possess, to have (an auxiliary verb); to take, to happen, to exist; **habérselas con** to have it out with; **ha de llegar mañana** he is to arrive tomorrow; **ha de ser verdad** it must be true; **hay (había, hubo, etc.)** there is, there are (there was, there were, etc.); **hay que** it is necessary; **no hay de qué** you are welcome?; **¿qué hay?** what's the mater?; m. property; income, fortune; credit, credit side (in bookkeeping); **—es** property, goods, cash, assets.

habichuela f. bean; **— verde** string bean.

hábil adj. skilful, capable, able; clever, dexterous, expert; apt; learned.

habilidad f. ability, skill, cunning, cleverness.

habilitar v. to enable; to equip; to provide; to supply.

habitación f. apartment; room; lodging.

habitante m. inhabitant, resident, dweller.

habitar v. to inhabit, to live, to reside.

hábito m. habit; custom; dress; garment.

habitual adj. habitual, customary, inveterate.

habla f. speech; language; dialect; idiom; **al — within** speaking distance; **perder el —** to be speechless.

hablador m. talker; gossip; adj. talkative.

habladuría f. gossip, rumor, empty talk; impertinent remark.

hablar v. to speak, to talk, to converse; **— alto (or en voz alta)** to speak loud; **— bajo (quedo or en voz baja)** to speak softly; **— por los codos** to chatter constantly.

hablilla f. gossip, tale, rumor, malicious tale.

hacedero adj. feasible.

hacedor m. maker; **el Supremo Hacedor** the Maker.

hacendado m. landholder; Am. owner of a farm, plantation or ranch.

hacendoso adj. industrious, diligent, assiduous.

hacer v. irr. to do, to make, to form; to accustom; to cause; to order; to produce; to practice; to perform; to effect; to create; to be, to exist; to mould, to form; **— caso** to mind, to pay attention; **— frío (calor)** to be cold (warm); **— la maleta** to pack one's suitcase; **— un papel** to play a part; **— aprecio** Am. to pay attention; **— caras (or caritas)** Am. to flirt; **no le hace** it makes no difference; **—se** to become; to grow; to get to be; **—se a** to get used to; **—se de rogar** to want to be coaxed.

hacia prep. toward, about, in a direction to, near to; **— adelante** forward; **— atrás** backward.

hacienda f. estate; finance, property, lands, tenements, fortune; Am. cattle, livestock.

hacina f. shock (of grain), stack, pile.

hacinar v. to shock (grain); to pile up; to stack; to accumulate.

hacha f. ax; hatchet, torch.

hachero m. axman, woodcutter.

hada f. fairy.

hado m. fate, fortune, destiny.

halagar v. to coax; to flatter; to allure, to attract.

halago m. flattery; caress, allurement.

halagüeño adj. alluring, attracting, flattering.

halar See **jalar**.

halcón m. falcon.

hálito m. breath, vapor.

hallar v. to find, to discover, to find out; **—se** to be; to fare; to get along.

hallazgo m. find, discovery; reward.

hamaca f. hammock.

hambre f. hunger, famine; appetite; **tener —** to be hungry.

hambrear v. to starve, to be hungry.
hambriento adj. hungry, greedy; Am. stingy.
hambruna f. Am. great hunger, starvation.
hampa f. underworld.
hangar m. hangar.
haragán adj. lazy, indolent; m. loafer, idler.
haraganear v. to lounge, to loaf, to be lazy.
haraganería f. laziness.
harapiento adj. tattered, ragged.
harapo m. rag, tatter; **andar hecho un —** to be in tatters.
haraposo adj. tattered, ragged.
harina f. flour; **eso es — de otro costal** that is something entirely different.
harinoso adj. floury; flourlike.
harmonía f. harmony.
hartar v. to fill up, to gorge, to sate, to satiate; **—se** to have one's fill; to overeat, to eat too much.
harto adj. full; sated, satiated; fed up; adj. too much; Am. much, very much.
hasta prep. till, until, as far as, also, even; **— ahora, — aquí** hitherto; **— luego** good-bye, see you later.
hastiar v. to surfeit, to cloy, to disgust.
hastío m. surfeit, excess; boredom; loathing, disgust.
hato m. herd; flock, sheepfold; sheep's herd hut; gang, crowd; pile; Am. cattle ranch.
haya f. beech.
haz f. face, surface; m. fagot, bundle, bunch.
hazaña f. deed, exploit, feat.
he (used with aquí or allí) behold, here is, here you have; **heme aquí** here I am; **helo aquí** here it is.
hebilla f. buckle.
hebra f. thread, fiber; fine string; **de una —** Am. all at once, at one stroke; **ni una —** Am. absolutely nothing.
hebroso adj. fibrous, stringy.
hecatombe f. massacre, great slaughter, hecatomb.
hechicera f. witch, enchantress, hag.
hechicería f. witchcraft, witchery, magic, charm, enchantment.
hechicero adj. bewitching, charming; m. magician; charmer, sorcerer.

hechizar v. to bewitch; to charm; to enchant.
hechizo m. charm, enchantment; fascination.
hecho m. fact, act, deed; **de —** in fact.
hechura f. make, shape, cut, workmanship.
heder v. irr. to stink, to reek.
hediondez f. stink, stench.
hediondo adj. stinking, fetid, mephitical; m. Am. skunk.
hedor m. stink, stench.
helada f. frost.
heladería f. Am. ice-cream parlor.
helado adj. frozen; freezing, frosty; icy; m. ice cream; ice.
heladora f. freezer.
helar v. irr. to freeze, to congeal.
helecho m. fern.
hélice f. screw propeller; helix, spiral.
hembra f. female; staple, nut (of a screw); **macho y —** hook and eye.
hemisferio m. hemisphere.
henchir v. irr. to swell, to stuff, to fill.
hendedura f. crack, crevice, fissure, chink, cleft.
hender v. irr. to split, to crack, to cleave, to chink.
henequén m. sisal, sisal hemp.
henil m. hayloft.
heno m. hay.
heraldo m. herald.
herbazal m. field of grass; pasture, ground for cattle.
herboso adj. grassy, weedy, herby, herbous.
heredad f. parcel of land; rural property, estate.
heredar v. to inherit; to bequeath, to deed to another.
heredera f. heiress.
heredero m. heir; successor.
hereditario adj. hereditary.
hereje m. heretic; **cara de —** hideous or deformed aspect.
herejía f. heresy; offensive remark.
herencia f. inheritance; heritage; heredity; heirdom.
herida f. wound, injury, outrage, mischief.
herido adj. wounded; m. wounded man; Am. small drainage channel.
herir v. irr. to wound, to hurt; to strike, to offend.
hermana f. sister.
hermanastra f. stepsister, half sister.

hermanastro m. stepbrother, half brother.
hermandad f. brotherhood, fraternity.
hermano m. brother.
hermético adj. hermetic, airtight; tight-lipped; close-mouthed.
hermetismo m. complete silence.
hermosear v. to beautify, to embellish, to adorn.
hermoso adj. beautiful, handsome, neat, graceful.
hermosura f. beauty, handsomeness, goodliness.
héroe m. hero.
heroico adj. heroic, heroical.
heroína f. heroine.
heroísmo m. heroism.
herradura f. horseshoe.
herraje m. ironwork; iron trimmings; horseshoes and nails; Am. silver saddle trimmings; horseshoe.
herramienta f. set of tools or instruments; teeth, grinders.
herrar v. irr. to shoe (a horse); to brand; to trim with iron.
herrería f. blacksmith's shop or trade; forge.
herrero m. smith, one who forges.
hervidero m. bubbling sound; bubbling spring; swarm, crowd; ebullition; un — de gente a swarm of people.
hervir v. irr. to boil; un — de gente a swarm of people.
hervor m. boiling, boiling point; ebullition; fervor, heat, fret; soltar el — to come to a boil.
hez f. scum, lee; la — del pueblo the scum of society; heces dregs, sediments.
hidalgo m. hidalgo; adj. noble, courteous.
hidalguía f. nobility; generosity, courtesy; nobleness of mind.
hidráulico adj. hydraulic; fuerza hidráulica water power; ingeniero — hydraulic engineer.
hidroavión m. hydroplane, seaplane.
hidrógeno m. hydrogen.
hiedra f. ivy.
hiel f. gall, bile; bitterness; asperity.
hielo m. ice, frost; coolness; indifference.
hierba f. grass; herb; weed; Am. mate (Paraguayan tea); marihuana (a narcotic); Am. ciertas —s so-and-so (person not named).
hierbabuena f. mint. Also yerbabuena.
hierro m. iron, any iron tool, instrument or weapon; brand; — colado or fundido cast iron.
hígado m. liver; courage, valor, bravery; malos —s ill will.
higiene f. hygiene.
higiénico adj. hygienic, sanitary.
higo m. fig.
higuera f. fig tree.
higuerilla f. castor-oil plant.
hija f. daughter, native daughter.
hijo m. son, native son; offspring; fruit, result.
hilacha f. filament or thread ravelled out of cloth; mostrar uno la — to show one's worse side or nature.
hilachos m. pl. Am rags, ratters.
hilado m. yarn; spun flax, hemp, wool, silk or cotton.
hilar v. to spin, make into thread; to argue, to discuss; — delgado to be very careful; to be very subtle.
hilaza f. coarse thread, yarn.
hilera f. file, row, line; beam of a roof; — de perlas strand or string of pearls.
hilo m. thread, wire; fine yarn; string; filament; linen; a — without interruption; — a drop by drop; ¡—! Am. scram!; al — along the thread; Am. very well, all right; de un — Am. constantaly; tener el alma en un — to be frightened to death; to be in great anxiety or suspense.
hilván m. basting stitch; basting; Am. hem.
hilvanar v. to baste; to put together; to act or perform in a hurry; Am. to hem.
himno m. hymn, anthem.
hincapié: hacer — to emphasize, to stress; to dwell (upon).
hincar v. to thrust in; —se (or —se de rodillas) to kneel down.
hinchado adj. swollen; inflated; presumptuous, vain, arrogant.
hinchar v. to swell; to inflate; to be tumefied; —se to swell up, to puff up.
hinchazón f. swelling; inflation; tumefaction; conceit; ostentation, vanity; bombast, inflated style.
hinojos: de — on one's knees.
hipo m. hiccough; sob; wish; longing; anxiety; grudge; anger; ill will, displeasure.

hipocresía f. hypocrisy.
hipócrita adj. hypocritical, insincere; m. & f. hypocrite.
hipódromo m. race track, hippodrome, circus.
hipoteca f. mortgage.
hipótesis f. hypothesis, theory; assumption.
hirviente adj. boiling.
hispano adj. Hispanic, Spanish; m. Spaniard.
hispanoamericano adj. Spanish-American.
histérico adj. hysterical, hysteric.
historia f. history; story, tale; fable; **dejarse de —s** to stop fooling and come to the point.
historiador m. historian.
historial m. record, data; adj. historical, historic.
historieta f. story, anecdote.
histórico adj. historic, historical.
hocico m. snout; **meter el —** to meddle, stick one's nose in anything; **caer de —** to fall on one's face.
hogaño adv. nowadays; this present year.
hogar m. hearth, fireplace; home.
hogareño adj. home-loving, domestic, homelike.
hoguera f. bonfire.
hoja f. leaf; petal; sheet of paper or metal; blade (of a sword or knife); **— de ventana** shutter; **— de lata** tin plate.
hojaldre m. & f. puff pastry.
hojarasca f. fallen leaves; dry foliage; superfluos ornament; trash; useless words.
hojear v. to leaf, to turn the pages of; to browse; to form metal into sheets.
hojuela f. leaflet, small leaf; thin leaf (of metal); flake; thin pancake; **— de estaño** tin foil; **—s de maíz** corn flakes.
¡hola! interj. hello!; ho!; ha!
holandés adj. Dutch; m. Dutchman; Dutch language.
holgado adj. loose, wide, lax; roomy, spacious; well off; free, at leisure.
holgar v. irr. to rest, to loaf; to cease from labour; to live or be at ease; **—se** to be glad of, to relax, to have a good time, to be pleased with; **huelga decir** needless to say.
holgazán m. idler, loafer, loiterer, vagabond; adj. lazy, idle.
holgazanear v. to loiter, to lounge, to idle, to bum around.
holgazanería f. idleness, laziness, indolence.
holgorio m. spree.
holgura f. ease, rest, repose; width, breadth; country feast.
holocausto m. holocaust, burnt sacrifice.
hollar v. to tread, to trample upon; to humble, to depress.
hollejo m. skin, peel, pellicle; husk.
hollín m. soot.
hombrada f. manly act; show of bravery.
hombre m. man; husband.
hombría f. manliness; manly strength; **— de bien** probity, honesty.
hombro m. shoulder; **arrimar (or meter) el —** to help.
hombruno adj. mannish, masculine.
homenaje m. homage, honor service, obeisance.
homicida m. murderer; f. murderess; adj. homicidal, murderous.
homicidio m. homicide, manslaughter; murder.
homogéneo adj. homogeneous.
honda f. sling, slingshot.
hondo adj. deep, profound; low; m. bottom, depth.
hondonada f. hollow, dip, gully, ravine, dale; dingle, valley.
hondura f. depth, profundity; **meterse en —s** to go beyond one's depth; to get in trouble.
honestidad f. chastity, modesty, decency, decorum, propriety; urbanity.
honesto adj. chaste, modest, decent; just, honest, honourable; pure, virtuous.
hongo m. mushroom; fungus, derby hat.
honor m. honor, glory, dignity, fame.
honorario m. fee (for professional services); adj. honorary.
honorífico adj. honorary; **mención honorífica** honorable mention.
honra f. honor, reputation, respect; chastity in women; **—s** obsequies, funeral rites.
honradez f. honesty, honor, probity, integrity.
honrado adj. honest, honorable, honored.
honrar v. to honor; **—se** to be honored.
honroso adj. honorable, honoring.
hora f. hour, time; **—s canonical hours**, office (required daily

— 130 —

horadar v. to pierce, to bore, to perforate.
horario m. schedule, timetable; horary, horal; hour hand.
horca f. gallows; pitchfork; forked prop; Am. birthday present; — **de ajos** string of garlic.
horcajadas: **a —** astride; **ponerse a —** to straddle.
horcón m. forked pole, forked prop; Am. post, roof support; roof.
horda f. horde.
horizontal adj. horizontal.
horizonte m. horizon.
horma f. form, block, mold (for shaping a hat); shoe last; shoe tree.
hormiga f. ant.
hormigón m. concrete.
hormiguear v. to swarm; to be crawling with ants; **me hormiguea el cuerpo** I itch all over.
hormigueo m. itching, creeping sensation; tingle, tingling sensation.
hormiguero m. ant hill; ant nest; crowd of people; **oso —** anteater;
hornada f. batch of bread, baking.
hornear v. to bake.
hornilla f. grate of a stove, burner.
horno m. furnace; oven; kiln; **alto —** blast furnace.
horquilla f. hairpin; forked pole; small pitchfork.
horrendo adj. horrible, hideous, dreadful.
horrible adj. horrible.
horror m. horror; atrocity; **dar —** to cause fright, to horrify; **tenerle — a uno** to feel a strong dislike for one.
horrorizar v. to horrify, to shock, to terrify; **—se** to be terrified.
horroroso adj. horrid; frightful; hideous.
hortaliza f. vegetables; vegetable garden.
hortelano m. gardener.
hosco See **fosco**.
hospedaje m. board and lodging; lodging.
hospedar v. to lodge, to give lodging; to room; to stop (at).
hospedero m. innkeeper.
hospiciano m. inmate of a poorhouse or asylum.
hospicio m. asylum; orphanage; orphan asylum; poorhouse; alm's house.

hospital m. hospital; **— de primera sangre** first aid hospital.
hospitalidad f. hospitality.
hostia f. host.
hostigar v. to harass, to vex, to beat; to lash; Am. to cloy.
hostil adj. hostile.
hostilidad f. hostility.
hotel m. hotel, villa.
hotelero m. hotel keeper.
hoy adv. today; **— día** nowadays; **de — en adelante** from now on; **— por —** at present; **de — más** henceforth, henceforward.
hoya f. pit, hole, grave; valley; cavity; Am. river basin.
hoyuelo m. dimple; tiny hole.
hoz m. sickle; narrow ravine.
hozar v. to root, to turn up the earth with the snout (as hogs).
huacal See **guacal**.
huarache See **guarache**.
huaso See **guaso**.
hueco adj. hollow, empty; vain, ostentatious; tumid, resonant, inflated, affected, puffed up; high sounding; m. gap, space, hole.
huelga f. labor strike; rest, repose, relaxation from work; **declararse en —** to strike.
huelguista m. striker.
huella f. trace, footprint; track; impression.
huérfano adj. & m. orphan.
huero adj. empty, rotten, spoiled (egg).
huerta f. orchard and vegetable garden; irrigated land.
huerto m. small orchard and vegetable garden; garden patch.
hueso m. bone; stone; **la sin —** the tongue; **soltar la sin —** to talk too much; **no dejarle un — sano** to pick him to pieces.
huésped m. guest; host; lodger; **ser un — en su casa** to be seldom at home.
hueste f. host, army, multitude.
huesudo adj. bony.
huevo m. egg; **— duro** hard-boiled egg; **— estrellado** fried egg; **— pasado por agua** soft boiled egg; **—s revueltos** scrambled eggs; **—s tibios** soft boiled eggs; **—s pericos** Am. scrambled eggs.
huida f. flight, escape.
huir v. irr. to flee, to escape, to avoid, to shun, to run away.
huizache m. Am. huizache (a species of acacia).
hule m. rubber; oilcloth; Am. rubber tree; gum, elastic.

hulla f. soft coal; pit coal.

humanidad f. humanity, mankind; humaneness; —**es** philology, grammatical studies.

humanitario adj. humanitarian, humane, kind, charitable.

humano adj. human; humane, benevolent; m. man, human being.

humareda f. cloud of smoke; confusion.

humeante adj. smoking, smoky, fuming.

humear v. to smoke, to give off smoke; to steam; Am. to fumigate.

humedad f. humidity, moisture, dampness.

humedecer v. irr. to moisten, to wet, to dampen, to humectate.

humildad f. humility; humbleness; meekness; modesty.

humilde adj. humble, lowly, meek, modest.

humillación f. humiliation, submission.

humillar v. to humiliate, to humble, to lower; to subdue, to degrade; —**se** to humiliate oneself, to bow humbly.

humillos m. pl. airs, conceit, vanity, petty pride.

humo m. smoke, fume, vapor; —**s** conceit, vanity, petty pride.

humorada f. pleasantry, witty remark; caprice, notion.

humorismo m. humor, humorous style, humorism.

humorístico adj. humorous.

humoso adj. smoky.

hundimiento m. sinking, collapse, submersion; cave-in.

hundir v. to sink, to submerge; to immerge; to crush, to oppress; to destroy, to fall down; —**se** to sink; to collapse, to cave-in.

huracán m. hurricane.

huraño adj. unsociable, shy, bashful; intractable.

¡hurra! interj. hurrah!

hurtadillas : a — on the sly, secretly, stealthily.

hurtar v. to steal, to rob; —**se** to withdraw, slip away; to hide; — el cuerpo to dodge, to flee.

hurto m. robbery, theft, stealing, stolen article; a — stealthily, on the sly.

husmear v. to scent, to smell; to follow the track of; to nose; to pry into; to peep.

husmeo m. sniff, sniffing, smelling, prying.

huso m. spindle.

I

ibérico adj. Iberian.

ibero adj. See **ibérico**.

iberoamericano adj. Ibero-American (Spanish or Portuguese American).

ida f. departure; sally; impetuosity; billete de — y vuelta round trip ticket; —**s** y venidas goings and comings.

idea f. idea, notion, conception; contrivance.

ideal m. & adj. ideal; mental.

idealismo m. idealism.

idealista adj. idealistic; m. & f. idealist; dreamer.

idear v. to form an idea; to think, to contrive, to invent, imagine; to devise; to plan.

ídem idem (abbreviation: id.); ditto, the same.

idéntico adj. identical, identic.

identidad f. identity, sameness.

identificar v. to identify; —**se** to identify oneself.

idilio m. idyl, pastoral poem.

idioma m. language, tongue, idiom.

idiota m. & f. idiot; adj. idiotic, foolish.

idiotismo m. idiotism; idiocy.

idolatrar v. to idolize, to worship, to idolatrize.

ídolo m. idol.

idóneo adj. fit, suitable, proper, convenient; qualified.

iglesia f. church, temple, diocese.

ignición f. ignition.

ignominia f. infamy, shame, disgrace, opprobrium.

ignominioso adj. ignominious, infamous, shameful, disgraceful, opprobrious.

ignorancia f. ignorance, folly, darkness.

ignorante adj. ignorant.

ignorar v. to be ignorant of, not to know.

ignoto adj. unknown, undiscovered.

igual adj. equal, even, smooth; uniform; constant; similar, like; alike; resembling; serle — a uno to be all the same to one, to make no difference to one; m. equal; al — equally.

igualar v. to equal, to equalize; to match; to flatten, to make even; to level, to smooth; to adjust; to be equal.

igualdad f. equality.

igualitario adj. equalitarian.

ijada f. loin, flank of an animal; pain in the side, colic.
ijar m. flank of an animal.
ilegal adj. illegal, unlawful.
ilegítimo adj. illegitimate, illegal, unlawful.
ileso adj. unharmed, uninjured, unhurt; safe and sound.
ilícito adj. illicit, unlawful.
ilimitado adj. unlimited.
iluminación f. illumination.
iluminar v. to illuminate, to light, to enlighten.
ilusión f. illusion.
ilusivo adj. illusive.
iluso adj. deluded, deceived, ridiculed; m. visionary, dreamer.
ilusorio adj. illusive; deceptive; worthless.
ilustración f. illustration; elucidation, explanation.
ilustrador m. illustrator.
ilustrar v. to illustrate.
ilustre adj. illustrious, noble, distinguished, celebrated, noted, renowned.
imagen f. image.
imaginable adj. imaginable, conceivable.
imaginación f. imagination.
imaginar v. to imagine, to fancy.
imaginativa f. imagination.
imaginativo adj. imaginative, fancy.
imán m. magnet; charm, attraction.
imbécil adj. imbecile, stupid; weak, feeble.
imborrable adj. indelible, not erasable, unforgettable.
imbuir v. irr. to imbue, to instill, to infuse.
imitación f. imitation.
imitador m. imitator; follower; adj. imitative, imitating.
imitar v. to imitate, to follow, to copy, to counterfeit.
impaciencia f. impatience, disinquietude.
impaciente adj. impatient.
impar adj. odd; número — odd number.
imparcial adj. impartial, equitable.
imparcialidad f. impartiality, fairness, justice.
impasible adj. impassive, insensitive, insensible, unfeeling, unmoved.
impávido adj. fearless; calm; dauntless, undaunted; Am. impudent, brazen.
impedimento m. impediment, hindrance, obstacle.

impedir v. irr. to impede, to prevent, to hinder, to obstruct; to prevent.
impeler v. to impel, to push; to incite, to spur; to stimulate, to press.
impenetrable adj. impenetrable.
impensadamente adv. offhand, without thinking; unexpectdly.
impensado adj. unforeseen, unexpected; offhand; done without thinking.
imperar v. to rule, to command, to dominate; to reign.
imperativo adj. imperative; urgent, compelling; m. imperative mood.
imperceptible adj. imperceptible.
imperdible m. safety pin; adj. safe, that cannot be lost.
imperecedero adj. imperishable, enduring, everlasting.
imperfecto adj. imperfect; m. imperfect tense.
imperial adj. imperial; f. coach top; top seats in a coach or bus.
impericia f. inexperience, unskilfulness.
imperio m. empire; command, rule; dominion; sway, influence.
imperioso adj. imperious, arrogant; domineering; urgent.
impermeable adj. waterproof, water-repellent, impervious, rainproof; m. raincoat.
impersonal adj. impersonal.
impertinencia f. impertinence; impudence; insolent remak or act, folly; nonsense; decir —s to talk nonsense; to make insolent remarks.
impertinente adj. impertinent, impudent; meddlesome; irrelevant, not to the point; —s lorgnette.
ímpetu m. impetus; violent force; impulse, fit; — de ira fit of anger.
impetuoso adj. impetuous, violent; fierce, vehement, passionate.
impío adj. impious; irreligious; profane.
implacable adj. implacable, relentless.
implantación f. implantation, establishment, introduction (of a system, ideas, etc.).
implantar v. to implant, to establish, to introduce.
implicar v. to imply; to implicate, to involve.
implorar v. to implore, to entreat, to beg.

— 133 —

imponente adj. imposing.
imponer v. irr. to impose; to invest (money); to lay, put, or set in or upon; — **miedo** to inspire fear; — **respeto** to inspire or command respect; —**se** to inspire fear or respect; to dominate; —**se a** Am. to get accustomed or used to.
importancia f. importance.
importar v. to import; to be important, to matter; to amount to; to be necessary; to concern.
importe m. amount, price, value, cost.
importunar v. to importune, to nag, to tease, to pester, to vex, to molest.
importuno adj. annoying; persistent; troublesome, heavy.
imposibilidad f. impossibility.
imposibilitado p.p. & adj. disabled; unfit, helpless.
imposibilitar v. to make impossible, to disable.
imposible adj. impossible; intolerable; unbearable, impracticable, unfeasible; Am. slovenly, untidy.
imposición f. imposition, burden, tax.
impostor m. impostor, cheat.
impostura f. imposture, fraud, deceit.
impotencia f. impotence.
impotente adj. impotent, powerless.
impreciso adj. vague, indefinite; inaccurate.
impregnar v. to impregnate, to saturate.
imprenta f. press, printing, printing shop.
imprescindible adj. essential, indispensable.
impresión f. impression; printing; mark; footprint.
impresionante adj. impressive.
impresionar v. to impress; to move; to affect, to stir; to fix in the mind; —**se** to be stirred, to be moved.
impreso p. p. printed, impressed, imprinted; m. printed matter.
impresor m. printer.
imprevisión f. carelessness, lack of foresight; inadvertency.
imprevisto adj. unforeseen, unexpected.
imprimir v. to print, to imprint, to impress.
improbable adj. unlikely, improbable.
improperio m. affront, insult.

impropio adj. improper, unsuitable; unfit.
improvisar v. to improvise.
improviso adj. unforeseen; **de —** suddenly; **en un —** Am. in a moment, in the twinkling of an eye.
imprudencia f. imprudence, indiscretion, rash act.
imprudente adj. imprudent; unwise; indiscreet.
impuesto p.p. imposed; informed; **estar — a** Am. to be used or accustomed to; m. tax, duty.
impulsar v. to impel, to push, to move, to force; to urge on.
impulso m. impulse, push.
impureza f. impurity.
impuro adj. impure.
imputar v. to impute, to attribute.
inacabable adj. unending, endless, interminable.
inacabado adj. unfinished.
inaccesible adj. inaccessible, unobtainable.
inacción f. inaction, inactivity; idleness.
inaceptable adj. unacceptable, unsatisfactory.
inactividad f. inactivity.
inactivo adj. inactive.
inadecuado adj. inadequate.
inadvertencia f. oversight; inattention, heedlessness.
inadvertido adj. careless, heedless; unnoticed.
inafectado adj. unaffected.
inagotable adj. inexhaustible.
inaguantable adj. insufferable, unbearable.
inalámbrico adj. wireless.
inalterable adj. unalterable; unchangeable.
inalterado adj. unchanged.
inamovible See **inmovible**.
inanición f. starvation.
inanimado adj. inanimate, lifeless.
inapetencia f. lack of appetite.
inaplicable adj. inapplicable, unsuitable; **— al caso** irrelevant.
inapreciable adj. invaluable, inappreciable; too small to be perceived, very slight.
inasequible adj. inaccessible, not obtainable; hard to attain or obtain.
inaudito adj. unheard-of; unprecedented, strange.
inauguración f. inauguration.
inaugurar v. to inaugurate, to begin, to open.

incaico adj. Incan (of or pertaining to the Incas).
incalculable adj. incalculable, innumerable, untold.
incandescente adj incandescent.
incansable adj. untiring, tireless, indefatigable.
incapacidad f. incompetence, inability, unfitness.
incapacitar v. to cripple, to disable, to handicap, to unfit, to make unfit, to incapacitate.
incapaz adj. incapable, unable.
incauto adj. unwary, heedless, reckless, incautious.
incendiar v. to set on fire; —se to catch fire.
incendio m. conflagration, fire, burning.
incentivo m. incentive, inducement.
incertidumbre f. uncertainty, uncertitude, doubt.
incesante adj. incessant, continual, uninterrupted.
incidental adj. incidental, casual.
incidente adj. incidental; m. incident.
incienso m. incense.
incierto adj. uncertain, doubtful, unstable; unknown; untrue; inconstant.
incisión f. incision, cut, slit, gash.
incitamiento m. incitement, incentive, inducement.
incitar v. to incite, to rouse, to stir up.
incivil adj. uncivil, rude, impolite; unpolished.
inclemencia f. inclemency, severity, harshness.
inclemente adj. unmerciful, merciless.
inclinación f. inclination, affection, tendency, bent, bow, incline, slope, bending, stooping, propensity, attachement.
inclinar v. to incline; to influence; to persuade; —se to bow, stoop, incline, slope, slant, lean, to bend; to be favorably disposed to.
incluir v. irr. to include, inclose, comprise, contain.
inclusive adv. inclusive, including.
inclusivo adj. inclusive, comprehensible.
incluso adj. inclosed, included; including; even.
incógnita f. unknown quantity (mathematics).
incógnito adj. unknown; de — incognito.
incoherente adj. incoherent, disconnected, rambling, inconsistent.
incoloro adj. colorless.
incombustible adj. incombustible; fireproof.
incomodar v. to inconvenience; to disturb, trouble, annoy; to incommode.
incomodidad f. inconvenience, bother, discomfort, annoyance.
incómodo adj. inconvenient, bothersome; uncomfortable.
incomparable adj. incomparable; peerless; matchless.
incompasivo adj. merciless, pitiless, incompassionate.
incompatible adj. incompatible; unsuitable, uncongenial, inconsistent.
incompetencia f. incompetence, inability, unfitness.
incompleto adj. incomplete.
incomprensible adj. incomprehensible.
incondicional adj. unconditional.
inconexo adj. unconnected; incoherent, disconnected.
inconfundible adj. unmistakable.
incongruente adj. unsuitable, incongruous, incongruent.
inconquistable adj. unconquerable.
inconsciencia f. unconsciousness; unawareness.
inconsciente adj. unconscious; unaware.
inconsecuente adj. inconsistent; illogical.
inconsiderado adj. inconsiderate; thoughtless.
inconstancia f. inconstancy, fickleness, changeableness.
inconstante adj. inconstant, fickle, changeable, variable.
incontable adj. countless, innumerable.
inconveniencia f. inconvenience, trouble.
inconveniente adj. inconvenient; improper; m. obstacle, objection.
incorporar v. to incorporate; to unite; to embody; to include; to form into a corporation; —se to sit up; —se a to join.
incorrecto adj. incorrect.
incredulidad f. incredulity, unbelief.
incrédulo adj. incredulous, unbeliever, miscreant.
increíble adj. incredible, unbelievable.
incremento m. increment, increase.
incrustar v. to inlay; to encrust,

inculcar to incrustate; —se en to penetrate, to impress itself deeply into.
inculcar v. to inculcate, to instill, to impress.
inculto adj. uncultured; uncultivated; unrefined.
incumbencia f. concern, duty, obligation; no es de mi — it does not concern me, it is not within muy province.
incurable adj. incurable.
incurrir v. to incur, to fall (into); to deserve.
incursión f. raid; invasion.
indagación f. investigation, inquiry, inquest, search.
indagador m. investigator; inquirer; detective; examiner: adj. investigating, inquiring.
indagar v. to find out, to investigate, to inquire.
indebidamente adv. unduly; illegally.
indebido adj. undue, improper, illegal, unlawful.
indecencia adj. indecency, obscenity, indecorum.
indecible adj. unexpressible, untold; unutterable.
indeciso adj. undecided, doubtful, uncertain.
indefectible adj. unfailing; —mente unfailingly; indefectibly.
indefenso adj. defenseless, unprotected.
indefinible adj. indefinable.
indefinido adj. indefinite.
indeleble adj. indelible.
indemnización f. indemnity, compensation.
indemnizar v. to indemnify, to compensate.
independencia f. independence.
independiente adj. independent.
indeseable adj. undesirable, unwelcome.
indiada f. Am. community, group or crowd of Indians; an Indian-like remark or act; an uncontrollable fit of anger.
indianista m. & f. student of Indian culture; adj. pertaining to Indian culture.
indiano adj. of or pertaining to the West or East Indies; m. Spaniard who goes back to settle in his country after having lived for some time in Spanish America.
indicación f. indication.
indicar v. to indicate, to show, to point out.

indicativo adj. indicative; m. indicative, indicative mood.
índice m. index; catalogue; sign; pointer; forefinger.
indicio m. indication, sign, mark, token.
indiferencia f. indifference.
indiferente adj. indifferent.
indígena adj. indigenous, native; m. & f. native inhabitant; Am. Indian.
indignación f. indignation, anger.
indignado p.p. & adj. indignant, irritated, angry.
indignar v. to irritate, to anger, to provoke, to tease; —se to become indignant, angry.
indignidad f. indignity, affront, insult; unworthy or disgraceful act.
indigno adj. unworthy, low, contemptible; undeserving.
indio adj. & m. Indian; Hindu.
indirecta f. hint, indirect remark, innuendo, insinuation, cue, surmise.
indirecto adj. indirect; oblique.
indisciplinado adj. undisciplined, untrained, untaught.
indiscreto adj. indiscreet, imprudent, unwise, rash.
indiscutible adj. indisputable, unquestionable.
indispensable adj. indispensable.
indisponer v. irr. to indispose; to make ill; — a uno con otro to prejudice someone against another; —se to become ill; —se con to fall out with, to quarrel with.
indisposición f. indisposition, upset, slight illness, reluctance, unwillingness.
indispuesto p.p. & adj. indisposed, unwilling; ill.
indisputable adj. unquestionable.
indistinto adj. indistict, dim, vague, not clear.
individual adj. individual.
individualidad f. individuality.
individuo adj. individual; indivisible; m. individual; person; member.
indócil adj. unruly, disobedient, headstrong.
indocto adj. uneducated, ignorant.
índole f. disposition, temper, inclination; kind, class.
indolencia f. indolence, laziness, indifference, insensitiveness.
indolente adj. indolent, lazy, indifferent, insensitive.
indomable adj. indomitable; un-

conquerable, unmanageable; untamable.
indómito adj. untamed; uncontrollable; unruly.
inducir v. irr. to induce; to persuade.
indudable adj. certain, unquestionable.
indulgencia f. indulgence, tolerance, forbearance, forgiveness, leniency.
indulgente adj. indulgent, lenient, tolerant.
indultar v. to pardon, to forgive, to free; to exempt.
indulto m. pardon, forgiveness; exemption; privilege.
indumentaria f. costume, dress, manner of dressing.
industria f. industry; cleverness; skill; **de —** intentionally, on purpose; **caballero de —** swindler.
industrial adj. industrial; m. industrialist, manufacturer.
industrioso adj. industrious.
inédito adj. unpublished.
inefable adj. ineffable, inexpressible.
ineficaz adj. ineffective; inefficient.
inepto adj. incompetent, unsuitable; useless.
inequívoco adj. unmistakable.
inercia f. inertia, lifelessness; inertness; inactivity, indolence.
inerme adj. unarmed, defenseless, disarmed.
inerte adj. inert, inactive, sluggish, slow, dull, motionless.
inesperado adj. unexpected.
inestable adj. unstable; unsettled; unsteady.
inestimable adj. inestimable, invaluable.
inevitable adj. inevitable, unavoidable.
inexacto adj. inexact, inaccurate.
inexperiencia f. inexperience.
inexperto adj. unskilful, unskilled, inexperienced.
inexplicable adj. inexplicable.
inextinguible adj. inextinguishable, unquenchable.
infalible adj. infallible.
infame adj. infamous, vile, despicable; m. scoundrel.
infamia f. infamy, dishonor, wickedness.
infancia f. infancy.
infante m. infant; infante; infantryman.
infantería f. infantry.

infantil adj. infantile, childlike, childish.
infatigable adj. tireless, untiring.
infausto adj. unfortunate; unhappy.
infección f. infection.
infeccioso adj. infectious.
infectar v. to infect; to corrupt; to vitiate; **—se** to catch, to become infected.
infeliz adj. unhappy, unfortunate; luckless, miserable; m. poor wretch.
inferior adj. inferior; lower; m. inferior.
inferioridad f. inferiority.
inferir v. irr. to infer; to imply; to inflict, to deduce.
infernal adj. infernal, hellish.
infestar v. to infest, to invade, to overrun, to plague; to corrupt; to infect.
inficionar v. to infect; to contaminate.
infiel adj. unfaithful, faithless; infidel; unaccurate; godless.
infierno m. hell; **en el quinto —** very far away.
infiltrar v. to filter through; **—se** to leak (into), filter (through); to infiltrate.
infinidad f. infinity; **una — de** a large number of.
infinito adj. infinite; adv. infinitely; m. infinity.
inflamación f. inflammation.
inflamado p.p. & adj. inflamed, sore, swollen.
inflamar v. to inflame, to excite; to kindle, to set on fire; **—se** to become inflamed.
inflar v. to inflate; to elate; to exaggerate; **—se** to become inflated; to swell up with pride.
inflexible adj. inflexible, stiff, rigid; unbending.
inflexión f. inflection.
infligir v. to inflict.
influencia f. influence.
influenza f. influenza, grippe, flu.
influir v. irr. to influence; to modify; to prevail upon.
influjo m. influence; influx, inward flow.
influyente adj. influential.
información f. information.
informal adj. informal; unconventional; unreliable, not dependable, not punctual.
informar v. to inform; to instruct; to acquaint; to report; to give form to; to give a report; to

informe — **innecesario**

present a case; —**se** to find out; to ask for information.
informe m. report, account; information; brief; adj. formless, shapeless.
infortunio m. misfortune, mishap; misery.
infracción f. infraction, breach; trespass.
infractor m. transgressor, violator, lawbreaker.
infrascrito m. undersigned, subscriber, signer.
infringir v. to infringe, to break, to violate.
infructuoso adj. fruitless.
ínfulas f. pl. airs, false importance; **darse** — to put on airs.
infundado adj. groundless, without foundation.
infundir v. to infuse, to inspire; to instill.
infusión f. infusion; inspiration; **poner en** — to steep (as tee leaves).
ingeniería f. engineering.
ingeniero m. engineer.
ingenio m. talent; ingenuity; mentality; mental power, mind, wit; — **de azúcar** sugar refinery; sugar plantation.
ingeniosidad f. ingenuity, cleverness.
ingenioso adj. ingenious, clever.
ingenuidad f. candor, frankness; unaffected simplicity.
ingenuo adj. frank, sincere; simple, unaffected.
ingerir See injerir.
inglés adj. English; **a la inglesa** in the English fashion; **ir a la** — Am. to go Dutch treat; m. Englishman; the English language.
ingobernable adj. ungovernable, unruly; uncontrollable.
ingratitud f. ingratitude.
ingrato adj. ungrateful, thankless; harsh; cruel; disdainful.
ingrediente m. ingredient.
ingresar v. to enter; to ingress; — **en** to join.
ingreso m. entrance, entry, ingress, —**s** receipts, profits, revenue.
inhábil adj. unskilled; unskilful; unfit.
inhabilidad f. inability; unfitness.
inhabilitar v. to disqualify, to unfit, to disable, to deprive of a right or claim.
inherente adj. inherent.
inhospitalario adj. inhospitable.
inhumano adj. inhuman, cruel.

iniciador m. initiator; pioneer; adj. initiating.
inicial adj. & f. initial.
iniciar v. to initiate, to begin, to start.
iniciativa f. initiative.
inicuo adj. wicked.
iniquidad f. iniquity, wickedness; sin.
ingerir v. irr. to inject, to insert; —**se** to interfere, to meddle; Am. to drink, to eat.
injertar v. to graft, to ingraft.
injuria f. affront, insult; harm, damage.
injuriar v. to insult, to offend; to harm, to damage.
injurioso adj. insulting, offensive, harmful.
injusticia f. injustice.
injustificado adj. unjustified; unjustifiable.
injusto adj. unjust, unfair.
inmaculado adj. immaculate, clean, pure.
inmediación f. vicinity; nearness; —**es** environs, outskirts.
inmediato adj. near, close; **de** — Am. immediately; suddenly.
inmensidad f. immensity, vastnes, infinity; vast number.
inmenso adj. immense, vast, huge, infinite; boundless.
inmersión f. immersion, dip.
inmigración f. immigration.
inmigrante adj. m. & f. immigrant.
inmigrar v. to immigrate.
inminente adj. imminent.
inmiscuir v. irr. to mix; —**se** to meddle, to interfere.
inmoble adj. motionless, unshaken.
inmoral adj. immoral.
inmoralidad f. immorality.
inmortal adj. immortal.
inmortalidad f. immmortality.
inmovible adj. inmovable, fixed; steadfast; firm; constant.
inmundicia f. filth, filthiness, dirt; impure, nasty, nastiness; uncleanness, uncleanliness.
inmundo adj. filthy, dirty; impure; nasty; unclean.
inmune adj. immune; exempt; free.
inmunidad f. immunity.
inmutable adj. unchangeable, immutable, invariable.
inmutar v. to alter; to change; —**se** to show emotion; to change one's appearance.
innato adj. innate, natural, inborn.
innecesario adj. unnecessary.

innegable adj. undeniable, incontestable, incontrovertible.
innocuidad. f. harmlessness.
innocuo adj. innocuous, harmless.
innovación f. innovation; novelty.
innumerable adj. innumerable.
inobservancia f. nonobservance.
inocencia f. innocence; sincerity; simplicity.
inocente adj. innocent, pure, candid, simple; m. innocent person.
inocentón adj. very foolish or simple; simpleton; easily fooled; m. dupe, unsuspecting victim.
inocular v. to inoculate.
inodoro adj. odorless, inodorous, without smell; Am. toilet, water closet.
inofensivo adj. inoffensive; harmless.
inolvidable adj. unforgettable.
inopinado adj. unexpected, inopinate.
inoportuno adj. inopportune, untimely, unsuitable.
inquietar v. to worry, to disturb, to make uneasy; to disquiet; to molest; —**se** to become uneasy, disturbed or restless.
inquieto adj. restless, uneasy, anxious, turbulent; noisy, troublesome.
inquietud f. restlessness; anxiety, uneasiness, fear.
inquilino m. tenant, renter; inmate, lodger.
inquina f. aversion, grudge, dislike, hatred.
inquirir v. irr. to inquire, to investigate, to find out; to look for carefully; to look after; to search out.
inquisición f. inquisition; inquiry, investigation; inquest.
insaciable adj. insatiable, greedy, craving.
insalubre adj. unhealthy, insalubrious; unwholesome.
inscribir v. to inscribe; to register, to enroll; to record; —**se** to register.
inscripción f. inscription; registration.
insecto m. insect.
inseguro adj. insecure; unsafe; doubtful, uncertain.
insensato adj. senseless; foolish; insensate, stupid, mad.
insensibilidad f. insensibility, unconsciousness; lack of feeling.
insensible adj. insensible, callous, stupid; imperceptible; unfeeling, cold, loveless.

inseparable adj. inseparable.
inserción f. insertion; insert.
insertar v. to insert.
inservible adj. useless.
insidioso adj. insidious, sly, guileful, crafty.
insigne adj. famous, notable, noted, remarkable.
insignia f. badge, medal, decoration; flag, pennant; —**s** insignia.
insignificante adj. insignificant.
insinuación f. insinuation; intimation; hint.
insinuar v. to insinuate, to hint; —**se** to insinuate oneself; to creep (into) gradually.
insipidez f. flatness, tastelessness, dullness.
insípido adj. insipid, tasteless.
insistencia f. insistence, persistence, obstinacy.
insistente adj. insistent, persistent.
insistir v. to insist, to persist.
insociable adj. unsociable.
insolación m. sunstroke.
insolencia f. insolence.
insolentarse v. to sauce, to become insolent, to act with insolence.
insolente adj. insolent.
insólito adj. unusual; uncommon; insolite.
insolvente adj. insolvent, bankrupt.
insomne adj. sleepless.
insondable adj. fathomless, deep, impenetrable.
insoportable adj. unbearable, insupportable, intolerable.
insospechado adj. unsuspected.
inspector m. inspector, overseer.
inspiración f. inspiration; breathing in.
inspirar v. to inspire, to inhale, to breathe in.
instalación f. installation, instalment.
instalar v. to install; to give possession of a rank or employment.
instancia f. instance, urgent request; instancy, importunity, persistency; petition; **a —s de** at the request of.
instantánea f. snapshot.
instantáneo adj. instantaneous; sudden.
instante adj. instant, moment, a point in duration; **al —** at once, immediately; **por —s** continually; from one moment to another; adj. instant, urgent.
instar v. to urge, to press; to be urgent.

instigar v. to instigate, to urge, to incite.
instintivo adj. instinctive.
institución f. institution, establishment, foundation; —es institutes, collection of precepts and principles.
instituir v. irr. to institute, to establish, to found; — **por heredero** to appoint as heir.
instituto m. institute; established principle, law, or custom; a body of learned man; — **de segunda enseñanza** high school.
institutriz f. governess.
instrucción f. instruction, education; teaching; —es directions, orders, mandate.
instructivo adj. instructive.
instruir v. irr. to instruct, to teach, to lecture; to inform.
instrumento m. instrument.
insuficiencia f. insufficiency, deficiency, incompetence; dearth, scarcity.
insuficiente adj. insufficient.
insufrible adj. insufferable, unbearable.
ínsula f. island.
insultante adj. insulting, abusive, insolent.
insultar v. to insult, to treat with insolence or contempt; —se to be seized with a fit.
insulto m. insult; a sudden and violent fit.
insuperable adj. insuperable; insurmountable.
insurgente adj. insurgent.
insurrección f. insurrection, revolt, uprising.
insurrecto m. insurgent, rebel; adj. rebellious.
intacto adj. intact, untouched, entire.
intachable adj. faultless, irreproachable.
integral adj. integral; f. integral.
integrante adj. integral; integrating.
integridad f. integrity; wholeness, honesty; purity; completeness.
íntegro adj. whole, complete; honest; upright.
intelecto m. intellect.
inteligencia f. intelligence; mind; knowledge.
inteligente adj. intelligent.
intemperancia f. intemperance, excess.
intemperie f. open air, intemperateness, intemperature; bad weather; **a la —** unsheltered, outdoors, in the open air; exposed to the weather.
intención f. intention.
intencional adj. intentional.
intendente m. manager, intendent; quartermaster; supervisor; Am. governor of a province, police commissioner.
intensidad f. intensity.
intenso adj. intense, intensive; ardent, vehement.
intentar v. to attempt, to try; to intend, to design.
intento m. intent, purpose, intention; **de —** on purpose.
intercalar v. to insert between; to intercalate.
interceder v. to intercede.
interceptar v. to intercept.
intercesión f. intercession, mediation.
interés m. interest.
interesante adj. interesting.
interesar v. to interest; to give an interest or share; —se to be or to become interested.
interferencia f. interference.
ínterin m. interim, meantime; **en el —** in the meantime.
interino adj. acting, temporary, provisional.
interior adj. inner, interior; internal, inward; m. the interior, inside part.
interjección f. interjection, exclamation.
interlocutor m. interlocutor.
intermedio adj. intermediate; intervening; m. intermission; interval; interlude; **por — de** by means of, through the intervention of.
interminable adj. interminable, unending, endless.
intermisión f. intermission, interruption, pause, interval.
intermitente adj. intermitten.
internacional adj. international.
internar v. to intern, to confine; to pierce, to penetrate; —se to go into the interior.
interno adj. internal; interior; inward.
interoceánico adj. interoceanic; transcontinental.
interpelar v. to interrogate, to question; to appeal to; to summon.
interponer v. irr. to interpose; to put between; to insert; —se to mediate.
interpretación f. interpretation.
interpretar v. to interpret.

intérprete m. & f. interpreter.
interrogación f. interrogation, question; **signo de —** question mark.
interrogador m. questioner; adj. questioning.
interrogar v. to interrogate, to question.
interrogativo adj. interrogative.
interrogatorio m. interrogation.
interrumpir v. to interrupt.
interrupción f. interruption.
interruptor m. interrupter, electric switch.
intersección f. intersection.
intervalo m. interval.
intervención f. intervention; mediation, participation, auditing of accounts.
intervenir v. irr. to intervene, to mediate; to audit.
interventor m. comptroller, supervisor, inspector, overseer, auditor.
intestino m. intestine; adj. intestine, internal.
intimación f. intimation; hint; insinuation.
intimar v. to announce, to notify; to make known; to become intimate, friendly.
intimidad f. intimacy, privacy, friendship.
intimidar v. to intimidate, to daunt.
íntimo m. intimate.
intitular v. to entitle; to give a title; to name, to dignify; **—se** to be entitled, to be called; to call oneself by a certain name.
intolerable adj. intolerable, unbearable.
intolerancia f. intolerance.
intolerante adj. intolerant, narrow-minded.
intranquilo adj. disturbed, uneasy.
intranquilidad f. uneasiness, restlessness.
intransigencia f. uncompromising act or attitude; intolerance.
intransigente adj. uncompromising, intransigent; intolerant.
intratable adj. unsociable; intractable, rude, stubborn; unruly.
intravenoso adj. intravenous.
intrepidez f. fearlessness; courage; intrepidity.
intrépido adj. intrepid, fearless; daring.
intriga f. intrigue, scheme, plot.
intrigante m. & f. intriguer; plotter; adj. intriguing.

intrigar v. to intrigue, to form plots.
intrincado adj. intricate, complicated; entangled.
introducción f. introduction.
introducir v. irr. to introduce, to lead in; to bring into notice or practice; to induce, to facilitate; **—se** to get in, to penetrate.
intromisión f. meddling; insertion; intromission.
intruso adj. intrusive, intruding; m. intruder.
intuición f. intuition.
intuir v. irr. to sense, to feel by intuition.
inundación f. inundation, flood.
inundar v. to inundate, to flood; to overflow.
inusitado adj. unusual, rare, not in use.
inútil adj. useless.
inutilidad f. uselessness.
inutilizar v. to render useless; to put out of commission; to disable; to ruin, spoil.
invadir v. to invade.
invalidar v. to render invalid; to void, to annul; to invalidate; to nulify.
inválido adj. invalid; void; null; sickly; weak; feeble; cripple.
invariable adj. unchangeable, invariable.
invasión f. invasion; raid.
invasor m. invader; adj. invading.
invencible adj. invincible, unconquerable.
invención f. invention; device.
invendible adj. unsaleable.
inventar v. to invent, to discover; to find out.
inventariar v. to inventory.
inventario m. inventory.
inventiva f. inventiveness; the faculty of invention.
inventivo adj. inventive.
invento m. invention, device.
inventor m. inventor; storyteller; fibber.
invernáculo m. greenhouse, hothouse; conservatory.
invernadero m. winter quarters; winter resort; winter pasture; greenhouse; hothouse.
invernal adj. wintry, winter; hibernal.
invernar v. irr. to winter, to pass the winter.
inverosímil adj. unlikely, improbable.
inversión f. inversion, investment.
inverso adj. inverse, inverted; re-

verse; a (or por) la inversa on the contrary.
invertir v. irr. to invert, to reverse; to invest.
investigación f. investigation, inquiry.
investigador m. investigator, inquirer; detective; adj. investigating.
investigar v. to investigate, to inquire.
invicto adj. unconquered; unvanquished.
invierno m. winter.
invisible adj. invisible.
invitación f. invitation.
invitar v. to invite.
invocar v. to invoke.
involuntario adj. involuntary.
inyección f. injection.
inyectado p.p. injected; adj. bloodshot, inflamed.
inyectar v. to inject.
ir v. irr. to go, to move, to walk; to leave; to be; — **corriendo** to be running; — **entendiendo** to understand gradually, to begin to understand; — **de compras** to go shopping; — **a pie** to walk; — **a caballo** to ride; — **en automóvil** to drive, to ride in automobile; — **a medias** to go halves; no difference to one; **¿cómo le va?** how are you?; **no me va nada en eso** that doesn't concern me; **¡vamos!** let's go!, come on!; **¡vaya!** well now!; **¡vaya un hombre!** what a man!; **—se** to go, to go away; to escape; **—se abajo** to fall down, to topple over; to collapse; **—se a pique** to founder, to sink.
ira f. ire, anger, fury, choler, rage.
iracundo adj. irritable, angry; enraged.
iris m. iris (of the eye); **arco —** rainbow.
irisado adj. iridiscent, rainbow-hued.
ironía f. irony.
irónico adj. ironic, ironical.
irracional adj. irrational, unreasonable.
irradiar v. to irradiate, to radiate.
irreal adj. unreal.
irreflexión f. thoughtfulness; rashness.
irreflexivo adj. thoughtless; inconsiderate.
irrefrenable adj. uncontrollable.
irregular adj. irregular, abnormal.
irreligioso adj. irreligious.

irremediable adj. irremediable; hopeless; incurable.
irreprochable adj. irreproachable, flawless.
irresistible adj. irresistible.
irresoluto adj. undecided, irresolute, hesitating.
irrespetuoso adj. disrespectful.
irreverencia f. irreverence.
irreverente adj. irreverent.
irrigación f. irrigation.
irrigar v. to irrigate.
irrisión f. mockery, ridicule, derision.
irritación f. irritation, commotion, agitation.
irritante adj. irritating, irritatory, stimulating.
irritar v. to irritate, to exasperate.
irrupción f. sudden attack, raid, invasion; irruption, inroad.
isla f. island.
isleño m. islander.
islote m. islet, small island.
istmo m. isthmus.
italiano adj. & m. Italian.
itinerario m. itinerary; timetable, schedule; railroad guide.
izar v. to hoist, to heave.
izquierda f. left hand; left side; left wing (in politics); **a la —** to the left.
izquierdista m. & f. leftist, radical.
izquierdo adj. left; left-handed.

J

jabalí m. wild boar.
jabón m. soap; Am. fright, fear; **dar —** to soft-soap, to flatter; **dar un —** to give a good scolding, to beat, to thrash.
jabonadura f. washing, soaping; **—s** suds, lather; **dar a uno una —** to reprimand or scold someone.
jabonar v. to lather, to soap, to cleanse with soap; to reprimand severely.
jabonera f. soap dish; woman soap vendor or maker; box or case for a wash ball.
jaca f. small horse; pony; nag.
jacal m. shack, adobe hut.
jacalucho m. Am. poor ugly shack.
jacinto m. hyacinth.
jaco m. small nag; poor horse.
jactancia f. boast, brag; boasting.
jactancioso adj. braggart, boastful, vainglorious.
jactarse v. to brag, to boast, to vaunt.
jaculatoria f. short prayer; ejaculation.

jadeante adj. breathless, panting, out of breath.
jadear v. to pant, to palpitate.
jadeo m. pant, panting, palpitation.
jaez m. harness; kind, sort; **jaeces** trappings.
jalar v. to pull, to haul; to jerk; Am. to court, to make love; to flunk (a student); ¡jala (or jálale)! Am. get going! get a move on there!; —se Am. to get drunk; to go away; to move away.
jalea f. jelly.
jalear v. to shout (to hunting dogs); to rouse, to beat up (game); to shout and clap; to encourage (dancers, actors, etc.).
jaleo m. shouting and clapping; an Andalusian dance; revelry; jesting, gracefulness.
jaletina f. gelatin; calf's foot jelly.
jalón m. marker for boundaries; Am. pull, jerk, tug; swallow of liquor; stretch, distance.
jalonear v. Am. to pull, to jerk.
jamás adv. never, at no time; **para siempre —** forever.
jamón m. ham; Am. fix, difficulty.
japonés adj. & m. Japanese.
jaque m. check (chess); braggart, bully; **— mate** checkmate (chess); **tener a uno en —** to hold someone under a threat.
jaqueca f. headache; megrim.
jara f. rockrose (shrub); Am. reed m. bramble of rockroses; Am. reeds, clump of reeds.
jarabe m. syrup, sweet beverage; Am. a kind of tap dance; song, a musical accompaniment of the jarabe.
jarana f. merrymaking, revelry; trick; fib; jest; Am. small guitar; **ir de —** to go on a spree.
jarcia f. rigging of a ship; fishing tackle; pile, heap; heap of things; parcel of a variety of things laid by for use.
jardín m. flower garden; privy on board of ships.
jardinero m. gardener.
jarra f. jar, vase, pitcher; **de (or en) —s** akimbo.
jarro m. jar, jug, pitcher.
jarrón m. large vase or jar.
jaspe m. jasper; veined marble.
jaspeado adj. veined, streaked, mottled.
jaula f. cage; cagelike cell or prison; Am. roofless cattle car or freight car.

jauría f. pack of hounds.
jazmín m. jasmine.
jefatura f. dignity of chief; headquarters of a chief.
jefe m. chief, leader, head; superior; **— de escuadra** rear admiral.
jengibre m. ginger.
jerez m. cherry wine; Jerez.
jerga f. thick hoarse cloth; jargon, gibberish, unintelligible talk; slang; Am. saddle pad; poncho made of hoarse cloth.
jergón m. straw mattress; ill-fitting suit or dress; big, clumsy fellow; Am. cheap coarse rug; paunch, belly.
jerigonza f. jargon, slang, gibberish; **andar en —s** to quibble.
jeringa f. syringe.
jeringar v. to inject, to syringe, to squirt; to bother, to molest, to vex, to annoy.
jeringazo m. squirt.
jesuíta m. jesuit.
jeta f. snout; thick and projecting lips.
jiba See **giba**.
jíbaro adj. Am. rustic, rural, rude, uncultured; wild (said of domestic animals); m. Am. bumpkin, peasant.
jícara f. chocolate cup; Am. small bowl made out of a gourd; any small bowl; bald head; gourd tree.
jilguero m. linnet.
jinete m. horseman, rider.
jineteada f. Am. roughriding, horsebreaking.
jinetear v. to ride horseback; to perform on horseback; Am. to break in (a horse); to ride a bronco or bull.
jira f. excursion, tour, outing, picnic; sample of stuff or cloth; feast, a banquet among friends.
jirafa f. giraffe, camelopard.
jitomate m. Am. tomato. Also **gitomate**.
jofaina f. basin; a china jug, whasbowl.
jolgorio See **holgorio**.
jornada f. day's journey; military expedition; journey, travel by land; act (of a Spanish play).
jornal m. day's wages; bookkeeping journal; **a —** by the day.
jornalero m. day laborer.
joroba f. hump; nuisance, annoyance; importunity.
jorobado adj. hunchbacked; crooked; gibbcus; humpbacked; annoyed; bothered, in a bad fix.

jorobar v. to bother, to pester, to annoy, to importune, to worry.
jorongo m. Am. Mexican poncho.
jota f. name of the letter j; iota; Aragonese and Valencian dance and music; Am. leather sandal; **no saber una —** no to know anything.
joven adj. young, youthful, juvenile; m. & f. youth; young man; young woman.
jovial adj. jovial, jolly, merry, gay, airy, cheerful.
jovialidad f. gaiety, merriment, fun, jollity, joviality.
joya f. jewel; **—s** jewels; trousseau.
joyería f. jeweler's shop.
joyero m. jeweler; jewel box.
juanete m. bunion.
jubilación f. retirement from a position or office; pension.
jubilar v. to pension, to retire, to superannuate; **—se** to be pensioned or retired; to rejoice; Am. to decline; to fall into decline; to play hooky or truant.
jubileo m. jubilee; time of rejoicing.
júbilo m. joy, glee, merriment, festivity.
jubiloso adj. jubilant, joyful.
jubón m. jacket; bodice, doublet.
judía f. bean; string bean; jewess; **—s tiernas** (or **verdes**) string-beans.
judicial adj. judicial; juridical.
judicialmente adv. judicially.
judío adj. Jewish; m. Jew.
juego m. play, amusement, sport, game, gambling; pack of cards; set; manner of acting of an engine; a number of things suited to each other; **— de palabras** pun, quibble; **— de té** tea set; **hacer —** to match; **poner en —** to coordinate; to set in motion.
juerga f. spree, revelry, wild festivity; **irse de —** to go out on a spree.
juerguista m. & f. merrymaker.
jueves m. Thursday.
juez m. judge; juror, member of a jury; **— arbitrador** (or **árbitro**) arbitrator, umpire; **— de primera instancia** judge of the primary court of claims.
jugada f. play, move; stroke, trick; **me ha hecho una mala —** he has played me a bad turn or trick.
jugador m. player; gambler; **— de manos** juggler.

jugar v. irr. to play, to sport, to frolic, to trifle, to gamble; **— a la pelota** to play ball; **— a dos cartas** Am. to be double-faced.
jugarreta f. bad play, wrong play; tricky deal; Am. noisy game.
jugo m. juice; sap.
jugosidad f. juiciness.
jugoso adj. juicy.
juguete m. plaything, toy; jest, joke; **— cómico** skit; **por** (or **de**) **—** jockingly.
juguetear v. to play around, to trifle, to frolic, to dally.
juguetón adj. playful.
juicio m. judgment; sense, soundness of faculties; trial; **perder el —** to lose one's mind; to go crazy; **sano de —** sound of mind.
juicioso adj. judicious; sensible.
julio m. July.
jumento m. ass, donkey.
junco m. rush, reed, junk.
jungla f. jungle.
junio m. June.
junquillo m. jonquille, jonquil; bamboo.
junta f. meeting, conference, board.
juntar v. to join, to connect, to unite; to convoke, to couple; **—se** to assemble, to gather, to associate with.
junto adj. joined, united; **—s** together; adv. near; **— a** near to; **en —** all together, in a lump, wholesale.
juntura f. juncture, junction, joint.
jurado m. jury, juror, juryman.
juramentar v. to swear in; **—se** to take an oath, to be sworn in.
juramento m. oath, vow, curse.
jurar v. to swear, vow; to take oath.
jurisconsulto m. jurist, counsellor, lawyer; expert in law.
jurisdicción f. jurisdiction.
jurisprudencia f. jurisprudence, law.
juro: de — adv. certainly, of course.
justa f. joust, tournament; contest.
justicia f. justice; court of justice; judge; police.
justiciero adj. strictly just, austere (in matters of justice).
justificación f. justification.
justificante adj. justifying; m. voucher; written excuse; proof.
justificar v. to justify; to vindicate, to clear of blame.
justo adj. just; pious; exact, correct, tight; adv. duly; exactly;

juvenil adj. juvenile, young, youthful.
juventud f. youth; young people.
juzgado m. court, tribunal.
juzgar v. to judge.

K

kerosena f. coal oil, kerosene.
kilo m. kilo, kilogram.
kilogramo m. kilogram.
kilometraje m. number of kilometers.
kilómetro m. kilometer.

L

la def. art. f. the; — de the one with; obj. pron. her, it; — que rel. pron. she who, the one that; which.
laberinto m. labryrinth, maze; labyrinth, internal ear.
labia f. sweet, winning eloquence; fluency, talkativeness; **tener mucha —** to be a good talker.
labio m. lip.
labor f. labor, task, work, embroidery; needlework; tillage; cultivation; **— de punto** knitting.
laborable adj. workable; tillable; **día —** work day.
laboral adj. pertaining to labor.
laboratorio m. laboratory.
laboriosidad f. laboriousness, industry.
laborioso adj. laborious; industrious.
labrado p.p. & adj. tilled, cultivated, wrought; carved, manufactured; m. carving; **— en madera** woodwork, carving; **—s cultivated lands.**
labriego m. peasant.
laca f. lacquer, shellac.
lacayo m. lackey, footman, flunky.
lacio adj. withered; languid; limp; straight (hair).
lacra f. mark left by some wound or disorder; fault, vice, wickedness; blemish, defect; Am. sore, ulcer, scab, scar.
lacre m. red sealing wax; adj. Am. red.
lactar v. to nurse, to suckle; to feed with milk.
lácteo adj. lacteous, milky, lacteal; **fiebre láctea** milk fever; **régimen — milk** diet; **Vía Láctea** Milky Way.
ladear v. to tilt, to incline, to tip; to go along the slope or side of; to turn aside (from a way or course); **—se** to tilt, sway; to incline or lean (towards), to move to one side; Am. to fall in love.
ladeo m. inclination, tilt.
ladera f. slope.
ladino adj. crafty, sly, shrewd; conversant with two or three languages; m. Am. Spanish-speaking person (as opposed to one who speaks an Indian language); mestizo, half-breed; talker; talkative person.
lado m. side, flank; **al —** near, at hand, at one side; **de —** tilted, obliquely, sideways; **— a —** side by side; **¡a un —!** gang way! **hacerse a un —** to move over, to step aside, to move to one side; **echérsela de —** Am. to boast.
ladrar v. to bark.
ladrido m. bark, barking.
ladrillo m. brick.
ladrón m. thief, robber, highwayman.
ladronzuelo m. petty thief.
lagartija f. small lizard.
lagarto m. lizard; rascal, sly fellow.
lago m. lake.
lágrima f. tear; **llorar a — viva** to weep abundantly.
lagrimear v. to weep, to shed tears.
laguna f. lagoon; gap, marsh, blank space.
laico adj. lay; m. layman.
laja f. slag, flat stone.
lamedero m. saltlick.
lamentable adj. lamentable, pitiful.
lamentación f. lamentation.
lamentar v. to lament, to deplore; to mourn; **—se** to moan, to complain, to wail.
lamento m. lament, moan, cry, lamentation.
lamer v. to lick; to lap.
lamida f. Am. lick.
lámina f. plate; sheet; engraving, book illustration.
lámpara f. lamp.
lampiño adj. hairless; beardless.
lana f. wool; Am. tramp, vagabond; money.
lanar adj. wool-bearing; of wool.
lance m. occurrence, event; cast; throw, move, turn; accident, quarrel, predicament.
lancear v. to lance, to spear.
lancha f. launch, boat; slab.
lanchón m. barge.

langosta f. lobster; locust.
languidecer v. irr. to languish.
languidez f. languor, faintness, weakness.
lánguido adj. languid.
lanudo adj. wooly; Am. coarse, crude, ill-bred, fleecy; dull, slow, weak-willed.
lanza f. spear, lance; Am. swindle; cheat.
lanzada f. thrust with a spear.
lanzadera f. shuttle.
lanzar v. to fling, to throw, to eject, to launch; —se to rush, fling oneself; to dart out.
lanzazo m. thrust with a lance.
lapicero m. pencil holder.
lápida f. slab, tombstone.
lapidar v. to stone, to cast stones; Am. to cut precious stones.
lápiz f. pencil; crayon; — **para los labios** lipstick.
lapso m. lapse.
lardo m. lard.
largar v. to loosen; to let go; to set free; to unfold (a flag or sail); Am. to hurl, to throw; to strike (a blow); to give, hand over; —se to go away, slip away; to leave.
largo adj. long; generous; m. length; largo (music); **a la larga** in the long run, slowly; **a lo —** along; lengthwise; **¡— de aquí!** get out of here!
largor m. length.
largucho adj. lanky.
largueza f. generosity, liberality; length.
larguísimo adj. the longest, very long.
largura m. length.
laringe f. larynx.
larva f. larva.
las def. art. f. pl. the; obj. pron. them; — **que** rel pron. those which, which.
lascivia f. lewdness.
lascivo adj. lascivious, lewd.
lástima f. pity; compassion, grief, condolence.
lastimadura f. sore, hurt.
lastimar v. to hurt; to offend; —se to get hurt; —se de to feel pity for.
lastimero adj. pitiful; mournful; doleful, sad.
lastimoso adj. pitiful.
lastre m. ballast, weight.
lata f. tin plate; tin can, can, thin board; small log; boring speech; annoyance, embarrassment; Am. gaucho saber; prop.

latente adj. latent.
lateral adj. lateral, side.
latido m. palpitation, throb, beat; bark; howl, pant.
latifundio m. large landed state.
latigazo m. lash, stroke with a whip; crack of a whip; harsh reprimand; unexpected blow or offense; **dar —s** to lash.
látigo m. whip; Am. whipping, beating; end or goal of a horse race; thong of a whip.
latín m. Latin language.
latino adj. Latin; m. Latinist, Latin scholar; Latin; a native of Latium.
latir v. to throb, to beat, to palpitate; to bark; to flutter; to yelp.
latitud f. latitude; extent, breadth, width.
latón m. brass, latten; — **en hojas** latten brass.
latrocinio m. larceny, theft, robbery.
laúd m. lute; catboat.
laudable adj. laudable, praiseworthy.
laurel m. laurel; laurel wreath; honor.
lauro m. laurel, glory, fame, honor, triumph.
lava f. lava; washing of minerals.
lavable adj. washable.
lavabo m. washroom, lavatory, washstand, washbowl.
lavadero m. washing place; washing machine.
lavado m. wash, washing; laundry, laundry work.
lavador m. washer; cleaner; adj. washing, cleaning.
lavadora f. washer, washing, washing machine.
lavadura f. washing; slops, dirty water.
lavamanos m. lavatory, washbowl; washstand.
lavandera f. laundress, washerwoman.
lavandería f. laundry.
lavar v. to wash, to launder; to whitewash.
lavativa f. enema; clyster, clyster pipe; syringe.
lavatorio m. washing, lavation; washbowl, washstand; ceremony of washing the feet on Holy Thursday; Am. washroom.
lavazas f. pl. slops, dirty water; foul water.
lazada f. bow, bowknot; Am. throwing of the lasso, lassoing.

lazar v. to rope, to lasso; to noose; Am. to catch with a lasso.
lazarillo m. blind's man guide.
lazo m. bow, knot; slipknot; lasso, lariat, tie, bond; snare, trick; trap.
le obj. pron. him, you (formal); to him; to her; to you (formal).
leal adj. loyal.
lealtad f. loyalty.
lebrel m. greyhound.
lebrillo m. earthenware basin or tub.
lección f. lesson; reading; **dar la —** to recite the lesson; **dar — to** teach; **tomarle a uno la — to** have someone recite his lesson.
lector m. reader; lecturer, teacher, professor.
lectura f. reading; lecture; a discourse delivered in public examination; **libro de —** reader.
lechada f. whitewash; Am. milking; lime slaked in water; mortar made in slaked lime.
leche f. milk; **cochinillo de —** sucking pig; **vaca de —** milk cow; **hermano de —** foster brother; **— de los viejos** old wine; Am. luck (in game).
lechera f. milkmaid; milk can; milk pitcher; dairy maid.
lechería f. dairy, creamery.
lechero adj. milk, milch, giving milk (applied to animals); cow house, lactary; Am. lucky (in games of chance); m. milkman.
lecho m. bed; river bed; a couch; litter; layer.
lechón m. suckling pig; a dirty fellow.
lechosa f. papaya.
lechoso adj. milky; m. papaya tree.
lechuga f. lettuce.
lechuza f. screech owl, barn owl; owl.
leer v. to read, to lecture, to instruct.
legación f. legation.
legado m. legacy, legate; representative; deputy, ambassador.
legal adj. legal, lawful, constitutional; loyal, true, truthful; reliable; Am. excellent, best; just, honest.
legalizar v. to legalize; to authorize.
legar v. to will, to bequeath; to depute.
legendario adj. legendary; legend, chronicle of the lives of saints.
legión f. legion.
legislación f. legislation.
legislador m. legislator, lawmaker; adj. legislating, legislative.
legislar v. to legislate.
legislativo adj. legislative, lawmaking.
legislatura f. legislature, legislative assembly.
legítimo adj. legitimate; true, certain; legal; lawful; authentic, real.
lego adj. laical, lay, ignorant; m. layman, laic.
legua f. league (linear measure of length).
leguleyo m. a bad legist, shyster.
legumbre f. pulse, leguminous plants, vegetables, herbs.
leída f. Am. reading. See **lectura**.
adj. having read much; learned.
lejanía f. distance, remoteness; distant place.
lejano adj. distant, remote, far.
lejía f. lye; severe reprehension.
lejos adv. far, far away; far off; **a lo —** in the distance; **a un —** Am. in the distance; **de (or desde) —** from afar; m. view; perspective; distant prospect; background.
lelo adj. silly, stupid, foolish; crazy.
lema m. motto; theme; slogan; argument; lema.
lencería f. dry goods; dry-goods store; linen room or closet; linen trade.
lengua f. tongue, language; idiom; interpreter; speech, discourse; **— de tierra** point, neck of land; **de — en —** from mouth to mouth.
lenguado m. flounder, sole.
lenguaje m. language, speech; style.
lenguaraz adj. talkative, loose-tongued; fluent, voluble; talkative.
lengüeta f. small tongue; languet.
lengüetada f. lick, the act of licking.
lente m. & f. lens; **—s** m. pl. eyeglasses.
lenteja f. lentil; lentil seed.
lentejuela f. spangle.
lento adv. slow, dull, sluggish; tardy.
leña f. firewood; kindling; beating; wood; timber.
leñador m. woodcutter; woodman.
leñera f. woodshed, woodbox.
leño m. log; timber; piece of firewood; the trunk of a tree.
león m. lion.

LEONA **LICENCIAR**

leona f. lioness.
leonera f. lion's den or cage; dive; gambling joint; disorderly room.
leontina f. Am. watch chain.
leopardo m. leopard.
leopoldina f. Am. watch chain.
lerdo adj. dull, heavy, stupid, slow.
les obj. pron. to them; to you (formal).
lesión f. wound, injury.
lesionar v. to injure; to wound; to hurt; to damage.
lesna See lezna.
letargo m. lethargy, stupor, drowsiness.
letra f. letter (alphabet); printing type; hand writing; letter (exact wording or meaning); words of a song; motto, inscription; — **abierta** letter of credit; — **de cambio** bill of exchange; — **mayúscula** capital letter; — **minúscula** small letter; **al pie de la** — literally; —**s** letters; —**s Sagradas** the Holy Scriptures.
letrado adj. learned, erudite, lettered; m. lawyer; advocate, counsellor.
letrero m. notice, poster, sign, legend under an illustration; advertisement.
leva f. levy, draft, weighing anchor, setting sail; **echar** — to draft, to conscript; **echar** —**s** Am. to boast; —**s** tricks, artful devices.
levadura f. leaven, yeast, ferment.
levantamiento m. uprising, revolt, riot, insurrection; elevation; lifting; rising; adjournment (of a meeting).
levantar v. to raise, to lift; to set up; to erect; to rouse; to stir up, to recruit; to heave, to get up; Am. to break land, to plow; — **el campo** to break camp; — **la mesa** to clear the table; — **la sesión** to adjourn the meeting; — **un plano** to survey, to map out.
levante m. East; East wind.
levantisco adj. turbulent, rebellious.
levar v. to weigh; — **el ancla** to weigh anchor, —**se** to weigh anchor, to set sails.
leve adj. light, slight, unimportant.
levita f. frock coat; m. Levite.
léxico m. lexicon, dictionary, vocabulary, glossary, thesaurus.
ley f. law; rule; loyalty; standard, quality; **de buena** — of good quality; **plata de** — sterling silver; —**es** jurisprudence; law; system of laws.
leyenda f. legend; reading; inscription.
lezna f. awl.
liar v. to tie, to bind, to roll up; to fagot; to deceive; —**se** to get tied; to get tangled up.
libelo m. libel.
libélula f. dragon fly.
liberación f. liberation; deliverance.
liberal adj. liberal; generous.
liberalidad f. liberality, generosity.
libertad f. liberty.
libertador m. liberator, deliverer.
libertar v. to liberate, to free, to set free; to exempt, to acquit; to clear from; to preserve; —**se** to get free, to escape.
libertinaje m. license, licentiousness; lack of moral restraint; libertinism.
libertino m. libertine, disolute, impudent.
libra f. pound; — **esterlina** sterling pound.
librador m. drawer (of a bill, draft, etc.); deliverer, liberator; measuring scoop.
libranza f. bill of exchange, draft; warrant.
librar v. to free, to set free; to issue, to draw (a draft); to deliver, to exempt; to dispatch; to commit; to instruct; — **guerra** to wage war; —**se** to save oneself; to escape; —**se de** to get rid of, escape from.
libre adj. free, unmarried; independent; exempt; libertine; loose.
librea f. livery (uniform).
librería f. bookstore.
librero m. bookseller; Am. bookcase; bookshelves.
libreta f. notebook; memorandum book.
libro m. book; — **de caja** cashbook; — **mayor** ledger.
licencia f. license; permission; furlough; leave; looseness; licentiousness; wantonness; degree of licentiate.
licenciado m. licenciate. Am. lawyer.
licenciar v. to license, to give a license or permit; to licenciate, to dismiss; to break out; to disband; to discharge (from the army); to confer the degree of licenciado; —**se** to get the degree of licenciado.

— 148 —

LICENCIATURA — LITERA

licenciatura f. degree of licenciado.
licencioso adj. licentious, lewd, disolute.
lícito adj. lawful; permissible; allowable.
licor f. liquid, liquor, strong drink, spirits.
lid f. fight, contest, conflict, dispute.
líder m. Am. leader.
lidiar v. to fight, to combat; to contend.
liebre f. hare; coward.
lienzo m. cotton or linen cloth; canvas; painting.
liga f. league; alliance; garter; alloy (mixture of metals); birdlime.
ligadura f. binding, tie, bond, ligature.
ligar v. to tie, to bind; to alloy; to league, to coalesce, to confederate; —se to unite, to combine, to form an alliance.
ligereza f. lightness; swiftness; flipancy; frivolity; levity, inconstance, flirtation.
ligero adj. light, slight; thin; nimble; adv. Am. quickly; a la ligera quickly, superficially.
lija f. sandpaper.
lila f. lilac; pinkish-purple.
lima f. file, lime (fruit); finish, polishing.
limar v. to file; to file down; to smooth, to polish.
limeño adj. of or from Lima, Peru.
limitación f. limitation, district.
limitar v. to limit; to restrict; to restrain, to circumscribe; to bound.
límite m. limit, boundary.
limo m. slime.
limón m. lemon; lemon tree.
limonada f. lemonade.
limonero m. lemon tree; lemon dealer, or lemon vendor.
limosna f. alms, charity.
limpiabotas m. bootblack; Am. bootlicker, flatterer.
limpiadientes m. toothpick.
limpiar v. to clean; to wipe; to scour; to cleanse; to purify; to steal; Am. to beat up, to whip, to lash.
límpido adj. limpid, clear.
limpieza f. cleanliness, cleanness, limpidness; purity, honesty.
limpio adj. clean; limpid; neat; pure; poner en — to make a clean copy; — y soplado Am. absolutely broke, wiped out.
linaje m. lineage, family, race; offspring.

linaza f. linseed.
lince m. lynx; sharp-sighted person.
linchar v. to lynch.
linde m. & f. limit, border, boundary.
lindero adj. bordering upon; m. Am. landmark; boundary.
lindeza f. prettiness; exquisiteness; neatness; witty act or remark.
lindo adj. pretty, neat, handsome, fine, genteel; de lo — wonderfully; very much; to the utmost.
línea f. line, limit.
lineal adj. lineal, linear.
lino m. linen; flax.
linón m. lawn; thin linen or cotton.
linterna f. lantern.
lío m. bundle; fib; mess; parcel; pack; confusion; armar un — to raise a rumpus; to cause confusion; hacerse un — to be confused; to get tangled up; meterse en un — to get oneself into a mess.
liquidación f. liquidation; settlement, balance.
liquidar v. to liquidate; to settle (an account).
líquido m. liquid.
lira f. lyre, small harp; a type of metrical composition; lira (Italian coin).
lírico adj. lyric, lyrical; Am. fantastic; m. Am. visionary; dreamer.
lirio m. lily.
lirismo m. lyricism, lyric quality; Am. idle dream, fantasy.
lisiado adj. lame, hurt, injured; crippled.
liso adj. smooth, even, flat; plain, clear, evident; Am. crafty, sly; fresh, impudent.
lisonja f. flattery.
lisonjear v. to flatter; to please; to fawn on.
lisonjero adj. flattering, pleasing; m. flatterer.
lista f. list, catalogue, strip; stripe; pasar — to call the roll, to call over, to muster; to review troops.
listado adj. striped.
listar v. to register, to enter a list; Am. to stripe, to streak, to strip.
listo adj. ready, prompt; clever; Am. mischievous.
listón m. ribbon, tape, strip.
lisura f. smoothness; sincerity; frankness; Am. freshness, impudence; insulting or filthy remark.
litera f. berth; litter.

LITERARIO   **LUCHAR**

literario adj. literary.
literato adj. literary, learned; m. literary man, writer, literate, lettered.
literatura f. literature.
litigio m. litigation, lawsuit.
litoral adj. seaboard, coastal; m. coast, shore.
litro m. liter.
liviandad f. lightness, frivolity; lewdness.
liviano adj. light; slight; unimportant; frivolous; fickle; lewd; unchaste.
lívido adj. livid, pale.
lo obj. pron. him; you (formal); it; so; dem. pron. — **de** that of, that affair of, that matter of; — **bueno** the good, what is good; — **que** that which, what.
loable adj. laudable, worthy of praise.
loar v. to praise.
lobanillo m. growth, tumor.
lobo m. wolf.
lóbrego adj. dark, gloomy.
lobreguez f. darkness, gloominess.
local adj. local; m. place, quarters, site, premises.
localidad f. location, locality; town; place; seat, in a theatre.
localización f. localization, localizing.
localizar v. to localize.
loco adj. insane, mad, crazy; — **de remate** stark mad; m. lunatic, insane person.
locomotor adj. locomotive.
locomotora f. locomotive.
locuaz adj. loquacious, talkative.
locución f. phrase, diction.
locura f. madness, insanity.
locutor m. radio announcer, speaker.
lodazal m. muddy place, mire.
lodo m. mud.
lodoso adj. muddy, miry.
logia f. lodge.
lógica f. logic, reasoning.
lógico adj. logical; reasonable.
lograr v. to gain, to obtain, to accomplish; — (and inf) to succeed in; —**se** to succeed; to turn out well.
logrero m. usurer; profiteer.
logro m. profit, gain; usury; attainment; realization.
loma f. small hill.
lombriz f. earthworm.
lomerío m. Am. group of hills.
lomo m. back (of an animal, book, knife, etc); loin; ridge between two furrows; **hacer** — Am.

to, bear with patience; to resign oneself.
lona f. canvas.
lonche m. Am. lunch.
lonchería f. Am. lunchroom.
longaniza f. pork sausage.
longevidad f. longevity, long life; span of life, length of life.
longitud f. longitude, length.
longitudinal adj. longitudinal; lengthwise; —**mente** longitudinally, lengthwise.
lonja f. exchange; market; slice of meat; leather strap; Am. raw hide.
lontananza f. background; **en** — in the distance, in the background.
loro m. parrot.
los def. art. m. pl. the; obj. pron. them; — **que** those which; which.
losa f. flagstone; slab; gravestone.
lote m. lot, share, part; fortune, chance; Am. remnant lot; swallow of liquor; blockhead, dunce.
lotear v. Am. to subdivide into lots; to divide into portions.
lotería f. lottery; raffle.
loza f. fine earthenware; crockery; — **fina** chinaware.
lozanía f. luxuriance; vigor; elegance.
lozano adj. luxuriant; exuberant, vigorous, lusty; elegant.
lubricar v. to lubricate, to oil, to grease.
lucero m. morning star; any bright star; star on the forehead of certain animals; splendor, brightness.
lúcido adj. lucid, clear, shining, bright.
luciente adj. shining, bright.
luciérnaga f. firefly, glowworm.
lucimiento m. splendor; brilliance; lucidity, brightness; lustre; success.
lucir v. irr. to shine, to excel; to glitter, to glow; to illuminate, to enlighten; to outshine, to exceed; —**se** to shine, to be brilliant; to show off; to be successful.
lucrativo adj. lucrative, profitable.
lucro m. profit, gain, lucre.
luctuoso adj. sad, mournful, dismal.
lucha f. fight, struggle, dispute; wrestling match, strife.
luchador m. fighter, wrestler.
luchar v. to fight, to wrestle, to struggle; to contend, to discuss, to debate.

luego adv. soon, presently; afterwards, then, next; **desde —** immediately, at once; naturally; **— de** after; **— que** as soon as; **hasta —** good-bye, so long; **— —** right away.

luengo adj. long; **—s años** many years.

lugar m. place, spot, situation, position, site, town, space, time, occasion, opportunity; cause, motive, reason; **— común** privy, water closet; **en — de** intead of; **dar — a** to give cause or occasion for; **hacer (or dar) —** to make room.

lúgubre adj. mournful, gloomy.

lujo m. luxury, extravagance, excess or profuseness in pomp, dresses, fare, etc.

lujoso adj. luxurious; elegant; showy.

lujuria f. lust, lewdness, sensuality.

lujurioso adj. lustful, lewd, sensual.

lumbre f. fire, brightness, splendor.

luminoso adj. luminous, lucid, bright, shining.

luna f. moon; mirror, glass for mirrors.

lunar adj. lunar; m. mole; blemish, spot; stain.

lunático adj. & m. lunatic.

lunes m. Monday; **hacer San Lunes** Am. to lay off on Monday.

lustre m. luster, shine, glory.

lustroso adj. lustrous, glossy, shining.

luto m. mourning; sorrow, grief, condolement.

luz f. light, clearness, clarity; hint, guidance; **dar a —** to give birth; to publish; **entre dos luces** at twilight; **luces** notice, information.

LL

llaga f. wound; ulcer, sore.

llama f. flame; fire; llama (South American beast of burden).

llamada f. call; beckon, sign; knock; marginal note; reference mark (as an asterisk).

llamador m. knocker (of a door); caller.

llamamiento m. call, calling; calling together; appeal; convocation.

llamar v. to call; to summon, to cite; to name, to invoke: to denominate; **— a la puerta** to knock at the door; **—se** to be called, named; **—se a rajado** to break one's word or promise.

llamarada f. flash; sudden flame or blaze of fire; sudden blush, flush.

llamativo adj. showy, loud, gaudy, flashy; thirst-exciting.

llameante adj. flaming.

llana f. mason's trowel.

llanero m. Am. plainsman.

llaneza f. simplicity; frankness; sincerity, plainnes.

llano adj. plain, simple, even, level, smooth, flat, frank; m. plain, flat ground.

llanta f. tire; tire casing; rim of a wheel; Am. large sunshade used in Peruvian markets.

llanto m. crying, weeping; tears; **anegarse en —** to burst into a flow of tears.

llanura f. extensive plain, prairie; evenness; flatness.

llave f. key; faucet; clef; winch of a stocking-frame; **— de tuercas** wrench; **— inglesa** monkey wrench; **— maestra** master key; **ama de —s** housekeeper.

llavera f. Am. housekeeper.

llavín m. small key.

llegada f. arrival.

llegar v. to arrive; to reach, to fetch; to amount to; **— a ser** to get or come to be; **— a las manos** to come to blows; **—se** to approach, to get near.

llenar v. to fill, to stuff; to satisfy, to content; **—se de** to fill up; to overeat; **—se de** to get filled with; to get covered with.

lleno adj. full; m. fullness, completeness; **de —** totally, completely; **un — completo** a full house (said of a theatre).

llenura f. fullness; abundance.

llevadero adj. bearable, tolerable.

llevar v. to carry, to convey, to transport; to bear, to wear, to have about one; to take to, to have with one; to keep accounts, to charge a certain price; **— un año a** to be one year older than; **— un mes aquí** to have been here one month; **— un castigo** to suffer a punishment; **—se to** carry away; **—se bien con** to get along with.

llorar v. to cry, to weep, to lament.

lloriquear v. to whimper, to whine, to weep.

lloriqueo m. whimper, whining.
lloro m. weeping, cry; tears.
llorón adj. weeping; sauce — weep-whiner.
llorona f. weeping woman; —s Am. large spurs.
ing willow; m. weeper, crybaby;
lloroso adj. tearful, weeping.
llovedizo adj. rain (used as adj.); agua llovediza rain water.
llover v. irr. to rain, to shower.
llovizna f. drizzle, sprinkle.
lluvia f. rain; shower.
lluvioso adj. rainy.

M

macana f. Am. club, cudgel, stick; lie, absurdity, nonsense.
macarrón m. macaroon; —es macaroni.
maceta f. flowerpot; small mallet; stonecutter's hammer; handle of tools; Am. head; adj. Am. slow.
macilento adj. lean, thin, extenuated, emaciated, decayed, pale.
macizo adj. solid, firm, massive; m. masiveness; firmness; m. thicket; clump.
machacar v. to pound, to crush; to insist, to harp on.
machacón adj. persistent; tenacious, monotonous.
machetazo m. large machete; blow with a machete.
machete m. machete; large, heavy knife.
macho m. male; he-mule; hook (of a hook and eye); abutment; pillar; stupid fellow; pararle a uno el — Am. to halt or repress a person; adj. masculine, strong, vigorous, robust, male; Am. he-man.
machucar v. to pound, to beat; to bruise; Am. to cruise; to break (a horse).
machucón m. smash, bruise.
madeja f. skein; mass of hair; limp, listless person.
madera f. wood; timber; lumber.
maderaje m. timber, lumber; timber work; woodwork.
maderamen m. timber; timberwork; woodwork.
maderero m. lumberman, lumber dealer.
madero m. beam; plank; timber, piece of lumber; blockhead, dunce.
madrastra f. stepmother.
madre f. mother; basis, foundation, origin; womb; root; river bed; sewer, sink; **salirse de** — to overflow (said of a river).
madrepeña f. Am. moss.
madreperla f. mother-of-pearl.
madreselva f. honeysuckle.
madriguera f. burrow; den; lurking place, lair.
madrileño adj. Madrilenian, from or pertaining to Madrid; m. Madrilenian.
madrina f. godmother; bridesmaid; sponsor; prop; strap for yoking two horses; leading mare; stanchion; Am. small herd of tame cattle (used for leading wild cattle).
madrugada f. dawn; early morning; **de** — at daybreak.
madrugador m. early riser.
madrugar v. to rise early; to be ahead of others.
madurar v. to mature, to ripen, to mellow.
madurez f. maturity; ripeness; mellowness.
maduro adj. mature, ripe, full-grown, prudent; Am. bruised, sore.
maestría f. mastery; mastership; great skill.
maestro m. master, teacher; chief craftsman; adj. master, masterly, skilful; llave maestra master key; obra maestra masterpiece.
magia f. magic, charm; enchantment.
mágico adj. magic; m. magician.
magín m. imagination, fancy; mind.
magisterio m. mastery, mastership; teaching profession.
magistrado m. magistrate, judge.
magistral adj. masterly; masterful; authoritative.
magnánimo adj. magnanimous, noble, generous.
magnético adj. magnetic; attractive.
magnificencia f. magnificence, splendor.
magnífico adj. magnificent, splendid.
magnitud f. magnitude, greatness; grandeur.
mago m. magician, wizard; los tres Reyes Magos the Three Wise Men.
magra f. slice of ham.
magro adj. lean.
maguey m. maguey, century plant.
magullar v. to bruise; to maul; to mangle; Am. to crumple.

mahometano adj & m. Mahomedan.
maíz m. corn, maize.
maizal m. cornfield.
maja f. belle.
majada f. sheepfold; dung; manure; Am. flock of sheep or goats.
majadería f. foolishness, nonsense.
majadero adj. foolish, bothersome; silly.
majar v. to pound; to crush; to bruise; to crumple; to mash; to annoy, bother.
majestad f. majesty, dignity.
majestuoso adj. majestic, stately.
majo adj. gaudy, gallant, gay, spruce; showy, gaily attired; pretty; m. dandy; boaster; bragger.
mal m. evil; illness; harm; wrong. See malo.
malabarista m. & f. juggler; Am. sly thief.
malacate m. hoist, hoisting machine; winch; Am. spindle (for cotton); parecer uno un — Am. to be constantly on the go, to be in constant motion.
malandanza f. misfortune.
malaventura f. misfortune, disaster.
malazo adj. perverse, evil, wicked, vicious.
malbaratar v. to undersell, to sell at a loss; to squander.
malcontento adj. discontented; m. malcontent, troublemaker.
malcriado adj. ill-bred, rude.
maldad f. badness, evil, wickedness.
maldecir v. irr. to curse, to accurse, to damn, to execrate; to detract.
maldición f. curse; malediction, execration, imprecation.
maldispuesto adj. unwilling, not inclined.
maldito p.p. & adj. cursed; perverse, damned, wicked; Am. tricky; bold, boastful.
maleante m. crook, rogue, rascal, villain.
malecón m. mole, dike.
maledicencia f. slander, calumny, obloquy.
maleficio m. spell, charm, witchery, enchantment.
maléfico adj. evil, harmful, mischievous, malicious.
malestar m. indisposition; slight illness, discomfort, uncomfortableness.

maleta f. travelling bag, suitcase; Am. bundle of clothes; hump (on the back); saddlebag; rogue, rascal; lazy fellow.
maletín m. small valise, satchel.
malevo adj. Am. bad, wicked.
malévolo adj. bad, evil, wicked; malevolent.
maleza f. underbrush, thicket; weeds.
malgastar v. to squander, to waste; to misspend.
malhechor m. malefactor, misdoer, evildoer, criminal.
malhora f. Am. trouble, misfortune.
malhumorado adj. ill-humored; peevish.
malicia f. malice, perversity; wickedness; shrewdness; suspicion; apprehension; Am. bit of brandy or cognac added to another drink.
maliciar v. to suspect.
malicioso adj. malicious; wicked; shrewd; suspicious.
maligno adj. malign, malignant, pernicious, harmful.
malmandado adj. disobedient, stubborn.
mal(o) adj. bad, evil, wicked; ill; difficult; Am. a la mala treacherously; de malas Am. by force; estar de malas to be out of luck; por la mala unwillingly, by force; venir de malas to come with evil intentions; estar — to be ill, to be sick.
malograr v. to waste, to lose; — el tiempo to misspend life; —se to turn out badly; to fail; to be disappointed.
malón m. mean trick; Am. surprise, Indian raid; tin-pan serenade, boisterous surprise party.
malpagar v. to underpay, to pay poorly.
malparto m. miscarriage, abortion.
malquerencia f. aversion, dislike, ill will, hatred.
malsano adj. unhealthy; sickly; unwholesome.
malta f. malt.
maltratar v. to treat badly; to misuse, to abuse; to maltreat, to spoil.
maltrato m. mistreatment, abuse, ill treatment.
maltrecho adj. battered, bruised, injured.
malvado adj. wicked, malicious, insolent.
malversación f. graft, corruption,

misuse of public funds, embezzlement.

malversar v. to misuse (funds in one's trust); to embezzle.

malla f. mesh; coat of mail; Am. species of potato; **hacer —** to knit.

mamá f. mamma.

mamada f. suck, sucking; Am. ill action.

mamar v. to suckle; to suck; to gorge; **—se** Am. to get drunk; to go back in one's promise; to fold up, to crack up; **—se a uno** Am. to get the best of someone, to deceive someone; to kill someone.

mamífero m. mammal; adj. mammalian, of mammals.

mamón adj. suckling (very young animal or child); shoot, sucker (of a tree); Am. cherimoya (tree and fruit); papaya (tree and fruit); kind of cake.

mampara f. screen.

mampostería f. masonry, stone masonry.

manada f. herd; flock; pack; drove of cattle; handful of corn.

manantial m. spring, source, origin, heap.

manar v. to spring; to flow (from); to bound.

manaza f. large hand.

manazo m. Am. slap. See manotazo.

mancarrón m. one-armed or one-handed man; cripple; old nag; Am. crude, clumsy fellow; disabled workman; dike, small dam.

mancebo m. young, young man; bachelor.

mancera f. handle of a plough.

mancilla f. stain, spot, blemish; dishonor.

manco adj. one-armed; one-handed; maimed; defective, imperfect; m. Am. nag.

mancha f. spot, stain, blemish; blot, macula; Am. roving herd of cattle.

manchar v. to stain, to corrupt; to daub; to darken; to cloud; to soil; to spot; to tarnish.

manchego adj. of or pertaining to La Mancha (region of Spain); m. inhabitant of La Mancha.

manchón m. large stain or spot; spot where grain grows rank or thick.

mandadero m. messenger, errand boy.

mandado m. command, order, errand; **bien —** well-behaved; **mal —** ill-behaved.

mandamiento m. command, order, mandate, precept, writ, commandment.

mandar v. to command, order; to ordain; to send; to bequeath, will; to rule, govern; Am. to throw, hurl; **— hacer** to have made, to order; **— una bofetada** to give a slap; **— una pedrada** Am. to throw a stone; **—se** Am. to be impudent; **—se mudar** to go away.

mandatario m. attorney, representative; Am. magistrate, chief, governor.

mandato m. mandate, order, precept, command.

mandíbula f. jaw, jawbone.

mando m. command, authority, power.

mandón adj. bossy, domineering, imperious; m. bossy person; Am. boss or foreman of a mine; race starter.

maneador m. Am. hobble, leather lasso for the legs of an animal; whip; halter.

manear v. to hobble; to lasso; to tie the legs of an animal; to chain; to fasten with fetters or shackles; **—se** Am. to get tangled up.

manecilla f. small hand, hand of a clock or watch.

manejable adj. manageable.

manejar v. to manage; to handle; to drive; to wield; to conduct; to govern; **—se** to move about, get around; Am. to behave oneself.

manejo m. handling, management, conduct; horsemanship; trick, intrigue.

manera f. manner, form, way, figure, method, mode, kind, guise; **—s** customs, manners, behavior; **a — de (o a la — de)** like, in the style of; **de — que** so that; **sobre—** exceedingly; extremely.

manga f. sleeve; bag; hose for watering; body of troops; fishing net; Am. multitude, herd, swarm; cattle shute; corral; **— de agua** waterspout, whirlwind over the ocean; **— de hule** Am. raincape; **por angas o por —s** by hook or crook, in one way or another.

mangana f. lariat, lasso.

manganeso m. manganese.

mango m. handle; Am. mango (tropical tree and its fruit).
manguera f. hose (for water); waterspout; Am. large corral (for livestock).
manguito m. muff; knitted half-sleeve (worn in the forearm); oversleeve.
maní m. Am. peanut.
manía f. mania, frenzy; craze; whim.
maniatar v. to tie the hands; to handcuff; to hobble (an animal).
maniático m. crank, queer fellow; adj. cranky, queer, odd.
manicero m. Am. peanut vendor.
manicomio m. insane asylum.
manicura f. manicure, manicurist.
manicurar v. to manicure.
manido adj. rotting; Am. trite, commonplace.
manifestación f. manifestation, demonstration.
manifestar v. irr. to manifest, to show.
manifiesto adj. manifest, clear, plain, open, obvious; m. manifesto; public declaration; customhouse manifest.
manigua f. Cuban jungle or thicket; **coger** — Am. to get feverish; **irse a la** — Am. to rise up in rebellion.
manija f. handle; crank; fetter.
manilla f. small hand; bracelet; **—s de hierro** handcuffs.
maniobra f. maneuver, operation.
maniobrar v. to maneuver.
manipulación f. manipulation.
manipular v. to manipulate; to handle.
maniquí m. manikin, model dummy; figure of a person; puppet.
manivela f. crank.
manjar m. dish, food; choice bit of food.
mano f. hand; forefoot; pestle; hand of a clock or watch; first hand at play; coat of paint or varnish; quire; Am. adventure, mishap; handful; **— de obra** workmanship; labor; **a —** at hand; by hand; **estamos a —** Am. we are even, we are quits; **doblar las —s** Am. to give up; **ser —** (or **ser la —**) to be first (in a game); to lead (in a game); **venir a las —s** to come to blows.
manojo m. handful; bunch.
manopla f. gauntlet; heavy glove; coachman's whip; huge hand.
manosear v. to handle, to touch,
to feel with the hand; Am. to fondle, to pet, to caress.
manotada f. slap, blow, sweep of the hand; Am. handful, fistful.
manotazo m. slap.
manotear v. to gesticulate, to move the hands from emotion; to strike with the hands; Am. to embezzle, to steal; to snatch away (what is given).
mansalva : a — without danger; treacherously; **matar a —** to kill without warning or without danger.
mansedumbre f. mildness, meekness, manageableness; gentleness.
mansión f. sojourn; stay; abode; dwelling, residence, habitation.
manso adj. meek; mild, gentle, tame, tractable, soft, quiet; Am. cultivated (plant); civilized (Indian); m. leading sheep, goat or ox.
manta f. a woolen mantle; tapestry; large shawl; Am. coarse cotton cloth; poncho; **— mojada** Am. dull person, dunce; **darle a uno una —** to toss someone in a blanket.
mantear v. to toss someone in a blanket.
manteca f. fat, lard, butter; **— de cacao** Am. cocoa butter; **— de coco** coconut oil.
mantecado m. ice cream; buttercake.
mantel m. tablecloth; altar cloth; **levantar los —es** to clear the table; **estar de —es largos** to dine in style.
mantener v. irr. to maintain, support; to nourish, keep, feed; to continue; to keep up; to sustain; to defend; **—se firme** to remain firm; **—se quieto** to stay or keep quiet.
mantenimiento m. maintenance, subsistence, livelihood, living, ration, sustenance.
mantequilla f. butter.
mantequillería f. Am. creamery, dairy (for making butter).
mantilla f. mantilla; saddlecloth.
manto m. silken veil for ladies; mantle, cloak, robe; cape; large mantilla; mantel, mantelpiece; cover.
mantón m. large shawl; **— de Manila** embroidered silk shawl.
manuable adj. handy, easy to handle.
manual adj. manual; handy; m. manual, handbook.

manubrio m. crank, handle.
manufacturar v. to manufacture.
manufacturero adj. manufacturing; m. manufacturer.
manuscrito adj. manuscript.
manutención f. maintenance; support, conservation.
manzana f. apple; block of houses; Am. Adam's apple.
manzano m. apple tree.
maña f. skill, knack; cunning; **malas —s** bad tricks or habits.
mañana f. morning; **media —** Am. mid-morning snack; adv. tomorrow, in the near future; **pasado —** day after tomorrow; **muy de —** very early in the morning; m. morrow.
mañanero m. early riser; adj. early rising.
mañanista m. & f. Am. procrastinator, one who puts things off untill tomorrow.
mañero adj. astute, dexterous, skilful, artful; clever; sly; tricky; Am. slow, lazy; greedy, gluttonous (child).
mapa m. map, chart.
mapache m. Am. raccoon.
mapurite m. Am. skunk. See zorrillo.
máquina f. machine, engine; **— de coser** sewing machine; **— de escribir** typewriter.
maquinación f. machination, contrivance, scheming, plotting; plot, scheme.
maquinador m. schemer, plotter.
maquinal adj. mechanical, automatic; **—mente** adv. mechanically, automatically, in a mechanical manner.
maquinar v. to plot, to scheme, to plan.
maquinaria f. machinery; mechanism; mechanics.
maquinista m. engineer, locomotive engineer, machinist, mechanician.
mar m. & f. sea; **— alta** rough sea; **pleamar** high tide; **— de fondo** swell; **baja —** low tide; **en alta —** on the high seas or waters; **la — de cosas** a lot of things.
maraña f. tangle; snarl; thicket; maze; plot, intrigue; mess; entanglement.
maravedí m. maravedi (old Spanish coin).
maravilla f. wonder, marvel; marigold; **a las mil —s** wonderfully, perfectly.

maravillar v. to astonish, to dazzle; **—se** to wonder, to marvel.
maravilloso adj. marvelous, wonderful.
marbete m. label, stamp; baggage tag or check.
marca f. mark, make, stamp, sign, brand; gauge, rule; march, frontier province; **— de fábrica** trademark; **de —** of excellent quality.
marcar v. to mark; to brand; to observe, to note; to stamp.
marcial adj. martial, warlike; frank, abrupt.
marco m. frame; mark (German coin); mark (unit of weight).
marcha f. march, course, progress, speed; gait; running, functioning; **sobre la —** on the spot.
marchamo m. customhouse mark; Am. tax on each slaughtered animal.
marchante m. merchant, dealer, customer, regular client.
marchar v. to march; to go, to go away, to go off; to depart; to walk; to parade; to run (machinery); **—se** to go away.
marchitar v. to wither; **—se** to wither, to fade; to shrivel up.
marchito adj. withered; faded; shriveled up.
marea f. tide; Am. sea fog.
mareado adj. seasick; dizzy.
marear v. to navigate, to sail; to annoy, to upset a person; **—se** to get seasick, nauseated.
mareo m. seasickness; nausea, vexation, annoyance.
marfil m. ivory; Am. fine toothed comb.
margarita f. marguerite, daisy; pearl.
margen m. & f. margin, border, edge, fringe; river bank; **dar —a** to give an occasion to.
maricón adj. sissy, effeminate; m. sissy.
marido m. husband.
marina f. seacoast, shore, marine, fleet; navy; seamanship; seascape; **— de guerra** navy; **— mercante** merchant marine.
marinero f. mariner, seaman, sailor.
marino adj. marine; m. mariner, seaman, sailor.
mariposa f. butterfly, moth; Am. blindman's buff (a game).
mariscal m. marshal; blacksmith; **— de campo** field marshal.
marisco m. shellfish.
marítimo adj. maritime, marine.

marmita f. kettle, boiler, tea kettle.
mármol m. marble.
marmóreo adj. marble, of marble, like marble.
maroma f. rope; Am. somersault; acrobatic performance; sudden change of political views; **andar en la —** to walk in the tightrope.
maromero m. Am. acrobat.
marqués m. marquis.
marquesa f. marquise; Am. couch.
marrano adj. m. pig, hog, filthy person.
marrazo m. Am. bayonet, dagger.
marrullero adj. sly, wily.
martes m. Tuesday; **— de carnestolendas** Shrove Tuesday (Tuesday before Lent).
martillar v. to hammer, to pound.
martillo m. hammer.
martinete m. pile driver; drop hammer; hammer of a piano.
mártir m. & f. martyr.
martirio m. martyrdom; torture, torment.
martirizar v. to martyr; to torture; to torment.
marzo m. March.
mas conj. but.
más adj. more; most; adv. more, most; plus; **— bien** rather; **— de** more than, over; **— que** more than; **no — que** only; **a — de** in addition to; **a lo —** at the most; **está de —** it is superfluous, unnecessary; **no — Am.** only; **no quiero — nada** Am. (instead of **no quiero nada**) I don't want anything more.
masa f. mass, volume; crowd; dough; paste, mortar; coral glee club; choral society; **agarrarle a uno con las manos en la —** to catch someone in the act.
masaje m. massage.
mascada f. chewing; Am. mouthful; chew or quid of tobacco; reprimand, scolding; silk handkerchief, scarf.
mascar v. to chew, to masticate, to pronounce with difficulty.
máscara f. mask; **—s** masquerade; m. & f. masquerader.
mascarada f. masquerade.
masculino adj. masculine.
mascullar v. to mumble, to munch; to falter.
masilla f. putty.
masón m. mason, freemason.
masonería f. masonry, freemasonry.
masticar v. to chew, to masticate.

mástil m. upright post of a bed or loom; mast, post.
mastín m. mastiff.
mastuerzo m. nasturtium; simpleton, fool; **dar — a alguien** Am. to kill someone.
mata f. shrub, plant, bush; spring, blade; lock of matted hair; Am. thicket, jungle.
matadero m. slaughterhouse; hard work.
matador m. killer, murderer; bullfighter who kills the bull.
matanza f. massacre, butchery; slaughter; Am. slaughterhouse.
matar v. to kill, to murder; to put to death, to execute; to put out a light; to worry, to vex, to molest; **—se** to commit suicide; to overwork; **—se con alguien** to fight with somebody.
matasanos m. quack, quack doctor; charlatan, empiric.
mate m. mate or checkmate in chess; Am. Paraguayan tea (used also in Argentina and Uruguay); teapot (for mate); any small pot; bald head; adj. unpolished, dull surface; **dar —** to scoff at anyone.
matear v. to plant seeds or shoots; to hunt among the bushes; Am. to drink mate; to checkmate, to make the winning move in chess.
matemáticas f. pl. mathematics.
matemático adj. mathematical; m. mathematician.
materia f. matter; ingredient; material; equipment; **— prima** raw material; subject, cause; purulent running; **de —** Am. made of adobe.
material adj. material, rude, uncouth; coarse; m. ingredient.
maternal adj. maternal.
maternidad f. maternity, motherhood.
materno adj. maternal, motherly.
matinal adj. morning, of the morning; matutinal.
matiné m. Am. matinée.
matiz m. tint, shade, color, hue; shading.
matizar v. to blend (colors); to tint; to shade; to tone down; to beautify.
matón m. bully.
matorral m. thicket.
matoso adj. bushy; weedy, full of weeds.
matrero adj. astute, shrewd, sly,

cunning; m. Am. tickster, swindler; bandit, outlaw, cattle thief.
matrícula f. register, list; matriculation, registration; certificate of registration.
matricular v. to matriculate, to enroll, to register.
matrimonio m. matrimony, marriage; married couple.
matriz f. matrix, mold, form; womb; matrice, screw nut; female screw; adj. main, principal, first, chief.
matungo m. Am. nag; old, worn-out horse.
matutino adj. morning, of the morning.
maullar v. to mew.
maullido m. mew.
máxima f. maxim, rule, proverb, sentence.
máxime adv. principally, especially.
máximo adj. & m. maximum.
maya f. daisy; May queen; m. & f. Maya, Mayan Indian; m. Mayan language.
mayo m. May; maypole; Am. Mayo Indian (form Sonora, Mexico); Mayo language.
mayonesa f. mayonnaise; dish served with mayonnaise.
mayor adj. greater, larger; superior; mayor or chief of a community; main, high (altar, mass); —es elders, ancestors; — de edad of age; por — (or al por —) wholesale.
mayoral m. head shepherd; stagecoach driver; foreman, overseer, boss; leader.
mayorazgo m. primogeniture (right of inheritance by the first-born); first-born son and heir; family state left to the eldest son.
mayordomo m. majordomo, butler, steward; manager of a state; superintendent.
mayorear v. Am. to wholesale, to sell or buy at wholesale.
mayoreo m. Am. wholesale.
mayoría f. majority.
mayorista m. Am. wholesale dealer.
mazmorra f. dungeon.
mazo m. mallet; sledge hammer; bunch, handful.
mazorca f. ear of corn; Am. tyrannical government; cruel torture (imposed by tyrants).
me obj. pron. me; to me; for me; myself.
mecánico adj. mechanical; m. mechanic, machinist, driver, chauffeur.

mecanismo m. mechanism.
mecanografía f. typewriting.
mecanógrafo m. typist.
mecate m. Am. rope, cord.
mecedor m. swing; adj. swinging; rocking.
mecedora f. rocking chair.
mecer v. to swing, to rock, to sway; to shake.
mecha f. wick; lock of hair; match, matchrope; fuse, strip of salt pork or bacon (for larding meat); Am. tip of a whip; scare, fright; fib; jest, joke; trifle, worthless thing.
mechar v. to lard (meat or fowl).
mechero m. lamp burner; gas jet; tube for the wick of a lamp; candlestick holder; pocket lighter; large wick; Am. disheveled hair; jocker, jester.
mechón m. large wick; large lock of hair.
medalla f. medal.
médano m. dune, sand hill, sand bank; Am. sandy marshland.
media f. stocking — corta (or —) sock.
mediación f. mediation.
mediador m. mediator.
mediados : a — de about the middle of.
medianero m. mediator; go-between; adj. mediating; intermediate; pared medianera partition wall.
medianía f. mediocrity, average.
mediano adj. middle-sized, moderate; average; mediocre.
medianoche f. midnight.
mediante adj. intervening; Dios — God willing; prep. by mean of, trough, with the help of.
mediar v. to mediate, to intervene; to intercede; to arrive at, or to be in, the middle.
medible adj. measurable.
medicamento m. medicament, medicine.
medicastro m. quack, quack doctor.
medicina f. medicine.
medicinar v. to doctor, to treat, to prescribe, to medicine, to administer medicines; —se to take medicine.
medición f. measurement; measuring.
médico m. doctor, physician; adj. medical.
medida f. measure, measurement, mensuration; gauge, rule, scale, height, lenght, breadth, time;

— para áridos dry measure; **a — del deseo** according to one's desire; **a — que** as, in proportion as; at the same time as.

medio adj. half, middle; intermediate; medium, average; way; **medianoche** midnight; **hacer una cosa a medias** to do something halfway; **ir a medias** to go halves; adv. half, not completely; middle, means, way; medium, environment; **—s** means, resources; **meterse de por —** to intervene, to meddle in a dispute.

mediocre adj. mediocre.
mediocridad f. mediocrity.
mediodía m. midday, noon, noonday; noontide; meridian; South.
medioeval adj. medieval.
medir v. irr. to measure, to scan (verses); **— las calles** Am. to walk the streets; to be out of a job; **—se** to measure one's words or actions; **—se con otro** to try one's strength or ability against another; to fight with another.
meditación f. meditation.
meditar v. to meditate, to muse; to consider.
medrar v. to flourish, to thrive; to prosper.
medroso adj. timid, faint-hearted; fearful, dreadful.
médula f. marrow; pith; **— oblongada** medulla oblongata.
megáfono m. megaphone, loudspeaker.
mejicano adj. Mexican; the Aztec language; inhabitant of Mexico. Also **mexicano**.
mejilla f. cheek.
mejor adj. better; **el —** the best; adv. better; more perfect, more advantageous; **tanto —** so much the better.
mejora f. betterment; improvement; melioration.
mejoramiento m. improvement.
mejorar v. to better, to improve; **—se** to get better, to recover.
mejoría f. betterment, improvement, superiority.
melado adj. honey-colored; m. sugar cane syrup; honey cake.
melancolía f. melancholy, gloom; gloominess.
melaza f. molasses.
melena f. mane.
melindre m. affectation; affected act or gesture; whim; marzipan.
melindroso adj. affected; too particular; fussy; dainty; prudish.
melocotón m. peach.

melocotonero m. peach tree.
melodía f. melody.
melodioso adj. melodious.
melón m. melon; cantaloupe; muskmelon; melon vine.
melosidad f. sweetness; softness; gentleness.
meloso adj. honeyed; soft, sweet; m. Am. honey-voiced person; over-affectionate person.
mella f. nick, dent; **hacer —** to make a dent or impression; to cause pain, worry or suffering.
mellar v. to notch; to nick; to dent; to impair; to damage.
mellizo adj. & m. twin.
membrete m. heading; letterhead; memorandum.
membrillo m. quince (tree and its fruit).
membrudo adj. sinewy, robust, strong, muscular.
memorable adj. memorable, notable, famous.
memorándum m. memorandum, note; memorandum book, notebook.
memoria f. memory, remembrance; memoir, note, account; memorandum; **de —** by heart; **hacer —** to remember, to recollect; **— de gallo** poor memory; **—s** regards, memoirs.
memorial m. memorandum book; memorial, brief; petition.
mención f. mention.
mendigar v. to ask alms; to beg.
mendigo m. beggar.
mendrugo m. crumb of bread.
menear v. to move; to shake; to stir; to manage; to wriggle; to waddle; **—se** to hustle about; to be brisk and active.
meneo m. shaking, swaying; waddling; wagging.
menester m. neccessity, need, want; job, occupation.
mengua f. diminution, decrease, waning.
menguar v. to diminish, to decrease; to wane.
menjurje m. stuff, mixture; beverage.
menor adj. smaller, lesser; minor, under age; younger; smallest, least, youngest; m. minor (music); Minorite, Franciscan; **por —** (al por **—**) at retail, in small quantities.
menoría See **minoría**.
menos adv. less; least; except; adj. & pron. less, least; m. minus; **— de** (or **— que**) less than; **al —**

(or por lo —) at least; a — que unless; echar de — to miss; to feel or notice the absence of; no puede — de hacerlo he cannot help doing it; venir a — to decline; to become weak or poor.

menoscabar v. to impair; to lessen; to reduce, to deteriorate; to damage; to diminish; — la honra de to undermine the reputation of.

menoscabo m. impairment; diminution, loss; injury.

menospreciar v. to despise, to underrate, to undervalue.

menosprecio m. scorn, contempt; neglect.

mensaje m. message, errand.

mensajero m. messenger; errand boy.

menstruo m. menstruation.

mensual adj. monthly.

mensualidad f. monthly allowance; monthly payment.

mensurable adj. measurable.

menta f. mint, peppermint; Am. rumor, hearsay; de — Am. by hearsay; persona de — Am. famous person.

mentado adj. famous.

mental adj. mental.

mentalidad f. mentality.

mentar v. irr. to mention, to record, to name.

mente f. mind; intellect, sense; will.

mentecato adj. foolish, silly, crackbrained; m. fool.

mentir v. irr. to lie, to tell lies; to deceive.

mentira f. lie, falsehood, mendacity; fib.

mentiroso adj. lying; deceptive; false; mendacious.

mentís: dar un — to give the lie (to).

mentón m. chin.

menú m. menu.

menudear v. to occur frequently; to repeat; to detail; to fall incessantly (as rain, projectiles, etc.); Am. to retail, to sell at retail; to meet together often.

menudeo m. act of repeating minutely; retail; vender al — to retail, to sell at retail.

menudo adj. small, slender of body; minute, insignificant; exact, deatailed; dinero — change; m. entrails, change; small coins.

meñique adj. tiny, wee; dedo — little finger.

meollo m. marrow; pith; kernel; the substance or essential part of a thing; brain, brains.

meple m. Am. maple.

merca f. purchase.

mercachifle m. peddler, vendor, hawker.

mercader m. trader, merchant; shopkeeper.

mercadería f. merchandise; commodity; trade; —s goods.

mercado m. market, market place; mart.

mercancía f. merchandise, goods; trade, traffic.

mercantil adj. mercantile, commercial.

mercar v. to purchase; to buy; to commerce.

merced f. favor; present, gift, grace, mercy; Vuestra **Merced** Your Honor; a — de at the mercy of; at the expense of.

mercería f. trade of a haberdasher; mercery; notions, notions store; Am. dry goods store.

mercurio m. mercury; quicksilver.

merecedor adj. worthy, deserving.

merecer v. irr. to deserve.

merecido adj & p.p. deserved; m. condign punishment.

merecimiento m. merit.

merendar v. irr. to have an afternoon snack or refreshment; —se uno a alguien Am. to fleece or skin someone (in a game or business deal); to kill someone.

merendero m. lunchroom.

meridional adj. Southern; m. Southerner.

meridiano adj. & m. meridian.

merienda f. light afternoon meal; afternoon refreshments.

mérito m. merit, desert, excellence; de — notable.

meritorio adj. worthy, deserving, meritorious; m. a supernumerary in a public office.

merluza f. hake.

merma f. leakage; reduction, decrease.

mermar v. to dwindle, to decrease; to reduce.

mermelada f. marmalade.

mero adj. mere, pure, simple; Am. exact, real, precise; very, very same, exactly; soon; only; la mera verdad the real truth; una mera de las tres only one of the three; ya — (or ya merito) very soon; allí — (or merito) right there; m. species of perch; Am. species of thrust.

merodear v. to pillage, to maraud.

mes m. month; catamenia, menses, courses.

mesa f. table; executive board; staircase landing; mesa, plateau; **levantar la —** to clear the table; **poner la —** to set the table; **sentarse a — puesta** to live at other people's expenses.

mesada f. monthly pay, wages or allowance; stipend.

mesarse v. to pluck off the hair or beard with the hands.

mesero m. waiter.

mesón m. inn, hostry.

mesonero m. innkeeper.

mestizo adj. half-breed, hybrid, hybridous; **perro —** mongrel dog; Am. mestee or mustee.

mesura f. moderation; serious countenance; composure; grave deportment, dignity, civility, politeness.

mesurado adj. moderate, circumspect, temperate, regulated, modest, dignified.

meta f. goal, objective; boundary; limit.

metáfora f. metaphor.

metal m. metal.

metálico adj. metallic; **pago en —** payment in cash.

metalurgia f. metallurgy.

metate m. Am. flat stone, used for grinding corn, etc.

meteoro m. meteor; shooting star.

meteorología f. meteorology.

meteorológico adj. meteorological; **oficina meteorológica** weather bureau.

meter v. to put in, to get in; to insert; to smuggle; to cause (fear); to make (noise); Am. **—le** to hurry up.

metódico adj. methodical.

método m. method.

métrico adj. metric; of or relating to the metric system.

metro m. meter, metre; unit of length.

metrópoli f. metropolis.

metropolitano adj. metropolitan; archbishop.

mexicano See **mejicano**.

mezcal m. mescal, a species of maguey, and an alcoholic beverage made from it.

mezcla f. mixture; mortar; mixed cloth.

mezclar v. to mix; to stir together; to mingle; to associate; to compound.

mezclilla f. cloth made of yarns of different colors; tweed.

mezcolanza f. jumble, mess, mixture.

mezquindad f. meanness; stinginess; dire poverty.

mezquino adj. poor, needy, scanty; mean; stingy; Am. wart (usually on a finger).

mi adj. my.

mí pers. pron. me, myself.

miaja See **migaja**.

miau m. mew.

microbio m. microbe.

micrófono m. microphone.

microscópico adj. microscopic.

microscopio m. microscope.

miedo m. fear; dread; **tener —** to be afraid.

miedoso adj. afraid, fearful, timid.

miel f. honey; molasses.

miembro m. member; limb.

mientes f. pl. thought, mind; **parar — en** to consider, to reflect on; **traer a las —** to recall; **venírsele a uno a las —** to occur to one, come to one's mind.

mientras conj. while; **— que** while; **— tanto** in the meanwhile, meantime.

miércoles m. Wednesday.

mies f. ripe grain; harvest; **—es** fields of grain.

miga f. crumb; soft part of bread; **hacer buenas —s** (or **malas —s**) to get along well (or badly) with.

migaja f. crumb bit, small particle.

migración f. migration.

milagro m. wonder, miracle.

milagroso adj. miraculous.

milicia f. militia; military science; military profession.

militar adj. military; m. soldier; military man; v. to serve in the army, to militate, to fight.

milpa f. Am. cornfield.

milla f. mile.

millar m. thousand; **—es** thousands, lots, a great number.

millón m. million.

millonario adj. millionaire.

millonésimo adj. & m. millionth.

mimar v. to pamper, to spoil, to humor; to pet.

mimbre m. wicker.

mimbrera f. willow.

mimo m. pampering; caress; coaxing.

mimoso adj. tender, sensitive; delicate.

mina f. mine; source.

minar v. to mine; to undermine; to dig; to excavate; to lay explosive mines.

mineral m. mineral; mine; source; **agua —** mineral water.
minería f. mining; miners.
minero m. miner; source; wealth, fortune; adj. mining; **compañía minera** mining company.
miniatura f. miniature.
mínimo adj. least, smallest; m. minimum.
minino m. kitten, kitty, pussy.
ministerio m. ministry; ministering; portfolio; office of a cabinet member; minister's office.
ministrar v. to minister; to supply.
ministro m. minister, cabinet member; clergyman, pastor; officer of justice.
minoría f. minority.
minucioso adj. minute, detailed; thorough.
minúsculo adj. very small; **letra minúscula** small letter.
minuta f. minute; first draft; **a la —** breaded and fried meat or fish.
mío poss. adj. my, of mine; poss. pron. mine; **detrás —** Am. behind me.
miope adj. shortsighted, nearsighted, miope, myops.
mira f. sight; gunsight; guiding point; aim of a gun; care, vigilance; expectation, design; **estar a la — de** to be on the look out for; **poner la — en** to fix one's eyes on; to aim at.
mirada f. glance, gaze, look.
mirador m. spectator, onlooker; gallery, enclosed balcony; watchtower.
miramiento m. consideration, respect, regard; awe, reverence, dread; prudence.
mirar v. to watch, to observe, to spy; to see; to glance; to behold; **— por alguien** to take care of someone; ¡**mira**! (or ¡**mire**!) look!
miríada f. myriad, multitude, crowd, great number.
mirlo m. blackbird.
mirón m. bystander, onlooker, looker-on; busybody, gazer; adj. curious.
mirto m. myrtle.
misa f. mass; **— de gallo** midnight mass.
misceláneo adj. miscellaneous; f. miscellany.
miserable adj. miserable, wretched; covetous; u n h a p p y; forlorn; niggard, stingy.
miseria f. misery; poverty; calamity; wretchedness; bit, trifle.

misericordia f. mercy, clemency, pity.
misericordioso adj. merciful, compassionate.
misero adj. miserable, unhappy; forlorn; stingy.
misión f. mission.
misionero m. missionary.
mismo adj. same; self, very; **ahora —** right away.
misterio m. mystery, secret.
misterioso adj. mysterious.
místico adj. mystical, mystic; m. mystic.
mitad f. half, moiety; middle.
mitigar v. to mitigate, to soften; to mollify; to soothe.
mitin m. meeting.
mito m. myth.
mitología f. mythology.
mitra f. mitre; the dignity of a bishop.
mixto adj. mixed, mingled; halfbreed; m. composite.
mobiliario m. furniture.
moblaje See **mueblaje.**
mocedad f. youth; youthfulness; juvenility.
mocetón m. tall, young, robust person.
moción f. motion, movement.
mocoso adj. sniffling; m. brat, scamp; sniffling boy.
mochar v. Am. to cut off, to chop off, to lop off, to cut, to trim. (See **desmochar**). Am. to snitch; to pilfer; to depose.
mochila f. a kind of caparison or cover for a horse, knapsack; soldier's kit.
mocho adj. cut off; cropped, shorn; lopped, maimed, mutilated; Am. conservative.
muda f. mode, custom, style, fashion, form; **de —** fashionable.
modelar v. to model, to form.
modelo m. model, copy, pattern, exemplar; m. & f. l'fe model.
moderación f. moderation, temperance.
moderado adj. moderate; conservative.
moderar v. to moderate, to regulate, to adjust; to temper; to restrain; **—se** to become moderate.
moderno adj. modern, fashionable, new, late.
modestia f. modesty.
módico adj. scanty, moderate, reasonable.
modificación f. modification.
modificar v. to modify.

modismo m. idiom.
modo m. mode, method, manner, form; way, mood (grammar); moderation, civility; a — (or al —) in a similar manner; de — so that; de — que so that; sobre — extremely; de todos —s at any rate, anyway.
modorra f. drowsiness, heaviness; gid (disease of sheep).
modular v. to modulate, to sing with harmony, to tone down.
mofa f. mockery, scoff, jeer.
mofar v. to mock, to deride, to jeer, to scoff, to ridicule, to flirt; —se de to make fun of.
moflete m. fat cheek.
mofletudo adj. fat-cheeked.
mohín m. grimace; wry face.
mohíno adj. fretful, peevish; sad; discontented.
moho n. moss; mold, rust.
mohoso adj. moldy, rusty, musty.
mojada f. drench; wetting.
mojado adj. wet, damp, moist.
mojadura f. wetting; moistening.
mojar v. to dampen, to wet, to moisten, to damp; to meddle; Am. to bribe; to celebrate by drinking; **mojársele a uno los papeles** Am. to get things mixed up.
mojicón m. blow in the face with the clenched fist; punch; muffin; bun.
mojigatería f. hypocrisy; prudery; religious fanatism.
mojigato adj. prudish, dissembler; deceitful; hypocritical; overzealous in matters of religion; m. prude.
mojón m. landmark; heap; milestone; pile; kind of game.
molde m. mold, pattern, mould; block; form which contains the types ready for printing; venir de — to come pat, to be to the point; escrito de — writing in characters of print; letras de — printed letter; de — in print, printed or published; fitting.
moldear v. to mold, to mould, to make moulds; to cast; to decorate with moldings.
moldura f. molding.
mole f. mass, bulk; adj. soft, mild; m. Am. — **de guajolote** a Mexican dish of turkey served with a chili gravy
molécula f. molecule.
moler v. irr. to grind, to pound, to mill; to molest; to fatigue; to waste, to consume by use; to chew; — **a palos** to give a severe beating.
molestar v. to vex, to disturb, to molest, to bother, to annoy.
molestia f. bother, molestation, injury, grievance.
molesto adj. grievous, vexatious, molestful.
molicie f. tenderness, softness; effeminacy.
molienda f. grinding; mill in which anything is ground; grind, milling; bother, weariness, fatigue.
molinete m. windlass, turnstile; small mill; ventilating fan.
molinillo m. little mill; hand mill; churn staff, chocolate beater.
molino m. mill; restless person; — **de viento** windmill; — **de agua** watermill; — **de mano** hand mill.
mollera f. crown or top of the head; judgment, good sense; ser duro de — to be obstinate; no tener sal en la — to be dull, stupid.
momentáneo adj. momentaneous; sudden; quick.
momento m. moment; importance; momentum; al — immediately; a cada — continually.
mona f. female monkey or ape; drunkenness, drunkard; **dormir la** — to sleep it off; **pillar una** — to get drunk.
monada f. monkeyshine; grimace; monkey face.
monarca m. monarch.
monarquía f. monarchy.
monasterio m. monastery.
mondadientes m. toothpick.
mondar v. to clean, cleanse; to husk; to peel; to prune; Am. to beat, to thrash; —se los dientes to pick one's teeth.
moneda f. coin, coinage; money; — **corriente** currency; — **menuda** (or **suelta**) change; **casa de** — mint.
monería f. grimace; trifle; bauble.
monetario adj. monetary; financial.
monigote m. puppet; ridiculous figure; lay brother; dunce.
monje m. monk.
monja f. nun.
mono m. monkey; silly fool; mimic, imitator; **meterle a uno los** —**s en el cuerpo** Am. to frighten; to terrify someone; adj. Am. sorrel, reddish-brown; blond.

monologar v. to soliloquize; to talk to oneself.
monólogo m. monologue, soliloquy.
monopolio m. monopoly.
monopolizar v. to monopolize; to corner (a market).
monosílabo adj. monosyllabic; m. monosyllable.
monotonía f. monotony.
monótono adj. monotonous.
monserga f. gabble.
monstruo m. monster.
monstruosidad f. monstruosity.
monstruoso adj. monstrous.
monta f. amount, sum, total; value, worth, price, importance; de poca — of little value or importance.
montaje m. assembly; assembling; mount.
montante m. broadsword; transom; post; Am. sum, amount; cost; f. high tide.
montaña f. mountain; — rusa roller coaster.
montañés adj. mountain, mountainous, highlandish; m. mountaineer; native of the province of Santander, Spain.
montañoso adj. mountainous.
montar v. to mount; to amount to; to set jewels; to cock a gun; to assemble, to set up; Am. to organize, to establish; —se en su macho Am. to be stubborn.
montaraz adj. wild, untamed; mountaineer; m. forester.
monte m. mount, mountain; forest; wood; difficulty, obstruction; game at cards; Am. grass, pasture; country, outskirts.
montepío m. pawnshop.
montera f. cap; Am. coneshaped Bolivian hat worn by Indians.
montés adj. wild.
montículo m. mound.
montón m. pile, heap; crowd, multitude; a —es in great number; in heaps, by heaps.
montonera f. Am. band of rebellious riders; pile of wheat, hay, straw, etc.; pile or heap of anything.
montuoso adj. hilly, mountainous.
montura f. riding horse or mule; saddle and trappings.
monumental adj. monumental.
monumento m. monument.
moño m. hair on the crown of the head tied together; bow of ribbon; crest, tuft of feathers; Am. forelock (lock of hair in the fore part of the head);

whim; estar con el — torcido Am. to be in an ugly humor.
mora f. blackberry; mulberry; brambleberry; Am. blood pudding sausage.
morada f. dwelling, residence, abode, habitation.
morado adj. purple.
morador m. dweller, resident.
moral adj. moral; f. ethics, morality.
moraleja f. moral, lesson, maxim.
moralidad f. morality.
moralista m. & f. moralist.
morar v. to live, to inhabit, to dwell, to reside, to lodge.
morbidez f. softness, mellowness.
mórbido adj. morbid, soft; diseased.
morboso adj. morbid, diseased, unhealthy.
morcilla f. blood pudding, blood sausage; black pudding; gag (amusing remark by an actor).
mordacidad f. mordacity, roughness.
mordaz adj. biting, cutting, sarcastic.
mordaza f. gag.
mordedor adj. biting; snappy; m. biter, slandering.
mordedura f. bite, sting.
mordelón adj. Am. biting, snappy; m. Am. biter; public official who accepts a bribe.
morder v. irr. to bite, to nip; to be pungent to the taste; to seize or stick fast; to gnaw, to wear away gradually; to taunt, to nibble, to satirize; Am. to swindle; to exact a bribe; —se los dedos to be vexed from desire of revenge.
mordida f. Am. bite; graft; money obtained by graft.
mordiscar v. to nibble, to gnaw.
mordisco m. bite, nibble.
moreno adj. brown; dark; tawny, brunette; m. Am. colored person.
moretón m. bruise, black-and-blue mark.
morfina f. morphine.
morfinómano adj. morphine addict, drug fiend.
moribundo adj. dying.
morir v. irr. to die, to perish; to hanker, to desire excessively; —se to die, to die out, to be extinguished.
morisco adj. Moorish; Moresque; m. Morisco, Christianized Moor; language of the Moriscos.
moro adj. Moorish; m. Moor.

morral m. nose bag; game bag; knapsack.
morriña f. melancholy, blues, sadness.
mortaja f. mortise; shroud, winding sheet.
mortal adj. mortal, deadly, fatal; m. mortal.
mortalidad f. mortality; death rate.
mortandad f. mortality, death rate; massacre, slaughter.
mortecino adj. deadly pale; low, weak, exhausted; dying a natural death.
morterete m. small mortar, small cannon.
mortero m. mortar.
mortífero adj. deadly, mortiferous, fatal.
mortificar v. to mortify; to torment, vex, annoy; —se to do penance, to be grieved; Am. to be embarrassed.
mortuorio adj. burial, funeral, mournful; m. funeral, burial.
mosaico adj. & m. mosaic.
mosca f. fly; impertinent, intruder; Am. sponger, parasite; bull's eye (center of a target).
moscón m. large fly; ir de — Am. to go along as a chaperone.
mozalbete m. youth, lad.
mozo adj. young, youthful; m. unmarried person; bachelor; manservant; waiter; porter; bellboy; buen — handsome man.
mozuela f. lass, young girl.
mozuelo m. lad, young boy.
mucama f. Am. servant girl.
mucamo m. Am. servant.
mucoso adj. mucous; slimy; membrana mucosa mucous membrane.
muchacha f. girl, lass; child.
muchacho m. boy, lad, child.
muchedumbre f. multitude, crowd.
mucho adj. much; large (quantity); long (time); many (number); abundant, plentiful; no ha — not long since; no es — que it is not wonder that; ni con — not by far, not by a long shot; ni — menos not by any means, nor anything like it; por — que no matter how much.
muda f. change, alteration; change of clothes; mute letter; mewing; the time of moulting; roost of birds of prey.
mudable adj. changeable, fickle, variable.
mudanza f. alteration, change, mutation; inconstancy, levity; removal.
mudar v. to change, to remove, to deviate; to vary, to alter; to moult, to shed the feathers; —se to change linen or clothes; to move to another house.
mudez f. dumbness, muteness.
mudo adj. mute, dumb, silent, still.
mueblaje m. furniture.
mueble m. piece of furniture; —s furniture, household goods; adj. movable; bienes —s chattels; movable possessions.
mueca f. grimace, wry face, grin.
muela f. runner, the upper millstone; grindstone; molar tooth; back tooth; — cordal (or del juicio) wisdom tooth.
muelle adj. soft, voluptuous, tender, delicate; m. spring; wharf; loading platform; — real main spring of a watch.
muerte f. death, mortality; murder, assassination.
muerto p.p. & adj. dead; extinguished, withered; faded; lifeless; naturaleza muerta still life; m. corpse.
muesca f. notch, groove, hack, nick, mortise.
muestra f. sample; pattern; the fag end of a piece of stuff; specimen; design.
muestrario m. book or collection of samples.
mugido m. moo; mooing, lowing of cattle.
mugir v. to bellow; to low; to moo.
mugre f. dirt, grime.
mugriento adj. grimy, dirty.
mujer f. woman, wife, mate.
mujeril adj. womanly, feminine; womanish.
mula f. mule; Am. cushion for carrying loads; worthless merchandise; cruel, treacherous person; echar a uno la — Am. to scold someone.
muladar m. heap of dung, pile of manure.
mulato adj. & m. mulatto.
muleta f. crutch, prop, support; red cloth draped over a rod used in bullfights.
muletilla f. cane with a crutchlike handle; red cloth draped over a rod used by bullfighters; refrain, repetitious word or phrase; braid, frog.
mulo m. mule.
multa f. fine.

multicolor adj. many-colored, motley.
múltiple adj. multiple.
multiplicación f. multiplication.
multiplicidad f. multiplicity.
múltiplo m. multiple number.
multitud f. multitude, crowd.
mullido adj. soft, fluffy; stuffing for mattresses or pillows; soft cushion or mattress.
mullir v. to fluff; to soften.
mundanal adj. wordly.
mundial adj. universal; **la guerra —** the World War.
mundo m. world; trunk; **todo el —** everybody.
munición f. ammunition; buckshot; **—es de guerra** war supplies.
municipal adj. municipal.
municipalidad f. municipality; town hall, city hall; city government.
municipio m. municipality.
muñeca f. doll; wrist; manikin.
muñeco m. boy doll; dummy, puppet.
muñón m. stump (of a limb).
muralla f. surrounding wall; rampart.
murciano adj. of or from Murcia, Spain; native of Murcia.
murciélago m. bat.
murga f. brass band.
murmullo m. murmur, rumor, whisper, muttering.
murmuración f. slander, gossip, grumbling.
murmurar v. to murmur; to slander; to gossip; to whisper; to grumble.
muro m. wall.
murria f. sulkiness, sullenness; melancholy; blues; **tener —** to be sulky; to have the blues.
musa f. Muse; muse, poetic inspiration; poetry; **—s** fine arts.
muscular adj. muscular.
musculatura f. muscles; muscular system.
músculo m. muscle.
musculoso adj. muscular; sinewy.
muselina f. muslin.
museo m. museum.
musgo m. moss.
musgoso adj. mossy.
música f. music.
musical adj. musical.
músico adj. musical; m. musician.
musitar v. to mutter, to mumble; to whisper.
muslo m. thigh.

mustio adj. sad, musty; parched; withered; humble.
mutilar v. to mutilate; to butcher; to mar; to maim; to cripple.
mutismo m. muteness, silence, mutism.
mutuo adj. mutual, reciprocal.
muy adv. very, greatly; most; **— ilustre** most illustrious.

N

nabo m. turnip.
nácar m. mother-of-pearl; nacre, pearl color.
nacarado adj. pearly, set with mother-of-pearl.
nacer v. irr. to be born, to come into the world; to blossom; to bud; to shoot, to grow; to rise; to appear in the horizon; to take its rise; to begin; to originate; **— de pie (or de pies)** to be born lucky.
naciente adj. rising; orient, East.
nacimiento m. birth, origin; beginning; nativity; descent; source; representation of the Nativity.
nación f. nation.
nacional adj. national; m. national citizen.
nacionalidad f. nationality.
nada f. nothingness; indef. pron. nothing; adv. not at all; **de —** you are welcome, don't mention it; **a cada —** Am. constantly; **una nadita** a trifle, just a little.
nadada f. swim.
nadador m. swimmer; Am. fish-net float.
nadar v. to swim, to float.
nadería f. a mere nothing; trifle; worthless thing.
nadie indef. pron. nobody, no one.
nafta f. naphtha.
naipe m. playing card.
nalgada f. spank; **—s** spanking.
nalgas f. pl. buttocks, rump.
nana f. grandma; lullaby; Am. child's nurse; nice old lady.
naranja f. orange; **— tangerina** tangerine.
naranjada f. orangeade; orange juice; orange marmalade.
naranjal m. orange grove.
naranjo m. orange tree.
narciso m. narcissus; daffodil; fop, dandy.
narcótico adj. & m. narcotic.
narcotizar v. to dope, to narcotize.
nariz f. nose; nostril; **narices** nostrils.

narración f. narration, account, tale, story.
narrar v. to narrate, relate, tell.
narrativa f. narrative.
narrativo adj. narrative, narratory.
nata f. cream, prime part; scum; —s whipped cream with sugar; custard.
natal adj. natal, native.
natalicio m. birthday.
natalidad f. birth rate.
natillas f. pl. custard; composition of flour, milk, eggs, and sugar.
nativo adj. native, natal.
natoso adj. creamy.
natural adj. natural; according to nature; native; pertaining to the place of birth; common, usual, regular; ingenuous; temper, genius, disposition; m. & f. native; al — without affectation; del — from nature, from life.
naturaleza f. nature, instinct; property, inclination; sex; nationality; naturalization; — muerta still life.
naturalidad f. naturalness; ingenuity, candour; simplicity; birthright.
naturalista adj. naturalistic; m. & f. naturalist.
naturalización f. naturalization.
naturalizar v. to naturalize; to acclimatize; to accustom to a new climate; —se to become naturalized.
naufragar v. to be stranded or shipwrecked; to suffer shipwreck; to suffer wreck or ruin in one's affairs.
naufragio m. shipwreck, failure, ruin.
náusea f. nausea; **dar** —s to nauseate, to sicken; to disgust; tener —s to be nauseated; to be sick to one's stomach.
nauseabundo adj. nauseating, loathsome.
náutica f. navigation.
navaja f. jackknife, pocketknife, penknife; razor.
navajazo m. stab with a jackknife; stab wound.
naval adj. naval.
navarro adj. Navarrese; of or pertaining to Navarre, Spain m. Navarrese.
nave f. ship, boat, vessel, nave; aisle.
navegable adj. navigable.

navegación f. navigation; sea voyage; — aérea aviation.
navegante m. navigator; adj. navigating.
navegar v. to navigate, to sail.
navidad f. Nativity, Christmas; —es Christmas season.
navío m. vessel, ship; — de guerra warship.
necesidad f. necessity, need, want; ..— mayor o menor evacuation of the body by stool or water.
necesitado adj. compelled, needy, necessitated, in need, in want; poor; m. needy person.
necio adj. stupid, ignorant; imprudent, injudicious; foolish, stubborn; Am. touchy.
nefando adj. abominable, base, nefarious; wicked.
negación f. negation, denial; want or total privation; negative particle.
negar v. irr. to deny, to contradict; to refuse; to forbid; to prohibit; to disown, to disclaim; to disregard; —se to refuse, to decline.
negativa f. negative, denial, refusal.
negativo adj. negative.
negligencia f. negligence, neglect, heedlessness, idleness, carelessness.
negligente adj. negligent, neglectful, careless, heedless.
negociación f. negotiation, management; business; business house; deal, transaction.
negociante m. merchant, trader, dealer; businessman; adj. negotiating.
negociar v. to negotiate, to trade; to transact.
negocio m. business, occupation, employment, management; affair; pretention, treaty, agency; commerce; utility in trading; hombre de —s businessman.
negra f. negress; Am. dear, darling.
negrear v. to become black; to grow black, to appear black.
negro adj. black; dark; jetty; gloomy, dismay, melancholy, sad, unfortunate; m. black color; negro; Am. dear, darling.
negrura f. blackness.
nena f. baby girl.
nene m. baby boy; infant.
nervio m. nerve.
nervioso adj. nervous; sinewy, strong; nervously.
nerviosidad f. nervousness; flexibility, vigor.

nervudo adj. sinewy, tough, powerful; nervous.
netamente adv. clearly, distinctly.
neto adj. clear, pure, net.
neumático m. tire; adj. pneumatic.
neutralidad f. neutrality.
neutralizar v. to neutralize; to counteract.
neutro adj. neutral, neuter; sexless.
nevada f. snowfall.
nevado adj. snowy; white as snow; covered with snow.
nevar v. irr. to snow; to make white as snow.
nevera f. icebox; refrigerator; ice house; ice or ice-cream vendor (woman).
ni conj & adv. nor; not even; neither; — **siquiera** not even.
nicho m. niche; recess; hollow in a wall.
nidada f. nestful of eggs; brood of chicks; hatch brood; covey, nide.
nido m. nest; abode; **patearle el —** **a alguien** Am. to upset someone's plans.
niebla f. fog, mist; confusion; haze, damp; disease of the eyes; mildew which blasts.
nieta f. granddaughter; descendant.
nieto m. grandson; grandchild.
nieve f. snow; Am. sherbet; ice cream, **tiempo de —s** snowy season.
nimio adj. miserly, stingy; excessive, too much; Am. very small, insignificant.
ninfa f. nymph, chrysalis.
ningun(o) indef. adj. & pron. no one, none; nobody; **de ninguna manera** by no means; **ninguna cosa** nothing.
niña f. baby girl; pupil of the eye; Am. lady, mistress (title of respect and endearment given to adults).
niñada f. childishness, childish act or remark; puerility.
niñera f. child's nurse; nursery maid.
niñería f. childish act; child's play; trifle; foolishness; bauble, plaything.
niñez f. infancy; childhood.
niño m. child; boy, infant; Am. master (title of respect given to a young man by his servants); adj. childlike, childish; very young; immature; **desde —** from infancy.
níquel m. nickel.

niquelado adj. nickel-plated; m. nickel plating; nickel plate.
nitidez f. clarity, clearness.
nítido adj. clear, bright; shining, nitid.
nitrato m. nitrate; saltpeter.
nitro m. niter; saltpeter.
nitrógeno m. nitrogen.
nivel m. level; **a —** perfectly level.
nivelar v. to level; to grade; to equalize; to make even.
no adv. no; not; nay; — **bien as soon as**; **un — sé qué** something indefinable; **por si o por —** just in case, anyway; **— vale nada** it is worth nothing.
noble adj. noble; highborn; illustrious, eminent; honourable; respectable; m. nobleman, noble.
nobleza f. nobility; nobleness; body of noblemen.
noción f. notion, idea; acceptation, meaning of a word.
nocivo adj. noxious, harmful, injurious, hurtful, mischievous.
nocturno adj. nocturnal, night; nightly; m. nocturne (musical or lyrical composition).
noche f. night; darkness; **a la —** tonight; **de —** by (at) night; **por (en) la —** at night, in the evening; **dejar a uno a buenas —s** to leave a person in the lurch.
Nochebuena f. Christmas Eve.
nocherniego m. night owl (person).
nodriza f. child's nurse; wet nurse.
nogal m. walnut (tree and wood).
nombradía f. renown, fame.
nombramiento m. nomination; naming, appointment, creation, commission.
nombrar v. to nominate; to name; to appoint; to mention by name.
nombre m. name; fame; noun; watchword; reputation; nickname **— de pila** (or **— de bautismo**) Christian name.
nomeolvides m. forget-me-not.
nómina f. list (of names); payroll; catalogue.
nominación f. nomination, appointment.
nominal adj. nominal; **valor —** small, insignificant value.
nominar v. to nominate; to name.
non adj. odd, uneven; m. odd number, uneven number; **estar (or quedar) de —** to be left alone, be left without a partner or companion; **ha dicho —es** he has said no, he has refused.

nonada f. trifle, mere nothing; nothingness.
nopal m. nopal; prickly pear tree (species of cactus).
nordeste adj. & m. Northeast.
noria f. draw well; chain pump; deep well.
norma f. norm; standard; model.
normal adj. normal, standard; f. perpendicular line.
normalizar v. to normalize; to standardize.
noroeste adj. & m. Northwest.
nortada f. strong North wind.
nortazo m. sudden gust of wind, strong North wind.
norte m. North; North wind; the arctic pole; rule, law, guide; clue.
norteamericano adj. North American; American; of or from America.
norteño adj. Northern; m. Northerner.
noruego adj. & m. Norwegian.
nostalgia f. nostalgia, longing, reverie, revery.
nostálgico adj. homesick; lonesome; nostalgic.
nota f. note; mark; fame.
notable adj. notable; famous, noticeable.
notar v. to note, to observe; to mark; to write down.
notario m. notary.
noticia f. notice, information; news; knowledge, note; **recibir** —s to receive word, to hear from.
noticiario m. news sheet, news column, news bulletin; news reel.
noticioso adj. newsy, full of news; well informed.
notificación f. notification, judicial intimation, summons.
notificar v. to notify.
notorio adj. notorious, well-known; obvious, evident.
novedad f. novelty; latest news; newness, modernness, fashion; ¿cuál es la —? what is cooking?; **sin** — as usual, well.
novel adj. new, inexperienced.
novela f. novel, fiction, fictious story, tale.
novelesco adj. novelistic, fictional, fantanstic.
novelista m. & f. novelist.
novia f. fiancée; sweetheart; bride.
noviazgo m. betrothal, engagement, courtship.
novicio m. novice; beginner, apprentice; adj. inexperienced, probationer.
noviembre m. November.

novilla f. heifer, cow between three and six years of age.
novillada f. herd of young bulls or bullocks; bullfight, using young bulls.
novillo m. young bull or ox; steer; cuckold; **hacer** —s to play truant.
novio m. bridegroom; fiancée; sweetheart.
nubarrón m. a large cloud; stormy cloud.
nube f. cloud; film on the eyeball; shade in precious stones.
nublado m. gloominess, storm cloud; imminent danger; adj. cloudy.
nubloso adj. cloudy, dark, overcast; gloomy, ill-fated.
nuca f. nape, nucha.
núcleo m. nucleus; kernel of a nut.
nudillo m. small knot; loop; knitted stitch; knuckle, the joint of the fingers; nodule.
nudo m. knot, knuckle, articulation; joint of plants; knag; tie, union, bond of association; intricacy, difficulty; nautical mile; **— ciego** hard knot.
nudoso adj. knotty, gnarled, knotted.
nueva f. new, news; **buena —** good news.
nuevecito adj. nice and new, brand new.
nuevo adj. new, novel, modern, fresh; renovated, repaired; anew, recently, of late; newly arrived; **— y flamante** spick and span; **de —** again; ¿que hay de **—**? what's new? what's the news? what's cooking?
nuez f. walnut, nut; **— o manzana de Adán** Adam's apple; **— moscada** (or **— de especia**) nutmeg.
nulidad f. nullity; incompetence; nonentity, a nobody; of no binding force.
nulo adj. null, void; useless; void of effect.
numeral adj. & m. numeral.
numerar v. to number; to enumerate; to numerate; to calculate; to cipher.
numeroso adj. numerous, containing many.
nunca adv. never; **más que —** more than ever; **— jamás** never, never more.
nuncio m. messenger; envoy or ambassador from the Pope.

nupcial adj. nuptial, relating to marriage or weddings; hymeneal.
nupcias f. pl. nuptials, wedding.
nutria f. otter.
nutrición f. nutrition; nourishment.
nutrido adj. full, abundant; substantial.
nutrimiento m. nutrition; nourishment; food; aliment.
nutrir v. to nourish, to feed; to fatten; to foment.
nutritivo adj. nutritious, nourishing; nutritive.

Ñ

ñapa f. Am. additional amount, something extra; **de — Am.** to boot, in addition, besides.
ñato adj. Am. flat-nosed; pug-nosed; snub-nosed; deformed; ugly; insignificant.
ñoñería f. old age, silly remark or action; Am. dotage.
ñoño adj. feeble-minded; decrepit; impaired by age; silly; Am. old. decrepit, feeble; old-fashioned, out of style.

O

o conj. or, either.
oasis m. oasis.
obedecer v. irr. to obey; to yield to; **— a cierta causa** to arise from, be due to, a certain cause.
obediencia f. obedience.
obediente adj. obedient.
obertura f. overture.
obispo m. bishop.
objeción f. objection.
objetar v. to object, to oppose.
objetivo adj. objective; m. objective, aim.
objeto m. object, purpose, design, aim, end.
oblea f. wafer.
oblicuo adj. slanting; bias.
obligación f. obligation; contract; duty; bond; security; debenture; engagement.
obligar v. to oblige, to compel, to bind; **—se** to bind oneself, to obligate oneself.
obligatorio adj. obligatory, compulsory, binding.
óbolo m. mite, small contribution.
obra f. work; act; labor, toil, book, building (under construction); repair; **— de** approximately; **por — de** through, by virtue or power of; **hacer mala — to** interfere, to hinder; **poner por — to** undertake, to begin; to put into practice.
obrar v. to work, to operate; to act; to manufacture; to put into practice, to execute; to ease nature; to perform; to make; to do; **obra en nuestro poder** we are in recepit of; **la carta que obra en nuestro poder** the letter that is in our possession.
obrero m. workman, laborer, day laborer; missionary.
obscenidad f. obscenity.
obsceno adj. obscene.
obscurecer v. irr. to obscure; to darken; to impair the lustre of things; to denigrate; **—se** to disappear, to be lost; to get dark or cloudy.
obscuridad f. obscurity, darkness; dimness; cloudiness, gloominess; insignificance.
obscuro adj. obscure, dark, gloomy; dim; **a obscuras** (See **a oscuras**) in the dark; unintelligible; confused; m. shade (in painting).
obsequiar v. to regale, to give; to entertain; to court; to wait upon; Am. to make a present of; to serve; to obey.
obsequio m. attention, courtesy; obsequiousness, complaisance; **en — de** for the sake of, in honor of.
obsequioso adj. attentive, obsequious, officious, servile.
observación f. observation, remark; note.
observador m. observer, remarker; adj. observing.
observancia f. respect, reverence, regard; attentive practice; obedience; observance.
observante adj. observing; obedient; observant.
observar v. to observe; to regard; to notice; to mind; to heed; to obey; to remark.
observatorio m. observatory.
obsesión f. obsession.
obsesionar v. to obsess.
obstáculo m. obstacle.
obstante: no — notwihstanding; nevertheless.
obstar v. to hinder; to impede; to obstruct.
obstinación f. obstinacy, stubornness; obduracy.
obstinado adj. obstinate, opinionated, stubborn.

obstinarse v. to obstinate; to persist (in); to be stubborn (about).
obstrucción f. obstruction, obstacle.
obstruir v. irr. to obstruct; to block.
obtener v. irr. to obtain, to get; to attain.
obtenible adj. obtainable, available.
obturador m. choke (automobile); throttle; plug; stopper; shutter (camera).
obviar v. to obviate, to clear away; to remove.
obvio adj. obvious.
ocasión f. occasion, opportunity; cause; danger; risk; de — bargain, reduced; avisos de — want advertisements; esta — Am. this time.
ocasional adj. occasional.
ocasionar v. to occasion, to cause.
ocaso m. sunset; setting (of any star or planet); West; decadence, decline; end.
occidental adj. Occidental, Western.
occidente m. Occident, West.
océano m. ocean.
ocio m. leisure, idleness; recreation, pastime.
ociosidad f. idleness, leisure.
ocioso adj. idle; useless; lazy; fruitless.
octubre m. October.
ocular adj. ocular; testigo — eye witness; m. eyepiece, lens.
oculista m. & f. oculist; Am. flatterer.
ocultar v. to hide, to conceal; to disguise.
oculto adj. hidden, concealed.
ocupación f. occupation; employment; concern.
ocupante m. & f. occupant.
ocupar v. to occupy; to employ; **ocuparse en** (Am. **ocuparse de**) to be engaged in; to pay attention to; to be interested in; to follow business.
ocurrencia f. occurrence, event; witty remark, joke; bright or funny idea.
ocurrente adj. witty, funny, humorous; occurring.
ocurrir v. to occur, to happen; to obviate.
ocurso m. Am. petition, application.
oda f. ode.
odiar v. to hate; to abhor; to detest.
odio m. hatred.
odioso adj. odious, hateful.

oeste m. West; West wind.
ofender v. to offend, to displease; to harm, to injure, to make angry; —se to get offended; to be vexed or displeased.
ofensa f. offense, injure, harm, transgression.
ofensiva f. offensive, attack.
ofensivo adj. offensive; obnoxious; attacking.
ofensor m. offender; adj. offending; attacking.
oferta f. offer; promise; gift.
oficial m. official, officer; skilled workman; adj. official.
oficiar v. to officiate, to serve, to minister; to communicate officially; — de to serve, act as.
oficina f. office; shop; workshop; working house.
oficinesco adj. clerical, pertaining to an office.
oficio m. office, employ, work, trade; function, opperation; official letter; trade; business; craft; position; religious office (prayers).
oficioso adj. officious, diligent; meddlesome.
ofrecer v. irr. to offer; to promise; to hold out; to present; to exhibit; to manifest; to dedicate; —se to offer; to occur, to present itself; to offer oneself, to volunteer; ¿qué se le ofrece a usted? what can I do for you?
ofrecimiento m. offer; offering; gift.
ofrenda f. offering, gift.
ofuscamiento m. clouded vision, blindness; obfuscation; confused reason; cloudiness of the mind; bewilderment.
ofuscar v. to confuse, to darken, to cast a shadow on; to blind; to render obscure; to cloud; to bewilder.
ogro m. ogre.
oído m. hearing; ear; al — confidentially; de (or al) — by ear; de —s (or de oídas) by hearsay or rumor.
oidor m. hearer, listener; one of the judges of Colonial America.
oir v. irr. to hear; to listen; to understand; to comprehend; — misa to attend, assist or hear mass; — decir que to hear that; — hablar de to hear about.
ojal m. buttonhole; hole.
¡ojalá! interj. God grant!; I hope

ojazo / **opositor**

so! — **que** would that; I hope that.
ojazo m. large eye.
ojeada f. glimpse, quick glance; ogle.
ojear v. to eye; to stare; to bewitch; to beat up; to rouse (wild game).
ojera f. dark circle under the eye; eyecup.
ojeriza f. grudge, ill will, spite.
ojeroso adj. with dark rings under the eyes.
ojiva f. pointed arch; adj. ojival pointed (arch); **ventaja ojival** window with a pointed arch.
ojo m. eye, sight, keyhole; eye of a needle; hole; arch of a bridge; ¡—! careful!, look out!; **a —** by sight, by guess; **a —s vistas** visibly, clearly; **mal (or mal de) —** evil eye; **hacer —** Am. to cast the evil eye; **pelar el —** Am. to be alert, to keep one's eye peeled; **poner a uno los —s verdes**, Am. to deceive someone; **tener entre —s a** to have ill will toward; to have a grudge against; **en un abrir y cerrar de —s** in the twinkling of an eye.
ojota f. Am. leather sandal worn by Indian women.
ola f. wave.
oleada f. surge; swell of the sea; big wave.
oleaje m. succession of waves; swell, surge.
óleo m. oil; holy oil; **al —** in oil colors.
oleoso adj. oily.
oler v. irr. to smell, to scent; to search, to discover; to pry; **— a** to smack of; to smell like; **olérselas** Am. to suspect it.
olfatear v. to scent, to sniff, to smell.
olfateo m. sniff, sniffing.
olfato m. the smell, sense of smell; odour; scent, chase followed by the smell.
oliva f. olive; olive tree; owl.
olivar m. olive grove.
olivo m. olive tree.
olmo m. elm.
olor m. odour, scent, smell, fragrance; smack, trace, suspicion; hope, promise, offer; fame, reputation; Am. spice.
oloroso adj. fragant, odoriferous, perfumed, scented.
olote m. Am. cob; corncob.
olvidadizo adj. forgetful, oblivious.

olvidar v. to forget, to neglect, to omit; **—se de** to forget.
olvido m. forgetfulness; carelessness; heedlessness; neglect; oblivion; **echar al —** to cast into oblivion; to forget on purpose.
olla f. pot, kettle; olla (vegetable and meat stew); **— podrida** Spanish stew.
ombligo m. navel; navel string; center, middle.
omisión f. omission; oversight; neglect; carlessness.
omiso adj. careless; neglectful, remiss, heedless; Am. guilty; **hacer caso —** to omit.
omitir v. to omit, to overlook, to neglect.
ómnibus m. omnibus; bus.
omnipotente adj. omnipotent, almighty.
onda f. wave; reverberation; ripple; fluctuation; scallop; agitation.
ondear v. to wave; to waver; to undulate; to ripple; to sway, to swing.
ondulación f. undulation, waving motion; wave; **— permanente** permanent wave.
ondulado p.p. & adj. wavy; scalloped.
ondulante adj. wavy, waving.
ondular v. to undulate, to wave.
onza f. ounce, wildcat; Am. small tiger.
opaco adj. opaque, dim, dull.
ópalo m. opal.
ópera f. opera.
operación f. operation; business transaction.
operador m. operator, surgeon.
operar v. to operate, to act, to work, to take effect; to speculate; to manipulate, to handle.
operario m. laborer, operator, workman, worker.
opereta f. operetta.
opinar v. to express an opinion; to argue; to judge; to think.
opinión f. opinion, reputation.
opio m. opium.
oponer v. irr. to oppose; to contradict; **—se a** to disapprove; **—se a** to oppose, to be against.
oporto m. port wine.
oportunidad f. opportunity.
oportuno adj. opportune; convenient; timely.
oposición f. oppossition; competition; **—es** competitive examinations.
opositor m. opponent, competitor.

opresión f. oppression.
opresivo adj. oppressive.
opresor m. oppressor.
oprimir v. to oppress; to crush; to press down; to overpower; to subdue.
oprobio m. infamy, insult, opprobrium; shame, dishonor.
optar v. to select, to elect; to choose; — por to decide upon; to select.
óptica f. optics.
óptico adj. optical, optic; m. optician.
optimismo m. optimism.
optimista m. & f. optimistic; adj. optimistic.
óptimo adj. very good; best; eminently best.
opuesto adj. opposite, contrary.
opulencia f. opulence, abundance; wealth.
opulento adj. opulent, rich, wealthy.
oquedad f. hollow, cavity; chasm.
ora conj. now; then; whether; either.
oración f. oration, prayer; sentence.
oráculo m. oracle.
orador m. orator, speaker.
oral adj. oral, verbal.
orar v. to pray.
oratoria f. oratory, eloquence.
oratorio m. oratory, private chapel; adj. oratorial, rhetorical; oratorical.
orbe m. orb, sphere, globe; the earth; world; universe.
órbita f. orbit.
orden m. order, regularity; method; class; succession; series; group; relation; proportion; f. order, command; honorary or religious order; m. & f. sacrament of ordination; a sus —es at your service.
ordenado p.p. & adj. ordered; ordained; orderly, neat; tidy.
ordenanza f. ordinance, decree, law; orderly.
ordenar v. to arrange, to class; to enact; to ordain, to regulate, to direct; —se to become ordained.
ordeña f. milking.
ordeñar v. to milk.
ordinariez f. commonness, lack of manners.
ordinario adj. ordinary, usual, common, customary, familiar, plain, coarse; m. ordinary (bishop or judge); ordinary mail; de — usually, ordinarily.
orear v. to air; —se to be exposed to the air; to dry in the air; to cool; to refresh.
oreja f. ear; loop; small flap; Am. handle.
orejera f. ear muff, ear flap.
orejón m. pull by the ear; Am. rancher or inhabitant of the sabana; adj. Am. coarse, crude; uncouth.
orfandad f. orphanage.
orfanato m. orphanage, orphan asylum.
orfanatorio m. Am. See **orfanato**.
orfebre m. goldsmith; silversmith.
orfeón m. glee club, choir.
orgánico adj. organic, organical, harmonious.
organismo m. organism.
organización f. organization.
organizador m. organizer.
organizar v. to organize, to arrange.
organillo m. hand organ.
órgano m. organ.
orgía f. orgy; wild revel; frantic revel.
orgullo m. pride, haughtiness; loftiness, arrogance.
orgulloso adj. haughty, proud, lofty, arrogant.
orientar v. to orientate; to give the right direction to; to orient; —se to orient oneself, to find one's bearings.
oriente m. Orient, East, Levant; source, origin.
orificación f. orifice, small hole; mouth, aperture, outlet.
origen m. origin, source, motive; family lineage.
original adj. original, strange, quaint; primitive; m. original, first copy, archetype, manuscript; queer person.
originalidad f. originality.
originar v. to originate; to cause to be; to bring into existence; —se to originate, to take existence.
orilla f. shore, bank, beach; edge, border, margin; —s outskirts, environs.
orillar v. to border; to trim the edge of; to skirt; to go along the edge of; to leave a selvage on cloth; to force, to compell.
orín m. rust; stain, taint of guilt; defect; —es urine.
orina f. urine.
orinar v. to urinate.
oriol m. oriole.
oriundo adj. native; originated, derived from; ser — de to come from.

orla f. list, selvage, border, fringe; trimming; orle.
orlar v. to border; to edge; to trim with a border. or fringe.
ornado adj. ornate.
ornamentar v. to adorn, to ornament, to embellish.
ornamento m. ornament, decoration; —s sacred vestments; frets, mouldings, etc.
ornar v. to adorn.
oro m. gold; ornament; wealth, riches; —s gold coins; Spanish card suit; **no todo lo que reluce es —** all that glitters is not gold.
orondo adj. self-satisfied; puffed up; pompous; showy; vain; Am. serene, calm.
óvalo m. oval.
oveja f. sheep.
ovejero m. shepherd; sheepdog.
ovejuno adj. sheep, pertaining or relating to sheep.
overo adj. peach-colored, applied to horses and cattle; Am. mottled, spotted; multicolored; **ponerle a uno —** Am. to insult someone.
overol or **overoles** m. Am. overalls.
ovillar v. to ball; to hank; to wind or form into a ball; **—se** to curl up into a ball.
ovillo m. ball of yarn or thread; clew, thread wind upon a bottom; tangle; **hacerse uno un —** to curl up into a ball; to become entangled; to confuse.
oxidado p.p. rusted; adj. rusty.
oxidar v. to oxidize; to rust; **—se** to become oxidized, to rust.
oxígeno m. oxygen.
oyente m. & f. listener, auditor, hearer; adj. listening.

P

pabellón m. pavilion; canopy, fieldbed; banner, flag; shelter, covering; external ear.
pabilo m. wick; snuff of a candle.
pacer v. irr. to pasture, to graze, to gnaw, to feed.
paciencia f. patience, endurance.
paciente adj. patient; m. & f. patient.
pacienzudo adj. patient, tolerant.
pacificar v. to pacify; to appease.
pacífico adj. pacific; peaceful, calm.
pacto m. pact, agreement, contract, covenant.
padecer v. irr. to suffer, to be liable to.

padecimiento m. suffering, sufferance.
padrastro m. stepfather; hangnail.
padre m. father; male of animals; source, origin; principal author; **—s** parents, ancestors; **— de familia** householder, housekeeper; **— santo** the Pope; **— nuestro** the Lord's prayer; Am. very great, stupendous.
padrenuestro m. paternoster, the Lord's Prayer; Our Father.
padrino m. godfather; second in a duel; protector, assistant, sponsor, patron; best man at a wedding.
paella f. a popular rice dish, with chicken, vegetables, etc.
paga f. payment; fee; pay; salary.
pagadero adj. payable; m. time and place of payment.
pagado p.p. & adj. paid; **— de sí mismo** pleased with oneself.
pagador m. payer; paymaster; paying teller (bank).
paganismo m. paganism, heathenism.
pagano adj. pagan, heathen; m. pagan; payer; dupe; sucker.
pagar v. to pay, to pay for; to requite, to return; to please, to give pleasure; to reward; **—se de** to be proud of; to boast of; to be pleased with; **—se de palabras** Am. to let oneself be tricked; **—se a nueve** Am. to pay in excess.
pagaré m. a note of hand, a promissory note; I.O.U.
página f. page.
paginar v. to page.
pago m. payment, fee, reward; **suspender el —** to stop payment; **pronto —** prompt payment.
país m. country, land, region; ground; soil.
paisaje m. landscape.
paisanaje m. peasantry; country people; civilians; Am. gang of farm laborers.
paisano m. fellow countryman; peasant; civilian.
paja f. straw; chaff; rubbish; beard of grain; blade of grass; froth; **por quítame allá estas —s** for a small trifle; **en un quítame allá esas —s** in a jiffy, in a second; **a humo de —s** thoughtlessly; lightly.
pajar m. straw loft, barn; place where straw is kept.
pájaro m. bird; shrewd, sly fellow;

paje Am. absent-minded person; person of suspicious conduct; — **carpintero** woodpecker; — **mosca** humming bird; **más vale — en mano que ciento volando** a bird in the hand is worth two in the bush.

paje m. page, valet, attendant; cabin boy.

pajizo adj. made of straw; covered with straw; straw-colored.

pajonal m. plain or field of tall, coarse grass.

pala f. shovel, trowel; scoop; paddle; blade of an oar; racket; cunning; craftiness; **meter la —** to deceive with cunning; to stall; to pretend to work; to flatter.

palabra f. word; affirmation; promise; offer; **— de matrimonio** promise of marriage; **—s mayores** offensive or insulting words; **de —** by word of mouth; **cuatro —s** few words; **empeñar la —** to promise; **tener la —** to have the floor; **¡—!** Am. I mean it, it is true!

palabrero adj. wordy, talkative.

palabrita f. a little word, a few words, a word of advice.

palaciego m. courtier; adj. relating to a palace or court.

palacio m. palace.

paladar m. palate, taste, relish; longing desire.

paladear v. to relish, to taste with relish.

paladín m. knight; champion.

palanca f. lever; crowbar; bar used for carrying a load.

palangana f. washbowl, basin; Am. platter; large wooden bowl; m. Am. bluffer, charlatan.

palco m. theatre box; scaffold raised for spectators at any exhibition; **— escénico** stage.

palenque m. palisade, fence; enclosure; Am. hitching post or plank.

paleta f. small flat shovel; mason's trowel; shoulder blade; painter's palette; Am. candy, sweetmeat or ice cream attached to a little stick; wooden paddle to stir with.

paletilla f. shoulder blade.

palidecer v. irr. to pale; to grow pale.

palidez f. pallor, paleness; ghastliness.

palizada f. palisade, stockade.

palma f. palm tree; palm leaf; palm of the hand; ferule; **llevarse la —** to carry the day; **batir —s** to clap.

palmada f. slap, clap.

palmario adj. clear, evident.

palmatoria f. ferule; small candlestick.

palo m. stick, cudgel; timber; wood; log; mast; blow with a stick; execution on the gallows; suit in a deck of cards; stalk of fruit, pedicle; **— de Campeche** logwood; Am. reprimand; large swallow of liquor; **a medio —** Am. half drunk.

paloma f. dove, pigeon; a mild, meek, dovelike person; **— torcaz** ringdove; **—s** whitecaps.

palomar m. dovecot, pigeon house.

palomilla f. little dove; moth; backbone of a horse; Am. gang; **—s** small whitecaps.

palomita f. little dove; **—s** popcorn.

palpable adj. palpable adj. palpable, evident, clear; obvious.

palpar v. to feel, to touch; to grope in the dark.

palpitación f. palpitation, panting, heaving; beat, throb.

palpitante adj. palpitating; vibrating; throbbing; exciting; trembling; **la cuestión —** the burning question.

palpitar v. to palpitate, to pant, to flutter, to throb, to beat.

palta f. Am. avocado, alligator pear.

palúdico adj. marshy; **fiebre palúdica** malarial or marsh fever; malaria.

pampa f. Am. vast, treeless plain of South America; prairie; m. & f. pampa, Indian of Argentina; m. language of the pampa Indian; adj. pertaining to the pampa Indian; **caballo —** Am. horse with head and body of different color; **trato —** Am. dubiously honest deal; **estar a la —** Am. to be in the open; **quedar en la —** Am. to be left in the lurch.

pampeano adj. Am. of, or pertaining to the pampas; m. Am. inhabitant of the pampas.

pampero m. Am. pampero, inhabitant of the pampa; violent wind of the pampa.

pan m. bread, a loaf; food in general; **— de boda** honeymoon; wedding cake; **echar —es** Am. to brag, to boast.

pana f. corduroy.
panadería f. bakery.
panadero m. baker; Am. flatterer.
panal m. honeycomb; sweet meat made of sugar, egg white and lemon.
panamericano adj. Pan-American.
pandearse v. to bulge, to warp, to sag.
pandeo m. sag, bulge.
pandilla f. gang, band, league, party.
panfleto m. pamphlet.
pánico m. panic; adj. panic, panicky.
panne f. accident, car trouble.
panocha f. ear of corn; Am. Mexican raw sugar; kind of tamale.
panqué m. Am. small cake; cup cake; pancake.
pantalón m. trousers; pants.
pantalla f. sconce; any screen or shelter.
pantano m. swamp; dam; difficulty, obstacle.
pantanoso adj. swampy, marshy, muddy.
pantera f. panther.
pantorrilla f. calf of the leg.
pantufla f. slipper.
panza f. paunch, belly.
panzón adj. big-bellied.
pañal m. diaper; swaddling-cloth; estar en —es to have little knowledge of anything.
pañero m. clothier.
paño m. cloth; blotch or spot in the skin; spot in the looking-glasses; film on the eyeball; Am. parcel of tillable land; kerchief; — de manos towel; — de mesa tablecloth; al — off-stage; —s clothes; —s menores underwear.
pañolón m. scarf, large shawl.
pañuelo m. handkerchief.
papa m. Pope; f. potato; fib; lie; —s pap, a soup for infants; echar —s Am. to fib, to lie; no saber ni — Am. to be ignorant.
papá m. father, papa; — grande grandfather.
papagayo m. parrot; talker; chatterer.
papal adj. papal.
papalote m. Am. kite.
papamoscas m. flycatcher (bird); ninny; simpleton.
papanatas m. simpleton, fool, dunce, ninny.
paparrucha f. silliness.
paparruchero m. fibber.
papel m. paper; treatise, discourse; part acted in a play; actor, actress; — avitelado vellum paper; — de estraza brown paper; — de lija sandpaper; — moneda paper money; hacer el — de to play the role of; hacer un buen (or mal) — to cut a good (or bad) figure.
papelera f. folder, file, case or device for keeping papers; wastepaper basket.
papelero m. paper manufacturer or vendor; newsboy.
papelería f. stationery store; stationery.
papeleta f. card, file card; slip of paper.
papelucho m. worthless piece of paper.
papera f. goiter; —s mumps.
paquete m. package; parcel; bundle; dandy; adj. Am. dolled up; insincere.
par adj. even; equal; alike; sin — matchless; m. pair, couple; peer of the realm; —es o nones odd or even (a play); de — en — wide open.
para prep. for; to; toward; in order to; ¿— qué? what for? para que so that; — siempre forever; — mis adentros to myself; sin qué ni — qué without reason; m. Am. Paraguayan tobacco.
parabién m. congratulation; dar el — to congratulate.
parabrisa m. windshield.
paracaídas m. parachute.
paracaidista m. & f. parachutist.
parachoques m. bumper.
parada f. stop; halt; halting; pause, suspension; fold for cattle; relay; dam; stake, set, bet; parade; Am. boastfulness.
paradero m. whereabouts; end; stopping place.
parado p.p. & adj. inactive; stopped; unoccupied; fixed; motionless; Am. stiff, proud; caer uno — Am. to land on one's feet; to be lucky; estar bien — Am. to be well-fixed; well-established.
paradoja f. paradox.
parafina f. paraffin.
paraguas m. umbrella.
paragüería f. umbrella stand or shop.
paragüero m. umbrella maker or vendor.
paraguayo adj. & m. Paraguayan.
paraíso m. paradise, heaven; upper gallery in a theatre.
paraje m. place, spot, situation.

paralelismo m. parallelism.
paralelo adj. parallel; similar; m. parallel, comparison.
parálisis f. paralysis.
paralizar v. to paralyze; to stop.
páramo m. paramo, desert, wilderness; any place extremely cold.
parangón m. comparison.
parangonar v. to compare.
paraninfo m. paranymph, assembly hall; auditorium; harbinger of felicity.
parapeto m. parapet.
parar v. to stop, to halt, to desist, to give over; to detain; to end; to parry (fencing); to set up (type); — **mientes en** to observe; to notice; — **las orejas** Am. to pay close attention; —**se** Am. to stand up.
pararrayos m. lightning rod.
parásito m. parasite; adj. parasitic.
parasol m. parasol.
parcela f. parcel of land; small particle; small part.
parcial adj. partial, partisan, follower.
parcialidad f. partiality; faction, party.
parche m. mending patch; sticking plaster; drum.
pardal m. sparrow; linnet; sly fellow.
pardear v. to grow dusky; to appear brownish-grey.
pardo adj brown; dark-grey; dark; cloudy.
pardusco adj. greyish; brownish.
parear v. to pair, couple, match, mate.
parecer v. irr. to seem; to appear; to judge; to show up; —**se** to resemble each other, to look alike; m. opinion, advise, counsel; appearance; looks; **al —** apparently, seemingly.
parecido adj. alike, similar; resembling; **bien —** good looking; m. similarity, likeness, resemblance.
pared f. wall; — **maestra** main wall; — **medianera** partition wall.
pareja f. pair; couple; match; partner; brace; Am. horse race.
parejero m. Am. race horse; overfamiliar person, backslapper, hail-fellow-well-met.
parejo adj. equal, similar, smooth; adv. Am. hard.
parentela f. relatives, kin, parentage; kindred.
parentesco m. kinship; kindred, relationship.

paréntesis m. parenthesis; digression; **entre —** by the way.
paria m. & f. outcast; paria.
paridad f. par, equality, parity.
pariente m. & f. relative, relation by birth or marriage.
parir v. to give birth; to bear (children); to be productive; to publish.
parlamentar v. to converse; to talk; to parley.
parlamentario adj. parliamentary; parliamentarian.
parlamento m. speech; parliament; parley.
parlanchín adj. talkative, chatterer; jabberer; m. talker.
parlero adj. talkative, loquacious; chirping.
parlotear v. to prate; to prattle; to chatter; to gossip.
parloteo m. chatter, prattle, idle talk.
paro m. work suspension; lockout; Am. throw, in the game of dice; — **y pinta** Am. game of dice.
parodia f. parody.
parodiar v. to parody; to imitate.
parótidas f. pl. mumps.
parpadear v. to wink; to blink; to twinkle.
parpadeo m. winking; blinking.
párpado m. eyelid.
parque m. park; ammunition.
parra f. grapevine; earthenware jug.
parrafada f. chat.
párrafo m. paragraph; **echar un —** to have a chat with.
parranda f. revel; orgy; spree; Am. gang, band; **andar (or ir) de —** to go on a spree.
parrandear v. to revel, to make merry, to go on a spree.
parrilla f. grill, gridiron, broiler, grate.
párroco m. parson.
parroquia f. parish, parochial church; clientele, customers.
parroquiano m. client, customer; parishioner; adj. parochial.
parsimonia f. thrift; parsimony, economy, moderation; prudence.
parsimonioso adj. thrifty; stingy; cautious, slow.
parte f. part, portion; share, lot; district, territory, place; party; interest; report, return; **de algún tiempo a esta —** for some time past; **de — de** on behalf of; **de — a —** through, from one side to the other; **dar — to inform**; to share; **echar a mala —**

to take amiss; **en —** partly; **por todas —s** everywhere; m. telegram; message.

partera f. midwife.

partición f. partition, division.

participación f. participation, share; notice.

participante m. & f. sharing, participant; adj. participating, sharing.

participar v. to participate, to share; to inform; to notify; to partake.

partícipe m. & f. participant; sharing; adj. participating.

participio m. participle.

partícula f. particle.

particular adj. particular, peculiar, special; private; personal, individual; strange; odd; **en —** specially; m. private citizen; individual; point; detail; matter.

partida f. departure, leave; charge, item, anotation; record; band; group, party; squad; shipment; game; set, in tenis; Am. part in the hair; **— de bautismo (de matrimonio** or **de defunción)** birth (marriage or death) certificate; **— de campo** picnic; **— de caza** hunting party; **— doble** double-entry bookkeeping; **confesar la —** Am. to tell the truth, to speak plainly; **jugar una mala —** to play a mean trick.

partidario m. partisan, follower; party man; supporter.

partido m. party, faction, group; contest, game; profit, advantage; district; **a** (or **al) —** Am. in equal shares; **dar —** Am. to give a handicap or advantage (in certain games); **darse a —** to yield, give up; **sacar — de** to derive advantage from, make the best of; **tomar un —** to decide, make a decision.

partir v. to split, to divide; to cut; to part; to break; to depart; to leave; to distribute; **a — de hoy** starting today; from this day on; **a** (or **al) —** Am. in equal parts; **— a uno por el eje** Am. to ruin someone.

partitura f. musical score.

parto m. childbirth, delivery; product; offspring; parturition; **estar de —** to be in labor.

parvada f. pile of unthreshed grains; place for unthreshed corn.

parvedad f. smallness; trifle; bit of food, snack; littleness; minuteness.

párvulo m. child; very small; innocent.

pasa f. raisin; woolly hair of negroes; passage of birds.

pasada f. passing, passage; Am. stay; embarrassment; shame; **una mala —** a mean trick; **de —** on the way; incidentally; by the way; **dar una — por** to pass by, walk by.

pasadizo m. aisle, narrow hall; narrow passage or covered way.

pasado m. past; adj. overripe; spoiled; Am. dried (fruits); Am. thin, bony (animal); **— mañana** day after tomorrow; **el año —** last year; **en días —s** in days gone by.

pasaje m. passage, fare, ticket; total number of passengers; road, way, straight; narrow pass; event, accident; Am. private alley; anecdote.

pasajero adj. passing; temporary; transient, transitory, fugitive, traveller, passenger, fleeting.

pasamano m. railing; handrail; gangplank; gangway (of a ship); balustrade; lace or edging for clothes.

pasaporte m. passport; furlough.

pasar v. to pass; to cross; to surpass; to exceed; to pierce; to go forward; to go over (in, by, to); to enter; to carry over; to take across; to happen; to get along; to swallow; to overlook; to tolerate, suffer; to ascend; to be promoted to a higher post; to pass away; to penetrate; to pass beyond the limit; **— las de Caín** to have a hard time; **— por alto** to omit; to overlook; **— por las armas** to execute; **—se** to transfer, change over; to get overripe, spoiled; to exceed, go beyond; **se me pasó decirle** I forgot to tell you; **pasársela a uno** Am. to deceive someone, break someone's confidence; **un buen —** enough to live on.

pasarela f. gangplank.

pasatiempo m. pastime; amusement; Am. cookie.

pascua f. Easter; Jewish Passover; **— florida** (or **de resurrección**); Easter Sunday; **— de Navidad** Christmas; **estar como una —** to be as merry as a cricket; **santas —s** be it so.

— 178 —

pase m. pass, permit; thrust (in fencing); permission; passport.

pasear v. to walk; to take a walk; to ride; to exercise; —se to take a walk; to parade; —se en automóvil to take an automobile ride; —se a caballo to go horseback riding.

paseo m. walk, ride; parade; public park; boulevard; — en automóvil automobile ride; dar un — to take a walk.

pasillo m. aisle; hallway; corridor; short step; short skit; Am. a type of dance music; runner, hall carpet; basting stitch.

pasión f. passion, suffering; the last suffering of the Redeemer.

pasivo adj. passive; inactive; not acting; unresisting; m. liabilities, debts, debit; debit side (in bookkeeping).

pasmar v. to astound, to stun; to benumb; to stupefy; to chill, to deaden; to marvel; to wonder; —se to be amazed; to be stunned; Am. to become dried up, shriveled up; to get bruised by the saddle or pack (said of horses and mules).

pasmo m. amazement; astonishment; wonder; awe.

pasmoso adj. astonishing, astounding; marvellous, wonderful.

paso m. pass, step; passage (act of passing); gait; pace, pacing, (motion of horses); flight of steps; lobby; narrow entrance; footstep; progress, advance, improvement; de — by the way; al — que while; salir del — to get out of a difficulty; marcar el — Am. to obey humbly.

pasta f. paste; dough; noodles; bullion; book cover, binding; cookie, cracker; de buena — of good temper or disposition.

pastal m. Am. range, grazing land, large pasture.

pastar v. to pasture, to graze, to feed cattle.

pastear v. to pasture, to graze, to feed cattle.

pastel m. pie; pastry roll; filled pastry; blotted print; trick, fraud; secret pact; plot; pintura al — pastel painting.

pastelería f. pastry shop, bakery; pastry.

pastelero m. pastry cook; Am. turncoat.

pasterizar v. to pasteurize.

pastilla f. tablet (medicine, candy, etc.); bar (chocolate); cake (soap).

pastizal m. pasture, grassland.

pasto m. pasture; grassland; grazing, nourishment; Am. grass; a — without restrain.

pastor m. shepherd; pastor (clergyman).

pastoral adj. pastoral; f. pastoral play; idyll; pastoral letter.

pastorela f. pastoral, pastoral play.

pastoril adj. pastoral.

pastoso adj. pasty, soft; mellow (voice); Am. grassy.

pastura f. pasture; fodder, feed; pasture ground.

pata f. foot, leg (of an animal); female duck; flap; pocket flap; a — on foot; — de gallo wrinkle at the corner of the eye; — de perro Am. wanderer; meter la — to make an embarrassing blunder; —s arriba head over heels upside down.

patacón m. Am. silver coin worth about one peso.

patada f. kick; step, pace; footprint; intoxicating effect; a —s with kicks; in great abundance; en dos —s Am. in a jiffy, in a second.

patalear v. to kick around; to stamp.

pataleo m. kicking, stamping.

pataleta f. convulsion; fainting fit.

patán m. boor, ill-mannered person; rustic; adj. rude, boorish, ill-mannered.

patata f. potato.

patear v. to kick, to stamp the foot; to tramp about; to trample on; to humiliate; Am. to kick, to spring back (as a gun); to have a kick or intoxicating effect.

patentar v. to patent

patente adj. patent, evident, clear; manifest, obvious, palpable; f. patent, grant, warrant, commission, privilege; de — Am. excellent, of best quality.

patentizar v. to evidence, to render evident, to reveal, to show.

paternal adj. paternal, fatherly.

paternidad f. paternity, fatherhood, fathership; authorship.

paterno adj. paternal, fatherly.

patético adj. pathetic.

patibulario adj. harrowing, frightful; criminal.

patíbulo m. scaffold, gallows.

patilla f. whiskers; small foot;

Am. railing of a balcony; slip of a plant; —s the Devil.
patín m. skate; small court or yard; goosander; **— de ruedas** roller skate.
patinadero m. skating ring.
patinar v. to skate; to skid.
patio m. patio, court, courtyard; Am. railway switchyard; **pasarse uno al —** Am. to take undue liberties.
patituerto adj. crook-legged; knock-kneed; bow-legged.
patizambo adj. knock-kneed.
pato m. duck; **pagar el —** to be the goat; to get the blame; **andar —** Am. to be flat broke; penniless; **hacerse —** Am. to play the fool; **pasarse de — a ganso** Am. to take undue liberties; **ser el — de la boda** Am. to be the life of the party.
patochada f. stupidity; blunder; nonsense.
patraña f. fabulous tale; lie; falsehood.
patria f. fatherland, native country.
patriarca m. patriarch.
patriarcal adj. patriarchal.
patrimonio m. patrimony; inheritance.
patrio adj. native; paternal.
patriota m. & f. patriot.
patriótico adj. patriotic.
patriotismo m. patriotism.
patrocinar v. to favour, to patronize; to sponsor; to protect.
patrocinio m. patronage, protection.
patrón m. patron; boss; patron saint; sponsor; master; proprietor; landlord; host; skipper; pattern, standard, model; sample, copy.
patrona f. landlady, patroness; hostess.
patronato m. board of trustees; foundation (for educational, cultural, or charitable purposes); patronship.
patrono m. patron, protector; trustee; patron saint.
patrulla f. patrol; squad; gang.
patrullar v. to patrol.
pausa f. pause, stop, rest.
pausar v. to pause.
pauta f. norm, rule, standard; guide lines for writing; model; example.
pava f. turkey hen; Am. kettle; tea pot; tea kettle; jest, coarse joke; **pelar la —** to talk by night at the window (said of lovers).

pavesa f. cinder; small firebrand; burnt wick or snuff of a candle; **—s** cinders.
pavimentar v. to pave.
pavimento m. pavement.
pavo m. turkey; Am. sponged, parasite; **— real** peacock; **comer —** to be a wallflower at a dance; adj. silly; foolish; vain.
pavón m. peacock.
pavonearse v. to strut; to swagger.
pavoneo m. strut, swagger.
pavor m. awe, dread, fear, terror.
pavoroso adj. frightful, dreadful; hair-rising.
payasada f. clownish act or remark.
payasear v. to clown; to play the fool.
paz f. peace.
pazguato adj. simple, dumb, stupid; m. simpleton.
peaje m. toll (for crossing a bridge or ferry).
pealar See **pialar**.
peal See **pial**.
peatón m. pedestrian.
peca f. freckle.
pecado m. sin.
pecador m. sinner; adj. sinful.
pecar v. to sin; **— de bueno** to be too good; **— de oscuro** to be exceedingly unclear, too complicated.
pecera f. fish bowl.
pecoso adj. freckly, freckled.
peculado adj. embezzlement, peculation.
peculiar adj. peculiar; appropriate.
peculiaridad f. peculiarity.
pechada f. Am. bump, push, shove with the chest; bumping contest between two riders.
pechar v. Am. to bump, to push, to shove with the chest.
pecho m. chest, breast, bossom; courage, fortitude; heart; conscience; **dar el —** to nurse, to suckle; **hombre de pelo en —** firm, spirited man; **tomar a —s** to take to heart.
pechuga f. breast of a fowl; bossom; Am. courage, nerve; audacity, impudence.
pedagogía f. pedagogy.
pedagógico adj. pedagogic.
pedagogo m. pedagogue, teacher, schoolmaster, educator.
pedal m. pedal; treadle.
pedalear v. to pedal.
pedante adj. pedantic, pedant, affected, vain, superficial.
pedantesco adj. pedantic.

pedazo m. piece, bit, part of a whole; lump; **hacer —s** to tear or break into pieces; **a —s** (or **en —s**) in fragments, in pieces, in bits.

pedernal m. flint.

pedestal m. pedestal, base.

pedestre adj. pedestrian, pedestrious, going on foot, walking; commomplace, low.

pedido m. commercial order; wares, goods set for sale; request, petition.

pedigüeño adj. begging, demanding, craving.

pedir v. irr. to solicit; to beg; to ask; to demand; to require; to crave; to beg alms; to claim; **— cuentas** to call to account; **a — de boca** exactly as desired.

pedrada f. hit with a stone; lapidation; **a —s** by stoning; with stones; **echar a alguien a —s** to stone somebody out; **matar a —s** to stone to death.

pedregal m. rocky ground; place full of stones.

pedregoso adj. rocky, stony, pebbly; afflicted with the gravel.

pedrusco m. boulder.

pedúnculo m. stem, stalk; peduncle.

pegajoso adj. sticky; contagious; adhesive.

pegar v. to join, to unite; to clap; to chastise; to punish; to beat; to infect; to communicate a distemper; to cleave; to cling; Am. to tie; to fasten; **— fuego** to set on fire; **— un chasco** to play a trick; to disappoint; **— un susto** to give a scare; **— un salto (una carrera)** to take a jump (a run); **pegársela a uno** to fool somebody.

pegote m. plaster made of pitch; sticky thing; clumsy patch; sponger; thick, sticky concotion; clumsy addition or insertion in a literally or artistic work.

peinado m. coiffure, hairdo; hairdressing; adj. combed, curled, dressed; effeminate; **bien —** spruce, trim.

peinador m. hairdresser; short wrapper or dressing gown.

peinadora f. woman hairdresser.

peinar v. to comb; Am. to flatter.

peine m. comb.

peineta f. large ornamented comb.

peladilla f. small pebble.

pelado p.p. & adj. plumed; bared; decorticated; peeled; plunked; skinned; hairless; featherless; treeless; barren; bare; penniless, broke; m. Am. ragged fellow; ill-bred person.

pelafustán m. tramp, vagabond.

pelagatos m. ragged fellow, tramp; vagrant, ragamuffin.

pelaje m. nature and quality of the hair and of wool.

pelar v. to pull out the hair; to strip off the feathers; to shell; to cheat; to rob; to boil; to scald; Am. to beat, to thrash; to slander; **— los dientes** Am. to smile affectedly; **— los ojos** Am. to open one's eyes wide; **—se** to cast the hair; to loose one's hair; to peel off; Am. to slip away; to die; **—selas por algo** to be dying for something, to want something very much.

peldaño m. step of a flight of stairs.

pelea f. battle, fight; quarrel, dispute, conflict; struggle; **— de gallos** cockfight.

pelear v. to fight, quarrel, combat, contend, dispute; to toil; **—se** to scuffle; to come to blows.

peletería f. trade of a furrier or skinner; fellmonger's shop; Am. leather goods, leather shop; shoe store.

película f. pellicle, thin skin; membrane, film; motion picture film.

peligrar v. to be in danger.

peligro m. danger.

peligroso adj. dangerous.

pelillo m. short, fine, tender hair; **—s** trouble, nuisance; **echar —s a la mar** to become reconciled; **no pararse en —s** not to stop at small details, not to bother about trifles; **no tener —s en la lengua** to speak frankly.

pelirrojo adj. redheaded, redhaired.

pelo m. hair; nap; soft fibres of plants; any slender thread of wool, silk, etc; pile; color of the coat of animals; flaw in precious stones or crystals; trifle; **venir al —** to come to the purpose, timely; **con todos sus —s y señales** with every possible detail; **por (or en) un —** Am. on the point of, almost, by a hair's breadth; **tomar el — a** to kid, to make fun of; **no aflojar un —** Am. no to yield an inch.

pelota f. ball; ball game; Am. boat made of cowhide; **en —** (or **en**

— 181 —

—s) stark naked; darle a la — Am. to hit upon by chance.
pelotera f. brawl, row, riot, Am. crowd.
pelotón m. platoon of soldiers; crowd, gang, heap, pile; large ball.
peluca f. wig.
peludo adj. hairy; shaggy; m. shaggy mat of an oval shape.
peluquería f. barbershop; hairdresser's shop.
peluquero m. hairdresser, barber.
pelusa f. down; fuzz; nap.
pellejo m. hide; skin; peel; felt; pelt; **salvar el —** to save one's life; **jugarse el —** to gamble one's life.
pellizcar v. to pinch; to nip; to wound artfully; to gripe.
pellizco m. pinching, nipping; pinch, nip.
pena f. punishment, pain, penalty, correction; painfulness, affliction, sorrow, grief; labor; hardship; difficulty; toil; Am. embarrassment; **a duras —s** with great difficulty or trouble; scarcely, hardly; **valer la —** to be worthwhile.
penacho m. tuft, crest; plume.
penal adj. penal; **código —** penal code.
penalidad f. hardship, trouble, penalty.
penar v. to suffer pain; to crave; to linger; to chastise; to worry; to fret; **— por** to long for.
penca f. leaf of a cactus plant; Am. **coger una —** to get drunk.
pendencia f. quarrel; scuffle, fight.
pendenciero adj. quarrelsome.
pender v. to hang; to dangle; to depend.
pendiente f. slope; m. earring; pendant; adj. hanging, dangling; pending.
pendón m. banner; standard.
péndulo m. pendulum.
penetración f. penetration; acuteness; keen judgment.
penetrante adj. penetrating; acute; keen.
penetrar v. to penetrate, to pierce, to force in; to fathom; to comprehend.
península f. peninsula.
peninsular adj. peninsular.
penitencia f. penance, penalty; fine.
penitenciaría f. penitentiary.
penitente adj. repentant, penitent; m. & f. penitent.

penoso adj. painful; hard; difficult; grievous; laborious; tormenting; fatiguing, embarrassing; Am. shy; timid.
pensador m. thinker; adj. thinking.
pensamiento m. thought, mind; idea; meditation; pansy.
pensar v. irr. to think; to consider, to meditate; to imagine; to intend; to mean.
pensativo adj. pensive.
pensión f. pension; board; scholarship for study; boardinghouse; **— completa** room and board.
pensionado m. pensioner (person receiving a pension); adj. & p.p. pensioned.
pensionar v. to pension.
pensionista m. & f. boarder; pensioner (person receiving a pension).
pentagrama m. musical staff.
penúltimo adj. next to the last.
penumbra f. partial shadow, dimness.
penumbroso adj. dim.
peña f. rock.
peñasco m. large rock.
peñascoso adj. rocky.
peón m. unskilled laborer; foot soldier; spinning top; pawn (in chess); Am. farm hand; apprentice; **— de albañil** mason's helper.
peonada f. gang of laborers or peons.
peor adj. & adv. worse; worst; **— que** worse than; **— que —** that is even worse; **tanto —** so much the worse.
pepa f. Am. seed (of an apple, melon, etc.); marble (to play with).
pepenar v. Am. to pick up; to seize, to grab.
pepino m. cucumber.
pepita f. seed (of an apple, melon, etc.); pip (disease of birds); nugget, lump of gold or other minerals; Am. fruitstone, pit.
pequeñez f. smallness; childhood; trifle; meanness; parvity.
pequeño adj. small, little; young; low, humble; m. child.
pera f. pear; goatee; sinecure, easy job.
peral m. pear tree; pear orchard.
percal m. percale.
percance m. misfortune, accident; occurrence.
percepción f. perception; idea.

perceptible adj. perceptible, noticeable.
percibir v. to perceive; to collect; to receive.
percudido adj. dirty, grimy.
percudir v. to soil, to make dirty or grimy; to tarnish; —se to get grimy.
percha f. perch; clothes or hat rack; pole; roost.
perchero m. clothes or hat rack.
perder v. irr. to lose; to forfeit; to squander away; to lavish; to misspend; to ruin; to harm; to miss; —se to lose one's way; to get lost; to go astray; to get spoiled; to become ruined.
perdición f. perdition, damnation, hell, ruin.
pérdida f. loss; damage.
perdidamente adv. excessively.
perdido p.p. & adj. lost, strayed, misguided; profligate, disolute; mislaid; ruined; estar — por alguien to be crazy about, or very fond of, someone; m. rake, dissolute fellow; bum, vagabond.
perdigón m. young partridge; bird shot, buckshot; losing gambler.
perdiz f. partridge.
perdón m. pardon; forgiveness, absolution, mercy, grace; remission of a debt.
perdonar v. to pardon, to forgive; to exempt; —se to spare; to excuse.
perdulario m. rake, dissolute person; reckless fellow; good-for-nothing tramp.
perdurable adj. lasting, everlasting; perpetual.
perdurar v. to last, to endure.
perecedero adj. perishable.
perecer v. irr. to perish, to die; to be destroyed; to suffer toil, damage or fatigue; —se to long for, to pine for.
peregrinación f. pilgrimage; peregrination; long journey.
peregrino m. pilgrim; adj. foreign; strange, rare; beautiful, perfect; travelling, wandering; ave peregrina migratory bird, bird of passage.
perejil m. parsley; —es showy dress or apparel.
perenne adj. perennial, enduring, perpetual.
pereza f. laziness; idleness; negligence.
perezoso adj. lazy, indolent, slothful, negligent, idle.
perfección f. perfection; a la — to perfection, perfectly.

perfeccionamiento m. perfecting, perfection; completion.
perfeccionar v. to perfect, to finish, to complete.
perfecto adj. perfect.
perfidia f. perfidy, treachery.
pérfido adj. perfidious, treacherous; faithless.
perfil m. profile; outline; Am. pen or pen point.
perfilar v. to silhouette; to outline; to draw profiles; to sketch outlines; —se to be silhouetted; to show one's profile.
perforación f. perforation, hole; puncture; perforating, boring, drilling.
perforar v. to perforate, pierce, drill, bore.
perfumar v. to perfume, to scent.
perfume m. perfume, scent, fragrance.
perfumería f. perfumery, perfume shop.
pergamino m. parchment.
pericia f. expertness, skill.
perico m. parrakeet, small parrot.
perifollos m. pl. frippery, finery; showy ornaments.
perifrasear v. to periphrase.
perilla f. small pear; ornament in form of a pear; knob; pommel of a saddle; goatee; de — apropos, to the purpose.
perímetro m. perimeter.
periódico m. newspaper; periodical; adj. periodic, periodical.
periodismo m. journalism.
periodista m. & f. journalist; newspaper editor or publisher.
periodístico adj. journalistic.
período m. period; cycle; sentence.
peripecia f. vicissitude; unforeseen incident.
peripuesto adj. very gay, very spruce on dress; dressed up, dolled up; decked out.
perito adj. learned; experienced; skilful; skilled; m. expert.
perjudicar v. to damage; to impair; to harm; to prejudice.
perjudicial adj. harmful, injurious.
perjurar v. to perjure; to swear falsely; to commit perjure; to curse.
perjurio m. perjury.
perla f. pearl; de —s perfectly, just right.
perlino adj. pearly, pearl-colored.
permanecer v. irr. to remain; to stay; to persist; to endure; to last.
permanencia f. permanence, dura-

tion, stability, stay, sojourn; permanency, perseverancy.
permanente adj. permanent.
permiso m. permission; permit; leave, license, allowance.
permitir v. to permit, let, grant; to consent, agree to; to give leave.
permuta f. exchange, barter.
permutar v. to exchange; to barter; to permute.
pernetas : en — barelegged.
pernicioso adj. harmful.
perno m. bolt; spike; hook of a hinge; Am. tricks, frauds.
pero conj. but, except, yet; m. exception, objection; defect; variety of apple tree; variety of apple.
perogrullada f. platitude; trite or common-place remark.
perón m. Am. a variety of apple.
peroración f. peroration, speech, harangue.
perorar v. to make an impassioned speech; to declaim, to harangue; to plea.
perorata f. harangue, speech.
perpendicular adj. m.& f. perpendicular.
perpetuar v. to perpetuate.
perpetuo adj. perpetual, everlasting.
perplejidad f. perplexity.
perplejo adj. perplexed, bewildered.
perra f. bitch, female dog; drunkenness; — **chica** five-centime copper coin; — **grande** (or **gorda**) ten-centime copper coin.
perrada f. pack of dogs; **hacer una — ** to play a mean trick.
perrera f. kennel; toil; hard work, hard job; tantrum; Am. brawl, dispute.
perrilla f. Am. sty (on the eyelid). See orzuelo.
perro m. dog; — **de muestra** pointer; — **de presa** or **dogo** bulldog; — **de lanas** poodle; adj. dogged, tenacious; Am. hard, selfish, mean, stingy.
perruno adj. canine, doglike, doggish, currish.
persecución f. persecution; pursuit.
perseguidor m. pursuer; persecutor.
perseguimiento m. pursuit; persecution.
perseguir v. irr. to pursue; to persecute; to dun; to importune; to beset; to harass; to annoy.
perseverancia f. perseverance.
perseverar v. to persevere.

persiana f. Venetian blind; window shade.
persistencia f. persistence.
persistente adj. persistent.
persistir v. to persist.
persona f. person; personage.
personaje m. personage; character (in a book or play).
personal adj. personal; m. personnel.
personalidad f. personality; individuality; person, personage.
perspectiva f. perspective; view; appearance.
perspicacia f. perspicaciousness, perspicacity, keenness of mind; penetration.
perspicaz adj. keen, perspicacious; shrewd.
persuadir v. to persuade.
persuación f. persuasion.
persuasivo adj. persuasive.
pertenecer v. irr. to belong to; to appertain; to concern; to behoove; to become; to relate to.
perteneciente adj. pertaining, belonging, concerning.
pértiga f. pole, bar, rod.
pertinente adj. pertinent, to the point, apt, fitting.
pertrechos m. pl. military supplies; tools, implements.
perturbación f. uneasiness, agitation, disturbance.
perturbar v. to perturb, to disturb.
peruano adj. & m. Peruvian.
perversidad f. perversity, wickedness, malignity.
perverso adj. perverse, wicked; mischievous; m. pervert.
pervertir v. irr. to pervert, corrupt; to turn from the right; to crook; to seduce; to distort; **—se** to become pervert; to go wrong.
pesa f. weight; — **de reloj** clock weight; **—s y medidas** weights and measures.
pesadez f. heaviness; dullness; drowsiness; slowness; gravity; weight.
pesadilla f. nightmare.
pesado adj. heavy; sound (sleep); tiresome; boring; annoying; slow; dull.
pesadumbre f. grief, sorrow; weight, heaviness.
pésame m. condolence.
pesantez f. gravity; heaviness.
pesar v. to weigh; to consider; to examine; to have weight, value or importance; to cause grief,

pesaroso sorrow or regret; m. grief, sorrow; a — de in spite of.
pesaroso adj. grieved, sad, repentant; restless.
pesca f. fishing; catch; fish caught.
pescadería f. fish market.
pescadero m. fishmonger, dealer in fish.
pescado m. fish; salted codfish.
pescador m. fisherman.
pescar v. to fish; to catch fish; to pick up anything.
pescozón m. slap on the neck with an open hand.
pescuezo m. neck.
pesebre m. manger.
peseta f. peseta, monetary unit of Spain.
pesimismo m. pessimism.
pesimista m. & f. pessimist; adj. pessimistic.
pésimo adj. very bad; the worst.
peso m. weight; weighing; burden; importance; Am. peso, monetary unit or several Spanish American countries.
pesquera f. fishery, place for catching fish.
pesquería f. fishery; fishing.
pesquero adj. fishing; **buque** — fishing boat; **industria pesquera** fishing industry.
pesquisa f. investigation, inquiry; m. Am. police investigator.
pestaña f. eyelash; edging, fringe; **quemarse las —s** to burn the midnight oil; to study hard at night.
pestañear v. to blink; to wink; to flicker.
peste f. pest, pestilence, plague; epidemic; corruption; stink, foul odor; plenty or abundance; **echar —s** to utter insults.
pestillo m. bolt, latch; lock.
petaca f. tobacco pouch; cigar case; Am. leather-covered trunk, suitcase; adj. Am. heavy, clumsy.
pétalo m. petal.
petate m. bundle; impostor; Am. mat of straw or palm leaves; dunce; coward; liar el — to pack up and go; Am. to die; **dejar a uno en un —** Am. to ruin a person; to leave him penniless.
petición f. petition, request.
petirrojo m. robin redbreast.
petiso adj. small, short, dwarfish; Am. small horse, pony.
pétreo adj. stone, stony.
petróleo m. petroleum.
petrolero m. oil man; dealer in petroleum.
petulancia f. flippancy; insolence; petulance.
petulante adj. pert; petulant; insolent; flippant.
pez m. fish; f. rosin, pitch, tar; **— griega** colophony; **— rubia** rosin.
pezón m. nipple; stem, stalk (of a fruit, leaf of flower); point of land.
pezuña f. hoof.
piadoso adj. pious, godly, clement, merciful.
pial m. Am. lasso, lariat (thrown in order to trip an animal); Am. snare, trap.
pialar v. to lasso by tripping with a pial.
piano m. piano; **— de cola** grand piano; **— vertical** upright piano.
piar v. to peep, to chirp, to pule, to call, to whine, to cry.
pica f. pike; spear; picador's goad or lance; stone cutter's hammer; Am. tapping of rubber trees; trail; pique, resentment.
picada f. prick; bite (insect or fish); puncture; sharp pain; dive (of a plane); Am. path, trail (cut through a forest); narrow ford; peck.
picadillo m. minced meat.
picador m. picador, mounted bullfighter armed with a goad; horse-breaker; chopping block; tree tapper.
picadura f. biting, pricking; bite; prick; puncture; sting; cut tobacco.
picante adj. pricking; piquant; high seasoned, acrid, hot, pungent; m. strong seasoning; Am. highly seasoned sauce with chili pepper.
picapleitos m. quarrelsome person; litigious person; pettifogging lawyer; shyster.
picaporte m. latch; latchkey; door knocker.
picar v. to prick; to pierce, to bite; to sting; to peck; to nibble; to itch; to spur, goad; to incite, stimulate; to mince, chop up; to stick; to poke; to hew, to chisel; to pique; to vex; to smart; to burn; to pick; to piddle; Am. to chop (wood); **— muy alto** to aim very high; **— en** to border on; to be somewhat of; **¡pícale!** Am. hurry!; **— se** to be piqued, to be angry; to be moth-

PICARDIA **PINTA**

eaten; to begin to sour; —se to boast of.
picardía f. knavery, roguery, roguishness; malice; wantonness; mischief.
picaresco adj. roguish, knavish, picaresque.
pícaro m. rogue, knavish, vile, low, rascal; adj. mischievous, malicious.
picarón m. big rascal.
picazón f. itch, itching; peevishness.
pico m. beak, bill; sharp point; nib; peak; top; summit; mouth; additional amount, a little over: Am. a small balance; **de —** by the mouth; **tener el — de oro** to be very eloquent; **tener mucho —** to be very talkative.
picoteada f. peck.
picotear v. to peck; to strike with the beak; to chatter; to gossip; Am. to mince; to cut into small pieces.
pichel m. pitcher; mug; pewter tankard.
pichón m. pigeon; Am. any male bird (except roosters); dupe, easy mark; novice, inexperienced person; apprentice; adj. timid, shy.
pie m. foot; leg; base; trunk of trees and plants; sediment; foot (measure of length); motive, occasion; **a — juntillas** steadfastly, firmly; **al — de la letra** to the letter; **no tiene —s ni cabeza** that has neither rhyme nor reason; **ir a —** to walk.
piedad f. piety; pity; mercy; **monte de —** pawnshop.
piedra f. stone; gravel; hailstone; gunflint; **— de amolar** whetstone, grinding stone; **— angular** corner stone; **a — y lodo** shut tight; **— de toque** touchstone.
piel f. skin; hide; leather; fur.
piélago m. high sea; sea; great abundance.
pienso m. feed; daily feed given to horses; **ni por —** not even by a thought.
pierna f. leg; honey jar; **dormir a — suelta** to sleep like a log; **en —s** bare-legged.
pieza f. piece, fragment; coin; part; room in a house; buffoon, wag, jester; **de una —** solid, in one piece; **ser de una —** Am. to be an honest man.
pigmento m. pigment.
pijama m. pajamas.

pila f. trough for cattle; basin; Baptismal font; pile; heap; electric battery; **— de agua bendita** holy water basin; **nombre de —** Christian name; **tener las —s (or por —s)** to have a lot, to have heaps.
pilar m. pillar, column, basin of a fountain; post; milestone.
pilcha f. Am. any article of clothing; mistress; **—s** Am. belongings.
píldora f. pill.
pilmama f. Am. child's nurse, wet nurse.
pilón m. large watering trough; basin of a fountain; drop or ball of a steelyard; counterpoise in an olive press; heap of grapes ready to be pressed; heap of mortar; **— de azúcar** loaf of refined sugar; Am. additional amount; premium given to a buyer.
pilotar or **pilotear** v. to pilot.
pilote m. pile for building.
piloto m. pilot; mate of a ship; Am. generous entertainer or host.
pillaje m. pillage, plunder, foray, marauding.
pillar v. to pillage, plunder, foray; to lay hold of; to chop at; **— un catarro** to catch a cold.
pillo adj. roguish, sly, crafty; m. rogue, rascal, vagabond; Am. species of heron.
pilluelo m. little rascal, scamp.
pimentero m. pepper plant; pepper box; pepper shaker.
pimentón m. large pepper, ground pepper; Cayenne; paprika.
pimienta f. black pepper.
pimiento m. green pepper; red pepper.
pimpollo m. rosebud; bud; shoot, sprout; sucker; attractive youth.
pináculo m. pinnacle, top, summit.
pinar m. pine grove.
pincel m. artist's brush; painter.
pincelada f. stroke of the brush.
pinchar v. to prick; to puncture; to wound.
pingajo m. a rag or patch hanging from clothes; tatter.
pingo m. Am. saddle horse; devil.
pingüe adj. abundant; fat, greasy, oily.
pino m. pine; Am. filling for a meat pie; **hacer —s (or hacer pinitos)** to begin to walk (said of a baby); to begin to do things (said of a novice).
pinta f. spot, mark, blemish, scar; outward sign, aspect; pint (liq-

pintar — **placer**

uid measure); **irse de —** Am. to play hooky, to cut class.

pintar v. to paint; to picture; to describe; to fancy; to imagine; to show; to give signs of; to depict; to feign; Am. to play hooky, to play truant; **no — nada** to be worth nothing; to count for nothing; **las cosas no pintaban bien** things did not look well; **— venados** to play hooky, to cut class; **—se** to put on make-up.

pintarrajear v. to daub, to paint without skill; to smear with paint.

pinto adj. Am. spotted, speckled.

pintor m. painter, artist; **— de brocha gorda** house painter; poor artist.

pintoresco adj. picturesque.

pintura f. painting; picture; paint, color; description; **— al temple** size painting; **— al óleo** oil painting.

pinzas f. pl. pincers, nippers; tweezers; claws (lobsters, crabs, etc.); Am. pliers, tongs.

piña f. pineapple; cone or nut of the pine tree; piña cloth; cluster; Am. pool (billiard game).

piñata f. Am. hanging fancy dressed pot containing fruit, candy, etc., to be broken by children at Christmas time.

piñón m. pine nut; nutpine; pinion.

pío adj. pious, devout; kind, merciful; dappled, spotted (horse).

piojo m. louse.

piojoso adj. lousy, mean, miserable, stingy.

pipa f. tobacco pipe; keg, barrel; reed pipe (musical instrument); **estar —** Am. to be drunk.

pipiar v. to peep, to chirp, to pule.

pipiolo m. novice, beginner; Am. child, youngster.

pipiripao m. a splendid feast.

pique m. pique, resentment; chigger (insect); **a — de** in danger of; on the point of; **echar a —** to sink (a ship); to destroy; **irse a —** to capsize.

piquete m. prick; bite, sting of insects; small hole; picket, stake; Am. cutting edge of scissors.

piragua f. Am. Indian canoe, pirogue.

pirámide f. pyramid.

pirata m. pirate.

piratear v. to pirate.

piropo m. flattery, compliment; variety of garnet; **echar un —** to "throw a bouquet", to compliment.

pirueta f. whirl; somersault; caper; **hacer —s** to cut capers; to turn somersaults; to do stunts.

pisada f. footstep; footprint; **dar una —** to step on, to stamp on; **seguir las —s de** to imitate.

pisapapeles m. paperweight.

pisar v. to step on; to tread; to trample; to stamp on the ground; to pound; to cover (said of a male bird).

piscina f. swimming pool, swimming tank; fish pond.

pise m. Am. rut; tread of a wheel. See **rodadura**.

piso m. floor, story, pavement; apartment, flat; tread, trampling, footing.

pisón m. heavy mallet (for pounding, flattening, crushing).

pisotear v. to tramp, to tramp on; to tread under foot; to trample.

pisotón m. stamp, hard step; **dar un —** to step hard, to stamp (upon).

pista f. track, trace, trail, clue; race track; **— de aterrizaje** landing strip.

pistola f. pistol.

pistolera f. holster.

pistón m. piston; Am. cornet.

pita f. Am. agave or century plant; fiber or thread made from the fiber of the agave, century plant or maguey.

pitar v. to toot, to whistle; to pipe; Am. to hiss; to escape; **—se una cosa** Am. to steal something; **salir pitando** Am. to leave on the run.

pitazo m. toot, whistle, blast.

pitillera f. cigarette case.

pitillo m. cigarette.

pito m. whistle; cigarette; Am. tick (insect); **no valer un —** it is not worth a straw; **no saber ni — de una cosa** Am. not to know anything about a subject.

pizarra f. slate; blackboard.

pizarrín m. slate pencil.

pizarrón m. blackboard.

pizca f. pinch, small bit; Am. harvest.

placa f. badge, insignia; plaque, tablet.

placentero adj. pleasant, agreeable; joyful, merry.

placer v. irr. to please, to content; m. pleasure; sand bank, shoal; placer, place where gold is ob-

placero m. market vendor.
plácido adj. placid, calm.
plaga f. plague, calamity; pest.
plagar v. to plague, to infest, to overrun with; —se de to become plagued or infested with.
plagiar v. to kidnap; to plagiarize, to steal and use as own the ideas, writings, etc. of another; to abduct.
plan m. plan; design; project; drawing; draught.
plana f. page; plain; flat country; mason's trowel; tally sheet; **enmendar la —** a uno to correct a person's mistakes.
plancha f. flatiron; metal plate; gang plank; blunder; Am. railway flatcar; dental plate; **— de blindaje** armor plate; **hacer una —** to make a ridiculous blunder; **tirarse una —** to place oneself in a ridiculous situation.
planchado m. ironing; clothes ironed or to be ironed; adj. Am. smart, clever; brave; dolled up; broke, penniless.
planchar v. to iron; to smooth out; Am. to leave (someone) waiting; to strike with the flat of a blade; to flatter; **— el asiento** Am. to be a wallflower at a dance.
planeador m. glider airplane.
planear v. to plan; to glide (said of an airplane or bird).
planeo m. planning; glide, gliding of an airplane.
planeta m. planet.
plano adj. plane, flat, level, plain; m. plan, design, draft; plane; **dar de —** to hit with the flat of anything.
planta f. plant, plantation; sole of the foot; plan of a building; project, disposition; **— baja** ground floor; **buena —** good looks; **echar —s** to brag.
plantación f. plantation, planting.
plantar v. to plant; to set up; to strike a blow; to put; **—se** to stand firm, to balk; Am. to doll up, to dress up; **dejar a uno plantado** to keep someone waiting indefinitely.
plantear v. to plan; to establish; to carry out; to state; to present a problem; to try.
plantío m. planting; plantation; tree nursery.
plasma m. plasma.

plástico adj. plastic.
plata f. silver; silver coins; silver money; **hablar en —** to speak in plain language.
plataforma f. platform.
platanal m. grove of banana trees; banana plantation.
plátano m. banana; banana tree; plane tree.
platea f. main floor of a theatre.
plateado adj. silverplated; silvery.
platear v. to silver; to plate; to cover with silver.
platel m. platter; tray.
platero m. silversmith; jeweler.
plática f. conversation, talk, chat; discourse; colloquy; speech.
platicador m. talker, talkative.
platicar v. to converse; to talk; to chat.
platillo m. saucer; pan; cymbal; stew; dish.
plato m. plate, dish; dinner course; daily fare.
platón m. large plate; platter.
platudo adj. wealthy, rich.
playa f. beach, shore; Am. wide, open space in front of a ranch house; **— de estacionamiento** Am. parking lot.
plaza f. plaza, public square; market place; job, employment; position; room, space, stall; Am. park, promenade; **— de armas** military parade ground; public square; **— fuerte** fortress; **— de gallos** cockpit for cockfights; **— de toros** bullring; **sentar —** to enlist.
plazo m. term, time; **a —s** on credit; in installments.
pleamar f. flood tide, high tide.
plebe f. rabble; masses; common people.
plebeyo adj. plebeian.
plebiscito m. plebiscite, direct vote.
plegadizo adj. folding; pliable; easily bent.
plegar v. to fold; to pleat; to crease; to plait; to double; to crimple, to purse up; **—se** to bend, to yield, to submit.
plegaria f. supplication, prayer; bell rung at noon for prayer.
pleitista m. & f. quarrelsome person.
pleito m. dispute, controversy, debate, litigation, lawsuit; **— de acreedores** bankruptcy proceedings.
plenipotenciario m. plenipotenciary; adj. plenipotenciary, having full power.

PLENITUD — **POLITICO**

plenitud f. plenitude, fullness, completeness; abundance.

pleno adj. full, complete; **sesión plena** joint sesion; **en — día** in broad daylight, openly; **en — rostro (or en plena cara)** right on the face.

pliego m. sheet of paper; sealed letter or document.

pliegue m. fold, crease, pleat; plait.

plomada f. plumb; lead weight, plumb bob.

plomazo m. Am. shot, bullet.

plomería f. the trade of a plumber; plumber's shop; plumbing; lead roof.

plomero m. plumber.

plomizo adj. leaden, lead-colored.

plomo m. lead; plumb; plummet, lead weight; bullet; **a — vertical**; vertically; adj Am. lead-colored.

pluma f. feather; pen; penmanship; writer, author; **— estilográfica (or fuente)** fountain pen.

plumada f. dash, stroke of the pen, flourish.

plumaje m. plumage; plume.

plumero m. feather duster; box for feathers; feather ornament.

plumón m. down; feather mattress.

plumoso adj. down, feathery.

plural adj. plural.

pluvial adj. rain, rainy; **capa —** cope, long cape used by priests during certain religious ceremonies.

población f. population; populating; town, city; Am. house.

poblado m. inhabited place; village; adj. populated; covered with growth.

poblador m. settler of a colony.

poblar v. irr. to people, to found a town; to populate; to colonize; to settle; to fill; to occupy; to breed; to bud; **—se** to become covered.

pobre adj. poor; m. poor man; beggar.

pobrete m. poor devil, poor wretch.

pobretón m. poor old fellow, poor wretch.

pobreza f. poverty; need; lack; want; scarcity; barrenness; indigence; poorness, lowness or littleness of spirit.

pocilga f. pigsty, pigpen.

pocillo m. cup.

poco adj. little, scanty, limited, small in quantity or extent, not much, few, some; m. a little, a bit; adv. little, shortly, briefly, in a short time; **a — presently**, after a short time; **a — rato (or al — rato)** after a short while; **— a —** gently, softly; stop!; little by little; **a los —s meses** after a few months; **por — me caigo** I almost fell; **tener en — a** to hold in low esteem.

podar v. to prune, to trim, to cut off.

podenco m. hound.

poder v. irr. to be able; may or can; to have force or energy to act or resist; in geometry, to value, produce; **no — más** not to be able to do more; to be exhausted; **no puede menos de hacerlo** he cannot help doing it; **no — con la carga** not to be able to lift the load; **—le a uno algo** Am. to be worried or affected by something; **él puede mucho (or poco)** he has much (or little) power; **puede que** it is possible that, it may be that, perhaps; **hasta más no —** to the utmost, to the limit; m. power, authority, dominion, mastery, force; power or letter of attorney.

poderío m. power, dominion; might, wealth.

poderoso adj. powerful, wealthy.

podre f. pus; decayed matter.

podredumbre f. corruption, decay; pus, rotten matter.

podrido adj. rotten.

podrir See **pudrir**.

poema m. poem.

poesía f. poetry; poem; poesy; **—s** poetical works.

poeta m. poet.

poetastro m. poor poet.

noética f. poetics.

poético adj. poetic.

poetisa f. poetess.

polaco adj. Polish; m. Polish, Polish language; Pole.

polaina f. legging; spatterdashes.

polar adj. polar.

polea f. pulley; tackle-block.

polen m. pollen.

policía f. police; m. policeman.

policial m. Am. policeman.

polilla f. moth; consumer; waster.

política f. politics, policy; politeness, civility; **— de campanario** Am. politics of a clique.

politicastro m. bad or incapable politician.

político adj. political, politic; polite, courteous; **madre política or suegra** mother-in-law.

— 189 —

póliza f. policy, written contract; draft; customhouse certificate.
polizonte m. policeman; cop.
polo m. pole.
poltrón adj. lazy, idle, lubberly; commodious, easy; **silla poltrona** easy chair, elbow chair.
polvareda f. cloud of dust; **armar** (or **levantar**) **una —** to kick up the dust; to raise a rumpus.
polvera f. powderbox; compact; powder puff.
polvo m. dust; powder; pinch of snuff or powder; **limpio de — y paja** entirely free; **tomar el —** Am. to escape.
pólvora f. gunpower; fireworks.
polvorear v. to powder, sprinkle with powder.
polvoriento adj. dusty.
polvorín m. powder magazine; priming powder; powder flask; priming horn; Am. spitifire, quick-tempered person.
polla f. pullet (young hen); young lass; pool (in cards).
pollada f. flock of young fowls; hatch; brood; covey.
pollino m. young, untamed ass; stupid fellow.
pollo m. young chicken; nestling; young bird; artful, clever man.
polluelo m. chick.
pompa f. pomp; pageant; splendor, parade, grandeur, procession; bubble, pump.
pomposo adj. pompous.
pómulo m. cheek bone.
ponche m. punch.
ponchera f. punch bowl.
ponderación f. pondering, careful consideration; weighing; exaggeration.
ponderar v. to weigh, to ponder; to exaggerate, to extol.
ponderoso adj. ponderous, heavy; weighty.
poner v. irr. to put; to place; to set; to lay a thing in a place; to dispose; to arrange; to suppose; to impose; to wager; to appoint; to leave; to lay eggs; to contribute; to bear a part; **al — del sol** at sunset; **— como nuevo a alguien** to cover somebody with insults; **— al sol** to expose to the sun; **— colorado a alguien** to make somebody blush; **— en claro** to clarify; **— todo de su parte** to do one's best; **pongamos que...** let us suppose that...; **—se** to place oneself; to become; **—se a** to begin to;
—se de pie to stand up; **—se bien con alguien** Am. to ingratiate oneself with someone; **ponérsela** Am. to get drunk; **—se pálido** to grow pale.
poniente m. West; West wind; **el sol —** the setting sun.
pontón m. pontoon or ponton; mudscow; log bridge; ponton bridge.
ponzoña f. venom, poison.
ponzoñoso adj. venomous, poisonous.
popa f. poop, stern; **viento en —** before the wind, going well; speedily.
popote m. Am. straw for brooms; drinking straw or tube.
populacho m. populace, mob, rabble, crowd.
popular adj. popular.
popularidad f. popularity.
populoso adj. populous.
poquito adj. very little; **a —s** in minute portions; **ser —** to be pusillanimous.
por prep. by, for, about; through; between; to; as; **tomar — esposo** to take as a husband; **está — venir, — ver, — saber** that is to come, to be seen, to be known; **— encima** over; upon; slightly, superficially; **— acá** or **— allá** here or there; **— más que** or **— mucho que** ever so much; **— si acaso** if by chance; **¿— qué?** interr. adv. why? for what reason?
porcelana f. porcelain; chinaware; enamel.
porcentaje m. percentage.
porción f. portion; part, share; **una — de gente** a lot of people.
porche m. porch.
pordiosero m. beggar.
porfía f. stubborness, obstinacy; persistence; obstinate dispute or quarrel; **a —** in competition; with great insistence.
porfiado adj. obstinate, stubborn; persistent.
porfiar v. to persist; to contend; to wrangle; to insist; to argue.
pormenor m. detail, minute account.
pormenorizar v. to detail; to tell in detail; to itemize.
poro m. pore.
poroso adj. porous.
poroto m. Am. bean; runt.
porque conj. beause, for that reason, on this or that account;
porqué m. cause, reason, motive.

porquería f. filth; filthy act or word; nastiness; hoggishness; trifle.
porra f. club, stick; **mandar a uno a la —** Am. to send someone to the devil.
porrazo m. blow; knock; bump.
porta f. porthole; cover for a porthole; goal, in football.
portaaviones m. airplane carrier.
portada f. facade, front of a building, title page.
portador m. bearer, carrier; tray.
portal m. portal, entrance, porch, entry; vestibule; portico; Am. Christmas creche; **—es** arcades; galleries.
portalón m. large portal; gangway (of a ship).
portamonedas m. coin purse.
portapapeles m. briefcase.
portaplumas m. penholder.
portar v. Am. to carry; **—se** to behave, to comport, to act.
portátil adj. portable.
portavoz m. megaphone, mouthpiece.
portazgo m. toll.
portazo m. bang or slam of a door; **dar un —** to bang or slam a door.
porte m. portage, cost of a carriage; freight; postage; deportment, demeanour, conduct, manner; size, capacity.
portear v. to carry, to heave; Am. to get out in a hurry.
portento m. portent, wonder, marvel; prodigy.
portentoso adj. portentous, wonderful, marvelous, prodigious, amazing.
porteño adj. from a port; Am. from Buenos Aires.
portero m. doorkeeper, doorman; janitor.
pórtico m. portico, porch, doorway.
portilla f. porthole; small gate.
portón m. gate.
portugués adj. Portuguese; m. Portuguese; Portuguese language.
porvenir m. future.
pos : en — after, in pursuit of.
posada f. lodging, inn; boarding house, dwelling, home; **las —s** Christmas festivity lasting nine days.
posaderas f. pl. posterior, buttocks, rump.
posadero m. innkeeper.
posar v. to lodge; to board; to rest, to repose; to perch (said of birds); **—se** to settle (said of sediment); to perch (said of birds).
posdata f. postscript.
poseedor m. possessor, holder, owner.
poseer v. to possess; to own; to hold; to master; to have; **—se** to have control of oneself.
posesión f. possession.
posesivo adj. & m. possessive.
posesor m. possessor, owner, holder.
posibilidad f. possibility.
posible adj. possible; **hacer lo —** to do one's best; **—s** m. pl. wealth, income, capital, means; goods; property.
posición f. position; posture; status; rank; standing; place; situation.
positivo adj. positive; effective; true; practical; sure; certain; real.
posponer v. irr. to postpone; to put off; to put after; to subordinate.
posta f. small bullet; slug of lead; mould shot; bet; wager; relay of post horses; post house; stage house; **—s** buckshot; m. postboy; courier, messenger.
postal adj. postal; **tarjeta —** postcard.
postdata See **posdata**.
poste m. post, pillar.
postergar v. to delay; to leave behind; to postpone; to disregard someone's right.
posteridad f. posterity.
posterior adj. posterior, back, rear, later.
postigo m. wicket; sally port, postern; small door or gate; peep window; shutter.
postizo adj. false, artificial; **false hair.**
postración f. postration, collapse, exhaustion, dejection, depression, lowness of spirit.
postrar v. to prostrate; to humble, humiliate; to debilitate, weaken, exhaust; **—se** to kneel on the ground; to prostrate oneself; to be extremely debilitated, weakened or exhausted; to collapse.
postre m. dessert; **a la —** at last.
postrer(o) adj. last; hindmost, nearest the rear; last in order.
postulante m. & f. petitioner; applicant, candidate; postulant.
póstumo adj. posthumous.
postura f. posture, position; bid;

wager; pact; agreement; egg laying.
potable adj. drinkable.
potaje m. pottage, thick soup; porridge; mixed drink.
pote m. pot, jar, jug, flask; Am. buzzard.
potencia f. potency; power; faculty; authority, dominin; possibility; kingdom, state; powerful nation; —s beligerantes belligerent powers or nations.
potente adj. potent, powerful, strong.
potestad f. power; dominion; authority.
potranca f. filly, young mare.
potrero m. herdsman of colts; fenced-in pasture land; Am. cattle ranch, stock farm.
potro m. colt; rack, torture; Am. wild horse; stallion.
poyo m. stone or brick bench usually built against a wall.
pozo m. well; hole, pit; mine shaft; puddle; pond; Am. spring fountain; hold of a ship.
práctica f. practice; exercise; custom, habit, method; manner, mode.
practicante m. & f. doctor's assistant; hospital intern; practiser; practitioner in surgery.
practicar v. to practice; to put into practice; to perform; to do; to make.
práctico adj. practical; skilful; experienced; m. practitioner, practiser; — de puerto harbor pilot.
pradera f. prairie; meadow; mead; rich pasture ground.
prado m. lawn, field, meadow.
preámbulo m. preamble, introduction, prologue, exordium, preface.
precario adj. precarious, uncertain.
precaución f. precaution.
precaver v. to prevent; to obviate; to guard (against); to keep from; to warn; to caution; —se to be on one's guard.
precavido adj. cautious, on guard; sagacious.
precedencia f. precedence, priority; preference.
precedente adj. preceding; m. precedent.
preceder v. to precede; to have precedence; to have priority.
precepto m. precept, rule, order; mandate.
preceptor m. teacher, tutor.

preciado adj. prized, esteemed, valued, appraised; precious, valuable.
preciar v. to appraise, to value; —se de to boast; to be proud of.
precio m. price, value, worth, esteem; cost.
precioso adj. precious, valuable, fine, exquisite; beautiful; excellent.
precipicio m. precipice; sudden fall; ruin.
precipitación f. precipitation, rush, haste, hurry, precipitancy.
precipitado adj. precipitate, haste, rash; m. precipitate (chemistry).
precipitar v. to precipitate; to hasten; to hurl; to throw headlong; —se to throw oneself headlong; to rush into.
precipitoso adj. precipitous, steep, rash, slippery.
precisar v. to determine precisely; to compel, to oblige; to necessitate; to be necessary or urgent; Am. to need.
precisión f. precision, exactness, accuracy; compulsion, force, necessity; preciseness; Am. haste.
preciso adj. necessary; precise, exact, clear; needful; distinct; Am. small travelling bag.
precoz adj. precocious.
precursor m. precursor, forerunner.
predecir v. irr. to predict; to prophecy; to forecast; to foretell.
predestinar v. to predestine; to predestinate.
predicación f. preaching.
predicado adj. & m. predicate.
predicador m. preacher.
predicar v. to preach.
predicción f. prediction.
predilección f. predilection, preference; liking.
predilecto adj. favorite, preferred; darling.
predisponer v. irr. to predispose, to bias, to prejudice.
predispuesto p.p. & adj. predisposed, prejudiced; biased.
predominante adj. predominant; ruling, prevailing.
predominar v. to predominate; to prevail.
predominio m. predominance; sway, influence.
prefacio m. preface.
prefecto m. prefect.
preferencia f. preference; de — with preference; preferably.

preferible adj. preferable, preeminent, preferred, preferential.
preferir v. irr. to prefer.
prefijar v. to prefix; to set beforehand.
prefijo m. prefix.
pregonar v. to proclaim, to cry out; to make known.
pregunta f. question.
preguntar v. to ask; to inquire.
preguntón adj. inquisitive.
prejuicio m. prejudice.
prelado m. prelate.
preliminar adj. & m. preliminary.
preludiar v. to be the beginning or prelude of; to initiate; to introduce; to try out (a musical instrument).
preludio m. prelude, introduction.
prematuro adj. premature, untimely, precocious.
premeditado adj. premeditated, deliberate.
premiar v. to reward, to remunerate.
premio m. prize; reward, recompense; premium; a — with interest, at interest.
premisa f. premise (either of the first two propositions of a syllogism).
premura f. pressure, urgency, haste
prenda f. pledge, token, security; piece of furniture put up at sale; present or gift made as a pledge of love or friendship; —s good qualities; gifts, talents; — de vestir garment; juego de —s game of forfeits; en — de as a proof of.
prendar v. to pawn; to pledge; to charm; to please; —se de to get attached to; to fall in love with.
prendedor m. clasp; stickpin; tie pin; brooch; Am. lighter.
prender v. to seize; to grasp; to catch; to imprison; to adorn; to set off; to take root; to begin to burn; to catch fire; —las Am. to take to one's heels; —se to dress up, to doll up.
prendero m. pawnbroker; secondhand dealer.
prensa f. press, printing press.
prensar v. to press.
preñado adj. pregnant; full.
preñez f. pregnancy.
preocupación f. preocupation; worry; bias; prejudice.
preocupar v. to preoccupy; to prejudice; to worry.

preparación f. preparation.
preparar v. to prepare; —se to be prepared; to get ready.
preparativo adj. preparatory. privilege.
preposición f. preposition.
prerrogativa f. prerogative, right.
presagiar v. to foretell.
presagio m. presage, omen, sign.
presbítero m. priest.
prescindir v. to disregard; to prescind; to abstract; to set aside; to omit; to dispense (with).
prescribir v. to prescribe.
presencia f. presence; figure; — de ánimo serenity, coolness; presence of mind.
presenciar v. to see; to witness; to be present at; to assist.
presentación f. presentation; personal introduction; Am. petition.
presentar v. to present; to exhibit; to view; to offer; to give; to introduce; —se to appear; to present onesef; Am. to file suit.
presente adj. present; m. gift, keepsake; al — now, at the present time; por el (la or lo) — for the present; mejorando lo — present company excepted; tener — to bear in mind.
presentimiento m. presentiment; foreboding; hunch.
preservación f. preservation.
preservar v. to preserve, guard; protect; to keep; to save.
presidencia f. presidency; office of president; presidential term; chairmanship.
presidencial adj. presidential.
presidente m. president; chairman; presiding judge.
presidiario m. prisoner, convict.
presidio m. penitentiary; prison; garrison; fortress.
presidir v. to preside, to direct.
presilla f. loop, fastener; clip.
presión f. pressure.
preso m. prisoner.
prestado adj. & p.p. loaned, lent; dar — to lend; pedir — to borrow.
prestamista m. & f. moneylender.
préstamo m. loan.
prestar v. to loan, to lend; to credit, to give credit; Am. to borrow; — ayuda to give help; — atención to pay attention; presta acá Am. give it, give it to me; —se to lend oneself.
presteza f. promptness, speed; haste.

prestidigitación f. juggling; sleight of hand.
prestidigitador m. juggler.
prestigio m. prestige; influence; authority; fame; good reputation.
presto adj. quick; nimble; prompt; ready; diligent, disposed; **de —** quickly.
presumido adj. conceited, presumptuous.
presumir v. to presume; to boast; to show off; Am. to court, to woo; **— de valiente** Am. to boast of one's valor.
presunción f. presumption, assumption; conceit; arrogance.
presunto adj. presumed; supposed; prospective; **— heredero** heir apparent.
presuntuoso adj. presumptuous, conceited.
presuponer v. irr. to presuppose; to estimate; to take for granted; to imply.
presupuesto m. budget; estimate.
presuroso adj. quick, prompt; hasty.
pretencioso adj. presumptuous; conceited.
pretender v. to pretend; to solicit; to seek; to claim; to try; to court.
pretendiente m. pretender, claimant; candidate; suitor; office seeker.
pretensión f. pretension; claim; presumption; pretense.
pretérito adj. m. preterite, past.
pretexto m. pretext, pretense, excuse.
pretil m. stone or brick railing; Am. ledge; stone or brick bench (built against a wall).
pretina f. belt, girdle; waistband.
prevalecer v. irr. to prevail.
prevaleciente adj. prevalent, current.
prevención f. prevention; foresight; preparedness; bias; prejudice; provision, supply; admonition, warning; police station; guardhouse.
prevenido adj. & p.p. prepared, provided; provident, careful; cautious.
prevenir v. irr. to prepare; to foresee; to prevent; to advise; to impede, hinder; to preoccupy; to supervene; **—se** to get prepared; to get ready.
prever v. irr. to foresee.

previo adj. previous; m. Am. preliminary examination.
previsión f. foresight.
prieto adj. dark, black; tight; compact; Am. dark-complexioned, swarthy.
prima f. female cousin; premium; prime.
primacía f. priority, precedence; superiority; mastership.
primario adj. primary, principal.
primavera f. spring.
primaveral adj. pertaining to spring.
primer(o) adj. first; former; chief, principal, leading; superior; **primera enseñanza** grammar school; **materia prima** or **primera raw material**; **de buenas a primeras** all of a sudden; **a primera luz** at dawn; adv. first, rather, sooner.
primicia f. first fruit; first profit.
primitivo adj. primitive; primary; original.
primo m. cousin; simpleton, dupe; sucker; **— hermano** (or **carnal**) first cousin; **coger a uno de —** to deceive someone easily; adj. first; **número —** prime number.
primogénito adj. & m. first born.
primogenitura f. birthright; rights of the first born.
primoroso adj. excellent, neat, elegant, graceful, dexterous; exquisite.
prímula f. primrose.
princesa f. princess.
principal adj. principal, chief, capital; renowned; famous; m. stock, principal, capital, funds.
príncipe m. prince; adj. princeps, first (edition).
principiante m. beginner, learner.
principiar v. to begin, to commence.
principio m. principle, beginning; origin; source; entrée (main dinner course); element; motive; fountain; **a —s** towards the beginning of.
prioridad f. priority; precedence.
prisa f. speed; haste; celerity; promptness in executing; **a toda —** with the greatest speed; **eso corre —** that is urgent; **darse —** to hurry; **tener (or estar de) —** to be in a hurry.
prisión f. prison, imprisonment; seizure; shackle; **—es** shackles, fetters; chains.
prisionero m. prisoner.
prisma f. prism.

prístino adj. first, early, former; primitive.
privación f. privation; want, lack, loss.
privado adj. private; personal; unconscious; m. favorite.
privar v. to deprive; to enjoy the favor of someone; to be in vogue; —**le a uno del sentido** to stun, daze; —**se** to lose consciousness; —**se de** to deprive oneself of.
privativo adj. exclusive; particular, distinctive.
privilegiado adj. privileged.
privilegiar v. to favor; to give a privilege to; to privilege.
privilegio m. privilege; exemption; patent, copyright; immunity, grant, concession; grace; franchise; faculty.
pro m. & f. profit; advantage; **en — de** in behalf of; **en — y en contra** pro and con, for and against; **hombre de —** man of worth.
proa f. prow.
probabilidad f. probability.
probable adj. probable.
probar v. irr. to prove; to try; to examine; to give evidence; to taste; to suit; to agree with.
probeta f. test tube; pressure gauge.
probidad f. integrity, probity; uprightness; honesty.
problema m. problem.
procedente adj. proceeding (from); originating; according to law.
proceder v. to proceed; to originate; to behave; to take action (against); m. behavior, procedure, conduct; management.
procedimiento m. procedure; method; process; conduct.
prócer m. distinguished person; hero; great statesman; tall; lofty, elevated.
procesado p.p. & adj. relating to, or included in, a law suit; accused, prosecuted; m. defendant.
procesar v. to prosecute; to indict; to accuse; to sue.
procesión f. procession, parade.
proceso m. process, law suit, legal proceedings; lapse of time; progress; — **verbal** minutes, record.
proclama f. proclamation; ban; marriage bans.
proclamación f. proclamation.
proclamar v. to proclaim.
procurador m. attorney.
procurar v. to procure; to manage; to transact; to get; to obtain; to solicit; to try; to acquire; to endeavor.
prodigar v. to lavish; to bestow upon; to squander; to waste.
prodigio m. prodigy; wonder; marvel; miracle.
prodigioso adj. prodigious; marvelous; fine; exquisite.
pródigo adj. prodigal, wasteful, lavish, generous; m. spendthrift.
producción f. production; produce; output.
producir v. irr. to produce; to bring about; to yield; —**se** to express oneself, to explain oneself; Am. to occur, to happen.
productivo adj. productive; fruitful; profitable.
producto m. product; yield; result; proceed, produce, fruit, growth.
productor m. producer; adj. producing, productive.
proeza f. prowess, bravery; Am. boast, exaggeration.
profanación f. profanation.
profanar v. to profane; to defile; to violate.
profano adj. profane, irreverent; lay; uninformed.
profecía f. prophecy; prediction; foretelling.
proferir v. irr. to utter, express, speak, pronounce, name.
profesar v. to profess; to avow, to confess, to exercise.
profesión f. profession; avowal; declaration; calling; occupation; assurance.
profesional adj. m. & f. professional.
profesionista m. & f. Am. professional.
profesor m. professor, teacher.
profesorado m. professorship; body of teachers.
profeta m. prophet.
profético adj. prophetic.
profetizar v. to prophecy.
proficiente adj. proficient, skilled.
profilaxis f. prophylaxis, disease prevention.
prófugo adj. & m. fugitive, vagabond.
profundidad f. profundity, depth.
profundizar v. to deepen; to go deep into; to penetrate; to fathom; to explore.
profundo adj. profound; deep; low; intense.
profuso adj. profuse; lavish; plentiful, prodigal.
programa m. program; plan.

progresar v. to progress.
progresista adj. m. & f. progressive.
progresivo adj. progressive.
progreso m. progress.
prohibición f. prohibition; ban; interdict.
prohibir v. to prohibit; to forbid; to interdict.
prójimo m. fellow creature, fellow being, neighbor; ese — Am. that fellow.
prole f. progeny, offspring.
proletariado m. proletariat, working class.
proletario adj. proletarian, belonging to the working class; plebeian; m. proletarian.
prolijo adj. prolix, too long, drawn out, too detailed; boring.
prologar v. to preface, to write a preface for.
prólogo m. prologue; preface.
prolongación f. prolongation, extension, lengthening.
prolongar v. to prolong, to protract, to lengthen, to extend.
promediar v. to average; to divide, or distribute in equal parts; to mediate; antes de — el mes before the middle of the month.
promedio m. average, middle.
promesa f. promise.
prometedor adj. promising, hopeful.
prometer v. to promise; to assure; to insure; to affirm; to give a promise of marriage; to become engaged.
prometido adj. & p.p. betrothed; m. promise, offer; outbidding, fiancé, betrothed.
prominente adj. prominent, protuberant.
promisorio adj. promissory.
promoción f. promotion, advancement.
promontorio m. promontory, headland, foreland, cape; anything bulky; bulge.
promotor m. promoter, advancer, forwarder.
promovedor m. promoter.
promover v. irr. to promote, advance; to forward.
promulgación f. promulgation, publication, proclamation of a law.
promulgar v. to promulgate; to publish; to announce publicly; to proclaim.
pronombre m. pronoun.
pronosticar v. to prognosticate; to predict; to prophecy.

pronóstico m. prognostic, prediction, divination, omen, forecast.
prontitud f. promptitude, promptness; readiness; activity, celerity, diligence, quickness.
pronto adj. prompt, ready, hasty, quick, speedy; adv. soon, promptly, quickly, expeditiously; m. sudden impulse; quick motion; de — suddenly; al — at first; por de (or por lo) — for the present; por el — provisionally.
pronunciación f. pronunciation.
pronunciar v. to pronounce; to utter; —se to make a declaration of insurrection; to rise up in rebellion.
propagación f. propagation, offspring, spread, spreading; increase.
propaganda f. propaganda.
propagar v. to propagate, diffuse, extend; to reproduce; to spread.
propalar v. to publish, divulge; to spread news.
propasarse v. to go too far; to be deficient in good breeding; to overstep one's bounds; to exceed one's authority.
propensión f. propensity, tendency, inclination, bent.
propenso adj. propense, inclined, disposed, prone, susceptible; liable.
propicio adj. propitious, favorable.
propiedad f. property; dominion, possession; right of property; landed estate; ownership; attribute; quality; appropriateness, propriety.
propietario m. proprietor; owner.
propina f. drink money, gratuity, tip, voluntary gift of money for sevices.
propinar v. to prescribe, to give, to tip; Am. to give a tip to.
propio adj. proper, one's own; suitable, adapted, fit, convenient, peculiar; natural, original, genuine; same; m. Am. messenger, postman; amor — vanity, pride, self-esteem.
proponer v. irr. to propose; to hold out; to represent; to resolve, determine; to mean; to present; —se to resolve, to make a resolution.
proporción f. proportion; simetry; aptitude; similarity; opportunity, occasion, chance; ratio; a — proportionally.
proporcionar v. to proportion; to

proposición f. proposition, proposal, scheme, overture, assertion.

propósito m. purpose, design, intention; aim; a — apropos, for the purpose; suitable, fitting; knowingly; by the by; de — on purpose, purposely; fuera de — irrelevant; untimely.

propuesta f. proposal, proposition, offer; representation.

propulsar v. to propel.

propulsor m. propeller; adj. propelling.

prorratear v. to divide; to prorate; to distribute; to assess proportionally; to average; to apportion.

prorrateo m. division into shares; distribution; average; apportionment, proportional distribution.

prórroga f. prorogation; prolongation; renewal, extension of time.

prorrogar v. to put off, postpone; to adjourn; to extend (time limit); to prorogue.

prorrumpir v. to break forth; to burst out.

prosa f. prose; tedious conversation.

prosaico adj. prosaic, dull, tedious, common.

proscribir v. to proscribe; to outlaw; to banish.

proscripción f. proscription, banishment.

proscripto m. outlaw, exile.

proseguir v. irr. to pursue; to prosecute; to follow; to continue.

prosperar v. to prosper; to make happy.

prosperidad f. prosperity, success.

próspero adj. prosperous, successful, fortunate.

prostituir v. to prostitute; to expose in vile terms; to corrupt.

prostituta f. prostitute.

protagonista m. & f. protagonist; character or actor.

protección f. protection, support.

proteccionista adj. protective; m. protectionist.

protector m. protector, guardian; adj. protecting, protective.

protectorado m. protectorate.

proteger v. to protect; to defend; to shelter.

proteína f. protein.

protesta f. protest; solemn promise; protestation.

protestación f. protestation, threat, menace; solemn declaration; protest.

protestar v. to protest; to assure, to assert; to avow publicly.

protoplasma m. protoplasm.

protuberancia f. protuberance; bulge.

provecho m. profit, benefit, advantage, utility, gain; improvement, proficiency, progress; hombre de — worthy man; mucho — much good may it do you.

provechoso adj. profitable; beneficial, gainful, useful; advantageous.

proveedor m. provisioner, provider; supply man.

proveer v. irr. to provide, furnish, supply; to confer, bestow; to decide; —se de to supply oneself with.

provenir v. irr. to arise; to proceed, originate, come from.

proverbio m. proverb.

providencia f. providence; foresight; Providence, God; legal decision, sentence; provision, measure.

providencial adj. providential.

provincia f. province.

provincial adj. provincial.

provinciano adj. & m. provincial.

provisión f. provision, supply, stock.

provisionario adj. provisional, temporary.

provocación f. provocation, dare, defiance.

provocador adj. provoking; m. provoker.

provocar v. to provoke, to excite; to rouse; to stimulate.

proximidad f. proximity, nearness.

próximo adj. next, neighboring; near.

proyección f. projection; jut.

proyectar v. to project; to plan; to throw; to cast; —se to be cast (as a shadow).

proyectil m. projectile.

proyectista m. & f. designer; schemer, planner.

proyecto m. project; plan; — de ley bill (in a legislature).

prudencia f. prudence, practical wisdom, discretion.

prudente adj. prudent, wise, discreet.

prueba f. proof; trial, test, fitting, sample, evidence; Am. acrobatic performance, stunt, trick.

prurito m. itch, keen desire.

psicología f. psychology.

psicológico adj. psychological.
psicólogo m. psychologist.
psiquiatra m. & f. psychiatrist, alienist.
psiquiatría f. psychiatry.
púa f. prick, barb, prong, thorn; quill (of a porcupine, etc.); sharp, cunning person; Am. cock's spur.
publicación f. publication.
publicar v. to publish; to reveal; to announce; to proclaim; to print a book.
publicidad f. publicity.
público adj. & m. public, notorious; vulgar, general; en — publicly.
puchero m. pot, kettle; meat and vegetables stew; pout; hacer —s to pout.
pudiente adj. powerful; rich, wealthy; m. man of means.
pudín m. pudding.
pudor m. modesty; shyness.
pudrir v. to rot; to vex; to annoy; —se to rot.
pueblero m. Am. townsman (as opposed to countryman).
pueblo m. town, village; people, race; nation; populace, common people.
puente m. bridge; Am. dental bridge; knife and fork rest; — colgante suspension bridge; — volante flying bridge; — giratorio turn table; — levadizo draw bridge.
puerca f. sow; nut of a screw.
puerco adj. nasty, filthy, dirty, foul; coarse, mean, ill-bred; m. hog, pig; — espín porcupine; — jabalí wild boar.
pueril adj. childish, puerile.
puerta f. door, doorway, gate; entrance; duty pay at the entrance of the gates in towns; llamar a la — to knock at the door; a — cerrada secretely, behind closed doors; en — Am. in view, in sight, very near.
puerto m. port, harbor; refuge; mountain pass; — franco free port.
pues conj. since; because; for; in as much as; then; adv. then, well; — bien well then; well; — que since.
puesta f. set, setting of a star or planet; stake at cards; — del sol sunset.
puestero m. Am. vendor, seller at a stand; man in charge of livestock on Argentina ranches.

puesto p.p. placed; put; set; mal bien) — badly or well dressed.
pugilato m. boxing.
pugilista m. boxer, prize fighter.
pugna f. struggle; conflict.
pugnar v. to fight; to struggle; to strive; to persist.
pujanza f. push, force, power.
pujar v. to make a strenuous effort; to grope for words; to falter; to outbid; Am. to grunt; to reject; to dismiss; — para adentro Am. to forbear, keep silent; andar pujando Am. to go around crestfallen; to be in disgrace.
pujido m. Am. grunt (due to strenuous effort).
pulcritud f. neatness; trimness; excellence, perfection.
pulcro adj. neat; trim; beautiful.
pulga f. flea; Am. small and insignificant person; tener malas —s to be ill-tempered; ser de pocas —s Am. to be touchy, oversensitive.
pulgada f. inch.
pulgar m. thumb.
pulgón m. blight, plant louse.
pulido adj. polished; refined; polite; neat; exquisite.
pulimentar v. to polish.
pulimento m. polish, gloss.
pulir v. to polish.
pulmón m. lung.
pulmonar adj. pulmonary, pertaining to the lungs.
pulmonía f. pneumonia.
pulpa f. pulp.
pulpería f. Am. country general store; tavern.
pulpero m. Am. owner of a country store or tavern.
púlpito m. pulpit.
pulque m. Am. pulque (fermented juice of the maguey).
pulsación f. pulsation, beat; throb, pulse; beating.
pulsar v. to pulsate; to throb; to beat; to sound out; to examine; Am. to judge or try the weight of (by lifting).
pulsera f. bracelet; wrist bandage; reloj de — wrist watch.
pulso m. pulse; steadiness; tact; Am. bracelet; wrist watch; un hombre de — a prudent, steady man; beber a — Am. to drink straight down; gulp down; levantar a — to lift with the strength of the wrist or hand;

— 198 —

sacar a — un negocio to carry out a deal by sheer perseverance.
pulular v. to swarm; to multiply rapidly; to sprout; to bud.
pulverizar v. to pulverize.
pulla f. taunt; quip; cutting remark; filthy word or remark.
puma m. puma, mountain lion.
puna f. Am. cold, arid tableland of the Andes; desert; sickness caused by high altitude.
pundonor m. point of honor; punctilliousness.
punta f. point, tip; extremity; summit; bull's horn; cigar or cigarette butt; Am. gang, band, herd, a lot (of things, people, etc.); a small part (of anything); **de —** on end; **de —s** (or **de puntillas**) on tiptoe; **a — de** by means of; **estar de —s con** to be in bad terms with; **sacar — a un lápiz** to sharpen a pencil.
puntada f. stitch; hint; careless word.
puntal m. prop; support, basis; fulcrum; stanchion; Am. snack (between meals).
puntapié m. kick (with the tip of the shoe).
puntazo m. Am. stab, jab.
puntear v. to pluck or play (a guitar); to make dots; to punctuate, to mark; to sew.
puntería f. aim.
puntero m. pointer; chisel; graver; blacksmith punch; Am. leader of a parade; clock or watch hand; leading animal; guide; adj. good shot.
puntiagudo adj. sharp, sharp-pointed.
puntilla f. small point; narrow lace ending; tip; small dagger; tracing point; Am. penknife; toe rubber; ridge (of a hill); **de —s** softly, gently, on tiptoe; **ponerse de —s** to persist obstinately in one's opinion.
puntillazo m. stab (with a dagger).
punto m. point of time or space; point, subject under consideration; end or design; dot, period, stop; stitch; state; opportunity; **a buen —** opportunely; **— de admiración** exclamation mark; **— y coma** semicolon; **— de interrogación** question mark; **dos —s** colon; **al —** at once, immediately; **al — de** on the point of; **de — knitted**; porous knit; stockinet or jersey weave; **en —** exactly, on the dot; **a — fijo** with cer-

tainty; **subir de —** to increase or get worse; **—s stitches** to close a wound.
puntuación f. punctuation.
puntual adj. punctual, prompt, exact, accurate; certain, convenient.
puntualidad f. punctuality, promtness; preciseness; certainty.
puntuar v. to punctuate.
punzada f. puncture; prick; sharp pain; push; sting.
punzante adj. sharp; pointing; pricking; piercing; penetrating.
punzar v. to puncture; to sting; to prick; to punch; to perforate; to bore.
punzón m. punch, puncher; pick; awl; puncheon; typefounder's punch.
puñada f. punch, box blow with the fist.
puñado m. fistful; handful; a few; **un — de hombres** a handful of men; **a —s** abundantly; plentifully.
puñal m. dagger; poniard.
puñalada f. stab; sharp pain, sudden shock of pain; **coser a —s** to stab to death.
puñetazo m. punch; blow with the fist.
puño m. fist; handful; grasp; scantiness; wristband; handruffle; cuff, mittens; hilt, guard of a sword; handle; head of a staff or cane; Am. blow with the fist; **a — cerrado** firmly; **ser como un —** to be stingy; **tener —s** to be strong, courageous; **apretar los —s** to exert the utmost efforts.
pupila f. eyeball, pupil; orphan girl.
pupilo m. ward; boarding-school pupil; boarder.
pupitre m. desk, school desk.
puré m. purée, thick soup.
pureza f. purity, innocence, chastity; purity of diction; pureness.
purga f. purge, laxative, physic.
purgante adj. purgative, laxative; m. purgative, purge, physic, laxative.
purgar v. to purge; to purify; to atone for, expiate; to evacuate the body; **—se** to clear oneself from guilt; to take a laxative.
purgatorio m. purgatory.
purificar v. to purify; to clean, cleanse; **—se** to be purified.
puro adj. pure, clean, neat, clear, free; chaste, modest, innocent, incorrupt; mere, only, sheer; **a**

pura fuerza by sheer force; **a —s gritos** by just shouting; m. cigar.
púrpura f. purple, purple cloth; royalty; rock-shell.
purpúreo adj. purple, puniceous.
pus m. pus; gleet.
puta f. whore, prostitute.
putativo adj. reputed, supposed; **padre —** foster father.
putrefacción f. putrefaction, decay, rotting.
putrefacto adj. putrid, rotten, decayed, putrefied.

Q

que rel. pron. that; which; who; whom; **el —** who; which; the one who; the one which; conj. that; for; because; **más (menos) —** more (less) than; **el mismo —** the same as; (with subj.) let, may you, I hope that; **por mucho — no matter how much;** **quieras —** no wheter you wish or not.
qué interr. adj & pron. what?; **what a!;** interr. adv. how; **¡— bonito!** how beautiful!; **¿a —?** what for?; **¿para —?** what for?; **¿por —?** why?; **¿— tal?** how?; hello!; **¡— más da!** what's the difference!; **¡a mí —!** so what! and what's that to me!
quebrada f. ravine; gorge; deep pass; failure, bankruptcy; Am. brook.
quebradizo adj. breakable; delicate; crisp; brittle, fragile.
quebrado adj. broken; debilitated; enervated; weakened; ruptured; bankrupt; rough or rugged (ground); m. arithmetical fraction; ruptured person; Am. navigable waters between reefs.
quebrantar v. to break, to crack, to crash; to pound; to move to pity; to transgress a law; to debilitate; to revoke to break a will; to violate (a law); to weaken; to vex; to crush; Am. to tame; to break in (a colt); **— el agua** to take the chill off the water.
quebranto m. weakness, lassitude; commiseration, pity; great loss; severe damage; grief; affliction; discouragement.
quebrar v. irr. to break; to double; to twist; to intercept; to transgress a law; to temper; to moderate; to fail; to become bankrupt; to crush; to wither (said of the complexion); **—se to break;** to be ruptured; to get broken; **—se la cabeza** to rack one's brain.
quebrazón m. Am. breakage, breaking.
quechua adj. Quichuan; m. & f. Quichua, Quichuan Indian; Quichuan language.
quedar v. to stay; to remain; to hold; to last; to subsist; to be left over; to be left (in a state or condition); **—se** to remain; **— bien** to acquit oneself well, to behave or come off well in an affair; Am. to suit; **—se con una cosa** to keep something; to take something (buy it); **—se como si tal cosa** Am. to act as if nothing had happened.
quedo adj. quiet, still; gently; adv. softly; in a low voice.
quehacer m. work; occupation; task, duty, chore.
queja f. complaint; groan; moan; grudge.
quejarse v. to complain, to grumble; to moan; to lament.
quejido m. moan; groan.
quejoso adj. complaining, whining.
quejumbre f. whine, moan, murmur, complaint; **—s** m. Am. grumbler; whiner.
quejumbroso adj. whining, complaining.
quemada f. burned forest; Am. burn.
quemado m. burned portion of a forest; Am. burned field; hot alcoholic drink; adj. dark, tan; Am. peeved; piqued; ruined.
quemadura f. burn, scald; smut (plant disease).
quemar v. to burn; to scald; to scorch; to sell at a loss; to annoy; Am. to deceive; to swindle; **—se** to burn; to be hot.
quemazón f. burn, combustion, conflagration; excessive heat; eagerness, covetousness; fire; pique, anger; bargain sale; Am. mirage on the pampas.
querella f. complaint, fray; petition in a court of justice; quarrel, controversy.
querellarse v. to complain, to lament; to bewail.
querencia f. affection; longing; favorite spot; haunt; stable; frequent place or resort.
querer v. irr. to want; to wish; to desire; to will, to love; to cher-

ish; to like; to conform; to agree; to cause; — **decir** to mean; **sin —** unwillingly; undesignedly; **quiere llover** it is about to rain; **como quiera** in any way; **como quiera que** since; no matter how; **cuando quiera** whenever; **—se** to love each other; Am. to be on the point of, to be about to; **quiero comer** I have an apetite; **— más** to have rather.

querida f. darling, mistress.

querido p.p. wanted, desired; adj. beloved, dear; wished; m. lover, darling, fondling, sweetheart.

quesera f. dairy, cheese factory; dairy maid; cheese dish; woman cheese vendor or maker; cheese board, cheese vat.

quesería f. dairy; creamery; cheese factory; season for making cheese.

queso m. cheese; **— de higos** Am. fig paste; **dos de —** a trifle.

quicio m. hinge of a door; hook binge; **sacar a uno de —** to exasperate someone; **fuera de —** violently, unnaturally.

quichua See **quechua**.

quiebra f. break; crack; fissure; fracture; damage; loss; bankruptcy, failure.

quien rel. pron. who, whom; he who; she who; **quién** interr. pron. who?; whom? **¿quién vive?** who goes there?

quienquiera pron. whoever, whosoever; whomsoever; whatever.

quieto adj. quiet, still; calm; pacific.

quietud f. quiet, stillness, calmness; quietude; repose; tranquillity.

quijada f. jaw; jawbone.

quilate m. carat; **—s** qualities; degree of perfection or purity.

quilla f. keel of a ship.

quimera f. absurd idea, wild fancy; chimera.

química f. chemistry.

químico adj. chemical; m. chemist.

quina f. quinine; Peruvian and Jesuit's bark.

quincalla f. hardware.

quincallería f. hardware; hardware store; hardware trade.

quincena f. fortnight; semi-monthly pay.

quinta f. villa, country house; draft, military conscription; sequence or five cards; drawing lots for the army.

quintaesencia f. quintessence; pure essence; purest form.

quiosco m. kiosk, small pavilion.

quirúrgico adj. surgical.

quisquilloso adj. touchy, oversensitive.

quisto: bien — well-liked, well-received, welcome; **mal —** disliked, unwelcome.

quitamanchas m. cleaner, stain remover.

quitar v. to remove; to take away; to take off; to take from; to deprive of; to parry (in fencing); **—se** to take off (clothing); to remove oneself, to withdraw; **—se de una cosa** to give up something, to get rid of something; **—se a alguien de encima** to get rid of someone; **¡quita allá!** don't tell me that!; **¡quítese de aquí!** get out of here!

quitasol m. large sunshade, parasol.

quite m. parry (in fencing); dodge, dodging; **andar a los —s** Am. to be on the defensive; to take offence easily; to be afraid of one's own shadow; **eso no tiene —** that cant' be helped.

quizá adv. perhaps, maybe.

R

rabadilla f. end of the spinal column; tail of a fowl; rump.

rábano m. radish; **tomar el — por las hojas** to take one thing for another.

rabia f. rabies; hydrophobia; rage, fury; **tener — a alguien** to hate someone; **volarse de —** Am. to get furious, angry.

rabiar v. to have rabies; to rage; to rave; to labour under hydrophobia; **— por** to be dying to or for; to be very eager to; **quema que —** it burns terribly.

rabieta f. tantrum, fit of temper.

rabioso adj. rabid; mad; furious; angry; violent.

rabo m. tail; **de cabo a —** from beginning to end; **mirar con el — del ojo** to look out of the corner of one's eye.

racimo m. bunch; cluster.

raciocinio m. reasoning.

ración f. ration; allowance; supply.

racional adj. rational; reasonable.

racionamiento m. rationing.

racionar v. to ration.

radiador m. radiator.

radiante adj. radiant; shining; beaming.
radiar v. to radiate; to broadcast.
radical adj. radical; fundamental; extreme; m. radical; root of a word.
radicar v. to take root; to be, to be found (in a certain place); —se to take root; to locate; to settle.
radio m. radius, radium; m. & f. radio.
radiodifundir v. to broadcast by radio. See **difundir**.
radiodifusión f. broadcasting. See **difusión**.
radiodifusora f. broadcasting station.
radioescucha m. & f. radio listener.
radiofónico adj. radio (used as adj); **estación radiofónica** radio station.
radiografía f. radiography, X-ray photography; X-ray picture.
radiografiar v. to take X-ray pictures.
radiolocutor m. radio announcer. See **locutor**.
radiotelefonía f. radiotelephony, radio, wireless.
radiotelegrafía f. radiotelegraphy; radio, wireless, telegraphy.
radioyente See **radioescucha**.
raer v. irr. to scrape off; to rub off; to scratch off; to fray; to erase.
ráfaga f. gust of wind; flash of light.
raído p.p. & adj. scraped off; rubbed off; frayed; worn out; threadbare.
raigón m. large root; root of a tooth.
raíz f. root; origin; foundation; a — de close to; right after; de — by the roots; completely; **echar raíces** to take root, to become firmly fixed.
raja f. slice; splinter; crack; split; crevice; **hacer** —s to slice; to tear into strips; to cut into splinters; **hacerse uno** —s to wear oneself out (by dancing, jumping, or any violent exercise).
rajadura f. crack, crevice.
rajar v. to split; to crack; to cleave; to slice; to chatter; to brag; Am. to defame, to insult; to flunk; to fail (a student); —se to split open, to crack; Am. to get afraid; to back down.
rajatabla m. Am. reprimand; scolding; **a** — in great haste.

ralea f. breed, race, stock; species, kind.
ralear v. to thin out; to make less dense; to become less dense.
ralo adj. sparse, thin, thinly scattered.
rallador m. grater.
rallar v. to grate; to grate on; to annoy; Am. to goad, to spur.
rama f. branch, limb; **en** — crude, raw; **andarse por las** —s to beat about the bush, not to stick to the point.
ramada f. branches, foliage; arbor; Am. shed; tent.
ramaje m. foliage; branches.
ramal m. strand (of a rope); branch; branch railway line; halter.
ramera f. harlot, prostitute.
ramificarse v. to branch off; to divide into branches.
ramillete m. bouquet, flower cluster.
ramo m. bunch (of flowers), bouquet; line; branch (of art, science, industry, etc.); branch bough; **domingo de** —s Palm Sunday.
ramonear v. to cut off twigs or tips of branches; to nibble grass, twigs, or leaves; Am. to eat scraps or lefts-overs.
ramplón adj. coarse, crude, uncouth; slovenly.
ramplonería f. coarse act or remark; crudeness; coarseness; slovenliness.
rana f. frog.
rancio adj. rancid, stale; old (wine); **linaje** — old, noble lineage.
ranchería f. group of huts; Am. inn (for arrieros).
ranchero m. Am. rancher, farmer.
rancho m. camp; hamlet; mess; (meal for a group and the group itself); Am. hut; country house; ranch, small farm (usually for cattle raising).
rango m. rank, position.
ranura f. grove, slot.
rapar v. to shave off; to crop (hair); to strip bare; to rob of everything.
rapaz adj. rapacious, grasping, greedy; m. lad.
rapaza f. lass, young girl.
rapé m. snuff.
rapidez f. rapidity, speed.
rápido adj. rapid, swift; m. rapids.
rapiña f. plunder; **ave de** — bird of prey.

rapiñar v. to plunder; to steal.
raposa f. fox.
raptar v. to kidnap; to abduct.
rapto m. abduction, kidnapping; ecstasy, rapture; outburst.
raqueta f. racket (used in games); tennis.
raquítico adj. rickety; feeble; weak; skinny; sickly.
rareza f. rarity; oddity; strangeness; freak; curiosity; queer act or remark; peculiarity; **por —** seldom.
ras : a — de flush with, even with; **al — con** flush with; **estar — con —** to be flush, perfectly even.
rascacielos m. skyscraper.
rascar v. to scratch, to scrape; Am. to dig up potatoes; **— uno para adentro** Am. to seek one's own advantage, to look out for oneself.
rasete m. sateen.
rasgado adj. torn; open; Am. generous; outspoken; **ojos —s** large, wide open eyes.
rasgadura f. tear, rip, rent.
rasgar v. to tear, to rip.
rasgo m. trait, characteristic; stroke of the pen; flourish; feat; Am. irrigation ditch; **un — de terreno** a parcel of land; **—s** features; traits.
rasgón m. large tear, rent, rip.
rasguñar v. to scratch; to claw.
rasguño m. scratch.
raso adj. plain; flat, smooth; clear, cloudless; Am. even, level (when measuring wheat, corn, etc.); scarce, scanty; **soldado —** private; **al —** in the open air; m. satin.
raspadura f. scrape; scrapings; erasure; shaving (of wood or metal).
raspar v. to scrape, to scrape off; to steal; Am. to scold, to upbraid.
rastra f. drag, sled; large rake; harrow; **a —s** dragging; unwillingly.
rastreador m. trailer, tracker, tracer.
rastrear v. to trail, to track, to trace; to rake; to harrow; to drag (a dragnet); to skim; to scrape the ground.
rastrero adj. low, vile.
rastrillar v. to rake; to comb (flax or hemp); Am. to scrape; to shoot; to barter; to exchange; to pilfer; to steal (in stores).
rastrillo m. rake; Am. barter, exchange; business deal.

rastro m. track, trail, scent; trace, sign; rake; harrow; slaughterhouse.
rastrojo m. stubble.
rasura f. shave, shaving.
rasurar v. to shave.
rata f. rat; m. pickpocket.
ratear v. to pilfer; to pickpocket; to creep, crawl.
ratería f. petty larceny; meanness.
ratero m. pickpocket; adj. contemptible; mean.
ratificar v. to ratify.
rato m. short time, little while; **buen —** pleasant time; long time; **—s perdidos** pleasure hours; **a —s** at intervals, form time to time; **pasar el —** to while away the time; to kill time; **¡hasta el —!** so long!; see you later.
ratón m. mouse; **tener un —** Am. to have hangover.
ratonera f. mousetrap.
raudal m. torrent, downpour; flood; Am. rapids.
raudo adj. rapid, swift.
raya f. line; dash; stripe; boundary line; part in the hair; Am. pay, wage; **día de —** Am. pay day; **tener a —** to keep within bounds; to hold in check; **pasar de la —** to overstep one's bounds; to take undue liberties; m. sting ray (a fish).
rayador m. Am. paymaster; umpire in a game.
rayar v. to line, to make lines on; to streak; to scratch; to mark; to cross out; Am. to pay or collect wages; to stop a horse all of a sudden; to spur a horse to run at top speed; **— el alba** to dawn; **— en** to border on; **—se uno** Am. to help oneself; to get rich.
rayo m. ray, beam; lightning; thunderbolt; spoke; **—s X** X-rays.
raza f. race; clan; breed; fissure, crevice; **caballo de —** thoroughbred horse.
razón f. reason; right, justice; ratio; account; information, word, message; **—** social firm, concern; **a — de** at the rate of; **¡con razón!** no wonder!; **dar —** to inform; **dar la —** a una persona to admit that a person is right; **perder la —** to lose one's mind; **poner en — —** to pacify; **tener —** to be right.
razonable adj. reasonable.
razonamiento f. reasoning.
razonar v. to reason; to discourse, talk; to argue.
reabrir v. to re-open.

reacción f. reaction.
reaccionar v. to react.
reaccionario adj. & m. reactionary.
reacio adj. stubborn, obstinate.
reajustar v. to readjust.
reajuste m. readjustment.
real adj. real; royal; m. army camp; fair ground; real (Spanish coin); —**es** Am. money (in general); **levantar el —** (or los —es) to break camp.
realce m. embossment; raised work; relief; prestige; lustre, splendour; **dar —** to enhance; to emphasize.
realeza f. royalty.
realidad f. reality; truth; fact; **en —** really, truly, in fact.
realismo m. realism; royalism.
realista adj. realistic; rolayist; m. realist; royalist.
realización f. realization; fulfilment; conversion into money; sale.
realizar v to realize; to fulfil; to make real; to convert into money; to sell out.
realzar v. to emboss; to raise; to enhance; to make stand out; to emphasize.
reanimar v. to revive; to comfort; to cheer; to encourage.
reanudación f. renewal.
reanudar v. to renew; to resume; to begin again.
reaparecer v. irr. to reappear.
reasumir v. to resume.
reata f. lariat, rope, lasso.
reavivar v. to revive.
rebaja f. deduction; reduction; discount.
rebajar v. to diminish; to lower, to reduce; to tone down; to humiliate; —**se** to lower or humble oneself.
rebanada f. slice.
rebanar v. to slice.
rebaño m. flock, herd.
rebatir v. to beat over and over; to repel; to resist; to refute; to rebut; to argue; to parry.
rebato m. alarm; call to emergency.
rebelarse v. to rebel.
rebelde adj. rebellious; m. rebel; defaulter.
rebeldía f. rebelliousness; defiance; default; failure to appear in court; **en —** in revolt.
rebelión f. rebellion, revolt.
rebencazo m. Am. crack of a whip; lash, stroke with a whip.
rebenque m. rawhide whip.
reborde m. edge, border.

rebosante adj. brimming, overflowing.
rebosar v. to overflow, to brim over; to abound.
rebotar v. to rebound; to bounce back or again; to make rebound; to repel; to reject; to annoy; to vex; —**se** to become vexed, upset; Am. to become cloudy or muddy; —**sele a uno la bilis** Am. to get angry, to become upset.
rebote m. rebound, bounce; **de —** on the rebound, indirectly.
rebozar v. to muffle up; —**se** to muffle oneself up; to wrap oneself up.
rebozo m. shawl; **sin —** frankly, openly.
rebullir v. irr. to stir, to move, to boil up.
rebusca f. research, search; searching; gleaning, residue.
rebuscar v. to search thoroughly; pry into; to glean.
rebuznar v. to bray.
rebuzno m. bray.
recabar v. to obtain, to gain by entreaty.
recado m. message; errand; gift; daily supply of provisions; daily marketing; precaution; tools, implements; Am. saddle and trappings; **— de escribir** writing materials; **— a** regards to.
recaer v. irr. to fall (upon); to fall again; to fall back; to relapse; to have a relapse.
recaída f. relapse; falling again; second fall.
recalar v. to saturate; to soak through; to reach port; to stand in shore; to land; to end up; to stop at; **— con alguien** Am. to take it out on somebody.
recalcar v. to emphasize; to stuff; to reiterate.
recalcitrante adj. obstinate; disobedient, stubborn.
recalentar v. irr. to reheat; to heat again; to rekindle; to warm over.
recamar v. to embroider.
recámara f. dressing room; wardrobe; Am. bedroom; chamber of an explosive charge.
recapitular v. to recapitulate, to sum up.
recargo m. overload; extraload; new charge or accusation.
recatado adj. cautious; modest; shy, coy, prudent, circumspect.
recatar v. to cover, to conceal; to secrete; —**se** to take care; to be cautious.

recato m. caution, prudence; modesty; honor.
recaudación f. collection, collecting; office of tax-collector.
recaudador m. tax-collector; tax-gatherer.
recaudar v. to collect; to gather rents or taxes.
recaudo m. collection, collecting; gathering; provision, supply; caution; **estar a buen —** to be safe; **poner a buen —** to place safely.
recelar v. to doubt, to suspect; to mistrust; **—se de** to be afraid of.
recelo m. suspicion; fear; imagination of something ill.
receloso adj. suspicious; mistrustful.
recepción f. reception, admission; aceptation.
receptáculo m. receptacle.
receptivo adj. receptive; capable of receiving.
receptor m. receiver; adj. receiving.
receta f. recipe; prescription.
recetar v. to prescribe (medicines).
recibidor m. receiver; reception room.
recibimiento m. reception; welcome; receipt; reception room; parlor.
recibir v. to accept; to receive; to take charge of; to suffer; to admit; to go out to meet; **— noticias de** to hear from; **—se de** to receive a title or degree of.
recibo m. reception; receipt, discharge; reception room; parlor; **sala de —** reception room; **estar de —** to be at home for receiving callers; **ser de —** to be acceptable, to be fit for use.
reciedumbre f. strength, force, vigor.
recién adv. recently, lately, newly (used before a past participle); Am. just now; a short time ago; **— entonces** Am. just then; **— nacido** Am. new born.
reciente adj. recent, new, fresh; just made; modern.
recinto m. enclosure; precinct, district.
recio adj. strong, robust, stout; coarse; rude; arduous; impetuous.
recipiente m. receptacle, container; receiver, recipient.
recitación f. recitation, recital, reciting.
recital m. musical recital.
recitar v. to recite; to rehearse.

reclamación f. protest, complaint; reclamation; remonstrance; claim, demand.
reclamador m. claimant; complainer.
reclamante m. & f. claimant; complainer; adj. complaining; claiming.
reclamar v. to claim; to demand; to complain; to decoy; to contradict; to protest; to oppose.
reclamo m. protest; claim; decoy bird; advertisement; enticement; call; catchword.
reclinar v. to recline; to lean; to lean back; **—se** to recline; to lean back; **—se en** (or **sobre**) to lean on or upon.
recluir v. irr. to seclude, to shut up; **—se** to isolate oneself.
recluso m. recluse, hermit; adj. shut in, shut up.
recluta f. recruiting; supply; Am. roundup of cattle; m. recruit.
reclutamiento m. recruiting; levy, draft.
reclutar v. to recruit, to enlist; Am. to round up (cattle).
recobrar v. to recover, regain; **—se** to recover, to recuperate.
recobro m. recovery.
recodo m. bend, turn; elbow (of a road); corner or angle.
recoger v. to gather, to collect; to pick up; to retake; to hoard; to receive; to shelter; to take in; **—se** to retire, go home; to withdraw; to seclude oneself; to take shelter.
recogimiento m. seclusion; retreat; concentration of thought; collecting; gathering.
recolección f. collecting, gathering; harvest, crop; summary, abridgment.
recolectar v. to harvest; to gather; to gather in a crop.
recomendable adj. praiseworthy, laudable; advisable; commendable.
recomendación f. recommendation; request.
recomendar v. irr. to recommend; to commend; to enjoin; to urge; to advise.
recompensa f. recompense; compensation.
recompensar v. to recompense, to reward.
reconcentrar v. to concentrate, to concentre; to bring together; **—se** to become absorbed in thought; to collect one's thoughts.

reconciliación f. reconciliation.
reconciliar v. to reconcile; —se to become reconciled.
recóndito adj. hidden, secret, recondite.
reconocer v. irr. to recognize; to confess; to acknowledge; to admit; to scout; to explore, scouting, exploring.
reconocimiento m. recognition; gratitude; acknowledgement;
reconstruir v. irr. to reconstruct; to rebuild.
recontar v. irr. to recount; to tell; to relate.
recopilar v. to compile, to abridge; to digest.
recordación f. recollection; remembrance.
recordar v. irr. to remember, remind; to awaken from sleep; —se to wake up.
recordativo m. reminder; adj. reminding.
recordatorio m. reminder.
recorrer v. to go over; to run over; to survey; to mend, repair; to recur; Am. to overhaul.
recorrido m. trip, run; mileage; distance traveled.
recortar v. to trim; to cut away; to shorten; —se to project itself; to outline itself.
recorte m. clipping; cutting; outline; Am. gossip, slander.
recostar v. to recline, to lean; —se to repose.
recoveco m. turn, bend; nook; sly or underhanded manner.
recreación f. recreation.
recrear v. to entertain; to amuse; to delight; to recreate; —se to amuse oneself.
recreo m. recreation, entertainment; place of amusement.
recrudecer v. to recur; to relapse; to become worse.
rectángulo m. rectangle; adj. rectangular.
rectificar v. to rectify; to make right; to redistil; to refine (liquors).
rectitud f. rectitude, uprightness; righteousness; straightness; accuracy.
recto adj. straight; erect; right; just, upright; fair; honest; m. rectum.
rector m. rector of a university or college; principal, curate; priest.
recua f. drove of pack animals or beasts of burden; crowd.
recuento m. recount.

recuerdo m. remembrance; recollection; memento; recognition; souvenir, keepsake, memory; —s regards; adj. Am. awake.
reculada f. recoil.
recular v. to recoil; to spring back; to fall back; to retreat; to yield, back down.
recuperación f. recovery.
recuperar v. to recuperate, recover; to rescue, regain; to gather strength; —se to recover one's health.
recurrir v. to resort; to recur; to have recourse to.
recurso m. recourse; appeal; resort, petition; —s means, wealth; sin — definitively; without appeal; without remedy.
recusar v. to reject, to decline; to refuse to admit.
rechazar v. to reject; to repel; to repulse; to rebuff.
rechifla f. hooting; hissing; ridicule.
rechiflar v. to hoot; to hiss; to ridicule.
rechinamiento m. creak, creaking; squeak, squeaking; gnashing.
rechinar v. to creak, to clash; to hurtle; Am. to be furious, to be angry; to grumble; to growl; — los dientes to gnash one's teeth.
rechino See rechinamiento.
rechoncho adj. plump; chubby; squat.
rechuparse v. to smack one's lips.
red f. net; netting; network; wile, fraud, snare.
redacción f. wording; editing; newspaper offices; editorial department, editorial staff; city room (in newspaper offices); jefe de — city editor.
redactar v. to write; to word; to compose; to edit.
redactor m. editor; compiler.
redargüir v. irr. to retort; to answer back; to reply; to contradict, to call in question; to reargue.
rededor m. surroundings; al (or en) — around, about.
redención f. redemption.
redentor m. redeemer, savior; el Redentor the Savior.
redil m. sheepfold.
redimir v. to redeem; to ransom; to set free.
rédito m. interest, revenue, yield; rent.
redituar v. to produce or yield any benefit or profit; to rent.

redoblar v. to double; to increase; to clinch; to rivet.
redoble m. roll (of a drum).
redoma f. flask, phial.
redomón m. Am. halft-tame horse or bull; adj. half-civilized; rustle.
redonda f. circle; neighbourhood; pasture ground; whole note in music; a la — all around, roundabout.
redondear v. to round; to make round; to round off; to round out.
redondel m. arena; bull ring; circle.
redondo adj. round, circular, spherical; clear, manifest, straight; Am. honest; stupid; en — all around.
redopelo: a — rubbing cloth against the grain.
redor m. round mat; en — around.
reducción f. reduction; cut, discount, decrease.
reducido p.p. & adj. reduced, diminished, compact, small; narrow.
reducir v. irr. to reduce; to diminish; to barter; to convert; to exchange; to adapt oneself; to be constrained.
reedificar v. to rebuild, reconstruct.
reelección f. re-election.
reelegir v. to re-elect.
reembolsar v. to reimburse; to pay back; —se to recover money advanced.
reembolso m. reimbursement; refund.
remitir v. to emit again; to issue again; to rebroadcast; to relay (a broadcast).
reemplazable adj. replaceable.
reemplazar v. to replace; to substitute.
reemplazo m. replacement; substitute, substitution.
refacción f. light lunch; refaction; refreshment; repair, reparation; Am. spare part.
refajo m. underskirt; shortskirt.
referencia f. reference; narration, account, relation to.
referente adj. referring.
referir v. irr. to refer; to relate, narrate; —se to refer to; to relate to.
refinamiento m. refinement.
refinar v. to refine; to purify.
refinería f. refinery.
reflector m. reflector; flood light.
reflejar v. to reflect; to think over; —se to be reflected.

reflejo m. reflex, reflection; image; adj. reflected.
reflexión f. reflection; meditation, consideration.
reflexionar v. to reflect; to meditate; to think over.
reflexivo adj. reflexive; reflective; thoughtful.
reflujo m. ebb; ebbtide.
reforma f. reform, correction; amendment.
reformador m. reformer.
reforzar v. irr. to reinforce; to strengthen.
refracción f. refraction.
refractario adj. refractory; impervious, rebellious; unruly; stubborn.
refrán m. popular proverb or saying.
refrenar v. to restrain; to keep in check; to curb; to coerce; to rein.
refrendar v. to legalize by signing; to countersign.
refrescante adj. refreshing.
refrescar v. to refresh; to renew; to cool; to refrigerate; —se to get cool, to cool off.
refresco m. refreshment.
refresquería f. Am. ,refreshment
refriega f. strife, fray; scuffle; affray.
refrigeración f. refrigeration; light meal or refreshment; refrigerating.
refrigerador m. Am. refrigerator; freezer; adj. refrigerating; freezing.
refrigerio m. refreshment; light meal or refreshment; relief; comfort.
refuerzo m. reinforcement.
refugiado m. refugee.
refugiar v. to shelter; —se to take shelter.
refugio m. shelter, refuge.
refulgente adj. refulgent, radiant, shining.
refundir v. to remelt, refound, recast; to contain, include; to convert to anything; to reconstruct.
refunfuñar v. to grumble; to mumble; to growl.
refunfuño m. grumble, growl.
refunfuñón adj. grouchy, grumbly; grumbling.
refutar v. to refute.
regadío adj. irrigable; m. irrigated land.
regalar v. to give; to present as a gift; to regale; to entertain; to

delight, to please; —se to treat oneself well.

regalo m. present; gift; pleasure; delight; dainty; delicacy; luxury; comfort.

regañadientes: a — much against one's wishes; unwillingly; reluctantly.

regañar v. to growl; to grumble; to quarrel.

regaño m. scold, scolding; reprimand.

regañón adj. grumbling; scolding; quarrelsome; snarling; snarler; m. growler, grumbler; scolder.

regar v. irr. to irrigate; to water; to sprinkle; to scatter; Am. to spill, to throw off (said of a horse); —se Am. to scatter; to disperse.

regatear v. to haggle; to bargain; to discute.

regazo m. lap.

regentear v. to direct; to conduct; to manage; — **una cátedra** to teach a course.

regente m. regent; manager; adj. ruling.

regidor m. councilman, alderman; adj. governing, ruling.

régimen m. régime; government; rule; management; — **lácteo** milk diet.

regimiento m. regiment of soldiers; corps; administration; municipal council.

regio adj. regal, royal; splendid; magnificent.

región f. region.

regir v. irr. to rule; to govern; to direct; to manage, administer; to move.

registrador m. register, registrary, recorder; searcher; toll gatherer; comptroller.

registrar v. to examine, inspect, scrutinize; to register; to record.

registro m. search, inspection registration, census; enrolling office; record; watch regulator; bookmark; organ stop; Am. wholesale textile store.

regla f. rule, ruler; rule of religious order; law, statute; precept; moderation, measure; order; catamenia; a — regularly; prudently.

reglamento m. regulations; rules; rule; bylaw.

regocijado adj. joyful, merry, gay; rejoicing.

regocijar v. to gladden; to delight; to cheer; to rejoice; —se to be glad.

regocijo m. joy, rejoicing, pleasure, merriment.

regordete adj. plump.

regresar v. to return.

regreso m. return; **estar de** — to be back.

reguero m. stream, rivulet; trickle; irrigation ditch.

regulación f. regulation; adjustment; computation.

regulador m. regulator; comptroller; governor of a machine; adj. regulating.

regular v. to regulate; to adjust; to put in order; adj. regular; ordinary, orderly, moderate; common, frequent; **por lo** — commonly, as a rule.

regularidad f. regularity, punctuality.

regularizar v. to regulate; to make regular.

rehacer v. irr. to remake; to mend, repair, to make again; to make over; —se to recover one's strength; to rally; to add new strength.

rehén m. hostage.

rehuir v. irr. to shun; to avoid; to withdraw.

rehusar v. to refuse; —se a to refuse to.

reina f. queen.

reinado m. reign; kingdom.

reinante adj. reigning; prevailing; ruling.

reinar v. to reign; to rule; to prevail.

reincidir v. to relapse; to slide back into.

reino m. kingdom.

reintegro m. reimbursement; refund.

reir v. irr. to laugh; to smile; —se **de** to laugh at; — **de dientes para afuera** to laugh outwardly, hypocritically.

reiterar v. to reiterate; to repeat.

reja f. grate, grating; plowshare; plowing; Am. jail.

rejilla f. small grating, lattice; small lattice window; cane upholstery.

rejuvenecer v. irr. to rejuvenate; to make young; to grow young again; —se to be rejuvenated.

relación f. relation; story, account; long speech in a play; Am. verse recited alternately by a couple in a folk dance; —**es personal**

relations; connections; acquaintances.

relacionar v. to relate; to connect; to report; —se to be related, connected; to establish friendly connections.

relajación f. relaxation; laxity; slackening; hernia.

relajar v. to relax, to slacken; to release from a vow or oath; to remit; —se to get a hernia or rupture; to be relaxed or dilated; to grow vicious; to be corrupted; to become weakened; to become lax.

relamerse v. to lick one's lips; to gloat; to boast; to slick oneself up.

relámpago m. lightning, flash.

relampaguear v. to lighten; to flash; to sparkle.

relampagueo m. flashing; lightning.

relatar v. to relate; to narrate; to tell.

relativo adj. relative; relating; — a relative to; regarding.

relato m. narration, story, account.

relegar v. to relegate; to banish, exile; to postpone; to set aside.

relente m. night dampness; Am. fresh night breeze.

relevar v. to relieve; to release; to absolve; to emboss; to exonerate; to disburden.

relevo m. relief.

relicario m. reliquary; Am. locket.

relieve m. relief, relieve, embossment, raised work.

religión f. religion.

religiosidad f. religiousness, piety; faithfulness.

religioso adj. religious, faithful; punctual; m. friar, monk.

relinchar v. to neigh.

relincho m. neigh.

reliquia f. relic, vestige; —s relics, remains.

reloj m. clock, watch; — de pulsera wrist watch; — de sol (or — solar) sundial; — despertador alarm clock.

reluciente adj. shining, sparkling; relucent.

relucir v. irr. to glitter, sparkle, shine, glow.

relumbrante adj. brilliant, flashing, resplendent.

relumbrar v. to glare, glitter, shine.

relumbre m. glare, glitter.

rellenar v. to refill; to fill up; to pad; to stuff.

relleno adj. stuffed; m. meat stuffing; filling.

remachar v. to clinch; to flatten; to rivet.

remache m. clinching, fastening; securing; riveting; rivet.

remanente m. remainder, balance; remnant; residue.

remar v. to row, to struggle.

rematado adj. & p.p. finished; sold at auction; loco — completely crazy.

rematar v. to finish, end; to give the final or finishing stroke; to auction; to fasten; Am. to stop suddenly; —se to be finished.

remate m. finish, end; highest bid at an auction; sale at auction; pinnacle, spire; Am. salvage; edge of a fabric; de — absolutely, without remedy; loco de — completely crazy.

remedar v. to imitate; to mimic; to copy.

remediar v. to remedy; to mend; to assist.

remedio m. remedy; amendment; help; reparation; resort; sin — hopeless; no tiene — it can't be helped.

remedo m. imitation, mockery, copy, mimic.

remembranza f. remembrance, memory.

rememorar v. to remember; to call to mind.

remendar v. irr. to mend; to patch; to correct.

remendón m. cobbler, shoe repairman; patcher.

remero m. rower.

remesa f. shipment; remittance; payment.

remesar v. to remit, to ship.

remiendo m. mend, mending; patch, amendment, addition; repair; a —s piecemeal, piece by piece.

remilgado adj. prudish, prim; affected.

remilgo m. prudery; primness, affectation.

reminiscencia f. reminiscence.

remisión f. remission; forgiveness; remittance; remitment; remitting; abatement; slackening.

remitente m. & f. sender; shipper; remittent.

remitir v. to remit; to send; to transmit; to pardon; to forgive; to suspend; to defer; to refer; to abate.

remo m. oar; long and hard labor;

remojar v. to soak; to steep; Am. to tip; to bribe.

remojo m. soaking; steeping; Am. steep, bribe.

remolacha f. beet.

remolcador m. towboat, tug, tugboat.

remolcar v. to tow, to tug; to take (a person) in tow.

remolino m. swirl; whirl; whirlwind; whirlpool.

remolón adj. indolent, lazy.

remolque m. tow; towrope; **llevar a —** to tow.

remontar v. to elevate; to raise; to patch up; to repair; Am. to go up; to go upstream; **—se** to raise; to soar; to fly upward; to date (from); to go back (to); Am. to take to the woods or hills.

remora f. impediment, obstacle; hindrance.

remordimiento m. remorse.

remoto adj. remote; distant; improbable.

remover v. irr. to remove; to dismiss; to stir.

rempujar v. to hostle; to push.

rempujón m. hostle, push.

remuda f. change; substitution; replacement; change of clothes; spare tire; relay of horses; Am. spare horse; spare pack animal.

remudar v. to change; to replace; to move again.

remuneración f. remuneration, compensation, pay; reward.

remunerar v. to remunerate; to compensate; to pay.

renacer v. irr. to be reborn; to spring up; to grow up again.

renacimiento m. renascence; revival; rebirth.

renco adj. lame.

rencor m. rancor, resentment, hatred, grudge.

rencoroso adj. resentful, spiteful, rancorous.

rendición f. surrender, submission; yield, profit.

rendido p.p. & adj. tired out, fatigued, devoted; obsequious, servile.

rendija f. crack, crevice.

rendimiento m. yield, output, profit; surrender, submission; fatigue.

rendir v. irr. to subdue; to subject; to surrender; to render; to hand over; to yield; to produce; to vomit, to fatigue; **— la jornada** Am. to end or suspend the day's work; **—se** to be tired; to be worn out with fatigue; to yield; to submit to another.

renegado m. renegade, traitor; apostate; adj. renegade, disloyal, wicked.

renegar v. irr. to deny; to detest; to blaspheme; to curse; **— de** to deny; to renounce; Am. to hate, to protest against.

renglón m. line, written or printed; item; part of one's revenue or income; Am. line of business; specialty.

renombrado adj. renowned, famous; celebrated.

renombre m. renown, fame; surname; family name.

renovación f. renovation, renewal; restoration.

renovar v. irr. to renew, to renovate; to reform.

renquear v. to limp.

renta f. rent, tax, revenue, rental; income.

renuencia f. reluctance, unwillingness.

renuente adj. reluctant, unwilling.

renuevo m. sprout, shoot; renovation, restoration.

renunciar v. to renounce, to resign, to disown; to abnegate; to leave; to refuse.

reñidor adj. quarrelsome.

reñir v. irr. to quarrel, to fight, to scold; to dispute; to reprimand.

reo m. guilty, offender, criminal; defendant.

reojo: mirar de — to look out of the corner of one's eye; to look scornfully.

repantigarse v. to lounge; to stretch out.

reparación f. reparation, repair; compensation.

reparar v. to repair; to restore; to observe; to consider; to compensate.

reparo m. repair; restoration; observation; notice; doubt; objection; protection; shelter; parry; Am. sudden bound or leap of a horse.

repartimiento m. distribution, division; assessment; apportionment.

repartir v. to distribute; to allot; to divide.

reparto m. distribution; mail delivery; cast of characters.

repasar v. to review; to look over;

to reprimand; to mend; to pass by again.
repaso m. review, revision; reprimand, chastisement.
repelente adj. repellent; repulsive; repugnant.
repeler v. to repel, to reject; to refute.
repente m. sudden movement; unexpected event.
repentino adj. sudden, unforeseen; unexpected.
repercutir v. to resound; to repercuss; to rebound; to drive back; to reverberate.
repetición f. repetition.
repetido p.p. repeated; **repetidas veces** often.
repetir v. irr. to repeat; to belch.
repicar v. to chime; to chop; to reprick; Am. to drum; to tap; —**se** to boast; to be conceited.
repique m. chime, ringing, peal, mincing, chopping.
repiquetear v. to chime, to ring, to jingle; Am. to tap (with fingers or heels).
repiqueteo m. chiming, ringing; jingling; tinkling; Am. clicking sound of heels.
repisa f. shelf, ledge; sill; wall bracket; pedestal; — **de ventana** window sill.
replegar v. irr. to fold; to pleat; to redouble; —**se** to retreat, to fall back.
réplica f. reply, answer, retort, replica, copy; Am. examiner.
replicar v. to reply; to retort; to answer back.
repliegue m. fold, crease; retreat of troops.
repollo m. cabbage.
reponer v. irr. to replace; to put back; to reply; to restore; —**se** to recover one's health or fortune; to collect oneself; to become calm.
reportaje m. newspaper report; reporting.
reportar v. to check; to report; to control; to restrain; to attain; to carry; to bring; to reach; Am. to report; —**se** to control oneself.
reporte m. report, news; notice; proof.
repórter or **reportero** m. reporter.
reposado p.p. & adj. reposed; quiet, calm, restful.
reposar v. to repose; to rest; to lie buried; to settle; —**se** to settle (said of sediment).

reposición f. replacement; recovery of one's health.
reposo m. repose, rest; calm.
repostada f. sharp answer, back talk.
reprender v. to reprimand, to scold, to censure.
reprensible adj. reprensible, deserving reproof.
reprensión f. reproof, rebuke, blame, censure.
represa f. dam; damming; stopping; Am. reservoir.
represalia f. reprisal.
represar v. to bank; to dam; to recapture a ship from the enemy; to retain; to stop, detain; to repress; to check.
representación f. representation; play; performance; authority, dignity; petition, plea; remonstrance.
representante adj. representing, representative; m. & f. representative; actor.
representar v. to represent; to manifest; to express; to declare; to state; to show; to play; —**se** to imagine; to picture to oneself.
representativo adj. representative.
represión f. repression, control, restraint.
reprimenda f. reprimand, rebuke.
reprimir v. to repress; to refrain; to curb; —**se** to repress oneself; to refrain.
reprobar v. irr. to reprove, to blame; to condemn; to flunk; to fail.
reprochar v. to reproach.
reproche m. reproach.
reproducción f. reproduction.
reproducir v. irr. to reproduce.
reptil m. reptile.
república f. republic.
republicano adj. & m. republican.
repudiar v. to repudiate; to disown.
repuesto m. stock, supply, provisions, sideboard; **de —** spare, extra; adj. recovered (from illness, etc.); replaced; restored.
repugnancia f. repugnance, disgust; aversion, dislike, reluctance; resistance.
repugnante adj. repugnant, disgusting, loathsome.
repugnar v. to be repugnant; to disgust; to oppose; to contradict.
repulido adj. polished up; slick; shiny.

repulsa f. repulse; rebuff, rebuke; refusal.
repulsar v. to repulse; to reject; to repel.
repulsivo adj. repulsive, repugnant.
reputación f. reputation.
reputar v. to repute.
requebrar v. irr. to compliment; to flatter; to flirt with; to court; to woo; to break again.
requemado p.p. & adj. burned; parched; tanned; sunburnt.
requemar v. to parch; to dry up; to burn; to overcook; —se to become overheated; to burn inwardly; to get tanned, sunburnt.
requerimiento m. requisition, requirement; summons; —s amorous advances; insinuations.
requerir v. irr. to require; to need; to intimate; to investigate; to take care; — de amores to court; to woo.
requesón m. cottage cheese.
requiebro m. flattery; compliment; love tale.
requisito m. requirement, requisite; — previo prerequisite.
res f. head of cattle; any large animal.
resabio m. disagreeable aftertaste; vicious habit, bad custom.
resaca f. undertow; surge; surf; redraft (of a bill of exchange); Am. beating, thrashing; mud and slime.
resaltar v. to stand out; to project; to rebound; to bounce or spring back; to be evident, obvious.
resarcir v. to indemnify; to compensate; to repay; to make amends for; —se de to make up for.
resbaladero m. slide, slippery place.
resbaladizo adj. slippery.
resbalar v. to slip; to slide; to fail in the performance of an engagement; —sele a uno una cosa to let a thing slide off one's back; to be impervious to a thing.
resbalón m. sudden or violent slip; slide; error; **darse un —** to slip.
resbaloso adj. slippery.
rescatar v. to ransom; to redeem; to barter; to exchange; to trade; Am. to resell.
rescate m. ransom; redemption; barter.
rescoldo m. embers, hot cinders, hot ashes; doubt; scruple.
resecar v. to dry up; to parch.

reseco adj. very dry; dried up; parched; thin; skinny.
resentimiento m. resentment; impairment; damage; flaw; crack; cleft.
resentirse v. irr. to show resentment, hurt or grief; to resent; to begin to give away; to fail.
reseña f. review of soldiers; book review; brief account; signal; muster.
reseñar v. to review (a book); to review (troops); to outline briefly; to give a short account of.
resero m. cowboy, herdsman; Am. dealer in livestock.
reserva f. reserve; reservation; exception; reservedness; circumspection, prudence; **a — de** intending to.
reservación f. reservation.
reservar v. to reserve; to defer; to put aside; to postpone; to separate; to exempt; to keep secret; to conceal; to hide; —se to conserve one's strength.
resfriado m. cold (illness).
resfriar v. to cool; to chill; —se to catch cold; to cool.
resguardar v. to guard; to defend; to shield; —se de to guard oneself against.
resguardo m. defense; security; guarantee; guard.
residencia f. residence; office or post of a resident foreign minister; Am. luxurious dwelling.
residente adj. resident; residing; m. & f. resident, dweller, resident foreign minister; Am. alien resident.
residir v. to reside; to live; to dwell; to be inherent; to belong to.
residuo m. residue; remainder.
resignación f. resignation.
resignar f. to resign; to hand over; —se to resign oneself.
resina f. resin.
resistencia f. resistance.
resistente adj. resistant; resisting.
resistir v. to resist; to tolerate; to endure; —se to resist; to struggle.
resolución f. resolution; courage; determination; **en —** in brief.
resolver v. irr. to resolve; to decide; to solve; to dissolve; —se to resolve; to be reduced to; to dissolve into.
resollar v. irr. to breathe hard; to pant.
resonar v. irr. to resound.

resoplar v. to puff; to breathe hard; to snort.
resoplido m. puff, pant, snort.
resorte m. spring; elasticity; means (to attain an object); Am. elastic, rubber band; **no es de mi —** Am. it doesn't concern me.
respaldar v. to indorse; **—se** to lean back; Am. to protect one's rear; m. back of a seat.
respaldo m. back part of anything; protecting wall; indorsement; Am. protection, security, guarantee.
respective adj. respective.
respecto m. relation, proportion; respect; reference; point; matter; **con — a** (or **con — de**) with regard to.
respetable adj. respectable.
respetar v. to respect.
respeto m. respect; reverence, regard, consideration, veneration, attention.
respetuoso adj. respectful; respectable.
respingar v. to bulk; to balk; to jerk.
respingo m. buck, balking; muttering; kick; jerk.
respiración f. respiration; breathing.
respirar v. to breathe.
respiro m. breathing; breath; respite; pause; cessation; stoppage.
resplandecer v. irr. to shine; to glitter.
resplandeciente adj. resplendent; shining.
resplandor m. splendor, brilliance; brightness.
responder v. to respond, answer; to acknowledge; to be responsible for.
respondón adj. saucy, pert, insolent (in answering).
responsabilidad f. responsibility.
responsable adj. responsible.
respuesta f. response; answer; reply.
resquebradura f. fissure, crevice, crack.
resquebrajar See **resquebrar**.
resquebrar v. irr. to crack; to split.
resquicio m. crack; slit; crevice; opening; Am. vestige; sign; trace.
resta f. substraction; remainder.
restablecer v. to re-establish; to restore; **—se** to recover.
restante adj. remaining; m. residue, remainder.
restañar v. to stanch; to check the flow of.

restar v. to deduct; to substract; to remain; to be left over; to strike back a ball; to rest.
restauración f. restoration.
restaurante m. restaurant.
restaurar v. to restore; to recover; to repair.
restitución f. restitution, return; restoration.
restituir v. irr. to return; to give back; **—se** to return to the place of departure.
resto m. remainder, residue, balance, rest; **—s** remains.
restorán m. Am. restaurant.
restregar v. irr. to rub hard; to scrub.
restricción f. restriction; restraint; curb.
restringir v. to restrain; to restrict; to restringe; to l!mit.
resucitar v. to resuscitate; to bring to life; to come to life; to revive.
resuelto p.p. resolved; resolute, audacious, bold, steady, determined.
resuello m. breath; breathing; panting.
resulta f. result; effect; consequence; **de —s as** a result, in consequence.
resultado m. result, effect; consequence.
resultante adj. resulting; f. resultant.
resultar v. to result; to spring; to follow; to proceed from; to turn out to be; **resulta que** it turns out that.
resumen m. résumé, summary; **en —** summing up, in brief.
resumidero m. Am. See **sumidero**.
resumir v. to summarize; to sum up; to abridge; to conclude.
resurgir v. to arise again; to reappear.
retablo m. altarpiece, picture drawn on a board and hung near the altars as a votive offering; series of pictures that tell a story.
retaguardia f. rear guard.
retal m. remnant.
retar v. to challenge; to defy; to impeach; to repehend; Am. to offend.
retardar v. to retard; to delay; to defer.
retazo m. remnant; piece; fragment; cuttings.
retener v. irr. to retain; to keep; to withhold; to detain; to suspend.

retintín m. jingle; tingle; affected tone of voice.
retirada f. retreat; withdrawal; retirement.
retirado p.p. & adj. retired, distant, remote; isolated; solitary; pensioned.
retirar v. to withdraw; to take away; to take off; —se to retire; to retreat.
retiro m. retreat; retirement; withdrawal; privacy; place of refuge; pension of a retired officer.
reto m. challenge; defiance; Am. scolding.
retobado adj. Am. saucy, stubborn; unruly.
retobar v. Am. to cover with leather, oilcloth or burlap; —se Am. to rebel, to talk back; to act saucy; to become disagreeable and aloof.
retocar v. to retouch; to touch up; to finish.
retoñar v. to sprout; to bud; to reappear.
retoño m. sprout; shoot; bud.
retoque m. retouching; finishing touch.
retorcer v. irr. to twist; to retort; to distort; to contort; —se to wriggle; to squirm.
retorcimiento m. twisting; squirming.
retórica f. rethoric.
retornar v. to return; to give back; to contort.
retorno m. return; repayment; barter; exchange.
retozar v. to gambol; to frisk about; to frolic; to romp; to stir within (passions).
retozo m. frolic.
retozón adj. frisky; playful; wanton; rompish.
retractarse v. to retract; to take back one's word.
retraer v. irr. to withdraw; to draw back; to retract; to reclaim; to retrieve; to refer; —se to take refuge; to flee; —se de to withdraw from.
retraimiento m. retirement; reserve; aloofness.
retranca f. Am. brake.
retrancar v. Am. to brake; to put the brake on; **se ha retrancado el asunto** Am. the affair has come to a standstill.
retrasado p.p. & adj. behind, behind time; backward; postponed; delayed.
retrasar v. to delay; to set back; to go backward; to defer; —se to fall behind; to be late, behind time.
retraso m. delay.
retratar v. to portray; to photograph; to copy, imitate; —se to be portrayed; to be photographed; to be reflected.
retrato m. portrait; photograph; copy, picture; imitation; reflection.
retrete m. toilet, water closet; place of retreat.
retroceder v. to turn back; to fall back; to retrograde; to retrocede; to recede.
retroceso m. retrogression; backward step; retrocession; setback; relapse.
retruécano m. pun.
retumbar v. to resound; to rumble.
retumbo m. loud echo or sound; rumble.
reuma m. & f. rheumatism.
reumatismo m. rheumatism.
reunión f. reunion; meeting.
reunir v. to reunite; to unite; to group; to gather; to assemble; to congregate; to collect; —se to join; to meet.
revancha f. revenge; return game or match.
revelación f. revelation.
revelador adj. revealing; m. developer (photography).
revelar v. to reveal; to develop (a film); to manifest; to communicate.
revendedor m. retailer; reseller; hawker; buckster; peddler.
reventa f. resale, second sale.
reventar v. irr. to burst; to burst forth; to crack; to drugde; to break loose; to explode; to smash; to sprout; to shoot; to harass; —se to burst; to blow out.
reventón m. burst, bursting; blowout; steep declivity; toil, drudgery; severe labor; adj. bursting.
reverdecer v. irr. to grow green again; to sprout again; to gain new strength.
reverencia f. reverence, veneration, homage; bow.
reverenciar v. to reverence, to revere, to venerate.
reverendo adj. reverend; respectful. Am. large, big (ironically).
reverente adj. reverent.
reverso m. reverse; back side.
revertir v. irr. to revert.
revés m. reverse; back; wrong side; stroke with the back of the

hand; back stroke or slap; disappointment, cross; thrust (fencing); misfortune; al — backward.

revestir v. irr. to dress; to cloth; to coat; to cover with a coating; —se to dress, to be invested with; —se de paciencia to arm oneself with patience.

revisar v. to revise; to review; to examine; to inspect; to check.

revisión f. revision; review; new trial.

revisor m. corrector; inspector; overseer; reviewer.

revista f. review; magazine; second trial or hearing; pasar — to pass in review; to review troops.

revistar v. to revise a suit at law; to review; to inspect troops.

revivir v. to revive; to return to life.

revocación f. repeal, cancellation; abrogation.

revocar v. to revoke, to annul; to abrogate, abolish; to repeal; to reverse.

revolcar v. to turn over and over; to floor; —se to wallow in mire or anything filthy; to roll over and over; to flounder.

revolotear v. to fly about; to flutter around; to hover; to circle around.

revoltijo m. mixture, mess; tangle; muddle; — de huevos scrambled eggs.

revoltoso adj. turbulent, unruly, rebellious; mischievous; intricate; m. agitator, troublemaker, rebel.

revolución f. revolution.

revolucionario adj. revolutionary; m. revolutionist, revolutionary.

revolver v. irr. to revolve; to turn over; to stir over; to mix up; to revert; to ecxite commotions; —se to move back and forth; to roll over and over.

revólver m. revolver, pistol; gun.

revuelo m. whirl; stir, commotion; flying around.

revuelta f. revolt, revolution; second turn; turn, bend; quarrel, fight; Am. sudden turning of a horse.

revuelto p.p. & adj. confused; mixed up; complicated; intricate; choppy (sea); changeable (weather); huevos —s scrambled eggs.

rey m. king.

reyerta f. quarrel, dispute; difference.

rezagado adj. back, behind; m. straggler; latecomer.

rezagar v. to leave behind; to separate the weak cattle from the herd; Am. to reserve; to set aside.

rezar v. to pray; to say or recite a prayer; to mutter; to grumble; asi lo reza el libro so the book says.

rezo m. prayer.

rezongar v. to grumble, to growl; to mutter.

rezongón adj. growling, grumbling; m. grumbler; growler; scolder.

rezumar v. to ooze; to leak; to run gently.

ria f. mouth of a river, estuary.

riachuelo m. rivulet, brook, streamlet.

ribazo m. a sloping bank or ditch.

ribera f. shore, bank, beach; strand.

ribereño adj. belonging to a river bank.

ribete m. ribbon or tape sewed to the edge of a cloth; seam, border, fringe; binding; tiene sus —s de poeta he is something of a poet.

ribetear v. to bind; to hem; to border; to fringe.

ricacho adj. quite rich, very rich.

ricachón adj. extremely rich, disgustingly rich.

rico adj. rich, wealthy; delicious; opulent.

ridiculizar v. to ridicule; to burlesque; to laugh at; to deride.

ridículo adj. ridiculous; queer; strange; odd, eccentrinc; m. ridicule, mockery; hacer el — to be ridiculous.

riego m. irrigation, watering.

riel m. rail; —es track, railroad track.

rienda f. rein, bridle; moderation, restraint; a — suelta with free rein; soltar la — to let loose; tirar las —s to draw rein; to restrain.

riente adj. laughing, smiling.

riesgo m. risk, danger, peril, hazard.

rifa f. raffle; scuffle; a species of lottery; quarrel, dispute, contest.

rifar v. to raffle; to scuffle; to quarrel.

rifle m. rifle.

rigidez f. rigidity, asperity, stiffness.

rígido adj. rigid, rigorous, severe, strict.

rigor m. rigor, severity; sternness;

harshness; **en —** in reality; **ser de —** to be required by custom.
rigoroso adj. rigorous, strict, austere, rigid, harsh; severe.
rima f. rhyme; **—s** poems.
rimar v. to rhyme.
rimbombante adj. high sounding; resounding.
rimero m. pile, heap.
rincón m. corner; nook; place of privacy; Am. narrow valley.
rinconada f. corner formed by two houses, streets or roads.
rinconera f. corner cup board; corner table.
ringlera f. tier, row, line; series.
rinoceronte m. rhinoceros.
riña f. quarrel, fight, dispute, contest.
riñón m. kidney; center; interior.
rio m. river.
ripio m. rubble, stone or brick fragments; useless word.
riqueza f. riches, wealth.
risa f. laugh, laughter; **reventar de —** to burst with laughter; **tomar a —** to take lightly; to laugh of.
risada f. gale of laughter, loud laugh.
risco m. rocky cliff; crag; honey fritter.
risible adj. laughable, ridiculous.
risotada f. guffaw, big laugh.
ristra f. string of onions, garlic, etc.
risueño adj. pleasant, delightful; agreeable.
rítmico adj. rhythmical.
ritmo m. rhythm.
rito m. rite, ceremony.
rival m. & f. rival, enemy, competitor.
rivalidad f. rivalry, competition; enmity.
rivalizar v. to vie with; to compete.
rizado p.p. & adj. wavy, curly; m. curling, curls; waves.
rizar v. to curl; to ripple; to plait.
rizo m. curl, frizzle, curlet; adj. curly.
roano adj. roan, sorrel.
robar v. to robe, steal; to abduct, kidnap.
roble m. oak, oak tree.
robledal m. oak grove.
robo m. robbery; theft; loot; plunder.
robusto adj. robust, vigorous.
roca f. rock; boulder; cliff; crag.
rocalloso adj. rocky.
roce m. graze; friction, contact; **no tener — con** to have no contact with a person.

rociada f. sprinkling; aspertion; spray; shower; volley of harsh words; slander.
rociar v. to sprinkle; to strew; to slander; to spray.
rocín m. nag; hack; draft horse; coarse; ill-bread man; working horse; Am. riding horse.
rocío m. dew; sprinkle; shower; spray, sprinkling; sligth shower of rain; adj. Am. reddish roan (horse).
rodada f. rut, wheel track; Am. tumble, fall.
rodado adj. dapple (horse); round, fluent.
rodadura f. rolling; rut; **— del neumático** tire tread.
rodaja f. disk; small wheel; round slice; rowel of a spur; jagging iron.
rodar v. irr. to roll; to revolve; to roam; to wander about; to run on wheels.
rodear v. to make a detour; to surround; to encircle; to encompass; to girdle; Am. to round up cattle.
rodela f. round shield; round buckler; Am. padded ring for carrying things on the head; kettle lid.
rodeo m. detour, roundabout way; circumlocution, roundabout expression; delay, protraction; subterfuge.
rodilla f. knee; **de —s** on one's knees; **hincarse de —s** to kneel down.
roer v. irr. to gnaw; to corrode; to detract; to backbite; to eat away.
rogar v. irr. to pray, beg, beseech; to implore; to crave; **hacerse de —** to let oneself be coaxed.
rojez f. redness.
rojizo adj. reddish.
rojo adj. red; ruddy; radical.
rojura f. redness.
rollizo adj. plump, round, robust, sturdy.
rollo m. roll, bundle; rolling pin; log.
romadizo m. nasal catarrh; head cold; hay fever.
romance adj. Romance, Romanic (language); m. Romance language; Spanish language; romance; chivalric novel; love affair; ballad; **en buen —** in plain language.
románico adj. Romanesque (architecture); Romance (language).
romano adj. & m. Roman.

romanticismo m. romanticism.
romántico adj. romantic; sentimental; m. romantic, sentimentalist.
romería f. pilgrimage.
romero m. pilgrim; rosemary (shrub).
romo adj. blunt; obtuse; flat-nosed.
rompecabezas m. puzzle, riddle.
rompeolas m. breakwater; mole.
rompe: de — y rasga resolute, bold; **al — Am.** suddenly.
romper v. to break; to dash; to fracture; to tear; to wear out; Am. to leave suddenly or on the run; **— el alba** to dawn; **— a** to start to; **—se** to break.
rompiente m. shoal, sand bank, reef; surge; **—s** breakers, surf.
rompimiento m. rupture, break; aperture, crack, cleft, fracture; quarrel.
ron m. rum.
roncar v. to snore; to brag; to roar.
ronco adj. hoarse, hard sounding.
roncha f. hive; welt; pustule.
ronda f. night patrol; night serenaders; round of a game, of drinks, etc.; Am. ring-around-a-rosy (children's game); **hacer la —** to court; Am. to surround, to trap (an animal).
rondar v. to go around; to hover around; to patrol; to make the rounds; to give night serenades; to haunt.
ronquera f. hoarseness.
ronquido m. snore, snort.
ronronear v. to purr.
ronzal m. halter.
roña f. scab, mange; filth; infection; stinginess; trickery; Am. ill will, grudge; **hacer — Am.** to fake an illness.
roñoso adj. scabby, mangy; dirty, filthy; stingy, miser; Am. spiteful; fainthearted, cowardly.
ropa f. clothing, clothes; **— blanca** linen; **— vieja** stew made with leftover meat; **a quema —** at close range; suddenly, without warning.
ropaje m. clothes, clothing; robe; apparel.
ropero m. clothier; wardrobe; wardrobe keeper; clothespress; Am. clothes rack.
roqueño adj. rocky.
rosa f. rose; rose diamond; red spot on the skin; rose color; Am. rosebush; **— de los vientos** (or **— náutica**) mariner's compass.

rosado adj. rosy, rosed, crimsoned; flushed; Am. reddish brown horse.
rosal m. rosebush.
rosario m. rosary; **— de desdichas** chain of misfortunes.
rosbif m. roast beef.
rosca f. screw and nut; anything round and spiral.
roseta f. rosette; small rose; the bloom of the cheeks.
rosillo adj. light red; roan (horse).
rostro m. face; **hacer —** to face.
rota f. rout, defeat; course of a ship; **de —** on a sudden.
rotación f. rotation.
rotatorio adj. rotary.
roto p.p. & adj. broken, destroyed; shattered; leaky; debauched, ragged; worn out; Am. person of the lower class.
rotular v. to label; to letter; to inscribe.
rótulo m. title, inscription; label; showbill.
rotundo adj. round; sonorous; **una negativa rotunda** a flat denial.
rotura f. breach; opening; rupture; fracture.
roturar v. to break ground; to plow; to letter.
rozadura f. friction; frication, clashing, clash.
rozamiento m. friction; rubbing.
rozar v. to graze; to scrape; to chafe; to stub up; to clear the ground; **—se con alguien** to have connections.
rozón m. graze; sudden or violent scrape.
ruano See roano.
rubí m. ruby.
rubicundo adj. reddish, red, rubicund.
rubio adj. blond, blonde.
rubor m. blush; bashfulness; flush; shame.
ruborizarse v. to blush; to feel ashamed.
rúbrica f. scroll, flourish added to a signature; rubric; **de —** according to a rule or custom.
rucio adj. grey (horse or donkey); **— rodado** dapple-grey.
rudeza f. rudeness; coarseness;
rudo adj. rude; coarse; rough; stupid.
rueca f. distaff.
rueda f. wheel; circle; crown; turn; time; succession; **hacer la — a** to court, to flatter.
ruedo m. circuit, tour; rim; border.

— 217 —

ruego m. prayer; supplication; request.
rufián m. ruffian; bully; pimp; rascal.
rugido m. roar; rumbling; roaring of a lion.
rugir v. to roar; to bellow; to halloo.
rugoso adj. wrinkled; furrowed; rugose.
ruibarbo m. rhubarb.
ruidazo m. big noise.
ruido m. noise; din; clamor, clatter; murmur; dispute; rumor, report; talk; hacer (or meter) — to make a noise; to create a sensation; to cause a disturbance.
ruidoso adj. noisy; clamorous; sensational.
ruin adj. vile, base, despicable; petty; puny; stingy; vicious; decayed; wicked; malicious; covetous.
ruina f. ruin; destruction; downfall.
ruindad f. baseness; meanness; stinginess; mean or vile act; malice.
ruinoso adj. ruinous; worthless; decayed.
ruiseñor m. nightingale.
rumba f. Am. rumba (dance and music); spree; irse de — Am. to go on a spree.
rumbear v. Am. to head (towards); to take a certain direction; to cut a path through a forest; to go on a spree; to dance rumba.
rumbo m. direction; road, route, way; course; pomp; ostentation; course of a ship; Am. cut on the head; revel, noisy spree; **hacer** — **a** to head or sail towards; **ir al** — to be going in the right trail, on the right track.
rumboso adj. generous, splendid, liberal.
rumiar v. to ruminate; to chew the cud; to ponder, meditate, muse.
rumor m. rumor, whispering, report; murmur.
runfla f. series of things of the same kind; sequence (in cards); Am. lots.
runrún m. rumor, murmur; report; gossip.
ruptura f. rupture; break; fracture.
rural adj. rural.
ruso adj. Russian; m. Russian; Russian language.
rústico adj. rustic, rural; m. peasant; en (or a la) rústica unbound, paper bound.

ruta f. route, course, way.
rutina f. routine.

S

sábado m. Saturday.
sábana f. bed sheet; altar cloth.
sabana f. Am. savanna; treeless plain, **ponerse en la** — Am. to become suddenly rich.
sabandija f. small reptile; small lizard.
sabañón m. chilblain.
sabedor adj. knowing, aware, informed.
saber v. irr. to know; to experience; to be able; to find out; Am. to be in the habit of; — **a** to taste of; to taste like; **a** — namely; that is; **¡a — si venga!** who knows whether he will come; **un no sé que an** indefinable something; **¿sabe usted a la plaza?** do you know the way to the square? m. knowledge, learning, lore.
sabiduría f. wisdom, kowledge; learning, sapience.
sabiendas: a — knowingly, consciously.
sabio adj. wise; learned; sage; judicious; m. **savant**, scholar, wise man.
sablazo m. blow with a saber; **dar un sablazo** Am. to strike for a loan.
sable m. saber.
sabor m. savor, flavor, relish; pleasure; **a** — at pleasure; — local local color.
saborear v. to savor; to taste with pleasure; to give a relish; to give a zest; —**se** to smack one's lips.
sabotaje m. sabotage.
sabotear v. to sabotage.
sabroso adj. savory, tasty, delicious.
sabueso m. hound.
sacabocados m. punch (tool).
sacacorchos m. corckscrew.
sacamuelas m. & f. tooth puller; quack dentist.
sacar v. to draw out; to extract; to remove; to deduce; to pull out, get out, or take out; to copy; to take (a snapshot or picture); to serve (a ball); — **a bailar** to ask a dance; — **a la luz** to publish; — **el cuerpo** to dodge; — **de madre** to make one lose patience; — **en claro** (or **en limpio**) to deduce, to conclude; — **fruto** to reap the fruit of

one's labor; ¡sáquese de ahí! Am. get out of here!
sacerdocio m. priesthood.
sacerdote m. priest.
saciar v. to satiate, to satisfy; —se to be satiated.
saco m. sack, bag; a coarse stuff worn by country people; Am. suit coat; — **de noche** overnight bag.
sacramento m. sacrament.
sacrificar v. to sacrifice.
sacrilegio m. sacrilege.
sacrílego adj. sacrilegious.
sacristán m. sacristan, sexton; Am. busybody, meddler.
sacro adj. sacred.
sacrosanto adj. sacrosant, holy and sacred.
sacudida f. shake, jolt, jerk.
sacudimiento m. shaking, shake, jerk; shock; jolt.
sacudir v. to shake; to beat; to jerk; to beat the dust from; to dart; to discharge; —se de alguien to shake someone off, to get rid of someone.
sádico adj. sadistic, cruel.
saeta f. arrow, dart; gnomon; hand of a watch or clock.
sagacidad f. sagacity.
sagaz adj. sagacious; shrewd.
sagrado adj. sacred; consecrated; holy; m. asylum, refuge.
sahumar v. to perfume with incense; to fumigate.
sahumerio m. vapor, fume, smoke, steam; fumigation.
sainete m. one-act comedy or farce; delicacy; flavor, relish; high flavored sauce.
sajón adj. & m. Saxon.
sal f. salt; wit, humor; wisdom; Am. misfortune; bad luck.
sala f. parlor; hall, large room; — **de justicia** court room.
salado adj. salty; salted; witty, facetious; **estar —** Am. to be unlucky; m. Am. salt pit, salt mine.
salar v. to salt; to cure or preserve with salt; to season with salt; to cure; to preserve; to corn.
salario m. salary, wages.
salchicha f. sausage.
salchichón m. large sausage.
saldar v. to balance, to settle an account.
saldo m. balance, settlement of an account; bargain sale.
saledizo See **salidizo**.
salero m. saltcellar; salt mine; salt pan; wit, gracefulness; charm. Am. salt dealer.
salida f. departure; exit; start; oulet; issue; result; projection. prominence; witty remark; — **de pie de banco** silly remark.
salidizo m. jut, ledge, projection; adj. salient, jutting, projecting.
saliente adj. salient, standing out, outjutting; m. salient, salient angle.
salina f. salt mine or pit; salt works.
salir v. irr. to go out, leave; to depart; to come out; to sprout; to turn out to be; — **bien** to turn out well; — **de la dificultad** to extricate oneself from a difficulty; — **a su padre** to turn out to be or look like his father; — **a mano** Am. to come out even; —se to get out; —se con la suya to get one's own way.
salitral m. saltpeter bed or works.
salitre m. saltpeter.
salitrera f. saltpeter mine or works.
salitroso adj. nitrous, abounding in saltpeter.
saliva f. saliva.
salmo m. psalm.
salmodiar v. to chant; to talk in a monotone or singsong.
salmón m. salmon.
salmuera f. brine.
salobre adj. briny, salty; brackish; saltish.
salón m. salon, hall, large room; salted meat or fish.
salpicadura f. spatter, splash; dab, dash of dirt.
salpicar v. to bespatter with dirt; to sprinkle; spray, spatter.
salpimentar v. irr. to salt and pepper.
salpullido m. rash, skin eruption.
salsa f. sauce; gravy; condiment; Am. sound whipping or beating.
saltamontes m. grasshopper.
saltar v. to jump; to leap; to hop; to frisk, to skip; to rebound; — **a la vista** to be evident; — **en tierra** to land; — **las trancas** Am. to lose one's patience; to lose one's head.
salteador m. bandit, highway robber; highwayman, footpad.
saltear v. to assault, attack, hold up; to rob on the highway; to take by surprise.
salto m. jump; leap; precipice, gap; — **de agua** waterfall; **a —s** by jumps; **dar (or pegar) un —** to jump

saltón adj. jumping, hopping, leaping; skipping; jumpy; protruding. Am. half-cooked; **ojos —es** popeyes; m. grasshopper.

salubre adj. healthy; healthful.

salubridad f. healthfulness; health; salubrity, sanitation.

salud f. health; welfare; salvation; **beber a la —** to drink to one's health; **¡—!** greetings; to your health.

saludable adj. wholesome, healthful, beneficial

saludador m. greeter; healer; quack.

saludar v. to greet; to salute; to hail; to fire a salute.

saludo m. salute, nod, greeting; salutation.

salutación f. salutation; salute; greeting.

salva f. salvo, salute with guns; greeting; welcome.

salvación f. salvation.

salvado m. bran.

salvador m. savior, rescuer; Savior; adj. saving.

salvaguardar v. to safeguard; to defend; to protect.

salvaguardia m. safeguard, security; protection, guard; f. safe-conduct paper, passport; password.

salvajada f. rude behavior; savage act or remark.

salvaje adj. savage, wild, barbarous, ignorant; m. savage.

salvajez f. wildness, savagery, savageness.

salvajismo m. savagery; Am. savage act or remark. See **salvajada**.

salvamento m. salvation, place of safety, salvage; rescue of property; **bote de —** lifeboat.

salvar v. to save; to clear; to jump over; to except; to exclude; **—se** to be saved; to save oneself; to escape.

salvavidas m. life preserver; life guard; **lancha —s** lifeboat; **¡salve!** inter. hail!

salve f. salve regina, prayer to the Virgin Mary.

salvia f. sage.

salvo adj. saved; safe; prep. save, except, but; **a —** safe, without injury; **en —** in safety; out of danger.

salvoconducto m. safe-conduct; pass, passport.

san adj. (contr. of **santo**) saint.

sánalotodo m. cure-all.

sanar v. to heal; to cure; to recover from sickness; to get well.

sanatorio m. sanitarium, sanatorium.

sanción f. sanction.

sancionar v. to sanction; to authorize, to ratify.

sandalia f. sandal.

sandez f. stupidity; folly; foolish act or remark.

sandía f. watermelon.

sandio adj. silly, foolish, stupid.

saneamiento m. sanitation; drainage of land; surety, guarantee, indemnification.

sanear v. to make sanitary; to drain; to give security; to indemnify.

sangrar v. to bleed; to drain; to tap a tree; to pilfer; to exploit someone; to indent a line; **—se** to be bled.

sangre f. blood; gore; **— fría** calmness, coolness of mind; **a — fría** in cold blood.

sangriento adj. bleeding, bloody; bloodstained; bloodthirsty; cruel.

sanguijuela f. leech.

sanguinario adj. bleeding, bloodthirsty; murderous, cruel; sanguinary.

sanidad f. health, soundness; healthfulness; sanitation.

sanitario adj. sanitary; hygienic; preservative of health.

sano adj. sound, healthy, healthful; safe, sane, sensible, whole, unbroken, undamaged; harmless; entire, complete; **— y salvo** safe and sound.

sanseacabó that's all; that's the end.

santiamén: en un — in a jiffy; in a moment.

santidad f. santity, holiness; saintliness; **su Santidad** his Holiness; the Pope.

santificar v. to sanctify; to hallow; to consecrate.

santiguar v. to bless; to make the sign of the cross; to chastise; to beat; to hit; to punish; **—se** to cross oneself; to show astonishment by crossing oneself.

santísimo adj. most holy; m. the Holy Sacrament.

santo adj. saintly, holy; sacred; **esperar todo el — día** to wait the whole blessed day; **— y bueno** well and good; **¡santa palabra!** Am. that's my final and last word!; m. saint; saint's day; **tener el — de espaldas** Am. to have a streak of bad luck.

santuario m. sanctuary; Am. buried treasure; Indian idol.
santurrón m. religious hypocrite, affectedly pious person.
saña f. fury, rage, anger, passion.
sañudo adj. furious, enraged; angry.
sapo m. toad; Am. despicable little man; chubby person; sly person; **echar —s y culebras** to swear, to curse.
saque m. serve, service in tennis, server.
saquear v. to sack, to plunder, to pillage; to loot.
saqueo m. sacking, pillaging, plunder; loot, booty.
saquillo m. small bag, handbag, satchel.
sarampión m. measles.
sarao m. soirée, evening party or entertainment.
sarape m. sarape, blanket.
sarcasmo m. sarcasm.
sarcástico adj. sarcastic.
sardina f. sardine.
sargento m. sergeant.
sarmentoso adj. vinelike, full of vine-shoots; gnarled; knotty.
sarmiento m. shoot or branch of a vine.
sarna f. itch, mange.
sarnoso adj. itchy, scabby; mangy; scaly.
sarpullido See **salpullido**.
sarro m. tartar on teeth; crust, sediment in utensils.
sarta f. string of beads, series.
sartén f. frying pan.
sastre m. tailor.
satánico adj. satanic, devilish.
satélite m. satellite.
satén m. sateen.
sátira f. satire.
satírico adj. satirical.
satirizar v. to satirize.
satisfacción f. satisfaction; apology; excuse; **tomar —** to vindicate oneself; to take revenge; **dar una —** to offer an apology; to apologize.
satisfacer v. irr. to satisfy; to pay a debt; **—se** to be satisfied; to be satiated.
satisfactorio adj. satisfactory.
satisfecho p.p. adj. content, contented.
saturar v. to saturate; to satiate; to glut.
sauce m. willow.
savia f. sap.
saxófono m. saxophone.
sazón f. season, opportune moment; ripeness, taste, flavor; **a la —** then, at that time; **en —** in season; ripe; opportunely; adj. Am. ripe.
sazonado adj. & p.p. seasoned; mellow; ripe; expressive (said of a phrase).
sazonar v. to season; to flavor; **—se** to become seasoned; to ripen; to mature.
se obj. pron. (before le, la, lo, las, and los) to him, to her, to it, to you (formal), to them; refl. pron. himself, herself, itself, yourself (formal), yourselves (formal), themselves; reciprocal pron. each other, one another.
sebo m. tallow, fat; candle grease.
secante adj. drying, blotting; **papel —** blotter; f. secant (math).
secar v. to dry, to exsiccate; to wipe dry; **—se** to dry or wipe oneself; to dry up; to wither; to get thin.
sección f. section; division; cutting.
seccionar v. to section; to cut; to divide.
seco adj. dry; dried; withered; harsh; barren, arid, sapless; plain, unadorned; **en —** on dry land; out of the water; **parar en —** to stop short; to stop suddenly; **a secas** plain; alone; without anything else; Am. simply, straight to the point; **comer pan a secas** to eat just bread; **bailar a secas** Am. to dance without musical accompaniment.
secreción f. secretion.
secretar v. to secrete.
secretaría f. secretary's office; position of secretary.
secretario m. secretary; confidant; f. woman secretary; secretary's wife.
secretear v. to whisper; **—se** to whisper to each other; to gossip.
secreto adj. secret, hidden; secretive; m. secret; secrecy; secret place; **— a voces** open secret; **en —** secretly; **hablar en —** to whisper.
secta f. sect.
secuaz m. partisan, follower; sequacious.
secuela f. sequel, outcome, consequence.
secuencia f. sequence.
secuestrador m. kidnapper, confiscator.
secuestrar v. to seize, to kidnap; to confiscate; to sequestrate.

secuestro m. kidnapping; seizure; sequestration.
secular adj. secular; lay, laical; wordly, centennial; m. secular, secular priest.
secundar v. to second; to favor; to back up; to aid; to assist.
secundario adj. secondary; subordinate.
sed f. thirst, craving, desire; eagerness; **tener —** to be thirsty.
seda f. silk; **como una —** soft as silk; **sweet tempered —** smoothly, easily.
sedán m. sedan.
sedativo adj. & m. sedative.
sede f. seat; See; **Santa Sede** Holy See.
sedentario adj. sedentary.
sedeño adj. silky, silken.
sedería f. silk goods; silk shop.
sedero m. silk dealer or weaver; adj. silk, pertaining to silk; **industria sedera** silk industry.
sedición f. sedition.
sedicioso adj. seditious, turbulent; factious.
sediento adj. thirsty, dry, parched; anxious, desirous; eagerly.
sedimento m. dregs, grounds; sediment.
sedoso adj. silken, silky.
seducción f. seduction.
seducir v. irr. to seduce; to mislead; to deceive; to entice; to charm.
seductivo adj. seductive, alluring; inviting, enticing; charming; deceiving.
seductor adj. tempting, fascinating; m. seducer, corrupter, tempter; charming person.
segador m. reaper, harvester.
segar v. irr. to mow; to reap; to cut off.
seglar adj. secular, lay; m. layman.
segmento m. segment.
seguida f. succession, series; continuation; **de —** without interruption, continuously; successively; **en —** at once; immediately.
seguido p.p. & adj. continuous; straight; direct; adv. without interruption; Am. often; **de —** Am. at once, immediately.
seguidor m. follower.
seguimiento m. pursuit.
seguir v. irr. to follow; to pursue; to continue; to prosecute; to accompany; to come after; to march in; **—se** to follow as a consequence.
según prep. according to; conj. as; according to; **— y conforme** (or **— y como**) exactly as, just as, that depends.
segundar v. to repeat a second time; to second; to be second.
segundero m. second hand (of a watch or clock).
segundo adj. & m. second.
seguridad f. security; surety; certainty; **alfiler de —** safety pin.
seguro adj. secure, sure, certain; assured; safe; firm, constant; Am. honest; trustworthy; m. tumbler of a gun-lock; assurance; insurance, safety device; **a buen — (al —** or **de —)** truly, certainly; **en —** in safety; **sobre —** without risk; without taking a chance; **irse uno del —** Am. to lose one's temper; **a la segura** Am. without risk.
selección f. selection, choice.
seleccionar v. to select; to choose.
selecto adj. select; choice.
selva f. forest, jungle.
sellar v. to seal, to stamp; to conclude; to close tightly.
sello m. seal; stamp; official stamped paper.
semana f. week; week's wages; **días de —** week days; **entre —** during week.
semanal adj. weekly.
semanalmente adv. weekly, every week.
semanario m. weekly publication; adj. weekly.
semblante m. countenance; facial expression; appearance; feature; look; **hacer —** to pretend; to feign.
semblanza f. portrait, literary sketch.
sembrado m. sown ground; cultivated field.
sembrar v. irr. to sow, to scatter; to spread.
semejante adj. similar, like; such a; m. fellowman; **nuestros —s** our fellowmen.
semejanza f. resemblance, similarity; simile; **a — de** in the manner of.
semejar v. to resemble; to be like; **—se** to be like.
semilla f. seed.
semillero m. seed bed; seed plot; plant nursery; **— de vicios** hotbed of vice.
seminario m. seminary; seed plot, plant nursery.
sempiterno adj. everlasting, evergreen; sempiternal.

senado m. senate.
senador m. senator.
sencillez f. simplicity; plainness.
sencillo adj. simple, unmixed, easy, plain; unadorned, unaffected.
senda f. path; way, course; footpath.
sendero m. path, footpath.
senectud f. senility; old age; senescence.
senil adj. senile.
seno m. cavity; hollow; breast; bosom; womb; lap of a woman; cove, hole; sinus; bay, gulf; innermost recess; sine (math).
sensación f. sensation.
sensacional adj. sensational.
sensatez f. prudence, judgment, common sense.
sensato adj. sensible, wise, prudent.
sensibilidad f. sensibility; sensitiveness.
sensible adj. sensitive, perceptible; regrettable.
sensitivo adj. sensitive.
sensual adj. sensual, sensuous; lewd.
sensualidad f. sensuality, lewdness.
sentada f. sitting; **de una —** at one sitting.
sentado adj. seated; sitting; **dar por —** to take for granted.
sentar v. irr. to seat; to set up; to establish; to become; to suit; to fit; to agree with one; **—se** to sit down; to settle down; to sink; to subside; **—se en la palabra** Am. to do all the talking; to monopolize the conversation.
sentencia f. sentence, verdict; judgment; maxim; proverb; opinion.
sentenciar v. to sentence; to pass judgment on; to decide.
sentido adj. heartfelt, filled with feeling; sensitive; touchy; **darse por —** to take offense; to have one's feelings hurt; **estar — con alguien** to be offended or peeved at someone; m. sense; meaning; judgment; **aguzar el —** to prick up one's ears; **perder el —** to faint; **— común** common sense.
sentimental adj. sentimental.
sentimentalismo m. sentimentalism; sentimentality.
sentimiento m. sentiment, sensation, feeling, regret; perception, resentment.
sentir v. irr. to feel; to sense; to hear; to regret; **—se** to feel (well, strong, sad, etc.); to feel oneself; to consider oneself; to feel resentment; to feel a pain; **sin —** without being realized or felt.

señá familiar contraction of **señora**.
seña f. sign, mark; signal; password; **—s** address, name and place of residence; **por más —s** as an additional proof.
señal f. sign, mark, signal, reminder; indication; trace, vestige, scar; token; pledge; Am. earmark, brand (on the ear of livestock); **en — de** in proof of; in token of.
señalar v. to stamp; to mark out; to signalize; to name; to fix; to determine; to make signals; to point out; to indicate; to appoint; Am. to earmark; to brand (cattle); **—se** to distinguish oneself; to excel.
señor m. mister, sir; owner; master; lord; gentleman; **el Señor** the Lord; God.
señora f. lady, madam; mistress.
señorear v. to lord it over, domineer; to dominate; to master; to control; to excel.
señoría f. lordship.
señoril adj. lordly.
señorío m. dominion, rule; domain of a lord; lordship; divinity; mastery; control; body of noblemen.
señorita f. miss; young lady.
señorito m. master, young gentleman.
señuelo m. decoy, lure; bait; Am. leading oxen.
separación f. separation.
separado p.p. & adj. separate, separated; **por —** separately.
separar v. to separate; to divide; to cut; to divorce; to set aside; to remove from; to dismiss from; **—se** to separate; to retire; to resign; to withdraw; to leave; to part; to be disunited.
septentrional adj. Northern.
septiembre m. September.
sepulcral adj. sepulchral; **lápida —** tombstone.
sepulcro m. sepulcher, tomb, grave.
sepultar v. to bury, to hide.
sepultura f. burial; grave; **dar —** to bury.
sequedad f. aridity, dryness; gruffness.
sequía f. drought; dryness; thirst.
séquito m. retinue; following; suite.

ser v. irr. to be; to exist; to happen; to occur; to fall out; to be worth; to belong; to become: — de (or para) ver to be worth seeing; m. being, the entity, essence or nature of things; existence; estar en un — Am. to be always in the same condition.

serenar v. to pacify, to tranquilize, to calm down; Am. to drizzle, to rain gently; —se to clear up; to become serene; to settle; to grow clear.

serenata f. serenade.

serenidad f. serenity; serene highness (title given to princes); calm.

sereno adj. serene, clear, cloudless; calm, quiet; m. night dew; night-watch; watchman; al — in the night air.

serie f. series; order; suite.

seriedad f. seriousness; gravity; sternness.

serio adj. serious, grave; important, weighty; grand, majestic; solemn.

sermón m. sermon; reproof, homily.

sermonear v. to preach; to lecture; to reprimand.

serpentear v. to wind; to twist; to turn; to serpentine.

serpiente f. serpent, snake; — de cascabel rattlesnake.

serrado adj. toothed, notched, dentated.

serrana f. mountain girl.

serranía f. mountainous region; ridge of mountains, mountainous country.

serranilla f. lyric poem with a rustic theme.

serrano m. mountaineer, highlander.

serrar See aserrar.

serrucho m. handsaw.

servible adj. serviceable, useful; fit for service.

servicial adj. helpful, obliging; obsequious.

servicio m. service; table service; favor, kind office; divine service; utility, benefit; tea or coffee set; Am. toilet, water closet.

servidor m. servant, waiter; — de usted at your service, your servant; su seguro — yours truly.

servidumbre f. domestic help, attendance, servitude; slavery; privy.

servil adj. servile.

servilismo m. servility, servileness.

servilleta f. napkin.

servir v. irr. to serve; to hold an employment; to perform another's functions; to serve as, to act as; to be used as; — para to be good for; —se to serve or help oneself; —se de to make use of; sírvase usted hacerlo please do it.

sesgado adj. slanting, oblique, bias.

sesgar v. to slant; to cut on the bias; to slope.

sesgo m. bias; slant; slope; diagonal cut; al — on the bias; diagonally.

sesión f. session; meeting, conference.

seso m. brain; wisdom; intelligence, understanding; devanarse los —s to rack one's brains.

sestear v. to snooze, to take a nap.

sesudo adj. sensible, wise, prudent; judicious; Am. stubborn.

seta f. mushroom.

seto m. fence, hedge, defense, inclosure.

seudónimo m. pseudonym, pen name; adj. pseudonimous.

severidad f. severity; strictness; seriousness.

severo adj. severe, strict, stern; grave, serious.

sevillano adj. of, from or pertaining to Sevilla, Spain.

sexo m. sex; el bello — the fair sex.

sexual adj. sexual.

si conj. if; whether; ¡— ya te lo dije! but I already told you!; — bien although; por — acaso just in case.

sí adv. yes; — que certainly; un — es no es somewhat; m. asent, consent; refl. pron. (used after a prep.) himself, herself, itself, yourself (formal), themselves; de por — separately, by itself; estar sobre — to be on the alert.

sidra f. cider.

siega f. reaping, mowing; harvesting; harvest time.

siembra f. sowing; seedtime; cornfield.

siempre adv. always; at all times; por — jamás for ever and ever; Am. in any case; anyway; para (or por) — forever; — que whenever; provided that; — si me voy Am. I'll go anyway.

siempreviva f. evergreen; everlasting.

sien f. temple.

sierpe f. serpent, snake.

sierra f. saw; — de mano hand-

saw; ridge of mountains; **sawfish**.
siervo m. serf; slave; servant.
siesta f. siesta, afternoon nap; early afternoon; the hottest part of the day; **dormir la —** to take an afternoon nap.
sifón m. siphon, siphon bottle.
sigilo m. secret, secrecy.
siglo m. century; age; a very long time; period, epoch; the world; worldly matters.
significación f. meaning; significance, signification.
significado m. significance, meaning.
significar v. to signify; to mean; to make known; to declare; to show; to matter; to have importance.
significativo adj. significant.
signo m. sign, mark; fate, destiny; notarial signet; type emblem; symbol.
siguiente adj. following.
sílaba f. syllable.
silabario m. speller, spelling book.
silbar v. to whistle, to hiss; to whiz.
silbato m. whistle.
silbido m. whistle; hiss.
silenciador m. silencer; muffler of an automobile.
silencio m. silence; pause; secrecy; adj. Am. silent, quiet; motionless.
silencioso adj. silent, quiet.
silueta f. silhouette.
silvestre adj. wild, uncultivated; rustic.
silvicultor m. forester.
silvicultura f. forestry.
silla f. chair; seat; saddle; **— de montar** saddle; **— de balanza** Am. rocking chair. See **mecedora**.
sillón m. large chair; easy or elbow chair; **— de hamaca** Am. rocking chair.
sima f. chasm, abyss.
simbólico adj. symbolic.
simbolismo m. symbolism.
símbolo m. symbol; **— de la fe** (or **de los Apóstoles**) the Apostle's creed.
simetría f. symmetry.
simétrico adj symmetrical.
simiente f. seed.
símil m. simile; similarity, resemblance; adj. similar.
simpatía f. sympathy; accord, harmony; liking.
simpático adj. sympathetic, congenial; pleasant; agreeable; nice.

simpatizar v. to sympathize; to have a liking or sympathy (for), to be congenial (with); **no me simpatiza** I don't like him.
simple adj. single, simple, pure; silly, foolish, crazy, mere; plain; unmixed, naive, innocent; m. simpleton.
simpleza f. simplicity; simpleness; stupidity, foolishness; rusticity, rudeness.
simplicidad f. simplicity, candor, ingenuity.
simplificar v. to simplify.
simplón m. simpleton.
simulacro m. mimic battle; sham or mock battle; image, vision.
simular v. to simulate, to feign.
simultáneo adj. simultaneous.
sin prep. without, besides, not counting; **— embargo** nevertheless; notwithstanding, however; **— que** conj. without; **— qué ni para qué** without rhyme or reason.
sinapismo m. mustard plaster; irritating person; nuisance, pest, bore.
sincerar v. to square, to justify, to excuse; **—se** to square oneself with, to justify oneself with.
sinceridad f. sincerity.
sincero adj. sincere.
sindicar v. to syndicate; **—se** to syndicate, to form a syndicate.
sindicato m. syndicate.
síndico m. receiver (person appointed to take charge of property under litigation or to liquidate a bankrupt business); trustee.
sinecura f. sinecure; easy and well paid position.
sinfonía f. symphony.
singular adj. singular, single, unique; striking; odd, strange; individual, particular.
singularizar v. to single out; to distinguish; to singularize; **—se** to distinguish oneself; to be singled out.
siniestra f. left hand; left-hand side.
siniestro adj. sinister; left (side); m. unforeseen loss, damage.
sinnúmero m. great number, endless number, numberless quantity.
sino conj. but; if not; prep. except; **no hace — lo que le mandan** he only does what he is told; **— que** conj. but: m. fate, destiny.

sinónimo m. synonym; adj. synonymous.
sinrazón f. injustice, wrong.
sinsabor m. displeasure; trouble, disgust, pain.
sintaxis f. syntax.
síntesis f. synthesis.
sintético adj. synthetic.
síntoma m. symptom, indication, sign.
sintonizar v. to tune in (on).
sinuoso adj. sinuous, winding, wavy.
sinvergüenza m. & f. shameless person; scoundrel.
siquiera adv. at least; even; **ni —** not even; conj. even though, though, although, or; scarcely; otherwise; **ni — quiso escucharle** he would not eve listen to him.
sirena f. siren; whistle; foghorn; syren; mermaid.
sirvienta f. waitress; housemaid.
sirviente m. servant; waiter.
sisa f. petty theft; dart (made in a garment).
sisal m. Am. sisal or sisal hemp, fiber used in rope making.
sisar v. to take in (a garment); to pilfer; to filch; to curtail; to size.
sisear v. to hiss.
siseo m. hissing, hiss.
sistema m. system.
sistemático adj. systematic.
sitial m. chair of a presiding officer; place of honor.
sitiar v. to besiege; to surround.
sitio m. siege; site, location; place, spot, space; Am. cattle ranch; taxicab station; **poner — a** to lay siege to.
situación f. situation, position, location; state; condition; **hombre de la —** Am. man of the hour, man of influence.
situar v. to locate; to place; **—se** to station oneself; to place oneself; to be located, placed, situated.
so: **— capa de** under the guise of; **— pena de** under penalty of; **— pretexto de** under the pretext of; prep. under, below; **¡—!** interj. used to stop horses or cattle.
sobaco m. armpit.
sobar v. to rub; to touch; to handle; to knead; to massage; to fondle; to pet; to bother; to beat, to slap; Am. to set bones; to flay, to skin; to win in a fight; to tire out a horse.
soberanía f. sovereignty.
soberano adj. & m. sovereign.

soberbia f. pride, arrogance; ostentation, pomp.
soberbio adj. proud, haughty, arrogant, pompous; superb, magnificent; spirited (horse).
sobornar v. to bribe.
soborno m. bribery, bribe; Am. overload on a pack animal, extra load.
sobra f. surplus, excess; **—s** leftovers, leavings; **de —** more than enough; superfluous, unnecessary
sobrado m. attic; loft; Am. pantry shelf; **—s** Am. leftovers, leavings; adj. leftover; excessive, superfluous, forward, brazen; **sobradas veces** many times, repeatedly.
sobrante adj. leftover, surplus, excess, spare; m. surplus, remainder.
sobrar v. to exceed; to remain; to be leftover; to be more than enough.
sobre prep. over, above, on, upon, about; approximately; besides; moreover; **— manera** excessively; **estar — sí** to be cautious; to be on the alert; **— que** besides, in addition to the fact that; m. envelope; address on an envelope.
sobrecama f. bedspread.
sobrecarga f. overload; overburden; overweight.
sobrecargar v. to overload; to overburden, to overweight; to surcharge.
sobrecoger v. to surprise, to catch unaware; to startle; **—se** to be startled; **—se de miedo** to be seized with fear.
sobreexcitación f. overexcitement; thrill.
sobreexcitar v. to overexcite; to cause commotion.
sobrehumano adj. superhuman.
sobrellevar v. to endure; to bear; to tolerate; to carry; to lighten another's burden.
sobremesa f. table runner; after dinner conversation at the table; **de —** during the after dinner conversation.
sobrenadar v. to float.
sobrenatural adj. supernatural.
sobrenombre m. surname, nickname.
sobreentender v. irr. to assume; to understand; **—se** to be assumed, to be obvious, to be understood.
sobrepasar v. to exceed, to excel; **—se** to overstep; to go too far.

sobreponer v. irr. to lay on top; —**se** to dominate oneself; —**se a** to overcome; to dominate.

sobrepuesto m. appliqué (trimming laid on a dress); Am. mend, patch.

sobrepujar v. to exceed, to excel, to surpass; to outweigh.

sobresaliente adj. outstanding; excellent; m. & f. substitute.

sobresalir v. irr. to surpass, to stand out; to project; to jut out; to excel.

sobresaltar v. to startle; to frighten; to assail; —**se** to be startled; to be surprised.

sobresalto m. start, scare, fright, shock; sudden dread; **de —** suddenly.

sobrescrito m. address of an envelope.

sobrestante m. overseer, boss, comptroller; foreman.

sobresueldo m. overtime pay; extra payment; extra wage.

sobretodo m. overcoat; adv. above all.

sobrevenir v. irr. to happen, to occur; to fall out; to supervene; to follow; to happen after.

sobreviviente m. & f. supervivor; adj. surviving.

sobrevivir v. to survive.

sobriedad f. sobriety, soberness, abstinence; moderation.

sobrina f. niece.

sobrino m. nephew.

sobrio adj. sober; temperate; frugal.

socarrón adj. cunning, sly, crafty.

socarronería f. craftiness, slyness, cunning.

socavar v. to dig, to undermine; to excavate.

socavón m. tunnel, cave, cavern; underground passageway.

social adj. social; sociable; friendly.

socialista adj. socialist, socialistic; m. & f. socialist.

sociedad f. society, partnership; familiar intercourse; company; friendship; firm, corporation; **— anónima** stock company.

socio m. associate, partner, member; pal.

sociología f. sociology.

socorrer v. to help; to aid; to assist; to succour.

socorro m. help, aid, assistance, support.

sodio m. sodium.

soez adj. low, mean, vile, base, vulgar.

sofá m. sofa, davenport.

sofocante adj. suffocating, stifling.

sofocar v. to suffocate, choke; to smother; to bother; to embarrass; to stifle.

sofoco m. suffocation, choking; upset; annoyance; embarrassment.

sofrenar v. to check; to control; to reprehend durely; to reprimand.

soga f. rope; Am. leather lasso or rope; halter, cord.

sojuzgamiento m. subjugation, subjection.

sojuzgar v. to subjugate; to subdue; to subject.

sol m. sun; sunshine; sol (fifth note of the scale); Am. sol (monetary unit of Peru); **de — a —** from sunrise to sunset; **hace —** it is sunny; **tomar el —** to bask in the sun; to enjoy the sunshine.

solana f. sunny place; sun room; sun porch; intense sunlight.

solanera f. sunburn; sunny place; open gallery.

solapa f. lapel; color, pretext.

solapado adj. sly, crafty, cunning; crafty, artful; deceitful; underhanded.

solar m. lot, plot of ground; ancestral mansion, manor; Am. tenement house; backyard; town lot, field (for growing alfalfa, corn, etc.); adj. solar, solary.

solar v. irr. to sole (shoes); to pave; to floor.

solariego adj. manorial, pertaining to a manor; **casa solariega** ancestral manor or mansion.

solaz m. solace, comfort; relaxation; recreation.

solazar v. to console; to cheer; to comfort; —**se** to seek relaxation or pleasure; to enjoy oneself; to be comforted.

soldado m. soldier; **— raso** private; **— de línea regular** soldier; **—de infantería** foot soldier.

soldadura f. soldering; welding; solder.

soldar v. irr. to solder; to weld; to mend.

soleado adj. sunny.

solear See **asolear**.

soledad f. solitude; loneliness; homesickness; lonely retreat; solitariness.

solemne adj. solemn; imposing; **— disparate** downright foolish-

SOLEMNIDAD   **SOPA**

ness, huge blunder; **es un — bobo** he is a downright booby.

solemnidad f. solemnity; solemn ceremony; solemness.

soler v. irr. to accustom; to be used to; to be in the habit of.

solferino adj. reddish, purple.

solicitante m. & f. solicitor; applicant.

solicitar v. to solicit; to entreat; to urge; to court; to apply for; to beg.

solícito adj. solicitous, careful; anxious.

solicitud f. solicitude; care; anxiety.

solidaridad f. solidarity; union; community of interests.

solidez f. solidity; compactness; integrity.

solidificar v. to solidify.

sólido adj. solid; firm, strong; consistent; m. solid; compact.

soliloquio m. soliloquy, monologue.

solista m. & f. soloist.

solitaria f. tapeworm.

solitario adj. solitary, lonely; m. recluse, hermit; solitaire (card game).

solo adj. sole, only; single; alone; lonely; **a solas** alone; m. solo.

sólo adv. only.

solomillo m. sirloin; loin; loin of pork.

soltar v. irr. to loosen, untie, unfasten; to discharge; **—se** to get loose; to grow expeditious; to set oneself free.

soltera f. spinster.

soltero adj. single, unmarried; m. bachelor.

solterón m. old bachelor.

solterona f. old maid.

soltura f. looseness; freedom; release; agility; ease; laxity; nimbleness.

solución f. solution; loosening; resolution.

solventar v. to pay; to settle an account.

sollozar v. to sob.

sollozo m. sob.

sombra f. shadow; shade; blind; darkness; spirit; ghost, manes; shelter; Am. wide lines under writing paper; awning; sunshade; **hacer —** to shade.

sombreado adj. shady; shaded.

sombrear v. to shade; **—se** Am. to seek the shade; to stand in the shade.

sombrerería f. hat shop.

sombrero m. hat; **— de copa** top hat; high hat; **— hongo** derby; **— de jipijapa** Panama hat; **— de pelo** Am. top hat.

sombrilla f. parasol, sunshade; umbrella.

sombrío adj. somber; shady; gloomy; hazy.

somero adj. superficial, shallow; concise.

someter v. to submit; to subject; **—se** to humble oneself.

sometimiento m. submission; subjection.

somnolencia f. drowsiness; sleepiness; **con —** sleepily.

son m. sound; tune; rumor; song; **en — de guerra** in a warlike manner; **sin ton ni —** without rhyme or reason.

sonaja f. jingles, tambourine (to accompany certain dances); rattle.

sonajero m. child's rattle.

sonante adj. sounding; ringing; sonorous; **en dinero contante y —** in hard cash.

sonar v. irr. to sound; to ring; to like or dislike; to pronounce; to allude, to refer; **—se** to blow one's nose; **se suena que** it is rumored that.

sonda f. plumb; catheter; borer; sounding.

sondar See sondear.

sondear v. to sound; to fathom; to sound out; to probe; to examine into.

sondeo m. sounding, fathoming.

soneto m. sonnet.

sonido m. sound.

sonoro adj. sonorous; pleasant; harmonious.

sonreír v. irr. to smile.

sonriente adj. smiling, beaming, radiant.

sonrisa f. smile.

sonrojarse v. to blush, to flush.

sonrojo m. blush.

sonsacar v. to lure away; to draw (someone) out; to obtain by cunning and craft a secret; to take on the sly.

sonsonete m. singsong; noise; sneer; rhythmical tapping sound.

soñador m. dreamer.

soñar v. irr. to dream; **— con** (or **— en**) to dream of; **— despierto** to daydream.

soñoliento adj. sleppy, drowsy.

sopa f. soup, sop; **estar hecho una —** to be wet; **es un —s** Am. he is a fool.

— 228 —

sopapo m. chuck, blow or slap with the hand.
sopetón m. box, slap; **de —** all of a sudden.
soplar v. to blow; to rob or steal; to inflate; **— una bofetada** Am. to strike a blow; **—se** to gulp down; **se sopló el pastel** he gobbled up the pie.
soplete m. blowtorch; blowpipe.
soplo m. blowing; puff; gust of wind; breath; advice; information.
soplón m. informer; squealer; talebearer.
soportal m. arcade.
soportar v. to support, to hold up; to suffer; to tolerate; to bear; to stand.
soporte m. support.
sorber v. to sip; to suck; to absorb; to imbibe.
sorbete m. sherbet; fruit ice; Am. cone; ice cream cone; silk top hat.
sorbo m. sip, swallow, gulp; sup; draught.
sordera f. deafness.
sórdido adj. sordid.
sordina f. mute (of musical instrument).
sordo adj. deaf; silent; still; quiet; noiseless; dull; muffled; m. deaf person.
sordomudo m. deaf-mute.
sorna f. slyness, cunning; sneer; sluggishness.
soroche m. Am. shortness of breath; sickness caused by high altitude; Am. blush, flush.
sorprendente adj. surprising.
sorprender v. to surprise; to overtake; to astonish; **—se** to be surprised.
sorpresa f. surprise; deceit; amazement.
sortear v. to draw lots; to raffle; to dodge; to shun; Am. to fight bulls.
sorteo m. drawing or casting of lots; sortition; raffle.
sortija f. ring, ringlet; curl.
sosa f. soda.
sosegado adj. calm, quiet, peaceful.
sosegar v. to calm; to pacify; to appease; **—se** to quiet down.
sosiego m. calm, peace; quiet; tranquility.
soslayar v. to do or place a thing obliquely.
soslayo: **al —** obliquely; slanting; askew, sidewise; **mirada de —** side glance.

soso adj. flat, tasteless, insipid; dull.
sospecha f. suspicion, mistrust.
sospechar v. to suspect, to mistrust, to conjecture.
sospechoso adj. suspicious, suspected; m. suspect.
sostén m. support; steadiness; brassiere.
sostener v. irr. to sustain, to support; to maintain; to bear; to endure; to suffer; **—se** to maintain oneself.
sostenido p.p. & adj sustained; supported; m. sharp (in music).
sota f. knave (at cards); deputy, substitute; Am. foreman.
sotana f. cassock of a priest; flogging.
sótano m. cellar, basement.
soto m. grove, thicket; prep. under, beneath, below.
sotreta m. Am. nag, old horse.
soviet m. soviet.
soviético adj. soviet.
suave adj. soft; smooth; mild; bland; delicate; mellow; easy; docile.
suavidad f. softness; smoothness; mildness; delicacy; sweetness; meekness.
suavizar v. to smooth; to soften; to mollify; to mitigate.
subalterno adj. & m. subordinate; inferior.
subasta f. public auction; judicial sale.
subastar v. to sell at auction
súbdito m. subject; inferior.
subida f. rise; ascension; mounting; ascent, acclivity; enhancement; **muchas —s y bajadas** much going up and down.
subir v. to ascend; to mount; to climb; to increase; to raise; to go up; to carry up; **— al tren** to get on the train.
súbito adj. sudden, unexpected; adv. suddenly, unexpectedly; **de —** suddenly.
sublevación f. revolt; insurrection; sedition.
sublevar v. to excite a rebellion; **—se** to revolt.
sublime adj. sublime.
submarino m. & adj. submarine; Am. U-boat.
subordinado adj. & m. subordinate, inferior.
subordinar v. to subordinate; to subject.
subrayar v. to underline; to underscore; to emphasize.

subsanar v. to mend; to remedy; to exculpate; to excuse; to make up for.
subscribir See suscribir.
subscripción See suscripción.
subscriptor See suscritor.
subsecretario m. undersecretary.
subsecuente adj. subsequent.
subsistencia f. living, subsistence, livelihood.
subsistir v. to subsist; to live; to last.
substancia See sustancia.
substancial See sustancial.
substancioso See sustancioso.
substituible See sustituible.
substantivo See sustantivo.
substitución See sustitución.
substituir See sustituir.
substituto See sustituto.
substracción See sustracción.
substraer See sustraer.
subteniente m. sublieutenant; second lieutenant.
subterráneo adj. subterraneous; m. subterrane, underground; cave.
suburbano adj. suburban; resident.
suburbio m. suburb, outskirt.
subvención f. subsidy; help, aid.
subvencionar v. to subsidize; to help; , to aid; to subvention; to hold in pay.
subyugar v. to subdue.
succión f. suction.
suceder v. to happen; to occur; to succeed; to follow in order; to inherit.
sucesión f. succession; series; offspring.
sucesivo adj. successive; **en lo —** hereafter.
suceso m. event; outcome; incident; success.
sucesor m. successor; succeeder.
suciedad f. dirt, filth, nastiness; filthy act or remark.
sucinto adj. compact, succinct; girded, tucked up.
sucio adj. dirty; foul; obscene; obscure.
suculento adj. juicy, succulent.
sucumbir v. to succumb; to yield; to yield under a difficulty.
sucursal f. branch; branch office of a bank, etc.
suche adj. Am. sour, unripe; m. Am. pimple; office boy; suche, a tree.
sud m. south; south wind.
sudamericano adj. & m. South American.
sudar v. to sweat, to perspire; to toil.

sudeste m. & adj. southeast.
sudoeste m. & adj. southwest.
sudor m. sweat, perspiration; toil.
sudoroso adj. sweaty, sweating; perspiring.
sueco adj. Swedish; Swede; Swedish language; **hacer el —** to pretend not to see or understand.
suegra f. mother-in-law.
suegro m. father-in-law.
suela f. sole of a shoe; sole leather.
sueldo m. salary; wages; stipend; penny.
suelo m. soil, ground; floor, surface; earth, world.
suelto adj. loose, free, light; easy, disengaged; m. small change, change, short newspaper article.
sueño m. sleep; dream; vision; drowsiness; **tener —** to be sleepy.
suero m. serum.
suerte f. fate, chance, lot, luck, doom, haphazard; kind, sort, species; manner, mode, way; **de la misma —** the same way; **echar —s** to cast lots; **tocarle a uno la —** to fall in one's lot.
suéter m. Am. sweater.
suficiente adj. sufficient, enough, apt, fit, able.
sufragar v. to defray; to favor; to aid; to suffice; **— por** Am. to vote for.
sufragio m. suffrage, vote; aid, assistance.
sufrido adj. suffering; patient; **mal —** impatient.
sufridor m. sufferer; adj. suffering.
sufrimiento m. suffering; patience; tolerance.
sufrir v. to suffer; to endure; to tolerate; to sustain, to undergo; **— un examen** to take an examination.
sugerencia f. Am. suggestion, hint.
sugerir v. irr. to suggest, to hint, to instigate.
sugestión f. suggestion, hint, instigation.
sugestivo adj. suggestive.
suicida m. & f. suicide.
suicidarse v. to commit suicide.
suicidio f. suicide.
suizo adj. & m. Swiss.
sujeción f. subjection; coercion; control.
sujetapapeles m. paper clip.
sujetar v. to subject; to subdue; to fasten; to hold; **—se** to subject oneself; to submit.
sujeto adj. subject, liable; m. subject matter; topic; fellow; individual.

sulfato m. sulphate.
sulfurarse v. to get angry.
sulfúrico adj. sulphuric.
sulfuro m. sulphide.
sultán m. sultan.
suma f. addition; sum; total; summary; en — in short.
sumador adj. adding.
sumar v. to add; to add up; to cast up accounts; —se a to join.
sumario m. summary; indictment; compendium, abridgement.
sumergible adj. submergible; m. submarine.
sumergir v. to submerge; to sink; to immerse; to embarrass; —se to submerge.
sumidero m. sink; sewer, drain.
suministrar v. to give; to supply with; to furnish.
sumir v. to sink; to submerge; Am. to dent; —se to sink; to shrivel; to crouch in fear.
sumisión f. submission; obedience; compliance.
sumiso adj. submissive; obedient; meek.
sumo adj. supreme, high, highest; greatest; — pontífice Sovereign Pontiff, the Pope; a lo — at the most.
suntuoso adj. sumptuous, magnificent, expensive.
superabundancia f. superabundance; overflow.
superar v. to surpass; to exceed; to overcome.
superávit m. surplus.
superficial adj. superficial, shallow.
superficialidad f. superficiality, shallowness, frivolity.
superficie f. surface, area.
superfluo adj. superfluous.
superintendente m. superintendent; supervisor, overseer; inspector.
superior adj. superior, paramount, higher, greater; upper; m. superior.
superioridad f. superiority; pre-eminence.
superlativo adj. & m. superlative.
superstición f. superstition.
supersticioso adj. supertitious.
supervivencia f. survival.
superviviente See sobreviviente.
suplantar v. to supplant; to displace; to falsify.
suplementar v. to supplement.
suplementario adj. supplementary, extra.
suplemento m. supplement; supply; supplying.

suplente adj., m. & f. supplent, substitute.
súplica f. entreaty; request; memorial; supplication.
suplicante adj. supplicant, beseeching; m. & f. suppliant, petitioner.
suplicar v. to beg, entreat, implore; to supplicate; to appeal.
suplicio m. torture; punishment; anguish; execution; scaffold; gallows.
suplir v. to supply; to fill up; to furnish.
suponer v. irr. to suppose; to possess authority.
suposición f. supposition; surmise; assumption.
supremacía f. supremacy.
supremo adj. supreme; final, last; highest, paramount, excessive.
supresión f. suppression; elimination, omission.
suprimir v. to suppress; to abolish; to omit.
supuesto p.p. & adj. supposed; supposititious, suppositive; por — of course; m. supposition.
supuración f. suppuration.
supurar v. to fester; to suppurate.
sur m. south, south wind.
suramericano See sudamericano.
surcar v. to furrow; to plow; to plough.
surco m. furrow; rut; groove; wrinkle.
sureño adj. southern.
sureste m. southeast.
surgir v. to surge; to rise; to appear.
suroeste m. southwest.
surtido m. assortment; stock; adj. assorted.
surtidor m. supplier; spout, jet; purveyor, caterer.
surtir v. to provide; to supply; to furnish; — efecto to have the desired affect.
susceptible adj. susceptible; sensitive; touchy.
suscitar v. to raise; to excite; to provoke.
suscribir v. to subscribe; to endorse; —se to subscribe.
suscripción f. subscription.
suscritor m. suscriber.
susodicho adj. aforesaid, forementioned; above-mentioned.
suspender v. to suspend; to hang; to stop; to delay; — el fuego to stop the fire.
suspensión f. suspension, delay; uncertainty.

— 231 —

suspenso adj. suspended; pending; astonished; m. suspense; **failure in an examination**.
suspicaz adj. suspicious.
suspirar v. to sigh; to long for.
suspiro m. sigh.
sustancia f. substance, essence; Am. broth; yolk-egg.
sustancial adj. substantial.
sustancioso adj. substantial; nourishing.
sustantivo m. noun; adj. substantive; real, independent.
sustentar v. to sustain; to feed; to maintain, to uphold.
sustento m. sustenance; food, maintenance.
sustitución f. substitution.
sustituible adj. replaceable.
sustituir v. irr. to substitute.
sustituto m. substitute.
susto m. scare, fright; sudden terror.
sustracción f. substraction.
sustraer v. irr. to substract; to remove; —se a to evade; to avoid; to give the slip.
susurrar v. to whisper; to rustle; to whiz gently; —se to be rumored about.
susurro m. whisper; murmur, rustle.
sutil adj. subtle; subtile; thin; slender; delicate.
sutileza f. subtlety; cunning, sagacity; delicacy; fineness.
suyo adj. his, of his; hers, of her; your, yours, of you; one's, his, her or its own or their own; **de —** spontaneously.

T

tabaco m. tobacco; cigar; snuff; rapee; Am. blow with the fist.
tábano m. horsefly, gadfly.
tabaquería f. tobacco and snuff shop.
taberna f. tavern, bar; liquor store.
tabernáculo m. tabernacle.
tabique m. partition, partition wall; Am. brick.
tabla f. board; table; butcher's block; index prefixed to a book; plant in a garden; list, catalogue; **a raja —** cost what it may; **—s** stage.
tablado m. platform, stage; scaffold; floor boards.
tablero m. board; panel; ckeckerboard; store counter; gambling house; gambling table; money table; Am. blackboard.

tableta f. tablet; small board; **estar en —s** to be in suspense.
tabletear v. to rattle; to move tables or boards; to make a tapping sound.
tableteo m. rattling sound.
tablilla f. tablet; small board; small bulletin board; **—s** wooden clappers.
tablón m. plank; large, thick board.
taburete m. stool, chair without arms.
tacañería f. stinginess, niggardness; miserliness.
tacaño adj. stingy, miser; sly; mean.
tácito adj. tacit, silent, implied.
taciturno adj. taciturn; sullen; sad.
taco m. wad; wadding; stopper; rammer; volley of oaths; mace of a billiard table; swear word; Am. short, fat person; heel of a shoe; **echar —s** Am. to curse; **darse uno —** Am. to put on airs.
tacón m. heel of a shoe.
taconear v. to click the heels; to walk hard on one's heels.
taconeo m. clicking of the heels.
táctica f. tactics.
tacto m. tact; touching, sense of touch.
tacha f. flaw, defect, fault, macula, blemish.
tachar v. to cross out; to censure; to accuse; to blot, to dash.
tachón m. stud; line drawn through a writing to blot it out; lace trimming.
tachonar v. to stud, to ornament with studs; to adorn with trimmings.
tachuela f. tack, small nail; Am. metal dipper; runt.
tafetán m. taffeta; **— inglés** court plaster.
tahúr m. gambler; cardsharp.
taimado adj. sly, crafty; Am. sullen, gloomy, gruff.
tajada f. slice; cut.
tajalápiz m. pencil sharpener.
tajar v. to slice, to cut; to sharpen a pencil.
tajo m. cut; gash; cutting edge; sheer cliff; shopping block.
tal adj. such, so, as; such a; similar; as much; so great; **— cual** such as; so-so; fair; **— vez** perhaps; **el — Pedro** that fellow Peter; **un — García** a certain Garcia; **— para cual** two of a kind; **un — por cual** a so-and-

talabarte m. sword belt.

taladrar v. to bore; to drill; to pierce; to penetrate.

taladro m. auger, drill, bore, drill hole; Am. mine tunnel.

tálamo m. bridal bed or chamber.

talante m. disposition, mode, manner, appearance, aspect.

talco m. talc; **— en polvo** talcum powder.

talega f. money bag, sack.

talento m. talent, ability, natural gift.

talentoso adj. talented, gifted, doted.

talismán m. talisman, charm.

talón m. heel, stub, check; coupon.

talonario m. stub book.

talonear v. to tap with one's heels; to walk briskly.

taloneo m. tapping with the heels.

talla f. stature, height; round of a card game; ransom; Am. chat; thrashing, beating.

tallar v. to carve; to cut stone; to appraise; to deal; Am. to court; to make love; to bother; to disturb.

tallarín m. noodle.

talle m. figure, form, waist; fit of a dress; looks; appearance; Am. bodice.

taller m. workshop, laboratory; studio; factory.

tallo m. stalk; stem; shoot; sprout.

tamal m. Am. tamale; vile trick; intrigue; clumsy bundle.

tamaño m. size; adj. such a; of the size of; **— disparate** such a (big) mistake; **— como un elefante;** big as an elephant.

tambalearse v. to totter; to stagger; to sway; to reel.

también adv. also; too; likewise.

tambor m. drum; drum-like object; drummel; pair of embroidery hoops; Am. bedspring; spring mattress.

tambora f. bass drum.

tamboril m. small drum.

tamborilear v. to drum; to extol.

tamborilero m. drummer.

tamiz m. fine sieve.

tamizar v. to sift; to blend.

tampoco conj. either (after a negative); **no lo hizo —** he did not do it either; **ni yo — nor I** either.

tan adv. (contr. of **tanto**) so, as; such a.

tanda f. turn; round; task, gang; group; shift; relay; Am. theatrical performance.

tangente adj. & f. tangent; **salirse por la —** to go off a tangent; to avoid the issue.

tangible adj. tangible.

tango m. tango.

tanque m. tank; reservoir; Am. pond; swimming pool.

tantán m. clang; knock! knock!; sound of a bell, drum, etc.

tantear v. to probe; to test; to sound out; to feel out; to estimate.

tanteo m. trial, test; calculation; estimate; score; **al —** by guess.

tanto adj., pron. & adv. so much, as much; so; **—s** so many, as many; m. certain amount; counter, chip (to keep score); **cuarenta y —s** forty odd; **el — por ciento** percentage; rate; **un — (or algún —)** somewhat; **como la mitad** as well as; as much as; **— en la ciudad como en el campo** both in the city and in the country; **entre (or mientras) —** meanwhile; **por lo —** therefore.

tañer v. to play an instrument; to ring; to ring the bell.

tañido m. tune, sound, clink, ring, twang of a guitar.

tapa f. lid, cover; horny part of a hoof; heel-piece of a shoe; **— de los sesos** top of the skull.

tapadera f. lid, cover; one who shields another.

tapar v. to cover; to stop up; to obstruct; to occlude; to conceal; to hide; Am. to fill a tooth; to crush, to crumple; to cover with insults.

tapera f. Am. ruins, abandoned room or house.

tapete m. rug; table scarf

tapia f. adobe wall; mud fence.

tapiar v. to stop up with a mud wall; to block up a door or window.

tapicería f. tapestry, upholstery; tapestry shop; tapestry trade.

tapiz m. tapestry.

tapón m. plug, stopper, cork; bung; stopple.

taquigrafía f. shorthand.

taquígrafo m. stenographer.

taquilla f. ticket office; box office;

tararear file for letters, papers, etc.: Am. tavern, liquor store.
tararear v. to hum.
tarareo m. hum, humming.
tarascada f. snap, bite; snappy or harsh answer.
tardanza f. slowness; delay, tardiness, lingering.
tardar v. to delay; to put off; to be late; —se to delay oneself; to be delayed; **a más —** at the very latest.
tarde f. afternoon; evening; adv. late; past the time; **de — en —** now and then; occasionally; seldom; **hacerse —** to grow late.
tardío adj. late, too late; tardy; dilatory.
tardo adj. slow, tardy; dull, lazy; stupid.
tardón adj. very slow; m. solwpoke.
tarea f. task, job; toll; drudgery.
tarifa f. tariff, book of rates or duties.
tarima f. wooden platform; low bench, table, footstool.
tarjeta f. card; **— de visita** visiting card; **— postal** post card.
tarro m. earthen jar; glazed earthen pan; Am. top hat.
tarta f. tart; pan for baking tarts.
tartamudear v. to stutter; to fumble; to stammer.
tartamudeo m. stammer, stuttering, stammering.
tartamudo m. stutterer; stammerer; adj. stuttering, stammering.
tartera f. griddle; pan for baking tarts.
tarugo m. wooden peg or pin, stopper, plug, bung; adj. Am. mischievous, devilish.
tasa f. measure, rule, standard; rate; appraisal, valuation.
tasación f. assessment, valuation; appraisement.
tasajo m. piece of jerked beef.
tasar v. to measure; to value; to rate.
tata m. daddy, dad; Am. chief (said by Indians to a superior).
tataranieto m. great-great-grandson.
tatita m. daddy; Am. dear chief or daddy.
taxear v. to taxi (said of a plane).
taxi See **taxímetro**.
taxímetro m. taxi, taxi cab; taximeter.
taza f. cup, bowl; basin of a fountain; large wooden bowl.

té m. tea; f. T-square, T-shaped ruler.
te obj. pron. you (fam. sing.); to you; for you; yourself.
teatral adj. theatrical.
teatro m. theater; stage; playhouse; scene; **hacer —** to put on airs.
tecla f. key of a piano, typewriter, etc.; delicate point; **dar en la —** to hit the mark.
teclado m. keyboard.
técnica f. technique.
técnico adj. technical; m. technical, expert.
tecolote m. Am. owl; policeman.
techado m. roof; shed; ceiling.
techar v. to roof.
techumbre f. roof, shed, ceiling.
tedio m. tediousness; boredom; disgust, bother.
tedioso adj. tedious, boring; disgusting.
teja f. roof tile; linden tree; Am. rear part of a saddle.
tejado m. roof covered with tiles; shed.
tejamanil m. shingle; small thin board.
tejedor m. weaver.
tejer v. to weave; to knit; to discuss; to devise.
tejido m. texture, weaving, fabric; web.
tejón m. badger; yew; bar of gold.
tela f. cloth; textile; fabric; web; **— de araña** cobweb; **— metálica** wire screen; **poner en — de juicio** to call in question.
telar m. loom.
telaraña f. cobweb.
telefonear v. to telephone.
telefónico adj. telephonic.
telefonista m. & f. telephone operator.
teléfono m. telephone.
telegrafía f. telegraphy.
telegrafiar v. to telegraph.
telegráfico adj. telegraphic.
telégrafo m. telegraph; **— sin hilos** wireless.
telegrama m. telegram.
telescopio m. telescope.
televisión f. television.
telón m. theater curtain.
tema m. theme; subject matter; topic.
temblar v. irr. to tremble; to shake; to quake.
temblón adj. tremulous, shaking, trembling.
temblor m. trembling; **— de tierra** earthquake.

tembloroso adj. trembling; shivering; shaking.
temer v. to dread; to fear; to aprehend.
temerario adj. bold, reckless; daring.
temeroso adj. fearful; suspicious; timid.
temible adj. terrible, dreadful; awful.
temor m. dread; fear; aprehension; suspicion.
témpano m. flitch of bacon; — **de hielo** iceberg.
temperamento m. temperament; temper; climate.
temperatura f. temperature.
tempestad f. tempest, storm.
tempestuoso adj. tempestuous, stormy.
templado p.p. & adj. tempered, temperate, moderate; tepid; lukewarm; brave; bold; Am. half-drunk; hard, severe.
templanza f. temperance; moderation; temperament.
templar v. to temper; to moderate; to calm; —**se** to be moderate; to control oneself.
temple m. temper, temperament; disposition of the mind; harmony of musical instruments.
templo m. temple, church.
temporada f. certain space of time; season.
temporal adj. temporal, temporary; secular; wordly; m. tempest; storm.
tempranero adj. early, prematurely; soon.
temprano adj. early, very early; soon.
tenacidad f. tenacity, viscosity; pertinacity.
tenacillas f. pl. small tongs; pincers; snuffers.
tenaz adj. tenacious; sticking; firm; obstinate.
tenazas f. pl. tongs, pincers; forceps.
tendedero m. place where washed linen is set up to dry; stretcher.
tendencia f. tendency, inclination.
tender v. irr. to stretch or stretch out; to unfold; to expand; to direct; to tend; to hang to dry; to lay out; —**se** to stretch oneself at full length.
ténder m. tender of a locomotive.
tendero m. strorekeeper; shopkeeper.
tendón m. tendon; — **de Aquiles** the tendon of Achilles.

tenducho m. wretched little shop or store.
tenebroso adj. tenebrous; dark, gloomy.
tenedor m. table fork; holder; keeper; tenant; guardian; — **de libros** bookkeeper.
teneduría f. store house; — **de libros** bookkeeping.
tener v. irr. to have; to hold; to keep; to retain; to take; to gripe; to possess; to maintain; to support; to contain; — **miedo, hambre, frío sueño, etc,** to be afraid, hungry, cold, sleepy, etc.; — ... **años to be**... years old.
tenería f. tannery.
teniente m. first lieutenant; deputy.
tenis m. tennis.
tenor m. tenor, contents, sense contained; nature.
tensión f. tension, strain.
tenso adj. tense; strained; tight; taut.
tentación f. temptation.
tentáculo m. tentacle, feeler.
tentador adj. tempting; tempter, the devil.
tentalear v. to feel around; to finger, to fumble.
tentar v. irr. to tempt; to touch; to try; to examine; to grope; to incite; to attempt, to procure; to hesitate.
tentativa f. attempt, trial.
tentativo adj. tentative.
tenue adj. delicate, thin; flimsy; slender.
teñir v. irr. to dye; to tinge; to stain.
teologal adj. theological.
teología f. theology.
teológico adj. theological.
teoría f. theory.
teórico adj. theoretical.
tequila m. & f. Am. tequila, strong liquor made from the **maguey** plant.
tercero adj. third; m. third person, mediator; pimp, bawd; tertiary, a member of the third order of St. Francis.
terciar v. to sling; to divide into three parts; to mediate; to arbitrate; to join, to share; Am. to carry on the back; to adulterate; to add water; to mix.
tercio adj. third; m. one third; half of a mule load; military corps; Am. bale, bundle; **hacer**

terciopelo uno mal — to hinder, to interfere.
terciopelo m. velvet.
terco adj. obstinate; pertinacious; firm.
tergiversar v. to distort; to twist; to stuffle.
terminación f. end, ending, final, termination.
terminal adj. terminal, final, ending.
terminante adj. closing, decisive; final.
terminar v. to end; to finish; to terminate.
término m. end; term; completion; boundary; landmark; limit; goal; manner; aim; object; — **medio** average.
termómetro m. thermometer.
termos f. thermos bottle.
ternera f. calf, veal.
terneza f. tenderness, affection; delicacy, softness; affectionate word or caress; fondness; suavity.
terno m. ternary number; group of three; Am. cup and saucer; **echar** (or **soltar**) **un** — to swear excessively.
ternura f. tenderness, affection; love.
terquedad f. obstinacy; stubborness; tenacity.
terrado m. terrace, flat roof; platform.
terraplén m. railroad embankment; mound; terrace.
terrateniente m. & f. landholder; master of land or property.
terraza f. terrace, veranda, flat roof.
terrenal adj. earthly, worldly.
terreno m. land, ground, soil; field; adj. earthly, wordly.
terrestre adj. terrestrial, wordly, earthly.
terrible adj. terrible, dreadful; horrible.
terrífico adj. terrific.
territorio m. territory, district; precint.
terrón m. clod, lump.
terror m. terror.
terso adj. polished, smooth, pure; correct, terse.
tertulia f. evening party; social gathering.
tertulio m. member of a tertulia.
tesis f. thesis.
tesón m. grit, endurance, pluck; persistence.
tesonero adj Am. tenacious, stubborn.

tesorería f. treasury.
tesorero m. treasurer.
tesoro m. treasure; treasury; riches, wealth.
testa f. head, crown of the head; front.
testamento m. testament, will.
testarudez f. stubborness; obstinacy; inflexibility.
testarudo adj. obstinate, stubborn; inflexible.
testigo m. & f. witness; — **ocular** eye witness; m. testimony, proof; evidence.
testimoniar v. to give testimony; to testify; **levantar falso testimonio** to bear false witness.
testuz m. nape; crown of the head of animals.
teta f. teat, nipple, breast; udder; dug.
tetera f. teapot, kettle.
tétrico adj. sad, melancholic, gloomy.
textil adj. textile.
texto m. text; quotation; textbook.
tez f. complexion, skin.
ti pers. pron. used after a prep. you; yourself.
tía f. aunt; good old woman; — **rica** Am. pawn shop; **no hay tu** — there is not use or hope.
tibio adj. tepid, lukewarm, remiss; indifferent.
tiburón m. shark.
tico adj & m. Am. Costa Rican (nickname).
tiempo m. time; weather; tense; season; opportunity, occasion; temperature, climate; age; musical measure; **a** — timely, on time; **a su** (or **a su debido**) — in due time; **andando el** — in time, as the time goes on.
tienda f. store, tent; — **de campaña** army tent, camping tent.
tienta, probe, surgical instrument; **a** —**s** groppingly.
tiento m. touch, tact; blind man's stick; tentacle, feeler; Am. saddle strap, leather strap, thong; **hacer algo con mucho** — to do something with great care or caution.
tierno adj. tender; soft, recent, young; delicate; fond; mild; Am. green, unripe.
tierra f. earth; land, ground; soil; the globe; country, region; — **firme** continent; — **adentro** inland; **echar por** — to knock down; **tomar** — to land.

tieso adj. stiff, rigid, firm; stubborn.
tiesto m. flower pot; Am. pot.
tiesura f. stiffness.
tifo m. typhus.
tifoidea f. typhoid fever.
tigre m. tiger.
tigresa f. tigress.
tijera(s) f. scissors; sawhorse; **silla de —** folding chair; **tener buena — or buenas —s** to be a gossiper; to have a sharp tongue.
tijeretada f. snip, cut, clip with scissors.
tijeretear v. to snip, cut, clip with scissors; to gossip; to criticize.
tilde f. tilde, mark over an n; bit; blemish.
timbrar v. to stamp; Am. to mail a letter.
timbre m. stamp; revenue stamp; sound of a bell; timbre, quality of tone; glorious deed.
timidez f. timidity, shyness.
tímido adj. timid, shy.
timón m. rudder, helm; beam of a plow.
timonear v. to steer.
timorato adj. timorous, timid, shy.
tímpano m. eardrum; kettledrum.
tina f. bathtub; vat, tank, tub; large earthen jar.
tinaco m. tank, vat, tub, reservoir.
tinaja f. large earthen jar.
tinieblas f. pl. darkness; obscurity; ignorance, confusion; **príncipe de las —** Satan.
tino m. acumen, keen insight, good judgment; tact; accurate aim; good sense.
tinta f. ink; dye; tint, hue; **—s** paints; **— simpática** invisible ink; **saber de buena —** to know from good authority.
tinte m. tint, ink; hue; tinge; color; dye; dyeing.
tinterillo m. shyster. See **picapleitos**.
tintero m. inkwell; inkstand; Am. writing materials, desk set.
tintinear v. to tinkle.
tintineo m. tinkle, tinkling.
tinto adj. tinged; red; **vino — red wine;** Am. dark red.
tintorería f. cleaner's and dyer's shop.
tintorero m. dyer.
tintura f. tincture, tint, color, dye.
tinturar v. to tincture, to tinge; to dye.
tiñoso adj. scabby, mangy; stingy.
tío m. uncle; old man; good old man; fellow; guy; **el cuento del —** Am. deceitful story told to extract money.
tiovivo m. merry-go-round.
típico adj. typical.
tiple m. & f. high soprano singer; m. treble; soprano voice; treble guitar.
tipo m. type; class; model, standard; fellow, guy; Am. rate of interest; **— de cambio** Am. rate of exchange; **buen —** good-looking fellow.
tipografía f. typography; printing press; printing shop.
tira f. strip, stripe; **estar hecho —s** Am. to be in rags; **sacar a uno las —s** Am. to tan one's hide; beat one to pieces.
tirabuzón m. corkscrew.
tirada f. throw; issue, edition; printing; Am. tirade; sly trick; dash on horseback; **de una —** all at once.
tirador m. shooter; thrower; slingshot; bell cord; handle; printer; Am. leader belt with pockets; **— de goma** sling shot.
tiranía f. tyranny.
tiránico adj. tyrannical.
tirano adj. tyrannical; m. tyrant.
tirante adj. pulling; stretched; taut; strained; m. trace (of a harness); brace; **—s** suspenders; supporter for stockings.
tirantez f. tension, tightness; strain; pull.
tirar v. to throw; to throw away; to shoot; to fire; to draw; to attract; Am. to cart; **— a** to tend toward; to resemble; to aim at; **— de** to pull, to tug; **ir tirando** to get along; **—sela de** to boast of.
tiritar v. to shiver.
tiro m. throw, shot, piece of artillery; range of a gun; team of horses; chimney draft; mine shaft; Am. issue, printing; cartage, transport; **—s** Am. suspenders; **— al blanco** target practice; **al —** Am. at once; **de a —** (or **de al —**) Am. all at once; completely; **caballo de —** draft horse; **ni a —s** absolutely not.
tirón m. jerk; sudden push; **de un —** all at once.
tironear v. Am. to push, to jerk; to attract.
tirotear v. to shoot around; to shoot at random; **—se** to exchange shots.

tiroteo m. shooting; exchange of shots.
tirria f. aversion, grudge; **tenerle — a una persona** to have a strong dislike for someone.
tísico adj. tubercular.
tisis f. tuberculosis, consumption.
títere m. puppet; ridiculous little fellow; **—s** puppet show.
titilación f. flicker; twinkle.
titilar v. to flicker; to twinkle; to glimmer.
titubear v. to hesitate; to totter; to stagger; to grope; to stutter; to stammer.
titubeo m. hesitation, reluctance, wavering.
titular v. to entitle; to name; **—se** to be called or named; to receive a title; adj. titular, in name only.
título m. title, heading; sign; inscription; claim, legal right; degree; credential; diploma; merit; bond; certificate; **a — de** under the pretext of.
tiza f. chalk.
tiznado adj. sooty, covered with soot; smutty; Am. drunk.
tiznar v. to smudge; to smut; to smear with soot.
tizne m. soot, smut.
tiznón m. smudge.
tizón m. firebrand, piece of burning wood; rust, blight on plants; stain on one's honor.
toalla f. towel.
tobillo m. ankle.
tocado m. headdress, hairdo, coiffure; adj. half-crazy.
tocador m. dressing table; boudoir, dressing room; dressing case; player of a musical instrument.
tocar v. to touch; to play (an instrument); to ring; to knock; to rap; **— en** to stop over in; **—le a uno** to fall to one's lot; **—se** to fix one's hair.
tocayo m. namesake.
tocino m. bacon; salt pork; lard.
tocón m. stub; stump of a tree, arm or leg.
todavía adv. still, yet, even.
todo adj. all, whole; every; each; **— hombre** everyman; **—s los días** everyday.
todopoderoso adj. almighty.
toga f. gown, robe worn by a judge, professor, etc.; Roman toga.
toldería f. Am. Indian camp; Indian village.

toldo m. awning; pomp, vanity; Am. Indian hut.
tolerancia f. tolerance, toleration, indulgence.
tolerante adj. tolerant.
tolerar v. to tolerate; to allow; to overlook; to let pass; to permit.
tolete m. Am. stick, club, cudgel; raft.
toma f. taking, seizure, capture; dose; tap of a water main; Am. irrigation ditch; **— de corriente** electric outlet.
tomar v. to take; to have; to catch; to seize; to grasp; to understand; to aprehend; to buy; to eat or drink; to intercept; to rob; to choose; to undertake; **— a pechos** to take to heart; **— a mal** to take it amiss; **— el pelo a** to make fun of; **— por la derecha** to turn to the right; **—se con** to quarrel with.
tomate m. tomato.
tomillo m. thyme.
tomo m. tome, volume; Am. heavy person; dull, silent person; **de — y lomo** bulky, important.
ton: **sin — ni son** without rhyme or reason.
tonada f. tune, song; Am. singsong; local accent.
tonadilla f. little tune; short popular song.
tonel m. keg, cask, barrel.
tonelada f. ton.
tonelaje m. tonnage.
tónico adj. & m. tonic.
tono m. tone; tune, key, pitch; accent; manner; vigor, strength; **de buen —** of good taste; **subirse de —** to put on airs.
tontera See **tontería**.
tontería f. foolishness, foolery, folly, nonsense; stupidity.
tonto adj. foolish, stupid, silly; **a tontas y a locas** recklessly; m. fool; dunce; Am. a game of cards.
topar v. to collide with; to run or strike against; to bump into; to encounter; to find; to meet; to run across; to butt; Am. to gamble.
tope m. butt; bump; collision; encounter; bumper; **hasta el —** up to the top; **estar hasta los —s** to be filled up.
topetada f. butt; bump; blow on the head.
topetear v. to butt, to bump.
topetón m. hard bump; collision; butt.

tópico m. topic, subject; subject matter.

topo m. mole, small animal; dunce; awkward person.

toque m. touch, ringing, beat of a drum; tap; sound of a trumpet, clarinet, etc; assay; **piedra de —** touch stone; **¡ahí está el —!** there is the difficulty.

torbellino m. whirlwind; rush; bustle; confusion; lively, boisterous, restless person.

torcedura f. twist, sprain, strain; twisting.

torcer v. irr. to twist; to turn; to bend; to sprain; to distort; to deflect; to crook; to pervert; to dissuade; to retort; **—se** to become twisted, bent or sprained.

torcido p.p. & adj. oblique, tortuous, twisted; crooked; angry; resentful; Am. unfortunate, unlucky; **estar — con** to be on unfriendly terms with; m. a kind of twisted sweetmeat.

tordillo adj. greyish, grizzled.

tordo adj. dapple, grey; m. thrush; dapple-grey horse.

torear v. to perform in a bullfight; to incite; to provoke a bull; to tease.

torero m. bullfighter; adj. relating to bullfighting.

tormenta f. storm, tempest; misfortune.

tormento m. torment; torture; rack (instrument of torture); anguish; pain.

tornar v. to return; to turn; to come back again; to repeat; to change; to alter; **— a hacerlo** to do it again.

tornasolado adj. iridiscent, rainbow-colored; changeable.

tornear v. to turn in a lathe; to do lathe work; to turn; to wind round about; to fight in a tournament.

torneo m. tournament.

tornillo m. screw; clamp; vise; **faltarle a uno un —** to have little sense.

torno m. lathe, turn; turnstile; revolving server; circumvolution; axeltree; **en —** around, round about.

toro m. bull; difficult question; **—s** bullfight.

toronja f. grapefruit.

torpe adj. stupid, dull; clumsy; slow, lewd.

torpedear v. to torpedo.

torpedero m. torpedo boat.

torpedo m. torpedo.

torpeza f. stupidity; torpidness; clumsiness.

torre f. tower, turret; castle (in chess).

torrente m. torrent; flood; **— de voz** powerful voice.

torreón m. large tower of a fortress, castle, etc.

tórrido adj. torrid.

torsión f. twist; sprain.

torta f. torte, round cake, round loaf.

tortilla f. omelette; Am. tortilla (flat, thin cornmeal cake).

tórtola f. turtledove.

tortuga f. tortoise; turtle.

tortuoso adj. tortuous; twisting, winding.

tortura f. torture; grief; affliction; pain.

torturar v. to torture.

torvo adj. grim, stern, severe.

tos f. cough; **— ferina** whooping cough.

tosco adj. coarse, rough; harsh; ill bred.

toser v. to cough; Am. to brag, to boast.

tosquedad f. coarseness, crudeness, roughness.

tostada f. toast; toasted bread; boring visit or conversation; Am. toasted tortilla; **dar (or pegar) una — a uno** to play a mean trick on someone.

tostado p.p. & adj. roasted, toasted, tanned; Am. worn out; m. toasting; Am. roasted corn.

tostador m. toaster.

tostar v. irr. to toast; to tan; to overheat; to roast coffee.

tostón m. toast dipped in oil; small roasted pig; coin worth half a Mexican peso.

total adj. & m. total.

totalidad f. totality; entirety; whole.

totalitario adj. totalitarian.

tóxico adj. toxic.

toxina f. toxin, poison produced within animals and plants.

toza f. wooden block; stump; log; piece of bark.

traba f. ligament, ligature; obstacle, impediment; trammel; fetter.

trabajador adj. industrious, painstaking; m. laborer; worker.

trabajar v. to work; to labor; to manufacture; to make; to travail; to act; to endeavor.

trabajo m. work, labor, difficulty; obstacle, hardship; hindrance; fatigue.

trabajoso adj. laborious, difficult, troublesome; painful; Am. unobliging; demanding.

trabar v. to join; to unite; to connect; to quarrel; to scuffle; to seize; to take hold of; to fetter; to thicken; —**se** to stammer in conversation; —**se de palabras** to get into an argument.

tracción f. traction.

tractor m. tractor.

tradición f. tradition.

tradicional adj. traditional.

traducción f. translation.

traducir v. irr. to translate; to interpret in another language.

traductor m. translator, interpreter.

traer v. irr. to fetch; to carry; to conduct; to bring; to come; to manage; to use; to wear; to bring over; to bring about; to cause; to contract; — **a uno inquieto** to keep one disturbed; — **y llevar cuentos** to carry tales backwards and forwards; — **a uno a mal** — to bother someone.

trafagar v. to traffic; to trade; to roam about; to bustle; to hustle; to toil.

tráfago m. bustle; trade; commerce; hustle; toil.

traficante m. trader, dealer, tradesman.

traficar v. to traffic, to trade; Am. to pass or move back and forth (as traffic).

tráfico m. traffic; trade; commerce.

tragaluz m. skylight.

tragar v. to swallow; to gulp; to engulf; to glut; to dissemble; to pocket an affront.

tragedia f. tragedy.

trágico adj. tragic.

trago m. swallow, gulp; — **amargo** misfortune; Am. brandy, hard liquor; **a —s** slowly; **echar un** — to have a drink.

tragón m. glutton; adj. gluttonous.

traición f. treason; treachery; **a** — treacherously; deceitfully.

traicionar v. to betray.

traicionero adj. treacherous; deceitful; m. traitor.

traído adj. used, old, worn out; **muy — y llevado** very worn out.

traidor adj. treacherous; m. traitor; betrayer.

traje m. dress; suit; gown; — **de etiqueta** formal gown; — **de luces** bullfighter's costume; — **sastre** Am. woman's tailor-made suit.

trajeado p.p. & adj. dressed, clothed.

trajín m. traffic, going and coming; hustle, bustle, commotion.

trajinar v. to carry; to cart back and forth; to go back and forth; to bustle; to hustle.

trama f. plot, scheme, conspiracy; woof (horizontal thread of a fabric).

tramar v. to weave; to plot; to hatch.

tramitar v. to transact; to take legal steps; to negotiate.

trámite m. transaction; procedure; step, formality.

tramo m. stretch, lap; span; short distance, regular interval; flight of stairs.

trampa f. trap, snare; trap door; fraud, deceit; debt fraudulently contracted; trick.

trampear v. to trick; to cheat; to swindle.

trampista m. & f. cheat, crook; swindler.

trampolín m. springboard.

tramposo adj. deceitful; tricky; m. swindler.

tranca f. crossbar, pole, prop; club; stick; Am. rustic gate; **tener una** — Am. to be drunk.

trance m. critical moment; dangerous situation; peril, danger; **el último** — the last stage of life; **a todo** — resolutely, at any cost.

tranco m. stride, long step; threshold; **a —s** hurriedly; **en dos —s** in a jiffy.

tranquear v. to stride along.

tranquera f. stockade, wooden fence; Am. large gate made with trancas.

tranquilidad f. tranquility; peacefulness.

tranquilizar v. to calm; to tranquilize; to quiet; to pacify; —**se** to become tranquil.

tranquilo adj. tranquil, peaceful, calm.

transacción f. transaction, negotiation, compromise, dealing, deal.

transar v. Am. to compromise; to yield; to give in.

transatlántico adj. transatlantic; m. transatlantic steamer.

transbordar See **trasbordar**.

transbordo See **trasbordo**.
transcendencia f. trascendency, consequence, importance, penetration.
transcendental adj. consequential, important.
transcurrir v. to go off; to pass; to elapse.
transcurso m. passing, lapse of time.
transeúnte m. passer-by, pedestrian; transient; adj. transient.
transferencia f. transference, transfer.
transformación f. transformation.
transformar v. to transform.
transgredir v. to transgress.
transgresión f. transgression.
transgresor m. transgressor, offender.
transición f. transition.
transigente adj. yielding, pliable, compromising.
transigir v. to compromise; to yield; to make concessions; to settle by compromise.
transitable adj. passable (road).
transitar v. to pass or move back and forth (as traffic).
tránsito m. transit; traffic; passing; passage; transition; **de —** on the way; in transit.
transitorio adj. transitory.
transmisión f. transmission.
transmisor m. transmitter; adj. transmitting.
transmitir v. to transmit.
transparencia f. transparency.
transparente adj. transparent, lucid, clear; m. window shade; stained-glass window.
transponer v. irr. to transpose; to transfer; to transplant; to go beyond; to go over to the other side; **—se** to hide from view.
transportación f. transportation, transport.
transportar v. to transport; to transpose music; **—se** to be transported.
transporte m. transport, transportation; transport vessel; ecstasy; **— de locura** fit of madness.
transversal adj. transversal, transverse; **sección —** cross section.
transverso adj. transverse, cross.
tranvía m. street car; street car track.
trapacear v. to swindle; to cheat; to racketeer.
trapacería f. racket, fraud, swindle.
trapacero m. racketeer; cheat, swindler; adj. cheating, deceiving.
trapacista m. & f. racketeer, swindler; cheat.
trapeador m. Am. mopper; mop.
trapear v. Am. to mop; to beat up; to give someone a licking.
trapiche m. sugar mill; press for extracting juices; Am. grinding machine for pulverizing minerals.
trapisonda f. escapade, prank; brawl; noisy spree.
trapo m. rag; Am. cloth; **—s** clothes; **a todo —** at full sail; **poner a uno como un —** to make one feel like a rag; **sacarle a uno los —s al sol** to exhibit somebody's dirty linen; **soltar el —** to burst out laughing or crying.
traposo adj. Am. ragged, tattered, in rags.
tráquea f. trachea, windpipe.
traquetear v. to rattle; to shake; to jolt; to crack; to crackle.
traqueteo m. rattling; shaking; jolting, cracking; crackling; Am. uproar; din; noisy, disorderly traffic.
tras prep. after; in search of; behind; in back of; **— de** behind; **¡—!** interj. bang!
trasbordar v. to transfer.
trasbordo m. transfer.
trascendencia See **transcendencia**.
trascendental See **transcendental**.
trasegar v. irr. to upset; to overturn; to change from one place to another; to pour from one container to another.
trasero adj. rear; hind, back; m. rump.
trasladar v. to move; to remove; to transfer; to postpone; to translate; to transcribe; to copy.
traslado m. transfer; transcript, written copy.
traslucirse v. irr. to be translucent; to be transparent, clear, evident.
trasnochar v. to sit up all night; to stay awake all night; to spend the night out.
traspalar v. to shovel.
traspapelar v. to mislay, misplace a paper, letter, document, etc.; **—se** to become mislaid among other papers.
traspasar v. to pass over; to cross over; to go beyond; to pass through; to pierce; to transfer property; to trespass.
traspaso m. transfer; transgression; trespass.

traspié m. stumble, slip; **dar un —** to stumble or trip.
trasponer See **transponer**.
trasplantar v. to transplant.
trasquila f. shearing, clip, clipping; bad hair cut.
trasquilar v. to shear; to clip; to crop; to cut badly (hair).
trastazo m. thump, blow.
traste m. fret, stop of a guitar; Am. tray, implement; **dar al — con** to destroy.
trasto m. household utensil; piece of junk; rubbish, trash; **—s** utensils; implements; **—s de pescar** fishing tackle.
trastornar v. to overturn; to upset.
trastorno m. upset; disorder; disturbance.
trastrocar v. irr. to invert; to change; to upset.
trasudar v. to perspire; to sweat slightly.
trasudor m. slight perspiration or sweat.
tratable adj. friendly, sociable, manageable.
tratado m. treaty; treatise.
tratamiento m. treatment; title of courtesy, form of address.
tratante m. & f. dealer, tradesman; trader.
tratar v. to treat; to discuss; to confer; to traffic; to trade; to manage; to conduct; **— con** to deal with; **— de** to try to; **—le a uno de** to address someone as; **— en** to deal in; **—se bien to** treat oneself well; **no se trata de eso** that is not the question.
trato m. treatment; behavior, conduct; manner, address; pact, agreement; treat; trade; traffic, commerce; friendly intercourse, conversation; **— hecho** it is a deal.
través m. crossbeam, reverse, misfortune; **a** (or **al**) **— de** through; **dar al — con** to ruin; to destroy; **mirar de —** to squint in a sinister manner.
travesaño m. cross piece, cross bar; bolster; Am. railway tie.
travesear v. to romp; to frisk; to frolic; to fool around; to misbehave.
travesía f. crossing; sea voyage; wind blowing towards a coast; Am. wasteland, desert land; partition wall or fence; mid-year crop.

travesura f. mischief, prank; lively wit.
traviesa f. railway tie; rafter; crossbeam.
travieso adj. mischievous; lively, restless; **a campo traviesa** cross country.
trayecto m. run, stretch, lap, distance traveled over.
trayectoria f. path of a bullet, missile, etc.
traza f. plan, design; scheme; plot, invention; appearance; semblance; aspect; indication; sign; **darse —s** to use one's wits.
trazado m. draft, plan, sketch, outline, drawing; p.p. & adj. traced, sketched; outlined.
trazar v. to contrive; to plan out; to design; to trace; to sketch; to draw.
trébol m. clover.
trecho m. space, distance, lapse in a race; **a —** by, or at intervals; **de — en —** at certain points or intervals.
tregua f. truce, rest, respite; repose.
tremedal m. quagmire; bog; marsh.
tremendo adj. tremendous; huge; terrible.
trementina f. turpentine.
tremolar v. to flutter; to wave a flag.
trémolo m. tremolo of the voice, quaver.
trémulo adj. tremulous, trembling, quivering; flickering.
tren m. train; Am. traffic; **— correo** mail train; **— de aterrizaje** landing gear.
trenza f. tress; braid; Am. string of garlics, onions, etc.
trenzar v. to braid; **—se** to braid one's hair; Am. to fight hand to hand.
trepar v. to climb; to clamber; **—se** to climb.
trepidación f. jar, vibration; shaking; trembling.
trepidar v. to shake; to vibrate; to tremble; to jar.
treta f. trick, wile; **malas —s** bad tricks.
triángulo m. triangle.
tribu f. tribe.
tribulación f. tribulation, trouble.
tribuna f. rostrum, speaker's platform.
tribunal m. tribunal; court of justice; body of judges.
tributar v. to pay tribute, to pay homage.

tributo m. tribute, contribution; tax.

trifulca f. fight; quarrel; revolt; riot.

trigo m. wheat.

trigueño adj. swarthy; brunette; dark.

trillado p.p. & adj. trite, hackneyed; commonplace; camino — beaten path.

trillar v. to thresh; to beat; to mistreat; Am. to put apart.

trimestral adj. quarterly.

trimestre m. quarter; period of three months; quarterly payment, income or salary.

trinar v. to trill (in singing); to wardle; to quaver (said of the voice); to get furious.

trinchante m. carving fork; carving knife; carver.

trinchar v. to carve meat.

trinche m. fork; Am. table fork; plato — Am. carving plate.

trinchera f. trench; ditch; Am. stockade, fence; curved knife.

trinchero m. carving table; plato — carving platter.

trineo m. sleigh; sled.

trino m. trill (in singing).

tripa f. intestine, bowel, paunch; belly; —s entrails, inside.

triple adj. & m. triple.

triplicar v. to triplicate; to triple; to treble.

tripulación f. crew, ship's company.

tripular v. to man a ship.

trique m. crack; snap; Am. utensil; trinket; clever trick in a game; —s Am. poor household utensils.

triscar v. to romp; to frisk; to frolic; to stamp or shuffle the feet; Am. to tease, to make fun of.

triste adj. sad; sorrowful; Am. bashful, backward; melancholy love song.

tristeza f. sadness; sorrow; Am. tick fever.

tristón adj. wistful, quite sad; melancholy.

triunfal adj. triumphal.

triunfante adj. triumphant.

triunfar v. to triumph; to trump (at cards).

triunfo m. triumph; trump card, trophy.

trivial adj. trivial, commonplace, trite.

triza f. shred, fragment, small piece, cord, rope for sails; hacer —s to tear into shreds.

trocar v. irr. to change; to barter; to exchange; to be transformed; to exchange.

trocha f. path, trail; Am. gauge (of a railway); trot; slice or serving of meat.

trofeo m. trophee, booty; spoils.

troje m. barn, granary.

trole m. trolley.

tromba f. waterspout.

trombón m. trombone.

trompa f. trumpet; trunk of an elephant; large spinning top; Am. snout; cowcatcher (of a locomotive).

trompada f. blow with the fist; bump.

trompeta f. trumpet; m. trumpeter; useless individual; Am. drunk, drunkard; bold, shameless fellow.

trompetear v. to trumpet, to blow the trumpet.

trompo m. spinning top; stupid fellow; dunce.

tronada f. thunderstorm.

tronar v. irr. to thunder; to explode.

tronco m. trunk; log; stem; trunk of the human body; team of horses.

tronchar v. to break a stalk or trunk; to chop off; to break off; —se to break off or get bent (said of a stalk or trunk).

tronera f. opening, porthole (through which to shoot); small, narrow window; pocket of a billiard table; m. madcap, reckless fellow.

tronido m. thunder; detonation; sharp, sudden sound.

trono m. throne.

tropa f. troop; crowd; Am. herd of cattle, drove of horses; often tropilla.

tropel m. throng, bustle, rush; confusion.

tropezar v. irr. to stumble; to be obstructed; to meet; to discover; to come across; to encounter; to wrangle.

tropezón m. stumbling; slip; a —es falteringly; tripping frequently; darse un — to stumble, to trip.

tropical adj. tropical.

trópico m. tropic.

tropiezo m. stumble, trip; obstacle, impediment; slip, fault; quarrel; difficulty.

tropilla f. small troop; Am. drove of horses guided by the madrina (leading horse); pack of dogs; group of spare saddle horses.

tropillero m. Am. horse wrangler; herdsman.
trotar v. to trot; to make a horse trot; to hurry.
trote m. trot; **al —** quickly, in a haste.
trovador m. troubadour, poet, minstrel.
troza f. log; parrel.
trozar v. to cut off; to break or cut into pieces; to haul taught the parrel.
trozo m. piece of anything cut off; passage, selection.
truco m. clever trick; Am. a card game; **—s** game of pool.
truculencia f. cruelty, ferocity, ruthlessness.
truculento adj. truculent, cruel; fierce.
trucha f. trout; crane; Am. vendor's portable stand.
trueno m. thunder; thunder-clap; report of fire arms; troublemaker; Am. firecracker, rocket.
trueque m. exchange, barter; **a** (or **en**) **— de** in exchange for.
truhán m. scoundrel; swindler; buffoon, juggler.
tú pers. pron. thou, you.
tu poss. pron. thy, thine; your. See **tuyo**.
tuberculosis f. tuberculosis.
tuberculoso adj. tuberculous; tubercular.
tubería f. tubing, piping; pipe line.
tubo m. tube, pipe; lamp chimney; **— lanzatorpedos** torpedo tube; **— de ensayo** test tube.
tuerca f. nut, or female screw; **llave de —s** wrench.
tuerto adj. one-eyed; squinteyed; m. wrong, injustice; **a —s** on the wrong side; **— o derecho** thoughtlessly.
tuétano m. marrow; innermost part; **hasta los —s** through and through.
tufo m. vapor; disagreeable odor; locks of hair which fall over the ear.
tul m. tulle; **—** (or **tule**) m. Am. a kind of bulrush used in the manufacture of seats and backs of chairs.
tulipán m. tulip.
tullido adj. crippled; numb; **estar —** to be crippled.
tullirse v. irr. to become crippled, numb or paralized.
tumba f. tomb, grave, vault.
tumbar v. to knock down; Am. to fell timber.

tumbo m. tumble; somersault; **dar —s** to jump.
tumor m. tumor.
tumorcillo m. boil, small tumor.
tumulto m. tumult; revolt; riot; commotion; uproar; faction; mob; throng.
tumultuoso adj. tumultuous, uproaring.
tuna f. prickly pear; prickle Indian fig; **andar a la —** Am. to play the truant; to loiter.
tunante m. & f. rascal, leading a licentious life.
tunda f. whipping, thrashing; the act of shearing cloth.
tundir v. to lash; to beat; to whip; to shear cloth.
túnel m. tunnel.
túnica f. tunic, gown, robe; tunicle, pellicle, or tegument.
tupido adj. dense, compact, thick; stuffed.
tupir v. to press close; to pack; to squeeze together; to clog; **—se** to get stuffed up; to over-eat; to become dense (as a forest).
turba f. mob, throng; confused multitude.
turbación f. disturbance, confusion; embarrassment.
turbamulta f. mob, throng; confused multitude.
turbar v. to perturb; to alarm; to disturb; **—se** to be uneasy, discomposed, embarrased.
turbio adj. muddy, turbid; troubled, unhappy.
turbulento adj. turbulent; disorderly; turbid, muddy.
turco adj. Turkish; m. Turk, Turkish; Turkish language; Am. peddler.
turismo m. tourist travel; touring; sightseeing; **oficina de —** travel bureau.
turista m. & f. tourist.
turnar v. to alternate; **—se** to alternate, to take turns.
turno m. turn; successive or alternate order.
turrón m. nougat; nut confection; **romper el —** Am. to break formalities, to decide to use the **tú** form of address as a mark of close friendship.
tusa f. Am. corncob; corn silk, tassel of an ear of corn.
tusar v. Am. to shear; to crop; to cut badly the hair.
tutear v. to address familiarly, using the **tú** form; to thou.
tutela f. guardianship, tutelage.

tutelar v. to guide; adj. tutelar, tutelary.
tutor m. tutor, guardian.
tuyo poss. adj. your, of yours (fam. sing.); poss. pron. yours.

U

u conj. used in the place of o to avoid cacophony (before o or ho)
ubicar v. Am. to locate; —se to be situated or located.
ubre f. udder.
ufanarse v. to glory in; to boast; to be haughty.
ufano adj. proud, gay; haughty; cheerful.
ujier m. usher, doorman.
úlcera f. ulcer.
ulterior adj. ulterior; later.
ultimar v. to put an end; to end; to finish; Am. to give the finishing touch; to kill.
último adj. last, latest, later, latter; remote, extreme; final; por — lastly, finally; estar en las últimas to be on one's last legs; to be at the end of one's resources. [to abuse
ultrajar v. to outrage; to offend;
ultraje m. outrage, insult.
ultramar m. country or place across the sea; de — overseas.
ulular v. to howl; to cry aloud; to shriek. [ginning, rudiment.
umbral m. threshold; lintel; be-
único a. 1. only, sole. 2 unique, unmatched, singular; rare.
untar v. to anoint; to smear; to grease; to oint; to bribe; to suborn; —se to embezzle; to cheat; to get smeared.
unto m. grease, fat, ointment; unguent.
untuosidad f. greasiness, unctuosity.
untuoso adj. unctuous, greasy; oily.
uña f. fingernail; toenail; hoof, claw; fang; pointed hook; cara de beato y —s de gato the face of a devotee, and the deeds of a rogue; largo de —s prone to stealing; —s largas thief; echar la — Am. to steal; ser — y carne to be close friends; vivir de sus —s to live by stealing.
urbanidad f. courtesy; urbanity, civility, politeness, refinement, courteousness.
urbano adj. urban, urbane, polite; courteous, civilized.
urbe f. metropolis, large city.

urdimbre f. warp of a fabric; scheme; chain.
urdir v. to warp (in weaving); to contrive; to plot; to scheme; to invent.
urgencia f. urgency; pressing need; exigence.
urgente adj. urgent, pressing; exigent.
urgir v. to urge; to be urgent.
urna f. urn, glass case; — electoral ballot box.
urraca f. magpie.
usado p.p. & adj. used; accustomed; employed, worn; worn out; threadbare, experienced; skilful, fashionable, frequent; second-hand articles.
usanza f. usage, custom, habit.
usar v. to use; to wear; to accustom, to practise; to enjoy a thing; —se to be in use; to be accustomed; to be in fashion; to be in vogue; to be wont.
uso m. use, employment, service, usage; wearing, wear; practice; habit; custom; style; common law; experience; assiduousness; al — de la época according to the custom or usage of the period; estar en buen — to be in good condition (said of a thing).
usted pers. pron. (abbreviated as Ud., Vd., or U.) you.
usual adj. usual; ordinary, customary; moneda — currency.
usufructo m. use, enjoyment, profit; usufruct.
usufructuar v. to enjoy the use or usufruct of anything; to make use of.
usura f. interest; gain; profit; usury.
usurero m. usurer, loan shark; miser.
usurpar v. to usurp.
utensilio m. utensil; implement; tool.
útero m. uterus; womb.
útil adj. useful, profitable, commodious; m. utility; —es m. pl. tools; implements, instruments.
utilidad f. utility; profit; usefulness.
utilizar v. to utilize; to use; to profit; to take advantage of.
uva f. grape; wart on the eyelid; tumor on the epiglotis; fruit of the barberry bush; — espina gooseberry; — pasa raising; estar hecho una — to be tipsy; to be drunk.

V

vaca f. cow; carne de — beef; cuero de — cowhide; — de leche milk cow; hacer — Am. to play hooky; to join in a quick business deal.
vacación f. vacation, intermission; (usually —es).
vacada f. herd of cows.
vacancia f. vacancy.
vacante adj. vacant, disengaged; vacancy of a post or employment; f. vacancy.
vaciar v. to empty; to evacuate; to mould; to form; to cast into a mold; —se to spill; to divulge what should be kept secret.
vaciedad f. emptiness; nonsense; frothiness.
vacilación f. hesitation, staggering; perplexity.
vacilante adj. vacillating; irresolute; unsteady.
vacilar v. to vacillate; to waver; to hesitate; to fluctuate; to doubt.
vacío adj. empty; void; unoccupied; concave, hollow; vain, arrogant; m. vacancy; gap; vacuity; cavity; hollowness.
vacuna f. vaccine; vaccination; ulcer on cow's teats; cowpox; vaccine virus.
vacunación f. vaccination.
vacunar v. to vaccinate.
vadear v. to ford; to wade; to surmount; to try.
vado m. ford, shallow part of a river.
vagabundear v. to tramp around; to wander.
vagabundo adj. vagabond; m. tramp; wanderer.
vagar v. to wander; to loiter; to rove; m. leisure; slowness.
vago adj. vague; idle; errant; vagrant; m. loose, tramp.
vagón m. railway car or coach, wagon; — tolva hopper wagon.
vagonada f. carload.
vaguear See vagar.
vahído m. dizziness, vertigo; giddiness.
vaho m. vapor, fume, steam, mist; odor.
vaina f. sheath; scabbard of a sword; case; Am. bother, nuisance.
vainilla f. vanilla.
vaivén m. sway, fluctuation; coming and going; —es ups and downs; inconstancy.
vajilla f. tableware, set of dishes; — de plata silverware; — de porcelana chinaware.
vale m. bond, promisory note; voucher; I.O.U.; m. & f. Am. comrade, pal, chum.
valedero adj. valid, binding, effective.
valedor m. defender, protector; Am. pal, chum.
valenciano adj. Valencian; of or from Valencia, Spain; m. Valencian.
valentía f. courage; heroic exploit; brag, boast.
valentón adj. blustering, boastful, arrogant; m. bully, braggart.
valer v. irr. to be valuable; to be marketable; to be worth; to amount to; to protect; to have power; to cost; — la pena to be worth; —se de to avail oneself of; más vale it is better; más vale tarde que nunca better late than never; ¡válgame Dios! good heavens!
valeroso adj. valiant, courageous; brave.
valía f. influence; credit; value; faction.
validez f. validity; stability; soundness.
válido adj. valid; firm; prevalent; binding.
valiente adj. valiant, courageous; brave; m. brave man.
valija f. valise; cloak bag; mail bag.
valimiento m. favor, protection; gozar de — to enjoy protection or favor.
valioso adj. valuable; worthy; wealthy.
valor m. value; price; courage; boldness; —es stocks, bonds.
valoración f. valuation, appraisal.
valorar v. to evaluate; to value; to appraise.
valorizar v. to value; to appraise; Am. to convert into money.
vals m. waltz.
valsar v. to waltz.
valuación f. valuation; appraisal; appraisement.
valuar v. to value; to price; to appraise; to rate.
válvula f. valve; valvule.
valla f. stockade, barrier, barricade, intrenchment; Am. cockpit (for cock fights).
vallado m. stockade, fenced-in place, fence.
valle m. valley, vale.

vanagloria f. vainglory, vanity; vaingloriousness.
vanagloriarse v. to be vainglorious; to boast of.
vanaglorioso adj. vain, boastful; conceited.
vanguardia f. vanguard, van.
vanidad f. vanity; conceit; ostentation.
vanidoso adj. vain, conceited; haughty, foppish.
vano adj. vain, empty; inane; fallacious; m. opening, vacuum in a wall, door or window.
vapor m. vapor, steam; steamer; steamship.
vaporoso adj. vaporous, steamy; vaporlike.
vapulear v. to beat; to whip; to thrash; to lash.
vapuleo m. beating, whipping; thrashing.
vaquería f. herd or drove of cows; dairy.
vaqueriza f. stable for cows.
vaquerizo m. herdsman; relating to cows.
vaquero m. cowherd, cowkeeper; cowboy; Am. milkman; relating to cows.
vaqueta f. sole leather; cowhide; ramrod; sonar a uno la — to tan someone's hide; to beat someone up.
vara f. twig; stick; rod; wand; staff; yard, yardstick; thrust with a picador's lance; — de pescar fishing rod.
varadero m. shipyard.
varar v. to run aground; to ground; to be stranded.
varear v. to whip; to beat; to beat down the fruit of trees; to measure or sell by the yard; Am. to exercise a horse before a race.
variable adj. variable, unstable, changeable; m. & f. variable.
variación f. variation.
variado p.p. & adj. varied, variegated, colored.
variar v. to vary; to change; to differ.
variedad f. variety; variation; change.
varilla f. small rod; wand; curtain rod; spindle, pivot; long, flexible twig; rib of an umbrella or fan; Am. peddler's wares.
varillero m. Am. peddler.
vario adj. various; different; changeable; inconstant; vague; —s several, various, some.
varón m. male, man; man of respectability; Am. long beam; timber.
varonil adj. manly, strong; brave; masculine.
vasallo adj. & m. vassal, subject; feudatory.
vasco adj. & m. Basque.
vascuence m. & f. Basque.
vasija f. vessel, container; any butt, pipe or cask for liquors; receptacle.
vaso m. drinking glass; glassful; vase; vessel; hull of a ship; — de elección person chosen by God.
vástago m. stem, bud, shoot; offspring; Am. trunk of a banana tree.
vasto adj. vast, extensive, large; huge; immense.
vate m. bard, poet.
vaticinar v. to prophecy; to foretell; to divine.
vaticinio m. prophecy, prediction, vaticination.
vecindad f. vicinity; neighborhood; casa de — tenement.
vecindario m. neighborhood, vicinity; neighbors.
vecino m. neighbor; resident; adj. adjoining, near, next; nearby.
vedar v. to prohibit; to impede.
vega f. fertile lowland or plain; Am. tobacco plantation.
vegetación f. vegetation.
vegetal adj. vegetable; m. vegetable plant.
vegetar v. to vegetate.
vehemente adj. vehement, impetuous, violent.
vehículo m. vehicle.
veintena f. score, twenty.
vejestorio m. old trumpery; old person.
vejete m. little old man.
vejez f. old age; decay.
vejiga f. bladder; blister; —s pustules of smallpox; — or vesícula biliar gall bladder.
vela f. vigil, watch, attendance without sleep; watchfulness, vigilance; candle; sail, ship; — mayor mainsail; — de trinquete foresail; — de mesana mizzen; hacerse a la — to set sail; a la — or en — vigilantly.
velada f. watch, vigil; evening party, function or meeting.
velador m. night watchman; lamp table; Am. lamp shade.
velar v. to keep vigil; to watch; to wake; to be attentive; to give the nuptial benediction; to veil;

to cover; to hide; to attend at night.
velatorio m. wake (vigil over a corpse). See velorio.
veleidoso adj. inconstant; fickle; changeable.
velero m. sailboat; sailmaker; candlemaker; tallow chandler; **buque —** sailboat.
veleta f. weathervane, weathercock; fickle person.
velís m. Am. valise.
velo m. curtain, veil, covering; cover, disguise; **— del paladar** velum, soft palate; **tomar el —** to become a nun.
velocidad f. velocity, speed.
velocímetro m. speedometer.
velorio m. wake, vigil over a corpse; Am. a dull party; **cara de —** Am. sad face.
veloz adj. swift, quick, fast, sepeedy.
vello m. down; fleece; tuft of wool; sheepskin with fleece; copper coin of Castile.
velloso adj. downy, hairy, fuzzy.
velludo adj. hairy, downy, fuzzy; m. plush; velvet.
vena f. vein; lode; vein of metal ore; mood, disposition; **estar en —** to be in the mood.
venado f. deer; venison, deer meat; **pintar —** Am. to play hooky.
vencedor adj. conquering, winning; victorious; m. winner, victor.
vencer v. to conquer; to subdue; to vanquish; to surmount; to overcome; to prevail upon; **—se** to control oneself; to fall due; **se venció el plazo** the time limit expired.
vencido p.p. & adj. conquered; defeated; due, fallen due.
vencimiento m. conquering, defeat; maturity; falling due; expiration of a period of time.
venda f. bandage.
vendar v. to bandage; to dress a wound.
vendaval m. strong wind; gale.
vendedor m. vendor, seller; peddler; trader.
vender v. to sell; to betray; **—se** to be sold; to denounce oneself; to accept a bribe.
vendimia f. vintage; profit.
venduta f. Am. auction; small fruit and vegetable store.
veneno m. venom, poison.
venenoso adj. poisonous.
venerable adj. venerable.
veneración f. veneration, reverence; worship.
venerado adj. venerable.
venerar v. to venerate; to revere; to worship.
venero m. water spring; source; vein of metal in a mine; origin.
venezolano adj. Venezuelan; m. Venezuelan; Am. Venezuelan silver coin.
vengador adj. avenging, avenger; revenger; m. avenger.
venganza f. vengeance, revenge.
vengar v. to avenge; to revenge; **—se de** to take avenge of.
vengativo adj. vindictive, revengeful.
venia f. pardon; permission, leave, bow, nod; Am. military salute.
venida f. arrival; return; river flood.
venidero adj. coming, future; **en lo —** in the future; **—s** m. pl. successors.
venir v. irr. to come; to happen; to pass; to follow; to proceed from; to originate in; to be occasioned by; to deduce; to yield; to suit; to grow; to shoot up; to arrive; **—le a uno bien** (or **mal**) to be becoming (or unbecoming); **— a menos** to decline; **— al pelo** to come just in the right moment; **¿a qué viene eso?** what is the point of that?; **—se abajo** to collapse; to fall down; to fail.
venoso adj. veined; venous, veiny.
venta f. sale; roadside inn; **— pública** auction.
ventaja f. advantage; gain, profit; bonus.
ventajoso adj. advantageous, beneficial; profitable; Am. self seeking; profiteering.
ventana f. window; window shutter; nostril; **arrojar** or **echar por la —** to waste; to dissipate.
ventarrón m. gale, strong wind.
ventear v. to smell, scent, sniff; to expose to the air; **—se** to expel air; to break wind; Am. to stay outdoors.
ventero m. innkeeper.
ventilación f. ventilation.
ventilador m. ventilator; fan, for ventilation.
ventilar v. to ventilate, to air; to fan.
ventisca f. blizzard, snowstorm; snowdrift.
ventiscar v. to snow hard and blow; to drift.
ventisquero m. blizzard, snowstorm; glacier; snow-capped mountain.

ventolera f. gust of wind; pride, vanity; whim; **darle a uno la —** to take the notion to.

ventoso adj. windy.

ventura f. happiness, fortune, chance; **a la —** at random; **buena —** good luck; **por —** perchance.

venturoso adj. fortunate, lucky, happy.

ver v. irr. to see; to observe; to judge; to explore; to find out; to look; to look at; to look into; **— de** to try to; **no — la hora de** to be anxious to; **no tener nada que —** not to have anything to do with; **a mi modo de —** in my opinion; **de buen —** good-looking; **ser de —** to be worth seeing.

vera f. edge.

veracidad f. truthfulness.

veraneante m. & f. summer resorter; vacationist.

veranear v. to spend the summer.

veraneo m. summering, summer vacation.

veraniego adj. summer, of summer.

verano m. summer.

veras f. pl. reality, truth; **de —** in reality.

veraz adj. truthful.

verbal adj. verbal, oral.

verbena f. verbena, a plant; festival or carnival.

verbigracia adv. for instance, for example.

verbo m. verb; **el Verbo** the Word, second person of the Trinity.

verboso adj. wordy, verbose.

verdad f. truth; **¿—?** really?; is that so?; insn't that so?; **— de Perogrullo** an evident truth; **de —** in truth; **en —** really.

verdadero adj. real; true; truthful; sincere.

verde adj. green; unripe; young; unexperienced; indecent; m. green, verdure.

verdinegro adj. drak green.

verdor m. verdure, greenness.

verdugo m. excutioner; cruel person.

verdugón m. large welt.

verduiera f. woman vendor of green vegetables.

verdulería f. green vegetable store or stand.

verdura f. verdure; greenness; green vegetables.

vereda f. path; Am. sidewalk.

veredicto m. verdict.

vergonzoso adj. shameful, disgraceful, shy.

vergüenza f. shame, disgrace; shyness; **tener —** to be ashamed.

vericueto m. rough, wild place, often rocky.

verídico adj. truthful; true.

verificar v. to verify; to confirm; to test; to check; to carry out; to fulfill; **—se** to be verified.

verijas f. pl. Am. groin, hollow between lower part of abdomen and thigh; flanks of a horse.

verja f. grate, grating.

verruga f. wart; nuisance.

versado adj. versed, skilled, expert.

versar v. to deal with; to treat of; **—se en** to become versed in.

versión f. version; translation.

verso m. verse; meter; **— suelto** or **— libre** free or blank verse.

verter v. irr. to pour; to empty; to spill; to translate; to flow down.

vertical adj. vertical.

vértice m. top, apex, summit.

vertiente f. slope; watershed; adj. flowing.

vertiginoso adj. whirling, dizzy, giddy.

vértigo m. dizzinness, giddiness, fit of madness.

vestíbulo m. vestibule, lobby.

vestido m. dress, clothing, apparel; garment; suit.

vestidura f. vestment; attire; apparel; raiment.

vestigio m. vestige, sign, trace.

vestir v. irr. to dress; to clothe; to wear; to put on; to adorn; to cover; **—se** to be clothed.

vestuario m. wardrobe, apparel; theatrical costumes; cloakroom; dressing room; vestry (room for church vestments).

veta f. vein; seam of mineral; streak; grain in wood; stripe; Am. rope.

veteado adj. veined; striped; streaked.

veterano adj. & m. veteran.

veterinario m. veterinary.

veto m. veto.

vetusto adj. old, ancient.

vez f. time, occasion, turn; **a la —** at the same time; **cada — más** more and more; **cada — que** whenever; **de — en cuando** once in a while; **de una —** all at once; **en — de** instead of; **otra —** again; **tal —** perhaps; **a veces** sometimes; **raras veces** seldom; **hacer las veces de** to take the place of.

vía f. way; road; track; railroad track; conduit; — **crucis** The Way of the Cross; — **Láctea** the Milky Way.

viaducto m. viaduct.

viajante m. traveler; — **de comercio** traveling salesman.

viajar v. to travel.

viaje m. voyage; trip; travel; — **de ida y vuelta** (or — **redondo**) round trip.

viajero m. traveler; adj. traveling.

vianda f. viand, food; meal.

viandante m. & f. wayfarer, walker; pedestrian; passer-by; vagabond; wanderer.

viático m. provisions for a journey; viaticum, communion given to dying persons.

víbora f. viper.

vibración f. vibration.

vibrante adj. vibrant, vibrating.

vibrar v. to vibrate.

vicepresidente m. vice-president.

viceversa adv. viceversa, conversely.

viciado adj. contaminated, foul, corrupt.

viciar v. to vitiate, to corrupt; to adulterate; to falsify; —**se** to become corrupt.

vicio m. vice; bad habit; fault; craving; **de** — as a habit; **hablar de** — to talk too much; —**s** Am. articles and ingredients for serving mate.

vicioso adj. vicious, evil; wicked; having bad habits; licentious; faulty, incorrect gramatical construcction, reasoning, etc.

vicisitud f. vicissitude.

víctima f. victim.

victoria f. victory; triumph, victoria (carriage).

victorioso adj. victorious.

vicuña f. vicuña (Andean animal allied to the alpaca and llama); vicuña wool; vicuña cloth.

vid f. vine, grapevine.

vida f. life, living, livelihood; — **mía** dearest; **hacer** — to live together; **pasar a mejor** — to die; **tener la** — **en un hilo** to be in great danger.

vidalita f. Am. melancholy song of Argentina and Chile.

vidente m. seer; prophet; adj. seeing.

vidriado m. glaze, glazed earthenware; p.p. & adj. glazed.

vidriar v. to glaze earthenware.

vidriera f. glass window; glass door; Am. show case, show window; — **de colores;** stained-glass window.

vidriero m. glazier (one who installs windowpanes); glass blower; glass maker; glass dealer.

vidrio m. glass; any glass article.

vidrioso adj. glassy; brittle; slippery ice; touchy, irritable.

viejo adj. old; ancient; worn-out; m. old man; — **verde** old man who boasts of his youth and vigor; **los** —**s** Am. the old folks.

viento m. wind; scent; **hace** — it is windy; **a los cuatro** —**s** in all directions.

vientre m. abdomen, belly; bowels; entrails; womb.

viernes m. Friday.

viga f. beam; rafter.

vigencia f. operation (of a law); **entrar en** — to take effect a law; **estar en** — to be in force (said of a law).

vigente adj. effective, in force (as a law).

vigía f. lookout; watchtower; watch, act of watching; reef; m. lookout; watchman.

vigilancia f. vigilance.

vigilante adj. vigilant, watchful; m. watchman.

vigilar v. to keep guard; to watch over.

vigilia f. vigil, watch, wakefulness, sleeplessness, night hours spent in study; eve before certain church festivals; vesper service; **día de** — day of abstinence; **comer de** — to abstain from meat.

vigor m. vigor; strength; **en** — in force (said of a law); **entrar en** — to become effective (as a law, statute, etc.).

vigorizar v. to invigorate; to tone up; to give vigor to; to strengthen.

vigoroso adj. vigorous.

vihuela f. guitar.

vil adj. vile, base, low, mean.

vileza f. villainy; baseness; vile act or remark.

vilipendiar v. to revile.

vilo: en — in the air; suspended; undecided; in suspense; **llevar en** — to waft.

villa f. village; villa, country house.

villancico m. carol; Christmas Carol.

villanía f. villainy; lowliness.

villano adj. rustic, uncouth; villainous, mean, base; m. villain; rustic, peasant.

villorrio m. small village, hamlet.
vinagre m. vinegar.
vinagrera f. vinegar cruet.
vincular v. to tie; to bind; to unite.
vínculo m. bond, tie, chain; entailed inheritance.
vindicar v. to vindicate.
vino m. wine; — **amontillado** good grade of pale sherry, originally from Montilla; — **tinto** red wine.
viña f. vineyard.
viñedo m. vineyard.
violación f. violation.
violado adj. violet; violated; m. violet, violet color.
violar v. to violate; to rape.
violencia f. violence.
violentar v. to force; to break into; —**se** to force oneself.
violento adj. violent, impetuous; strained.
violeta f. violet.
violín m. violin; m. & f. violinist; **estar hecho un —** Am. to be very thin.
violinista m. & f. violinist.
virada f. tack, change of direction; turn.
virar v. to turn; to change direction; to tack.
virgen adj. & f. virgin.
viril adj. virile, manly.
virilidad f. virility, manhood; strength.
virreinato m. viceroyalty.
virrey m. viceroy.
virtud f. virtue.
virtuoso adj. virtuous; m. virtuoso, person skilled in an art.
viruela f. smallpox; pock, mark left by smallpox; —**s locas** or **bastardas** chicken pox.
viruta f. wood shaving.
visa f. visa, visé.
visado m. visa, visé.
visaje m. grimace; wry face; **hacer —s** to make faces.
visar v. to visé, to approve; to O.K.
viscoso adj. slimy; sticky.
visera f. visor, eyeshade; Am. blinder.
visible adj. visible; conspicuous; notable.
visillo m. window curtain.
visión f. vision; sight; fantasy; apparition.
visionario adj. & m. visionary.
visita f. visit, call; visitor; caller, company; **— de cumplimiento** (or **— de cumplido**) formal courtesy call.
visitación f. visitation, visit.

visitador m. visitor, inspector.
visitante m. & f. caller, visitor; adj. visiting.
visitar v. to visit; to call; to inspect.
vislumbrar v. to catch a glimpse of; to guess; to surmise; —**se** to be faintly visible.
vislumbre f. glimmer; glimpse, vague idea, faint appearance.
viso m. appearance, semblance; pretense.
víspera f. eve, evening or day before; time just before.
vista f. sight; vision; landscape; glance; **a — de** in the presence of; **pagadero a la —** payable at sight; **¡hasta la —!** good by!; **bajar la —** to lower one's eyes; **conocer de —** to know by sight; **hacer la — gorda** to pretend not to see; **pasar la — por** to glance over.
vistazo m. glance; **dar un — a** to glance over.
visto p.p. & adj. evident, clear; **bien —** well thought of; **mal —** improper; **— bueno (VºBº)** approved (O.K.); **dar el — bueno** to approve, to O.K.; **— que** whereas, considering that.
vistoso adj. showy, colorful.
vital adj. vital, important, necessary.
vitalicio adj. for life; m. life insurance policy; lifetime pension.
vitalidad f. vitality.
vitamina f. vitamin.
vítor m. cheer, applause; **¡—!** hurrah!
vitorear v. to cheer, to applaud.
vitrina f. glass case; show window.
vituallas f. pl. victuals, provisions.
vituperar v. to insult, to revile.
vituperio m. affront, insult; censure.
viuda f. widow.
viudez f. widowhood.
viudo m. widower.
vivac m. bivouac, military encampment; Am. police headquarters.
vivacidad f. vivacity; brightness; liveliness.
vivaracho adj. lively; vivacious, gay.
vivaz adj. vivacious, lively, bright; keen, witty.
víveres m. pl. food supplies, provisions.
vivero m. fish pond, fish hatchery; tree nursery.
viveza f. vivacity, liveliness, animation.

vívido adj. vivid, colorful.
vivienda f. dwelling, apartment.
viviente adj. living.
vivir v. to live; to endure; to last; ¡viva! hurrah!, long live!; ¿quién vive? who goes there?; m. existence, living.
vivo adj. alive, living, active; lively; efficacious; acute, ingenious; vivid, bright, smart, diligent, nimble; constant, enduring; tío — merry-go-round; al — vividly; de viva voz by word of mouth; carne viva quick flesh in a wound.
vizcacha f. Am. viscacha, South American rodent about the size of a hare.
vizcachera f. Am. viscacha burrow or hole; room filled with junk.
vizcaíno adj. Biscayan, of or from Biscay, Spain.
vocablo m. word, term.
vocabulario m. vocabulary.
vocación f. vocation; aptness; talent.
vocal adj. vocal; vowel; f. vowel; voter, in an assembly or council.
vocear v. to shout; to cry out; to hail.
vocecita f. sweet little voice.
vocería f. clamor, shouting.
vocerío m. Am. clamor, shouting.
vocero m. spokesman.
vociferar v. to shout; to clamor; to yell; to boast loudly of.
vodevil m. vaudeville.
volante adj. flying, floating; **papel** (or **hoja**) — handbill; m. ruffle, frill, balance wheel.
volar v. irr. to fly; to fly away; to pass through the air; to make rapid progress; to irritate; to pique; to rouse (bird game); —se to fly off the handle.
volátil adj. volatile, fickle, changeable; flying.
volcán m. volcano; Am. precipice; swift torrent.
volcánico adj. volcanic.
volcar v. irr. to overturn; to capsize; to upset; —se to upset.
volear v. to volley; to hit a ball in the air.
volición f. valition.
voltaje m. voltage.
voltear v. to turn, to turn around; to overturn; to turn a somersault; Am. to go prying around; — la espalda Am. to turn one's back; —se to turn over.
voltereta f. somersault, tumble.
voltio m. volt.

voluble adj. fickle, moody; twining (as a climbing vine).
volumen m. volume.
voluminoso adj. voluminous, huge; bulky.
voluntad f. will, benevolence; consent; de (or de buena) — willingly.
voluntario adj. voluntary; willful; m. volunteer.
voluntarioso adj. willful.
voluptuoso adj. voluptuous; sensual.
voluta f. scroll, spiral-like ornament; —s de humo spirals of smoke.
volver v. irr. to return; to turn; to turn up, over, or inside out; to restore; — loco to drive crazy; — a (and inf.) to do again; — en sí to come to; to recover one's senses; — por to return for; —se to change one's ideas; —se atrás to go back; —se loco to go crazy.
vomitar v. to vomit.
vómito m. vomit; vomiting.
voracidad f. voraciousness, greediness.
vorágine f. vortex, whirlpool.
voraz adj. voracious, ravenous, greedy.
vórtice m. vortex, whirlpool; whirlwind, tornado; center of a cyclone.
votación f. voting; vote, total number of votes.
votante m. & f. voter.
votar v. to vote; to vow; to curse; ¡voto a tal! by Jove!
voto m. vote; vow; prayer; votive offering; oath; wish.
voz f. voice; sound; shout; outcry; word; rumor; — común common rumor or gossip; a — en cuello (or a — en grito) shouting; at the top of one's lungs; en — alta aloud; a voces shouting; with shouts; secreto a voces open secret; dar voces to shout, yell.
vozarrón m. loud, strong voice.
vuelco m. upset; overturning; tumble, capsizing.
vuelo m. flight; width; fulness (of a dress or cloak); frill, ruffle, jut; projection (of a building); a (or al) — on the fly; quickly; levantar (or alzar) el — to fly away; to soar.
vuelta f. turn; return; repetition; reverse side; cuff, facing of a sleeve; cloak lining; change (money returned); a la — around the corner; on returning;

a la — de los años within a few years; **otra —** Am. again; **dar —s** to turn over and over; **dar una — to take a walk**; **estar de — to be back**; **no tiene — de hoja** there are no two ways about it.

vuelto m. Am. change (money returned).

vuestro poss. adj. your, of yours (fam. pl.); poss. pron. yours.

vulgar adj. common, ordinary, in common use; low; vile; base.

vulgaridad f. vulgarity, coarseness, commonness.

vulgarismo m. slang, slang expression; vulgar or ungrammatical expression.

vulgo m. populace, the common people; adv. commonly, popularly.

Y

y conj. and.

ya adv. already, now; finally; soon; presently, in time; **¡— lo creo!** I should say so!; **— no** no longer; **— que** since; **— se ve de** course; **— voy** I am coming.

yacer v. irr. to lie down, to lie down in the grave; to lie; to be situated.

yacimiento m. bed, layer of ore; **— de petróleo** oil field.

yanqui m. & f. of or from the United States; native of the United States; yankee.

yantar v. to eat.

yarará f. Am. Argentine poisonous snake.

yarda f. yard, unit of measure.

yate m. yatch.

yedra See **hiedra**.

yegua f. mare; Am. cigar butt.

yeguada f. herd of breeding mares and stallions.

yelmo m. helmet.

yema f. egg yolk; bud; shoot; **— del dedo** finger tip.

yerba See **hierba**.

yerbabuena f. mint; peppermint.

yerbero m. Am. herb vendor.

yerno m. son-in-law.

yerro m. error, fault, mistake; defect.

yerto adj. stiff, motionless; rigid, inflexible; tight.

yesca f. tinder; anything highly inflamable; spunk; **estar hecho una — to** be in great anger.

yeso m. gypsum, gypse, sulphate of lime; chalk; plaster; **— blanco** whitewash; **— mate** plaster of Paris.

yesoso adj. gypseous; chalky.

yo pers. pron. I; **— mismo** myself.

yodo m. iodine.

yugo m. yoke of oxen; nuptial tie; marriage ceremony; oppressive authority; transom.

yunque m. anvil.

yunta f. yoke of oxen; couple, pair of draft animals.

yuyo m. Am. wild grass, weeds; an herb sauce; garden stuff; **estar — to** be lifeless, insipid; **volverse uno — Am.** to faint.

Z

zacate m. Am. grass, forage; hay.

zafado adj. impudent, brazen; shameless; Am. smart, wide awake, keen; touched, half crazy.

zafar v. to release; to disembarrass; to lighten a ship; Am. to exclude; **—se** to slip away; to run away; to escape; to dodge; to get rid of; to decline; to excuse; to get loose; Am. to get dislocated (said of a bone); Am. to go crazy.

zaflo adj. coarse, uncouth; rude; clownish, uncivil.

zafir(o) m. sapphire.

zafra f. sugar-making season; sugar making; sugar crop.

zaga f. rear; load packed on the back part of a carriage; **a la (o en la) — in** the extremity behind.

zagal m. young shepherd; lad; stout spirited young man; subordinate coachman.

zagala f. young shepherdess; lass; maiden; young girl.

zagalejo m. young shepherd; short skirt, petticoat.

zaguán m. vestibule; porch; entrance; hall.

zaherir v. irr. to hurt the feelings; to censure; to blame; to reproach; to reprove.

zaino adj. treacherous; vicious; chestnut-colored horse.

zalamería f. flattery, scraping and bowing.

zalamero m. fawner, flatterer, servile.

zalea f. pelt, undressed sheepskin; sheepskin mats.

zambo adj. knock-kneed; m. Indian and negro half-breed; Am. a

species of South American monkey.
zambullida f. dive, dip, plunge; ducking.
zambullir v. to plunge; to dip; to duck; to dive; —se to dive; to plunge.
zambullón m. quick, sudden dip or dive.
zanahoria f. carrot.
zanca f. shank, a long leg of any fowl; long leg; long prop.
zancada f. stride, long step.
zanco m. stilt; andar en —s to walk on stilts.
zancón adj. lanky, long-legged; Am. too short skirt or dress.
zancudo adj. long-legged; m. Am. mosquito.
zángano m. drone, loafer; sponger; Am. rogue, rascal.
zangolotear v. to shake; to piggle; —se to shake; to waddle; to sway from side to side.
zangoloteo m. jiggle, jiggling; shaking; waddling.
zanguanga f. feigned illness; **hacer la —** to pretend to be ill.
zanguango adj. lazy; silly; m. fool.
zanja f. ditch; trench; Am. irrigation ditch.
zanjar v. to excavate; to dig ditches in; to settle disputes.
zapapico m. pickaxe.
zapateado m. a Spanish tap dance.
zapatear v. to tap with the feet; to tap dance.
zapateo m. tapping with the feet; Am. a popular tap dance.
zapatería f. shoe store; shoemaker's shop.
zapatero m. shoemaker; shoe dealer.
zapatilla f. slipper, pump.
zapato m. shoe.
zarandajas f. pl. trifles, trinkets, worthless things.
zarandear v. to winnow (separate the chaff from the grain); to sift; to wiggle; to jiggle; Am. to whip; to lash; to mistreat; to abuse; —se to wiggle.
zarandeo m. jiggle, wiggle; jiggling; waddling; strutting.
zarcillo m. earring, tendril, coil of a climbing vine; Am. earmark, on the ear of an animal.
zarpa f. paw; claw; weighing anchor; **echar la —** to grasp.
zarpazo m. blow with the paw.
zarpar v. to weigh anchor; to set sail.
zarza f. bramble; blackberry bush.

zarzamora f. blackberry.
zarzuela f. Spanish musical comedy.
zigzag m. zigzag.
zigzaguear v. to zigzag.
zinc See cinc.
zócalo m. base of a pedestal; Am. public square.
zodiaco m. zodiac.
zona f. zone, band, girdle; shingles, a disease.
zonzo adj. dull, stupid, silly, foolish.
zoología f. zoology.
zoológico adj. zoological; **jardín —** zoo.
zopenco adj. stupid; dull, thickheaded; m. bolckhead.
zopilote m. Am. buzzard.
zoquete m. block; chunk of wood; hunk of bread; blockhead; ugly, fat person.
zorra f. fox; foxy person; prostitute; **pillar una —** to get drunk.
zorro m. fox; foxy person; —s foxskins; **estar echo un —** to be drowsy; **hacer uno el —** to pretend to be stupid or not to hear; adj. foxy.
zorrillo m. Am. skunk.
zorruno adj. foxy.
zorzal m. thrush; crafty fellow; Am. scapegoat.
zozobra f. foundering, anxiety, worry.
zozobrar v. to founder; to capsize; to be in great danger, to worry.
zumbar v. to buzz; to hum; to scoff at; — **una bofetada** to give a slap; —se Am. to slip away.
zumbido m. buzzing, humming; ringing in one's ears; hit, blow, whack.
zumbón adj. funny, playful, sarcastic; m. jester.
zumo m. juice; profit.
zumoso adj. juicy.
zurcido m. darn; darning.
zurcir v. to darn; to invent; to make up lies.
zurdo adj. left-handed, left; **a zurdas** with the left hand; clumsily.
zuro m. cob, corn cob.
zurra f. beating, flogging; tanning of leather.
zurrar v. to flog, to thrash; to tan leather.
zurrón m. pouch, bag; leather bag; Am. big coward.
zutano m. so-and-so; a certain person (used often with **fulano** and **mengano**).

PARTE SEGUNDA

INGLÉS
ESPAÑOL

PARTE SEGUNDA

INGLÉS
ESPAÑOL

GRAMATICA INGLESA

PRONUNCIACIÓN: El alfabeto inglés consta de veintiséis letras: a, b, c, d, e, f, g, h, i, j, k, l, m, n, o, p, q, r, s, t, u, v, w, x, y, z; pero en la lengua inglesa existe un número mucho mayor de sonidos: 32 según algunos, 43 en opinión de otros, y hay quien los hace ascender a 46. Por ello, no es suficiente con saber cómo se pronuncia cada una de las letras del alfabeto, ya que con una misma letra se representan dos o más sonidos y, por otra parte, las excepciones son muy numerosas. Esta es la causa de que aun personas para quienes el inglés es idioma vernáculo se vean precisadas a recurrir a diccionarios de pronunciación, cosa de todo punto innecesaria en el idioma castellano, cuyas letras representan siempre el mismo sonido, salvo pequeñas y contadas excepciones.

Se han ideado diversos sistemas para representar gráficamente la pronunciación de las palabras inglesas; es decir, se han ideado varios alfabetos fonéticos en los que haya siempre un sonido para cada signo y un signo para cada sonido. Si bien es cierto que cualquiera de dichos sistemas obvia las dificultades de la pronunciación, obliga, en cambio, a aprender un nuevo alfabeto o una nueva serie de símbolos que, en la mayor parte de los casos, hacen más difícil el aprendizaje de quien, urgido por las diarias necesidades, requiere un instrumento práctico y fácil que resuelva sus problemas sin aumentar las dificultades, ya en sí mismas considerables, que son propias del estudio de un idioma extraño.

En consecuencia, hemos resuelto presentar en este DICCIONARIO DE BOLSILLO [INGLES-ESPAÑOL] la forma más aproximada de pronunciación aprovechando únicamente los recursos que nos ofrece nuestro propio albabeto. A continuación de cada palabra inglesa ofrecemos, entre paréntesis, la forma aproximada en que la escribiría un hispanoamericano que la oyera pronunciar sin saber cómo se escribe en inglés.

En dicha pronunciación, todas las letras conservan su sonido hispanoamericano propio, con las siguientes excepciones: la combinación *th* se pronunciará siempre como la *z* española, no hispanoamericana; la *y* se usa para representar el sonido de la *j* francesa; la combinación *sh* tendrá el sonido de la *ch* francesa o la *sch* alemana, y la *h* se usará después de una vocal para indicar que esta última se alarga considerablemente. Por último, debemos aclarar que la *c*, antes de *e* o *i*, se pronunciará como *s*, y que el sonido *k* se representa indistintamente con las letras *c* (antes de *a, o* y *u*) o *k*.

ARTICULO: Se divide en definido *(definite)* e indefinido *(indefinite)*.

El primero, *the*, es invariable en todos los números, géneros y casos, y corresponde a las formas españolas *el, la, los, las* v.gr.: *the man* el hombre, *the men* los hombres, *the woman* la mujer, *the women* las mujeres, *the book* el libro, *the books* los libros, (*I saw the book* vi el libro). El artículo definido se omite cuando el sustantivo singular se refiere a todo el género o a todo un grupo de seres humanos (v. gr.: *man is the lord of the earth* el hombre es el señor de la tierra), cuando el sustantivo en plural llevaría artículo indefinido si estuviera en singular (v. gr.: *horses are noble brutes* los caballos son nobles brutos), con sustantivos abstractos tomados en sentido general (v. gr.: *necessity is the mother of invention* la necesidad es la madre de la invención), y si se habla de una sustancia en sentido ilimitado (v. gr.: *honey is sweet* la miel es dulce). Tampoco se usa el artículo definido cuando va delante de títulos, empleos, dignidades, etc., si éstos preceden al nombre de la persona sin estar, a su vez, precedidos por un adjetivo (v. gr.: *General Washington* el general Washington; pero: *the good General Washington* el buen general Washington).

El artículo indefinido, que equivale en español a *un, una*, tiene dos formas: *a* delante de palabras que comienzan con consonante o *s aspirada* (v. gr.: *a tree* un árbol, *a house* una casa) y *an* cuando precede a una palabra que empieza con vocal o *h* muda (v. gr.: *an elephant* un elefante, *an hour*, una hora); pero suele usarse *an* delante de *h* aspirada si no está acentuada la primera sílaba de la siguiente palabra (v. gr.: *an hotel* un hotel).

SUSTANTIVO: El sustantivo *(noun)* puede ser *masculino* o *femenino, singular* o *plural*.

Género: Todo nombre de varón o animal macho es masculino (v. gr.: *man* hombre, *tiger* tigre); todo nombre de mujer o animal hembra es femenino (v. gr.: *girl* muchacha, *cow* vaca). Los demás son neutros (v. gr.: *book* libro, *pride* orgullo).

Algunos sustantivos que designan objetos inanimados pueden personificarse y se usan como masculinos o femeninos (v. gr.: *the moon* la luna, femenino; *the sun* el sol, masculino). Otros se consideran poéticamente como femeninos (v. gr.: *nature* naturaleza).

Otros nombres, que permanecen invariables, pueden ser masculinos o femeninos según su significado (v. gr.: *child* niño o niña, *teacher* maestro o maestra), y lo mismo sucede con algunos terminados en *er* y derivados de un verbo (v. gr.: *reader* lector o lectora, *thinker* pensador o pensadora).

En algunos casos, el género se indica con diferente palabra (v. gr.: *king* rey, *queen* reina; *husband* esposo, *wife* esposa; *son* hijo, *daugther* hija).

Otros más lo expresan añadiendo una palabra (v. gr.: *male-child* niño, *female-child* niña; *he-bear* oso, *she-bear* osa).

Número: Generalmente, el plural se forma añadiendo una *s* al singular (v. gr.: *tiger* tigre; *tigers* tigres). Los nombres terminados en *s*, *sh*, *ch* y *x* forman el plural añadiendo *es* al singular (v. gr.: *press* prensa, *presses* prensas; *dish* plato, *dishes* platos; *watch* reloj, *watches* relojes; *fox* zorra, *foxes* zorras). Si terminan en *y* precedida por consonante, cambian su terminación a *ies* (v. gr.: *fly* mosca, *flies* moscas); pero si la *y* final sigue a vocal, sólo aumentan *s* (v. gr.: *day* día, *days* días). Muchos sustantivos terminados en *o* aumentan *es* para formal el plural (v. gr.: *hero* héroe, *heroes* héroes). Algunos de los que acaban en *f* o *fe* mudan la terminación a *ves* (v. gr.: *leaf* hoja, *leaves* hojas, *life* vida, *lives* vidas).

Hay otros nombres de plural irregular (v. gr.: *man* hombre, *men* hombres; *child* niño, *children* niños), y otros más se usan siempre en singular (v. gr.: *hair* cabello o cabellos, *business* negocio o negocios) o siempre en plural (*troussers* pantalón o pantalones, *goods* mercado o mercaderías).

CASOS: En inglés sólo hay tres casos: nominativo (*nominative*), posesivo (*possessive*) y objetivo (*objective*). El nominativo y el objetivo se distinguen sólo por su colocación en la frase. En cuanto al posesivo, se forma agregando un apóstrofo y la letra *s* a las palabras que no terminan en *s*, y sólo un apóstrofo a las que terminan en dicha consonante (v. gr.: *the king's palace* el palacio del rey, *my brother's wife* la esposa de mi hermano, *the ladies' hats* los sombreros de las señoras).

Es preciso observar que nunca se hace uso de esta inversión con los adjetivos empleados sustantivamente (v. gr.: *the happiness of the wicked is transitory* la felicidad de los malvados es pasajera).

ADJETIVO: Los adjetivos ingleses no admiten variación de género o número y suelen preceder al sustantivo (v. gr.: *an interesting man* un hombre interesante, *an interesting woman* una mujer interesante, *an interesting book* un libro interesante, *interesting men* hombres interesantes, *interesting women* mujeres interesantes, *interesting books* libros interesantes).

Los adjetivos de dimensión (tales como *long* largo, *wide* ancho, *thick* grueso, *deep* profundo, etc.) siguen siempre a los nombres de medida sin expresar el *de* castellano (v. gr.: *a wall six feet long* una pared de seis pies de largo, *a carpet two yards wide* una alfombra de dos yardas de ancho).

La mayor parte de los adjetivos ingleses se forman de los sustantivos y toman diversas terminaciones. Mencionaremos las siguientes: *ful*, que expresa abundancia de lo que anuncia la palabra simple y equivale a la terminación castellana *oso* (v. gr.: *joy* júbilo, *joyful* jubiloso; *grace* gracia, *graceful* gracioso); *less*, que significa privación de lo que expresa el sustantivo (v. gr.: *end* fin, *endless* interminable o sin fin); *ish*, que indica semejanza (v. gr.: *child* niño, *childish* pueril).

En inglés suele usarse como adjetivo la forma del participio presente (v. gr.: *to run* correr, *running water* agua corriente; *to read* leer, *reading room* sala de lectura).

Comparativos y superlativos: La única variación que admiten los adjetivos monosílabos y algunos disílabos de fácil pronunciación es la de los grados de comparación; dichos adjetivos forman el comparativo de aumento y el superlativo añadiendo las terminaciones *er* y *est*, respectivamente (v. gr.: *black* negro, *blacker* más negro, *the blackest* el más negro). Si terminan en y, ésta se transforma en *i* (v. gr.: *dry* seco; *drier* más seco, *the driest* el más seco). Si terminan en *e* muda, basta con añadir las terminaciones *r* y *st*, respectivamente (v. gr.: *polite* cortés, *politer* más cortés, *the politest* el más cortés). Si terminan en consonante precedida de una sola vocal, dicha consonante se duplica (v. gr.: *hot* caliente, *hotter* más caliente, *the hottest* el más caliente).

Hay también comparativos y superlativos irregulares (v. gr.: *good* bueno, *better* mejor, *the best* el mejor; *bad* malo, *worse* peor, *the worst* el peor).

Los demás adjetivos van precedidos de *more* y *most*, respectivamente (v. gr.: *careful* cuidadoso, *more careful* más cuidadoso, *the most careful* el más cuidadoso).

El comparativo y el superlativo de inferioridad se forman anteponiendo los adverbios *less* y *least*, respectivamente (v. gr.: *less careful* menos cuidadoso, *the least careful* el menos cuidadoso).

El comparativo de igualdad se forma con el adverbio *as* (v. gr.: *as careful as* tan cuidadoso como).

El superlativo absoluto se forma anteponiendo los adverbios *very* o *most* (v. gr.: *very careful* muy cuidadoso, cuidadosísimo).

Adjetivos sustantivados: Cuando el sustantivo ha de sobrentenderse después del adjetivo, se usa la palabra *one*, uno o *ones*, unos v. gr.: *I don't like the new book; I like the old one* no me gusta el nuevo libro; me gusta el viejo).

El adjetivo puede usarse sustantivamente para expresar una cualidad abstracta (v. gr.: *I seek the good of others* busco el bien de otros) o cuando se habla de todo un género o de toda una especie (v. gr.: *the lazy are generally poor* los holgazanes generalmente son pobres), en cuyo caso se emplean en su forma singular a pesar de referirse a una pluralidad; pero otros adjetivos se han convertido ya en nombres y pueden tomar la forma plural (v. gr.: *the Romans* los romanos; *the Catholics* los católicos). En los adjetivos sustantivos no se puede prescindir del artículo definido *the*.

PRONOMBRE: Los pronombres pueden ser *personales, reflexivos, relativos, interrogativos y adjetivos*.

Pronombres personales: Son de tres clases, a saber: 1) de *primera persona*, 2) *de segunda persona* y 3) *de tercera persona*, y admiten variaciones de género, número y caso.

Los pronombres personales toman las siguientes formas:

PRIMERA PERSONA

Género masculino o femenino
Singular

Nom.	I	yo
Pos.	mine	mío, mía, míos, mías
Obj.	me	me, a mí

Plural

Nom.	we	nosotros, nosotras
Pos.	ours	nuestro, nuestra, nuestros, nuestras
Obj.	us	nos, a nosotros, a nosotras

SEGUNDA PERSONA

Género masculino o femenino
Singular

Nom.	you	usted
Pos.	yours	suyo, suya, suyos, suyas, de usted
Obj.	you	le, a usted

Plural

Nom.	you	ustedes
Pos.	yours	suyo, suya, suyos, suyas, de ustedes
Obj.	you	a ustedes

TERCERA PERSONA

Género masculino
Singular

Nom.	he	él
Pos.	his	suyo, suya, suyos, suyas, de él
Obj.	him	lo, le, a él

Plural

Nom.	they	ellos
Pos.	theirs	suyo, suya, suyos, suyas, de ellos
Obj.	them	los, les, a ellos

Género femenino
Singular

Nom.	she	ella
Pos.	hers	suyo, suya, suyos, suyas de ella
Obj.	her	la, le, a ella

Plural

Nom.	they	ellas
Pos.	theirs	suyo, suya, suyos, suyas, de ellas
Obj.	them	las, les, a ellas

Género neutro
Singular

Nom.	it	ello
Pos.	its	suyo, suya, suyos, suyas, de ello
Obj.	it	lo, la, le

Plural

Nom.	they	ellos, ellas
Pos.	theirs	suyo, suya, suyos, suyas, de ellos, de ellas
Obj.	them	a ellos, a ellas

Pronombres reflexivos: Los pronombres reflexivos se usan cuando el sujeto es la misma persona o cosa que el objeto; son los siguientes: *myself, yourself, himself, herself, itself, ourselves, yourselves* y *themselves* (v. gr.: *they wash themselves* ellos se lavan; *I said to myself,* me dije).

Para indicar *reciprocidad* se usa la expresión *each other* cuando son dos personas, animales o cosas, y *one another* si son más de dos (v. gr.: *John and Peter help each other* Juan y Pedro se ayudan, *they were shouting one another in the street* se gritaban en la calle, se estaban gritando en la calle).

Pronombres relativos: Son *who* (que, quien) para personas; *which* (que, cual) para animales y cosas; *that* (que), el cual se usa en lugar de *who* o *which* antes de una cláusula o frase, y *what* (lo que), relativo compuesto que comprende tanto el relativo simple como el antecedente (v. gr.: *this is what they found* esto es lo que ellos encontraron, frase que equivale a *this is the thing which they found*).

Los pronombres relativos son invariables en género y número, y sólo *who* varía en los diversos casos gramaticales: Nominativo, *who* (que, quien, quienes); posesivo, *whose* (de quien, de quienes, cuyo, cuya, cuyos, cuyas); objetivo *whom* (a quien, a quienes).

El pronombre *that* sólo puede usarse al hablar de una persona o cosa que no sea la única de su especie (v. gr.: *the man that read the book* el hombre que leyó el libro; pero: *Charles, who read the book* Carlos, que leyó el libro).

Suele omitirse el pronombre relativo en el caso objetivo (v. gr.: *the man I saw* el hombre que vi, *the book you read* el libro que leíste).

Pronombres interrogativos: Son *who* (quién, quiénes); *whose* (de quién, de quiénes, cúyo, cúya, cúyos, cúyas); *whom* (a quién, a quiénes); *which* (cuál, cuáles), y *what* (qué).

Pronombres adjetivos: Hay cuatro clases de pronombres adjetivos, a saber: pronombres *posesivos,* pronombres *distributivos,* pronombres *demostrativos* y pronombres *indefinidos.*

Posesivos: Son los siguientes: *my* (mi), *your* (su, sus, de usted), *his* (su, sus, de él), *her* (su, sus, de ella), *its* (su, sus, de ello), *our* (nuestro, nuestra, nuestros, nuestras), *your* (su, sus, de ustedes) y *their* (su, sus, de ellos, de ellas).

Cuando se habla de una parte del cuerpo o de alguna facultad del alma, se usa el posesivo en lugar del artículo definido que se emplearía en español (v. gr.: *I have cut my fingers* me he cortado los dedos, *she washes her face* ella se lava la cara).

Distributivos: Son *each* (cada uno, cada una), *every* (todo, toda), *either* (uno u otro) y *neither* (ni uno ni otro).

Demostrativos: Son dos, *this* (este, esta, esto) y *that* (ese o aquel, esa o aquella, eso o aquello), y sus plurales *these* y *those* (v. gr.:

what does that mean? ¿qué significa eso?, *this is the age of revolutions* ésta es la época de las revoluciones).

Pueden usarse indistintamente como pronombres o adjetivos, y en este último caso van seguidos por un sustantivo (v. gr.: *those women are not so good as these men* aquellas mujeres no son tan buenas como estos hombres).

Indefinidos: Son: *whole* (todo, toda), *all* (todos, todas), *some* (alguno, alguna, algunos, algunas), *any* (cualquier, cualquiera, cualesquier, cualesquiera), *both* (ambos, ambas), *one* (uno, una), *other* (otro, otra, otros, otras), *none* (ninguno, ninguna, ningunos, ningunas), *such* (tal, tales, el que, la que, los que, las que).

ADVERBIO: Los adverbios de modo se forman en inglés agregando al adjetivo el sufijo *ly* (que no es sino la contracción de *like*), del mismo modo que en castellano se aumenta la terminación *mente* (v. gr.: *rich* rico, *richly* ricamente). Cuando el adjetivo termina en *y*, ésta se muda en *i* (v. gr.: *easy* fácil, *easily* fácilmente).

Algunas palabras conservan la misma forma como adjetivos y como adverbios (v. gr.: *a fast train* un tren rápido, *the train runs fast* el tren corre rápidamente).

No puede darse regla fija sobre el lugar que ocupa el adverbio en la frase, pues depende del énfasis, la eufonía o la significación.

Los adverbios admiten los grados de comparación, que son semejantes a los del adjetivo (v. gr.: *soon* pronto, *sooner* más pronto, *the soonest* lo más pronto). Los que terminan en *ly* forman el comparativo con *more* y el superlativo con *most*.

PREPOSICION: Son muchos los verbos ingleses que modifican su significación según la preposición que los acompañe. Esto sucede no sólo con el significado más evidente de la preposición (v. gr.: *to go* ir, *to go in* entrar, *to go out* salir, *to go up* subir, *to go down* bajar, etc.), sino también de una manera menos patente (v. gr.: *to do* hacer, *to do with* disponer, usar en provecho de, *to do without* pasar sin, dispensar de, *to do on* meter, etc.). Es por esta razón que el uso de las preposiciones puede dar a los verbos ingleses matices muy definidos que no se encuentran en español.

VERBO: Los verbos tienen cuatro modos: *infinitive* (infinitivo), *indicative* (indicativo), *imperative* (imperativo) y *subjunctive* (subjuntivo). (El *conditional* no es, en realidad, más que el subjuntivo de los verbos auxiliares defectivos).

Tiempos. En inglés sólo hay dos inflexiones para indicar el tiempo, pero, mediante el uso de adverbios o frases adverbiales, pueden expresarse seis o más relaciones temporales, que son: *present* (presente), *past* (pasado), *future* (futuro), *present perfect* (pretérito perfecto), *past perfect* (pretérito pluscuamperfecto) y *future perfect* (futuro perfecto).

Participios. Son dos: *present participle* (gerundio), que termina en *ing*, y *past participle* (participio pasivo), que termina en *d* o *ed* (como el pasado), a no ser que pertenezca a un verbo irregular.

OBSERVACIONES SOBRE LA CONJUGACION DE LOS VERBOS REGULARES

Modo infinitivo. Es la raíz de que se forman los demás tiempos y personas, y se distingue porque le precede la preposición *to* (*to see* ver, *to sing* cantar).

Modo indicativo. En el presente, el único cambio que sufre el verbo es en la tercera persona singular, que toma una *s* (v. gr.: *to eat* comer, *he eats* él come); si el verbo termina en *o, s, sh, ch* o *x*, se agrega la terminación *es* (v. gr.: *to do* hacer, *she does* ella hace); si el verbo termina en *y*, se cambia ésta en *ie* antes de agregar la *s* (v. gr.: *to reply* responder, *he replies* él responde); pero en los diptongos se conserva la *y* (v. gr.: *to pay* pagar, *she pays* ella paga). En los verbos auxiliares *shall, will, can, may* y *must* (y el verbo *need* cuando se usa como auxiliar), no se modifica la tercera persona singular. En el pasado, se agrega la terminación *d* si el verbo termina en *e*, y *ed* si termina en consonante (v. gr.: *to decide* decidir, *they decided* decidieron; *to form* formar, *she formed* ella formó); en los verbos terminados en *y*, ésta se cambia por *ie* antes de agregar la *d* (v. gr.: *to reply* responder, *we replied* respondimos); pero en los diptongos se conserva la *y* (*to pay* pagar, *you payed* ustedes pagaron). Para formar el futuro, si se quiere expresar simplemente un acontecimiento o una acción futura, se pone *shall* en la primera persona y *will* en la segunda y tercera (v. gr.: *I shall go* iré, *they will go* irán); pero si se trata de alguna promesa, amenaza, mandato o prohibición, se invierte el uso de los verbos auxiliares (v. gr.: *I will go* iré; *they shall go* irán). En cuanto a las formas compuestas (*present perfect*, y *future perfect*), se forman, como en español, agregando la conjugación del verbo *to have* (haber o tener) en presente, pasado o futuro, respectivamente.

Modo imperativo. Su forma es la misma que el infinitivo, pero sin la partícula *to* (*to love* amar, *love your neighbor* ama a tu prójimo). Para la primera y tercera persona se usa el auxiliar *let* (v. gr.: *let us go* vayamos).

Modo subjuntivo. El presente se forma por medio de los auxiliares *may* o *can*, o de las conjunciones *if, though* o *whether*. El pasado se forma con los auxiliares *might, could, would* o *should*, según su respectiva significación. El futuro se forma con el futuro de indicativo, al que preceden las mismas conjunciones *if, though* o *whether* a que nos hemos referido al hablar del presente subjuntivo. Los tiempos compuestos se forman con el presente perfecto de indicativo.

Para mayor claridad, ofrecemos la conjugación completa del verbo *to love* como ejemplo de la conjugación de los verbos regulares.

INFINITIVO

to love — amar

Gerundio

loving — amando

Participio pasado

loved — amado

INDICATIVO

Presente

I love	yo amo
you love	tú amas, usted ama
he loves	él ama
we love	nosotros amamos
you love	ustedes aman
they love	ellos aman

Pasado

I loved	yo amaba, amé
you loved	tú amas, amaste
he loved	él amaba, amó
we loved	nosotros amábamos, amamos
they loved	ellos amaban, amaron

Pretérito perfecto

I have loved	yo he amado
you have loved	tú has amado, usted ha amado
he has loved	él ha amado
we have loved	nosotros hemos amado
you have loved	ustedes han amado
they have loved	ellos han amado

Pretérito pluscuamperfecto

I had loved	yo había amado
you had loved	tú habías o usted había amado
he had loved	él había amado
we had loved	nosotros habíamos amado
you had loved	ustedes habían amado
they had loved	ellos habían amado

Futuro

I shall o will love	yo amaré
you will o shall love	tú amarás o usted amará
he will o shall love	él amará
we shall o will love	nosotros amaremos
you will o shall love	ustedes amarán
they will o shall love	ellos amarán

Futuro perfecto

I shall o will have loved	yo habré amado
you will o shall have loved	tú habrás amado o usted habrá [amado
he will o shall have loved	él habrá amado
we shall o will have loved	nosotros habremos amado
you will o shall have loved	ustedes habrán amado
they will o shall have loved	ellos habrán amado

IMPERATIVO

love	ama tú, ame usted
let him love	ame él
let us love	amemos
love	amad, amen ustedes
let them love	amen ellos

SUBJUNTIVO

Presente

that I may love	que yo ame
that you may love	que tú ames, que usted ame
that he may love	que él ame

XIII

that we may love	que nosotros amemos
that you may love	que ustedes amen
that they may love	que ellos amen

Pasado

I migt, could, would, should love	yo amara, amaría, amase
you might, could, would, should [love	tú o usted amara, amaría, amase
he might, could, would, should [love	él amara, amaría, amase
we might, could, would, should [love	nosotros amáramos, amaríamos, [amásemos
you might, could, would, should [love	ustedes amaran, amarían, amasen
they might, could, would, [should love	ellos amaran, amarían, amasen

Pretérito perfecto

that I may have loved	que yo haya amado
that you may have loved	que tú o usted haya amado
that he may have loved	que él haya amado
that we may have loved	que nosotros hayamos amado
that you may have loved	que ustedes hayan amado
that they may have loved	que ellos hayan amado

Pretérito pluscuamperfecto

I might, could, would, should [have loved	yo hubiera, habría, hubiese amado
you might, could, would, [should have loved	tú o usted hubiera, habría, hu- [biese amado
he might, could, would, should [have loved	él hubiera, habría, hubiese amado
we might, could, would, should [have loved	nosotros hubiéramos, habríamos, [hubiésemos amado
you might, could, would, [should have loved	ustedes hubieran, habrían, hubie- [sen amado
they might, could, would, [should have loved	ellos hubieran, habrían, hubiesen [amado

Futuro

if I shall *o* will love	si yo amare
if you will *o* shall love	si tú o usted amare
if he will *o* shall love	si él amare
if we shall *o* will love	si nosotros amáremos
if you will *o* shall love	si ustedes amaren
if they will *o* shall love	si ellos amaren

Futuro perfecto

if I shall *o* will have loved	si yo hubiere amado
if you will *o* shall have loved	si tú o usted hubiere amado
if he will *o* shall have loved	si él hubiere amado
if we shall *o* will have loved	si nosotros hubiéremos amado
if you will *o* shall have loved	si ustedes hubieren amado
if they will *o* shall have loved	si ellos hubieren amado

Verbos irregulares. Se da este nombre a los verbos que no forman el pasado y el participio pasado agregando *ed* al presente (v. gr.: *to see* ver, *I saw* yo vi, *he has seen* él ha visto).

Ofrecemos a continuación una lista de los principales verbos irregulares, en la que figuran sus principales partes:

Presente	*Pretérito*	*Participio pasado*
abide	abode	abode
arise	arose	arisen
awake	awoke	awaked
be (am, is, are)	was, were	been
bear	bore	born
beat	beat	beaten
become	became	become
befall	bhefell	befallen
beget	begot, begat	begotten
begin	began	begun
behold	beheld	beheld
belay	belayed, belaid	belayed, belaid
bend	bent	bent
bereave	bereaved, bereft	bereaved, bereft
beseech	besought, beseeche	beseeched, beseeched
beset	beset	beset
bestrew	bestrewed	bestrewed, bestrewn
bestride	bestrode	bestridden
bet	bet, betted	bet, betted
bid	bid	bid, bidden
bide	bided, bode	bided

bind	bound	bound
bite	bit	bit, bitten
bleed	bled	bled
blend	blent, blended	blent, blended
bless	blest, blessed	blest, blessed
blow	blew	blown
break	broke	broken
breed	bred	bred
bring	brought	brought
build	built	built
burn	burnt, burned	burnt, burned
burst	burst	burst
buy	bought	bought
can	could	—
cast	cast	cast
catch	caught	caught
chide	chid	chid, chidden
choose	chose	chosen
cleave	clove, clef	cloven, cleft
cling	clung	clung
clothe	clothed, clad	clothed, clad
come	came	come
cost	cost	cost
creep	crept	crept
crow	crew, crowed	crowed
curse	cursed, curst	cursed, curst
cut	cut	cut
dare	dared, durst	dared
deal	dealt	dealt
dig	dug, digged	dug, digged
dive	dived, dove	dived
do (does)	did	done
draw	drew	drawn
dream	dreamed, dreamt	dreamed, dreamt
drink	drank	drunk
drive	drove	driven
dwell	dwelt, dwelled	dwelt, dwelled
eat	ate	eaten
fall	fell	fallen
feed	fed	fed
feel	felt	felt
fight	fought	fought
find	found	found
flee	fled	fled
fling	flung	flung
fly	flew	flown
forbear	forbore	forborne
forbid	forbade	forbidden
forecast	forecast	forecast

foresee	foresaw	foreseen
foretell	foretold	foretold
forget	forgot	forgotten
forgive	forgave	forgiven
forsake	forsook	forsaken
freeze	froze	frozen
geld	gelded, gelt	gelded, gelt
get	got	got, gotten
gild	gilt, gilded	gilt, gilded
gird	girt, girded	girt, girded
give	gave	given
go (goes)	went	gone
grave	graved	graved, graven
grind	ground	ground
grow	grew	grown
hang	hung, hanged	hung, hanged
have	had	had
hear	heard	heard
heave	hove, heaved	hove, heaved
hew	hewed	hewn, hewed
hide	hid	hidden
hit	hit	hit
hold	held	held
hurt	hurt	hurt
keep	kept	kept
kneel	knelt, kneeled	knelt, kneeled
knit	knit, knitted	knit, knitted
know	knew	known
lade	laded	laded, laden
lay	laid	laid
lead	led	led
lean	leaned, leant	leaned, leant
leap	leapt, leaped	leapt, leaped
learn	learnt, learned	learn, learned
leave	left	left
lend	lent	lent
let	let	let
lie	lay	lain
light	lit, lighted	lighted, lit
load	loaded	loaded, laden
lose	lost	lost
make	made	made
may	might	—
mean	meant	meant
meet	met	met
melt	melted	melted, molten
mistake	mistook	mistaken
mow	mowed	mown, moved
must	—	—

ought	—	—
pay	paid	paid
pen	penned, pent	penned, pent
prove	proved	proven, proven
put	put	put
quit	quit, quitted	quit, quitted
read	read	read
rend	rent	rent
rid	rid, ridded	rid, ridded
ride	rode	ridden
ring	rang	rung
rise	rose	risen
run	ran	run
saw	sawed	sawn
say	said	said
see	saw	seen
seek	sought	sought
sell	sold	sold
send	sent	sent
set	set	set
sew	sewd	sewn, sewed
shake	shook	shaken
shall	should	—
shave	shaved	shaved, shaven
shear	sheared	shorn, sheared
shed	shed	shed
shine	shone	shone
shoe	shod	shod
shoot	shot	shot
show	showed	shown
shred	shred, shredded	shred, shredded
shrink	shrank	shrunk
shut	shut	shut
sing	sang	sung
sink	sank	sunk
sit	sat	sat
slay	slew	slain
sleep	slept	slept
slide	slid	slid
sling	slung	slung
slink	slunk	slunk
slit	slit	slit
smell	smelt, smelled	smelt, smelled
smite	smote	smitten
sow	sowed	sown, sowed
speak	spoke	spoken
speed	sped, speeded	sped, speeded
spell	spelt, spelled	spelt, spelled
spend	spent	spent

spill	spilt, spilled	spilt, spilled
spin	spun	span
spit	spat	spat
split	split	split
spoil	spoiled, spoilt	spoiled, spoilt
spread	spread	spread
spring	sprang	sprung
stand	stood	stood
stave	staved, stove	staved, stove
steal	stole	stolen
stick	stuck	stuck
sting	stung	stung
stink	stank	stunk
strew	strewed	strewn, strewed
stride	strode	stridden
strike	struck	struck, stricken
string	strung	strung
strive	strove	striven
swear	swore	sworn
sweat	sweat, sweated	sweat, sweated
sweep	swept	swept
swell	swelled	swollen, swelled
swim	swam	swum
swing	swung	swung
take	took	taken
teach	taught	taught
tear	tore	torn
tell	told	told
think	thouht	thought
thrive	throve	thriven
throw	threw	thrown
thrust	thrust	thrust
tread	trod	trodden
understand	understood	understood
uphold	upheld	upheld
upset	upset	upset
wake	woke, waked	woken, waked
wear	wore	worn
weave	wove, weaved	woven, weaved
wed	wedded, wed	wedded, wed
weep	wept	wept
wet	wet, wetted	wet, wetted
will	would	—
win	won	won
wind	wound	wound
work	worked, wrought	worked, wrought
wrap	wrapt, wrapped	wrapt, wrapped
wring	wrung	wrung
write	wrote	written

ABREVIATURAS USADAS EN ESTE DICCIONARIO

adj.	adjetivo
adv.	adverbio
alb.	albañilería
Arq.	arquitectura
art.	artículo
aux.	auxiliar
Bot.	botánica
Carp.	carpintería
com.	comercio
comp.	comparativo
conj.	conjunción
contr.	contracción
defect.	defectivo
fig.	figurado
ger.	gerundio
Gram.	gramática
Ig.	Iglesia
indef.	indefinido
imperf.	imperfecto
indic.	indicativo
interj.	interjección
	interrogativo
mec.	mecánica
Mús.	música
pers.	personal
part.	participio
pl.	plural
pos.	posesivo
p.p.	participio pasado
prep.	preposición
pret.	pretérito
pron.	pronombre
Quím.	química
s.	sustantivo
sing.	singular
subj.	subjuntivo
superl.	superlativo
v.	verbo
Zool.	zoología

A

a (e) art. indef. un, una.
abandon (abándon) v. abandonar, dejar; s. abandono, entrega, desahogo, cesión.
abandoned (abándond) adj. abandonado, dejado, inmoral.
abashed (abásht) adj. humillado, avergonzado, corrido.
abate (abéit) v. disminuir, reducir, menguar, ceder, mitigar(se), calmarse.
abatement (abéitment) s. reducción, disminución, merma, rebaja; mitigación.
abbey (ábi) s. abadía, monasterio.
abbot (ábot) s. abad.
abbreviation (abriviéishon) s. abreviatura, contracción.
abdicate (ábdikeit) v. abdicar, renunciar, dimitir.
abdomen (abdómen) s. abdomen, vientre.
abduct (abdóct) v. raptar, secuestrar.
aberration (aberréishon) s. aberración, extravío, error.
abhor (abjór) v. aborrecer, detestar, abominar.
abhorrence (abjórrens) s. aborrecimiento, odio, aversión.
abide (abáid) v. quedar, permanecer, morar, habitar, residir; soportar, tolerar; to — by conformarse a; atenerse a.
ability (abíliti) s. habilidad, aptitud.
abject (abyéct) adj. abatido; vil; despreciable, bajo.
able (éibl) adj. hábil, capaz, apto; **able-bodied** robusto, fornido; **to be — to** poder; saber.
ably (éibly) adv. hábilmente.
abnormal (abnórmal) adj. anormal.
aboard (abórd) adv. a bordo; en el tren; **to go — embarcarse**, ir a bordo.
abode (abóud) s. domicilio, morada, casa; estancia, permanencia.
abolition (abolíshon) s. abolición.
abominable (abóminabl) adj. abominable, execrable, detestable.
abortion (abórshon) s. aborto.
abound (abáund) v. abundar; **to — with** abundar en; estar lleno de; adj. copioso.
about (abáut) prep. acerca de, tocante a, alrededor, encima; adv. casi; **at — six o'clock** a eso de las seis; **to be — to** estar a punto de; **to face —** dar media vuelta **to beat — the bush** andarse por las ramas; **to set — emprender**; **week —** semanas alternas, turnando por semanas.
above (abóv) prep. por encima de; sobre; adv. arriba, en lo alto; **— all** sobre todo; **— board** abiertamente, a la vista de todos; **from —** del cielo.
abroad (abród) adv. por el mundo; en el extranjero; **to be all —** perder la brújula; **to set — divulgar**, publicar.
abrupt (abrópt) adj. brusco, repentino, precipitado; rudo, escarpado; **—ly** bruscamente.
abscess (ábses) s. absceso, apostema, tumor.
absence (ábsens) s. ausencia, falta, distracción; **— of mind** abstracción; **leave of —** licencia.
absent (ábsent) adj. ausente, distraído; **absent-minded** absorto; enajenado o fuera de sí; **to — oneself** ausentarse.
absolute (ábsolut) adj. absoluto; amplio, completo; **—ly** adv. absolutamente, en absoluto.
absolution (absolúshon) s. absolución; perdón.
absolve (absólv) v. absolver, dispensar, perdonar.
absorb (absórb) v. absorber, chupar.
absorbent (absórbent) adj. absorbente; **— cotton** algodón hidrófilo.
absorption (absórshon) s. absorción; preocupación; embebecimiento.
abstain (abstéin) v. abstenerse, pasar sin, privarse de.
abstinence (ábstinens) s. abstinencia.
abstract (ábstract) adj. abstracto, ideal; s. sumario, compendio, epítome. v. abstraer, resumir, separar, considerar aisladamente; substraer.
abstraction (abstrácshon) s. abstracción; retraimiento; concepto.
absurd (absórd) adj. absurdo; irracional; ridículo; disparatado.
absurdity (absórditi) s. absurdo; disparate.
abundance (abóndans) s. abundancia, exuberancia, caudal.

— 1 —

abundant (abóndont) adj. abundante, pingüe, feraz, caudaloso.
abuse (abiús) s. abuso, maltrato, injuria; v. abusar, ultrajar, violar.
abusive (abiúsiv) adj. abusivo, ofensivo, insultante, injurioso; — language palabras injuriosas.
abyss (abís) s. abismo, sima.
academic (académic) adj. académico, escolar.
academy (académi) s. academia, universidad, colegio, gimnasio.
accede (acsíd) v. acceder, asentir, consentir.
accelerate (acséiereit) v. acelerar.
acceleration (acseleréshon) s. aceleración, prisa, apresuración.
accelerator (acsélereitor) s. acelerador.
accent (ácsent) s. acento, inflexión de voz. v. acentuar, recalcar.
accentuate (acséntchueit) v. acentuar, dar énfasis.
accept (acsépt) v. aceptar, recibir, acoger; aprobar.
acceptable (acséptabl) adj. aceptable, admisible, grato.
acceptance (accéptans) s. aceptación; (com.) giro; aprobación.
access (ácses) s. acceso, entrada, arrebato de cólera.
accessible (accésibl) adj. accesible, conquistable, asequible.
accessory (acsésori) adj. accesorio, secundario; s. cómplice; adminículo, dependencia.
accident (ácsident) s. accidente, percance (gram.) desinencia, modo: by — por casualidad, accidentalmente.
accidental (acsidéntal) adj. accidental, fortuito, casual; (Mús.) bemol o sostenido accidental; —ly adv. accidentalmente.
acclaim (acléim) v. aclamar, vitorear, aplaudir; s. aplauso.
acclamation (acleméshon) s. aclamación, celebración.
acclimatize (acláimatais) v. aclimatar(se).
accommodate (acómodeit) v. acomodar, servir, hospedar, alojar; proveer, surtir; com. prestar dinero; to — oneself adaptarse, convenir, conformarse.
accommodation (acomodéshon) s. servicio, favor, conveniencia, alojamiento; — train (en E. U.) tren de escala.

accompaniment (acómpaniment) s. acompañamiento.
accompanist (acómpanist) s. acompañante.
accompany (acómpani) v. acompañar, ir con, asociarse con.
accomplice (acómplis) s. cómplice.
accomplish (acómplish) v. llevar a cabo, cumplir, lograr, realizar, desempeñar; completar.
accomplished (acómplish) adj. cumplido, acabado, realizado, consumado, perfecto, diestro.
accomplishment (acómplishment) s. cumplimiento, consumación, logro, éxito; habilidad; mérito, proeza.
accord (acórd) s. acuerdo, armonía, convenio; of one's own — espontáneamente; with one — por unanimidad; v. otorgar; acordar; convenir, concertar, avenirse.
accordance (acórdans) s. conformidad, buena inteligencia; in — with de acuerdo con, de conformidad.
according (acórding) part. según, conforme; — to de conformidad con — as según (que), a medida que.
accordingly (acórdingli) adv. de consiguiente; en conformidad, en efecto; por lo tanto; así.
accost (acóst) v. dirigirse a una persona, abordarla para hablarle. Acosar, molestar. Ofrecerse (una mujer).
account (acáunt) s. cuenta, cálculo, relato; dignididad, importancia; on — of debido a; por motivo de; por; on my — por mí; on joint — de cuenta a mitad; on no — de ninguna manera; to turn to — sacar provecho account of sales cuenta de ventas; people of no — gente de poca importancia; v. dar cuenta; considerar; tener por; to — for dar cuenta o razón de; to keep an — tener cuenta abierta.
accountable (acáuntebl) adj. responsable, explicable.
accountant (acáuntant) s. contador, perito mercantil.
accounting (acáunting) s. contabilidad, arreglo de cuentas.
accredit (acrédit) v. acreditar, dar credenciales.

accrue (acrú) v. acumular, incrementar.

accumulate (akiúmiuleit) v. acumular(se), atesorar, juntar.

accumulation (akiumuléshon) s. acumulación, hacinamiento.

accuracy (ákiuraci) s. precisión, cuidado, exactitud, corrección.

accursed (acórst) adj. maldito, detestable, excomulgado, infame.

accusation (akiuséshon) s. acusación.

accuse (akiús) v. acusar, delatar.

accuser (akiúser) s. acusador.

accustom (acóstom) v. acostumbrar, habituar; to — oneself acostumbrarse; to be —ed to tener hábito, soler, estar hecho a.

ace (éis) s. as (de la baraja), el mejor de su clase; within an — of en un tris, a punto de.

ache (éik) s. dolor, dolencia mal; head – — dolor de cabeza; tooth — dolor de muelas. v. doler.

achieve (achív) v. llevar a cabo, ejecutar; realizar; lograr, obtener, alcanzar.

achievement (achívment) s. ejecucución, logro, realización; hecho; hazaña, proeza.

acid (ácid) adj. ácido, agrio, acedo.

acidity (acíditi) s. acidez, agrura.

acknowledge (acnóledy) v. reconocer; confesar; agradecer; to — receipt acusar recibo.

acorn (écorn) s. bellota.

acoustics (acústics) s. acústica.

acquaint (akuéint) v. enterar, informar, instruir, familiarizar; to — oneself with ponerse al corriente de; familiarizarse; to be —ed with conocer a (una persona), conocer (un país), etc.

acquaintance (akuéintens) s. conocimiento, familiaridad; —s amistades.

acquiesce (akuiés) v. asentir, allanarse; someterse, quedar conforme.

acquiescence (akuiésens) s. aquiescencia, asentimiento, conformidad.

acquire (acuáir) v. adquirir, ganar, contraer (vicios, hábitos), etc.

acquisition (akuisíshon) s. adquisición.

acquit (akuít) v. absolver, descargar, exonerar; pagar, librar, dispensar; to — oneself well quedar bien, portarse bien.

acquittal (akuítal) s. absolución; descargo, pago.

acre (éiker) s. acre, medida agraria.

acrobat (ácrobat) s. acróbata.

across (acrós) prep. a través de, al otro lado de, por, por medio de; v. to go — atravesar; to come —, to run — encontrarse con, tropezar con.

act (act) s. acto, hecho, acción, efecto. v. representar en el teatro; to — of servir de, estar de, — of faith auto de fe.

acting (ácting) s. representación, actuación; en funciones de; adj. suplente.

action (ácshon) s. acción, obra, funcionamiento.

active (áctiv) adj. activo, diligente.

activity (activiti) s. actividad.

actor (áctor) s. actor, cómico.

actress (áctres) s. actriz.

actual (ácchual) adj. actual, verdadero, real, existente; —ly adv. realmente, de hecho.

acumen (akiúmen) s. cacumen, tino, agudeza, perspicacia.

acute (akiút) adj. agudo, ingenioso, penetrante, fino, sutil.

adamant (ádamant) adj. adamante, duro, firme, inflexible.

adapt (adápt) v. adaptar, ajustar, acomodar.

adaptation (adaptéshon) s. adaptación, ajuste.

add (ad) v. sumar, añadir, adicionar, agregar.

addict (ádict) s. adicto; drug — drogadicto.

addicted (adicted) adj. adicto, afecto a, dado a, habituado.

addition (adíshon) s. suma, adición; in — to además de.

additional (adíshonal) adj. adicional.

address (adrés) s. dirección; petición; sobrescrito; discurso; trato; form of — tratamiento; v. dirigir, arengar, hablar a: to — oneself to a task dedicarse a una tarea.

addressee (adresí) s. destinatario.

adequate (ádekueit) adj. adecuado, proporcionado.

adhere (adjír) v. adherirse, unirse, allegarse; pegarse.

adherence (adjírens) s. adherencia, adhesión.

adhesion (adjíshon) s. adhesión, adherencia.

adhesive (adjísiv) adj. adhesivo, adherente, pegajoso; — **tape** tela adhesiva; — **plaster** tafetán inglés.

adjacent (adyácent) adj. adyacente, colindante, contiguo.

adjective (adyéctiv) s. adjetivo.

adjoin (adyóin) v. lindar, unir, estar contiguo o adyacente.

adjourn (adyórn) v. diferir, suspender, aplazar; **to — a meeting** suspender una sesión; **meeting —ed** se levanta la sesión.

adjournment (adyóurment) s. aplazamiento, traslación, suspensión, levantamiento de una sesión.

adjunct (adyónct) s. adjunto, auxiliar, añadidura, adj. unido, subordinado.

adjustment (adyóstment) s. ajuste; transacción; arreglo; regulación.

administer (admínister) v. administrar; proveer, regir, gobernar; aplicar (medicina); **to — an oath** tomar juramento.

administration (administréshon) s. administración, gobierno; intendencia.

administrative (admínistretiv) adj. administrativo, gubernativo.

admirable (admírabl) adj. admirable; **admirably** adv. admirablemente.

admiral (ádmiral) s. almirante.

admiration (admiréshon) s. admiración, pasmo.

admire (admáir) v. admirar, contemplar.

admirer (admáirer) s. admirador, amante, pretendiente.

admission (admíshon) s. admisión, acceso; concesión; precio de entrada.

admit (admít) v. admitir; aceptar; permitir; reconocer; confesar; asentir.

admittance (admítans) s. entrada; derecho de admisión.

admonish (admónish) v. amonestar, exhortar, reprender.

admonition (admoníshon) s. amonestación, consejo; advertencia.

ado (edú) s. bullicio, tumulto, **without more —** ni más acá ni más allá.

adobe (adóbi) s. adobe.

adolescence (adolésens) s. adolescencia.

adopt (adópt) v. adoptar, prohijar.

adoption (adópshon) s. adopción.

adoration (adoréshon) s. adoración.

adore (adóur) v. adorar, idolatrar.

adorn (adórn) v. adornar, ornamentar, embellecer, ataviar.

adornment (adórnment) s. adorno.

adrift (adríft) adj. y adv. a la deriva, al garete.

adroit (adrólt) adj. hábil, diestro.

adult (adólt) adj. y s. adulto.

adulterate (adóltereit) v. adulterar.

adulterer (adólterer) s. adúltero.

adultery (adólteri) s. adulterio.

advance (adváns) v. avanzar, adelantar; acelerar; anticipar dinero; pagar por adelantado; insinuar; encarecer; s. avance; progreso; alza; **—s** requerimiento, pretenciones, insinuaciones; **in — por adelantado**, con anticipación.

advanced (advánst) adj. adelantado, anticipado; **— in years** entrado en años, anciano.

advancement (advánsment) s. adelantamiento, progresión, mejora; ascenso; promoción.

advantage (advántey) s. ventaja, superioridad; ganancia, provecho; beneficio; **to have the — over** llevar ventaja a; **to take — of** aprovecharse de, valerse de; **take — of a person** abusar de la confianza de alguien.

advantageous (advantéyos) adj. ventajoso, lucrativo, útil.

advent (ádvent) s. advenimiento, llegada; adviento.

adventure (advénchur) s. aventura, casualidad, riesgo; lance.

adventurer (advénchurer) s. aventurero; (com.) pacotillero.

adventurous (advénchuros) adj. aventurero, audaz, atrevido, arrojado, arriesgado, intrépido.

adverb (ádverb) s. adverbio.

adversary (ádversari) s. adversario, enemigo, antagonista, contrario; **the Adversary** satanás.

adverse (advérs) adj. adverso, contrario, hostil; funesto.

adversity (advérsiti) s. adversidad, desgracia, calamidad.

advertise (ádvertais) v. anunciar, publicar, dar aviso, informar.

advertisement (advertáisment) s. anuncio, notificación, aviso.

advertiser (advertáiser) s. anunciante, anunciador, avisador.

advertising (ádvertaising) s. publicidad, arte de anunciar.

— 4 —

ADVICE

AGILE

advice (adváis) s. consejo, advertencia; aviso, informe, noticia.
advisable (adváisabl) adj. aconsejable, prudente, indicado.
advise (adváis) v. aconsejar, advertir, informar, apercibir, avisar; pedir o tomar consejo.
adviser, advisor (adváiser) s. consejero, consultor, asesor.
advocate (ádvokeit) s. abogado, casuista, intercesor, defensor (advokéit) defender, interceder.
aerial (érial) adj. aéreo, s. antena; **frame** — antena de cuadro.
aeroplane (érplein) s. avión.
aesthetic (eszétic) adj. estético, s. estética.
afar (afár) adv. lejos, distante, a gran distancia; **from** — desde lejos; — **off** muy remoto.
affable (áfabl) adj. afable, atento.
affair (afér) s. asunto, negocio; tertulia; convite; **love** — amorío; — **of honor** lance de honor.
affect (aféct) v. afectar, impresionar, conmover; aparentar, fingir, hacer ostentación.
affectation (afectéshon) s. afectación.
affected (afécted) adj. afectado, impresionado, emocionado; artificioso, fingido.
affection (afécshon) s. afecto, cariño, amor, inclinación; dolencia.
affectionate (afécshoneit) adj. afectuoso, expresivo, cariñoso.
affiliate (afíliet) v. afiliar(se), asociarse; prohijar; adoptar.
affinity (afíniti) s. afinidad.
affirm (afírm) v. afirmar, asegurar, declarar, asentar.
affirmative (afírmativ) adj. afirmativo; s. aserción, afirmativa.
affix (afíx) v. añadir, fijar, pegar; s. afijo, añadidura.
afflict (aflíct) v. afligir, angustiar; acongojar, atribular.
affliction (aflícshon) s. aflicción, tribulación, calamidad, pena, dolor, angustia.
affront (afrónt) s. afrenta, provocación, insulto, ultraje; v. agraviar.
afire (afáir) adj. ardiendo, quemándose; en llamas.
afloat (aflóut) adj. y adv. a flote, a flor de agua; a la deriva, sin rumbo; **the rumor is** — corre la voz.
afoot (afút) adv. a pie, en movimiento; en preparación.
aforesaid (afórsed) adj. susodicho, precitado, ya mencionado.

afraid (afréid) adj. miedoso, atemorizado, espantado; **to be** — **of** tener miedo de.
afresh (afrésh) adv. otra vez, de nuevo, desde el principio.
African (áfrican) adj. y s. africano, negro.
after (áfter) prep. después de; tras (de); en busca de; por; según; adv. en seguida, adj. subsiguiente; **day** — **to morrow** pasado mañana; — **all** después de todo; **soon** — poco después; — **hope** esperanza renovada; — **math** segunda siega; — **thought** ocurrencia o idea tardía; — **wise** discreto o prudente; **pasada la ocasión**.
afternoon (áfternún) s. tarde; después de mediodía.
aftertaste (áfterteist) s. dejo, sabor.
afterwards (áfteruerds) adv. después; **long** — mucho tiempo después.
again (aguén) adv. otra vez, aun, de nuevo; segunda vez; además, por otra parte; — **and** — muchas veces; **now and** — de vez en cuando; **never** — nunca jamás; **come** — vuelva usted; **do it** — vuelva a hacerlo.
against (aguénst) prep. contra; enfrente; — **the grain** a contrapelo; — **a rainy day** para cuando llueva; — **time** para ganar tiempo.
age (eiy) s. edad; época, período, evo, siglo, generación; **of** — mayor de edad; **old** — vejez, ancianidad; **under** — minoridad; **the golden** — el Siglo de Oro; v. envejecer.
agency (éiyensi) s. agencia, sucursal; gestión; medio; mediación, órgano, fuerza.
agent (éiyent) s. agente, intermediario, delegado, comisionado, encargado.
aggrandize (ágrandaiz) v. agrandar; elevar, exaltar, engrandecer.
aggravate (ágreviet) v. agravar; exasperar, irritar.
aggregate (ágregueit) v. agregar, unir; ascender a; s. colección, conjunto; adj. agregado; **in the** — en conjunto.
aggression (agréshon) s. agresión.
aggressive (agrésiv) adj. agresivo.
aggressor (agrésor) s. agresor.
aghast (agást) adj. espantado, pasmado.
agile (áyil) adj. ágil, vivo, ligero.

agitate (áyiteit) v. agitar; turbar, soievantar, discutir acaloradamente.
agitation (eyitéshon) s. agitación.
agitator (éyitetor) s. agitador, perturbador, revoltoso.
ago (agó) adj. y adv. pasado; en el pasado; **many years —** hace muchos años; mucho tiempo ha; **long —** tiempo ha; mucho; **a week —** la semana pasada; **a long time —** hace mucho tiempo.
agonize (ágonais) v. agonizar, luchar desesperadamente; retorcerse de dolor.
agony (ágoni) s. agonía; angustia, zozobra; dolor; lucha; paroxismo; tormento.
agree (agrí) v. acordar, concordar, convenir; concertar; estar de acuerdo; sentarle bien a uno (dícese del clima); sentar; aprobar.
agreeable (agríabl) adj. agradable, afable; grato; conveniente; ameno; satisfactorio; proporcionado; conforme, lo que agrada.
agreement (agríment) s. acuerdo, convenio, concordancia, ajustamiento, pacto; **to be in —** estar de acuerdo, **to come to an —** ponerse de acuerdo, acomodamiento, transacción.
agricultural (agricólchoral) s. agrícola.
agriculture (ágricolchor) s. agricultura.
agriculturist (agricólchurist) s. agricultor.
ahead (ajéd) adv. delante, a la cabeza; por la proa; **— of time** adelantado; antes de tiempo; **to go —** adelantar(se); hacia adelante.
aid (éid) s. ayuda, auxilio, favor, amparo, v. ayudar, auxiliar, socorrer, conllevar; sufragar.
ail (éil) v. adolecer, padecer, afligir; **what —s you?** ¿qué tienes?
ailment (éilment) s. achaque, dolencia.
aim (éim) s. puntería; tino; fin; blanco; v. dirigir, largar, aspirar a; pretender; apuntar un arma; **to — to please** proponerse, o tratar de agradar.
aimless (éimles) adj. sin propósito.
air (er) s. aire, atmósfera, brisa; **in the —** en el aire; incierto; **in the open —** al raso; aire libre; **— brake** freno neumático; **— line** línea aérea; **by — mail** por correo aéreo, por vía aérea, por avión; **— conditioner** de aire acondicionado; v. airear; orear; ventilar; publicar; pregonar, ostentar.
aircraft (ercraft) s. avión, aeroplano, aeronave.
airplane (érplein) s. aeroplano; **— carrier** portaaviones.
airport (éport) s. aeropuerto, aeródromo.
airship (érship) s. aeronave.
airtight (értaigt) adj. hermético.
airy (éri) adj. etéreo, aéreo, vaporoso, ventilado, ligero, tenue.
aisle (éil) s. pasillo, pasadizo; (arq.) (arq.) nave lateral, ala.
ajar (ayár) adj. entreabierto, entornado.
alarm (alárm) s. alarma; sobresalto, arrebato; **— clock** despertador; v. alarmar; inquietar.
alcohol (álcojol) s. alcohol.
alcoholic (alcojólic) s. alcohólico.
alcove (álcov) s. alcoba, retrete.
alderman (ólderman) s. consejal; regidor.
ale (éil) s. cerveza.
alert (alért) adj. alerta, vigilante, vivo, activo; s. rebato; **to be on the —** estar alerta.
alfalfa (alfálfa) s. alfalfa.
algebra (ályebra) s. álgebra.
alien (élien) s. extranjero; forastero; adj. extraño, ajeno.
alienate (élieneit) v. enajenar; apartar, alejar (a una persona)
alienist (élienist) s. psiquiatra.
alight (aláit) v. apearse, bajar de un coche; bajar de; posarse (dícese de pájaros, mariposas, etc.).
alike (aláik) adj. semejante, parecido; **to be —** parecerse, semejarse, a la par, adv. del mismo modo.
alive (aláiv) adj. vivo, viviente; activo; **— with** lleno de.
all (ol) adj. todo, todos; s. todo el mundo; adv. enteramente.
allegation (aleguéshon) s. alegación, alegato; aseveración.
allege (aléy) v. alegar; declarar; afirmar, sostener.
allegiance (alíyans) s. lealtad, fidelidad; homenaje, sumisión.
allergy (áleryi) s. alergia (sensibilidad anormal a ciertos alimentos).
alleviate (alíviet) v. aliviar; mitigar, aplacar.
alley (áli) s. callejón, callejuela. **blind —** callejón sin salida; **bowling —** boliche, bolera, boleo.
alliance (aláians) s. alianza.

allied (aláid) adj. aliado; relacionado.
alligator (áliguetor) s. lagarto, caimán; — **pear** aguacate.
allot (alót) v. asignar, distribuir, adjudicar, destinar.
allow (aláu) v. permitir, dejar, consentir; admitir, confesar, com. rebajar, descontar, reducir.
allowable (aláuabl) adj. lícito, permisible, tolerable.
allowance (aláuans) s. asignación; pensión, alimentos; permiso, concesión; gaje, salario; indulgencia, com. rebaja, descuento; **monthly —** mesada; **to make — for** tener en cuenta, hacerse cargo de.
alloy (álol) s. amalgama, aleación; liga (de metales), v. alear, ligar, amalgamar metales.
allude (allúd) v. aludir, referirse.
allure (allúr) v. seducir, fascinar, halagar; s. señuelo.
allurement (allúrment) s. seducción, tentación, atractivo; añagaza.
alluring (alúring) adj. seductivo, tentador, atrayente, encantador.
allusion (alúshon) s. alusión, insinuación; indirecta.
ally (alái) v. aliarse; confederarse, **to — oneself with** aliarse con; s. aliado.
almanac (ólmanac) s. almanaque, calendario.
almighty (olmáiti) adj. omnipotente, todopoderoso.
almond (ámond) s. almendra; alloza; **— tree** almendro; **sugar —** almendra garapiñada.
almost (ólmost) adv. casi, cerca de, **I — fell down** por poco me caigo.
alms (ams) s. limosna, caridad; **— box** cepo, alcancía para limosna.
aloft (alóft) adv. arriba, en alto.
alone (alóun) adj. solo, solitario; solamente; **all — a solas,** solito; **to let —** dejar en paz, no molestar; **let — a letter** mucho menos una carta.
along (alóng) prep. a lo largo, adelante; con, en compañía de, junto; **all —** todo el tiempo; de un extremo a otro; **all — the coast** por toda la costa; **to carry — with one** llevar consigo; **to go — with** acompañar a; **to get —** llevarse bien con una persona; **come — with me** venga conmigo.
alongside (alóngsaid) prep. y adv. al lado de; **— a ship** al costado de un buque.

aloof (alúf) adj. aislado, apartado; adv. lejos, de lejos, a distancia; **to stand —** no mezclarse en.
aloofness (alúfnes) s. alejamiento, aislamiento.
aloud (aláud) adv. alto, recio, en voz alta, fuerte.
alphabet (álfabet) s. alfabeto.
already (olrédi) adv. ya; antes de ahora.
also (ólso) adv. también, aun, del mismo modo, así, igualmente.
altar (óltar) s. altar, ara; **high — altar** mayor; **— cloth** sabanilla, mantel, palia; **— piece** retablo.
alter (ólter) v. alterar, modificar, reformar, cambiar, variar.
alteration (olteréshon) s. alteración, modificación, cambio, mudanza; reforma.
alternate (ólterneit) adj. alterno, recíproco; s. suplente, sustituto; **—ly** adv. alternativamente; v. alternar, turnar.
alternative (oltérnetiv) adj. alternativo. s. alternativa.
although (olzó) conj. no obstante, aunque, si bien que, aun cuando
altitude (áltitiud) s. altitud, cumbre, elevación, altura.
altogether (oltoguéder) adv. del todo, enteramente, en conjunto.
aluminum (alúminum) s. aluminio.
alumnus (alómnus) s. graduado, ex alumno.
always (óluels) adv. siempre.
am (am) primera persona del presente de indic. del v. **to be:** soy, estoy.
amalgamate (amálgameit) v. amalgamar, combinar, unir.
amass (amás) v. amontonar, juntar, apilar; Am. amasar.
amateur (ámater) s. aficionado; novicio, principiante.
amaze (améis) v. asombrar, dejar bonito, maravillar, confundir.
amazement (améisment) s. asombro, aturdimiento.
amazing (améising) adj. asombroso, extraño; **—ly** asombrosamente.
ambassador (ambásador) s. embajador.
amber (ámber) s. ámbar; electro; adj. ambarino; de ámbar.
ambiguity (ambigüiti) s. ambigüedad.
ambiguous (ambíguous) adj. ambiguo.
ambition (ambíshon) s. ambición; aspiración.
ambitious (ambíshos) adj. ambicioso.

— 7 —

amble (ámbl) v. andar, vagar.
ambulance (ámbiulans) s. ambulancia.
ambush (ámbush) s. emboscada, sorpresa; acecho; **to lie in —** estar emboscado, estar al acecho; v. emboscar; poner celada a.
amend (aménd) v. enmendar; corregir; **—s** s. pl. satisfacción, recompensa; **to make — for** resarcir, compensar por, reparar.
amendment (améndment) s. enmienda.
American (américan) adj. y s. americano; norteamericano.
amethyst (ámezist) s. amatista.
amiable (émiebl) adj. amable, afable, afectuoso.
amicable (ámicabl) adj. amigable, amistoso.
amid (amíd) **amidst** prep. en medio de; mezclado con; entre.
amiss (amís) adj. errado, equivocado; adv. mal; fuera de caso; impropiamente; **to make —** llevar a mal; equivocadamente.
ammonia (amónia) s. amoniaco; álcali volátil.
ammunition (amiuníshon) s. munición; pertrechos.
amnesty (ámnesti) s. amnistía, indulto.
among (amóng) prep. entre, mezclado con; enmedio de.
amorous (ámoros) adj. enamorado, amoroso, tierno, apasionado.
amount (amáunt) s. suma; cantidad, total; monto; cuantía. v. montar, importar, ascender (a); **that —s to stealing** eso equivale a robar.
amphitheatre (ámfiziater) s. anfiteatro, circo.
ample (ámpl) adj. amplio; extensivo, dilatado; suficiente, bastante.
amputate (ámpiuteit) v. amputar.
amuse (amiús) v. divertir, recrear, solazar; **to — oneself** divertirse.
amusement (amiúsment) s. diversión, pasatiempo, entretenimiento, distracción, recreo.
amusing (amiúsing) adj. recreativo, entretenido; gracioso, chistoso.
analogous (análogos) adj. análogo.
analogy (análoyi) s. analogía, correlación, afinidad, semejanza.
analysis (análisis) s. análisis.
analyze (ánalais) v. analizar.
anarchy (ánarki) s. anarquía.
anatomy (anátomi) s. anatomía.
ancestor (áncestor) s. antepasado; ascendientes, antecesores.
ancestral (ancéstral) adj. solariego, hereditario.
ancestry (áncestri) s. linaje, abolengo, alcurnia.
anchor (áncor) s. ancla; **to drop —** anclar, echar anclas, dar fondo, fondear; **— cross** cruz del ancla; **foul —** ancla enredada.
anchovy (ánchovi) s. anchoa.
ancient (énshent) adj. antiguo, viejo; vetusto; **the —s** antepasados, los antiguos; la antigüedad.
and (and) conj. y; e (delante de i o de hi); **— so forth** etcétera; y así sucesivamente; **better — better** cada vez mejor, o mejor que mejor.
Andalucian (andalúshan) adj. andaluz.
anecdote (ánecdot) s. anécdota.
anesthetic (aneszétic) adj. y s. anestésico.
anew (aniú) adv. otra vez, de refresco, nuevamente.
angel (ányel) s. ángel.
angelic (anyélic) adj. angélico.
anger (ánguer) s. ira, cólera, saña; v. enojar, enfadar.
angina (ányina) s. angina; **— pectoris** angina de pecho.
angle (ángl) s. rincón, esquina; recodo, cornijal; punto de vista.
Anglo-Saxon (ánglo-sáxon) adj. y s. anglosajón.
angry (ángri) adj. colérico, irritado.
anguish (ángüish) s. ansia, pena, angustia, aflicción, tormento.
angular (ánguiular) adj. esquinado.
animal (ánimal) s. y adj. animal.
animate (ánimeit) adj. viviente, vigoroso, animado. v. alentar, animar.
animation (animéshon) s. viveza, animación; (fig.) calor, fuego.
animosity (animósiti) s. animosidad, mala voluntad, ojeriza, tema, odio.
ankle (ánkl) s. moléolo o tobillo.
annals (ánals) s. pl. anales.
annex (anéx) s. añadidura; aditamento; adición, apéndice; ala de un edificio; v. anexar.
annexation (anexéshon) s. anexión.
annihilate (anáijilet) v. aniquilar, anonadar.
anniversary (anivérsari) s. y adj. aniversario.
annotation (anotéshon) s. nota, acotación, apostilla, apunte.
announce (anáuns) v. proclamar; anunciar; publicar; pregonar.
announcement (anáunsment) s.

anuncio, aviso; declaración; pregón.
announcer (anáunser) s. anunciador; publicador; **radio** — locutor.
annoy (anói) v. fastidiar; molestar, enfadar; incomodar; aburrir.
annoyance (anóians) s. fastidio; molestia, enfado.
annual (ániual) adj. anual; cadañal; s. anuario, aniversario; **—ly** adv. anualmente; todos los días.
annuity (anúiti) s. prima, anualidad, pensión.
annul (anól) v. anular; invalidar, abolir; derogar; abrogar.
anoint (anóint) v. ungir; untar; administrar la extremaunción.
anon (anón) adv. pronto, luego, inmediatamente; en seguida.
anonymous (anónimos) adj. anónimo.
another (anóder) adj. y pron. otro; **one** — a otro, unos a otros.
answer (ánser) s. contestación, refutación; solución; v. replicar; contestar; responder; refutar; to — **for** ser responsable de (o por); **no, that will never** — eso no saldrá bien.
ant (ánt) s. hormiga; — **eater** oso hormiguero; — **hill** hormiguero.
antagonism (antágonism) s. oposición, antagonismo; rivalidad; hostilidad.
antagonist (antágonist) s. antagonista; rival; adversario.
antagonize (antágonais) v. contrariar; contender; competir.
antecedent (antecídent) adj. y s. antecedente; precedente.
antelope (ánteloup) s. antílope, gacela; gamuza.
antenna (anténa) (pl.) **antennae** (anténi) s. antena; (radio) antena.
anterior (antírior) adj. anterior, delantero, precedente.
anteroom (ánterrum) s. antecámara; sala de espera.
anthem (ánzem) s. himno; motete.
anthracite (ánzrasait) s. antracita; carbón de piedra.
antiaircraft (antiércraft) adj. antiaéreo.
anticipate (anticípeit) v. anticipar prevenir; adelantarse; impedir.
anticipation (anticipéshon) s. anticipación, adelantamiento.
antics (ántics) s. pl. travesuras, cabriolas.
antidote (ántidot) s. antídoto, contraveneno; triaca, preservativo.

antipathy (antípazi) s. antipatía; repugnancia.
antiquated (ánticueitid) adj. anticuado; desusado; añejo; viejo.
antique (antic) adj. antiguo, anticuado; s. antigualla.
antiquity (antíkuiti) s. antigüedad; vetustez; vejez; ancianidad
antiseptic (antiséptic) adj. y s. antiséptico; desinfectante; antipútrido.
antisocial (antisóshal) adj. antisocial.
anxiety (angsáieti) s. ansiedad, desasosiego; anhelo; afán.
anxious (ánkshos) adj. ansioso. inquieto; preocupado; impaciente; **—ly** adv. con vehemencia; con ansia.
anybody (énibodi) pron. alguien, **any** (éni) adj. y pron. cualquier(a), cualesquier(a); alguno(s), alguno; nadie; ninguno; **he does not know** — no conoce a nadie.
anyhow (énijau) adv. de todos modos, en cualquier caso.
anyone (éniuan) véase **anybody**.
anything (énizing) pron. alguna cosa, cualquier cosa; **not** — nada; — **you choose** todo lo que usted quiera; **not to know** — no saber nada.
anyway (éniuei) adv. de todos modos; en cualquier caso.
anywhere (énijuéar) adv. dondequiera; en todas partes; en cualquier parte o lugar **not**... — no... en ninguna parte; **not to go** — no ir a ninguna parte.
apart (apárt) adv. aparte; a un lado; separadamente; adj. aislado, separado; **to take** — desarmar, desmontar.
apartment (apártment) s. apartamiento, piso; vivienda; habitación; cuarto.
apathy (ápazi) s. apatía, indolencia, flema, indiferencia.
ape (éip) s. (zool) mono, simio, mico; v. remedar, imitar.
aperture (ápershur) s. abertura, paso, rendija, buco, portillo.
apex (épeks) s. ápice, cumbre, punta; cima; fastigio.
apiece (epís) adv. por barba, por cabeza, por persona, cada uno.
apologetic (apoloyétik) adj. apologético; que se excusa o disculpa
apologize (apóloyais) v. disculparse, excusarse.
apology (apóloyi) s. apología, excusa, disculpa; satisfacción.
apoplexy (ápoplecsi) s. apoplejía.

apostolic (apostólic) adj. apostólico.
appall (epól) v. aterrorizar, aterrar; desmayar, desanimar.
appalling (epólin) adj. espantoso, aterrador, asombroso.
apparatus (aparétus) s. aparato, tren.
apparel (apárel) s. ropa, traje, vestido, ropaje.
apparent (apárent) adj. aparente; visible, obvio, evidente; manifiesto; **heir** — presunto heredero; **—ly** adv. aparentemente.
apparition (aparíshon) s. aparición; aparecido, fantasma, espectro.
appeal (apíl) s. apelación, súplica, petición, instancia, recurso; llamamiento; v. clamar, recurrir, apelar; atraer; poner por testigo; llamar la atención.
appear (apír) v. aparecer(se); manifestar(se); comparecer.
appearance (apírans) s. apariencia, semejanza, aspecto, talante.
appease (apís) v. apaciguar, aplacar; calmar, sosegar, conciliar.
appeasement (apísment) s. apaciguamiento; pacificación.
appendix (apéndics) s. apéndice.
appertain (apertéin) v. pertenecer.
appetite (ápetait) s. apetito; gana, hambre, deseo; anhelo.
appetizer (ápetaiser) s. aperitivo; apetitivo.
appetizing (ápetaising) adj. apetecible, apetitoso; tentador.
applaud (aplód) v. aplaudir, palmotear; aclamar; celebrar.
applause (aplós) s. aplauso, palmoteo.
apple (apl) s. manzana, poma; **— tree** manzano; **Adam's** — nuez (de la garganta); **— yard** huerto; **— of my eye**, pupila o niña del ojo, globo del ojo.
applesauce (áplsos) s. compota de manzana.
appliance (apláians) s. herramienta, utensilio; instrumento.
applicable (áplicabl) adj. aplicable, conforme, pertinente.
applicant (éplikent) s. suplicante, aspirante, candidato.
application (eplikéshon) s. aplicación; medicamento aplicado; súplica, petición, memorial; Am. ocurso; estudio, esmero, atención.
applied (apláid) adj. y p.p. aplicado, adaptado; utilizado; **— for** pedido, solicitado, encargado.

apply (aplái) v. aplicar(se); apropiar; acomodar; adaptar, destinar; **to — to** dirigirse a, acudir a, recurrir a; **to — for** solicitar, pedir; **to — oneself** aplicarse.
appoint (apóint) v. designar, señalar, equipar, amueblar, asignar.
appointment (apóintment) s. nombramiento; designación, descripción.
apportionment (apórshonment) s. prorrateo, distribución, rateo.
appraisal (apréisal) s. tasación, aforamiento, valuación, tasa.
appraise (apréis) v. avaluar, aforar.
appreciable (apríshabl) adj. apreciable, apreciativo, perceptible, sensible, notable.
appreciate (aprishieit) v. apreciar, estimar; agradecer; **to — in value** subir de valor.
appreciation (aprishiéishon) s. apreciación, estimación, valuación, agradecimiento, alza.
apprehend (apréjend) v. aprehender, asir, prender, capturar, apiolar.
apprehension (aprejénshon) s. aprehensión, recelo, temor; captura.
apprehensive (aprejénsiv) adj. aprensivo, receloso, tímido.
apprentice (apréntis) s. aprendiz, novicio, tirón; v. poner de aprendiz.
apprenticeship (apréntiship) s. aprendizaje, noviciado.
approach (apróuch) s. acercamiento; aproximación; entrada, acceso; **method of** — técnica o modo de plantear (un problema); v. acercarse, aproximarse; abordar (a alguien).
approbation (aprobéshon) s. aprobación, aceptación, beneplácito.
appropriate (aprópr:eit) adj. apropiado, apto, conveniente, a propósito v. apropiar.
appropriation (apropriéshon) s. apropiación; asignación, suma asignada.
approval (aprúval) s. aprobación; asentimiento.
approximate (aprócsimeit) adj. aproximado; aproximativo, próximo; v. aproximar, acercarse.
apricot (épricot) s. albaricoque, damasco. Am. chabacano.
April (épril) s. abril.
apron (épron) s. delantal, excusali, mandil; batiente de un dique.

apropos (apropó) adv. a propósito, oportunamente; pertinente.
apt (ápt) adj. apto, capaz; — **to** propenso a.
aptitude (áptitiud) s. aptitud, capacidad; habilidad.
aquarium (akuériom) s. acuario; pecera.
aquatic (akuátic) adj. acuático.
aqueduct (ákueduct) s. acueducto; Am. cañería.
Arab (árab) adj. y s. árabe, arábico.
arbiter (árbiter) s. árbitro, juez árbitro; arbitrador.
arbitrary (árbitreri) adj. arbitrario, despótico.
arbitrate (árbitreit) v. arbitrar, decidir, someter al arbitraje.
arbitration (arbitréshon) s. arbitraje, arbitración.
arbitrator (árbitretor) s. arbitrador; medianero, tercero, ponente.
arbor (árbor) s. emparrado, enramada, glorieta; (mec) eje, tambor.
arc (ark) s. arco, — **lamp** lámpara de arco.
arcade (arkéid) s. arcada, galería, soportal, pasaje.
arch (arch) s. arco, bóveda; v. arquear, encorvar, enarcar, abovedar; **semicircular** — arco de medio punto; —**enemy** enemigo acérrimo; adj. travieso, inquieto, picaresco, socarrón, astuto.
archaic (arkéic) adj. arcaico, desusado, anticuado.
archbishop (archbíshop) s. arzobispo, metropolitano.
archipelago (arkipélago) s. archipiélago.
architect (árkitect) s. arquitecto.
architectural (arkitékchural) adj. arquitectónico.
architecture (árkitekchur) s. arquitectura.
archway (árchuei) s. pasadizo (bajo un arco); pasaje abovedado.
arctic (árctic) adj. ártico.
ardent (árdent) adj. ardiente; apasionado, fogoso.
ardor (árdor) s. ardor; enardecimiento; pasión.
arduous (árduous) adj. arduo, difícil.
are (ar) 2ª persona y pl. del presente de indic. del verbo **to be:** eres, estas; somos, estamos; sois.
area (érea) s. área, superficie; espacio; patio, corral.
arena (arína) s. arena, liza, redondel, plaza.

Argentine (áryentin) adj. y s. argentino.
argue (árguiu) v. argüir, debatir; disceptar; **to** — **into** persuadir a.
argument (árguiument) s. argumento, tema, asunto; razonamiento.
arid (árid) adj. árido, seco, enjuto.
arise (aráis) v. levantarse, ponerse en pie; elevarse, surgir.
arisen (arálsen) p.p. de **to arise.**
aristocracy (aristócraci) s. aristocracia.
aristocrat (arístocrat) s. aristócrata.
aristocratic (aristokrátik) adj. aristocrático.
arithmetic (arízmetic) s. aritmética.
ark (ark) s. arca; — **of Convenant** arca del testamento; arca de la alianza; **Noah's** — arca de Noé.
arm (arm) s. brazo, arma; pata delantera; miembro; brazo de mar, vara o rama; Am. de brazo, de brazos; **at** —**'s length** a una brazada; **arm's reach,** alcance, **fore** — antebrazo.
armada (armáda) s. armada, flota.
armament (ármament) s. armamento.
armature (ármachur) s. armadura.
armchair (ármchear) s. sillón, butaca, silla de brazos.
armful (ármful) s. brazada.
armistice (ármistis) s. armisticio.
armor (ármor) s. armadura, arnés, blindaje, coraza; v. acorazar.
armored p.p. blindado, acorazado.
armory (ármory) s. armería; arsenal, maestranza.
armpit (ármpit) s. sobaco.
army (ármi) s. ejército; muchedumbre; **Salvation** — Ejército de Salvación; — **doctor** médico militar: **regular** — tropa de línea.
aroma (aróma) s. aroma, fragancia.
aromatic (aromátic) adj. aromático.
arose (aróus) pret. de **to arise.**
arouse (aráus) v. despertar, mover, recordar (al dormido); excitar.
arraign (arréin) v. acusar, procesar criminalmente (a un criminal).
arrange (arréiny) v. arreglar; disponer, poner en orden, coordinar, hacer planes (para).
arrangement (arrényment) s. arreglo; disposición, preparativo, colocación, orden; convenio.
array (arréi) s. arreglo, formación, orden (de batalla), pompa; **to**

challenge the — poner en orden de batalla; ataviar, adornar.
arrears (arrírs) s. pl. atrasos, pagos o rentas vencidos y no cobrados; **in —** atrasado en el pago de una renta.
arrest (arrést) s. arresto, prisión, aprehensión; detención; v. impedir, detener, retener, atajar; reprimir, arrestar.
arrival (arráival) s. llegada, arribo; logro; **the new —s** los recién llegados.
arrive (arráiv) v. llegar, arribar, llevar a cabo, lograr; **to — at a result** lograr (o conseguir).
arrogance (árrogans) s. arrogancia;
arrogant (árrogant) adj. arrogante.
arrow (árrou) s. saeta, flecha.
arsenal (ársenal) s. arsenal.
arsenic (ársenik) s. arsénico.
art (art) s. arte, destreza; maña; **fine —s** bellas artes; **master of —s** licenciado en letras.
artery (árteri) s. arteria.
artichoke (ártichok) s. alcachofa.
article (ártikl) s. artículo; **— of clothing** prenda de vestir; **to be under —s** estar escriturado.
articulate (artíkiuleit) adj. articulado, claro, distinto; capaz de hablar; v. articular; enunciar, enlazar.
articulation (artikiuléshon) s. articulación.
artifice (ártifis) s. artificio; ardid.
artificial (artifíshal) adj. artificial.
artillery (artíleri) s. artillería.
artisan (ártisan) s. artesano; artífice.
artist (artist) s. artista.
artistic (artístic) adj. artístico; **—ally** adv. artísticamente.
as (as) adv. y conj. como; mientras; como, tan, igualmente; según, a medida que; **— you please** como usted quiera; **— good —** tan bueno como; **— I was writing** mientras yo escribía; **— much —** tanto como; **— long — you wish** todo el tiempo que usted quiera; **— for me** por lo que a mí me toca; **strong — he is** aunque es tan fuerte; **all such — went there** todos los que fueron allí.
ascend (asénd) v. ascender, subir; adelantar; elevarse.
ascension (asénshon) s. ascensión, (Ig.) la Ascensión de N. S. Jesucristo.
ascent (asént) s. ascenso, subida, elevación.
ascertain (ascertéin) v. averiguar.
ascribe (ascráib) v. atribuir, achacar, aplicar.
ash (ash) s. ceniza; **— tray** cenicero; **— pan** cenicero, cenizal; **— tree** fresno; **Ash Wednesday** Miércoles de Ceniza.
ashamed (ashéimd) adj. avergonzado, vergonzoso; **to be —** avergonzarse, tener vergüenza.
ashore (ashór) adv. a tierra, en tierra; **to run —** encallar, varar.
Asiatic (asiátic) adj. asiático.
aside (asáid) adv. aparte, al lado; a un lado; s. aparte (en un drama).
ask (ask) v. preguntar; pedir, rogar, solicitar; demandar; **to — in, up, down** rogar (a una persona) que entre, suba o baje.
askance (askáns) adv. de soslayo; al sesgo, oblicuamente, de reflejón; con desdén.
asleep (aslíp) adj. dormido, durmiendo; **to fall —** dormirse, quedarse dormido; **my arm is —** se me ha dormido el brazo.
asparagus (aspáragos) s. espárrago.
aspect (áspect) s. aspecto, cara.
asphalt (ásfalt) s. asfalto.
aspiration (aspiréshon) s. aspiración; anhelo, deseo.
aspire (aspáir) v. aspirar; anhelar, desear, ambicionar.
ass (as) s. asno, burro, borrico, jumento, pollino.
assail (aséil) v. asaltar, invadir, acometer, agredir, atacar.
assailant (aséilant) s. asaltador.
assassin (asésin) s. asesino.
assassination (asesinéshon) s. asesinato.
assault (asólt) s. asalto, acometida, ataque; insulto; ultraje; **— at arms** asalto de armas.
assay (aséi) s. (metal) ensayo, ensaye, toque, aquilatación, contraste v. ensayar (metales); analizar; examinar; contrastar.
assemble (asémbl) v. reunir(se), congregar(se), allegar(se); convocar; montar.
assembly (asémbli) s. asamblea; reunión, junta, congreso; montaje (de maquinaria)
assent (asént) s. asentimiento; consentimiento; aquiescencia; v. asentir, convenir, consentir.
assert (asért) v. afirmar, asegurar,

ASSERTION **ATTEND**

aseverar; **to — oneself** hacerse valer; sostener, defender.

assertion (asérshon) s. aserción, aserto, aseveración.

assess (asés) v. avaluar; tasar; asignar, amillarar; **to — damages** fijar los daños y perjuicios.

assessment (asésment) s. avalúo; tasa de tributación; impuesto; imposición.

asset (áset) s. cualidad, ventaja; cada partida del activo; **—s** (com.) activo; haber; capital, caudal.

assiduous (asíduous) adj. asiduo, constante, diligente.

assign (asáin) v. asignar; señalar, fijar, destinar; exponer.

assignment (asáinment) s. asignación; designación, señalamiento, cesión.

assimilate (asímileit) v. asimilar, asemejar, comparar; asimilarse.

assist (asíst) v. asistir, ayudar.

assistance (asístans) s. asistencia.

assistant (asístant) s. asistente, auxiliar, ayudante; adj. subordinado, auxiliar.

associate (asóshiet) s. socio, compañero, consocio, aparcero, colega, v. asociar(se), relacionar.

association (asociéshon) s. asociación, unión, asamblea, conexión.

assorted (asórtid) adj. surtido, ordenado, clasificado, coleccionado.

assortment (asórtment) s. variedad; colección ordenada; surtido.

assume (asiúm) v. asumir; tomar; arrogar, apropiar, usurpar; dar por supuesto; arrogarse, apropiarse.

assumption (asúmshon) s. suposición; toma, apropiación, presunción, asunción (de la Virgen).

assurance (ashúrans) s. seguridad, certeza; certidumbre, convicción; firmeza; arrojo, resolución.

assure (ashúr) v. asegurar, acreditar, afirmar, certificar; infundir confianza.

assuredly (ashúerdli) adv. ciertamente, seguramente, indubitablemente.

asterisk (ásterisk) s. asterisco.

astonish (astónish) v. asombrar, sorprender, enajenar, pasmar.

astonishing (astónishing) adj. asombroso, maravilloso, pasmoso.

astonishment (astónishment) s. asombro, espanto, sorpresa.

astound (astáund) v. pasmar; aterar, aturdir; confundir.

astride (astráid) adv. a horcajadas.

astronomer (astrónomer) s. astrónomo, planetario.

astronomy (astrónomi) s. astronomía.

Asturian (astiúrian) adj. y s. asturiano.

astute (astiút) adj. astuto, agudo, sagaz.

asunder (asónder) adj. separado; **to cut —** separar, apartar; dividir en dos.

asylum (asáilom) s. asilo; refugio; hospicio, retiro, sagrado; **orphan —** orfanato, casa de huérfanos; Am. orfanatorio.

at (at) prep. a; en.

atheist (ézeist) s. ateo, ateísta.

athlete (ázlit) s. atleta; gimnasta.

athletic (azlétic) adj. atlético.

athletics (azlétics) s. gimnasia; atletismo; deportes.

Atlantic (atlántic) adj. atlántico; s. el mar Atlántico.

atlas (átlas) s. atlas; (Arq.) atlante o telamón.

atmosphere (átmosfir) s. atmósfera; aire, medio ambiente, alcance.

atmospheric (atmosféric) adj. atmosférico.

atom (átom) s. átomo, molécula, corpúsculo; **— bomb** bomba atómica.

atomic (atómic) adj. atómico.

atone (atóun) v. expiar, purgar.

atonement (atóunment) s. expiación.

atrocious (atróshos) adj. atroz.

atrocity (atrósiti) s. atrocidad.

attach (atách) v. unir, juntar, pegar, adherir; asignar; atribuir.

attachment (atáchment) s. adhesión, apego, cariño, fidelidad, aficción.

attack (aták) s. ataque, agresión, acometimiento; arremetida.

attain (atéin) v. conseguir, ganar, lograr, procurar; alcanzar.

attainment (atéinment) s. logro, consecución; obtención; adquisición.

attempt (atémpt) s. intento, ensayo; experimento, esfuerzo. v. intentar; procurar; probar; ensayar; **to — the life of** atentar contra la vida de.

attend (aténd) v. atender; servir, acompañar, concurrir; asistir a.

ATTENDANCE

attendance (aténdans) s. asistencia; presencia; comparecencia.
attendant (aténdant) s. acompañante; sirviente, secuaz; cortesano; galán; adj. acompañante.
attention (aténshon) s. atención; miramiento; cuidado; urbanidad; **to pay or give —** prestar atención.
attentive (aténtiv) adj. atento, curioso; cortés, solícito, aplicado.
attest (atést) v. atestar; atestiguar; dar fe; certificar.
attic (átic) s. desván, sotabanco, camarachón.
attire (atáir) s. atavío; vestidura; adorno, ropa. v. ataviar.
attitude (átitiud) s. actitud, postura, ademán, posición.
attorney (atórni) s. apoderado; abogado; procurador; **— general** fiscal (de una nación o estado); **power of —** procuración, poder; **district —** fiscal de distrito.
attract (atráct) v. atraer; cautivar, llamar, captar, interesar.
attraction (atrécshon) s. atracción; atractivo, interés, aliciente; **—s** diversiones; lugares de interés.
attractive (atráctiv) adj. atractivo, seductor, simpático, atrayente.
attractiveness (atráctivnes) s. fuerza atractiva; gracia; atractivo.
attribute (atríbiut) s. atributo; honra. v. atribuir, aplicar, dar.
auction (ócshon) s. subasta, remate, almoneda; v. subastar, rematar.
audacious (odéshos) adj. audaz, osado, atrevido.
audacity (odásiti) s. audacia, osadía, descaro.
audible (ódibl) adj. oíble, perceptible, audible.
audience (ódiens) s. auditorio, público, concurrencia; audiencia, entrevista.
audit (ódit) s. intervención y ajuste de cuentas, comprobación; v. intervenir (cuentas).
auditor (óditor) s. interventor, revisor de cuentas; oyente; auditor.
auditorium (aditórium) s. auditorio, salón de conciertos o conferencias.
auger (óguer) s. barrena, taladro.
aught (ót) pron. algo, alguna cosa.
augment (ógment) v. aumentar.
augur (ógor) s. agorero; v. augurar, pronosticar; predecir.

AVOW

August (ógost) s. agosto.
aunt (ánt) s. tía.
auspicious (ospíshos) adj. próspero, benigno, propicio, favorable.
austere (ostír) adj. austero, adusto, riguroso, severo, rígido.
austerity (ostériti) s. austeridad, severidad; rigorismo.
Austrian (óstrian) adj. y s. austriaco.
authentic (ozéntic) adj. auténtico, legítimo, fehaciente, original.
author (ózor) s. autor; escritor.
authoritative (azóritetiv) adj. autorizado, autoritario, positivo, perentorio, terminante.
authority (azóriti) s. autoridad; potestad; poder legal, facultad; **to have on good —** saber de buena tinta.
authorize (ózorais) v. autorizar, facultar; acreditar, sancionar.
auto (óto) s. auto, automóvil.
automatic (otomátic) adj. automático; **—ally** adv. automáticamente.
automobile (otomobíl) s. automóvil.
autonomy (otónomi) s. autonomía.
autumn (ótem) s. otoño.
autumnal (otémnal) adj. otoñal, estival.
auxiliary (ogsíliari) adj. y s. auxiliar, auxiliador.
avail (avéil) v. aprovechar, beneficiar; **to — oneself** aprovecharse de, s. provecho, ventaja.
available (avéilabl) adj. útil, disponible, aprovechable, obtenible.
avalanche (ávalansh) s. avalancha, alud, torrente.
avarice (ávaris) s. avaricia, codicia, sordidez.
avaricious (avaríshos) adj. avaro; avariento, miserable.
avenge (avény) v. vengar, vindicar.
avenger (avényer) s. vengador.
avenue (áveniu) s. avenida, calzada.
aver (avér) v. asegurar, afirmar.
averse (avérs) adj. renuente, adverso.
aversion (avérshon) s. aversión.
avert (avért) v. apartar, desviar, evitar, impedir, conjurar.
aviation (aviéishon) s. aviación.
aviator (aviétor) s. aviador.
avocado (avocado) s. aguacate.
avoid (avóid) v. evitar, esquivar, eludir.
avow (aváu) v. confesar, reconocer, declarar, profesar, admitir.

avowal (aváual) s. declaración, confesión, profesión.
await (auéit) v. esperar, aguardar.
awake (auéik) adj. despierto, alerto. v. despertar.
awaken (auéiken) v. despertar(se).
award (auórd) s. sentencia, laudo, adjudicación; premio. v. asignar, otorgar, juzgar; adjudicar.
aware (auér) adj. cauto, consciente, orejeado, sabedor, enterado.
away (auéi) adv. lejos, fuera, adj. ausente; **to send —** despedir; **right —** ahora mismo; **to go —** irse; **to take — quitar; — with you** ¡márchate, vete de aquí!
awe (oh) s. pavor, miedo, espanto, temor; **to stand in —** tener miedo v. atemorizar, aterrar, amedrentar; maravillar; infundir miedo.
awful (óful) adj. tremendo, terrible, horroroso; impresionante, horrendo, terrorífico.
awhile (ajuáil) adv. (por) un rato; (por) algún tiempo.
awl (ól) s. lesna, punzón.
awning (óning) s. toldo, entalamadura.
awoke (auóc) pret. de **to awake**.
ax, axe (acs) s. hacha, segur.
axis (ácsis) s. eje, centro de rotación, pibote; (Bot.) centro.
axle (acsl) s. eje (de una rueda); **front —** eje delantero; **rear —** eje trasero; **— box** collarín.
Aztec (ástec) adj. y s. azteca.
azure (áyur) **azured** (áyurd) adj. azul, s. azur, azul celeste.

B

babble (bábl) s. balbuceo, charla; v. balbucear, parlotear, charlar.
babe (béib) **baby** s. nene.
baboon (babún) (zool) mandril.
baby (béibi) s. nene, criatura, bebé; adj. de niño; infantil; **— girl** nena.
bachelor (báchelor) s. bachiller, soltero, mancebo, célibe.
bacillus (bacílos) s. bacilo, microbio.
back (bac) s. espalda; lomo; espinazo; revés, respaldo (de silla), espaldar; reverso; **behind one's — a** espaldas de uno; **in — of** detrás de, tras; **to turn one's —** volver las espaldas; adj. posterior, trasero; retrasado; rezagado; **— pay** sueldo atrasado; **— and forth** de aquí para allá; **to come — regresar, volver; to give — devolver; respaldar, endosar; sostener, apoyar; retroceder; hacer retroceder; to — down** hacerse (para) atrás; de espaldas; **to take a — seat** humillarse; interj. ¡atrás!
backbone (bácboun) s. espinazo, espina dorsal; entrecuesto, cerro, firmeza, apoyo, sostén.
backer (báker) s. fiador, sostenedor, defensor, apostador.
background (bákgraund) s. fondo, último término; experiencia; lontananza; **to keep in the —** dejar en último término, mantenerse retirado.
backhand (bácjand) s. revés; escritura inclinada a la izquierda; irónico; **—ed remark** una ironía.
backing (báking) s. sostén, apoyo, garantía; avío, endoso, respaldo, forro, espaldar.
backward (bácuard) adj. atrasado, retrógrado; lerdo; tardo; huraño, perezoso; tímido, esquivo.
backwardness (bácuardnes) s. torpeza, timidez; negligencia; atraso.
backwards (bácuards) adv. hacia (o para) atrás; de espaldas; **to go — retroceder, andar hacia atrás.
bacon (béicon) s. tocino; lacón, **flitch of —** lonja de tocino.
bacteria (bactíria) s. pl. bacterias.
bacteriology (bacterióloyi) s. bacteriología, microbiología.
bad (bad) adj. malo; dañoso, perverso; podrido; depravado, nocivo, **to go from — to worse** ir de mal en peor; **to look — tener** mal aspecto; **—ly** adv. mal, malamente.
bade (béid) pret. del v. **to bid**.
badge (bady) s. distintivo, escarapela, insignia; condecoración, divisa; símbolo.
badger (bádyer) s. tejón; v. molestar, acosar, atormentar.
badness (bádnes) s. maldad; demasía.
baffle (báfl) v. frustrar, impedir, desconcertar, desbaratar, contrariar.
bag (bag) s. saco, costal, talega, bolsa, maleta, zurrón; **— pipe** gaita gallega; v. ensacar, cazar, agarrar; inflarse, entalegar.
baggage (báguey) s. bagaje, equipaje; coqueta, maula, buena al-

— 15 —

haja; — **car** vagón de equipajes; — **tag** marbete, etiqueta.

bail (béil) s. fianza, caución, fiador; asa, cogedero (de cubo o caldero); división entre los compartimientos de un establo, achicador; **to let out on** — poner en libertad bajo fianza; v. dar fianza; salir fiador.

bait (béit) s. cebo; anzuelo, añagaza, señuelo; atractivo, aliciente; v. tentar, atraer; cebar.

bake (béik) v. hornear, cocer al horno; desecar, endurecer.

baker (béiker) s. panadero, tahonero, pastelero.

bakery (béikeri) s. panadería, tahona, pastelería.

baking (béiking) s. hornada, cocimiento; — **pan** tortera o tartera; — **powder** levadura.

balance (bálans) s. balanza, balance; cotejo, comparación; equilibrio; péndula, volante de reloj; saldo (de una cuenta).

balcony (bálkoni) s. balcón, antepecho; galería (de teatro).

bald (bold) adj. calvo; pelón, escueto; sin vegetación; — **headed** calvo; — **spot** calva.

bale (béil) s. bala, paca, fardo. v. embalar, empacar, enfardar.

balk (bók) v. oponerse, frustrar, rebelarse, resistirse; encabritarse un caballo; **to** — **someone's plans** frustrar los planes de alguien.

ball (bol) s. bola, pelota, esfera, ovillo; bala (de cañón); **eye** — globo del ojo; **fancy** — baile de trajes; v. **to** — **up** enredar, confundir.

ballad (bálad) s. balada, copla, trova, cantinela.

ballast (bálast) s. lastre, balastre, grava; **to go in** — ir en lastre.

balloon (balún) s. globo aerostático; (quím.) redoma.

ballot (bálot) s. balota, papeleta para votar; voto, escrutinio; v. votar; — **box** urna electoral.

balm (bam) s. bálsamo, ungüento; v. embalsamar.

balmy (bámi) adj. balsámico, untuoso, fragante, calmante; algo loco.

balsam (bólsam) s. bálsamo; especie de abeto.

bamboo (bambú) s. bambú.

ban (ban) bando, pregón, edicto, proclama; excomunión, prohibición; —**s of marriage** amonestaciones; v. proscribir, prohibir, condenar.

banana (banána) s. banana, plátano; — **tree** banano; plátano.

band (band) s. banda; fleje, venda, lista, tira, cinta, franja; gavilla, cuadrilla, pandilla; **to** — **together** confederarse, unirse; — **saw** sierra de hoja sin fin.

bandage (bándey) s. vendaje, venda, faja; v. vendar.

bandit (bándit) s. bandido, bandolero.

bang (bang) s. golpe, detonación, estallido, porrazo; fleco de cabello sobre la frente; **to** — **the door** dar un portazo; v. golpear con estrépito; —! ¡pum!; salto, brinco; v. saltar.

banish (bánish) desterrar, deportar, proscribir; **to** — **fear** ahuyentar el temor.

banishment (bánishment) s. destierro, deportación, expulsión.

banister (bánister) s. barandal, pasamano, balaustre.

bank (bank) s. banco, banca; orilla, ribera, margen; terrero, loma, cuesta, escarpa; bajo, bajío, alfaque; adj. bancario; v. depositar en un banco; ladear (un aeroplano); **savings** — banco de ahorro; — **note** billete de banco; **to** — **upon** contar con.

bankbook (bánkbuk) s. libreta de banco.

banker (bánker) s. banquero.

banking (bánking) s. transacciones bancarias, la banca; adj. bancario; — **house** casa de banca.

banknote (bánknout) s. billete de banco.

bankrupt (bánkropt) adj. en quiebra, insolvente, quebrado, arruinado; v. quebrar.

bankruptcy (bánkroptsi) s. bancarrota, quiebra; **to go into** — declararse en quiebra.

banner (báner) s. bandera, insignia, estandarte, pendón; primero, principal, sobresaliente.

banquet (bánkuet) s. banquete, festín; v. banquetear.

baptism (báptism) s. bautizo, bautismo.

Baptist (báptist) s. bautista.

baptize (báptais) v. bautizar.

bar (bar) s. barra, barrote, tranca; v. atrancar; estorbar.

barbarian (barbérian) s. y adj. bárbaro, salvaje.

barbarous (bárbarus) adj. bárbaro, salvaje, troglodita, cruel.
barbecue (bárbekiu) s. Am. barbacoa; v. hacer barbacoa. Am. churrasco, v. churrasquear.
barbed (bárbd) adj. con púas; — **wire** alambre de púas.
barber (bárber) s. peluquero.
barbershop (bárbershop) s. peluquería, barbería.
bard (bard) s. bardo, vate, poeta; v. poner barda a un caballo.
bare (bér) adj. desnudo, raso, descubierto; mero, puro, solo; vacío, desamueblado; **to lay —** poner de manifiesto, descubrir; **— majority** escasa mayoría; **to ride — back** montar en pelo.
barefoot (bérfut) adj. descalzo, con los pies desnudos.
bareheaded (berjéded) adj. descubierto, sin sombrero.
barelegged (bérlegued) adj. en pernetas, sin medias.
barely (bérli) adv. apenas, puramente, escasamente; **— three pounds** escasamente tres libras.
bareness (bérnes) s. desnudez, flaqueza, miseria.
bargain (barguen) s. convenio, pacto, contrato; ganga, chiripa; trato o compromiso de compra o venta; **— sale** barata; **into the — de ganancia; to make a —** cerrar un trato; v. regatear o negociar; **— driver** regateador.
barge (bary) lanchón, barcaza, chalán.
bark (bark) s. ladrido, corteza de árbol; barco de vela; v. descortezar, raer, raspar; ladrar.
barley (bárli) s. cebada.
barn (barn) s. granero, troje, pajar, cuadra.
barnyard (bárniard) s. era, corral, patio de granja.
barometer (barómeter) s. barómetro.
baron (báron) s. barón.
barracks (bárraks) s. cuartel, barraca.
barrel (bárrel) s. barril, barrica, tonel, cuba; cañón de escopeta; v. embarrilar, envasar.
barren (bárren) adj. estéril, árido infructuoso; erial.
barrenness (bárrenes) s. aridez, infecundidad, esterilidad.
barrette (barrét) s. broche, prendedor para sujetar el pelo.
barricade (bárrikeid) s. barricada, empalizada, estacada; v. obstruir, cerrar con barricadas.
barrier (bárrier) s. barrera, cerca, valla, obstáculo.
barter (bárter). v. permutar, trocar, cambiar; s. trueque, tráfico, permuta.
base (béis) s. base, pedestal, fundamento; v. basar, apoyar, fundar; adj. bajo, vil, ruin, inferior.
baseball (beisbol) beisbol.
basement (béisment) s. sótano.
baseness (béisnes) s. bajeza, infamia, ruindad, vileza.
bashful (báshful) adj. tímido, corto, vergonzoso, modesto.
bashfulness (báshfulnes) s. timidez, vergüenza, cortedad, apocamiento.
basic (béisic) adj. básico.
basin (béisn) s. palangana, jofaina; estanque; dársena; tazón de fuente; **river —** cuenca de río.
basis (béisis) pl. **bases** (béisis) s. base, cimiento, pedestal, fundamento.
bask (bask) v. asolear, calentar al sol; tomar el sol.
basket (básket) s. cesta, canasta.
basketball (básquetbol) s. juego de basquetbol.
bass (bás) s. bajo (en música); esparto; **— drum** tambora, bombo; **— horn** tuba.
bastard (bástard) s. y adj. bastardo.
baste (beist) v. hilvanar, bastear, embastar; pringar, lardar.
bat (bat) s. palo; Am. bate (de beisbol); murciélago; v. apalear; garrotear, volear con un bat; pestañear.
batch (batch) s. hornada; colección; cochura.
bath (baz) s. baño, lavatorio.
bathe (bez) v. bañar(se), lavar.
bather (bézer) s. bañista.
bathhouse (bázjaus) s. casa de baños; bañadero.
bathrobe (bázrob) s. bata de baño.
bathroom (bázrum) s. baño, cuarto de baño.
bathtub (báztob) s. bañera, tina.
battalion (batálion) s. batallón.
batter (báter) s. batido, masa; talud; **to — down** demoler; v. apalear, cañonear.
battery (báteri) s. batería; acumulador; agresión, asalto.
battle (bátl) s. batalla, lucha, pelea, combate; acción de lucha; v. batallar, luchar; combatir.

battlefield (bátlfild) s. campo de batalla.

battleship (bátlship) s. buque de guerra, acorazado.

bawl (bol) s. aullido, grito; v. aullar; pregonar; vocear; chillar, desgañitarse.

bay (béi) s. bahía, rada, cala; ladrido, balido, aullido; laurel; adj. bayo; v. dar aullidos; **to hold at —** tener a raya; **— window** ventana saliente, mirador.

bayonet (béionet) s. bayoneta; v. cargar a la bayoneta.

be (bi) v. ser; estar.

beach (bich) s. playa, ribera, costa, orilla; v. varar, poner en seco (una embarcación), encallar; **— comber** ola de grandes dimensiones que avanza y rompe sobre la playa.

beacon (bíkon) s. faro, fanal.

bead (bid) s. cuenta (de rosario o collar, etc.), canutillo, mostacilla, chaquira; **—s** rosario; v. adornar.

beak (bik) s. pico (de ave); espolón (de nave).

beam (bim) s. rayo (de luz o de calor); sonrisa; madero, trabe; brazo de balanza; radio — línea de radiación, radiofaro; v. emitir (luz); brillar; sonreír, estar radiante de alegría; destellar, fulgurar.

beaming (bíming) adj. radiante, resplandeciente; alegre; vivo.

bean (bín) s. judía, habichuela; frijol; string **—s** ejotes; **to give a person —s** hacer pasar mal rato a una persona.

bear (ber) s. oso, osa; bajista (el que hace bajar los valores de la bolsa) Great **—** Osa Mayor; Little **—** Osa Menor; v. soportar, llevar, tolerar, aguantar, portar, cargar; producir; parir; dar a luz; sufragar; **to — down** deprimir, apretar; **to — a grudge** guardar rencor; **to — in mind** tener en cuenta; **to — on a subject** tener relación con un asunto; **to — oneself with dignity** portarse con dignidad.

beard (bírd) s. barba o barbas; aristas (de trigo o maíz); lengüeta de flecha; **—ed** adj. barbado; barbudo.

bearer (bérer) s. portador, mensajero.

bearing (béring) s. aguante; paciencia; parte, presencia; relación; conexión; rumbo; orientación; valor de una expresión; ball **— cojinete de bolas; beyond —** inaguantable, insufrible.

beast (bist) s. bestia, cuadrúpedo, animal.

beat (bít) s. golpe, pulsación, latido; compás; toque repetido; toque de tambor; v. pegar, batir, golpear, cascar, sacudir, azotar, pulsar, moler, marcar, latir, vencer, derrotar; **to — around the bush** andarse por las ramas; pret. y p.p. de **to beat**.

beaten (bíten) adj. batido, fatigado, trillado, asendereado.

beating (bíting) s. paliza, zurra, soba, pulsación, latido.

beatitude (biátitiud) s. beatitud; bienaventuranza.

beau (bo) s. galán, pretendiente.

beauteous (biútius) adj. hermoso, bello.

beautiful (biútiful) adj. bello, hermoso; adv. hermosamente.

beautify (biútifai) v. hermosear, acicalar, embellecer, adornar.

beauty (biúti) s. primor, belleza, hermosura, preciosidad; **— parlor** salón de belleza.

beaver (bíver) s. castor; piel de castor; sombrero de copa.

became (bikéim) pret. del v. to become.

because (bicós) conj. porque; **— of** prep. por, a causa de.

beckon (békon) s. seña, llamada; v. llamar a señas.

become (bicóm) v. convenir, parecer, sentar, hacerse, ponerse, llegar a ser; convertirse en; **to — crazy** volverse loco, enloquecer; **to — warm** enardecerse, acalorarse.

becoming (bicóming) adj. conveniente, correcto, decoroso, propio; that dress is **— to you** le sienta bien ese traje.

bed (bed) s. cama, lecho; capa, estrato, yacimiento; madre; álveo; armadura, macizo (de jardín) yacimiento (mineral); **— of state** cama de respeto; **to go to —** acostarse; **to put to —** acostar.

bedbug (bédbog) s. chinche.

bedclothes (bétclozs) s. pl. ropas de camas.

bedding (béding) s. colchones, ropa de cama; paja que se pone en el suelo para que descansen las caballerías.

bedroom (bédrum)s. alcoba, recámara.
bedside (bédsaid) lado de cama; at the — al lado de la cama; — table mesilla de noche.
bedspread (bédspred) s. colcha, sobrecama, telliza.
bedtime (bédtaim) s. hora de acostarse, hora de dormir.
bee (bí) s. abeja; reunión, tertulia; queen — abeja reina; worker — abeja obrera; to have a — in one's bonnet tener una idea metida en la cabeza.
beech (bích) s. haya, — nut nuez de haya, fabuco.
beef (bif) s. carne de res; dry — cecina; roast — rosbif.
beefsteak (bífstec) c. bistec o bisté.
beehive (bíjaiv) s. abejera, colmena, arna, abejar.
been (bín) p.p. del v. to be.
beer (bír) s. cerveza, cold — cerveza fría; — tavern cervecería.
beet (bít) s. remolacha, betabel.
beetle (bítl) s. escarabajo; pisón.
befall (bifól) v. sobrevenir, suceder, acontecer.
befallen (bifólen) p.p. de to befall.
befell (bifél) pret. de to befall.
befit (bifít) v. convenir; venir bien, cuadrar, ser propio o digno.
before (bifór) adv. delante, al frente; antes; con prioridad, ante; conj. antes (de) que.
beforehand (bifórjand) adv. de antemano, por adelantado, con anticipación, previamente; adj. acomodado; con recursos.
befriend (bifrénd) v. favorecer, patrocinar, amparar, proteger.
beg (beg) v. mendigar, pordiosear, rogar, suplicar; to — the question dar por sentado lo mismo que se arguye; I — your pardon perdone.
began (bigán) pret. de to begin.
beget (biguét) v. engendrar; causar, suscitar, producir.
beggar (béguer) s. mendigo, pordiosero, pobre, infeliz.
begin (biguín) v. comenzar, principiar, iniciar, empezar.
beginner (biguíner) s. autor, originador, principiante, novato.
beginning (biguining) s. origen, principio, comienzo; — with comenzando con o por; a partir de; at the — al principio.
begot (bigót) pret. y p.p. del v. to beget.
begotten (bigótn) p.p. de to beget.

beguile (bigáil) v. engañar, defraudar, seducir, pasar el tiempo.
begun (bigón) p.p. del v. to begin.
behalf (bijáf) s: a favor, en nombre, en defensa de; in my — en mi nombre, a mi favor; por mí; in his — en su defensa.
behave (bijéiv) v. portarse, conducirse, proceder (bien o mal); — yourself! ¡pórtese bien!
behavior (bijévior) s. proceder, conducta, comportamiento; modo de funcionar, marcha.
behead (bijéd) v. degollar, decapitar, descabezar.
beheld (bijéld) pret. y p.p. de to behold.
behind (bijáind) adv. atrás, detrás, en zaga; prep. tras, detrás de; después de; — one's back a espaldas o en ausencia de uno; — the scenes entre bastidores; to fall — atrasarse, retrasarse; — the times anticuado.
behold (bijóld) v. contemplar, ver, considerar, observar; —! he aquí.
behoove (bijúv) v. tocar, corresponder, atañer (a uno), incumbir.
being (bíing) s. existencia, ser o esencia; estado o condición; well — bienestar, bienandanza.
belated (biléited) adj. tardío, trasnochado.
belch (belch) v. vomitar, arrojar, echar de sí, eructar.
Belgian (bélyian) s. belga.
belief (bilíf) s. creencia, fe, confianza, opinión; credo; religión, parecer, opinión.
believable (bilívabl) adj. creíble.
believe (bilív) v. creer, confiar en, fiarse de; to make — pretender, fingir.
believer (bilíver) s. creyente, fiel.
belittle (bilítl) v. deprimir, menospreciar, dar escasa importancia, achicar.
bell (bel) s. campana, timbre, cow — cencerro, esquila; jingle — cascabel; clipper of — badajo.
bellboy (bélboi) s. botones, mozo de hotel.
belle (bel) s. beldad, mujer bella.
belligerent (belíyerent) adj. belicoso, beligerante, guerrero.
bellow (bélou) s. bufido, bramido, rugido; v. mugir, vociferar, gritar.
bellows (bélous) s. fuelle.
belly (beli) s. vientre, barriga, panza, estómago, entrañas.

belong (bilóng) v. pertenecer; atañer; concernir; ser natural de; it does not — here está fuera de lugar.
belongings (bilónguings) s. pl. posesiones, bienes, efectos, bártulos.
beloved (bilóvd) adj. caro, dilecto, querido, amado.
below (bilóu) adv. bajo, abajo, debajo, más abajo; en el infierno; — par a descuento, con pérdida; here — en este mundo.
belt (belt) s. cinturón, cinto, faja; correa; zona; sword — biricú; talabarte.
bemoan (bimóun) v. lamentar(se), quejar(se), deplorar.
bench (bench) s. banco, banca; tribunal; banqueta; asiento.
bend (bend) s. curva, vuelta, recodo; comba, encorvadura; codillo; nudo; v. torcer, combar; inclinar(se); someter(se), doblegar (se).
beneath (biníz) prep. debajo de, abajo, inferior a, indigno de.
benediction (benedícsho⁻) s. bendición.
benefactor (benefáctor) s. benefactor, bienhechor; fundador.
beneficent (benéfisnt) adj. benéfico.
beneficial (benefísal) adj. benéfico, ventajoso, útil, provechoso.
benefit (bénefit) s. beneficio; provecho, ventaja; pro, bien, privilegio, gracia; — performance función de beneficio; — by the advice aprovecharse de un consejo.
benevolence (benévolens) s. benevolencia, caridad, merced.
benevolent (benévolent) adj. benévolo, humano, gracioso.
benign (bináin) adj. benigno, afable, generoso, liberal.
bequeath (bikuíz) v. heredar, legar; trasmitir a la posteridad.
bequest (bikuést) v. legado, donación.
berate (biréit) v. regañar, reprender; reñir; zaherir.
berry (bérri) s. baya (como mora, fresa, etc.) grano (de café, etc.).
berth (berz) s. litera; espacio de almacenamiento; muelle; to give a wide — to apartarse de, pasar de lejos.
beseech (bisích) v. rogar, implorar.
beside (bisáid) prep. al lado de, cerca de, además de, fuera de.
besides (bisáids) adv. también, además, asimismo; prep. tras de, amén de; ultra; sobre.
besiege (bisíy) v. sitiar, asediar acosar, importunar.
besought (bisót) pret y p.p. de to beseech.
best (best) adj. mejor; óptimo, superior; superlativo de good (bueno); the — el mejor; lo mejor; — man padrino de boda; at — dado o supuesto lo mejor; a lo más; for the — con la mejor intención; to do one's — hacer todo lo posible; to make the — of sacar el mejor partido de.
bestow (bistóu) v. dar, conferir, otorgar, conceder; regalar; time well —ed tiempo bien empleado.
bet (bet) s. apuesta, v. apostar.
betake (bitéik) v. recurrir, acudir; to — oneself encaminarse, dirigirse, trasladarse.
betaken (bitéiken) p.p. de to betake.
betray (bitréi) v. traicionar, vender a uno; descubrir, revelar (un secreto); to — one's ignorance hacer patente su ignorancia.
betrayer (bitréier) s. traidor, traicionero.
betrothal (bitrózal) s. desposorio, compromiso, mutua promesa de matrimonio.
betrothed (bitrózt) adj. prometido, novio, futuro; desposado.
better (béter) adj. mejor, adv. mejor; — half media naranja; so much the — tanto mejor; to be — off estar en mejor posición o mejores condiciones; you had — más vale que, sería mejor que; to change for the — mejorar; to get — mejorar d⁻ salud, aliviarse; ser de mejor conducta; to — oneself mejorarse, mejorar de situación.
betterment (béterment) s. mejora, adelantamiento, mejoría.
between (bituín) prep. entre; adv. en medio de.
beverage (béverey) s. brebaje, bebida, potación.
bewail (biuéil) v. llorar, lamentar, sentir, plañir; quejarse de.
beware (biuér) v. cuidarse de, precaverse, guardarse de.
bewilder (biuílder) v. aturdir, confundir, perturbar, azorar, dejar perplejo; to be —ed estar aturdido o turbado, estar perplejo.
bewilderment (biuílderment) s.

perplejidad, azoramiento, aturdimiento.
bewitch (biuích) v. hechizar, embrujar, aojar; arrobar, fascinar, embelesar.
beyond (biyónd) adv. más allá, alliende, allá lejos; — **my reach** fuera de mi alcance; — **measure** desmesuradamente.
bias (báias) s. prejuicio, predisposición, sesgo, oblicuidad; v. predisponer, influir en; **to cut on the** — cortar al sesgo.
bib (bib) s. babero, pechero.
Bible (báibl) s. biblia.
bicker (bíker) v. altercar, reñir.
bicycle (báisikl) s. bicicleta, biciclo; v. andar en bicicleta.
bid (bid) s. postura, oferta; cotización; v. pujar, ofrecer, licitar; rogar, pedir, convidar; envidar (en naipes); **to** — **good-bye** decir adiós; **to** — **up** alzar la oferta en una subasta.
bidden (biden) p.p. **to bid** y **to bide**.
bide (báid) v. esperar, aguardar; sufrir, aguantar; **to** — **one's time** esperar su oportunidad.
bier (bir) s. féretro, ataúd; andas.
big (big) adj. grande, grueso, voluminoso; importante, imponente; — **Dipper** Osa Mayor; — **game** caza mayor; **to talk** — darse bombo; — **sister** hermana mayor; — **with child** encinta; **big-bellied** ventrudo, panzón, barrigón; — **hearted** magnánimo.
bigamy (bígami) s. bigamia.
bigot (bígot) s. fanático.
bigotry (bígotri) s. fanatismo, intolerancia.
bile (báil) s. bilis, hiel, cólera, enojo; mal genio.
bill (bil) s. cuenta, nota, factura; proyecto de ley; programa; cartel; billete de banco; pico de ave; — **of exchange** libranza, letra de cambio; — **of fare** la carta en un restaurant; — **of lading** talón o conocimiento de embarque; — **of rights** declaración de derechos; — **of sale** escritura de venta; **to** — **and coo** acariciarse y arrullarse como palomas.
billboard (bilbord) s. cartelera.
billfold (bilfold) s. cartera.
billiards (biliards) s. billar.
billion (bilion) s. billón; mil millones en Francia y Estados Unidos.

billow (bilou) s. oleada, ola grande, alzarse en olas.
bin (bin) s. hucha, arcón, depósito; **coal** — **carbonera**; **grain** — granero.
bind (báind) v. atar; unir, juntar; ligar, amarrar; obligar, precisar; vendar; ribetear; encuadernar; empastar; escriturar o contratar a alguno.
binding (báinding) s. encuadernación; cinta, faja, ribete; **cloth** — encuadernación en tela; **paper** — encuadernación a la rústica; adj. obligatorio.
biography (baiógrafi) s. biografía.
biology (baióloyi) s. biología.
birch (berch) s. abedul.
bird (bérd) s. ave, pájaro; persona extraña o mal vista; — **of prey** ave de rapiña; — **seed** alpiste; — **shot** perdigones.
birth (bérz) s. nacimiento; principio, origen; linaje; — **certificate** certificado o acta de nacimiento; — **control** control de la natalidad; **to give** — **to** dar a luz.
birthday (bérzdei) s. cumpleaños, natalicio.
birthplace (bérzpleis) s. lugar de origen; suelo natal.
birthright (bérzrait) s. derechos de nacimiento, naturalidad; primogenitura, mayorazgo.
biscuit (bískit) s. galleta, bizcocho, mollete, panecillo.
bishop (bíshop) s. obispo; alfil en el juego de ajedrez.
bison (báison) s. bisonte, búfalo.
bitch (bitch) s. perra, ramera, prostituta.
bite (báit) s. mordisco, bocado; picadura (de insecto); tarascada; v. morder, mordiscar, picar; **to** — **the dust** morder el polvo.
bitten (bitn) p.p. de **to bite**.
bitter (bíter) adj. amargo, agrio, acre; mordaz, satírico, rudo; enconado, encarnizado; **to figth to the** — **end** luchar hasta morir; —**ly** adv. amargamente, severamente.
bitterness (biternes) s. amargura, rencor, odio, inquina, tirria.
black (blak) adj. negro, obscuro; tétrico; horrible; funesto; atroz; — **and blue** cardenal, contusión; — **mark** estigma, mancha, deshonra; **to put down in** — **and white** poner por escrito; **lamp** — negro de humo; **ivory** — negro

— 21 —

marfil: — list lista de personas ~~sospechosas. [mora.
blackberry (blákberri) s. zarzamora, mora.
blackbird (blákberd) mirlo.
blackboard (blákbord) s. pizarrón, pizarra, encerado.
blacken (bláken) v. ennegrecer, teñir de negro, embetunar; difamar, denigrar.
blackhead (blákjed) s. espinilla.
blackish (blákish) adj. negrusco, bruno, oscuro.
blackmail (blákmeil) s. chantaje, extorsión; v. ejercer el chantaje.
blackness (blákness) s. negrura, oscuridad. |— shop herrería
blacksmith (bláksmiz) s. herrero;
bladder (bláder) s. vejiga; ampolla
blade (bléid) s. hoja de navaja, etc.; pala de remo; — of a propeller aspa de hélice; shoulder — espaldilla o paletilla.
blame (bléim) s. culpa, falta, delito; v. culpar, acusar.
blameless (bléimles) adj. intachable, inculpable.
blanch (blanch) v. blanquear, palidecer; pelar, mondar; escaldar.
bland (bland) adj. blando, suave.
blank (blánk) adj. en blanco, vacío; turbado, desconcertado; — cartridge cartucho vacío; — face cara sin expresión; — form esqueleto, forma en blanco; application — forma en blanco para hacer una solicitud; — verse verso libre; s. blanco, espacio, hueco, intermedio.
blare (bler) s. fragor, son de trompetas; clarinada; v. trompetear, proclamar; hacer estruendo.
blaspheme (blasfím) v. blasfemar, vilipendiar; renegar. [reniego
blasphemy (blásfemi) s. blasfemia.
blanket (blænkat) s. 1. manta frazada (Am.) 2. (fig.) manto. 3. to throw a wet b. on, echar un jarro de agua fría a; aguar (la fiesta, etc.).
blast (blast) s. ráfaga de viento, golpe de aire; resoplido; soplo; sonido de trompetas; silbido; explosión; — hole barreno de mina; v. barrenar, explotar, volar (con explosivos); — furnace alto horno.
blaze (bléis) s. llama, fuego, incendio; ardor, acceso; — of anger arrebato de cólera; v. arder, resplandecer; to — a trail marcar una senda.
bleach (blich) v. blanquear al sol desteñir(se); s. blanqueador.

bleachers (blíchers) s. pl. graderías; Am. glorietas.
bleak (blík) adj. yermo, raso, desierto, desabrigado; helado.
blear (blir) v. nublar(se) los ojos.
bleary (blíri) adj. lagrimoso, lagañoso; nublado, inflamado.
bleat (blit) s. balido; v. balar.
bled (bled) pret. y p.p. de to bleed.
bleed (blíd) v. sangrar, extorsionar; exudar (las plantas).
blemish (blémish) s. mancha, tacha, defecto, imperfección; deshonra; v. manchar, empañar.
blend (blend) mezcla, mixtura; gradación de colores, sonidos, etc. v. entremezclarse, graduar, armonizar colores o sonidos.
bless (bles) v. bendecir; God — you! ¡Que Dios te bendiga!
blessed (blésed) adj. bendito, santo, bienaventurado; feliz; the whole — day todo el santo día.
blessing (blésing) s. bendición, gracia divina; don, beneficio.
blest (blest) adj. blessed.
blight (bláit) s. tizón; pulgón; quemadura; roña; añublo; alheña, malogro; ruina; v. abrasar; marchitar, agostar; frustrar (esperanzas), atizonar, añublarse, agotarse.
blind (bláind) adj. ciego; oculto, escondido; oscuro, tenebroso; hecho a ciegas; — alley callejón sin salida; — flying vuelo a ciegas; — side el lado flaco; — of one eye tuerto; s. persiana, biombo, cortinilla; to be a — for some one ser tapadera de alguien; v. cegar, quitar la vista, ofuscar, obcecar; deslumbrar; —s blindajes, blinda.
blinder (bláinder) s. anteojera; Am. visera para caballos de tiro.
blindfold (bláindfold) v. vendar los ojos; adj. vendado (de ojos); s. ardid, engaño.
blindly (bláindli) adv. ciegamente, sin reflexión.
blindness (bláindnes) s. ceguedad; ofuscación, obcecación.
blink (blínk) s. pestañeo, guiño; parpadeo; v. parpadear, mirar con los ojos entreabiertos; guiñar.
bliss (blís) s. beatitud, bienaventuranza; arrobamiento, deleite, felicidad.
blister (blister) s. ampolla, vejiga;

BLIZZARD

v. ampollarse; avejigarse; —ing plaster epispástico.
blizzard (blísard) s. ventisca, ventisquero; desastre repentino.
bloat (blóut) v. inflar(se), hinchar; ahumar (arenques); entumecerse.
block (blók) s. bloque, trozo de piedra; zoquete; manzana de casas; Am. cuadra; horma de sombrero; obstrucción, obstáculo, estorbo; polea; **chopping** — tajo de cocina; **to — in o out delinear**, esbozar; bloquear, obstruir; **to — up a door** tapiar una puerta; parar la pelota; conformar o planchar un sombrero sobre la horma.
blockade (blokéid) s. bloqueo; obstrucción.
blockhead (blókjed) s. bruto, necio, tonto, zoquete.
blond(e) (blónd) adj. y s. rubio, blondo; Am. güero.
blood (blód) s. sangre; alcurnia, linaje, parentesco; vida, vitalidad, temperamento; **— count** análisis cuantitativo de la sangre; **— relative** pariente consanguíneo; **— vessel** vena; arteria; **in cold — a sangre fría.**
bloodshed (blódshed) s. matanza, derramamiento de sangre.
bloodshot (blódshot) adj. ensangrentado o inyectado de sangre.
bloodthirsty (blódzersti) adj. sanguinario, cruel, carnicero.
bloody (blódi) adj. sangriento, cruento, sanguinario, feroz.
bloom (blúm) s. floración, florecimiento, flor; lozanía; frescura; color rosado (en las mejillas); v. florear, florecer.
blooming (blúming) adj. floreciente, fresco, lozano, vigoroso.
blossom (blósom) s. flor, capullo, botón; niñez, juventud.
blot (blót) v. emborronar o manchar de tinta; secar con papel secante; manchar; **to — out** borrar, tachar, **this pen —s esta pluma echa borrones; blotting paper** papel secante.
blotch (blótch) v. emborronar o borronear, manchar.
blotter (blóter) s. papel secante, libro borrador.
blouse (bláus) s. blusa.
blower (blóuer) s. ventilador, soplador, fuelle; tapadera de chimenea.

BOARD

blown (blóun) p.p. y adj. soplado; inflado; **full — rose** rosa abierta.
blowout (blóaut) s. reventón de neumático; explosión de gas.
blowpipe (blóupaip) s. soplete; **glass blower's pipe** caña de soplar vidrio.
blue (blú) adj. azul; **the —s** tristeza; melancolía; fiel, leal; **— paper** papel heliográfico; **— print** copias heliográficas; v. teñir de azul, pavonar.
bluebell (blubel) s. campanilla (flor).
bluebird (blúberd) s. azulejo; pájaro azul.
bluejay (blúyei) s. azulejo; gayo.
bluff (blóf) s. escarpa, risco, farallón, acantilado; adj. francote, fanfarrón, farsante, enhiesto; v. alardear, hacer alarde, embaucar.
bluffer (blófer) s. fanfarrón, farsante; bravucón.
bluing (bluing) s. azul para la ropa; pavón; adj. pavonado.
bluish (blúish) adj. azulado, azulino, azulenco.
blunder (blónder) v. desatinar, disparatar, errar, equivocarse, hacer una pifia; s. despropósito, dislate; error craso; pifia.
blunt (blont) adj. romo, embotado; brusco, áspero, rudo, lerdo; Am. claridoso; v. despuntar, embotar.
blur (blór) s. borrón, mancha, nube, trazo confuso; v. empañar, manchar, nublar, ofuscar, ponerse borroso, indistinto.
blush (blósh) s. rubor, bochorno, sonrojo; v. ruborizarse, sonrojarse, ponerse colorado.
bluster (blóster) v. ventear, soplar con furia; fanfarronear, bravear; s. ruido, tumulto; ventolera, ventarrón; jactancia, fanfarria.
blustering (blóstering) adj. fanfarrón; **— style**, estilo hinchado.
boar (bour) s. jabalí; verraco.
board (bord) s. tabla, tablero; mesa, comida, manutención, pupilaje; junta, tribunal, consejo; cartón; **the —s** las tablas, escenario; **— and room** cuarto y comida; asistencia; **— of directors o of trustees** junta directiva; **free on — (f.o.b.)** franco a bordo; **to go by the —** caer al mar; arruinarse por completo; v. abordar, acometer, acercarse a; entablar; tomar a pensión, dar asis-

— 23 —

tencia; residir o comer (en casa de huéspedes).
boarder (bóurder) s. huésped, pupilo, pensionista.
boardinghouse (bórdingjaus) s. posada, casa de huéspedes, pensión.
boast (bóust) s. jactancia, vanagloria; ostentación, baladronada; alarde, bravata; v. jactarse, vanagloriarse; blasonar; ponderar; exaltar.
boastful (bóustful) adj. jactancioso
boastfulness (bóustfulnes) s. jactancia, ostentación, alarde.
boat (bóut) s. bote, buque, barco, lancha, batel, chalupa; ferry — vapor de río; tow o tug boat remolcador; — races regatas.
boathouse (bóutjaus) s. casilla o cobertizo para botes.
boating (bóuting) s. paseo en lancha, a bote; to go — pasear en bote.
boatman (bóutman) s. barquero, botero, lanchero.
bob (bob) s. meneo, sacudida; balancín; to wear a — llevar el pelo cortado a la romana; to — up aparecer de repente; to — up and down saltar, brincar; cabecear una embarcación.
bobwhite (bobjuáit) s. codorniz, perdiz.
bode (boud) pret. y p.p. de to bide.
bodice (bódis) s. corpiño, jubón.
bodily (bódili) adj. corpóreo, corporal; real, verdadero; adv. todos juntos, colectivamente; they rose — se levantaron todos a una, se levantaron todos juntos.
body (bódi) s. cuerpo; gremio, corporación; densidad, consistencia; carrocería de automóvil; fuselaje de aeroplano; — of water extensión de agua; politic — grupo político; estado.
bog (bog) s. pantano, fangal, ciénaga; v. sumergir en un pantano, hudirse; atascarse.
Bohemian (Bojímian) adj. y s. bohemio.
boil (boil) s. hervor, ebullición; tumorcillo, furúnculo; to come to a — soltar el hervor; v. hervir, cocer; bullir; to — down reducir por medio de cocción.
boiler (bóller) s. caldera, marmita, olla; palla; calorífero central.
boisterous (bóisteros)• adj. turbulento, ruidoso, bullicioso, estrepitoso; borrascoso.

bold (bold) adj. atrevido, osado, intrépido, arrojado; audaz; insolente; temerario; — cliff risco, escarpado; — faced descarado, desvergonzado.
boldness (bóldnes) s. atrevimiento, arresto, arrojo, intrepidez; audacia, descaro, desvergüenza.
bologna (bolón) s. especie de embutido.
Bolshevik (bólshevik) adj. y s. bolchevique.
bolster (bólster) s. travesero, larguero, almohadón; refuerzo, sostén, soporte; apoyo, puntal; v. sostener, apoyar, apuntalar; to — someone's courage infundir ánimo a alguien.
bolt (bolt) s. cerrojo, pasador, pestillo, perno, clavija; pieza o rollo de paño o papel; salida repentina; centella, rayo; fuga; v. cerrar con cerrojo; lanzarse, correr; to — out salir de golpe.
bomb (bómb) s. bomba; v. bombardear.
bombard (bombárd) v. bombardear, cañonear.
bombardier (bombardír) s. bombardero.
bombardment (bombárdment) s. bombardeo, cañoneo.
bombastic (bombástic) adj. ampuloso, altisonante, retumbante.
bomber (bómber) s. bombardero, avión de bombardeo.
bonbon (bónbon) s. bombón, confite.
bond (bond) s. lazo, atadura, ligadura; parentesco, unión, bono.
bondage (bóndey) s. cautiverio, servidumbre, esclavitud, obligación.
bondsman (bóndsman) s. fiador, dita.
bone (bóun) s. hueso; espina, raspa; cuesco de fruta; barba de ballena; restos, osamenta; to have a — to pick with any one tener que habérselas con alguno; — of contention materias de discordia.
bonfire (bónfair) s. hoguera, fogata.
bonnet (bónet) s. gorra, toca, capota, sombrero (de mujer).
bonus (bónos) s. prima, premio, gratificación; adehala.
bony (bóni) adj. huesudo, osudo.
boo (bu) v. mofarse, burlarse de; —! interj. ¡bu!; —s s. pl. rechifla, gritos de mofa.

BOOK

book (buk) s. libro, tomo; libreta donde se escriben las apuestas; **cash —** libro de caja; **day —** diario; **invoice —** libro de facturas; **memorandum —** libreta; **on the —s** cargado a cuenta; **to keep —s** llevar los libros de contabilidad; **paper —** libro en blanco.
bookcase (búkeis) s. armario o estante para libros, estantería.
bookkeeper (búkiper) s. tenedor de libros, contador.
bookkeeping (búkiping) s. teneduría de libros, contabilidad; **doubly entry —** partida doble.
booklet (búklet) s. librillo, librito, cuaderno, folleto, opúsculo.
bookseller (búkseler) s. librero.
bookshelf (búkshelf) s. estante, repisa para libros.
bookshop (búkshop) s. librería.
bookstore (búkstor) s. librería.
boom (bum) s. estampido; alza, auge (en el mercado o bolsa); botalón; botavara; cadena para cerrar un puerto; v. rugir, resonar, hacer estampido; estar en auge, medrar, florecer; fomentar, dar bombo; prosperar; anunciar.
boon (bun) s. don, dádiva, regalo; gracia, merced; adj. jovial.
boor (bur) s. patán, aldeano, villano, hombre zafio, grosero, rústico.
boorish (búrish) adj. agreste; zafio.
boost (bust) s. empuje; empujón (de abajo arriba), alza, ayuda, asistencia; **— in prices** alza de precios; v. empujar, alzar, levantar, hacer subir.
boot (but) s. bota, calzado; **to —** de ganancia, de pilón, de ñapa; provecho, utilidad, ventaja; **to — out** echar a puntapiés, a patadas.
bootblack (bútblak) limpiabotas.
booth (buz) s. casilla, puesto, mesilla en una feria o mercado.
bootlegger (bútleguer) s. contrabandista, traficante clandestino de bebidas alcohólicas.
bootlicker (bútliker) s. servilón, zalamero.
booty (búti) s. botín, presa, saqueo.
border (bórder) s. borde, orilla, margen; frontera, límite, confín; orla, cenefa, ribete; v. orlar, guarnecer (el borde); lindar, **to — on o upon** confinar con, colindar, limitar; **it —s on madness** rayar en locura.

BOUND

bore (bor) s. taladro, barreno, perforación; calibre; persona o cosa aburrida; v. taladrar, barrenar, horadar; molestar, incomodar, aburrir, fastidiar.
bored (bórd) adj. fastidio, aburrido, cansado. p.p. de **to bore**.
boredom (bórdom) s. aburrimiento, tedio, fastidio, hastío.
boring (bóring) adj. aburrido, hastiado, fastidioso, tedioso.
born (born) adj. nacido, destinado; **to be —** nacer; **first —** primogénito.
borne (born) p.p. de **to bear**.
borough (bóro) s. suburbio, distrito de municipio; villa.
borrow (bórrou) v. pedir prestado, tomar fiado; hacerse suyo; copiar.
borrower (bórrouer) s. prestatario.
bosom (búsom) s. seno, pecho, corazón; afecto; íntimo, querido; pechera; **in the — of the family** en el seno de la familia; **— friend** amigo íntimo.
boss (bos) s. jefe, amo, patrón, capataz, cabecilla; **political —** cacique político; v. mandar, dominar, dirigir; regentear.
bossy (bósi) adj. mandón, autoritario.
botany (bótani) s. botánica.
both (boz) adj. y pron. ambos, entrambos, los dos; **— this and that** tanto esto como aquello; **— of us** nosotros dos, **— his** sons sus dos hijos.
bothersome (bódersom) adj. molesto, cargante, fastidioso.
bottle (bótl) s. botella, frasco, redoma; v. embotellar, enfrascar.
bottom (bótom) s. fondo, base, fundamento; asiento (de una silla); **to stand on one's own —** depender de uno mismo.
boudoir (buduár) s. tocador.
bough (bau) s. rama de un árbol.
bought (bot) pret y p.p. de **to buy**.
boulder (bóulder) s. peña, roca, guijarro grande, canto rodado.
bounce (báuns) s. salto, brinco; bote, rebote; v. saltar, brincar; despedir de un empleo; jactarse.
bound (báund) s. límite, término, confín; adj. ligado; atado; ceñido; encuadernado; obligado; destinado; **to be — for** ir con destino a; **to be — up in one's work** estar absorto o enfrascado en su trabajo; **it is — to happen** tiene que suceder; **homeward —** en

— 25 —

viaje de regreso; I am — to do it estoy resuelto o decidido a hacerlo; v. botar, saltar; deslindar, parcelar, limitar, ceñir; cercar; pret y p.p. de to bind.

boundary (báundari) s. límite, linde, frontera; término, coto.

boundless (báundles) adj. ilimitado, infinito, sin término.

bountiful (báuntiful) adj. dadivoso, generoso, bienhechor, liberal.

bounty (báunti) s. largueza, generosidad, munificencia; merced, gracia; premio, recompensa.

bouquet (buké) s. ramo, ramillete; aroma de los vinos; fragancia.

bourgeois (buryuá) adj. y s. burgués; común, ordinario; comerciante, industrial.

bout (báut) s. combate, lucha, contienda, asalto; vez, turno; a — of pneumonia un ataque de pulmonía.

bow (bou) s. arco (de violín o flecha) lazo, moño (de corbata o listón); — legged patizambo; v. arquear, encorvar; tocar con arco.

bowels (báuels) s. pl. entrañas, intestinos, tripas.

bower (báuer) s. enramada, glorieta, cenador; morada, domicilio; músico de arco; arquero.

bowl (boul) s. cuenco, tazón, escudilla; jícara; bolo, boliche; wash — palangana; lavamanos; —s juego de bolos; v. jugar al boliche; derribar, hacer rodar.

box (bóks) s. caja, estuche, cofre, arca; palco de teatro; bofetada; — car furgón; — office taquilla; v. encajonar; boxear; cambiar de opinión o color político.

boxer (bóxer) s. boxeador, púgil.

boxing (bóksing) s. boxeo, pugilato.

boy (boi) s. niño, muchacho, mozo.

boycott (bóikot) v. boicotear, coaligarse para no tener tratos con alguien o comprarle mercancías.

boyhood (bóijud) s. niñez, mocedad.

boyish (bóish) adj. infantil, pueril; amuchachado.

brace (breis) s. traba, abrazadera, tirante; apoyo, refuerzo; llave; herbiquí; v. trabar, apuntalar, reforzar, apoyar; estimular, vigorizar (los nervios); to — up animarse, cobrar ánimo.

bracelet (bréislet) s. brazalete, pulsera.

bracket (bráket) s. ménsula, soporte, rinconera; puntal; —s paréntesis; v. poner entre paréntesis; agrupar.

brag (brag) s. jactancia, bravata; v. jactarse, alardear.

braggart (brágart) adj. y s. jactancioso, fanfarrón.

braid (bréid) s. trenza, cordón, galón alamar; v. trenzar, galonear.

brain (brein) s. cerebro, seso; entendimiento, juicio, cordura, to rack one's —s devanarse los sesos, romperse la cabeza.

brake (bréik) v. freno, retranca, garrote; — lining forro de freno; to apply the —s frenar, enfrenar; Am. retrancar; dar garrote.

brakeman (bréikman) s. guardafreno, retranquero, garrotero.

bramble (brambl) s. zarza, breña.

bran (bran) s. salvado.

branch (branch) s. rama; ramo; sucursal, dependencia; bifurcación; ramal, empalme; afluente; — railway ramal; ramificarse, bifurcarse; to — off dividirse, separarse; to — out ampliar, extenderse.

brand (brand) s. sello o marca de fábrica; — iron hierro de marcar reses; estigma; — new nuevecito, flamante, acabado de hacer o comprar; difamar, infamar; to — as motejar de.

brandish (brándish) v. blandir, cimbrar; floreo, molinete, blandear.

brandy (brandi) s. aguardiente, coñac.

brass (bras) s. latón, bronce; descaro, desvergüenza; desfachatez; —es utensilios de latón; instrumentos musicales de metal; — foundry fundición de bronce.

brassiere (brasír) s. portabusto, corpiño.

brat (brat) s. rapaz, mocoso.

bravado (bravédo) s. bravata, baladronada; jactancia.

brave (bréiv) adj. bravo, valiente, denodado, bizarro, esforzado, animoso, atrevido; v. desafiar, hacer frente a.

bravery (bréveri) s. valor, ánimo.

brawl (brol) v. alboroto; reyerta; v. armar camorra, alborotar, reñir; vociferar, vocinglear.

bray (brei) s. rebuzno; v. majar.

brazen (brésn) adj. bronceado; descarado, desvergonzado.

breach (brich) s. brecha, abertura; fractura, rotura; infracción; rom-

BREAD — **BRIGHTNESS**

bread pimiento; contravención; disensión, escisión; — **of trust** abuso de confianza; v. abrir brecha.
bread (bred) s. pan, sustento; **slice of** — rebanada de pan.
breadth (bredz) s. anchura, holgura, extensión, amplitud.
break (bréik) s. rompimiento, desgarro; grieta; pausa; interrupción; baja en el mercado; v. romper, quebrar; infringir, violar; arruinar, to — **away** fugarse, escaparse; to — **into** allanar, forzar la entrada; to — **out** estallar (una guerra); to — **a promise** faltar a la palabra; to — **up** desmenuzar, despedazar; to **make a bad** — cometer un disparate; to **have a good** — tener suerte; to — **open** forzar, fracturar; to — **upon** comprender repentinamente; to — **forth** brotar; to — **the law** infringir la ley.
breakable (bréikabl) adj. quebradizo, frágil.
breaker (bréiker) s. rompimiento, roturador; infractor; quebrantador.
breakfast (brékfast) s. desayuno, almuerzo; **to eat** — tomar el desayuno; v. desayunar(se).
breakwater (bréikuoter) s. rompeolas, tajamar, malecón, escollera.
breast (brest) s. pecho, seno; peto; pechuga (de ave); corazón, interior del hombre.
breath (brez) s. aliento, respiración, resuello; hálito, soplo; vida; instante; pausa, demora; un momento; **foul** — mal aliento; **out of** — sin aliento.
breathe (briz) v. respirar, alentar; tomar aliento; resollar; aspirar; to — **into** infundir; **he —ed his last** exhaló el último suspiro; to — **upon** empañar.
breathless (brézles) adj. jadeante; sin aliento, desalentado.
bred (bred) pret. y p.p. de **to breed**.
breeches (bríches) s. y pl. bragas; calzones, pantalones (cortos).
breed (brid) s. casta, raza; ralea, progenie; generación; v. criar, procrear, engendrar, multiplicarse; reproducirse.
breeder (bríder) s. criador, animal de cría.
breeding (bríding) s. cría, crianza, educación, urbanidad, modales.
breeze (bris) s. brisa, airecillo.
breezy (brísi) adj. airoso, oreado,

animado, jovial, vivaz; **it is** — hace brisa.
brethren (brézren) s. pl. hermanos (los fieles de una religión o de una sociedad).
brevity (bréviti) s. brevedad, concisión.
brew (brú) s. cerveza; mezcla; v. fermentar, hacer cerveza; fomentar, tramar, urdir; fraguar; **a storm is brewing** amenaza una tormenta.
brewery (brúri) s. cervecería, fábrica de cerveza.
briar o **brier** (bráiar) s. zarza; rosal silvestre.
bribe (braib) s. soborno, cohecho; v. sobornar, cohechar.
bribery (bráiberi) s. soborno, cohecho.
brick (brik) s. ladrillo; v. enladrillar.
brickbat (bríkbat) s. pedazo de ladrillo; tejoleta.
bridal (bráidal) adj. nupcial; de bodas, de novia; — **dress** vestido de novia.
bride (braid) s. novia, desposada.
bridegroom (bráidgrum) s. novio, desposado.
bridesmaid (bráidsmeid) s. madrina de boda.
bridge (bridy) s. puente; caballete de la nariz; **draw** — puente levadizo; **suspension** — puente colgante; v. construir o levantar un puente; to — **a gap** llenar un vacío.
bridle (braidl) s. brida o freno de caballo; freno, sujeción; — **path** camino de herradura; v. embridar, enfrenar, reprimir, refrenar, erguir o levantar la cabeza.
brief (brif) adj. breve, conciso, corto, sucinto; s. epítome, resumen, sumario; escrito, memorial; —**ly** brevemente, en resumen, en breve.
briefcase (brífkeis) s. portafolio, portapapeles, maletín de cuero.
brigade (briguéid) s. brigada.
bright (bráit) adj. brillante, resplandeciente, reluciente, radiante; esclarecido, inteligente; — **color** color subido.
brighten (bráiten) v. pulir, bruñir, pulimentar; abrillantar, dar lustre; avivar(se); aclarar; animar(se).
brightness (bráitnes) s. brillo, resplandor, lustre, claridad, viveza, inteligencia, agudeza de ingenio.

— 27 —

brilliance (brílians) s. brillantez, brillo, resplandor, fulgor, lustre.
brilliant (bríliant) adj. brillante, refulgente, radiante, esplendoroso; talentoso; s. brillante.
brim (brim) s. borde, margen, orilla; ala (de sombrero); **to fill to the —** llenar hasta el borde; **to be filled to the —** estar hasta los topes; v. **to — over** rebosar.
brine (brain) s. salmuera.
bring (bring) v. llevar o traer, acarrear; ocasionar, causar; inducir, persuadir; **to — about** efectuar; producir; **to — down** bajar; deprimir, humillar; **to — forth** dar a luz; poner de manifiesto; parir; **to — to** sacar de un desmayo; **to — up** criar, educar; **to — up a subject** traer a colación un asunto.
brink (brink) s. borde, orilla, margen; **on the — of** al borde de.
brisk (brisk) adj. vivo, activo, animado, fuerte, rápido; **—ly** aprisa, vivamente.
bristle (bristl) s. cerda; v. erizar(se); **to — with** estar erizado o lleno de.
bristly (brístli) adj. cerdoso, hirsuto, erizado.
British (brítish) adj. británico.
brittle (britl) adj. quebradizo, frágil.
broach (brouch) v. traer a colación, mencionar por primera vez.
broadcast (bródcast) s. radiodifusión, difusión, transmisión; v. esparcir, diseminar, propalar.
broadcloth (bródkloz) s. paño fino de algodón o de lana.
brocade (brokéid) s. brocado.
broil (broil) v. asar; soasar, padecer calor.
broke (brouk) pret. de **to break**; adj. quebrado, arruinado; hacer de corredor; **to go —** quebrar, arruinarse.
broken (bróken) adj. roto, quebrado; arruinado; chapurrado, mal pronunciado.
broker (bróker) s. corredor, agente, cambista.
bronchitis (bronkáitis) s. bronquitis.
bronco, broncho (brónkou) s. potro o caballo bronco; **— buster** domador.
bronze (brons) s. bronce; color de bronce; v. broncear.
brooch (bruch) s. broche, prendedor, imperdible.

brood (brud) s. pollada, cría; casta, ralea; v. empollar; **to — over** cavilar.
brook (bruk) s. arroyuelo, arroyo; cañada, quebrada; v. aguantar, tolerar.
broom (brúm) s. escoba; retama (arbusto); **— stick** palo de escoba.
broth (broz) s. caldo.
brother (bróder) s. hermano, cofrade.
brotherhood (bróderjud) s. hermandad, fraternidad, cofradía, congregación.
brother-in-law (bróderinlo) s. cuñado.
brotherly (bróderli) adv. fraternalmente; adj. fraternal.
brought (bröt) pret. y p.p. **to bring**.
brow (brau) s. ceja, sien, frente.
brown (braun) adj. moreno, castaño, pardo, oscuro, tostado; v. tostar(se), broncear(se); **— paper** papel de estraza.
browse (braus) v. hojear, ramonear, tascar, pacer (el ganado).
bruise (brus) s. moretón, contusión, cardenal; v. magullar, estropear.
brunet o **brunette** (brunét) adj. moreno, trigueño.
brush (brosh) s. cepillo, brocha, pincel; escaramuza, pelea; matorral, breñal; v. acepillar, rozar; **— aside** desechar, echar a un lado; **— away** restregar duro.
brushwood (bróshud) s. matorral, breñal, zarzal; maleza.
brusque (brusk) adj. brusco, rudo.
brutal (brútal) adj. brutal, bestial, inhumano, salvaje.
brutality (brutáliti) s. brutalidad.
brute (brút) s. bruto, bestia; adj. montaraz, irracional, feroz.
bubble (bóbl) s. burbuja, ampolla, borbollón; v. bullir, hervir; hacer burbujas; **to — over with joy** rebosar de gozo.
buck (bok) s. gamo; macho cabrío; macho (del ciervo, liebre, conejo, etc.); respingo (de un caballo); embestida; **— private** soldado raso; **to pass the —** Am. pasar el fardo; v. cabriolar, respingar, embestir; **to — up** cobrar ánimo, apresurarse; **the horse —ed the rider** el caballo tiró al jinete.
bucket (bóket) s. cubo, cubeta, balde; **to pass the —** poner a alguien en aprietos.

— 28 —

buckle (bócl) s. hebilla; bucle; v. abrochar con hebilla; doblarse, encorvarse; to — down to aplicar(se) con empeño; to — with luchar con, encontrarse con.

buckshot (bócshot) s. posta, perdigón.

buckwheat (bókjuit) s. trigo, alforfón, sarracena.

bud (bod) s. botón, yema; pimpollo; brote, cogollo; capullo de una flor; v. florecer, brotar.

buddy (bódi) s. camarada.

budge (body) v. mover(se); hacer lugar; menearse.

budget (bódyet) s. morral, saco, mochila, presupuesto.

buff (bof) s. piel de ante o búfalo; pulidor cubierto de cuero.

buffalo (bófalou) s. búfalo.

buffet (bufét) s. aparador; repostería, copero; caja de órgano; mostrador para refrescos.

buffoon (bufún) s. bufón, payaso.

bug (bug) s. insecto, chinche.

buggy (búgui) s. cochecillo.

bugle (biúgl) s. clarín, corneta.

build (bild) s. estructura; talle, forma, figura; to — up one's health reconstruir su salud; v. edificar, construir, fabricar, erigir, labrar; formar.

builder (bílder) s. constructor.

building (bílding) s. edificio; obra; fábrica, construcción.

built (bilt) pret. y p.p. de to build.

bulb (bulb) s. bulbo (cebolla y otras plantas); cubeta del barómetro; ampolleta del termómetro, v. hincharse formando ampolla o bulto.

bulge (boly) s. pandeo, comba, bulto, protuberancia.

bulgy (bólyi) adj. abultado.

bulk (bolk) s. bulto, volumen; masa, balumba, magnitud, grosor.

bulky (bólki) adj. abultado, voluminoso, corpulento.

bull (bul) s. toro; Tauro; bula pontificia; disparate, despropósito; alcista (el que hace subir los valores de la bolsa); — fight corrida de toros; v. especular en alza.

bulldog (búldog) s. perro dogo.

bullet (búlet) s. bala (de fusil).

bulletin (búletin) s. boletín; — board tablilla.

bullfrog (búlfrog) s. rana grande.

bullion (búlion) s. oro (o plata) en barras; lingotes de oro o plata; — fringe galón o franja de oro.

bully (búli) s. espadachín, camorrista, matón; jaque, rufián; adj. excelente, magnífico; v. intimidar, echar bravatas.

bulwark (búlwarc) s. baluarte.

bum (bom) s. holgazán, vagabundo, sablista, gorrón; borracho; to go on a — irse de juerga; adj. malo, mal hecho, de ínfima calidad; inútil, inservible; to feel — estar indispuesto.

bumblebee (bómblbi) s. abejorro, abejón, moscón.

bump (bomp) s. tope, choque; golpe; chichón; giba; abolladura; barriga, comba; protuberancia; v. chocar, topetar; abollar; to — along zarandearse, ir zarandeándose; to — off matar; derribar.

bumper (bómper) s. defensa, parachoques; tope; copa o vaso lleno — harvest cosecha abundante.

bun (bon) s. bollo (de pan).

bunch (bónch) s. manojo, puñado, atado, hacecillo, mazo, racimo (de uvas); grupo; — of flowers ramillete de flores; v. juntar(se), agrupar(se), hacer racimos.

bundle (bondl) s. bulto, lío, fardo, hato, haz, paquete, envoltorio; v. liar, atar, envolver, empaquetar; to — up taparse, abrigarse bien.

bungalow (bóngalou) s. casita de un piso; casita de campo.

bungle (bóngl) v. chapucear; estropear, echar a perder.

bunion (bónion) s. juanete del pie.

bunk (bonk) s. litera, camilla (fija en la pared); embuste, tontería, paparrucha, papa.

bunny (bóni) s. conejito; ardilla.

buoy (bói) s. boya; boyar, mantener a flote; to — up sostener, apoyar.

buoyant (bóiant) adj. boyante, animado, alegre, vivaz.

burden (bórden) s. carga, peso, cuidado, gravamen; v. cargar, agobiar.

burdensome (bórdnsom) adj. gravoso, pesado, oneroso, molesto.

bureau (biúro) s. oficina, división, ramo; cómoda, papelera; travel — oficina de turismo; weather — oficina u observatorio de meteorología.

burglar (bórglar) s. ladrón.

burglary (bórglari) s. robo.

burial (bérial) s. entierro, sepelio.
burlap (bérlap) s. harpillera, guata; tela burda de cáñamo.
burly (bérli) adj. corpulento, nudoso, voluminoso, grandote.
burn (bern) s. quemadura; v. quemar, abrasar, incendiar, arder; **to — up** consumir con fuego.
burner (bérner) s. quemador, mechero, hornilla.
burnish (bérnish) s. bruñir, lustrar, pulir; s. bruñido, pulimento; satinado.
burnt (bernt) pret. y p.p. de **to burn**.
burst (berst) s. reventón, estallido, explosión; **— of laughter** carcajada; reventar, estallar; prorrumpir; **to — into** entrar de repente; **to — in tears** deshacerse en lágrimas; **to — with laughter** reventar de risa; **to — open** forzar, abrir con violencia; pret. y p.p. de **to burst**.
bury (béri) v. enterrar, sepultar, inhumar; **to be buried in thought** estar absorto, meditabundo.
bus (bos) s. autobús, ómnibus; camión de pasajeros, camioneta.
bush (bush) s. arbusto, mata, manigua; matorral, breñal; **rose —** rosal; **to beat around the —** andarse por las ramas.
bushel (búshel) s. fanega (medida de áridos).
bushy (búshi) adj. matoso, espeso, lleno de arbustos.
busily (bísli) adv. diligentemente.
business (bísnes) s. negocio, ocupación, empleo, quehacer, trabajo; comercio, asunto; **— house** casa o establecimiento comercial; **— transaction** transacción comercial; **to do — with** comerciar o negociar con; **he has no — doing it** no tiene derecho a hacerlo; **not to be one's —** no concernirle o importarle a uno; **to make a — deal** hacer un trato.
businesslike (bísneslaik) adj. práctico, eficiente, formal.
bust (bost) s. busto, pecho de mujer; **to go out on a —** ir de parranda; v. reventar, quebrar, domar, desbravar.
bustle (bóstl) s. bullicio, animación, alboroto, bulla; polisón; v. bullir; menearse; trajinar.
busy (bísi) adj. ocupado, activo, atareado; **— body** entrometido; **— street** calle de mucho tráfico.
but (bót) conj. prep. y adv. pero,

burial ... **bypath**

mas; sino, sin embargo, excepto; sólo, solamente; no más que; **— for** a no ser por; **not only... but also** no sólo... sino que también; **— little** muy poco; **— yet** sin embargo; **I cannot help —** no puedo menos de; **she is — a child** no es más que una niña; **last — one** penúltimo.
butcher (bútcher) s. carnicero; hombre cruel o sanguinario; v. matar (reses); **—'s shop** carnicería, hacer una matanza o carnicería.
butchery (bútcheri) s. matanza o carnicería.
butler (bótler) s. despensero, mayordomo; **—'s pantry** despensa.
butter (bóter) s. mantequilla; v. untar con mantequilla.
buttercup (bótercop) s. botón de oro (flor).
butterfly (bóterflai) s. mariposa.
buttermilk (bótermilk) s. suero de mantequilla.
butterscotch (bóterscotch) s. jarabe de azúcar y mantequilla.
buttocks (bótoks) s. pl. nalgas, asentaderas; ancas.
button (bótn) s. botón **— hook** abotonador; v. abotonar(se).
buttonhole (bótonjol) s. ojal; presilla; v. hacer ojales; **to — someone** detener, demorar a uno (charlando).
buttress (bótres) s. contrafuerte, estribo; sostén, apoyo; v. sostener, reforzar; poner contrafuerte.
buy (bai) v. comprar; **to — off** sobornar; **to — up** acaparar.
buyer (báier) s. comprador.
buzz (bós) s. zumbido, susurro, murmullo; v. zumbar, murmurar; **to — the bell** tocar el timbre.
buzzard (bósard) s. buitre, aura, zopilote; carancho; gallinazo.
by (bai) prep. por, a, en, junto, al lado de; de; con; según; **— and — luego**, pronto; **— dint of a** fuerza de; **— far** con mucho; **— then** para entonces; **— the way** a propósito; **— this time** en ese momento, ya; **—'s two o'clock** para las dos; **— day** de día; **day — day** días tras día.
bygone (báigon) adj. pasado; **let —s be —s** lo pasado pasado.
bylaw (báilo) s. estatuto, reglamento.
bypath (báipaz) s. senda, vereda, atajo.

by-product (báiprodoct) s. subproducto, derivados, producto secundario.
bystanders (báistanders) s. mirones, circunstantes, presentes.

C

cabbage (cábey) s. col, repollo, berza.
cabin (cábin) s. cabaña, choza, bohío, camarote; **airplane** — cabina de aeroplano.
cabinet (cábinet) gabinete, ministerio; armario, vitrina, escaparate.
cable (kéibl) s. cable, amarra; cablegrama; — **address** dirección cablegráfica; v. cablegrafiar.
cablegrama (kéiblgram) s. cablegrama.
cabman (cábman) s. cochero, chofer.
cackle (kákl) s. cacareo, charla, risotada; v. cacarear, parlotear.
cactus pl. **cacti** (kaktus) s. cacto.
cad (cad) s. canalla, malcriado.
cadence (cádens) s. cadencia, modulación, ritmo.
cadet (cádet) s. cadete.
café (café) s. café, restaurante.
cafeteria (cafetéria) s. restaurante (donde se sirve uno mismo).
cage (kéiy) s. jaula; v. enjaular.
calamity (calámiti) s. calamidad.
calcium (cálcium) s. calcio.
calculate (cálkiulet) v. calcular; computar, contar; **to — on** contar con.
calculation (kalculéshon) s. cálculo, cómputo, cuenta.
calculus (cálkiulos) s. cálculo.
calendar (kálender) s. calendario, almanaque; — **year** año corriente.
calf (káf) s. ternero, becerro; cervatillo; pantorrilla; — **skin** piel de becerro.
caliber (káliber) s. calibre.
calico (kálico) s. calicó, percal.
call (col) s. llamada; convocatoria; visita, pedido; aviso, señal; **within** — al alcance de la voz; v. llamar, gritar; convocar, citar; hacer una visita; nombrar; **to —at a port** hacer escala en un puerto; **to — for** requerir; ir por; **to — on** visitar; **to — together** convocar; **to — up** llamar por teléfono; **to — off** disuadir; revocar.
caller (cóler) s. visita; llamador.

callous (kélous) adj. calloso; duro; córneo, endurecido.
callus (kélos) s. callo, dureza.
calm (kám) s. calma, serenidad, sosiego; adj. quieto, sereno, calmado, sosegado, tranquilo; v. calmar, tranquilizar, sosegar, serenar; **to — down** calmarse; —**ly** adv. sosegadamente, con calma.
calmness (kámnes) s. calma, sosiego, tranquilidad, serenidad.
calorie (kálori) s. caloría.
calumny (kálomni) s. calumnia.
came (kéim) pret. de to come.
camel (cámel) s. camello.
camera (kámera) s. cámara fotográfica.
camouflage (kámuflay) s. camuflaje, disfraz; desfiguración; v. encubrir, disfrazar.
camp (kamp) s. campo, campamento; — **chair** silla de tijera; **political —** partido político; v. acampar.
campaign (campéin) s. campaña; v. salir a campaña; hacer propaganda.
camphor (cámfor) s. alcanfor.
campus (kémpus) s. patio o campo de una universidad, de un colegio.
can (can) s. lata, bote, envase; — **opener** abrelatas; v. enlatar, envasar; —**ned goods** conservas alimenticias enlatadas; v. defect. y aux. (usado sólo en las formas can y could), poder, saber.
Canadian (canédian) s. canadiense.
canal (canál) s. canal, acequia.
canary (canéri) s. canario.
cancel (cáncel) v. cancelar, anular, revocar, rescindir, tachar, borrar.
cancellation (kanseléshon) s. cancelación, revocación, rescisión.
cancer (kánser) s. cáncer.
candid (cándid) adj. sincero, franco, cándido, ingenuo.
candidacy (kéndidasi) s. candidatura.
candidate (kéndideit) s. candidato; aspirante, pretendiente.
candle (kándl) s. candela, vela, bujía, cirio; — **power** potencia lumínica (en bujías); — **wick** pabilo.
candlestick (kándlstik) s. candelero, palmatoria, candil.
candor (cándor) s. candor, sinceridad, sencillez, ingenuidad, franqueza.
candy (kándi) s. dulce, confite,

CANE **CARD**

bombón; — **shop** dulcería; v. confitar, azucarar, almibarar; garapiñar, cristalizarse (el almíbar); **candied almonds** almendras garapiñadas.

cane (kéin) s. caña, bejuco; — **field** cañaveral; — **chair** silla de bejuco; — **juice** guarapo; **walking** — bastón; — **mill** ingenio azucarero; **head of a** — puño de bastón.

canine (kénain) adj. canino, perruno.

canned (kánd) adj. enlatado, envasado, conservado en lata o frasco.

cannery (kéneri) s. fábrica de conservas alimenticias.

cannibal (cánibal) s. caníbal.

cannon (kánon) s. cañón.

cannonade (kánoneid) s. cañoneo; v. cañonear.

cannot (cánot) **can not** no puedo, no puede, no podemos, etc.

canoe (kanú) s. canoa, piragua, chalupa.

canon (kánon) s. canon; ley, regla, estatuto; norma, canónigo.

canopy (cánopi) s. dosel, pabellón, palio, baldaquín.

cantaloupe (cántalup) s. melón.

canteen (kantín) s. cantimplora.

canton (kánton) s. cantón, región, distrito.

canvas (cánvas) s. lona; lienzo; cañamazo; toldo.

canvass (kánvas) s. inspección, indagación; examen, escrutinio; encuesta; solicitación (de votos); v. escudriñar, examinar; solicitar votos o pedidos comerciales; hacer una gira solicitando votos.

canyon (kánion) s. cañón, desfiladero, garganta.

cap (cap) s. gorro, boina, capelo; tapa, tapón; cima, cumbre; capitel; **percussion** — cápsula fulminante; v. tapar, poner tapón a; **that** —**s the climax** eso es el colmo.

capability (kepebíliti) s. capacidad, idoneidad, aptitud.

capable (képebl) adj. capaz, apto, idóneo, competente.

capacious (kepéshus) adj. capaz, amplio, holgado, espacioso, extenso.

capacity (kepéciti) s. capacidad; cabida; aptitud, suficiencia; habilidad; **in the** — **of a teacher** en calidad de maestro.

cape (kéip) s. capa; cabo; promontorio; punta de tierra.

caper (kéiper) s. cabriola, voltereta; travesura; **to cut** —**s** cabriolar, retozar, hacer travesuras.

capital (cápital) s. capital, principal; caudal; chapitel de una columna; letra mayúscula; — **punishment** pena capital, pena de muerte; adj. capital, principal, excelente, magnífico.

capitalism (cápitalism) s. capitalismo.

capitalist (cápitalist) s. capitalista; —**ic** adj. capitalista.

capitalization (cápitaliséshon) s. capitalización.

capitalize (cápitalais) v. capitalizar; sacar provecho de; principiar una palabra con mayúscula.

capitol (cápitol) s. capitolio.

caprice (keprís) s. capricho, antojo.

capricious (kepríshos) adj. caprichoso, antojadizo.

capsize (cápsais) v. zozobrar; volcar(se).

capsule (cápsul) s. cápsula, cajilla, vaina.

captain (cápten) s. capitán; v. capitanear, mandar; servir de capitán.

captivate (káptiveit) v. cautivar.

captive (cáptiv) s. y adj. cautivo, prisionero; esclavo.

captivity (cáptiviti) s. cautiverio, prisión; obsesión.

captor (cáptor) s. aprehensor.

capture (cápchur) s. captura; aprehensión; presa, apresamiento, prisión; v. capturar; prender, tomar.

car (car) s. coche, automóvil, vagón, coche de ferrocarril; tranvía; carro; caja de ascensor; barquilla del globo aerostático; **dining** — carro comedor.

caramel (cáramel) s. caramelo.

carat (cárat) s. quilate.

caravan (cáravan) s. caravana.

carbolic (karbálik) adj. carbólico.

carbon (kárbon) s. corbono; — **paper** papel carbón; — **monoxide** monóxido de carbón.

carburetor (cárburetor) s. carburador.

carcass (cárcas) s. esqueleto; cuerpo descarnado; res (muerta); casco o armazón, carcasa.

card (card) s. tarjeta; naipe, cartar; carda (para cardar lana); almohaza; **visiting** — tarjeta de visita; **court** — figura; — **sharp**

fullero; **file** — ficha, papeleta; **post** — tarjeta postal; — **table** mesa de juego; **trump** — triunfo; **to play** —**s** jugar a la baraja.
cardboard (cárbord) s. cartón; **fine** — cartulina.
cardinal (cárdinal) adj. cardinal, fundamental, primero; rojo, bermellón; cardenal; púrpura; — **number** número cardinal; — **bird** cardenal.
care (ker) s. cuidado, cautela; ansiedad; inquietud; atención; cargo, custodia; **to take** — **of** cuidar de; **to** — **about** tener interés, preocuparse por; **to** — **for** tener cariño a, simpatizarle a uno (una persona); **to** — **to** querer, desear, tener ganas de; **what does he** — ? ¿a él qué le importa? **to cast away** — olvidar penas; — **worn** devorado de inquietud.
career (kerír) s. carrera, profesión, curso, corrida.
carefree (kérfri) adj. libre de cuidado, sin cuidados.
careful (kérful) adj. cuidadoso; esmerado, cauteloso, próvido; ansioso, lleno de cuidados, inquieto; —**ly**; adv. con esmero, cuidadosamente.
carefulness (kérfulnes) s. cuidado, cautela; atención, vigilancia.
careless (kérles) adj. descuidado, negligente; omiso; indiferente; —**ly** adv. descuidadamente, sin esmero.
carelessness (kérlesnes) s. descuido, abandono, indiferencia, dejadez, negligencia.
caress (carés) s. caricia, mimo.
caretaker (kérteiker) s. cuidador, vigilante, celador, guardián.
carfare (cárfer) s. pasaje de tranvía.
cargo (cárgo) s. carga, flete, cargamento, consignación.
caricature (kéricachur) s. caricatura; v. hacer caricaturas, parodiar.
carload (cárloud) s. carro entero, furgonada; flete por carro entero.
carnal (kárnal) adj. carnal; lascivo.
carnation (carnéshon) s. clavel, color encarnado.
carnival (kárnival) s. carnaval.
carnivorous (karnívoros) adj. carnívoro, carnicero.
carol (károl) s. villancico; **Christmas** —**s** villancicos de Navidad; v. cantar villancicos.
carouse (caráus) v. andar de parranda, andar de juerga, embriagarse.
carpenter (cárpenter) s. carpintero.
carpentry (cárpentri) s. carpintería.
carpet (cárpet) s. alfombra, tapiz, **small** — tapete; v. alfombrar.
carriage (kárriy) s. carruaje, coche, vehículo; porte, acarreo, conducción; — **paid** porte pagado; **good** — buen porte, garbo.
carrier (kérrier) s. portador, carretero, mandadero, transportador; cargador; **airplane** — portaavión; **disease** — transmisor de gérmenes contagiosos; — **pigeon** paloma mensajera.
carrot (kárrot) s. zanahoria.
carry (kárri) v. llevar, conducir, acarrear, transportar; sostener una carga; dirigir; ganar, lograr (una elección, un premio) **to** — **away** llevarse, entusiasmar, arrebatar; **to** — **on** continuar, no parar; **to** — **oneself well** andar derecho, airoso; **to** — **out** llevar a efecto, realizar; **to** — **over** o **forward** pasar al frente; a la otra hoja.
cart (cart) s. carro, carreta, vagoncillo; v. acarrear.
cartage (cártey) s. carretaje, porteo.
carter (cárter) s. carretero.
carton (cárton) s. caja de cartón.
cartoon (cartún) s. caricatura, boceto.
cartoonist (cartúnist) s. caricaturista.
carve (karv) v. esculpir, tallar, cincelar; grabar; tajar carne.
carver (cárver) s. tallista, grabador; trinchante (cuchillo), escultor, entallador.
carving (cárving) s. escultura, tallado; — **knife** trinchante.
cascade (káskeid) s. cascada, catarata.
case (kéis) s. caso, suceso; caja, funda, cubierta, estuche; **window** — marco de ventana; **in** — si acaso; **a** — **in law** un proceso, una causa; **in any** — en todo caso.
casement (kéisment) s. puerta ventana.
cash (cash) s. dinero en efectivo, numerario; pago al contado; — **on delivery** (c.o.d.) reembolso, cóbrese al entregar; — **register** caja registradora; **petty** — gastos menores de caja; v. cambiar

o cobrar un cheque; hacer efectivo.
cashier (cashier) s. cajero.
cask (kask) s. barril, tonel, cuba.
casket (cásket) s. atúd, cofrecito, joyelero, arquilla.
casserole (cáserol) s. cacerola.
cassock (cások) s. sotana.
cast (cast) lanzamiento, tirada; molde; matiz, tinte, tono; apariencia; defecto (del ojo); reparto de papeles; elenco; — **iron** hierro fundido o colado; v. echar, tirar, lanzar; fundir, vaciar, moldear; repartir (papel dramático); **to — lots** echar suertes; **to — a ballot** votar; **to — about** esparcir; considerar, hace planes; **to — aside** desechar; **to be — down** estar abatido; **to — away** abandonar, arrojar; **to — out** echar fuera, arrojar; pret. y p.p. **to cast**.
castanets (kástenets) s. pl. castañuelas.
caste (kast) s. casta, clase social; **to lose —** perder el prestigio.
Castilian (Castilian) s. castellano.
castle (kasl) s. castillo, fortaleza; torre de ajedrez, enroque.
castor oil (cástor oil) s. aceite de ricino.
casual (késuel) adj. casual, accidental, fortuito, inusitado.
casualty (késuelti) s. baja (en el ejército); accidente, desastre, muerte violenta; contingencia.
cat (cat) s. gato; **to bell the —** poner el cascabel al gato.
catalogue (cátalog) s. catálogo.
cataract (káterakt) s. catarata.
catarrh (ketár) s. catarro.
catastrophe (ketástrofi) s. catástrofe.
catch (ketch) s. presa; botín; pesca; tomadura, asimiento, cogedura; captura, prisión; enganche; — **phrase** frase llamativa; — **bolt** picaporte; **he is a good —** es un buen partido; **to play —** jugar a la pelota; v. coger, agarrar; atrapar; alcanzar; detener; capturar; **to — at** tratar de coger; **to — cold** resfriarse; **to — up** coger, asir, empuñar; **to — sight of** avistar; **to — unaware** sorprender, coger desprevenido; **to — it** ganarse una zurra, una reprimenda; **to — up with** alcanzar a, emparejarse con.
catching (cáching) s. engranaje.

catechism (cátekism) s. catecismo.
category (cátegori) s. categoría.
caterpillar (cáterpiler) s. oruga; — **tractor** tractor.
cathedral (cazídral) s. catedral; adj. episcopal; dogmático.
Catholic (cázolic) s. y adj. católico.
Catholicism (cazólisism) s. catolicismo.
catsup (cátsup) s. salsa de tomate.
cattle (cátl) s. ganado, ganado vacuno; gentuza; **neat —**, **black —**, **horned —** ganado vacuno; — **ranch** hacienda de ganado; — **bell** esquila.
caught (cot) pret. y p.p. del v. **to catch**.
cauliflower (cóliflauer) s. coliflor.
cause (cos) s. causa, origen, principio; v. causar, originar.
caution (cóshon) f. precaución, prevención, cautela; amonestación —! ¡cuidado! ¡atención! v. prevenir.
cautious (cóshus) adj. cauto, prevenido, precavido, cuidadoso.
cavalier (cavalír) s. caballero; galán, cortejo; jinete; adj. caballeresco.
cavalry (cávalri) s. caballería.
cave (kéiv) s. cueva, caverna; sibil.
cavern (cávern) s. caverna.
cavity (cáviti) s. cavidad, hueco.
caw (có) s. graznido; v. graznar.
cease (sís) v. cesar; parar, desistir, dejar de; fenecer.
ceaseless (sísles) adj. incesante.
cedar (sídar) s. cedro; tuya.
cede (sid) v. ceder, traspasar.
celebrate (sélebreit) v. celebrar.
celebrated (sélebreited) adj. célebre, famoso, afamado, renombrado.
celebration (celebréshon) s. celebración, fiesta, solemnidad.
celebrity (selébriti) s. celebridad, renombre, fama; persona célebre.
celery (séleri) s. apio.
celestial (celéschal) adj. celestial.
cell (sel) s. celda; célula; pila eléctrica; cavidad, alvéolo.
cellar (sélar) s. bodega, sótano.
celluloid (sélluloid) s. celuloide.
cemetery (sémeteri) s. cementerio.
censor (sénsor) s. censor; crítico, censurador; v. censurar (cartas, periódicos, etc.).
censorship (sénsorship) s. censura.
censure (sénshur) s. censura, crítica, reprobación, reprensión, reprimenda.
census (cénsos) s. censo.

cent (sént) s. centavo (de-peso o dólar); **per —** por ciento.
centennial (senténial) adj. y s. centenario.
center (sénter) s. centro; v. centrar; colocar en el centro.
centigrade (séntigred) adj. centígrado.
centipede (séntipid) s. ciempiés, escolopendra.
central (séntral) s. central; céntrico; **(la) central de teléfonos.**
centralize (séntralais) v. centralizar.
century (sénchuri) s. siglo.
cereal (círial) adj. cereal; s. grano.
ceremonial (seremónial) adj. ceremonial s. rito externo o ritual.
ceremony (céremoni) s. ceremonia, ceremonial; cumplido.
certain (sérten) adj. cierto, seguro; **—ly** adv. ciertamente; determinado, fijo, inevitable; un tal.
certainty (sértanti) s. certeza; certidumbre, seguridad.
certify (cértifai) v. certificar, dar fe, atestiguar; afirmar.
cessation (seséshon) s. suspensión, paro.
cesspool (séspul) s. cloaca, sumidero, letrina.
chafe (chéif) s. rozadura, excoriación, irritación; molestia; v. rozar, frotar, irritar.
chaff (chaff) s. hollejo, cáscara; ahechadura; broza; v. embromar, bromear; fisgar, dar matraca.
chain (chein) s. cadena; sucesión; **— of mountains** cordillera; **— store** tienda sucursal; v. encadenar, aherrojar, esclavizar.
chair (cher) s. silla; cátedra; presidencia.
chairman (chérman) s. presidente de una junta.
chalice (chális) s. cáliz.
chalk (chók) s. greda, marga, tiza, yeso; marcar con yeso, enyesar; **to — down** apuntar con tiza; **to — out** bosquejar con tiza.
chalky (chóki) adj. gredoso, blanco.
challenge (cháleny) s. desafío, reto, duelo; v. desafiar, demandar, retar, poner a prueba, disputar.
chamber (chémber) s. cámara, aposento.
chambermaid (chámbermeid) s. camarera; sirvienta.
chamois (chami) s. ante, gamuza.
champion (champion) s. campeón, adalid; defensor; v. defender, abogar.

championship (chámpionship) s. campeonato.
chance (cháns) s. oportunidad, ocasión; ventura, suerte; probabilidad, posibilidad; acaso, casualidad; riesgo, peligro; **by —** por casualidad; **there is no —** no hay esperanza; **to take the —** correr el riesgo o el albur; **to — to** acertar a, hacer algo por casualidad.
chancellor (chánselor) s. canciller, magistrado; rector de universidad; **— of the Exchequer** Ministro de Hacienda en Inglaterra.
chandelier (chándilir) s. candil, araña de luces.
change (cheiny) s. cambio, permuta, mudanza, alteración; reemplazo; vuelta o sobrante de un pago; moneda fraccionaria; **the — of life** la menopausia; v. cambiar, variar, transformar, mudar, alterar, permutar; **to — clothes** mudar de ropa; **to — trains** transbordar de tren.
changeable (chényabl) adj. voluble, inconstante, veleidoso; **— silk** seda tornasolada.
channel (chanl) s. canal, cauce.
chant (chant) s. canto llano, sonsonete; salmo; cantar salmos.
chaos (kéos) s. caos, desorden, confusión.
chaotic (kéotic) s. caótico.
chap (chap) s. grieta, raja, hendidura; mozo, chico; v. hender, rajar; agrietarse, cuartearse; (chop) s. mandíbula, quijada.
chaperon (cháperon) s. acompañante, dueña; persona de respeto; **to go along as a —** ir de moscón; v. acompañar, escudar a una señorita.
chaplain (cháplen) s. capellán; **army —** capellán castrense.
chapter (chápter) s. capítulo; cabildo; **— house** sala capitular.
char (char) v. requemar, carbonizar.
character (káracter) s. carácter, índole, genio; personaje en el teatro; v. caracterizar; grabar, esculpir.
characteristic (karaterístic) adj. característico; típico, propio; s. característica, rasgo distintivo, peculiaridad.
characterize (kárácterais) v. caracterizar.
charcoal (charkol) s. carbón de le-

ña; carboncillo para dibujar; — **drawing** dibujo al carbón.
charge (chary) s. carga; cargo; precio, gasto, partida; gravamen; asalto, embestida; comisión, encargo; acusación; — **account** cuenta abierta; — **prepaid** porte pagado; **under my** — a mi cargo; **to be in** — **of** estar encargado de; v. cargar; gravar; encargar; mandar, exhortar; atacar, embestir; acusar, imputar; **to** — **with murder** acusar de homicidio.
charger (cháryer) s. cargador de batería; corcel.
chariot (chériot) s. carroza, carruaje.
charitable (cháritabl) adj. caritativo.
charity (cháriti) s. caridad, limosna; beneficencia.
charlatan (chárlatn) s. charlatán, farsante.
charm (charm) s. encanto, embeleso, atractivo; talismán, amuleto; dije; v. encantar, cautivar, arrobar.
charming (chárming) adj. encantador, **agradable, fascinante**, hechicero.
chart (chart) s. carta de navegación, mapa, gráfica; v. cartografiar, delinear mapas; **to** — **a course** trazar una ruta o derrotero.
charter (chárter) s. cédula, título, carta de privilegio; constitución; — **member** socio fundador; v. estatuir; fletar un barco; alquilar (un ómnibus).
chase (chéis) s. caza; persecución; partida de caza; v. cazar, perseguir; **to** — **away o off** ahuyentar.
chasm (kásm) s. abismo, precipicio.
chaste (chéist) s. casto, honesto, puro.
chastise (chestáis) v. castigar, reformar, corregir.
chastisement (chéstisment) s. castigo, escarmiento, pena, corrección.
chastity (chéstiti) s. castidad, pureza, continencia.
chattels (chétls) s. pl. enseres, efectos, bienes muebles; **goods and** — bienes muebles.
chatter (cháter) s. charla, parloteo; rechinido; castañeteo de los dientes; v. charlar, parlotear, rechinar los dientes.
chauffeur (chófer) s. chofer.

cheap (chíp) adj. barato, cursi, de pacotilla; **to feel** — sentir vergüenza; —**ly**; adv. barato, a poco precio.
cheapen (chípn) v. abaratar.
cheapness (chípnes) s. baratura, cursilería.
cheat (chít) s. fraude, timo, trampa, engaño; trampista, timador, estafador; v. engañar, timar, embaucar, estafar.
check (chék) s. cheque (de banco); talón, contraseña; marbete; cuenta (de restaurante); restricción, obstáculo, comprobación de cuentas; jaque en ajedrez; — **room** depósito de equipajes; v. reprimir, refrenar; confrontar, revisar; facturar; depositar; marcar (con una señal); **to** — **out of a hotel** desocupar el cuarto de un hotel; dar jaque en el juego de ajedrez.
checkbook (chékbuk) s. chequera o libreta de cheques, talonario de cheques.
checker (chéker) s. comprobador, inspector; cuadro o casilla (en ajedrez o de damas); —**board** tablero de ajedrez o de damas; v. cuadricular; formar escaques o cuadros; diversificar; —**ed career** vida azarosa o llena de variedad; —**ed cloth** paño o tela de cuadros.
cheek (chik) s. mejilla, carrillo, cachete; desvergüenza, descaro, desfachatez; **fat** — mejilla gorda, moflete; — **bone** pómulo.
cheer (chír) s. alegría, regocijo, jovialidad; —**s** vivas, vítores, aplausos; consuelo; v. alegrar, vitorear, aplaudir; animar, confortar; **to** — **up** alentar, dar ánimo.
cheerful (chírful) adj. animado, alegre, jovial, placentero; —**ly** alegremente, con júbilo; de buena gana, de buen grado.
cheerfulness (chírfulnes) s. alegría, jovialidad, buen humor.
cheerily (chírili) ver **cheerfully**.
cheerless (chírles) adj. abatido, desalentado, desanimado, triste, sombrío.
cheery (chíri) ver **cheerful**.
cheese (chís) s. queso; **cottage** — requesón; — **curds** cuajadas — **monger** quesero.
chemical (kémical) adj. químico; s. producto químico.
chemist (kémist) s. químico.
chemistry (kémistri) s. química.
cherish (chérish) s. acariciar, abri-

gar una esperanza; apreciar, estimar, fomentar.
cherry (chérri) s. cereza; — **tree** cerezo.
chess (chés) s. ajedrez; — **board** tablero de ajedrez.
chest (chest) s. cofre, arca; pecho, tórax; — **of drawers** cómoda.
chew (chú) v. mascar, masticar; s. mascadura, mordisco, bocado.
chewing gum (chúingom) s. goma de mascar; chicle.
chick (chik) s. pollo, polluelo, pajarito; jovencito, niño; — **pea** garbanzo.
chicken (chíken) s. ver **chick**; — **pox** viruelas locas; — **hearted** cobarde, gallina.
chide (chaid) v. increpar, reprender, regañar; refunfuñar.
chief (chif) s. jefe, principal; caudillo, cacique; **commander in** — comandante en jefe; — **clerk** oficial mayor; — **justice** presidente de una sala de la Suprema Corte; —**ly** principalmente, sobre todo.
chiffon (shífon) s. gasa.
chilblain (chílblein) s. sabañón.
child (cháild) s. niño, niña, hijo, hija; **child's play** cosa de niños; **to be with** — estar encinta; **this** — el hijo de mi padre, yo.
childbirth (cháildberz) s. parto, alumbramiento.
childhood (cháildjud) s. niñez, infancia.
childish (cháildish) adj. aniñado, pueril, frívolo, infantil, trivial; — **action** niñería.
childlike (cháildlaik) adj. como niño, pueril, infantil.
children (chíldren) s. pl. niños.
Chilean (Chilean) adj. y s. chileno.
chili (chíli) s. chile, ají.
chill (chil) s. frío, calosfrío; resfriado, enfriamiento; —**s and fever** escalofríos; v. resfriar(se); templar o endurecer al frío; **chilled iron** hierro endurecido.
chilly (chíli) adj. frío, friolento adv. fríamente.
chime (chaim) s. repique, campaneo; tañer de campanas; conformidad, analogía; —**s** órgano de campanas; v. tocar, sonar, tañer, repicar; **to** — **with** estar en armonía con.
chimney (chímnl) s. chimenea; cañón de chimenea; bombilla; **lamp** — tubo de lámpara.
chin (chin) s. barba, mentón.
china (cháina) s. loza de china; porcelana; loza fina; vajilla; — **closet** chinero.
chinaware (cháinauer) ver **china**.
Chinese (chainís) adj. chino; s. chino; idioma chino.
chink (chink) s. grieta, hendedura.
chip (chip) s. astilla, brizna, pedacito, fragmento; desconchadura, desportilladura; ficha (de póker); v. desmenuzar, picar, astillar, desportillar; tajar (con cincel o hacha); **to** — **in** contribuir con su cuota.
chirp (cherp) s. gorjeo, canto, chirrido, pío v. chirriar, gorjear, piar, pipiar.
chisel (chisl) s. cincel, formón, escoplo; v. cincelar, sisar; estafar.
chivalrous (chívalros) adj. caballeresco, galante, cortés, gentil.
chivalry (chívalri) s. caballerosidad, hidalguía; caballería.
chlorine (klórin) s. cloro.
chloroform (clóroform) s. cloroformo.
chocolate (chócoleit) s. chocolate; — **pot** chocolatera.
choice (chóis) s. elección, selección, preferencia, opción; cosa elegida; adj. selecto, escogido, delicado; **to have no other** — no tener otra alternativa.
choir (kuáir) s. coro.
choke (chóuk) s. sofocamiento, ahogo, estrangulación; obstrucción; v. ahogar, sofocar, estrangular; regularizar (el motor).
cholera (kólera) s. cólera (m).
choose (chús) v. escoger, elegir, seleccionar; preferir; optar; **I do not** — **to do it** no se me antoja o no quiero hacerlo; **to pick and** — elegir cuidadosamente.
chop (chop) s. chuleta, tajada (de carne); —**s** quijadas, mandíbulas; v. tajar, cortar, picar carne, desbastar.
choppy (chópi) adj. rajado, picado, agitado (el mar).
choral (córal) adj. coral.
chord (cord) s. cuerda, acorde.
chorus (kóros) s. coro, masa coral; v. corear, contestar a una voz.
chose (chous) pret. de **to choose**.
chosen (chosn) p.p. de **to choose**.
christen (krisn) v. bautizar.
christening (krísning) s. bautizo adj. bautismal.
Christian (kristchan) s. y adj. cristiano; — **name** nombre de pila.
Christianity (kristchániti) s. cristiandad, cristianismo.

Christmas (krismas) s. Navidad, Pascua; aguinaldo; — **Eve** Nochebuena; — **gift** regalo de Navidad; **Merry** — ¡Feliz Navidad! ¡Felices Pascuas! — **carol** villancico.

chronic (krónic) adj. crónico, inveterado.

chronicle (krónikl) s. crónica; v. escribir una crónica; relatar.

chronicler (krónikler) s. cronista.

chronological (kronolóyical) adj. cronológico.

chronometer (cronómeter) s. cronómetro.

chrysanthemum (krisénzemon) s. crisantema, crisantemo.

chubby (chóbi) adj. rechoncho, regordete, gordiflón.

chuck (chok) s. mamola, caricia en la barba; mordaza de torno; v. echar, arrojar; mandrilar; cacarear.

chuckle (chokl) s. risa ahogada; v. reír entre dientes.

chum (chom) s. camarada, compañero, **to — up with** intimar con alguien.

chunk (chonk) s. trozo, pedazo.

church (chorch) s. iglesia, templo.

churchman (chórchman) s. clérigo, sacerdote, eclesiástico.

churchyard (chórchiard) s. cementerio de parroquia.

churn (chorn) s. mantequera v. batir manteca; agitar, menear.

cider (sáider) s. sidra.

cigar (sigár) s. puro, tabaco, — **store** tabaquería; estanquillo; — **holder** boquilla.

cigarette (sigarét) s. cigarrillo, pitillo, cigarro, — **case** cigarrera; — **lighter** encendedor.

cinch (cinch) s. cosa segura, ganga v. cinchar, apretar; s. cincho.

cinder (sínder) s. ceniza, carbón, pavesa, rescoldo, ascua.

cinnamon (sínamon) s. canela; — **tree** canelo.

cipher (sáifer) s. cero, cifra; clave.

circle (serkl) s. círculo, cerca, circunferencia; anillo, rueda; v. cercar, circundar, rodear, circular.

circuit (sérkit) s. circuito, rodeo.

circular (sérkiular) adj. circular, redondo; s. circular, hoja volante.

circulate (sérkiuleit) v. circular, propalar, divulgar, diseminar; poner en circulación.

circulation (sérkiuléshon) s. circulación.

circumference (serkómferens) s. circunferencia; periferia, perímetro.

circumlocution (sérkumlokiúshon) s. circunlocución, circunloquio.

circumscribe (sercumscráib) v. circunscribir, limitar.

circumspect (sérkumspect) adj. circunspecto, prudente, discreto.

circumspection (sérkumspécshon) s. circunspección, prudencia.

circumstance (sérkumstans) s. circunstancia, incidente; detalle; ceremonia, pompa.

circus (sércus) s. circo.

cistern (sístern) s. cisterna.

citadel (sitadl) s. ciudadela.

citation (saitéshon) s. cita; citación, mención, comparendo.

cite (sáit) v. citar, citar a juicio; hacer comparecer, mencionar.

citizen (sitisn) s. ciudadano.

citizenship (sítisnship) s. ciudadanía.

citron (sitron) s. acitrón; limón.

city (síti) s. ciudad, población; adj. municipal, urbano; — **council** ayuntamiento; — **hall** casa municipal, o del ayuntamiento.

civic (sívic) adj. cívico.

civics (síviks) s. derecho político.

civil (sivil) adj. civil; cortés; afable; urbano; — **engineer** ingeniero civil; — **service** servicio público.

civilian (sivílian) s. paisano.

civility (sivíliti) s. civilidad, urbanidad, cortesía; afabilidad.

civilization (sivilishéshon) s. civilización.

civilize (sívilais) v. civilizar.

civilized (sívilaisd) adj. civilizado.

clad (klad) pret. y p.p. de **to clothe**.

claim (kléim) s. demanda, pedimento, reclamación; pretensión, título, reclamo; pertenencia, denuncia; v. demandar, pedir en juicio, exigir; **to — be** pretender ser.

claimant (kléimant) s. reclamante; pretendiente (a un trono); actor.

clairvoyant (clervóiant) s. vidente, lúcido.

clam (clam) s. almeja, tellina.

clamber (clámber) v. trepar, gatear o encaramarse.

clamor (clámor) s. clamor, gritería, algarabía, alboroto; v. clamar, vociferar, gritar.

clamorous (clámoros) adj. clamoroso.

clamp (clamp) s. grapa, tornillo de banco; abrazadera, manija; v. afianzar, sujetar; empalmar.

clan (klan) s. clan, familia, tribu.

clandestine (klandéstin) adj. clandestino, secreto, furtivo.

clang (klang) s. tantán, retintín, sonido metálico; v. sonar, resonar, replicar, tocar fuerte.

clarify (clárifai) v. aclarar, clarificar; esclarecer.

clarinet (clerinét) s. clarinete.

clarity (claríti) s. claridad, luz.

clasp (klasp) s. broche, presilla, traba, hebilla, cierre; apretón, apretón de mano; v. abrochar, asir, abrazar, asegurar, enganchar.

class (clas) s. clase; v. clasificar.

classic (klásic) adj. clásico; — scholar humanista, autor clásico.

classical (klásical) adj. clásico.

classification (klasifikéshon) s. clasificación.

classify (klásifai) v. clasificar.

classmate (klásmeit) s. condiscípulo.

classroom (klásrum) s. clase, aula.

clatter (kléter) s. estrépito; gresca, alboroto, bulla; v. hacer boruca; traquetear; gritar, charlar.

clause (clós) s. cláusula, párrafo; período; estipulación.

claw (cló) s. garra, zarpa; gancho; — hammer martillo de orejas; v. desgarrar; arañar; rasgar, despedazar; s. arañazo.

clay (kléi) s. barro, arcilla, greda; — ground tierra arcillosa.

clean (klin) s. limpio, claro, puro, aseado; — cut bien definido; v. limpiar, asear; to — up asearse, limpiarse; adv. limpiamente, enteramente, completamente.

cleaner (klíner) s. limpiador, sacamanchas.

cleanliness (clínlines) s. limpieza, aseo; aliño, tersura.

cleanly (klínli) adj. limpio, aseado; adv. aseadamente.

cleanness (klínes) s. limpieza, aseo.

cleanse (klins) v. limpiar; lavar, purificar, depurar, purgar.

cleanser (klínser) s. limpiador.

clear (klir) adj. claro, transparente, diáfano; libre (de culpa, estorbos, deudas, etc); perspicuo, evidente, indisputable; — profit ganancia neta; **to pass — through** atravesar, traspasar de lado a lado; **to be in the —** estar sin deudas, estar libre de culpa; v. aclarar, disipar; despejar; despachar en la aduana; pasar (un cheque) por un banco de liquidación; desmontar; saltar por encima de; **to — up** aclarar.

clearance (clírans) s. espacio libre entre dos objetos; despacho de aduana; — **sale** saldo, barata.

clearing (clíring) s. aclaramiento, claro; despejo; liquidación de balances; — **house** cámara de compensación.

clearness (clírnes) s. claridad.

cleave (clív) v. rajar, hender; tajar; partir.

cleaver (clíver) s. cuchilla; hacha de carnicero.

clef (clef) s. llave (de música).

cleft (cleft) s. rajadura, hendedura, fisura; adj. partido, agrietado, hendido, pret. y p.p. de **to cleave**.

clemency (clémenci) s. clemencia.

clement (clément) adj. clemente.

clench (clénch) s. agarrón; apretón; v. agarrar, asir; cerrar el puño o los dientes.

clergy (cléryi) s. clero.

clergyman (cléryiman) s. clérigo, sacerdote, padre, cura.

clerical (clérikal) adj. clerical, eclesiástico; oficinesco; de escribiente; — **error** error de pluma.

clerk (clerk) s. empleado, escribiente; **law —** escribano; sacristán; v. estar de dependiente.

clever (cléver) adj. diestro, experto, hábil, inteligente, talentoso, mañoso; **—ly** adv. diestramente, hábilmente, con talento, con maña.

cleverness (clévernes) s. talento, destreza, habilidad, maña.

clew (klu) s. indicio, (para resolver un misterio o problema), pista, huella.

click (clik) s. golpe seco; chasquido de la lengua; sonido del gatillo; taconeo; v. sonar con golpe seco; tic-tac; **to — the heels** taconear al cuadrarse.

client (cláient) s. cliente.

clientele (claientél) s. clientela.

cliff (klif) s. risco, precipicio, farallón, escarpa, peñasco.

climate (cláimet) s. clima.

climax (cláimax) s. clímax, colmo, culminación, cenit; v. culminar, llegar al clímax.

climb (claim) s. subida, ascenso, v. trepar, subir, escalar, encara-

CLIMBER   **CLUB**

marse; to — **down** bajar a gatas; desprenderse (de un árbol).

climber (cláimer) s. trepador; enredadera; planta trepadora.

clime (kláim) s. clima; región.

clinch (clinch) v. remachar; afirmar, fijar, afianzar; sujetar; asegurar bien; cerrar (un trato); s. forcejeo, lucha cuerpo a cuerpo; abrazo; **to be in a —** estar agarrados o abrazados.

cling (cling) v. adherirse, pegarse, unirse.

clinic (clínic) s. clínica.

clip (clip) s. broche, presilla; tijeretada; trasquila; **paper —** sujeta papeles; v. cortar a raíz, cercenar, recortar; trasquilar; **to — together** sujetar; moverse o deslizarse con rapidez; **to go at a good —** ir a paso rápido, andar de prisa.

clipper (clíper) s. velero o avión de gran velocidad; trasquilador, cercenador; —**s** tijeras, maquinilla (para cortar el pelo).

clipping (clíping) s. recorte.

cloak (klóuk) s. capa, manto; palio, v. encapotar, tapar, embozar, encubrir.

cloakroom (klóukrrum) s. guardarropa, vestuario.

clock (klók) s. reloj; **alarm —** reloj despertador.

clockwork (klókuerk) s. maquinaria de reloj; **like —** con precisión, puntualmente; sin dificultad.

clod (klod) s. terrón; tierra, suelo, césped; tonto, necio; zoquete.

clog (clog) s. estorbo, traba, impedimento, obstáculo; zueco, zoclo; **— dance** zapateado; v. estorbar, embarazar; entorpecer; apiñarse; agolparse; atascarse, azolvarse; obstruirse (un caño, una acequia).

cloister (klóister) s. claustro, monasterio, convento; v. enclaustrar proveer de claustros.

close (klóus) s. fin, término, conclusión; cierre; v. cerrar(se), concluir, terminar; **to — an account** saldar una cuenta; **to — in** o **upon** cercar, rodear; **to — out** liquidar, vender en liquidación.

close (klóus) adj. cerrado, apretado, ajustado; próximo; íntimo, estrecho; compacto, denso; inmediato, contiguo; mezquino, tacaño; sofocante; limitado, restringido; **— attention** suma atención; **—**

questioning interrogatorio detallado o minucioso; **at — range** de cerca, cerca; **—ly** adv. estrechamente, contiguamente; aproximadamente; con sumo cuidado o atención.

closeness (klóusnes) s. cercanía, proximidad; estrechez, densidad; apretamiento; solidez, firmeza; tacañería, avaricia; mala ventilación; falta de aire; fidelidad (de una traducción).

closet (klóset) s. ropero, alacena, armario, gabinete; letrina, retrete, excusado; v. encerrar una cuarto, conferenciar a puerta cerrada; **to —oneself** encerrarse.

clot (klót) s. grumo, coágulo, cuajarón; coagular(se), cuajar(se); **— of blood** trombosis.

cloth (klóz) s. tela, paño, género; tejido; mantel, vestido o ropa clerical; **— nipper** desmontador.

clothe (clóz) v. vestir; cubrir, arropar; trajear; investir.

clothes (clózs) s. pl. ropa; ropaje; vestido, vestidura, vestuario; **suit of —** terno; **cast of —** ropa usada; **— line** tendedero; **— pin** pinzas (para ropa).

clothier (klózier) s. comerciante en ropa o paño; ropero.

clothing (clózing) s. ropa, ropaje, vestidos; pelaje.

cloud (cláud) s. nube; nublado, nubarrón; mancha, acumulación, hacinamiento; **storm —** nubarrón.

cloudless (cláudles) adj. claro, despejado; sin nubes, sereno.

cloudy (cláudi) adj. nublado, nuboso; vaporoso; obscuro; sombrío.

clove (klov) s. clavo, (especia); **— of garlic** diente de ajo.

clover (klóver) s. trébol; **to be** o **live in —** vivir en la abundancia; sentirse próspero.

clown (klaun) s. payaso, bufón; patán, paleto; v. payasear.

cloy (kloi) v. empalagar; saciar.

club (clob) s. club, círculo; casino; clava, porra, cachiporra, garrote; tertulia; **— house** casino; **— together** formar club; escotar; pagar la cuota que le toca a cada uno.

clubhouse (clóbjaus) s. club, casino.

cluck (klok) s. cloqueo; v. cloquear, enclocar.

clue ver **clew** (clú) guía, norte.

clump (klomp) s. terrón; bosquecillo; grupo de árboles; pisada fuerte; — of bushes matorral; v. apiñar, amontonar; to — along andar pesadamente.

clumsy (clómsi) adj. torpe, desmañado; incómodo; chapucero; zompo; difícil de manejar; mal hecho.

clung (clong) pret. y p.p. de to cling.

cluster (clóster) s. racimo, macolla, piña; grupo; v. agrupar(se), arracimarse (formar un racimo).

clutch (cloch) s. apretón fuerte; agarrón; embrague, presa; —es garras, uñas; grapa, garra, mano; nidada; — pedal palanca del embrague; to step on the — pisar el embrague; to throw in the — embragar; v. agarrar, asir, apretar.

clutter (klóter) v. obstruir; atestar (de cosas); poner en desorden; s. barahúnda, batahola, confusión.

coach (cóuch) s. coche, carruaje, carroza; entrenador (en deportes); maestro particular; v. amaestrar, guiar; to — with entrado por.

coachman (cóuchman) s. cochero.

coagulate (coágoleit) v. coagular; cuajarse, espesarse.

coal (kóul) s. carbón de piedra; braza, tizón; — oil aceite mineral, petróleo; — gas gas de carbón; — coal box o bin o hole carbonera; cápsula de obús grande de alemán; hard — antracita; v. carbonizar, proveerse de carbón.

coalition (coalíshon) s. coalición.

coarse (kors) adj. tosco; burdo, basto; ordinario; rústico; vulgar; soez, descortés; — sand arena gruesa.

coarseness (córsnes) s. tosquedad; vulgaridad, grosería.

coast (kóust) s. costa, litoral; — guard guarda de costa; the — is clear ha pasado el peligro; v. deslizar(se), resbalar(se), cuesta abajo.

coastal (kóustal) adj. costero, de la costa.

coastline (cóustlain) s. costa.

coat (kóut) s. chaqueta; Am. saco; lana; levita, pelaje; cubierta o envoltura; — of paint capa de pintura; v. cubrir; vestir, revestir, dar una mano (de pintura); to — with sugar azucarar.

coax (kóuks) v. rogar o persuadir con halagos, engatusar, tentar.

cob (cob) s. carozo, zuro (de la mazorca del maíz); bulto, montón.

cobbler (kóbler) s. remendón, zapatero de viejo; chapucero; pudín de bizcocho y fruta.

cobweb (kóbueb) s. telaraña.

cocaine (kókein) s. cocaína.

cockroach (kókrrouch) s. cucaracha.

cocktail (cócteil) s. coctel, aperitivo (de ostras, almejas, etc.).

cocky (kóki) adj. arrogante, Am. retobado.

cocoa (kokóa) s. cacao; bebida de cacao; cocotero, chocolate.

coconut (kókonot) s. coco (fruta).

cocoon (kokún) s. capullo (del gusano de seda); v. ovillar, embozarse; ovillarse.

cod (kod) s. bacalao, abadejo; vaina, vainilla; — liver oil aceite de hígado de bacalao.

coddle (kodl) v. mimar, consentir.

code (kóud) s. código; clave; cifra; civil — código civil; signal — código de señales.

codfish (kódfish) ver cod.

coerce (koérs) v. forzar, obligar.

coffee (cófi) s. café (bebida) — bean grano de café; black — café solo.

coffeepot (cófipot) s. cafetera.

coffer (cófer) s. cofre, arca, caja.

coffin (cófin) s. ataúd, féretro.

coherent (cojírent) adj. coherente; consecuente; conexo.

cohesion (cojíshon) s. cohesión.

coiffure (cuaflúr) s. tocado, peinado.

coin (coin) s. moneda; v. acuñar; amonedar; to — words inventar palabras.

coinage (cóiney) s. acuñación, sistema monetario; moneda.

coincide (coinsáid) v. coincidir.

coincidence (coínsidens) s. coincidencia; casualidad.

coke (kouk) s. coque.

cold (could) adj. frío, frígido; enfriado, helado; — cream crema cosmética; — meat fiambre; to be — tener frío; to take — resfriarse; to catch a — resfriarse.

coldness (cóuldnes) s. frialdad, frigidez; tibieza; despego.

collaborate (coláboreit) v. colaborar.

collaboration (colaboréshon) s. colaboración.

collapse (coláps) s. desplome, de-

COLLAR   **COMMAND**

rrumbe, hundimiento; colapso, fracaso; ruina; v. hacer derrumbarse, contraerse o decaer; doblar(se), plegar(se); hundirse; desbaratarse; desplomarse.

collar (cólar) s. collar; cuello (de vestido; camisa, etc.); collera (para mulas o caballos de tiro); cabezada; aro, anillo; v. apercollar; poner cuello; coger o agarrar por el cuello.

collateral (coláteral) adj. colateral; subordinado; auxiliar; subsidiario, accesorio; — **security** garantía subsidiaria.

colleague (cólig) s. colega.

collect (coléct) v. recoger; congregar, juntar; coleccionar; cobrar; recaudar; **to — oneself** calmarse.

collection (colécshon) s. colección; cobro, recaudación; cuestación o colecta.

collective (coléctiv) adj. colectivo.

college (cóley) s. colegio; **medical —** colegio o escuela de medicina; **electoral —** colegio electoral.

collide (coláid) v. chocar; estar en conflicto, contradecir.

collie (cóli) s. perro pastor.

collision (colíshon) s. choque, colisión; encuentro, topetazo; oposición.

colloquial (colócuial) adj. familiar, dialogístico o dialogal.

colon (cólon) s. colon (del intestino); dos puntos.

colonel (cólonel) s. coronel.

colonial (colónial) adj. colonial.

colonist (cólonist) s. colono, colonizador.

colonization (coloniséshon) s. colonización.

colonize (cólonais) v. colonizar, poblar; establecerse en colonia.

colony (cóloni) s. colonia.

color (cólor) s. color; matiz; colorido; color de la tez; **the —s** la bandera; v. colorar, colorear; teñir; dar color.

colored (cólord) adj. colorado, teñido; colorido; pintado; pardo, de color (negro o mulato).

colorful (cólorful) adj. lleno de color; colorido; vistoso; pintoresco.

coloring (cóloring) s. colorido; coloración; estilo o aire particular.

colorless (cólorles) adj. incoloro; descolorido.

colossal (colósal) adj. colosal.

colt (colt) s. potro.

Columbian (colómbian) adj. colombiano, de Colombia; relativo a Cristóbal Colón; colombino.

column (cólumn) s. columna.

combat (cómbat) s. combate, pelea; v. combatir, pelear.

combatant (cómbatant) adj. y s. combatiente.

combination (combinéshon) s. combinación, unión, liga; mezcla.

combine (combáin) v. combinar(se); formar(se), mezclar(se).

combustible (combóstibl) adj. y s. combustible.

combustion (combóschon) s. combustión.

come (kom) v. venir; llegar, provenir; acercarse, aproximarse; avanzar; adelantarse, aparecer, salir; **to — about** suceder; **to — again** volver; **to — across** atravesar; **to — asunder** deshacerse, desunirse; **to — in** entrar; **to — at** alcanzar; **to — away** retirarse, irse; **to — up** subir; surgir (una cuestión); **to — home** volver a casa; **to — in the away** presentarse al paso.

comedian (comídian) s. comediante, cómico.

comedy (cómedi) s. comedia.

comely (cómli) adj. agradable a la visita, gentil.

comet (cómet) s. cometa.

comfort (cómfort) s. comodidad; bienestar, alivio; animar, alentar, consolar; confortar.

comfortable (cómfortabl) adj. cómodo; confortable, confortativo, consolador; **— life** vida holgada; **— income** un buen pasar; **comfortably** adv. cómodamente; con comodidad; holgadamente.

comforter (cómforter) s. consolador; confortador; el Espíritu Santo.

comfortless (cómfortles) adj. incómodo; desconsolado.

comic (cómic) adj. cómico; chistoso; burlesco, bufo, gracioso **—s** s. pl. caricaturas, historietas cómicas.

comical (cómical) s. cómico, gracioso.

coming (cóming) adj. próximo, venidero, que viene; s. venida, llegada; **— of Christ** advenimiento de Cristo.

comma (kóma) s. coma.

command (kománd) s. mando, orden, dominio, poder; comandancia; comando; autoridad; dominación; **at your —** a sus órdenes;

— 42 —

he has a good — of English domina bien el inglés; v. mandar, ordenar, dominar, comandar; to — respect inspirar respeto, imponerse.

commander (coménder) s. jefe, comandante; teniente de navío; capitán; — in chief generalísimo; comandante en jefe.

commandment (comándment) s. mandamiento; precepto, mandato.

commemorate (komémoreit) v. conmemorar; recordar; celebrar.

commence (coméns) v. comenzar, empezar, iniciar.

commencement (koménsment) s. comienzo, principio, inauguración; exámenes de fin de curso.

commend (koménd) v. alabar, ensalzar, elogiar; recomendar; encargar.

commendation (komendéshon) s. encomio, alabanza; recomendación.

comment (kóment) s. comentario, observación; explicación; nota; v. comentar, glosar, anotar; hacer observaciones o comentarios.

commentary (kómentari) s. comentario.

commentator (kómentetor) s. comentarista; **radio —** comentarista de radio.

commerce (kómers) s. comercio.

commiseration (komiseréshon) s. compasión, piedad, conmiseración.

commissary (kómisari) s. comisario, delegado.

commission (comíshion) s. comisión, encargo, cometido; nombramiento; junta o grupo de comisionados; v. comisionar, autorizar, encargar, apoderar, facultar, diputar; **—ed officer** oficial autorizado; **to put out of —** inutilizar, descomponer; retirar del servicio un navío.

commissioner (comíshoner) s. comisionado, comisario; apoderado; factor; **police —** comisario de policía.

commit (comít) v. cometer, perpetrar; encargar, encomendar; **to — to memory** aprender de memoria; **to — to prison** encarcelar; **to — oneself** comprometerse, expresarse abiertamente.

committee (comiti) s. comité, comisión, delegación, diputación; junta; **standing —** comisión permanente; **— of one** comisionado o delegado único.

commodity (comóditi) s. mercancía; mercadería, producto, artículo; interés, ventaja, utilidad.

common (kómon) adj. común, ordinario, corriente; público; vulgar; bajo — **law** derecho consuetudinario; **— sense** sentido común; **— soldier** soldado raso; **—s** pl. refectorio (de un colegio); ejido; el vulgo; **—ly** comúnmente, por lo común.

commonness (kómones) s. vulgaridad, ordinariez; frecuencia.

commonplace (kómonpleis) adj. común, trivial, vulgar; **—s** s. pl. lugares comunes.

commonwealth (cómonuelz) s. el estado, la nación, pueblo, colectividad, comunidad de naciones.

commotion (comóshon) s. conmoción, agitación, tumulto, bullicio.

commune (comiún) v. comunicarse (con); departir; comulgar; s. comuna.

communicate (comiúnikeit) v. comunicarse; transmitir; notificar; abrir, dar a; comulgar.

communication (comiunikéshon) s. comunicación; despacho, mensaje; participación, notificación.

communicative (comiúnketiv) adj. comunicativo; expansivo.

communion (comiúnion) s. comunión.

communism (cómiunism) s. comunismo.

communist (cómiunist) s. comunista.

community (comiuniti) s. comunidad, el público, la sociedad, vecindario, barrio; **— chest** caja o fondo de beneficencia.

compact (kompáct) adj. compacto; macizo; denso; apretado, conciso; sucinto; breve, compendioso; s. pacto, convenio, concierto, trato; pólvora.

compactness (kompáctnes) s. solidez; firmeza; densidad; concisión.

companion (compánion) s. compañero; consorte, camarada; acompañante.

companionship (kompánionship) s. compañerismo, camaradería.

company (kómpani) s. compañía, sociedad; visita; **ship's —** tripulación; **to keep — with** acompañar; frecuentar; asociarse con;

cortejar; **to part — with** separarse (de).
comparable (kómparabl) adj. comparable.
comparative (kompárativ) adj. comparativo, respectivo, relativo.
compare (compér) v. comparar, cotejar, confrontar, parangonar, equiparar; **beyond —** sin igual, incomparable, sin comparación.
compartment (compártment) s. compartimiento, división, departamento; tablero, cajoncito, gaveta; sección.
compass (cómpas) s. círculo, ámbito, alcance; compás; brújula; circunferencia.
compassion (kompéshon) s. compasión, piedad, conmiseración, lástima.
compassionate (kompéshoneit) adj. compasivo, misericordioso.
compatible (kompátibl) adj. compatible.
compatriot (kompéitriot) s. compatriota, paisano.
compel (kompél) v. compeler, obligar, constreñir; exigir; forzar.
compensate (cómpenseit) v. compensar, indemnizar, resarcir; remunerar; recompensar.
compensation (kompenséshon) s. compensación, resarcimiento, remuneración; recompensa.
compete (kompít) v. competir.
competence (kómpetens) s. competencia; suficiencia; aptitud, capacidad.
competent (kómpetent) adj. competente, calificado, capaz, apto.
competition (kompetíshon) s. competencia; concurso, contienda.
competitive (kompétitiv) adj. en competencia; **— examination** oposición; concurso.
competitor (compétitor) s. competidor, opositor, rival, antagonista.
compile (compáil) v. compilar, recopilar.
complacency (komplésensi) s. complacencia, contentamiento.
complacent (komplésent) adj. complaciente, satisfecho.
complain (kompléin) v. quejarse, lamentarse, querellarse.
complaint (kompléint) s. queja; lamento; agravio; dolencia; demanda; **to lodge a —** hacer una reclamación.
complement (kómplement) s. complemento; apéndice; v. complementar, completar.
complete (complít) adj. completo, acabado; v. completar, concluir; **—ly** adv. completamente, enteramente.
completeness (complítnes) s. perfección, totalidad, integridad.
completion (complíshon) s. terminación, consumación; cumplimiento.
complex (kómplex) s. complejo; (kompléx) adj. complejo, compuesto, complicado.
complexion (complékshon) s. cutis, tez; aspecto; carácter, calidad.
complexity (compléxiti) s. complejidad.
compliance (compláians) s. complacencia, condescendencia, docilidad, conformidad; cumplimiento; **in — with** de acuerdo con.
complicate (cómplikeit) v. complicar; enredar, embrollar.
complicated (cómplikeited) adj. complicado.
complication (komplikéshon) s. complicación.
compliment (cómpliment) s. cumplido, lisonja, galantería, piropo; **to send one's —s** enviar saludos; v. cumplimentar, galantear, felicitar; alabar.
comply (complái) v. cumplir, satisfacer, consentir, someterse, conformarse; obrar de acuerdo (con).
component (compónent) adj. y s. componente.
compose (compóus) v. componer, formar; sosegar, apaciguar; escribir.
composed (compóusd) adj. compuesto, sosegado, sereno, tranquilo; **to be — of** estar compuesto de, constar de.
composer (compóser) s. autor, escritor, compositor.
composite (compósit) adj. compuesto, mixto; s. compuesto, mezcla, mixtura.
composition (composíshon) s. composición, compuesto, mezcla, pasta.
composure (compóshur) s. compostura, serenidad, tranquilidad, calma.
compound (cómpaund) adj. y s. compuesto, mezcla; (compáund) v. componer, mezclar, combinar; **— interest** interés compuesto.
comprehend (comprejénd) v. com-

COMPREHENSIBLE   **CONDITIONAL**

prender, entender, penetrar; contener, encerrar; abarcar, abrazar, incluir.

comprehensible (comprejénsibl) adj. comprensible, inteligible.

comprehension (comprejénshon) s. comprensión, inteligencia.

comprehensive (comprejénsiv) adj. comprensivo, amplio, inclusivo.

compress (kómpres) s. compresa, defensivo; (comprés) v. comprimir, apretar, condensar; abreviar, reducir; —ed air aire comprimido.

compression (compréshon) s. compresión.

comprise (compráis) v. comprender, contener, incluir, abarcar, constar de, abrazar.

comptroller (kontróuler) s. interventor, contralor, inspector.

compulsion (kompólshon) s. compulsión, apremio, coacción.

compulsory (kompólsori) adj. compulsivo; obligatorio.

computation (compiutéshon) s. cómputo, cálculo, cuenta.

compute (compiút) v. computar, calcular, contar; estimar.

comrade (kómred) adj. camarada.

concave (cónkeiv) adj. cóncavo.

conceal (konsíl) v. ocultar, esconder, encubrir; tapar, disimular.

concealment (consílment) s. ocultación; encubrimiento.

concede (consíd) v. conceder; asentir; otorgar; reconocer.

conceit (consít) s. amor propio, presunción, arrogancia, engreimiento; vanagloria; concepto, agudeza.

conceited (consíted) adj. presuntuoso, presumido, vanidoso, engreído.

conceivable (consívabl) adj. concebible, imaginable, comprensible.

conceive (consív) v. concebir, imaginar; pensar; sentir; crear.

concentrate (cóncentreit) v. concentrar(se); reconcentrar(se).

concentration (concentréshon) s. concentración, reconcentración.

concept (cóncept) s. concepto, idea, noción, opinión.

conception (consépshon) s. concepción, idea; imagen; conocimiento; pensamiento.

concern (consérn) s. compañía, negociación, negocio, empresa; establecimiento mercantil; interés, incumbencia; preocupación, ansiedad; to be of no — no ser de consecuencia; v. concernir, importar, atañer; preocupar; in all that —s him en cuanto le concierne.

concerned (consérnd) adj. interesado, comprometido; inquieto; preocupado; intranquilo, ansioso; to be —ed about interesarse por, preocuparse por; as far as I am — por lo que a mí atañe o respecta.

concert (cónsert) s. concierto; (consért) v. concertar, acordar.

concession (conséshon) s. concesión.

conciliate (consílieit) v. conciliar, propiciar, armonizar.

concise (consáis) adj. conciso, sucinto, breve, lacónico.

conciseness (consáisnes) s. concisión; brevedad, laconismo.

conclude (conclúd) v. concluir, acabar; determinar, decidir; deducir, inferir.

conclusion (conclúshon) s. conclusión.

conclusive (conclúsiv) adj. concluyente, terminante, decisivo.

concoct (concóct) v. confeccionar, mezclar; proyectar, urdir; inventar.

concoction (concócshon) s. cocimiento; mezcla; maquinación, trama.

concord (cóncord) s. concordia, armonía, acuerdo, pacto; unión.

concrete (concrít) s. concreto; hormigón; adj. de hormigón, de cemento.

concur (konkér) v. concurrir, coincidir, estar de acuerdo; convenir; ser del mismo parecer.

condemn (condém) v. condenar; desaprobar, censurar, culpar; to — a building condenar un edificio.

condemnation (condemnéshon) s. condenación.

condensation (condenséshon) s. condensación; resumen, compendio.

condense (condéns) v. condensar; reducir; comprimir.

condescend (condesénd) v. condescender; consentir, dignarse.

condescension (condesénshon) s. condescendencia; deferencia.

condiment (cóndiment) s. condimento; aderezo, guiso, salsa, sazón.

conditional (condíshonal) adj. condicional.

— 45 —

condole (condól) v. condolerse; to — with dar el pésame a; consolar a.
condolence (condóulens) s. pésame.
conduce (condiús) v. conducir; tender.
conducive (condiúsiv) adj. conducente.
conduct (cóndoct) s. conducta; proceder, comportamiento; gobierno, escolta, conducta; dirección, manejo; (condóct) v. conducir, guiar, dirigir; gestionar; comportarse; to — oneself well portarse bien.
conductor (condóctor) s. conductor, guía; **orchestra —** director de orquesta; **train —** revisor; cobrador.
conduit (kóndit) s. conducto, caz, cañería, atarjea; tubería.
cone (kóun) s. cono; cucurucho; **pine —** piña.
confection (confécshon) s. confección; confitura, dulce.
confectionary (confékshoneri) s. confitería, dulcería; dulces.
confederacy (confédèrasi) s. confederación; alianza, liga.
confederate (confédèreit) adj. y s. confederado; v. confederar(se).
confederation (confederéshon) s. confederación.
confer (confér) v. conferir, conceder; consultar, tratar, conferenciar.
conference (cónferens) s. conferencia, consulta, entrevista.
confess (confés) v. confesar(se); reconocer; admitir; hacer una confesión.
confession (conféshon) s. confesión.
confessional (conféshonal) s. confesionario.
confessor (confésor) s. confesor.
confidant (cónfidant) s. confidente.
confide (confáid) v. confiar; fiar.
confidence (cónfidens) s. confianza; fe; crédito; **— game** estafa; **— man** estafador; **— trick** timo.
confident (cónfident) adj. confiado, seguro, resuelto, cierto; **—ly** adv. confiadamente.
confidential (confidénshal) adj. confidencial; íntimo, reservado; secreto; **—ly** adv. en confianza.
confine (cónfain) s. confín; límite, término, frontera; v. confinar, encerrar; to — oneself to limitarse a.
confinement (confáinment) s. prisión, clausura, encierro.
confirm (conférm) v. confirmar.
confirmation (confirméshon) s. confirmación, corroboración.
confiscate (cónfiskeit) v. confiscar.
conflagration (conflagréshon) s. conflagración, incendio.
conflict (cónflict) s. conflicto, pugna, lucha, combate, pelea; (conflíct) v. chocar, contender, luchar, combatir, oponerse.
conform (confórm) v. conformar (se), ajustar, concordar.
conformity (confórmiti) s. conformidad.
confound (confáund) v. confundir, enredar, embrollar; perturbar, desconcertar; aturdir; **— it!** ¡caramba!
confront (confrónt) v. confrontar, carear, arrostrarse; encararse con; cotejar, comparar.
confuse (confiús) v. confundir, turbar; trastornar, aturdir; desconcertar.
confused (confiúsd) adj. confuso; turbio; indistinto; revuelto; perplejo; **to become —** confundirse, desconcertarse.
confusing (confiúsing) adj. confuso, revuelto, desconcertante.
confusion (confiúshon) s. confusión, desorden, caos; tumulto, vergüenza.
congenial (conyínial) adj. congenial, simpático.
congestion (conyéschion) s. congestión; aglomeración.
congratulate (congráchuleit) v. felicitar; congratular; dar el parabien.
congratulation (congrachuléshon) s. congratulación, felicitación, enhorabuena.
congregate (cóngregueit) v. congregar(se), convocar, reunir, juntarse.
congregation (congreguéshon) s. congregación; asamblea, auditorio, reunión; agregado, colección, masa, fieles, feligreses.
congress (cóngres) s. congreso, asamblea; convención, concilio.
congressional (congréshonal) adj. del congreso.
congressman (cóngresman) s. congresista, diputado; representante.
conjecture (conyékchur) s. conje-

— 46 —

tura, suposición; v. conjeturar, suponer.
conjugate (cónyugueit) v. conjugar.
conjugation (conyuguéshon) s. conjugación.
conjunction (conyónkshon) s. conjunción; unión, liga.
conjure (cónyur) v. conjurar; to — up evocar; (conyúr) rogar, implorar.
connect (conéct) v. conectar, unir, enlazar, trabar, acoplar; relacionar; asociarse; juntarse.
connection (conécshon) s. conexión; enlace; unión, engarce; afinidad, parentesco; pariente, amigo, amistad; relación.
conniption (conípshon) s. pataleta; to have a — darle a uno una pataleta.
connive (konáiv) v. conspirar, disimular; hacerse de la vista gorda.
connoisseur (konisér) s. conocedor, perito; inteligente; juez.
conquer (cónker) v. conquistar, sojuzgar; vencer, rendir.
conqueror (cónkeror) s. conquistador; vencedor.
conquest (kónkuest) s. conquista.
conscience (cónshiens) s. conciencia.
conscientious (conshiénshus) adj. concienzudo, escrupuloso.
conscious (kónshus) adj. consciente; —ly adv. conscientemente; a sabiendas.
consciousness (cónshusnes) s. conciencia; estado consciente; to lose — perder el conocimiento.
conscript (konscrípt) v. reclutar;
consecrate (cónsekreit) v. consagrar, ungir, santificar; dedicar.
consecration (consekréshon) s. consagración, dedicación, unción.
consecutive (consékiutiv) adj. consecutivo, consiguiente, sucesivo.
consent (consént) s. consentimiento; anuencia, aquiescencia; v. consentir, permitir, condescender.
consequence (cónsekuens) s. consecuencia.
consequent (cónsekuent) adj. consecuente, consiguiente, lógico; s. consecuente, consiguiente; —ly adv. por consiguiente.
conservation (coservéshon) s. conservación; preservación.
conservative (consérvativ) adj. conservador; conservativo; preservativo s. conservador.
conservatory (consérvatori) s. conservatorio, invernáculo, invernadero; academia.
conserve (consérv) v. conservar, cuidar, guardar, preservar; s. conserva, dulce, compota.
consider (consider) v. considerar.
considerable (considerabl) adj. considerable, respetable, importante, cuantioso; adv. considerablemente; bastante más.
considerate (considereit) adj. considerado; prudente, mirado; discreto.
consideration (consideréshon) s. consideración, reflexión, deliberación; respeto; importancia; remuneración; in — of en atención a; en vista de; en razón de.
considering (considering) prep. en atención a; visto que, considerando.
consign (consáin) v. consignar, enviar; ceder, traspasar, relegar.
consist (consíst) v. consistir en, constar de, componerse de.
consistency (consistensi) s. consistencia, conformidad; firmeza, solidez.
consistent (consistent) adj. consecuente, lógico; conveniente, compatible, conforme; coherente.
consolation (consoléshon) s. consolación; consuelo; confortación.
console (consóul) v. consolar, confortar.
consolidate (consólideit) v. consolidar; unir, combinar.
consonant (kónsonant) adj. consonante, conforme; s. consonante.
consort (kónsort) s. consorte, cónyuge; to — with asociarse con.
conspicuous (conspíkiuos) adj. visible, conspicuo, sobresaliente notorio, manifiesto; eminente, ilustre.
conspiracy (conspírasi) s. conspiración, complot, conjuración.
conspirator (conspíretor) s. conspirador, conjurado.
conspire (conspáir) v. conspirar, maquinar; conjurarse.
constable (cónstabl) s. alguacil, policía; condestable (título).
constancy (cónstansi) s. constancia.
constant (cónstant) adj. constante, invariable; s. constante; —ly adv. siempre, a menudo.

constellation (constelésohn) s. constelación, pléyade.

consternation (consternésohn) s. consternación, terror, espanto.

constipate (cónstipeit) s. estreñir, cerrar, tupir, obstruir.

constipation (constipéshon) s. estreñimiento.

constituent (constítiuent) adj. constituyente, elemental, esencial; s. elector, votante, mandante.

constitute (cónstitiut) v. constituir, formar, componer, establecer.

constitution (constitiúshon) s. constitución, complexión; físico.

constitutional (constitúshonal) adj. constitucional; s. caminata, paseo.

constrain (constréin) v. constreñir, compeler, obligar, forzar, restringir; estrechar, comprimir, apretar.

construct (constróct) v. construir, edificar; fabricar; erigir.

construction (constrókshon) s. construcción, estructura, obra.

constructive (constróctiv) adj. constructivo; tácito, provechoso.

construe (constrú) v. interpretar, explicar.

consul (cónsl) s. cónsul.

consulate (cónsiuleit) s. consulado.

consult (consólt) v. consultar, examinar, estudiar.

consultation (consoltéshon) s. consulta.

consume (consiúm) v. consumir, acabar, gastar, disipar; perder (el tiempo).

consumer (consiúmer) s. consumidor.

consummate (cónsumeit) v. consumar, acabar, completar; (consómeit) adj. consumado, completo, cabal.

consumption (consómpshon) s. tisis, tuberculosis, consunción; consumo.

consumptive (consómptiv) adj. tísico, consuntivo.

contact (cóntact) s. contacto, tocamiento; v. tocar, ponerse o estar en contacto con.

contagion (contéyon) s. contagio.

contagious (contéyos) adj. contagioso.

contain (contéin) v. contener, tener cabida para; comprender, abarcar; reprimir, refrenar(se), contener(se); ser divisible exactamente.

container (contéiner) s. envase, caja, recipiente.

contaminate (contámineit) v. contaminar, infestar; viciar, manchar.

contemplate (contémpleit) v. contemplar; meditar; proyectar, tener intención de.

contemplation (contempléshon) s. contemplación, meditación, proyecto; expectación, propósito.

contemporary (contémporari) adj. contemporáneo, coetáneo.

contempt (contémpt) s. desprecio, menosprecio; rebeldía; desdén; — of court contumacia.

contemptible (contémptibl) adj. despreciable, vil.

contemptuous (contémpchus) adj. desdeñoso, despreciativo.

contend (conténd) v. contender, porfiar; disputar; pretender; competir; altercar.

content (contént) s. contenido, sustancia, cabida, capacidad, volumen; table of —s tabla de materias, índice general.

contented (conténted) adj. contento, satisfecho.

contention (conténshon) s. contención, contienda, pugna, pendencia, disputa; controversia; tema, argumento; aseveración.

contentment (conténtment) s. contentamiento, contento, satisfacción.

contest (contést) s. concurso, certamen; debate; pugna, lucha, lid, torneo; v. contender; disputar; competir; luchar por.

context (cóntekst) s. contexto, contenido.

contiguous (contíguiuos) adj. contiguo; junto, inmediato, adyacente.

continent (cóntinent) s. continente; the — Europa, el continente europeo.

continental (continéntal) adj. y s. continental.

contingency (contínyenci) s. contingencia, eventualidad.

contingent (contínyent) adj. y s. contingente.

continual (contíniual) adj. continuo, frecuente; —ly adv. de continuo; incesante.

continuance (contíniuans) s. continuación; aplazamiento.

— 48 —

continuation (continuéshon) s. continuación, prolongación.
continue (contíniu) v. continuar; prolongar, perpetuar; durar, seguir, permanecer, quedar.
continuity (continiúiti) s. continuidad; continuación.
continuous (contíniuos) adj. continuo; sin parar, sin cesar.
contortion (contórshon) s. contorsión.
contour (contúr) s. contorno; perímetro; perfil.
contraband (kóntraband) s. contrabando; v. contrabandear.
contraction (contrákshon) s. contracción.
contractor (contráctor) s. contratista.
contradict (contradíct) v. contradecir.
contradiction (contradíkshon) s. contradicción; contrariedad.
contradictory (contradíktori) adj. contradictorio; opuesto, contrario.
contrary (cóntrari) adj. contrario.
contrast (cóntrast) contraste; (contrást) v. contrastar.
contribute (contríbiut) v. contribuir.
contribution (contribiúshon) s. contribución; cooperación; cuota.
contributor (contríbiutor) s. contribuyente, colaborador.
contrite (cóntrait) adj. contrito.
contrivance (contráivans) s. traza, maquinación; idea, plan, designio, invención; artificio.
contrive (contráiv) v. tramar, maquinar; inventar, ideař; imaginar, ingeniar; discurrir, arbitrar; urdir, darse maña.
control (contróul), s. mando, manejo; dirección; inspección, intervención; sujeción, freno; Am. control; —s mandos, controles; —ling interest mayoría, interés predominante; — stick palanca (de un aeroplano); to lose — of one's temper perder la paciencia; v. gobernar, manejar; Am. controlar; dominar, dirigir, gobernar; regular, restringir, reprimir, contener.
controller (kontróler) s. interventor, contralor, supervisor; regulador; aparato de manejo y control.
controversy (cóntroversi) s. controversia, disputa, debate, polémica.

conundrum (konóndrom) s. adivinanza, acertijo.
convalesce (convalés) v. convalecer.
convene (konvín) v. convocar, citar, juntar(se); reunirse.
convenience (convíniens) s. conveniencia, comodidad, oportunidad, at one's — cuando le convenga a uno, cuando tenga oportunidad.
convenient (convínient) adj. conveniente; cómodo, útil, oportuno; a propósito; —ly adv. convenientemente, cómodamente.
convent (cónvent) s. convento.
convention (convénshon) s. convención, congreso, asamblea, junta; costumbre, regla.
conventional (convénshonal) adj. convencional, tradicional.
converge (convéry) v. converger.
conversant (convérsant) s. versado, experimentado.
conversation (converséshon) s. conversación.
converse (convérs) v. conversar, platicar, hablar; departir.
conversion (convérshon) s. conversión.
convert (cónvert) s. converso, neófito; catecúmeno; (convért) v. convertir, transformar, cambiar.
convex (cónveks) adj. convexo.
convey (convéi) v. transportar, llevar, conducir; transmitir, comunicar; to — thanks expresar las gracias o el agradecimiento.
conveyance (convéyans) s. conducción, transporte, vehículo; entrega, comunicación; transmisión, traslación de dominio, escritura de traspaso.
convict (cónvict) s. presidiario, reo, convicto; (convíct) v. probar la culpabilidad de un reo; declarar culpable.
conviction (convíkshon) s. convicción; convencimiento; prueba y fallo de culpabilidad.
convince (convíns) v. convencer, persuadir.
convincing (convínsing) adj. convincente, persuasivo.
convocation (convokéshon) s. convocación; asamblea.
convoke (convóuk) v. convocar.
convoy (cónvoi) s. convoy, escolta, guardia; (convói) v. convoyar.
convulsion (convólshon) s. convulsión, espasmo, conmoción, agitación.
coo (ku) s. arrullo; v. arrullar.

cook (kuk) s. cocinero; v. cocinar, guisar; cocer; aderezar; **to — up a plan** urdir un plan.

cookery (kúkeri) s. cocina, arte de cocinar.

cookie, cooky (kúki) s. bizcochito, pasta seca, pastelillo.

cooking (kúking) s. arte culinario; **— stove** cocina de gas, cocina eléctrica; **— utensils** batería de cocina; trastos de cocina.

cool (kul) adj. fresco, frío, indiferente, tibio; sereno; s. frescura; v. enfriar, refrescar, entibiar, atemperar; **to — off** calmarse, serenarse.

coolness (kúlnes) s. frescura, tibieza; indiferencia; calma, serenidad.

coon (kun) s. coatí; negro; **a — 's age** una eternidad, mucho tiempo; **— song** canción de negros.

coop (kup) s. jaula; gallinero; v. enjaular; encarcelar; **to — up** encerrar.

cooperate (koóperait) v. cooperar.

cooperation (cooperéshon) s. cooperación.

cooperative (koóperativ) adj. cooperativo; s. cooperativa, sociedad cooperativa.

coordinate (koórdineit) v. coordinar, clasificar; adj. coordinado.

coordination (koordinéshon) s. coordinación.

cop (kop) s. polizonte, policía.

cope (koup) s. arco, bóveda, cúpula; v. contender, rivalizar, competir; **to — with** tener suficiente fuerza para; **I cannot — with this** no puedo con esto.

copious (kópius) adj. copioso, abundante, prolijo.

copper (kóper) s. cobre; policía; **— kettle** marmita o caldera de cobre; adj. cobrizo, de cobre.

copy (kópi) s. copia, duplicado; ejemplar; número (de periódico); muestra, modelo, plana; manuscrito; v. copiar, trasladar, imitar, remedar.

copyright (cópirrait) s. derechos de propiedad literaria; v. registrar, adquirir el título de propiedad literaria.

coquette (kokét) s. coqueta.

coral (kóral) s. coral; adj. coralino, de coral.

cord (kórd) s. cuerda, cordón, cordel; torzal; cuerda de leña; tendón; **—s** pantalones de pana; **spinal —** espina dorsal.

cordial (kórdial) adj. y s. cordial.

corduroy (kórdiuroi) s. pana; **— road** camino hecho de troncos o maderos.

core (kor) s. centro, alma, núcleo, corazón; ánima; substancia; esencia; v. quitar el corazón o centro; despepitar.

cork (kórk) s. corcho, tapón; **— tree** alcornoque; v. tapar con corcho.

corkscrew (kórkscru) s. tirabuzón; adj. espiral, en forma de espiral.

corn (korn) s. maíz, grano, cereal; callo (de los pies o manos); **— bread** pan de maíz; **— meal** harina de maíz; v. salar, curar, acecinar.

corned beef (kórnd bif) s. carne de res curada (en salmuera y salitre).

cornet (kórnet) s. corneta.

cornfield (kórnfild) s. maizal; Am. milpa.

cornice (kórnis) s. cornisa.

coronation (koronéshon) s. coronación.

coronet (kóronet) s. guirnalda, cintillo, coronilla.

corporal (kórporal) adj. corpóreo; s. cabo (militar).

corporation (korporéshon) s. corporación; sociedad, cuerpo, gremio.

corps (kor) s. cuerpo; **air —** cuerpo de aviación; **army —** cuerpo de ejército.

corpse (kórps) s. cadáver.

corpulent (kórpiulent) adj. corpulento; gordo, grueso, obeso.

corpuscle (kórposl) s. corpúsculo.

corral (corrál) s. corral; v. acorralar.

correct (korréct) v. corregir, rectificar, enmendar; adj. correcto; **it is —** está bien; **— ly** adv. correctamente; **—ly done** bien hecho.

correction (korrékshon) s. corrección.

correctness (corréktnes) s. corrección.

corrector (corréktor) s. corrector, revisador.

correlate (kórreleit) v. correlacionar; v. tener correlación.

correspond (korrespónd) v. corresponder; convenir, adaptar; mantener correspondencia.

correspondence (correspóndens) s. correspondencia.

correspondent (correspóndent) adj. correspondiente; s. corresponsal.

corresponding (correspónding) adj. correspondiente, conforme, similar.

corridor (kórridor) s. corredor, pasillo, pasadizo.

corroborate (korróboreit) v. corroborar, confirmar.

corrode (korród) v. corroer, roer.

corrupt (korrópt) adj. corrompido, corrupto, podrido, putrefacto; perverso, depravado; **to become —** corromperse; v. corromper, malear, pervertir, seducir; podrir.

corruption (korrópshon) s. corrupción; descomposición; putrefacción; cohecho; depravación.

corset (kórset) s. corsé.

cosmetic (kosmétic) adj. y s. cosmético.

cosmopolitan (kosmopólitan) adj. cosmopolita.

cost (kost) s. precio, costo, coste; **at all —s** a toda costa; **to sell at —** vender al costo; v. costar.

costly (kóstli) adj. costoso.

costume (kóstium) s. vestido, traje, atavío, indumentaria; disfraz.

cot (kot) s. catre; cabaña, choza; **folding —** catre de tijera.

cottage (kótey) s. casa de campo; quinta; **— cheese** requesón.

cotton (kóton) s. algodón; **raw — algodón en rama; — yarn** hilaza.

couch (káuch) s. diván, canapé; v. acostarse, recostarse, tenderse; explicar, indicar, expresar; estar escondido; **—ed in difficult language** expresado en lenguaje difícil.

cough (kof) s. tos; **whooping —** tosferina; v. toser; **to — up** expectorar; **fit of —ing** acceso de tos.

council (káuncil) s. concilio, consejo; junta; sínodo; **—man** concejal.

councilor (káunslor) s. concejal.

counsel (káunsl) s. consejo; parecer, dictamen; abogado, asesor; v. aconsejar, dirigir, guiar.

counselor (káunslor) s. consejero, abogado consultor.

count (káunt) s. cuenta, cómputo, cálculo; demanda, cargo; conde; v. contar, considerar; valer; **to — on** contar con o confiar en.

countenance (káuntenans) s. semblante, rostro, aspecto; **to give — to** favorecer, proteger; apoyar, amparar.

counter (káunter) s. calculista; mostrador, barra; ficha, tanto; adj. contrario; adv. al contrario; **to run — to** ser contrario a; v. oponerse, contradecir.

counteract (kaunteráct) v. contrarrestar, frustrar, impedir.

counterbalance (kaunterbálans) s. contrapeso, equilibrio.

counterfeit (káunterfit) s. falsificación; adj. falso, falsificado; **— money** moneda falsa; v. falsificar, falsear.

counterpart (káunterpart) s. contraparte; duplicado, copia, imagen.

counterpoise (káunterpois) s. contrapeso; v. equilibrar, contrapesar.

countess (káuntes) s. condesa.

countless (káuntles) adj. incontable, innumerable, sin cuento.

country (kóntri) s. país, patria, nación; campo, campiña; adj. campestre, rústico, agreste, rural.

countryman (kóntriman) s. compatriota, paisano; campesino; Am. ranchero; aldeano, guajiro.

countryside (kóntrisaid) s. campiña, campo.

county (káunti) s. condado.

coupé (kupé) s. cupé.

couple (kopl) s. par, pareja; v. acoplar, unir, juntar, parear.

couplet (kóplet) s. copla; cuplé.

coupling (kópling) s. junta, unión, acoplamiento, enganche, conexión.

coupon (kúpon) s. cupón, talón.

courage (kórey) s. valor, ánimo, coraje, denuedo, intrepidez.

courageous (keréyos) adj. valeroso, intrépido, animoso, valiente.

courier (kúrier) s. mensajero, estafeta.

course (kors) s. curso; marcha; trayecto; rumbo; vía, ruta; progreso, método, regla; asignatura; plato; **the last —** los postres; **golf —** campo de golf; **in the — of years** en el transcurso de los años; **of —** por supuesto; **matter of —** cosa de cajón; **to follow a straight —** seguir una línea recta.

court (kort) s. tribunal, corte, juzgado; séquito, cortejo; patio, atrio; **tennis —** cancha para tenis; **— plaster** tela adhesiva, tafetán; **to pay — to** hacer la corte, galantear; enamorar, cortejar; buscar; **to — danger** exponerse al peligro.

— 51 —

courteous (kórteus) adj. cortés, afable, atento, político.
courtesy (kórtesi) s. cortesía, finura; reverencia; gracia; atención.
courtier (kórtier) s. cortesano, palaciego.
court martial (kortmárshal) s. consejo de guerra.
courtship (kórtship) s. cortejo, galanteo.
courtyard (kórtiard) s. patio.
cousin (kósn) s. primo; **first —** primo carnal.
cove (kouv) s. cala, ensenada; abra.
covenant (kóvenant) s. convenio, pacto; **the New —** el Nuevo Testamento.
cover (kóver) s. cubierta, tapa; sobre; capa; abrigo; cobertor; envoltura; funda; tapete; **table —** mantel; **to send under separate —** enviar por separado; v. cubrir, tapar; abrigar, compensar; proteger; **to — a distance** recorrer una distancia.
covering (kóvering) s. cubierta; abrigo; arropamiento; envoltura.
covet (kóvet) v. codiciar, anhelar.
covetous (kóvetos) adj. codicioso, ambicioso, avariento.
cow (káu) s. vaca; v. acobardar, intimidar.
coward (káuard) adj. y s. cobarde.
cowardice (káuardis) s. cobardía.
cowardliness (káuardlines) s. cobardía.
cowardly (káuardli) adv. cobardemente; adj. cobarde.
cowboy (káuboi) s. vaquero.
cower (káuer) v. agacharse; encogerse (de miedo), acobardarse.
cowhide (káujaid) s. vaqueta; cuero de vaca.
cowl (kaul) s. capucha, capuz.
coy (koi) adj. recatado, modesto, tímido, esquivo; v. acariciar, engatusar, embaucar; recatarse.
coyote (kaióti) s. coyote.
cozy (kóusi) adj. cómodo, agradable; abrigado.
crab (krab) s. cangrejo; Cáncer; **— apple** manzana silvestre; malacate.
crack (krak) s. hendedura, grieta, raja; cuarteadura; crujido, estallido, estampido; chiste, chanza; adj. excelente, de calidad superior; v. rajar, hender, crujir; decir o contar chistes; **to — nuts** cascar nueces.
cracked (krakt) adj. hendido, rajado, agrietado, cuarteado; loco.
cracker (cráker) s. galleta.
crackle (krákl) s. crepitación; chasquido; v. crepitar, crujir.
cradle (kréidl) s. cuna.
craft (kráft) s. artificio, arte; maña, destreza; habilidad, pericia; gremio; barco, embarcación.
craftsman (kráftsman) s. artífice, artesano.
crafty (kráfti) adj. mañoso, astuto, taimado; artificioso.
crag (krag) s. despeñadero, risco.
cram (kram) v. rellenar, henchir, atestar; hartar; s. atracón.
cramp (kramp) s. calambre, retortijón; v. acalambrar; comprimir; sujetar (con grapa); apretar.
cranberry (kránberri) s. arándano.
crane (krein) s. grulla (ave); grúa, cabria v. **to — ones neck** estirar el cuello.
cranium (krénium) s. cráneo.
crank (krank) s. biela, cigüeña, manubrio; chiflado; v. voltear el manubrio o cigüeña; **he is a —** es un maniático.
cranky (kránki) adj. lunático, cascarrabias, venático, enojadizo.
cranny (kréni) s. grieta, hendedura, rendija.
crape (kreip) s. crespón.
crash (krash) s. estallido, estampido, estruendo; choque; fracaso; quiebra, bancarrota; v. estrellar(se); estallar; chocar; **to — an airplane** aterrizar de golpe un aeroplano; **to — into** estrellarse con.
crate (kreit) s. canasto, jaula; huacal; v. embalar en jaula.
crater (kréiter) s. crater.
cravat (kravát) s. corbata.
crave (kréiv) s. ansiar, anhelar, apetecer; implorar, pedir; **to — mercy** pedir misericordia.
crawl (krol) v. arrastrarse, serpear; andar a gatas; s. arrastramiento; **to — up** trepar; **to be —ing with ants** estar lleno de hormigas.
crayon (kréion) s. lápiz de color; creyón, gis, tiza, yeso.
craze (kréis) s. locura, demencia, manía; delirio; antojo; v. enloquecer.
crazy (créisi) adj. loco; exageradamente deseoso; trastornado; **to go —** perder el juicio.
creak (krik) s. crujido, rechina-

miento, chirrido; v. crujir, rechinar, chirriar.
cream (krim) s. crema, nata; — of tomato soup puré de tomate; cold — crema cosmética; ice — helado; v. desnatar, batir; preparar legumbres con crema.
creamery (krímeri) s. cremería, lechería.
creamy (krími) adj. cremoso, natoso.
crease (kris) s. pliegue, doblez, arruga; v. plegar, doblar, acanalar; arrugar.
create (kriéit) v. crear, producir; procrear; constituir.
creation (kriéshon) s. creación.
creative (kriéitiv) adj. creativo.
creator (kriéitor) s. creador.
creature (krichur) s. criatura, ser viviente; animal; our fellow — nuestro semejante.
credence (krídens) s. creencia, fe.
credentials (kridénshals) s. credenciales.
credible (krédibl) adj. creíble, verosímil.
creditable (kréditabl) adj. fidedigno; loable.
creditor (créditor) s. acreedor.
credulous (krédiulos) adj. crédulo.
creed (krid) s. credo, creencia.
creeper (kríper) s. enredadera, trepadora:
crepe (krep) ver **crape**.
crescent (krésent) adj. creciente; luna creciente; media luna.
crest (krest) s. cresta; copete; penacho; cima, cumbre; cresta de una ola; timbre (de un escudo de armas).
crestfallen (créstfolen) adj. cabizbajo, abatido, alicaído.
cretonne (kritón) s. cretona.
crevice (krévis) s. raja, grieta, hendedura, abertura.
crew (krú) s. tripulación; cuadrilla; pret. de to **crow**.
crib (krib) s. pesebre; camita de niño; arcón; armazón (usado en la construcción de edificios); clave o acordeón fraudulento (en un examen); v. enjaular; plagiar.
cricket (kríket) s. grillo, vilorta (juego).
crime (kráim) s. crimen, delito.
criminal (kríminal) adj. y s. criminal, culpable, reo.
crimp (krimp) v. rizar, encrespar; s. rizo.

crimson (krimsn) adj. y s. carmesí.
cripple (krípl) s. inválido, baldado, tullido; cojo, manco; v. lisiar, mutilar; baldar, incapacitar; adj. lisiado, baldado.
crisis (kráisis) s. crisis.
crisp (krisp) adj. frágil; crespo, rizado; tostado; quebradizo; — answer contestación aguda; — wind brisa refrescante.
criterion (kraitírion) s. criterio.
critic (krític) s. crítico; crítica.
critical (krítical) adj. crítico; escrupuloso; difícil.
criticize (krítisais) v. criticar, censurar.
croak (krouk) v. graznar, croar; gruñir; s. graznido, canto de rana.
crochet (choshé) v. hacer crochet; — hook gancho de tejer.
crock (krok) s. vasija de loza.
crockery (krókeri) s. loza; trastes.
crocodile (krókodail) s. cocodrilo, Am. caimán.
crony (króni) s. compadre, camarada, compañero.
crooked (krúked) adj. encorvado, torcido; ladeado. Am. chueco, falso, fraudulento.
croon (krun) v. canturrear; cantar tristemente, con patetismo.
crop (krop) s. cosecha, recolección, agosto; buche (de ave); látigo; cuarta; — of hair cabellera; v. segar, cosechar; rapar, trasquilar; pacer; to — out aparecer, asomar; to — up brotar, manifestarse inesperadamente.
cross (crós) s. cruz; pena; cruzamiento; mezcla; revés; v. cruzar, atravesar(se); encontrarse, contrariar; adj. malhumorado, transversal; en cruz; arisco; enfadado; — country a campo traviesa; — examine interrogar; — eyed bizco
crossbar (krosbar) s. travesaño.
crossing (krósing) s. cruce; vado; paso; encrucijada; crucero; railroad — cruce de F. C.
crossroad (krósrod) s. crucero, encrucijada, vía transversal.
crouch (krauch) v. agacharse, agazaparse.
crow (krou) s. cuervo, corneja; cacareo, canto del gallo; crow's foot pata de gallo (arrugas en el rabo del ojo); v. cacarear; jactarse; hacer alarde de.
crowbar (króbar) s. barra, palanca de hierro.
crowd (kráud) s. multitud, muche-

— 53 —

grupo, pandilla; v. amontonar, atestar; apiñar(se); empujar, estrujar.
crowded (kráuded) adj. atestado, aglomerado, lleno, apiñado.
crown (kráun) s. corona, diadema; copa (de sombrero); cima; v. coronar.
crucible (krúsibl) s. crisol.
crucifix (krúsifix) s. crucifijo.
crucify (krúsifai) v. crucificar.
crude (krud) adj. crudo, tosco, rudo, inculto; — oil petróleo crudo; — sugar azúcar no refinada.
cruel (krúel) adj. cruel, inhumano.
cruelty (krúelti) s. crueldad, atrocidad; ensañamiento.
cruet (krúet) s. ampolleta; vinajera; oil — aceitera; vinegar — vinagrera.
cruise (kruz) s. travesía; viaje por mar; v. navegar.
cruiser (krúzer) s. crucero (buque), guardacosta.
crumb (krom) s. miga, migajón; pizca, mendrugo; v. desmenuzar, migar.
crumble (krombl) v. desmoronar(se), desmigajar.
crumple (krompl) v. arrugar, ajar; contraerse; encogerse.
crunch (kronch) v. cascar, crujir.
crusade (kruséid) s. cruzada; hacer una campaña.
crusader (kruséider) s. cruzado.
crush (krosh) v. aplastar, machacar, quebrar; triturar; estrujar; s. quebrantamiento; apretura; apiñamiento; agolpamiento; compresión; to — stone moler piedra.
crust (krost) s. costra, corteza; mendrugo; v. encostrar(se); incrustar.
crusty (krósti) adj. costroso.
crutch (krotch) s. muleta.
cry (krai) s. grito, alarido, lamento, lloro, llanto; gritería; clamor; v. gritar, llorar, vocear, exclamar; lamentarse; to — for help pedir socorro.
crystal (crístal) s. cristal; — clear cristalino.
crystallize (krístalais) v. cristalino, claro, transparente.
crystallize (krístalais) v. cristalizar(se).
cub (kob) s. cachorro.
Cuban (kiúban) adj. y s. cubano.
cube (kiub) s. cubo; — root raiz cúbica; v. cubicar.
cubic (kiúbic) adj. cúbico.

cuckoo (kúkú) s. cuco, cuclillo; adj. tocado, chiflado, medio loco.
cucumber (kiúkamber) s. pepino.
cud (kod) s. rumia; panza; to chew the — rumiar.
cuddle (kodl) v. abrazar, tener en brazos; estar abrazados.
cudgel (kódyel) s. garrote, porra, tranca; v. garrotear, apalear.
cue (kiu) s. cola, rabo; coleta; indicación, señal; billiard — taco de billar; s. apunte en el teatro.
cuff (kof) s. puño (de camisa, etc.), doblez (del pantalón); revés, bofetada; v. abofetear.
culminate (kólmineit) v. culminar.
culprit (kólprit) s. reo, delincuente, criminal; culpable.
cult (kolt) s. culto, secta religiosa; homenaje, devoción.
cultivate (kóltiveit) v. cultivar, ejercer, practicar; consagrarse a.
cultivated (kóltiveited) adj. culto, cultivado.
cultivation (koltivéshon) s. cultivo, cultura; labor; adelantamiento.
cultivator (kóltiveitor) s. cultivador, labrador; cultivadora.
culture (kóltchor) s. cultura; ilustración; v. enseñar, educar.
cultured (kóltchord) adj. culto.
cumbersome (kómbersom) adj. engorroso, enfadoso, incómodo.
cup (kop) s. taza, pocillo, copa que se da como premio en los partidos.
cupboard (kóbord) s. armario, alacena, aparador; chinero.
cur (kér) s. perro de mala ralea; hombre vil; villano, cobarde.
curate (kiúret) s. cura, vicario.
curb (kerb) s. reborde, encintado o cordón de la acera; freno con barda; restricción; brocal de pozo; v. refrenar, contener, moderar.
curd (kord) s. cuajada, requesón; v. cuajar, coagular, condensar.
curdle (kordl) v. cuajar, coagular.
cure (kiur) s. curación; remedio; v. curar, sanar.
curio (kiúrio) s. curiosidad, objeto curioso y raro (de arte).
curiosity (kiuriósiti) s. curiosidad, rareza.
curious (kiúrios) adj. curioso; singular; extraño, raro; entrometido.
curl (kerl) s. rizo, bucle; espiral (de humo) v. rizar, encrespar,

— 54 —

ensortijar, torcer; enroscar; alzarse en espirales (el humo).
curly (kérli) adj. rizado, encrespado; crespo; chino.
currant (kórrant) s. grosella; — **bush** grosellero.
currency (kórrensi) s. moneda corriente o en circulación, dinero; **paper** — papel moneda.
current (kórrent) adj. corriente, común; en boga; del día; prevaleciente; de actualidad; popular; s. corriente (eléctrica).
curse (kors) s. maldición, imprecación; v. maldecir; jurar; blasfemar.
cursed (korst) adj. maldito.
curt (kort) adj. corto, conciso, brusco.
curtail (kortéil) v. restringir, reducir; abreviar, acortar, cercenar.
curtain (kórtn) s. cortina, telón; poner cortinas.
curvature (kórvachur) s. curvatura.
curve (kerv) s. curva, comba; v. encorvar, torcer, combar.
curved (kervd) adj. encorvado, combado; curvo, torcido; chueco.
cushion (kúshon) s. cojín, almohadón, almohadilla; amortiguador (para sonidos o choques).
custard (kóstard) s. flan, natilla.
custody (kóstodi) s. custodia, guardia, cuidado; **to hold in** — custodiar.
custom (kóstom) s. costumbre, hábito, uso, usanza; —s derechos de aduana; — **made** hecho a la medida; —. **tailor** maestro sastre.
customary (kóstomeri) adj. usual, habitual, ordinario, acostumbrado.
customer (kóstomer) s. cliente, parroquiano, marchante.
customhouse (kóstomjaus) s. aduana; — **official** vista de aduana; — **mark** marchamo.
cute (kiut) adj. lindo, mono, cuco.
cuticle (kiútikl) s. cutícula.
cutlery (kótleri) s. cuchillería.
cutlet (kótlet) s. chuleta.
cutter (kóter) s. cortador; máquina para cortar; trineo; **wood** — leñador; grabador, tallador.
cutting (kóting) adj. cortante; mordaz; satírico; sarcástico.
cycle (sáicl) s. ciclo, período.
cyclone (sáiclon) s. ciclón; huracán.
cylinder (cílinder) s. cilindro.

cylindrical (cilíndrikl) adj. cilíndrico.
cymbal (símbal) s. címbalo, platillo; **to play the** — tocar los platillos.
cynical (sínical) adj. cínico.
cynicism (sínisism) s. cinismo.
cypress (sáipres) s. ciprés.

D

dad (dad) s. papá, tata; **daddy** papaíto, papacito.
daffodil (dáfodil) s. narciso.
dagger (dáguer) s. daga, puñal; **to look** —s **at** traspasar con la mirada.
daily (déili) adj. diario; s. diario, periódico; adv. diariamente.
dainty (déinti) adj. delicado, refinado; exquisito; s. regalo, golosina; manjar.
dairy (déiri) s. lechería, quesería; — **man** lechero, quesero.
daisy (déisi) s. margarita; primor.
dale (déil) s. cañada; valle.
dally (dáli) v. juguetear; holgazanear; tardarse, rezagarse, entretenerse; perder tiempo; malgastar el tiempo.
dam (dam) s. presa; madre (en ganadería); yegua; v. represar.
damage (dámey) s. daño; perjuicio; detrimento, estropeo, empecimiento; **to pay for** —s indemnizar; v. dañar(se); averiar(se); empecer.
dame (deim) s. dama, señora, ama, dueña; **old** — vieja.
damn (damn) v. maldecir; condenar; infernar; condenar a pena eterna; — **it!** ¡maldito sea!
damnation (damnéshon) s. condenación, damnación, maldición.
damp (damp) adj. húmedo; mojado; liento; s. humedad; v. humedecer.
dampen (dámpen) v. mojar, humedecer; **to** — **down a fire** cubrir el fuego con cenizas para que la combustión sea lenta.
dampness (dámpnes) s. humedad.
damsel (dámsel) s. damisela.
dance (dáns) s. baile, danza; v. danzar, bailar.
dancer (dánser) s. bailador, bailarín.
dandelion (dándelaion) s. diente de león o amargón.
dandruff (dándrof) s. caspa.
dandy (dándi) s. currutaco, majo.

dangerous (dányeros) adj. peligroso, arriesgado; espinoso, grave;—**ly** adv. peligrosamente; —**ly ill** gravemente enfermo.

dangle (dángl) v. prender, colgar, suspender, bambolear(se) (en el aire).

dapple (dápl) adj. rodado, con manchas (dícese de los caballos); habado; — **grey** rucio moteado, tordo.

dare (der) s. desafío, reto, provocación; — **devil** atrevido, osado; v. retar, desafiar, provocar.

daring (déring) s. atrevimiento, osadía; adj. osado, atrevido.

dark (dark) adj. obscuro, opaco, moreno; — **horse** caballo desconocido (que gana una carrera inesperadamente); candidato (nombrado inesperadamente) — **secret** enigma; — **lantern** linterna sorda; s. obscuridad; sombra.

darken (dárkn) v. oscurecer(se); poner obscuro, sombrío.

darkness (dárknes) s. obscuridad; tinieblas; sombra, lobreguez.

darky (dárki) s. negro (persona).

darling (dárlin) adj. y s. amado, querido; el predilecto, el querido.

darn (darn) s. zurcido; **it is not worth a** — vale un comino; v. zurcir; —! ¡caramba! ¡canastos! —**ing needle** aguja de zurcir.

dart (dart) s. dardo, flecha, saeta, venablo; tragacete; sisa (en un vestido); movimiento rápido; v. lanzar(se); flechar; arrojar; **to — out** salir como una flecha; **to — in and out** entrar y salir precipitadamente.

dash (dash) s. raya; arranque, incursión; ímpetu; garbo; pizca (de sal o azúcar); roceada (de agua); — **board** tablero de instrumentos; — **of a pen** rasgo, rúbrica; v. lanzar(se), echar(se); estrellar; reprimir; frustrar; **to — with** salpicar; mezclar; sazonar; **to — out** salir a la carrera.

data (déta) s. pl. datos.

date (deit) s. fecha, data, plazo; cita; compromiso; dátil; **up to — al** día; moderno; **up to this —** hasta la fecha; v. fechar; **to — from** datar de; remontarse a; computar.

daub (dob) v. embadurnar, untar; pintarrajear; ensuciar.

daughter (dóter) s. hija; — **in law** nuera.

daunt (dont) v. acobardar, desanimar, espantar, intimidar.

dauntless (dóntles) adj. intrépido, impertérrito, denodado.

davenport (dávenport) s. sofá.

dawn (don) s. alba; amanecer, madrugada; v. amanecer; alborear, rayar (el día); **it just —ed upon me** acabo de darme cuenta.

day (dei) s. día; luz del día; tiempo o período; — **after tomorrow** pasado mañana; — **before yesterday** anteayer o antier; **by —** de día; **from — to —** de día en día, de un día para otro; **every other —** cada tercer día; **by the —** por día.

daybreak (déibreik) s. amanecer, alba, **at —** al amanecer, al romper el día, al rayar el día.

daylight (déilait) s. luz del día.

daytime (déitaim) s. día (tiempo de luz natural); de sol a sol; **in the —** durante el día.

daze (déis) s. deslumbramiento, ofuscamiento; **to be in a —** estar aturdido; v. aturdir, ofuscar, deslumbrar.

dazzle (dásl) s. brillantez; v. encandilar, deslumbrar, ofuscar.

deacon (dícon) s. diácono.

dead (ded) adj. muerto; inerte; apagado, sordo; que no transmite corriente; — **air** aire viciado; — **letter** carta no reclamada; —**loss** pérdida absoluta; —**ly** adv. completamente, absolutamente, sumamente, — **calm** calma profunda; — **certainty** certeza completa; — **head** gorrero; — **hours** quietud de la noche; — **point** punto muerto.

deaden (déden) v. amortiguar.

deadly (dédli) adj. mortal; fatal; como la muerte; cadavérico; destructivo; letal; grave; mortalmente; — **dull** sumamente aburrido.

deaf (def) adj. sordo; **to make —** aturdir; — **mute** s. y adj. sordomudo.

deafen (défen) v. ensordecer; amortiguar, asordar.

deafening (défening) adj. ensordecedor, estruendoso.

deafness (défnes) s. sordera.

dealer (díler) s. negociante, comerciante; tallador (en el juego de naipes); **plain —** hombre sincero; **false —** hombre de dos caras.

dealings (dílings) s. pl. relaciones

(comerciales o amistosas); negocios; tratos.
dean (din) s. deán (dignidad eclesiástica), decano (de la Universidad).
dear (dir) adj. querido, amado; predilecto, caro; my — querido mío, querida mía; — Sir muy señor mío; —ly adv. cariñosamente; a precio alto; my —ly beloved muy amado mío; — me! ¡Dios mío! oh —! ¡ay!
dearth (derz) s. escasez, carestía, hambre, esterilidad.
death (dez) s. muerte; mortandad; defunción; — rate mortalidad.
deathbed (dézbed) s. lecho de muerte.
debase (dibéis) v. rebajar el valor de; degradar, humillar, prostituir, adulterar.
debatable (debéitabl) adj. discutible, disputable.
debate (debéit) s. debate, discusión; contienda, disputa, controversia; v. debatir, discutir.
debit (débit) s. débito; adeudo; cargo; debe (una cuenta); saldo deudor.
debris (debris) s. escombros; ruinas.
debt (det) s. deuda; adeudo; débito; obligación; **bad —** cuenta incobrable; **to run into —** endeudarse.
debtor (détor) s. deudor; cargo, "Debe".
debut (debiú) s. estreno; **to make a —** debutar, estrenarse.
decade (déked) s. década, decena.
decadence (dekédens) s. decadencia.
decanter (dekánter) s. garrafa; ampolla; **large —** garrafón.
decay (dikéi) s. decaimiento; decadencia; ruina, menoscabo, desmedro, perecimiento; caries (de la dentadura); v. decaer, venir a menos.
decease (disís) s. muerte, fallecimiento, defunción; óbito; v. morir, fallecer.
deceased (disíst) adj. y s. muerto, difunto, finado.
deceit (disít) s. engaño; fraude.
deceitful (disítful) adj. engañador; tramposo, engañoso, falso.
deceive (disív) v. engañar.
December (décémber) s. diciembre.
decency (dísensi) s. decencia.

decent (disnt) adj. decente, decoroso.
decide (disáid) v. decidir, resolver; determinar, juzgar; **to — to** resolverse a, decidirse a.
decided (disáidid) adj. decidido, resuelto.
decimal (décimal) adj. decimal; s. decimal, fracción decimal.
decipher (disáifer) v. decifrar.
decision (desíshon) s. decisión, resolución, determinación.
decisive (disáisiv) adj. decisivo, terminante, conclusivo.
deck (dek) s. cubierta (de un buque), baraja; techo de un vagón; albergue; **to — oneself out** emperifollarse.
declaration (declaréshon) s. declaración.
declare (dicler) v. declarar.
decline (dicláin) s. declinación; decadencia, menoscabo, descaecimiento; consunción; enfermedad que va cediendo de su violencia.
declivity (diclíviti) s. declive.
decompose (dicompóus) v. descomponer(se).
decorate (décoreit) v. decorar, adornar; hermosear.
decoration (decoréshon) s. decoración, adorno, ornamentación.
decorative (décorativ) adj. decorativo, ornamental.
decorum (dicórum) s. decoro; circunspección.
decoy (dicói) s. reclamo, señuelo, figura de ave (que sirve para atraer aves); cebo (artificio para atraer con engaño); estruchada; trampa; v. atraer con señuelo.
decree (dikrí) s. decreto, ley, edicto; v. decretar; mandar.
decrepit (dikrépit) adj. decrépito.
dedicate (dédikeit) v. dedicar.
dedication (dedikéshon) s. dedicación, consagración, dedicatoria.
deduce (didiús) v. deducir, inferir.
deduct (didóct) v. deducir, descontar, rebajar, restar.
deduction (didókshon) s. deducción; corolario; descuento, rebaja.
deed (did) s. hecho, acción, acto, realidad, hazaña, proeza; escritura (de venta o compra).
deem (dim) v. juzgar, creer, considerar.
deep (dip) adj. hondo; profundo; recóndito, abstruso; sagaz; perspicaz; **— in debt** cargado de deudas **— in thought** absorto; —

— 57 —

drawing de mucho calado; **— musing** pensativo; **— sea alta mar; — mourning** luto riguroso; **—ly** adv. profundamente, hondamente, intensamente; **— sea line** sonda o plomada.

deepen (dípen) v. ahondar.

deer (dír) s. ciervo, venado; **fallow — gamo, gama; red —** ciervo común; **— skin** piel de venado.

deface (diféis) v. desfigurar, estropear, mutilar, deteriorar.

defame (diféim) v. difamar, calumniar, desacreditar, deshonrar, denigrar.

default (difólt) s. falla, falta, negligencia, omisión, descuido; culpa, delito; deficiencia; v. fallar, faltar (en el cumplimiento de un deber, pago, obligación); no comparecer a la cita de un tribunal.

defeat (difít) s. derrota, vencimiento; frustración, rota, destrozo, v. derrotar, vencer, desechar.

defect (difect) s. defecto.

defective (diféctiv) adj. defectuoso; incompleto; defectivo, imperfecto; **— verb** verbo defectivo.

defend (difénd) v. defender.

defendant (diféndant) s. acusado, demandado, procesado, defensor.

defender (difénder) s. defensor; abogado defensor; campeón.

defense (diféns) s. defensa, amparo, protección, escudo, apoyo.

defenseless (difénsles) adj. indefenso, inerme, desarmado.

defensive (difénsiv) adj. defensivo; s. defensiva.

defer (difér) v. diferir, posponer, aplazar; ceder, condescender; **to — to another's opinion** remitirse o ceder dictamen a otro.

defiance (difáians) s. reto, desafío; provocación; oposición.

deficiency (difíshenci) s. deficiencia; defecto, falta.

deficient (difíshent) adj. deficiente; defectuoso, falto, incompleto.

deficit (défisit) s. déficit.

defile (difáil) v. viciar, corromper, profanar, manchar, ensuciar, violar.

define (difáin) v. definir.

definite (définit) adj. definido; claro, preciso; fijo, exacto, terminante; **— article** artículo determinado o definido; **—ly** adv. definidamente; **—ly not** terminantemente no.

definition (definíshon) s. definición.

definitive (definítiv) adj. definitivo.

deform (difórm) v. deformar, afear.

deformed (difórmed) adj. deforme, desfigurado.

deformity (difórmiti) s. deformidad, deformación, fealdad.

defraud (defród) v. defraudar.

defray (difréi) v. sufragar, costear; pagar (gastos).

deft (deft) adj. diestro, ágil.

defy (defái) v. desafiar, retar, oponerse a, resistirse a, arrostrar.

degenerate (deyénereit) adj. y s. degenerado; v. degenerar.

degradation (degradéshon) s. degradación; envilecimiento.

degrade (digréid) v. degradar; envilecer, privar, deponer.

degree (digrí) s. grado; rango; **by —s** gradualmente; **to get a —** graduarse.

deign (dein) v. dignarse, condescender.

deity (díiti) s. deidad.

dejected (diyécted) adj. abatido.

dejection (deyékshon) s. abatimiento, melancolía, depresión, evacuación.

delay (diléi) s. demora, tardanza, dilación; detención, retraso, v. diferir, tardar.

delegate (délegueit) s. delegado, comisario, representante.

delegation (deleguéshon) s. delegación, diputación, comisión.

deliberate (delíbereit) adj. deliberado, premeditado; cauto, pensado, reflexionado; v. deliberar, discutir, considerar, aconsejarse.

deliberation (deliberéshon) s. deliberación, reflexión, premeditación.

delicacy (délikasi) s. delicadeza, suavidad, finura, ternura.

delicate (délikeit) adj. delicado; tenue; frágil; exquisito, fino.

delicatessen (delicatésn) s. tienda de fiambres, manjares delicados.

delicious (delíshos) adj. delicioso.

delight (diláit) s. deleite; delicia; placer, gozo, encanto; regocijo; v. deleitar(se); encantar; agradar; regocijar; causar placer.

delighted (deláited) adj. encantado **to be —** alegrarse de, tener mucho gusto en.

delightful (deláitful) adj. deleitoso; delicioso, ameno, agradable, grato, encantador; exquisito.

delineate (delíniet) v. delinear, trazar, diseñar, describir.
delinquent (delínkuent) adj. y s. delincuente, pecador.
delirious (delírios) adj. delirante; desvariado; to be — v. desvariar.
delirium (delíriom) s. delirio.
deliver (delíver) v. entregar; librar; libertar; dar; comunicar; recitar; sacudir; tirar.
deliverance (delíverans) s. deliberación, rescate, salvación.
deliverer (delíverer) s. libertador; portador; salvador; relator.
dell (del) s. cañada, hondonada.
deluge (délioy) s. diluvio; golpe, calamidad; v. diluviar, inundar abrumar.
delusion (delúshon) s. ilusión; engaño; error; decepción.
demand (dimánd) s. demanda, exigencia; solicitud; petición; on — a solicitud; v. demandar, reclamar.
demanding (dimánding) adj. exigente.
demeanor (demínor) s. conducta, comportamiento; porte; proceder.
demented (deménted) adj. demente
demobilize (demóbilais) v. demovilizar, licenciar.
democracy (demócrasi) s. democracia.
democrat (démocrat) s. demócrata.
democratic (democrátic) adj. democrático.
demolish (demólish) v. demoler, derribar; destruir.
demon (démon) s. demonio.
demonstrate (démonstreit) v. demostrar.
demonstration (demonstréshon) s. demostración; prueba, evidencia.
demonstrative (demónstrativ) adj. demostrativo; efusivo.
den (den) s. guarida; escondrijo; cueva, antro, latebra.
denial (denáial) s. negación; negativa; self — abnegación.
denomination (denominéshon) s. denominación; nombre, título; designación; secta religiosa.
denote (denóut) v. denotar.
denounce (denáuns) v. denunciar, delatar, acusar, amenazar.
dense (dens) adj. denso; espeso, compacto, apretado; estúpido.
density (dénsiti) s. densidad; estupidez.
dent (dent) s. abolladura; mella; diente, indentación; v. abollar.
dental (déntl) adj. dental; s. dental. consonante dental.
dentist (déntist) s. dentista.
denunciation (denonciéshon) s. denuncia, acusación, denunciación.
deny (denái) v. negar; rehusar; desmentir; renunciar; negarse a, no dejarse ver de; to — oneself sacrificarse.
depart (depárt) v. partir, salir, irse; desviarse, diferir de, salirse de.
departed (depárted) adj. ido; ausente, difunto.
department (depártment) s. departamento; distrito; ramo, división, subdivisión; ministerio, negociado, despacho.
departure (depárchur) s. salida, partida; desviación, divergencia; muerte; diferencia de meridiano.
depend (depénd) v. depender.
dependable (depéndabl) adj. seguro.
dependence (depéndens) s. dependencia, confianza, sostén, apoyo.
dependency (depéndensi) s. dependencia, pertenencia, sucursal.
dependent (depéndent) adj. dependiente; subordinado; subalterno; s. dependiente, familiar.
depict (depíkt) v. pintar, describir; representar; retratar.
deplete (deplít) v. agotar, vaciar.
deplorable (deplórabl) adj. deplorable, lamentable; lastimoso.
deplore (deplór) v. deplorar, lamentar, llorar.
deportment (depórtment) s. conducta.
depose (depóus) v. deponer; declarar, destronar; destituir.
deposit (depósit) s. depósito, sedimento, precipitado; v. depositar.
deposition (deposíshon) s. disposición, testimonio, declaración.
depositor (depósitor) s. depositador.
depot (dípo) s. depósito; almacén; estación de ferrocarril.
depreciate (depríshieit) v. depreciar, bajar, rebajar, menospreciar.
depress (diprés) v. deprimir.
depressed (diprést) adj. abatido.
depressing (diprésing) adj. deprimente.
depression (dipréshon) s. depresión; decaimiento, abatimiento.
deprive (dipráiv) v. privar; despojar.
depth (depz) s. profundidad; hon-

dura, fondo; espesor, grueso, parte interior o recóndita; gravedad (de los sonidos); viveza de los colores; **in the — of the night** en las tinieblas de la noche; **in the — of winter** en lo más crudo del invierno.

deputation (deplutéshon) s. diputación; delegación; comisión.

depute (depiút) v. delegar, diputar.

deputy (dépiuti) s. diputado, delegado; agente; comisario.

derange (derény) v. trastornar, desordenar; desarreglar.

derby (dérbi) s. sombrero hongo o de bola; llana; famosa carrera anual de caballos.

deride (diráid) v. escarnecer; ridiculizar; burlar; mofar; burlarse de; zumbar o dar zumba.

derision (diríshon) s. mofa, irrisión.

derive (deráiv) v. derivar(se); provenir; sacar provecho; recibir.

derrick (dérrik) s. grúa de pescante, armazón (en explotación de petróleo).

descend (desénd) v. descender, bajar; **— upon** caer sobre.

descendant (deséndant) adj. y s. descendiente; nieto.

descent (desént) s. descenso, bajada, descendimiento; alcurnia, linaje; pendiente, declive.

describe (diskráib) v. describir.

description (descrípshon) s. descripción; clase; **of all —s** de todas clases.

descriptive (descríptiv) adj. descriptivo.

desert (désert) adj. desierto, despoblado; inhabitado; solitario; estéril; s. páramo; v. abandonar, desamparar, desertar.

deserter (desérter) s. desertor.

desertion (desérshon) s. deserción; abandono; defección.

deserve (disérv) v. merecer.

deserving (desérving) adj. meritorio; merecedor; acreedor.

design (desáin) s. diseño, dibujo, trazo; proyecto; designio, propósito; intención; v. diseñar, trazar; proyectar.

designate (dézigneit) v. designar; señalar; indicar; distinguir.

designer (disáiner) s. diseñador; dibujante, proyectista, tracista.

desirability (desairability) s. conveniencia; utilidad.

desirable (desáirabl) adj. deseable,

agradable, conveniente, apetecible.

desire (disáir) s. deseo, anhelo, aspiración; v. anhelar, ansiar.

desirous (disáiros) adj. deseoso.

desist (desíst) v. desistir(se).

desk (desk) s. escritorio, bufete, pupitre, mesa de escritorio, carpeta.

desolate (désoleit) adj. desolado, despoblado, desierto; solitario; v. desolar, talar, devastar.

desolation (desoléshon) s. desolación; soledad; aflicción.

despair (dispér) s. desesperación; desesperanza; v. desesperar, perder la esperanza.

despairing (dispéring) s. desesperado; sin esperanza.

desperate (déspereit) adj. desesperado, arriesgado, temerario; arrojado; irremediable; **— illnes** enfermedad gravísima; **—ly** adv. desesperadamente.

desperation (desperéshon) s. desesperación, temeridad, furor.

despise (despáis) v. despreciar; desdeñar; menospreciar.

despite (despáit) s. despecho; prep. a despecho; a pesar ae; no obstante; sin embargo de; v. enfadar.

despoil (despóil) v. despojar; robar.

despondency (despóndensi) s. abatimiento, decaimiento del ánimo, descaecimiento.

despondent (despóndent) adj. abatido, decaído, desalentado, desesperado; desesperanzado.

despot (déspot) s. déspota.

despotic (despótic) adj. despótico.

despotism (déspotism) s. despotismo.

dessert (desért) s. postre.

destination (destinéshon) s. destino, paradero, meta.

destine (déstin) v. destinar; dedicar, consagrar; **—ed for** con rumbo a; con destino a.

destiny (déstini) s. destino, sino.

destitute (déstitiut) adj. destituido, necesitado, desamparado, desprovisto; v. destituir, desamparar.

destroy (destrói) v. destruir, devastar.

destroyer (destróier) s. destructor, cazatorpederos, destróyer.

destruction (destrókshon) s. destrucción, ruina, asolamiento.

destructive (destróctiv) adj. destructivo, destructor.

detach (ditách) v. separar, despegar, desprender; destacar (una porción de tropa).
detachment (ditáchment) s. separación; desprendimiento, despegadura; alejamiento; destacamento (de tropas).
detail (ditéil) s. detalle, pormenor; destacamento (militar); **to go into** — detallar, pormenorizar; v. detallar, circunstanciar.
detain (ditéin) v. detener, entretener, retardar, contener.
detect (detékt) v. descubrir.
detective (detéctiv) s. detective, policía secreto, espía asalariado.
detention (deténshon) s. detención.
deteriorate (detérioreit) v. deteriorar, desmejorar.
determine (detérmin) v. determinar, decidir, resolver.
determined (detérmind) adj. determinado, decidido, resuelto.
detest (ditést) v. detestar, aborrecer.
detour (dítur) s. rodeo, desvío, desviación, vuelta.
devastate (dévasteit) v. devastar, arruinar, asolar.
develop (devélop) v. desarrollar(se); revelar (una película o placa fotográfica), desenvolver, fomentar.
development (divélopment) s. desarrollo, desenvolvimiento; crecimiento, fomento, explotación, progreso, revelado (de una película); evolución.
deviate (díviet) v. desviarse.
deviation (deviéshon) s. desviación, extravío, divergencia.
device (diváis) s. artificio; mecanismo, aparato, ardid, invento, proyecto; **left to one's own** —s abandonado a sus propios recursos.
devil (dévl) s. diablo, demonio; **the** —, ¡demonio! ¡diantre!
devilish (dévilish) adj. diabólico, endiablado, demoníaco, excesivo; travieso.
deviltry (déviltri) s. diablura.
devious (dévios) adj. desviado; tortuoso; descarriado, extraviado.
devise (diváis) v. idear, trazar, proyectar.
devoid (devóid) adj. exento, libre, falto, privado.
devote (devóut) v. dedicar; consagrar; asignar; **to** — **one's self** consagrarse a.
devoted (devóted) adj. dedicado, consagrado; leal; adicto, afecto; — **friend** amigo fiel.
devotion (devóshon) s. devoción; piedad, fervor; afecto, lealtad.
devour (diváur) v. devorar.
devout (diváut) adj. devoto, piadoso; religioso, sincero, pío.
dew (diú) s. rocío, sereno; v. rociar.
dewdrop (diúdrop) s. gota de rocío.
dewy (diúi) adj. rociado, húmedo de rocío, lleno de rocío.
dexterity (dekstériti) s. destreza.
dexterous (dékstrous) adj. diestro.
diadem (dáiadem) s. diadema, corona.
diagnose (daiagnóus) v. diagnosticar.
diagonal (daiágonal) adj. diagonal, s. inglete; diagonal.
diagram (dáiagram) s. diagrama.
dialect (dáialect) s. dialecto.
dialogue (dáialog) s. diálogo.
diameter (daiámeter) s. diámetro.
diamond (dáiamond) s. diamante; rombo (figura geométrica).
diaper (dáiaper) s. pañal.
diarrhea (daiarría) s. diarrea.
diary (dáiari) s. diario.
dice (dais) s. pl. de **die** dados; v. cuadricular, jugar los dados.
dictate (dícteit) s. dictado.
dictation (dictéshon) s. dictado, mando absoluto; mando arbitrario.
dictator (dícteitor) s. dictador.
dictatorship (dictéitorship) s. dictadura.
diction (díkshon) s. dicción.
dictionary (dícshonari) s. diccionario.
did (did) pret. de **to do**.
die (dai) v. morirse; marchitarse, secarse (las flores).
die (dai) s. (pl. **dice**) dado (para jugar) (pl. **dies**); matriz, molde, troquel, cubo; — **sinker** entallador.
diet (dáiet) s. dieta; régimen; alimento; v. estar a dieta; **to put on a** — adietar, ponerse a dieta.
differ (dífer) v. diferir, diferenciarse, distinguirse, discrepar, disentir.
difference (díferens) s. diferencia, distinción, desigualdad, disparidad; disensión; **makes no** — no importa, es igual.
different (díferent) adj. diferente; distinto, diverso.

differentiate (diferénshieit) v. diferenciarse, distinguir(se).
difficult (dificolt) adj. difícil; dificultoso; peliagudo.
difficulty (dificolti) s. dificultad; apuro, aprieto, reparo.
diffidence (dífidens) s. timidez, cortedad, apocamiento.
diffident (dífident) adj. huraño.
diffuse (difiús) adj. prolijo; v. difundir, derramar, propagar.
diffusion (difiúshon) s. difusión.
dig (dig) v. cavar; excavar, ahondar; escarbar, minar; extraer, trabajar duro; **to — again** binar; **to — deeper** profundizar; **to — up** desenterrar; s. piquete.
digest (dáiyest) s. sumario; compendio; digesto; recopilación; código; v. digerir; recopilar; descocer; meditar; rumiar.
digestible (diyéstibl) adj. digestible, digerible.
digestion (diyéschon) s. digestión; descocedura.
digestive (diyéstiv) adj. digestivo.
dignified (dígnifaid) adj. digno, mesurado, serio; enaltecido.
dignitary (digniteri) s. dignatario.
dignity (digniti) s. dignidad.
digress (digrés) v. divagar.
digression (digréshon) s. digresión; divagación.
dilate (diléit) v. dilatar(se), extender(se), ensanchar(se); espaciarse.
diligence (dílyens) s. diligencia, aplicación, esmero, asiduidad.
diligent (dílyent) adj. diligente, activo, aplicado, solícito.
dilute (dilút) v. diluir, aguar; adj. diluído, disuelto.
dim (dim) adj. penumbroso, obscuro; nublado; confuso; caliginoso; deslustrado; sin brillo; v. obscurecer, anublar.
dime (dáim) s. moneda de diez centavos.
dimension (diménshon) s. dimensión.
diminish (diminish) v. disminuir.
diminution (diminiúshon) s. disminución, mengua, merma.
diminutive (dimíniutiv) adj. diminutivo; diminuto; s. diminutivo; nombre diminutivo.
dimness (dímnes) s. semi-obscuridad, penumbra, ofuscación.
dimple (dímpl) s. hoyuelo.
din (din) s. estruendo, fragor, estrépito, barahúnda.

dine (dáin) v. comer; festejar u obsequiar una comida.
diner (dáiner) s. coche-comedor; comida principal.
dingy (dínyi) adj. negruzco; manchado, sucio, deslustrado, deslucido.
dining (dáining) ger. de **to dine**; **—car** carro-comedor; **— room** comedor.
dinner (díner) s. comida; **— coat** smokin, esmoquin.
dint (dint); **by — of** a fuerza de.
dip (dip) s. zambullida; inmersión; bajada; declive, baño corto; inclinarse hacia abajo; depresión; v. mojar (una pluma en el tintero), teñir; agachar (la cabeza); saludar (con la bandera); meterse en el agua; empeñarse o meterse en algún negocio; dar un bajón (un avión).
diphtheria (difzíria) s. difteria.
diploma (diplóma) s. diploma.
diplomacy (diplómaci) s. diplomacia.
diplomat (díplomat) s. diplomático
dipper (díper) s. cucharón, cazo; sumergidor; **the Big —** la Osa Mayor.
dire (dáir) adj extremo; horrendo; de mal agüero; espantoso, terrible.
direct (dirékt) adj. directo; derecho, en línea recta; claro, patente; **— current** corriente continua; **— object** acusativo; **—ly** adv. directamente; inmediatamente; v. dirigir, poner el sobrescrito, encaminar, dar direcciones u órdenes.
direction (dirécshon) s. dirección; administración; curso, rumbo, gobierno.
directive (diréctiv) adj. directivo; s. orden, mandato.
directness (diréctnes) s. derechura; franqueza; lo directivo; **with —** sin rodeos.
director (diréctor) s. director.
directory (diréctori) s. directorio; junta directiva; anuario.
dirigible (díriyibl) adj. y s. dirigible.
dirt (dert)s. suciedad, mugre, tierra, cieno, barro.
dirty (dérti) adj. sucio; mugriento; cochino, inmundo, enlodado; v. enlodar, ensuciar, manchar.
disable (diséibl) v. incapacitar.
disadvantage (disadvántay) s. des-

ventaja; to be at a — estar en una situación desventajosa.
disagree (disagrí) v. diferir, disentir; no convenir; no estar de acuerdo; — with no ser conveniente; no sentarle a uno bien (el clima).
disagreeable (disagríabl) adj. desagradable, de mal genio, ofensivo.
desagreement (disagríment) s. desavenencia, desacuerdo, disensión; discordia, discordancia.
disappear (disapír) v. desaparecer.
disappearance (disapírans) s. desaparición; desaparecimiento.
disappoint (disapóint) v. chasquear; contrariar; decepcionar; faltar a lo prometido; faltar a una cita o promesa; desilusionar; to be —ed estar desilusionado o decepcionado; estar desengañado; verse contrariado.
disappointing (disapóinting) adj. desilusionante, desengañador.
disappointment (disapóintment) s. desilusión, desengaño; chasco; contratiempo; camelo, jaquimazo.
disapproval (disaprúval) s. desaprovación, censura.
disapprove (disaprúv) v. desaprobar.
disarm (disárm) v. desarmar(se).
disarray (disarréi) s. desarreglo, confusión, desorden, desatavio; paños menores; v. desarreglar, desordenar.
disaster (disáster) s. desastre.
disas rous (disástros) adj. desastroso, calamitoso, funesto, fatal.
disband (disbánd) v. dispersar, licenciar (las tropas); despedirse.
disbelieve (disbelív) v. descreer.
disburse (disbérs) v. desembolsar.
disbursement (disbúrsment) s. desembolso, gasto.
disc (dis) ver disk.
discard (discárd) s. descarte; desecho, cosa desechada; v. descartar; desechar, deponer.
discern (disérn) v. discernir, distinguir, descubrir, percibir.
discernment (disérnment) v. discernimiento, criterio.
discharge (dischári) s. descarga (de artillería); descargo (de una obligación) finiquito, carta de pago; exoneración; desempeño (de un deber), remoción, deposición; licencia (militar); desagüe; supuración; v. descargar, exonerar, poner en libertad, de-

poner; despedir; arrojar; desaguar; dar de baja.
disciple (disáipl) s. discípulo.
disclose (disklóus) v. descubrir, destapar; exponer.
discolor (discólor) v. decolorar(se), desteñir(se).
discomfort (diskómfort) s. incomodidad; molestia, malestar.
disconcert (diskoncért) v. desconcertar.
disconnect (diskonékt) v. desconectar, desunir, separar, desacoplar.
disconnected (diskonékted) p.p. y adj. desconectado, desunido; inconexo, incoherente.
disconsolate (diskónsoleit) adj. desconsolado; inconsolable.
discontent (diskontént) s. descontento; disgusto, desagrado; v. descontentar; desagradar, disgustar.
discontented (diskonténted) adj. descontento; disgustado.
discontinue (discontíniu) v. descontinuar; parar, cesar, suspender; interrumpir; abandonar.
discord (dískord) s. discordia, disonancia; desavenencia; disensión, discordancia; desacuerdo.
discount (diskáunt) s. descuento; rebaja; — rate tipo de descuento; v. descontar; rebajar.
discourage (diskórey) v. desanimar, desalentar, abatir; descorazonar; to — from disuadir de.
discouragement (discóureyment) s. desaliento, abatimiento, desmayo.
discourse (diskórs) s. discurso; conversación; plática; v. disertar, discurrir, platicar.
discourteous (discórteus) adj. descortés, desatento, grosero.
discourtesy (diskórtesi) s. descortesía, desatención, grosería.
discover (diskóver) v. descubrir.
discoverer (diskóverer) s. descubridor.
discovery (diskóveri) s. descubrimiento.
discredit (diskrédit) s. descrédito; deshonra; desconfianza, oprobio; v. desacreditar; deshonrar, no creer.
discreet (discrít) s. discreto.
discrepancy (diskrépansi) s. discrepancia, diferencia, variación.
discriminate (diskrímineit) v. discriminar, discernir, distinguir, diferenciar; entresacar; hacer fa-

voritismos; to — against hacer favoritismos en perjuicio de.
discuss (diskós) v. discutir.
disdain (disdéin) s. desdén, menosprecio; v. desdeñar, menospreciar, despreciar, desdeñarse.
disdainful (disdéinful) adj. desdeñoso.
disease (disís) s. enfermedad.
diseased (disísd) adj. enfermo.
disembark (disembárk) v. desembarcar.
disentangle (disentángl) v. desenredar, deshacer (una maraña o enredo); desenmarañar, desligar.
disfigure (disfíguiur) v. desfigurar.
disgrace (disgréis) s. ignominia, deshonra, vergüenza, afrenta; to be in — estar desacreditado; haber perdido la gracia o el favor; v. deshonrar, degradar, avergonzar.
disguise (disgáis) s. disfraz; v. disfrazar.
disgust (disgóst) s. asco, repugnancia; desazón; v. repugnar.
disgusted (disgósted) adj. disgustado, asqueado, descontento.
disgusting (disgósting) adj. asqueroso, repugnante, ofensivo.
dish (dish) s. plato; manjar, vianda; vajilla; v. servir.
dishearten (disjártn) v. desalentar desanimar, descorazonar.
disheveled (disjéveled) adj. desgreñado, desaliñado, desaseado.
dishonest (disónest) adj. engañoso, falso, tramposo, falto de honradez, pícaro, malo, ímprobo.
dishonesty (disónesti) s. fraude, falta de honradez, picardía, dolo.
dishonor (disónor) s. deshonra; afrenta; ignominia; infamia; v. deshonrar; recusar (un giro o cheque).
dishonorable (disónorabl) adj. deshonroso; infame; afrentoso.
disillusion (disilúshon) s. desilusionar, decepcionar, desengañar.
disinfect (disinféct) v. desinfectar.
disinfectant (disinféctant) s. desinfectante.
disinterested (disínterested) adj. desinteresado.
disk (disk) s. disco.
dislike (disláik) s. antipatía, aversión; aborrecimiento; v. sentir o tener aversión por; I — it me repugna, no me gusta, me desagrada.
dislocate (díslokeit) v. dislocar, descoyuntar.

dislodge (dislódy) v. desalojar.
disloyal (dislóial) adj. desleal.
dismal (dísmal) adj. lúgubre, sombrío; tétrico, funesto.
dismantle (dismántl) v. desmantelar; desmontar, desarmar, desguarnecer.
dismay (dísmei) s. desmayo, desaliento, pavor; v. desalentar, desanimar, espantar, aterrar.
dismiss (dismís) v. despedir, expulsar, destituir, desechar; deponer; licenciar; descartar; dar por terminado (un pleito o caso jurídico); to — the meeting disolver la junta, levantar la sesión.
dismissal (dismísal) s. despedida, expulsión, destitución (de un cargo), liberación, acción de desechar.
dismount (dismáunt) v. desmontar; apear(se); desarmar (un cañón, una máquina).
disobedience (disobídiens) s. desobediencia, rebeldía.
disobedient (disobídient) adj. desobediente, malmandado, refractario.
disobey (disobéi) v. desobedecer.
disorder (disórder) s. desorden; trastorno; confusión; enfermedad; desarreglo; irregularidad; v. desordenar; desarreglar, trastornar.
disorderly (disórderli) adj. desordenado; desarreglado; revoltoso; escandaloso; adv. desordenadamente.
disown (disóun) v. repudiar; desconocer, negar, renegar.
dispassionate (dispáshoneit) adj. desapasionado, imparcial, recto.
dispel (dispél) v. disipar.
dispensary (dispénsary) s. dispensario.
dispensation (dispenséshon) s. dispensa, exención, dispensación; revelación.
dispense (dispéns) v. dispensar, dar, repartir; distribuir; administrar (la justicia); despachar (recetas, medicamentos); eximir; to — from dispensar de; to — with omitir; pasarse sin.
dispersal (dispérsal) s. dispersión, desbandada.
disperse (dispérs) v. dispersar(se) disipar(se), esparcir.
display (displéi) s. manifestación; exhibición; ostentación; despliegue; v. desplegar, exhibir.

displease (displís) v. desagradar; disgustar, ofender, descontentar
displeasure (displéshur) s. desagrado, disgusto, descontento, desgracia.
disposal (dispóusal) s. disposición; arreglo; venta (de bienes).
dispose (dispóus) v. disponer; arreglar; influir; inclinar el ánimo; **to — of** deshacerse de.
disposition (disposíshon) s. disposición, orden, método; arreglo; aptitud; **good (bad) —** buen (mal) genio.
disprove (disprúv) v. refutar.
dispute (dispiút) s. disputa.
disqualify (diskuálifai) v. inhabilitar; incapacitar; descalificar.
disrespect (disrespékt) s. desacato, falta de respeto, desatención.
disrespectful (disrespéktful) adj. irrespetuoso, irreverente.
dissatisfied (disátisfaid) adj. descontento, malcontento.
dissatisfy (disátisfai) v. descontentar, no satisfacer, desagradar.
dissect (disékt) v. disecar, hacer una disección, anatomizar.
dissemble (disémbl) v. disimular, fingir, encubrir.
dissension (disénshon) s. disensión, discordia, desunión, pendencia.
dissent (disént) v. disentir; s. desacuerdo; disensión, disidencia.
dissimulation (disimiuléshon) s. disimulo, disimulación.
dissipate (dísipeit) v. disipar.
dissipation (disipéshon) s. disipación.
dissolute (dísolut) adj. disoluto.
dissolution (disolúshon) s. disolución.
dissolve (disólv) v. disolver; anular.
dissuade (disuéid) v. disuadir.
distaff (distaf) s. rueca.
distance (dístans) s. distancia; lejanía; alejamiento; intervalo; **in the —** a lo lejos.
distant (dístant) adj. distante; apartado, lejano, remoto, serio, esquivo; **to be — from** distar de; **—ly** adv. de lejos, en lontananza.
distaste (distéist) s. disgusto, aversión, repugnancia; hastío.
distasteful (distéistful) adj. desagradable, repugnante, desabrido.
distend (disténd) v. dilatar.
distil (distíl) v. destilar.
distillation (distiléshon) s. destilación; alambicamiento.

distillery (distíleri) s. destilería.
distinct (distínkt) adj. distinto, claro, diferente; preciso; **—ly** adv. distintamente.
distinction (distínkshon) s. distinción.
distinctive (distínktiv) adj. distintivo.
distinguish (distíngüish) v. distinguir; discernir, diferenciar.
distinguished (distíngüisht) adj. distinguido, eminente.
distinguishing (distíngüishing) adj. distintivo, característico.
distort (distórt) v. desfigurar, deformar, torcer, retorcer; falsear, pervertir.
distract (distrákt) v. distraer.
distraction (distrácshon) s. distracción; diversión; perturbación.
distress (distrés) s. angustia, aflicción, congoja, pena, dolor; zozobra; calamidad, miseria, apuro, embargo, secuestro; **estar apurado; estar en zozobra** (un navío); **to be —ed** estar afligido o apurado.
distribute (distríbiut) v. distribuir, repartir; clasificar, arreglar.
distribution (distribiúshon) s. distribución; repartimiento, división.
distributor (distríbiutor) s. distribuidor.
district (dístrikt) s. distrito.
distrust (distróst) s. desconfianza; recelo; sospecha; v. recelar.
distrustful (distróstful) adj. desconfiado, sospechoso, receloso, modesto, difidente.
disturb (distórb) v. turbar, perturbar, inquietar; desarreglar; alterar; estorbar; desasosegar; **don't — yourself!** ¡no se moleste Ud.!
disturbance (distórbans) s. disturbio; perturbación; desorden; confusión; molestia.
disuse (disiús) s. desuso; deshabituación; **to fall into —** caer en desuso.
ditch (dich) s. zanja; foso; **irrigation —** acequia; presa; badén; v. abrir zanjas; **to — someone** deshacerse de alguien.
ditto (díto) s. ídem, lo mismo.
divan (diván) s. diván, canapé.
dive (daiv) v. zambullida; picada, descenso rápido de un avión; garito, leonera; enfrascamiento; lupanar; sumergirse (un submarino); **to — into someone** abalan-

zarse sobre alguien; v. **bucear**, **zambullir**.
diver (dáiver) s. buzo, clavadista.
diverge (divéry) v. divergir, irse apartando, separarse, desviarse.
divergence (divéryens) s. divergencia.
divers (dáivers) adj. diversos, varios.
diverse (divérs) adj. diverso.
diversion (divérshon) s. diversión, recreo, entretenimiento.
diversity (divérsiti) s. diversidad, diferencia; desemejanza.
divert (divért) v. divertir, recrear; distraer, desviar, apartar.
divide (diváid) v. dividir.
dividend (dívidend) s. dividendo.
divine (diváin) adj. divino; sagrado; v. adivinar.
divinity (díviniti) s. divinidad; deidad, numen; teología; atributo divino.
division (divishon) s. división.
divorce (divórs) s. divorcio; repudio; desunión; v. divorciarse.
divulge (divólj) v. divulgar.
dizziness (dísines) s. vahído o vaguido; vértigo; mareo.
dizzy (dísi) adj. desvanecido, mareado, aturdido; — **speed** velocidad vertiginosa.
do (du) v. hacer, ejecutar, finalizar, concluir, rematar; producir; **to — away with** deshacerse de; **to — one's hair** peinarse, arreglarse el pelo; **how — you —?** ¿cómo está Ud.? **I did go** ciertamente que fui; **make haste —,** vamos, dese usted prisa; **to — the dishes** lavar los platos; **to — up** envolver; limpiar; arreglar; **to — over** hacer de nuevo; **to have nothing to — with** no tener nada que ver con; **that will —** basta, bastará; **that wont —** eso no sirve, eso no resultará; **to — one's best** esmerarse; **to — with** manejárselas, componérselas; disponer de; aprovechar; **well to —** acomodado, de buena posición.
docile (dósil) adj. dócil.
dock (dok) s. muelle, desembarcadero; dársena; muñón de la cola cercenada de un caballo; **dry —** carenero, dique de carena; v. entrar en el muelle; meter (una embarcación) en el muelle o dique.
doctor (dóctor) s. doctor; médico, facultativo; v. medicinar, recetar, curar; practicar la medicina.

doctrine (dóktrin) s. doctrina.
document (dókiument) s. documento; v. documentar; probar con documentos.
dodge (dody) s. evasión, evasiva; regate; v. escabullirse, regatear; seguir con disimulo; hurtar el cuerpo; **to — around a corner** dar un esquinazo.
doe (do) s. cierva (hembra del antílope, del gamo, de la liebre).
dog (dog) s. perro, perra; can; macho de algunos cuadrúpedos; **hot —** salchicha caliente; Am. perro caliente; **to put on a lot of —** emperifollarse; darse mucho tono; **dog bane** matacán — **brier** zarza perruna; v. seguir, acosar; seguir los pasos o pisadas de alguno; — **tired** cansadísimo.
dogma (dógma) s. dogma, axioma.
dogmatic (dogmétik) adj. dogmático.
doily (dóili) s. mantelito (para platos, vasos, etc.); adorno.
doings (dúings) s. pl. hechos, acciones, acontecimientos; eventos; **great —** mucha actividad.
dole (dóul) s. reparto gratuito (de dinero o alimento); limosna, distribución; repartimiento; v. repartir.
doleful (dóulful) adj. lúgubre, triste, lastimoso, dolorido, lastimero.
doll (dol) s. muñeca, muñeco; **—y muñequita; — shop** muñequería; v. **to —up** emperifollarse, ataviarse.
dollar (dólar) s. dólar.
domain (doméin) s. dominio; heredad.
dome (doum) s. cúpula; media naranja (de iglesia), dombo, domo.
domestic (doméstik) adj. doméstico; hogareño; nacional, del país, casero, familiar; s. criado, sirviente.
dominant (dóminant) adj. dominante.
dominate (dómineit) v. dominar.
domination (dominéshon) s. dominación.
domineer (dominír) v. dominar, señorear; mandar; gobernar.
domineering (dominíring) adj. tiránico, dominador, mandón, imperioso.
dominion (dominion) s. dominio.
domino (dóminou) s. dominó, traje de máscara; disfraz; ficha del juego del dominó; **dominoes** dominó (juego).

don (don) s. don (título); caballero; v. vestirse, ponerse, calar.

donate (dóneit) v. donar, regalar, hacer donación; contribuir.

donation (donéishon) s. donación; regalo, dádiva, donativo.

done (dón) p.p. de to do; **to be —** in estar rendido de cansancio; fatigado; interj. ¡hecho! ¡muy bien! ¡ya está! **the meat is well —** está bien asada la carne.

donkey (dónki) s. burro, asno.

doom (dum) s. hado, sino, destino; mala suerte; sentencia de muerte; perdición; **the day of —** el día del juicio final; v. condenar; sentenciar.

door (dor) s. puerta; entrada, pasillo.

doorbell (dórbel) s. campanilla o timbre (de llamada).

doorknob (dórnab) s. tirador de puerta; perilla, manija.

doorman (dórman) s. portero.

doorstep (dórstep) s. escalón de la puerta, umbral.

doorway (dóruei) s. puerta, entrada, vano (de la puerta).

dope (dóup) s. opio; narcótico; droga, menjurje, medicamento; información; grasa para lubricar; pasta de opio; **— fiend** morfinómano; **he is a —** es un zoquete; v. narcotizar, medicinar, administrar drogas; conjeturar.

dormitory (dórmitori) s. dormitorio.

dose (dous) s. dosis; píldoras, mal trago; **to — oneself** medicinarse.

dot (dot) s. punto; tilde, virgulilla; v. marcar con puntos; poner el punto (sobre la i); tildar.

dotage (dótay) s. chochez, chochera, ñoñez; **to be in one's —** chochear.

dote (daut) v. chochear; caducar; **to — on** estar loco por; **to — upon** amar con exceso.

double (dóbl) adj. doble; doblado; duplo, dúplice, duplicado; ambiguo; engañoso; **— boiler** baño de María; **— deal** trato doble; s. doble; **—s** juego de dobles (en tenis); adv. doblemente; **double breasted** cruzado; **— faced** de dos caras; **— minded** indeciso; **doubly** doblemente; por duplicado.

doubt (daut) s. duda; v. dudar.

doubtful (dáutful) adj. dudoso; dudable.

doubtless (dáutles) adj. indudable, cierto, seguro; confiado; adv. sin duda; indudablemente; probablemente.

douche (duch) s. ducha, jeringa.

dough (dóu) s. pasta, masa.

doughnut (dóunot) s. buñuelo.

dove (dóv) s. paloma.

downcast (dáuncast) adj. cabizbajo, abatido; inclinado; **with — eyes** con los ojos bajos.

downfall (dáunfol) s. caída, ruina.

downpour (dáunpor) s. aguacero, chaparrón.

downright (dáunrait) adj. claro, categórico, absoluto; franco, abierto, llano, liso; positivo; **— foolishness** solemne disparate; adv. absolutamente, enteramente.

downstairs (dáunstérs) adv. abajo; en el piso bajo; adj. del piso bajo; piso inferior.

downstream (dáunstrim) adv. río abajo, aguas abajo.

downtown (dáuntaun) adv. el centro, en el centro (de una población) adj. del centro; s. centro.

downward (dáunuord) adj. descendente; inclinado; pendiente; adv. **(downwards)** hacia abajo.

downy (dáuni) adj. suave, blando; velloso; felpudo; plumoso; dulce, tranquilo.

dowry (dáuri) s. dote; arras.

doze (dous) s. siestecita, sueño ligero; sopor; v. dormitar.

dozen (dósen) s. docena.

drab (drab) pardo, pardusco; monótono; s. color entre gris y amarillento.

draft (draft) s. corriente de aire; aire colado; trago; libranza; letra de cambio; tiro de chimenea; giro bancario; plan; leva; succión; aspiración; calado (de un barco); **— beer** cerveza de barril; **— horse** caballo de tiro; **rough —** borrador.

draftsman (dráftsman) s. dibujante.

drag (drag) s. rastra; traba, obstáculo; draga; rastrillo; galga; **to have a — with someone** tener buenas aldabas con alguien; **— sail** ancla flotante; v. arrastrar (se); rastrear; tirar; dragar; moverse despacio.

dragon (drágon) s. dragón.

drainage (dréiney) s. desagüe; drenaje; avenamiento; desecación, desecamiento; cuenca de un río; arroyada.

drake (dréik) s. pato.

drama (dráma) s. drama.
dramatic (dramátic) adj. dramático.
dramatist (drámatist) s. dramaturgo; dramático.
dramatize (drámatais) v. dramatizar.
drank (drank) pret. de to drink.
drape (dreip) s. colgadura, cortina, tapiz; formar pliegues artísticos en un ropaje o colgadura.
drapery (dréiperi) s. tapicería, colgaduras, cortinas; pañería; paños.
drastic (drástik) adj. extremo, fuerte, violento; **to take — steps** tomar medidas enérgicas.
draught (draft) véase draft.
drawback (dróbak) s. desventaja; obstáculo, inconveniente; rebaja.
drawer (dróer) s. cajón, gaveta; naveta; —s calzoncillos.
drawer (dróer) s. librador, girador, extractor; dibujante.
drawing (dróing) s. dibujo; delineación; tiro, tirante; sorteo; — **paper** papel de dibujo; — **room** recibidor; estrado; sala.
dread (dred) s. pavor, temor, aprensión; miedo, terror, espanto; adj. terrible, temido; v. temer, sentir aprensión de; tener miedo o temor.
dreadful (drédful) adj. horrendo, espantoso, terrible, horrible.
dream (drím) s. sueño; ensueño; visión; ilusión; v. soñar con.
dreamer (drímer) s. soñador.
dreamland (drímland) s. tierra del ensueño; región de los sueños; país del sueño.
dreamy (drími) adj. soñoliento, soñador; melancólico; desvariado; **a — recollection** un vago recuerdo.
dreary (dríri) adj. melancólico.
dredge (dredy) s. draga; rastra.
dregs (dregs) s. pl. heces, sedimento; pozo; asiento, suelo.
drench (drench) s. mojada, mojadura; empapada; tragantada; inundación; v. mojar, empapar, remojar.
dress (dres) s. vestido, traje; vestidura; vestido o túnica de mujer o niña; atavío, tocado, tuniía, compostura; — **rehearsal** ensayo general y último (antes de una función); — **suit** traje de etiqueta; **citizen's —** vestido de paisano; v. vestir(se), arreglarse, adobar (carne o pieles); curar (heridas).
dresser (dréser) s. tocador.
dressing (drésing) s. aderezo; salsa (para ensaladas); aderezamiento; relleno (para carne, etc.); condimento, aliño; vendajes (para heridas) **a — down** regaño; — **room** tocador; trasalcoba; — **case** neceser; — **table** tocador.
dressmaker (drésmeiker) s. modista.
dribble (dríbl) v. gotear; dejar caer en gotas; babear; regatear; s. goteo; chorrito.
driblet (dríblet) s. gota, gotita; trozo, pedacito, pizca; **en pequeñas cantidades**.
dried (draid) pret. y p.p. de **to dry** adj. seco; paso; — **fig** higo seco.
drift (drift) s. dirección, rumbo; tendencia; montón, amontonamiento (de arena, nieve, etc.); todo objeto llevado por una corriente (nubes, restos de un naufragio, etc.); deriva, desvío (de un barco o avión); **to get the — of a conversation** enterarse a medias de una conversación; v. flotar; ir(se) a la deriva; impeler; llevar; apilar, amontonar; abrir un socavón o galería.
driftwood (dríftud) s. madera o leña flotante; madera de deriva.
drill (dril) s. taladro, barrena; ejercicio; adiestramiento, broca, perforador; Am. entrenamiento; disciplina; dril (tela); v. taladrar.
drink (drink) s. bebida; trago; poción; v. beber; absorber; embeber; **to — down** tragar; — **it down!** ¡bébaselo! ¡tráguéselo!
drinkable (drínkabl) adj. potable.
drip (drip) s. goteo; gotera; v. caer gota a gota; chorrear.
drive (draiv) s. paseo en coche o automóvil; calzada para coches; urgencia, presión, exigencia; manada de reses; campaña; tirada; tiro; montón de leños o trozos de árboles; v. impulsar, impeler; empujar; arrear animales; conducir, guiar (un auto); inducir; esclavizar; forzar a; lanzar (una pelota); **to — away** ahuyentar; **to — in** o **into** meter a macha martillo; **to — a good bargain** hacer un buen trato; **to be —n**

to the wall verse entre la espada y la pared; **to — mad** volver loco.
drivel (drivl) s. baba; ñoñería, tontería; cháchara; v. babear, chochear.
driveling (drivling) adj. baboso.
driven (drivn) p.p. de **to drive**.
driver (dráiver) s. cochero, chofer, mecánico, conductor (de un automóvil); carretero; maquinista; uno de los palos de golf; **pile —** martinete (para clavar pilotes).
driveway (dráivuei) s. calzada o carretera de entrada.
drizzle (drisl) v. lloviznar; s. llovizna, mollina, cernidillo.
drone (droun) s. zángano; holgazán; zumbido; abejón; roncón de gaita; v. zumbar, hablar con monotonía.
droop (drup) v. doblarse, andar o estar alicaído; estar abatido; inclinarse; caer; colgar, pender; bajar (los hombros); **his shoulders —** tiene los hombros caídos; **—ing eyelids** párpados caídos.
drop (drop) s. gota; declive; bajada; caída; pizca; pendiente; **cough —** pastilla para la tos; **— scene** telón de foro; **letter —** buzón; **— hammer** martinete; v. dejar caer; verter a gotas; dejar (un asunto, una amistad); **to — a line** poner unos renglones; **to — off** decaer; **to — sleep** quedarse dormido, dormirse; **to — out** desaparecer; **to —** in hacer una visita inesperada; **to — the curtain** bajar el telón; **to — a courtesy** hacer una cortesía.
drought (dráut) s. sequía, seca.
drove (drouv) s. manada, recua, rebaño; hato, muchedumbre; pret. de **to drive**.
drown (dráun) v. ahogar(se), anegar(se), sumergir; apagar, sofocar; **to — sorrow in wine** ahogar las penas en vino.
drowse (dráus) v. dormitar; estar amodorrado, adormecerse.
drowsiness (dráusines) s. modorra, somnolencia, soñera.
drowsy (dráusi) adj. soñoliento; adormilado, amodorrado; soporífero; **to become —** amodorrarse.
drudge (dródy) v. afanarse, atarearse; fatigarse; insudar; s. esclavo del trabajo.
drug (drog) s. droga; narcótico, artículo invendible; **to be a — on the market** ser invendible (una mercancía); v. jaropar; narcotizar; mezclar con drogas.
druggist (dróguist) s. boticario. droguista, droguero, especiero.
drugstore (drógstor) s. botica, droguería, farmacia.
drum (drom) s. tambor; tímpano (del oído); barril, tonel, caja redoblante; **bass —** tambora, bombo; **—stick** bolillo de tambor; **to — out** expeler a tambor batiente; **to — a lesson into someone** meterle a uno la lección en la cabeza.
drummer (drómer) s. tambor, tamborilero; viajante de comercio.
drunk (drónk) p.p. de **to drink** adj. borracho, ebrio, beodo; emborrachado, bebido; **to get —** emborracharse, embriagarse.
drunkard (drónkard) s. borracho, borrachín; borrachón, bebedor; odre.
drunken (drónken) adj. borracho.
drunkenness (drónknes) s. borrachera, embriaguez; crápula.
dry (drái) adj. seco, árido; sequizo; **a — book** un libro aburrido; **— cleaner** quitamanchas; **— cupping** ventosa seca; **— cleaning** lavado o limpieza en seco; **— goods** lencería, géneros, tejidos; v. secar(se) desecar; pasar (fruta).
dryness (dráines) s. sequedad.
dubious (diúbios) adj. dudoso.
duchess (dóches) s. duquesa.
duck (dók) s. pato, pata; ánade; dril; zambullida; acción de agacharse; capuz o chapuz; v. zambullir(se), chapuzar(se); dar chapuz; agachar (la cabeza).
duckling (dókling) s. patito.
due (diú) adj. debido; vencido; pagadero; caído; devengado; **in — time** a su debido tiempo; **the bill is —** se ha vencido la cuenta; **— west** poniente derecho; **the train is — at two o'clock** el tren debe llegar a las dos; **give the devil its —** ser justo hasta con el diablo; **— East** hacia el Este.
duel (diúel) s. duelo, desafío, certamen; v. batirse en duelo.
duet (diuét) s. dúo, dueto; pieza a cuatro manos.
dug (dog) pret. y p.p. de **to dig**.
duke (diuk) s. duque.
dukedom (diúkdom) s. ducado.
dull (dol) adj. opaco, empañado; mate; embotado, obtuso; apagado, sordo; lerdo, torpe; negado;

sin punta, sin filo; — pain dolor sordo; **— of hearing** duro de oído;**— sound** sonido sordo o apagado; v. embotarse; empeñar (se), enromar.

dullness (dólnes) s. falta de brillo, estupidez, torpeza; embotamiento; somnolencia; falta de punta o filo; zoquete; tonto; aburrimiento; entorpecimiento.

duly (diúll) adv. debidamente.

dumb (domb) adj. mudo; silencioso; callado; torpe; oculto; latente; **— creature** animal.

dumbness (dómbnes) s. mudez; mutismo; estupidez; silencio.

dummy (dómi) s. maniquí, figurón; testaferro; personaje que no habla; zoquete; tonto; adj. fingido, falseado, imitado.

dump (domp) s. montón (de tierra, carbón, etc); locomotora de calles; **garbage —** muladar, basurero; v. echar, vaciar, descargar, verter.

dunce (dóns) s. zopenco, zote, tonto.

dune (diún) s. duna o médano.

dung (dóng) s. boñiga, estiércol, fiemo; freza, bosta, hienda.

dungeon (dónyon) s. mazmorra, calabozo, bartolina.

dunghill (dónjil) s. muladar, estercolero, basurero.

dupe (diúp) s. inocentón, incauto, primo, víctima de engaño o dolo; v. embaucar.

duplicate (diúplikeit) adj. y s. doble, duplicado, copia; **en pares**; v. duplicar, copiar, reproducir.

duplicity (diupliciti) s. duplicidad, doblez, engaño.

durable (diúrabl) adj. durable.

duration (diuréshon) s. duración.

during (diúring) prep. durante.

dusk (dosk) s. crepúsculo (vespertino); anochecida; obscuridad; **at — of day** al atardecer.

dusky (dóski) adj. oscuro, negrusco; sombrío; fusco, moreno.

dust (dost) s. polvo; tierra; polvareda, cisco, altercado, restos mortales; v. sacudir el polvo; empolvar, llenar de polvo, despolvar.

duster (dóster) s. limpiador; quitapolvo; **feather —** plumero.

dusty (dósti) adj. polvoriento; empolvado, lleno de polvo, polvoroso.

Dutch (Dótch) adj. y s. holandés; mujer, esposa.

Dutchman (Dóchman) s. holandés.

duty (diúti) s. deber, obligación; derechos aduanales; derechos de aduana o de puertas; **— free** libre de derechos aduanales.

dwarf (duórf) s. y adj. enano diminuto; v. impedir el crecimiento o desarrollo de; achicar.

dwell (duél) v. residir, morar, habitar; vivir; (con **on** o **upon**) espaciarse en un asunto.

dweller (duéler) s. habitante.

dwelling (duéling) s. morada; habitación, domicilio, casa.

dwelt (duelt) pret. y p.p. de **to dwell**.

dwindle (duindl) v. menguar, mermar, disminuir(se); degenerar, decaer; consumirse(se).

dye (dái) s. tinte, tintura; color; matiz; v. teñir, tinturar.

dyer (dáier) s. tintorero; **—'s shop** tintorería.

dying (dáing) adj. moribundo, agonizante.

dynamic (dainámik) adj. dinámico; eficaz; **—s** s. dinámica.

dynamite (dáinamait) s. dinamita; v. dinamitar, volar con dinamita.

dynamo (dáinamo) s. dínamo.

dynasty (dáinasti) s. dinastía.

dysentery (dísenteri) s. disentería.

E

each (ich) adj. cada, todo; pron cada uno, todos; **— other** el uno al otro, mutuamente.

eager (íguer) adj. anhelante, ansioso, deseoso, vehemente; **—ly** adv. con anhelo; con ahínco; ansiosamente.

eagerness (íguernes) s. anhelo, ansia, deseo vehemente, avidez; ardor.

eagle (ígl) s. águila, moneda de oro.

ear (ir) s. oreja; oído; atención, asa, asidero; espiga, mazorca; **— drum** tímpano, **— muff** orejera; **—ring** pendiente, arete, arillo; **— of wheat** espiga; **by — de** oído.

earl (erl) s. conde, título de nobleza.

early (érli) adv. temprano; adj primitivo, remoto; avanzado, pre coz; **— riser** madrugador, tempranero; **to rise —** madrugar.

earn (ern) v. ganar; merecer, devengar.

earnest (érnst) adj. serio, formal, extremo, fervoroso, ansioso.

earnestness (érnstnes) s. seriedad, formalidad, buena fe; sinceridad; **in all** — con todo ahínco; con toda formalidad; — **borer** barrena.

earnings (érnings) s. ganancias; sueldo; estipendio, jornal.

earring (írring) s. arete, zarcillo; arracada, pendiente.

earth (érz) s. tierra; suelo, terreno; gente, mundo; madriguera.

earthen (érzen) adj. de tierra.

earthenware (érzenuer) s. loza de barro; trastos, cacharros.

earthly (érzli) adj. terrenal, terrestre, mundano, temporal; terreno; **to be of no** — úse no servir para nada.

earthquake (érzkueik) s. terremoto, temblor de tierra.

earthworm (érzuorm) s. lombriz.

ease (is) s. facilidad; naturalidad; soltura; comodidad; quietud; ocio, reposo; despejo; desahogo; **at** — tranquilo; cómodo; **with** — con facilidad.

easel (isl) s. caballete (de pintor).

easily (ísili) adv. fácilmente; sin duda; cómodamente, tranquilamente.

east (ist) s. Este, Oriente; Levante; Leste; — **wind** viento del Este; adv. al Este, en el Este.

Easter (íster) s. Pascuas, Pascua Florida o de Resurrección — **tide** Sábado Santo.

eastern (ístern) adj. oriental.

eastward (ístuord) adv. y adj. hacia el Este u Oriente.

easy (ísi) adj. fácil; cómodo; dócil; tranquilo; holgado; asequible; — **chair** silla cómoda, poltrona; — **sail** poca vela; — **going man** hombre cachazudo o calmo; **at an** — pace a paso moderado.

eat (it) v. comer; **to** — **away** corroer, destruir; **to** — **breakfast** desayunarse, tomar el desayuno; **to** — **up** devorar, hartarse; destruir, arruinar; **to** — **one's words** retractarse; **to** — **one's heart out** sufrir en silencio.

eaten (ítn) p.p. de **to eat**.

eaves (ivs) s. pl. alero (de un tejado).

ebb (eb) s. reflujo; decadencia; — **tide** marea menguante; — **of life** vejez; v. menguar, decaer.

ebony (éboni) s. ébano.

eccentric (excéntric) adj. y s. excéntrico.

ecclesiastic (eclesiástic) adj. y s. eclesiástico; clérigo.

echo (éko) s. eco; v. repetir, resonar, repercutir; hacer eco.

eclipse (iklíps) s. eclipse; v. eclipsar; extinguir, anublar.

economic (icónómik) adj. económico.

economical (icónómical) adj. económico.

economics (icónómics) s. economía política; crematología.

economist (ikónomist) s. economista.

economize (ikónomais) v. economizar.

economy (ikónomi) s. economía; parsimonia; baratura de costo.

ecstasy (éxtasi) s. éxtasis.

eddy (edi) s. remolino; regolfo; v. regolfar.

Eden (íden) s. paraíso, edén.

edge (edy) s. orilla, borde; filo; esquina; ángulo; **to be on** — estar nervioso.

edgewise (édyuais) adv. de lado.

edible (édibl) adj. y s. comestible.

edifice (édifis) s. edificio.

edify (édifai) v. edificar (moral y espiritualmente); instruir.

edit (édit) v. redactar; preparar o corregir (un manuscrito) para la imprenta; dirigir un periódico.

edition (edishon) s. edición.

editor (éditor) s. redactor, director de un periódico; revisor.

editorial (editórial) adj. editorial; s. artículo de fondo.

educate (édiukeit) v. educar, instruir.

education (ediukéshon) s. educación; crianza; instrucción, enseñanza; ilustración; pedagogía.

educational (ediukéshonal) adj. educativo, relativo a la enseñanza.

educator (ediukéitor) s. educador.

eel (il) s. anguila.

effect (eféct) s. efecto; resultado, consecuencia; —**s** bienes, efectos; v. efectuar; ejecutar, poner por obra.

effective (eféctiv) adj. efectivo, eficaz, vigente (de una ley); —**ly** adv. eficazmente; s. persona activa y eficaz.

effeminate (eféminit) s. afeminado.

efficacy (éficaci) s. eficacia.

efficiency (efishensi) s. eficiencia.

efficient (efíshent) adj. eficiente, eficaz.
effort (éfort) s. esfuerzo, empeño.
effrontery (efrónteri) s. descaro, desvergüenza, impudencia.
effusive (efíúsiv) adj. efusivo, demostrativo, comunicativo.
egg (eg) s. huevo; **fried** — huevo frito o estrellado; **— glass** reloj de arena de tres minutos para cocer huevos; **scrambled —s** huevos revueltos.
eggplant (égplant) s. berenjena.
egotism (ígotism) s. egoísmo.
Egyptian (iyípshan) s. egipcio; egipsíaco.
either (íder) adj. pron. uno u otro; **— of the two** cualquiera de los dos; **— you or I** o tú o yo, o usted o yo.
eject (iyéct) v. echar, arrojar.
elaborate (eláboreit) adj. elaborado, primoroso; esmerado, detallado, trabajado.
elapse (eláps) v. transcurrir, pasar.
elastic (elástic) adj. elástico; s. elástico; **— gum** caucho.
elasticity (ilasticíti) s. elasticidad, resorte.
elated (eléited) adj. exaltado, gozoso, triunfante, alborozado.
elbow (élbou) s. codo; recodo, ángulo; codillo; brazo de sillón; **to be within — reach** estar a la mano; **at one's** — muy cerca; v. rodear, dar codazos.
elder (élder) adj. mayor, más grande, más viejo; s. anciano, señor mayor; dignatario (de ciertas iglesias); **— berry** baya del saúco; **our —s** nuestros mayores.
elderly (élderli) adj. viejo.
eldest (éldest) adj. mayor, primogénito, el mayor.
elect (iléct) adj. y s. electo, elegido; v. elegir, escoger.
election (ilécshon) s. elección.
elector (iléctor) s. elector.
electoral (iléctoral) adj. electoral.
electric (eléctric) adj. eléctrico; vivo, fogoso, magnético; **— meter** electrómetro; contador eléctrico; **— action** mecanismo de un órgano electrico; s. tranvía eléctrico.
electrical (eléctrical) adj. eléctrico; **— engineering** electrotecnia; ingeniería eléctrica; **— engineer** ingeniero electricista.
electrician (electríshan) s. electricista.

electricity (electrisiti) s. electricidad.
electrify (eléctrifai) v. electrizar.
electrocute (eléctrokiut) v. electrocutar.
elegance (élegans) s. elegancia.
elegant (élegant) adj. elegante.
element (élement) s. elemento.
elemental (eleméntal) adj. elemental.
elementary (eleméntari) adj. elemental.
elephant (élefant) s. elefante.
elevate (éleveit) v. elevar, alzar, levantar; encumbrar, exaltar.
elevation (eléveshon) s. elevación, altura; altitud; exaltación.
elevator (éleveitor) s. elevador, ascensor; **grain** — almacén de granos.
elicit (ilísit) v. sacar, atraer, sonsacar; **to — admiration** despertar admiración; **to — applause** suscitar el aplauso.
eligible (éliyibl) adj. elegible.
eliminate (ilímineit) v. eliminar.
elimination (iliminéshon) s. eliminación.
elk (elk) s. alce.
elm (elm) s. olmo.
elope (elóup) v. fugarse (con su novio).
eloquence (élokuens) s. elocuencia.
eloquent (élokuent) adj. elocuente.
else (els) adj. y adv. (úsase sólo en ciertas combinaciones; **nothing** — nada más; **or** — de otro modo; si no; en su lugar; **somebody** — algún otro, otra persona; **what** —? ¿qué más?
elsewhere (élsjuer) adv. en otra parte, de otra parte.
elucidate (ilúsidet) v. elucidar.
elucidation (ilusidéshon) s. elucidación, esclarecimiento, aclaración.
elude (ilúd) v. eludir, evadir.
emaciated (iméshieted) adj. demacrado, escuálido, enflaquecido, flaco.
emanate (émaneit) v. emanar, brotar.
emanation (imanéshon) s. emanación, efluvio, extenuación, demacración.
emancipate (iménsipeit) v. emancipar.
emancipation (imensipéshon) s. emancipación; ahorramiento.
embalm (embám) v. embalsamar.
embankment (imbánkment) s. terraplén; dique, presa.

embargo (embárgou) s. embargo; prohibición; v. embargar, detener.

embark (embárk) v. embarcar(se).

embarrass (embárras) v. turbar, desconcertar, aturdir; apenar; avergonzar; embarazar, poner en aprieto; **to be financially —ed** encontrarse escaso de fondos.

embarrassing (embárrasing) adj. embarazoso, penoso; desconcertante; angustioso.

embarrassment (embárrasment) s. turbación, vergüenza, perplejidad, compromiso, embarazo, dificultad, estorbo, apuro.

embassy (émbasi) s. embajada.

embellish (embélish) v. embellecer, hermosear, adornar, aderezar.

ember (émber) s. ascua; pavesa, chispa; **—s** rescoldo, ascuas.

embezzle (embésl) v. desfalcar.

embezzlement (embéslment) s. desfalco, peculado.

embitter (embíter) v. amargar.

emblem (émblem) s. emblema.

embody (embódi) v. encarnar, dar cuerpo a; incorporar, incluir.

emboss (embós) v. realzar, grabar en relieve; abollonar.

embrace (embréis) s. abrazo; v. abrazar(se); abarcar, contener, comprender, admitir, recibir.

embroider (embróider) v. bordar, recamar; ornar, embellecer.

embroidery (embróideri) s. bordado; bordadura, recamo.

emerald (émerald) s. esmeralda.

emerge (eméry) v. emergir, surgir.

emergency (eméryensi) s. caso fortuito; emergencia, aprieto, necesidad urgente.

emigrant (émigrant) adj. y s. emigrante.

emigrate (émigreit) v. emigrar.

emigration (emigréshon) s. emigración.

eminence (éminens) s. eminencia.

eminent (éminent) adj. eminente.

emit (emít) v. emitir; exhalar, arrojar, despedir.

emotion (emóshon) s. emoción.

emotional (emóshonal) adj. emocional; emotivo; sentimental, sensible.

emperor (émperor) s. emperador.

emphasis (émfasis) s. énfasis.

emphasize (émfasais) v. dar énfasis; hacer hincapié en; subrayar; recalcar; acentuar.

emphatic (emfátik) adj. enfático; recalcado; categórico.

empire (émpair) s. imperio.

employ (emplói) v. emplear, dar empleo; ocupar, dar trabajo a; servir de; **to be in his —** ser su empleado.

employer (emplóier) s. patrón, amo, principal, dueño, jefe.

employment (emplóiment) s. empleo; ocupación, trabajo.

empower (empáuer) v. autorizar, apoderar (dar poder a un abogado).

empress (émpres) s. emperatriz.

emptiness (émptines) s. vaciedad, futilidad, vanidad; ayuno; vacío.

empty (émpti) adj. vacío; vacante, desocupado, hueco; vano; inútil; v. vaciar, desaguar, evacuar, agotar, desembocar.

enable (enéibl) v. capacitar, hacer capaz; habilitar, proporcionar, permitir, hacer posible.

enact (enákt) v. decretar, promulgar; hacer el papel de; efectuar; desempeñar la parte de.

enamel (enáml) s. esmalte; v. esmaltar.

encamp (enkámp) v. acampar.

enchant (enchánt) v. encantar; embelesar; hechizar; deleitar.

enchanter (enchánter) s. encantador; hechicero, mago, brujo.

enchantment (enchántment) s. encanto; encantamiento, hechicería.

enchantress (enchántres) s. encantadora; bruja, seductora.

encircle (ensérkl) v. cercar, rodear.

enclose (enclóus) v. encerrar; cercar, rodear, circundar, incluir.

enclosure (enclóshur) s. recinto, cercado, vallado, remesa, corral anexo; contenido, encerramiento.

encompass (encómpas) v. abarcar; encuadrar; **to — the globe** dar la vuelta al mundo.

encounter (encáunter) s. encuentro; combate, choque; v. encontrar(se); tropezar con, atacar.

encourage (encóurey) v. alentar, animar; incitar; fomentar.

encouragement (encóureyment) s. aliento, ánimo, estímulo, fomento, incentivo.

encroach (encróuch) v. pasar los límites; **to — upon** usurpar, invadir; quitar (el tiempo); menguar.

encyclopedia (ensaiclopídia) s. enciclopedia.

end (end) s. fin; cabo; término; v. acabar; terminar.
endear (endíar) v. hacer amar.
endeavor (endévor) s. esfuerzo, empeño; tentativa; tarea; conato; v. empeñar; tratar de, procurar, intentar.
ending (énding) s. final; terminación, conclusión, cesación.
endless (éndles) adj. sinfín, infinito, interminable, perpetuo, eterno.
endorse (endórs) véase **indorse**.
endorsement (endórsment) véase **indorsement**.
endow (endáu) v. dotar; fundar.
endowment (endáument) s. dotación; don; dote, fundación.
endurance (endiúrans) s. resistencia; aguante; paciencia; sufrimiento; duración.
endure (endiúr) v. aguantar, soportar, sufrir; durar, sostener, resistir, perdurar.
enema (énema) s. lavativa.
enemy (énemi) s. enemigo.
energetic (eneryétik) adj. enérgico.
energy (éneryi) s. energía.
enervate (énerveit) v. enervar.
enfold (enfóld) véase **infold**.
enforce (enfórs) v. dar fuerza a; hacer cumplir (una ley); exigir u obtener por fuerza; **to — obedience** hacer obedecer.
enforcement (enfórsment) s. coacción.
engage (enguéy) v. ocupar; emplear, contratar; atraer (la atención); ajustar, apalabrar; tomar en alquiler; acoplar; **to — in battle** trabar batalla; **to be —d** estar comprometido a; **to be —ed to be married** estar comprometido para casarse.
engagement (enguéyment) s. compromiso; cita; noviazgo; empeño, ajuste; palabra de casamiento; obligación; traba, engrane; batalla, combate.
engender (enyénder) v. engendrar, producir; procrear.
engine (ényin) s. máquina, motor, locomotora, ingenio; mecanismo, aparato; instrumento, agente.
engineer (enyinír) s. ingeniero; maquinista (de locomotora); v. dirigir; ejercer la carrera de ingeniero.
engineering (enyiníring) s. ingeniería; ingeniatura, manejo, planeo.
English (ínglish) adj. inglés; s. idioma inglés; **the —** los ingleses.

Englishman (ínglishman) s. inglés.
engrave (engréiv) v. grabar, esculpir.
engraving (engréiving) s. grabado; lámina, estampa.
engrossed (engróst) adj. absorto, ensimismado.
engulf (engólf) v. engolfar, absorber, tragar.
enhance (enjáns) v. realzar; engrandecer, mejorar, acrecentar.
enigma (enígma) s. enigma.
enjoin (enyóin) v. mandar, ordenar; encargar; **to — from** prohibir.
enjoy (enyói) v. gozar de; disfrutar de; gozarse en; tener; poseer; **to — one's self** divertirse, gozar, deleitarse; fruir.
enjoyable (enyóiabl) adj. agradable, deleitable, fruitivo.
enjoyment (enyóiment) s. placer, goce; usufructo; fruición.
enlarge (enláry) v. agrandar(se); ensanchar; aumentar; ampliar; **to — upon** explayarse en.
enlighten (enláitn) v. alumbrar; iluminar; instruir, ilustrar, aclarar.
enlist (enlíst) v. alistar(se); sentar plaza (de soldado); poner empeño en algo.
enlistment (enlístment) reclutamiento; alistamiento; enganche.
enliven (enláiven) v. avivar, animar, alegrar, alentar; regocijar.
enmity (énmiti) s. enemistad.
ennoble (enóbl) v. ennoblecer.
enormous (enórmus) adj. enorme.
enough (enóf) adj. y adv. bastante; suficiente; asaz; s. lo bastante, lo suficiente; **—!** ¡basta!
enquire véase **inquire**.
enrage (enreiy) v. enrabiar, hacer rabiar, enfurecer, irritar.
enrapture (enrápchur) v. extasiar; embelesar, enajenar, transportar.
enrich (enrích) v. enriquecer.
enroll (enról) v. alistar(se); empadronar; envolver, enrollar.
enrollment (enrólment) s. alistamiento; registro; empadronamiento, matrícula, padrón.
ensign (énsain) s. alférez (de la marina); bandera, pabellón, enseña.
enslave (ensléiv) v. esclavizar.
ensnare (ensnér) v. enredar, entrampar; embaucar; tender un lazo.
ensue (ensiú) v. sobrevenir, seguir(se); resultar, perseguir.

enter (énter) v. entrar en; ingresar en; salir (al escenario); penetrar; ingerir, insertar.
enterprise (énterprais) s. empresa.
enterprising (énterpraising) adj. emprendedor, atrevido.
entertain (entertéin) v. divertir, agasajar; obsequiar; acariciar (una idea); hospedar; divertir; abrigar (una esperanza); dar comidas o saraos.
entertaining (entertéining) adj. entretenido, divertido, chistoso, alegre.
entertainment (entertéinment) s. entretenimiento; pasatiempo; diversión; hospedaje; convite, festín.
enthusiasm (enzúsiasm) s. entusiasmo.
enthusiast (enzúsiast) s. entusiasta.
enthusiastic (enzusiástik) adj. entusiasta, entusiástico; caluroso; **to be —** estar entusiasmado
entice (entáis) v. atraer, tentar, seducir, inducir.
entire (entáir) adj. entero, cabal; todo, íntegro; **the — world** todo el mundo; **—ly** adv. enteramente.
entirety (entáirti) s. totalidad, entereza, integridad, conjunto, todo.
entitle (entáitl) v. titular, intitular, dar derecho, autorizar.
entity (éntiti) s. entidad, ente.
entrails (éntreils) s. pl. entrañas.
entrance (éntrans) s. entrada.
entreat (entrít) v. suplicar, rogar.
entreaty (entríti) s. súplica, ruego, petición, instancia, solicitud.
entrench véase **intrench**.
entrust (entróst) v. confiar; depositar, entregar.
entry (éntri) s. entrada; ingreso; partida, vestíbulo, portal; **double — partida doble.**
enumerate (eniúmereit) v. enumerar.
enunciate (enónsieit) v. articular; enunciar; hablar, declarar.
envelop (envélop) v. envolver.
envelope (énveloup) s. sobre, cubierta (de una carta), funda.
enviable (énviebl) adj. envidiable.
envious (énvios) adj. envidioso.
environment (enváironment) ambiente, medio ambiente, cercanía
environs (enváirons) s. pl. cercanías, contornos, alrededores, inmediaciones, afueras.
envoy (énvoi) s. enviado.

envy (énvi) s. envidia; v. envidiar.
epic (épik) s. epopeya, poema épico; adj. épico.
epidemic (epidémic) s. epidemia; peste, plaga; adj. epidémico.
episode (épisod) s. episodio.
epistle (epísl) s. epístola, carta.
epitaph (épitaf) s. epitafio.
epoch (épok) s. época.
equality (ikuáliti) s. igualdad.
equalize (ikualais) v. igualar; emparejar, nivelar.
equation (ekuéshon) s. ecuación.
equator (ekuéitor) s. ecuador.
equilibrium (ekulíbriom) s. equilibrio. inhabilitar; pertrechar.
equip (ekuip) v. equipar; proveer.
equipment (ekuípment) s. equipo; aparatos; avíos; habilitación, armamento, apresto; vestuario.
equity (ékuiti) s. equidad; justicia
equivalent (ekuívalent) adj. y s. equivalente.
equivocal (ekuívocal) adj. equivoco, ambiguo, de doble sentido.
era (íra) s. era, época, edad, tiempo. ¡var. raspar
erase (erréis) v. borrar; tachar, raser (erréiser) s. goma, raspador; Am. borrador; **blackboard —** cepillo. ¡raspadura.
erasure (erréshur) s. borradura.
ere (ér) prep. antes de; conj. antes (de) que; dentro de poco.
erect (iréct) adj. erguido; derecho; levantado; Am. parado; v. erguir, alzar, enaltecer, levantar.
ermine (érmin) s. armiño.
erosion (eróshon) s. erosión.
err (err) v. errar, equivocarse.
errand (érrand) s. mandado, recado.
errant (érrant) adj. errante.
erroneous (errónius) adj. erróneo.
error (érror) s. error.
eruption (erópshon) s. erupción.
escapade (eskepéid) s. trapisonda, travesura, escapada.
escape (eskéip) s. escape; fuga, huida, escapada, escapatoria, evasión, zafada; v. escaparse; eludir; **it —s me** se me escapa.
escort (éskort) s. escolta; acompañante; convoy; (eskórt) v. escoltar, convoyar, acompañar.
escutcheon (iskótchon) s. escudo de armas, blasón.
espionage (éspionev) s. espionaje
essay (ései) s. ensayo.
essence (esens) s. esencia.
essential (csénshal) adj. esencial.
establish (estáblish) v. establecer

ESSENCE   **EVOLVE**

establisnment (estáblishment) s. establecimiento, fundación.
estate (estéit) s. hacienda, heredad; bienes, propiedades, patrimonio; condición; country — finca rural.
esteem (estím) s. estima, estimación, aprecio, crédito; v. estimar, apreciar, tener en o por.
estimable (éstimebl) adj. estimable.
estimate (éstimeit) s. tasa, cálculo aproximado; presupuesto; opinión; cómputo; v. apreciar, estimar, tasar, calcular aproximadamente; hacer un presupuesto, juzgar, opinar, computar, presuponer.
estimation (estiméshon) s. juicio, opinión; estima; estimación, valuación, suposición, análisis cualitativo.
estuary (éschueri) s. estuario o estero, desembocadura de un río.
etch (etch) v. grabar al agua fuerte.
etching (étching) s. agua fuerte, grabado al agua fuerte.
eternal (itérnal) adj. eterno.
eternity (itérniti) s. eternidad.
ether (ízer) s. éter.
ethereal (izérial) adj. etéreo.
ethical (ézical) adj. ético, moral.
ethics (ézics) s. ética, moral.
etiquette (étiket) s. etiqueta (regla de conducta social).
etymology (etimóloyi) s. etimología.
eucalyptus (iukalíptus) s. eucalipto. [ropeo.
European (iuropían) adj. y s. eu-
evacuate (evákiuet) v. evacuar; desocupar, vaciar.
evade (evéid) v. evadir.
evaluate (evélíueit) v. valorar.
evaporate (eváporeit) v. evaporar(se).
evaporation (evaporéshon) s. evaporación.
evasion (evéshon) s. evasión.
evasive (evéisiv) adj. evasivo.
eve (iv) s. víspera, vigilia; Christmas — Nochebuena; New Year's — víspera del Año Nuevo; on the — of en vísperas de.
even ('ivan) a. 1. plano, llano. 2. liso. 3. a nivel, paralelo. 4. parejo, regular, uniforme. 5. balanceado, constante.
evening (ivining) s. tarde, noche (las primeras horas); last — ayer noche; — star estrella vespertina; good — buenas noches.
evenness (ívenes) s. lisura; igualdad; uniformidad; — of temper apacibilidad o suavidad de genio.
event (evént) s. suceso, acontecimiento, incidente, evento, hecho, caso; éxito, consecuencia; in any — en todo caso.
eventful (evéntful) adj. lleno de sucesos, memorable, importante.
eventual (evéntchual) adj. eventual; consiguiente, fortuito; final, terminal; acaecedero; —ly adv. finalmente, por fin, con el tiempo.
ever (éver) adj. siempre; jamás; alguna vez; en cualquier tiempo; for — more para siempre jamás; — and anon o every now and then de cuando en cuando, de vez en cuando; — since desde entonces, después; the best friend I — had el mejor amigo que en mi vida he tenido.
evergreen (évergrin) s. siempreviva, sempiterna, adj. siempre verde.
everlasting (everlásting) adj. sempiterno, eterno, perpetuo, perdurable; s. eternidad; ser eterno; sempiterna (planta); siempreviva.
evermore (evermór) eternamente, para siempre jamás.
every (évri) adj. cada; todo; todos los, todas las; cada uno o cada una; — day todos los días; — bit of it todo, todito; — other day todos los días; — whit eternamente.
everybody (éribodi) pron. todos, todo el mundo, cada uno.
everyone (évriuan) pron. todos; todo el mundo; cada uno.
everything (évrizing) pron. todo, cada cosa.
everywhere (évrijuer) adv. por (o en) todas partes; a todas partes.
evict (ivict) v. desalojar; expulsar.
evidence (évidens) s. evidencia; prueba; demostración, testimonio; señal, declaración; to be in — mostrarse; v. hacer evidente.
evident (évident) adj. evidente, patente, claro, notorio.
evil (ívl) adj. malo, malvado, maligno, depravado, perverso; aciago; de mal agüero; the — one el diablo, Satanás; s. mal, maldad.
evildoer (ívldúer) s. malhechor.
evoke (evók) v. evocar; llamar; to — laughter provocar la risa.
evolution (evolúshon) s. evolución.
evolve (evólv) v. desarrollar(se),

desenvolverse(se); desplegar, urdir.
ewe (iu) s. oveja.
exact (egsáct) adj. exacto; cabal; v. exigir; —ly adv. exactamente; en punto.
exacting (egsácting) adj. exigente.
exaggerate (egsáyereit) v. exagerar.
exalt (egsólt) v. exaltar, ensalzar.
exaltation (egsoltéshon) s. exaltación.
examination (egsaminéshon) s. examen, reconocimiento (médico).
examine (egsámin) v. examinar, investigar, inspeccionar.
example (egsámpl) s. ejemplo.
exasperate (egsáspereit) v. exasperar, irritar, enojar, provocar.
excavate (ékskeveit) v. excavar.
exceed (eksíd) v. exceder; sobrepasar; propasarse; aventajar, descollar.
exceedingly (eksídingli) adv. sumamente, extremadamente; excesivamente; — well extremadamente bien.
excel (eksél) v. sobresalir (en o entre); aventajar.
excellence (ékselens) s. excelencia.
excellency (ékselensi) s. excelencia.
excellent (ékselent) adj. excelente.
except (eksépt) prep. excepto, menos, con exclusión de; v. exceptuar.
excepting (eksépting) prep. excepto, salvo, menos, fuera de.
exception (eksépshon) s. excepción; objeción, salvedad; with the — of excepción de; to take — objetar; ofenderse; resentirse.
exceptional (eksépshonal) adj. excepcional.
excess (eksés) s. exceso; sobrante; superabundancia; — baggage exceso de equipaje (de paseo); to drink — beber con exceso.
excessive (eksésiv) adj. excesivo; sobrado, demasiado; —ly adv. excesivamente, en exceso.
exchange (ekschéiny) s. cambio; trueque; permuta; canje; bolsa; lonja; rate of — cambio; telephone — central de teléfonos; v. cambiar, trocar, canjear; permutar; to — words tener un intercambio de palabras; to — greetings saludarse, mandarse felicitaciones.
excite (eksáit) s. excitar, incitar.
excited (eksáited) adj. excitado, acalorado; animado; to get —en-

tusiasmarse; sobreexcitarse; —ly adv. con acaloramiento, agitadamente.
excitement (eksáitment) s. excitación; acaloramiento; estímulo, incitamiento; agitación, alboroto; animación.
exciting (eksáiting) adj. excitante; incitante; estimulante; conmovedor.
exclaim (eskléim) v. exclamar.
exclamation (eksklaméshon) s. exclamación; grito; clamor.
exclude (eksklúd) v. excluir; exceptuar.
exclusion (eksklúshon) s. exclusión.
exclusive (eksklúsiv) adj. exclusivo; privativo; — of sin contar.
excommunicate (ekscomiúnikeit) v. excomunicar; excomulgar.
excommunication (ekscomiunikéshon) s. excomunión; descomunión; anatema.
excrement (ékskrement) s. excremento.
excursion (ekscórshon) s. excursión, expedición, romería.
excusable (eksklúsabl) adj. excusable, disculpable, disimulable.
excuse (eksklús) s. excusa, disculpa; defensa; v. excusar, disculpar; perdonar; — me dispense usted.
execute (éksekiut) v. ejecutar; ajusticiar; llevar a cabo.
execution (eksekiúshon) s. ejecución; desempeño; mandamiento judicial; legalización de documento.
executioner (eksekiúshoner) s. verdugo; ejecutor.
executive (eksékiutiv) s. Poder Ejecutivo; gerente, administrador; adj. ejecutivo.
executor (eksékiutor) s. albacea, ejecutor testamentario.
exemplary (eksémpleri) adj. ejemplar.
exempt (eksémpt) adj. exento, libre; v. eximir; libertar; franquear.
exemption (eksémpshion) s. exención, dispensa; inmunidad.
exert (eksért) v. ejercer; esforzar; empeñarse; esforzarse.
exertion (ekséršhon) s. esfuerzo, empeño.
exhale (eksjéil) v. exhalar, emitir, despedir, vahar; expirar, soplar.
exhaust (egsóst) s. escape (de gas o vapor); emisión; — fan expulsor de aire; v. apurar, extraer,

vaciar, agotar; acabar, gastar, consumir; I am —ed no puedo más.

exhaustion (egsóschon) s. agotamiento, evacuación, vaciamiento, fatiga.

exhibit (egsíbit) v. exhibir; mostrar, exponer, presentar; ofrecer.

exhibition (egsibíshon) s. exhibición, presentación, exposición; manifestación.

exhilarate (egsílareit) v. alborozar; alegrar, regocijar; animar.

exhort (egsórt) v. exhortar.

exile (egsáil) s. destierro, exilio; expatriación; v. desterrar, expatriar.

exist (egsíst) v. existir.

existence (egsístens) s. existencia.

existent (egsístent) adj. existente.

exit (égsit) s. salida; partida, muerte; v. vase (un personaje o personajes al fin de una escena).

exodus (égsodos) s. éxodo.

exonerate (egsónereit) v. exonerar.

exorbitant (egsórbitant) adj. exorbitante, excesivo.

exotic (egsótic) adj. exótico; raro; extranjero, extraño.

expand (ekspánd) v. ensanchar(se); dilatar(se); extender(se); alargar, esparcir; desplegar.

expanse (ekspáns) s. espacio.

expansion (ekspánshon) s. expansión; ensanche, distensión; desarrollo (de una ecuación).

expansive (ekspánsiv) adj. expansivo, efusivo.

expect (ekspéct) v. esperar; contar con; aguardar; suponer; I — so supongo que sí.

expectation (ekspectéshon) s. expectación; expectativa; esperanza.

expectorate (ekspéctoreit) v. expectorar, desgarrar.

expedient (ekspídient) adj. conveniente, oportuno; prudente, propio; maravilloso; s. expediente, medio.

expedition (ekspedíshon) s. expedición.

expeditionary (ekspedíshonari) adj. expedicionario.

expel (ekspél) v. expeler, expulsar.

expend (ekspénd) v. gastar, consumir.

expenditure (ekspéndichur) s. gasto, desembolso.

expense (ekspéns) s. gasto; costo; desembolso; at any — a toda costa.

expensive (ekspénsiv) adj. costoso.

expensiveness (ekspénsivnes) s. precio subido, costo elevado.

experience (ekspíriens) s. experiencia; aventura, lance; conocimiento; práctica; mundo; v. experimentar.

experienced (ekspírienst) adj. experimentado, ducho, perito; versado.

experiment (ekspériment) s. experimento, prueba, ensayo; v. experimentar; hacer un experimento, ensayar.

experimental (eksperiméntal) adj. experimental.

expert (ekspért) s. experto, perito; juez, adj. experto, hábil, perito.

expiration (ekspiréshon) s. terminación, vencimiento (de un plazo); cumplimiento; muerte.

expire (ekspáir) v. expirar; morir; acabar; expeler (el aire respirado).

explain (ekspléin) v. explicar.

explainable (ekspléinabl) adj. explicable.

explanation (eksplanéshon) adj. explicación.

explanatory (eksplánatori) adj. explicativo.

explode (eksplóud) v. estallar, hacer explosión; volar, hacer saltar (una mina); dar un estallido; desacreditar (una teoría).

exploit (eksplóit) s. hazaña, proeza; v. sacar partido o utilidad de.

exploitation (eksploitéshon) s. explotación.

exploration (eksploréshon) s. exploración.

explore (eksplór) v. explorar.

explorer (eksplórer) s. explorador.

explosion (eksplóshon) s. explosión; estallido, voladura.

explosive (eksplósiv) adj. y s. explosivo, fulminante.

export (ekspórt) s. exportación, artículo exportado; mercancía exportada; v. exportar.

exportation (eksportéshon) s. exportación, extracción.

expose (ekspóus) v. exponer, exhibir, mostrar, poner a la vista; poner en peligro.

exposition (eksposíshon) s. exposición, exhibición.

exposure (ekspóshur) s. exposición; revelación, situación; orientación; to die of — morir por efecto de la intemperie.

expound (ekspáund) v. exponer.

express (eksprés) adj. expreso; explícito, claro; categórico; s. correo, mensajero; — company compañía de expreso; Am. exprés; v. expresar; enviar por expreso.
expression (ekspréshon) s. expresión.
expressive (eksprésiv) adj. expresivo.
expulsion (ekspólshon) s. expulsión.
exquisite (ékskuísit) adj. exquisito.
exquisiteness (ekskuísitnes) s. exquisitez; primor, gentileza.
extant (ekstánt) adj. existente.
extend (eksténd) v. extender(se); tender; prolongar(se); alargar; ensanchar; agrandar; amplificar; proyectar; dilatar.
extended (eksténded) adj. extenso; prolongado; estirado; diferido.
extension (eksténshon) s. extensión; prolongación, dilatación; prórroga; añadidura; anexo.
extensive (eksténsiv) adj. extenso, ancho, dilatado; extensivo; espacioso; —ly adv. extensamente, por extenso.
extent (ekstént) s. extensión; grado; dimensión; tamaño; amplitud; to a great — en gran parte; generalmente; to a certain — hasta cierto punto; to the full — en toda su extensión.
extenuate (éksteniueit) v. atenuar; mitigar, disminuir.
exterior (ekstíriour) adj. exterior; externo; s. lo exterior, porte.
exterminate (ekstérmineit) v. exterminar, destruir por completo.
extermination (eksterminéshon) s. exterminio.
external (ekstérnal) adj. externo; exterior; extranjero; s. lo externo.
extinct (ekstínkt) adj. extinto; apagado, destruido, desaparecido.
extinguish (ekstíngüish) v. extinguir; apagar, sofocar.
extol (ekstól) v. enaltecer.
extort (ekstórt) v. obtener por fuerza o amenaza; extorsionar; exigir dinero sin derecho.
extortion (extórshon) s. extorsión.
extra (ékstra) adj. extraordinario; de sobra, de más, adicional; suplementario; adv. inusitadamente; de un modo especial; — tire neumático de repuesto o de recambio; — workman obrero supernumerario; — work, — pay trabajo, paga extraordinaria; s. extra; extraordinario (de un periódico), actor suplente.
extract (ekstrákt) s. extracto; cita, trozo (entresacado de un libro); v. hacer un extracto.
extraordinary (extrórdinari) adj. extraordinario; extraordinarily adv. de manera extraordinaria; extraordinariamente.
extravagance (ektrávagans) s. despilfarro, derroche, gasto, lujo desmedido; gasto excesivo; extravagancia; capricho; disparate, locura; desarreglo, desorden.
extravagant (ekstrávagant) adj. gastador, despilfarrado; extravagante, singular; disparatado; — praise elogios excesivos.
extreme (ekstrim) adj. extremo; último, extremado, excesivo; sumo; postrero; riguroso; radical; — opinons opiniones extremadas; s. extremo, extremidad; ápice; v. hacer extremos; tomar las medidas más extremas; adv. extremadamente.
extremity (ekstrémiti) s. extremidad, extremo, agudeza, rigor; medida extrema; in — en gran peligro.
exuberant (egsiúberant) adj. exuberante.
exult (egsólt) v. alborozarse.
eye (ai) s. ojo; vista, mirada; atención, observación, vigilancia; corcheta, cada agujero del pan; — shade visera; in a twinkling of an — en un abrir y cerrar de ojos; blind of one — tuerto; before one's eyes a la vista, en presencia de alguno; to keep an — on cuidar, vigilar; to see — to — estar completamente de acuerdo.
eyeball (áibol) s. globo del ojo.
eyebrow (áibrau) s. ceja.
eyeglass (aiglás) s. lente, anteojo; ocular (del microscopio o telescopio); —es lentes, anteojos.
eyelash (ailásh) s. pestaña.
eyelid (ailíd) s. párpado.
eyesight (aisáit) s. vista; poor — mala vista.

F

fable (féibl) s. fábula.
fabric (fábric) s. género; tela; tejido; ropa; fábrica, obra, edificio; mano de obra.
fabulous (fébiulos) adj. fabuloso.
facade (feséd) s. fachada.

face (féis) s. cara, rostro; fachada, frente, efigie; haz, superficie, semblante, facciones, facha, frontis; aspecto, cariz; apariencia; conocimiento inmediato; ojo de la letra; **to fly in the — of** ir contra viento y marea; **— ache, — ague** neuralgia facial, **to make —s** hacer muecas o gestos; **to save one's —** salvar el amor propio; **— value** valor nominal; **to lose —** perder el prestigio; v. enfrentarse, encararse; forrar; cubrir, guarnecer; **to — the music** arrostrar las consecuencias; **to — about** volverse, voltear; **it —s the street** da a la calle.

facilitate (facíliteit) v. facilitar.

facility (fasíliti) s. facilidad.

fact (fáct) s. hecho; dato; verdad, realidad; destreza, habilidad.

faction (fácshon) s. facción, bando, partida, liga, pandilla, bandería.

factor (fáctor) s. factor; elemento, agente; comisionado; v. descomponer en factores.

factory (fáctori) s. fábrica.

faculty (fácolti) s. facultad.

fad (fad) s. novedad, manía.

fade (féid) v. decolorar(se), desteñir(se); marchitar(se); poner(se)

fagged (fágd) adj. agotado, rendido de cansancio.

fail (féil) v. faltar; fallar; fracasar; decaer; abandonar, dejar; frustrar; engañar; fracasar; **to — in an examination** fallar un examen, salir mal en un examen; **to — a student** reprobar o suspender a un estudiante; **not to — no** dejar de; **without —** sin falta; **has —ed to appear** no compareció.

failure (féiliur) s. fracaso, malogro; falta, descuido, fiasco, falla, quiebra, negligencia.

faint (féint) adj. débil; lánguido; abatido; v. desmayarse, perder el conocimiento; desfallecer; desanimarse, desalentarse; acobardarse; languidecer; adj. **to feel o grow — sentir un desfallecimiento; to be — with** morirse de, estar muerto de hambre; **— heartedly** medrosamente.

faintness (féintnes) s. languidez; debilidad; ahilo, flaqueza; desaliento, lasitud.

fair (fer) adj. claro, despejado, sereno; justo, equitativo, honrado, imparcial; rubio, blondo, sincero, razonable; corriente, mediano, ordinario; **— play** proceder leal, juego limpio; **— chance** buena probabilidad; **— complexion** tez blanca; **— and square** honrado a carta cabal; **— weather** buen tiempo; **—ly** adv. imparcialmente, honradamente, justamente; **—ly difficult** medianamente difícil; **to make a — copy** sacar en limpio; **— hair** pelo rubio; **— name** reputación sin mancha; **— sex** el bello sexo.

fairness (férnes) s. hermosura, belleza; justicia, imparcialidad, rectitud; equidad; blancura de la tez.

fairy (féri) s. hada; duende; **— land** tierra de los duendes; **— tale** cuento de hadas; **— godmother** hada madrina.

faith (féiz) s. fe, creencia; crédito; fidelidad, lealtad; **in good —** de buena fe; **to have —** in tener fe en; **upon my —!** ¡a fe mía!

faithful (féizful) adj. fiel, leal, justo, recto; **—ly** adv. fielmente, firmemente, puntualmente; **—ly yours** suyo afectísimo.

faithfulness (féizfulnes) s. fidelidad; honradez; lealtad.

faithless (féizles) adj. infiel, pérfido; falso; desleal; sin fe.

fake (féik) s. fraude, patraña; engaño; falsedad; adj. falso, fingido; v. falsear, simular, fingir.

falcon (félcon) s. halcón.

fall (fol) s. caída; desolación; ruina; bajada; muerte violenta; otoño; catarata, cascada, salto de agua; v. caer; disminuir; decaer; **to — asleep** dormirse; **to — back** retroceder; retirarse; **to — behind** rezagarse, quedarse atrás; **to — off** enflaquecer, menguar; **to — out with** reñir con, querellarse; **to — due** vencerse una letra o giro; **to — through** malograrse, salir mal una cosa.

fallen (fólen) p.p. de **to fall**.

fallow (fálou) adj. flavo; baldío; s. barbecho; v. barbechar; **to let lie —** dejar en barbecho.

false (fóls) adj. falso; postizo; falaz; cuasi, seudo; fingido; simulado; discordante.

falsehood (fólsjud) s. falsedad, embuste; mentira, engaño.

falseness (fólsnes) s. falsedad.

FALSIFY   **FASHIONABLE**

falsify (fólsifai) v. falsificar, adulterar; mentir.

falsity (fólsiti) s. falsedad, mentira.

falter (fólter) v. balbucear, vacilar, titubear; to — an excuse balbucear una excusa; s. vacilación, temblor.

fame (feim) s. fama; celebridad.

famed (feimd) adj. afamado, famoso, renombrado; celebrado.

familiar (famíliar) adj. familiar; íntimo; muy conocido; confianzudo; to be — with acostumbrado a; versado o ducho en; s. familiar.

familiarity (familiáriti) s. familiaridad; llaneza; intimidad.

family (fámli) s. familia; linaje, cuna; — name apellido; — tree árbol genealógico; — way encinta.

famine (fámin) s. hambre, carestía, escasez.

famished (fámishd) adj. hambriento, to be — morirse de hambre.

famous (féimos) adj. famoso, célebre, afamado; preclaro, eximio.

fan (fan) s. abanico; ventilador; bieldo; aficionado, admirador; v. abanicar, ventilar, soplar; — wheel rueda de paletas.

fanatic (fanátic) adj. y s. fanático.

fanaticism (fanáticism) s. fanatismo.

fanciful (fánciful) adj. fantástico; antojadizo, caprichoso, imaginativo.

fancy (fánsi) s. fantasía; antojo; imaginación; idea, concepto, capricho, inclinación, gusto; adj. fantástico, caprichoso, imaginario, ideal; bello, elegante; v. imaginar; apasionar(se), aficionar(se), figurarse, encapricharse; — monger hombre fantástico; to take a — to prendarse de; — work labor, bordado fino; — goods artículos de fantasía; to strike one's — antojársele a uno; — free libre de cuidados; sin amor; — ball baile de fantasía; just — the idea! ¡figúrate qué idea!

fang (fang) s. colmillo; garras, uña.

fantastic (fantástic) adj. fantástico, estrambótico, extravagante; ilusorio; caprichoso.

fantasy (fántasi) s. fantasía, ensueño, imagen; dibujo fantástico.

far (far) adv. lejos, a distancia, lejano; — away muy lejos; — better mucho mejor; by — con mucho; thus — hasta aquí; as — as I know según parece; que yo sepa; so — hasta ahora; how —? ¿hasta dónde?; adj. lejano, distante, remoto; — other muy diferente; — reaching de mucho alcance, que llega a lo lejos — and wide por todas partes; — off a gran distancia, a lo lejos.

faraway (fáreuéi) adj. lejano, alejado, distante, abstraído, distraído.

farce (fars) s. farsa, sainete.

fare (fer) s. pasaje, precio del pasaje; vianda, comida; viaje; v. pasarla o irle a uno bien o mal; he —s like a prince se trata a cuerpo de rey; to — forth salir.

farewell (féruel) s. despedida, adiós; to bid — to despedirse de.

farfetched (farfétcht) adj. traído de muy lejos; forzado; alambicado, apurado; improbable; no obvio.

farm (farm) s. hacienda, granja; estancia; finca de labranza, rancho; — house alquería, cortijo; — hand peón; — produce productos agrícolas; v. cultivar o labrar la tierra; to — out arrendar; repartir.

farmer (fármer) s. agricultor, ranchero, hacendado; labriego; arrendador; granjero.

farmhouse (fármjaus) s. finca, cortijo, alquería; granja.

farming (fárming) s. labranza, cultivo; beneficio de una heredad; agricultura; adj. agrícola.

farmyard (farmyard) s. corral (de una casa de campo o alquería).

far-off (faróf) adj. distante, remoto.

farther (farder) adv. más lejos, a mayor distancia; más adelante; adj. ulterior; más distante o más remoto; v. adelantar, promover.

farthest (fardest) adj. remotísimo; adv. mucho muy lejano.

fascinate (fásineit) v. fascinar.

fascination (fasinéshon) s. fascinación.

fashion (fáshon) s. moda, boga, estilo; uso, costumbre; the latest — la última moda; after a — a la manera de; no muy bien; — plate figurín; **English** — a la inglesa; v. formar, forjar, amoldar, adaptar, ajustar, idear.

fashionable (fáshonabl) adj. hecho

a la moda, elegante, de buen estilo; acostumbrado, usado.

fast (fast) adj. veloz; rápido, de prisa; adelantado (el reloj); firme, seguro, apretado; fiel; disipado, derrochador; adv. aprisa; firmemente, para siempre; fijamente; — **asleep** profundamente dormido; s. ayuno; v. ayunar.

fasten (fasn) v. asegurar, trabar, fijar, sujetar, abrochar, unir.

fastener (fásener) s. broche.

fastidious (fastídius) adj. melindroso; descontentadizo; desdeñoso.

fat (fat) adj. gordo; grasiento; pingüe; opulento; rico; s. grasa, manteca, gordura; v. engordar.

fatal (féitl) adj. fatal mortal.

fatality (fatéliti) s. fatalidad; predestinación; desgracia, infortunio.

fate (feit) s. hado, destino, sino; suerte, fortuna; providencia.

father (fáder) s. padre.

fatherhood (fáderjud) s. paternidad.

father-in-law (faderinló) s. suegro.

fatherland (fáderlard) s. patria; madre patria; tierra natal.

fathom (fézom) v. sondar, sondear; penetrar; profundizar; s. braza.

fathomless (fézomles) adj. insondable.

fatigue (fatig) s. cansancio, fatiga; v. fatigar, cansar(se).

fatness (fatnes) s. gordura.

fatten (fátn) v. engordar; nutrir.

faucet (fócet) s. llave, grifo, espita, canilla, bitoque.

fault (folt) s. falta, culpa, defecto, falla; **to find** — criticar.

faultfinder (fólfainder) s. criticón.

faultless (fóltles) adj. intachable, perfecto; cumplido; acabado.

faulty (folti) adj. culpable, defectuoso, imperfecto.

favor (féivor) s. favor, fineza, beneficio; gracia; carta; grata; patrocinio; v. favorecer, ayudar, amparar, proteger; socorrer.

favorable (féivorabl) adj. favorable, propicio, benévolo; benigno.

favorite (féivorit) adj. y s. favorito.

favoritismo (féivoritism) s. favoritismo.

fawn (fón) s. cervato; gamo en su primer año; v. lisonjear, adular.

fear (fir) s. miedo, temor, recelo; v. temer, mirar con respeto.

fearful (fírful) adj. medroso, miedoso; temeroso; pusilánime.

fearless (fírles) adj. osado, intrépido; atrevido, arrojado, bravo.

fearlessness (fírlesnes) s. osadía, intrepidez, arrojo, atrevimiento.

feasible (físibl) adj. factible, acequible, hacedero, practicable.

feast (físt) s. fiesta; banquete, festín; convite; v. festejar, agasajar; gozarse, entretenerse.

feat (fit) s. proeza, hazaña; acto de destreza; suerte; juego de manos; valentía.

feather (feder) s. pluma; especie; —s plumaje; **birds of a** — **flock together** cada oveja con su pareja; v. emplumar; enriquecer, adornar.

feathery (féderi) adj. plumoso, ligero como una pluma.

feature (fíchur) facción; semblante, rostro; película principal en el cine; rasgo; carácter distintivo; cara; — **article** artículo sobresaliente; v. destacar; hacer sobresalir; dar realce; asemejarse, parecerse.

February (fébruari) s. febrero.

fed (fed) pret. y p.p. de **to feed**; **to be** — **up** estar harto, hasta el copete; estar fastidiado.

federal (féderal) adj. federal.

federation (federéshon) s. federación; confederación; liga.

fee (fí) s. honorario(s); salario; derechos; gratificación; estipendio; **admission** — derecho de admisión; cuota de entrada.

feeble (fíbl) adj. débil; lánguido; endeble; **feebly** adv. débilmente.

feed (fid) s. comida, alimento; forraje, pasto, pienso; v. alimentar; pacer, pastar; nutrir; proveer, suplir.

feeler (fíler) s. tentáculo; antena (de los insectos), tentativa, prueba para averiguar algo.

feeling (filing) s. sensación palpamiento; tacto; percepción, sentimiento; sensibilidad, ternura; compasivo; **to hurt someone's** —s herir la sensibilidad de alguien.

feet (fit) s. plural de **foot**.

feign (féin) v. fingir; pretextar.

fell (fel) v. derribar, cortar árboles; acogotar; derrocar; pret. de **to fall**.

fellowship (féloushlp) s. camaradería, compañerismo; confraternidad; **to get a** — **ganar** u obtener una beca.

felony (féloni) s. crimen, felonía.

felt (felt) s. fieltro; adj. de fieltro.
female (fímell) s. hembra; mujer; adj. femenino; mujeril, propio de la hembra o mujer; — **cat** (dog, etc.) gata (perra, etc); — **screw** tuerca, hembra de tornillo.
feminine (féminin) adj. femenino; femenil; tierno; delicado.
fence (fens) s. cerca, palizada, vallado; resguardo; receptor de cosas robadas; **to be on the —** estar indeciso; v. cercar, avallar un sitio o heredad; esgrimir, pelear.
fencing (fénsing) s. esgrima; cercado.
fender (fénder) s. guardafango; salpicadera; defensa; trompa.
ferment (férment) s. fermento; fermentación; (fermént) v. fermentar, estar en conmoción, estar excitado.
fern (fern) s. helecho.
ferocious (feróshius) adj. feroz, fiero, salvaje, rapaz, voraz.
ferocity (feróciti) s. ferocidad, fiereza.
ferret (férret) v. rastrear, indagar; averiguar; **to — out** cazar, buscar.
ferry (férri) s. vapor de río; embarcadero; v. cruzar un río en barca; transportar de una a otra orilla en barca de pasaje.
fertile (fértil) adj. fértil, fecundo.
fertility (fertíliti) s. fertilidad.
fertilize (fértilais) v. abonar, fertilizar, fecundar.
fertilizer (fértilaiser) s. abono para la tierra.
fervent (férvent) adj. ferviente.
fervor (férvor) s. fervor; ardor.
fester (féster) v. supurar; enconarse (una llaga); ulcerarse.
festival (féstival) s. fiesta.
festive (féstiv) adj. festivo.
festivity (festíviti) s. júbilo, regocijo, festividad, fiesta.
fetch (fétch) v. ir a buscar, coger.
fete (fet) s. fiesta; v. festejar.
fetter (féter) v. engrillar, meter en grillos, encadenar, aprisionar, trabar.
feud (fiúd) s. riña, pelea, contienda; pendencia; **old —** enemistad antigua.
feudal (fiúdal) adj. feudal.
fever (fíver) s. fiebre.
feverish (fíverish) adj. calenturiento, febril, febricitante.

feverishness (fívrishnes) s. calentura; agitación febril, desasosiego.
fiancé (fiansé) s. novio; **fiancée** f. novia.
fib (fib) s. bola, mentirilla, paparrucha, embuste, filfa; v. decir mentirillas.
fibber (fíber) s. cuentero, mentirosillo, embustero.
fiber (fáiber) s. fibra.
fibrous (fáibros) adj. fibroso.
fickle (fikl) adj. inconstante, voluble, veleidoso, **mudable**.
fiction (fíkshon) s. ficción.
fictional (fíkshonal) adj. novelesco.
fictitious (fictíshius) adj. ficticio.
fiddle (fidl) s. violín, v. tocar el violín; **to — around** malgastar el tiempo.
fidelity (fidéliti) s. fidelidad.
fidget (fídyet) v. estar inquieto, agitarse, molestar, inquietar.
field (fild) s. campo, cancha (de deportes); — **artillery** artillería de campaña; — **day** día de ejercicios atléticos o militares.
fiend (fínd) s. demonio, diablo; espíritu malo; furia, arpía; **dope —** morfinómano.
fiendish (fíndish) adj. diabólico.
fierce (firs) adj. feroz, fiero, furioso, torvo; violento; vehemente; impetuoso, espantoso.
fierceness (fírsnes) s. ferocidad; fiereza; vehemencia.
fiery (fáiri) adj. fogozo, ardiente, vehemente, caliente.
fig (fig) higo; — **tree** higuera.
fight (fáit) s. lucha; pelea; riña; pleito; v. guerrear, combatir, reñir, pugnar, luchar (con); dirigir una batalla; contender, lidiar, pelear (gallos); hacer la guerra; **to — it out** decirlo a golpes o con argumentos.
fighter (fáiter) s. luchador; combatiente, guerrero, batallador; — **airplane** aeroplano de combate.
fighting (fáiting) s. lucha, combate; querella; adj. aguerrido.
figure (figuiur) s. figura, forma, talle (de una persona); cifra, número; valor; precio; presencia; representación, dibujo, estatua; pintura o imagen; tipo; papel; viso; guarismo o número; **—s** cuentas, cálculos; — **of speech** figura de dicción; **to be good at —s** saber hacer bien las cuentas; **to — out** hallar por cálculo, resolver; **to — up** computar, calcular, sumar, hacer papel o figura.

filament (fílament) s. filamento.
file (fáil) s. fichero; archivo; registro, lista; guardapapeles; lima, escofina; — **card** ficha, papeleta; v. archivar, guardar en el fichero; asentar en el registro; marcar en filas; **to — off** desfilar.
filial (fílial) adj. filial.
fill (fil) v. llenar(se); ocupar (un puesto); empastar (un diente); rellenar, hendir; satisfacer, servir, atender, despachar, hartar; terraplenar; saciarse, atracarse; despachar (un pedido); inflar (un neumático); **to — out a blank** llenar un formulario (forma o esqueleto).
fillet (filét) s. filete; cinta, lista de adornos, prendedero.
filling (fíling) s. relleno; empaste (dental); henchimiento; **gold —** orificación.
filly (fíli) s. potranca.
film (film) s. película, membrana, tela (formada sobre la superficie de un líquido); nube (en el ojo); v. cubrir una película; formarse una película; **her eyes ed with tears** se le arrasaron los ojos de lágrimas.
filter (fílter) s. filtro; v. filtrar.
filth (filz) s. suciedad; porquería.
filthiness (fílzines) s. suciedad, porquería, inmundicia.
filthy (fílzi) adj. sucio, puerco.
fin (fín) s. aleta (de pez).
final (fáinal) adj. final; terminante, definitivo; último.
finance (fináns) s. teoría bancaria; Am. finanza; hacienda pública; pl. rentas; fondos, recursos monetarios; v. hacer operaciones bancarias, administrar rentas.
financial (finánshal) adj. financiero; monetario, rentístico.
financier (financír) s. financiero; Am. financista, rentista.
financing (finánsing) s. Am. financiamiento.
find (fáind) v. hallar; encontrar; declarar; **to — fault with** criticar a, censurar a; **to — out** solver, resolver; **to — guilty** declarar o encontrar culpable.
finding (fáinding) s. descubrimiento, hallazgo; fallo, decisión; sentencia; **—s** resultados.
fine (fáin) adj. fino, perfecto, excelente; superior, refinado, puro; primoroso; bello, hermoso; — **arts** bellas artes; — **sand** arena fina o menuda; — **champagne** coñac; **in —** finalmente, en conclusión; en resumen; v. multar; afinar, refinar; clarificar, purificarse; adelgazarse, derretirse; **—ly** adv. finamente; con primor; excelentemente, muy bien; perfectamente.
fineness (fáines) s. finura; fineza; primor; excelencia, ingenio.
finery (fáineri) s. galas, atavíos.
finger (fínguer) s. dedo (de la mano); ancho o largo del dedo como medida; — **print** impresión o huella digital; **the little —** el dedo meñique; — **stall** dedal, apoyadedos; v. tocar, manosear; tener destreza en los dedos.
fingernail (fínguernel) s. uña.
finicky (fíniki) adj. melindroso.
finish (fínish) s. fin, término, conclusión, remate, cima, fenecimiento, acabamiento, colmo; **to have a rough —** estar sin pulir; v. acabar con, terminar, finalizar, consumar.
finished (fínisht) adj. acabado; pulido, pulimentado, excelente.
fir (fer) s. abeto, pino.
firecracker (fairkráker) s. cohete; petardo; triquitraque.
firefly (fáirflai) s. luciérnaga.
fireman (fairman) s. bombero.
fireplace (fáirpleis) s. chimenea; hogar.
fireproof (fairpruf) adj. incombustible; a prueba de incendio.
fireside (fairsaid) s. hogar.
firewood (fáirud) s. leña.
fireworks (fáiruerks) s. fuegos artificiales.
firm (ferm) adj. firme, fuerte, seguro, estable, fijo; constante; s. firma, razón social; compañía; **—ly** firmemente; fuertemente.
firmament (férmament) s. firmamento.
firmness (férmnes) s. firmeza.
fish (fish) s. pez, pescado; — **pond** nansa, estanque de peces, vivero; — **market** pescadería; — **story** patraña, cuento chino; **neither — nor fowl** ni chicha ni limonada; **flying —** pez volador; v. pescar, buscar en; intentar una cosa.
fisher (físher) s. pescador.
fisherman (físherman) s. pescador.
fishhook (físhjuk) s. anzuelo.
fishing (físhing) s. pesca, pesquería; — **rod** caña de pescar; — **line** cordel de pescar; — **tackle**

avíos de pesca; **to go —** ir de pesca.
fissure (físhur) s. grieta, hendedura; abertura; rajadura.
fist (fist) s. puño; **to shake one's — at** amenazar con el puño; **with clenched — a** puño cerrado.
fit (fit) adj. apto, idóneo, a propósito, conveniente; justo; juicioso, decente; sano, de buena salud; en buen estado; **— to be tied** frenético; **not to see — to do it** no estar dispuesto a hacerlo; s. talle; forma; corte; ajuste; conveniencia; conformidad; **by —s and starts** a tontas y a locas; **if you think —** si a usted le parece; **the suit —s you** el traje le viene, le queda bien; v. ajustar, adaptar, acomodar; entallar; surtir; venir bien; ser a propósito, caer bien; **to — out** equipar; tripular; armar; **to — in with** armonizar con; llevarse bien; **to — up** ajustar una cosa con otra, acomodar, componer; **to — the facts** estar de acuerdo con los hechos.
fitness (fítnes) s. aptitud, capacidad; idoneidad; conveniencia; proporción; **physical —** buena salud; propiedad.
fitting (fíting) adj. apropiado, adecuado, conveniente; s. ajuste; **dress —** prueba de un traje; **—s** avíos; herrajes, guarniciones, accesorios.
fix (fiks) v. fijar; asegurar; decidir; determinar; arreglar; reparar; componer; establecer(se); **to — up** arreglar(se), componer(se), s. apuro, dificultad, dilema.
fixed (fikst) adj. fijo, firme.
fixture (fíkschur) s. accesorio fijo; **gas —** cañerías y lámparas de gas; **electric light —** instalaciones eléctricas (como brazos de lámparas, arañas, etc.).
flabby (flebi) adj. blando, flojo.
flag (flag) s. bandera, pabellón, banderola; **— stone** losa; v. hacer señales con banderolas; adornar con banderas; flaquear, amilanarse; debilitarse; embaldosar.
flagrant (flégrant) adj. flagrante; encendido; notorio; escandaloso.
flagstaff (flágstaf) s. asta de bandera o pabellón.
flair (fler) s. instinto, penetración; aptitud natural.
flake (fleik) s. copo (de nieve);

vedija de algodón; escama; hojuela; **corn —s** hojuelas de maíz; v. descostrarse; descascararse.
flame (flem) s. llama, flama, fuego; llamarada; v. flamear; arder, encenderse; inflamar(se), enardecer.
flaming (fléming) adj. flameante; llameante, excitante; apasionado; llamativo; fautoso.
flank (flank) s. flanco, lado, costado; ijar; v. flanquear; orillar, rodear.
flannel (flánel) s. franela.
flap (flap) s. aleta; falda; cubierta; oreja de zapato; revés; v. golpear; aletear; batir; sacudir; hojear con violencia (las páginas).
flare (fler) s. llamarada, fulgor, brillo, destello; **arranque de ira**; vuelo de una falda; v. llamear, fulgurar; brillar, deslumbrar; **to — up** enfurecerse; **the illness —d up** recrudeció la enfermedad.
flash (flash) s. relámpago; destello, fogonazo; chispazo; **— of hope** rayo de esperanza; **in a —** en un instante; **news —** última noticia enviada por radio o telégrafo; v. relampaguear, brillar, centellear, radiar, telegrafiar noticias; **to — by** pasar como relámpago.
flashing (fláshing) s. relampagueo; centelleo; adj. relumbrante, flameante.
flashlight (fláshlait) s. linterna sorda o eléctrica.
flashy (fláshi) adj. llamativo en apariencia, pero de relumbrón; chillante; ostentoso.
flask (flask) s. frasco.
flat (flat) adj. plano, llano, bajío, chato, aplanado; liso, raso, aplastado; mate, sin lustre; insípido; monótono; desinflado; **— note** nota desentonada; **— denial** negativa terminante; **— rate** precio o número redondo; bemol; **— car** plataforma del ferrocarril; **to be — broke** estar sin dinero; **to fall —** caer mal un chiste; **to sing —** desafinar; s. plano, palma de la mano, apartamento, piso; v. bajar un tono; achatar; aplastar; allanar la superficie de algo; atontarse; aplanarse.
flatiron (flátairon) s. plancha.
flatness (flátnes) s. llanura; lisura; insipidez; insulsez; frialdad.

flatten (fláten) v. aplanar, allanar; achatar; aplastar; atontarse.
flatter (fláter) v. lisonjear, adular.
flatterer (fláterer) s. adulador.
flattering (flátering) adj. lisonjero; adulador; halagüeño
flattery (fláteri) s. lisonja halago; adulación; zalamería.
flavor (fléivor) s. sabor. salsa o condimento; v. sazonar, dar sabor a; condimentar.
flavorless (fléivorles) adj. insípido; soso, sin sabor.
flaw (fló) s. falta, defecto, tacha; hendedura, grieta; pelo; paño.
flawless (flóles) adj. sano, entero, irreprochable, sin defecto.
flax (flax) s. lino.
flay (flei) v. desollar; descortezar.
flea (fli) s. pulga.
flee (fli) v. huir; escapar; apartarse de; fugarse; desaparecer.
fleece (flis) s. vellón, lana; v. trasquilar, esquilar; desnudar; despojar; estafar, defraudar.
fleet (flit) s. flota, armada.
fleeting (flíting) adj. fugaz, transitorio; momentáneo; efímero.
Flemish (flémish) adj. flamenco; s. flamenco; idioma flamenco; the — los flamencos.
flesh (flesh) s. carne; cuerpo; — **and blood** carne y hueso; **in the** — en persona; — **color** encarnado.
fleshy (fléshi) adj. gordo; carnoso; pulposo; suculento; carnal.
flew (flú) pret. de to fly.
flexibility (flexibíliti) s. flexibilidad; docilidad.
flexible (fléxibl) adj. flexible.
flicker (flíker) s. parpadeo, llama vacilante; temblor momentáneo; luz trémula; aleteo; v. titilar, aletear; temblar, vacilar, fluctuar; **to** — **one's eyelash** pestañear.
flier (fláier) s. aviador; volador; tren rápido; cosa veloz; escalón; volante.
flight (fláit) s. vuelo, bandada (de pájaros); escuadrilla (de aviones); arranque, arrebato; huída, fuga; — **of stairs** tramo de escaleras.
flimsy (flímsi) adj. endeble, débil; insubstancial, fútil; frívolo; **a** — **excuse** una excusa baladí.
fling (fling) v. arrojar(se); lanzar (se); tirar; echar; **to** — **about** desparramar, esparcir; **to** — **open** abrir de repente, de golpe; s. tiro; brinco; bravata; mofa; tentativa.
flint (flint) s. pedernal.
flip (flip) v. arrojar, lanzar al aire, soltar, dar un golpe rápido; dar un Jedazo.
flippancy (flípansi) s. petulancia; locuacidad; ligereza; frivolidad.
flippant (flípant) adj. petulante; ligero (en sus acciones); frívolo; impertinente; locuaz.
flirt (flert) s. coqueteo; coqueta; v. coquetear, flirtear.
flirtation (flértéshon) s. coquetería; galanteo; flirteo.
flit (flit) v. volar, deslizarse rápidamente; revolotear.
float (flóut) s. balsa, boya, salvavidas, flotador, corcho de una caña de pescar; v. flotar, mantener o llevar a flote; lanzar al mercado, emitir, circular (valores, etc.); fluctuar; cernerse, nadar.
flock (flak) s. parvada; manada; rebaño; grey; multitud, muchedumbre; **to** — **to acudir en masa**; v. congregarse, juntarse, reunirse.
flog (flag) v. azotar, vapular, tundir; s. azotaina, tunda, zurra.
flood (flod) s. avenida, desbordamiento, diluvio, inundación, creciente; torrente; — **tide** pleamar; — **gate** compuerta de esclusa, arbollón; — **light** reflector, proyector de luz; v. inundar, diluviar, anegar; apantanar.
floor (flor) s. suelo, piso, pavimento; fondo, plan; era; — **cloth** hule para cubrir el suelo; **to have the** — tener la palabra; v. solar, entarimar, enladrillar, tillar, echar al suelo; vencer, derrotar, poner en el suelo, derribar, asombrar.
flop (flap) v. caer o colgar flojamente, batir, sacudir, aletear; menearse (una cosa) de uno a otro lado; venirse abajo, desplomarse; **to** — **down** dejarse caer; **to** — **over** voltear(se); s. fracaso.
florist (flórist) s. florero, florera; —'s **shop** florería.
floss (flos) s. seda floja; pelusa; **dental** — seda dental; penacho del maíz.
flounder (fláunder) v. patear, tropezar, vacilar; patalear en el lodo o la nieve; forcejear para salir de cualquier aprieto; revolcarse; s. lenguado, rodaballo.

FLOUR   **FOLLOW**

flour (fláur) s. harina; v. enharinar.

flourish (flóurish) v. florear, blandir; menear; sacudir; vibrar; florecer; medrar; prosperar; s. floreo, rasgo, plumada, rúbrica; adorno.

floury (flaurí) adj. harinoso.

flow (fló) s. corriente; creciente; flujo; torrente; chorro, desagüe; v. fluir, manar; ondear, flotar; to — into desembocar, desaguar en; inundar; deslizarse; derramar.

flower (fláuer) s. flor; — bed cuadro de jardín, macizo; — leaf pétalo; — bud capullo; — vase florero; v. florecer, dar flor, florear.

flowerpot (fláuerpot) s. florero, maceta de flores, tiesto.

flowery (fláueri) adj. florido; poético; adornado.

flowing (flóuing) adj. corriente; fluido, ondeante, colgante; suelto; s. derrame; creciente del agua.

flu (flú) s. influenza, gripe.

fluctuate (flókchueit) v. fluctuar.

fluctuation (flokchuéshon) s. fluctuación.

flue (flú) s. cañón (de chimenea).

fluency (flúensi) s. fluidez.

fluent (flúent) adj. fluente; fluido; to speak —ly hablar con facilidad.

fluff (flóf) v. mullir, esponjar.

fluffy (flófi) adj. mullido, suave, blando; — hair cabello sedoso.

fluid (flúid) adj. y s. fluido.

flung (flóng) pret. y p.p. de to fling.

flunk (flónk) s. reprobación (de un examen o asignatura); fracaso; retirada vergonzosa; v. reprobar, suspender, fracasar, salir mal.

flunky (flónki) s. lacayo; ayudante servil; adulón, lavacaras.

flush (flósh) s. sonrojo, rubor, color (en las mejillas); bochorno; vuelo súbito de un pájaro o bandada; flujo rápido; flux (de naipes); adj. lleno, igual, parejo, ras, nivelado; copioso, abundante; rico, al mismo nivel; v. sonrojar, abochornar; igualar, emparejar, nivelar.

flute (flut) s. flauta; estría (de una columna); rizado; v. acanalar.

flux (flóks) s. flujo, fusión.

fly (flái) s. mosca, pliegue (para cubrir botones); mosca artificial (cebo para pescar); cabriolé; calesín, volanta; fruslería, bagatela; uno de varios objetos de movimiento rápido; bragueta (abertura en los pantalones); on the — al vuelo; to — about cambiar el viento con frecuencia; to — at arrojarse o lanzarse sobre alguno; to hit a — pegar una planchita o elevar una palomita (en beisbol); v. volar, pasar velozmente; huir.

flyer (fláier) véase flier.

flyleaf (fláilif) s. guarda (hoja en blanco al principio y al fin de un libro).

foam (foum) s. espuma; v. espumar.

focus (fókos) s. foco; distancia focal; v. enfocar, afocar.

fodder (fóder) s. forraje.

foe (fóu) s. enemigo.

fog (fóg) s. niebla, neblina, bruma; velo; cerrazón, brua, calina; — horn sirena; v. anublar, ofuscar; obscurecer; velar(se); ponerse brumoso.

foggy (fógui) adj. brumoso, nublado; confuso, nebuloso.

foil (fóil) s. oropel, hojuela, laminita de metal; chapa; pan u hoja de oro o plata; florete (de esgrima); realce, contraste; azogado de un espejo; hoja, lóbulo.

fold (fóuld) s. pliegue, doblez; redil; grey; repliegue, arruga; rebaño, rebaño; three — tres veces; v. doblar(se), plegar(se); abrazar, velar(se) (una película); to — one's arms cruzarse de brazos.

folder (fóulder) s. folleto, circular; papelera; plegador, plegadera (máquina para plegar).

folding (fóulding) adj. plegadizo; plegable; — chair silla plegadiza; silla de tijera; — screen biombo; — seat asiento levadizo.

foliage (fólley) s. follaje.

folio (fóulio) s. folio, infolio; página; libro en folio; pliego.

folk (fólk) s. gente, pueblo, nación, raza; parientes, parentela; —s familia, allegados, personas, amigos; — dance danza o baile tradicional; — lore tradiciones, creencias y costumbres del vulgo; — song canción popular; cantar de gesta, canción típica o tradicional.

follow (fólou) v. seguir; ejercer

follower (un oficio o profesión); seguir el hilo de (un argumento); suceder; ir detrás; acompañar; escoltar; to — suit seguir el ejemplo.
follower (fólouer) s. seguidor, imitador, acompañante, criado.
following (fólouing) s. séquito, comitiva; oficio, carrera; adj. siguiente, subsiguiente.
folly (fóli) s. locura; necedad, tontería, sandez, desatino.
foment (fomént) v. fomentar.
fondle (fóndl) v. acariciar, mimar.
fondness (fóndnes) s. cariño, afecto; ternura, terneza: afición, apego; inclinación.
font (fónt) s. pila bautismal.
food (fúd) s. alimento, sustento, comida; nutrimiento, vianda, víveres, manjar; sea — mariscos.
foodstuff (fúdstof) s. alimento; producto alimenticio; comestibles.
fool (ful) s. tonto, necio, zonzo; payaso; badulaque, bufón; to play the — payasear, hacer el payaso; v. chasquear, chancear (se); bromear, engañar, defraudar, hacer el mono; tontear, divertirse.
foolish (fúlish) adj. tonto, necio, bobo, simple, sandio, zonzo.
foolishness (fúlishnes) s. tontería, necedad, mentecatada.
foot (fút) s. pie; pata (de animal); base, parte inferior; on — a pie; — soldier soldado de infantería; fróm head to — de pies a cabeza; to put one's — in it meter la pata; v. andar a pie; hollar, pisar; to — the bill pagar la cuenta.
football (fútbol) s. futbol.
footing (fúting) s. base; posición firme; fundamento; piso, paso; baile; danza; **to be on a friendly —** with tener relaciones amistosas con.
footlights (fútlaits) s. pl. candilejas.
footman (fútman) s. lacayo.
footnote (fútnot) s. nota al pie de una página.
footpath (fútpaz) s. vereda, senda, trocha, (para gente de a pie).
footprint (fútprint) s. huella.
footstep (fútstep) s. pisada, huella; paso; **to follow in the —s** seguir las pisadas o huellas de.
footstool (fútstul) s. banquillo, taburete; escabel.

fop (fop) s. mentecato, petimetre, currutaco.
for (for) prep. por, para; durante, por espacio de, no obstante, a pesar de; muy; porque, puesto que; but — a no ser por; — fear por el momento; as — him en cuanto a él; to know — a fact saber de cierto, saber de hecho; —dry muy seco; —ever para siempre; — all that no obstante.
forage (fórey) s. forraje, pastura; v. forrajear, apasturar; saquear.
foray (fórei) s. irrupción, pillaje, saqueo, correría; v. pillar, saquear.
forbade (forbéid) pret. de to forbid.
forbear (forbér) v. abstenerse, contenerse, reprimirse; tener paciencia; s. antepasado.
forbid (forbid) v. prohibir, vedar.
forbidden (forbidn) adj. prohibido, vedado; impedido, estorbado.
forbidding (forbíding) adj. prohibitivo; reservado; austero; repulsivo.
forbore (forbór) pret. de to forbear.
forborne (forbórn) p.p. de to forbear.
force (fors) s. fuerza, vigor, fortaleza; cuerpo (de policía, de empleados); in — en vigor, vigente; v. forzar, compeler, constreñir; obligar; to — back hacer retroceder; to — out arrancar; echar a la fuerza; to — one's way abrirse paso a la fuerza.
forced (forst) adj. forzado, obligado.
forceful (fórsful) adj. fuerte, potente; vigoroso; enérgico; violento.
forceps (fórseps) s. pinzas, tenazas.
forcible (fórsibl) adj. fuerte, potente; enérgico; eficaz; violento; hecho a la fuerza; **forcibly** adv. forzadamente, por la fuerza.
ford (ford) s. vado; v. vadear.
fore (for) adj. anterior, delantero; proel, de proa; adv. anteriormente; delante, antes; interj. ¡cuidado! (en el juego de golf).
forearm (fóram) s. antebrazo.
forebode (forbód) v. pronosticar; presagiar, presentir; antever.
foreboding (forbóding) s. presentimiento; corazonada; presagio.
forecast (fórkast) v. prever, predecir; pronosticar, proyectar, trazar.
forefather (fórfader) s. antepasado.

forefinger (fórfinguer) s. dedo índice.
forefoot (fórfut) s. mano o pata delantera; gorja, tajamar.
forego (forgó) v. abstenerse de.
foregone (forgón) p.p. de to forego; a — conclusion una conclusión inevitable.
foreground (fórgraund) s. frente, primer plano, primer término.
forehead (fórjed) s. frente (f).
foreign (fóreln) adj. extranjero; foráneo; exótico, exterior; — to his nature ajeno a su índole; — trade comercio exterior; — office ministerio de relaciones exteriores; — products productos extranjeros; — built construido en el extranjero.
foreigner (fóreiner) s. extranjero.
forelock (fórlok) s. guedeja.
foreman (fórman) s. capataz; presidente (de un jurado); mayoral; Am. caporal (de un rancho o hacienda).
foremost (fórmost) adj. primero, delantero; principal, más notable, más distinguido.
forenoon (fórnun) s. la mañana.
forerunner (forróner) s. precursor; presagio; pronóstico.
foresaw (forsó) pret. de to foresee.
foresee (forsí) v. prever.
foreseen (forsín) p.p. de to foresee.
foresight (fórsait) s. previsión.
forest (fórest) s. bosque, selva; monte, floresta; — ranger guardabosques; v. arbolar, plantar árboles.
forester (fórester) s. guardabosques; silvicultor, guardamonte.
forestry (fórestri) s. silvicultura.
foretell (fortél) v. predecir, pronosticar, profetizar, presagiar.
foretold (fortóld) pret. p.p. de to foretell.
forever (foréver) adv. por (o para) siempre; — more por siempre jamás.
forfeit (fórfit) s. multa; pena; prenda, pérdida; pérdida legal de un derecho; decomiso; v. perder.
forgave (forguéiv) pret. de to forgive.
forge (fóry) s. fragua; forja; hornaza; herrería; v. fraguar; tramar; falsificar; to — ahead abrirse paso, avanzar.
forgery (fóryeri) s. falsificación.
forget (forguét) v. olvidar; descuidar; to — one's self perder el tino o la paciencia; cometer un desmán impensadamente.
forgetful (forguétful) adj. olvidadizo; negligente; descuidado.
forgetfulness (forguétfulnes) s. olvido, negligencia, descuido.
forget-me-not (forguétminot) s. nomeolvides; miosota.
forgive (forguív) v. perdonar.
forgiven (forguívn) p.p. de to forgive.
forgiveness (forguívnes) s. perdón.
forgiving (forguíving) adj. perdonador, misericordioso, de buen corazón.
forgot (forgót) pret. p.p. de to forget.
forgotten (forgótn) p.p. de to forget.
fork (fork) s. tenedor; Am. trinche; horquilla (para heno); horca, horcón; horcadura; bifurcación; confluencia de un río; v. bifurcarse, levantar o arrojar (heno) con horquilla.
forlorn (fórlorn) adj. desamparado; desdichado, abandonado.
form (form) s. forma; condición, estado; hechura, modelo; orden, disposición; **blank** — forma en blanco; v. formar(se); construir, labrar.
formal (fórmal) adj. formal; perteneciente a la forma; metódico; convencional; solemne, ceremonioso; — **party** reunión de etiqueta; **—ly** adv. con ceremonia, solemnemente.
formality (formáliti) s. formalidad; ceremonia; etiqueta.
formation (forméshon) s. formación; desarrollo, disposición, arreglo.
former (fórmer) adj. primero; precedente; anterior, pasado; antiguo; **in** — **times** en otro tiempo; en días de antaño; antiguamente; anteriormente; **the** — aquél (aquélla, aquéllos); s. molde; matriz.
formidable (fórmidabl) adj. formidable.
formula (fórmiula) s. fórmula.
formulate (formiuléit) v. formular.
forsake (forséik) v. abandonar, desamparar, desertar.
forsaken (forséikn) p.p. de to forsake y adj. desamparado, abandonado.
forsook (forsúk) pret. de to forsake.
fort (fort) s. fuerte, fortín, fortaleza.

forth (forz) adv. adelante; hacia adelante; fuera, afuera; **to go —** salir; **and so —** etcétera.

forthcoming (forzcóming) adj. venidero, próximo, futuro, que viene; **funds will not be —** until no habrá fondos disponibles hasta.

forthwith (fórzuiz) adv. en seguida.

fortification (fortifikéshon) s. fortificación; plaza; fuerte.

fortify (fórtifai) v. fortificar.

fortitude (fórtitiud) s. fortaleza.

fortnight (fórtnait) s. quincena.

fortress (fórtres) s. fortaleza.

fortuitous (fortiúitos) adj. fortuito; inopinado, accidental.

fortunate (tórchuneit) adj. afortunado; **—ly** adv. afortunadamente.

fortune (tórchun) s. fortuna; suerte, ventura; lote, sino; **— teller** agorero, adivino.

forum (fórum) s. tribunal, foro.

forward (fóruard) adj. delantero, proel, precoz; progresista, atrevido; adv. adelante, hacia adelante; v. **to go —** ir hacia adelante; **to — a plan** fomentar un plan.

fossil (fósil) adj. fósil; s. fósil.

foster (fóster) v. criar, nutrir, fomentar; dar alas; adj. adoptivo.

fought (fót) pret. y p.p. de **to fight**.

foul (fául) adj. sucio, asqueroso; puerco, impuro, cochino, inmundo, fétido, vil; injusto; **— air** aire viciado; **— ball** pelota foul (en beisbol); **— weather** mal tiempo; **— breath** aliento fétido; **— dealings** dolo, mala fe; s. acción de ensuciar, enredarse una cosa en otra; mala jugada (contraria a las reglas del juego); trampa.

found (fáund) v. fundar, establecer; pret. p.p. de **to find**.

foundation (faundéshon) s. fundación, base, fundamento, principio.

founder (fáunder) s. fundador, fundidor (de metales); despeadura; v. zozobrar, irse a pique, fracasar, desplomar.

foundry (fáundri) s. fundición, fundería, ferrería.

fountain (fáunten) s. fuente; manantial; fontana, principio; **— pen** pluma fuente, pluma estilográfica.

fourscore (fórskór) adj. cuatro veintenas, ochenta, octogenario.

fourth (fóurz) adj. cuarto, cuarta parte; **the — of July** el cuatro de julio.

fowl (fául) s. ave, gallina.

fox (fox) s. zorra; zorro.

foxy (fóxi) adj. zorro, astuto.

fraction (frácshon) s. fracción.

fracture (frácchur) s. fractura; quiebra; v. fracturar, romper.

fragile (fréyil) adj. frágil.

fragment (frágment) s. fragmento.

fragrance (frágrans) s. fragancia.

fragrant (frágrant) adj. fragante, oloroso, aromático.

frail (fréil) adj. frágil; endeble.

frailty (fréilti) s. debilidad.

frame (fréim) s. armazón, armadura, esqueleto; marco (de un cuadro, puerta, etc.); composición, estructura; **embroidery —** bastidor para bordar; **— house** casa con armazón de madera; **— saw** sierra montada; v. formar, forjar, fabricar, construir, armar; componer, ajustar; arreglar, dirigir; **to — someone** conspirar contra una persona.

framework (fréimuerk) s. armazón, esqueleto, entramado.

franc (frank) s. franco (moneda de Francia).

franchise (francháis) s. franquicia; derecho o privilegio político; inmunidad, exención; voto, sufragio.

frank (frank) adj. franco, sincero; abierto, ingenuo; **very — francote**; s. sello de franqueo; carta franca; v. franquear, enviar carta exenta de franqueo.

frankfurter (fránkforter) s. salchicha.

frankness (fránknes) s. franqueza; sinceridad; ingenuidad, candor.

frantic (frántik) adj. frenético; enfurecido; **—ally** adv. frenéticamente.

fraternal (fratérnal) adj. fraternal.

fraternity (fretérniti) s. fraternidad.

fraud (fród) s. fraude, engaño, artificio, timo; Am. chapuza.

fraudulent (fródiulent) adj. fraudulento, engañoso.

fray (fréi) s. reyerta, riña, pelea; disputa; v. raer(se); deshilacharse.

frayed (fréid) adj. raído.

freak (frik) s. capricho, rareza.

freckle (frékl) s. peca; v. ponerse pecoso.

freckled (fréklt) adj. pecoso.

freckly (frékli) adj. pecoso.
free (fri) adj. libre; suelto; gratuito; exento, independiente, emancipado, manumiso, horro, liberal, generoso; **— of charge** gratis; **— on board** libre a bordo; **— agency** libre albedrío; **— and easy** despreocupado; **— port** puerto libre; **to give someone a — hand** dar rienda suelta o libertad de acción a una persona; **—ly** adv. libremente; con soltura; v. librar; exentar, soltar, eximir.
freedom (frídom) s. libertad; libre uso, independencia.
freezing (frísing) adj. helado, glacial; frigorífico.
freight (fréit) s. flete, carga; cargazón; **— train** tren de carga; tren de mercancías; v. fletar, cargar, enviar por carga.
French (French) adj. francés; idioma francés; **to take — leave** marcharse a la francesa; s. francés; **— horn** bocina; **the —** los franceses.
Frenchman (Frénchman) s. francés.
frenzy (frénsi) s. frenesí.
frequency (frikuensi) s. frecuencia.
frequent (fríkuent) adj. frecuente; habitual; v. frecuentar; **—ly** adv. frecuentemente, a menudo.
fresh (fresh) adj. fresco, reciente; nuevo; flamante; puro (aire, agua); impertinente; **— water** agua dulce; **—ly** adv. frescamente; con frescura; recientemente.
freshen (freshn) v. refrescar(se).
freshman (fréshman) s. novato, novicio, estudiante de primer año.
freshness (fréshnes) s. frescura; frescor; lozanía; descaro.
fret (fret) v. irritar(se); apurar(se); estar nervioso, gastar estregando; s. agitación, apuro, preocupación, roce, rozamiento; **— work** calado.
fretful (frétful) adj. descontentadizo, malhumorado, mohíno.
friar (fráiar) s. fraile.
friction (fríkshon) s. fricción; rozamiento, roce, frote, ludimiento.
Friday (fráidei) s. viernes.
fried (fráid) adj. frito; freído; p.p. de **to fry**.
friend (fréad) s. amigo, amiga.
friendless (fréndles) adj. sin amigos.

friendliness (fréndlines) s. afabilidad, amistad.
friendly (fréndli) adj. amistoso, afable, amigable; servicial, favorable; adv. amistosamente.
friendship (frénship) s. amistad.
frigate (frígueit) s. fragata.
fright (fráit) s. espanto, susto, terror; espantajo; pavor; **she is a —** es un adefesio.
frighten (fráiten) v. espantar, asustar, amedrentar, **to — away** espantar, ahuyentar.
frightened (fráitend) adj. espantado, asustado, amedrentado.
frightful (fráitful) adj. espantoso, terrible, pavoroso, horrendo.
frigid (fríyid) adj. frígido, frío.
fringe (friny) s. fleco, flequillo; orla; v. guarnecer el fleco.
frippery (fríperi) s. perifollos, moños, fruslería, trapería.
frisk (frisk) v. retozar, saltar, brincar, cabriolar, registrar (los bolsillos), escular.
frisky (fríski) v. retozón, alegre.
fritter (fríter) s. fritura, fruta de sartén; v. desperdiciar poco a poco, desmenuzar.
frivolity (frivóliti) s. frivolidad.
frivolous (frívolos) adj. frívolo.
fro (fró) **to and —** de una parte a otra; de aquí para allá.
frock (frok) s. vestido (de mujer); túnica, **— coat** levita.
frolic (frólik) s. retozo, juego; holgorio; diversión; travesura; v. retozar, travesear, juguetear.
from (from) prep. de; desde; de parte; **to take something away —** a person quitarle algo a una persona.
front (front) s. frente (m); fachada; faz, cara, atrevimiento, descaro; frontispicio; **in — of** enfrente de; delante de; **— door** puerta de entrada; **shirt —** pechera; **— view** vista al frente; v. estar al frente o de frente.
frontier (frontír) s. frontera; adj fronterizo, limítrofe.
frost (frost) s. escarcha; helada hielo, rosada; v. cubrir de escarcha, congelar, helar.
frosting (frósting) s. escarche, confitura (para cubrir un pastel); capa de clara de huevo batida con azúcar.
frosty (frósti) adj. escarchado, congelado, helado; canoso.
froth (fróz) s. espuma, espumara

— 91 —

jos, bambolla; to — at the mouth echar espuma por la boca.
frown (fráun) s. ceño, entrecejo; v. fruncir el ceño, mirar con ceño.
frozen (frósn) adj. helado, congelado, frío.
frugal (frúgal) adj. frugal.
fruit (frut) s. fruto (en general); fruta (comestible); producto; efecto, resultado, prole; **to eat —** comer fruta; **— knife** cuchillo de postres; v. fructificar, producir frutas.
fruitful (frútful) adj. fructuoso, productivo, feraz, fértil.
fruitless (frútles) adj. infructuoso, improductivo, estéril, inútil.
frustrate (fróstreit) v. frustrar.
frustration (frostréshon) s. frustración, contratiempo.
fry (frái) v. freír; achicharrarse; s. fritada; brete; **small —** pececillos; gente menuda; **—ing pan** sartén.
fudge (fody) s. dulce (usualmente de chocolate y nueces); embuste.
fuel (fiúel) s. combustible.
fugitive (fiúyitiv) adj. fugitivo, transitorio, prófugo; s. tránsfuga.
fulfill (fulfíl) v. cumplir; realizar, colmar, llenar; llevar a cabo.
fulfillment (fulfílment) s. cumplimiento, desempeño, ejecución.
fullness (fúlnes) s. plenitud.
fumble (fómbl) v. tentalear, buscar a tientas; chapucear, parar una pelota desmañadamente.
fume (fiúm) v. exhalar vapor o gas; rabiar; **—s** s. pl. vapores; emanaciones, gases.
fumigate (fiúmigueit) v. fumigar, sahumar, perfumar; Am. humear.
fun (fon) s. diversión; burla, broma, chanza, chirigota, guasa; Am. choteo; **for —** en (o de) broma; **to make — of** burlarse de, chancearse con; v. hacer chistes, gastar bromas, divertirse; Am. chotear, chotearse con.
function (fónkshon) s. función; desempeño, oficio, ocupación, acto, ceremonia; v. funcionar.
fund (fond) s. fondo; caudal; capital, acopio, reserva; **—s** fondos públicos, prorrogar el plazo (de una deuda).
fundamental (fondaméntal) adj. fundamental; cardinal; esencial; s. fundamento, principio.

funeral (fiúneral) adj. funeral, fúnebre; funerario, exequias.
fungus (fóngos) s. hongo.
funnel (fónel) s. embudo; humero (cañón o chimenea); túnel, boca de carga; **— shaped** infundibuliforme.
funny (fóni) adj. chistoso, cómico, gracioso, divertido, burlesco; extraño, raro; bufón; **the funnies** sección cómica (de un periódico).
fur (fer) s. piel (de animales peludos o lanudos); sarro (en la lengua); **— coat** abrigo de pieles; v. forrar o adornar con pieles finas.
furious (fiúrios) adj. furioso.
furl (ferl) v. plegar, enrollar.
furlough (férlou) s. licencia militar; v. dar licencia militar.
furnace (fórnes) s. horno.
furnish (fórnish) v. proveer, suministrar, surtir, deparar, proporcionar; **to — a room** amueblar un cuarto.
furniture (fórnichur) s. muebles, mobiliario; ajuar, equipo, aderezo.
furrow (fórrou) s. surco; arruga, zanja, reguera; v. zanjar, surcar.
further (fórder) adj. adicional; más lejano, más remoto; adv. además, más allá, ulterior; v. promover, fomentar.
furthermore (fórdemor) adv. además.
furthest (fórdest) adj. (el) más lejano; (el) más remoto; extremo; adv. más lejos, remotamente.
furtive (fértiv) adj. furtivo.
fury (fiúri) s. furia; frenesí.
fuse (fiús) s. fusible; v. fundir.
fuselage (fiúseley) s. fuselaje.
fussy (fósi) adj. melindroso; minucioso (en demasía); remilgado; inquieto, exigente.
futile (fiútil) adj. fútil, vano.
future (fiúchur) adj. futuro; ventura, s. porvenir.
fuzz (fos) s. vello, pelusa, tamo.
fuzzy (fósi) adj. velloso; cubierto de plumón fino, cubierto de peluca.

G

gab (gab) charlar, parlotear; picotear; s. **gift of —** labia.
gabardine (gáberdín) s. gabardina.
gabble (gabl) s. charla, cotorreo, algarabía; v. charlar, comentar.
gable (guéibl) s. gablete (de un

tejado); faldón; — **roof** tejado de caballete o de dos aguas.
gad (gad) v. vagar, callejear; andar de aquí para allá, andorrear.
gadget (gádyet) s. adminículo, artefacto, chisme.
gag (gag) s. mordaza; acial; burla, broma; asco; lo que produce bascas; chiste (improvisado por un actor); v. amordazar, dar náuseas, hacer callar.
gage (guéiy) véase **gauge**.
gaiety (guéiti) s. alegría, gozo.
gaily (guéili) adj. alegremente, vistosamente, jovialmente.
gain (guéin) s. ganancia; v. ganar.
gait (guéit) s. paso, andadura.
gale (guéil) s. ventarrón; viento fuerte; — **of laughter** carcajada.
gall (gol) s. bilis, hiel; amargura; odio; descaro; aspereza, rencor; — **bladder** vejiga de la bilis, v. irritar, hostigar.
gallant (gálant) adj. valiente; noble; intrépido, galante, cortés.
gallantry (gálantri) s. galantería, gallardía, valor, bizarría.
gallery (gáleri) s. galería, balcón.
galley (gálei) s. galería; cocina (de buque); falúa; — **proof** galerada; — **slave** galeote.
gallon (gálon) s. galón (aproximadamente cuatro litros).
gallop (gálop) s. galope, ful¹ — **a** galope tendido, a rienda suelta; v. galopar.
gallows (gálous) s. horca.
galoshes (galóshes) s. pl. chanclos, zapatos fuertes, zapatones.
gamble (gámbl) v. jugar, apostar, aventurar (algo) en el juego; jugar por dinero; **to — away** perder en el juego; **to — everything** jugar el todo por el todo; **gambling hell** o den garito, casa de juego; s. jugada (en juegos de azar).
gambol (gámbol) v. retozar; cabriolar, brincar, saltar; s. retozo.
gander (gánder) s. ánsar, ganso.
gang (gang) s. cuadrilla, pandilla; juego (de herramientas o máquinas); pelotón, banda; v. agrupar (se); **to — up against** conspirar contra.
gangplank (gángplank) s. plancha, pasamanos (de un buque).
gangrene (gángrin) s. gangrena; v. gangrenar(se).
gangster (gángster) s. bandolero, malhechor, maleante, pistolero, atracador.

gangway (gángüei) s. paso, pasadizo, plancha, pasamanos, portalón; —; ¡a un lado! ¡ábranse!
gantlet (gántlet) véase **gauntlet**.
gap (gap) s. brecha, abertura, claro, espacio, intervalo.
gape (guéip) s. bostezo, boqueada, v. estar con la boca abierta, abrirse o estar abierta una cosa; estar embobado.
garage (garash) s. garaje.
garb (garb) s. vestido, vestidura; aspecto; v. vestir, ataviar.
garbage (gárbey) s. desperdicios.
garden (gardn) s. jardín; huerta, huerto; — **balsam** balsamina de jardín; v. cultivar un jardín.
gardener (gárdner) s. jardinero, hortelano, horticultor.
gargle (gargl) s. gargarismo; Am. gárgaras; enjuague; v. hacer gárgaras; Am. gargarear.
garland (gárland) s. guirnalda.
garlic (gárlik) s. ajo. |vestir.
garment (gárment) s. prenda (de
garnish (gárnish) s. aderezo, adorno; v. ornar, ataviar, aderezar.
garret (gárret) s. desván, buhardilla.
garrison (gárrison) s. guarnición; v. guarnecer o guarnicionar (una fortaleza).
garter (gárter) s. liga (para sujetar las medias); v. sujetar con ligas.
gas (gas) s. gasolina; gas; **gas de alumbrado**; — **fitter** instalador o aparejador de gas; — **fixture** tubo de derivación con su brazo, — **stove** estufa o cocina de gas; v. asfixiar con gas.
gaseous (gáseous) adj. gaseoso.
gash (gash) s. cuchillada, herida, incisión, cicatriz; v. dar una cuchillada, acuchillar, hacer una incisión.
gasoline (gáslin) s. gasolina.
gasp (gasp) s. boqueada, grito sofocado; v. boquear, jadear, emitir sonidos entrecortados.
gate (guéit) s. portón, entrada; puerta; portillo, rastrillo.
gateway (guéituei) s. paso, entrada
gathering (gádering) s. junta, reunión, amontonamiento, asamblea. |tivo, chillón, lucido
gaudy (gódi) adj. vistoso, llama-
gather ('gaedtar, B - J) v.t. 1. recoger (flores, etc.); cosechar, recolectar. 2. recaudar (dinero). 3. acumular, reunir (a gente, dinero, etc.); acopiar (provisiones).

gauge (guéy) s. calibrador; indicador; instrumento para medir, calibrador; escantillón; calado, manómetro; calibre (de un cañón, pistola, etc.); v. medir, calibrar; estimar, calcular, apreciar |macrado, flaco, delgado.

gaunt (gónt) adj. maciliento, degauntlet (góntlet) s. guantelete; manopla; v. **to throw down the —** retar, desafiar.

gave (guéiv) pret. de **to give**.

gawk (gók) v. bobear, mirar embobado; cometer torpezas; s. bobo. |do, bobo, desgarbado.

gawky (góki) adj. torpe, desmaña-

gay (guéi) adj. vivo, alegre, vistoso.

gayety (guéiti) véase **gaiety**.

gaze (guéis) s. mirada (fija); contemplar; v. clavar la mirada.

gazette (gasét) s. gaceta.

gear (guír) s. aperos; herramientas; aparejo; equipo, rueda dentada; engranaje; encaje, transmisión de movimiento; **foot —** calzado; **low —** primera velocidad; **— block** cuadernal de paloma; **to shift —** cambiar el engrane o velocidad; **— shift lever** palanca de engrane; **to throw into —** poner en juego; v. aparejar, enjaezar; montar, armar, engranar, encajar, conectar; endentar.

geese (guis) pl. de **goose**.

gelatin (yélatin) s. gelatina.

gem (yem) s. gema, piedra preciosa; joya, joyel, alhaja, preciosidad.

gender (yénder) s. género.

general (yéneral) adj. y s. general, **in —** en general; indeterminado; por lo común, por lo general.

generality (yeneráliti) s. generalidad. |lizar.

generalize (yéneralais) v. generagenerate (yénereit) v. engendrar; producir, originar, procrear.

generation (yeneréshon) s. generación; producción, linaje.

generosity (yenerósiti) s. generosidad, liberalidad.

generous (yéneros) adj. generoso; magnánimo, liberal, dadivoso.

genial (yínial) adj. genial.

genius (yínius) s. genio; ingenio; talento; ángel, cupidillo.

gentile (yéntail) adj. gentil.

gentle (yentl) adj. suave, afable; apacible; gentílico.

gentleman (yentlman) s. caballero,

gentlemen pl. caballeros.

gentlemanly (yéntlmanli) adj. caballeroso, caballero, cortés, galante, civil, urbano; hidalgo; adv. caballerosamente, galantemente.

gentleness (yéntlnes) s. suavidad, dulzura, apacibilidad.

gently (yentli) adj. suavemente; despacio, dulcemente; mansamente.

genuine (yéniuin) adj. genuino.

geographical (yiográfical) adj. geográfico.

geography (yiógrafi) s. geografía.

geological (yiolóyical) adj. geológico.

geology (yióloyi) s. geología.

geometric (yiométric) adj. geométrico.

geranium (yeránium) s. geranio.

germ (yerm) s. germen; microbio, embrión, yema, botón, simiente.

German (yérman) adj. y s. alemán.

germinate (yérmineit) v. germinar.

gesticulate (yestíkiuleit) v. gesticular, accionar, hacer gestos o ademanes, manotear.

gesture (yéschur) s. gesto, ademán, **a mere —** una pura formalidad; v. gesticular, hacer gestos.

get (guet) v. obtener, adquirir, lograr, conseguir, recibir, ganar, llegar (a); traer, coger, atrapar, granjear, alcanzar, llevar (premio, ventaja, etc.); reportar, recibir, aprender de memoria; **to — along** llevarse bien con alguien; ir pasándola; **to have got** tener; poseer; **to have got to** haber de o tener que; **to — away** huir, irse; **to — away with** salirse con la suya; **to — by heart** aprender de memoria; **to — down** bajar; **to — ill** enfermar(se); **to — in** entrar, meter(se); **to — married** casarse; **to — near** acercarse; **to — off the train** bajar del tren; **to — on** subir a; ponerse encima de; **to — out** salir; sacar; irse; divulgarse (un secreto); **to — over** recuperarse de (una enfermedad); olvidar una ofensa; pasársele a uno el susto; **to — ready** disponerse a; alistarse; **to — rid of** deshacerse de, desprenderse de; **to — through with** terminar, acabar; **to — together** reunirse; ponerse de acuerdo; **to — somebody to do some thing** hacer que alguien haga algo; **I — you** le entiendo.

ghastly (gástli) adj. horrible, pálido, lívido, cadavérico, espantoso.

ghost (gost) s. espectro, fantasma; alma, espíritu; aparecido, ánima en pena; **Holy —** el Espíritu Santo; **not to have the — of a notion** of no tener la más remota idea de.

ghostly (góstli) adj. como un espectro; perteneciente a duendes.

giant (yáiant) s. gigante; adj. gigantesco, enorme.

giddy (guidi) adj. ligero de cascos; frívolo, vertiginoso; **— speed** velocidad vertiginosa.

gift (guift) s. regalo; obsequio; dote, talento, gracia, favor.

gifted (guifted) adj. talentoso.

gigantic (yaigántik) adj. gigantesco.

giggle (guigl) s. risita, risilla; risa falsa; v. reírse tratando de suprimir u ocultar la risa; reírse falsamente.

gild (guild) v. dorar.

gill (guil) s. agalla (de pez).

gilt (guilt) adj. y s. dorado; pret. y p.p. de **to gild**.

gin (yin) s. ginebra (licor).

ginger (yínyer) s. jengibre; **— ale** cerveza de jengibre.

gingerbread (yínyerbred) s. pan de jengibre, ornato de mal gusto.

gingham (guíngam) s. guinga (tela de algodón); carrancián.

gipsy (yípsi) véase **gypsy**.

giraffe (yiráf) s. jirafa.

gird (guerd) v. ceñir; rodear; cercar, **to — oneself for** prepararse para; mofarse, burlarse.

girdle (guerdl) s. ceñidor, cinto; faja; cíngulo; v. fajar.

girl (guerl) s. niña, muchacha, joven.

girlhood (guérljud) s. niñez; mocedad, doncellez.

girlish (guérlish) adj. pueril, de niña; de muchacha, juvenil.

girt (guert) pret. y p.p. de **to gird**; v. véase **gird**.

girth (guerz) s. cincha, fajo, cinto; periferia; **— away** correas de cincha; v. fajar, ceñir.

gist (yist) s. substancia, punto.

give (guiv) v. dar, regalar, ceder, dar de si, donar, entregar, traspasar, conferir; **to — away** regalar, entregar; revelar (un secreto); **to — again** volver a dar, **to — birth** dar a luz, parir; **a — away** revelación indiscreta; **to — in** ceder, darse por vencido; **to — fire** mandar hacer fuego; **to — up** abandonar, renunciar a, perder la esperanza; s. elasticidad.

giver (guiver) s. dador, donador.

glacial (gléshial) adj. glacial.

glacier (gléshier) s. glaciar, helero.

glad (glad) adj. alegre; contento, gozoso, agradable, **to be — to** alegrarse de, tener mucho gusto en, **—ly** adv. alegremente, con mucho gusto, de buena gana.

gladden (gladn) v. regocijar.

glade (gléid) s. claro herboso (en un bosque), raso, páramo.

gladness (gládnes) s. alegría, regocijo.

glamour (glámor) s. encanto, hechizo, fascinación, encantamiento; embrujo; **— girl** niña hechicera.

glamorous (glámoros) adj. fascinador; hechicero.

glance (glans) s. mirada, vistazo, ojeada; vislumbre, intuito, fulgor, desviación (por choque); v. pegar de soslayo, ver o mirar de prisa, dar un vistazo o una ojeada.

gland (gland) s. glándula.

glare (glér) s. resplandor, relumbre; v. resplandecer, relumbrar, tener colores chillones.

glass (glass) s. vidrio, cristal, vaso, cualquier objeto de vidrio; copa (de cristal); lente; **looking —** espejo, **—es** anteojos, lentes, **crown —** vidrio ordinario.

glassware (glásuer) s. vajilla de cristal, cristalería.

glassy (glási) adj. vidrioso.

glaze (gleis) s. vidriado, lustre, superficie lustrosa o glaseada, v. poner vidrios en la ventana.

glazier (gleisír) s. vidriero.

gleam (glim) s. destello, rayo, fulgor, resplandor, brillo, viso; v. fulgurar, destellar, relampaguear

glean (glin) v. recoger, espigar.

glee (gli) s. regocijo; júbilo; gozo; **— club** orfeón, masa coral.

glib (glib) adj. locuaz; de mucha labia, suelto de lengua.

glimmer (glimer) s. vislumbre, viso, titileo, luz débil; **— of hope** rayo de esperanza; v. titilar, rielar, centellear.

glimpse (glimps) s. vislumbre, vistazo, ojeada, relámpago; v. vislumbrar.

glisten (glisn) v. relucir, brillar.

glitter (gliter) s. lustre, brillo, v. relumbrar, rutilar, lucir.

GLOAT   **GOOD**

gloat (glóut) v. gozarse (en), deleitarse en el daño ajeno.
globe (glóub) s. globo; esfera.
gloom (glum) s. lobreguez, sombra; abatimiento, melancolía, tristeza.
gloomy (glúmi) adj. lóbrego, sombrío, obscuro, lúgubre.
glorify (glórifai) v. glorificar.
glorious (glórius) adj. glorioso, espléndido, ilustre.
glory (glóri) s. gloria; v. gloriarse, vanagloriarse, jactarse.
gloss (glos) s. lustre, brillo, pulimento; glosa, comentario; barniz; apariencia; paliativo; v. lustrar, dar brillo, pulir; glosar; to — over dar colorido de bueno (a algo que no lo es).
glossary (glóseri) s. glosario.
glossy (glósi) adj. lustroso.
glove (glóv) s. guante; v. poner guantes.
glow (glóu) s. incandescencia; brillo (de un ascua); calor vivo; fosforescencia; v. lucir, fosforescer, dar luz o calor sin llama.
glowing (glóuing) adj. encendido.
glowworm (glóuuorm) s. luciérnaga.
glue (glu) s. cola (para pegar); v. encolar; pegar (con goma); aglutinar.
glutton (glotn) s. glotón.
gluttonous (glótnos) adj. goloso.
gluttony (glótni) s. gula.
gnarled (narld) adj. nudoso, torcido.
gnash (nash) v. crujir, rechinar (los dientes).
gnat (net) s. jején (insecto).
gnaw (noh) s. roer, corroer.
go (go) v. ir(se), interesar, contribuir; marchar; funcionar; acudir; tener participaciones en; responder por; to — around andar alrededor de; dar vueltas; to — halves ir a medias; to — abroad ir de viaje a otro país; to — back on one's word faltar a la palabra; to — after seguir, ir tras de; to — by pasar por; to — away irse, marcharse, to — to the back of mirar más allá de; to — on proseguir, continuar; to — along continuar; to — along with one acompañar a alguno; to — to sleep dormirse; to — under ir o pasar por debajo de; to — astray extraviarse, descarriarse; to — beyond sobrepujar, exceder, ir más allá; s. energía; moda, usanza; actividad, empuje; it is a — trato hecho; to be on the — estar en continuo movimiento.
goad (góud) s. aguijón; aguijonada, pincho, v. aguijonear, pinchar, incitar, picar, estimular.
goat (goút) s. cabra; chivo; **male —** macho cabrío; **young —** cabrito, chivo, choto.
goatee (gouti) s. perilla.
gobble (góbl) v. tragar, engullir, hacer ruido en la garganta como los pavos, to — up engullirse.
gobbler (góbler) s. pavo.
go-between (gobituín) s. mediánero.
goblet (góblet) s. copa grande.
goblin (góblin) s. duende.
god (god) s. dios; **God** Dios.
godchild (gódchaild) s. ahijado(a)
goddess (gódes) s. diosa.
godfather (gódfader) s. padrino.
godless (gódles) adj. impío, ateo.
godlike (gódlaik) adj. como Dios.
godly (gódli) adj. pío, devoto.
godmother (gódmoder) s. madrina.
goggles (gogls) s. pl. antiparras, gafas, anteojos de camino.
going (góing) ger. y adj. que anda, marcha o funciona bien; s. paso, andadura; to be — ir, irse; s. ida, partida, marcha.
goiter (gólter) s. papera; **Am.** buche.
gold (gold) s. oro; dinero; — **standard** patrón de oro.
golden (goldn) adj. de oro, áureo; dorado, brillante, excelente.
goldfinch (góldfinch) s. jilguero amarillo, cardelina, pintacilgo.
goldfish (góldfish) s. carpa dorada.
goldsmith (góldsmiz) s. orfebre.
golf (golf) s. golf, juego escocés.
gondola (góndola) s. góndola; cabina (de una aeronave); — **car** vagón de mercancías (sin techo); Am. jaula.
gone (gon) p.p. de to go y adj. ido; perdido; arruinado, pasado; **he is** — se fue; **it is all** — se acabó.
gong (gong) s. gong, batintín.
good (gud) adj. bueno, válido, verdadero, excelente; apto; útil; genuino; — **afternoon** buenas tardes; — **day** buenos días; adiós; **a — turn** un favor, una gracia; **in — time** a tiempo, a propósito; — **morning** buenos días; **Good Friday** Viernes Santo; **a — way** un buen trecho. **to have a —**

— 96 —

time pasar un buen rato; divertirse; **to hold —** subsistir; continuar en toda su fuerza; s. bien, beneficio, provecho; ventaja; utilidad; servicio; **—s** bienes; mercancías, efectos.
good-bye (gudbái) interj. adiós.
good-looking (gudlúking) adj. bien parecido, guapo.
goodly (gudli) adj. grande; considerable; de buena apariencia; hermoso, guapo, bien parecido.
good-natured (gudnéchurd) adj. de buen genio, bonachón, afable.
goodness (gúdnes) s. bondad; **—!** ¡Dios mío! ¡cielos!
goody (gúdi) s. golosina, bombón, dulce; bonachón, interj. ¡qué bueno! **goody-goody** beato, santurrón.
goose (gus) s. ganso; bobo, tonto; ánsar, ánade, oca; plancha de sastre; **— flesh** carne de gallina.
gooseberry (gúsberri) s. grosella, grosellero (arbusto); uva espina o crespa.
gopher (gófer) s. roedor semejante a la ardilla; variedad de topo.
gore (gor) s. cuajarón de sangre; cruor, cuchillo (Am. cuchilla); pedazo de terreno triangular; sesgue; v. cortar en triángulo; herir con arma blanca; cornar.
gorge (gory) s. garganta, cañada, desfiladero, barranca; v. engullir.
gorgeous (góryus) adj. primoroso, vistoso, brillante, esplendoroso.
gorilla (goríla) s. gorila.
gory (góri) adj. sangriento, ensangrentado.
gospel (góspl) s. evangelio; cosa cierta e indubable.
gossip (gósip) s. chisme, chismería, murmuración, hablilla, picotería, chismografía, murmurador, chismero, v. chismear, murmurar.
goossipy (gósipi) adj. chismero.
gotten (gótn) p.p. de **to get**.
gouge (gáuy) s. gubia (especie de formón o escoplo curvo); mediacaña; ranura, canal o estría; v. escoplear con una gubia; **to — someone's eyes out** sacarle los ojos a alguien.
gourd (gord) s. calabaza.
gout (gáut) s. gota (enfermedad).
govern (góvern) v. gobernar, regir.
governess (góvernes) s. institutriz.
government (góvernment) s. gobierno.
governmental (góvernméntal) adj. gubernativo, gubernamental.

governor (góvernor) s. gobernador, regulador (de una máquina); administrador.
gown (gáun) s. vestido (de mujer); toga (de un juez, profesor, etc.) túnica; **dressing —** bata; v. poner o ponerse toga o vestido de mujer.
grab (grab) v. agarrar; asir; arrebatar, coper; s. agarrón, presa.
grace (greis) s. gracia; favor, donaire, garbo; elegancia, despejo; indulgencia, perdón, remisión; **to say —** dar gracias o bendecir la mesa. v. agraciar, adornar.
graceful (gréisful) adj. gracioso, agraciado, garboso; donoso; **—ly** adv. graciosamente, con gracia.
gracefulness (gréisfulnes) s. gracia; donaire, gentileza, gallardía.
gracious (gréshus) adj. afable; cortés; **—!** ¡válgame Dios!
gradation (gradéshon) s. graduación; grado; paso gradual.
grade (gréid) s. grado, nota, calificación; cuesta; rango, declive y su rasante; Am. gradiente; **— crossing** cruce a nivel (de un ferrocarril con una carretera); **— down —** cuesta abajo; **to — up** cruzar castas de animales; **— up** cuesta arriba; v. graduar, clasificar.
gradual (grádyual) adj. gradual; graduado; **—ly** adv. gradualmente.
graduation (gradyuéshon) s. graduación.
graft (graft) s. injerto; tejido injertado; acodo, cosa que se ingiere en otra; v. injertar; malversar fondos ajenos; exigir pago ilegal; Am. morder.
grafter (gráfter) s. malversador (de fondos públicos), estafador, injertador; Am. coyote, mordelón.
grain (gréin) s. grano; fibra (de la madera), veta (del mármol o madera); cualquier cereal, pizca; granilla del paño.
gram (gram) s. gramo.
grammar (grámar) s. gramática.
grammatical (gramátikal) adj. gramatical, gramático.
granary (gráneri) s. granero.
grand (grand) d. grande; grandioso, admirable; magnífico, sublime, comprensivo, ilustre.
grandchild (grándcháild) s. nieto.
grandchildren (grándchildren) s. nietos.
granddaughter (grándóter) s. nieta.

— 97 —

grandeur (grándiur) s. grandeza, grandiosidad, magnificencia.
grandfather (grándfader) s. abuelo.
grandiose (grándios) adj. grandioso, magnífico, imponente.
grandma (grándma) s. abuela, abuelita; Am. mamá grande.
grandmother (grándmoder) s. abuela.
grandness (grandnes) s. grandeza, grandiosidad, magnificencia.
grandpa (grándpa) s. abuelo, abuelito; Am. papá grande.
grandparent (grándperent) s. abuelo, abuela; —s abuelos.
grandson (grándson) s. nieto.
grandstand (grándstand) s. andanada; gradería, cubierta.
grange (grény) s. granja, asociación de agricultores, cortijo, alquería, hacienda para el fomento de la agricultura.
granite (gránit) s. granito (roca).
granny (gráni) s. abuelita; viejecita, viejita, comadre.
grant (grant) s. concesión, subvención, donación, cesión, don, dádiva, merced; asenso, asentimiento; v. conceder; dar, otorgar, dispensar, permitir; ceder, conferir; **to take for** —ed dar por supuesto; dar por sentado.
granulate (grániuleit) v. granular.
grape (gréip) s. uva.
grapefruit (gréipfrut) s. toronja.
grapevine (gréipvain) s. vid; parra.
graph (graf) s. diagrama, gráfica; v. hacer una gráfica o diagrama.
graphic (gráfic) adj. gráfico.
graphite (gráfait) s. grafito.
grapple (grápl) v. luchar, pelear cuerpo a cuerpo, aferrar, agarrarse, agarrar, asir, atracarse.
grasp (grasp) v. agarrar; asir, apretar, abarcar; comprender, apoderarse de, usurpar, tomar; s. agarro, asimiento, apretón de manos, puño, puñado; **to be within one's** — estar al alcance de uno; **to have a good** — **of a subject** estar fuerte en una materia.
grass (gras) s. hierba; césped.
grasshopper (grásjoper) s. saltón.
grassy (grási) adj. herboso, gramíneo; Am. pastoso.
grate (gréit) s. reja, verja, enrejado; — **bar** cada barra de la parrilla; v. enrejar, poner enrejado, emparrillar, rechinar, chirriar, molestar, irritar.
grateful (gréitful) adj. agradecido, grato, agradable, reconocido.

grater (gréiter) s. rallador, rallo, raspador.
gratify (grátifai) v. complacer, dar gusto, agradar, satisfacer, premiar, recompensar.
grating (gréiting) s. reja, enrejado, verja; emparrillado.
gratis (grátis) adj. gratis, de balde, gratuitamente.
gratitude (grátitiud) s. gratitud.
gratuitous (gratíuitos) adj. gratuito, sin fundamento, gratis, dado; — **statement** afirmación arbitraria.
grave (gréiv) adj. grave; serio; circunspecto; s. tumba, sepulcro; sepultura, fosa, huesa, cárcava; — **stone** losa o lápida sepulcral.
gravel (grávl) s. grava, guijo, cascajo, sábulo, litiasis.
graveyard (gréivyard) s. cementerio.
gravity (gráviti) s. gravedad.
gravy (gréivi) s. salsa, jugo.
gray (gréi) adj. gris; cano, entrecano (que empieza a encanecer); pardo; animal gris; — **horse** rucio, tordo, tordillo; v. poner o volverse gris o cano, encanecer, ponerse gris.
grayish (gréish) adj. grisáceo, pardusco, gríseo, agrisado; entrecano, — **hair** pelo entrecano.
grayness (gréines) s. grisura, gris.
graze (gréis) s. pacer, apacentar; pastar, herbajar; pastorear; rozar, s. roce, rozón, raspadura, pasto.
grease (gris) s. grasa; saín, gordura; v. engrasar, untar; lubricar; **to** — **the palm** untar la mano.
greasy (grísi) adj. grasiento.
great (gréit) adj. gran(de); eminente; magnífico, magno, grueso, vasto, excelente; mucho, numeroso; **a** — **deal** una gran cantidad; **a** — **many** muchos; **a** — **while** largo rato o tiempo; **—ly** adv. grandemente, mucho, muy; en gran parte.
great-grandchild (greitgrandchaild) s. biznieto.
great-grandfather (greitgrandfader) s. bisabuelo.
great-grandmother (greitgranmoder) bisabuela.
greatness (gréitnes) s. grandeza.
Grecian (gríshan) adj. y s. griego.
greed (grid) s. codicia, avaricia.
greedily (grídli) adv. vorazmente, con avaricia, ansiosamente, vehemente, con gula.

greediness (grídines) s. codicia, avaricia, voracidad, gula, anhelo.
greedy (grídi) adj. codicioso; avaro; goloso, voraz, insaciable.
Greek (grik) adj. y s. griego.
green (grin) adj. verde; novato, inexperto, crudo, nuevo, fresco; pálido, reciente, acabado de hacer; **to grow —** verdear; **bottle —** verde botella; s. verdor, césped, campo de golf.
greenhouse (grínjaus) s. invernáculo, invernadero, conservatorio.
greenish (grínish) adj. verdoso.
greenness (grínes) s. verdor, verdura, inmadurez; falta de experiencia, novedad.
greet (grit) v. saludar; dar la bienvenida, **to — each other** saludarse.
greeting (gríting) s. saludo, salutación; **—s!** ¡salud! ¡saludos!
grenade (grenéid) s. granada, bomba pequeña.
greyish véase **grayish**.
greyness véase **grayness**.
greyhound (gréijaund) s. lebrel.
griddle (grídl) s. tartera, plancha (para tapar el hornillo).
grief (grif) s. dolor, pesar, pesadumbre; **to come to —** sobrevenirle a uno una desgracia.
grievance (grívans) s. queja, resentimiento, agravio, injusticia, perjuicio, entuerto, motivo de queja, ofensa.
grieve (griv) v. afligir(se); lamentar(se); agraviar; lastimar, oprimir; apesadumbrarse.
grievous (grívous) adj. doloroso, penoso; grave, atroz, aflictivo.
grill (gril) s. parrilla; manjar asado en parrillas; **men's —** restaurante para hombres; v. asar en parrillas; interrogar (un sospechoso).
grim (grim) adj. austero, áspero, fiero, torvo, feo, ceñudo, horrendo.
grimace (grimés) s. mueca, gesto; v. hacer muecas o gestos.
grime (gráim) s. mugre; v. ensuciar.
grimy (gráimi) adj. mugriento.
grin (grin) s. sonrisa abierta; sonrisa maliciosa; visaje; sonrisa burlona; v. sonreír.
grinder (gráinder) s. moledor, molino para café; amolador; afilador; diente molar; muela, piedra para afilar.
grip (grip) v. agarrar, asir, apretar, agarrarse con fuerza; empuñar; conmover, impresionar; s. agarro, asimiento; apretón de manos; saco de mano; **to have a — on someone** tener agarrado a alguien.
grippe (grip) s. gripe.
gritty (gríti) adj. arenoso, valeroso, arenisco, esforzado, firme.
grizzly (grísli) adj. grisáceo, pardusco; mezclilla; **— bear** oso pardo.
groan (groun) s. gemido, quejido, mugido; v. gemir, quejarse; lanzar gemidos.
grocer (gróser) s. abacero; Am. abarrotero, bodeguero, especiero.
grocery (gróseri) s. abacería, tienda de abarrotes, lonja; bodega; pl. **groceries** comestibles, especierías.
groom (grum) s. novio, caballerizo, mozo de caballería, caballerango, establero, palafrenero, lacayo, v. almohazar, limpiar con la almohaza (los caballos); cuidar; **to — oneself** asearse, peinarse, componerse; **— of the chamber** gentil hombre de cámara.
groove (gruv) s. estría, ranura, acanaladura; surco (de un camino); encaje, rebajo, encastre; v. acanalar, estriar, hacer muescas, rufiar.
grope (group) v. tentalear, tentar, andar a tientas; buscar tentando; **to — for** buscar a tientas.
gross (gros) adj. grueso, burdo, tosco, grosero, espeso, denso; **— earnings** ganancias totales; grueso, gruesa (doce docenas).
grotesque (grotésk) adj. y s. grotesco.
grotto (gróto) s. gruta.
grouch (gráuch) s. malhumor; gruñón, descontento, cascarrabias; descontento, cascarrabias; **to have a — against someone** tenerle ojeriza (o mala voluntad) a una persona; v. gruñir, estar de mal humor.
grouchy (gráuchi) adj. gruñón, refunfuñón, malhumorado, cascarrabias.
ground (gráund) s. suelo, tierra, terreno; motivo, razón, fundamento, base; piso, pavimento, solar, heredad, **—s** heces, desperdicios, sedimento; **— floor** piso

bajo, planta baja; **to break —** desmontar; roturar, empezar un trabajo; arar; cavar; **to give —** retroceder, ceder; **to gain —** ganar terreno; v. conectar (un alambre) con la tierra; encallar (una embarcación). |cado.
groundless (gráundles) adj. infundado.
group (grup) s. grupo; v. agrupar.
grove (gróuv) s. arboleda, bosquecillo, alameda, soto.
grow (grou) v.i. (pret., Grew [gru]; p.p. **GROWN** [groun]; p. pr. **GROWING**) 1. crecer. 2. medrar prosperar, florecer. 3. desarrollarse, crecer (en tamaño), aumentar (en cantidad).
growl (grául) s. gruñido; v. gruñir |gañón; tarro de cerveza
growler (gráuler) s. gruñón; regrown (gróun) adj. crecido; desarrollado, espigado; cubierto de hierbas; prevalente, dominante; **— man** hombre maduro;
grown-up (gróunop) adj. crecido, adulto; s. adulto.
growth (gróuz) s. crecimiento; vegetación, acrecencia; aumento, desarrollo.
grudge (grody) s. resentimiento, rencor, inquina, rencilla; mala voluntad; v. envidiar, codiciar; dar de mala gana.
gruff (grof) adj. áspero, ceñudo, arisco, malhumorado; rudo, grosero.
grumble (grómbl) s. gruñido, queja; v. quejarse, gruñir, murmurar; rezongar, regañar.
grumbler (grómbler) s. gruñón.
grumpy (grómpi) adj. malhumorado, gruñón; quejoso, áspero.
grunt (gront) s. gruñido; pez americano; v. gruñir; pujar.
guarantor (gárantor) s. fiador.
guaranty (gáranti) s. garantía, fianza, caución.
guard (gard) s. guarda; guardia, vigilante, custodio, resguardo; **to be on —** estar alerta o en guardia; **to keep —** vigilar; resguardar, defender, custodiar, vigilar.
guardian (gárdian) s. guardián, custodio; tutor; **— angel** ángel custodio o de la guarda.
guardianship (gárdianship) s. tutela, guarda, custodia; amparo.
Guatemalan (Guatemálan) adj. y s. guatemalteco.

guess (gues) s. suposición, adivinación, conjetura; v. pensar, juzgar, creer, conjeturar. suponer
guest (guest) s. huésped, pensionista, visita; inquilino; convidado.
guffaw (gufó) s. carcajada, risotada.
guidance (gáidans) s. guía, gobierno, dirección, conducta. |delo.
guide (gáid) s. guía, mentor, mo-
guidebook (gáidbuk) s. guía de viajero; **railway —**. guía de ferrocarril.
guild (guild) s. gremio, cuerpo, hermandad, cofradía, asociación.
guile (gáil) s. engaño, dolo, fraude.
guilt (guilt) s. delito, culpa, falta.
guiltless (guíltles) s. inocente, sin culpa; puro, sin tacha.
guilty (guílti) adj. culpable, reo, delincuente; convicto.
guise (gáis) s. aspecto, modo, manera; apariencia; **under the — of** disfrazado de; **in this —** de este modo.
guitar (guitár) s. guitarra.
gulf (golf) s. golfo, seno; sima.
gull (gol) s. gaviota; engaño; timo.
gullet (gólet) s. fauces, gaznate.
gully (góli) s. barranca, hondonada, **— hole** sumidero, albañal.
gulp (golp) s. trago; v. tragar.
gum (gom) s. goma; encía; pegamento; **chewing —** chicle; **— drop** pastilla de goma; v. engomar, pegar con goma; **— lac** goma laca.
gun (gon) s. pistola, cañón, fusil, escopeta; v. disparar con arma de fuego; **— reach** alcance del arma. |lancha cañonera.
gunboat (gónbout) s cañonero:
gunner (góner) s. artillero; ametralladorista.
gunpowder (gónpauder) s. pólvora.
gurgle (gorgl) v. gorgorear, hacer borbollones; s. borbotón.
gush (gósh) s. chorro, borbotón; efusión; v. derramar, verter, chorrear; fluir, manar; borbotar, hacer borbollón; ser muy efusivo o extremoso.
gust (gost) s. ráfaga, racha; ventolera; gusto, sentido del paladar.
gut (got) s. tripa, intestino; **to have —s** tener agallas, ánimo.
gutter (góter) s. gotera, cuneta; arroyo de la calle; zanja, acequia; v. acanalar, estriar, zanjar.
guy (gái) s. sujeto, tipo, individuo; tirante; alambre; cadena de sostén; mofarse, burlarse de.

gymnasium (yimnésium) s. gimnasio.
gymnastics (yimnástics) s. gimnasia; **Sweedish —** gimnasia sueca.
gypsy (yípsi) s. y adj. gitano.

H

habit (jábit) s. hábito; uso; rutina; costumbre; estado; condición; **riding —** traje de montar.
habitual (abíchual) adj. habitual, inveterado, usual, acostumbrado.
hack (jek) s. corte; tajo; tos seca; caballo de alquiler; escritor que se vende; v. alquilarse; venderse; tajar; picar; acuchillar.
hackneyed (jéknid) adj. trillado, manoseado; gastado; muy común.
had (jad) pret. y p.p. de to have; **you — better do it** mejor sería que lo hiciese usted.
hag (jag) s. bruja, hechicera; v. aterrar, acosar, atormentar.
haggard (jágard) adj. macilento, flaco; ojeroso; s. halcón; fiera.
haggle (jágl) v. regatear; cavilar.
hail (jéil) s. granizo; pedrisco; saludo, grito; llamada; ¡salve!; v. granizar; saludar, aclamar, llamar; **to — from** ser originario de; **to — a ship** saludar, ponerse al habla con una nave.
hailstorm (jéilstorm) s. granizada.
hair (jer) s. pelo, vello, cabello; hebra, fibra, filamento; **to a —** exactamente, perfectamente; **— dresser** peluquero; peinadora.
hairbrush (jérbrosh) s. cepillo para la cabeza.
haircut (jércot) s. corte de pelo; **to have a —** hacerse cortar el pelo; ir a pelarse.
hairdo (jérdu) s. peinado.
hairless (jérles) adj. pelado, lampiño; sin pelo; pelón.
hairpin (jérpin) s. horquilla; pasador para el pelo; gancho.
hairy (jéri) adj. peludo, velludo; hirsuto; peloso, cabelludo.
hale (jéil) adj. sano, robusto, fuerte; v. arrastrar; jalar; llevar por la fuerza a una persona.
half (jaf) s. mitad; **— an orange** media naranja; adj. medio; semi; **— away** equidistante; **— past two** las dos y media; **— seas over** medio borracho.
half-breed (jáfbrid) adj. y s. mestizo.

half-hour (jáfaur) s. media hora; adj. de media hora.
half-mast (jafmast) v. poner a media asta la bandera.
half-open (jáfopen) adj. entreabierto; entornado.
halfway (jáfuei) adj. y adv. a medio camino; **— between** equidistante de; **— finished** a medio acabar; **to do something —** hacer alguna cosa a medias.
half-witted (jafuíted) adj. bobo, imbécil, zonzo, tonto.
halibut (jálibot) s. mero; hipogloso (pez sin espinas).
hall (jol) s. vestíbulo; antecámara; corredor; sala de sesiones; edificio público; **City —** casa del Ayuntamiento; sala de un tribunal.
hallo (jaló) véase hello.
hallow (jálou) v. santificar, consagrar; reverenciar.
Halloween (jálouin) s. víspera de Todos Santos.
halo (jélo) s. halo, nimbo, aureola; corona; cerco.
halt (jolt) s. parada, alto; cojera; v. pararse, detenerse; vacilar.
halter (jólter) s. cabestro; ronzal; dogal; v. cabestrar.
halting (jólting) adj. vacilante; **—ly** con vacilación.
halve (jav) v. partir a la mitad; machihembrar.
halves (havs) pl. de **half**; **to go —** ir a medias.
ham (jam) s. jamón, pernil.
hamburger (jámberguer) s. hamburguesa; carne picada.
hamlet (jámlet) s. aldea, villorrio; caserío; aldehuela.
hammer (jámer) s. martillo, martinete; **sledge —** macho de herrero.
hammock (jámock) s. hamaca.
hamper (jámper) s. cuévano, canasta, cesto grande; traba; impedimento; v. estorbar, impedir, dificultar; enredar.
hand (jand) s. mano; manecilla (de reloj); operario, obrero; carácter de letra; **clean —s** honradez, integridad; **— over head** inconsideradamente; **at —** a la mano; **— made** hecho a mano; **on —** en existencia; **off —** repentino, imprevisto; **on the other —** por otra parte; **to — down** transmitir; **to — over** entregar; **to shake —s** estrechar la mano; **to keep one's —s off** no tocar; v.

— 101 —

dar; pasar; entregar; to have one's —s ful estar ocupadísimo; in — de contado.
handbag (jándbag) s. bolsa o bolso de mano; maletín.
handball (jándbol) s. pelota; juego de pelota.
handbill (jándbil) s. cartel pequeño; prospecto; volante.
handcuff (jándcof) s. manilla, esposas; v. maniatar, esposar.
handful (jándful) s. puñado, manojo; manípulo.
handicap (jándicap) s. ventaja o desventaja en ciertas competencias; igualar a los competidores; obstáculo, impedimento, traba; — race carrera de handicap.
handiwork (jándiuerk) s. artefacto; trabajo hecho a mano; labor.
handkerchief (jándkerchif) s. pañuelo.
handmade (jándmeid) adj. hecho a mano.
handsaw (jándso) s. serrucho.
handshake (jándsheik) s. apretón de mano.
handsome (jándsom) adj. hermoso; guapo; primoroso; liberal; generoso; elegante; distinguido; a — sum una suma considerable.
handwriting (jándráiting) s. carácter de letra; modo de escribir.
handy (jándi) adj. manual; fácil de manejar; próximo, a la mano; diestro, hábil; mañoso.
hang (jang) v. colgar; ahorcar; suspender; pender; pegarse o agarrarse a uno; colgarse al cuello de uno; to — around rondar, haraganear; esperar sin hacer nada; to — back rehusar a ir adelante; to — on colgarse de; depender de; apoyarse en; insistir, persistir; to — paper on a a wall empapelar una pared; to — with tapestries entapizar; s. caída, modo como cuelga una cosa; modo de manejar un mecanismo o de resolver un problema; I don't care a — no me importa un comino; to — off no decidirse, hacerse remolón; to — together permanecer unidos; tener cohesión.
hangar (jángar) s. hangar, cobertizo.
hanger (jánguer) s. soporte colgante, percha, clavijero.
hanging (jánguing) s. ahorcadura; —s colgaduras, cortinajes, tapices; adj. colgante, colgado.

hangman (jángman) s. verdugo.
hangnail (jángneil) s. padrastro (en las uñas).
hang-over (jángover) s. sobrante, remanente; resto; estar crudo después de una borrachera; malestar que se siente después de la embriaguez.
haphazard (jápjasard) s. suerte, accidente, lance; el azar, al acaso; adj. casual, impensado.
haphazardly (jápjasardli) adv. véase **haphazard**.
hapless (jáples) adj. desgraciado, desaventurado; miserable.
happen (jápen) v. acontecer, acaecer, suceder, sobrevenir, pasar, ocurrir; whatever —s suceda lo que suceda; to — to hear (do, be, etc.) oir, hacer, estar, por casualidad; to — on encontrarse con, tropezar con alguna persona o cosa.
happening (jápening) s. acontecimiento, suceso, sucedido.
happily (jápili) adv. dichosamente, afortunadamente, felizmente.
happiness (jápines) s. felicidad, dicha, prosperidad, ventura.
happy (jápi) adj. feliz, dichoso, contento, afortunado, alegre; to be — to alegrarse de.
harangue (jaréng) s. arenga, perorata, alocución; v. arengar, pronunciar un discurso.
harass (járas) v. acosar, fatigar, molestar; cansar, vejar.
harbor (járbor) s. puerto; abrigo; asilo; albergue; v. abrigar, albergar, hospedar; resguardar; amparar.
hard (jard) s. duro, arduo, trabajoso, penoso, difícil; tieso; sólido; firme; rígido, severo; — by inmediato; — cash dinero en efectivo; — coal antracita; — pressed falto de recursos; — to deal with intratable; — luck mala suerte; — water agua cruda; — working muy trabajoso, industrioso.
harden (járdn) v. endurecer.
hardening (járdning) s. endurecimiento; temple.
hardly (járdli) adv. apenas; difícilmente; no del todo; ásperamente; duramente; severamente.
hardness (járdnes) s. dureza, aspereza; crueldad, severidad.
hardship (járdship) s. penalidad, apuro, aflicción; fatiga; opresión.

hardware (járduer) s. ferretería, quincalla.
hardy (járdi) adj. robusto, fuerte, bravo, intrépido; recio; endurecido.
hare (jér) s. liebre.
harebrained (jérbreind) adj. atolondrado, cabeza de chorlito.
harlot (járlot) s. ramera, prostituta.
harm (járm) s. daño, detrimento, perjuicio; mal; v. dañar, perjudicar; hacer mal; ofender; herir.
harmful (jármful) adj. dañino, nocivo; perjudicial; pernicioso.
harmless (jármles) adj. innocuo, inofensivo; libre de daño, sano y salvo; inocente.
harmonic (jarmónic) adj. armónico.
harmonize (jármonais) v. armonizar, concordar, ajustar, hermanar.
harnomy (jármoni) s. armonía, consonancia, concordancia.
harness (járnes) s. guarniciones (de caballería); jaez; aparejo; atelaje; **to get back in —** volver al servicio activo; **—** maker talabartero; v. poner guarniciones (a un caballo, una mula, etc.).
harp (jarp) s. arpa; lira; v. tocar o tañer el arpa; **to — on** repetir constantemente (una nota, palabra; etc.); machacar.
harpoon (jarpún) s. arpón, rastrillo; v. rastrear, arponear.
harrow (járrou) s. rastro, rastrillo; trilla; escarificador; grada; v. rastrear, rastrillar, atormentar.
harrowing (járrouing) adj. horrendo; horripilante, que pone los cabellos de punta.
harry (járri) v. acosar, molestar.
harsh (jársh) adj. tosco, áspero; severo, agrio, austero, bronco.
harshness (járshnes) s. aspereza; tosquedad, rudeza, austeridad.
harvest (járvest) s. recolección; cosecha, siega, v. cosechar; segar.
hash (jásh) s. picadillo, salpicón.
haste (jéist) s. prisa, presteza, diligencia, apresuramiento, premura; **to make —** darse prisa; **to be in —** estar o tener prisa.
hasten (jéisn) v. apresurar(se); precipitarse; acelerar, avivar.
hastily (jéistili) adv. aceleradamente, apresuradamente.
hasty (jéisti) adj. pronto, apresurado, precipitado; ligero, vivo.
hat (jat) s. sombrero.
hatch (játch) v. empollar, aclocar; criar pollos; fraguar; incubar; s. cría, nidada, pollada; escotilla, compuerta.
hatchet (játchet) s. hacha; destral; machado; **to bury the —** hacer la paz, olvidar rencillas.
hate (jéit) s. odio, aversión, aborrecimiento; v. odiar, detestar.
hateful (jéitful) adj. odioso, detestable, aborrecible.
hatred (jéitred) s. odio, aversión.
haughtily (jótili) adv. con arrogancia, altaneramente, altivamente.
haughtiness (jótines) s. altanería; altivez; soberbia, orgullo; ínfulas, humos.
haughty (jóti) adj. altivo, vanidoso; altanerc, arrogante.
haul (jol) v. acarrear; transportar; arrastrar, tirar de; **to — down the flag** arriar la bandera; s. acarreo, transporte; arrastre; tirón; botín.
haunch (jonch) s. anca, grupa, culata.
haunt (jont) v. frecuentar, rondar; obsesionar; **that idea —s him** le persigue esa idea; **haunted house** casa de espantos; s. hábito, costumbre, querencia; guarida.
have (jav) v. haber o tener; poseer; comprender; efectuar; procurar; comer; **to — a mind** tener ganas, deseo de hacer algo; **to — a look at** dar un vistazo a; **to — to** tener que; deber; **to — on** vestir; **what will you —?** ¿qué quiere usted comer (o beber)?
haven (jévn) s. puerto; abra; abrigo, refugio, asilo.
havoc (jávok) s. estrago; destrucción; desolación; ruina; **to cause —** hacer estragos; asolar.
hawk (jok) s. halcón; v. pregonar mercancías; arrojar flemas.
hawthorn (józorn) s. espino.
hay (jéi) s. heno, paja, hierba para forraje; zacate; **— fever** romadizo; **— fork** bieldo.
hayloft (jéiloft) s. henil, pajar.
haystack (jéistak) s. montón de heno o paja.
hazard (jásard) s. azar, suerte; peligro, riesgo; v. arriesgar; aventurar; exponer; correr un albur.
hazardous (jásardus) adj. arriesgado, peligroso.
haze (jeis) s. niebla, bruma; ofuscamiento mental; v. atormentar, hostigar con bromas estudiantiles.
hazel (jéisl) s. avellano; **— nut**

avellana; adj. castaño; color de avellana; avellanado.
hazy (jéisi) adj. nublado, brumoso; confuso; vago.
he (ji) pron. pers. él; — **who** el que, aquel que; quien; — **bear** oso.
head (jed) s. cabeza; cabezal; testa; cabecera; — **over heels** desmesuradamente; **to make** — avanzar, adelantar; **to be out of one's** — delirar; **to come to a** — madurar, supurar; **it goes to his** — se le sube a la cabeza; adj. principal; primero; proel; — **cook** primer cocinero; v. encabezar, mandar, dirigir, adelantarse; poner título o epígrafe; **to** — **off** atajar, detener; **to** — **towards** dirigirse a; encaminarse a; **to make** — **against one** hacer frente o resistir a alguno; **to bring a business to a** — ultimar un negocio.
headache (jédeik) s. dolor de cabeza.
headdress (jédres) s. tocado, adorno para la cabeza.
headgear (jédguir) s. sombrero, gorro, toca; cabezada de guarnición para caballo.
heading (jéding) s. encabezado; título.
headland (jédland) s. cabo, promontorio; farallón.
headlight (jédlait) s. fanal o faro delantero.
headlong (jédlong) adj. temerario; arrojado; adv. precipitadamente.
headquarters (jédkuorters) s. cuartel general; jefatura; oficina matriz.
headstrong (jédstrong) adj. terco, obstinado, testarudo, rehacio, aferrado, porfiado.
headway (jeduei) s. avance, progreso; **to make** — avanzar, adelantar, progresar.
heal (jil) v. curar, sanar, cicatrizar; remediar; reconciliar.
health (jelz) s. salud; sanidad; salubridad.
healthful (jélzful) s. sano, salubre, saludable.
healthfulnes (jélzfulnes) s. salud; salubridad, sanidad.
healthy (jélzi) s. sano, saludable.
heap (jip) s. montón, hacinamiento; pila; acervo; v. amontonar, apilar, acumular.
hear (jir) v. oír, escuchar, dar audiencia; atender; otorgar; tener noticias; saber de; **I** —**d that** oí decir que.
heard (jerd) pret. y p.p. de **to hear**.
hearer (jírer) s. oyente, oidor.
hearing (jíring) s. oído, audiencia, examen de testigos, **hard of** — algo sordo; **within** — al alcance del oído.
hearsay (jírsei) s. rumor, hablilla; fama.
hearse (jirs) s. carroza funeraria, ataúd, féretro.
heart (jart) s. corazón, valor, ánimo; **at** — esencialmente; **by** — de memoria; **from the bottom of on's** — con toda sinceridad; — **break** corazón, aflicción; **to take to** — tomar en serio, tomar a pecho.
heartache (jártek) adj. dolor de corazón, angustia, congoja, pesar.
heartbroken (jártbroken) s. transido de dolor, de angustia, acongojado; desanimado.
hearten (jártn) v. alentar, animar; abonar (la tierra).
heartfelt (jártfelt) adj. cordial; sincero; de corazón; **my** — **symphaty** mi más sentido pésame.
hearth (jarz) s. hogar, fogón.
heartless (jártles) s. inhumano, cruel, sin corazón; insensible.
heart-rending (jártrending) adj. angustioso; agudo; aflictivo.
hearty (járti) adj. cordial, sincero, fuerte, sano, vigoroso; — **food** alimento nutritivo; — **meal** comida abundante; — **laugh** sonora carcajada.
heat (jit) s. calor, ardor, fogosidad; vehemencia; celo en los animales; calefacción; **white** — incandescencia; — **unit** caloría; carrera de prueba (de caballos); v. calentar(se), acalorar(se); fermentar; hervir.
heater (jíter) s. calentador.
heathen (jízen) s. pagano, gentil, ateo, idólatra; adj. pagano, irreligioso, ateísta.
heating (jíting) s. calefacción.
heaven (jéven) s. cielo; firmamento.
heavenly (jévenli) adj. celeste, divino; adv. divinamente; celestialmente.
heavily (jévili) adv. pesadamente, lentamente; excesivamente.
heaviness (jévines) s. pesadez, peso, gravedad; tardanza, torpeza.
heavy (jévi) adj. pesado, lento, opresivo; grueso; burdo; — **rain**

aguacero; macizo, fuerte; denso, espeso; triste, melancólico.
hectic (jéctic) adj. ético o hético; febril, inquieto.
hedge (jédy) s. seto, cerca, vallado, barrera; v. cercar, poner seto o valla; ponerse el abrigo; evitar o eludir contestaciones.
hedgehog (jédyjog) s. erizo.
heed (jíd) v. atender, escuchar, observar, hacer caso; s. cuidado, atención, cautela, precaución to pay — v. prestar atención a.
heel (jíl) s. talón; tacón: **head over** —**s** patas arriba; v. poner tacones; escorar; asir, agarrar.
heifer (jéifer) s. novilla, vaquilla.
height (jáit) s. altura, elevación; estatura; alzada; collado, loma; colmo; excelencia.
heighten (jáitn) v. realzar, elevar, aumentar(se); sublimar, exaltar.
heinous (jénos) adj. odioso, atroz, nefando, malvado, horrible.
heir (er) s. heredero.
heiress (éres) s. heredera.
hell (jél) s. infierno.
hello (jaló) interj. ¡hola! ¡oiga!
helm (jelm) s. timón, gobernalle.
helment (jélmet) s. yelmo, casco.
help (jelp) s. ayuda, socorro, auxilio; alivio, remedio; apoyo, protección, amparo; criado, sirviente; servidumbre, empleado; v. ayudar, socorrer, auxiliar; alliviar; servir (de comer); **to — down** ayudar a alguien a bajar; **to — one another** favorecerse mutuamente; **— yourself** sírvase usted (de comer o beber); **he cannot — it** no puede evitarlo.
helper (jélper) s. ayudante, asistente.
helpful (jélpful) adj. útil, provechoso; sano, saludable; servicial.
helping (jélping) s. ayuda; porción que se sirve en la mesa.
helpless (jélples) adj. desamparado, desvalido, imposibilitado, abandonado; irremediable; **— situation** una situación irremediable.
helplessness (jélplesnes) s. incapacidad; debilidad; impotencia; desamparo; abandono.
hem (jem) s. dobladillo, bastillas; v. dobladillar, bastillar; **to — in** rodear, cercar; **to — and haw** toser y retoser fingidamente; tartamudear, vacilar.
hemisphere (jémisfir) s. hemisferio.

hemlock (jémlok) s. cicuta; abeto, pícea; pinabete.
hemp (jemp) s. cáñamo, sisal; sisal — henequén.
hemstitch (jémstitch) s. dobladillo de ojo; hacer o echar dobladillo de ojo; hacer una vainica.
hen (jen) s. gallina; hembra de cualquier ave; **broad —** gallina clueca; **turkey —** pava; **— coop** gallinero.
hence (jens) adv. de aquí, desde aquí; desde ahora; por lo tanto; por consecuencia; **two years —** de aquí a dos años; **far —** lejos de aquí.
henceforth (jénsforz) adv. de hoy en adelante, en lo futuro; desde ahora.
her (jer) pron. la, le, ella, a ella, adj. su(s), de ella.
herald (jérald) s. heraldo, precursor, pregonero; publicador; v. anunciar, proclamar, publicar.
herb (jerb) s. hierba, yerba; **sweet —s** hierbas aromáticas.
herd (jerd) s. hato, grey, rebaño; manada, tropel, muchedumbre; chusma; **the common —** la gentuza, el populacho, la chusma; v. reunir el ganado en hatos o rebaños.
herdsman (jérdsman) s. pastor, zagal.
here (jír) adv. aquí, acá; ahí; por aquí; ahora, en este momento, en este punto; **— it is** aquí está; **— is to you!** ¡a la salud de usted! **— goes** ahí va; **that is neither — nor there** no viene al caso.
hereafter (jírafter) adv. en lo futuro; de aquí o de hoy en adelante; **the —** la otra vida.
hereby (jírbai) adv. por la presente, por este medio; por éstas.
hereditary (jeréditeri) adj. hereditario.
heredity (jeréditi) s. herencia.
herein (jíarin) adv. aquí dentro, incluso; en esto.
heresy (jéresi) s. herejía.
heretic (jéretic) adj. herético; s. hereje.
herewith (jíruiz) adv. adjunto, incluso, con esto, aquí dentro.
heritage (jéritey) s. herencia.
hermit (jérmit) s. ermitaño, eremita.
hernia (jernie) s. hernia, relajamiento, ruptura, quebradura.
hero (jíro) s. héroe, protagonista

HEROIC   **HISTORY**

heroic (jiróic) adj. heroico, épico.
heroine (jéroin) heroína.
heroism (jéroism) s. heroísmo.
heron (jéron) s. garza; airón.
herring (jérring) s. arenque.
herself (jersélf) pron. ella misma; se (como reflexivo) **by —** sola; **she — did it** fue ella quien lo hizo; **she spoke of —** ella habló de sí misma.
hesitant (jésitant) véase **hesitating**.
hesitate (jésiteit) v. titubear, dudar, vacilar, tardar, tartamudear.
hesitating (jesitéiting) adj. indeciso, irresoluto; vacilante; **—ly** con indecisión; con vacilación.
hesitation (jesitéshon) s. irresolución, titubeo, perplejidad, vacilación, duda; hesitación.
hew (jiu) v. tajar, cortar, picar; desvastar; **to — a stone** labrar una piedra; **to — out** hachear, cortar.
hewn (jiún) p.p. de **to hew**.
hey (jei) interj. ¡oiga! ¡oye! ¡eh!
hiccup (jícop) s. hipo; v. tener hipo; hipar.
hickory (jícori) s. nogal americano; **— nut** nuez.
hid (jid) pret. y p.p. de **to hide**.
hidden (jíden) p.p. de **to hide**, oculto, escondido, recóndito, secreto; **—ly** adv. secretamente, ocultamente.
hide (jáid) v. ocultar, esconder, encubrir, disimular; **to play — and seek** jugar a las escondidillas; s. cuero, piel.
hideous (jídius) adj. horrible, espantoso, horripilante, deforme, feo.
high (jai) adj. alto, elevado, enhiesto, noble; altivo, orgulloso; **— altar** altar mayor; **— treason** alta traición; **— explosive** explosivo de alta velocidad; **— tide** pleamar; **in — gear** en tercera velocidad; **— priced** caro; **— spirited** gallardo, bizarro; **— grade** de calidad superior, **— handed** magnánimo; **— pressure** alta presión; **— seasoned** picante; **— strung** agudo; impresionable, sensitivo; **it was — time to do so** ya era hora de hacerlo; **— and dry** en seco, enjuto; borrascoso.
highland (jáiland) s. país montañoso; **the —s** las montañas de Escocia.
highly (jáili) adv. altamente, elevadamente, sumamente; en sumo grado; arrogantemente; muy; **— paid** muy bien pagado.
highness (jáines) s. Alteza; altura, elevación.
highway (jáiuei) s. carretera, camino real; calzada.
highwayman (jáiueiman) s. salteador de caminos, forajido, bandolero, ladrón.
hike (jáik) v. echar, tirar, arrastrar; s. marcha, caminata, andada, paseo muy largo a pie.
hill (jil) s. loma, colina, cerro; cuesta, otero, collado, montecillo; **ant —** hormiguero; **down —** cuesta abajo; **up —** cuesta arriba.
hillock (jílok) s. mogote, montecillo, otero, altillo.
hillside (jílsaid) s. ladera.
hilltop (jíltop) s. cumbre, cima de una colina.
hilly (jíli) adj. montañoso, accidentado, montuoso.
hilt (jilt) s. puño (de una espada o daga); empuñadura, guarnición.
him (jim) pron. le, lo, a él, **I saw —** le vi.
himself (jimsélf) pron. él mismo; se (como reflexivo); a sí mismo; **he is kidding —** se hace tonto solo, se engaña a sí mismo.
hind (jáind) adj. trasero, zaguero; posterior; s. cierva; **— most** el último, postrero.
hinder (jínder) v. estorbar, detener; obstruir, impedir, oponerse; poner obstáculos o trabas.
hindrance (jíndrans) s. estorbo; obstáculo; traba, cortapisa; perjuicio.
hinge (jiny) s. gozne, bisagra; v. engoznar, poner bisagras; **to — on** depender de; **— joint** coyuntura.
hint (jint) s. indirecta, alusión, sugestión, insinuación; **not to take the —** no darse por aludido; v. insinuar, aludir, intimar.
hip (jip) s. cadera.
hippopotamus (jipopótamus) s. hipopótamo.
his (jis) pron. pos. suyo(a, os, as); de él, el, la, lo, las, los suyos; **this table is —** esta mesa es suya; adj. su(s), de él.
hiss (jis) s. silbido, siseo; v. sisear, silbar; chiflar.
historian (jistórian) s. historiador.
historic (jistórik) adj. histórico.
historical (jistórikal) adj. histórico.
history (jístori) s. historia.

— 106 —

hit (jit) v. pegar; golpear; atinar, acertar; encontrar, dar con o en; acaecer, acontecer felizmente; chocar; **to — the mark** dar en el blanco; **to — upon encontrarse con; they — it off well** se llevan bien, cogenían; pret. y p.p. de **to hit**; s. golpe, choque, rasgo de ingenio; **a lucky —** golpe de fortuna; ocurrencia feliz; **to be a great —** ser un gran éxito; **to make a — with someone** caerle en gracia a una persona.

hitch (jitch) v. uncir, enganchar, acoplar; atar, unir, ligar; mover a tirones; s. alto; parada; tirón; tropiezo, impedimento, obstáculo; enganche, enganchamiento.

hitchhike (jítchjaik) v. viajar de gorra en automóvil; irse a viajar de mosca.

hither (jíder) adv. acá, hacia acá; **— and thither** acá y allá.

hitherto (jidertú) adv. hasta hoy, hasta ahora, hasta aquí.

hive (jaiv) s. colmenar, enjambre; **—s** ronchas (de la piel), urticaria.

hoard (jord) s. atesorar, amontonar, acumular, almacenar en secreto provisiones; s. tesoro escondido, acumulamiento secreto; repuesto.

hoarse (jors) adj. ronco, áspero; bronco; enronquecido.

hoarseness (jórsnes) s. ronquera, carraspera; enronquecimiento.

hoary (jóri) adj. cano, encanecido; blanquecino; carchado.

hobble (jóbl) v. cojear, renquear, manear (un animal); impedir, estorbar; s. cojera, traba, maniota; dificultad; atolladero.

hobby (jóbi) s. afición, manía, ocupación o trabajo hecho por gusto.

hobo (jóbo) s. vago, vagabundo.

hodgepodge (jódypody) s. mezcolanza; almodrote, batidillo.

hoe (jo) s. azada, azadón; v. cavar, limpiar con azadón; escardar.

hog (jóg) s. cerdo, puerco, marrano, cochino; v. apropiárselo todo; arquearse, combarse, torcerse.

hoist (jóist) s. cabria, malacate; v. izar, levantar, alzar.

hold (jold) s. presa, agarradero; mango, asidero; prisión; bodega; escondite; apresamiento; v. asir, detener, retener; tener; sostener; opinar; celebrar una junta; ocupar un puesto; valer, ser válido; durar; continuar; **to —**
back resistir, detener a alguien; **to — forth** arengar, hablar, perorar; **to — in hand** entretener; **to — off** alejar, mantener(se) apartado; **to — on** aferrarse, asir (se), persistir; **to — someone responsible** hacer a uno responsable; **to — out** proponer, ofrecer; no ceder; durar, alargar; **to — someone to his word** obligar a uno a cumplir su palabra; **to — a wager** apostar, hacer una apuesta; **to — oneself erect** mantenerse erecto o derecho; **to — one's own** mantenerse firme; **to — one's tongue** callar(se); **to — a meeting** celebrar una asamblea; **to — tight** apretar; **to — up** asaltar, cometer un atraco; detener en alto, alzar; **how much does it —?** ¿cuánto le cabe?; **to — with one** ser partidario de; **to get — of** asir; agarrar, hacerse de; **— it!** interj. ¡deténte! ¡quieto!

holder (jólder) s. poseedor; arrendador; vasija o receptáculo; mango; puño; asa; a veces se traduce por porta, como **pen —** portaplumas; **cigarette —** boquilla, pipa.

holdup (jóldop) s. asalto, atraco.

hole (jól) s. agujero, hoyo; cueva, cavidad; atolladero, dilema; orificio, boquete; **swimming —** charco, remanso; **to be in a —** hallarse en un aprieto, en un apuro; **arm —** axila, sobaco.

holiday (jólidei) s. día festivo, festividad; **—s** vacaciones; días de descanso.

holiness (jólines) s. santidad, beatitud; perfección de costumbres.

hollow (jólou) adj. hueco; vacío; cóncavo, hundido; cavernoso; falso, insincero; s. depresión, cañada, hondonada; v. ahuecar, ahondar; excavar; escotar.

holly (jóli) s. acebo, agrifolio.

holster (jólster) s. pistolera; funda de pistola; **— cap** caperuza, tapafundas.

holy (jóli) adj. santo; pío; sacro, sagrado; **— cup** cáliz; **— day** festividad; **— water** agua bendita; **— writ** La Sagrada Escritura.

homage (jómey) s. homenaje, reverencia; respeto, acatamiento; v. reverenciar, rendir homenaje a.

home (jóm) s. hogar, casa propia; habitación; domicilio; país, patria; adj. doméstico, casero; na-

tal; at — casa de usted (en cartas); **— office** oficina matriz, oficina central; **— rule** autonomía; **— stretch** la recta final en las carreras; *adv.* íntimamente, estrechamente; a casa; en casa; **to hit** o **strike —** dar en el blanco, herir en lo más hondo.

homeland (jóumland) *s.* suelo patrio; tierra natal; país de origen.

homeless (jóumles) *adj.* destituido; sin casa ni hogar.

homelike (jómlaic) *adj.* hogareño, sosegado, cómodo.

homely (jómli) *adj.* liso, llano; feo; ignorante; sencillo; doméstico; vulgar; sin elegancia.

homemade (jómeid) *adj.* en casa, fabricado en el país.

homesick (jómsik) *adj.* nostálgico.

homesickness (jómsiknes) *s.* nostalgia.

homestead (jómsted) *s.* heredad; casa y terrenos adyacentes, sitio de la casa.

homeward (jómuord) *adv.* hacia la casa; hacia el país natal; **— bound** de regreso, de vuelta, retorno.

homework (jómuerk) *s.* trabajo hecho en casa.

homicide (jómisaid) *s.* homicidio; homicida; asesino.

homogeneous (jomoyínious) *adj.* homogéneo.

hone (jón) *v.* afilar, asentar, amolar; *s.* piedra de afilar.

honest (ónest) *adj.* honrado, recto, justo; honesto, recatado; genuino; **—ly** honradamente, de veras; **to deal —ly** tratar honradamente.

honesty (ónesti) *s.* honradez, integridad; rectitud.

honey (jóni) *s.* miel, dulzura; tratamiento de cariño; querido(a).

honeycomb (jónicomb) *s.* panal.

honeymoon (jónimun) *s.* luna de miel, viaje de novios o de bodas; *v.* pasar la luna de miel.

honeysuckle (jónisókl) *s.* madreselva.

honk (jonk) *s.* pitazo de automóvil; graznido; *v.* sonar la bocina; graznar.

honor (ónor) *s.* honor; reverencia; probidad; **Your — Su Señoría;** *v.* honrar; venerar; glorificar.

honorable (ónorabl) *adj.* honrado; ilustre, noble; esclarecido.

honorary (ónorari) *adj.* honorario; honorífico.

hood (júd) *s.* caperuza, capucha; tapa, cubierta; *v.* cubrir, tapar; encapuchar.

hoof (júf) *s.* casco, pezuña; *v.* andar bailar.

hooky (júki) *v.* pintar venado; jubilarse; **to play —** hacer novillos.

hoop (júp) *s.* aro, arco, argolla; arete, zarcillo; *v.* ceñir, cercar.

hoot (jút) *v.* ulular; gritar; burlarse; vociferar; rechiflar, ridiculizar; *s.* alarido, grito, chillido; clamor.

hooting (júting) *s.* gritería; rechifla; vociferación.

hop (jop) *s.* salto, brinco; baile; *v.* saltar, brincar.

hope (jóup) *s.* esperanza, confianza; expectativa; *v.* esperar; anhelar; confiar; **to — against —** esperar lo imposible, lo que no puede ser.

hopeful (jóupful) *adj.* esperanzado, anhelante; **—ly** *adv.* con esperanza, con ansias; lleno de esperanza.

hopeless (jóuples) *adj.* desesperanzado; desahuciado; irremediable; **— cause** causa perdida; **— illness** enfermedad incurable; **it is — es** irremediable, no tiene remedio; **—ly** *adv.* sin esperanza; sin remedio.

hopelessness (jóuplesnes) *s.* desesperanza; falta de remedio.

horde (jórd) *s.* horda, muchedumbre; gentío; aduar; ranchería.

horizon (joráisn) *s.* horizonte.

horizontal (horisóntal) *adj.* horizontal.

hornet (jórnet) *s.* avispón; **—'s nest** avispero; **to stir up a —'s nest** meterse en un avispero.

horrible (jórribl) *adj.* horrible; **horribly** *adv.* horriblemente.

horrid (jórrid) *adj.* horrendo, espantoso; ofensivo.

horrify (jórrifai) *v.* horrorizar; aterrorizar; espantar, horripilar.

horror (jórror) *s.* horror, espanto.

horse (jors) *s.* caballo; caballete de madera; borriquete, bastidor; **saddle —** caballo de silla; **race —** caballo de carreras; **— sense** sentido común; **— way** camino de herradura; **carriage —** caballo de tiro.

horseback (jórsbak) *s.* lomo de caballo; **to ride —** montar caballo; cabalgar, jinetear.

— 108 —

horsefly (jórsflai) s. tábano; moscarda.

horselaugh (jórslaf) s. carcajada, risotada.

horseman (jórsman) s. jinete.

horsemanship (jórsmanship) s. equitación.

horsepower (jórspauer) s caballo de fuerza.

horseradish (jórsradish) s. rábano picante o rústico.

horseshoe (jórsshú) s. herradura.

hose (jos) s. medias; calceta; manguera para riego; men's — calcetines; — pipes tubos de manguera.

hosiery (jósiri) s. calcetería.

hospitable (jóspitabl) adj. hospitalario; caritativo.

hospital (jóspital) s. hospital, sanatorio.

hospitality (jospitáliti) s. hospitalidad.

host (jost) s. huésped, anfitrión; hostelero, hospedero, posadero; hueste, ejército, multitud; hostia; sacred — hostia sagrada.

hostage (jóstey) s. rehén, prenda, gaje.

hostess (jóstes) s. hospedera, hostelera; la que convida.

hostile (jóstil) adj. hostil.

hostility (jostility) s. hostilidad.

hot (jot) adj. caliente; tórrido; fogoso, ardiente; picante; furioso, colérico; — headed irascible, vehemente, exaltado; — house invernadero; it is — today hace calor hoy; piping — hirviendo.

hotel (jotél) s. hotel.

hotel-keeper (jotelkíper) s. hotelero.

hotly (jótli) adv. calurosamente; vehementemente; lascivamente.

hound (jáund) s. perro de caza, sabueso; galgo; lebrel; podenco; v. azuzar; perseguir; incitar; soltar los perros tras una presa.

hour (áuar) s. hora; trance; momento; — hand horario; after —s horas extraordinarias de trabajo.

hourly (áurli) adv. a cada hora; frecuentemente; a menudo.

house (jáus) s. casa; residencia, domicilio; cámara; asamblea legislativa; country — casa de campo; a full — un lleno completo en el teatro; v. alojar, albergar; residir, tener alojamiento.

household (jáusjold) s. casa, familia; adj. casero, doméstico.

housekeeper (jáuskiper) s. ama de llaves; to be a good — ser mujer hacendosa.

housekeeping (jáuskiping) s. manejo o cuidado de la casa; quehaceres domésticos.

housetop (jáustop) s. techo, azotea.

housewife (jáusualf) s. ama de casa; madre de familia.

housework (jáusuerk) s. quehaceres domésticos.

hovel (jóvl) s. cobertizo; choza, cabaña, bohío; jacal.

hover (jóver) v. revolotear, cernerse; rondar; hovering revoloteo.

however (jauéver) adv. y conj. sin embargo; no obstante, empero; de cualquier modo; — difficult it may be por muy difícil que sea; — much por mucho que.

howl (jául) s. aullido; alarido; gemido; rugido; bramido; grito; chillido; v. aullar, dar alaridos; gemir; rugir; bramar; gritar.

hub (job) s. maza de la rueda; eje, centro de actividad.

hubbub (jóbob) s. ajetreo, barullo.

huckster (jókster) s. vendedor ambulante; revendedor; mercachifle.

huddle (jódl) s. tropel; confusión; alboroto; desorden; v. amontonar; confundir; mezclar(se); agrupar(se); acurrucarse.

hue (jiú) s. color, tinte, matiz.

huff (jóf) s. enfado, enojo, rabieta; v. maltratar, injuriar; hinchar(se), inflar(se).

hug (jog) v. abrazar, estrechar; to — the coast costear; s. abrazo.

huge (jiúy) adj. vasto, enorme; inmenso; descomunal; tremendo.

hull (jól) s. cáscara, corteza; casco de una nave; armazón de aeronave; vaina; hollejo; v. pelar, descortezar; descascarar; mondar.

hum (jóm) v. canturrear, tararear; zumbar; to — to sleep arrullar; s. zumbido, susurro; tarareo; interj. ¡hum! ¡ejem! ¡ya!

human (jiúman) adj. humano; s. mortal, ser humano.

humane (jiuméin) adj. humanitario; compasivo, afable; benigno.

humanitarian (jiumanitérian) adj. humanitario; s. filántropo.

humanity (jiumániti) s. humanidad.

humble (jombl) adj. humilde, modesto; v. humillar; abatir; humbly adv. humildemente; rendidamente.

humbleness (jómblnes) s. humildad.
humid (jiúmid) adj. húmedo.
humidity (jiumíditi) s. humedad.
humiliate (jiumílieit) v. humillar.
humiliation (jiumiliéshon) s. humillación; mortificación.
humility (jiumíliti) s. humildad.
hummingbird (jómingberd) s. colibrí, pájaro mosca; chupamiel; chuparrosa; chupaflor; guainambí.
humor (jiúmor) s. humor, carácter, genio; humorismo, gracia; agudeza; **aqueous — humor** ácueo; **out of —** malhumorado, disgustado; v. complacer, mimar; dar gusto; consentir; acomodarse a.
humorous (jiúmoros) adj. humorístico; jocoso; gracioso; cómico, festivo; chistoso; caprichoso.
hump (jómp) s. joroba, giba, corcova; v. encorvarse, doblar la espalda.
humpback (jómpbak) véase **hunch back**.
hunch (jónch) s. joroba, giba, corcova; corazonada; presentimiento; v. empujar, dar empellones; corcovear.
hunchback (jónchbak) s. jorobado.
hundred (jóndred) adj. cien(to); s. ciento; centena; **per — weight** por cien libras; quintal.
hundredth (jóndredz) adj. centésimo.
hung (jóng) pret. y p.p. de to **hang**.
hunger (jónguer) s. hambre; deseo vehemente; anhelo; v. tener hambre; **to — for** anhelar, ansiar.
hungrily (jóngrili) adv. hambrientamente, con hambre, con ansia.
hungry (jóngri) adj. hambriento, famélico; deseoso; **to be —** tener hambre.
hunk (jónk) s. pedazo grande, rebanada gruesa; mendrugo de pan.
hunt (jónt) v. cazar, perseguir; escudriñar; buscar una cosa; registrar; **to — down** dar caza a; seguir la pista; **to — for** buscar; s. caza, cacería; búsqueda; persecución; acosamiento.
hunter (jónter) s. cazador; montero, podenco; buscador.
huntsman (jóntsman) s. cazador.
hurl (jerl) v. lanzar; arrojar, tirar; s. tiro, lanzamiento.
hurrah (jorréi) interj. ¡hurra! ¡viva!; v. aclamar, vitorear, aplaudir; **—'s nest** el caos.

hurricane (jórrikein) s. huracán.
hurried (jórried) adj. precipitado; apresurado; **—ly** precipitadamente; de prisa; apresuradamente.
hurry (jórri) v. acelerar; precipitar(se); dar(se) prisa; acuciar; apurar(se); correr; **to — in (out)** entrar (salir) de prisa; **to — after** correr en pos de; **to — up** apresurarse, darse prisa; s. prisa; premura; festinación.
hurt (jert) s. mal, daño, perjuicio, dolor; v. hacer daño, hacer mal; perjudicar; herir; doler, magullarse, lastimarse; **to — one's feelings** darle a uno que sentir; adj. lastimado, herido, perjudicado; dañado.
husband (jósband) s. esposo, marido.
hush (jósh) v. acallar, sosegar, aquietar, callar(se); **to — up** ocultar, mantener en secreto; s. silencio, quietud, sosiego.
husk (jósk) s. cáscara, hollejo; pellejo; vaina, bagazo; v. mondar, pelar, despellejar.
husky (jóski) adj. fuerte, forzudo; ronco, enronquecido; s. esquimal.
hustle (jósl) v. apresurar(se); afanarse; moverse atropelladamente; activar; s. prisa, actividad; apresuramiento; **and bustle** vaivén.
hut (jót) s. choza, cabaña, barraca.
hyacinth (jáiasinz) s. jacinto.
hybrid (jáibrid) adj. híbrido.
hydraulic (jáidrolic) adj. hidráulico.
hydrogen (jáidroyen) s. hidrógeno.
hydroplane (jáidroplein) s. hidroavión.
hygiene (jáiyini) s. higiene.
hymn (jimn) s. himno.
hyphen (jáifen) s. guión.
hypocrite (jipócrit) s. hipócrita.
hypocritical (jipocrítical) adj. hipócrita; falso; disimulado.
hypothesis (jaipózesis) s. hipótesis.
hysterical (jistérikal) adj. histérico.

I

I (ai) pron. pers. yo; s. el yo.
Iberian (aibírian) adj. ibérico.
ice (áis) s. hielo; helado; sorbete; **— cream** helado; **ice-cream parlor** nevería; **ice-pick** picahielo; v. helar; escarchar; congelar.

iceberg (áisberg) s. montaña o témpano de hielo flotante.
icebox (áisbox) s. refrigerador; nevera.
iceman (áisman) s. vendedor de hielo.
icicle (áisikl) s. carámbano.
icy (áisi) adj. helado, frío, álgido; cubierto de hielo; congelado.
idea (aidía) s. idea.
ideal (aidíal) adj. s. ideal.
idealism (aidíalism) s. idealismo.
idealist (aidíalist) s. idealista.
idealistic (aidialístik) adj. idealista.
identical (aidéntikal) adj. idéntico.
identify (aidéntifai) v. identificar.
identity (aidéntiti) s. identidad.
idiom (ídiom) s. modismo, lengua, jerga; locución; idiotismo.
idiot (ídiot) adj. idiota, imbécil.
idle (áidl) s. ocioso, haragán; perezoso; desocupado; v. haraganear, holgar, estar de ocioso o desocupado, perder el tiempo; funcionar el motor en desembrague; **idly** adv. ociosamente; vanamente; inútilmente.
idleness (áidlnes) s. ocio; pereza; haraganería; inutilidad, futilidad.
idler (áidler) s. haragán; holgazán; gandul; poltrón; vago.
idol (áidl) s. ídolo.
idolatry (aidólatri) s. idolatría.
idolize (áidolais) v. idolatrar.
idyl (áidl) s. idilio.
if (if) conj. si; adv. aunque, aun cuando; as — como si; — so be con tal que; supuesto que.
ignite (ignáit) v. prender, encender; pegar fuego; inflamar(se).
ignition (ignishon) s. ignición; encendido de un motor; — switch interruptor de encendido.
ignoble (ignóbl) adj. innoble, indigno.
ignorance (ígnorans) s. ignorancia.
ignorant (ignorant) adj. ignorante.
ignore (ignór) v. ignorar; no hacer caso; no darse por aludido.
ill (il) adj. enfermo; malo; malsano; inhábil; funesto; — natured de mal genio; — will mala voluntad; tirria, aversión; inquina; s. mal; desgracia, infortunio, calamidad; adv. malamente, calamitosamente; — at ease intranquilo, inquieto; — favoured disforme, feo; — humored malhumorado; mal genioso.
illegal (ilígal) adj. ilegal; ilícito.
illegitimate (ileyítimet) adj. ilegítimo; bastardo; falso, erróneo.

illicit (ilícit) adj. ilícito.
illiteracy (iliteresi) s. analfabetismo; falta de instrucción.
illiterate (ilitereit) adj. y s. analfabeto; iletrado; ignorante.
illness (ílnes) s. enfermedad, mal.
illuminate (ilúmineit) v. iluminar; dar luz; alumbrar; esclarecer.
illumination (iluminéshon) s. iluminación; alumbrado; brillo.
illusion (ilúshon) s. ilusión.
illusive (ilúsiv) adj. ilusorio, falaz; engañoso, falso.
illusory (ilúsori) adj. fantástico, aparente; engañoso; ilusivo.
illustrate (ilostréit) v. ilustrar.
illustration (ilostréshon) s. ilustración; elucidación; grabado; estampa; dibujo.
illustrator (ilostréitor) s. ilustrador.
illustrious (ilóstrios) adj. ilustre.
image (imey) s. imagen, efigie.
imagery (ímeyeri) s. conjunto de imágenes; fantasía; aprehensión.
imaginary (iméyineri) adj. imaginario.
imagination (imeyinéshon) s. imaginación; invención; visión.
imaginative (iméyinetiv) adj. imaginativo.
imagine (iméyin) v. imaginar(se), suponer(se); figurarse.
imbecile (ímbesil) adj. y s. imbécil.
imbibe (imbáib) v. embeber; chupar; absorber; empapar(se); empinar el codo.
imbue (imbiú) v. imbuir; infundir; teñir, impregnar.
imitate (ímiteit) v. imitar, emular.
imitation (imitéshon) s. imitación; emulación; remedo.
imitator (ímiteitor) s. imitador; emulador.
immaculate (imákiuleit) adj. inmaculado; puro; sin mancha.
immaterial (imatírial) adj. inmaterial; fútil; indiferente; que no tiene la menor importancia.
immediate (imídiet) adj. inmediato; próximo; instantáneo; intuitivo; **—ly** adv. inmediatamente; al punto; en seguida; desde luego.
immense (iméns) adj. inmenso.
immensity (iménsiti) s. inmensidad.
immerse (imérs) v. sumergir, zambullir; meter dentro del agua.

immigrant (ímigrant) adj. y s. inmigrante.
immigrate (ímigret) v. inmigrar.
immigration (imigréshon) s. inmigración.
imminent (íminent) adj. inminente.
immodest (imódest) adj. deshonesto; indecoroso, impúdico; indecente.
immoral (imóral) adj. inmoral; corrompido; licencioso; vicioso.
immorality (imoráliti) s. inmoralidad.
immortal (imórtal) adj. y s. inmortal.
immortality (imortáliti) s. inmortalidad.
immovable (imúvabl) adj. inamovible, inmóvil; fijo, inmutable, firme.
immune (imiún) adj. inmune.
immunity (imiúniti) s. inmunidad.
imp (imp) s. diablillo; duende.
impair (impér) v. dañar; deteriorar; echar a perder; perjudicar; menoscabar; desvirtuar.
impairment (impérment) s. menoscabo; deterioro; empeoramiento.
impart (impárt) v. impartir; conferir; dar; comunicar; hacer saber.
impartial (impárshal) adj. imparcial.
impartiality (imparsháliti) s. imparcialidad, equidad.
impassible (impásibl) adj. impasible.
impassioned (impéshond) adj. apasionado; vehemente, ardiente.
impatience (impéshens) s. impaciencia; desasosiego.
impatient (impéshent) adj. impaciente; inquieto; irritable.
impede (impíd) s. impedir; obstruir, retardar; poner obstáculos.
impediment (impédiment) s. impedimento; obstáculo; estorbo; traba.
impel (impél) v. impeler, impulsar.
impending (impénding) adj. inminente; pendiente; amenazador.
imperative (impérativ) adj. imperativo; perentorio; imperioso.
imperceptible (imperséptibl) adj. imperceptible.
imperfect (impérfekt) adj. imperfecto; incompleto; defectuoso.
imperial (impírial) adj. imperial.

imperil (impéril) v. poner en peligro; someter a un riesgo.
impersonal (impérsnl) adj. impersonal.
impersonate (impérsneit) v. personificar, representar, hacer el papel de; fingirse otro; imitar.
impertinence (impértinens) s. impertinencia; insolencia; absurdo.
impertinent (impértinent) adj. impertinente; insolente.
impervious (impérvios) adj. impermeable; impenetrable.
impetuous (impéchus) adj. impetuoso.
impetus (ímpetos) s. ímpetu.
impious (ímpios) adj. impío.
implacable (implácabl) adj. implacable; irreconciliable.
implant (implánt) v. implantar; fijar; plantar; ingerir; inculcar.
implement (ímplement) s. herramienta; instrumento; útil; apero.
implicate (ímplikeit) v. implicar, enredar; embrollar; envolver.
implore (implór) v. implorar; rogar, suplicar; pedir insistentemente.
imply (implái) v. implicar; insinuar; dar a entender; denotar.
impolite (impoláit) adj. descortés.
import (ímport) s. tendencia; sentido; significado; importancia; —s artículos importados; (impórt) v. importar; denotar; significar.
importance (impórtans) s. importancia.
important (impórtant) adj. importante.
impose (impóus) v. imponer; colocar; engañar; hacer creer una cosa falsa; to — upon abusar de (la amistad, confianza, etc.).
imposing (impóusing) adj. impresivo; imponente; tremendo.
imposition (imposíshon) s. imposición, tributo, obligación, impuesto.
impossibility (imposibílity) s. imposibilidad; imposible.
impossible (impósibl) adj. imposible.
impostor (impóstor) s. impostor; embaucador; embustero.
imposture (impóschur) s. impostura; fraude, engaño, falsedad.
impotence (ímpotens) s. impotencia.
impotent (ímpotent) adj. impotente.
impoverish (impóverish) v. empobrecer; deteriorar.

impregnate (imprégneit) v. impregnar; fecundar; imbuir, penetrar.
impress (imprés) v. imprimir; impresionar; influir; fijar; marcar; grabar; s. impresión; marca; divisa; lema; figura; imagen; leva.
impression (impréshon) s. impresión; edición; marca; señal, huella.
impressive (imprésiv) adj. impresionante; imponente; admirable.
imprison (imprísn) v. encarcelar, poner preso; encerrar.
imprisonment (imprísnment) s. reclusión, prisión, encarcelamiento.
improbable (impróbabl) adj. improbable; inverosímil.
improper (impróper) adj. impropio.
improve (imprúv) v. mejorar; perfeccionar; embellecer; aprovechar; corregir; explotar una hacienda.
improvement (imprúvment) s. mejora; progreso; adelanto; mejoría (de salud); aumento.
improvise (ímprovais) v. improvisar; hablar o componer de repente.
impudence (impíudens) s. impudencia; insolencia; descaro; inmodestia.
impudent (impíudent) adj. desvergonzado; descarado; insolente.
impulse (impols) s. impulso; ímpetu; instigación; motivo; inclinación; **to act on** — obrar impulsivamente.
impunity (impiúniti) s. impunidad; falta de castigo; exención de daño.
impure (impiúr) adj. impuro; inmundo; adulterado; deshonesto; impúdico.
impurity (impiúriti) s. impureza.
impute (impiút) v. imputar, atribuir; achacar; incusar.
in (in) prep. en, de, por, con, dentro de; — **a hurry** de prisa; — **the evening** por la noche; — **writing** por escrito; — **a few days** dentro de unos días; — **order to** a fin de; — **the meantime** entre tanto **a week — advance** una semana de anticipación; **to be — and out** estar entrando y saliendo; **to be all** — no poder más; estar rendido de cansancio; **to be — for it** no tener medios para evitar una cosa, un castigo; **to come (go) in** entrar; **to be — with someone** disfrutar del favor o aprecio de alguien; **to have it — for someone** tenerle mala voluntad a una persona; **to put — meter; is the train —?** ¿llegó ya el tren?; **in-and-in** de una misma casta; **to be — it** participar en una cosa.
inability (inebíliti) s. incapacidad; inhabilidad; ineptitud.
inaccessible (inaksésibl) adj. inaccesible; inasequible.
inaccurate (inákiureit) adj. inexacto; erróneo; impreciso.
inactive (ináktiv) adj. inactivo; indolente; inerte; negligente.
inactivity (inaktíviti) s. inactividad; ociosidad; inacción; inercia.
inadequate (inádekueit) adj. inadecuado; insuficiente; incompleto.
inadvertent (inadvértent) adj. inadvertido; accidental; descuidado; —**ly** adv. inadvertidamente.
inanimate (inánimeit) adj. inanimado.
inasmuch (inasmóch) adv. — **as** en cuanto; visto que; puesto que.
inattentive (inaténtiv) adj. desatento.
inaugurate (inógiureit) v. inaugurar instalar; investir; principiar, iniciar; consagrar, dedicar.
inauguration (inogiuréshon) s. inauguración; instalación; exaltación.
inborn (inbórn) adj. ínsito, innato.
incandescent (incandésnt) adj. incandescente; candente; hecho ascua.
incapable (inképabl) adj. inhábil, incapaz; inepto.
incense (insens) s. incienso; v. exasperar; irritar; inflamar.
incentive (incéntiv) s. incentivo; interés; estímulo; motivo.
incessant (insésnt) adj. incesante; constante.
inch (inch) s. pulgada; **by —es** poco a poco; gradualmente; **every — cabalmente**; **inch by inch** palmo a palmo; **to be within an — of** estar a punto de; estar muy cerca; v. avanzar o retirarse poco a poco; muy despacio
incident (insident) s. incidente; suceso; acontecimiento; casualidad.
incidental (insidéntal) adj. contingente; casual; accidental; —**s** pl. gastos imprevistos; —**ly** adv

casualmente; de paso; incidentalmente; a propósito.
incision (insíshon) s. incisión.
incite (insáit) v. incitar; estimular.
inclination (inclinéshon) s. inclinación; tendencia.
incline (incláin) v. inclinar(se); ladearse; s. declive; pendiente.
inclose véase **enclose**.
inclosure véase **enclosure**.
include (inklúd) v. incluir; abrazar; contener; comprender; encerrar.
inclusive (inklúsiv) adj. inclusive;
incoherent (incojírent) adj. incoherente; inconexo; suelto.
incomparable (inkómparabl) adj. incomparable; sin igual; sin par.
incompatible (inkompátibl) adj. incompatible.
incompetent (inkómpetent) adj. incompetente; insuficiente.
incomplete (inkomplít) adj. incompleto; inconcluso.
incomprehensible (inkomprijénsibl) adj. incomprensible.
inconsiderate (inkonsídereit) adj. desconsiderado; irreflexivo.
inconsistent (inconsístent) adj. inconsistente; voluble.
inconstancy (inkónstansi) s. inconstancia; diversidad; mudanza.
inconstant (inkónstant) adj. inconstante; diverso; voluble; mudable.
inconvenience (inkonvíniens) s. inconveniencia; molestia; dificultad; v. molestar, incomodar; estorbar.
inconvenient (inkonvínient) adj. inconveniente; molesto: inoportuno.
incorporate (inkórporeit) adj. incorporado; asociado; incorpóreo; inmaterial; v. incorporarse, asociarse; organizar una corporación.
incorrect (inkorrékt) adj. incorrecto; erróneo; inexacto.
increase (incrís) s. aumento; incremento; acrecentamiento; v. aumentar; acrecentar; engrandecer; crecer; multiplicarse.
increasingly (incrísingli) adv. más y más; en creciente, en aumento.
incredible (inkrédibl) adj. increíble; que no se puede creer.
incredulity (inkrediúliti) s. incredulidad; escepticismo.

incredulous (inkrédiulos) adj. incrédulo; descreído; escéptico.
inculcate (inkólkeit) v. inculcar; infundir.
incur (inkór) v. incurrir; merecer.
incurable (inkiúrabl) adj. incurable; irreparable; s. incurable.
indebted (indéted) adj. endeudado; obligado; agradecido.
indebtedness (indétednes) s. deuda; obligación.
indecency (indísnsi) s. indecencia.
indecent (indísnt) adj. indecente.
indeed (indíd) adv. de veras, realmente; en verdad; bien que.
indefinite (indéfinit) adj. indefinido.
indelible (indélebl) adj. indeleble.
indelicate (indélikeit) adj. indecoroso; grosero; falto de urbanidad.
indemnify (indémnifai) v. indemnizar.
indemnity (indémniti) s. indemnización; resarcimiento.
indent (indént) v. dentar; endentar; sangrar (empezar una línea más adentro que las otras).
independence (indepéndens) s. independencia.
independent (indepéndent) adj. independiente; separado; desunido.
indescribable (indiskráibabl) adj. indescriptible; inenarrable.
index (índeks) s. índice; v. ordenar alfabéticamente; poner índice.
indicate (índikeit) v. indicar.
indication (indikéshon) s. indicación.
indicative (indíketiv) adj. y s. indicativo.
indict (indáit) v. acusar por escrito ante un juez; demandar; enjuiciar.
indictment (indáitment) s. acusación formulada por el Gran Jurado; denuncia; proceso judicial.
indifference (indífrens) s. indiferencia; frialdad; despego; desinterés.
indifferent (indífrent) adj. indiferente; apático; descuidado; desinteresado.
indigenous (indíyenos) adj. indígena; autóctono; nativo.
indigestion (indiyéschon) s. indigestión.
indignant (indígnant) adj. indignado; —ly adv. con indignación.
indignation (indignéshon) s. indignación.

indignity (indígniti) s. indignidad; ultraje; oprobio; afrenta.
indigo (índigo) s. índigo, añil; — **blue** azul índigo.
indirect (indirékt) adj. indirecto.
indiscreet (indiskrít) adj. indiscreto; incauto.
indiscretion (indiscréshon) s. indiscreción; imprudencia.
indispensable (indispénsabl) adj. indispensable.
indispose (indispóus) v. indisponer.
indisposed (indispóusd) adj. indispuesto.
indisposition (indisposíshon) s. indisposición, malestar.
indistinct (indistínkt) adj. indistinto.
individual (indivíyual) adj. individual; particular; s. individuo, sujeto, persona.
individuality (indiviyuáliti) s. individualidad; individuo, persona.
indivisible (indivísibl) adj. indivisible.
indoctrinate (indóktrineit) v. doctrinar, enseñar; instruir.
indolence (índolens) s. indolencia; desidia; pereza; apatía.
indolent (índolent) adj. indolente; desidioso, perezoso; apático.
indomitable (indómitabl) adj. indomable.
indoor (índor) adj. interior.
indoors (índórs) adv. dentro, adentro; en casa; **to go —** entrar al interior de la casa, de un edificio.
indorse (indórs) v. endosar, avalar; garantizar un documento.
indorsement (indórsment) s. endoso; aval; garantía; respaldo.
indorser (indórser) s. endosante.
induce (indiús) v. inducir; instigar.
inducement (indiúsment) s. móvil, aliciente; incentivo.
induct (indókt) v. instalar; iniciar; dar posesión de un cargo.
induction (indókshon) s. inducción; instalación; introducción.
indulgence (indólyens) s. indulgencia; complacencia en el vicio.
indulgent (indólyent) adj. indulgente.
industrial (indóstrial) adj. industrial.
industrialist (indóstrialist) s. industrial; fabricante.
industrious (indóstrios) adj. industrioso; laborioso; aplicado.
ineffable (inéfabl) adj. inefable.
ineffective (ineféktiv) adj. ineficaz; vano, inútil; inefectivo.

inequality (inikuáliti) s. desigualdad; desemejanza; disparidad.
inert (inért) adj. inerte, inanimado; carente de vida.
inertia (inersha) s. inercia.
inestimable (inéstimabl) adj. inestimable; inapreciable.
inevitable (inévitabl) adj. inevitable.
inexhaustible (inegsóstibl) adj. inagotable.
inexpensive (inexpénsiv) adj. económico; barato.
inexperience (inexpíriens) s. inexperiencia; impericia.
inexperienced (inexpírienst) adj. inexperto; falto de experiencia.
inexplicable (inéxplicabl) adj. inexplicable.
inexpressible (ineksprésibl) adj. indecible; que no puede expresarse; inefable.
infallible (infálibl) adj. infalible; seguro; cierto.
infamous (ínfemos) adj. infame; vil; ignominioso; infamante.
infamy (ínfemi) s. infamia.
infancy (ínfansi) s. infancia.
infant (ínfant) s. infante; bebé; menor; criatura; nene.
infantile (infantail) adj. infantil.
infantry (ínfantri) s. infantería.
infect (infékt) v. infectar; contaminar; corromper; inficionar.
infection (infékshon) s. infección; contagio; corrupción.
infectious (inféksios) adj. infeccioso; contagioso; corrupto.
infer (infér) v. inferir; deducir; implicar; colegir.
inference (ínferens) s. inferencia; deducción; consecuencia.
inferior (infírior) adj. y s. inferioridad; subordinación.
infernal (inférnal) adj. infernal.
inferno (inférno) s. infierno.
infest (infést) v. infestar; plagar.
infidel (ínfidl) adj. y s. infiel; pagano; gentil.
infinite (infinit) adj. y s. infinito.
infinitive (infinitiv) adj. y s. infinitivo.
infinity (infíniti) s. infinidad; inmensidad; infinito.
infirm (inférm) adj. enfermizo; débil, enclenque, achacoso.
infirmary (inférmeri) s. enfermería.
infirmity (inférmiti) s. enfermedad; flaqueza; mal; falta de salud.

inflame (infléim) v. inflamar, encender; azuzar; enardecer(se).
inflammation (inflaméshon) s. inflamación; enardecimiento.
inflate (infléit) v. inflar, hinchar.
inflation (infléshon) s. inflación.
inflection (inflékshon) s. inflexión.
inflict (inflíkt) v. castigar, infligir.
influence (ínfluens) v. influir; intervenir; tener ascendiente sobre; s. influencia; influjo.
influential (influénshal) adj. influyente.
influenza (influénza) s. influenza.
influx (inflóks) s. flujo, afluencia; instilación, intromisión.
infold (infóuld) v. envolver; abrazar; incluir.
information (informéshon) s. información; informe; aviso, noticia, conocimientos; saber; instrucción.
infringe (infríny) v. infringir; violar; contravenir.
infuriate (infiúriet) v. enfurecer.
infuse (infiús) v. infundir, inculcar; instilar; hacer infusión de algo.
ingenious (inyínios) adj. ingenioso.
ingenuity (inyinuiti) s. ingeniosidad; destreza; maña; habilidad.
ingratitude (ingrátichud) s. ingratitud.
ingredient (ingrídient) s. ingrediente.
inhabit (injábit) v. habitar; vivir; residir en; ocupar una casa.
inhabitant (injábitant) s. habitante.
inhale (injéil) v. inhalar, inspirar; aspirar.
inherent (injírent) adj. inherente.
inherit (injérit) v. heredar.
inheritance (injéritans) s. herencia.
inhibit (injíbit) v. inhibir, contener; impedir; cohibir; vedar.
inhibition (injibíshon) s. inhibición; impedimento; prohibición; veda.
inhospitable (injóspitabl) adj. inhospitalario.
inhuman (injiúman) adj. inhumano.
inimitable (inímitabl) adj. inimitable.
iniquity (iníkuiti) s. iniquidad.
initial (iníshal) adj. y s. inicial; incipiente; v. siglar.
initiative (iníshietiv) s. iniciativa.
inject (inyéct) v. inyectar; introducir; echar sobre, aglomerar.

injection (inyékshon) s. inyección.
injunction (inyónkshon) s. requerimiento; mandato; orden judicial.
injure (ínyur) v. injuriar, ofender; dañar; herir; lastimar; lisiar.
injurious (inyúrios) adj. injurioso; ofensivo; dañoso, hiriente.
injury (ínyuri) s. injuria, daño, agravio, ofensa, perjuicio, mal.
injustice (inyóstis) s. injusticia.
ink (ink) s. tinta; v. entintar.
inkling (ínkling) s. indicación; insinuación; indicio; idea vaga.
inkstand (ínkstand) s. tintero.
inkwell (ínkuel) s. tintero.
inlaid (inléid) adj. incrustado; embutido; — **work** embutido; pret. y p.p. de to inlay.
inland (ínland) s. interior del país; tierra adentro; — **commerce** comercio interior.
inlay (inléi) v. incrustar; embutir.
inmate (ínmeit) s. inquilino; recluso; huésped; asilado; presidiario.
inmost (ínmost) adj. íntimo, recóndito; el más secreto; el más profundo.
inn (in) s. posada, mesón, fonda; —**s of court** colegio de abogados.
innate (inéit) adj. innato, ingénito, connatural.
inner (íner) adj. interior; íntimo; recóndito; — **most** véase inmost.
inning (íning) s. entrada en el juego de beisbol; turno en el mando.
innkeeper (ínkiper) s. posadero, mesonero, hospedero; fondista.
innocence (ínosens) s. inocencia; pureza; sencillez.
innocent (ínocent) adj. inocente; cándido; simple; inofensivo; libre de culpa.
innocuous (inókious) adj. innocuo; inofensivo; inocente.
innovation (inovéshon) s. innovación; novedad.
innuendo (iniuéndo) s. indirecta; insinuación; pulla.
innumerable (iniúmerabl) adj. innumerable; incontable.
inoculate (inókiuleit) v. inocular; contaminar; infectar; inficionar.
inoffensive (inofénsiv) adj. inofensivo; pacífico.
inopportune (inoporchún) adj. inoportuno, inconveniente.
inquire (inkuáir) v. inquirir; preguntar; averiguar; indagar; to

— **for (about)** preguntar por; **to — into** investigar; indagar; examinar.
inquiry (incuáiri) s. pregunta; indagación; investigación; pesquisa.
inquisition (inkuisíshon) s. inquisitivo; preguntón; curioso.
inroad (ínroud) s. incursión, irrupción; ataque; v. **to make —s upon** atacar; mermar.
insane (inséin) adj. loco; demente; **— asylum** manicomio.
insanity (insániti) s. locura.
insatiable (inséshiabl) adj. insaciable.
inscribe (inscráib) v. inscribir.
inscription (inscripshon) s. inscripción; rótulo; letrero.
insect (insekt) s. insecto.
insecure (insekiúr) adj. inseguro.
insensible (insénsibl) adj. insensible; impasible; imperceptible.
insensitive (insénsitiv) adj. insensible.
inseparable (inséparabl) adj. inseparable; indivisible.
insert (insert) s. inserción; circular; folleto; (insért) v. insertar; intercalar; encajar; meter; introducir.
insertion (insérshon) s. inserción; introducción; metimiento.
inside (insáid) adj. interior; interno; s. el interior; la parte de dentro; **— out** al revés; de dentro afuera; adv. dentro; adentro.
insight (insait) s. discernimiento; perspicacia; percepción; comprensión; penetración.
insignia (insignia) s. pl. insignias.
insignificant (insignificant) adj. insignificante; despreciable.
insinuate (insíniuet) v. insinuar.
insinuation (insiniuéshon) s. insinuación, indirecta.
insipid (insípid) adj. insípido.
insist (insíst) v. insistir; instar; empeñarse; porfiar; persistir.
insistence (insístens) s. insistencia; empeño; porfía.
insistent (insístent) adj. insistente; persistente; porfiado.
insolence (ínsolens) s. insolencia.
insolent (ínsolent) adj. insolente.
inspect (inspékt) v. reconocer; examinar; inspeccionar; registrar.
inspection (inspékshon) s. inspección; registro; examen.
inspector (inspéktor) s. inspector.
inspiration (inspiréshon) s. inspiración.

inspire (inspáir) v. inspirar.
install (instól) v. instalar.
installation (instoléshon) s. instalación; montaje.
installment (instólment) s. instalación; abono en pago; entrega periódica de una publicación o novela; **to pay in —s** pagar en abonos.
instance (ínstans) s. ejemplo; caso; vez; ocasión; instancia; **for —** por ejemplo.
instant (ínstant) s. instante; inminente, inmediato; urgente; perentorio; **the 10th —** el 10 de los corrientes; **—ly** al instante.
instantaneous (instenténeos) adj. instantáneo.
instead (instéd) adv. en lugar de; en vez de.
instep (ínstep) s. empeine (del pie o del zapato).
instigate (ínstigueit) v. instigar.
instill (instíl) v. infundir.
instinct (ínstinkt) s. instinto.
instinctive (instínktiv) adj. instintivo; **—ly** instintivamente.
institution (institiúshon) s. institución, instituto; establecimiento.
instruct (instrókt) v. instruir; educar; enseñar; dar órdenes o instrucciones; mandar.
instructive (instróktiv) adj. instructivo.
instructor (instróktor) s. instructor.
instrument (ínstrument) s. instrumento.
instrumental (instruméntal) adj. instrumental; **to be — in** ayudar a; servir de instrumento para.
insufferable (insófrabl) insufrible; inaguantable, insoportable.
insufficiency (insofíshensi) s. insuficiencia; incapacidad.
insufficient (insofíshent) adj. insuficiente; incapaz; inepto.
insulate (ínsoleit) v. aislar.
insulation (insoléshon) s. aislamiento.
insulator (insoléitor) s. aislador.
insult (insólt) s. insulto, ultraje; denuesto; v. insultar; ultrajar.
insure (inshúr) v. asegurar; afianzar.
insurgent (insóryent) adj. y s. insurgente, insurrecto.
insurmountable (insormáuntabl) adj. insuperable; incontrastable.
insurrection (insorrékshon) s. insurrección; sublevación; rebelión.

— 117 —

intact (intákt) adj. intacto; íntegro.
integral (íntegral) adj. integral; integrante; total; perfecto.
integrity (intégriti) s. integridad; probidad; entereza.
intellect (intelekt) s. intelecto; entendimiento.
intelligence (intéliyens) s. inteligencia; entendimiento; noticia; acuerdo; — service policía secreta.
intelligent (intéliyent) adj. inteligente; talentoso; ilustrado.
intemperance (intémperans) s. intemperancia; exceso en la bebida.
intend (inténd) v. intentar; tener intención de; proyectar; proponerse; destinar; aplicar; to — to do it pensar hacerlo.
intense (inténs) adj. intenso.
intensity (inténsiti) s. intensidad.
intensive (inténsiv) adj. intensivo; entero; enfático.
intent (intént) s. intento; propósito; designio; ánimo; significado; to all intents and purposes en todos sentidos; prácticamente; adj. atento; asiduo; dedicado; — on decidido o resuelto a.
intention (inténshon) s. intención; designio; finalidad; propósito.
intentional (inténshonal) adj. intencional; —ly adv. intencionalmente; con propósito deliberado.
inter (intér) v. enterrar; sepultar; inhumar.
intercede (intersíd) v. interceder; mediar, abogar por.
intercept (intersépt) v. interceptar; detener; atajar.
interception (intersépshon) s. interceptación; atajo.
intercession (interséshon) s. intercesión.
interchange (intercheiny) s. intercambio; cambio; trueque; v. alternar; trocar; permutar; cambiar.
intercourse (ínterkours) s. comunicación; comercio; trato; roce; intercambio de ideas.
interest (ínterest) s. interés; rédito; participación; provecho, utilidad; beneficio; lucro; v. interesar; interesarse; tomar parte.
interested (ínterested) adj. interesado; to be — in interesarse en o por.
interesting (ínteresting) adj. interesante; atractivo.

interfere (interfír) v. interponerse; intervenir; estorbar; poner obstáculos; to — with estorbar, frustrar; entremeterse.
interference (interfírens) s. intervención; interferencia.
interior (intírior) adj. interior; interno, s. el interior.
interjection (interyékshon) s. interjección, exclamación, intervención.
interlace (interléis) v. entrelazar; enlazar, entremezclar.
interlock (interlók) v. entrelazar(se); trabar(se); unir uno con otro con mutua acción.
intermediate (intermídieit) adj. intermedio.
interminable (intérminabl) adj. interminable, ilimitado.
intermingle (intermíngl) v. entremezclar(se); entreverar(se).
intermission (intermíshon) s. intermisión; intermedio, tiempo intermedio; entreacto.
intermittent (intermítent) adj. intermitente.
intern (intérn) v. internar, confinar, encerrar, en un lugar determinado; s. médico cirujano residente en un hospital.
internal (intérnal) adj. interno.
international (internéshonal) adj. internacional.
interoceanic (interoshiánik) adj. interoceánico.
interpose (interpóus) v. interponer.
interpret (intérpret) v. interpretar.
interpretation (interpretéshon) s. interpretación.
interpreter (intérpreter) s. intérprete.
interrogate (intérrogueit) v. interrogar.
interrogation (interroguéshon) s. interrogación.
interrupt (interrópt) v. interrumpir.
interruption (interrópshon) s. interrupción.
intersect (intersékt) v. cortar(se); cruzar(se); intersecarse.
intersection (intersékshon) s. intersección; street — bocacalle.
intersperse (interspérs) v. entremezclar; esparcir.
intertwine (intertuáin) v. entrelazar, entretejer; trenzar.
interval (ínterval) s. intervalo.
intervene (intervín) v. intervenir; interponerse; mediar.

intervention (intervénshon) s. intervención.
interview (ínterviu) s. entrevista; conferencia; v. entrevistar.
intestine (intéstin) s. intestino; adj. intestino, interno, interior.
intimacy (íntimasi) s. intimidad.
intimate (íntimeit) adj. íntimo, interior, cordial; v. insinuar, intimar.
intimation (intiméshon) s. insinuación; indirecta; intimación.
intimidate (intímideit) v. intimidar; amedrentar; acobardar.
into (intu) prep. en, dentro de; hacia el interior; por.
intolerable (intólerabl) adj. intolerable; inaguantable; insufrible.
intolerance (intólerans) s. intolerancia.
intolerant (intólerant) adj. intolerante.
intonation (intonéshon) s. entonación.
intoxicate (intóxikeit) v. embriagar; intoxicar; envenenar.
intoxication (intoksikéshon) s. embriaguez; intoxicación; envenenamiento; estado tóxico.
intravenous (intravínous) adj. intravenoso.
intrench (intrénch) v. atrincherar; to — oneself atrincherarse; to — upon another's rights infringir los derechos de otro.
intrepid (intrépid) adj. intrépido.
intricate (íntrikeit) adj. intrincado; enredado; complicado; revuelto.
intrigue (intríg) s. intriga; trama; lío; embrollo; v. intrigar; tramar; maquinar; tener intrigas amorosas.
intriguer (intríguer) s. intrigante.
introduce (introdiús) v. introducir; insertar; presentar una persona a otra; hacer adoptar.
introduction (introdókshon) s. introducción; prólogo; proemio; presentación.
intrude (intrúd) v. entremeterse; inmiscuirse.
intruder (intrúder) s. intruso; entremetido.
intrusion (intrúshon) s. intrusión; impertinencia.
intrusive (intrúsiv) adj. intruso.
intrust véase **entrust**.
intuition (intuíshon) s. intuición.
inundate (ínondeit) s. inundar.
inure (iniúr) v. habituar; avezar; acostumbrar; tener afecto.

invade (invéid) v. invadir.
invader (invéider) s. invasor.
invalid (inválid) adj. inválido; nulo; que no tiene valor.
invalid (ínvalid) adj. inválido; baldado; enfermo; achacoso; — **diet** dieta para inválidos; — **chair** sillón para inválido.
invaluable (inváliuabl) adj. inestimable; inapreciable, de gran valor.
invariable (invériabl) adj. invariable; invariably adv. invariablemente; sin falta, sin excepción.
invasion (invéshon) s. invasión.
invention (invénshon) s. invención; invento, descubrimiento, facultad para inventar.
inventive (invéntiv) adj. inventivo.
inventiveness (invéntivnes) s. inventiva.
inventor (invéntor) s. inventor.
inventory (ínventori) s. inventario; catálogo; v. inventariar.
invert (invért) v. invertir; trastrocar, volver al revés, trasponer.
invest (invést) v. invertir, colocar (fondos); interesar; investir (de una dignidad o cargo).
investigate (invéstigueit) v. investigar, indagar, examinar.
investigation (investiguéshon) s. investigación, indagación, pesquisa, escrutinio.
investment (invéstment) s. inversión (de fondos); cerco, sitio.
investor (invéstor) s. el que invierte fondos.
invigorate (invígoreit) v. vigorizar, fortalecer, confortar.
invincible (invínsbl) adj. invencible.
invisible (invísibl) adj. invisible.
invitation (invitéshon) s. invitación, convite, envite.
invite (inváit) v. invitar.
inviting (inváiting) adj. atractivo, seductivo, tentador, incitante.
invoice (ínvois) s. factura; envío; mercancías enviadas; v. facturar.
invoke (invóuk) v. invocar.
involuntary (invólunteri) adj. involuntario.
involve (invólv) v. complicar, enredar, enrollar; comprometer; torcer, retorcer; **to get —d in difficulties** meterse en embrollos.
inward (ínuard) adj. interior; interno; secreto, oculto; adv. hacia el interior; hacia dentro; —s adentro.
iodine (áiodain) s. yodo.

ire (áir) s. ira.
iridescent (iridésnt) adj. iridiscente, tornasolado, irisado.
iris (áiris) s. iris, arco iris.
Irish (áirish) adj. irlandés; s. idioma irlandés; **the —** los irlandeses; **— man** irlandés.
irksome (érksom) adj. fastidioso, engorroso, molesto, cansado.
ironical (airónikal) adj. irónico.
ironing (áironing) s. planchado.
irony (áironi) s. ironía.
irregular (irréguiular) adj. irregular; anómalo; extraño.
irrelevant (irrélevant) adj. fuera de razón o propósito; desatinado; que no viene al caso; inaplicable; inoportuno.
irreligious (irrelíyos) adj. irreligioso, impío; profano.
irremediable (irremídiabl) adj. irremediable, irreparable, incurable.
irreproachable (irrepróchabl) adj. intachable; incensurable; irreprochable.
irresistible (irresístibl) adj. irresistible.
irresolute (irrésolut) adj. irresoluto; indeciso.
irreverence (irréverens) s. irreverencia; desacato.
irreverent (irréverent) adj. irreverente; irrespetuoso.
irrigate (írrigueit) v. irrigar; regar; mojar; bañar.
irrigation (irriguéshon) s. riego, irrigación; **— canal** acequia.
irritable (írritabl) adj. irritable.
irritate (írriteit) v. irritar.
irritating (irritéiting) adj. irritante.
island (áiland) s. isla; **—er** isleño.
isle (áil) s. isla, ínsula.
isolate (áisoleit) v. aislar.
isolation (aisoléshon) s. aislamiento.
issue (íshu) s. edición; emisión, impresión; problema, discusión; consecuencia; fin; término; prole; sucesión; v. **to take — with** disentir o diferir de; publicar; **point at —** punto a discusión; librar; emitir, poner en circulación; salir, nacer, surgir.
isthmus (ísmos) s. istmo.
it (it) pron. lo, la; ello, él, ella; **— is there** está allí; **— is raining** está lloviendo; **he saw — all** él lo vio todo; **what time is —?** ¿qué hora es? **who is —?** ¿quién es?
Italian (itálian) adj. y s. italiano.
italic (itálik) adj. itálico; **—s** letra bastardilla.
italicize (itálisais) v. poner en letra bastardilla; dar énfasis; subrayar.
itch (itch) s. comezón; picazón, sarna; urticaria; v. picar; sentir comezón o picazón; tener prurito por algo, antojarse.
itchy (itchi) adj. sarnoso, picante, hormigoso.
item (áitem) s. artículo; detalle; suelto (de un periódico); partida; párrafo, ítem.
itemize (áitemais) v. pormenorizar, detallar, especificar, hacer una lista de.
itinerary (aitínereri) s. itinerario, ruta, guía de viajeros.
its (its) pos. neutro su(s), de él; de ella, de ello.
itself (itsélf) pron. neutro mismo (a); la misma, lo mismo; **by —** por sí, de por sí; **in —** en sí.
ivory (áivori) s. marfil.
ivy (áivi) s. hiedra (yedra).

J

jab (yab) v. picar, pinchar; s. hurgonazo; pinchazo, piquete.
jackass (yákas) s. asno, burro, borrico; tonto, necio; garañón.
jacket (yáket) s. chaqueta, envoltura; forro (de un libro); jubón, jaquet; cubierta del cilindro.
jackknife (yáknaif) s. navaja.
jagged (yágd) adj. serrado, mellado, dentado.
jail (yéll) s. cárcel; v. encarcelar.
jailer (yéiler) s. carcelero.
jam (yam) v. estrujar, apachurrar; atorar(se); estrechar, golpearse; apretar, acuñar, apiñar; atascar (se); **to — on the brakes** frenar de golpe; **to — one's fingers** machucarse los dedos; s. conserva, compota; apretura, atascamiento, agolpamiento, apiñadura.
janitor (yánitor) s. conserje; portero, casero (encargado de un edificio); bedel.
January (yénuari) s. enero.
Japanese (yapanís) adj. y s. japonés.
jar (yar) s. jarra, jarro, tarro; choque, sacudida; tinaja, cántaro; orza, botija; vibración, trepidación; pendencia, disensión, riña; chirrido, ruido desagradable; **large earthen —** tinaja; v. trepidar, ha-

cer vibrar; reñir; desentonar; agitar, sacudir; chocar.
jargon (yárgon) s. jerga.
jasmine (yásmin) s. jazmín.
jasper (yásper) s. jaspe.
jaunt (yont) s. caminata, excursión; paseata; v. dar un paseíto; hacer una corta caminata.
jaw (yoh) s. quijada, mandíbula; Am. carretilla; hueso maxilar.
jawbone (yóboun) s. mandíbula.
jay (yéi) s. grajo; rústico, bobo; torpe, patán, chova; blue — azulejo; — walker el que cruza las bocacalles descuidadamente.
jazz (yas) s. jazz (cierta clase de música sincopada; v. tocar el jazz; bailar el jazz; to — up sincopar; animar, alegrar.
jealous (yélous) adj. celoso; envidioso, receloso; to be — of someone tenerle celos a una persona.
jealousy (yélousi) s. celos, envidia.
jeer (yir) s. mofa, befa; v. mofar.
jelly (yéli) s. jalea; v. convertir (se) en jalea.
jerk (yerk) s. tirón, sacudida; sacudimiento; jalón, espasmo muscular; v. sacudir, dar un tirón; arrojar; mover a tirones.
jersey (yérsei) s. tejido de punto, tejido elástico, estambre fino; toro o vaca de la isla de Jersey.
jest (yest) s. broma; chanza; chiste; v. bromear, chancearse; bufonearse, burlarse, jaranear.
jester (yéster) s. chancero, bufón.
Jesuit (yésuit) s. jesuita.
jet (yet) s. chorro, surtidor (de fuente); caño de salida; gas — mechero de gas; adj. de azabache; — black negro como el azabache; v. chorrear, salir en chorro.
Jew (yu) s. judío.
jewel (yúel) s. joya, alhaja, gema; prenda; presea; venera; piedra preciosa; — box estuche, joyero.
jeweler (yúeler) s. joyero; platero; —'s shop taller de joyería.
jewelry (yúelri) s. joyas; alhajas; pedrería; — store joyería, aderezo.
Jewish (yúish) adj. judío.
jiffy (yífi) s. instante; periquete; in a — en un instante; en dos paletas; en un decir Jesús.
jig (yig) s. jiga (música y baile); chasco, bromazo; — saw sierra mecánica (para recortar figuras); conductor o guía para fabricar piezas idénticas; — saw puzzle rompecabezas (de recortes).
jiggle (yigl) v. zangolotear(se), zarandear(se), menear(se); s. zarandeo, meneo.
jilt (yilt) v. desairar, dar calabazas, dejar plantado o colgado.
jingle (yingl) s. retintín; verso o rima infantil; retiñir; — bell cascabel; v. hacer retintín.
jockey (yóki) s. jockey; chalán; v. maniobrar (para sacar ventaja o ganar un puesto); trampear.
join (yóin) v. juntar(se); enlazar; unir, acoplar, asociarse a, anexar.
joint (yóint) s. coyuntura; juntura; junta; unión, empalme; ensambladura; conexión, enganche, bisagra; garito (casa de juego); fonducho; out of — descoyuntado; desunido; adj. unido, asociado; agrupado; combinado, colectivo; — action acción colectiva; — committee comisión mixta; — pipe manguito, golilla; — heir coheredero; —ly adv. juntamente, colectivamente.
joke (yóuk) s. broma, chiste; chanza; guasa; v. chancear; bromear.
joker (yóuker) s. bromista; chancero; guasón; burlón; comodín de la baraja; choteador.
jokingly (yóukingli) adv. en (o de) chanza; de chiste; burlonamente.
jolly (yóli) adj. jovial; alegre; festivo; divertido; v. bromear.
jolt (yolt) s. sacudida; sacudimiento; choque; v. sacudir; traquetear.
jostle (yostl) v. empujar o rempujar; dar empellones, codear; s. rempujón, empujón.
jot (yot) v. to — down apuntar, tomar apuntes, tomar notas; s. pizca, ápice; tilde.
journal (yórnal) s. diario; periódico; revista; jornal.
journalism (yórnalism) s. periodismo.
journalist (yórnalist) s. periodista.
journalistic (yornalístik) adj. periodístico.
journey (yórni) s. viaje, jornada; viaje por tierra; v. viajar.
joy (yói) s. júbilo; regocijo; gusto, deleite, alborozo.
joyful (yóiful) adj. regocijado, jubiloso; alegre; gozoso; —ly adv. regocijadamente, alegremente.

joyous (yóious) adj. alegre, gozoso, jubiloso.
jubilant (yúbilant) adj. regocijado.
jubilee (yúbili) s. jubileo, júbilo.
judge (yody) s. juez; magistrado; perito; conocedor; v. juzgar.
judgment (yódyment) s. juicio; sentencia; fallo; discreción; opinión; discernimiento; dictamen; — **day** día del juicio final.
judicial (yudíshal) adj. judicial.
judicious (yudíshus) adj. juicioso.
jug (yog) s. cántaro, jarro, jarra; cacharro; chirona (cárcel); porrón.
juggle (yogl) v. hacer juegos de manos, hacer suertes; **to — the accounts** barajar (o manipular las cuentas); s. juego de manos, engaño.
juggler (yógler) s. prestidigitador; malabarista, juglar, truhán.
juice (yus) s. jugo, zumo.
juiciness (yúsines) s. jugosidad.
juicy (yúsi) adj. jugoso; zumoso; suculento, **a — story** un cuento picante.
July (yulái) s. julio.
jumble (yombl) v. revolver(se); mezclar confusamente unas cosas con otras; s. mezcla, revoltillo.
jump (yomp) v. saltar, brincar, cruzar una distancia; salvar (de un salto); hacer saltar; sacudirse, moverse a saltos; comerse una pieza (en el juego de damas); convenir, concordar; **to — at the chance** aprovechar la oportunidad; **to — over** saltar de un lado a otro por encima de alguna cosa; **to — bail** perder la fianza por evasión; s. salto, brinco; **to be always on the —** andar siempre de un lado a otro, ser muy activo, trafagar.
jumper (yómper) s. saltador, chaquetón holgado (de obrero); vestido sin mangas (puesto sobre la blusa de mujer); traje de juego (para niños).
jumpy (yómpi) adj. saltón; asustadizo, nervioso.
junction (yónkshon) s. unión, juntura, empalme (de ferrocarriles); paraje de unión.
June (yún) s. junio.
jungle (yongl) s. selva, jungla, matorral; manigua.
junior (yúnior) adj. menor, joven; más joven que otro; — **college** colegio para los dos primeros años del bachillerato; hijo; s. estudiante del tercer año (en escuela superior, colegio o universidad).
junk (yonk) s. basura, desperdicios; trastos viejos; junco, trozos de cable viejo; v. desechar, echar la basura.
jurisdiction (yurisdíkshon) s. jurisdicción.
jurisprudence (yurisprúdens) s. jurisprudencia, derecho.
juror (yúror) s. jurado, miembro de un jurado.
jury (yúri) s. jurado; **grand —** jurado de acusación.
just (yost) adj. justo; recto; exacto, equitativo, imparcial, verdadero; íntegro, honrado; adv. no más ni menos; exactamente, justamente, precisamente, sólo; cabalmente; tasadamente; casi, no más que, apenas; nada más; — **now** ahora mismo; **he — left** acaba de salir; — **as you please** como usted guste.
justice (yóstis) s. justicia; juez, magistrado; equidad, razón.
justification (yostifikéshon) s. justificación, descargo.
justify (yóstifai) v. justificar.
justly (yóstli) adv. justamente; con razón, rectamente, exactamente.
jut (yot) v. sobresalir, proyectarse, extenderse; s. salidizo.
juvenile (yúvenil) adj. juvenil.

K

kangaroo (kangarú) s. canguro.
keel (kil) s. quilla; v. dar de quilla (voltear un barco); **rabbit of the —** alefriz de quilla; **to — over** zozobrar; caerse patas arriba.
keen (kin) adj. agudo; afilado; perspicaz, ansioso, penetrante.
keenness (kínes) s. agudeza; perspicacia; anhelo; sutileza; viveza; aspereza, ansia.
keep (kip) v. guardar; tener guardado; tener; retener; conservar(se); preservar(se); mantener(se); librar, custodiar, cuidar, defender, proteger, entretener; atender a una tienda; dirigir (llevar el manejo de una casa o los libros de comercio); **to — accounts** llevar las cuentas; **to — at it** seguir dale que dale; **to — at home** quedarse en casa; **to —**

down sujetar, oprimir; **to — from** abtener(se) de; **to — going** seguir andando, seguir adelante; **to — off** estar o tener a distancia; no arrimarse; **to — one's hands off** no tocar; **to — one's temper** refrenarse, contenerse; **to — out** impedir a uno que entre; estar o mantenerse fuera de algún sitio; **to — out of sight** esconder, quitar de adelante; estar o mantenerse oculto; **to — something up** seguir o continuar haciendo algo; s. manutención, subsistencia, mantenimiento; guarda; guardia; custodia, cuidado.

keeper (kíper) s. guardián, custodio; defensor; **jail —** carcelero.

kernel (kérnl) s. simiente; grano (de trigo o maíz); meollo (de ciertas frutas como la nuez); almendra.

kerosene (kérosin) s. kerosina; petróleo para lámparas.

kettle (ketl) s. caldera, paila, marmita; **— drum** tímpano; **tea —** tetera, marmita; Am. pava (para el mate).

key (ki) s. llave; clave (tecla del piano); clavija; destornillador; chaveta; cuña; cayo, isleta; **dental — forceps** de dentista; **— ring** llavero; **to be in — estar a tono; — tone** nota tónica; **to — up** v. elevar el tono de; **to be all —ed up** estar sobreexcitado; estar en tensión nerviosa; calzar, acuñar.

keyboard (kíbord) s. teclado.

keyhole (kíjoul) s. ojo de cerradura.

keynote (kínout) s. nota tónica; idea o principio fundamental.

keystone (kístoun) s. clave (de un arco); fundamento principal, dovela.

khaki (káki) s. kaki; adj. de kaki.

kick (kik) s. coz, patada, puntapié; puntillazo; fuerza (de una bebida); estímulo; queja; protesta; v. acocear; cocear; **to have a —** patear (dícese del licor); v. dar coces o patadas; dar patadas o puntapiés; **to — out** echar a patadas; echar; expulsar; **to — the bucekt** estirar la pata, morir; fallecer; **to — one out** echar a alguno a puntapiés; **to — up a lot of dust** levantar una polvareda.

kid (kid) s. cabrito; cabritilla (piel curtida de cabrito); chivo, chivato; niño, niña; **— gloves** guantes de cabritilla; v. bromear, chancearse con.

kidnap (kídnap) v. secuestrar, raptar, plagiar.

kidnapper (kídnaper) s. secuestrador; robachicos, ladrón de niños.

kidnapping (kídnaping) s. secuestro.

kidney (kídni) s. riñón; temperamento, índole; **— bean** judía, frijol; **— stones** cálculos.

kill (kil) v. matar, destruir, amortiguar; neutralizar, descartar, anular, parar (el motor); s. animal o animales (matados en la caza).

killer (kíler) s. asesino.

kiln (kiln) s. horno.

kilo (kílo) **kilogram** (kilogram) s. kilo.

kilometer (kilómiter) s. kilómetro.

kimono (kimóno) s. quimono, bata.

kin (kin) s. parentela, parientes, familia; vínculo; **to notify the nearest of —** avisar al pariente o deudo más cercano.

kind (káind) adj. bondadoso, benévolo; benigno, cariñoso; amable; **to send one's — regards to** enviar afectuosos saludos a; **— hearted** de buen corazón; **in a —** en cierto modo, en cierta manera; s. clase, especie, género; **to pay in —** pagar en la misma moneda o especie.

kindle (kindl) v. encender(se); inflamar(se); quemar, pegar fuego.

kindling (kíndling) s. encendimiento; leña ligera; astillas, charamuscas.

kindly (káindli) adj. bondadoso; benigno, benévolo; amable; blando, suave, tratable; adv. apaciblemente; bondadosamente; benignamente; cariñosamente, amablemente.

kindness (káindnes) s. bondad, amabilidad, gentileza, buena voluntad.

kindred (kíndred) adj. emparentado; allegado; semejante; s. sangre; **— facts** hechos relacionados; **— spirits** espíritus afines.

kingdom (kíngdom) s. reino.

kingly (kíngli) adj. regio, real, majestuoso; adv. majestuosamente.

kinky (kínki) adj. crespo, ensortijado, encarrujado, grifo.

kinship (kínship) s. parentesco, afinidad, semejanza.
kinsman (kínsman) s. pariente.
kiss (kis) s. beso; v. besar.
kit (kit) s. estuche, caja de herramientas; violín de tres cuerdas; envoltura (para guardar instrumentos, herramientas, etc.); gatito; marquito.
kitchen (kítchen) s. cocina; fogón portátil.
kite (káit) s. cometa; Am. papalote; milano, sobrejuanete.
kitten (kitn) s. gatito.
kitty (kíti) s. gatito, minino.
knack (nak) s. destreza, maña, habilidad, tino, don.
knapsack (nápsak) s. mochila, morral, alforja, barjuleta.
knave (neiv) s. bribón, bellaco, pícaro, sota (de naipes), truhán.
knead (níd) v. amasar.
knee (ni) s. rodilla, codo, codillo; — deep hasta la rodilla.
kneel (nil) v. arrodillarse, hincarse.
knell (nel) s. doble (de campanas por los difuntos); tañido fúnebre; v. tocar a muerto, doblar.
knelt (nelt) pret. y p.p. de to kneel.
knew (niú) pret. de to know.
knickknack (níknak) s. chuchería; baratija, chisme; bujería.
knife (naif) s. cuchillo, navaja; carving — trinchante; chopping — cuchilla de carnicero; v. acuchillar, frustrar o arruinar por medio de intrigas.
knight (náit) s. caballero; campeón; caballo (de ajedrez); — errantry caballería andante.
knighthood (náitjud) caballería; orden de la caballería; encomienda.
knit (nit) v. tejer (a punto de aguja); hacer malla, hacer media o calceta; enlazar, soldarse (un hueso); to — one's brow fruncir las cejas; pret. y p.p. de to knit.
knitting (níting) s. labor de punto; unión, junta.
knives (náivs) pl. de knife.
knock (nok) v. golpear, chocar, topar, llamar o tocar la puerta; criticar, aporrear; macerar; censurar o hablar mal; to — down desmontar (una máquina o aparato); to — off hacer saltar una cosa a fuerza de golpes; descontinuar; suspender; s. golpe, toque, llamada; aldabonazo; choque, porrazo; crítica, censura; —kneed zambo, patizambo.
knocker (nóker) s. llamador; criticón, murmurador; aldabilla.
knoll (nol) s. colina; loma.
knot (not) s. nudo; v. anudar(se).
knotty (nóti) adj. nudoso; dificultoso, enredado, duro, áspero, intrincado, difícil.
know (nóu) v. conocer; saber; reconocer; distinguir; hacerse cargo; to — how to swim saber nadar; to — how saber la manera, saber cómo.
knowingly (nóuingli) adv. a sabiendas, adrede, conocidamente.
knowledge (nóuledy) s. conocimiento; sabiduría; ciencia, erudición; not to my — no que yo sepa.
knuckle (nókl) s. nudillo; coyuntura; articulación; artejo, charnela; v. someterse; to — down aplicarse con empeño al trabajo.

L

label (léibl) s. etiqueta, marbete; rótulo, letrero; v. etiquetar, marcar, rotular; clasificar.
labor (léibor) s. trabajo; labor; obra, apuro; pena, fatiga; tarea; faena; — union unión de obreros; v. trabajar, afanarse, estar de parto; elaborar (un punto).
laboratory (léibratori) s. laboratorio.
laborer (léiborer) s. trabajador; obrero; peón; gañán; bracero.
laborious (labórios) adj. laborioso, trabajoso; afanoso, difícil, industrioso; ímprobo, arduo.
labyrinth (lábirinz) s. laberinto.
lace (léis) s. encaje, cordón; cordoncillo; cinta (de zapato, de corsé, etc); blonda, puntilla; galón de oro o plata; pasamano; gold — galón de oro (para guarnecer uniformes); v. atar, ajustar, abrochar; acordonar, enlazar; entrelazar.
lack (lak) s. falta; escasez; carencia; menester; v. carecer; faltarle a uno; necesitar.
lacking (láking) adj. falto, carente.
lacquer (láker) s. laca; v. barnizar con laca; dar laca.
lad (lad) s. rapaz, chico, mozo.
ladder (láder) s. escalera de mano.
laden (léidn) adj. cargado; ago-

— 124 —

LADIES   **LAST**

biado, abrumado; v. cargar, agobiar.
ladies (léidis) pl. de **lady**.
ladle (léidl) s. cucharón; cazo; v. servir con cuchara grande.
lady (léidi) s. señora, dama; young — señorita; —like con fineza; elegante; — love amada.
lag (lag) v. rezagarse; quedarse atrás; postrero; s. último; retardo, retraso; retardación de movimiento.
lagoon (lagún) s. laguna.
laid (léid) pret. y p.p. de **to lay**; **to be** — **up** estar incapacitado.
lain (léin) p.p. de **to lie**.
lair (lér) s. guarida, cueva de fieras.
lake (léik) s. lago, laguna.
lamb (lamb) s. cordero; —**kin** corderito; borrego.
lame (léim) adj. cojo, lisiado, estropeado; zopo; derrengado; — **excuse** disculpa falsa; v. hacer cojo.
lament (lamént) s. lamento; queja; v. lamentar(se); llorar; dolerse.
lamentable (lámentebl) adj. lamentable, doloroso; deplorable; flébil.
lamentation (lamentéshon) s. lamentación, lamento; duelo.
lamp (lamp) s. lámpara; linterna; farol; candil, velón; — **post** poste (de farol); — **shade** pantalla de lámpara; **safety** — lámpara de seguridad.
lance (lans) s. lanza, lanceta, lancero; v. herir con lanza.
land (land) s. tierra, terreno, suelo; bienes raíces; v. desembarcar; aterrizar (un avión); coger (un pez); **to** — **a job** conseguir una colocación, lograr un empleo.
landholder (lándjolder) s. terrateniente, propietario, hacendado.
landing (lánding) s. desembarco, desembarque, aterrizaje (de un avión); — **place** desembarcadero; — **field** campo de aterrizaje; — **strip** pista de aterrizaje.
landlady (lándleidi) s. patrona, casera, dueña (de la casa); ama.
landlord (lándlord) s. amo, patrón; propietario, arrendador.
landmark (lándmark) s. mojón, señal (para fijar los confines); marca; coto; linde.
landowner (lándouner) s. terrateniente; propietario, hacendado.

landscape (lándskeip) s. paisaje.
landslide (lándslaid) s. derrumbe; desprendimiento de tierra; desplome; gran mayoría de votos.
lane (léin) s. senda, vereda; callejuela; ruta, calle, derrotero (de vapores o aviones).
languid (lángüid) adj. lánguido, flojo, débil, flaco.
languish (lángüish) v. languidecer.
languor (lángor) s. languidez.
lank (lank) adj. alto y delgado.
lanky (lánki) adj. larguirucho, zancón; zancudo, delgaducho.
lantern (lántern) s. linterna.
lap (lap) s. falda, regazo; aleta; etapa; trecho (de una carrera); parte sobrepuesta de una cosa sobre otra; — **over** entrecruzar(se).
lapel (lapél) s. solapa.
lapse (láps) s. lapso, transcurso, desliz; intervalo de un tiempo; error; v. deslizarse; pasar; transcurrir; caer en algún defecto; prescribir.
larboard (lárbord) s. babor; adj. de babor.
larceny (lárceni) s. latrocinio; hurto; ratería.
lard (lard) s. lardo; manteca de puerco; aceite de manteca de cerdo; v. mechar, entreverar, guarnecer.
large (lary) adj. grande; abultado, grueso; **at** — sin trabas, suelto; —**ly** adv. grandemente, en gran parte.
lariat (láriet) s. reata.
lark (lark) s. alondra; diversión; holgorio; calandria; **to go on a** — ir o andar de jarana.
larva (lárva) s. larva.
larynx (lárinks) s. laringe.
lascivious (lacívos) adj. lascivo.
lash (lash) s. látigo; azote; latigazo; fuetazo; pestaña; v. fustigar; chasquear el látigo; azotar.
lass (las) s. moza, muchacha.
lassitude (lásitiud) s. dejadez, flojedad; decaimiento de fuerzas; languidez, lasitud.
lasso (láso) s. lazo, reata; mangana; v. manganear; lazar.
last (last) adj. último; final; pasado; postrero; — **night** anoche; — **year** el año pasado; **at** — por fin; — **but two** antepenúltimo; s. fin, término; horma (de zapato); v. durar; perdurar; —**ly**

adv. finalmente, en conclusión; al fin.
lasting (lásting) adj. duradero; perdurable; perpetuo.
latch (latch) s. pestillo, picaporte; aldaba, cerrojo; v. cerrar con aldaba; colar con lejía.
late (leit) adj. tardío; remoto, lejano; lento, último; reciente; — **comer** recién llegado; — **in years** de edad provecta; a — **hour** una hora avanzada; the — **Mr. X** el finado (o difunto) Sr. X; **to have a — supper** cenar tarde; **to be —** llegar tarde; **to keep — hours** retirarse o acostarse a deshora; **of —** de poco tiempo a esta parte; —**ly** adv. poco ha, últimamente, antes; recientemente, hace poco; — **in the night** a una hora avanzada de la noche; — **in the week** a fines de la semana; — **in the year** al fin del año.
latent (létent) adj. latente.
later (léiter) adv. y adj. (comp. de late) más tarde; después, luego, posterior, subsecuente.
lateral (láteral) adj. lateral.
latest (léitest) adv. y adj. (superl. de late) más tarde; más reciente; más nuevo; el último; fresco; novísimo; **the — fashion** la última moda; las últimas novedades; **the — news** las últimas noticias.
lathe (léiz) s. torno (de carpintero o mecánico), marco de telar.
lather (lázer) s. jabonadura, espuma de jabón; v. enjabonar para afeitar, hacer espuma.
Latin (látin) adj. latino; latín.
latitude (látitud) s. latitud; libertad; amplitud; anchura.
latter (láter) adj. último; el último de quien se habla; **towards the — part of the week** a (o hacia) fines de la semana; **the — éste.**
lattice (látis) s. celosía, rejilla.
laud (lod) v. loar, encomiar, alabar; s. laudes.
laudable (lódabl) adj. laudable, loable, recomendable.
laugh (laf) v. reír(se); **to — at** reírse de; estar alegre; mofar, burlar, encarnecer; **to — at one to his face** reírsele a uno en las barbas; s. risa; risada; **loud —** carcajada, risotada.
laughable (láfabl) adj. risible, ridículo, reídero, divertido.

laughter (láfter) s. risa.
launch (lonch) v. botar o echar (un barco) al agua; lanzar, dar principio, llevar adelante; poner en operación; **to — forth on a journey** emprender un viaje; s. lancha.
launder (lónder) v. lavar y planchar (la ropa).
laundress (lóndres) s. lavandera.
laundry (lóndri) s. lavandería; lavado, ropa (lavada); tren de lavado; v. lavar y planchar la ropa.
laurel (lórel) s. laurel, honor.
lava (láva) s. lava.
lavatory (lávatori) s. lavabo; lavamanos; lavatorio, retrete.
lavender (lávender) s. espliego, lavándula; adj. lila, morado claro.
lavish (lávish) adj. gastador, pródigo; dadivoso; abundante; manirroto, despilfarrado; copioso; v. despilfarrar; prodigar, malgastar; malbaratar; **to — praise upon** colmar de alabanzas a.
law (loh) s. ley; derecho; jurisprudencia; regla; estatuto; código de leyes; leyes (en general); norma de conducta; — **student** estudiante de leyes.
lawbreaker (lóhbréiker) s. infractor, transgresor, el que viola la ley.
lawful (lóhful) adj. legal; lícito; válido; permitido, conforme a la ley, según derecho.
lawless (lóhles) adj. sin ley; ilegal; desenfrenado; desaforado.
lawmaker (lóhmeiker) s. legislador.
lawn (lohn) s. césped, prado, linón (tela de hilo o algodón); dignidad de obispo anglicano.
lawsuit (lóhsiut) s. pleito, litigio.
lawyer (lóhier) s. abogado.
lax (lax) adj. flojo; suelto.
laxative (láksativ) adj. y s. laxante; purgante; laxativo.
laxity (láksiti) s. flojedad, flojera; flaccidez.
lay (léi) pret. de **to lie.**
lay (léi) v. colocar, poner; tender; extender; poner (huevos); echar (la culpa); instalar; tumbar, derribar, abatir; asentar (el polvo); **to — a wager** apostar; **to — aside** poner a un lado, ahorrar; **to — about** dar palos de ciego; **to — away** (o **by**) dejar; guardar; **to — bare** revelar, exponer; **to — down** acostar, abatir, abandonar; entregar, rendir; dimitir; **to — down the law**

— 126 —

mandar, dictar; to — **hold of** asir, agarrar; to — **off a workman** suspender a un obrero; to — **open** exponer a la **vista**; to — **up** guardar, atesorar, acumular, almacenar; obligar a guardar cama; encerrar; to — **waste** asolar, s. lay, balada; adj. lego, laico, profano; (no iniciado en una ciencia).

layer (léier) s. capa; estrato; gallina ponedora, lecho, cama.

layman (léiman) s. lego, seglar.

lazily (léisili) adv. perezosamente.

laziness (léisines) s. pereza.

lazy (léisi) adj. perezoso, holgazán.

lead (led) s. plomo, plomada; pesa, escandallo, regleta.

leaden (ledn) adj. plomizo; aplomado, pesado, — **hearted** insensible.

leader (líder) s. jefe, caudillo; líder; guía, conductor; capitán, comandante; caballo delantero; —s puntos suspensivos.

leadership (lídership) s. dirección; mando; iniciativa.

leading (líding) adj. principal; delantero; capital; — **man** primer actor.

leaf (lif) s. hoja (de un libro, mesa, puertas, etc.); v. cubrir (se) de hojas.

leafless (lífles) adj. deshojado, sin hojas.

leaflet (líflet) s. hojilla, folleto, volante; circular.

leafy (lífi) adj. frondoso.

league (lig) s. liga, confederación; sociedad; alianza, v. asociarse; ligarse, unirse.

leak (lik) s. gotera (en un techo); agujero, grieta (por donde se escapa el agua o el gas); vía de agua; goteo, filtración; v. gotear (se); hacer agua, derramarse.

lean (lin) v. inclinar(se); recostar(se), torcerse, ladearse; adj. magro, flaco; — **year** año estéril, improductivo.

leap (lip) v. saltar, brincar, corvetear; s. salto, brinco; — **year** año bisiesto.

leapt (lépt) pret. y p.p. de to leap.

learn (lern) v. aprender; saber, averiguar; tener noticia de.

learned (lérned) adj. erudito.

learner (lérner) s. principiante, estudiante, aprendiz.

learning (lérning) s. erudición, saber; literatura, letras.

learnt (lernt) pret. y p.p. de **to learn**.

lease (lis) v. arrendar, dar o tomar en arriendo; s. arriendo; escritura de arrendamiento.

least (list) adj. (el) mínimo; (el) más pequeño; el menor; adv. menos; **at** — **al** menos, por lo menos; **not in the** — de ninguna manera.

leather (leder) s. cuero, piel; adj. de cuero, de piel, — **belt** correa.

leave (liv) v. dejar, abandonar; salir (de); dejar estar; dejar o legar; **to** — **out** dejar fuera; omitir; s. permiso; licencia, venia; **to take** — **of** despedirse de.

leaven (léven) s. levadura; fermento; v. fermentar, leudar.

leaves (livs) pl. de **leaf**.

leavings (lívings) s. sobras.

lecture (lékchur) s. conferencia; reprensión, disertación, lección explicada en una clase; v. explicar.

lecturer (lékchurer) s. conferenciante; lector (de la Universidad); s. disertante; catedrático.

led (led) pret. y p.p. de **to lead**.

ledge (ledy) s. borde, salidizo.

ledger (lédyer) s. libro mayor (en contabilidad); adj. ligero.

leech (lich) s. sanguijuela.

leer (lir) s. mirada de soslayo; mirada lujuriosa; templador; v. mirar de soslayo o reojo.

left (left) pret. y p.p. de **to leave**; I have two books — me quedan dos libros; adj. izquierdo; s. izquierda; — **handed** zurdo; — **off** desechado.

leftist (léftist) s. izquierdista.

leftover (léftover) adj. sobrante, —s s. pl. sobras.

leg (leg) s. pierna; pata (de animal, mesa, etc.); etapa, trecho (de una carrera); pata de las aves y animales; **to take** — **bail** tomar las de Villadiego; **to be on one's last** —**s** estar en las últimas; **to get on one's legs** levantarse para hablar.

legacy (légasi) s. legado, herencia, manda.

legal (lígal) adj. legal, lícito.

legalize (lígalais) v. legalizar; sancionar, autorizar.

legate (léguiet) s. legado, delegado.

legation (leguéshon) s. legación.

legend (léyend) s. leyenda, letrero; fábula, saga, inscripción.

leggings (léguings) s. pl. polainas.

legion (líyon) s. legión.
legislate (léyisleit) v. legislar.
legislation (leyisléshon) s. legislación, legislativo.
legislative (léyisletiv) adj. legislativo.
legislator (léyisleitor) s. legislador.
legislature (léyislechur) s. legislatura, asamblea.
legitimate (leyítimeit) adj. legítimo.
leisure (líyur) s. ocio; vagancia; desocupación; — **hours** horas de ocio; **to be at** — estar desocupado; **do it at your** — hágalo Ud. en sus ratos de ocio.
leisurely (líyurli) adj. lento, deliberado; adv. sin prisa.
lemon (lémon) s. limón; — **tree** limonero; adj. de limón.
lemonade (lemonéd) s. limonada.
lend (lend) v. prestar.
lender (lénder) s. prestamista; logrero.
length (lenz) s. largo; largura; largueza; longitud; cantidad (de una sílaba); **at** — largamente; detenidamente; finalmente; **to go to any** — hacer cuanto esté de su parte.
lengthen (lénzen) v. alargar(se); prolongar(se); estirar, extender; dilatar; aumentarse.
lengthwise (lénzuais) adv. a lo largo; longitudinalmente; adj. longitudinal.
lengthy (lénzi) adj. largo.
lenient (línient) adj. indulgente; clemente; benigno.
lens (lens) s. lente; cristalino.
lent (lent) pret. p.p. de **to lend**.
Lent (lent) s. cuaresma.
leopard (lépard) s. leopardo.
less (les) adj. menor; menos, inferior; adv. y prep. — **and** — cada vez menos.
lessen (lesn) v. aminorar, mermar.
lesser (léser) adj. más pequeño.
lesson (léson) s. lección.
lest (lest) conj. no sea que; por miedo de que; para que no.
let (let) v. dejar, permitir; alquilar; dar arrendamiento o alquiler; — **us** (o **let's**) **do it** vamos a hacerlo; hagámoslo; — **him go** que se vaya; — **us fly** huyamos; **to** — **be** no molestar; dejar en paz; **to** — **in** dejar entrar; admitir; **to** — **know** avisar, enterar; — **the children play** que jueguen los niños; **house to** — casa por alquilar; pret. p p. de **to let**.

letnargy (lézaryi) s. letargo; estupor, entorpecimiento.
letter (léter) s. letra, carta; comunicación, epístola; — **box** buzón; — **of advise** carta de aviso; v. rotular; hacer a mano letras de molde; estampar con letras.
lettuce (létis) s. lechuga.
level ('leval) s. 1. nivel (instrumento) 2. nivel, altura. 3. grado, rango, categoría, posición (social, moral, intelectual, etc.)
lever (léver) s. palanca; leva; barra; **control** — palanca de mano.
levy (lévi) s. imposición; recaudación (de tributos, impuestos); v. embargar; ejecutar; imponer; exigir; recaudar; **to** — **on someone's property** embargar la propiedad de alguien.
lewd (lud) adj. lujurioso, lascivo, deshonesto; sensual.
lewdness (lúdnes) s. lujuria.
liability (laiabíliti) s. responsabilidad; riesgo, exposición; desventaja; **liabilities** obligaciones, pasivo. obligado; propenso.
liable (láiabl) adj. responsable.
liar (láiar) s. mentiroso.
libel (láibl) s. libelo; difamación; v. satirizar, difamar.
liberal (líberal) adj. y s. liberal.
liberality (liberáliti) s. liberalidad; largueza; dadivosidad.
liberate (líbereit) v. libertar; librar, soltar, redimir. ción.
liberation (liberéshon) s. liberación.
liberator (liberéitor) s. libertador.
libertine (líbertin) adj. y s. libertino, disoluto.
liberty (líberti) s. libertad.
librarian (laibrérian) s. bibliotecario.
library (láibreri) s. biblioteca.
lice (láis) pl. de **louse**.
license (láisens) **licence**; s. licencia; permiso; título, venia; facultad; autorización; **driver's** — licencia de chofer; título de conductor; — **plate** placa de circulación; v. licenciar, permitir, autorizar.
licentious (laisénshos) adj. licensioso, disoluto, desenfrenado.
lick (lik) v. lamer; dar una tunda o zurra; absorber; chupar; vencer; **to** — **someone's boots** adular a uno con servilismo; **to** — **the dust** morder el polvo; adular; s. lamedura; lamida; lengüetada; saladar, lamedero; **not to**

do a — of work no hacer absolutamente nada.
licking (líking) s. zurra, tunda.
lid (lid) s. tapadera, tapa; guardapolvo de reloj; **eye —** párpado.
lie (lái) s. mentira; embuste; ficción, falsedad; desmentida; caída; cubil; **to give the — to** dar un mentís; desmentir; v. mentir; echarse, tenderse; yacer; descansar; estar recostado; **to — in wait** acechar, espiar; **to — at stake** estar muy interesado en algo; **to — by** reposar.
lieutenant (liuténant) s. teniente; **second —** subteniente.
life (láif) s. vida; existencia; modo de vivir; relación o historia biográfica; **from —** del natural; **still —** naturaleza muerta; **— insurance** seguro de vida; **— boat** bote de salvamento, lancha salvavidas; **— belt** cinturón salvavidas; **— imprisonment** prisión perpetua; **— line** cuerda salvavidas.
lifeless (láifles) adj. sin vida; muerto; exánime.
lifelike (láiflaik) adj. como la vida; que parece vivo, natural.
lifelong (láiflong) adj. perpetuo; de toda la vida.
lifetime (láiftaim) s. vida, transcurso de la vida.
lift (lift) v. levantar; alzar; elevar; disiparse (las nubes, la niebla, las tinieblas); sopesar; exaltar, enlazar; quitar la presión; **to — one's hat** quitarse el sombrero (para saludar); s. elevación; esfuerzo para levantar; alzamiento; elevador, ascensor; **to give one a —** ayudar a uno a levantar algo.
light (láit) s. luz, lumbre; lumínico, claridad; bujía, lámpara; **tail —** farito trasero; farol de cola; adj. claro; con luz; de tez blanca; ligero, leve, sutil; boyante; llevadero; **— complexion** tez blanca; **— armed** armado a la ligera; **— keeper** torrero; **— headed** frívolo, ligero de cascos; **— heared** alegre; **to make — of** dar poca importancia a; v. encender; iluminar; alumbrar; dar luz; prender (fuego la luz); **to — upon** caer sobre; posarse en (dícese de los pájaros).
lighten (láitn) v. aligerar; iluminar; aclarar, hacer más claro.
lighter (láiter) s. encendedor.

lighthouse (láitjaus) s. faro.
lighting (láiting) s. iluminación; alumbrado; **electric —** alumbrado eléctrico.
lightly (láitli) adv. ligeramente; levemente.
lightness (láitnes) s. ligereza, frivolidad; agilidad, velocidad.
lightning (láitning) s. relampagueo; relámpago, centella; **— rod** pararrayos.
likable (láikebl) adj. agradable, simpático; atrayente, placentero.
like (láik) adv. y prep. como; del mismo modo que; semejante a; verosímilmente; adj. semejante, parecido; lo mismo que; **in — manner** de manera semejante, del mismo modo; **to look —** someone parecerse a alguien; **to give — for—** pagar en la misma moneda; s. semejante, igual; **—s** gustos, preferencias; v. gustarle a uno; hallar agrado en; contentarse con.
likely (láikli) adj. probable, creíble; prometedor; verosímil; adv. ligeramente; probablemente; prometedoramente.
liken (láikn) s. asemejar.
likeness (láiknes) s. semejanza; parecido; igualdad; viso, forma, retrato.
likewise (láikuais) adv. igualmente; asimismo; además.
liking (láiking) s. simpatía; afición; preferencia, gusto.
lilac (láilak) s. lila; adj. de color lila; aberenjenado, morado claro.
lily (líli) s. lirio; azucena.
limb (limb) s. rama; miembro del cuerpo, especialmente pierna, brazo; limbo, orilla, extremo.
limber (límber) flexible, blando; v. ablandar, hacer flexible.
lime (láim) s. cal; lima; v. encalar; unir con argamasa.
limelight (láimlait) s. proscenio; **to be in the —** estar en escena.
limestone (láimstoun) s. piedra de cal.
limit (límit) s. límite, término, fin; lindero; confín.
limitation (limitéshon) s. limitación; restricción, acotamiento.
limited (límited) adj. limitado, escaso; restringido; finito.
limitless (límitles) adj. ilimitado.
limp (limp) s. cojera; v. cojear; adj. flojo; flexible.

LIMPID — LOAF

limpid (límpid) adj. límpido, claro, transparente; limpio.
lineage (líney) s. linaje.
linear (línier) adj. lineal.
lined (láind) adj. rayado; forrado.
linen (línen) s. lino; ropa blanca
liner (láiner) s. vapor, buque; air — avión, transporte aéreo.
linger (línguer) v. tardar(se), demorar(se); andar ocioso; consumirse; padecer poco a poco o lentamente; vagar; perdurar; prolongarse. [de mujer.
lingerie (línyeri) s. ropa interior
lining (láining) s. forro.
link (link) s. eslabón; enlace; cuff —s gemelos; v. eslabonar.
linnet (línet) s. jilguero.
linoleum (linólium) s. linóleo (tela impermeable para cubrir el suelo).
linseed (línsid) s. linaza; — oil aceite de linaza.
lint (lint) s. hilaza; plumón.
lion (láion) s. león.
lioness (láiones) s. leona.
lip (lip) s. labio. ["billet".
lipstick (lipstik) s. lápiz labial;
liquid (líkuid) adj. líquido; fluido; blando; claro; — assets valores líquidos o irrealizables; s. líquido, licor.
liquidate (líkuideit) v. liquidar; saldar cuentas.
liquidation (likuidéshon) s. liquidación; saldo de cuentas.
liquor (líkr) s. licor, bebida espiritosa; como aguardiente, etc. malt — cerveza.
lisp (lisp) s. ceceo; v. cecear.
list (list) s. lista, registro; nómina; cédula de personas o cosas; escora; v. alistar, registrar; poner o apuntar en una lista; escorar; inclinarse a la banda.
listen (lisn) v. escuchar; atender; dar oídos; seguir un consejo; obedecer; atender una opinión; to — in escuchar por radio; escuchar a hurtadillas una conversación.
listener (lisner) s. oyente; oidor; radio — radioescucha, radiooyente.
listless (listles) adj. abstraído; indiferente; omiso; desatento.
listlessness (lístlesnes) s. indiferencia; descuido; omisión.
lit (lit) pret. y p.p. de **to light** alumbrado; algo borracho.
literal (líteral) adj. literal; exacto; —ly adv. literalmente.

literary (líterери) adj. literario.
literature (líterechur) s. literatura; impresos, folletos, circulares.
litigation (litiguéishon) s. litigio.
litter (líter) s. litera; camilla; parihuela; andas; cama de paja; cosas en desorden; v. desarreglar; revolver; desordenar; parir los animales.
little (lítl) adj. pequeño; chico; diminuto; menudo; breve; poco; a — while un ratito; — by — poco a poco; adv. poco, escasamente.
live (lív) v. vivir; existir; to — down borrar una falta; olvidar lo pasado; to — up to vivir de acuerdo con; cumplir una promesa.
live (láiv) adj. vivo; activo; eficaz; ardiente; dinámico; — coal ascua encendida; — oak encina; — question cuestión de actualidad palpitante; — wire circuito o alambre cargado; persona activa.
livelihood (láivlijud) s. vida; alimento; subsistencia; mantenimiento.
liveliness (láivlines) s. viveza; actividad; agilidad; despejo.
lively (láivli) adv. vivamente, vigorosamente; de prisa; adj. vivo; vivaz; vigoroso; enérgico; airoso; apresurado; animado; intensivo.
liver (líver) s. hígado.
livery (líveri) s. librea; caballeriza; — coach (horse) carruaje (caballo) de alquiler; auto — garaje para autos de alquiler.
lives (láivs) pl. de **life**.
livestock (láivstok) s. ganado; bienes semovientes; animales de granja.
livid (lívid) adj. lívido, amoratado.
living (líving) s. modo de vivir o de ganarse la vida; subsistencia; manutención; adj. vivo, viviente; animado; vigoroso; — room estancia; sala; the — los vivos.
lizard (líserd) s. lagarto; saurio; small — lagartija.
load (lóud) s. carga; peso; agobio; ship — cargamento de un barco; — water line línea de flotación; v. cargar; agobiar; colmar.
loaf (lóuf) s. hogaza de pan; — of sugar pan de azúcar; small — panecillo; v. haraganear; holgazanear
loafer (lóufer) s. haragán; holgazán.

loan (lóun) s. préstamo; empréstito; — **shark** usurero; v. prestar.
loath (lóuz) adj. renuente; opuesto; mal dispuesto; contrario.
loathe (lóuz) v. repugnarle a uno; aborrecer; detestar; abominar.
loathsome (lóuzsom) adj. repugnante; detestable, aborrecible; abominable; asqueroso.
loaves (lóuvs) pl. de loaf.
lobby (lóbi) s. vestíbulo; antecámara; camarilla; salón de entrada; v. cabildear (procurar ventajas en una asamblea o cuerpo legislativo).
lobster (lóbster) s. langosta.
local (lókal) adj. local, regional; — **train** tren ordinario o de escalas; circuito local.
locality (lokáliti) s. localidad.
localize (lókalais) s. localizar.
locate (lókeit) v. colocar; situar; averiguar la posición; avecindarse; radicarse; trazar la vía.
location (lokéshon) s. situación; ubicación; sitio; localidad.
lock (lók) s. cerradura; gatillo; esclusas; represa; cerca; vallado; guedeja; bucle; rizo; trenza; **pad** — candado; v. cerrar con llave, echar la cerradura; trabajar; juntar; entrelazar; **to — in** encerrar; **to — out** cerrar la puerta a uno para que no entre; **to — up** encarcelar; encerrar bajo llave.
locket (lóket) s. guardapelo.
lockout (lókaut) s. paro (suspensión de trabajo por parte de la empresa), cierre de una fábrica.
locksmith (lóksmiz) s. cerrajero.
locomotive (lokomótiv) s. locomotora; — **engineer** maquinista.
locust (lókost) s. langosta, saltamontes, cigarra; — **tree** algarrobo; acacia falsa.
lodge (loy) s. casa de guarda; pabellón; casa de campo; casita accesoria; logia; v. alojar, albergar; hospedar; colocar; habitar; vivir.
lodger (lódyer) s. huésped; inquilino.
lodging (lódying) s. posada; albergue, alojamiento; vivienda; hospedaje.
loft (loft) s. desván; galería; balcón interior de un templo; **choir —** coro; **hay —** pajar.
lofty (lófti) adj. alto; elevado; sublime; altivo; orgulloso.
log (lóg) s. leño, palo; tronco; troza; — **book** cuaderno de bitácora; diario de navegación; — **cabin** cabaña rústica; v. cortar árboles o leños y transportarlos.
logic (lóyic) s. lógica.
logical (lóyikal) adj. lógico.
loin (lóin) s. ijada, ijar; lomo.
loiter (lóiter) v. malgastar el tiempo; vagar; holgazanear; **to — behind** rezagarse.
loll (lol) v. recostarse; arrellanarse; ponerse cómodo.
lone (lóun) adj. solo; aislado; solitario; soltero(a).
loneliness (lóunlines) s. soledad.
lonely (lóunli) adj. solo, solitario; abandonado; triste; desamparado.
lonesome (lóunsom) adj. solitario; desierto; triste; nostálgico.
long (long) adj. largo; prolongado; tardo, lento; adv. mucho; durante; continuamente; **the whole day —** todo el santo día; — **after** mucho después; **three feet —** tres pies de largo; — **ago** (since) hace mucho tiempo; **do not be —** no se tarde en regresar; **as** (o) **so — mientras que, en tanto que; how — is it since?** ¿cuánto tiempo hace que...?; v. anhelar, ansiar; **to — for** anhelar, suspirar por.
longer (lónguer) adj. más largo; adv. más tiempo; **no —** ya no.
longevity (lonyéviti) s. longevidad.
longing (lónguing) s. anhelo, ansia; deseo vehemente; añoranza; adj. anhelante, ansioso, nostálgico; —**ly** adv. con vehemencia; impacientemente; con ansia.
longitude (lónyitiud) s. longitud.
longshoreman (lóngshorman) s. estivador; cargador de muelle.
look (luk) v.i. 1. mirar. 2. tener aspecto o cara de, \ej., 1. **ill** parecer enfermo 3. indicar, señalar, tender.
looking (lúking) s. mirada; — **glass** (lúkinglas) s. espejo; **good —** guapo.
lookout (lúkaut) s. vigía; vigilancia; atalaya; mirador; garita; **to be on the —** estar alerta; estar a la mira de.
loom (lum) s. telar; — **shuttle** lanzadera mecánica; v. asomar(se), aparecer; destacar; descollar; lucir.
loop (lup) s. lazo, gaza, ojal, presilla; vuelta; onda; abrazadera; curva; circuito; v. hacer gazas, formar festones; atar con una gaza o presilla.

loophole (lúpjou!) s. agujero; abertura; escapatoria; excusa; salida.
loose (lús) adj. suelto, desatado, flojo, holgado; v. desatar; soltar; aflojar; aliviar; — change moneda suelta, suelto; **to let —** soltar; **—ly** adv. flojamente; con soltura; holgadamente.
loosen (lúsn) v. aflojar(se); soltar(se); desatar(se); desligar; relajar(se); ablandar; librar.
looseness (lúsnes) s. flojedad, soltura; holgura; relajación; flujo; diarrea.
loot (lút) s. botín, pillaje, saqueo; v. saquear, pillar, robar.
lop (lop) v. desmochar, descabezar; s. rama podada; oreja gacha.
loquacious (lokuéshus) adj. locuaz; hablador, lenguaraz.
lord (lord) s. señor, amo, patrón, dueño; marido; lord; **Lord's Prayer** Padre Nuestro; **Our Lord** Nuestro Señor; v. mandar despóticamente; señorear; gobernár.
lordly (lórdli) adj. señoril; altivo; orgulloso; imperioso; adv. altivamente; imperiosamente.
lordship (lórdship) s. señorío, dominio; señoría, excelencia; **your —** Su señoría, Vuecencia.
lose (lús) v. perder; malograr; perderse; extraviarse; disipar.
loss (los) s. pérdida; daño; detrimento; **to be at a —** estar perplejo; no saber qué hacer; **to sell at a —** vender con pérdida.
lost (lost) pret. y p.p. de to lose perdido, extraviado, malogrado; perplejo, confuso; **— to insensible** a.
lot (lot) s. lote; suerte; fortuna; solar; porción de terreno; **a — of** (o **—s of**) una gran cantidad de, mucho; **to draw —s** echar suertes; **a — better** mucho mejor; v. asignar, repartir.
lotion (lóshon) s. loción.
lottery (lóteri) s. lotería.
loud (láud) adj. recio, ruidoso, fuerte, clamoroso; chillón (dícese de los colores); adv. ruidosamente; en voz alta.
loudspeaker (láudspiker) s. magnavoz; alto parlante.
lounge (láuny) s. sala de descanso; canapé, sofá, diván; v. arrellanarse; recostarse cómodamente; sestear; haraganear; gandulear.
louse (láus) s. piojo.
lousy (láusi) adj. piojoso; asqueroso; astroso; miserable.

lovable (lóvabl) adj. amable.
love (lóv) s. amor, cariño, afecto; persona amada; galanteo; **— affair** amorío; **to be in —** estar enamorado; **to fall in —** with enamorarse de; **to make — to** enamorar, cortejar; v. amar, querer, adorar, gustarle a uno mucho; tener inclinación o afición por algo.
loveliness (lóvlines) s. belleza, amabilidad, hermosura, agrado.
lovely (lóvli) adj. amable, cariñoso; lindo; bello; encantador.
lover (lóver) s. amante; **music —** aficionado o amante de la música.
loving (lóving) adj. amante, amoroso; cariñoso; aficionado; benigno; apacible; **—ly** con cariño, con ternura; amorosamente.
low (lóu) adj. bajo, profundo; módico; humilde; abatido; débil; gravemente enfermo; vulgar; vil, servil; **— comedy** farsa, sainete; **— gear** primera velocidad; **— necked** escotado; **— spirited** abatido; adv. bajo, en voz baja; quedo, quedito; a bajo precio; s. mugir, berrear.
lower (lóuer) adj. más bajo, inferior; v. bajar, disminuir, abatir; mirar ceñudo; **— case letter** letra minúscula; **— house** cámara de diputados; **to — the sails** arriar las velas.
lowland (lóuland) s. tierra baja.
lowliness (lóulines) s. bajeza; vileza; humildad.
lowly (lóuli) adv. humildemente; adj. vil, ruin, despreciable; inferior, humilde, sumiso.
lowness (lóunes) s. bajeza; humildad; abatimiento, postración; baratura; gravedad de tono; suavidad de sonido.
loyal (lóial) adj. leal, constante; fiel.
loyalty (lóialti) s. lealtad, fidelidad; constancia.
lubricant (lúbricant) adj. y s. lubricante.
lubricate (lúbrikeit) v. lubricar; engrasar.
lucid (lúsid) adj. lúcido, diáfano; claro; transparente, luminoso.
luck (lók) s. suerte, fortuna; acaso, azar; **good —** fortuna, dicha; **in bad —** de mala suerte; **for —** para que traiga suerte.
luckily (lókili) adv. afortunadamente; felizmente; dichosamente.

lucky (lóki) adj. afortunado, feliz, venturoso; propicio; **to be —** tener suerte; ser afortunado.
lucrative (lúkrativ) adj. lucrativo.
ludicrous (lúdikros) adj. ridículo.
lug (log) v. llevar, tirar de una cosa; **to — away** cargar con, llevarse (una cosa pesada).
luggage (lóguey) s. equipaje.
lukewarm (lúkuorm) adj. tibio, templado; seco, frío.
lull (lol) v. arrullar, sosegar; calmar; adormecer.
lullaby (lólabai) s. arrullo; canción de cuna.
lumber (lómber) s. madera; tablazón; maderaje; **— man** maderero; negociante en madera; **— room** cuarto de trastos; v. cortar y aserrar madera; explotar los bosques.
luminous (lúminos) adj. luminoso.
lump (lomp) s. terrón; bulto; hinchazón; masa; burujón; chichón; **— of sugar** terrón de azúcar; v. amontonar, consolidar (gastos); trabajar como estibador.
lumpy (lómpi) adj. aterronado.
lunatic (lúnatik) adj. y s. lunático.
lunch (lonch) s. almuerzo; merienda; refacción; lonche; **— room** merendero; v. merendar, tomar un bocado; almorzar.
luncheon (lónchon) s. almuerzo, merienda; ambigú.
lung (long) s. pulmón.
lurch (lorch) s. sacudida; tambaleo repentino; vaivén; **to give a — tambalearse; to leave one in the —** dejar a uno en las astas del toro; v. tambalearse, dar un tambaleo repentino, cabecear.
lure (lur) s. aliciente; señuelo; tentación; v. atraer (con cebo o reclamo); persuadir, seducir; entruchar; tentar.
lurk (lerk) v. estar oculto; espiar, acechar, estar en acecho; moverse furtivamente.
luscious (lóshus) adj. exquisito; grato, sabroso, meloso.
lust (lost) s. lujuria, deseo vehemente; codicia.
luster (lóster) s. lustre, brillo.
lustrous (lóstros) adj. lustroso.
lusty (lósti) adj. vigoroso, fornido, robusto, lozano.
lute (lut) s. laúd.
luxuriant (logshúriant) adj. lozano; frondoso, exuberante.

luxurious (logshúrios) adj. lujoso, dado al lujo; fastuoso.
luxury (lókshuri) s. lujo.
lye (lái) s. lejía.
lynx (links) s. lince.
lyre (láir) s. lira.
lyric (líric) s. poema, lírico; adj. lírico.
lyrical (lírikal) adj. lírico.
lyricism (líricism) s. lirismo.

M

macaroni (macaróni) s. macarrón o macarrones.
macaroon (macarún) s. macarrón pasta hecha con almendras.
machine (mashín) s. máquina, automóvil, ingenio, aparato; **— man** negociante en máquinas; **— gun** ametralladora; **— shop** taller de maquinaria.
machinery (mashíneri) s. maquinaria.
machinist (mashínist) s. mecánico, maquinista.
mackerel (mákerel) s. escombro; caballa (pez).
mad (mad) adj. loco; rabioso; furioso; demente, lunático, maníaco; enojado; **to drive —** enloquecer; volver loco; **— doctor** alienista; adv. locamente.
madam, madame (mádam) s. madama, señora.
madcap (mádcap) s. calavera; botarate; temerario; atolondrado.
madden (madn) v. enloquecer(se).
madman (mádman) s. loco, orate.
madness (mádnes) s. locura; demencia; furor, arrebato, rabia.
magazine (magasín) s. revista; almacén de explosivos; **powder —** polvorín.
magic (máyic) s. magia; adj. mágico.
magician (mayíshan) s. mago, brujo.
magistrate (máyistreit) s. magistrado.
magnanimous (magnánimos) adj. magnánimo; noble.
magnet (mágnet) s. imán; magneto.
magnetic (magnétic) adj. magnético.
magnificence (magnifísens) s. magnificencia; grandiosidad, esplendor.
magnificent (magnifísent) adj. magnífico; suntuoso, grandioso.
magnify (mágnifai) v. amplificar; engrandecer; exaltar; exagerar.

magnitude (mágnitiud) s. magnitud.

magpie (mágpai) s. urraca; cotorra; hablador.

mahogany (majógani) s. caoba.

maid (méid) s. sirvienta; criada; camarera; recamarera; mucama; doncella; soltera; virgen; **old —** solterona; **— of honor** dama de honor; **— servant** criada; fámula.

maiden (méidn) s. doncella; virgen; joven soltera; adj. virginal, primer(o), inicial; **— lady** mujer soltera; **— voyage** primer viaje.

mail (méil) s. correo; correspondencia; **air —** correo aéreo; **— bag** valija; **— train** tren correo; v. mandar una carta por correo.

mailbox (méilboks) s. buzón.

mailman (méilman) s. cartero.

maim (meim) v. mutilar, cortar, lisiar.

main (méin) adj. principal; mayor; importante; esencial; gran (de); s. océano; alta mar; cañería principal; **—ly** adv. principalmente; primeramente; **in the —** en su mayor parte; en general; en conjunto.

mainland (méinland) s. continente; tierra firme; tierra adentro.

maintain (meintéin) v. mantener; sostener; sustentar; afirmar; tener; guardar; conservar.

maintenance (méintenans) s. mantenimiento; sostenimiento; sustento; apoyo; protección; manutención.

maize (méis) s. maíz, zara.

majestic (mayéstic) adj. majestuoso.

majesty (máyesti) s. majestad; poder.

major (méyor) s. mayor; más grande; comandante; principal; mayor de edad; **— key** tono mayor; curso o asignatura de especialización; v. especializarse (en un curso de estudios).

majority (mayóriti) s. mayoría; mayoría de edad.

make (méik) v. hacer, producir, fabricar; formar; ejecutar; pronunciar un discurso; relatar; obtener; ganar; obligar, compeler; calcular; sacar una suma; tender la cama; aderezar; **to — a clean breast of** confesar; **to — a train** alcanzar un tren; **to — a turn** dar vuelta; **to — after** tratar de coger, seguir; **to — away with** derrochar; llevarse; hurtar; matar; **to — believe** fingir, pretender; **to — headway** progresar, adelantar, avanzar; **to — much of** dar demasiada importancia a; **to — nothing out of** no comprender, no sacar nada en claro de; **to — out** llegar a comprender; establecer; probar; **to — over** rehacer; transferir; ceder; confiar; **to — sure** asegurarse, cerciorarse; **to — the most of** aprovecharlo todo; sacar toda la ventaja posible; **to — to, for** (o) **toward** dirigirse a, encaminarse a; **to — up** hacer las paces, contentarse; compensar por una pérdida; pintarse, maquillarse; resolverse; s. hechura, forma manufactura, marca.

maker (méiker) s. artífice, constructor; fabricante; autor.

make-up (méikop) s. maquillaje; afeites; cosméticos; conjunto; carácter; modo; compostura; naturaleza.

malady (máladi) s. enfermedad, mal.

malaria (maléria) s. malaria, paludismo.

malcontent (malkontént) adj. y s. malcontento; descontento.

male (méil) adj. masculino; macho; varonil; de hombre; s. macho; varón; hombre; animal macho.

malice (mális) s. malicia.

malicious (malishus) adj. malicioso; perverso; maléfico; ruin; malévolo.

malign (maláin) adj. maligno; dañino; pernicioso; v. envidiar; perjudicar; calumniar.

malignant (malignant) adj. maligno; malévolo; nocivo.

mallet (málet) s. mazo; mallete; maceta.

malt (molt) s. malta; **—ed milk** leche malteada.

mama, mamma (máma) s. mamá.

mammal (mámal) s. mamífero.

mammoth (mámoz) adj. mamut, enorme, gigantesco.

mammy (mámi) s. mamita; niñera negra; nana.

man (man) s. hombre; varón; alguien; cualquiera; marido; **to a —** unánimemente; todos a una; **officers and men** oficiales y soldados; **man-of-war** buque de guerra; **— cook** cocinero; v. tripular; armar; guarnecer; manhater misántropo; merchant — buque mercante.

manage (máney) v. manejar; conducir; gobernar; dirigir; regentear; to — to do something arreglárselas para hacer algo.

manageable (máneyebl) adj. manejable; dócil, tratable; domable.

management (máneyment) s. gerencia; administración; dirección; manejo; gobierno, régimen.

manager (mánayer) s. gerente, director, administrador; empresario.

mandate (mándeit) s. mandato; orden; precepto; mandamiento.

mane (méin) s. melena de león; crin del caballo.

maneuver (manúver) s. maniobra; evolución; v. maniobrar; hacer evoluciones; intrigar; tramar.

manful (mánful) adj. valiente; varonil, viril; bravo.

manganese (manganís) s. manganeso.

mange (méiny) s. sarna, roña.

manger (méinyer) s. pesebre.

mangle (mangl) v. mutilar, destrozar; magullar; satinar, lustrar; planchar a máquina; s. máquina de planchar.

mangy (méinyi) adj. sarnoso, roñoso.

manhood (mánjud) s. virilidad; edad viril; masculinidad; fortaleza.

mania (ménia) s. manía.

manicure (mánikiur) s. manicura; v. manicurar; arreglarse las uñas.

manifest (mánifest) adj. manifiesto; s. manifiesto; v. manifestar, declarar, hacer patente; expresar; demostrar; revelar.

manifestation (manifestéshon) s. manifestación; declaración.

manifesto (manifésto) s. manifiesto; declaración; bando; proclama.

manifold (mánifould) s. exhaust — tubo de escape; adj. múltiple; variado; diverso.

manikin (ménikin) s. maniquí; muñeco.

manila (manila) s. abacá (cáñamo de Manila); — **paper** papel Manila.

manipulate (manípiuleit) v. manipular; manejar; trabajar con las manos.

manipulation (manipiuléshon) s. manipulación.

mankind (mankáind) s. humanidad; género humano; los hombres.

manly (mánli) adj. varonil; viril; valiente; valeroso; adv. varonilmente.

manner (máner) s. manera, modo, forma; costumbre; hábito; aire; ademán; porte; —s modales, comportamiento; conducta; **in this** — así, de este modo; **by no** — **of means** de ninguna manera o modo; **he has no** —**s es un** malcriado.

mannish (mánish) adj. hombruno.

manoeuvre véase **maneuver**.

manor (mánor) s. finca solariega; feudo; solar.

mansion (mánshon) s. mansión, residencia; palacio.

manslaughter (mánsloter) s. homicidio impremeditado o casual.

mantel (mántl) s. manto (de una chimenea), repisa de chimenea.

mantle (mantl) s. manto, capa; v. cubrir, tapar, ocultar.

manual (mániual) adj. manual; — **training school** escuela de artes y oficios; s. manual; teclado de órgano.

manufacture (maniufákchur) s. manufactura; fabricación; v. fabricar; manufacturar; elaborar.

manufacturer (maniufákchurer) s. manufacturero; fabricante; industrial.

manufacturing (maniufákchuring) s. industria, fabricación; adj. fabril, fabricante, manufacturero.

manure (maniúr) s. abono, estiércol.

manuscript (mániuskript) adj. y s. manuscrito; códice.

many (méni) adj. muchos; varios; diversos; — **a time** muchas veces; **a great** — muchísimos; **as** — **as** tantos como; **too** — demasiados; **one too** — uno de más; **twice as** — el doble, otros tantos, tantos.

map (map) s. mapa; carta geográfica; **to** — **out** proyectar; planear.

maple (mépl) s. arce; maple.

mar (mar) v. echar a perder, estropear; desfigurar; s. mancha.

marble (marbl) s. mármol, canica; adj. de mármol, marmóreo.

march (march) s. marcha, caminata; v. marchar; hacer mar-

char; to — up adelantar, avanzar.
March (march) s. marzo.
mare (mer) s. yegua.
margin (máryin) s. margen, borde, orilla; reserva; sobrante.
marginal (máryinl) adj. marginal; — **note** acotación, apostilla.
marigold (mérigould) s. caléndula, maravilla.
marine (marín) adj. marino; marítimo; s. marino, soldado de marina; — **corps** cuerpo de marinos; **merchant** — marina mercante.
mariner (máriner) s. marinero.
maritime (máritim) adj marítimo.
marker (márker) s. marcador; marca; señal; ficha, colme; jalón.
market (márket) s. mercado, plaza; emporio; bazar; — **place** mercado; — **day** día de mercado; — **rate** tipo de mercado; v. vender o comprar en el mercado; llevar a vender al mercado; mercar; **to go** —**ing** ir de compras.
marmalade (mármeleid) s. mermelada.
maroon (marún) s. y adj. rojo obscuro; v. abandonar a uno en costa desierta.
marooned (marúnd) adj. abandonado (en lugar desierto); aislado; **to get** — encontrarse aislado, perdido o incomunicado.
marquis (márkuis) s. marqués.
marquise (markís) s. marquesa.
marriage (márriey) s. matrimonio; casamiento, boda; nupcias; unión, enlace; — **license** licencia para casarse.
married (márrid) adj. casado, matrimonial; conyugal; — **couple** pareja de casados.
marrow (márrou) s. meollo; médula (de los huesos); substancia; esencia.
marry (márri) v. casar, casarse; casarse con; unir en matrimonio.
marsh (marsh) s. pantano, ciénaga.
marshal (márshal) s. mariscal; alguacil; bastonero o maestro de ceremonias; jefe de policía (en ciertas regiones); **fire** — jefe de bomberos; **town** — alguacil mayor; v. poner en orden; arreglar.
marshmallow (márshmalou) s. pastilla o bombón de altea; malvavisco.

marshy (márshi) adj. pantanoso; cenagoso; lagunoso.
mart (mart) s. mercado.
martial (márshal) adj. marcial; militar; bélico; — **law** estado de guerra.
martin (mártin) s. avión (pájaro).
martyr (mártir) s. mártir; v. martirizar; torturar, atormentar.
martyrdom (mártirdom) s. martirio. [digio; v. maravillarse.
marvel (marvl) s. maravilla; prodigio;
marvelous (márvelous) adj. maravilloso.
masculine (máskiulin) adj. masculino
mash (mash) s. amasar, machacar; triturar, estrujar; magullar; —**ed potatoes** patatas majadas.
mask (mask) s. máscara, antifaz; disfraz; mascarilla de una persona muerta; v. disfrazar, enmascarar; disimular; ocultar.
mason (méisn) s. albañil; abeja albañila; **Mason** masón, francmasón.
masonry (mésonri) s. albañilería; mampostería; masonería; **Masonry** francmasonería.
masquerade (maskeréd) s. mascarada; disfraz; comparsa; v enmascararse; andar disfrazado; ir disfrazado.
mass (mas) s. **masa**; montón, mole; mayoría; misa; — **meeting** mitin popular; — **book** libro de misa; v. reunir(se) en masa.
massacre (másaker) s. hecatombe; matanza, carnicería; mortandad, destrozo; v. hacer matanza.
massage (masáy) v. friccionar, dar masaje; s. masaje.
massive (másiv) adj. sólido; macizo, voluminoso; pesado, abultado.
mast (mast) s. mástil, palo.
master (máster) s. amo; señor, maestro; director; gobernador, jefe; experto; perito; **band** — director de orquesta; — **of arts** maestro en artes; licenciado; — **jest** chiste notable; — **key** llave maestra; — **builder** maestro de obras; v. dominar; domar; gobernar; ser superior en alguna cosa.
masterful (másterful) adj. magistral; dominante; imperioso; perito
masterly (másterli) adj. magistral; maestro; adv. magistralmente
masterpiece (másterpis) s. obra maestra; obra magistral

mastery (másteri). s. maestría, arte, destreza, dominio; poder, gobierno.

mastiff (mástif) s. mastín, alano.

mat (mat) s. estera; esterilla; petate; felpudo; colchoncillo (de gimnasia); cartón de estereotipia; borde de cartón (para hacer resaltar una pintura).

match, s. 1. fósforo, cerillo. 2. mecha, cuerda (combustible, para prender fuego a cañón, mina, etc.).

matchless (mátchles) adj. sin par; sin igual; incomparable.

mate (méit) s. consorte; compañero; pareja; macho o hembra; piloto; oficial subalterno de la marina; v. casar; aparear; competir.

material (matírial) adj. material, esencial; s. material, ingrediente materia; género; **raw** — materia prima.

maternal (matérnal) adj. maternal.

maternity (matérniti) s. maternidad.   [matemático.

mathematical (mazemátikal) adj.

mathematician (mazematíshan) s. matemático.   [temáticas.

mathematics (mazemátiks) s. matemáticas.

matinée (matiné) s. función de la mañana o la tarde; matiné.

matriculate (matríkiuleit) v. matricular(se).

matriculation (matrikiuléshon) s. matriculación.

matrimony (mátrimoni) s. matrimonio; casamiento.

matrix (métriks) s. matriz, molde.

matron (métron) s. matrona, madre de familia; ama de llaves; directora de instituto; celadora, vigilante; cuidadora de un asilo o cárcel para mujeres, etc.

matter (máter) s. materia, cuerpo, sustancia; material; sujeto, asunto, objeto o cuestión de que se trata; negocio; cosa; pus; **— for complaint** motivo de queja; **— of hours** cosa de horas; **a — of fact** un hecho, cosa positiva, realidad; **business —s** asuntos de negocios; **printed —** impresos; **a — of course** una cosa de cajón, de rutina; **what is the —?** ¿Qué pasa? ¿Qué tiene usted? **— of fact person** persona que sólo toma en cuenta los hechos; **it does not —** no importa; v. importar; hacer caso; convenir; hacer al caso alguna cosa.

mattress (mátres) s. colchón; cojín grande; **spring —** colchón de resortes o muelles.

mature (matiúr) adj. maduro, sazonado; vencido; **a — note** un pagaré o letra vencida; v. madurar; sazonar; cumplir o vencerse un plazo.

maturity (matiúriti) s. madurez; sazón; vencimiento.

maul (mol) v. apalear; aporrear; magullar; tratar con rudeza.

maxim (máksim) s. máxima.

maximun (máksimum) adj. y s. máximo.

may (méi) v. irr. y defec. poder; tener permiso para; ser lícito o posible; serle permitido a uno; **— I come in?** ¿puedo entrar?; **it — be** puede ser, es posible; quizás; **it — rain** puede ser que llueva; **if I — say so** si se me permite decirlo; **— you have a good time** que se divierta usted; **she — be late** puede ser que llegue ella tarde.

May (méi) s. mayo, quinto mes del año; **— Queen** Reina de las fiestas de mayo, maya; **— Day** Primero de Mayo.

maybe (méibi) adv. quizás, tal vez; acaso; probablemente; es posible.

mayonnaise (maionés) s. mayonesa.

mayor (méior) s. alcalde principal.

maze (méis) s. laberinto; enredo; confusión; **to be in a —** estar perplejo o confundido.

me (mi) pron. pers. me, mí, yo; **as for —** en cuanto a mí; **give it to —** démelo; **for —** para mí; **with —** conmigo; **do — the favor** hágame favor.

meadow (médou) s. pradera, prado, vera; henar.

meager (míger) adj. magro, flaco; insuficiente; escaso; seco; pobre.

meal (mil) s. comida; harina (medio molida); **corn —** harina de maíz; **— time** hora de comer.

mean (mín) adj. humilde, mediano; inferior; pobre; bajo; vil; ruin; tacaño, mezquino; de mal genio, malo; medio, intermedio; **in the — time** entre tanto, mientras; interin; **— distance** distancia media; s. medio; término medio; **—s** medios, recursos; **by all —s** positivamente; sin falta; **by no —s** de ningún modo, de

ninguna manera; v. pensar, proponerse, tener la intención de; querer decir, significar; what do you —? ¿qué quiere usted decir? he did not — to do it lo hizo sin querer, sin intención.

meaning (míning) s. significado, sentido; ánimo; intención; designio; adj. significativo.

meaningless (míningles) adj. sin o vacío de sentido, sin objeto.

meanness (mínes) s. bajeza, vileza; infamia; ruindad; tacañería.

meant (ment) pret. y p.p. de **to mean**.

meantime (míntaim) adv. mientras tanto, entre tanto; en el intervalo.

meanwhile (mínjuail) véase **meantime**.

measles (mísls) s. sarampión.

measurable (méshurabl) adj. mensurable; limitado en cantidad; **measurably** adv. mesuradamente.

measure (méshur) s. medida; compás; metro, cadencia; modo, grado; expediente; propuesta de ley; **dry —** medida para áridos; **beyond —** con exceso, sobremanera; v. medir, juzgar; valuar; proporcionar.

measured (méshurd) adj. medido, calculado; moderado; acompasado.

measurement (méshurment) s. medida; dimensión; medición; tamaño.

meat (mit) s. carne, vianda; meollo; sustancia; **stewed —** estofado; **— ball** albóndiga; **— market** carnicería; **cold —** fiambre; **chopped, hashed, minced —** picadillo.

meaty (míti) adj. carnoso; sustancioso.

mechanic (mekánic) adj. y s. mecánico; maquinal; s. obrero mecánico.

mechanical (mekánikl) adj. mecánico; maquinal.

mechanism (mékanism) s. mecanismo.

medal (médal) s. medalla.

meddle (medl) v. inmiscuirse, entremeterse; ingerirse.

meddler (médler) s. entremetido.

meddlesome (médlsom) adj. entremetido.

median (mídian) adj. del medio; mediano; s. punto, línea o número del medio; mediana.

mediate (mídiet) v. mediar; intervenir; arbitrar; adj. mediato; interpuesto; medio.

mediation (midiéshon) s. mediación; intervención; intercesión; tercería.

mediator (mídietor) s. mediador; intercesor; medianero; árbitro.

medical (médikal) adj. médico; curativo **— school** escuela de medicina.

medicine (médicin) s. medicina, medicamento; droga; remedio; **— chest** botiquín; **— man** curandero indio; **patent —** medicina de patente.

medieval (midíval) adj. medieval, de la edad media.

mediocre (midióker) adj. mediocre; mediano; ordinario; vulgar; trivial.

mediocrity (midiókriti) s. mediocridad; medianía.

meditate (méditeit) v. meditar.

meditation (meditéshon) s. meditación; reflexión; cogitación.

medium (mídium) s. medio, expediente; instrumento; medio ambiente; adj. mediano, intermedio; a medio cocer, a medio asar.

medley (médli) s. miscelánea, mezcla; mezcolanza; revoltijo.

meek (mik) adj. manso, dócil, sumiso; apacible; sufrido.

meekness (míknes) s. mansedumbre; docilidad; humildad; suavidad.

meet (mit) v. encontrar; hallar; tropezar con; reunir(se); conocer; ser presentado a; ir a esperar un barco, un tren; satisfacer; llenar; pagar; saldar; refutar; batirse; enfrentarse a; **to — expenses** hacer frente a los gastos; **to — with** encontrarse con; topar con alguien; **to — half way** partir la diferencia; adj. apto, idóneo, propio; s. concurso, contienda; **track —** competencia de atletas.

meeting (míting) s. reunión, mitin; asamblea; junta; congreso; entrevista; conferencia.

megaphone (mégafon) s. megáfono, bocina, altoparlante.

melancholy (mélankoli) s. melancolía; adj. melancólico.

mellow (mélou) adj. maduro, sazonado; meloso; tierno, blando, suave; v. madurar(se); ablandar(se), suavizar(se).

melodious (melódios) adj. melodioso.

melody (mélodi) s. melodía.
melon (mélon) s. melón.
melt (melt) v. fundir, derretir, disolver; **to — into tears** deshacerse en llanto.
member (mémber) s. miembro, socio.
membership (mémbership) s. calidad de miembro o socio; número de socios de un club o asociación.
membrane (mémbren) s. membrana.
memento (memento) s. memento, memoria, recuerdo.
memoir (mémuar) s. memoria, relación; pl. memorias, autobiografías.
memorable (mémorabl) adj. memorable.
memorandum (memorándum) s. memorándum; nota, apunte, minuta; **— book** agenda; libro de memorias.
memorial (memórial) s. conmemorativo; monumento conmemorativo; memorial, petición; ocurso; nota.
memorize (mémorais) v. aprender de memoria; recordar, memorar.
memory (mémori) s. memoria; recuerdo.
men (men) pl. de **man**.
menace (ménes) s. amenaza. v. amenazar.
mend (mend) v. componer, reparar, remendar; corregir; enmendar; reformar; **to — one's way** enmendarse; s. reparación; mejoría; reforma.
menial (mínial) adj. doméstico; servil; bajo; s. criado, lacayo.
menstruation (menstruéshon) s. menstruación.
mental (méntal) adj. mental.
mentality (mentáliti) s. mentalidad; ingenio.
mention (ménshon) s. mención; alusión; recuerdo; v. mencionar, mentar, aludir; **don't — it** no hay de qué (contestación a "thank you").
menu (méniu) s. menú, la carta o lista de platillos que se sirven.
meow (miau) véase **mew**.
mercantile (mércantil) adj. mercantil; comercial.
mercenary (mérsneri) adj. mercenario; venal, interesado.
merchandise (mérchandais) s.
mercancía; mercadería; efectos; géneros; **piece of —** mercancía.
merchant (mérchant) s. comerciante; negociante; mercader; adj. mercante; mercantil; **— marine** marina mercante; **— commission —** comisionista, corredor.
merciful (mérsiful) adj. misericordioso; piadoso, clemente.
merciless (mérciles) adj. impío; cruel, inhumano, desalmado.
mercury (mérkiuri) s. mercurio, azogue.
mercy (mérsi) s. misericordia, clemencia; merced, favor, gracia; **to be at the —** of estar a merced de; **for —!** ¡por piedad!
mere (mír) adj. mero, puro, simple; solo, no más; **a — formality** una pura formalidad; **a — trifle** una nonada, una cosa sin importancia; **—ly** adv. meramente, puramente; solamente; simplemente.
merge (mery) v. unir(se); fundir(se); combinar(se); asociar(se); absorber(se).
meridian (meridian) adj. y s. meridiano.
merit (mérit) s. mérito; v. merecer.
meritorious (meritórios) adj. meritorio.
merrily (mérrili) adv. regocijadamente.
merriment (mérriment) s. alegría, regocijo; diversión; júbilo.
merry (mérri) adj. alegre, regocijado; gozoso; jovial, divertido; risueño, placentero; **— Christmas** Felices Pascuas.
merry-go-round (mérrigorráund) s. el carrusel, los caballitos.
merrymaker (mérrimeiker) s. fiestero; parrandero; juerguista.
merrymaking (mérrimeiking) s. regocijo; jolgorio; juerga; parranda; adj. regocijado; festivo; alegre.
mesh (mesh) s. malla de una red, **—es** redes; v. coger con red; enredar; **to — gears** engranar.
message (mésey) s. mensaje; aviso; parte, recado; comunicación.
messenger (mésenyer) s. mensajero; mandadero; nuncio.
met (met) pret. y p.p. de **to meet**.
metal (métal) s. metal; vidrio en fusión; cualidad, esencia; **Babbitt —** metal blando de antifricción.
metallic (metálik) adj. metálico.

metallurgy (métaloryi) s. metalurgia.
metaphor (métafor) s. metáfora.
meteor (mítior) s. meteoro; estrella fugaz; exhalación.
meteorological (mitiorolóyikal) adj. meteorológico.
meteorology (mitioróloyi) s. meteorología.
meter (míter) s. metro; medidor; contador (de gas, de agua, de electricidad, etc.).
method (mézod) s. método, técnica.
methodical (mezódikal) adj. metódico.
metre (mítr) véase **meter**.
metric (métrik) adj. métrico.
metropolis (metrópolis) s. metrópoli.
metropolitan (metropólitan) adj. metropolitano.
mettle (métl) s. temple, brío, valor, coraje; vivacidad, fuego.
mew (miú) s. maullido, maúllo, miau, v. maullar; enjaular; encerrar.
Mexican (méksican) adj. y s. mexicano.
mezzanine (mésanin) s. entresuelo.
mice (máis) pl. de **mouse**.
microbe (máikroub) s. microbio.
microphone (máikrofoun) s. micrófono.
microscope (máikroskoup) s. microscopio.
microscopic (maikroskópik) adj. microscópico.
midday (mídei) s. mediodía; adj. del mediodía.
middle (mídl) adj. medio, intermedio; **Middle Ages** Edad Media; — **finger** dedo del corazón; — **size** tamaño mediano; s. medio, centro, mitad; **in the** — **of** en medio de; a la mitad de; **towards the** — **of the month** a mediados del mes.
middle-aged (mídleyd) adj. de edad madura.
middleman (mídlman) s. intermediario; corredor; agente.
middle-sized (mídlsaisd) adj. de mediana estatura; de tamaño mediano.
middy (mídi) s. guardiamarina; — **blouse** blusa a la marinera.
midget (mídyet) s. enanito; mosquito.
midnight (mídnait) s. medianoche; adj. nocturno; — **blue** azul oscuro — **Mass** misa de gallo.

midshipman (mídshipman) s. guardiamarina.
midst (mídst) s. medio, centro; adv. en medio; **in the** — **of** en medio de, entre; **in our** — entre nosotros.
midstream (mídstrim) s. el medio de una corriente.
midsummer (mídsomer) s. pleno verano; solsticio estival; la mitad del verano.
midterm (mídterm) — **examination** examen a mitad del curso.
midway (míduei) adj. situado a mitad del camino; equidistante; adv. a medio camino; en medio del camino.
midwife (míduaif) s. partera, comadrona; matrona.
mien (min) s. semblante, aspecto; facha; porte; talante.
might (máit) imperf. de **may**; s. poder, fuerza, poderío.
mighty (máiti) adj. potente, poderoso; fuerte, vigoroso; enorme; adv. extremadamente, sumamente; muy.
migrate (máigreit) v. emigrar.
migration (maigréshon) s. migración.
mike (máik) véase **microphone**.
mild (máild) adj. suave, apacible, benigno, dócil, manso; templado; moderado.
mildness (máildnes) s. suavidad; lenidad; mansedumbre, apacibilidad; templanza, dulzura.
mile (máil) s. milla; — **stone** piedra miliaria; mojonera.
mileage (máiley) s. millaje; longitud en millas; recorrido (en millas), número de millas.
military (míliteri) adj. militar; de guerra; bélico; s. tropa; el ejército.
militia (milísha) s. milicia.
milk (mílk) s. leche; v. ordeñar; — **warm** tibio; — **diet** dieta o régimen lácteo.
milkmaid (mílkmeid) s. lechera.
milkman (mílkman) s. lechero; vaquero.
milky (mílki) adj. lácteo; lechoso; **Milky Way** La Vía Láctea.
miller (míler) s. molinero, mariposa nocturna.
milliner (míliner) s. modista de sombreros.
millinery (mílineri) s. sombreros de señora; artículos para sombreros de señora; oficio de modista; — **shop** sombrerería.

million (mílion) s. millón; **a — dollars** un millón de dólares.
millionaire (milioner) s. y adj. millonario.
millionth (milionz) adj. y s. millonésimo.
millstone (mílstoun) s. muela, piedra de molino; carga pesada.
mimic (mímik) adj. mímico; imitativo, burlesco; s. pantomima; remedo; imitador; v. imitar; remedar.
mince (mins) v. picar; desmenuzar; hacer picadillo; **— pie** pastel relleno de picadillo, fruta y especias.
mincemeat (mínsmit) s. picadillo de carne, pasas, manzanas y especies.
mind (maind) s. mente, entendimiento; pensamiento; ingenio; espíritu, ánimo; gusto, propensión; voluntad; gana; propósito, intención; opinión, parecer; **to make up one's —** resolverse, decidirse; **to be out of one's —** estar loco; haber perdido el juicio; **to have in —** tener presente, no olvidar, tener en cuenta; **whit one —** unánimemente; **to change one's —** cambiar de parecer o de opinión; **to have a —** tener ganas, estar dispuesto a; **to my —** a mi modo de ver; v. notar, considerar, observar, cuidar, observar, cuidar, vigilar; recordar; **I dont — no** tengo inconveniente; no me importa; **never — —** no importa; no se preocupe usted; no haga caso; **— your business** métase usted en lo que le importa; **— him** ten cuidado con él; **— reader** adivinador.
mindful (máindful) adj. atento; cuidadoso; diligente.
mine (máin) pron. pos. mío, mía, el mío, la, los, las mías; **a book of —** un libro mío; **it is —** es mío(a).
mine (máin) s. mina; v. minar; explotar una mina; extraer mineral; **— sweeper** dragaminas.
miner (máiner) s. minero.
mineral (míneral) s. mineral.
mingle (mingl) v. mezclar(se); confundir(se); juntar(se); unir(se).
miniature (míniechur) s. miniatura; en miniatura; diminuto.
minimize (mínimais) v. empequeñecer; reducir al mínimo; achicar.

minimum (mínimum) adj. y s. mínimo.
mining (máining) s. minería; explotación de minas; adj. minero, de mina; **— engineer** ingeniero de minas.
minister (mínister) s. ministro; pastor; clérigo; v. ministrar; suministrar; proveer de; socorrer; asistir; dar.
ministry (mínistri) s. ministerio; cargo, incumbencia; ayuda, intervención; socorro.
mink (mink) s. visón.
minnow (mínou) s. pez chico de río.
minor (máinor) adj. menor, de menor edad; secundario; inferior; **— key** tono menor; s. menor de edad; premisa menor de un silogismo; curso o asignatura menor.
minority (minóriti) s. minoría; los menos; minoridad.
minstrel (mínstrel) s. trovador; cantor cómico que remeda a los negros; bardo; vate.
mint (mint) s. menta; yerbabuena; casa de moneda; **a — of money** un montón de dinero; la mar de dinero; v. acuñar moneda; forjar.
minuet (miniuét) s. minué.
minus (máinus) adj. menos; negativo; falto de; sin; **three — two** tres menos dos; s. signo de menos.
minute (miniút) s. minuto; momento; instante; **—s** actas, minutas; **— hand** minutero del reloj.
minute (mínit) adj. menudo, diminuto; minucioso, detallado.
miracle (mírakl) s. milagro; maravilla, prodigio.
miraculous (mirákiulous) adj. milagroso; sobrenatural.
mirage (miráy) s. espejismo.
mire (máir) s. cieno, fango, lodo; limo; v. atascar(se) en el fango.
mirth (merz) s. júbilo; alegría, contento; regocijo.
mirthful (mérzful) adj. jubiloso; regocijado; alegre; gozoso.
miry (máiri) adj. cenagoso, fangoso; lodoso.
misbehave (misbijéiv) v. portarse u obrar mal; proceder mal.
miscarriage (miskérriey) s. aborto; mal parto; mala conducta; fracaso; extravío de correspondencia.

miscarry (miskérri) v. frustrarse; malograrse; abortar; extraviarse.

miscellaneous (miselénios) adj. misceláneo; diverso; mixto; mezclado.

mischief (míschif) s. mal, daño, perjuicio; travesura; diablura.

mischievous (míschivos) adj. travieso; dañino, perjudicial, perverso.

misconduct (miskóndokt) s. mala conducta, mal manejo, mala administración; v. mal administrar, desacertar; to — oneself portarse mal.

misdeed (misdíd) s. mala acción, iniquidad; transgresión; fechoría.

misdemeanor (misdemínor) s. mal comportamiento; mal proceder.

miser (máiser) s. mísero, avaro; tacaño; avariento.

miserable (míserabl) adj. miserable; infeliz, desdichado; pobre.

miserly (máiserli) adv. con avaricia; con tacañería; mezquinamente.

misery (míseri) s. miseria, desdicha; infortunio; desventura; pobreza.

misfortune (misfórchun) s. infortunio; desventura; desgracia; desastre.

misgiving (misguíving) s. recelo; presentimiento; duda; temor.

mishap (misjap) s. desgracia; calamidad; desastre; accidente; contratiempo.

mislaid (misléd) pret. y p.p. de to mislay.

mislay (misléi) v. colocar mal; poner una cosa fuera de su lugar; extraviar; traspapelar.

mislead (mislíd) v. descarriar; seducir; engañar; llevar por mal camino.

misled (misléd) pret. y p.p. de to mislead.

misplace (mispléis) v. colocar mal; poner fuera de sitio; traspapelar; extraviar.

misprint (misprínt) s. error tipográfico; error de imprenta.

misrepresent (misresprént) v. falsear; tergiversar; falsificar.

miss (mis) v. errar; fallar el tiro; no acertar; perder (el tren, la oportunidad, etc.); faltar; carecer; echar de menos; extrañar; a book is missing falta un libro; she —ed the train ella perdió el tren; he just —ed being killed por poco lo matan; s. error; falla; falta.

miss (mís) s. señorita; the misses Smith las señoritas Smith.

missile (mísil) s. proyectil; arma arrojadiza; adj. arrojadizo, que se puede arrojar o tirar.

missing (mísing) adj. extraviado; perdido; ausente; que falta.

mission (míshon) s. misión.

missionary (míshoneri) adj. y s. misionero.

misspell (mispél) v. deletrear mal; escribir con faltas de ortografía.

mist (mist) s. neblina, niebla; llovizna; v. anublar, obscurecer.

mistake (mistéik) s. equivocación; yerro; error; v. equivocar(se); engañar(se), tomar una cosa por otra; comprender mal.

mistaken (mistéiken) p.p. de to mistake; adj. equivocado; errado; erróneo, incorrecto; to be — estar equivocado.

mister (míster) s. señor.

mistook (mistúk) pret. de to mistake.

mistreat (mistrít) v. maltratar.

mistress (místres) s. señora; ama; dueña; querida; amante.

mistrust (mistróst) s. desconfianza; v. desconfiar; recelar de.

mistrustful (mistrósful) adj. desconfiado; receloso; sospechoso.

misty (místi) adj. nebuloso; nublado; empañado; indistinto; vago.

misunderstand (misondersténd) v. mal comprender; mal interpretar; tomar en sentido erróneo.

misunderstanding (misondersténding) s. mala interpretación; desavenencia; mala inteligencia.

misunderstood (misonderstúd) pret. y p.p. de to misunderstand.

misuse (misiús) s. abuso; mal uso; malversación; maltratar; mal aplicar; malversar; abusar de algo.

mite (máit) s. pizca; ardite; casi nada; friolera; pequeñez.

miter (máiter) s. mitra; dignidad de obispo; inglete; v. conferir una mitra; juntar con inglete.

mitigate (mítigueit) v. mitigar; moderar; aplacar; hacer menos rigoroso.

mitten (mitn) s. mitón (guante de una sola pieza, sin dedos).

mix (miks) v. mezclar(se); unir(se); juntar(se); asociar(se); to

— someone up confundir a uno; s. mezcla; confusión; lío.
mixture (míkschur) s. mezcla; mixtura; mezcolanza.
moan (móun) s. lamento, quejido, gemido; queja; v. lamentar(se); quejar(se); gemir.
moat (móut) s. foso.
mob (mob) s. populacho; muchedumbre; gentío; bola de gente; v. incitar a la plebe a cometer excesos; apiñarse en derredor de; atropellar.
mobile (móbil) s. móvil, inconstante; variable; movedizo.
mobilize (móbilais) v. movilizar.
moccasin (mókesin) s. mocasín. (zapato burdo de cuero).
mock (mok) v. mofar(se); escarnecer; burlarse de; remedar, imitar; **they mocked at him** se burlaron de él; s. mofa, escarnio, burla, remedo; adj. falso, fingido, cómico — **battle simulacro**.
mockery (mókeri) s. burla, mofa, escarnio, remedo; imitación, irrisión, ridículo.
mode (móud) s. moda; modo; manera; forma; accidente; método.
moderate (módereit) adj. moderado; templado; parco; quieto; tranquilo; módico; v. moderar(se); calmar; restringir; limitar; apaciguar; templar(se).
moderation (moderéshon) s. moderación; templanza.
modern (módern) adj. moderno.
modernize (módernais) v. modernizar.
modest (módest) adj. modesto; recatado; casto; púdico; sencillo.
modesty (módesti) s. modestia; decencia; pudor; reserva.
modification (modifikéshon) s. modificación.
modify (módifai) v. modificar; cambiar; templar.
modulate (módiuleit) v. modular.
Mohammedan (mojámedan) adj. y s. mahometano, islamita.
moist (móist) adj. húmedo, mojado.
moisten (móisn) v. humedecer, mojar ligeramente.
moisture (móischur) s. humedad.
molar (mólar) adj. molar; s. muela.
molasses (moláses) s. melaza, miel de caña.
mold (mold) s. molde, matriz; tierra, moho; v. moldear, modelar; enmohecer(se).
molder (mólder) v. desmoronarse.
molding (mólding) s. moldura.
moldy (móldi) adj. mohoso.
mole (móul) s. lunar; topo (animal); muelle; dique; malecón; rompeolas.
molecule (mólekiul) s. molécula.
molest (molést) v. molestar.
molten (móltn) adj. derretido; fundido; liquidado; disuelto.
moment (móment) s. momento; impulso; importancia; consecuencia.
momentary (mómentari) adj. momentáneo.
momentous (moméntous) adj. importante; grave; de consecuencia.
momentum (moméntum) adj. s. momento; ímpetu; impulsión.
monarch (mónark) s. monarca.
monarchy (mónarki) s. monarquía.
monastery (mónasteri) s. monasterio.
Monday (móndei) s. lunes.
monetary (móneteri) adj. monetario.
money (mónei) s. dinero; moneda; — **changer** cambista; — **order** giro postal; **paper** — papel moneda; **hard** — dinero acuñado, numerario; — **making** lucrativo, ganancioso.
mongrel (móngrel) adj. y s. mestizo; mixto, atravesado, cruzado.
monk (monk) s. monje.
monkey (mónki) s. mono; mico; grapa; trinquete; crisol para fundir el vidrio; — **shine** monada, monería; — **wrench** llave inglesa; v. hacer monerías; juguetear; **to** — **with** juguetear con; meterse con.
monogram (mónogram) s. monograma.
monologue (mónolog) s. monólogo; soliloquio.
monopolize (monópolais) v. monopolizar; acaparar.
monopoly (monópoli) s. monopolio.
menosyllable (monosílabl) s. monosílabo.
monotonous (monótonous) adj. monótono; uniforme en el tono.
monotony (monótoni) s. monotonía.
monster (mónster) s. monstruo;

— 143 —

pasmo; prodigio; adj. enorme; extraordinario; prodigioso.
monstrosity (monstrósiti) s. monstruosidad.
monstrous (mónstrous) adj. monstruoso.
month (monz) s. mes.
monthly (mónzli) adj. mensual; adv. mensualmente; s. revista mensual.
monument (móniument) s. monumento.
manumental (moniuméntal) adj. monumental; conmemorativo; grandioso.
moo (mu) s. mugido; v. mugir.
mood (mud) s. humor, genio, talante; disposición de ánimo; modo del verbo; to be in the — to estar dispuesto a; tener ganas de.
moody (múdi) adj. caprichoso; extravagante; melancólico; mohíno; fantástico; irritable.
moonlight (múnlait) s. luz de luna; — **dance** lunada, baile a la luz de la luna; — **night** noche de luna.
moor (mur) v. amarrar, atracar un buque; anclar; atar con cables; s. páramo; ciénaga; terreno inculto.
Moor (mur) s. moro.
Moorish (múrish) adj. morisco, moro.
mop (mop) s. trapeador; mechón, copete; estropajo; — **of hair** greñas; v. limpiar con estropajo mojado; sacudir; to — one's brow limpiarse la frente; to — up limpiar, acabar con; vencer.
mope (móup) v. estar abatido, atontado; quejumbroso.
moral (mórál) adj. moral, casto, púdico; virtuoso; —s moral, ética; s. moraleja.
morale (morál) s. entereza de ánimo.
moralist (móralist) s. moralista.
morality (moráliti) s. moralidad.
moralize (móralais) v. moralizar.
morbid (mórbid) adj. mórbido; morboso; insano, patológico.
more (mor) adj. y adv. más, mayor, numeroso, adicional; con mayor exceso o intensión; once — otra vez; — **or less** más o menos; never — nunca más, jamás; no — no más, lo que no existe o se acabó; he is no — ha muerto.

moreover (morover) adv. además; por otra parte; conj. también.
morning (mórning) s. mañana; good — ¡Buenos Días! tomorrow — mañana por la mañana; adj. matutino, matinal; — **star** lucero del alba.
morphine (mórfin) s. morfina.
morrow (mórrou) s. mañana; **day after to** — pasado mañana.
morsel (mórsl) s. bocado; manjar sabroso.
mortal (mórtal) adj. y s. mortal.
mortality (mortáliti) s. mortalidad, mortandad.
mortar (mórtar) s. mortero; argamasa, mezcla; cal y arena amasadas.
mortgage (mórguey) s. hipoteca; gravamen; v. hipotecar.
mortify (mórtifai) v. mortificar; humillar; avergonzar; herir el amor propio; afligir.
mosaic (moséik) s. y adj. mosaico.
mosquito (moskito) s. mosquito; — **net** mosquitero.
moss (mos) s. musgo, moho; tremedal; **Iceland** — liquen de Islandia; — **trooper** bandolero, bandido; — **grown** cubierto de musgo; anticuado.
mossy (mósi) adj. musgoso; mohoso.
most (móust) adv. más; sumamente; muy, en sumo grado; s. los más, el mayor número; la mayoría; — **people** la mayoría de la gente; **at** — a lo más; a lo sumo; **the** — I can do lo más que puedo hacer; **for the** — **part** generalmente; principalmente; — **amiable** sumamente amable; — **of his money** la mayor parte o casi todo su dinero.
mostly (móustli) adv. comúnmente, ordinariamente; generalmente; principalmente.
moth (móz) s. polilla; mariposa nocturna; — **ball** bolita de naftalina; — **eaten** apolillado.
mother (móder) s. madre; — **of pearl** madreperla, nácar; adj. natural, nativo, materno, vernáculo; natal; — **tongue** lengua madre; — **Superior** Madre Superiora; abadesa; — **church** Iglesia Metropolitana; v. servir de madre; criar; cuidar de.
motherhood (móderjud) s. maternidad.
mother-in-law (móderinlo) s. suegra.

motherly (móderli) adj. maternal; materno; adv. **maternalmente**.

motif (motíf) s. motivo, asunto, tema.

motion (móshon) s. moción, movimiento; aire; ademán; señal; seña; v. presentar una moción; hacer una señal o una seña.

motionless (móshonles) adj. inmóvil; yerto; inmoble.

motion picture (móshonpikchur) s. cinematógrafo; película de cine; adj. cinematográfico.

motive (móutiv) s. motivo, causa, móvil, razón; motor, motriz; tema, asunto; idea.

motley (mótli) adj. abigarrado; pintarrajeado; mezclado, variado, diverso; s. mezcla, mezcolanza.

motor (mótor) s. motor; automóvil; pasear en auto.

motorboat (mótorbout) s. lancha de gasolina; bote de motor.

motorcar (mótorcar) s. automóvil.

motorcoach (mótorkouch) s. autobús; ómnibus, camión de pasajeros.

motorcycle (mótorsaikl) s. motocicleta.

motorist (mótorist) s. motorista; automovilista.

motorman (mótorman) s. motorista.

mottled (mótled) adj. moteado, veteado, jaspeado; manchado.

motto (móto) s. mote, divisa, lema.

mould véase **mold**.

moulder véase **molder**.

moulding véase **molding**.

mouldy véase **moldy**.

mound (máund) s. montón de tierra; montículo; terraplén; atrincheramiento; terraplén.

mount (máunt) s. monte, cuesta; montura; cabalgadura; caballería; v. montar a caballo; subir, trepar; engastar piedras preciosas; alzar, elevar; armar una máquina.

mountain (máuntn) s. montaña; sierra; adj. montañés; — **chain** cadena de montañas; sierra; — **lion** puma; — **range** cordillera.

mountaineer (mauntenír) s. montañés; montaraz; serrano.

mountainous (máuntenos) adj. montañoso; peñascoso, enriscado.

mourn (móurn) v. lamentar; deplorar; vestirse de luto; estar de duelo.

mournful (móurnful) adj. fúnebre; lúgubre; lastimero; apesadumbrado; triste; funesto; luctuoso.

mourning (móurning) s. luto; duelo; dolor, desconsuelo; lamento, llanto; aflicción; **to be in** — estar de luto; **half** — medio luto.

mouse (máus) s. ratón; — **trap** ratonera.

moustache véase **mustache**.

mouth (máuz) s. boca; orificio; desembocadura; v. proferir voces.

mouthful (máuzful) s. bocado.

mouthpiece (máuzpis) s. boquilla; embocadura; portavoz.

movable (múvabl) adj. móvil, movible; —s bienes muebles, menaje.

movement (múvment) s. movimiento; meneo; marcha; evolución; paso; acto; acción; evacuación (del vientre); movimiento (de un reloj).

movie (múvi) s. cine; película; —s cinematógrafo.

mow (móu) v. segar; cortar el césped; hacer muecas; burlarse; s. mueca.

Mr. (míster) Sr., señor.

Mrs. (mísis) Sra., señora.

much (móch) adj. adv. y s. mucho; abundante; copioso; largo; excesivo; en gran manera; casi; tan; tanto; **as** — tanto, tan, otro tanto; **the same** casi lo mismo; **as** — **as** tanto como; **how** —?; ¿cuánto?; **so** — **that** tanto que; **too** — demasiado; **very** — muchísimo; **for as** — **as** por cuanto; **so** — **the better** tanto mejor.

muck (mók) s. abono, estiércol; suciedad; porquería.

mucous (miúkous) adj. mucoso; flemoso; — **membrane** membrana mucosa.

mud (mod) s. lodo, cieno, fango; limo, légamo; — **wall** tapia, barda.

muddle (modl) v. enturbiar; atontar; embotar; confundir; embrollar; s. embrollo, confusión; lío.

muddy (módi) adj. lodoso, cenagoso; fangoso; enturbiado; confuso; v. enlodar, encenagar; ensuciar; enturbiar; confundir.

muff (mof) s. manguito (para las manos); torpeza; falta, falla; error; v. no coger la pelota.

muffin (mófin) s. mollete, bollo, panecillo.

muffle (mófl) v. amortiguar el sonido; apagar; encubrir; tapar; ocultar; —d noise sonido sordo.
muffler (mófler) s. amortiguador, silenciador; embozo, bufanda.
mug (mog) s. pichel, vaso con asa.
mulatto (miuléto) s. mulato.
mulberry (mólberri) s. mora.
mule (miúl) s. mula.
muleteer (miuletír) s. arriero.
mull (mol) v. moler; pulverizar; meditar; ponderar; revolver en la mente; afanarse mucho sin resultado.
multiple (móltipl) s. múltiplo; adj. múltiple.
multiplication (moltiplikéshon) s. multiplicación.
multiplicity (moltiplíciti) s. multiplicidad.
multiply (móltiplai) v. multiplicar.
multitude (móltitiud) s. multitud.
mum (mom) adj. callado, silencioso; **to keep —** estarse callado.
mumble (mombl) v. musitar; barbotar; murmurar; gruñir; refunfuñar; mascullar; s. murmullo; gruñido; **to talk in a —** mascullar las palabras.
mummy (mómi) s. momia.
mumps (momps) s. parótidas; paperas.
munch (monch) v. mascar ruidosamente; mascullar.
municipal (miunícipal) adj. municipal.
municipality (miunicipáliti) s. municipio; municipalidad.
munition (miuníshon) s. munición; pertrechos, parque; **— plant** fábrica de municiones; arsenal; v. guarnecer; abastecer de municiones.
mural (miúral) adj. y s. mural.
murder (mé:der) s. asesinato; homicidio; crimen; v. asesinar, matar; exterminar.
murderer (mérderer) s. asesino.
murderess (mérderes) s. asesina; homicida.
murderous (mérderos) adj. asesino, homicida, sanguinario.
murmur (mérmer) s. murmullo, susurro; queja; rumor; descontento; v. murmurar; quejarse; rezongar; regañar, refunfuñar.
muscle (mosl) s. músculo.
muscular (móskiular) adj. muscular; musculoso; poderoso.
muse (miús) v. meditar; pensar; s. meditación; **Muse** musa; numen.
museum (miusíum) s. museo.
mush (mósh) s. potaje espeso de maíz; mineral de hierro de primera calidad; cualquier masa blanda; sentimentalismo.
mushroom (móshrum) s. seta, hongo.
music (miúsik) s. música; melodía; armonía; **— stand** atril.
musical (miúsikl) adj. musical, músico, melodioso; canoro; aficionado a la música; **— comedy** zarzuela; comedia musical.
musician (miusíshan) s. músico.
muskmelon (móskmelon) s. melón.
muskrat (móskrrat) s. rata almizclera.
muslin (móslin) s. muselina.
muss (mos) s. desarreglar; desordenar; arrugar, manosear.
must (most) v. defect. deber; haber de; ser preciso; **it — be late** debe ser tarde.
mustache (móstach) s. bigote.
mustard (móstard) s. mostaza; **— gas** cierto gas asfixiante con olor a mostaza que se empleó en la guerra europea; **— plaster** sinapismo.
muster (móster) v. pasar lista o revista; juntar, reunir; juntarse para una formación militar; **to — out** dar de baja; **to pass —** pasar revista; valer algo; ser aceptado; s. revista (de soldados o marinos); **— master** comisario de revistas.
musty (mósti) adj. mohoso; rancio.
mute (miút) adj. mudo, silencioso, callado; s. letra muda, mudo.
mutilate (miútileit) v. mutilar.
mutiny (miútini) s. motín; v. amotinarse; rebelarse.
mutter (móter) v. murmurar; refunfuñar; hablar entre dientes; s. murmullo, refunfuño.
mutton (móton) s. carne de carnero.
mutual (miúchual) adj. mutuo.
muzzle (mosl) s. hocico; bozal (para el hocico); jeta, mordaza; v. abozalar; poner bozal; acercar el hocico para husmear o ventear.
my (mái) adj. mi(s).
myriad (míriad) s. miríada, diez mil; millares; un gran número.

myrtle (mírtl) s. mirto, arrayán.
myself (maisélf) pron. yo mismo; me (como reflexivo); a mí mismo; by — solo; **I said to — me dije; I — did it** yo mismo lo hice. [rioso.
mysterious (mistírious) adj. miste-
mystery (místeri) s. misterio.
mystic (místic) adj. y s. místico.
mystical (místikal) adj. místico.
myth (miz) s. mito, fábula.
mythology (mizóloyi) s. mitología.

N

nab (nab) v. agarrar, coger, arrestar, prender.
nag (nag) s. rocín, caballejo; jaco; cuartago; v. importunar; irritar (con repetidos regaños).
nail (néil) s. clavo, uña (del dedo); pezuña, garra; v. clavar; guarnecer o adornar con clavos, tachonar.
naive (naív) adj. simple, ingenuo, candoroso, sencillo, natural.
naked (néiked) adj. desnudo. [dez
nakedness (néikednes) s. desnu-
name (neim) s. nombre, renombre, fama; título, reputación, crédito; — **sake** tocayo; **in God's —** en nombre de Dios; **por el amor de Dios; to call one —s** poner motes o apodos a uno; **what is your name?** ¿cómo se llama Ud.?; v. nombrar, mentar, mencionar, llamar; apellidar; especificar.
nameless (néimles) adj. sin nombre, anónimo, desconocido.
namely (néimli) adv. a saber; esto es; es decir; señaladamente.
nap (nap) s. siesta; pelo (de un tejido); vello de las plantas; **to take a —** echar un sueño, echar una siesta; v. dormitar, sestear.
nape (néip) s. nuca, cogote.
naphtha (náfza) s. nafta.
napkin (nápkin) s. servilleta.
narcissus (narcísos) s. narciso.
narcotic (narkótik) adj. y s. narcótico, soporífero.
narrate (narréit) v. narración.
narrative (nárrativ) adj. narrativo; s. narración, narrativa; relato; relación.
narrow ('naerou) a. 1. estrecho, angosto; reducido, apretado, ahogado, ajustado. 2. limitado (en extensión o número), restringido, circunscrito, ej., **in the narrowest sense,** en el sentido más restringido. 3. preciso, exacto, minucioso.

narrowness (nárrounes) s. estrechez; estrechura; pobreza; mojigatería; intolerancia.
nasal (násal) adj. nasal.
nastiness (nástines) s. suciedad; porquería, obscenidad.
nasturtium (nastérshum) s. mastuerzo, berro, capuchina.
nasty (násti) adj. sucio; asqueroso; indecente, puerco, nauseabundo; grosero; **a — fall** una caída terrible; **a — sea** mala mar.
nation (néshon) s. nación.
national (néshonal) adj. nacional; general; público; s. ciudadano, nacional.
nationality (neshonáliti) s. nacionalidad, nación; ciudadanía.
native (nétiv) adj. nativo; natal; natural; oriundo; vernáculo; indígena; del país; criollo; s. nativo, natural, producto nacional.
nativity (nativíti) s. nacimiento; natividad (de la Virgen María); natalicio, horóscopo; **Nativity** Navidad.
natural (néchural) adj. natural; sencillo; sin afectación; inafectado; s. **he is a — for that job** tiene aptitud natural para ese puesto. [turalismo.
naturalism (néchuralism) s. na-
naturalist (néchuralist) s. naturalista. [naturalización.
naturalization (nechuraliséshon) s.
naturalize (néchuralais) v. naturalizar. [turalidad, ingenuidad
naturalness (néchuralnes) s. na-
nature (néchur) s. naturaleza; natural; genio, índole; idiosincrasia; instinto, especie; laya, calidad; **from —** del natural.
naught (not) s. cero, nada.
naughty (nóti) adj. malo, desobediente; travieso, pícaro, perverso; — **boy** picaruelo.
nausea (nóshia) s. náusea.
nauseate (nóshiet) v. dar náuseas, dar bascas, asquear; causar aversión o antipatía; **to be —ed** tener náuseas.
nauseating (nóshieting) adj. nauseabundo, asqueroso, molesto.
naval (néval) adj. naval; — **officer** oficial de marina, capitán de puerto. [sia).
nave (néiv) s. nave (de una igle-
navel (névl) s. ombligo. ble.
navigable (névigabl) adj. navega-
navigate (névigueit) v. navegar

navigation (naviguéshon) s. navegación.

navigator (névigueitor) s. navegador; navegante; marino, piloto.

navy (néivi) s. marina de guerra, armada; **Navy Department** Ministerio de Marina; — **blue** azul marino.

nay (nei) adv. no; no sólo... sino (que) también; de ningún modo; s. voto negativo, no.

near (nir) adv. cerca; casi; inmediato a; junto a; — **at hand** a la mano; cerca; **I came — forgetting to do it** por poco se me olvida hacerlo; — **relation** pariente cercano; — **sighted** corto de vista; miope; — **the end of the month** hacia fines del mes; adj. cercano; próximo, íntimo; contiguo, vecino, propincuo; v. acercarse(a); acercar.

near-by (nirbai) adv. cerca, a la mano; adj. cercano, próximo.

nearly (nirli) adv. casi, cerca de; aproximadamente; cercanamente; estrechamente; **I — did it** estuve a punto de hacerlo.

nearness (nírnes) s. cercanía; proximidad; tacañería; ruindad; inminencia; mezquindad.

neat (nit) adj. pulcro, aseado, limpio; ordenado; esmerado; bonito; pulido, lindo; hábil, diestro; **—ly** adv. aseadamente; primorosamente; esmeradamente.

neatness (nítnes) s. pulcritud, aseo, limpieza, esmero; elegancia.

necessarily (nésesarili) adv. necesariamente.

necessary (néseceri) adj. necesario; decisivo; **—s** s. pl. necesidades, requisitos.

necessitate (necésiteit) v. necesitar, precisar, obligar, requerir.

necessity (necésiti) s. necesidad.

neck (nek) s. cuello; pescuezo; garganta; gollete (de una botella); — **of land** istmo; **low —ed** escotado.

necklace (nékleis) s. collar.

necktie (néktai) s. corbata.

need (nid) s. necesidad; pobreza; urgencia; carencia, falta; **for — of** por falta de; **if — be** si hubiese necesidad o si fuese necesario; v. tener necesidad de; ser menester.

needful (nídful) adj. necesario, necesitado, indispensable.

needle (nídl) s. aguja.

needless (nídles) adj. innecesario; inútil; superfluo.

needlework (nídluerk) s. labor, bordado, costura; bordado de aguja.

needy (nídi) adj. necesitado, menesteroso; indigente, apurado.

ne'er (ner) adv. contr. de **never**; **ne'er do-well** s. persona incompetente; haragán.

negation (niguéshon) s. negación, negativa, carencia.

negative (négativ) adj. negativo; s. negativa; negación; denegación; partícula o voz negativa; negativa (de una fotografía).

neglect (neglékt) s. negligencia; descuido; abandono; dejadez; v. descuidar; desatender; menospreciar; **to — to** dejar de; olvidarse de.

neglectful (negléktful) adj. negligencia.

negligent (néglivent) adj. negligente; descuidado, dejado, flojo, perezoso.

negotiate (negóshiet) v. negociar, agenciar; tratar, cambiar; vencer (un obstáculo o dificultad).

negotiation (negoshiéshon) s. negociación.

negro (nigro) s. y adj. negro.

neigh (ne) s. relincho; v. relinchar.

neighbor (néibor) s. vecino; prójimo; adj. vecino, cercano.

neighborhood (néiborjud) s. vecindad; vecindario; inmediación; cercanía; **in the — of a hundred dollars** cerca de cien dólares.

neighboring (néiboring) adj. vecino; cercano, colindante, rayano, adyacente.

neither (níder) pron. ninguno, ni (el) uno ni (el) otro; — **of the two** ninguno de los dos; — **girl was hurt** ninguna de las dos niñas se hizo daño; conj. ni; —... **nor**... ni... ni...; — **will I** tampoco yo.

nephew (néfiu) s. sobrino.

nerve (nerv) s. nervio, valor, ánimo; audacia; descaro; fortaleza, vigor; desfachatez; v. vigorizar; animar, alentar; **to strain every —** esforzarse hasta más no poder.

nervous (nérvous) adj. nervioso.

nervousness (nérvosnes) s. nerviosidad; agitación; vigor, fuerza.

nest (nest) s. nido; nidada; ponedero; — **egg nidal**; ahorros; madriguera, guarida; juego, serie; engranaje; **wasp's** — avispero; v. anidar, hacer un nido.

nestle (nésl) v. acurrucarse; abrigar(se); anidar, poner en un nido.

net (net) s. red; malla; tejido de mallas; adj. de mallas, de punto de malla; **mosquito** — mosquitero; v. redar, coger con red.

net (net) adj. neto; limpio; puro; — **price** precio neto; — **profit** ganancia neta o líquida; — **produce** producto neto; v. producir una ganancia neta o líquida.

nettle (nétl) s. ortiga; v. picar; irritar; enfadar; espinar.

network (nétuerk) s. red, malla; **radio** — cadena de difusoras.

neuter (niúter) adj. neutro.

neutral (niútral) adj. neutral.

neutrality (niutréliti) s. neutralidad.

never (néver) adv. nunca, jamás.

nevertheless (néverdeles) adv. y conj. sin embargo; no obstante, con todo; empero; a pesar de; aun así.

new (niú) adj. nuevo; fresco; reciente; moderno; novel; tierno; — **born baby** bebé recién nacido.

newcomer (niúcomer) s. recién llegado.

newly (niúli) adv. nuevamente; hace poco; recientemente; — **wed** recién casado.

newness (niúnes) s. novedad; innovación; calidad de nuevo.

news (niús) s. noticia, informe, novedad, nueva; **piece of** — noticia; — **boy** voceador, vendedor de periódicos; — **reel** noticiero; — **stand** puesto de periódicos.

newsmonger (niúsmonguer) s. gacetista; chismoso; cuentista.

newspaper (niúspeiper) s. periódico.

next (nekst) adj. próximo; siguiente, entrante; venidero; contiguo; sucesivo; futuro; **to be** — **in turn** tocarle a uno, ser su turno; adv. luego, inmediatamente después, en seguida; prep. junto a; al lado de; después de.

nibble (nibl) s. mordisco; probada; v. mordiscar, probar; **to** — **at a drink** dar una probada a la copa.

nice (náis) adj. fino, delicado;

bello; amable, simpático; lindo; primoroso; elegante, tierno, frágil; exquisito; —**ly** adv. con finura, delicadamente; con amabilidad; **to get along** —**ly with** llevarse bien con.

nicety (náiseti) s. finura, delicadeza; exactitud; esmero.

niche (nich) s. nicho; capilla.

nick (nik) s. muesca; mella; desportilladura, escote; **in the** — **of time** en el momento crítico; v. mellar; desportillar.

nickel (níkl) s. níquel; moneda de cinco centavos; — **plate** niquelar.

nickname (níkneim) s. mote, apodo; sobrenombre; v. poner apodo a.

niece (nis) s. sobrina.

niggardly (nígardli) adj. mezquino; ruin; tacaño; miserable; adv. mezquinamente.

nightfall (náitfol) s. anochecer; caída de la tarde.

nightgown (náitgaun) s. camisa de dormir, camisa de noche.

nightingale (náitingueil) s. ruiseñor.

nightly (náitli) adv. cada noche, todas las noches, por las noches; adj. nocturno, de noche.

nightmare (náitmer) s. pesadilla.

nimble (nimbl) adj. ágil, ligero, listo, vivo, activo.

nip (nip) v. pellizcar, mordiscar; coger, asir, sujetar; agarrar; helar (por la acción del frío); **to** — **in the bud** cortar en germen, destruir al nacer; s. pellizco.

nipple (nipl) s. teta, tetilla, chimenea de arma de percusión.

nitrate (náitret) s. nitrato.

nitrogen (náitroyen) s. nitrógeno.

no (no) adv. no; — **longer** ya no; **wheter or** — de un modo u otro; **there is** — **more** no hay más; **say** — **more** no digas más; adj. ningún(o); — **matter how much** por mucho que; — **one** ninguno, nadie; **by** — **means** de ninguna manera, de ningún modo; s. no, voto negativo.

noble (nóubl) s. y adj. noble.

nobleman (nóublman) s. noble.

nobleness (nóublnes) s. nobleza.

nobly (nóubli) adv. noblemente.

nobody (nóbodi) pron. nadie, ninguno.

nod (nod) v. inclinar la cabeza (para hacer una seña, saludar o asentir); cabecear; dar cabezadas; inclinar la cima o parte superior (de una rama, etc.); s. saludo, inclinación de cabeza, señal; reverencia; mocha.

noise (nois) s. ruido, barullo, sonido; són, estruendo; v. divulgar; esparcir, turbar con gritos o con estruendo.

noiseless (nóisles) adj. sin ruido, adv. silenciosamente.

noisily (nóisili) adv. ruidosamente.

noisy (nóisi) adj. ruidoso.

nominal (nóminal) adj. nominal.

nominate (nómineit) v. nombrar, designar, elegir, señalar.

nomination (nominéshon) s. nominación; nombramiento; propuesta.

none (non) pron. ninguno; ningunos; nada; — **attendance** falta de asistencia; — **of that** nada de eso; — **of his business** nada le importa (a él); adv. no, de ningún modo; — **the less** no menos; **he was** — **the worse** no se hallaba peor.

nonentity (nonéntiti) s. la nada; persona o cosa de ningún valor.

nonsense (nónsens) s. tontería, despropósito; disparate; desatino.

noodle (nudl) s. tallarín, fideo; pasta para sopas.

nook (nuk) s. rincón; escondrijo; **breakfast** — desayunador.

noon (nún) s. mediodía.

noonday (núndei) s. mediodía; adj. meridional; — **meal** comida de mediodía.

noontide (núntaid) s. mediodía; adj. meridional;—apogeo, culminación.

noontime (núntaim) s. mediodía.

noose (nús) s. dogal; gaza, nudo corredizo; v. lazar; coger con lazo corredizo o con trampa.

nor (nor) conj. ni; **neither...** — **ni... ni**; tampoco; — **was this all** pero esto no fue todo.

norm (norm) s. norma.

normal (nórmal) adj. normal; regular; perpendicular.

northeastern (norzístern) adj. del nordeste; nordeste.

northern (nórzern) adj. septentrional; boreal, ártico; del norte o hacia el norte; — **lights** aurora boreal.

northerner (nórzerner) s. norteño, habitante del norte.

northward (nórzuard) adv. hacia el norte; rumbo al norte.

northwest (norzuést) adj. y s. noroeste; adv. hacia el noroeste.

northwestern (norzuéstern) adj. noroeste; hacia el noroeste.

Norwegian (noruíyan) adj. y s. noruego.

nose (nóus) s. nariz; proa; pico de cafetera o jarra, etc.; — **dive** picada de un avión; v. olfatear; **to** — **around** husmear, curiosear; **to blow one's** — sonarse; **pug o snub nose** nariz respingada.

nostalgia (nostályia) s. nostalgia; añoranza.

nostrils (nóstrils) s. pl. ventanas de la nariz.

not (not) adv. no, de ninguna manera; — **at all** de ningún modo, de nada; — **to say** por no decir; — **so much as** ni siquiera; — **certainly** — por supuesto que no.

notable (nótabl) adj. notable.

notary (nóteri) s. notario.

notation (notéshon) s. anotación; apunte; sentido, significación.

notch (nótch) s. muesca; corte; gubiadura; ranura; rebajo; v. ranurar; muescar; rebajar; hender.

note (nóut) s. nota; apunte; comunicación; esquela; **bank** — billete de banco; **promissory** — pagaré; v. notar; distinguir; apuntar; registrar; poner por escrito.

notebook (nóutbuk) s. libreta, cuaderno; libro de apuntes; agenda.

noted (nóuted) adj. célebre, famoso, notable; eminente.

noteworthy (nóutuerzi) adj. notable; célebre; digno de ser anotado.

notice (nóutis) s. aviso, advertencia; anuncio; mención; notificación; **on short** — a última hora; v. notar; advertir; atender a; cuidar de; apercibirse de, hacer caso a; notificar.

noticeable (nótisebl) adj. notable; conspicuo; perceptible.

notify (nótifai) v. notificar, avisar.

notion (nóshon) s. noción; idea; parecer; entendimiento; capricho; —**s** mercería, novedades, baratijas.

notorious (notórius) adj. notorio.

notwithstanding (notuizstánding) prep. a pesar de; sin embargo; adv. y conj. no obstante; empe-

ro; — that a pesar de que; conj. aun cuando, aunque; por más que.
nought véase **naught**.
noun (naun) s. nombre, sustantivo.
nourish (nórish) v. nutrir, alimentar; sustentar; mantener; abrigar.
nourishing (nórishing) adj. nutritivo; substancial; alimenticio.
nourishment (nórishment) s. nutrición; alimentación; sustento.
novel (nóvl) s. novela; adj. novel, nuevo; original; reciente; raro.
novelist (nóvlist) s. novelista.
novelty (nóvlti) s. novedad; innovación; —s novedades.
November (novémber) s. noviembre.
novice (nóvis) s. novicio, novato; principiante; bisoño; neófito.
now (náu) adv. ahora, en este momento, actualmente; poco ha; ya, ora; — and then de vez en cuando; — that ahora que; — then pues bien, ahora bien; just — ahora mismo, inmediatamente; acabar de; until o till — hasta ahora; hasta el momento.
nowadays (náuedeis) adv. hoy día.
nowhere (nójuer) adv. en ninguna parte; — else en ninguna otra parte.
noxious (nóxius) adj. nocivo.
nucleus (niúklios) s. núcleo.
nude (niud) adj. desnudo.
nudge (nody) v. codear; tocar con el codo; empujar ligeramente con el codo; s. codazo ligero.
nuisance (niúsans) s. molestia, lata, fastidio; engorro; incomodidad; persona o cosa molesta o fastidiosa; what a —! ¡qué fastidio!
null (nol) adj. nulo, inválido; s. cosa sin validez ni eficacia.
numb (nom) adj. entumecido, aterido, paralizado; v. entumecer, baldar; entorpecer.
number (nómber) s. número, cifra; pl. aritmética; ritmo, cadencia; v. numerar; ascender o montar a.
numberless (nómberles) adj. innumerable, sin número, infinito.
numeral (niúmeral) s. número, cifra; guarismo; adj. numeral.
numerical (niumérikal) adj. numérico.
numerous (niúmeros) adj. numeroso; cuantioso; muchos.

nun (non) s. monja; religiosa.
nuptial (nópshal) adj. nupcial; —s s. pl. nupcias, boda, matrimonio.
nurse (ners) s. enfermera; enfermero; niñera; aya; nana, pilmama; wet — ama de cría, nodriza; v. criar; amamantar; lactar; asistir enfermos; fomentar; abrigar rencores.
nursery (nérseri) s. crianza; cuarto destinado a los niños; criadero; vivero; — garden plantel; — tales cuentos para niños.
nurture (nórchur) s. crianza; alimentación; nutrimiento; v. criar; nutrir; educar; fomentar; enseñar.
nut (not) s. tuerca; nuez; loco; tipo raro o extravagante; chest— castaña; hazel— avellana; walnuez de nogal.
nutcracker (nótkraker) s. cascanueces.
nutmeg (nótmeg) s. nuez moscada.
nutrition (nutríshon) s. nutrición; alimentación.
nutritious (nutríshios) adj. nutritivo; alimenticio.
nutritive (niútritiv) adj. nutritivo.
nutshell (nótshel) s. cáscara de avellana o nuez; in a — en pocas palabras; en suma.
nymph (nimf) s. ninfa.

O

oak (óuk) s. roble; encino; — grove robledal; live — encina siempre verde.
oar (óur) s. remo; v. remar, bogar.
oasis (oésis) s. oasis.
oat (óut) s. avena; wild —s excesos de juventud; wild — avena silvestre.
oath (óuz) s. juramento; blasfemia; reniego; upon — bajo juramento.
oatmeal (óutmil) s. harina de avena; gachas de avena.
obedience (obídiens) s. obediencia; sumisión.
obedient (obídient) adj. obediente; sumiso, dócil.
obesity (obésiti) s. obesidad.
obey (obéi) v. obedecer.
object (óbyekt) s. objeto, cosa, artículo; fin, propósito; (obyékt) v. objetar, aducir; oponerse; tener inconveniente.
objection (obyékshon) s. objeción;

reparo; inconveniente; dificultad.
objective (obyéktiv) adj. objetivo; s. punto, objetivo, propósito, fin; acusativo; meta.
obligate (óbligueit) v. obligar, comprometer; constreñir; precisar.
obligation (obliguéshon) s. obligación; deber; compromiso; deuda; to be under — to estar obligado a, estar agradecido; deber favores.
obligatory (obliguetori) adj. obligatorio, forzoso.
oblige (obláiy) v. obligar, compeler; complacer; agradar; you will — me le agradeceré a usted; much —d! ¡muchas gracias!; ¡muy agradecido!
obliging (obláiying) adj. complaciente; cortés; servicial; obsequioso.
oblique (oblík) adj. oblicuo, sesgado; indirecto; evasivo.
obliterate (oblítereit) s. borrar; tachar; destruir; arrasar.
oblivion (oblívion) s. olvido.
oblivious (oblívious) adj. olvidadizo; desmemoriado; absorto.
obnoxious (obnókshos) adj. ofensivo; odioso; detestable; molesto.
obscene (obsín) adj. obsceno.
obscenity (obséniti) s. obscenidad; impudicia; indecencia.
obscure (obskiúr) adj. obscuro; ininteligible; vago; indistinto.
obscurity (obskiúriti) s. obscuridad.
obsequies (óbsikuis) s. exequias, funerales; honras fúnebres.
obsequious (obsékios) adj. obsequioso; servicial; zalamero.
observance (obsérvans) s. observancia; acatamiento; rito o ceremonia; costumbre, práctica uso. [vador; obediente
observant (obsérvant) adj. observation (observéshon) s. observación; escrutinio.
observatory (obsérvetori) s. observatorio, mirador; atalaya.
observe (obsérv) v. observar; guardar (las fiestas religiosas); atisbar, mirar; notar, reparar.
observer (obsérver) s. observador.
obsess (obsés) v. obsesionar, causar obsesión.
obsession (obséshon) s. obsesión; idea fija; sitio (de una plaza).
obsolete (óbsolit) adj. anticuado; desusado; fuera de uso.
obstacle (óbstekl) s. obstáculo.

obstinacy (óbstinaci) s. obstinación, terquedad; persistencia.
obstinate (óbstineit) adj. obstinado, terco, persistente.
obstruct (obstrókt) v. obstruir.
obstruction (obstrókshon) s. obstrucción; impedimento; atasco.
obtain (ab'tein, ab—, Bab—) v.t. 1. obtener, conseguir, adquirir, poseer. 2. (ant.) lograr, alcanzar.
obviate (óbvieit) v. obviar; allanar (una dificultad), evitar.
obvious (óbvius) adj. obvio, evidente, manifiesto.
occasion (okéshon) s. ocasión; oportunidad; causa, motivo; lance; ocurrencia, casualidad; v. ocasionar, causar, producir, traer.
occasional (okéshonl) adj. ocasional; infrecuente; casual, contingente; v. ocasionar, causar.
occidental (oksidéntal) adj. y s. occidental; occiduo. [inquilino.
occupant (okiupant) s. ocupante;
occupation (okiupéshon) s. ocupación; trabajo, empleo; toma de posesión; empleo, oficio.
occupy (ókiupai) v. ocupar.
occur (okér) v. ocurrir; suceder; encontrarse o hallarse aquí y allí; to — to one ocurrírsele a uno.
occurrence (okérrens) s. ocurrencia; suceso; incidente, caso.
ocean (óshan) s. océano.
o'clock (oklók) contr. de **of the clock**; it is two — son las dos.
October (október) s. octubre.
oculist (ókiulist) s. oculista.
odd (od) adj. extraño, singular, raro; non; impar; tanto, pico, sobrante, excedente; — **change** suelto, cambio sobrante; **an — card** una carta sobrante; **twenty — pounds** veinte y tantas libras; **—ly** adv. singularmente; raramente; desigualmente; en forma extraña. [dad; particularidad.
oddity (óditi) s. rareza, singulari**odds** (ods) s. pl. o sing. desigualdad, diferencia; apuesta desigual; ventaja; — **and ends** sobrantes, pedacitos varios; **the — are against me** la suerte me es adversa; estoy de malas; **they are at —** riñen constantemente; s. ventaja, superioridad, exceso.
ode (óud) s. oda.
odious (ódious) adj. odioso; aborrecible; detestable.
odor (ódor) s. olor; fragancia; aroma; **bad —** mal olor, hedor.

odorous (ódorus) adj. oloroso.

o'er (ór) contr. de over.

of (of) prep. de; en; entre; sobre; según; a; — **course** por supuesto; **of custom** según costumbre; — **old** en otro tiempo; — **all things** entre todas las cosas; **a quarter — three** las tres menos cuarto.

off (of) adv. lejos, a distancia, fuera; (modifica los verbos indicando separación, ausencia); privación, distancia; — **and on** de vez en cuando; a intervalos; **far —** muy lejos; **five percent —** cinco por ciento de descuento; **way —** muy lejos, a gran distancia; — **hand** de repente, de improviso; **an — day** un día de descanso; adj. ausente, distante, más remoto; **he took his hat —** se quitó el sombrero; **to pull —** arrancar; **to send —** despachar, expedir; **to turn —** quitar (el agua, el gas, el vapor); — **the coast** lejos de la costa; **to be well —** estar en buenas condiciones económicas; **I saw him —** lo vi marcharse; **to be — in one's accounts** estar equivocado en sus cuentas; — **color** de mal color; — **the road** fuera del camino, desviado; **to be — duty** no estar de turno; estar libre.

offend (ofénd) v. ofender; agredir.

offender (ofénder) s. delincuente; transgresor; ofensor.

offense (oféns) s. ofensa; injuria; agravio; ataque; delito; **he took — se dio por sentido; no — was meant** lo hice o (lo dije) sin malicia.

offensive (oténsiv) adj. ofensivo; s. ofensiva, ataque.

offering (ófering) s. ofrecimiento; ofrenda; sacrificio.

offhand (ófjand) adv. repentinamente; de improviso; impensadamente; adj. sin premeditación, sin pensarlo; hecho de improviso; sin ceremonia; de sopetón.

office (ófis) s. oficio; ocupación; empleo, cargo; puesto; oficina, despacho; bufete; — **building** edificio comercial; **post —** oficina de correos; **box —** taquilla; **good —** favor.

officer (ófiser) s. oficial, funcionario, empleado de alta categoría; agente de policía; v. comandar; proveer de oficiales.

official (ofíshal) adj. oficial; s. oficial, funcionario.

officiate (ofíshieit) v. oficiar.

officious (ofíshios) adj. oficioso; solícito, entremetido.

offset (ófset) s. compensación, equivalencia; v. compensar por.

offspring (ófspring) s. hijos, prole, descendencia; vástago; resultado; consecuencia.

often (ófen) adv. a menudo, muchas veces.

ogre (óguer) s. ogro, monstruo.

oil (oil) s. aceite, petróleo; — **can** alcuza; — **well** pozo de petróleo; v. aceitar, lubricar; ungir; — **painting** pintura al óleo.

oilcloth (óilcloz) s. hule, encerado.

oily (óili) adj. aceitoso, oleoso; grasiento; — **grain** ajonjolí.

ointment (óintment) s. ungüento.

O. K. (okéi) adj. bueno, corriente, convenido; adv. bien; **it's —** está bien; **to give one's —** dar el visto bueno; aprobar.

old (old) adj. viejo, antiguo, añejo de edad; usado, gastado; familiar; — **man** anciano, viejo; — **wine** vino añejo; **of —** antiguamente; — **shoes** zapatos usados; — **fashioned** anticuado; **to be an — hand at** ser muy ducho, perito o experto en.

olden (óldn) adj. viejo, antiguo; v. envejecer; hacerse viejo.

old-fashioned (oldfáshiond) adj. pasado de moda; anticuado; chapado a la antigua.

old-time (oldtáim) adj. vetusto; de antaño.

old-timer (oldtáimer) s. veterano; antiguo concurrente o residente.

olive (óliv) s. olivo; aceituna; — **grove** olivar; — **oil** aceite de oliva; adj. aceitunado; verde aceituna; — **bearing** olivífero; — **branch** rama de olivo.

omelet (ómlet) s. tortilla de huevos.

omen (ómen) s. agüero; presagio.

ominous (óminos) adj. ominoso; siniestro; azaroso; amenazador.

omission (omíshon) s. omisión.

omit (omít) v. omitir; prescindir de; descuidar; dejar de; olvidar la inserción o mención de.

omnipotent (omnípotent) adj. omnipotente; todopoderoso.

on (on) prep. en, sobre, encima de; a; de; con; por; — **arriving** al llegar; — **all sides** por todos lados; — **the table** en, sobre o encima de la mesa; — **board** a bordo en el tren; — **pain of death** bajo pena de muerte; — **purpose** con intención, a propósito; adrede; — **credit** a crédito, fiado; — **foot** a pie; — **time** a tiempo; **later** — después; — **an average** por término medio; — **and** — continuamente, sin cesar; — **account of** a causa o debido a; **the light is** — está encendida la luz.

once (uóns) adv. una vez en otro tiempo; — **and for all** de una vez por todas; **at** — al mismo tiempo; simultáneamente; **in** — **mediatamente**; — **in a while** muy de vez en cuando; **just this** — siquiera esta vez; **por esta vez**; **all at** — de repente; repentinamente; conj. una vez que; luego que; cuando.

one (uán) adj. un, uno; solo; único; cierto; igual; — **thousand** mil, millar; — **day** cierto día; **his** — **chance** su única oportunidad; — **eyed** tuerto; — **sided** unilateral; parcial; s. y pron. uno; — **by** — uno por uno; **any** — alguien, quienquiera, cualquiera; **the** — who el que, la que; **this** — éste, ésta; **to love** — **another** amarse unos a otros.

oneself (uansélf) pron. se (reflexivo), sí, sí mismo; **to speak to** — hablar consigo mismo; **by** — por sí, por sí solo.

onion (ónion) s. cebolla.

onlooker (ónluker) s. espectador

only (ónli) adj. solo, único; adv. sólo, solamente; conj. sólo que.

onset (ónset) s. ataque, arrebato; ímpetu inicial, arranque.

onto (óntu) prep. a; sobre.

onward (ónuard) adv. adelante, progresivamente; en lo venidero.

ooze (us) v. sudar, exudar; manar; escurrir(se); s. fango, limo, cieno.

open (ópen) v. abrir; adj. abierto, franco, sincero.

opening (ópening) s. abertura, brecha; entrada; luz; claro; abra; comienzo; inauguración, principio; oportunidad; adj. primero; — **night of a play** noche de estreno, noche de "premier".

opera (ópera) s. ópera; — **bouffe** ópera bufa; — **house** teatro de la ópera; coliseo; — **glasses** gemelos; **grand** — ópera; drama lírico.

operation (operéshon) s. operación; dirección; manejo, funcionamiento; maniobra; procedimiento; **to be in** — estar funcionando.

operator (ópereitor) s. operario; operadora (de teléfonos); maquinista; **mine** — explotador de minas, minero; especulador en la Bolsa.

operetta (operéta) s. opereta; zarzuela.

opinion (opínion) s. opinión; parecer; dictamen, juicio.

opium (ópium) s. opio.

opponent (opónent) s. contrincante; adversario; antagonista.

opportune (oportiún) adj. oportuno; a propósito; conveniente.

opportunity (oportiúniti) s. oportunidad; ocasión.

oppose (opóus) v. oponer(se); resistir; objetar; hacer frente a; impugnar.

opposing (opóusing) adj. opuesto; frontero; contrario; encontrado; adverso; prep. frente a, enfrente de; — **to** frente a; **the** — **sex** el sexo contrario; **the** — **lo opuesto**.

opposition (oposíshon) s. oposición; resistencia; impugnación.

oppress (oprés) v. oprimir, gravar, agobiar; tiranizar; supeditar.

oppression (opréshon) s. opresión.

oppressive (oprésiv) adj. opresivo; duro, cruel, inhumano, abrumador, gravoso; sofocante.

oppressor (oprésor) s. opresor.

optic (óptik) adj. óptico; —**s** s. óptica.

optical (óptikal) adj. óptico.

optician (optíshan) s. óptico.

optimism (óptimism) s. optimismo.

optimist (óptimist) s. optimista.

optimistic (optimístik) adj. optimista.

option (ópshon) s. opción; derecho de escoger; elección; alternativa; plazo para determinar.

optional (ópshonal) adj. discrecional.

opulence (ópiulens) s. opulencia; riqueza; abundancia.

opulent (ópiulent) adj. opulento; rico; acaudalado, pudiente.

or (or) conj. o, u.

oracle (órakl) s. oráculo.

oral (óral) adj. oral, verbal, bucal.

orange (órany) s. naranja; — **blossom** azahar; — **grove** naranjal;

— tree naranjo (el árbol); adj. anaranjado, de naranja.
orangeade (oranyéd) s. naranjada.
oration (oréshon) s. oración; discurso; peroración; arenga.
orator (órator) s. orador.
oratory (óratori) s. oratoria; elocuencia; oratorio; capilla.
orb (orb) s. orbe; esfera; globo.
orbit (órbit) s. órbita.
orchard (órchard) s. huerto.
orchestra (órkestra) s. orquesta; — seat butaca; luneta; platea.
orchid (órkid) s. orquídea.
ordain (ordéin) v. ordenar; decretar; mandar; estatuir; instituir.
ordeal (ordíl) s. ordalía, prueba dura.
order (órder) s. orden; pedido; mandato; serie, clase; medida; forma; régimen; condecoración; pl. orden sacerdotal; sacramento; in — to a fin de, con objeto de; till further —s hasta nueva orden; to be out of — estar descompuesto; v. ordenar; mandar; disponer; arreglar; pedir (hacer un pedido); regularizar; to — in mandar entrar o mandar traer; to — away despedir; expulsar.
orderly (órderli) s. ordenanza; asistente; adj. ordenado; bien arreglado; metódico; adv. ordenadamente; metódicamente; en orden.
ordinance (órdinans) s. ordenanza; estatuto; ley; reglamento.
ordinarily (órdinarili) adv. ordinariamente; regularmente; por lo común.
ordinary (órdinari) adj. ordinario.
ore (or) s. mineral.
organ (órgan) s. órgano.
organic (orgánik) adj. orgánico; sistematizado; fundamental.
organism (órganism) s. organismo.
organist (órganist) s. organista.
organization (organiséshon) s. organización; organismo; sociedad.
organize (órganais) v. organizar(se).
organizer (órganaiser) s. organizador.
orgy (óryi) s. orgía.
orient (órient) s. oriente; v. orientar; adj. oriental.
oriental (oriéntal) adj. s. oriental.
orientate (órienteit) v. orientar.
orifice (órifis) s. orificio.
origin (óriyin) s. origen.
original (oríyinal) adj. original; —ly adv. originalmente; en principio.

originality (oriyináliti) s. originalidad.
originate (oríyineit) v. originar.
oriole (óriol) s. oriol (ave).
ornament (órnament) s. ornamento; adorno; ornato; atavío; v. ornamentar; adornar; ornar; ataviar.
ornamental (ornaméntal) adj. ornamental; decorativo; de adorno.
ornate (ornéit) adj. ornado; adornado en exceso; — style estilo florido.
orphan (órfan) adj. y s. huérfano; —age orfandad, asilo para huérfanos; hospicio; v. dejar huérfano.
ostentation (ostentéshon) s. ostentación, alarde; boato; pompa.
ostentatious (ostentéshos) adj. ostentoso; jactancioso; pomposo.
ostrich (óstrich) s. avestruz.
other (óder) adj. y s. otro; — than más que; otra cosa que; every — day cada tercer día.
otherwise (óderuais) adv. de otra manera; de otro modo; adj. otro, diferente.
otter (óter) s. nutria; piel de nutria.
ought (ót) defect. y aux. v. deber, ser menester; you — to know usted debía saber; it — to be so así debe ser; (tiene más fuerza que should).
ounce (áuns) s. onza.
our (áur) adj nuestro, nuestra, nuestros; nuestras.
ours (áurs) pron. pos. (el, la, los, las) nuestro, nuestra, nuestros, nuestras; a friend of — un amigo nuestro; this is — esto es nuestro.
ourselves (aursélvs) pron. nosotros mismos; nos (reflexivo); we — nosotros mismos; by — solos, por nosotros.
out (áut) adv. fuera; afuera; hacia fuera.
outbreak (áutbreik) s. erupción; ataque violento; tumulto; estallido; insurrección; at the — of war al estallar la guerra.
outburst (áutberst) s. explosión; erupción; arranque de pasión.
outcast (áutcast) s. proscripto, paria; desterrado; arrojado de; desechado.
outcome (áutcom) s. resultado, consecuencia.
outcry (áutkrai) s. clamor, alarido; alboroto; gritería.

outdoor (áutdor) adj. externo; fuera de la casa; — **sports** juegos o deportes al aire libre, al raso.

outdoors (áutdors) adv. puertas afuera; al aire libre; a campo raso; s. aire libre, campo raso.

outer (áuter) adj. exterior, externo.

outfit (áutfit) s. equipo, habilitación; avíos; pertrechos.

outing (áuting) s. salida, paseo, caminata; jira; excursión.

outlaw (áutloh) s. bandolero; bandido; forajido; malhechor; v. proscribir; declarar ilegal.

outlay (áutlei) v. gastar, desembolsar; s. gasto, desembolso.

outlet (áutlet) s. desagüe; salida, orificio de salida.

outline (áutlain) s. perfil; diseño; esbozo; croquis; v. perfilar; diseñar; esbozar; delinear; trazar.

outlive (autlív) v. sobrevivir.

outlook (áutluk) s. vista, perspectiva; aspecto; probabilidades; v. turbar con la mirada; desconcertar.

outlying (áutlaing) adj. circundante; extrínseco; distante del centro.

out-of-date (áutofdéit) adj. pasado de moda; anticuado.

outpost (áutpost) s. avanzada.

output (áutput) s. producción total; rendimiento.

outrage (áutrey) s. ultraje, afrenta.

outrageous (autréyus) adj. violento; ofensivo, atroz, ultrajante.

outran (autrrán) pret. de to outrun.

outrun (autrrón) v. correr más que otro, aventajarle; dejarlo atrás.

outset (áutset) s. principio, comienzo; inauguración.

outshine (autsháin) v. eclipsar; exceder en brillantez o esplendor.

outside (áutsaid) adj. exterior; superficial; aparente; extraño; ajeno; adv. fuera, afuera; s. exterior; parte de fuera; apariencia; **at the —** a lo sumo, a lo más; **to close on the —** cerrar por fuera.

outsider (autsáider) s. forastero; extraño; persona de fuera.

outskirts (áutskerts) s. pl. suburbios, inmediaciones, alrededores.

outspoken (autspóken) adj. franco, abierto; claridoso.

outstanding (autstánding) adj. prominente; destacado; sobresaliente; pendiente; — **bills** cuentas por cobrar; — **debts** cuentas por pagar.

outstretched (autstrétched) adj. extendido; alargado; **with —arms** con los brazos abiertos.

outward (áutuord) adj. exterior; superficial; aparente; extraño; adv. hacia fuera, fuera; superficialmente; exteriormente; — **freight** flete de ida; — **bound** con rumbo a puerto extranjero.

outweigh (autuéi) v. preponderar; pasar más que; sobrepujar.

oval (óval) adj. oval, ovalado.

ovation (овéshon) s. ovación.

oven (óven) s. horno.

over (óver) prep. sobre, por; por encima de; allende, al otro lado; a pesar de; más de; a través de; **all — the world** en todo el mundo; **all —** por todas partes, por todos lados; — **to** a; adv. al otro lado; otra vez, de nuevo; por lo tanto; encima; demás; completamente; enteramente; adj. acabado; terminado; **it is all —** se acabó; — **and above** además de, por sobre todo; — **again** otra vez, de nuevo; — **against** enfrente, en contraste con; — **and —** una y otra vez; en repetidas ocasiones; — **here** acá, aquí; **to run —** atropellar; **turn —** ciclo comercial; **a la vuelta**; **to do it —** hacerlo otra vez; adj. excesivo; — **generous** demasiado generoso, excesivamente generoso.

overalls (óverols) s. pl. pantalones, regularmente de mezclilla, para el trabajo; overoles.

overate (overéit) pret. de to overeat.

overboard (óverbourd) adv. al mar, al agua; **to fail —** caer fuera de la borda, caer al agua; **man —!** ¡hombre al agua!

overcame (overkéim) pret. de to overcome.

overcast (overcást) adj. nublado, cerrado (el cielo), sombrío; encapotado; **to become —** nublarse; sobrehilar (dar puntadas sobre el bordado de una tela).

overcoat (óverkout) s. abrigo; gabán.

overcome (overkóm) v. vencer; domar; subyugar; sujetar; conquistar; sobreponerse; adj. vencido, rendido; agobiado.

overeat (overít) v. hartarse.

overeaten (overítn) p.p. de to overeat.

— 156 —

overexcite (overeksáit) v. sobreexcitar.

overflow (overflóu) s. inundación; avenida; derrame; desbordamiento; superabundancia; v. inundar, rebosar; desbordarse, derramarse.

overgrown (overgróun) adj. cubierto de hierba o follaje; frondoso; — **boy** muchacho demasiado crecido.

overhang (overjáng) s. sobresalir; colgar; pender de; mirar a, dar a, caer a; amenazar, ser inminente (un desastre, una calamidad).

overhaul (overjól) v. reparar; remendar; alcanzar a otro en una carrera; registrar, revisar.

overhead (óverjed) s. gastos generales de administración; adj. de arriba, elevado; adv. en lo alto; encima de; arriba.

overhear (overjír) escuchar palabras no destinadas a quien las oye; oír por casualidad; alcanzar a oír.

overheard (overjérd) pret. y p.p. de **to overhear**.

overheat (overjít) v. recalentar; s. recalentamiento.

overhung (overjóng) pret. y p.p. de **to overhang**.

overland (óverland) adj. y adv. por tierra; — **route** por la vía terrestre, por tierra.

overload (overlóud) v. recargar, sobrecargar; s. sobrecarga.

overlook (overlúk) v. mirar desde lo alto; dominar con la vista; examinar; vigilar; pasar por alto; disimular, tolerar; perdonar o no hacer caso de alguna falta; hacerse de la vista gorda; s. altura; atalaya; mirada desde lo alto.

overly (óverli) adv. excesivamente.

overnight (óvernait) adv. durante la noche o por la noche; de noche; toda la noche; adj. nocturno; — **bag** saco de noche; — **trip** viaje de una noche.

overpower (overpáuer) v. predominar; subyugar; superar; sobrepujar.

overran (overrán) pret. de **to overrun**.

overrun (overrón) v. invadir; infestar; desbordarse, rebosar; traspasar los límites, excederse.

overseas (oversís) adv. ultramar; allende el mar.

oversee (oversí) v. dirigir, vigilar.

overseer (oversír) s. sobrestante, capataz; inspector; superintendente; mayoral, obrajero.

overshoe (óvershu) s. chanclo; zapato de goma, caucho o hule.

oversight (oversáit) s. inadvertencia, negligencia; yerro, equivocación; descuido.

overstep (overstép) v. sobrepasarse; propasarse; traspasar; transgredir; extralimitarse; excederse.

overtake (overtéik) v. alcanzar.

overtaken (overtéikn) p.p. de **to overtake**.

overthrew (overzrú) pret. de **to overthrow**.

overthrow (overzróu) s. derrocamiento, derrota, destrucción; v. echar abajo; derrocar, derribar; demoler, vencer; destronar.

overthrown (overzróun) p.p. de **to overthrow**.

overtime (óvertaim) adv. y adj. en exceso de las horas estipuladas; fuera del trabajo estipulado.

overtook (overtúk) pret. de **to overtake**.

overture (óverchur) s. obertura; preludio; propuesta; insinuación.

overturn (overtérn) v. volcar(se);

overwhelm (overjuélm) v. abrumar; agobiar, oprimir, arrollar, hundir.

overwhelming (overjuélming) adj. abrumador; opresivo, arrollador, preponderante; irresistible.

overwork (óveruérk) v. atarearse; afanarse; hacer trabajar con exceso; s. exceso de trabajo.

owe (óu) v. deber, adeudar.

owing (óuing) adj. debido.

owl (ául) s. lechuza, búho, tecolote.

own (óun) adj. propio; particular; peculiar; individual; verdadero, real; a **house of his** — una casa suya; **this is my** — esto me pertenece; **my** — **brother** mi propio hermano; **he is on his** — trabaja por su propia cuenta; **it is his** — **fault** es culpa suya; v. poseer; tener; reconocer; confesar; aseverar.

owner (óuner) s. dueño, amo; propietario; poseedor o posesor.

ownership (óunership) s. posesión, propiedad, dominio.

ox (ox) pl. **oxen** (óksn) s. buey

oxygen (óksivin) s. oxígeno.

P

pace (péis) s. paso; marcha, modo de andar; v. pasear, andar; marchar; recorrer o medir a pasos.
pacific (pasífik) adj. pacífico.
pacify (pásifai) v. pacificar; apaciguar; calmar; poner paz.
pack (pak) s. paquete; lío; fardo; paca; carga; hato; manada; cuadrilla; jauría; muchedumbre; baraja completa; — mule acémila de carga; v. empacar, empaquetar; envasar; enlatar; atestar; arreglar el equipaje; to — away largarse; to — off despedir; echar a la calle; — train recua; — saddle albarda, basto.
package (pákey) s. paquete; fardo; bulto; cajetilla (de cigarros); abarrote, envase.
packer (páker) s. empacador; embalador, envasador; arpillador.
packet (páket) s. paquetillo.
packing (páking) s. embalaje; envase; relleno; enfardeladura; — box caja para embalar o empacar; — house establecimiento frigorífico; establecimiento donde se embarrilan conservas alimenticias; empacadora.
pact (pakt) s. pacto, convenio.
pad (pad) s. almohadilla; cojincillo; tableta; caderillas; hoja grande de planta acuática; v. rellenar; forrar, acolchar.
padding (páding) s. relleno (de pelo, algodón, paja, etc.); guata; imprimación; palabras o frases inútiles; ripio.
paddle (pádl) s. pala, remo de canoa; canalete; — wheel rueda de paleta; v. remar con pala, apalear; bogar o remar con canalete.
padlock (pádlok) s. candado; v. cerrar con candado.
pagan (péigan) s. y adj. pagano.
paganism (péiganism) s. paganismo.
page (pey) s. página, paje, "botones" (de hotel); escudero; criado; v. paginar; vocear, llamar a voces.
pageant (péyant) s. manifestación; desfile; procesión; pompa; espectáculo, aparato escénico.
paid (péid) s. pret. y p.p. de to pay.
pail (péil) s. balde, cubo, cubeta.
painful (péinful) adj. doloroso; penoso; arduo, aflictivo; ímprobo.

painless (péinles) adj. sin dolor; libre de dolor.
painstaking (péinsteiking) adj. esmerado; cuidadoso; aplicado.
paint (peint) s. pintura; color; colorete; v. pintar; colorar; dar una capa o baño.
paintbrush (péintbrosh) s. pincel.
painter (péinter) s. pintor.
painting (péinting) s. pintura; coloración; cuadro o pintura al óleo, al temple etc.
pair (péir) s. par, pareja; marido y mujer; macho y hembra; a — of scissors unas tijeras; v. aparear; hacer pareja.
pajamas (payámas) s. pl. pijama.
pal (pal) s. compañero, camarada, confederado; codelincuente.
palace (pálas) s. palacio.
palate (pálet) s. paladar.
pale (péil) adj. pálido, descolorido; v. palidecer; ponerse pálido.
paleness (péilnes) s. palidez.
palisade (paliséid) s. palizada, estacada; empalizada; —s riscos.
pall (pol) s. paño mortuorio; palio; v. empalagar, aburrir; —s on me me empalaga, me aburre; desvirtuar; poner insípido; desalentar, desanimar; saciar, ahitar; perder el sabor o el atractivo.
pallid (pálid) adj. pálido.
pallor (pálor) s. palidez.
palm (pam) s. palma; palmera; victoria; palma de la mano; — Sunday Domingo de Ramos; — cabbage palmito; v. escamotear; engañar, defraudar; manosear.
palpable (pálpabl) adj. palpable; tangible; evidente; obvio.
palpitate (pálpiteit) v. palpitar.
palpitation (palpitéshon) s. palpitación; latido.
paltry (póltri) adj. mezquino, miserable, despreciable, vil.
pamper (pámper) v. mimar; consentir (a un niño), engordar.
pamphlet (pámflet) s. folleto; panfleto; impreso.
pan (pan) s. cazuela; cacerola; cazo; platillo (de balanza); perol; caldero; **dish** — cazo para lavar platos; **v. to** — **out (well)** salir bien; dar buen resultado o provecho.
pancake (pánkeik) s. tortita de harina; panqué; filló.
pander (pánder) s. alcahuete; encubridor; v. alcahuetear; servir de alcahuete.

pane (pein) s. vidrio; vidriera; cristal (de ventana o puerta).
panel (pánel) s. panel; tablero; cuarterón (de puerta, ventana, etc.); artesón; cara de una piedra labrada; **jury —** jurado; v. proveer de (o adornar con) paneles.
pang (pang) s. dolor, tormento, pena.
panic (pánik) adj. y s. pánico; miedo o terror ciego; **— struck** sobrecogido de terror.
pansy (pánsi) s. pensamiento (flor).
pant (pant) v. jadear, anhelar con vehemencia; palpitar; ansiar.
panther (pánzer) s. pantera.
panting (pánting) s. jadeo, palpitación; adj. jadeante.
pantry (pántri) s. despensa.
pants (pants) s. pl. pantalones.
papa (pápa) s. papá.
papal (péipal) adj. papal.
paper (péiper) s. papel, periódico.
par (par) s. paridad; igualdad; paridad de cambio; equivalente; **— value** valor a la par; **at — a** la par; **on a — with** a la par con, al igual que; **below — a** descuento; **to feel above** (o) **below par** sentirse mejor o peor que de ordinario.
parable (párabl) s. parábola (alegoría bíblica).
parachute (párachut) s. paracaídas.
parachutist (párachutist) s. paracaidista.
parade (paréid) s. desfile, parada; revista militar; procesión; marcha; paseo; **— ground** campo de maniobras; v. hacer ostentación de; desfilar; marchar; ir en procesión; pasear con pompa.
paradise (páradais) s. paraíso.
paradox (páradoks) s. paradoja.
paraffin (párafin) s. parafina.
paragraph (págraf) s. párrafo; v. dividir en párrafos.
Paraguayan (paraguáian) adj. y s. paraguayo.
parallel (páralel) adj. y s. paralelo; cotejo; v. correr en paralelo; cotejar; comparar.
paralysis (parálisis) s. parálisis.
paralyze (páralais) v. paralizar.
paramount (páramaunt) adj. importantísimo; principalísimo; superior; supremo, eminente; de primer orden.
parapet (párapet) s. parapeto.
parasite (párasait) s. parásito.

parasol (párasol) s. sombrilla; parasol; quitasol.
parcel (pársl) s. paquete, parcela; lote; porción; **— post parcela** postal; paquete postal **— of ground** parcela de tierra; v. parcelar; dividir en porciones; hacer paquetes; **to — out** repartir; hacer particiones.
parch (parch) v. desecar; tostar; abrasar; quemar.
parchment (párchment) s. pergamino.
pardon (párdn) v. perdonar; disculpar; indultar; hacer gracia; dispensar; **I beg your —** perdone usted; usted dispense.
pare (per) v. mondar, pelar frutas; cortar las uñas; cercenar; **to — potatoes** pelar papas.
parent (pérent) s. el padre o la madre; **—s** los padres; autor, causa.
parentage (pérentey) s. linaje, parentela; origen y descendencia.
parenthesis (parénzesis) s. paréntesis.
parish (párish) s. parroquia.
parishioner (paríshoner) s. parroquiano, feligrés; **—s** fieles.
park (párk) s. parque; v. estacionar; dejar un automóvil; estacionarse; **—ing lot** lote de estacionamiento; **free —ing** estacionamiento gratis; **no —ing** se prohíbe estacionarse.
parley (párli) s. parlamento; conferencia; plática; v. parlamentar; discutir; conferenciar.
parliament (párliament) s. parlamento; cuerpo legislativo.
parliamentary (parliaméntari) adj. parlamentario.
parlor (párlor) s. sala, salón; sala de recibo; **beauty —** salón de belleza.
parochial (parókial) adj. parroquial.
parody (párodi) s. parodia; v. parodiar.
parole (paról) s. palabra de honor; **to put on —** dejar libre bajo palabra de honor; libertad preparatoria.
parrot (párrot) s. loro, papagayo; cotorra; v. remedar, repetir como loro o perico.
parry (párri) v. parar, rechazar el golpe de un contrario.
parsley (pársli) s. perejil.
parsnip (pársnip) s. chirivía.

parson (párson) s. pastor; clérigo.
part (part) s. parte; porción; región; lugar; obligación; raya del cabello; papel dramático; **— and parcel** uña y carne; **— owner** condueño; **spare —s** refacciones; **for my part** por lo que a mi toca; **in foreign —s** en otros países, en el extranjero; **do your —** cumpla usted con su obligación; v. partir, separar(se); desprenderse; irse; tomar parte; **to — company** separarse de; **to — from** despedirse; decir adiós; **to — with** deshacerse de algo, ceder; **to — the hair** hacerse la raya en el pelo.
partake (partéik) v. participar; tener parte en; repartir.
partaken (partéiken) p.p. de **to partake**.
partial (párshal) adj. parcial; **—ly** adv. parcialmente; en parte.
partiality (parshálití) s. parcialidad.
participant (partisipant) adj. y s. partícipe; copartícipe.
participate (partisipeit) v. participar; tomar parte en algo.
participation (partisipéshon) s. participación; distribución.
participle (pártisipl) s. participio; **present —** gerundio.
particle (pártikl) s. partícula.
particular (partikiular) adj. particular; peculiar; privativo; singular; esmerado; preciso; minucioso; quisquilloso; raro; escrupuloso; s. particular, detalle, circunstancia; relación; dato; **—ly** adv. en particular.
parting (párting) s. despedida; bifurcación; separación; **the — of the ways** la encrucijada; la bifurcación, el cruce de caminos.
partisan (pártisn) adj. partidario; parcial; s. partidario, secuaz.
partition (partishon) s. división; pared; partición; separación; v. dividir, partir; separar.
partly (pártli) adv. en parte.
partner (pártner) s. socio; compañero, cómplice; camarada; pareja (en el baile).
partnership (pártnership) s. sociedad en participación.
partook (partúk) pret. de **to partake**.
partridge (pártriy) s. perdiz.
party (párti) s. partido; parte en un pleito; partida de gente; fiesta, convite; reunión; **a fishing —** una partida de pesca; **political —** partido político.
pass (pas) v. pasar; atravesar; cruzar; trasponer; aprobar; trasladar; cerner; aventajar; cesar; morir; ocurrir, suceder; pronunciar sentencia; adoptar una ley; dejar de hacer una jugada; **to come to —** acontecer, suceder; s. paso, pasillo; pasaje; desfiladero, garganta; pasaporte, salvoconducto, pase; estocada; **— parole** santo y seña.
passable (pásabl) adj. pasable, transferible; transitable; pasadero.
passage (pásey) s. pasaje; tránsito; travesía; callejón; ocurrencia; acontecimiento; lance; pasadizo.
passenger (pásenyer) s. pasajero; transeúnte; viajero; **the —s** el pasaje; los pasajeros.
passer-by (páserbai) s. transeúnte; viandante.
passion (páshon) s. pasión; ira, cólera; **Passion play** drama de la pasión; v. llorar, lamentar.
passionate (páshoneit) adj. apasionado.
passive (pásiv) adj. pasivo; quieto; inactivo; s. voz pasiva.
passport (pásport) s. pasaporte.
password (pásuerd) s. consigna; contraseña, santo y seña; palabra de pase.
past (past) adj. pasado; último; transcurrido; concluido, terminado; consumado; **— master** perito; **the — president** el expresidente, el último presidente; **woman with a —** mujer de malos antecedentes; **— tense** tiempo pasado, pretérito; **half — three** las tres y media; **woman — forty** mujer de más de cuarenta años; **— bearing** insoportable; infecundo; **to go — the house** pasar por (o por enfrente) de la casa; **— hope** sin esperanza; s. pasado; pretérito imperfecto; lo pasado; antecedentes, historia.
pasteboard (péistbourd) s. cartón; adj. de cartón, acartonado.
pasteurize (pásteris) v. pasterizar (o pasteurizar).
pastime (pástaim) s. pasatiempo.
pastor (pástor) s. pastor, clérigo, cura, pastor espiritual.
pastoral (pástoral) adj. pastoril;

PASTRY   **PEAK**

pastoral; pastoricio; s. pastoral; carta pastoral; bucólica, égloga.
pastry (péistri) s. pastelería, pasteles; pastas; — **cook** pastelero.
pasture (páschur) s. pastura; pasto; dehesa; apacentadero; v. pastar.
pat (pat) adj. apto, oportuno; conveniente, propio; **to have a lesson** — saber al dedillo la lección; **to stand** — mantenerse firme; adv. a propósito; oportunamente; justamente; s. palmadita; caricia, golpecito; mamola; v. dar palmaditas a; acariciar; pasar la mano.
patch (pátch) s. remiendo; parche; apaño; pedazo (de terreno); sembrado; v. remedar; echar remiendos; hacer labor de retazos.
pate (péit) s. coronilla (de la cabeza); la cabeza; **bald** — calva.
patent (pátent) adj. patente; evidente; manifiesto; visible, público; — **leather** charol; — **medicine** medicina de patente; s. patente; privilegio; v. patentar; obtener una patente o privilegio exclusivo.
paternal (patérnal) adj. paternal.
paternity (patérniti) s. paternidad.
path (paz) s. senda, sendero; vereda, ruta; camino; vía; huella.
pathetic (pazétik) adj. patético.
pathos (pázos) s. patetismo, cualidad patética, sentimiento.
pathway (pázwei) s. senda, vereda.
patient (péshent) adj. paciente; pacienzudo; s. paciente; doliente.
patriarch (pétriark) s. patriarca.
patrimony (pátrimoni) s. patrimonio.
patriot (pétriot) s. patriota.
patriotic (peitriótik) adj. patriótico.
patrol (patról) s. patrulla; ronda; v. patrullar, rondar; hacer la ronda.
patron (péitron) s. patrón, patrono; benefactor; patrocinador; cliente, parroquiano; santo patrón.
patronage (péitroney) s. patrocinio; amparo; clientela; protección; condescendencia; **political** — control de nombramientos políticos.
patroness (péitrones) s. patrona; protectora, patrocinadora.
patronize (péitronais) v. patrocinar; amparar; apadrinar; apoyar; tratar con condescendencia.

patter (páter) v. golpetear ligeramente; talonear; charlar; hacer ruido acompasado; s. golpeteo, golpecitos, pataleo.
pattern (pátern) s. modelo; dechado; muestra; ejemplo, patrón; molde; pauta, regla, norma; plantilla, escantillón; dibujo (en tejidos, telas, etc.); v. **to** — **oneself after** seguir el ejemplo de; copiar, imitar; **servir de** ejemplo.
paunch (pónch) s. panza, barriga, vientre; panza de los rumiantes.
pause (pos) s. pausa; suspensión; v. pausar, hacer pausa, cesar, parar; detener(se); interrumpirse.
pave (péiv) v. pavimentar; empedrar; adoquinar; **to** — **the way for** preparar o abrir bien el camino para; enladrillar.
pavement (péivment) s. pavimento; empedrado, adoquinado.
pavilion (pavílion) s. pabellón.
paw (poh) s. garra; zarpa; v. echar la zarpa; arañar; manosear; piafar; **to** — **the ground** patear la tierra (dícese del caballo).
pawn (pohn) s. prenda, empeño; peón (de ajedrez); — **broker** prestamista; — **shop** empeño; **in** — en prenda; v. empeñar.
pay (pei) v. pagar; remunerar; costear; recompensar; convenir, ser provechoso; **to** — **attention** prestar atención; **to** — **in cash** pagar al contado; **to** — **off** pagar y despedir a un empleado; **to** — **back** restituir, devolver; **to** — **by instalments** pagar en abonos; s. paga, sueldo, salario, compensación; — **day** día de pago; — **master** pagador; — **roll** nómina de sueldos.
payable (péiebl) adj. pagadero.
payment (péiment) s. pago; recompensa; — **in full** pago total.
pea (pi) s. chícharo, guisante; **chick-pea** garbanzo.
peace (pis) s. paz.
peaceable (písabl) adj. pacífico; sosegado, tranquilo, apacible.
peaceful (písful) adj. quieto, apacible, tranquilo.
peach (pích) s. durazno; melocotón; adj. bella, encantadora; **dried** — orejones.
peacock (píkok) s. pavo real; **to act like a** — pavonearse; hacer ostentación.
peak (pik) s. cima, cumbre, pica-

cho; cúspide; v. dar la impresión de estar enfermo.

peal (píl) v. repicar las campanas; s. repique; **— of laughter** risotada, carcajada; **to ring the bells in a —** tocar las campanas a vuelo.

peanut (pínot) s. maní, cacahuate.

pear (per) s. pera; **— tree** peral; **— shaped** piriforme; **alligator —** aguacate.

pearl (perl) s. perla; **mother of —** nácar; madreperla; **— eyed** que tiene una nube en un ojo.

pearly (pérli) adj. perlino; aperlado; aljofarado.

peasant (pésant) s. labriego, aldeano; campesino; jíbaro, patán.

pebble (pébl) s. guijarro, piedrecilla; adoquín; **— stone** lente de cristal de roca.

peck (pek) v. picar; picotear; to **— at** regañar de continuo; s. picotazo; gran cantidad; a **— of trouble** la mar de disgustos; medida de áridos (aproximadamente 9 litros).

peculiar (pekiúliar) adj. peculiar; singular, privativo, raro; extraño; extraordinario.

peculiarity (pekiuliáriti) s. peculiaridad; singularidad; rareza.

pedagogue (pédagog) s. pedagogo; maestro de escuela; dómine.

pedal (pédal) v. pedalear; ir en bicicleta, mover los pedales.

pedant (pédant) s. pedante.

pedantic (pedántik) adj. pedante; pedantesco.

peddle (pédl) v. ir vendiendo de puerta en puerta; escatimar, revender.

peddler (pédler) s. buhonero; revendedor; vendedor ambulante.

pedestal (pédestal) s. pedestal.

pedestrian (pedéstrian) s. peatón; transeúnte; caminante; peón; adj. pedestre; vulgar.

pedigree (pédigri) s. genealogía.

peek (pik) v. atisbar, espiar; s. atisbo; **— a boo** escondite, juego de niños.

peel (pil) s. corteza, cáscara (de algunas frutas); pellejo; telilla de cebolla; v. descortezar; mondar, pelar; deshollejar.

peep (pip) v. atisbar, espiar; mirar a hurtadillas; asomar; s. atisbo, ojeada; atisbadura.

peer (pír) s. par, igual, noble; compañero; grande; v. mirar con atención; escudriñar, atisbar, fisgar, husmear; asomar, salir.

peeve (piv) v. irritar; poner de mal humor; **to get —d** disgustarse.

peevish (pívish) adj. enojadizo; malhumorado, quisquilloso.

pellet (pélet) s. pelotilla; píldora; bolita; perdigón.

pell-mell (pelmél) adv. confusamente; atropelladamente, en tumulto; adj. confuso; tumultuoso.

pelt (pélt) s. piel; zalea, cuero; v. apedrear; llover; arrojar; golpear; caer con fuerza.

pen (pen) s. pluma (para escribir); corral, zahurda; gallinero; **— holder** portapluma; **— name** nombre de pluma, seudónimo; **fountain —** pluma fuente; **pig —** pocilga; v. escribir; componer; acorralar; encerrar.

penal (pínal) adj. penal.

penalty (pénalti) s. penalidad; pena; castigo.

penance (pénans) s. penitencia.

pencil (pénsil) s. lápiz; lapicero; **red lead —** lápiz rojo.

pendant (péndent) s. pendiente.

pending (pénding) adj. pendiente, colgante; prep. durante, mientras.

pendulum (péndiulum) s. péndulo.

penetrate (pénetreit) v. penetrar.

penetrating (pénetreiting) adj. penetrante, penetrativo.

penetration (penetréshon) s. penetración, filtración.

peninsula (penínsola) s. península.

penitent (pénitent) adj. arrepentido, penitente, contrito; s. penitente; arrepentida.

penitentiary (peniténshari) s. penitenciaría; presidio, cárcel modelo; penitenciario.

penknife (pénnaif) s. cortaplumas; navaja, cuchilla.

penmanship (pénmanship) s. escritura, caligrafía, carácter de letra.

pennant (pénant) s. banderola; gallardete, grímpola, insignia.

penniless (péniles) adj. pobre, sin dinero, sin blanca.

penny (péni) s. centavo (de dólar); dinero en general; **to cost a pretty —** costar un ojo de la cara.

pension (pénshon) s. pensión; retiro (de un militar); cesantía; v. pensionar, dar una pensión.

pensive (pénsiv) adj. pensativo.
pent (pent) adj. encerrado; acorralado; enjaulado; **pent-up emotions** sentimientos reprimidos.
people (pípl) s. gente, v. poblar.
pepper (péper) s. pimienta; **black** — pimienta negra; — **plant** pimentero; **red o Cayenne** — pimentón; pimiento; **green** —**s** pimientos verdes; v. sazonar con pimienta; sazonar una conversación o escrito con dichos picantes.
peppermint (pépermint) s. menta; hierba buena o yerbabuena.
percale (perkál) s. percal.
perceive (persív) v. percibir.
percentage (percéntey) s. porcentaje, tanto por ciento.
perceptible (percéptibl) adj. perceptible.
perception (persépshon) s. percepción.
perch (perch) s. percha (para pájaros); perca (pez); pértica (medida); alcántara; v. posarse (en una percha o rama).
perchance (percháns) adv. por ventura.
percolate (pércoleit) v. filtrar(se).
perdition (perdíshon) s. perdición.
perennial (perénial) adj. perenne.
perfect (pérfekt) adj. perfecto; completo; acabado, cabal; entero; s. tiempo perfecto (del verbo); v. perfeccionar, acabar, consumar, coronar; redondear, puntualizar.
perfection (perfékshon) s. perfección.
perfidious (perfídious) adj. pérfido.
perfidy (pérfidi) s. perfidia.
perforate (pérforeit) v. perforar.
performance (perfórmans) s. ejecución; desempeño; cumplimiento; composición, obra; acción, hecho, hazaña; representación; acto.
perfume (pérfium) s. perfume, fragancia, aroma; v. perfumar; sahumar.
perfumery (perfiúmeri) s. perfumería; perfumes.
perhaps (perjáps) adv. acaso, tal vez; quizá(s); puede ser, por ventura.
peril (péril) s. peligro; riesgo; exposición; trance; v. poner en peligro; estar en peligro, arriesgar.
perilous (périlous) adj. peligroso.
perimeter (perímeter) s. perímetro.

period (píriod) s. período, fin.
periodic (periódik) adj. periódico.
periodical (periódikal) adj. periódico; s. revista; publicación periódica.
perish (pérish) v. perecer.
perishable (périshabl) adj. perecedero; deleznable, frágil.
perjure (péryur) v. **to** — **oneself** perjurar.
perjury (péryuri) s. perjurio; **to commit** — jurar en falso.
permanence (pérmanens) s. permanencia, duración, fijeza.
permanent (pérmanent) adj. permanente, duradero.
permeate (pérmiet) v. penetrar, saturar; atravesar, pasar por medio.
permissible (permísibl) adj. lícito.
permission (permíshon) s. permiso, licencia, permisión.
permit (pérmit) s. permiso, pase; licencia; v. permitir, consentir.
pernicious (perníshos) adj. pernicioso, funesto, fatal.
perpendicular (perpendíkiular) adj. y s. perpendicular.
perpetrate (pérpetreit) v. perpetrar, cometer algún delito o culpa grave.
perpetual (perpéchual) adj. perpetuo.
perpetuate (perpéchueit) v. perpetuar.
perplexed (perplékst) adj. perplejo, irresoluto, confuso, dudoso.
perplexity (perpléksiti) s. perplejidad, duda, irresolución.
persecute (pérsekiut) v. perseguir, acosar, molestar, hostigar, vejar, importunar.
persecution (persekiúshon) s. persecución, vejación, acosamiento.
persecutor (pérsekiutor) s. perseguidor, acosador.
perseverance (persevírans) v. perseverancia, persistencia.
persevere (perservír) v. perseverar; persistir.
persist (persíst) v. persistir.
persistence (persístens) s. persistencia; porfía, constancia.
persistent (persístent) adj. persistente; porfiado, perseverante, firme, resuelto.
person (pérson) s. persona.
personage (pérsoney) s. personaje.
personal (pérsonal) adj. personal; en persona, particular, corporal.
personality (personáliti) s. perso-

nalidad; individualidad; personaje.
personnel (personél) s. personal.
perspective (perspéktiv) s. perspectiva; — drawing dibujo en perspectiva.
perspiration (perspiréshon) s. sudor.
perspire (perspáir) v. sudar.
persuade (persuéid) v. persuadir.
persuasion (persuéshon) s. persuasión; creencia; inducción, opinión fija.
persuasive (persuésiv) adj. persuasivo.
pert (pert) adj. insolente; descarado, atrevido; petulante.
pertain (pertéin) v. pertenecer.
pertinent (pértinent) adj. pertinente, al caso, atinado.
perturb (pertórb) v. perturbar.
peruse (perús) v. leer con cuidado.
Peruvian (perúvian) adj. y s. peruano.
pervade (pervéid) v. llenar, penetrar; compenetrarse; ocupar.
pervert (pervért) v. pervertir; falsear; corromper; s. perverso.
pessimism (pésimism) s. pesimismo.
pessimist (pésimist) s. pesimista; —ic adj. pesimista.
pest (pest) s. peste; plaga; pestilencia; persona revoltosa.
pester (péster) v. importunar.
pestilence (péstilens) s. pestilencia, peste.
pet (pet) s. animal mimado; animal casero o doméstico; favorito; niño mimado; adj. favorito; mimado; acariciado; — name nombre de cariño; v. mimar, acariciar.
petal (pétal) s. pétalo.
petition (petíshon) s. petición; súplica; instancia; recurso; representación; memorial, solicitud; v. solicitar, pedir; dirigir una instancia o memorial a; rogar.
petroleum (petrólium) s. petróleo; — ether nafta.
petticoat (péticout) s. enaguas.
petty (péti) adj. insignificante; pequeño; mezquino, despreciable; inferior; subordinado; — cash fondos para gastos menores; — wares géneros menudos; — larceny ratería; — officer oficial subordinado (en la marina).
pew (piú) s. banco de iglesia.
phantom (fántom) s. fantasma.
pharmacist (fármasist) s. farmacéutico, boticario.

pharmacy (fármasi) s. farmacia.
phase (feis) s. fase.
phenomena (fenómena) pl. de phenomenon.
phenomenon (fenómenon) s. fenómeno.
philosopher (filósofer) s. filósofo.
philosophical (filosófikal) adj. filosófico.
philosophy (filósofi) s. filosofía.
phone (fóun) s. teléfono; v. telefonear.
phonetics (fonétiks) s. fonética.
phonograph (fónograf) s. fonógrafo.
phosphate (fósfeit) s. fosfato.
phosphorous (fósforous) s. fósforo, elemento químico.
photo (fóto) s. fotografía.
photograph (fótograf) s. fotografía; retrato, v. fotografiar, retratar.
photographer (fotógrafer) s. fotógrafo.
photography (fotógrafi) s. fotografía.
phrase (fréis) s. frase; expresión; período, locución; v. frasear.
physic (físik) s. purga, purgante; medicina; v. purgar.
physical (físikal) adj. físico.
physician (fisishan)) s. médico.
physicist (físicist) s. físico.
physics (físiks) s. física.
physiological (fisiolóyikal) adj. fisiológico.
physiology (fisióloyi) s. fisiología.
physique (fisíc) s. físico; constitución física; figura, presencia.
piano (piáno) s. piano; pianoforte; — bench banqueta de piano; — cabinet — piano vertical; — stool taburete de piano; grand — piano de cola; upright — piano vertical.
picaresque (picarésk) adj. picaresco.
pickaxes (píkaks) s. pico, zapapicos.
picket (píket) s. piquete (estaca o palo clavado en la tierra); — guard piquete, centinela avanzada; v. estacionar piquetes cerca de (una fábrica, campamento, etc); poner o colocar de guardia.
pickle (píkl) s. encurtido; salmuera; adobo; pepinillo; to be in a — hallarse en un aprieto; to have a rod in — tenérsela guardada a uno; v. encurtir; escabechar, adobar; conservar.

pickpocket (píkpoket) s. ratero.
picnic (píknik) s. partida de campo; día de campo, jira, romería; Am. día de campo; v. hacer una comida campestre; ir de romería.
picture (píkchur) s. cuadro, pintura; retrato, ilustración, diseño; lámina; fotografía; — **frame** marco; v. pintar; dibujar, describir; hacer un cuadro.
picturesque (pikchurésk) adj. pintoresco.
pie (pai) s. pastel, empanada; marica; urraca.
piece (pis) s. pieza; pedazo, trozo, sección; triza, cacho; retazo; parte; — **of advice** consejo; **of a —** (with) de la misma clase o calidad; — **of money** moneda; **to give one a —** of **one's mind** decirle a uno las verdades del barquero; v. remendar; apedazar, echar pedazos; **to — on to** juntar a.
pier (pir) s. muelle, embarcadero; estribo, pilar, pilón.
pierce (pirs) v. atravesar, traspasar; penetrar, agujerear, taladrar.
piety (páieti) s. piedad, devoción.
pig (pig) s. puerco, cerdo, cochino; marrano; — **iron** hierro en lingotes; —**s might fly** cuando la rana críe pelo; **guinea —** conejillo de Indias.
pigeon (píyon) s. pichón; paloma.
pigeonhole (píyonjoul) s. casilla; v. encasillar.
pigment (pígment) s. pigmento, color.
pike (paik) s. pica, lanza; lucio (pez).
pile (páil) s. pila; montón; rimero; hacina; pelo (de ciertos tejidos); pilote; fibra, pelillo, pelusa; —**s** almorranas (enfermedad); — **drawer** aparato para arrancar pilotes.
pilfer (pílfer) v. pillar; ratear; hurtar, sisar.
pilgrim (pílgrim) s. peregrino.
pilgrimage (pílgrimey) s. peregrinación, romería, peregrinaje.
pill (pil) s. píldora; desazón.
pillage (piley) v. pillar, saquear; s. saqueo, pillaje.
pillar (pílar) s. pilar, columna; **to go from — to post** ir de la Ceca a la Meca.
pillow (pílou) s. almohada, cojín.
pollowcase (píloukeis) s. funda de almohada.
pilot (pállot) s. piloto, práctico; guía; — **light** o — **burner** mechero; piloto de estufa; **harbor —** práctico de puerto; v. pilotear; guiar; conducir una nave a puerto.
pimple (pímpl) s. grano, barro.
pin (pin) s. alfiler, prendedor, clavija, pasador, perno, bolo; — **money** dinero para alfileres; — **wheel** molinete, remolino; **to — down** asegurar; fijar, sujetar; **to — one's hope to** cifrar todas sus esperanzas en; v. prender con alfileres; fijar con tachuelas; colgar un retrato o un cuadro.
pincers (pínsers) s. pl. pinzas; tenazas; **small —** tenacillas.
pinch (pinch) v. pellizcar; apretar; estrechar; escatimar; prender; arrestar; ahorrar, economizar; **to — one's finger in the door** machucarse el dedo en la puerta; s. pellizco, pizca, apuro, aprieto; dolor, tormento; **upon a —** en caso necesario, de apuro.
pinchers (pínchers) véase **pincers**.
pine (pain) s. pino; — **cone** piña — **grove** pinar; v. languidecer; debilitarse; **to — oneself to death** morirse o consumirse de pena.
pineapple (páinapl) s. piña; ananá.
pink (pink) s. clavel, color de rosa, color rojo muy claro; v. hacer ojales en la ropa.
pinnacle (pínakl) s. pináculo; chapitel; cima, cumbre.
pint (páint) s. pinta (aproximadamente medio litro).
pioneer (páionir) s. explorador, colonizador, fundador, iniciador, precursor; v. explorar, fundar, colonizar.
pious (páius) adj. pío, devoto, religioso.
pipe (páip) s. tubo, caño, conducto; pipa o cachimba para fumar; pipa, casco, tonel; —**s** gaita; **gas —** tubería de gas; **water —** cañería de agua; **to — down** callarse la boca; v. tocar la gaita, entubar, desaguar por cañería.
piper (páiper) s. gaitero.
piping (páiping) adj. hirviente; pastoril, que silba, chillón; s. cañería, tubería; — **hot** muy caliente; hirviendo.
pippin (pipin) s. camuesa.
pique (pik) s. pique; desazón, desavenencia ligera; resentimiento;

— 165 —

enojo; v. picar, irritar, hacer enojar; excitar.

pirate (páiret) s. pirata, corsario; v. piratear, plagiar, hurtar.

pistol (pístol) s. pistola, revólver.

piston (piston) s. émbolo, pistón; — **ring** anillo de pistón; — **rod** biela.

pit (pit) s. hoyo, foso, abismo; hueso de ciertas frutas; **arm— sobaco; sand—** mina de arena; — **of the stomach** boca del estómago.

pitch (pitch) s. pendiente, declive, paso de rosca, cabeceo de una nave; término; lanzamiento; brea; alquitrán; resina; — **dark** oscurísimo; v. tirar, lanzar la pelota; cabecear un barco; dar el diapasón; echarse de cabeza, inclinarse; instalarse; fijarse; establecerse; **to — in o into** acometer, embestir; arremeter contra; — **in!** manos a la obra.

pitcher (pítcher) s. parra, cántaro; lanzador en beisbol; pichel; bocal; jarro.

pitchfork (pítchfork) s. horca, horquilla (para hacinar las mieses, levantar la paja, etc.).

piteous (pítios) adj. lastimoso, compasivo, tierno.

pith (piz) s. médula espinal, meollo, corazón; fuerza, vigor; substancia; esencia; parte esencial.

pitiful (pítiful) adj. lastimoso, lamentable, miserable.

pitiless (pítiles) adj. cruel, inhumano, despiadado; duro de corazón.

pity (píti) s. piedad, misericordia; conmiseración; lástima; **for —'s sake!** ¡por piedad! ¡por Dios!; **what a —!** ¡qué lástima!; v. apiadarse, tener compasión; compadecerse; enternecerse.

placard (plákard) s. letrero; anuncio; cartel; v. fijar carteles.

place (pleis) s. sitio, lugar, paraje; plaza; puesto militar; situación, colocación; empleo; asiento; finca; quinta — **of refuge** asilo; **market —** plaza, mercado; **in —of** en lugar de, en vez de; **out of —** impropio, fuera de lugar; **to take —** verificarse, efectuarse, celebrarse; v. colocar, situar, acomodar, fijar.

placid (plásid) adj. plácido, apacible, tranquilo, sosegado.

plague (pléig) s. plaga; peste; calamidad; v. plagar, infestar.

plaid (pléid) s. tela a cuadros, tartán; género o manta escocesa listada a cuadros; diseño a cuadros.

plain (pléin) llano, sencillo.

plaintive (pléintiv) adj. triste, quejumbroso; lamentoso.

plan (plan) v. idear, proyectar, urdir; tramar; proponerse, planear; s. proyecto, plan, idea, diseño.

plane (pléin) s. plano, superficie plana; aeroplano; cepillo de carpintero; **jack —** garlopa; **dovetail —** guillame de ensamblar; v. allanar; acepillar; alisar; planear.

planet (plánet) s. planeta.

plank (plank) s. tablón; tarima; madero; v. entablar, entarimar; cubrir con madera o tablas.

plant (plant) s. planta; fábrica; taller; instalación de maquinaria; v. plantar; sembrar, instalar; establecer; fundar; **electric —** planta eléctrica.

plantation (plantéshon) s. plantío; plantación; siembra, hacienda; ingenio; ostrera; pl. colonias; **coffee —** cafetal; **sugar —** ingenio azucarero; **cotton —** plantío de algodón.

planter (plánter) s. sembrador, cultivador.

plaque (plék) s. placa.

plasma (plásma) s. plasma.

plaster (pláster) s. yeso; emplasto; — **of Paris** yeso mate; sulfato calcinado de cal; **court —** esparadrapo; tafetán; **mustard —** sinapismo; v. enyesar; poner un emplasto; pegar anuncios.

plastic (plástic) s. plástico.

plat (plat) s. plano, parcela; v. entretejer; delinear o trazar un plano; baderna.

plate (pleit) v. cubrir con planchas de metal; dorar, platear; niquelar; s. placa, plancha, plato; lámina; chapa de metal.

plateau (plató) s. altiplanicie; meseta; rasa.

plateful (pléitful) s. plato lleno.

platform (plátform) s. plataforma; tribuna; andén; declaración de principios de un partido político.

platinum (plátinum) s. platino.

platitud (plátitud) s. perogrullada; adj. trivial, vulgar.

platter (pláter) s. plato grande; fuente, platón.
play (pléi) v. jugar, entretenerse; tocar música; representar un papel; manejar, manipular; usar o valerse de; arrojar, lanzar; ondular, flotar; to — a trick engañar, hacer una mala jugada; to — a joke gastar una broma; to — a game jugar una partida; to — havoc hacer estragos, arrasar, causar daño; to — at cards jugar a la baraja; to — out agotar las energías; s. juego, divertimiento, recreo; comedia, drama, función, representación; libertad de acción; movimiento libre, juego entre dos piezas; fair — juego limpio; in — turno para jugar.
player (pléier) s. jugador; actor; músico; comediante; **piano** — pianista; instrumentista.
playful (pléiful) adj. juguetón; travieso; bullanguero.
playground (pléigraund) s. campo deportivo, para juegos, de recreo.
playmate (pléimeit) s. compañero en el juego.
plaything (pléizing) s. juguete.
playwright (pléirrait) s. dramaturgo.
plea (pli) s. argumento; ruego; súplica; instancia; alegato; defensa; disculpa; excusa; pretexto; — **in abatement** instancia de nulidad.
plead (plid) v. defender en juicio; argüir; suplicar; rogar; to — **guilty** declararse o confesarse culpable; to — **not guilty** negar la acusación.
pleasant (plésnt) adj. placentero; grato, agradable, simpático.
pleasantry (plésntri) s. humorada; broma; chanza; chiste.
please (plís) v. complacer; agradar; dar gusto; satisfacer; tener gusto en; servirse; tener a bien; — **do it** haga usted el favor de hacerlo; tenga la amabilidad de hacerlo; **as you** — como usted quiera, como guste; **I am** —**d to see you** tengo mucho gusto en verle; — **be seated** sírvase tomar asiento, **I am** —**d with** estoy satisfecho de.
pleasing (plísing) adj. grato, placentero, agradable.
pleasure (pléshur) s. placer, gusto; satisfacción; deleite; alegría; — **trip** viaje de recreo; **with much** — con mucho gusto.

pleat (plit) s. pliegue, doblez, alforza; v. plegar, hacer pliegues.
plebeian (plebéian) adj. y s. plebeyo.
pledge (pledy) s. promesa; garantía; fianza; prenda; v. empeñar; dar en prenda; prometer; hacer firmar una promesa; to — **one's word** dar o empeñar la palabra de uno; to — **to secrecy** exigir promesa de sigilo.
plenipotentiary (plenipoténsheri) adj. y s. plenipotenciario.
plentiful (pléntiful) adj. copioso; abundante; fértil; feraz.
plenty (plénti) s. abundancia; copia; profusión; afluencia; demasía; — **of time** bastante tiempo; **that is** — con eso basta.
pliable (pláiabl) adj. flexible; dócil, manejable; transigente.
pliant (pláiant) adj. doblegable; dócil, blando; sumiso.
pliers (pláiers) s. alicates, pinzas, tenazas.
plight (pláit) s. compromiso solemne; promesa; esponsales; promesa de matrimonio.
plod (plod) v. bregar, afanarse, trabajar con ahínco.
plot (plot) s. conspiración; intriga; trama; estratagema; enredo; complot; parcela; solar; plano, esquema; diagrama; v. conspirar; tramar; urdir; hacer un plano; to — **a curve** hacer una gráfica.
plotter (plóter) s. conspirador; conjurado; intrigante.
plough véase **plow.**
plow (pláu) s. arado; **snow** — quitanieves; v. arar; labrar la tierra.
pluck (plók) v. tirar con fuerza de; arrancar; desplumar un ave; derribar; to — **up** cobrar ánimo; s. valor, resolución, arranque, ánimo; menudencias de un animal.
plucky (plóki) adj. valeroso, animoso.
plug (plóg) s. tapón; obturador; llave; enchufe; cualquier cosa que no sirve; se aplica especialmente a los caballos; — **of tobacco** tabaco curado o torcido; **electric** — tapón o clavija de conexión; **spark** — bujía para auto; **fire** — boca de agua para incendios; **to** — **in** enchufar; v. tapar; obturar; orificar; to — **along** atarearse, afanarse.

plum (plóm) s. ciruela; la parte óptima de una cosa; lo mejor; — **pudding** pudín de pasas; — **tree** ciruelo; — **pie** pastel de pasas.
plumage (plúmey) s. plumaje.
plumb (plom) s. plomada; sonda; **out of** — no vertical; adv. a plomo, verticalmente; — **crazy** completamente loco; v. sondear; aplomar; adj. perpendicular; recto; a plomo.
plumber (plómber) s. plomero.
plumbing (plómbing) s. instalación sanitaria de una casa o edificio; cañerías; tuberías; arte del plomero; emplomados.
plume (plium) s. pluma, plumaje; penacho; v. adornar con plumas; jactarse, vanagloriarse; pelar o quitar las plumas; emplumar; — **alum** alumbre de plumas.
plump (plomp) adj. gordiflón, rollizo; regordete; rechoncho; brusco; francote; adv. de golpe, de repente; v. engordar, hinchar; caer a plomo; desplomarse.
plunder (plónder) s. pillaje, saqueo; despojo; robo; botín; v. pillar, saquear, despojar.
plunge (plóny) v. sumergirse, zambullirse, lanzarse, arrojarse; precipitarse; **to** — **headlong** echarse de cabeza; s. sumersión, zambullida; salto de arriba abajo.
plus (plos) s. signo más; adv. más; — **value** plusvalía; **three** — **five** tres más cinco.
plush (plósh) s. felpa; tela afelpada.
ply (plái) v. trabajar con ahínco; dar que hacer; manejar con tesón; instar con importunidad; ir y venir; hacer viajecitos; **to** — **a trade** ejercer un oficio; s. hoja o capa; pliegue; **three** — de tres capas, o de tres hojas.
pneumatic (niumátik) adj. neumático.
pneumonia (niumónia) s. pulmonía.
poach (póuch) v. cocer, dar un hervor ligero; cazar en terrenos vedados; **to** — **eggs** pasar huevos por agua, rompiéndolos.
pocket (póket) s. bolsa, bolsillo, faltriquera; cavidad; receptáculo; buchaca; v. embolsar(se); apropiarse; tragarse una injuria; **airpocket** bolsa de aire; **in** — **con ganancia**; **to** — **up** tomar algo clandestinamente.
pocketbook (póketbuk) s. portamonedas; bolsa; cartera; libro de bolsillo.
pocketknife (póketnaif) s. cortaplumas; navaja de bolsillo.
pod (pod) s. vaina (de legumbres).
poem (póem) s. poema; poesía.
poet (póet) s. poeta; vate.
poetry (póetri) s. poesía.
point (póint) s. punto; punta; **it is not to the** — no viene al caso; v. apuntar, señalar.
pointed (póinted) adj. puntiagudo, agudo, aguzado; picante, satírico; directo; a propósito; al caso; — **arch** arco ojival.
pointer (póinter) s. indicador, índice; puntero; manecilla; buril.
poise (pois) s. equilibrio, contrapeso; reposo; porte; compostura; v. equilibrar; balancear, equiparar, contrapesar.
poison (póisn) s. veneno; ponzoña; — **nut** nuez vómica; v. envenenar.
poisonous (póisnus) adj. venenoso; deletéreo, tóxico, ponzoñoso.
poke (póuk) v. picar; picotear; aguijonear; hurgar; husmear; atizar; **to** — **along** andar perezosamente; **to** — **into** hurgar en; **to** — **fun at** burlarse de; mofarse; s. empuje; pinchazo, piquete; codazo; **slow** — tardón.
polar (pólar) adj. polar; — **bear** oso polar.
pole (póul) s. polo; asta; percha; poste; pértiga; palo largo; mástil; **Pole** polaco; **north** — polo norte; **south** — polo sur; — **vault** salto con garrocha.
police (polís) s. policía; v. vigilar; guardar el orden.
policeman (polísman) s. policía, vigilante; gendarme.
policy (pólici) s. norma de conducta en los negocios; política; prudencia, sagacidad; póliza de seguros; curso o plan de acción.
Polish (pólish) s. y adj. polaco; idioma polaco.
polish (pólish) v. pulir, bruñir, alisar, satinar, lustrar; s. lustre, pulimento; tersura; cortesía; urbanidad; **shoe** — grasa o betún para limpiar los zapatos.
polite (poláit) adj. político, fino, atento, cortés, bien educado.
politeness (poláitnes) s. cortesía; fineza; urbanidad.
politic (pólitik) adj. político, sa-

political (politikal) adj. político.
politician (politishan) s. político; politicastro.
politics (pólitiks) s. la política.
poll (pol) s. padrón; lista electoral, empadronamiento; votación; —s comicios; urnas electorales; casilla donde se vota; — **tax** impuesto personal; v. empadronar; matricular; votar; registrar los votos; recibir votos; hacer una encuesta.
pollen (pólen) s. polen.
pomegranate (pómgraneit) s. granada; — **tree** granado.
pomp (pomp) s. pompa, fausto, boato.
pompous (pómpos) adj. pomposo; aparatoso; ostentoso.
pond (pond) s. estanque, alberca; **fish** — piscina; **horse** — abrevadero.
ponder (pónder) v. ponderar; pesar; examinar; considerar; **to** — **over** reflexionar.
ponderous (pónderos) adj. pesado, importante; grave.
pontoon (pontún) s. pontón, barcaza; chalán; flotador de hidroavión; — **bridge** puente flotante.
pony (póni) s. jaca, caballito; clave usada ilícitamente (en un examen); vaso pequeño para licor.
poodle (púdl) s. perro lanudo.
pool (pul) v. mancomunar intereses; hacer una polla en el juego; combinación hecha para especular; s. charco; alberca; balsa; "trust"; **swimming** — piscina de natación; piña en el billar; rebalsa; pago a escote.
poor (pur) adj. pobre, menesteroso; de mala calidad; de poco mérito; escaso, incompleto; humilde; infeliz, desdichado; inútil, seco; — **little thing** pobrecito, pobrecillo; —**ly** adv. pobremente.
poorhouse (púrjáus) s. hospicio, casa de pobres o de beneficencia.
pop (pop) s. detonación, pistoletazo; estallido; tronido; taponazo; **soda** — bebida gaseosa; — **corn** palomitas de maíz; v. reventar, estallar; detonar; saltar (un **tapón**); **to** — **the question** pedir en matrimonio; **to** — **in and out** entrar y salir de sopetón dar un chasquido; **to** —

one's head out sacar o asomar de repente la cabeza.
Pope (póup) s. Papa.
popeyed (popáid) adj. de ojos saltones, desorbitado.
poplar (póplar) s. álamo o chopo, temblón; — **grove** alameda.
poppy (pópi) s. amapola.
populace (pópiules) s. pueblo, populacho; plebe; chusma.
popular (pópiular) adj. popular.
popularity (popiuláriti) s. popularidad.
populate (pópiuleit) v. poblar.
population (popiuléshon) s. población.
populous (pópiulos) adj. populoso.
porcelain (pórslin) s. porcelana.
porch (porch) s. pórtico, porche.
porcupine (pórkiupain) s. puerco espín.
pore (pór) s. poro; **to** — **over a book** hojear un libro.
pork (pork) s. carne de puerco; — **chop** chuleta de puerco; **salt** o **corned** — carne de puerco salada; **fresh** — tocino fresco.
porous (pórus) adj. poroso.
porridge (pórridy) s. potaje; gachas.
port (port) s. puerto; porta; babor (lado izquierdo de un barco); vino de Oporto.
portable (pórtabl) adj. portátil.
portal (pórtal) s. portal.
portent (pórtent) s. portento; prodigio; señal de mal agüero.
portentous (portéptos) adj. portentoso; prodigioso, de mal agüero.
porter (pórter) s. mandadero, portero; camarero de coche tren; mozo de cordel; portador.
portfolio (portfólio) s. **portafolio**; cartera; carpeta; ministerio.
portion (pórshon) s. porción, parte; cuota; dote; v. partir, dividir, distribuir, dotar.
portly (pórtli) adj. corpulento.
portrait (pórtreit) s. retrato.
portray (portréi) v. retratar; pintar, dibujar, esculpir o de cualquier modo representar una persona.
Portuguese (pórchugu.s) adj. y s. portugués.
pose (póus) s. pose, postura, actitud; posición; colocarse en determinada postura; afectar una actitud, proponer, plantear una cuestión; **to** — **as** hacerse pasar por; fingirse.

position (posíshon) s. posición, situación, colocación; ubicación; empleo, categoría, puesto.
positive (pósitiv) adj. positivo, real, verdadero, cierto, seguro.
possess (posés) v. poseer.
possession (poséshon) s. posesión.
possessive (posésiv) adj. posesivo.
possessor (posésor) s. poseedor, dueño; posesor.
possibility (posibílity) s. posibilidad, contingencia.
possible (pósibl) adj. posible; **possibly** adv. posiblemente; tal vez, quizá(s).
post (póust) s. posta; correo; estafeta; poste, pilar; puesto, empleo; asiento; **army —** guarnición militar; **— office** oficina de correos; correo; **— office box** apartado postal; **— paid** porte pagado; franco de porte; v. apostar; situar; anunciar; fijar anuncios o carteles; echar al correo; to **— an entry** hacer un asiento en los libros de contabilidad; **to be well —ed** estar al corriente, o bien informado.
postage (póstey) s. porte, franqueo; **— stamp** sello o estampilla de correos; timbre.
postal (póstal) adj. postal; **— money order** giro postal.
postcard (poustcard) s. tarjeta postal.
poster (póuster) s. cartel, anuncio desplegado; el que fija carteles.
posterior (postírior) adj. posterior, trasero, ulterior.
posterity (postériti) s. posteridad.
posthumous (pószumos) adj. póstumo.
postman (póustman) s. cartero.
postmaster (póstmaster) s. administrador de correos.
postpone (postpóun) v. posponer, aplazar; diferir; menospreciar.
postponement (postpóunment) s. aplazamiento; postergación.
postscript (póustscript) s. posdata.
posture (póschur) s. postura; posición; actitud; pie, disposición; v. adoptar una postura.
posy (póusi) s. flor, ramillete de flores.
pot (pot) s. olla, marmita, pote; crisol; bacinica (de cámara); **flower —** florero; **— bellied** panzón, barrigón; apuesta; pozo en la baraja.
potassium (potésium) s. potasio.
potato (potéito) s. patata, papa; **sweet —** camote, boniato.
potency (pótensi) s. potencia, poder, fuerza; autoridad.
potent (pótent) adj. potente, poderoso, fuerte, autoritario.
potential (poténshal) adj. y s. potencial.
pottage (pótey) s. potaje.
potter (póter) s. alfarero; **—'s field** cementerio de pobres.
pottery (póteri) s. alfarería, cerámica; vasijas de barro.
pouch (páuch) s. saco, bolsita; **mail —** valija de correo; **tobacco —** tabaquera, petaca.
poultice (póultis) v. poner cataplasmas.
poultry (póultri) s. aves de corral.
pounce (páuns) s. garra de ave; zarpazo; grasa; v. **to — into** entrar de sopetón; horadar; **to — upon** echarse encima; abalanzarse para atacar.
pound (páund) s. libra; depósito; golpazo; **— sterling** libra esterlina; v. golpear, machacar, aporrear.
pour (póur) v. verter, escanciar; vaciar; desparramar; fluir; llover a cántaros; diluviar; arrojar.
pout (páut) s. mueca; puchero; v. lloriquear; enfadarse; poner mala cara; fruncir el ceño.
poverty (póverti) s. pobreza.
powder (páuder) s. polvo; polvos para tocador; pólvora; medicamento en polvo; **— compact** polvera; **— magazine** polvorín; **— puff** borla; mota; v. polvear(se); espolvorear; ponerse polvo en la cara.
power (páuer) s. poder; poderío; potencia; gobierno; dominio; **motive —** fuerza motriz; **— house** planta de fuerza; **— of attorney** poder.
powerful (páuerful) adj. poderoso.
powerless (páuerles) adj. impotente.
practicable (práktikabl) adj. practicable; viable, accesible, transitable; factible.
practical (práktikal) adj. práctico; virtual; experto; avezado; **—ly** adv. prácticamente, virtualmente; en realidad; avezadamente.
practice (práktis) s. práctica; uso; ejercicio; experiencia; método; profesión; clientela; v. practicar; ejercer; hacer ejercicios.
prairie (préri) s. pradera, llanura.

praise (préis) v. alabar, loar; elogiar, aplaudir; s. alabanza; loa, elogio, encomio.
praiseworthy (préisuerzi) adj. laudable; encomiable; plausible.
prance (prans) v. cabriolear, hacer cabriolas.
prank (prank) s. travesura, extravagancia; **to play —s** hacer travesuras; v. hermosear; adornar.
prate (préit) v. parlotear; charlar.
prattle (prátl) v. parlotear, charlar; s. parloteo, charla, plática insubstancial.
pray (préi) v. rezar; orar; pedir; rogar, suplicar; invocar; **— tell me** le ruego que me diga.
prayer (préier) s. oración, rezo; deprecación; **— book** devocionario; **Lord's —** El Padre Nuestro.
preach (prich) v. predicar.
preacher (prícher) s. predicador.
preaching (príching) s. predicación; sermón.
preamble (príambl) s. preámbulo.
prearranged (priarrényd) adj. arreglado de antemano.
precarious (prikérios) adj. precario; arriesgado, peligroso; inseguro.
precaution (prikóshon) s. precaución; cautela, cuidado.
precede (prisíd) v. preceder.
precedence (presídens) s. prioridad; anterioridad, precedencia.
precedent (présedent) s. precedente.
preceding (presíding) adj. anterior, que precede.
precept (prísept) s. precepto.
precinct (prísinkt) s. distrito; zona; demarcación; **—s** inmediaciones.
precious (préshos) adj. precioso; muy estimado; caro; bastante; considerable; **— little** poquísimo.
precipice (présipis) s. precipicio.
precipitate (presípiteit) v. precipitar(se); s. precipitado; adj. apresurado; arrebatado.
precipitation (precipitéshon) s. precipitación; derrumbamiento; cantidad de agua pluvial; rocío.
precipitous (presípitos) adj. escarpado, precipitoso; pendiente.
precise (prisáis) adj. preciso, exacto.
precision (prisíshon) s. precisión; exactitud; limitación exacta.
preclude (preklúd) v. excluir, impedir; prevenir; echar fuera.
precocious (prikóshos) adj. precoz.
predecessor (predesésor) s. predecesor.

predestine (predéstin) v. predestinar.
predicament (predíkement) s. predicamento, aprieto, apuración.
predicate (prédikeit) adj. y s. predicado; afirmado; v. predicar, afirmar.
predict (predíkt) v. vaticinar.
prediction (predíkshon) s. predicción, vaticinio; pronóstico.
predilection (predilékshon) s. predilección, preferencia.
predispose (predispóus) v. predisponer.
predominance (predóminans) s. predominio; ascendiente, superioridad.
predominant (predóminant) adj. predominante.
predominate (predómineit) v. predominar; prevalecer.
preface (prífeis) s. prefacio, prólogo; discurso preliminar.
prefer (prifér) v. preferir; anteponer; exhibir; exaltar.
preferable (préfrebl) adj. preferible; preferente; **preferably** adv. preferentemente; preferiblemente; de preferencia.
preference (préfrens) s. preferencia.
preferred (prifér̃d) p.p. y adj. preferido; **— stock** acciones preferentes.
prefix (prifíks) s. prefijo; (prífiks) v. anteponer; poner un prefijo.
pregnancy (prégnansi) s. embarazo; preñez.
pregnant (prégnant) adj. preñada; encinta.
prejudice (préyudis) s. prejuicio; predisposición; perjuicio, daño; v. predisponer, prevenir, perjudicar.
prelate (prileit) s. prelado.
preliminary (prelimíneri) adj. y s. preliminar.
prelude (préliud) s. preludio; v. preludiar.
premature (primatiúr) adj. prematuro.
premeditated (priméditeited) adj. premeditado; resuelto anticipadamente.
premier (prímier) s. primer ministro; adj. primero, principal.
premise (prémis) s. premisa; aserción; asunto; **—s** predio, terreno, local.
premium (prímium) s. premio; **at a —** muy caro, muy escaso; **insurance —** prima de seguro.

preoccupy (priókiupai) v. preocupar; prevenir el ánimo.
prepaid (pripéid) adj. pagado con anticipación; — **freight** flete pagado; porte o franqueo pagado.
preparation (priparéshon) s. preparación; preparativo.
preparatory (prepáratori) adj. preparatorio; previo, antecedente.
prepare (pripér) v. preparar(se).
preparedness (pripérdnes) s. preparación; prevención.
preposition (preposishon) s. preposición.
preposterous (prepósteros) adj. absurdo; descabellado; insensato.
prerequisite (prirrékuisit) s. requisito previo.
prerogative (prirrógativ) s. prerrogativa; privilegio.
presage (présey) s. presagio; pronóstico; v. presagiar, pronosticar.
prescribe (prescráib) v. recetar; prescribir.
prescription (prescripshon) s. receta; prescripción; precepto; mandato.
presence (présens) s. presencia; porte; — **of mind** presencia de ánimo.
present (présent) s. presente, regalo; adj. presente, corriente, actual; **at** — por ahora, en los actuales momentos; — **company excepted** mejorando lo presente; **—s remove difficulties** dádivas quebrantan peñas; v. presentar; regalar; exhibir; manifestar.
presentation (presentéshon) s. presentación; obsequio; exhibición.
presentiment (priséntiment) s. presentimiento, corazonada.
presently (présentli) adv. en estos momentos; desde luego, pronto.
preservation (preservéshon) s. preservación, conservación.
preserve (presérv) v. preservar; proteger; conservar; guardar; mantener; s. conserva, compota.
preside (prisáid) v. presidir; dirigir; **to** — **at a meeting** presidir una asamblea.
presidency (présidensi) s. presidencia.
president (président) s. presidente.
presidential (presidénshal) adj. presidencial.
pressing (présing) adj. apremiante; importante; urgente; importuno.
pressure (préshur) s. presión, urgencia; apremio; aprieto, apuro, premura, prisa; — **gauge** manómetro.
prestige (préstiy) s. prestigio.
presumable (presúmebl) adj. presumible; razonable; probable.
presume (presiúm) v. presumir, suponer; jactarse, vanagloriarse; **to** — **on (upon)** contar con, imaginarse; **to** — **to** atreverse a; osar.
presumption (presómshon) s. presunción; sospecha; conjetura; pretensión, soberbia.
presumptuous (presómchuos) s. presumido.
presuppose (prisupóus) v. presuponer.
pretend (priténd) v. pretender, fingir; aparentar; disfrazar(se).
pretense (priténs) s. pretensión; afectación; simulación; pretexto; **under** — **of** so pretexto de.
pretension (priténshon) s. pretensión; pretexto.
pretext (pritékst) s. pretexto.
prettily (prítili) adv. bonitamente; lindamente; agradablemente.
prettiness (pritines) s. lindeza, gracia.
pretty (priti) adj. bonito, hermoso; dulce, encantador, agradable; chulo; adv. bastante, cerca, poco más o menos; un poco; algo; — **well** regular; así, así; medianamente.
prevail (privéil) v. prevalecer; influir, persuadir; estar en boga.
prevailing (privéiling) adj. predominante; generalizado, común.
prevalent (priválent) adj. prevaleciente; dominante, grandemente esparcido; común.
prevent (privént) v. prevenir; evitar; precaver; frustrar; estorbar.
prevention (privénshon) s. prevención, precaución; frustración; estorbo.
previous (privious) adj. previo; **—ly** previamente; antes; de antemano.
prey (préi) s. presa, víctima; despojo, rapiña; **to fall a** — **to** ser presa de; v. pillar, hurtar; hacer presa; consumir; pesar en el ánimo; oprimir; agobiar.
price (prais) v. valuar, tasar, fijar el precio; preguntar el precio de; s. precio; valor; costo; monto.
priceless (práisles) adj. inapreciable; sin precio.
prick (prik) v. picar, pinchar;

aguzar; estimular; aguijonear; sentir comenzón o picazón; to — up one's ears aguzar el oído; s. picadura, pinchazo; piquete; comezón; púa; aguijón; espina.

prickly (príkli) adj. espinoso, lleno de púas; **— pear tuna** (de nopal; **— heat** picazón causada por el calor.

pride (práid) s. orgullo, vanidad, soberbia; altivez; v. enorgullecerse.

priest (prist) s. sacerdote.

priesthood (pristjud) s. sacerdocio.

prim (prim) adj. ataviado, predispuesto; emperifollado; estirado.

primarily (práimarili) adv. en principio; principalmente; en primer lugar; sobre todo.

primary (práimari) adj. primario; elemental; fundamental; prístino; **— colors** colores elementales; **— school** escuela primaria; primario, inductor.

prime (práim) s. plenitud de vigor; flor de la vida; número primo; escogido, selecto; prístino; original; **— minister** primer ministro; **— cost** precio de fábrica; v. preparar, alistar, prevenir; cebar (un arma de fuego, un carburador); **to be in one's —** estar en la flor de la edad; informar, instruir de antemano; aparejar; cubrir con la primera capa de colores o de argamasa; imprimar.

primer (primer) s. abecedario; cartilla para aprender a leer; devocionario.

primeval (praimíval) adj. primitivo.

primitive (prímitiv) adj. primitivo.

primness (prímnes) s. escrupulosidad; remilgo; dengue; afectación; demasiada formalidad.

primp (primp) v. acicalar(se); adornar(se); arreglar(se).

primrose (prímrous) s. color amarillo-verdoso claro; primavera; **the — path** camino de rosas.

prince (príns) s. príncipe.

princely (prínsli) adj. regio, magnífico; principesco; augusto.

princess (prínces) s. princesa.

principal (prínsipal) adj. principal; primordial; esencial; s. jefe, director; capital puesto a interés.

principle (prínsipl) s. principio; norma; ley; base; fundamento.

printer (prínter) s. impresor.

printing (prínting) s. imprenta, impresión, tipografía; **— press** prensa para imprimir o para estampar telas; **— office** imprenta.

prior (práior) adj. anterior, antecedente; previo; precedente; s. prior; **— to** anterior a; con antelación a.

prority (praióriti) s. prioridad; procedencia; antelación.

prism (prísm) s. prisma.

prison (prison) s. prisión, cárcel.

prisoner (prísner) s. prisionero.

privacy (práivasi) s. retiro, aislamiento, soledad; secreto; reserva; **to have no —** carecer de sitio privado; estar a la vista de todos.

private (práivet) adj. privado, particular, personal, propio; secreto; solitario, retirado; confidencial; **a — citizien** un particular; s. soldado raso; **in —** en privado, a solas.

privation (praivéshon) s. privación.

privilege (príviley) adj. privilegio; prerrogativa, gracia.

privileged (privileyd) adj. privilegiado; exceptuado; exento.

prize (práis) s. premio, recompensa; botín; ganancia; **— fight** pelea de box; **— fighter** boxeador; v. apreciar; estimar; valuar; tasar.

probability (probabíliti) s. probabilidad.

probable (próbabl) adj. probable; **probably** adv. probablemente.

probation (probéshon) s. prueba, experiencia; evidencia; noviciado; **to put a prisoner on —** conceder a un prisionero la libertad preparatoria.

probe (próub) s. tocamiento, reconocimiento; prueba; ensayo; v. tocar, tentar; reconocer, escudriñar, indagar; examinar a fondo.

problem (próblem) s. problema.

procedure (prosídiur) s. procedimiento; manera de proceder.

proceed (prosíd) v. proceder, proseguir; recurrir; adelantar; echar mano de; comenzar a; portarse.

proceeding (prosíding) s. procedimiento; conducta; porte; acto; **—s** autos procesales.

proceeds (prósids) s. pl. ingresos, ganancias; producto; réditos.

process (próses) s. procedimiento; tratamiento; manipulación; progreso, continuación; adelantamiento; método; curso; serie; causa; proceso; expediente; **— of time** lapso o transcurso de

tiempo; v. **preparar mediante un procedimiento especial**; procesar ante un juez; manipular, tratar.
procession (procéshon) s. procesión; desfile; cabalgata; desfile de tropa; **funeral** — cortejo fúnebre.
proclaim (prokléim) v. proclamar; promulgar, publicar, pregonar.
proclamation (proclaméshon) s. proclamación.
procure (proklúr) v. procurar, conseguir, alcanzar; obtener.
prod (prod) v. aguijonear, picar.
prodigal (pródigal) adj. y s. pródigo, profuso, abundante.
prodigious (prodíyos) adj. prodigioso; enorme, vasto.
prodigy (pródiyi) s. prodigio.
produce (prodiús) s. producto; productos agrícolas, provisiones; v. producir; generar, criar.
producer (prodiúser) s. productor.
product (pródokt) s. producto.
production (prodókshon) s. producción; producto; composición; obra del ingenio; representación de una obra.
productive (pródóktiv) adj. productivo, fecundo.
profanation (profanéshon) s. desacato; profanación.
profane (proféin) adj. profano; v. profanar; violar, contaminar.
profess (profés) v. profesar.
profession (proféshon) s. profesión.
professional (proféshonal) adj. profesional; profesional, facultativo.
professor (profésor) s. profesor, catedrático, maestro, perito.
proffer (profer) s. oferta, propuesta; v. ofrecer; brindar, proponer.
proficiency (profíshensi) s. pericia; perfeccionamiento, habilidad.
proficient (profíshent) adj. proficiente, perito, adelantado, experto, hábil.
profile (prófail) s. perfil.
profit (prófit) s. provecho, utilidad; beneficio, ventaja, lucro; — **and loss** pérdidas y ganancias; **gross** — ganancia total o bruta; v. aprovechar; sacar utilidad o provecho; **to** — **by** sacar provecho de.
profitable (prófitabl) adj. provechoso; gananciosos: lucrativo.
profiteer (profitír) s. extorsionista; carero, explotador; acaparador; v. acaparar, extorsionar.

profound (profáund) adj. profundo.
profuse (profiús) adj. profuso, abundante; pródigo.
progeny (próyeni) s. prole.
program (prógram) s. programa, plan.
progress (prógres) s. progreso; adelanto (progrés) v. adelantar.
progressive progrésiv) adj. progresivo; s. progresista.
prohibit (projíbit) v. prohibir.
prohibition (projibíshon) s. prohibición, veda, acto prohibitorio.
project (proyékt) s. proyecto, plan; idea, pensamiento; v. proyectar(se).
projectile (proyéktil) s. proyectil; adj. proyectante, arrojadizo; — **weapon** arma arrojadiza.
projection (proyékshon) s. proyección; saliente; lanzamiento.
proletarian (proletérian) adj. y s. proletario; gañán, peón.
proletariat (proletériat) s. proletariado.
prologue (prólog) s. prólogo.
prolong (prolóng) v. prolongar.
prolongation (prolonguéshon) s. prolongación; dilatación.
promenade (prómeneid) s. paseo; baile (usualmente **prom**); v. pasearse.
prominent (próminent) adj. prominente; saliente, proyectante; turgente.
promiscuous (promískious) adj. promiscuo.
promise (prómis) s. promesa; oferta, ofrecimiento; v. prometer; dar o hacer concebir esperanzas.
promising (prómising) adj. prometedor.
promoter (promóuter) s. promotor; promovedor, gestor.
promotion (promóshon) s. promoción; ascenso; adelantamiento.
prompt (prómpt) adj. pronto, puntual; dispuesto, listo; presto; v. mover, incitar, inducir; excitar; soplar (sugerir a otro lo que debe decir en una clase o junta).
promptly (prómptli) adv. pronto; prontamente; prestamente; puntualmente; con presteza.
promptness (prómptnes) s. prontitud; presteza; diligencia.
promulgate (promólgueit) v. promulgar, publicar, proclamar.
prone (próun) adj. inclinado; propenso, dispuesto; inclinado.

prong (prong) s. púa; punta; pitón de asta.
pronoun (prónaun) s. pronombre.
pronounce (pronáuns) v. pronunciar; proferir, declarar.
pronounced (pronáunst) adj. pronunciado, marcado; fuerte, subido; — **opinions** opiniones decididas.
pronunciation (pronunciéshon) s. pronunciación, fonación.
proof (pruf) s. prueba; comprobación; evidencia; ensayo; experimento; — **against a prueba de**; **author's** — prueba limpia para el autor; **bomb** — a prueba de bomba; **fire** — a prueba de incendios; **burglar** — a prueba de ladrones; **water** — impermeable.
prop (prop) s. puntal; sostén; apoyo; paral; apeo; asnilla; v. sostener; apuntalar.
propaganda (propagánda) s. propaganda.
propagate (própagueit) v. propagar.
propagation (propaguéshon) s. propagación; multiplicación, reproducción.
propel (propél) v. propulsar.
propeller (propéler) s. hélice (de un buque, avión, etc.); tornillo.
proper (próper) adj. propio; conveniente; a propósito; idóneo; justo; — **noun** nombre propio; — **sense** sentido propio, justo o literal.
property (próperti) s. propiedad; posesión; heredad.
prophecy (prófesi) s. profecía.
prophet (prófet) s. profeta.
prophetic (profétic) adj. profético.
propitious (propíshos) adj. propicio; favorable; benéfico.
proportion (propórshon) s. proporción; correlación; **out of** — desproporcionado; v. proporcionar.
proposal (propósal) s. propuesta; proposición; ofrecimiento; declaración (de amor).
propose (propóus) v. proponer; declararse, hacer propuesta de matrimonio; tener intención de; pensar.
proposition (proposíshon) s. proposición; propuesta; oferta.
proprietor (propráietor) s. propietario, dueño; amo.
propriety (propráieti) s. propiedad, corrección; decoro, decencia.
prorate (prorréit) v. prorratear, repartir proporcionalmente.

prosaic (proséik) adj. prosaico.
prose (próus) s. prosa; adj. prosaico.
prosecute (prósekiut) v. procesar; seguir, continuar; enjuiciar; demandar ante un juez; seguir un pleito.
prosecution (prosekiúshon) s. prosecución; seguimiento; parte actora; fiscal.
prosecutor (prósekiutor) s. fiscal, acusador, actor.
prospect (próspekt) s. perspectiva; vista; paisaje; panorama, aspecto, traza; cliente (candidato a comprador); v. explorar, andar en busca de, descubrir, catear.
prospective (prospéctiv) adj. probable; anticipado, venidero.
prospector (prospéctor) s. explorador; operador, buscador.
prosper (prósper) v. prosperar.
prosperity (prospériti) s. prosperidad.
prosperous (prósperous) adj. próspero.
prostitute (próstitiut) s. ramera; prostituta; v. prostituir.
prostrate (próstreit) adj. postrado; humillado; v. humillar, postrar.
protect (protékt) v. proteger.
protection (protékshon) s. protección, amparo.
protective (protéktiv) adj. protector; s. resguardo, abrigo, amparo; — **tariff** tarifa proteccionista.
protector (protéktor) s. protector.
protectorate (protéctoreit) s. protectorado, protectoría.
protégé (proteyé) s. protegido, ahijado, paniaguado.
protein (prótein) s. proteína.
protest (protést) s. protesta; protestación; v. protestar, declarar.
protestant (prótestant) adj. y s. protestante.
protestation (protestéshon) s. protestación, protesta, declaración.
protoplasm (prótoplasm) s. protoplasma.
protract (protrákt) v. alargar, extender, prolongar; dilatar.
protrude (protrúd) v. sobresalir; resaltar; empujar, sacar fuera.
protuberance (protiúberans) s. protuberancia, prominencia.
proud (práud) adj. orgulloso, soberbio.
prove (prúv) v. probar; demostrar; resultar; substanciar, justificar.
proverb (próverb) s. proverbio; adagio; dicho, refrán.

provide (prováid) v. proveer, abastecer, proporcionar; surtir, dar; suministrar; to — for hacer provisión para; to — against precaver.
provided (prováidid) conj. con tal (de) que; a condición (de) que.
providence (próvidens) s. providencia, prudencia, previsión.
providential (providénshal) adj. providencial.
provider (prováider) s. proveedor.
province (próvins) s. provincia; jurisdicción; incumbencia; it ins't within my — no está dentro de mi jurisdicción.
provincial (provínshal) adj. provincial; s. provinciano.
provision (províshon) s. provisión; abastecimiento; víveres; ajuste, convenio, estipulación; tomar las medidas (o precauciones) necesarias; requisito.
proviso (prováiso) s. condición, caución, estipulación.
provocation (provokéshon) s. provocación; incitamiento.
provoke (provóuk) v. provocar; irritar; excitar, encolerizar.
prow (práu) s. proa.
prowess (práues) s. proeza.
prowl (prául) v. rondar en acecho; fisgonear.
proximity (proksímiti) s. proximidad.
proxy (próksi) s. apoderado; substituto; delegado; poderhabiente; by — mediante apoderado.
prude (prud) s. mojigato, remilgado; persona gazmoña.
prudence (prúdens) s. prudencia.
prudent (prúdent) adj. prudente.
prudery (prúderi) s. mojigatería, remilgo, melindrería.
prudish (prúdish) adj. gazmoño, remilgado, mojigato, denguero.
prune (prun) s. ciruela; ciruela pasa; v. podar, cortar.
pry (prai) v. atisbar; fisgar; espiar, acechar; curiosear; to — a secret out extraer (o arrancar) un secreto; to — into fisgar, fiscalizar; entremeterse; to — apart separar por la fuerza; to — into other people's affairs entremeterse en lo ajeno; s. palanca, barra.
psalm (sam) s. salmo.
pseudonym (siúdonim) s. seudónimo
psychiatrist (saikáiatrist) s. psiquiatra, alienista.

psychiatry (saikáiatri) s. psiquiatría.
psychological (saikolóyikal) adj. psicológico.
psychologist (saikóloyist) s. psicólogo.
psychology (saikóloyi) s. psicología.
public (póblik) adj. público; común; notorio, patente; s. público.
publication (poblikéshon) s. publicación.
publicity (pobliciti) s. publicidad; propaganda, notoriedad.
publish (póblish) v. publicar; editar; dar a luz; —ing house editorial o editora.
publisher (póblisher) s. publicador.
pucker (póker) v. fruncir.
pudding (púding) s. budín, pudín.
puddle (pódl) s. charco.
puff (pof) s. resoplido; bufido, soplo; bocanada (de humo, vapor, etc.); bullón (de vestido); mota de empolvarse; — of wind ráfaga; racha; Spanish — buñuelo; v. resoplar, hinchar, inflar; soplar; ensoberbecer; to — up ahuecar(se).
pug (pog) s. perro, dogo; torta; — nose nariz chata.
pull (pul) v. tirar de; tirar hacia sí; jalar (halar); sacar, arrancar, estirar; bogar, remar; sacar (una prueba) con la prensa de mano; to — apart desgarrar, descomponer, desmontar; to — down the curtain bajar la cortinilla; to — asunder o away separar o apartar con violencia; to — up arrancar; parar (un caballo, un auto); hacer alto; to — back tirar hacia atrás; hacer recular o cejar; to — through salir de un apuro; s. tirón; estirón, esfuerzo; arrancada, sacudimiento; jaladera (de una puerta); ejercicio de remos, boga.
pullet (púlet) s. polla.
pulley (púli) s. polea, garrucha; motón; cuadernal; tambor.
pulp (polp) s. pulpa; arilo; pasta.
pulsate (pólseit) v. pulsar, latir, batir.
pulse (pols) s. pulso; pulsación.
pulverize (pólverais) v. pulverizar.
pumice (pómis) s. piedra pómez.
pun (pon) s. equívoco; retruécano; juego de vocablos; v. decir retruécanos o equívocos.
punch (ponch) s. puñetazo; punzón; sacabocados; ponche (be-

bida); empuje; fuerza; — bowl ponchera; v. dar un puñetazo; dar una puñalada; horadar; punzar; **to — a hole** hacer un agujero o perforación.

punctual (pónkchual) adj. puntual, exacto, preciso.

punctuality (ponkchuáliti) s. puntualidad, exactitud, formalidad.

punctuate (pónkchueit) v. puntuar.

punctuation (ponkchuéshon) s. puntuación, atildadura.

puncture (pónkchur) v. picar, pasajerear, pinchar; perforar; s. puntura; picadura; pinchazo; **to have a tire —** tener una llanta o neumático picado.

punish (pónish) v. castigar.

punishment (pónishment) s. castigo.

puny (piúni) adj. endeble, débil; pequeño, diminuto, mezquino.

pup (pop) s. cachorro.

pupil (piúpil) s. discípulo; alumno; pupila; niña del ojo.

puppet (pópet) s. títere; maniquí; muñeco; **— show** títeres.

puppy (pópi) s. cachorrito.

purchase (pórches) v. comprar; mercar; feriar; lograr, ganar, obtener; s. compra, adquisición; palanca.

purchaser (pórcheser) s. comprador, marchante.

pure (piúr) adj. puro; **— ly** adv. puramente, meramente.

purée (piuré) s. puré.

purgative (pérgativ) adj. purgante; purgativo; s. purga, purgante.

purgatory (pérgatori) s. purgatorio.

purge (pery) v. purgar(se); limpiar; purificar; s. purga, purgante.

purify (piúrifai) v. purificar(se); purgar, defecar; depurar; limpiar, refinar, clarificar; explar; expurgar.

purity (piúriti) s. pureza.

purple (pérpl) s. púrpura; múrice; adj. purpúreo, morado, imperial.

purport (pérport) s. significado, tenor; sentido; substancia de un escrito; v. pretender, aparentar; significar, querer decir.

purpose (pórpos) s. propósito; intención, fin, objeto, mira; **for no — a sin** objeto; **to the — a** propósito; **al grano; on — adrede.**

purr (por) s. ronroneo (del gato);

zumbido (del motor); v. ronronear; decir murmurando.

purse (pers) s. bolsillo; portamonedas; bolso; hacienda; riqueza; v. embolsar, fruncir.

pursue (persú) v. proseguir; seguir; dar caza; dedicarse a.

pursuer (persúer) s. perseguidor.

pursuit (persút) s. perseguimiento; busca; ejercicio (de una profesión, cargo, etc.); acosamiento, persecución, caza.

pus (pos) s. pus, podre.

push (push) v. empujar; fomentar; promover, apresurar; impeler, empellar; **to — aside** hacer a un lado, rechazar; **to — down** abatir, derribar; **to — forward** empujar, abrirse paso; s. empuje, empujón; empellón; apuro, aprieto; energía; esfuerzo; **— button** botón eléctrico.

pushcart (púshcart) s. carretilla de mano.

pussy (púsi) s. minino; gatito; bichito, michito.

put (put) v. poner, colocar; disponer; confiar; exponer; presentar para ser discutido; arrojar; lanzar, dirigirse; **to — about** cambiar de rumbo; **to — away** apartar, quitar; **to — before** anteponer; proponer ante; **to — down** reprimir; humillar; anotar; registrar; **to — in** insertar; introducir; **to — in a claim** demandar; reclamar; **to — in writing** poner por escrito; **to — off** aplazar, posponer, diferir; **to — on** ponerse; vestir; **to — out** apagar, extinguir; **to — up** enlatar, envasar; **to — up with** aguantar, tolerar; **to — to bed** acostar; **to — up for sale** poner en venta; **to — a stop to** poner coto a; **to — to shame** avergonzar; **to — in practice** ejercitar; poner en práctica; **to — to rights** ordenar; **to — to the sword** pasar a cuchillo; pret. y p.p. de to put; **to — an end** poner término.

putrefy (piútrefai) v. corromper; podrir.

putrid (piútrid) s. podrido, corrompido, putrefacto.

putter (póter) s. incitador, instigador; v. ocuparse en cosas que no valen la pena.

putty (póti) s. mastique, masilla; v. tapar o rellenar con masilla.

puzzle (posl) s. rompecabezas,

acertijo; adivinanza; crossword — crucigrama; v. embrollar; confundir; dejar perplejo; **to — out** descifrar; **to — over** ponderar.

pyramid (píramid) s. pirámide.

Q

quack (kuak) s. graznido (del pato); curandero, matasanos; charlatán; adj. falso; v. graznar.

quagmire (kuágmair) s. tremedal, cenagal.

quail (kuéil) s. codorniz.

quaint (kuéint) adj. raro, extraño; curioso; singular; pintoresco.

quake (kueik) s. temblor, terremoto; v. temblar, estremecerse.

qualification (kualifikéshon) s. calificación; cualidad; idoneidad.

qualify (kuálifai) v. calificar; habilitar; modificar; restringir; diluir un licor; llenar los requisitos; **to — for a position** tener aptitud para el desempeño de un empleo; **qualified voter** elector habilitado. [lidad

quality (kuáliti) s. cualidad, calidad.

qualm (kuam) s. escrúpulo de conciencia; basca.

quantity (kuántiti) s. cantidad.

quarantine (kuórantin) s. cuarentena; v. poner en cuarentena.

quarrel (kuórrel) s. riña, reyerta, contienda, querella; pendencia; v. reñir, pelear, altercar; disputar; romper, desavenirse, contender.

quarrelsome (kuórrelsom) adj. refidor, rencilloso, pendenciero.

quarry (kuórri) s. cantera; presa; pedrera; caza; cuadrado, rombo (de vidrio, teja, etc.); v. trabajar en una cantera. [cuarta.

quart (kuórt) s. cuarto de galón

quarter (kuórter) s. cuarto, cuarta parte; trimestre; cuarto de hora; moneda de 25 centavos; barrio; distrito; —s morada, vivienda; alojamiento; semínima; **from all —s** de todas partes; **— day** día en que principia una estación del año; día en que se paga un trimestre; adj. cuarto; v. cuartear, dividir en cuartos.

quarterly (kuórterli) adv. trimestralmente, por trimestre; s. publicación trimestral.

quartet (kuortét) s. cuarteto.

quartz (kuórts) s. cuarzo.

quaver (kuéiver) v. temblar, vibrar; s. temblor; gorjeo, trino.

quay (ki) s. embarcadero, muelle.

queen (kuín) s. reina, soberana.

queer (kuír) adj. raro, extraño; excéntrico, estrafalario; **to feel —** sentirse raro, no sentirse bien; sospechoso; v. poner en ridículo; comprometer; poner a uno en mal lugar.

quell (kuél) v. reprimir; sofocar (una revuelta); subyugar.

quench (kuénch) v. apagar (el fuego, la sed); reprimir; ahogar; sofocar; templar el ardor de, extinguir; sosegar.

query (kuíri) s. pregunta; interrogación, duda; signo interrogante (?); v. preguntar; expresar duda; marcar con signo de interrogación.

quest (kuést) s. busca, pesquisa.

question (kuéschon) s. pregunta; cuestión, problema; interrogación; disputa; debate; controversia; **that is out of the —** ¡imposible! ¡ni pensar en ello! v. interrogar, preguntar, examinar; poner en tela de juicio.

questionable (kuéschonabl) adj. dudoso.

questioner (kuéschoner) s. interrogador, preguntón.

questionary (kuéschonary) s. cuestionario, lista de preguntas; interrogatorio.

questioning (kuéschoning) s. interrogatorio; adj. interrogador.

quibble (kuíbl) v. sutilizar, valerse de argucias o sutilezas; buscar escapatorias; s. sutileza; equívoco, argucia, subterfugio.

quick (kuík) adj. pronto, presto, listo; veloz, acelerado; vivo, diligente; ágil; **— temper** genio violento; **— fire** fuego ardiente; **— pulse** pulso irritable; s. carne viva; lo vivo; la sensibilidad.

quicken (kuíkn) v. acelerar(se); vivificar, dar vida; resucitar, urgir; aguzar (la mente, el entendimiento); animar.

quickly (kuíkli) adv. pronto, presto.

quickness (kuíknes) s. rapidez; presteza; vivacidad; prontitud; sagacidad; penetración, celeridad.

quicksand (kuíksand) s. arena movediza.

quicksilver (kuíksilver) s. mercurio, azogue; v. azogar.

quiet ('kwaiat) a. 1. quieto, quedo; sosegado, tranquilo, calmado. 2. callado, silencioso. 3. sencillo, modesto. 4. discreto (color).

quietness (kuáietnes) s. quietud, sosiego, calma, tranquilidad, paz.
quill (kuíl) s. pluma; cañón (de pluma de ave); cañón o pluma para escribir; púa (de puerco espín).
quilt (kuílt) s. colcha; v. acolchar.
quince (kuíns) s. membrillo.
quinine (kuáinain) s. quinina.
quip (kuíp) s. pulla, cuchufleta; agudeza.
quirk (kuérk) s. chifladura, extravagancia; desviación, vuelta corta; peculiaridad mental.
quit (kuít) v. dejar, abandonar; irse; cesar o desistir de; soltar; dejar ir; parar; to — doing something dejar de hacer algo; — your nonsense déjate de tonterías; —s adj. desquitado; descargado.
quite (kuáit) adv. bastante, del todo; completamente; enteramente; absolutamente; bastante, muy.
quitter (kuíter) s. el que deja fácilmente lo empezado; el que se da fácilmente por vencido, desertor.
quiver (kuíver) v. temblar, estremecerse; tembelequear; s. temblor; estremecimiento.
quiz (kuís) s. examen, interrogatorio; chanza, broma, guasa, v. examinar, interrogar; examinar a un discípulo o clase.
quota (kuóta) s. cuota.
quotation (kuotéshon) s. citación, cita; texto citado; cotización (de precios); — mark comillas (").
quote (kuóut) v. citar; cotizar (precios); repetir un texto; to — from entresacar una cita de; s. cita; comillas; in —s entre comillas.
quotient (kuóshent) s. cociente.

R

rabbi (rábai) s. rabí, rabino.
rabbit (rábit) s. conejo.
rabble (rábl) s. populacho, plebe; gentuza; canalla; chusma.
rabies (rébis) s. hidrofobia, rabia.
race (réis) s. raza; corrida; estirpe; casta; descendencia, carrera; contienda; — track (o — course) pista; — of Alderney corriente de aire producida por la hélice de un aeroplano; v. ir corriendo; correr de prisa; moverse aceleradamente; competir.
racer (réiser) s. corredor, caballo de carrera; auto de carreras.
racial (réshal) adj. racial.
rack (rak) s. percha, colgadero; bastidor, rambla; aparato para estirar; potro de tormento; — and pinion engranaje de cremallera y piñón; v. atormentar; torturar, afligir; agobiar, oprimir; amarrar, trasegar vino.
racket (ráket) s. raqueta; baraúnda; barullo; boruca, estrépito; parranda; bullicio; trapacería.
racketeer (raketír) s. trapacista, extorsionista, trapacero; v. extorsionar; trapacear.
raccoon (rakún) s. mapache, coatí.
radiance (rédians) s. resplandor.
radiant (rédiant) adj. radiante; resplandeciente; radioso, brillante.
radiate (rédieit) v. irradiar.
radiator (rédieitor) s. radiador.
radical (rádikal) adj. y s. radical.
radio (rédio) s. radio; radiotelegrafía; radiotelefonía; by — por radio; — commentator comentarista radial; — program programa radiofónico; — listener radioescucha; radioyente; v. radiar, emitir; radiodifundir o difundir.
radish (rádish) s. rábano, horse — rábano picante.
radium (rédium) s. quim. radio.
radius (rédius) s. radio (de un círculo), semidiámetro; rayo.
raffle (rafl) s. rifa, sorteo; v. rifar, sortear.
raft (raft) s. balsa; almadía; madera; a — of things un montón (o la mar) de cosas.
rafter (ráfter) s. viga (del techo).
rag (rag) s. trapo, harapo; andrajo; jirón; hilacho; bandera; vela; periódico; — doll muñeca de trapo; — money papel moneda.
ragamuffin (rágamofin) s. pelagatos; golfo, pillo, granuja, pícaro.
rage (reiy) s. rabia, ira; enojo, furor, arrebato; cólera; to be all the — estar en boga; estar de moda; intensidad, ardor, anhelo; v. anhelar; rabiar, enfurecer, bramar.
ragged (rágued) adj. andrajoso; roto; rasgado; trapajoso; desarrapado; — edge borde raído o deshilachado; mellado, escabroso; áspero; to be on the — edge estar al borde del precipicio.

raid (réid) s. incursión; invasión repentina; irrupción; correría; allanamiento (de un local); **air — ataque aéreo**; bombardeo aéreo; v. hacer una incursión; invadir.

railing (réiling) s. baranda, balaustrada; barandilla; pasamano, rastel; barrera, rieles.

railway (réiluei) s. ferrocarril; camino de hierro; empresa o línea de un ferrocarril; **— crossing** cruce.

raiment (réiment) s. vestidura.

rain (réin) s. lluvia; **— pour** aguacero; **— storm** tempestad, chubasco; v. llover.

rainbow (réinbou) s. arco iris.

raincoat (réincout) s. impermeable; capa de agua; manga o capa de hule.

raise (réis) v. levantar, alzar; erigir; criar, cultivar; **to — a question** suscitar una duda; s. aumento, subida.

raisin (réisn) s. pasa, uva seca.

rake (reik) s. rastro, rastrillo; mielga, libertino; perdulario; v. rastrear; barrer, raspar; enfilar, tirar a lo largo de; pasar el rastro o la mielga.

rally (ráli) v. reunir, reanimar; juntar(se); replegarse; rehacer(se); recobrar las fuerzas; revivir; s. reunión, recuperación, junta popular; junta libre.

ram (ram) s. carnero; martinete; ariete hidráulico; pisón; **battering — ariete**; v. apisonar; golpear; meter por la fuerza, apretar; rellenar; atacar un arma; **to — a boat** chocar con un barco.

ramble (rámbl) v. vagar, andar a la ventura; hablar sin sentido; callejear; serpentear; s. correría.

rampart (rámpart) s. baluarte; terraplén; muralla.

ran (ran) pret. de to run.

ranch (ranch) s. rancho, hacienda; estancia; **cattle — hacienda** ganadera; granja.

rancid (ránsid) adj. rancio, acedo.

rancor (ránkor) s. rencor, encono.

random (rándom) adj. a la ventura; al azar; casual, fortuito; s. desatino; desacierto.

rang (rang) pret. de to ring.

range (réiny) v. recorrer; rondar; colocar, ordenar, alinear; vagar; ir; arreglar; **to — ten miles** tener un alcance de diez millas (dícese de los proyectiles); variar; extenderse; tomar el mismo partido; s. extensión o espacio, duración; pastizal; distancia; alcance; fila; hilera; ringlera; clase, orden; variación (dentro de ciertos límites); **gas — cocina de gas**; **— of mountains** cordillera de montañas; **— of vision** campo visual; **in — with** en línea con; **—s cornamusas**.

rank (rank) s. fila, hilera, ringlera; clase, orden, categoría, dignidad; rango; grado en el ejército; **the — and file** la tropa; v. clasificar; colocar, ordenar; poner en fila; **to — above** ser de grado superior a; **to — high** tener un alto rango; ser de elevada categoría; **to — with** estar al nivel de; **to — second** ocupar o tener el segundo lugar.

ransack (ránsak) v. registrar; rebuscar; escudriñar; saquear; pillar.

ransom (ránsom) s. rescate; v. rescatar, redimir, libertar.

rant (rant) v. delirar, disparatar; hablar necedades.

rap (rap) v. golpear; llamar a la puerta, arrebatar; criticar; s. golpe ligero; **— on the nose** papirote; cosa sin valor.

rapacious (rapéshios) adj. rapaz; voraz; **—ly** con rapacidad.

rape (reip) s. estupro, violación; v. forzar, violar a una mujer.

rapid (rápid) adj. rápido, veloz, raudo; **—s** pl. raudal, rápidos de un río.

rapiditi (rapiditi) s. rapidez; velocidad, celeridad.

rapt (rapt) adj. extasiado; absorto.

rapture (ráptchur) s. éxtasis, rapto.

rare (rer) adj. raro; extraño; precioso; extraordinario; a medio asar; a medio freír; medio crudo; **—ly** adv. raramente; raras veces; muy de vez en cuando.

rarity (rériti) s. rareza; curiosidad; enrarecimiento atmosférico.

rascal (ráskal) s. pillo, bribón.

rash (rash) adj. irreflexivo, temerario, arrebatado; atrevido; imprudente; s. sarpullido, erupción de la piel.

rashness (ráshnes) s. temeridad.

rasp (rasp) s. escofina, limatón; ronquera, carraspera; v. chirriar; raspar, rallar.

raspberry (ráspberri) s. **frambuesa**.
raspy (ráspi) adj. ronco; áspero.
rat (rat) s. rata; esquirol; postizo para el pelo.
rate (réit) s. razón, proporción, tasa, tanto por ciento; precio; valor; tipo de interés; tarifa; — **of exchange** tipo de cambio; modo; manera; I — **of increase** incremento proporcional; **at any** — en todo caso, de cualquier modo; **at the** — **of a** razón de; **at that** — de ese modo; **first** — de primera clase o calidad; lo mejor; v. tasar, valuar, clasificar; **he —s as the best** se le considera como el mejor; **he —s high** se le tiene en alta estima.
rather (ráder) adv. mejor, más bien, tal vez, algo, un poco; antes bien; **I would** — preferiría, me gustaría más; — **expensive** algo caro.
ratify (rátifai) v. ratificar; revalidar, sancionar.
rating (réting) s. clasificación, rango, clase, categoría.
ratio (résho) s. razón, proporción; relación.
ration (réshon) s. ración; v. racionar.
rational (réshonal) adj. racional, razonable; cuerdo, juicioso.
rationing (réshoning) s. racionamiento.
rattle (rátl) v. traquetear; golpetear; aturdir; rechinar; sonar ruidosamente; confundir; desconcertar; **to** — **away** parlotear; tocar a distancia haciendo ruido; s. traqueteo, rechinido; golpeteo; **child's** — sonaja; **death** — estertor de la muerte.
rattlesnake (rátlsneik) s. víbora de cascabel; cascabel del crótalo.
raucous (rókos) adj. ronco, áspero, estentóreo.
ravage (révely) s. ruina, destrucción, destrozo, asolamiento; saqueo, pillaje; v. asolar, destruir; saquear, pillar.
rave (réiv) v. bramar, encolerizarse; ponerse fuera de sí; desvariar; delirar, disparatar.
raven (réivn) s. cuervo; v. apresar, hacer presa; devorar; rapiñar.
ravenous (rávnos) adj. voraz; rapaz; devorador; estar hambriento; **to be** — tener hambre canina.

ravine (ravin) s. **barranca**, hondonada; quebrada.
ravish (révish) v. encantar; cautivar; arrebatar; violar a una mujer.
raw (roh) adj. crudo; verde; raído, descarnado; nuevo; en su estado natural; novato, inexperto; — **silk** seda en rama; — **flesh** carne viva; — **meat** carne cruda, no asada o cocida.
rawhide (rójaid) s. cuero no curtido; — **whip** látigo; rebenque.
ray (réi) rayo; raya (pez).
rayon (rélon) s. **rayón**, seda artificial.
raze (réis) v. arrasar, demoler.
razor (reisor) s. navaja de rasurar; — **blade** hoja de rasurar; **safety** — navaja de seguridad para afeitarse.
reach (rich) v. alcanzar; lograr con esfuerzo; llegar a; extenderse; alargar; tender; **to** — **for** tratar de coger; echar mano; **to** — **into** penetrar; meter la mano en; **to** — **out one's hand** tender o alargar la mano; s. alcance, extensión; **beyond his** — fuera de su alcance.
react (riákt) v. reaccionar.
reaction (riákshon) s. reacción.
reactionary (riákshoneri) adj. y s. reaccionario.
read (rid) v. leer; indicar (como un termómetro, contador, etc); **to** — **law** estudiar derecho; **it —s thus** dice así, reza así; **it —s easily** se lee sin esfuerzo.
read (red) pret. y p.p. de **to read**.
reader (rider) s. lector.
readily (rédili) adv. con facilidad, sin esfuerzo; de buena gana.
readiness (rédines) s. buena disposición, buena voluntad; prontitud; v. estar listo, estar dispuesto; estar preparado; tener voluntad de.
reading (riding) s. lectura; indicación; lección, variante, texto; — **room** salón de lectura.
readjust (riadyóst) s. reajuste; v. reajustar; arreglar; readaptar.
readjustment (riadyóstment) s. reajuste, readaptación, arreglo nuevo; nueva disposición.
ready (rédi) adj. listo, pronto; dispuesto, útil, disponible sin dilación, propenso; preparado; — **cash** fondos disponibles.

ready-made (rédiméid) adj. hecho, ya hecho.

real (rial) adj. real; genuino; verdadero; sincero; **— estate** bienes raíces; **—ly** adv. realmente, genuinamente, verdaderamente.

realism (ríalism) s. realismo.

realist (ríalist) s. realista; **—ic** adj. realista, vivo, natural.

reality (riáliti) s. realidad.

realization (rialiséshon) s. realización, verificación; comprensión.

realize (ríalais) v. percibir como realidad; darse cuenta de; hacerse cargo de; vender, realizar.

realm (relm) s. reino, dominio, jurisdicción.

reap (rip) v. cosechar; segar; recoger las mieses; obtener, aprovechar; sacar fruto.

reaper (ríper) s. máquina segadora.

reappear (riapír) v. reaparecer.

rear (rir) adj. posterior, postrero; trasero, último; de atrás; **— admiral** contraalmirante; **— guard** retaguardia; s. parte posterior; fondo; espaldas; parte de atrás; cola de una fila; **in the —** atrás, detrás; v. levantar; erigir; criar; educar; encabritarse.

reason (rísn) s. razón, fundamento, causa, motivo; prueba, justicia; intuición; **it stands to —** es justo, es lógico; v. razonar; discurrir; probar; argüir; raciocinar.

reasonable (rísnabl) adj. razonable; justo, lógico, módico, racional; **reasonably** adv. con razón, con justicia; con moderación.

reasoning (rísning) s. razonamiento; argumento; discurso; raciocinio.

reassure (riashúr) v. alentar; asegurar una vez más; tranquilizar; restaurar la confianza.

rebate (ribéit) s. rebaja de precio; v. rebajar (precio).

rebel (rébel) s. y adj. rebelde; v. rebelarse, insurreccionarse.

rebellion (rebélion) s. rebelión.

rebellious (rebélios) adj. rebelde.

rebirth (rebérz) s. renacimiento.

rebound (ribáund) v. rebotar; saltar (la pelota); rechazar; s. rebote; **on the —** de rebote.

rebuff (ribóf) s. desaire; v. desairar; rechazar.

rebuild (ribíld) v. reconstruir; reedificar.

rebuilt (ribílt) pret. y p.p. de to rebuild.

rebuke (ribiúk) s. reprensión; amonestación; reprimenda; v. reprender, reprochar.

recall (ricól) v. recordar; revocar; retirar (a un diplomático); s. revocación; llamada; notificación (para hacer volver).

recede (risíd) v. retroceder; cejar.

receipt (risít) s. recibo; receta; **—s** ingresos; percepciones; **on — of** al recibo de; v. extender recibo de un pago; **we are in — of your favor...** obra en nuestro poder su grata...

receive (risív) v. recibir.

receiver (risíver) s. receptor; depositario; síndico; recipiente; receptáculo.

recent (rísnt) adj. reciente; moderno; **—ly** adv. recientemente; nuevamente, hace poco; **—ly married** recién casados.

receptacle (reséptakl) s. receptáculo.

reception (resépshon) s. recepción; recibimiento; acogida; besamanos.

recess (risés) s. nicho; alcoba; hueco; tregua, receso; vacación; retiro; escondrijo; soledad; asueto; v. suspender los trabajos; poner en receso; hacer un nicho o hueco en la pared.

recipe (résipi) s. receta, prescripción; fórmula.

recipient (risípient) s. recipiente; receptor; recibidor; adj. receptivo.

reciprocal (risíprokal) adj. recíproco; mutuo; alternado.

reciprocate (resíprokeit) v. corresponder.

recital (risáital) s. recital; narración; recitación; relato.

recitation (risitéshon) s. recitación.

recite (risáit) v. recitar, declamar, relatar, narrar; referir.

reckless (rékles) adj. osado, atrevido, temerario; precipitado; descuidado; indiferente; **to be — with money** ser derrochador.

recklessness (réklesnes) s. osadía; temeridad; atrevimiento; descuido; indiferencia; precipitación.

reckon (rékon) v. suponer; admitir; reconocer; contar, computar; juzgar; **to — on** contar con.

reckoning (rékoning) s. cuenta; tanteo; **the day of —** el día del juicio.

— 182 —

reclaim (rikléim) v. reclamar; domesticar; vindicar; recobrar; aprovechar; utilizar; pedir la devolución de algo.

recline (rikláin) v. reclinar(se); recostar(se); descansar.

recluse (riklús) adj. recluso; solitario; s. recluso, asceta.

recognition (rekognishon) s. reconocimiento; agradecimiento.

recognize (récognais) v. reconocer.

recoil (rikóil) v. recular, patear un arma de fuego; s. retroceso; rebote; repugnancia.

recollect (recolékt) v. recordar; recoger; recolectar; cosechar; acordarse.

recollection (rekolékshon) s. recuerdo; reminiscencia; memoria.

recommend (rikoménd) v. recomendar.

recommendation (rikomendéshon) s. recomendación.

recompense (rékompens) v. recompensar, retribuir; resarcir; indemnizar; s. recompensa, retribución, resarcimiento, indemnización.

reconcile (rékonsail) v. reconciliar; ajustar; avenirse; conformarse; to — oneself to resignarse a.

reconciliation (rekonsiliéshon) s. reconciliación; ajuste; avenencia; conformidad; resignación.

reconnoitre (rekonóiter) v. practicar un reconocimiento; hacer una exploración; inspeccionar.

reconsider (riconsíder) v. reconsiderar; volver a discutir.

reconstruct (riconstróct) v. reconstruir; reedificar.

reconstruction (rikonstrókshon) s. reconstrucción.

recount (rikáunt) s. recuento; (rikáunt) v. recontar, hacer un recuento; referir, narrar, relatar; detallar.

recourse (ríkors) s. recurso; remedio; auxilio; to have — to recurrir a.

recover (rikóver) v. recuperar; recobrar; rescatar; resarcirse; restablecerse; recobrar la salud.

recovery (rikóvri) s. convalecencia; recuperación; recobro; rescate.

recreation (rekriéshon) s. recreación; recreo; pasatiempo; esparcimiento.

recruit (rikrút) v. reclutar; enrolar en el ejército; alistar; s. recluta; novato; nuevo miembro.

rectangle (réktangl) s. rectángulo.

rectify (réktifai) v. rectificar.

rector (réktor) s. rector.

rectum (réktum) s. recto.

recuperate (rikiúpereit) v. recuperar; recobrar; restablecerse.

recur (rikór) v. repetirse, volver a ocurrir; to — to a matter volver a un asunto.

red (red) adj. rojo, encarnado.

redden (rédn) v. enrojecer(se); ponerse colorado; ruborizarse; teñir de rojo.

redeem (redím) v. redimir; rescatar; cumplir una promesa, resarcir; desempeñar; recompensar.

redeemer (redímer) s. redentor; salvador; the Redeemer El Redentor.

redemption (redémpshon) s. redención; amortización de una deuda; — of a note pago de un documento u obligación.

redness (rédnes) s. rojez, rojura; bermejura; inflamación.

redouble (redóbl) v. redoblar; aumentar; repetir; repercutir.

redress (ridrés) v. reparar, resarcir; compensar; desagraviar; s. reparación; compensación, desagravio; enmienda.

reduce (rediús) v. reducir; aminorar; contraer; adelgazar; rebajar; sojuzgar; subyugar.

reduction (ridókshon) s, reducción; merma; disminución; rebaja.

redwood (rédúd) s. pino o secoya, árbol gigantesco de California que tiene madera roja.

reed (rid) s. caña, junco; chirimía; cualquier instrumento de boquilla; caramillo.

reef (rif) s. arrecife; rizo; banco de arena (en el mar).

reek (rík) v. vahar, exhalar, oler mal; s. hedor, mal olor.

reel (ríl) s. devanadera; carrete; rollo de película cinematográfica; v. aspar, devanar, hilar; hacer eses; bambolearse.

re-elect (rielékt) v. reelegir.

re-election (rielékson) s. reelección.

re-enter (riénter) v. volver a entrar.

re-establish (riestáblish) v. restablecer; restaurar.

refer (refér) v. referir, remitir; trasladar; atribuir; aludir, referirse a; recurrir a; dar referencias; dejar al juicio o decisión de.

referee (réferi) s. árbitro; v. arbitrar; conducir un juego.
reference (réfrens) s. referencia; alusión; marca de referencia; fiador; el que recomienda a otro; — **book** libro de consulta; **commercial** —s referencias comerciales; **with** — **to** con relación a; con respecto a.
refill (rifíl) s. relleno; v. rellenar; rehenchir.
refine (rifáin) v. refinar; purificar; pulir; perfeccionar; **to be** —**d** ser muy cortés.
refined (rifáind) adj. refinado; pulido; clarificado; fino, culto.
refinement (rifáinment) s. refinamiento; buena educación, buenos modales; purificación; perfeccionamiento; cortesía, gentileza.
refinery (rifáineri) s. refinería.
reflect (riflékt) v. reflejar; reflexionar; deslucir; manchar; **to** — **on one's character** desdecir del carácter de uno.
reflection (reflékshon) s. reflexión; reflejo; meditación; censura; tacha; baldón.
reflex (rífleks) s. reflejo.
reflexive (rifléxiv) adj. reflexivo.
reform (rifórm) s. reforma; v. reformar; enmendar; corregir.
reformation (riforméshon) s. reforma.
reformer (rifórmer) s. reformador; reformista.
refraction (refrákshon) s. refracción.
refractory (rifráktori) adj. refractario; terco, obstinado, rebelde.
refrain (rifréin) v. refrenarse, abstenerse; s. refrán, estribillo.
refresh (rifrésh) v. refrescar; renovar; vivificar, confortar.
refreshing (rifréshing) adj. refrescante; renovador; vivificante.
refreshment (refréshment) s. refresco.
refrigeration (refriyeréshon) s. refrigeración; enfriamiento.
refrigerator (refríyereitor) s. nevera; refrigerador.
refuge (réfiuy) s. refugio; amparo; asilo; albergue; guarida; recurso.
refugee (refiuyí) s. refugiado.
refund (refónd) s. restitución; reembolso; reintegro; v. restituir, reembolsar; reintegrar.
refusal (refiúsal) s. negativa; denegación; desaire; opción para recusar un convenio provisional.

refuse (refiús) v. recusar; negar; rehusar; rehuir; desechar; **to** — **to** rehusarse a, negarse a.
refuse (refiús) s. desechos, basura, desperdicio; sobras.
refute (rifiút) v. refutar; rebatir.
regain (riguéin) v. recobrar, recuperar; volver a ganar lo perdido.
regal (rígal) adj. regio, real.
regale (riguéil) v. regalar; agasajar; festejar, recrear.
regalia (reguéilia) s. pl. galas; insignias reales; distintivos.
regard (rigárd) v. mirar; considerar; observar o mirar de cerca; reparar; atender; estimar; **as** —**s this** tocante a esto; en cuanto a esto; s. miramiento, atención, circunspección; consideración; respeto; —**s** recuerdos, memorias.
regarding (rigárding) prep. tocante a; relativamente a; en cuanto a.
regardless (rigárdles) — **of** sin hacer caso de; prescindiendo de.
regent (ríyent) s. regente.
regime (reyím) s. régimen; dieta; gobierno metódico.
regiment (réyiment) s. regimiento; gobierno.
region (ríyon) s. región.
register (réyister) s. registro; matrícula; rol; lista, archivo; protocolo; libro de parroquias; contador; indicador; — **of a ship** matrícula de un barco; v. registrar; certificar una carta; inscribir(se); marcar, matricular.
registrar (réyistrar) s. registrador; archivero.
registration (reyistréshon) s. registro; asiento, empadronamiento; matrícula, inscripción.
regret (regrét) s. pesadumbre; cuidado, sentimiento; remordimiento; pesar; compunción; **to send** —**s** enviar sus excusas (al rehusar una invitación); v. sentir, lamentar.
regrettable (rigrétabl) adj. lamentable, que ha de ser sentido.
regular (réguiular) adj. regular; metódico; arreglado; **a** — **fool** un verdadero necio; un tonto de capirote; que vuelve o se repite sin omisión; — **soldier** soldado de línea.
regulation (reguiuléshon) s. regulación, arreglo, método; orden; —**s** reglamento; — **size, length** tamaño, longitud de reglamento.
regulator (réguiuleitor) s. regulador; registro (de un reloj).

rehearsal (rijérsal) s. ensayo (de un drama, concierto, etc.); repetición; enumeración.
rehearse (rijérs) v. ensayar, repetir; recitar; referir, repasar.
reign (réin) s. reino, reinado.
reimburse (reimbérs) v. reembolsar.
reimbursement (reimbérsment) s. reembolso; reintegro.
rein (rein) s. rienda, gobierno, dirección; v. refrenar (un caballo).
reindeer (réindir) s. reno (especie de ciervo).
reinforce (reinfórs) v. reforzar.
reinforcement (reinfórsment) s. refuerzo.
reiterate (riítereit) v. reiterar.
reject (riyékt) v. rechazar; desechar; abatir, repulsar, rehusar.
rejoice (riyóis) v. regocijar(se).
rejoin (riyóin) v. reunirse con; volverse a unir; volver a la compañía de; v. replicar.
rejuvenate (reyúveneit) v. rejuvenecer, remozar.
relapse (reláps) s. recaída; reincidencia; v. recaer; reincidir.
relate (reléit) v. relatar, narrar, relacionar, referir, contar.
relation (reléshon) s. relación; narración; respecto, consonancia; interdependencia; —s parientes; parentela; **with — to** con relación a.
relationship (riléshonship) s. relación, parentesco.
relative (rélativ) adj. relativo; pertinente; s. relativo; pronombre relativo; pariente, deudo.
relax (riláks) v. relajar; aflojar; laxar, ablandar; recrearse.
relaxation (relakséshon) s. esparcimiento; aflojamiento; relajación; solaz, recreo; descanso, reposo; distracción; mitigación, lenidad; **— of discipline** relajación de la disciplina; **— of one's mind** esparcimiento del ánimo.
relay (riléi) s. relevo; relai; relai de teléfonos; **— race** carrera de relevos; tanda, muda, remuda; eleciric — relevador; v. transmitir; despachar; hacer cundir (una noticia).
release (relís) v. soltar; librar, poner en libertad; libertar; eximir de alguna obligación; ceder; relevar, apartarse; **to — a piece of news** hacer pública una nueva; exonerar; aliviar los dolores; s. liberación, soltura; alivio.

relegate (rélegueit) v. relegar; desterrar; apartar.
relent (relént) v. mitigar(se); apiadarse; aplacarse.
relentless (reléntles) adj. implacable; despiadado.
reliability (relaiabíliti) s. formalidad.
reliable (reláiabl) adj. formal; puntual; seguro, digno de confianza.
reliance (reláians) s. confianza; seguridad; **self —** confianza en sí; confianza en sus propias fuerzas.
relic (rélik) s. reliquia.
relief (relíf) s. alivio; descanso; consuelo; socorro, ayuda caritativa; realce; refuerzo; **to be on —** recibir manutención gratuita; **high —, low —** alto y bajo relieve.
relieve (relív) v. relevar; librar; remediar; socorrer; aliviar.
religion (relíyon) s. religión.
religious (relíyos) adj. y s. religioso; pío, devoto.
relinquish (relínkuish) v. abandonar; dejar, ceder; resignar.
relish (rélish) s. buen sabor; gusto; apetencia; sainete; cata; apetito; condimento; entremés (aceitunas; encurtidos, etc.); v. saborear; dar sabor; gustar de.
reluctance (relóktans) s. repugnancia; disgusto, mala gana.
reluctant (relóktant) adj. renuente; refractario; que no quiere; opuesto; **—ly** adv. renuentemente; con renuencia.
rely (reláí) v. confiar en, tener confianza en; fiarse de; **to — on** contar con.
remain (reméin) v. quedar(se); permanecer; restar, faltar; quedarse solo; estar(se).
remainder (reméinder) s. resto; restante; residuo, alcance.
remains (riméins) s. pl. restos; cadáver; reliquias, ruinas.
remake (riméik) v. rehacer, hacer de nuevo.
remark (remárk) s. observación; advertencia, nota; reparo; v. notar; observar; señalar, distinguir.
remarkable (remárkabl) adj. notable; reparable; interesante; extraordinario; considerable.
remedy (rémedi) s. remedio; medicamento; cura; v. remediar; curar.
remember (remémber) s. recordar; acordarse; tener presente; rememorar; hacer memoria; mentar

remembrance (remémbrans) s. recuerdo; memoria, retentiva; recordación; —s saludos.
remind (remáind) v. recordar, acordar; avisar.
reminder (remáinder) s. recordatorio, recordativo; advertencia; memorándum; memoria.
reminiscence (reminísens) s. reminiscencia; memoria, recuerdo.
remiss (remís) adj. descuidado; flojo; perezoso; negligente.
remission (remíshon) s. remisión.
remit (remít) v. remitir; remesar; enviar; enviar dinero de una parte a otra; perdonar.
remittance (remítans) s. remisión; envío; remesa (de fondos).
remnant (rémnant) s. resto; residuo; remanente.
remodel (remódl) v. rehacer, reconstruir; modelar de nuevo.
remorse (remórs) s. remordimiento.
remote (remóut) adj. remoto.
removal (remúval) s. mudanza; traslado; alejamiento; cambio de lugar; extracción.
remove (remúv) v. remover; alejar; desviar; mudar una cosa de un lugar a otro; deponer (de un empleo); apartar; sacar.
removed (remúvd) adj. remoto.
Renaissance (renesáns) s. Renacimiento.
rend (rend) v. desgarrar, rasgar.
render (rénder) v. dar; entregar; hacer, ejecutar; suministrar; prestar, rendir; interpretar; traducir; to — an account of rendir o dar cuenta de; to — thanks to God dar gracias a Dios; to — useless inutilizar, incapacitar; to — assistance to prestar auxilio.
renew (reniú) v. renovar; restaurar; hacer o hacerse de nuevo; reanudar; prorrogar (un préstamo).
renewal (reniúal) s. renovación; prórroga; reanudación.
renounce (renáns) v. renunciar.
renovate (rénoveit) v. renovar.
renown (renáun) s. renombre.
renowned (renáund) adj. renombrado.
rent (rent) s. alquiler, renta, arrendamiento; desgarrón, rasgón; rotura; cuarteadura; it is for — se alquila; se arrienda; v. arrendar; alquilar.
rent (rent) pret. y p.p. de to rend; s. grieta, cuarteadura; cisma.

rental (réntal) s. renta; arriendo.
reopen (riópen) v. reabrir(se); volver a abrir.
repair (ripér) v. reparar; remendar; componer, restaurar; aderezar, recorrer; s. reparo, reparación; to — to ir a alguna parte; encaminarse a; in — en buen estado.
reparation (reparéshon) s. reparación, renovación; satisfacción.
repay (ripéi) v. resarcir; volver a pagar, recompensar; retornar.
repayment (ripéiment) s. reintegro; pago; devolución.
repeal (ripíl) v. derogar; abrogar; anular; revocar; abolir (una ley); s. abrogación; revocación; anulación.
repeat (ripít) v. repetir; s. repetición.
repeated (ripíted) adj. repetido; —ly adv. repetidamente; reiteradamente; una y otra vez.
repel (ripél) v. repeler; rechazar, repulsar; repugnar; that idea —s me me repugna esa idea.
repent (ripént) v. arrepentirse (de).
repentance (ripéntans) s. arrepentimiento, compunción.
repentant (repéntant) adj. arrepentido; contrito; penitente.
repetition (repetíshon) s. repetición; reiteración; repaso.
replace (ripléis) v. reponer, volver a colocar; reemplazar; devolver; reembolsar; restituir.
replaceable (ripléisabl) adj. reemplazable, renovable.
replenish (riplénish) v. rellenar, llenar; rehenchir; reabastecer.
replete (riplít) adj. repleto.
replica (réplika) s. reproducción; duplicado; copia exacta.
reply (riplái) v. replicar, contestar; responder; s. contestación; respuesta; réplica.
reporter (ripórter) s. reportero.
repose (ripóus) v. reposar; descansar, reclinar, dormir; to — one's confidence in confiar en; s. reposo.
represent (represént) v. representar.
representation (representéshon) s. representación.
representative (represéntativ) adj. representativo; típico, representante; s. delegado, diputado, gestor, apoderado; símbolo.
repress (riprés) v. reprimir; sojuzgar; refrenar; cohibir.
repression (represhon) s. represión.

reprimand (reprimánd) v. reprender; regañar; reprochar, amonestar; s. reprimenda; amonestación.
reprisal (repráisal) s. represalia.
reproach (repróuch) v. reprochar, censurar; criticar; reconvenir; increpar; s. reproche, increpación.
reproduce (reprodiús) v. reproducir.
reproduction (reprodókshon) s. reproducción, copia, traslado.
reproof (riprúf) s. reprensión, reprobación; peluca; regaño.
reprove (riprúv) v. reprobar; culpar; censurar; reprender.
reptile (réptil) s. reptil.
republic (repóblik) s. república.
republican (repóblikan) adj. y s. republicano.
repudiate (repiúdiet) v. repudiar, renunciar; echar o lanzar de sí.
repugnance (repógnans) s. repugnancia; desgana, aversión.
repugnant (repógnant) adj. repugnante; contrario; antipático.
repulse (ripóls) v. repulsar, repeler; desechar; s. repulsa; rehuso.
repulsive (repólsiv) adj. repulsivo, repugnante, chocante.
reputable (répiutabl) adj. de buena reputación; honroso, decoroso.
reputation (repiutéshon) s. reputación; estimación, fama, renombre.
repute (repiút) v. reputar; estimar; juzgar, tener por; s. reputación; fama, crédito, estimación.
request (rikuést) s. solicitud; petición; pedimento, ruego, súplica; **at the — of** a solicitud de; v. solicitar, rogar, pedir, encargar, suplicar.
require (rikuáir) v. requerir; exigir, solicitar, pedir.
requirement (rikuáirment) s. requerimiento.
requisite (rékuisit) s. requisito; adj. requerido, necesario, indispensable; preciso.
requisition (rekuisíshon) s. requisición, demanda, petición; pedimento; v. demandar, pedir, ordenar.
rescue (réskiu) v. rescatar; librar; recobrar; salvar; s. rescate, libramiento; salvamento; socorro; **to go to the — of** acudir al socorro de.
research (risérch) s. rebusca; búsqueda; escudriñamiento; v. rebuscar; investigar.
resemblance (risémblans) s. semejanza, parecido, similitud.
resemble (risémbl) v. asemejarse a; semejar; parecerse a.
resent (risént) v. resentirse de, sentirse de; encolerizarse.
resentful (riséntful) adj. resentido; enfadadizo; vidrioso; rencoroso.
resentment (riséntment) s. resentimiento, desazón, pesar.
reservation (reservéshon) s. reservación; restricción mental.
reserve (resérv) v. reservar.
reservoir (réservor) s. depósito (de agua, aceite, gas, provisiones, etc.); **water —** alberca; aljibe; estanque.
reside (resáid) v. residir, vivir.
residence (résidens) s. residencia; morada, domicilio.
resident (résident) adj. y s. residente, permanente; inherente.
residue (résidiu) s. residuo, resto.
resign (resáin) v. renunciar; dimitir; ceder, rendirse.
resignation (resignéshon) s. renuncia; resignación; dimisión.
resin (résin) s. resina.
resist (resíst) v. resistir; oponerse; rechazar, repeler; imponerse.
resistance (resístans) s. resistencia; oposición, impedimento.
resistant (resístant) adj. resistente.
resolute (résoliut) adj. resuelto.
resolution (resolúshon) s. resolución, determinación; arresto.
resort (resórt) v. recurrir; acudir, frecuentar; concurrir; s. refugio; recurso; concurso; **to have — to** recurrir a.
resorter (resórter) s. **summer —** veraneante.
resound (risáund) v. resonar; repercutir; publicar; cantar; celebrar; repetir.
resource (risórs) s. recurso; arbitrio, medio, expediente.
respect (respékt) v. respetar; venerar; acatar, estimar; **as —s** por lo que respecta a; s. respeto; consideración; la razón.
respectable (respéktabl) adj. respetable, venerable.
respectful (respéktful) adj. respetuoso, lleno de respeto.
respecting (respékting) prep. con respecto a, en cuanto a.
respective (respéktiv) adj. respectivo; cada uno.

respiration (respiréshon) s. respiración, respiro.
respite (réspit) s. tregua, pausa, descanso; plazo, respiro.
resplendent (respléndent) adj. resplandeciente, brillante.
respond (respónd) v. responder.
response (respóns) s. respuesta; contestación; reacción.
responsibility (responsibiliti) s. responsabilidad, deber.
responsible (respónsbl) adj. responsable, solvente.
rest (rest) s. reposo; quietud; descanso; apoyo; soporte; resto; pausa; tregua; **at** — en paz; **the** — los demás, resto; v. posar; yacer; apoyarse en; confiar en; contar con, depender de; cesar; permanecer; proporcionar descanso.
restaurant (réstorant) s. restaurante, fonda, restorán.
restful (réstful) adj. reposado, sosegado, lleno de reposo, tranquilo; quieto.
restitution (restitiúshon) s. restitución; restablecimiento.
restless (réstles) adj. inquieto, inconstante, mudable.
restlessness (réstlesnes) s. inquietud; insomnio, vigilia.
restoration (restoréshon) s. restauración; restitución.
restore (restór) v. restaurar; restituir; reproducir, reedificar.
restrain (restréin) v. refrenar, contener; cohibir, restringir.
restraint (restréint) s. restricción; reserva, sujeción; circunspección; moderación.
restrict (restríkt) v. restringir.
restriction (restríkshon) s. restricción.
result (resólt) v. resultar; seguirse, inferirse; acabar, terminar en; **to — from** resultar de; tener un resultado; **as a —** como resultado, de resultas.
resumé (résumé) s. resumen, sumario.
resuscitate (resósiteit) v. resucitar; hacer revivir.
retail (ritéil) s. venta al por menor; v. revender, regatear; decir o relatar una cosa detalladamente; **at —** al por menor; **— merchant** detallista, comerciante al por menor; v. detallar, vender al menudeo (vender al por menor).
retailer (ritéiler) s. detallista, revendedor; lonjista; tendero

retain (retéin) v. retener.
retaliate (retáliet) v. desquitarse; castigar con la pena del talión.
retaliation (retaliéshon) s. desquite; despique; desagravio.
retard (retárd) v. retardar, retrasar, disminuir la velocidad.
retinue (rétiniu) s. comitiva; séquito; tren, serie de resultados.
retire (retáir) v. retirar(se); jubilar(se); retroceder, apartarse.
retirement (retáirment) s. retiro; retiramiento; lugar apartado.
retort (retórt) v. replicar, redargüir; s. réplica.
retouch (ritóch) v. retocar; s. retoque.
retrace (ritréis) v. repasar; desandar; volver a trazar; **to — one's steps** volver sobre sus pasos; retroceder.
retract (ritrákt) v. retractarse; desdecirse; retraer; retirar.
retreat (ritrít) s. retiro; soledad; refugio, asilo; retirada; retreta; v. retirarse; refugiarse; retroceder; retraerse; cejar.
retrench (retrénch) v. cercenar, acortar; disminuir; economizar.
retrieve (retrív) v. recuperar; resarcirse; cobrar (la caza); restaurar; componer; reparar una pérdida; desquitarse.
return (ritérn) v. volver; devolver; regresar; restituir; pagar; retornar; replicar; redituar; producir; **to — a favor** corresponder a un favor; **to — a report** rendir un informe; s. vuelta, regreso; retorno; respuesta, réplica; restitución; recompensa; rédito, ganancia; resultados; cambio; trueque; **in —** en cambio, en reciprocidad; **— ticket** boleto de ida y vuelta; **by — mail** a vuelta de correo; **election —s** resultados de las elecciones; **income tax —** declaración del impuesto sobre la renta; **many happy —s** muchas felicidades en su día.
reunion (riúnion) s. reunión, junta.
reunite (riunáit) v. reunir(se); reconciliarse.
reveal (revíl) v. revelar; divulgar.
de parranda; s. juerga, parranda; farra; jolgorio.
revelation (reveléshon) s. revelación; **Revelation** Apocalipsis.
revelry (révelri) s. juerga, parranda
revenge (revény) v. vengar; vindicar; s. venganza; desquite; desagravio.

revengeful (revényful) adj. vengativo; vindicativo.
revenue (réveniu) s. ingresos del Erario; rentas, réditos; beneficio.
revere (revír) v. venerar.
reverence (révrens) s. reverencia; veneración; acatamiento; v. reverenciar; venerar; honrar.
reverend (révrend) adj. reverendo; venerado; **Reverend** Reverendo (tratamiento).
reverent (révrent) adj. reverente.
reverie, revery (réveri) s. ensueño.
reverse (rivérs) v. invertir; trastocar; trastornar; revocar; abolir; adj. reverso; invertido, opuesto; contrario; s. revés; dorso; contratiempo; reversión; inversión.
revert (revért) v. retroceder; revertir; resurtir.
review (reviú) s. revista; reseña; examen, análisis, juicio crítico; v. revisar; criticar; reseñar; pasar revista a las tropas; repasar; escribir una revista.
revile (reváil) v. denigrar, vilipendiar; denostar; vituperar.
revise (reváis) v. revisar; corregir; repasar; releer.
revision (revishon) s. revisión; corrección de pruebas.
revival (riváival) s. renacimiento; restauración; renovación; nueva presentación de una obra; — **meeting** junta para revivir el fervor religioso.
revive (reváiv) v. revivir, renovar; reavivar; animar; excitar; volver en sí; resucitar.
revoke (revóuk) v. revocar; abrogar; derogar; abolir; anular; hacer un renuncio en los juegos de naipes.
revolt (rivólt) s. rebelión, revuelta; sublevación; v. rebelarse; sublevarse; sentir repugnancia; it —s me me repugna, me da asco.
revolution (revolúshon) s. revolución; rotación de una rueda; giro.
revolutionary (revolúshoneri) adj. y s. revolucionario.
revolutionist (revolúshonist) s. revolucionario.
revolve (rivólv) v. dar vueltas, girar; voltear; rodar; to — **in one's mind** revolver en la mente; ponderar, reflexionar.
revolver (rivólver) s. revólver.
reward (riuórd) v. recompensar; gratificar; premiar; s. recompensa; premio; gratificación; retribución; albricias.
rewrite (rirráit) v. volver a escribir; refundir un escrito.
rhetoric (rétorik) s. retórica.
rheumatism (rúmatism) s. reumatismo; reuma.
rhinoceros (rainóceros) s. rinoceronte, unicornio.
rhubarb (rúbarb) s. ruibarbo.
rhyme (ráim) s. rima; v. rimar.
rhythm (rizm) s. ritmo; cadencia; armonía.
rhythmical (rízmikal) adj. rítmico; acompasado, cadencioso.
rib (rib) s. costilla; listón; nervio, viga; varilla de paraguas.
ribbon (ríbon) s. cinta; listón; banda, tira; v. encintar.
rice (rais) s. arroz; — **field** arrozal; — **paper** papel de China.
rich (rich) adj. rico; precioso; costoso; abundante; pingüe; sabroso; fértil; empalagoso; — **food** alimento muy grasoso o muy dulce; — **hues** matices vivos.
riches (ríches) s. pl. riquezas; opulencia; bienes.
rickety (ríketi) adj. destartalado; desvencijado; raquítico.
rid (rid) v. desembarazar; librar; quitar de encima; **to get** — **of** librarse de; deshacerse de; pret. y p.p. de **to rid**.
riddle (ridl) s. adivinanza; acertijo, misterio; enigma; v. acribillar; hablar enigmáticamente.
ride (ráid) v. cabalgar, montar.
rider (ráider) s. jinete; pasajero de automóvil; ciclista; motociclista; volante pegado a un documento; cláusula agregada a un proyecto de ley.
ridge (ridy) s. cerro, loma; cordillera, serranía; arruga; camellón; caballete; intersección de dos planos; arrecife; escollo; cordoncillo de ciertos tejidos.
ridicule (rídikiul) s. ridículo; ridiculez; burla; mofa; v. ridiculizar; burlarse de; escarnecer.
ridiculous (ridíkiulos) adj. ridículo.
rifle (ráifl) v. robar, pillar; arrebatar; despojar; s. rifle.
rig (rig) v. aparejar; guarnir; equipar; enjarciar un barco de vela; **to** — **oneself up** emperifollarse; ataviarse; s. aparejo; equipo; apresto; burla, mala partida.

rigging (ríguing) s. aparejo, cordaje; jarcia; cordelería.

right (ráit) adj. recto, equitativo, honesto; idóneo, conveniente; derecho; propio; adecuado; correcto; sano; cuerdo; — **angle** ángulo recto; — **hand** mano derecha; de la mano derecha; **to be —** tener razón; **it is — that** está bien que, es justo que; **to be all —** estar bien de salud; adv. con rectitud, con justicia; perfectamente; muy; inmediatamente; — **about face** media vuelta; — **now** ahora mismo; — **there** ahí mismo; **to the —** a la derecha; **go — back** ¡regresa inmediatamente!; **it is in the — place** está en el lugar que le corresponde, está en su lugar; **to hit — in the eye** dar en el mero ojo; s. derecho; equidad; razón; autoridad; privilegio; — **of way** derecho de vía; **to be in the —** estar en lo justo, tener razón; v. enderezar; corregir; **to set to —s** poner en orden; componer; **to maintain one's —s** defender o sostener sus derechos.

righteous (ráichos) adj. recto, justo, equitativo; virtuoso.

righteousness (raichosnes) s. rectitud; equidad; honradez.

rightful (ráitful) adj. legítimo; justo; recto.

rightist (ráitist) s. derechista.

rightly (ráitli) adv. con razón; justamente; correctamente; perfectamente; propiamente; debidamente.

rigid (ríyid) adj. rígido.

rigidity (riyíditi) s. rigidez; inflexibilidad; rigor; tiesura.

rigor (rígor) s. rigor; severidad.

rigorous (rígorous) adj. rigoroso; estricto; severo.

rim (rim) s. borde; orilla; aro.

rime véase **rhyme**.

rind (ráind) v. descortezar, mondar; pelar; s. corteza; cáscara.

ring (ring) s. anillo, sortija; círculo, circunferencia; aro; argolla; circo; arena; redondel; corro; campaneo; tañido; sonido metálico; clamor; estruendo; — **leader** cabecilla; — **of defiance** tono de reto; **telephone —** llamada de teléfono; **wedding —** sortija de matrimonio; **ear— arete**; — **shaped** anular; v. rodear; cercar; tocar un timbre o una campanilla; tañer, sonar; zumbar los oídos; **to — up cn the telephone** llamar por teléfono; **to — for something** llamar con el timbre para pedir algo.

ringlet (rínglet) s. bucle, rizo; sortija; círculo pequeño.

rink (rink) s. cancha para patinar o superficie helada para jugar curling.

rinse (rins) v. lavar, enjuagar; aclarar; blanquear la ropa.

riot (ráiot) s. tumulto; alboroto; motín; desorden; bola; v. amotinarse; armar un tumulto, alborotar; — **of color** exceso de colores chillantes.

rip (rip) v. rasgar(se); romper(se); rajar; descoser; aserrar al hilo; **to — off a plank** cortar un tablón; **to — out a seam** descoser una costura; s. rasgadura, rasgón; descosido; rotura; — **saw** sierra de hender.

ripe (ráip) adj. maduro, sazonado; pronto; preparado; — **for** maduro para; sazonado para; bien preparado para; listo para.

ripen (ráipen) v. madurar(se); sazonar(se).

ripeness (ráipnes) s. madurez; sazón.

ripple (rípl) v. rizar(se), agitar(se); ondear; temblar (superficie del agua); murmurar (un arroyo); s. ola, onda, ondulación; murmullo de un arroyo.

rise (ráis) v. subir; levantarse; salir el sol; brotar; sublevarse; sobrevenir; ascender; encumbrarse; hincharse; aumentar de volumen; s. cuesta, nacimiento, altura, creciente; elevación; — **of a hill** pendiente de una colina; **to give — to** dar origen a, causar.

risen (rísn) p.p. de **to rise**.

risk (risk) s. riesgo; peligro; albur; v. arriesgar, poner en peligro; jugarse el albur; exponerse a; aventurar(se).

risky (ríski) adj. arriesgado, peligroso; expuesto; aventurado.

rite (ráit) s. rito, ceremonia.

ritual (ríchual) adj. y s. ritual; ceremonial.

rival (ráival) s. rival, competidor; contrario; adj. competidor; opuesto; v. competir, emular, rivalizar; **the — party** el partido opuesto.

rivalry (ráivalri) s. rivalidad.

river (ríver) s. río.

rivet (rívet) s. remache; v. remachar; fijar; asegurar.
rivulet (ríviulet) s. riachuelo; arroyo; cañada.
road (róud) s. camino, carretera; vía.
roadside (róudsaid) s. borde del camino.
roadway (róuduei) s. carretera; calzada; camino.
roam (róum) v. vagar, errar, andar sin rumbo.
roar (róur) s. rugido; bramido; — **of laughter** risotada, carcajada; v. rugir, bramar, mugir, roncar.
roast (róust) v. asar; tostar; ridiculizar; burlarse de; criticar; s. asado; carne asada; — **beef** rosbif; **to — coffee** tostar café.
rob (rob) v. hurtar, robar; saquear; quitar; privar de; **to — someone of something** robarle algo a alguien.
robber (róber) s. ladrón, ratero; **highway —** salteador de caminos.
robbery (róbri) s. robo; hurto; pillaje; saqueo.
robe (róub) s. bata, túnica, toga; traje talar; ropón; **automobile —** manta de automóvil.
robin (róbin) s. petirrojo.
robust (robóst) adj. robusto, fuerte.
rock (rok) s. roca, peña; peñasco; escollo; laja; piedra; — **crystal** cristal de roca; — **salt** sal de piedra; sal gema, sal mineral; — **crusher** trituradora; v. mecer; arrollar, balancear; estremecer; **to — to sleep** adormecer.
rocker (róker) s. mecedora; balancín; arco de una mecedora o cuna.
rocket (róket) s. cohete.
rocking (róking) s. balanceo; adj. vacilante; oscilatorio; — **chair** silla mecedora.
rocky (róki) adj. roqueño, rocoso; rocalloso; pedregoso; pétreo, duro, movedizo, tembloroso.
rod (rod) s. vara, varilla; cetro, bastón de mano; longitud (aproximadamente 5 metros).
rode (róud) pret. de **to ride**.
rogue (róug) s. pícaro, bribón; tunante, pillo; villano, ruin, **—s gallery** colección policíaca de retratos de criminales.
roguish (róguish) adj. pícaro, pillo; belitre; tuno.
role (rol) s. papel, parte.
roll (rol) v. rodar; girar; hacer rodar; balancearse (un barco); laminar; cilindrar, alisar; bambolearse; ondular, retumbar (el trueno, un cañón); redoblar (el tambor); poner los ojos en blanco; revolver(se); arrollar, envolver; vibrar la lengua para pronunciar (la rr); **to — up** enrollar; s. rollo (de papel, etc.); balanceo; redoble; lista; nómina, catálogo; ondulación; oleaje; bollo, rosca; **to call the —** pasar lista.
roller (róler) s. rodilla; cilindro; aplanadora; alisador; rollo; rodillo de pastelero; — **coaster** montaña rusa; — **skate** patín de ruedas; venda, faja.
romance (románs) s. romance; novela; cuento, fábula; amorío; lance amoroso; aventura romántica; v. contar o fingir fábulas; andar en amoríos o en aventuras; mentir; adj. romance; románico; neolatino.
romantic (romántik) adj. romántico, novelesco; fantástico.
romanticism (romántisism) s. romanticismo.
romanticist (romántisist) s. escritor romántico; romancero.
romp (romp) v. retozar; brincar; juguetear; hacer travesuras; s. muchacha retozona; saltabardales.
roof (ruf) s. tejado, techo; azotea; techado; hogar, casa, habitación; — **garden** azotea jardín; — **of the mouth** paladar; **flat —** terrado; azotea; **slate —** techo de pizarras; — **tile** teja; v. techar, abrigar, alojar.
room (rum) s. cuarto, pieza; sala; lugar, paraje, sitio; causa; habitación; espacio; motivo; **there is no — for more** no cabe(n) más; no hay lugar para más; v. vivir, hospedarse; alojarse; — **mate** compañero de cuarto.
roomer (rúmer) s. inquilino.
roominess (rúmines) s. holgura.
roomy (rúmi) adj. espacioso; amplio; dilatado; capaz; holgado.
roost (rust) s. gallinero; pértiga de gallinero; sueño, descanso, reposo de las aves; v. acurrucarse; estar alojado en alguna parte.
rooster (rúster) s. gallo.
root (rut) s. raíz; v. arraigar; echar o criar raíces; hocicar; hozar (los cerdos); inveterarse los males; **to — for** vitorear, aclamar; **root-**

stock rizoma; **to — up** o **out** arrancar la raíz; extinguir.

rosary (rósari) s. rosario.

rose (róus) s. rosa; color de rosa; rosal; roseta; rosetón; **honey of —s** miel rosada.

rosebud (róusbod) s. capullo o botón de rosa; niña adolescente; yema, pimpollo.

rosette (rosét) s. roseta, rosetón.

rostrum (róstrum) s. tribune

rosy (rósi) adj. rosado; color de rosa; sonrojado, agradable; alegre; risueño; optimista.

rot (rot) v. pudrir(se); corromperse; ir a menos; s. podre.

rotary (róteri) adj. rotario, giratorio; rotante; rotativo.

rotate (róteit) v. girar, dar vueltas; girar o hacer rodar sobre un eje; turnarse.

rotation (rotéshon) s. rotación.

rote (róut) s. rutina, repetición maquinal; **by —** maquinalmente.

rotten (rótn) adj. putrefacto.

rouge (ruy) s. colorete, afeite; v. pintarse la cara, ponerse colorete; adj. encarnado; rojizo.

rough (rof) adj. áspero, tosco; escabroso; erizado; encrespado; duro; agrio; bronco; cerril; rudo; ordinario; insolente; tempestuoso; **— diamond** diamante en bruto; **— sea** mar gruesa; **— wind** viento borrascoso; **— draft** boceto; bosquejo; **— estimate** cálculo aproximado; **at a — guess** a ojo de buen cubero; **to — it** vivir sin comodidades; pasar trabajos.

roughen (rófen) v. hacer o poner áspero o tosco; picar; rascar una superficie; agrietarse la piel; **to — a horse** domar un caballo.

roughly (rófli) adv. con aspereza; aproximadamente; rudamente; bruscamente; toscamente; groseramente; **to estimate —** tantear.

roughness (rófnes) s. aspereza, rudeza; tosquedad; severidad; dureza; grosería, ordinariez; tempestad; tormenta; **the — of the sea** lo picado del mar.

round (ráund) adj. redondo; circular, esférico; rotundo; cabal; grande, cuantioso; liberal; franco, claro; rápido, vivo; justo; honrado; **— assertion** afirmación clara y categórica; **— trip** viaje redondo; viaje de ida y vuelta; **— trip ticket** boleto de viaje redondo; s. vuelta, giro, rotación; ronda; turno; **peldaño;** travesaño de escalera de mano; andanada; salva; disparo; cartucho con bala; rondó; adv. alrededor; en derredor; **all —** ducho o experto en su profesión; **— of ammunition** carga de municiones; descarga; **— about** a la ronda; por todos lados; v. **to go — a corner** dar vuelta a la esquina; **to — out** redondear, completar; **to — up cattle** juntar el ganado; desarrollarse; perfeccionarse; rondar.

roundabout (ráundabaut) adj. indirecto; desviado.

roundup (ráundop) s. rodeo de ganado.

rouse (ráus) v. despertar; despabilar; excitar; incitar; provocar; levantar la caza; animarse; moverse; despertarse.

rout (ráut) s. derrota; huida; fuga; v. derrotar; poner en fuga.

route (rut) s. ruta; camino; curso; itinerario; trazado, línea.

routine (rutin) s. rutina.

rove (róuv) v. vagar, andar errante.

rover (róuver) adj. vagabundo.

row (rau) s. riña; pendencia; pelea; v. pelear; reñir; armar camorra.

row (róu) s. fila, hilera; línea; v. remar; bogar; conducir remando.

rowboat (róubout) s. bote de remos.

rower (róer) s. remero.

royal (róial) adj. real, regio, majestuoso; magnífico.

royalist (róialst) s. realista.

royalty (róialti) s. realeza, soberanía; dignidad real; regalía; derechos (pagados a un autor o inventor); prerrogativas reales.

rub (rob) v. frotar; restregar; fregar; limpiar; rozar; rascar; raspar; irritar; **to — out** borrar; **to — away** continuar frotando o estregando; **to — someone the wrong way** llevarle a uno la contraria; s. fricción; frotamiento, estregamiento.

rubbish (róbish) s. basura; desechos; desperdicios; tonterías.

rubble (róbl) s. escombros; ripio, cascajo; morrillo; piedras; cascajo; piedra en bruto.

ruby (rúbi) s. rubí.

rudder (róder) s. timón.

ruddy (ródi) adj. rojo, rojizo.

rude (rud) adj. rudo, grosero; áspero, brutal, rústico, tosco.

rudeness (rúdnes) s. rudeza; grosería; descortesía; dureza.

rueful (rúful) adj. triste; lastimoso; lamentable; terrible.

ruffian (rófian) s. rufián, hombre brutal; malhechor, ladrón.

ruffle (rofl) v. rizar; desordenar; confundir; desarreglar; fruncir (tela); molestar; s. volante; vuelta o puño de camisola; frunce; pliegue; ondulación (en el agua).

rug (rog) s. alfombra, tapete.

rugged (rógued) adj. escabroso; fragoso; áspero, desigual, tosco, recio, robusto; tempestuoso.

ruin (rúin) s. ruina; caída, decadencia; bancarrota; to go to — arruinarse, caer en ruinas; echar a perder, estropear.

rule (rul) s. regla; reglamento; precepto; mando; poder, autoridad, señorío; as a — por regla general; v. regir; gobernar; mandar; reprimir; subyugar; contener.

ruler (rúler) s. gobernante; regla (para medir o trazar líneas).

ruling (rúling) s. fallo, decisión de un juez o una persona; rayado.

rum (rom) s. ron.

rumble (rómbl) v. retumbar; hacer estruendo; alborotar; s. rumor, ruido sordo; estruendo; — seat pescante, asiento trasero de un cupé.

ruminate (rúmineit) v. rumiar; reflexionar, meditar.

rummage (rómey) v. revolver; explorar, escudriñar, revolverlo todo en busca de algo; s. búsqueda desordenada.

rumor (rúmor) s. rumor, run-run; v. murmurar; divulgar, propalar.

rump (rómp) s. rabadilla; anca.

rumple (rómpl) v. arrugar, ajar; estrujar; s. arruga en un traje.

rumpus (rómpos) s. bulla; disturbio, alboroto, boruca, alharaca.

run (ron) v. correr, andar; funcionar; marchar; meter, clavar; empujar, echar; atravesar; cruzar; derramar, fundir; deslizarse; volar; fluir, gotear; competir, ser candidato a; encontrar, tropezar; oponerse; ser contrario; encogerse; to — away huir, fugarse, escaparse; to — after perseguir; to — by ser conocido por, pasar por; to — across a person encontrarse una persona; to — off desviar; to — out of money quedarse sin dinero; to — over atropellar; to — to acudir, correr hacia; to — into debt endeudarse; to — something into meter algo en; clavar algo en; to — out salirse; esparcirse, derramarse; gastarse; to — through atravesar; traspasar; ojear; to — counter oponerse, ir en contra; to — down dar caza; aprehender; vilipendiar, difamar; to get — down in health quebrantársele a uno la salud; to — up hacer subir una cuenta; sumar, hacer una suma; s. carrera, curso; marcha; recorrido, movimiento, operación, funcionamiento; serie de representaciones; — on a bank demanda extraordinaria de fondos bancarios; in the long — a la larga; tarde o temprano; terreno de pasto; migración; discreción o libertad en el uso de una cosa; hilo de un discurso; duración, vida de alguna cosa; adj. extraído; vaciado; derretido; — metal metal derretido.

runaway (rónauei) adj. fugitivo; desertor; — horse caballo desbocado; — marriage casamiento de escapatoria; s. fugitivo, fuga.

rung (rong) s. barrote, travesaño, paso, escalón; varengas, planes; pret. y p.p. de to ring.

runner (róner) s. corredor; correo, mensajero; vástago; tapete (para un pasillo o mesa); pasillo; carrera (en una media).

running (róning) s. corrida, carrera; curso; corredor; dirección, flujo; — horse caballo de carreras; — rigging cabos de labor; to be out of the — estar fuera de combate; adj. corriente; — board estribo; for ten days — por diez días seguidos.

runt (ront) s. enano, hombrecillo.

runway (rónuei) s. senda, vía; pista (de aterrizaje).

rupture (rópchor) s. ruptura; rompimiento, rotura; riña, desavenencia; hernia; v. romper(se); reventar.

rural (rúral) adj. rural, campestre; campesino, rústico.

rush (rosh) v. lanzar(se); arrojarse; abalanzarse; dispararse; despachar; empujar o arrojar con violencia; acometer; empujar; ejecutar con precipitación; to — forward arrojarse con ímpetu; to — out salir a todo correr; to — past pasar a toda prisa; to — in entrar de rondón; — of business gran movimiento comercial; — order pedido urgente.

Russian (róshan) adj. y s. ruso.

rust (rost) s. moho; orín; herrumbre; robín (enfermedad de las plantas); v. oxidar(se), enmohecer(se); embotarse.

rustic (róstik) adj. y s. rústico; agreste, villano; campesino.

rustle (róstl) s. susurrar; crujir; menear; to — cattle robar ganado; s. rozamiento, susurro.

rusty (rósti) adj. mohoso; oriniento; herrumbroso; oxidado; rojizo; entorpecido, falto de uso.

rut (rot) s. rodada; carril, costumbre; sendero trillado; to be in a — hacer una cosa por rutina.

ruthless (rúzles) adj. despiadado; cruel, endurecido; insensible, falto de piedad, brutal.

ruthlessness (rúzlesnes) s. fiereza; crueldad; falta de miramiento.

rye (rai) s. centeno.

S

saber (séiber) s. sable.
sabotage (sábotey) s. sabotaje; v. sabotear.
sack (sak) s. saco, costal; talega; saqueo, pillaje; v. ensacar; saquear; pillar.
sacrament (sákrement) s. sacramento.
sacred (séikred) adj. sagrado, sacro.
sacredness (sélkrednes) s. santidad.
sacrifice (sákrifais) s. sacrificio; inmolación; víctima; pérdida; v. sacrificar; inmolar; renunciar; to sell at a — vender con pérdida.
sacrilege (sákriley) s. sacrilegio.
sacrilegious (sakriléyos) adj. sacrílego.
sad (sad) adj. triste, melancólico.
sadden (sádn) v. entristecer; contristar; apesadumbrar.
saddle (sádl) s. silla de montar; asiento de bicicleta o motocicleta; — bag alforja; — horse caballo de silla; v. ensillar; cargar; poner a cuestas.
sadistic sadistik) adj. sádico; cruel.
sadness (sádnes) s. tristeza.
safe (seif) adj. seguro, ileso, incólume; intacto; sin peligro; — and sound sano y salvo; — conduct salvoconducto; s. caja fuerte o de seguridad; —ly adv. con seguridad, sin peligro; to be — no correr peligro; to arrive —ly llegar sin contratiempo alguno.

safeguard (séifgard) s. salvaguardia; resguardo; escolta; v. resguardar; salvaguardar.

safety (séifti) s. seguridad; protección; in — con seguridad, sin peligro; adj. de seguridad; — device mecanismo de seguridad; — pin alfiler de seguridad, seguro.

saffron (sáfron) s. azafrán; adj. azafranado; color de azafrán.

sagacious (saguéshus) adj. sagaz; listo; vivo; perspicaz; ladino.

sagacity (saguésiti) s. sagacidad; astucia.

sage (séiy) s. sabio; adj. sabio, cuerdo, prudente; sagaz.

sail (séil) s. vela (de barco); excursión o paseo en barco de vela; to set — hacerse a la vela, zarpar; v. darse a la vela, navegar; ir embarcado; flotar; deslizarse; to — along the coast costear; to — before the wind navegar viento en popa; main — vela mayor.

sailboat (séilbout) s. bote o barco de vela.

sailor (séilor) s. marinero, marino.

saintly (séintli) adj. santo; pío; devoto; adv. santamente; piadosamente; con devoción.

sake (séik) s. causa, motivo, fin, razón; amor; consideración; for God's — por amor a Dios; for pity's — por piedad; for my — por mí.

salad (sálad) s. ensalada; — dressing aderezo para ensalada.

salary (sálari) s. salario, sueldo.

sale (séil) s. venta; barata; —s tax impuesto sobre ventas; for (on) — de venta; auction — almoneda, subasta.

salesman (séilsman) s. vendedor; empleado de mostrador de ventas; traveling — agente viajero.

saleswoman (séilsuman) s. vendedora; empleada de mostrador de ventas.

salient (séilient) adj. saliente; surgente; prominente.

saliva (saláiva) s. saliva.

sallow (sálou) adj. pálido; lívido.

sally (sáli) s. salida; excursión; ímpetu, arranque; agudeza; chis-

SALMON — **SAVAGE**

te; humorada; v. salir, hacer una salida; **to — forth** salir.
salmon (sálmon) s. salmón.
saloon (salún) s. salón (de un vapor); taberna; cantina; coche salón; **— keeper** tabernero.
salt (solt) s. sal, chiste; agudeza; cloruro de sodio; desconfianza; **smelling —s** sales aromáticas; **the — of the earth** la flor y nata de la humanidad; **with a grain of —** con un grano de sal; adj. salado; salobre; curado o conservado con sal; v. salar; arencar, curar con sal; **to — one's money away** guardar o ahorrar dinero.
saltpeter (sóltpíter) s. salitre, nitro; **— maker** salitrero.
salty (sólti) adj. salado, salobre.
salutation (saliutéshon) s. salutación, bienvenida, enhorabuena.
salute (salút) s. saludo; salva, honras militares o navales; v. saludar; besar; cuadrarse (militarmente).
salvation (salvéshon) s. salvación.
salve (salv) s. untura; ungüento; pomada; auxilio; v. aliviar, calmar.
same (seim) adj. mismo; igual; idéntico; **the —** el mismo, la misma; los mismos, las mismas; **it is all the — to me** me da lo mismo, me es igual; **much the — as** casi como.
sample (sámpl) s. muestra, prueba; espécimen, ejemplo, dechado; v. probar; calar; catar.
sanctify (sánktifai) v. santificar.
sanction (sánkshon) s. sanción, autorización; aprobación; ratificación; v. sancionar, ratificar.
sanctity (sánktiti) s. santidad.
sanctuary (sánkchueri) s. santuario; asilo, templo, refugio sagrado.
sand (sand) s. arena; fuerza de carácter; **— pit** arenal; v. enarenar; cubrir con arena; refregar con arena; mezclar con arena.
sandal (sándal) s. sandalia; abarca; guarache (huarache).
sandpaper (sandpéiper) s. papel de lija; v. lijar, pulir o alisar con papel de lija.
sandstone (sándstoun) s. piedra arenisca.
sandwich (sánduich) s. bocadillo, emparedado; v. meter (entre); colocar entre dos tapas.

sandy (sándi) adj. arenoso, arenisco.
sane (séin) adj. sano, sensato, cuerdo.
sanitarium (sanitérium) s. sanatorio.
sanitation (sanitéshon) s. saneamiento; aplicación práctica de la ciencia sanitaria.
sanity (sániti) s. cordura.
sank (sank) pret. de to sink.
sap (sap) s. savia; tonto, bobo; vitalidad, zapa; v. agotar, minar.
sapling (sápling) s. vástago, renuevo; serpollo, un joven.
sapphire (sáfair) s. zafiro; color de zafiro.
sarcasm (sárcasm) s. sarcasmo.
sarcastic (sarkástic) adj. sarcástico.
sardine (sardín) s. sardina.
sash (sash) s. faja (cinturón de lana, seda o algodón); banda, trena; ceñidor, cinto.
sat (sat) pret. y p.p. de to sit.
satchel (sátchel) s. valija; maletín; maleta; bolsa, saquito de mano; saco.
sate (séit) v. saciar.
sateen (satín) s. satén o rasete (raso de inferior calidad).
satellite (sátelait) s. satélite.
satiate (séshiet) v. saciar, hartar.
satin (sátn) s. raso.
satire (sátair) s. sátira.
satirical (satírikal) adj. satírico.
satirize (sátirais) s. satirizar.
satisfactory (satisfáktori) adj. satisfacción.
satisfactorily (satisfáktorili) adv. satisfactoriamente.
satisfactory (satisfáktri) adj. satisfactorio.
satisfied (sátisfaid) adj. satisfecho, contento.
satisfy (sátisfai) v. satisfacer.
saturate (sátiureit) v. saturar.
Saturday (sátordei) s. sábado.
sauce (sos) s. salsa; moje, aderezo; aliño; compota, verduras; v. aderezar, sazonar; condimentar.
saucepan (sóspan) s. cacerola.
saucer (sóser) s. platillo.
sauciness (sósines) s. descaro.
saucy (sósi) adj. descarado, respondón; desfachatado.
saunter (sónter) v. pasearse, vagar.
sausage (sósey) s. salchicha, salchichón; embutido, chorizo.
savage (sávey) adj. salvaje; fiero, bárbaro; silvestre, brutal, feroz.

— 195 —

savagery (sáveyri) s. salvajismo; crueldad, fiereza; saña.
savant (savánt) s. sabio.
save (seiv) v. salvar, ahorrar; economizar; librar, guardar, conservar; resguardar; **to — from** librar de; conj. sino, a menos que.
saver (séiver) s. salvador; ahorrador; **life —** salvavidas.
saving (séiving) adj. salvador, ahorrativo; frugal, económico; calificativo; **— clause** cláusula que contiene una salvedad o reserva; s. ahorro, economía; **—s** ahorros.
savior (sélvior) s. salvador.
savor (séivor) s. sabor, dejo; sainete; gusto; olor, perfume; v. saborear; sazonar; saber a, oler a; **it —s of treason** huele a traición.
savory (sélvori) adj. sabroso.
saw (soh) s. sierra; dicho, refrán; sentencia, proverbio; **— horse** caballete; v. aserrar, serrar; ser serrado.
sawdust (sóhdost) s. aserrín.
sawmill (sóhmil) s. aserradero.
sawn (son) p.p. de to saw.
Saxon (sáksn) adj. y s. sajón.
saxophone (sáksofon) s. saxófono.
say (sei) v. decir; hablar, recitar; declarar; **—!** ¡diga! ¡oiga usted! alegar, afirmar; **that is to —** es decir; **to — over again** volver a decir; repetir; **to — one's prayers** rezar, decir o recitar sus oraciones; **it is said, they —** se dice; dicen; s. afirmación, acierto; uso de la palabra, discurso; turno de hablar.
saying (séing) s. dicho, refrán; lo que se dice; **as the — goes** como dice el refrán.
scab (skab) s. costra (de una herida); escara; roña; esquirol; hombre ruin o roñoso; escabro; obrero no agremiado; obrero que acepta un jornal inferior; v. encostrarse (una herida), cubrirse de una costra.
scabbard (skábard) s. vaina; funda (de espada, puñal, etc.); cuchillera.
scabby (skábi) adj. costroso; roñoso; postilloso; sarnoso; tiñoso.
scabrous (skébros) adj. escabroso.
scaffold (skáfold) s. andamio; tablado; cadalso, patíbulo.
scaffolding (skáfolding) s. andamiada; castillaje; paral, armazón.

scald (skóld) v. escaldar; quemar; **to — milk** calentar la leche hasta que suelte el hervor; s. quemadura; escaldadura; escaldada.
scale (skéil) s. platillo de balanza; escala; báscula; escama (de pez o de la piel); hoja rudimentaria; incrustación de las calderas; v. escalar, trepar, subir por; desconcharse; pelarse; **pair of —s** peso de cruz; **money —s** pesillo para pesar el oro y la plata.
scallop (skálop) s. onda, pico (adorno); venera, pechina; molusco bivalvo; platillo en forma de concha para ostras; v. festonear; ondear; asar ostras empanadas.
scalp (skálp) s. cuero cabelludo; pericráneo; v. desollar el cráneo; revender boletos (de espectáculos).
scaly (skéili) adj. escamoso, lleno de escamas; conchado.
scamp (skamp) s. picaro, bribón.
scamper (skámper) v. correr, escabullirse; escaparse; s. escabullida; fuga; huida precipitada; carrera.
scan (skan) v. escudriñar; examinar; registrar; escandir; mirar detenidamente; medir (el verso).
scandal (skándal) s. escándalo; difamación; murmuración.
scandalize (skándalais) v. escandalizar; difamar, dar escándalo.
scandalous (skándalos) adj. escandaloso; difamatorio; ofensivo.
scant (skant) adj. escaso; corto; parco, limitado; v. escatimar, escasear, limitar.
scanty (skánti) adj. escaso, insuficiente, parco, corto, estrecho.
scar (skar) s. cicatriz; chirlo, costurón; marca (en una superficie pulida); v. marcar con una cicatriz; marcar, rayar.
scarce (skers) adj. escaso; raro; **—ly** adv. escasamente; apenas.
scarcity (skérciti) s. escasez; penuria; carestía, rareza.
scare (sker) v. asustar; espantar; **to — away** ahuyentar; amedrentar; s. susto, sobresalto, alarma.
scarecrow (skérkrou) s. espantajo; espantapájaros.
scarf (skarf) s. bufanda; mantilla; banda, corbata ya hecha; chalina; ensamble, empalme; ajuste.
scarlet (skárlet) s. escarlata; gra-

na; adj. bermejo, de color escarlata; — **fever** escarlatina.
scary (skéri) adj. miedoso, asustadizo; pusilánime.
scatter (skáter) v. esparcir; dispersar; disipar; — **brained** ligero de cascos, aturdido.
scene (sin) s. escena; paisaje; vista; perspectiva; escenario; **to make a —** provocar un escándalo.
scenery (síneri) s. paisaje; perspectiva; **stage —** decoraciones.
scent (sent) s. aroma, perfume; olor; fragancia; rastro, huella; **to be on the —** of seguir el rastro de; **to have a keen —** tener buen olfato; v. oler, olfatear; perfumar; seguir la pista.
scepter (sépter) s. cetro.
sceptic (sképtik) adj. y s. escéptico.
scepticism (sképtisism) s. escepticismo.
schedule (skédiul) s. itinerario, horario (de trenes); documento; lista; inventario; anexo; v. fijar el día y la hora; establecer el itinerario para trenes, autobuses, etc.
scheme (skim) s. plan, esquema, diseño, diagrama; bosquejo; proyecto; **trama,** maquinación; **color —** combinación de colores; **metrical —** sistema de versificación; v. proyectar; trazar un plan; tramar; urdir; maquinar.
schemer (skímer) s. maquinador, intrigante; proyectista.
scheming (skiming) adj. maquinador; intrigante; s. maquinación, trama.
scholar (skólar) s. estudiante; erudito; doctor en alguna ciencia; letrado; becario.
scholarly (skólarli) adj. erudito, docto; adv. como sabio; doctamente; con erudición.
scholarship (skólarship) s. saber, ciencia, erudición; beca; **to have a —** disfrutar de una beca.
scholastic (skolástik) adj. escolástico; escolar; estudiantil.
school (skúl) s. escuela, colegio, aulas; — **of fish** banco de peces; adj. escolar, de escuela; — **day** día de clases; — **board** consejo de enseñanza; v. enseñar, instruir, educar, aleccionar.
schoolboy (skúlboi) s. muchacho de escuela; escolar.

schoolgirl (skúlguerl) s. colegiala, muchacha de escuela.
schoolhouse (skúljaus) s. escuela.
schooling (skúling) s. instrucción; enseñanza; precio pagado por la escuela.
schoolmaster (skúlmaster) s. maestro de escuela.
schoolmate (skúlmeit) s. compañero de escuela, condiscípulo.
schoolroom (skúlrum) s. clase, aula.
schoolteacher (skúlticher) s. maestro o maestra de escuela.
schooner (skúner) s. goleta; tarro de cerveza; carreta con toldo; **prairie —** galera con toldo.
science (sáiens) s. ciencia.
scientific (saientífic) adj. científico; **—ally** adv. científicamente.
scientist (sáientist) s. científico; hombre de ciencia.
scion (sáion) s. vástago; trasplante; pie de una planta; descendiente; hijo.
scissors (sísors) s. tijeras.
scoff (skóf) v. mofarse, burlarse; escarnecer; s. mofa, burla, escarnio, befa.
scold (skold) v. regañar, reprender; reñir, rezongar; s. regañón.
scolding (skolding) s. regaño, reprimenda; adj. regañón.
scoop (skúp) s. cucharón; pala; cucharada; palada; buena ganancia; **newspaper —** primera publicación de una noticia; v. sacar con cucharón; vaciar; cavar; ahuecar; **to — in a good profit** sacar una buena ganancia.
scoot (skút) v. alejarse a toda prisa, irse corriendo; volar por encima (un ave).
scope (skóup) s. alcance; esfera de acción; propósito; intención, plan.
score (skor) s. cuenta; calificación; v. calificar; instrumentar.
scorn (skorn) s. desdeñar, despreciar; s. desdén, menosprecio.
scornful (skórnful) adj. desdeñoso.
scorpion (skórpion) s. alacrán.
Scotch (skótch) adj. y s. escocés.
scoundrel (skánudrel) s. pícaro; bribón; ruin; bellaco.
scour (skáur) v. fregar, estregar; limpiar; lavar; recorrer; explorar; **to — the country** recorrer la comarca; **to — about** vagar.
scourge (skóry) s. azote; látigo; castigo; v. azotar, castigar.

scout (skáut) v. explorar; reconocer; **to — at** burlarse, reírse de; **a good —** una buena persona, un buen amigo.

scowl (skául) s. ceño, v. fruncir el ceño; poner mala cara, enfurruñarse.

scramble (skrámbl) v. trepar, andar a gatas; hacer una tortilla de huevos; revolver, mezclar confusamente; **to — for something** pelear por coger alguna cosa; **— eggs** huevos revueltos; s. revoltillo; confusión; arrebatiña; lucha por conseguir una cosa.

scrap (skrap) s. fragmento, pedazo, recorte, migaja, mendrugo; riña, pleito, reyerta; **—s** desperdicios, desechos; **— iron** hierro viejo, pedacería de hierro; v. desechar, tirar a la basura; descartar; reñir.

scrape (skréip) v. raspar, rasguñar; raer; **to — off, out** o **from** quitar raspando; **to — along** ir pasándola; **to — together** amontonar; acumular poco a poco; **to bow and — ser** muy servil; s. raspadura; arañazo; lío, dificultad; enredo.

scraper (skréiper) s. raspador; estregadera; persona tacaña.

scratch (skrátch) v. arañar, rasguñar; rascar; raer; cavar; escarbar; hacer garabatos; tachar; s. araño, arañazo, rasguño, raya, marca; **to start from scratch** empezar sin nada; desde el principio, sin ventaja.

scrawl (skról) s. garabato; hacer garabatos; borronear.

scrawny (skróni) adj. flaco, huesudo.

screech (skrich) s. chillido; **— owl** lechuza; v. chillar.

screen (skrin) s. pantalla; biombo; cancel; mampara; persiana; cerca; resguardo; tamiz; cedazo; abrigo, defensa; **— door** antepuerta de tela de alambre; **motion picture —** pantalla de cinematógrafo; **— wire** tela metálica o tela de alambre; v. proteger; resguardar; cribar; cerner; ocultar, esconder; encubrir; proyectar sobre la pantalla; **to — windows** proteger las ventanas con tela metálica.

screw (skrú) s. tornillo; cilindro de metal; tuerca, rosca; **— eye** armella; **right handed —** tornillo de cuerda derecha; v. atornillar; torcer, retorcer; forzar; apretar, comprimir; oprimir.

screwdriver (skrudráiver) s. destornillador.

scribble (skríbl) v. garrapatear; hacer garabatos; escribir de prisa y sin cuidado; s. garabato.

script (skrípt) s. libreto; manuscrito (de un drama o comedia); escritura; carácter ordinario de letra.

scripture (skrípchur) s. escritura sagrada; **the Scriptures Las Sagradas Escrituras**; La Biblia.

scroll (skról) s. rollo de pergamino o papel; voluta; adorno encaracolado; rúbrica.

scrub (skrob) v. fregar, estregar; adj. achaparrado, bajo, inferior; **— oak** chaparro; **— pine** pino achaparrado; **— team** equipo de jugadores suplentes o menos bien entrenados; **— woman** fregona.

scruple (skrúpl) s. escrúpulo; duda; v. tener escrúpulos, vacilar.

scrupulous (skrúpiulos) adj. escrupuloso; delicado; riguroso.

scrutinize (skrútinais) v. escudriñar; escrutar; averiguar.

scrutiny (skrútini) s. escrutinio.

scuff (skof) v. ponerse áspera una superficie; arrastrar los pies.

scuffle (skófl) s. pendencia, contienda; riña; reyerta; pelea; v. contender; reñir; pelear; arrastrar los pies.

sculptor (skólptor) s. escultor.

sculpture (skólptchur) s. escultura; v. esculpir, entallar, cincelar.

scum (skóm) s. nata; espuma; escoria; hez; desecho; canalla, gente baja; v. espumar; desnatar.

scurry (skérri) v. escabullirse, poner en fuga; echar a correr; escaparse; s. apresuramiento, fuga precipitada; carrera; prisa.

scuttle (skótl) v. barrenar un barco; echar a pique; s. escotilla; balde o cubeta para carbón.

scythe (sáiz) s. guadaña.

sea (sí) s. mar, océano; oleaje; ola; **to put to —** hacerse a la mar; **to be at —** estar confuso, perplejo; **high swelling —** mar de leva; **high — mar gruesa**; **— fowl** ave marina; **— gull** gaviota; **— level** nivel del mar; **— power** potencia naval.

seaboard (síbourd) adj. costanero, litoral; vecino al mar.

seacoast (sícoust) s. costa, litoral.

seal (síl) s. sello; timbre; foca; león marino; v. sellar; poner fin a una cosa; estampar el sello; lacrar una carta o un paquete; to — in encerrar, cerrar herméticamente; guardar secreto; santiguar; bautizar; confirmar.

sealing wax (sílinguoks) s. lacre.

seam (sim) s. costura, sutura, juntura; grieta, hendedura; filón, veta; v. hacer una costura; juntar, señalar con cicatrices.

seaman (símán) s. marino, marinero.

seamstress (símstres) s. costurera.

seaplane (síplein) s. hidroavión.

seaport (síport) s. puerto de mar.

search (serch) v. registrar, buscar, indagar; escudriñar; to — for buscar, solicitar; procurar; to — into investigar, indagar; to — a house registrar una casa; s. registro; búsqueda; indagación; examen, investigación, pesquisa; — **warrant** mandato judicial para practicar un registro; **in —of** en busca de.

seashore (síshor) s. playa, orilla del mar.

seasick (sísik) adj. mareado; s. mareo; v. to get — marearse.

seasickness (sísiknes) s. mareo.

seaside (sísaid) s. costa, litoral.

season (sísn) s. estación del año; temporada; época; tiempo; sazón; ocasión; — **ticket** boleto de abono; **Christmas —** tiempo de Navidad; **harvest —** siega, tiempo de cosechar; **hunting —** temporada de caza; **close —** veda; v. sazonar; templar; aclimatar; madurarse.

seasoning (sísning) s. punto o madurez de las cosas; desecación de la madera; condimento; sazón.

seat (sit) s. asiento; situación; mansión; residencia; sede (episcopal o de gobierno, etc.); nalgas; parte trasera de los calzones o pantalones; — **back** respaldo, espaldar; v. asentar; dar asiento; to — **oneself** sentarse; **it —s a thousand people,** tiene cabida para mil personas.

seaweed (síuid) s. alga marina.

secede (sisíd) v. separarse.

seclude (siklúd) v. apartar; alejar; recluir; encerrar; aislar.

secluded (siklúdid) adj. apartado; retirado; solitario; alejado.

seclusion (siklúshon) s. reclusión; retiro; alejamiento; soledad.

second (sékond) adj. segundo; secundario; inferior; — **hand** segunda mano, segundero del reloj; — **lieutenant** subteniente; — **rate** de segunda clase; mediocre; de calidad inferior; **on — thought** después de pensarlo bien; **to play — fiddle** hacer un papel secundario; s. segundo, ayudante; defensor; padrino.

secondary (sékonderi) adj. secundario; subordinado; subsecuente; accesorio; — **battery** acumulador; — **school** escuela secundaria.

second-hand (sékondjánd) adj. de segunda mano; usado; indirecto; por intermedio de otro.

secondly (sékondli) adv. en segundo término, en segundo lugar.

secrecy (síkresi) s. sigilo, reserva; misterio; soledad, retiro.

secret (síkret) s. secreto; adj. secreto; recóndito; reservado; callado; oculto; — **service** policía secreta; —**ly** adv. secretamente; a puerta cerrada; reservadamente.

secretary (sekretéri) s. secretario; escritorio, pupitre; ministro.

secrete (sikrít) v. secretar; esconder; encubrir; ocultar.

secretion (sikríshon) s. secreción.

secretive (secrítiv) adj. callado; reservado; secretorio.

sect (sékt) s. secta.

section (sékshon) s. sección; departamento; división; v. seccionar; dividir en secciones.

secular (sékiular) adj. y s. secular.

secure (sekiúr) adj. seguro, confiado; firme; cierto; v. asegurar; proteger; afianzar; encerrar adquirir; —**ly** adv. con seguridad; sin riesgo; tranquilamente.

security (sekiúriti) s. seguridad; confianza; firmeza, certeza; garantía, fianza; protección; **securities** bonos, obligaciones, valores; acciones.

sedan (sidán) s. sedán.

sedate (sidéit) adj. sosegado, juicioso, sereno, tranquilo, serio.

sedative (sédativ) adj. y s. calmante, sedativo.

sedentary (sédnteri) adj. sedentario; inactivo.

sediment (sédiment) s. sedimento; residuo; asientos; heces.

sedition (sedíshon) s. sedición.

seditious (sedíshos) adj. sedicioso.

— 199 —

seduce (sediús) v. seducir; corromper, deshonrar, desvirtuar.
seduction (sedókshon) s. seducción.
see (sí) v. ver; mirar; discernir; atisbar; comprender; inquirir; indagar; examinar; visitar; reparar; — **that you do it** no deje usted de hacerlo; **I'll — to it** me encargaré de ello; **to — about** cuidar de; examinar; **let me —** veamos, vamos a ver; **to — a person home** acompañar a una persona a su casa; **to — one off** ir a despedir; **to — to** atender a; **to — military service** servir en el ejército; **to — through** comprender, reconocer; llevar a cabo; **you can — it clearly** usted comprende perfectamente; s. sede; silla; **Holy See** Santa Sede.
seed (sid) s. semilla, germen; principio generador; **— of a fruit** la pepita, el hueso de una fruta; v. sembrar, despepitar; producir semillas; descuidar de su persona; andar desaseado.
seedling (sídling) s. planta de semillero.
seedy (sídi) adj. lleno de semillas; andrajoso; desaseado.
seek (sík) v. buscar; solicitar; procurar, interrogar; recurrir; **to — to** esforzarse por, procurar; tratar de.
seem (sím) v. parecer; **it —s to me** me parece.
seemingly (símingli) adv. aparentemente, al parecer, en apariencia.
seemly (símli) adj. decente; decoroso, conveniente; adv. de una manera conveniente.
seen (sin) p.p. de to see.
seep (síp) v. colar, resumirse, escurrirse; filtrarse.
seer (sir) s. vidente; adivino; profeta.
seethe (siz) v. hervir, bullir.
segment (ségment) s. segmento.
seize (sis) v. agarrar, coger, asir; embargar; decomisar; apresar, apoderarse de, secuestrar; **to — upon** asir; **to become —d with fear** sobrecogerse de miedo.
seizure (síshur) s. aprehensión; captura; embargo; secuestro; ataque de una enfermedad.
seldom (séldom) adv. rara vez; muy de vez en cuando.
select (selékt) adj. selecto; escogido; v. elegir; entresacar; seleccionar.
selection (selékshon) s. selección; elección.
selfish (sélfish) adj. egoísta; **—ly** adv. interesadamente; por egoísmo.
selfishness (sélfishnes) s. egoísmo, amor propio.
selfsame (sélfseim) adj. mismísimo; idéntico.
sell (sel) v. vender; venderse; **to — at auction** subastar; **to — out** venderlo todo; **to — underhand** vender por trasmano.
seller (séler) s. vendedor.
semblance (sémblans) s. semejanza; apariencia; imagen.
semicircle (sémiserkl) s. semicírculo; hemiciclo.
semicolon (sémicolon) s. punto y coma.
seminary (sémineri) s. seminario.
senate (séneit) s. senado.
senator (sénotor) s. senador.
send (send) v. enviar; despachar, mandar, remitir; extender, propagar; conceder; lanzar una flecha, pelota; etc.; **to — away** despedir; **to — back** devolver; **to — someone up for 10 years** condenar a 10 años de prisión; **to — word** mandar aviso o recado; **to — down** suspender a un estudiante, expulsarlo.
sender (sénder) s. remitente, expedicionario; transmisor.
senile (sínail) adj. senil, caduco.
senility (seníliti) s. senilidad, senectud.
senior (sínior) adj. mayor, de más edad, decano; superior en dignidad o rango; s. persona o socio más antiguo; estudiante del último año en un colegio.
sensation (senséshon) s. sensación.
sensational (senséshonal) s. sensacional; emocionante.
sense (sens) s. sentido, entendimiento, juicio; sensatez, significado; interpretación; dirección; **common —** sentido común; **in a —** bajo un solo aspecto; **a man of —** hombre de juicio; **to make —** tener sentido; ser comprensible una cosa; **to be out of one's —** estar fuera de sí, estar loco, haber perdido el juicio; v. percibir; sentir, darse cuenta de.
senseless (sénsles) adj. sin senti-

do; insensible; insensato, absurdo; privado de sentido; estólido; necio; **— of insensible** a.

sensibility (sensibíliti) s. sensibilidad, precisión de un instrumento.

sensible (sénsibl) adj. sensato; sensible, convencido, persuadido; cuerdo, perceptible; razonable, juicioso; **sensibly** adv. sensatamente; con sensatez; perceptiblemente.

sensitive (sénsitiv) adj. sensitivo; sensible, impresionable; quisquilloso; s. sensitiva.

sensitiveness (sénsitivnes) s. sensibilidad.

sensual (sénshual) adj. sensual, carnal, lascivo, voluptuoso.

sensuality (senshuáliti) s. sensualidad; lujuria, lascivia.

sent (sent) pret. y p.p. de **to send**.

sentence (séntens) s. sentencia, fallo; dictamen; dicho grave o sucinto; período, frase; v. sentenciar.

sentiment (séntiment) s. sentimiento; afecto, sentido.

sentimental (sentimental) adj. sentimental, tierno.

sentimentality (sentimentáliti) s. sentimentalismo.

sentinel (séntinl) s. centinela.

sentry (séntri) s. centinela.

separate (sépareit) adj. separado; apartado, solitario; desunido, segregado, sin lazo, distinto; **—ly** adv. separadamente; v. separar (se); apartar(se); dividir, desunir.

separation (separéshon) s. separación, desunión, divorcio.

September (septémber) s. septiembre.

sepulcher (sépolker) s. sepulcro, sepultura.

sequel (síkuel) s. secuela; continuación; conclusión, resultado.

sequence (síkuens) s. secuencia, sucesión, serie; arreglo, efecto, consecuencia; runfla de naipes, continuación, modulación.

serenade (serenéid) s. serenata; v. dar serenata a.

serene (serín) adj. sereno; tranquilo; claro, sosegado, despejado.

serenity (seréniti) s. serenidad.

sergeant (sáryent) s. sargento, alguacil; **— at arms** oficial que guarda el orden (en un cuerpo legislativo).

serial (sírial) s. cuento o novela por entregas; adj. consecutivo a manera de serie.

series (síries) s. serie, series.

serious (sérios) adj. serio, grave, sensato, reflexivo, severo; **—ly** adv. seriamente, con seriedad.

seriousness (siríosnes) s. seriedad.

sermon (sérmon) s. sermón.

serpent (sérpent) s. serpiente.

serum (sirum) s. suero.

servant (sérvant) s. sirviente; criado; **— girl** criada.

serve (sérv) v. servir; ayudar, escanciar; surtir, entregar un requerimiento judicial, cumplir una condena; **to — an office** desempeñar algún cargo; **to — one right** merecer; **to — a warrant** ejecutar un auto de prisión, entregar una citación; **to — one's purpose** servir para el caso o al propósito; **to — in the army** prestar o hacer el servicio militar.

server (sérver) s. servidor; saque (el que saca la pelota en el juego de tenis).

service (sérvis) s. servicio, servidumbre; vajilla; favor, asistencia; oficio religioso; obligación de un arrendatario, entrega de un requerimiento judicial; **at your —** servidor de usted; **funeral —** exequias; honras fúnebres; **tea —** juego de té; **— entrance** entrada para el servicio; v. servir; reparar; surtir; prestar servicio; **out of —** sin acomodo.

serviceable (sérvisebl) adj. servible; útil, aprovechable, duradero.

servile (sérvil) adj. servil; abyecto, adulador; esclavo.

servitude (sérvitiud) s. servidumbre, esclavitud, vasallaje.

session (séshon) s. sesión.

set (set) v. colocar, fijar; poner; asentar, establecer, situar, determinar; destinar, preparar, arreglar; engastar; detener; solidificar; fraguar (el yeso, el cemento; etc.); ponerse (el sol, la luna); empollar; dedicarse; **to — a bone** componer un hueso manos a la obra; **to — on fire** prender fuego; **to — an example** dar el ejemplo; **to — aside** apartar; poner a un lado; ahorrar; **to — fast** sujetar, consolidar; **to — about** emprender, comenzar; **to — forth** exponer manifestar; exhibir; avanzar; **to — one's**

mind resolverse a; **to — out** ponerse en camino, partir, emprender un viaje; **to — right** rectificar, enmendar, corregir; **to — off** hacer estallar un explosivo; disparar; **to — one's heart on** poner o cifrar sus esperanzas en; **to — a razor** asentar, afilar una navaja de rasurar; **to — sail** hacerse a la vela; **to — the brake** frenar; aplicar el freno; **to — up** erigir; fundar, instituir; armar; montar una máquina; parar tipo de imprenta; s. juego; colección, serie; cuadrilla; terno; aderezo; ocaso; decoración; **dinner — vajilla** de mesa; **— out** arreglos y equipo para un viaje; **radio —** radio, receptor; **tennis —** partida de tenis; adj. resuelto; determinado, señalado, fijo; firme; sólido; prescrito, engastado; ajustado; puesto; colocado, rígido.

setback (sétbak) s. revés, contrariedad; retroceso inesperado.

settee (setí) s. canapé.

setting (séting) s. montadura o engaste de una joya; escenario; ocaso; **— sun** sol poniente.

settlement (sétlment) s. colonización; colonia; establecimiento; traspaso de propiedad; ajuste o liquidación de cuentas; sedimento; **— house** casa de beneficencia; **marriage —** dote; asiento de un edificio; empleo; destino.

settler (sétler) s. colono, poblador; fundador.

sever (séver) v. separar; apartar; desunir; cortar; partir; romper; entreabrirse; partirse.

several (sévral) adj. diversos; distintos; varios; diferentes.

severe (sevír) adj. severo; riguroso; inexorable; duro; cruel; austero; recio; fuerte.

severity (sevériti) s. severidad; rigor; opresión; dureza; crueldad; austeridad; seriedad.

sew (so) v. coser.

sewer (slúer) s. albañal, atarjea; cloaca; alcantarilla; sumidero.

sewing (sóing) s. costura; **— machine** máquina de coser; **— press** telar; **— bee** reunión de amigas para coser.

sewn (son) p.p. de to sew.

sex (seks) s. sexo.

sexton (sékston) s. sacristán.

shabby (shábi) adj. andrajoso; desaseado; desharrapado; raído; muy usado; **— genteel** cursi; **to treat someone shabbily** menospreciar a alguien; tratarlo injustamente.

shack (shák) s. cabaña, choza, bohío; jacal.

shackle (shákl) v. encadenar, poner grilletes; atar; trabar; estorbar; poner obstáculos; s. grillete, esposa; traba; impedimento.

shade (shéid) s. sombra, persiana; oscuro; cortinilla; pantalla de lámpara; visera; toldo; **a — longer** un poco más largo; **— of meaning** matiz; v. sombrear; obscurecer; resguardar de la luz; casar bien los colores; matizar.

shadow (shádou) s. sombra, oscuridad; fantasma, espectro; reclusión; traza, pizca; **not a — of doubt** sin la menor duda; v. sombrear; oscurecer; **to — someone** seguir los pasos a alguien por todas partes.

shadowy (shádoui) adj. umbrío; tenebroso; sombrío; vago; indistinto.

shady (shéidi) adj. sombreado; obscuro; sospechoso; **— character** persona de carácter dudoso, de mala fama; declinante.

shaft (shaft) s. eje; árbol de maquinaria; tiro de una mina; cañón de chimenea; túnel de un horno de fundición; fuste de columna.

shaggy (shégui) adj. peludo, velludo; lanudo; áspero; desaseado.

shake (shéik) v. sacudir(se); menear(se); agitar(se); temblar; arrojar; lanzar; desalentar; excitar; despertar; estrechar la mano; estremecerse; cimbrar; trepidar; vacilar; **to — off** sacudir; desembarazarse o deshacerse de, con una sacudida; **to — hands** estrecharse la mano; **to — one's head** mover la cabeza; s. meneo, sacudida; concusión; agitación; vibración; temblor, estremecimiento; escalofrío de la fiebre; apretón de manos.

shaken (shéiken) p.p. de to shake.

shaky (shéiki) adj. tembloroso; trémulo; vacilante.

shall (shál) v. aux. signo del futuro de indicativo en las primeras personas (I, we); en las demás expresa mayor énfasis; sin infinitivo; pretérito; participio imperativo; **thou shalt not steal** no hurtarás.

shallow (shálou) adj. vadoso, poco profundo; de poco calado; superficial; trivial; vano.

shallowness (shálounes) s. poca profundidad; superficialidad; frivolidad; vanidad; ligereza de juicio.

sham (shem) v. simular, fingir; disimular; s. impostura; pretexto; farsa; falsedad; fingimiento; adj. fingido, simulado, postizo, falso.

shame (shéim) s. vergüenza; it is a — es una lástima; — on you ¡debía darte vergüenza! v. deshonrar, avergonzar; afrentar; abochornar.

shameful (shéimful) adj. vergonzoso.

shameless (shéimles) adj. desvergonzado; descarado, sin vergüenza.

shamelessness (shéimlesnes) s. desvergüenza; descaro, impudicia, cinismo, desfachatez.

shampoo (shampú) s. champú; frotación; soba; lavado de la cabeza; v. lavar y limpiar la cabeza; dar un champú.

shamrock (shámrok) s. trébol; emblema de Irlanda.

shank (shank) s. canilla (parte inferior de la pierna); mango, caña.

shanty (shánti) s. choza; cabaña.

shape (shéip) s. forma, figura; contorno, conformación; talle, cuerpo; estado, condición; to be in a bad — estar mal; to — a course dar el rumbo; v. formar, dar forma a; ahormar; modelar; tallar; proporcionar, ajustar; to — one's life ajustar o disponer su vida; dar forma a.

shapeless (shéiples) adj. informe.

share (sher) s. porción; parte; acción; v. tomar parte en; gozar o disfrutar con otros; compartir; partir; alcanzar.

shareholder (shérjolder) s. accionista.

shark (shark) s. tiburón; estafador; perito; escualo, marrajo; pillastre, tunante; **to be a — at** ser un águila (o muy listo) para.

sharp (sharp) adj. agudo, puntiagudo; filoso; perspicaz; astuto; penetrante, mordaz; severo, violento; pronto; impetuoso; punzante; repentino; — **sight** vista penetrante; — **nosed** nariz aguileña; — **features** facciones bien marcadas; — **pointed** puntiagudo; — **temper** malgeniudo; — **turn** vuelta repentina; — **curve** curva muy cerrada; s. sostenido (en música); **card** — tahur; **at five o' clock — a las 5 en punto.**

sharpen (shárpen) v. afilar(se); aguzar, adelgazar; sacar punta a, hacer más severo, intenso.

sharply (shárpli) adv. agudamente; mordazmente; con filo, corte o punta; ásperamente; repentinamente; vivamente; sutilmente.

sharpness (shárpnes) s. agudeza; sutileza; perspicacia, acrimonia.

shatter (shátér) v. estrellar(se); destrozar, hacer pedazos; romper, trozar; hacer(se) añicos; astillar(se); **to — one's hopes** frustrar sus esperanzas; — **pated** aturdido; s. pl. pedazos, trozos, añicos; fragmentos.

shave (shéiv) v. afeitar(se); rasurar; acepillar, raspar; descarnar; desollar a uno en un negocio; s. rasura, afeitada; **he had a close —** por poco no se escapa; se salvó por milagro.

shaven (shéiven) p.p. de **to shave**; **clean-shaven** bien afeitado.

shaving (shéiving) s. rasura, afeitada; rasurada; virutas, alisaduras; acepilladura; pl. acepilladuras.

shawl (shohl)) s. mantón, chal.

she (shi) pron. pers. ella; — **who** la que; s. hembra.

sheaf (shif) s. haz, gavilla, manojo; garba, fajo, mostela; v. hacer gavillas.

shear (shir) v. trasquilar; cortar (con tijeras grandes); rapar.

shears (shirs) s. pl. tijeras grandes.

sheath (shiz) s. vaina, funda.

sheathe (shiz) v. envainar.

sheaves (shivs) pl. de **sheaf**.

shed (shed) s. cobertizo; tejadillo; galpón (de una estancia); efusión o derramamiento; **bloodshed** derramamiento de sangre; v. derramar; arrojar, quitarse; desprenderse de; difundir, esparcir; mudar (de piel, plumas, etc.).

sheen (shin) s. lustre, viso.

sheep (ship) s. oveja; carnero; rebaño; ovejas; — **fold** redil; — **dog** perro pastor; — **shearer** esquilador; — **skin** zalea; badana; pergamino.

sheepish (shípish) adj. vergonzoso;

corrido, timido; pusilánime.
sheer (shir) **adj.** puro; completo; claro, consumado; cabal; ligero, fino, delgado; enhiesto; transparente; diáfano; escarpado.

sheet (shit) s. sábana; hoja; pliego (de papel); lámina; un diario; extensión de agua, escota, vela; **to sail with flowing —s** navegar a escota larga.

shelf (shelf) s. estante, anaquel; entrepaño; banco de arena.

shellac (shelác) s. laca; goma laca en hojuelas; v. barnizar con laca.

shellfish (shélfish) s. marisco.

shelter (shélter) s. abrigo, refugio; asilo; resguardo, amparo; albergue; techo, hogar; protección; v. abrigar, guarecer, resguardar.

shelve (shelv) v. poner o guardar en un estante; poner a un lado; dar carpetazo; proveer de estantes o anaqueles, estar en declive.

shelves (shelvs) s. pl. estantes, anaqueles; estantería.

shepherd (shéperd) s. pastor; zagal; párroco, cura; **— dog** perro pastor.

sherbet (shérbet) s. sorbete, granizado.

sheriff (shérif) s. alguacil mayor (de un condado en los Estados Unidos); magistrado.

shield (shild) s. escudo, rodela; broquel; v. escudar, amparar.

shift (shift) v. cambiar; mudar (se); desviar, trasladar; alternar (se); transferir, transportar; mudar la ropa, cambiar de decoración; **to — for oneself** valerse o mirar por sí mismo; **to — about** revolverse; girar; s. cambio, desvío; mutación, desviación; sustitución; tanda; grupo de obreros; subterfugio.

shiftless (shíftles) adj. negligente.

shilling (shíling) s. chelín.

shin (shin) s. espinilla (de la pierna); canilla; v. trepar.

shine (sháin) v. brillar; resplandecer, lucir; relumbrar, rutilar; resaltar; exceder; rielar, sobresalir; dar brillo, lustre o bola; s. brillo, lustre; resplandor; **sunshine** claridad del sol; **rain or —** llueva o truene.

shingle (shingl) s. ripia, tabla delgada; hoja de madera; tejamaní o tejamanil; muestra o letrero de oficina; v. cubrir con ripia o tejamaniles; rapar el pelo.

shining (sháining) adj. brillante; radiante, resplandeciente.

shiny (sháini) adj. brillante.

ship (ship) s. buque; navío; nave, barco, bajel, embarcación; aeronave; **— of the line** navío de alto bordo o línea; **— builder** ingeniero naval, constructor de buques; v. embarcar(se); ir a bordo, engancharse como marinero.

shipment (shipment) s. embarque; cargamento; despacho, envío; remesa.

shipper (shiper) s. embarcador.

shipping (shiping) s. embarque; despacho, envío; buques, marina; **— charges** gastos de embarque; **— agent** consignatario de buques.

shipwreck (shíprek) s. naufragio; desastre, desgracia, ruina; v. echar a pique; hacer naufragar.

shirk (sherk) v. evadir.

shirt (shert) s. camisa; revestimiento de horno; **— waist** blusa; **— sleeve** manga de camisa; **— front** pechera de camisa.

shiver (shiver) v. tiritar; temblar; calofriarse; s. escalofrío; tiritón; cacho, pedazo; estremecimiento.

shoal (shóul) s. bajío; multitud muchedumbre; banco de arena.

shock (shok) s. choque; sacudida; golpe, colisión, encontronazo; susto, conmoción; sobresalto; desazón; postración nerviosa; **— absorber** amortiguador, silenciador; **— of hair** rizo; greña; guedeja v. chocar, sacudir; golpear; asustar; sobresaltar; ofender; horrorizar; hacinar.

shocking (shóking) adj. chocante, horrible, espantoso, ofensivo.

shod (shod) pret. y p.p. de **to shoe**.

shoe (shu) s. zapato; calzado, herradura; galga de carruaje; **brake —** zapata de freno; **— black** limpiabotas; **— store** zapatería; **to cast a —** desherrarse un animal; v. calzar, herrar (un caballo); **to — an anchor** calzar el ancla.

shoeblack (shúblak) s. limpiabotas.

shoehorn (shújorn) s. calzador.

shoelace (shúleis) s. lazo, cinta, agujeta, cordón de zapato.

shoemaker (shúmeiker) s. zapatero

— 204 —

shoestring (shústring) véase **shoelace**.

shone (shon) pret. y p.p. de **to shine**.

sook (shuk) pret. de **to shake**.

shoot (shut) v. herir o matar con arma de fuego; disparar; descargar; fusilar; tomar una instantánea; filmar; echar los dados; brotar; germinar; **to — an arrow** lanzar una flecha; **to — forth** lanzarse, abalanzarse; **to — up a place** entrar a balazos a un lugar; s. vástago, retoño; recial de un río; tiro al blanco; **to — up** crecer las plantas; **to — it out with someone** pelearse a balazos.

shooter (shúter) s. tirador.

shooting (shúting) s. tiroteo; **— match** concurso de tiro al blanco; **— pain** dolor agudo; punzada; **— star** estrella fugaz.

shop (shop) s. tienda; almacén; taller; cajón de ropa; comercio; **baker's —** panadería; tahona; **silversmith —** platería; **— window** escaparate, vitrina, aparador; **beauty —** salón de belleza; **— board** tabla de sastre; **to talk —** hablar de negocios o de la propia profesión; v. ir de compras.

shopkeeper (shópkiper) s. tendero.

shopper (shóper) s. comprador.

shopping (shóping) s. compra; **to go —** ir de compras.

shore (shor) s. costa, playa; ribera, borde, orilla de un río o lago; puntal; **ten miles off —** a diez millas de la costa; v. apuntalar, circundar.

shorn (shorn) p.p. de **to shear**.

short (short) adj. corto; bajo; escaso, breve; conciso, compendiado; chaparro, insuficiente; brusco; **— cut** atajo, método corto; **— nosed** chato; de nariz roma; **— sighted** miope; **— handed** que carece de un número suficiente de operarios, etc.; **— circuit** cortocircuito; **in —** en breve, en resumen; **in a — time** en poco tiempo; **to be — of** estar falto o carecer de; **to run — of something** irsele acabando a alguno algo; faltar.

shortage (shórtey) s. escasez; carestía, déficit; falta.

shortcoming (shórtkoming) s. falta, negligencia del deber; defecto.

shorten (shórtn) v. acortar(se); abreviarse; hacer más corto; abreviar; compendiar, resumir; recortar; disminuir(se).

shortening (shórtening) s. manteca; grasa (para hacer pasteles); disminución, acortamiento.

shorthand (shórtjand) s. taquigrafía.

shortly (shórtli) adv. brevemente; presto, luego, al instante, en breve; en pocas palabras.

shortness (shórtnes) s. cortedad; brevedad; pequeñez; flaqueza de memoria; escasez, deficiencia.

shorts (shórts) s. pl. pantalón corto de mujer; calzoncillos.

shortsighted (shórtsáited) adj. miope, corto de vista; **—ness** miopía; cortedad de vista.

shot (shot) pret. y p.p. de **to shoot** s. tiro, disparo; perdigón; proyectil, balazo, jugada de billar; barreno; **— of liquor** trago de aguardiente; **buck o beer — postas; not by a long —** ni por pienso; ni por asomo; ni con mucho; **a good —** un buen tirador; **to take a — at** disparar un tiro a; hacer una tentativa de; **within rifle —** a tiro de rifle.

shotgun (shótgon) v. escopeta.

should (shud) v. aux. para formar el condicional en las primeras personas; v. gr: **I said that I — go** dije que iría; **I would call him if I — want him** le llamaría si lo necesitase; **you — not do it** no debiera o no debería hacerlo.

shoulder (shólder) s. hombro, lomo; espaldilla de puerco o cordero; cuarto delantero; borde; saliente de un camino; omóplato; paletilla; **—s** espaldas; **straight from the —** con toda franqueza; **to give one the cold —** recibir a uno fríamente; v. echarse a la espalda, cargar al hombro; llevar en hombros; asumir; meter al hombro, cargar con.

shout (sháut) v. gritar; dar voces.

shove (shóv) v. empujar; impeler; dar empellones; **to — away** rechazar, alejar; **to — back** hacer retroceder; **to — off** alejarse de, dejar, partir, zarpar; s. empujón; empellón.

shovel (shovl) s. pala; v. traspalar.

show (shóu) v. mostrar; demostrar; enseñar; señalar; hacer ver;

SHOWER — **SIDE**

shower exponer; probar; indicar; guiar; parecer; asomar; dar señales; — him in hágale pasar; que pase; to — off alardear, hacer ostentación de; to — up comparecer; presentarse; to — someone up hacer subir; descorrer un velo, mostrar el camino; poner a alguien en evidencia; s. exhibición; demostración; exposición; espectáculo público, ostentación; función teatral; prosopopeya; indicación, apariencia; pretexto; — bill cartel, cartelón; — case aparador, vitrina; to go to the — ir al cine o al teatro.

shower (sháuer) s. chubasco, chaparrón; baño de regadera; bridal — fiesta para despedir de soltera; v. regar; derramar; llover; caer un chubasco.

showy (shóui) s. vistoso, llamativo, ostentoso.

shrew (shrú) s. harpía; mujer de mal genio.

shrewd (shrúd) adj. astuto; perspicaz; sutil; fino; agudo; sagaz.

shriek (shrik) v. chillar; gritar; desgañitarse; s. grito agudo; chillido.

shrill (shril) adj. agudo, penetrante, chillón; v. chillar.

shrimp (shrimp) s. camarón; enanillo, hombre insignificante.

shrine (shráin) s. relicario, santuario; altar, urna; lugar venerado; capilla.

shrink (shrink) v. encoger(se), contraer(se).

shrivel (shrivl) v. arrugar(se); fruncir(se); marchitar(se).

shroud (shráud) s. mortaja; cubierta; vestidura; v. amortajar, cubrir; guarecerse; refugiarse.

shrub (shrob) s. arbusto.

shrubbery (shróberi) s. arbustos.

shrug (shrog) v. encogerse de hombros; encoger, contraer.

shrunk (shronk) pret. y p.p. de **to shrink**.

shrunken (shronken) p.p. de **to shrink**.

shudder (shóder) v. estremecerse; temblar de miedo o de horror; s. estremecimiento; temblor.

shuffle (shófl) v. barajar; mezclar, eludir; evadir; desordenar; arrastrar los pies; to — along caminar arrastrando los pies; s. evasiva; embuste; confusión; to — up hacer una cosa de mala manera; it is your — a usted le toca barajar.

shun (shon) v. huir; rehuir; evadir; esquivar; apartarse de.

shut (shot) v. cerrar; impedir; negar la entrada; excluir; cerrar el abanico, el paraguas, etc.; to — down parar los trabajos; cerrar una fábrica; to — in encerrar; to — off cortar el gas, apagar la luz; desconectar la electricidad; to — from excluir; to — off from incomunicar; to — out impedir la entrada; to — up callarse; pret. y p.p. de **to shut**; adj. cerrado.

shutter (shóter) s. contraventana; postigo; obturador (de cámara fotográfica).

shuttle (shótl) s. lanzadera; ir y venir acompasadamente (como una lanzadera).

shy (shái) adj. tímido; cauteloso; prudente; esquivo; asustadizo; vergonzoso; to — off desviar, apartarse de; v. respingar, asustarse; to be — a couple of cents faltarle a uno dos centavos; to — at something retroceder; espantarse al ver algo; respingar un caballo al ver algo; s. sobresalto; respingo; prueba; ensayo.

shyness (sháines) s. timidez; recato; reserva; vergüenza; apocamiento.

shyster (sháister) s. tinterillo; leguleyo; picapleitos.

sick (sik) adj. enfermo, malo; cansado, fastidiado; angustiado; v. to be — at the stomach tener náuseas; to be — of estar fastidiado, estar harto de; to be — for suspirar, anhelar; to make — enfermar; causar lástima; dar pena; v. buscar, incitar, excitar, azuzar a (un perro).

sicken (síken) v. enfermar(se); dar asco; tener asco; sentir náuseas; fastidiarse, hartarse.

sickening (síkening) adj. nauseabundo; repugnante; asqueroso.

sickle (sikl) s. hoz.

sickly (síkli) adj. enfermizo; malsano, enclenque; achacoso.

sickness (síknes) s. enfermedad; malestar; náusea.

side (sáid) lado; cara; margen; falda; ladera; partido; fracción; banda; starboard — banda de estribor; — by — lado a lado; by the — of al lado de, por el

— 206 —

lado de; on all —s por todos lados; to take —s with ser partidario de, ponerse del lado de; on that — de aquel o de ese lado; adj. lateral, de lado; oblicuo; incidental, secundario; de menor importancia; — glance mirada de soslayo; — issue cuestión secundaria; v. to — track desviar, apartar; to — with declararse partidario de; ser de la opinión de; apoyar a.

sideboard (sáidbourd) s. aparador.

sidetrack (sáidtrak) s. desviadero de ferrocarril.

sidewalk (sáiduok) s. acera, banqueta; vereda.

sideways (sáidueis) adv. de lado; oblicuamente; hacia un lado; adj. lateral, oblicuo.

siege (siy) s. sitio, asedio, cerco; v. to lay — to poner sitio a.

sieve (siv) s. cedazo, harnero, criba; coladera; tamiz.

sift (sift) v. cerner, tamizar, cribar; separar, entresacar.

sigh (sái) v. suspirar; s. suspiro.

sight (sáit) s. vista; visión; perspectiva; cuadro; espectáculo; aspecto; parecer; mira de un arma de fuego; payable at — pagadero a la vista; at first — a primera vista; this room is a — este cuarto es un horror; v. to know by — conocer de vista; to lose — of perder de vista; v. avistar; alcanzar con la vista; ver; descubrir; vislumbrar.

sightseeing (sáitsiing) s. turismo; — tour paseo para ver puntos de interés.

sign (sáin) s. signo; seña, señal; nota, marca, indicación; síntoma; indicio, prueba; muestra; letrero; — board cartel; tablero (para fijar anuncios); to make the — of the cross hacer la señal de la cruz; v. firmar, contratar; hacer firmar; rubricar, signar; poner una marca o firma; to — up for a job firmar el contrato para un empleo.

signal (sígnal) s. señal, seña; indicio; aviso; signo; adj. insigne; señalar, hacer una señal; hacer seña; indicar; — beacon faro; — code código de señales.

signature (sígnachur) s. firma.

signer (sáiner) s. firmante.

significance (signífikens) s. significación; expresión, significado.

significant (signífikent) adj. significativo; expresivo, enfático.

signify (sígnifai) v. significar.

silence (sáilens) s. silencio; taciturnidad; quietud; v. acallar, apagar (un sonido); sosegar.

silent (sáilent) adj. silencioso; callado; taciturno, sigiloso; quieto; mudo; be — ¡cállese!

silhouette (siluét) s. silueta; v. dibujar una silueta; perfilar.

silk (silk) s. seda; adj. de seda, sedoso, sedeño; — hat sombrero de copa; — ribbon cinta de seda.

silken (sílken) adj. sedoso.

silkworm (sílkuorm) s. gusano de seda.

silky (sílki) adj. sedoso, sedeño; asedado; suave y lustroso.

sill (sil) s. umbral; solera; viga de carrera; window — antepecho de ventana.

silly (síli) adj. necio, tonto, bobo; memo, mentecato; simple.

silver (sílver) s. plata; vajilla de plata; monedas de plata; color de plata; adj. de plata; argentino, plateado; crude mass of — plata bruta o en bruto; plata virgen.

silversmith (sílversmiz) s. platero.

silverware (sílveruer) s. vajilla de plata; plata labrada.

silvery (sílveri) adj. plateado, argentino.

similar (símilar) adj. semejante; similar; homogéneo; —ly adv. similarmente; semejantemente.

similarity (similáriti) s. semejanza, parecido, conformidad.

simile (símile) s. símil, ejemplo.

simmer (símer) v. hervir a fuego lento.

simple (simpl) adj. simple; sencillo; puro, fácil, tonto, mentecato.

simpleton (símplton) s. simplón.

simplicity (simplísiti) s. sencillez, simplicidad; simpleza; candor.

simplify (símplifai) v. simplificar.

simply (símpli) adv. con sencillez, simplemente; solamente.

simultaneous (simolténios) adj. simultáneo; sincrónico.

sin (sin) s. pecado, culpa; falta; v. pecar; errar; faltar.

since (síns) adv. desde, desde que, desde entonces; hace tiempo; conj. puesto que, como, visto que; dado que; ever — desde entonces; long — hace mucho

tiempo; — **we arrived desde que llegamos;** — **it is so supuesto que es asi.**
sincere (sinsír) adj. sincero; franco.
sincerity (sinsériti) s. sinceridad.
sinecure (sinikiur) s. sinecura; canonjía; prebenda.
sinew (síniu) s. tendón, fibra, nervio, fortaleza; v. fortalecer.
sinewy (síniui) adj. fuerte, vigoroso, nervudo; robusto.
sinful (sínful) adj. pecaminoso.
sing (sing) v. cantar; to — out of tune desentonar(se), desafinar (se); to — to sleep arrullar.
singe (síny) v. chamuscar, sollamar; dañar; s. chamusquina; chamuscadura; chamuscada.
singer (sínguer) s. cantor, cantante; cantatriz.
single (singl) adj. único; solo; particular; individual; soltero; simple; — eyed tuerto; not a — word ni una sola palabra; — room cuarto para uno; — man soltero; s. billete de un dólar; v. to — out singularizar; distinguir; entresacar.
singlehanded (síngljanded) adj. solo; sin ayuda.
sinsong (síngsong) s. sonsonete, estribillo; cadencia; tonada monótona.
sinister (sínister) adj. siniestro; mal intencionado; aciago; funesto; s. siniestra, izquierda.
sink (sink) s. sumidero; vertedero; fregadero; v. hundir; sumergir (se), irse a pique; abrir o cavar un pozo; deprimir; abatir; humillar; enterrar o clavar un poste; to — into one's mind grabarse en la memoria; to — down caer por grados; to — under atribularse, anonadarse; —ing fund fondo de amortización; —ing spirit abatimiento.
sinner (síner) s. pecador.
sinuous (síniuos) adj. sinuoso; tortuoso; anfractuoso.
sinus (sáinos) s. seno, cavidad en un hueso; **frontal** — seno frontal.
sip (sip) v. sorber, chupar; s. sorbo.
siphon (sáifon) s. sifón, probeta; v. sacar (agua) con sifón.
sir (ser) s. señor.
siren (sáiren) s. sirena.
sirloin (sérloin) s. solomillo.
sirup (sírop) s. jarabe.

sissy (sisi) adj. y s. afeminado.
sister (síster) s. hermana; sor; monja; **step** — **media hermana.**
sister-in-law (sisterinloh) s. cuñada; hermana política.
sit (sit) v. sentar(se); tomar asiento; posarse (los pájaros); empollar (las aves); reunirse para celebrar una sesión; entallar bien o mal un traje; to — **down** sentarse; to — **by** sentarse al lado de; to — **close** sentarse cerca; to — **out** quedarse sentado durante una pieza de baile; to — **still** estarse quieto; to — **tight** mantenerse firme en su puesto; to — **up** velar, incorporarse; to — **up and take notice** despabilarse.
site (sait) s. sitio; local; situación; solar.
sitting (síting) s. sesión (de un cuerpo legislativo, tribunal, etc.); junta; sentada; anidada; adj. sentado; — **hen** gallina ponedora; — **room** sala de espera; antesala; estancia.
situated (sichuéited) adj. situado; sitio; ubicado, colocado.
situation (sichuéshon) s. situación; colocación; posición; localidad.
size (sais) s. tamaño; medida; dimensión, volumen; cuerpo, talla; corpulencia; v. clasificar según el tamaño; to — **up** tantear.
skate (skéit) s. patín; liza; **roller** — patín de ruedas; **ice** — patín de hielo; v. patinar.
skein (skéin) s. madeja.
skeleton (skéleton) s. esqueleto; armazón; esbozo, esquema; — **key** llave maestra.
skeptic véase sceptic.
sketch (skech) s. boceto; diseño, croquis; traza; dibujo; v. bosquejar; diseñar; dibujar.
ski (ski) s. esquí; patín largo de madera escandinavo; v. esquiar.
skid (skid) v. patinar; resbalarse; proveer de varaderas; deslizarse.
skill (skil) s. destreza; maña; habilidad; conocimiento práctico.
skilled (skild) adj. experto; instruido, hábil, diestro; práctico.
skillet (skílet) s. sartén, cacerola.
skillful, skilful (skílful) adj. experto, diestro, ducho, práctico, mañoso; perito.
skim (skim) v. desnatar; quitar la nata a; espumar, rasar, tocar ligeramente; to — **over the surface** rozar la superficie.
skimp (skimp) v. escatimar; eco-

nomizar; ejecutar con descuido; ser tacaño.
skimpy (skímpi) adj. escaso; tacaño.
skin (skin) s. piel, cutis, pellejo; tegumento; pellejo o cuero para vino; cáscara; hollejo; **to save one's —** salvar el pellejo; v. desollar; pelar; escorchar; mondar; cubrir superficialmente.
skinny (skíni) adj. flaco, descarnado.
skipper (skíper) s. patrón (del barco); capitán; gusanillo de queso.
skirmish (shérmish) s. escaramuza; v. escaramuzar.
skirt (skert) s. falda; pollera; orilla; saya; guardapiés; borde; **under — enaguas**; v. bordear; orillar, poner cenefa.
skit (skit) s. parodia; juguete o paso cómico; articulillo.
skull (skol) s. cráneo, calavera.
skunk (skonk) s. zorrillo o zorrino; mofeta; mapurito; golfo, truhán.
sky (skai) s. cielo, firmamento, atmósfera; **— blue** azul celeste.
skylark (skáilark) s. alondra, calandria; v. jaranear.
skylight (skáilait) s. claraboya.
skyrocket (skáirroket) s. cohete.
skyscraper (skáiscreper) s. rascacielos.
slab (slab) s. tabla, plancha, losa.
slack (slak) adj. flojo, laxo; tardo, lento; inactivo; poco, firme; perezoso; negligente, descuidado; **— season** temporada inactiva; s. flojedad, flojera; seno de un cabo; **take up the —** apretar, estirar.
slacken (sláken) v. aflojar(se); desapretar; soltar, lascar; moderar.
slag (slag) s. escoria.
slain (sléin) p.p. de **to slay**.
slam (slam) v. cerrar(se) de golpe; en los juegos de naipes, dar capote; cerrarse de golpe y con estrépito; **to — someone** decirle a alguien una claridad o grosería; **to — the door** darle un portazo; **to make a grand —** ganar todas las bazas en el juego de bridge.
slander (slánder) s. calumnia, descrédito, impostura; maledicencia.
slanderous (sláderos) adj. calumnioso; difamatorio; infamatorio.
slang (slang) s. jerga, caló, jerigonza; vulgarismo.
slant (slant) s. sesgo, declive, inclinación; punto de vista; adj. sesgado, inclinado; oblicuo; v. sesgar; inclinar(se); ladear(se).
slap (slap) s. manotada; bofetón; insulto, desaire; v. dar un manazo; dar una palmada; dar un sopapo.
slash (slash) v. dar de cuchilladas; cortar; hacer una rebaja de precio; s. cuchillada; corte; azote; latigazo; tajada.
slat (slat) s. tablilla, tira de madera; tabla.
slate (sléit) s. pizarra; pizarrón; lista de candidatos; **— pencil** pizarrín; **— coloured** color pizarra.
slaughter (slóter) s. carnicería; matanza; mortandad; **— house** matadero; v. hacer una carnicería o una matanza; carnear; destrozar.
slave (sléiv) s. esclavo; **— driver** capataz de esclavo; **— labor** trabajo de esclavos; v. trabajar como esclavo.
slaver (sléver) s. baba; v. babosear, babear.
slavery (sléivri) s. esclavitud.
slavish (sléivish) adj. servil.
slay (sléi) v. matar.
sled (sled) s. trineo; rastra.
sleek (slik) adj. liso; bruñido; suave; pulido; insinuante; mañoso; v. alisar; peinar; pulir; bruñir; sacar lustre.
sleep (slip) v. dormir; entumecerse un miembro por falta de circulación; **to — it off** dormir la mona; **to — over** consultar una decisión con la almohada; posponerla hasta pasada la noche; **to — upon** descuidarse en el cumplimiento de una obligación; **to go to —** dormirse.
sleeper (sliper) s. coche dormitorio; avión pullman; animal adormecido durante el invierno.
sleepily (slípili) adv. con somnolencia; con pesadez.
sleepiness (slípines) s. somnolencia; letargo; modorra; sueño.
sleeping (slíping) adj. durmiente; **— pills** píldoras para conciliar el sueño; **— sickness** encefalitis letárgica.
sleepless (slíples) adj. desvelado; insomne; sin sueño.
sleepy (slípi) adj. soñoliento.
sleet (slit) s. aguanieve.
sleeve (sliv) s. manga.
sleigh (sle) s. trineo.

— 209 —

sleight (sláit) s. **maña; ardid;** artificio; — **of hand** juego de manos.

slender (slénder) adj. delgado; sutil; tenue, débil; enclenque; ligero; escaso; falto de volumen.

slept (slept) pret. y p.p. de **to sleep.**

sleuth (slúz) s. detective.

slew (slú) pret. de **to slay.**

slice (sláis) s. rebanada; tajada; v. rebanar; cortar; tajar.

slick (slík) v. alisar, bruñir, lustrar; pulir; to — **up** acicalarse; ataviarse, componerse; adj. liso, terso, adulador, mañoso, astuto.

slicker (slíker) s. impermeable de hule o caucho; embaucador.

slid (slid) pret. y p.p. de **to slide.**

slidden (slídn) p.p. de **to slide.**

slide (sláid) v. resbalar(se); deslizar(se); patinar; escurrirse; errar; to — **into** meter(se); to — **out** colocarse; escabullirse; escaparse; **to let something** — no hacer caso de; s. resbalón; tapa corrediza; corredera; **microscope** — platina o portaobjetos para el microscopio; — **rule** regla de cálculo.

slight (sláit) adj. ligero, leve; pequeño, corto; negligente, descuidado; necio; débil; delgado; insignificante; —**ly** adv. ligeramente; levemente; apenas; un poco; s. desaire; descuido; indiferencia; desprecio; menosprecio.

slim (slim) adj. delgado, flaco; esbelto; escaso; falto de vigor.

slime (sláim) s. lama, légamo; fango; barro pegajoso; substancia viscosa.

slimy (sláimi) adj. viscoso, pegajoso; fangoso; mucoso.

sling (sling) s. honda; cabestrillo; eslinga; portafusil; v. tirar con honda; lanzar, tirar; arrojar; izar, poner en cabestrillo; oscilar; colgar; to — **a rifle over one's shoulder** echarse el rifle al hombro.

slink (slink) v. escabullirse, escaparse; escurrirse furtivamente; to — **away** deslizarse; huir.

slip (slip) s. resbalón; desliz; error; equivocación; escapada; funda de almohada; tira o pedazo de papel; papeleta; nota; — **knot** nudo corredizo; fondo (ropa interior de mujer); guía; — **of mind** olvido; v. deslizar(se); resbalar(se); cometer un deliz; equivocarse; salirse alguna cosa de su lugar; soltar un cable o un cabo; **to — away** escabullirse; huir precipitadamente; to — **out** salirse; sacar a hurtadillas; to — **out of joint** zafarse o dislocarse un hueso; to — **off** quitarse una cosa de encima; to — **down** dejarse caer; borrarse algo de la mente, olvidársele a uno algo; **to let an opportunity** — dejar pasar, escapársele a uno la oportunidad.

slipper (slíper) s. zapatilla; pantufla; babucha.

slit (slit) v. rajar, hender, cortar a lo largo; hacer una incisión o rendija; to — **into strips** cortar en tiras; pret. y p.p. de **to slit;** s. raja; hendedura; abertura larga y estrecha; rendija; incisión.

slobber (slóber) véase **slaver.**

slobbering (slóbering) adj. baboso.

slogan (slógan) s. lema, mote.

sloop (slup) s. chalupa.

slop (slóp) v. verter, derramar, ensuciar; mojar; s. agua sucia; desechos líquidos; desperdicios.

slope (slóup) s. sesgo, declive, descenso; bajada; cuesta; ladera; vertiente; escarpa; pendiente.

sloppy (slópi) adj. mojado, lodoso, cenagoso; sucio; desaseado.

slot (slot) s. muesca, ranura; hendedura; canal; — **machine** "tragalníqueles" "tragamonedas"; v. acanalar; cortar una hendedura o muesca; ajustar en una ranura.

sloth (sloz) s. pereza, dejadez, flojera; perezoso (animal cuadrúpedo de la América tropical).

slovenliness (slóvenlines) s. desaliño; descuido; dejadez; suciedad; porquería; desaseo.

slovenly (slóvenli) adj. desaliñado, descuidado; dejado; astroso; sucio; adv. astrosamente; desaliñadamente.

slow (slóu) adj. lento; pausado; tardo; flemático; calmudo; lerdo; torpe; —**ly** adv. lentamente; tardíamente; despacio; paulatinamente; v. **to — down** retardar; disminuir el paso, la marcha, la velocidad; **muy watch is — mi reloj anda atrasado; — witted** torpe, estúpido.

slowness (slóunes) s. lentitud, tardanza; pesadez; torpeza; cachaza.

— 210 —

slug (slóg) s. haragán, holgazán; bala; posta; porrazo; puñetazo; trago de aguardiente; v. aporrear; dar puñetazos.

sluggard (slógard) s. haragán; holgazán; zángano.

sluggish (slóguish) adj. flojo; tardo; indolente; perezoso.

sluice (slus) s. canal, acequia; compuerta; v. mojar, regar.

slum (slom) s. barrio bajo; v. visitar los barrios bajos.

slumber (slómbr) v. dormitar; s. sueño ligero.

slump (slómp) v. hundirse; desplomarse los valores en la bolsa; bajar repentinamente los precios; s. hundimiento; baja repentina; quiebra; desplome.

slung (slong) pret. y p.p. de to sling.

slunk (slonk) pret. y p.p. de to slink.

slush (slósh) s. aguanieve; fango; cieno; lodazal; v. engrasar, ensebar; embarrar (con up).

sly (slái) adj. astuto, socarrón; zorro; on the — a hurtadillas, a escondidas; — boots mosca muerta.

slyness (sláines) s. socarronería; disimulo; astucia.

smack (smák) s. sabor; gusto; beso tronado; chasquido del látigo; palmada; manotada; a — of something una pizca de algo; v. dar un beso tronado; chasquear el látigo; dar un manazo; saborear; to — of tener el sabor de; oler a; to — one's lips chuparse los labios tronando la boca.

small (smol) adj. pequeño; chico; bajo de estatura; escaso; mezquino; insignificante; — change dinero suelto; — hours primeras horas de la mañana; — talk chismografía, vulgaridades; s. cosa o cantidad pequeña.

smallness (smólnes) s. pequeñez; insignificancia; exigüidad.

smallpox (smólpoks) s. viruelas.

smart (smart) adj. vivo; ingenioso; despierto; sutil; mordaz; de buen tono; gallardo; astuto; ladino; — remark observación mordaz; — set gente de buen tono; s. escozor; dolor; ardor; v. escocer; picar.

smash (smásh) v. romper, quebrar; hacer pedazos; estrellar; aplastar; fracasar; quebrar; to — into topar, con; chocar con; s. quebrazón; bancarrota; ruina; destrozo; derrota completa.

smattering (smátering) s. conocimiento superficial y rudimentario.

smear (smir) v. manchar; ensuciar; untar; embarrar; to — with paint pintarrajear; embarrar de pintura; s. mancha.

smell (smel) v. oler, percibir con el olfato; s. olor, olfato; to — of oler a; to take a — oler.

smelly (sméli) adj. oloroso.

smelt (smelt) v. fundir metales; pret. y p.p. de to smell.

smile (smáil) v. sonreír; s. sonrisa.

smiling (smáiling) adj. sonriente; risueño; —ly adv. con cara risueña; sonriendo; con una sonrisa.

smite (smáit) v. herir; golpear; afligir; castigar; asolar; matar; cortar, partir a golpes.

smith (smiz) s. forjador; véase **blacksmith**, **goldsmith**, **silversmith**.

smithy (smízi) s. fragua, forja, hornaza, herrería.

smitten (smítn) p.p. de to smite y adj. afligido, castigado, asolado; to be — with a disease darle a uno una enfermedad.

smock (smók) s. bata corta, camisa de mujer.

smoke (smóuk) s. humo; v. to have a — fumar; humear; ahumar; to — out ahuyentar o hacer salir por medio de humo.

smoker (smóuker) s. fumador; vagón o carro fumador.

smokestack (smóukstak) s. chimenea.

smoking (smóuking) adj. humeante; de fumar; — car carro fumador; no — se prohibe fumar.

smoky (smóuki) adj. humeante, humoso; lleno de humo, ahumado.

smooth (smuz) adj. liso, pulido.

smoothness (smúznes) s. lisura; tersura; igualdad; blandura; suavidad; tranquilidad; afabilidad.

smother (smóder) v. asfixiar; sofocar; apagar; ocultar; estofar; ahogarse; estar latente; s. sofocación; humareda; supresión.

smudge (smody) v. tiznar; ensuciar; ahumar; fumigar; s. fumigación; ahumadura; nube espesa de humo.

smuggle (smógl) v. contrabandear;

— 211 —

to — in meter de contrabando; **to — out** sacar de contrabando.
smuggler (smógler) s. contrabandista; alijador; matutero.
smut (smot) s. mancha, obscenidad; dicho obsceno o indecente; tizón; suciedad; v. manchar; ensuciar; tiznar; añublar; mancillar; infamar; atizonar.
smutty (smóti) adj. tiznado; sucio; manchado; mancillado; añublado.
snack (snák) s. bocado; comida ligera; merienda; parte, porción; **to go —s** ir a medias.
snag (snag) s. nudo en la madera, protuberancia; tocón (tronco cortado casi a flor de tierra); raigón de diente; pitón; obstáculo; estorbo; v. rasgar, enredar.
snail (sneil) s. caracol.
snake (snéik) s. culebra; víbora; serpiente; **rattle —** víbora de cascabel; v. serpear, culebrear.
snap (snap) v. chasquear; hacer estallar una cosa; quebrar(se); cerrar de golpe; fotografiar en instantánea; atrapar; cortar la palabra; reventarse; fallar un tiro; **his eyes —** le chispean los ojos; **to — at** dar una tarascada; querer morder; **to — off** soltarse; saltar; abrirse de golpe; **to — one's fingers** tronar los dedos; castañetear con los dedos; burlarse de; **to — shut** cerrar de golpe; **to — together** abrochar; s. chasquido, estallido; cierre de resorte; garra; dentellada; broche de presión, mordisco, galleta; energía, vigor, ganga, instantánea; **cold —** descenso repentino de temperatura; **I dont care a —** me importa un comino; **— faster** broche de presión; **— look** cerradura de golpe; **— judgment** decisión atolondrada; adj. hecho de repente o de golpe.
snappy (snápi) adj. mordelón; violento, enojadizo; vivo; elegante; **— cheese** queso picante; **— eyes** ojos chispeantes.
snapshot (snápshot) s. instantánea fotográfica; v. sacar o tomar una instantánea.
snare (snér) s. cepo, trampa, celada; acechanza; lazo; red; v. enredar; atrapar; cazar con trampas o cepo; tender un lazo o una celada.
snarl (snarl) v. gruñir; refunfuñar; enredar, enmarañar; s. regaño, maraña; contienda; riña; pelo enmarañado o desgreñado; hilo enredado.
snatch (snatch) v. arrebatar; echar mano; agarrar; **to — at** tratar de asir o agarrar; s. arrebatiña; pedacito; bocado; rato; sandez; **by —s** a ratos; **to make a — at** tratar de arrebatar o asirse a.
sneak (sník) v. andar furtivamente; obrar solapadamente o con bajeza; **to — in** entrar o meterse a escondidas; colarse; **to — out** salirse sin ser visto; escurrirse; escabullirse; s. persona solapada.
sneer (snir) v. sonreírse con sorna; burlarse; mirar o hablar con desprecio; s. sorna; mofa; escarnio; risa falsa, gesto desdeñoso.
sneeze (snís) v. estornudar.
sniff (snif) v. husmear, olfatear, ventear; resollar; sorberse los mocos; **to — at** husmear; menospreciar; s. olfateo; cosa olfateada.
sniffle (snífl) v. sorber por las narices.
snip (snip) v. tijeretear; **to — off** cortar de un tijeretazo; s. tijeretada, recorte, retazo.
snipe (snáip) s. agachadiza.
snitch (snitch) v. arrebatar; ratear; hurtar.
snoop (snup) v. curiosear, fisgar; s. curioso, fisgón.
snooze (snus) v. sestear; dormitar; cabecear; s. siesta, sueño ligero; **to take a —** echar un sueñito.
snore (snor) v. roncar; s. ronquido; **snoring** ronquido.
snort (snort) v. resoplar, bufar; s. bufido, resoplido.
snout (snaut) s. hocico; jeta; trompa de elefante; tobera; boquerel de manguera; embocadura de un cañón.
snow (snou) s. nieve; nevasca; v. nevar; **to be —ed under, over, o up;** estar cubierto o aprisionado entre la nieve.
snowball (snóubol) s. bola de nieve.
snowdrift (snóudrift) s. ventisca; ventisquero.
snowfall (snóufol) s. nevada.
snowflake (snóufleik) s. copo de nieve; campanilla.
snowstomn (snóustorm) s. nevasca, ventisca, borrasca.
snowy (snóui) adj. nevado, níveo.
snub (snob) v. desairar; tratar con aspereza; reprender; **— nosed**

— 212 —

chato; s. reprensión, regaño, desaire.
snuff (snof) v. olfatear, ventear, husmear; aspirar por la nariz; despabilar; **to — at** olfatear; **to — out** apagar, extinguir; **to — up** sorber por la nariz; s. sorbo; rapé; **— box** caja de rapé; pabilo; mecha quemada; pavesa.
snug (snog) adj. ajustado; bien dispuesto; compacto; cómodo, abrigado; v. acomodar, ajustar, apretar; aparejar.
so (so) adv. así, tan, muy; tanto; de este modo, de esta manera; de modo o de manera que; por tanto, por lo cual; aproximadamente; cosa así; poco más o menos; **— — regular; it is not — no es cierto, no es así; if — si así es, o de ese modo; so-and-so** Fulano (de tal); **— as to** para; **— far** tan lejos; hasta ahora, hasta aquí; **I think — así lo** espero; **— many** tantos; **I belive — así lo creo; why —?** ¿por qué así? **is that —?** ¿de veras? **ten minutes or —** poco más o menos diez minutos, como diez minutos.
soak (sóuk) v. remojar; empapar; poner en remojo; (con **in o up**) chupar, embeber; absorber; beber con exceso; s. remojo, calada; líquido en que se empapa alguna cosa; borrachín; orgía.
soap (sóup) s. jabón; lisonja, adulación; dinero; **— bubble** pompa de jabón; bombita; **— boiler** jabonero; caldera para jabón; v. enjabonar; lavar con jabón; adular.
soapy (sóupi) adj. lleno de jabón.
soar (sóur) v. remontarse; encumbrarse; elevarse; sublimarse; remontar el vuelo; s. vuelo o remonte.
sob (sob) v. sollozar; s. sollozo.
sober (sóuber) adj. sobrio, moderado; templado; cuerdo, sano; en su juicio; sereno, tranquilo, de sangre fría; sensato; **to be — estar en su juicio, no estar borracho;** v. volverse sobrio, cuerdo, moderado, sensato; **to — down** sosegar(se); calmar(se).
soberly (sóuberli) adv. sobriamente; cuerdamente, con sensatez; con moderación; juiciosamente.
soberness (sóubernes) s. sobriedad; templanza, moderación.

sobriety (sobráieti) s. **sobriedad;** cordura, calma, **sangre fría.**
so-called (sokóld) adj. así llamado, llamado.
sociable (sóshebl) adj. sociable, amigable; tratable, social.
social (sóshal) adj. social; sociable; afable, franco; tratable; s. reunión social; tertulia.
socialism (sóshalism) s. socialismo.
socialist (sóshalist) adj. y s. socialista.
society (sosáieti) s. sociedad.
sociology (sociólöyi) s. sociología.
sock (sok) s. calcetín; porrazo; escarpín, zueco; comedia; reja de arado; v. pegar, golpear, batear.
socket (sóket) s. cuenca (del ojo); culto, caja, cajera.
sod (sod) s. césped; terrón (de tierra sembrada de césped); v. cubrir de césped.
soda (soda) s. **soda, sosa; — fountain** fuente de sodas; **— water** agua gaseosa; **baking — bicarbonato de sodio; óxido de sodio.**
sodium (sódium) s. sodio.
sofa (sófa) s. sofá.
soft (soft) adj. blando; muelle; tenue; dúctil; suave; dulce; tierno; apacible; jugoso; almibarado; condescendiente; **— boiled eggs** huevos tibios o pasados por agua; **— iron** hierro dulce; **— drink** bebida no alcohólica; **— water** agua dulce; **— skin** cutis terso, blando.
soften (sófen) v. ablandar; mitigar; calmar; suavizar; enternecer; endulzar; **to — one's voice** hablar quedo, bajar la voz.
softly (sóftli) adv. con blandura; suavemente; tiernamente; quedo.
softness (sóftnes) s. blandura; suavidad; ductilidad; ternura; dulzura; delicadeza; morbidez.
soil (soil) s. suelo; tierra, país; suciedad; mancha; v. ensuciar, manchar; empañar; abonar la tierra.
sojourn (soyórn) s. residencia, permanencia; estancia; estadía; v. permanecer; residir temporalmente; morar; quedarse; estar de paso.
solace (sóles) s. solaz; v. solazar.
solar (sólar) adj. solar; del sol.
sold (sould) pret. y p.p. de **to sell; to be — on an idea** estar casado con la idea de.

solder (sólder) v. soldar; —**ing** s. soldadura.
soldier (sóldier) s. soldado.
sole (sóul) adj. uno, único, solo; absoluto, exclusivo; s. suela; planta del pie; v. ensuelar; **to half —** poner medias suelas a los zapatos.
solely (sóuli) adv. únicamente, solamente; meramente.
solemn (sólem) adj. solemne.
solemnity (solémniti) s. solemnidad.
solicit (solísit) v. solicitar.
solicitor (solísitor) s. agente; solicitante; procurador.
solicitous (solísitos) adj. solícito.
solicitude (solísitiud) s. solicitud; afán; diligencia; avidez.
solid (sólid) adj. sólido, compacto; firme; macizo; efectivo; consistente; sensato; unánime; **— gold** oro puro; **for one — hour** por una hora entera; durante una hora sin parar; s. sólido.
solidarity (solidáriti) s. solidaridad; mancomunidad.
solidify (solídifai) v. solidificar.
solidity (solíditi) s. solidez.
soliloquy (solílokui) s. soliloquio.
solitary (sóliteri) adj. solitario; solo; s. solitario; ermitaño.
solitude (sólitiud) s. soledad.
solo (solo) s. solo.
soloist (sóloist) s. solista.
soluble (sóliubl) adj. soluble; que se disuelve con facilidad.
solution (solúshon) s. solución.
solve (sólv) v. resolver; desentrañar; aclarar; explicar.
somber (sómber) adj. sombrío.
some (som) adj. unos; algún, alguno; algunos; algo de; un poco de; ciertos; **— one** alguien, alguno; **— bread** un poco de pan; **— ten or more** unos diez o más; adj. unos y otros; una parte, una porción de.
somebody (sómbodi) pron. alguien, alguna persona; **— else** alguien más.
somehow (sómjau) adv. en cierto modo; de alguna manera; **— or other** de una manera u otra; por alguna razón.
someone (sómuan) pron. alguien; alguno.
somersault (sómersolt) s. salto mortal; voltereta.
somewhere (sómjuer) adv. en alguna parte; **— else** en alguna otra parte; en algún otro lugar o sitio.
son (son) s. hijo.
song (song) s. canción; canto, **the Song of Songs** el Cantar de los Cantares; **— bird** ave canora; **to sell for a mere —** vender algo casi regalado.
son-in-law (sóninloh) s. yerno.
sonnet (sónet) s. soneto.
sonorous (sonóros) adj. sonoro.
soon (sun) adv. pronto, luego; de inmediato; presto; de buena gana; **as — as** tan pronto como; **— after** poco después; **too —** demasiado pronto.
soot (sut) s. hollín.
soothe (suz) v. calmar; aliviar; mitigar; consolar.
soothsayer (súzseyer) s. adivino.
sooty (súti) ad. fuliginoso.
sop (sop) v. empapar; mojar; hacer sopas; **to — up** absorber; **to be sopping wet** estar empapado, hecho una sopa; s. sopa de pan u otra cosa mojada en leche, etc.
sophomore (sófomor) s. estudiante de segundo año.
soprano (soppráno) s. soprano; **high —** tiple; **— voice** voz de soprano.
sorcerer (sórserer) s. brujo, hechicero; mago.
sordid (sórdid) adj. sórdido; codicioso, vil; mezquino.
sore (sor) s. llaga, úlcera; inflamación; lastimadura; dolor; pena; disgusto; aflicción; adj. dolorido; enconado; inflamado; delicado; apesadumbrado; disgustado; sensible; **— throat** dolor de garganta; **to be — at** estar enojado o disgustado con; **—ly** adv. dolorosamente; penosamente; **to be —ly in need of** necesitar con urgencia.
sorrel (sórrel) adj. alazán; roano; caballo alazán.
sorrow (sórrou) s. pesar; pena; aflicción; amargura; pesadumbre; v. apenarse; afligirse.
sorrowful (sórrouful) adj. angustiado; afligido; apenado; doloroso; lastimoso; **—ly** adv. angustiosamente; con aflicción; con pena; desconsoladamente.
sorry (sórri) adj. triste, melancólico; apesadumbrado; arrepentido; **I am —** lo siento; me pesa; **I am** (o **feel**) **— for her** la compadezco; **— sight** triste espectáculo.

— 214 —

sort (sort) s. clase, género, especie; calidad; manera; modo; suerte; **all —s of people** todas clases de gente; **out of —s** malhumorado; indispuesto; v. clasificar; separar; **to — out** dividir en grupos; escoger, clasificar.
sought (sót) pret. y p.p. de **to seek**.
soul (sóul) s. alma; ánima; ser; **not a —** nadie, ni un alma.
sound (sáund) adj. sano; ileso; perfecto; seguro; firme; cuerdo; sensato; completo; solvente; **safe and —** sano y salvo; **— sleep** sueño profundo; **— business** negocio sólido, bien organizado; **— reasoning** raciocinio sólido; **— wave** onda sonora; s. sonido; són; tañido; estuario; brazo de mar; estrecho; v. sonar; tocar; entonar; tañer; aclamar; publicar; sondear; tantear; echar la plomada; resonar; divulgarse; auscultar; **to — out** tantear; sondear.
soundness (sáundnes) s. salud, vigor; fuerza; pureza; rectitud; solidez; firmeza; **— of body** buena salud corporal.
soup (sup) s. sopa.
sour (sáur) adj. agrio; ácido; acre; desabrido; rancio; huraño; malhumorado; **— milk** leche agria, leche cortada; v. agriar(se); acedar; irritar; desagradar; poner de mal humor; indisponer el ánimo.
source (sors) s. fuente; manantial, origen; causa; procedencia.
sourness (sáurnes) s. acidez; agrura; acedía.
south (sáuz) s. sur, sud; adj. del sur; meridional; austral; **South American** sudamericano; **— pole** polo sur; polo antártico; adv. hacia el sur.
southeast (sauzíst) s. y adj. sudeste; adv. hacia el sudeste.
southeastern (sauzístern) adj. del sudeste; sudeste.
southern (sáuzern) adj. meridional; del sur; austral; sureño; **— Cross** de la Cruz del Sur.
southerner (sáuzerner) s. sureño; habitante del sur.
southward (sáuzuord) adv. hacia el sur; rumbo al sur.
southwest (sáuzuest) s. y adj. sudoeste; adv. rumbo al sudoeste.
southwestern (sáuzuestern) adj. sudoeste; del sudoeste.
souvenir (suvenír) s. recuerdo.
sovereign (sóverin) s. y adj. soberano.
sovereignty (sóverinti) s. soberanía.
soviet (sóviet) s. soviet; adj. soviético.
sow (sáu) s. puerca.
sow (sou) v. sembrar.
sown (soun) p.p. de to sow.
space (spéis) s. espacio; v. espaciar.
spacious (spéshos) adj. amplio; espacioso; vasto; extenso.
spade (spéid) s. azada, azadón; espadas de la baraja; v. cavar con la azada.
span (span) s. palmo; lapso; trecho; luz de un puente; envergadura de un avión; v. medir a palmos; extenderse sobre; amarrar; ligar.
spangle (spángl) s. lentejuela; v. adornar con lentejuelas; **—d with stars** tachonado de estrellas.
Spaniard (spániard) s. español.
spaniel (spániel) s. perro de aguas.
Spanish (spánish) adj. español; s. idioma español.
spank (spank) v. dar una zurra; dar de nalgadas; dar una tunda; s. palmada; nalgada.
spanking (spánking) s. zurra; tunda; nalgadas.
spare (spér) v. ahorrar; guardar; escatimar; evitar molestias, trabajos, etc.; perdonar; dispensar; abstenerse; desistir; ser frugal; **I cannot — another dollar** no dispongo de otro dólar, no tengo más dinero disponible; **to — the life** perdonar la vida; **to have to —** tener de sobra; **to — no expense** no escatimar gastos; adj. disponible; sobrante; de repuesto; flaco; descarnado; mezquino; **— time** tiempo desocupado; **— hours** horas de recreo, de ocio; **— room** cuarto de sobra; **— tire** llanta de refacción; **— built** flaco, delgado.
spark (spark) s. chispa; **— plug** bujía para automóvil; v. chispear, chisporrotear.
sparkle (sparkl) s. centelleo; destello; chispa; brillo; viveza; animación; v. centellear; relucir.
sparkling (spárkling) adj. rutilante; chispeante; brillante; espumoso; **— wine** vino espumoso.

sparrow (spárrou) s. gorrión.
sparse (spars) adj. esparcido; desparramado; ralo; poco poblado; — **hair** pelo ralo.
spasm (spásm) s. espasmo.
spat (spat) pret. y p.p. de **to spit**; v. dar una palmadita; reñir ligeramente; disputar; dar un manazo o una bofetada; desovar los mariscos; s. palmada; manotada; sopapo; bofetada; gota grande de lluvia; huevas de mariscos; riña; desavenencia; —**s polainas** cortas.
speak (spik) v. hablar, decir, recitar; **to** — **one's mind** hablar sin rodeos.
speaker (spíker) s. orador; conferencista; locutor; **loud** — magnavoz; altoparlante; — **of the House** presidente de la cámara de diputados.
spear (spír) s. lanza; arpón; venablo; brote, retoño; — **grass** hierba de los prados; — **head** punta de lanza; v. alancear; brotar.
spearmint (spírmint) s. yerbabuena; menta verde.
special (spéshal) adj. especial, particular; singular; peculiar; — **delivery** entrega inmediata; s. tren o autobús especial; —**ly** adv. especialmente; sobre todo.
specialist (spéshalist) s. especialista.
specialize (spéshalais) v. especializarse.
specialty (spéshalti) s. especialidad.
specific (spesífik) adj. específico; expreso; formal; característico; — **gravity** peso específico; —**ally** expresamente; en particular; específicamente.
specify (spécifai) v. especificar; estipular; determinar.
specimen (spésimen) s. espécimen.
speck (spék) s. manchita; motita; nube en un ojo; lunar; punto; partícula; átomo; **not a** — **ni pizca**; véase **speckle**.
speckle (spekl) s. manchita; mota; v. motear; manchar; jaspear.
speckled (spékld) adj. moteado; — **with freckles** pecoso.
spectacle (spéktakl) s. espectáculo; —**s anteojos; to make a** — **of oneself** ponerse en la evidencia.
spectacular (spektákiular) adj. espectacular; ostentoso; aparatoso.
spectator (spektéitor) s. espectador.

specter (spékter) s. espectro, fantasma; visión; aparecido.
spectrum (spéktrum) s. espectro; — **analysis** análisis espectral.
speculate (spékiuleit) v. especular; meditar; reflexionar.
speculation (spekiuléshon) s. especulación; reflexión; teoría.
speculative (spékiuletiv) adj. especulativo; teórico.
speculator (spékiuletor) s. especulador; teórico.
sped (sped) p.p. y pret. de **to speed**.
speech (spích) s. lenguaje; discurso; arenga; alocución; conferencia; disertación, idioma; parlamento; **to make a** — pronunciar un discurso.
speechless (spíchles) adj. demudado; mudo; estupefacto; turbado.
speed (spid) s. rapidez, presteza; velocidad; prisa; apresuramiento; prontitud; — **limit** velocidad máxima; **at full** — a toda velocidad; v. acelerar; apresurar(se); progresar; adelantar; despachar; ir con exceso de velocidad.
speedily (spídili) adv. velozmente; rápidamente; de prisa; pronto; **a todo correr**.
speedometer (spidómeter) s. velocímetro.
speller (speler) s. silabario.
spelling (snéling) s. ortografía; — **book** silabario.
spend (spend) v. gastar; disipar; agotar; consumir; pasar; emplear; **to** — **a day** pasar un día haciendo.
spendthrift (spénzrift) s. maniroto; derrochador; pródigo.
spent (spent) pret. y p.p. de **spend**.
sphere (sfír) s. esfera; globo; orbe.
spherical (sférikal) adj. esférico.
spicy (spáisi) adj. condimentado; picante; aromático; sazonado.
spider (spáider) s. araña; cazo con pies; — **web** telaraña.
spigot (spígot) s. espita; grifo; llave; canilla.
spike (spáik) s. espiga, alcayata; perno; clavo grande; v. clavar.
spill (spil) v. verter, derramar(se), desparramar(se); divulgar un secreto; revelar una noticia; s. derrame; vuelvo; astilla; pajuela.
spin (spin) v. hilar; girar; dar

— 216 —

vuelta; bailar un trompo; **to —
out** prolongar; alargar; **to —
yarns** contar cuentos; s. giro,
vuelta; paseo en coche, bicicleta;
barrena de avión.
spinach (spínach) s. espinaca.
spinal (spáinal) adj. espinal; **—
cord** espina dorsal.
spindle (spindl) s. husillo; eje.
spine (spáin) s. espina; espinazo;
espina dorsal, columna vertebral.
spinner (spíner) s. hilandero; máquina de hilar.
spinning (spíning) s. hilandería;
arte de hilar; **— jenny** máquina
de hilar; **— top** trompo; **—
wheel** torno de hilar.
spinster (spínster) s. solterona.
spiral (spáiral) adj. espiral; helicoidal; **— staircase** escalera de
caracol; s. espiral.
spire (spáir) s. chapitel; cúspide;
ápice; punto más alto; **— of
grass** brizna de hierba.
spirit (spírit) s. espíritu; ánimo;
valor; viveza; temple; carácter;
low —s abatimiento; **to be in
good —** estar de buen humor;
— away hacer desaparecer; llevarse; arrebatar; **ardent —** bebidas espirituosas; **animal —** vivacidad, fogosidad.
spirited (spírited) adj. fogoso; vivo; valiente; brioso; animoso.
spiritual (spírichual) adj. espiritual; intelectual; santo; puro.
spit (spit) v. escupir; espectorar;
pret. y p.p. de **to spit**; s. esputo;
saliva; escupitina; asador.
spite (spáit) s. rencor; despecho;
mala voluntad; odio; **in — of** a
pesar de; a despecho de; **out of
—** por despecho; v. mostrar resentimiento; picar; irritar.
spiteful (spáitful) adj. rencoroso.
splash (splash) v. salpicar; rociar;
chapotear; chapalear; humedecer; s. rociada, salpicadura, chapoteo.
spleen (splin) s. bazo; resentimiento, mal humor; tristeza;
esplín.
splendid (spléndid) adj. espléndido.
splendor (spléndor) s. esplendor.
splice (spláis) v. empalmar; unir;
juntar; s. empalme, junta, gaza.
splint (splint) s. tablilla; astilla;
tira plana y delgada; v. entablillar.
splinter (splínter) s. astilla; raja;

v. astillar(se); hacerse pedazos;
romperse en astillas.
split (split) v. rajar(se); hender
(se); dividir, partir; agrietarse;
estrellarse; **to — the difference**
partir la diferencia; **to — upon
a rock** estrellarse contra una
roca; pret. y p.p. de **to split**; adj.
hendido; rajado; partido; dividido; resquebrajado; cuarteado.
s. hendidura; grieta; raja; cuarteadura; resquebradura; división:
cisma; rompimiento.
spoil (spoil) v. estropear, desbaratar; echar a perder; dañar(se);
podrir(se) o pudrir(se); deteriorar; mimar; s. botín, presa; robo,
despojo; saqueo.
spoke (spóuk) s. rayo de rueda;
escalón de escalera; pret. de **to
speak**.
spoken (spóuken) p.p. de **to speak**.
spokesman (spóuksman) s. portavoz, vocero, interlocutor.
sponge (spónỵ) s. esponja; gorrón;
parásito; escobillón; v. lavar o
limpiar con esponja; esponjar,
comer de gorra; estar a costa
ajena; chupar, embeberse.
spongecake (spónykeik) s. bizcocho esponjoso; panetela.
sponger (spónyer) s. esponja, gorrón; sablista; parásito; pavo.
spongy (spónyi) adj. esponjoso, esponjado, fofo, embebido; empapado.
sponsor (spónsor) s. padrino, madrina; fiador; patrocinador; promotor; defensor; v. apadrinar;
patrocinar; fomentar; ser fiador de; promover.
spontaneity (spontanieti) s. espontaneidad; voluntariedad.
spontaneous (spontáneos) adj. espontáneo; voluntario, natural.
spook (spuk) s. espectro; fantasma; aparición.
spool (spul) s. carrete, canilla; v.
devanar; ovillar, encanillar.
spoon (spún) s. cuchara; v. cucharear, sacar con cuchara; pescar con anzuelo de cuchara.
spoonful (spúnful) s. cucharada.
sport (sport) s. deporte; diversión; juego; entretenimiento,
recreo; **in —** en broma, de burla; **field —s** diversiones del campo; **to make — of** reirse de, burlarse de; **to be a good —** ser
buen perdedor (en el juego);
v. jugar, divertirse; ostentar;

hacer alarde de; bromear; lucir, holgar.

sportsman (spórtsman) s. deportista; — like aficionado al deporte; buen perdedor (en deportes).

spot (spot) s. mancha, mota; sitio; lugar, paraje; punto, parte, puesto; borrón, pinta; **in —** aquí y allí; **upon the —** en el mismo sitio; al instante, en el acto; v. manchar; abigarrar; echar de ver.

spotless (spótles) adj. sin mancha.

spotted (spóted) adj. manchado; moteado; pintojo; mosqueado.

spouse (spáus) s. esposo, esposa.

spout (spáut) v. chorrear; salir en chorro; surgir, brotar; correr a chorro; emitir, declamar; s. chorro; caño, pitón; conducto.

sprain (spréin) v. torcer (una coyuntura o músculo); torcerse; **to — one's anakle** torcerse el tobillo; s. torcedura.

sprang (spráng) pret. de **to spring.**

sprawl (spról) v. tender o tenderse; despatarrarse; estar despatarrado; s. postura floja (abiertos los brazos y piernas).

spray (spréi) s. rocío; rociada; espuma del mar; rociador; pulverizador; líquido para rociar; v. rociar; pulverizar un líquido.

spread (spréd) v. extender(se); esparcir(se); desplegar(se); diseminar(se); propalar (noticias); exhibir; espaciar; difundir; apartar; poner la mesa; **to — butter on** poner mantequilla en; **to — over** cubrir o untar con; **to — out the table cloth** extender el mantel; s. extensión, expansión; desarrollo; difusión; propagación; cobertor de cama; aderezo (para el pan); prt. y p.p. de **to spread;** comilona, festín, banquete.

spree (sprí) v. ir de parranda, emborracharse; andar de farra; s. parranda, juerga; holgorio.

sprig (spríg) s. ramita; vástago; espiga; tachuela.

sprigthly (spráitli) adj. alegre; vivo; despierto; animado; vivaracho, despejado, brioso.

spring (spring) v. saltar; brincar; brotar; manar un líquido; soltar un resorte; presentarse súbitamente; moverse como por resorte; combarse; torcerse; **to — a leak** hacer agua una embarcación; comenzar a gotearse la cañería o el techo; **to — forth** brotar; crecer; **to — at** lanzarse sobre, abalanzarse; **to — away** saltar a un lado; **to — something open** abrir algo haciendo saltar la tapa; **to — to one's feet** levantarse de un salto; s. primavera; resorte; elasticidad; salto; brinco; bote; móvil; impulso; manantial; fuente; surtidor; origen; adj. primaveral; **— board** trampolín; **— water** agua de manantial; **— mattress** colchón de muelles o resortes.

springtime (springtaim) s. primavera.

sprinkle (sprinkl) v. rociar; regar; salpicar; lloviznar; s. rocío; rociada; **— of salt** una pizca de sal; **it —s** está lloviznando.

sprint (sprint) v. echar una carrera; correr velozmente; s. carrera; corrida corta.

sprout (spráut) v. hacer germinar o brotar; quitar los botones o vástagos; germinar; retoñar; s. retoño; renuevo; **Brussels —s** coles de Bruselas.

spruce (sprus) s. abeto; adj. guapo; garboso; pulcro; elegante; aseado; v. **to — up** asearse; vestirse con esmero; emperifollarse.

sprung (sprong) pret. y p.p. de **to spring.**

spun (spon) pret. y p.p. de **to spin.**

spur (spér) s. espuela; acicate; aguijón; espolón; (uña puntiaguda); estribación; risco; **— track** ramal corto de ferrocarril, espuela; **— gear, — wheel** rueda dentada; v. espolear; avivar; incitar; estimular; **to — on** animar; incitar (a obrar o a seguir adelante).

spurn (spérn) v. cocear (a puntapiés); desdeñar; despreciar; menospreciar; s. coz; maltrato.

spurt (spert) v. brotar a chorros, a borbotones; chorrear; brotar; surgir; hacer un esfuerzo supremo; s. chorro, borbotón; esfuerzo repentino; arranque de ira; **—s of flame** llamaradas.

sputter (spóter) v. chisporrotear; farfullar; refunfuñar; s. chisporroteo; chispeo de saliva.

sputum (splútom) s. esputo.

spy (spái) espía; v. esplar; observar; atisbar; acechar.

spyglass (spáiglas) s. anteojo de larga vista.

squabble (skuábl) s. riña; disputa; tremolina; trifulca; reyerta; v. reñir; disputar; contender.
squad (skuád) s. escuadra, patrulla; pelotón; partida.
squadron (skuádron) s. escuadrón; escuadra; armada; flota.
squalid (skuálid) adj. escuálido.
squall (skuol) s. chubasco, turbonada; chillido; berrido; v. chillar.
squander (skuónder) v. malgastar; despilfarrar; disipar; derrochar.
square (skuér) s. cuadro; cuadrado; escuadra; nivel; proporción debida; manzana de casas; casilla de ajedrez o de damas; integridad; equidad; cuadratura; cuadrángulo; — **root** raíz cuadrada; — **dealing** obrar de buena fe; honradez en el trato; **on the** — de buena fe, honradamente; v. cuadrar; ajustar; saldar cuentas; cuadricular; elevar al cuadrado; estar en ángulos rectos; convenir; concordar una cosa con otra; **to** — **one's shoulders** enderezar los hombros; **to** — **oneself with** sincerarse con; justificarse ante; adj. cuadrado, en cuadro, en ángulo recto, a escuadra; saldado; justo; cabal; íntegro; honrado; de buena fe; opíparo; en paz; franco; — **mile** milla cuadrada.
squarely (skuérli) adv. equitativamente; honradamente; firmemente; de buena fe; derecho; en justicia.
squash (skuósh) s. calabaza; pulpa; v. aplastar; magullar; apachurrar; macerar.
squat (skuót) v. agacharse; agazaparse; sentarse en cuclillas; ocupar tierras baldías para ganarse el título de propietario; adj. agazapado; sentado en cuclillas; achaparrado; rechoncho.
squawk (skuók) v. graznar; chillar; s. graznido; chillido; queja.
squeak (skuík) v. crujir; rechinar; chirriar; chillar; s. rechinamiento; chirrido; chillido; crujido.
squeal (skuíl) v. delatar; chillar; quejar(se); protestar; soplar; s. delación; chillido; queja.
squeeze (skuís) v. exprimir; estrujar; apretar; comprimir; extorsionar; agobiar; apretar; v. pasar, entrar o salir apretando; **to** — **in** o **into** meterse a la fuerza, a estrujones; **to** — **through a crowd** abrirse paso a la fuerza entre una multitud; s. estrujón; apretón; presión; apretura.
squelch (skuélch) v. acallar; desconcertar; reprender; **to** — **out a revolt** sofocar una revuelta.
squint (skuínt) s. estrabismo; mirada de soslayo; mirada bizca; v. hacer el bizco; entornar los ojos; —**eyed** (skuintáid) adj. bizco.
squire (skuáir) s. escudero; v. escoltar; acompañar.
squirm (skuerm) v. retorcerse; serpear; **to** — **out of a difficulty** salir con grandes trabajos de una dificultad.
squirrel (skuérrel) s. ardilla.
squirt (skuírt) v. salir a chorros; echar chisguetes; jeringar; s. chisguete; chorro; jeringazo.
stab (stab) v. herir con arma blanca; dar de puñaladas; acuchillar; s. puñalada, cuchillada; pinchazo; estocada.
stability (stebíliti) s. estabilidad; solidez; consistencia.
stable (stéibl) adj. estable; permanente; durable; firme; s. establo, caballeriza; cuadra.
stack (sták) s. rimero; pila; hacina; montón; cañón de chimenea; v. hacinar; apilar; amontonar; **library** —**s** estanterías o anaqueles de libros.
stadium (stédium) s. estadio.
stage (stey) s. tablado; foro; escenario; teatro; jornada; etapa; diligencia; — **hand** tramoyista; **by easy** —**s** por grados; gradualmente; **to go on the** — adoptar la carrera del teatro; — **manager** director de escena; v. poner en escena; representar; viajar en diligencia; **to** — **a hold up** cometer un asalto; atracar; **to** — **a surprise** sorprender.
stagger (státguer) v. hacer eses; tambalearse; trastabillar; vacilar; estar incierto; hacer bambolearse; azorar; temblar; **to** — **working hours** escalonar las horas de trabajo; s. tambaleo, bamboleo.
stagnant (stágnant) adj. estancado; **to become** — estancarse.
staid (stéid) adj. grave, serio.
stain (stein) v. manchar; teñir; colorar; entintar; —**ed glass** vidrio de colores; s. mancha; tintura; materia colorante.
stainless (stéinles) adj. limpio; sin

— 219 —

mancha; inmaculado; — steel acero inoxidable.

stair (ster) s. escalón; peldaño; —s escalera; **flight of —s** tramo de escaleras.

staircase (stérkeis) s. escalera.

stairway (stéruei) s. escalera.

stake (steik) s. estaca; poste; jalón; pira; tas; apuesta; riesgo; peligro; **his future is at —** su porvenir está en peligro; **he died at the —s** murió en la hoguera; **to — all** aventurarlo todo; **to have much at —** haber aventurado o apostado mucho; v. estacar; apostar; aventurar; arriesgar; exponer; **to — off** señalar con estacas un perímetro.

stale (stéil) adj. añejo; rancio; deteriorado; gastado; improductivo.

stalk (stók) s. tallo; caña.

stall (stól) s. pesebre; puesto o tienda portátil; luneta en el teatro; v. meter o encerrar en el pesebre; atascar(se); detener (se); pararse (el motor); hacerse guaje; demorar un asunto.

stallion (stélion) s. garañón.

stammer (stámer) v. **tartamudear**; balbucear; s. tartamudeo, balbuceo.

stammerer (stámerer) s. tartamudo.

stammering (stámering) s. tartamudeo; adj. tartamudo.

stamp (stamp) v. patear; patalear; estampar; imprimir o señalar una cosa; sellar; timbrar; acuñar; troquelar; **machacar**; **to — out** borrar; extirpar; s. sello; timbre; estampilla de correos; **postage —** estampilla; **revenue —** timbre fiscal.

stampede (stampíd) s. estampida; tropel; huida con terror pánico, en desorden; éxodo repentino; v. ahuyentar; hacer huir con terror pánico (a un rebaño, una turba, etc.); obrar por común impulso; tomar un acuerdo repentinamente; escampar; huir en tropel; ir en tropel; moverse desordenadamente.

stanch (stánch) v. restañar; estancar; adj. firme; fiel; adicto; sano; fuerte; constante.

stand (stand) v. enderezar, poner o colocarse de pie; pararse; levantarse; soportar; sufrir; aguantar; sufragar; pagar el costo de algo; estar en pie; mantenerse acuerdo; **to — alone** estar solo; **to — aside** apartarse, mantenerse alejado; **to — by** sostenerse en, no retroceder; **to — back** erecto; durar; subsistir; estar situado; perseverar; quedar de salir fiador de; apoyar, garantizar; respaldar; **to — in the way** estorbar; **to — on end** ponerse de punta; **to — from under** alejarse de alguna cosa que está por caer; **to — six feet** tener seis pies de altura; **to — up** defender; sostener; ponerse de pie; **to — still** estarse quieto, no moverse; s. puesto; posición; pedestal; plataforma; tribuna; mesita; estante; término; inactividad; actitud; alto; parada; resistencia; armamento equipo completo; **music —** atril; **grand —** gradería; **flower —** jardinera; puesto para vender flores.

standing (stánding) s. posición; reputación; crédito; sitio; antigüedad; alto; paraje; **of long —** que ha prevalecido largo tiempo; adj. erecto; de pie; en pie; permanente, estable; estancado; **— water** agua estancada.

standpoint (stándpoint) s. punto de vista.

standstill (stándstil) s. parada; alto; detención; pausa; descanso; **to come to a —** hacer alto.

stank (stank) pret. de to stink.

stanza (stánza) s. estrofa.

staple (stéipl) s. grapa; argolla; armella; artículo o producto principal de un país; fibra de algodón, artículo de primera necesidad; materia prima; adj. principal; prominente; de consumo general; reconocido; admitido; vendible; v. engrapar; asegurar papeles.

star (star) s. estrella; astro; asterisco; hado; suerte; actor o actriz eminente; adj. **— spangled** estrellado; v. adornar con estrellas; marcar con asterisco; presentar como estrella a un actor, ya sea en el teatro o el cine; desempeñar el papel principal en una obra.

starboard (stárbourd) s. estribor; **— side** banda de estribor; adj. a estribor.

starch (starch) s. almidón, fécula; v. almidonar.

stare (ster) v. clavar o fijar la

vista; mirar azorado; mirar a la cara, descaradamente; abrir grandes ojos; s. mirada fija. encaro.

starfish (stárfish) s. estrella de mar.

stark (stark) s. tieso; rígido; escueto; muerto; — **and stiff** rígido, muerto; — **folly** pura tontería; — **narrative** narración escueta, sin adornos; adv. completamente, enteramente; — **naked** completamente desnudo; — **mad** loco de remate.

starlight (stárlait) s. candilejas; luz de las estrellas.

starry (stárri) adj. sembrado de estrellas; rutilante; sideral.

start (start) v. iniciar; empezar; principiar; comenzar; poner en movimiento; poner en marcha; partir; suscitar; emprender; estrenar; sobresaltarse; to — **after someone** salir en busca de alguien; to — **out on a trip** emprender un viaje; to — **the motor** poner en marcha el motor; to — **wine** trasegar el vino; s. sobresalto; respingo; susto; comienzo; principio; arranque; marcha; salida; delantera; ventaja; to get the — coger la delantera.

starter (stárter) s. arranque; iniciador; palanca de marcha; **self** — arranque automático.

startle (startl) v. sobrecoger; alarmar; dar un susto; espantar.

startling (stártling) adj. sorprendente; espantadizo; asombroso.

starvation (starvéshon) s. inanición; hambre; miseria; indigencia.

starve (starv) v. morir(se) de hambre; matar de hambre; hambrear.

state (stéit) s. estado; gobierno civil; posición; condición; pompa; **in** — con gran pompa o ceremonia; adj. de estado; político; público; v. manifestar, declarar; decir; expresar; enunciar; exponer.

stately (stéitli) adj. majestuoso; augusto, soberbio, imponente.

statement (stéitment) s. relación; declaración; exposición; informe; cuenta; relato; estado de cuenta.

stateroom (stéitrrum) s. camarote; salón de recepciones de un palacio.

static (státik) s. estática; adj. estático.

station (stéshon) s. estación; puesto de marca; posición social; lugar señalado; **broadcasting** — estación radiodifusora; v. estacionar, colocar; situar; disponer.

stationary (stéshoneri) adj. estacionario; fijo.

stationery (stéshoneri) s. papelería.

statistics (statístiks) s. estadística; adj. estadístico.

statuary (stéchueri) s. estatuaria; escultor; colección de estatuas.

statute (stéchu) s. estatua.

stature (stéchur) s. estatura.

status (stétos) s. estado legal; posición económica o social; estado que guardan las cosas.

statute (stéchut) s. estatuto; ordenanza.

staunch véase **stanch**.

stave (stéiv) s. duela de barril; v. poner duelas; desfondar; quebrantar; destrozar; to — **off** rechazar; mantener a distancia; retardar.

stay (stéi) v. sostener; apoyar; apuntalar; quedarse; hospedarse; to — **in** quedarse en casa, no salir; to — **away** no volver; to — **up all night** velar toda la noche; no acostarse; s. estancia; permanencia; espera; suspensión; sostén, apoyo; varilla de corsé; nervio; **to grant** — conceder una prórroga.

stead (sted) s. (precedido de **in**) lugar; sitio; las veces de; **in his** — en su lugar; **in** — **of** en lugar de; en vez de; **to stand in good** — serle a uno de provecho; serle útil.

steadfast (stédfast) adj. constante; inmutable; fijo; firme.

steadily (stédili) adv. constantemente; invariablemente; de continuo; sin vacilar.

steadiness (stédines) s. firmeza; constancia; estabilidad; entereza.

steady (stédi) adj. firme; estable; seguro; prudente; juicioso; uniforme; v. calmar los nervios; mantener firme; sostener; fijar.

steak (stek) s. bistec; tajada para asar o freír.

steal (stíl) v. robar; hurtar; andar furtivamente; colarse; escaparse sin ser visto; to — **away from** quitar de en medio; esconder; to — **into a room** entrar en una pieza sin ser visto; to — **over**

ganar insensiblemente; s. robo; hurto.

stealth (stélz) s. recato, cautela, reserva; **by — a hurtadillas; a escondidas; con reserva.**

stealthy (stélzi) adj. furtivo; cauteloso; escondido; secreto.

steam (stím) s. vapor; vaho; **— engine** máquina de vapor; **— heat** calefacción de vapor; v. cocer al vapor; **with all — on a** todo vapor; **to — into port** llegar a puerto un vapor; **— is on** hay presión.

steamboat (stímbout) s. buque de vapor, especialmente vapor de río.

steamer (stímer) s. buque de vapor; trasatlántico.

steamship (stímship) s. véase **steamer**; **— company** compañía naviera.

steed (stid) s. corcel; caballo brioso; caballo de combate.

steel (stil) s. acero; adj. acerado; v. acerar; revestir de acero; fortalecer; endurecer; acorazar; **cast —** acero colado o fundido.

steep (stíp) adj. escarpado; acantilado; precipitoso; s. precipicio; despeñadero; v. empapar, impregnar, poner en infusión.

steeple (stípl) s. chapitel; espira; campanario; cúspide.

steepness (stípnes) s. pendiente abrupta; calidad de escarpado; altura (de precios).

steer (stir) s. novillo; buey; v. guiar; conducir; gobernar; dirigir el rumbo; **— wheel** volante, rueda del timón; **the car —s easily** el auto es de fácil manejo.

stem (stem) s. tallo; vástago; pedúnculo; pecíolo; caña; espiga; raíz de una palabra; pie de copa; cañón de pipa; tajamar; proa; v. resistir; represar; contener; oponerse a; ir en contra de; **to — from** provenir de.

step (step) s. paso, pisada, peldaño, escalón.

stenographer (stenógrafer) s. taquígrafo; estenógrafo.

stepfather (stépfader) s. padrastro.

stepmother (stepmoder) s. madrastra.

steppe (step) s. estepa.

sterile (stéril) adj. estéril.

sterility (steríliti) s. esterilidad.

sterilize (stérilais) v. estirilizar; desinfectar.

sterling (stérling) s. vajilla de plata esterlina; adj. genuino; puro; verdadero; **— silver plata de ley; — pound** libra esterlina.

stern (stern) adj. austero; severo; s. popa de una nave; cola; rabo.

sternness (stérnes) s. austeridad; severidad; rigor; firmeza.

stethoscope (stézoskoup) s. estetoscopio.

stevedore (stívedor) s. estibador; cargador.

stew (stiú) s. estofar; preocuparse; apurarse; s. estofado; guisado; ansiedad; agitación mental; **to be in a —** estar preocupado.

steward (stiúard) s. mayordomo; administrador; camarero de barco o o avión; **—'s room** despensa.

stewardess (stiúardes) s. camarera en los barcos o aviones.

stick (stik) s. palo; garrote; vara; bastón; batuta; raja de leña; **— of dynamite** cartucho de dinamita; **control —** palanca de mando en un avión; **— up** atraco, asalto; v. hundir; clavar; hincar; pinchar; prender con alfileres; fijar con tachuelas; pegar; encolar; unir; **to — in the mud** atascarse en el fango; **to — by** sostener, apoyar; **to — to** pegarse; adherirse tenazmente; perseverar; persistir; **to — out** proyectar, sobresalir; **to — out one's head** asomar la cabeza; **to — one's hands up** alzar las manos; **to — at nothing** no pararse en pintas; no hacer caso de nada; **to — it out** soportar las consecuencias de algo.

sticker (stiker) s. marbete engomado.

sticky (stiki) adj. pegajoso; viscoso; tenaz.

stiff (stif) s. cadáver; adj. tieso; rígido, yerto; duro; firme; aterido; tenso; estirado; obstinado; terco; **— neck** torticolis; **— climb** subida ardua o difícil; **scared —** yerto, muerto de miedo.

stiffen (stifen) v. atiesar(se); entumecer(se); aterir(se); espesar; obstinarse; aumentar la resistencia; endurecerse.

stiffness (stífnes) s. tiesura; rigidez; inflexibilidad; rigor; terquedad; espesura.

stifle (stáifl) v. sofocar; ahogar; apagar; asfixiar(se); extinguir; suprimir; callar; ocultar.

stigma (stígma) s. estigma; baldón; afrenta.

still (stíl) adj. inmóvil; fijo; mudo; silencioso; quedo; quieto; apacible; inanimado; — born nacido muerto; — life naturaleza muerta; v. aquietar; acallar; calmar; apaciguar; adv. todavía; aún; sin cesar; siempre; conj. empero, no obstante; sin embargo; s. alambique; destiladera.

stillness (stílnes) s. quietud; calma; sosiego; tranquilidad.

stilt (stilt) s. zanco; trípode; pilote; puntal.

stilted (stílted) adj. afectado; ampuloso; altisonante.

stimulant (stímiulant) adj. y s. estimulante; pl. licores embriagantes.

stimulate (stímiuleit) v. estimular.

stimulation (stimiuléshon) s. estímulo; excitación.

stimulus (stímiulos) s. estímulo.

sting (sting) v. picar; pinchar; escocer; arder; atormentar; remorder la conciencia; s. picadura; piquete; mordedura; picazón; punzada; escozor.

stinginess (stínyines) s. avaricia; tacañería; ruindad; mezquindad.

stingy (stínyi) adj. tacaño; avaro;

stink (stink) v. oler mal, apestar; s. hedor; mal olor; hediondez.

stint (stint) v. limitar; escatimar; restringir; ser frugal; ser económico o parco; to — oneself privarse de lo necesario; s. tarea; cuota; destajo.

stipulate (stípiuleit) v. estipular; condicionar; pactar.

stipulation (stipiuléshon) s. estipulación; condición; cláusula; artículo; pacto.

stir (ster) v. agitar; batir; menear; mover; excitar; suscitar; atizar; revolver; conmover; bullir; s. movimiento; conmoción; excitación; alboroto; agitación; meneo; bullicio.

stirring (stírring) adj. conmovedor.

stirrup (stírrop) s. estribo.

stitch (stitch) s. puntada de costura; v. dar puntadas; coser; back — punto atrás; chain — punto de cadeneta; cross — punto de cruz; hem — vainica.

stock (stók) v. surtir; abastecer; proveer; llevar en existencia; almacenar; s. ganado; acciones; valores; tronco; injerto; capital comercial o consolidado; existencias; estirpe; linaje; enseres; in — en existencia; live — ganado; — on hand mercancías a la mano o en almacén; to take —s tomar un inventario; joint — company sociedad por acciones; sociedad anónima; — broker corredor de bolsa; — exchange bolsa de valores; — yard matadero; corral para ganado; — dove paloma torcaz.

stockade (stokéid) s. empalizada; vallado; estancada; v. empalizar; levantar un vallado.

stockbroker (stókbroker) s. corredor de bolsa.

stockholder (stókjolder) s. accionista.

stocking (stóking) s. media.

stoic (stóik) adj. y s. estoico.

stoke (stóuk) v. atizar; cebar; alimentar un horno.

stole (stóul) pret. de to steal.

stolen (stólen) p.p. de to steal.

stolid (stólid) adj. estólido.

stomach (stómak) s. estómago; pit of the — boca del estómago.

stone (stóun) s. piedra; hueso o cuesco de las frutas; — blind, deaf o dumb completamente ciego, sordo o mudo; — quarry pedrera; cantera; v. apedrear; lapidar; quitar los huesos a las frutas.

stony (stóuni) adj. pedregoso; pétreo; de piedra; duro.

stood (stud) pret. y p.p. de to stand.

stool (stúl) s. taburete, banquillo; inodoro; —s evacuación de vientre; — pigeon delator.

stoop (stúp) v. agacharse; encorvarse; inclinarse; humillarse; rebajarse; someterse; s. encorvamiento; declinación; abatimiento; gradería; escalinata de entrada; to walk with a — andar encorvado o caído de hombros; — shouldered cargado de espaldas.

stop (stop) s. detener; interceptar; parar; suspender; cesar; dejar de; paralizar; poner coto; contener; tapar algún agujero o abertura; estancar; obstruir; to — at alojarse, hospedarse; to — at nothing no tener escrúpulos; no detenerse por nada; to — from impedir; to — payment suspender el pago; to — over at hacer escala en; to — the way obstruir, cerrar el paso; hacer alto; alojarse por algún tiempo; quedarse; s. **parada; cesación;** alto; pausa; suspensión, paro de trabajo; obstáculo; impedimento; represión; traste de guitarra; full — punto final; — **consonant** consonante explosiva.

stopover (stópover) s. parada, escala; **to make a — in** hacer escala.

stoppage (stópey) s. detención; interceptación; obstrucción; **work —** paro; interrupción; cesación.

stopper (stóper) s. tapón.

storage (stórey) s. almacenaje; **battery —** acumulador; **to keep in —** almacenar.

store (stor) v. almacenar; surtir; abastecer; guardar; **to — up** acumular; s. tienda; almacén; depósito; **—s** víveres, municiones, provisiones, abastecimientos; **department —** almacén de departamentos; **dry goods —** lencería; cajón de ropa; mercería; **grocery —** tienda de abarrotes; **shoe —** zapatería; **to have in —** tener guardado; tener almacenado.

storehouse (stórjaus) s. bodega; depósito; almacén.

storekeeper (stórkiper) s. almacenista; bodeguero.

storeroom (stórrum) s. almacén; bodega; despensa.

stork (stórk) s. cigüeña.

storm (storm) s. tempestad; tormenta; vendaval; borrasca; temporal; arrebato; furia; tumulto; conmoción; **— troops** tropas de asalto; **rain and wind —** turbonada; **snow —** nevasca; v. asaltar; atacar; enfurecerse; rabiar.

stormy (stórmi) adj. tempestuoso; turbulento; borrascoso.

story (stóri) s. historia; cuento; narración; relato; anécdota; trama; piso de un edificio; rumor; **as the — goes** según se dice; **newspaper —** artículo de periódico.

stout (stáut) adj. fornido, robusto; sólido; resuelto; animoso; corpulento; intrépido.

stove (stóuv) s. estufa; hornillo; cocina de gas o eléctrica; pret. y p.p. de **stave.**

stow (stóu) v. estibar; acomodar la carga de un barco; hacinar; colocar; meter; esconder; guardar; **to — away on a ship** embarcarse clandestinamente, esconderse en un barco.

straddle (stradl) v. ponerse o estar a horcajadas; caminar con las piernas abiertas; cabalgar.

straggle (stra) v. extraviarse; dispersarse; desbandarse; rezagarse; andar perdido.

straight (stréit) adj. recto; derecho; en línea recta; lacio; erguido; tieso; justo; equitativo; franco; sincero; íntegro; correcto; **— hair** pelo lacio; **— run** ron puro; **— hand of five cards** runfla de cinco cartas del mismo palo; **— face** cara seria; **— out** sincero; adv. directamente; al punto; inmediatamente; con honradez; con sinceridad; en línea recta; **to talk — from the soulder** hablar con toda franqueza o sinceridad; **to set someone —** dar consejos a alguien, mostrarle el camino o la forma de hacer alguna cosa.

straighten (stréiten) v. enderezar; poner en orden; arreglar.

straightforward (stréitforuard) adj. recto; íntegro; sincero; honrado; adv. de frente, en línea recta.

straightness (stréitnes) s. rectitud; integridad; honradez.

straightway (stréituei) adv. inmediatamente; luego; al instante.

strain (stréin) s. tensión; estiramiento; esfuerzo; lesión; torcedura; contorsión; abuso; estilo; raza; linaje; tonada; aire; melodía; v. estirar demasiado; forzar; esforzarse; torcer; retorcer; estrechar; abrazar; colar.

strainer (stréiner) s. coladera, cedazo; tamiz; colador.

strait (stréit) s. estrecho; **—s** estrecho; apuro; aprieto; **— jacket** camisa de fuerza.

strand (strand) v. encallar; embarrancar; quedarse perdido, aislado en algún sitio; extraviarse; **to be —ed on the road** quedarse atascado, perdido o aislado en mitad del camino; s. costa; ribera; playa; ramal; hebra; cabo; **— of hair** trenza; guedeja; **— of pearls** hilo de perlas.

strange (stréiny) adj. extraño; raro; desconocido; extraordinario; singular; peregrino.

strangeness (stréinynes) s. extrañeza; rareza; alejamiento, reserva.

stranger (stréinyer) s. extranjero; extraño; forastero, desconocido.
strangle (strangl) v. estrangular.
strap (strap) s. tirante; correa; faja; precinto; trabilla; gaza; metal — banda de metal; v. atar; amarrar con correas; precintar; azotar con correa.
stratagem (stráteyen) s. estratagema; ardid; artimaña.
strategic (stratéyic) s. estratégico.
strategy (stráteyi) s. estrategia.
stratosphere (strátosfir) s. estratosfera.
straw (stroh) s. paja; nonada; fruslería; not to care a — no importarle a uno nada; adj. de paja; — hat sombrero de paja; — vote voto no oficial para averiguar la opinión pública; stack of — pajar.
strawberry (stróberri) s. fresa.
stray (stréi) v. extraviarse; descarriarse; perder el camino; errar; adj. extraviado, descarriado, perdido; s. persona descarriada o animal perdido.
streak (strik) s. raya; línea; rasgo de ingenio; traza; pizca; antojo; rayo de luz; v. rayar; listar.
stream (strim) s. corriente; arroyuelo; río; torrente; raudal; chorro, flujo; **down —, up —** río abajo, río arriba; v. manar, brotar; fluir; derramar con abundancia, salir a torrentes; ondear; flotar; flamear; pasar dejando un rayo de luz.
streamer (strímer) s. banderola; gallardete; listón.
street (strit) s. calle.
streetcar (strítcar) s. tranvía.
strength (strenz) s. fuerza; vigor; energía; potencia; pujanza; fortaleza; validez; on the — of his promise basado en su promesa.
strengthen (strénzen) v. fortalecer; fortificar; reforzar; infundir brío; alentar.
strenous (strénous) adj. tenaz; vigoroso; enérgico; persistente.
stress (stres) v. acentuar; recalcar; dar énfasis; hacer hincapié; s. fuerza; importancia; tensión; compulsión; acento tónico; énfasis.
stretch (stretch) v. alargarse; extenderse; estirarse; dar de sí; desplegarse; ensanchar; **to — oneself** estirarse; desperezarse; **to — out one's hand** tender la mano; s. extensión; tensión; esfuerzo; alcance; trecho; distancia; lapso; bordada; **home —** último trecho de una carrera.
stretcher (strétcher) s. atesador; dilatador; camilla; andas; (alb.) clave; (carp.) vigueta; madero; tirante; peana; pedestal de bote.
stricken (striken) p.p. de to strike; herido; agobiado; afligido.
strict (strikt) adj. estricto; riguroso; escrupuloso; severo; áspero; **—ly** exactamente, estrictamente confidencial; con toda reserva.
stridden (stridn) p.p. de to stride.
stride (stráid) v. caminar a paso largo; dar zancadas; s. paso largo; tranco; zancada.
strife (stráif) s. contienda; refriega; pleito; disputa.
strike (stráik) v. pegar; golpear; herir; chocar con; encontrar (oro, plata; petróleo, etc.); encender un fósforo; ocurrirle a uno una idea; causar una impresión, parecer; asumir una actitud o postura; arriar la bandera; declararse o ir a la huelga; sonar las campanas; **to — at** acometer; amagar; **to — out** borrar; tachar; **to — back** devolver golpe por golpe; **to — a vein** descubrir una veta; **to — into** comenzar repentinamente; **to — one's attention** atraer o llamarle a uno la atención; **to — upon** suceder por casualidad; **to — against** estrellarse, chocar con; **to — up a friendship** trabar amistad con; **to — down** derribar; arriar; **to — out in a certain direction** tomar determinado rumbo; encaminarse en cierta dirección; **to — through** atravesar; traspasar; s. golpe; descubrimiento; huelga; ganga; medida; **— breaker** esquirol, rompehuelgas; **general —** huelga general, paro.
striker (stráiker) s. huelguista.
striking (stráiking) adj. sorprendente; llamativo; notable; conspicuo; manifiesto; extraordinario; que está en huelga.
string (string) s. cuerda, cinta, sarta; v. ensartar, tender, encordelar, engañar.
strip (strip) v. desnudar; desvestir; robar; despojar; cortar en tiras; desmantelar; **to — the gears** estropear los engranes; **to — the skin from** desollar; pelar;

— 225 —

s. tira; listón; faja; jirón; — of land faja de tierra.
stripe (stráip) s. tira; franja; lista; raya; banda; barra; índole; género; v. rayar; listar.
striped (stráipt) adj. rayado, listado; adornado con rayas.
strive (stráiv) v. esforzarse, hacer lo posible; luchar; contender; procurar; **to — for** esforzarse por conseguir o lograr algo.
striven (stríven) p.p. de to strive.
strode (stróud) pret. de to stride.
stroke (stróuk) s. golpe; carrera (de un émbolo); golpe de remo; toque; rasgo; pincelada; plumada; campanada del reloj; ataque fulminante; jugada; hazaña; proeza; éxito; caricia con la mano; **— of lightning** rayo; **— of the hand** caricia; **— of a painter's brush** pincelada; v. pasar la mano por la espalda; acariciar; frotar con suavidad; ranurar la piedra con cincel.
stroll (stról) v. pasear a pie; vagar; s. paseo.
strong (strong) adj. fuerte; vigoroso; fornido; poderoso; sólido; recio; enérgico; pujante; firme; acérrimo; pronunciado; picante; concentrado (el vino); impetuoso; activo; **— cofee** café muy cargado; **— bodied** corpulento; **— market** mercado firme; adv. fuertemente.
stronghold (stróngjould) s. plaza fuerte; fuerte.
strop (strop) v. asentar navajas de afeitar; s. asentador.
strove (stróuv) pret. de to strive.
struck (strók) pret. y p.p. de to strike; **to be —** with a disease darle a uno una enfermedad; to be **— w** i terror estar sobrecogido de terror.
structural (strókchurel) adj. estructural.
structure (strókchur) s. estructura; construcción; edificio.
struggle (strógl) s. esfuerzo, contención; pugna; lucha; pelea; v. esforzarse; contender; pugnar; luchar; pelear.
strung (strong) pret. y p.p. de to string.
strut (strot) s. tirante; puntal; ademe; riostra; v. contonearse; pavonearse; por extensión: contoneo.
stub (stob) s talón (de un libro talonario, de un boleto; etc.); colilla de cigarro; pedazo; fragmento; **— book** libro talonario; v. tropezar con una cosa baja.
stubble (stóbl) s. rastrojo; cañón de la barba.
stubborn (stóborn) adj. necio, terco; obstinado; porfiado.
stubborness (stóbornes) s. terquedad; necedad, obstinación; porfía.
stucco (stóko) s. estuco; v. estucar, cubrir de estuco.
stuck (stók) pret. y p.p. de to stick; pegado; atorado; atascado; **— full of holes** agujereado; **— up** tieso; estirado; orgulloso.
stud (stód) s. tachón; pasador; perno, prisionero; botón postizo de camisa; **— horse** caballo padre; v. tachonar; clavetear.
student (stiúdent) s. estudiante.
studied (stódid) adj. estudiado; premeditado.
studio (stiúdio) s. estudio, taller.
studious (stiúdios) adj. estudioso; aplicado; asiduo, diligente.
study (stódi) s. estudio; asignatura; solicitud; aplicación; cuidado; v. estudiar; observar; investigar.
stuff (stóf) s. material; substancia; materia prima; cosa, objeto; baratija; desperdicio; fruslería; género; paño; tela; menjurje; pócima; **of good —** de buen material; v. henchir; rellenar; atestar; atiborrar; **—ed celery** apio relleno.
stuffing (stófing) s. relleno.
stumpy (stómpi) adj. rechoncho; cachigordete; lleno de tocones.
stun (ston) v. aturdir; atontar; atolondrar; s. choque, golpe o sacudimiento que aturde.
stung (stóng) pret. y p.p. del v. to sting.
stunk (stónk) pret. y p.p. del v. to stink.
stunning (stóning) adj. aplastante; elegante; bellísimo.
stunt (stónt) v. impedir el desarrollo o crecimiento de; achaparrar; hacer suertes, piruetas, malabarismos, acrobacias; s. suerte; acto acrobático; ejercicio de habilidad o destreza.
stupefy (stiúpefai) v. causar estupor; dejar estupefacto; atontar; pasmar; atolondrar.

stupendous (stiupéndos) adj. estupendo.
stupid (stiúpid) adj. estúpido; atontado; lelo; necio; estólido.
stupidity (stiupíditi) s. estupidez.
stupor (stiúpor) s. estupor; atontamiento; letargo; modorra.
sturdy (stórdi) adj. fornido; vigoroso; tenaz; fuerte; firme.
stutter (stóter) v. tartamudear; s. tartamudeo; tartamudez.
stutterer (stóterer) s. tartamudo.
stuttering (stótering) adj. tartamudo; s. tartamudeo.
sty (stái) s. zahurda, pocilga; orzuelo en el párpado; perrilla.
style (stáil) s. estilo; modo o manera; moda; género; tratamiento; estilete; to be in — estar de moda; v. intitular; nombrar.
stylish (stáilish) adj. elegante; a la moda.
subdivision (sobdivíshon) s. subdivisión; parcelación de terrenos.
subdue (sobdiú) v. subyugar; someter, sojuzgar; avasallar; domar; amasar; — tone tono sumiso.
subdued (sobdiúd) p.p. de to subdue; adj. sumiso; sujeto; manso; tenue.
subject (sóbyekt) s. súbdito; sujeto; materia; asunto; tema; individuo; — matter materia, asunto de que se trata; adj. sujeto, expuesto, propenso; inclinado; v. sujetar; someter; sojuzgar; avasallar.
subjection (sobyékshon) s. sujeción; yugo; dominación; sumisión.
subjugate (sóbyugueit) v. subyugar.
sublime (sobláim) adj. sublime.
submarine (sobmarín) s. submarino.
submerge (sobméry) v. sumergir (se); zambullirse; hundir; sumir(se).
submission (sobmíshon) s. sumisión; sometimiento; obediencia.
submissive (sobmísiv) adj. sumiso.
submit (sobmít) v. someter; presentar; rendir (un informe); to — to punishment someterse al castigo; to — a report rendir un informe.
subordinate (sobórdineit) adj. y s. subordinado; subalterno; inferior; v. subordinar; posponer; someter.
subscribe (sobscráib) v. subscribirse; firmar; rubricar; to — five dollars dar cinco dólares de cuota; to — for suscribirse a; abonarse a; to — to a plan aprobar un plan; consentir.
subscriber (sobcráiber) s. subscritor; abonado; infrascrito; el que subscribe; firmante.
subscription (sobskrípshon) s. subscripción; abono.
subsequent (sóbsikuent) adj. subsecuente; subsiguiente; posterior; —ly adv. subsecuentemente; después; posteriormente.
subservient (sobsérvient) adj. servil; servicial; útil.
subside (sobsáid) v. apaciguarse; calmarse; bajar de nivel (un fluido); menguar.
subsidize (sóbsidais) v. subvencionar.
subsidy (sóbsidi) s. subvención;
subsist (sobsíst) v. subsistir; perdurar; conservarse; existir.
substance (sóbtans) s. substancia; naturaleza de las cosas.
substantial (substánshal) adj. sustancial; sustancioso; sólido; resistente; cuantioso; importante; material; esencial; to be in — agreement estar de acuerdo substancialmente con.
substantive (sóbstantiv) adj. y s. sustantivo.
substitute (sóbstitiut) v. substituir; reemplazar; s. sustituto; suplente; reemplazo.
substitution (sobstitúshon) s. sustitución; reemplazo.
subterranean (sobterrénien) adj subterráneo.
subtle (sobtl) adj. sutil.
subtlety (sóbtleti) s. sutileza; agudeza; artificio; astucia.
subtract (sobtrákt) v. sustraer; restar.
subtraction (sobtrékshon) s. resta; sustracción.
suburb (sóborb) s. suburbio, arrabal.
suburban (sobórban) adj. y s. suburbano; arrabalero.
subversive (sobvérsiv) adj. subversivo; trastornador del orden; destructivo.
subway (sóbuei) s. ferrocarril subterráneo; metro.
succeed (soksíd) v. ser el sucesor

de; reemplazar; tener éxito; salir bien; lograr; conseguir.
success (soksés) s. éxito; triunfo.
successful (soksésful) adj. próspero; afortunado; venturoso; to be — tener éxito; —ly adv. felizmente; prósperamente; con éxito.
succession (sokséshon) s. sucesión.
successive (soksésiv) adj. sucesivo
successor (soksésor) s. sucesor.
succor (sókor) s. socorro; v. socorrer.
succumb (sokóm) v. sucumbir.
such (sóch) adj. tal, igual, semejante; — a thing cosa semejante; — as aquel que; cualquiera que; adv. tan; — a good man un hombre tan bueno.
suck (sók) v. chupar; mamar; sorber; s. chupada; mamada.
sucker (sóker) s. chupador; dulce que se chupa; pelele, primo; incauto.
suckle (sókl) v. mamar, amamantar; dar de mamar; lactar.
suction (sókshon) s. succión; aspiración; — pump bomba aspirante.
sudden (sódn) adj. repentino; súbito; imprevisto; inesperado; precipitado; all of a — de pronto; repentinamente; —ly adv. de repente; de súbito; inesperadamente.
suddenness (sódnes) s. precipitación; rapidez.
suds (sóds) s. jabonaduras; espuma.
sue (sú) v. demandar; entablar juicio; to — for damages demandar por daños y perjuicios.
suet (siúet) s. sebo; grasa en rama.
suffer (sófer) v. sufrir.
sufferer (sóferer) s. paciente, víctima.
suffering (sófering) s. sufrimiento; pena; dolor; padecimiento.
suffice (sofáis) v. bastar; alcanzar; ser bastante o suficiente.
sufficient (soféshent) adj. suficiente; bastante; amplio; —ly adv. suficientemente; asaz.
suffocate (sófokeit) v. sofocar(se); ahogar(se); asfixiar(se).
suffocation (sofokéshon) s. asfixia, sofocación; ahogo.
suffrage (sófrey) s. sufragio, voto.
sugar (shúgar) s. azúcar; — bowl azucarera; — cane caña de azúcar; lump of — terrón de azúcar; — beet remolacha; brown — piloncillo.

suggest (soyést) v. sugerir; indicar.
suggestion (soyéschon) s. sugestión; sugerencia; indicación.
suggestive (soyéstiv) adj. sugestivo.
suicide (siúisaid) s. suicidio; to commit — suicidarse.
suit (sút) s. traje, terno, flux; petición; súplica; cortejo; pleito; litigio; serie; colección; palo de la baraja; v. convenir; acomodar; venir bien; sentar; satisfacer; — yourself haga usted lo que le parezca, lo que le guste.
suitable (sútabl) adj. apropiado, conveniente; adecuado; propio; a propósito, satisfactorio.
suitably (sútabli) adv. de manera conveniente; satisfactoriamente.
suitcase (sútkeis) s. maleta, valija.
suite (suit) s. serie, séquito; comitiva; — of rooms apartamento; vivienda; habitación; bedroom — juego de muebles para recámara.
suitor (sútor) s. demandante; parte actora; galán, pretendiente.
sulk (sólk) v. amodorrarse, estar malhumorado; s. murria.
sulky (sólki) adj. arisco; amodorrado; malhumorado; huraño.
sullen (sólen) adj. hosco, adusto; sombrío; taciturno; tétrico.
sully (sóli) v. manchar; ensuciar; mancillar; empañar.
sulphate (sólfeit) s. sulfato.
sulphide (sólfaid) s. sulfito; sulfuro.
sulphuric (solfiúrik) adj. sulfúrico; — acid ácido sulfúrico.
sultan (sóltan) s. sultán.
sultry (sóltri) adj. bochornoso; sofocante; — heat bochorno.
sum (som) s. suma; total; monto; esencia; in — en suma; en breve; v. to — up sumar.
summarize (sómarais) v. resumir; compendiar; epitomar.
summary (sómeri) s. sumario; resumen; compendio; adj. sumario, breve.
summer (sómer) s. verano; estío; adj. veraniego; estival; de verano; — resort balneario; lugar de veraneo; v. veranear.
summit (sómit) s. cima; cumbre; pináculo; cúspide; ápice.
summon (sómon) v. citar; convocar; requerir; —s s. notificación;

cita judicial; emplazamiento; requerimiento; intimación.
sumptuous (sómpchuos) adj. suntuoso.
sun (son) s. sol; v. asolear.
sunburn (sónbern) s. quemadura de sol; v. asolear(se); requemarse al sol; tostarse al sol.
Sunday (sóndei) s. domingo.
sundial (sóndaial) s. cuadrante solar; reloj de sol.
sundown (sóndaun) s. puesta de sol.
sundry (sóndri) adj. varios, diversos.
sunflower (sónflauer) s. girasol.
sung (song) pret. y p.p. de to sing
sunk (sonk) pret. y p.p. de to sink.
sunken (sónken) adj. hundido; sumido.
sunlight (sónlait) s. luz de sol; luz solar.
sunny (sóni) adj. asoleado; soleado; resplandeciente; alegre; risueño; — **day** día de sol.
sunrise (sónrais) s. amanecer; salida del sol.
sunset (sónset) s. puesta de sol; crepúsculo vespertino.
sunshine (sónshain) s. luz del sol; solana; **in the —** al sol.
sunstroke (sónstrouk) s. insolación.
sup (sop) v. cenar.
superb (supérb) adj. soberbio; grandioso; magnífico; espléndido.
superficial (superfíshal) adj. superficial; aparente; somero.
superfluous (supérfluos) adj. superfluo; sobrante.
superhuman (superjiúman) adj. sobrehumano.
superintend (superinténd) v. inspeccionar; dirigir; vigilar.
superintendent (superinténdent) s. superintendente; inspector; capataz.
superior (supírior) adj. y s. superior.
superiority (superióriti) s. superioridad.
superlative (supérlativ) adj. y s. superlativo.
supernatural (supernáchural) adj. sobrenatural.
supersede (supersíd) v. reemplazar.
superstition (superstíshon) s. superstición.
superstitious (superstíshos) adj. supersticioso.

supervise (superváis) v. supervisar, inspeccionar, vigilar.
supervision (supervíshon) s. supervisión; inspección; vigilancia.
supervisor (superváisor) s. supervisor; sobrestante; inspector.
supper (sóper) s. cena.
supplant (soplánt) v. suplantar.
supple (sópl) adj. flexible, dócil.
supplement (sóplement) s. suplemento; apéndice; v. suplir, suplementar.
supplication (soplikéshon) s. súplica; ruego; petición; preces.
supply (soplái) v. proveer, surtir; s. provisión, surtido.
support (sopórt) v. sostener; mantener; soportar; aguantar; s. sostén, apoyo; puntal; sustento; manutención; **point of —** punto de apoyo; **in — of** en favor de.
supporter (sopórter) s. defensor; partidario; sostén; soporte.
suppose (sopóus) v. suponer.
supposed (sopóusd) adj. supuesto; presunto; **— ly** adv. supuestamente.
suppress (soprés) v. suprimir; sofocar; reprimir; eliminar; parar; suspender.
suppression (sopréshon) s. supresión; represión; extinción.
supremacy (soprémasi) s. supremacía.
supreme (supprím) adj. supremo.
sure (shúr) adj. seguro, indudable; efectivo, firme; certero; cierto; **be — and do it** hágalo sin falta; sin duda; ciertamente.
surety (shúrti) s. seguridad; garantía; fianza.
surf (sérf) s. rompiente; marejada; oleaje; resaca.
surface (sórfeis) s. superficie; cara; v. allanar, alisar.
surfeit (sórfit) s. empacho; hastío; exceso; indigestión; v. hastiarse; saciarse; empalagarse.
surge (séry) v. agitarse o embravecerse el mar; romper las olas; s. oleaje; oleada; marejada.
surgeon (séryon) s. cirujano.
surgery (séryeri) s. cirujía.
surgical (séryikal) adj. quirúrgico.
surly (sérli) adj. arisco, rudo; insolente; malhumorado.
surmise (sormáis) v. conjeturar; presumir; suponer; imaginarse; s. conjetura; suposición.
surmount (sormáunt) v. superar; vencer; sobrepujar.

surname (sérneim) s. sobrenombre; mote; **apellido**; v. apellidarse.
surpass (serpás) v. sobrepasar; exceder; superar; aventajar; ganar.
surpassing (serpásing) adj. sobresaliente; excelente; superior.
surplus (sérplos) s. sobrante, excedente; superávit; adj. sobrante; excedente; de sobra.
surprise (sorpráis) s. sorpresa; v. sorprender.
surprising (sorpráising) adj. sorprendente; asombroso.
surrender (sorrénder) v. rendir(se); entregar(se); darse, ceder; s. rendición; entrega; cesión, sumisión.
surround (sorráund) v. circundar; rodear; sitiar; asediar.
surrounding (sorráunding) adj. circundante; circunstante.
surroundings (sorráundings) s. pl. alrededores; cercanías; contornos; inmediaciones; ambiente.
surveyor (servéior) s. agrimensor.
survival (serváival) s. supervivencia; sobreviviente; resto.
survive (serváiv) v. sobrevivir; salvarse.
survivor (serváivor) s. sobreviviente.
susceptible (soséptibl) adj. susceptible; capaz; delicado; propenso; sensible.
suspect (sospékt) v. sospechar; recelar; s. sospechoso.
suspend (sospénd) v. suspender.
suspenders (sospénders) s. pl. tirantes (de pantalón).
suspension (sospénshon) s. suspensión; — **bridge** puente colgante.
suspicion (sospíshon) s. sospecha.
suspicious (sospíshos) adj. suspicaz; desconfiado; receloso.
sustain (sostéin) v. sostener; resistir; sustentar; aguantar; sufrir un daño o pérdida; apoyar.
sustenance (sóstenans) s. sustento; subsistencia; manutención; alimentos.
swagger (suáguer) v. pavonearse, contonearse; baladronear; s. pavoneo; contoneo; baladronada.
swain (suéin) s. galán; enamorado.
swallow (suálou) s. trago; deglución; golondrina; v. tragar, deglutir.
swam (suam) pret de to swim.
swamp (suámp) s. pantano; ciénaga; fangal; — **land** terreno pantanoso; v. sumergir(se); hundir (se); **to be —ed with work** estar abrumado de trabajo.
swampy (suómpi) adj. pantanoso; cenagoso; fangoso.
swan (suón) s. cisne.
swap (suóp) v. cambiar; permutar; trocar; s. cambio, permuta, trueque.
swarm (suórm) s. enjambre; multitud; hormiguero; v. pulular; bullir; hervir; hormiguear.
swarthy (suórzi) adj. trigueño; moreno; prieto.
swat (suót) v. pegar; aporrear; aplastar de golpe; s. golpe.
sway (suéi) v. ladearse, inclinarse; oscilar; mecerse; tambalear; balancearse; izar; guindar; inducir; s. vaivén; oscilación; balanceo; poder; predominio; influjo; preponderancia; **to hold —** regir.
swear (suer) v. jurar; renegar; blasfemar; maldecir; proferir palabras obscenas; juramentar; prestar juramento; **to — by** poner toda su confianza implícita en; **to — off** jurar no volver a hacer alguna cosa; renunciar a ella.
sweat (suét) v. sudar; exudar; s. sudor; fatiga; exudación.
sweater (suéter) s. suéter; sudadera; el que suda.
sweaty (suéti) adj. sudoroso.
Swede (suíd) s. sueco.
Swedish (suídish) adj. sueco.
sweep (suíp) v. barrer; deshollinar; arrebatar; dragar; extenderse; **to — down upon** caer sobre; asolar; **to — along** pasar majestuosamente, con garbo; **to — away** barrer con todo; s. barredura; extensión; recorrido; soplo; aspa de molino; curva descrita; vuelta; giro.
sweeper (suíper) s. barrendero; barredora; **carpet —** escoba mecánica.
sweeping (suíping) s. barrido; pl. barreduras; basura; adj. arrebatador; vasto; comprensivo; que lo abarca todo; — **victory** victoria completa.
sweet (suít) adj. dulce; sabroso; oloroso; melodioso; bello; hermoso; suave; afable; fresco; s. dulzura; deleite; persona querida; pl. dulces, golosinas; — **butter** mantequilla sin sal; — **oil**

aceite de oliva; — scented perfumado; **my —!** ¡mi vida!, ¡mi alma!

sweeten (suítn) v. endulzar; dulcificar; suavizar; aplacar.

sweetheart (suítjart) s. novia; prometida; querida; amante; galán; novio; pretendiente.

sweetmeat (suítmit) s. dulce, golosina; confitura.

sweetness (suítnes) s. dulzura; delicadeza; suavidad; bondad.

swell (suél) v. hinchar; inflar; henchir; distender; dilatar; engreír; abotagarse; hincharse; esponjarse; s. hinchazón; aumento de volumen; oleada, marejada; protuberancia; adj. elegante; excelente; magnífico; encantador; de buen tono.

swelling (suéling) s. hinchazón; tumefacción; turgencia; abotagamiento; **— brest** pecho turgente.

swept (suépt) pret. y p.p. de **to sweep**.

swerve (suérv) v. desviar(se); apartar(se); cambiar violentamente de rumbo; extraviarse; s. desvío brusco; cambio repentino de dirección; **to make a — to the right** torcer a la derecha.

swift (suíft) adj. veloz; vivo; rápido.

swiftness (suíftnes) s. ligereza; velocidad; prontitud; presteza.

swim (suím) v. nadar; flotar; padecer vahídos; **to — with the tide** dejarse llevar por la corriente; **my head is —ming** se me va la cabeza; estoy desvanecido.

swimmer (suímer) s. nadador.

swindle (suíndl) v. estafar; s. estafa.

swine (suáin) s. cerdo; marrano; cochino; puerco.

swing (suíng) v. columpiar(se); mecer(se); oscilar; hacer oscilar; balancear(se); girar; blandir; vibrar; dar vueltas; **to — a deal** llevar a cabo un negocio; **to — around** dar vueltas; girar; **to — open** abrirse repentinamente (una puerta); **to — clear** evitar un choque; s. oscilación; vaivén; balanceo; columpio; hamaca; mecedora; libertad de acción; **to give seomeone full —** darle a alguien completa libertad de acción; compás; golpe; puñetazo.

swipe (suáip) v. hurtar; dar o golpear duro.

swirl (suírl) v. arremolinar(se); girar; dar vueltas; s. remolino; torbellino; vueltas; movimiento giratorio.

Swiss (suis) adj. y s. suizo.

switch (suitch) s. latiguillo; azote; chicote; rebenque; bastoncillo; pelo postizo; **electric —** interruptor; conmutador; **railway —** aguja; cambio; **— man** cambiavía; v. azotar; desviar; cambiar; **to — off** apagar la luz; cortar la corriente; **to — on** the light encender la luz.

switchboard (suítchbourd) s. tablero de distribución; conmutador.

swollen (suólen) p.p. de **to swell**.

swoon (súun) v. desmayarse; desvanecerse; perder el sentido; s. desmayo; desvanecimiento; síncope.

swoop (súup) v. descender; precipitarse sobre algo; agarrar la presa al vuelo; acometer; **to — down upon** caer de súbito sobre; **to — up** arrebatar; **to — off** cortar de golpe; s. descenso súbito.

sword (sord) s. espada.

swore (suór) pret. de **to swear**.

sworn (suorn) p.p. de **to swear**.

swum (suom) p.p. de **to swim**.

swung (suong) pret. y p.p. de **to swing**.

syllable (sílabl) s. sílaba.

symbol (símbol) s. símbolo.

symbolic (simbólik) adj. simbólico.

symbolism (símbolism) s. simbolismo.

symmetrical (cimétrikal) adj. simétrico; proporcionado.

symmetry (símetri) s. simetría.

sympathetic (simpazétik) adj. simpático; que causa o experimenta simpatía; compasivo; **— towards** favorablemente dispuesto hacia.

sympathize (símpazais) v. simpatizar; compadecerse; condolerse; convenir; armonizarse.

sympathy (símpazi) s. simpatía; armonía; lástima; compasión; afinidad; conmiseración; **to extend one's —** dar el pésame.

symphony (símfoni) s. sinfonía; **— orchestra** orquesta sinfónica.

symptom (símptom) s. síntoma.

syndicate (síndikeit) s. sindicato; **newspaper —** sindicato de periodistas; v. sindicarse; formar un sindicato; asociarse para formar un sindicato; vender (un

SYNONYM   **TAKE**

cuento; caricatura; serie de artículos, etc.) a un sindicato o a través del mismo.
synonym (sínonim) s. sinónimo.
syntax (síntaks) s. sintaxis.
synthesis (sínzesis) s. síntesis; reunión de parte divididas.
synthetic (sinzétik) adj. sintético; lo contrario de analítico.
syringe (síriny) s. jeringa (para aplicar inyecciones).
syrup véase sirup.
system (sístem) s. sistema.
systematic (sistemátik) adj. sistemático.

T

tabernacle (tábernakl) s. tabernáculo.
table (téibl) s. mesa; cuadro sinóptico; meseta; tarima; tablero; — **cover** mantel, cubremesa; — **land** altiplanicie; meseta; v. catalogar; poner índice; tender sobre la mesa; **to — a motion** dar carpetazo a una moción.
tablecloth (téiblcloz) s. mantel.
tablespoon (téiblspun) s. cuchara grande; cuchara sopera.
tablespoonful (téiblspunful) s. cucharada grande.
tablet (táblet) s. tableta; pastilla; bloc de papel; plancha; lápida.
tableware (téibluer) s. vajilla; servicio de mesa.
tabulate (tábiuleit) v. tabular; formar tablas o listas.
tacit (tásit) adj. tácito.
taciturn (tásitorn) adj. taciturno; callado; silencioso.
tackle (takl) s. aparejo; maniobra; cuadernal; jarcia; avíos; equipo; agarrada (en futbol); **fishing —** avíos de pescar; v. agarrar; asir; atajar; atacar; acometer una empresa.
tact (takt) s. tacto, tino, diplomacia; tiento.
tactful (táktful) adj. cauto; prudente; diplomático.
tactics (táktiks) s. táctica.
tactless (táktles) adj. imprudente; incauto; falto de tacto.
taffeta (táfeta) s. tafetán.
tag (tag) s. etiqueta; marbete; marca; rótulo; apéndice; rabo; cabo; **to play —** jugar a la roña; v. pegar un marbete; poner una etiqueta; **to — after** pisar los talones a; **to — something**

on to juntar, añadir, agregar algo a.
tail (téil) s. cola; rabo; apéndice; extremidad; — **light** calavera de un automóvil; farol trasero.
tailor (téilor) s. sastre.
taint (teint) s. mancha, corrupción; máscula; v. manchar; corromper; podrirse; inficionar(se).
take (téik) v. tomar; coger; recibir; llevar; conducir; apropiarse; apoderarse de; restar; deducir; prender, hacer prisionero; escoger; interpretar de cierto modo; asumir; emplear; coger una enfermedad; prender la vacuna; adherirse; arraigar las plantas; **to — after** parecerse a; seguir el ejemplo de; **to — advantage of** aprovecharse de; **to — away** quitar; llevarse; **to — oath** prestar juramento; **to — back** retractarse; desdecirse; **to — cold** resfriarse, acatarrarse; **to — down** tomar nota de; asentar; **to — heed** hacer caso; **to — over** tomar posesión de; **to — offense** ofenderse; **to — up** alzar; levantar; tratar un asunto; **to — up space** ocupar espacio; **to — off** despegar un avión; parodiar; **to — leave** despedirse; **to — in** achicar un vestido; disminuir el gasto; encoger; abarcar; tragar; engañar; **to — the lead** tomar la directiva; **to — charge of** encargarse de; **to — to** dedicarse a; tomar afición a; retirarse; **to — aim** apuntar; **to — on a responsibility** asumir la responsabilidad; **to — place** efectuarse, verificarse; tener efecto; **to — a leap** dar un salto; **to — to one's bed** enfermar, caer en cama; **to — care of** atender; cuidar de; **to — a chance** aventurarse; correr un riesgo; **to — a look at** mirar; echar una mirada a; **to — stock** sacar inventario; **to — the floor** tomar la palabra; **to — to heart** tomar a pecho, tomar en serio; **to — to pieces** hacer pedazos; desarmar; refutar punto por punto; **to — to one's heels** poner pies en polvorosa; **to — a notion to** antojársele a uno; **to — for granted** dar por sentado; tomar por hecho; **to — hold** apropiarse; apoderarse de; dirigir; administrar; **to — pity** apiadarse o compade-

cerse de; I — it that supongo que; — **notice** aviso, advertencia; s. toma; redada; — **off** despegue de un aeroplano; caricatura; remedo, parodia.

taken (télkn) p.p. de to take.

talcum (tálkum) s. talco; talco pulverizado.

tale (teil) s. cuento; relato; fábula; rondalla; novela; chisme; **to tell —s** contar cuentos o chismes; murmurar.

talebearer (télberer) s. soplón.

talk (toc) v. hablar, charlar, platicar; s. conservación, charla.

talker (tóker) s. orador; platicador; hablador; conversador.

tall (tól) adj. alto; de elevada estatura; **six feet —** de seis pies de estatura; seis pies de altura.

tallow (tálou) s. sebo.

tally (táll) s. tarja, tara, cuenta; **— sheet** plana para llevar la cuenta; **to tally up** contar; sumar; v. corresponder con; estar conforme; cuadrar; concordar con.

tame (téim) v. amansar, domar; domeñar; domesticar; s. dócil; manso; humilde; sumiso; pálido; falto de colorido; poco animado.

tamper (támper) v. alterar o falsificar un documento; jugar con; meterse con; **to — with a lock** tratar de forzar una cerradura.

tan (tan) v. curtir; tostar; quemar; azotar; s. casca; color moreno amarillento que tira a rojo; color canela; **— yard** tenería; adj. tostado; requemado por el sol; bayo; de color canela; amarillento.

tangent (tányent) adj. y s. tangente, **to go off at a —** salirse por la tangente.

tangerine (tányerin) s. naranja mandarina; adj. tangerino.

tangible (tányibl) adj. tangible; palpable; corpóreo.

tangle (tángl) v. enredar; enmarañar; embrollar; confundir; s. enredo; maraña; embrollo; confusión.

tank (tank) s. tanque; depósito; cisterna; **swimming —** piscina.

tanner (táner) s. curtidor.

tannery (táneri) s. tenería.

tantalize (tántalais) v. atormentar; desesperar; exasperar.

tantrum (tántrum) s. berrinche; acceso de cólera; rabieta.

tap (tap) v. tocar ligeramente; dar golpecitos o palmadas; taladrar; extraer; **to — a tree** sangrar un árbol; s. palmada; golpecito; espita; grifo; **on —** que se saca de un barril; mostrador de taberna.

tape (téip) s. cinta; tira de metal; galoncillo; melindre; **— measure** cinta de medir; **— worm** solitaria; **adhesive —** tela adhesiva, esparadrapo; v. atar o vendar con cinta; medir con cinta.

taper (télper) s. bujía; cerilla; vela pequeña; cirio de una iglesia; disminución gradual; cono; v. adelgazar o disminuir gradualmente; **to — off** ahusarse, disminuir hasta rematar en punta.

tapestry (tápestri) s. tapiz; tapicería; cortinajes; colgaduras.

tapioca (tapióka) s. tapioca.

tar (tar) s. alquitrán; brea; **coal —** alquitrán de hulla; **mineral —** betún; v. alquitranar; embrear.

tardy (tárdi) adj. tardo; lento; tardío; negligente; que no sucede en tiempo oportuno.

target (tárguet) s. blanco; **— practice** tiro al blanco.

tariff (tárif) s. tarifa; arancel; derechos o impuestos.

tarnish (tárnish) v. empañar; deslustrar; manchar; enmohecerse; s. falta de lustre; empañamiento.

tarry (tárri) v. tardarse, demorarse; adj. embreado, alquitranado.

tart (tárt) adj. acre, ácido, acerbo; picante; agridulce; mordaz; s. tartaleta; torta rellena con dulce de frutas; pastelillo de frutas; **— reply** respuesta mordaz.

task (tásk) s. tarea; quehacer; labor; obra; faena; **to take to —** reprender; regañar.

tassel (tásel) s. borla; campanilla.

taste (téist) v. gustar; saborear; catar; probar; paladear; experimentar; ensayar; **it —s sweet** sabe dulce; tiene un sabor dulce; s. gusto; sabor; sorbo; prueba; ensayo; afición; **after —** dejo; **a matter of —** cuestión de gusto; **to have a — for** gustarle a uno algo.

tasteless (téistles) adj. insípido; desabrido; soso; de mal gusto.

tasty (téisti) adj. sabroso; agradable al paladar; gustoso.

tatter (táter) s. harapo; andrajo; hilacho; guiñapo.
tattered (táterd) adj. harapiento; andrajoso; roto.
tattle (tátl) v. chismear; murmurar; s. habladuría, murmuración, chisme; — **tale** chismoso; soplón.
taught (tót) pret. y p.p. de to teach.
taunt (tónt) v. vilipendiar; mofarse de; reprochar; s. mofa; vituperio.
tavern (távern) s. taberna; posada.
tax (taks) s. impuesto; tributo; gabela; contribución; exacción; v. imponer contribuciones, tributos, etc.; abrumar; abusar de; — **payer** contribuyente; — **collector** recaudador de rentas o impuestos.
taxation (takséshon) s. impuestos.
taxi (taksi) s. automóvil de alquiler; taxi.
taxicab (táksikab) véase taxi.
taxpayer (takspéyer) s. contribuyente.
tea (tí) s. té.
teach (tích) s. enseñar; instruir.
teacher (tícher) s. maestro, maestra.
teaching (tíching) s. enseñanza; instrucción; adj. docente.
teacup (tíkop) s. taza para té.
teakettle (tíketl) s. tetera; pava para el mate.
team (tím) s. equipo de jugadores; tronco (de caballos), yunta; partido; — **work** trabajo en cooperación; v. uncir; enganchar; acarrear; transportar; to — **up** unirse; formar un equipo.
teamster (tímster) s. cochero, carretero.
teapot (típot) s. tetera.
tear (ter) v. desgarrar; romper; hacer pedazos; rasguñar; arañar; arrancar o separar con violencia; atormentar; to — **to tatters** hacer garras o jirones; to — **one's hair** arrancarse los cabellos; to — **down** derribar, demoler (un edificio); to — **up** arrancar; desarraigar; to — **off in a hurry** salir a la carrera; **wear and** — desgaste; s. rasgón; rasgadura; desgarradura.
tear (tír) s. lágrima; gota; llanto; aflicción; — **gas** gas lacrimógeno; **to burst into** — **s** romper a llorar; deshacerse en llanto.

tearful (tírful) adj. lloroso; lagrimoso.
tease (tís) v. fastidiar; importunar; chotear; embromar.
teaspoon (tíspun) s. cucharita; cuchara chiquita.
teaspoonful (tíspunful) s. cucharadita.
teat (tít) s. teta.
technical (téknikal) adj. técnico.
technician (tekníshan) s. técnico.
tecnique (teknik) s. técnica; tecnicismo.
tedious (tídios) adj. tedioso; aburrido; pesado; fastidioso; molesto; cansado.
tediousness (tídiosnes) s. tedio; fastidio; aburrimiento.
teem (tím) v. estar rebosante; abundar en; estar lleno de.
teens (tíns) s. pl. edad de los trece a los diecinueve años; **to be in one's** — no llegar a los veinte años; tener de trece a diecinueve.
teeth (tíz) s. pl. de **tooth**; —**ing** dentición.
telegram (télegram) s. telegrama.
telegraph (télegraf) s. telégrafo; v. telegrafiar.
telegraphic (telegráfik) adj. telegráfico.
telegraphy (telégrafi) s. telegrafía.
telephone (télefon) s. teléfono; — **booth** caseta de teléfono; — **operator** telefonista; — **receiver** receptor; audífono; v. telefonear; llamar por teléfono.
telescope (téleskop) s. telescopio; v. enchufar; encajar un objeto en otro; telescopiar.
television (télevishon) s. televisión.
tell (tel) v. decir; contar; informar; revelar; explicar; expresar; adivinar; disponer; mandar; producir efecto; **every blow told** cada golpe produjo efecto; **his age is beginning to** — ya comienza a notársele la edad.
teller (téler) s. cajero de un banco; narrador; relator; escrutador de votos.
temerity (temériti) s. temeridad.
temper (témper) v. templar, atemperar; s. temple, genio; humor; carácter; disposición de ánimo; **to lose one's** — perder la cabeza; violentarse.
temperament (témperment) s. temperamento; disposición de ánimo.

temperance (témperans) s. templanza; temperancia; sobriedad.
temperate (témperet) adj. templado; sobrio; abstemio; moderado.
temperature (témperchur) s. temperatura; **to have a —** tener calentura.
temple ('tempal) s. 1. templo, santuario, iglesia. 2. (fig.) templo. 3. (anat.) sien.
tempter (témpter) s. tentador.
tempting (témpting) adj. tentador; atractivo; llamativo.
tenacious (tenáshos) adj. tenaz; pegajoso; adhesivo; fuerte; terco; porfiado; firme.
tenacity (tenásiti) s. tenacidad; aferramiento; porfía; terquedad.
tenant (ténant) s. inquilino; arrendatario; residente; morador.
tend (tend) v. propender; contribuir; tender; cuidar; atender; vigilar; inclinarse a; dirigirse a.
tendency (téndensi) s. tendencia; propensión; inclinación.
tender (ténder) adj. tierno; delicado sensible; benigno; afectuoso; cariñoso; **— hearted** de corazón tierno; s. oferta; proposición; ténder de un tren; **legal —** moneda corriente; v. ofrecer; hacer una oferta o propuesta.
tenderloin (ténderloin) s. filete.
tenderness (térdernes) s. ternura; benevolencia; delicadeza; cariño.
tendon (téndon) s. tendón.
tendril (téndril) s. zarcillo (tallito de una planta trepadora).
tenement (ténement) s. casa de vecindad. [cancha de tenis
tennis (ténis) s. tenis; **— court**
tenor (ténor) s. tenor; significado; **— voice** voz de tenor.
tense (téns) adj. tenso; estirado; tirante; tiempo del verbo.
tension (ténshon) s. tensión; tirantez; fuerza expansiva de un gas.
tent (tent) s. tienda de campaña; pabellón; v. acampar.
tentacle (téntakl) s. tentáculo.
tentative (téntativ) adj. tentativo.
tepid (tépid) adj. tibio; templado.
term (term) s. término; vocablo; tecnicismo; plazo; período; límite; confín; fin; **—s condiciones**; términos; palabras; expresiones; **to be on good —s** estar en buenas relaciones; **not on any —s** por ningún concepto

a ningún precio; **to come to —s** ponerse de acuerdo; llegar a un convenio; v. nombrar; llamar; denominar.
terminal (términal) adj. último; extremo; final; s. término; fin; estación terminal; **electric —** toma de corriente; borne.
terminate (términeit) v. terminar.
termination (terminéshon) s. terminación; fin; desinencia.
terrace (térres) s. terraza; terraplén; terrado; v. terraplenar.
terrestrial (terréstriel) adj. terrestre; terrenal.
terrible (térribl) adj. terrible.
terribly (térribly) adv. terriblemente.
terrier (térrier) s. perro de busca.
terrific (terrífik) adj. terrífico.
terrify (térrifai) v. aterrar.
territory (térritori) s. territorio.
terror (térror) s. terror, espanto.
test (test) s. prueba; ensayo; experimento; tentativa; **examen; — tube** probeta; tubo de ensayo; **to undergo a —** sufrir una prueba; v. probar; ensayar; experimentar; poner a prueba; examinar. [mento.
testament (téstament) s. testa**testify** (téstifai) v. atestiguar; atestar; testimoniar. [nio
testimony (téstimoni) s. testimo**text** (tekst) s. texto.
textbook (tékstbuk) s. libro de texto; tema; tesis.
textile (tékstl) adj. textil; hilable; **— mill** fábrica de hilados y tejidos; s. tejido, materia textil; tela.
texture (tékschur) s. textura; contextura; tejido; tela.
than (dan) conj. que (partícula comparativa); **more — once** más de una vez; **I am taller — he** soy más alto que él.
thank (zank) v. dar las gracias; agradecer; **—s heaven!** ¡gracias a Dios!; **— you** gracias; **many —s** muchas gracias; **—s to you** gracias a usted.
thankful (zánkful) adj. agradecido; **—ly** adv. con gratitud, reconocidamente; con agradecimiento.
thankfulness (zánkfulnes) s. gratitud; reconocimiento; agradecimiento.
thankless (zánkles) adj. ingrato; desagradecido.
thanksgiving (zánksguiving) s. ac-

ción de gracias; — **Day** día de dar gracias a Dios.
that (dat) adj. ese, esa, aquel, aquella; pron. ése, ésa, aquél, aquélla; aquello; pron. rel. que; — **which** el que, la que, lo que; — **way** por allí, por ese camino; — **is es decir; so** — por cuanto, de suerte que; — **far** tan lejos; hasta allá; — **long** así de largo; de este tamaño; tanto tiempo; **save** — salvo que; **supposing** — suponiendo que.
thatch (zátch) s. paja para techar; barda; bardear; **—ed roof** techo de paja.
thaw (zoh) v. derretir(se); deshelar; s. deshielo; derretimiento; **it —s** deshiela.
the (di) art. el, la, los, las, — **sooner** — **better** cuanto antes, mejor.
theater (zíater) s. teatro.
theatrical (ziátrical) adj. teatral.
thee (di) pron. te.
theft (zeft) s. robo, hurto.
their (deir) adj. sus, su de ellos o de ellas.
theirs (deirs) pron. pos. suyo(s) s. suya(s) de ellos o de ellas; el, la, los; las suyas, de ellos o de ellas; **a friend of** — un amigo suyo: un amigo de ellos.
them (dem) pron. los, las, ellos, ellas (con preposición).
theme (zim) s. tema, asunto, materia; ensayo; tesis; disertación
themeselves (demsélvs) pron. ellos mismos; ellas mismas; sí mismos; se (como reflexivo).
then (den) adv. entonces; en aquel tiempo; a la sazón; en aquella ocasión; luego, después, en seguida; en otro tiempo; conj. pues, en tal caso; **now** — ahora bien; **now and** — de cuando en cuando, de vez en cuando; **now...** — ora... ora; ya... ya; **well** — pues entonces.
thence (dens) adv. desde allí, de allí; desde aquel momento; de allí en adelante; por eso; por esa razón, por ese motivo.
theological (ziolóyical) adj. teológico; teologal.
theology (zióloyi) s. teología.
theoretical (ziorétical) adj. teórico.
theory (zíori) s. teoría.
there (der) adv. allí, allá, ahí; — **she is** héla allí; — **is,** — **are** hay.
thereabouts (derabáuts) adv. por allí, por ahí; por allá; en los contornos; aproximadamente: acerca de.
thereafter (deráfter) adv. después de eso; en seguida; conforme, de allí en adelante.
thereby (derbái) adv. en relación con eso; así, de ese modo.
therefore (dérfor) adv. por eso; por esto; por consiguiente.
therein (derín) adv. en eso, en ello; allí adentro.
thereof (deróf) adv. encima; encima de (o sobre) él, ella, ello.
thereupon (deropón) adv. luego, después, en eso, en esto; sobre o encima; por consiguiente; por lo tanto; por eso.
therewith (deruíz) adv. con eso, con ello; a eso, a ello.
thermometer (zermómeter) s. termómetro.
thermos (zérmos) — **bottle** termos.
these (dis) adj. estos, estas; pron. éstos, éstas.
thesis (zísis) s. tesis.
they (dei) pron. ellos, ellas.
thick (zik) adj. espeso; grueso, macizo; tupido; vasto; cerrado; brumoso; embotado; torpe; denso; — **voice** voz ronca; — **set** grueso, rechoncho; — **skinned** insensible, que no se avergüenza con facilidad; — **of hearing** duro de oído; **one inch** — una pulgada de espesor; s. espesor, densidad, grueso; **the** — **of the fight** lo más reñido de la pelea; **the** — **of the crowd** lo más denso de la muchedumbre; **through** — **and thin** por toda suerte de penalidades.
thicken (zíken) v. espesar; engrosar; condensar, aumentar.
thicket (zíket) s. espesura, maleza; soto; matorral; fosca.
thickly (zíkli) adv. espesamente; densamente; con frecuencia.
thickness (zíknes) s. espesor; espesura; densidad, grueso.
thief (zif) s. ladrón.
thieve (ziv) v. hurtar, robar.
thieves (zivs) pl. de **thief.**
thin (0in) a. (**THINNER: THINNEST**) 1. delgado, fino, tenue. 2. delgado, cenceño, flaco, enjuto, descarnado, magro. 3. claro, ralo, no denso, fluido (líquido).
thing (zing) s. cosa; objeto, substancia; **no such** — nada de eso: **the** — lo conveniente, lo que está de moda; lo necesario o lo que se desea.

think (zink) v. pensar; creer; juzgar; opinar; to — it over pensarlo; considerar, idear, reflexionar; to — well o ill of one tener buen o mal concepto de; — nothing of it no haga Ud. caso, no le dé Ud. importancia; as you — fit como Ud. guste; what do you — of her? ¿qué piensa Ud. de ella?
thinker (zínker) s. pensador.
thinly (zínli) adv. delgadamente, poco, en corto número; escasamente.
thinness (zínes) s. delgadez, flacura; tenuidad; raleza (del cabello); sutileza, rareza.
third (zerd) adj. tercero, tercer; s. tercio; tercera parte.
thirst (zerst) s. sed, anhelo, ansia; v. tener o padecer de sed; ansiar, anhelar. [— tener sed.
thirsty (zérsti) adj. sediento; to be this (dis) adj. este, esta; pron. éste, ésta, esto.
thistle (zestl) s. abrojo.
thither (zíder) adv. allá, hacia allá; a ese fin; para allá.
tho (dou) véase though.
thong (zong) s. correa, tira de cuero; guasca, zurriaga.
thorn (zorn) s. espina, púa, espino; pincho, pesadumbre, zozobra; abrojo. [duo; difícil.
thorny (zórni) adj. espinoso; arthorough (dórou) adj. completo, entero; cabal, esmerado; cumplido.
thoroughbred (dóroubred) adj. de pura casta; de pura raza; bien nacido; s. animal o persona de casta; caballo de casta.
thoroughfare (dóroufer) s. vía pública, carretera; pasaje; camino real.
thoroughly (dórouli) adj. completamente; cabalmente; a fondo.
those (dous) adj. esos, esas; aquellos, aquellas; pron. ésos, ésas; aquéllos, aquéllas; — of los de; las de; — who los que o las que.
thou (dau) pron. tú.
though (dou) conj. aunque, si bien; no obstante, sin embargo; aun cuando; as — como si.
thought (zot) s. pensamiento, idea; intención; juicio, dictamen, opinión; meditación; reflexión; cogitación; concepto; designio, proyecto; recordación; cuidado; solicitud, atención; to be lost in — estar abstraído; to

give it no — no pensar en ello; — strikes me me ocurre una idea.
thoughtful (zótful) adj. pensativo, considerado; atento; solícito; meditabundo; previsor; precavido; to be — of others pensar en los demás, tener consideración o solicitud por los demás; adv. con reflexión; consideradamente.
thoughtfulness (zótfulnes) s. consideración; meditación profunda.
thoughtless (zótles) adj. inconsiderado; atolondrado; irreflexivo, incauto; insensato, improvido; —ly adv. inconsideradamente; sin pensar; atolondradamente; irreflexivamente.
thoughtlessness (zótlesnes) s. irreflexión; descuido, omisión; inadvertencia; atolondramiento.
thrash (zrash) v. trillar, desgranar (las mieses); zurrar; batanear; arrojarse, trabajar; afanarse; agitarse.
thread (zred) s. hilo; hebra, fibra; filamento; paso de la rosca de un tornillo; v. ensartar, enhebrar; ensartar; colocarse a través de; pasar por; brujulear; enhilar; to — a screw roscar un tornillo.
threadbare (zrédber) adj. raido, gastado; muy usado.
threat (zret) s. amenaza; amago.
threaten (zréten) v. amagar; amenazar.
threatening (zrétening) adj. amenazante, terrible, amenazador.
thresh (zresh) véase thrash.
treshold (zréshjould) s. umbral.
threw (zru) pret. de to throw.
thrice (zrais) adv. tres veces.
thrift (zrift) s. economía.
thrifty (zrífti) adj. económico, próspero, frugal, floreciente.
thrill (zril) v. emocionar(se), conmover(se); causar una emoción viva; estremecerse de emoción; temblar; s. emoción, estremecimiento emotivo, sobreexcitación.
thrive (zraiv) v. medrar, prosperar; adelantar, tener éxito, florecer.
thriven (zriven) p.p. de to thrive.
throat (zrout) s. garganta.
throb (zrob) v. latir; palpitar, vibrar; s. latido, palpitación.
throe (zrou) s. angustia, dolor.
throne (zroun) s. trono, poder soberano; v. llevar al trono.
throng (zrong) s. muchedumbre,

multitud, tropel; gentío; caterva; v. agolparse; venir en tropel.

throttle (zrótl) s. válvula reguladora; traquearteria; gollete; obturador, regulador; v. ahogar; estrangular; ahogarse; **to — down** disminuir o reducir la velocidad; asfixiar.

through (zru) prep. por; a través de; por medio de; por entre, por causa de, gracias a; adj. directo, continuo; que va hasta el fin; **— train** tren directo; tren rápido; **to be — with** haber acabado con; no querer ocuparse más de; **to fall —** fracasar; **I am wet —** estoy calado hasta los huesos; adv. a través; de un lado a otro; de parte a parte; de cabo a rabo; **— design** adrede; expresamente; desde el principio hasta el fin; **loyal — and —** leal a toda prueba; **— ticket** boleto directo.

throughout (zruáut) prep. por todo; a lo largo de; por todas partes; adv. en todas partes; en todo; de principio a fin; **— the day** durante todo el día; de parte a parte.

throve (zróuv) pret. de to thrive.

throw (zróu) v. arrojar; echar, tirar, lanzar; derribar; apear; impeler; empujar; despojarse de; cambiar piel; dirigir la mirada; **to — away** disipar; malgastar; **to — back** rechazar, devolver; **to — by** arrinconar; **to — down** derribar; echar por tierra; **to — in gear** engranar; **to — open** abrir de par en par; **to — silk** torcer seda; **to — up** vomitar; elevar, echar al aire; renunciar a; **to — overboard** echar al mar, echar fuera de borda; s. tiro; golpe; esfuerzo; **whitin a stone's —** a tiro de piedra.

thrown (zróun) p.p. de to throw.

thrush (zrosh) s. tordo; zorzal.

thud (zod) s. sonido sordo; golpe; porrazo; golpe sordo.

thug (zog) s. asesino; salteador.

thumb (zomb) s. pulgar; **— nut** tuerca de mariposa; **under the — of** bajo el poder de; v. hojear con el pulgar; emporcar con los dedos.

thumbtack (zómbtak) s. chinche.

thump (zomp) s. golpe sordo; porrazo; golpazo; v. golpear; aporrear; cascar; golpear pesadamente.

thunder (zónder) s. trueno; estruendo; atronar; oírse el ruido del trueno.

thunderbolt (zónderboult) s. rayo.

thundering (zóndering) adj. atronador.

thunderous (zónderos) adj. atronador; estruendoso.

thunderstorm (zónderstorm) s. tempestad de truenos; tormenta en seco.

Thursday (zérsdei) s. jueves.

thus (dós) adv. así; de este modo; en estos términos; a ese grado; **— far** hasta aquí; hasta entonces; **— it is** así es que.

thwart (zuort) v. impedir; estorbar; poner obstáculos; frustrar.

thy (dai) adj. tu, tus.

thyme (táim) s. tomillo.

thyself (daisélf) pron. tú mismo; a ti mismo; te (como reflexivo).

tick (tik) s. sonido acompasado; tictac; garrapata; funda de colchón o almohada; cotí; v. marcar lo que se confronta; hacer sonido de tic-tac; latir el corazón.

ticket (tíket) s. boleto; billete; papeleta; boleta; licencia; permiso; **— office** taquilla; v. rotular; marcar.

tickle (tíkl) v. cosquillear; hacer cosquillas; halagar; lisonjear; divertir; tener cosquillas; **to be —d to death** morirse de gusto; estar muy contento; s. cosquilleo, cosquillas.

ticklish (tíklish) adj. cosquilloso; delicado; inseguro, incierto.

tidbit (tídbit) s. bocado, golosina, bocadito.

tide (taid) s. marea, corriente; curso, marcha; flujo; tiempo, estación; **Christmas —** navidades; temporada de navidades; v. navegar o flotar con la marea.

tidings (táidings) s. pl. noticias, nuevas.

tidy (táidi) adj. aseado, limpio; ordenado; pulcro, decente; **a — sum** una suma considerable; v. asear, arreglar; poner en orden.

tie (tai) v. atar, liar, amarrar; enlazar, vincular, ligar, trincar; sujetar, encadenar; restringir; limitar; confinar; empatar; **to — tight** amarrar bien, apretar fuerte; **to — up** atar, amarrar; asegurar; s. lazo, ligadura, atadura; enlace, vínculo, parentes-

co; corbata; adhesión; unión; empate.
tier (tir) s. fila, hilera.
tigress (táigres) s. tigre hembra.
tile (tail) s. teja; baldosa; azulejo; losa; **ridge —** teja acanalada; v. tejar; cubrir con tejas.
till (til) prep. hasta; conj. hasta que; v. cultivar, arar, labrar; s. cajón o gaveta para guardar dinero.
tillage (tíley) s. labranza.
tilt (tilt) s. ladeo, inclinación; declive; torneo, lanzada; toldo; altercado; tendal; v. ladear(se).
timber (timber) s. madera de construcción; palo; fuste; viga.
time (taim) s. tiempo; hora; era; época; plazo; período; vez, turno; edad; ocasión; coyuntura; respiro; espera; **at —s** a veces; **what — is it?** ¿qué hora es? **my — has come** ha llegado mi hora; **from — to —** de vez en cuando; **all —** todo el tiempo; **in — a** tiempo; **in our —s** en nuestros días; **on —** puntual; con puntualidad; **in a day's —** en el espacio de un día; **to buy on —** comprar a plazos; **to have a good —** divertirse; pasar un buen rato; v. cronometrar; medir el tiempo; regular; llevar el compás; hacer alguna cosa a tiempo oportuno.
timely (táimli) adj. oportuno.
timepiece (táimpis) s. reloj; cronómetro.
timetable (táimteibl) s. itinerario; horario.
timid (tímid) adj. tímido.
timidity (timíditi) s. timidez.
timorous (tímoros) adj. timorato; espantadizo; miedoso; asustadizo.
tin (tin) s. estaño; hojalata; lata; **— can** bote de hojalata; lata; **— foil** hoja de estaño; v. estañar, cubrir con estaño.
tincture (tínkchur) s. tintura; tinte; **— of iodine** tintura de yodo; v. teñir; colorar; tinturar.
tinder (tínder) s. yesca.
tinge (tiny) v. teñir; colorear; matizar; s. tinte, matiz; color ligero; gusto.
tingle (tíngl) v. picar; sentir picazón; hormiguear; **to — with excitement** estremecerse de entusiasmo; s. hormigueo, picazón; comezón.
tinkle (tinkl) v. tintinear; s. tintineo; retintín.
tinsel (tínsl) s. oropel; adj. de oropel; que tiene brillo falso.
tint (tint) s. tinte, matiz; v. teñir; matizar.
tiny (táini) adj. diminuto; muy pequeño; menudito.
tip (tip) s. punta; extremidad; casquillo; regatón; propina; informe o aviso que se da en secreto; consejo personal; v. ladear(se); inclinar(se); **to — a person off** dar aviso secreto a; **to — one's hat** tocarse el sombrero; **to — over** volcarse; voltearse.
tipsy (tipsi) adj. medio intoxicado; alumbrado; que hace eses.
tiptoe (típtou) s. punta del pie; **on —** de puntillas; v. andar de puntillas.
tire (táir) s. llanta, neumático; **flat —** llanta reventada, "ponchada"; v. cansarse, fatigarse; **to — out** extenuarse, agotarse por la fatiga.
tired (táird) adj. cansado, fatigado.
tireless (táirles) adj. incansable; infatigable.
tiresome (táirsom) adj. tedioso; fastidioso; cansado, aburrido.
tissue (tíshu) s. tejido.
tithe (táiz) s. diezmo.
title (táitl) s. título; **— page** portada; v. titular; intitular.
to (tu) prep. a, hacia, hasta, para; signo del infinitivo en inglés; (en estado normal) **he came —** volvió en sí; (por) **he came only — see me** vino sólo por verme; a verme o para verme; **a quarter — five** las cinco menos cuarto; **from place — place** de sitio en sitio; de lugar en lugar; (que) **he has — go** tiene que ir; adv. **— and for** de acá para allá.
toad (tóud) s. sapo.
toast (tóust) s. pan tostado; tostada; brindis; v. tostar; brindar por; beber a la salud de.
toaster (tóuster) s. tostador.
tobacco (tobáko) s. tabaco.
today (tudéi) adv. hoy, hoy día.
toe (tóu) s. dedo del pie; pezuña; puntera de un zapato; **great —** dedo gordo del pie; **from head to —** de pies a cabeza.
toenail (tóuneil) s. uña del dedo del pie.
together (tuguéder) adv. juntamente; en compañía de; a la

TOIL   **TORTUOUS**

vez; juntos; a un tiempo; sin interrupción; **all** — todos juntos; — **with** junto con; **to call** — convocar; juntar; simultáneamente.

toil (tóil) v. afanarse; fatigarse; trabajar mucho; aplicarse con desvelo.

toilet (tóilet) s. retrete; excusado; — **articles** artículos de tocador; — **case** neceser; — **paper** papel sanitario; papel higiénico.

token (tóuken) s. prueba de amistad; prenda; recuerdo; muestra de cariño; **as a** — **of** en señal de.

told (tould) pret. y p.p. de **to tell**.

tolerance (tólerans) s. tolerancia.

tolerant (tólerant) adj. tolerante.

tolerate (tólereit) v. tolerar.

toleration (toleréshon) s. tolerancia.

toll (toul) s. peaje; tañido de las campanas; portazgo; — **bridge** puente de peaje; **to pay** — pagar peaje o portazgo; v. tañer o doblar las campanas.

tomato (tométo) s. tomate; jitomate.

tomb (tum) s. tumba.

tombstone (túmstoun) s. lápida.

tomcat (tómkat) s. gato.

tomorrow (tumórrou) adv. mañana; — **morning** mañana por la mañana; — **noon** mañana al mediodía; **day after** — pasado mañana.

ton (ton) s. tonelada.

tone (tóun) s. tono; tonalidad; matiz; timbre; sonido; v. dar el tono a; modificar la expresión o el afecto; **to** — **down** suavizar; moderar; **to** — **up** subir de tono; tonificar; vigorizar.

tongs (tongs) s. pl. tenazas.

tongue (tong) s. lengua; idioma; **to be** — **tied** tener trabada la lengua; **to hold one's** — callarse.

tonic (tónik) adj. y s. tónico.

tonight (tunáit) adv. esta noche; a la noche.

tonnage (tóney) s. tonelaje.

tonsil (tónsil) s. amígdala.

tonsilitis (tonsiláitis) s. amigdalitis.

too (tu) adv. también; demasiado; aun; asimismo; — **many** demasiados; — **much** demasiado; **it is** — **bad!** ¡es una lástima!

took (tuk) pret. de **to take**.

tool (túl) s. herramienta; instrumento; utensilio.

toot (tút) s. toque o sonido de bocina, etc.; silbido; pitido; pitazo; v. tocar el claxon, la bocina **to** — **one's own horn** alabarse uno mismo.

tooth (tuz) s. diente, muela; **eye** — colmillo; — **brush** cepillo de dientes; **back** — muela.

toothache (túzeik) s. dolor de muelas.

toothed (túzt) adj. dentado.

toothless (túzles) adj. desdentado.

toothpaste (túzpeist) s. dentrífico, pasta para los dientes.

toothpick (túzpik) s. mondadientes; palillo de dientes.

top (top) s. cima; cumbre; cabeza; remate; copa de árbol; trompo; punta; ápice; auge; superficie; tupé, cofia; adj. superior; más alto; primero; principal; **from** — **to bottom** de arriba abajo; **from** — **to toe** de pies a cabeza; **on** — **of** encima de; sobre; — **hat** sombrero alto; sombrero de copa; — **coat** abrigo, sobretodo; **at** — **speed** a máxima velocidad; **to fill to the** — llenar hasta la tope; v. descabezar; cubrir; coronar; rematar; exceder; sobresalir; sobrepujar.

topaz (tópes) s. topacio.

toper (tóuper) s. bebedor, borrachín.

topic (tópik) s. asunto; tópico; tema; materia; sujeto.

topmost (tópmoust) adj. más alto; superior.

topple (topl) v. hacer caer; echar por tierra; derribar; venirse abajo; **to** — **over** volcarse; caer hacia delante.

topsy: — **turvy** (tópsitérvi) adj. y adv. patas arriba; en confusión; trastornado; con lo de abajo arriba; al revés.

torch (torch) s. antorcha; **blow** — soplete.

tore (tóur) pret. de **to tear**.

torment (tórment) s. tormento; pena; v. atormentar; angustiar.

torn (torn) p.p. de **to tear** roto; rasgado.

tornado (tornédo) s. tornado.

torpedo (torpído) s. torpedo; — **tube** tubo lanzatorpedos; v. torpedear.

torrent (tórrent) s. torrente.

torrrid (tórrid) adj. tórrido.

tortoise (tórtes) s. tortuga.

tortuous (tórchos) adj. tortuoso.

— 240 —

torture (tórchur) s. tortura, tormento; suplicio; v. torturar.

toss (tos) v. tirar, echar, arrojar; lanzar al aire; sacudir; agitar; mover; to — **aside** echar a un lado; s. tiro, tirada; sacudimiento; ajetreo.

tot (tot) s. chiquitín, niño, nene.

total (tótal) adj. cabal; total; completo; entero; s. suma; el todo; total.

totalitarian (totelitérian) adj. totalitario.

totter (tóter) v. tambalearse; bambolear(se); vacilar, titubear.

touch (toch) v. tocar, palpar, tentar; conmover, enternecer; tropezar; herir; probar, ensayar; compararse con; igualar; to — **at a port** hacer escala en un puerto; to — **off** descargar (un cañón); to — **off an explosive** prender la mecha de un explosivo; — **hole** fogón, oído del cañón; s. toque, tacto; sentido del tacto; palpamiento; pincelada; rasgo.

touching (tóching) adj. conmovedor; patético, enternecedor.

touchy (tóchi) adj. quisquilloso; susceptible; vidrioso.

tough (tof) adj. tenaz; fuerte; vigoroso; arduo; duro; difícil; resistente; correoso.

toughen (tófn) v. curtir(se); hacerse correoso; endurecer(se); empedernir(se).

toughness (tófnes) s. dureza; tenacidad, endurecimiento; tesura; rigidez; flexibilidad; resistencia; dificultad.

tour (tur) s. viaje; excursión; peregrinación; vuelta; jira; v. viajar; hacer una jira turística; hacer un viaje de paseo.

tourist (túrist) s. turista.

tournament (túrnament) s. torneo; certamen; justa; concurso.

tow (tóu) v. remolcar; halar; s. remolque; — **boat** remolcador; — **line** cabo de remolque, sirga; to **take in** — llevar a remolque; remolcar.

toward (tóard) prep. hacia; con dirección a; alrededor de; cerca de; — **four o'clock** a eso de las cuatro; con respecto a.

towards (tóards) véase toward.

towel (táuel) s. toalla.

tower (táuer) s. torre; campanario; torreón, ciudadela; v. sobresalir; destacarse; elevarse; remontarse.

towering (táuering) adj. encumbrado; elevado, muy alto; dominante.

town (táun) s. población, ciudad, pueblo; villa; lugar; aldea; **in** — en la ciudad; en la metrópoli.

township (táunship) s. unidad primaria de gobierno local; jurisdicción de una ciudad; extensión de terrenos públicos de seis millas cuadradas.

toxin (tóksin) s. toxina.

toy (toi) s. juguete; adj. de juguete; diminuto; v. juguetear.

trace (tréis) s. señal, indicio; rastro, huella, pisada; pizca; vestigio; trábea; v. trazar; calcar; delinear; rastrear, seguir; investigar; señalar, plantear.

trachea (trékia) s. tráquea.

track (trak) s. pista, huella, rastro; vestigio, pisada; estampa; rodada, carril; senda, vía; ruta; — **sports** deportes de pista; **double** — vía doble; **side** — desviadero; **railroad** — rieles, vía férrea o ferrovía; — **walker** guardavía; **to be off the** — estar extraviado, estar descarrilado; v. rastrear; seguir la huella de; seguir la pista; sirgar; to — **down** coger, atrapar; descubrir; to — **in mud** traer lodo en los pies.

tract (tract) s. área; terreno; trecho; folleto; **digestive** — canal digestivo.

traction (trákshon) s. tracción.

tractor (tráktor) s. tractor.

trade (treid) s. comercio, trato; industria; oficio; arte mecánica; trueque; cambio; clientela; contratación; actividad de los submarinos; convenio de mala ley; v. comerciar; negociar, traficar; tratar; contratar; cambiar.

trademark (tréidmark) s. marca de fábrica.

trader (tréider) s. mercader, comerciante; traficante; tratante.

tradesman (tréidsman) s. mercader; comerciante; tendero; artesano.

tradition (tradíshon) s. tradición.

traditional (tradíshonal) s. tradicional.

traffic (tráfik) s. tráfico; tráfago; tránsito; v. negociar, vender; traficar; comerciar.

tragedy (tráyedi) s. tragedia.

— 241 —

tragic (tráyic) adj. trágico.
trail (tréll) s. pista, rastro, huella; senda; pisada; traza; cola (de vestido, de cometa, etc.); v. arrastrar(se); rastrear; llevar arrastrando, andar atrás de.
train (tréin) s. tren; cola (de vestido); procesión, séquito; comitiva; v. amaestrar(se); ejercitar(se); entrenar(se); educarse; disciplinar, adiestrar.
trainer (tréiner) s. domador; entrenador; espaldera.
training (tréining) s. adiestramiento; disciplina; enseñanza, educación; instrucción; entrenamiento; — **camp** campo de entrenamiento o práctica.
trait (tréit) s. rasgo, característica, golpe, toque.
traitor (tréitor) s. traidor.
tram (tram) s. vagoneta (de una mina de carbón); tranvía.
tramp (tramp) v. pisotear; andar a pie; patrullar; corretear, vagabundear; s. vago, vagabundo.
trample (trámpl) v. pisar, hollar; atropellar, maltratar; **to — on** pisotear; s. pisadas; atropello.
trance (trans) s. rapto, arrobamiento; éxtasis; hechizo, síncope; **to be in a —** estar arrobado; estar distraído o ensimismado.
tranquil (tránkuil) adj. tranquilo.
tranquillity (trankuíliti) s. tranquilidad, sosiego.
transact (transákt) v. tramitar; llevar a cabo, hacer, ejecutar.
transaction (transákshon) s. transacción; trato, negocio; desempeño; gestión; **—s actas, memorias.**
transatlantic (transetlántik) adj. trasatlántico.
transcend (transénd) v. trascender, ir más allá de, superar.
transcontinental (trascontinéntal) adj. transcontinental.
transcribe (transkráib) v. transcribir, copiar, trasladar.
transcript (tránscript) s. transcripción; trasunto; copia, traslado; apógrafo.
transfer (tránsfer) s. transferencia; traslado, trasbordo; transporte; cesión; traspaso; **— of ownership** cesión o traspaso de propiedad; **street car —** transferencia, contraseña; v. transferir; transpor-

tar, trasladar; trasbordar, cambiar (de tren, de tranvía); traspasar (la propiedad).
transgressor (transgrésor) s. transgresor, infractor.
transient (tránshent) s. transeúnte; pasajero, transitorio.
transit (tránsit) s. tránsito, paso, pasaje, trámite.
transition (transíshon) s. transición; tránsito; paso, mudanza.
transitive (tránsitiv) adj. transitivo.
transitory (tránsitori) adj. transitorio, pasajero, transeúnte.
translate (transléit) v. traducir.
translation (transléshon) s. traducción, versión; remoción; traslación.
translator (transléitor) s. traductor.
translucent (translúsent) adj. traslúcido, trasluciente.
transmission (transmíshon) s. transmisión, caja de velocidades.
transmit (transmít) v. transmitir; emitir, remitir, enviar.
transmitter (transmíter) s. transmisor; emisor.
transom (tránsom) s. montante.
transparent (transpérent) adj. transparente.
transplant (transplánt) v. trasplantar.
transport (tránsport) s. transporte; acarreo; transportamiento; éxtasis; **— plane** aeroplano de transporte; v. transportar; acarrear, deportar, desterrar.
transportation (transportéshon) s. transportación, transporte.
transpose (transpóus) v. transponer.
transverse (transvérs) adj. transverso, transversal.
trap (trap) s. trampa, lazo, red; armadijo; sifón; **mouse —** ratonera; v. coger con trampa; atrapar; hacer caer en el lazo.
trapeze (trapís) s. trapecio.
trappings (trápings) s. pl. arreos; aderezos, adornos, galas.
trash (trash) s. basura; hojarasca; paja, escombros, plebe, gentuza.
travel (trávl) v. viajar; recorrer; andar; s. viaje, jornada, camino.
traveler (tráveler) s. viajero.
traveling (tráveling) adj. de viaje; para viaje; **— expenses** gastos de viaje; **— salesman** agente viajero; viajante de comercio.

— 242 —

traverse (trávers) v. atravesar; hacer vaivén; moverse de un lado a otro; s. travesaño.
travesty (trávesti) s. parodia; v. disfrazar, parodiar.
tray (trei) s. bandeja, batea.
treacherous (trécheros) adj. traicionero, traidor; alevoso.
treachery (trécheri) s. traición, perfidia; deslealtad, falsedad.
tread (tred) v. pisar, hollar; andar, caminar; pisotear; andar a pie; s. paso, huella; pisada; escalón de escalera; cara de rueda; centro del trono.
treason (trisn) s. traición.
treasonable (trísnebl) adj. traidor; desleal, pérfido; traicionero.
treasure (tréshur) s. tesoro; v. atesorar; acumular riquezas.
treasurer (tréshurer) s. tesorero.
treasury (tréshuri) s. tesorería; tesoro; erario; hacienda; **Secretary of the Treasury** ministro de hacienda.
treat (trit) v. tratar; curar; escribir o discurrir sobre alguna materia; s. obsequio, placer.
treatise (tritis) s. tratado.
treatment (tritment) s. trato; tratamiento; método curativo.
treaty (tríti) s. tratado, pacto.
treble (trébl) adj. triple; tríplice; — **voice** voz atiplada; s. tiple; v. triplicar.
tree (tri) s. árbol; palo, madero; horca; cruz; **apple —** manzano; **family —** árbol genealógico; — **of life** árbol de la vida; **to be up a —** estar en un gran aprieto.
treeless (tríles) adj. pelado, sin árboles; sin arboleda.
treetop (trítop) s. copa de árbol.
trellis (trélis) s. emparrado.
tremble (trémbl) v. temblar; estremecerse; s. temblor; estremecimiento.
tremendous (treméndos) adj. tremendo.
tremor (trémor) s. temblor.
tremulous (trémiulos) adj. trémulo; tembloroso; tremulante.
trench (trénch) s. trinchera, zanja.
trend (trend) s. tendencia; rumbo; curso, giro; dirección.
trespass (tréspas) v. invadir, traspasar; quebrantar; rebasar; violar; infringir; **to — on property** meterse sin derecho en la propiedad ajena; s. transgresión.
tress (tres) s. trenza; bucle, rizo.

trial (tráial) s. ensayo, prueba, tentativa; esfuerzo, experimento; aflicción, juicio; proceso; — **by jury** juicio por jurado.
triangle (tráiangl) s. triángulo.
triangular (traiángulular) adj. triangular; triangulado.
tribe (tráib) s. tribu.
tribulation (tribiuléshon) s. tribulación.
tribunal (tribiúnal) s. tribunal.
tributary (tríbiuteri) adj. y s. tributario; subalterno.
tribute (tríbiut) s. tributo.
trick (trik) s. treta; suerte; maña; ardid; petardo, timo; artería, truco, fraude; v. defraudar, timar; embaucar, hacer trampa; engañar; ataviar, componer, asear.
trickery (tríkeri) s. engaños.
trickle (tríkl) v. gotear; s. goteo.
tricky (tríki) adj. tramposo.
tried (traid), p.p. de **to try** y adj. probado.
trifle (tráifl) s. fruslería; bagatela; baratija, menudencia; v. chancear(se); bromear; jugar.
trigger (tríguer) s. gatillo (de pistola, rifle, etc.); disparador.
trill (tril) v. trinar; gotear, correr gota a gota; s. trino.
trim (trim) v. guarnecer; vacilar; titubear entre dos partidos; recortar; nadar entre dos aguas; estar bien equilibrado (buque); podar; mondar; despabilar (una vela); **to — up** adornar; s. adorno, franja; atavío, aderezo, compostura; traje, vestido, estilo.
trimming (tríming) s. adorno, aderezo; guarnición, galón; orla; ribete; pasamanería.
trinket (trínket) s. baratija.
trip (trip) s. viaje; travesía; recorrido; excursión; tropiezo; v. hacer caer a uno echándole la zancadilla; armar un lazo o zancadilla; bailar; hacer tropezar; soltar, disparar; zarpar, levar anclas.
triple (trípl) adj. y s. triple.
trite (trait) adj. trillado, vulgar.
triumph (tráionf) s. triunfo.
triumphal (traíomfal) adj. triunfal.
triumphant (traíónfant) adj. triunfante; victorioso; **—ly** adv. triunfalmente; en triunfo.
trivial (trívial) adj. trivial, insignificante; frívolo, vulgar.
trod (trod) pret. y p.p. de **to tread**.

trodden (tródn) p.p. de **to tread**.
trolley (tróli) s. trole.
trombone (trómboun) s. trombón.
troop (trup) s. tropa, cuadrilla.
trophy (trófi) s. trofeo.
trópic (trópik) s. trópico; adj. tropical.
tropical (trópical) adj. tropical.
trot (trot) v. hacer trotar; s. trote.
trouble (tróbl) v. perturbar, turbar; molestar, incomodar; revolver; enfadar; importunar; preocuparse; **to be in** — estar en un aprieto; tener dificultades; **it is not worth the** — no vale la pena; s. turbación; inquietud; desazón; pena; molestia; inconveniencia; avería; accidente; **heart** — enfermedad del corazón.
troublemaker (tróblmeiker) s. agitador; alborotador; malcontento.
troublesome (tróblsom) adj. molesto; gravoso; importuno; enfadoso; impertinente.
trough (tróf) s. artesa; batea; cubeta; **drinking** — abrevadero; — **eaves canal**, gotera de tejado.
trousers (tráusers) s. pl. pantalones.
trousseau (trusó) s. ajuar de novia.
trout (tráut) s. trucha.
trowel (tráuel) s. llana, cuchara de albañil.
truant (trúant) s. y adj. tunante; holgazán; haragán; **to play** — "pintar venado".
truce (trus) s. tregua; suspensión, interrupción; armisticio.
truck (trók) s. camión; carretón; carreta; troca; artículos sin valor; basura; baratijas; **garden** — hortalizas; legumbres; verduras; — **garden** hortaliza; huerta de legumbres; v. acarrear; transportar en camión; traficar; vender.
trudge (tródy) v. caminar con esfuerzo; caminata muy pesada.
true (trú) adj. verdadero; cierto; real; positivo; ingenuo; sincero; exacto; justo; a nivel; preciso; — **blue** fiel, leal.
truly (trúli) adv. exactamente; en verdad; en realidad; verdaderamente; **very** — **yours** su seguro servidor; su afectísimo.
trump (tromp) s. triunfo (en el juego de naipes); v. matar con un triunfo (en la baraja); **to** — **up an excuse** inventar una disculpa.
trust (trost) s. confianza, crédito;

cargo; depósito; **trust**; v. confiar, fiar, esperar; dar crédito a.
trustful (tróstful) adj. confiado.
trusting (trósting) adj. confiado.
trustworthy (tróstuerzi) adj. fidedigno; seguro; digno de confianza.
trusty (trósti) adj. fiel, leal, íntegro; firme; fuerte; seguro.
truth (trúz) s. verdad; **in** — en verdad; en realidad; seriamente.
truthful (trúzful) adj. verídico; veraz; exacto.
truthfulness (trúzfulnes) s. veracidad.
try (trái) v. probar; tratar de; intentar; poner a prueba; exasperar; cansar; fatigar; comprobar; procesar; purificar; refinar; **to** — **on a suit** probarse un traje; **to** — **one's luck** probar fortuna; **to** — **someone's patience** poner a prueba la paciencia de alguien; s. prueba; tentativa; ensayo.
trying (tráing) adj. penoso; irritante; molesto; fatigoso.
tub (tob) s. tina; bañera; baño; batea; cuba; cubeta; v. lavar en tina; bañarse en tina.
tube (tiúb) s. tubo; caño; sifón; conducto; **inner** — cámara de un neumático; **radio** — lámpara o tubo de radio.
tubercular (tiubérkiular) adj. tuberculoso; tísico.
tuberculosis (tiuberkiulósis) s. tuberculosis.
tuck (tók) v. arropar; arremangar; echar alforzas; recoger; **to** — **in bed** arropar en la cama; **to** — **under one's arm** meterse debajo del brazo; **to** — **up one's sleeves** arremangarse; s. alforza.
Tuesday (tiúsdei) s. martes.
tuft (tóft) s. copete; tupé; moño; penacho; ramillete; borla.
tug (tog) v. arrastrar; halar; remolcar; esforzarse; tirar con fuerza de; s. tirón; — **boat** remolcador; — **of war** lucha a tirones de cuerda.
tuition (tiuíshon) s. colegiatura; derechos de enseñanza.
tulip (tiúlip) s. tulipán.
tumble (tómbl) v. dar en tierra; venirse abajo; desplomarse; voltear; revolcarse; dar volteretas; **to** — **into someone** tropezar con alguien; **to** — **over** volcar; tumbar; derribar; s. tumbo; caída;

— 244 —

vuelco; voltereta; rodada; desorden.
tumbler (tómbler) s. vaso (de mesa); acróbata; cubilete.
tumor (tiúmor) s. tumor.
tumult (tiúmolt) s. tumulto.
tumultuous (tiumólchus) adj. tumultuoso; turbulento.
tuna (túne) s. atún (pez).
tune (tiun) s. tonada; tono; armonía; afinación; concordancia; **to be in —** estar a tono, estar afinado o templado; estar entonado; **out of —** destemplado, desafinado; desentonado; v. afinar, templar; acordar, entonar; ajustar, adaptar; armonizar, modular.
tunic (tiúnik) s. túnica.
tunnel (tónel) s. túnel, socavón; embudo, cañón de chimenea; v. socavar; abrir un túnel.
turbulent (térbiulent) adj. turbulento; revoltoso; agitado.
turf (terf) s. césped; terrón de tierra (con césped); tepe; turba; hipódromo, pista (para carreras).
Turk (terk) s. turco.
turkey (térki) s. pavo; guajolote; **— buzzard** aura, zopilote.
Turkish (térkish) adj. turco; turquesco; s. turco, idioma turco.
turmoil (térmoil) s. alboroto.
turn (tern) v. volver(se); voltear; dar vuelta, girar; rodar, virar; mudar; cambiar; tornear; volver del revés al derecho, desviar, verter; traducir; rechazar; doblar; aplicar; transferir; **to — aside** desviar(se); **to — away** despedir; **to — back** volver atrás, retroceder, restituir; **to — down an offer** rechazar una oferta; **to — in** recogerse, acostarse, entregar; **to — into** transformarse, convertirse; **to — off** cerrar una llave (de gas, etc.); **to — on** encender la luz, conectar (el gas, el agua, etc.); **to — off the main road** salirse o desviarse de la carretera; **to — over** transferir, trasladar, invertir; **to — to** acudir a; recurrir; **to — the stomach** volver el estómago; **to — on someone** volverse contra; caer sobre alguien; **to — out well** salir o resultar bien; **to — sour** agriarse; fermentarse; **to — the corner** doblar la esquina; **to — to the right** dar vuelta a la derecha; **to — up** presentarse, aparecer; **to — up one's sleeves** arremangarse; **to — upside down** trastornar, volcar; **to — short** dar media vuelta; s. vuelta; giro; rodeo, recodo; turno; vez; ocasión; mudanza; cambio, dirección, pase; aspecto; comportamiento; genio; propensión; **— of mind** actitud mental; **at every — a cada paso; by —s** por turno; **to be one's —** tocarle a uno su turno; **to take another —** cambiar de aspecto; **to do one a good —** hacerle a uno un favor.
turtle (tértl) s. tortuga.
tusk (tósk) s. colmillo.
tutor (tiútor) s. tutor; maestro particular; preceptor; v. enseñar; instruir; ser curador de.
tuxedo (toksído) s. esmóquin.
twang (tuáng) s. tañido (de la cuerda de una guitarra); nasalidad; tono gangoso; v. puntear las cuerdas de un instrumento; hablar con voz nasal; hablar gangoso.
twangy (tuángui) adj. gangoso; nasal.
tweed (tuíd) s. mezclilla de lana; **— suit** traje de mezclilla.
tweezers (tuísers) s. pl. pinzas; tenacillas.
twice (tuáis) adv. dos veces; doblemente; **— told** repetido.
twig (tuig) s. ramita; varita; vástago; ramal, derivación.
twilight (tuáilait) s. crepúsculo; **at —** entre dos luces; adj. crepuscular.
twin (tuín) adj. y s. gemelo mellizo; cuate.
twine (tuaín) s. cuerda; cordel; mecate; enroscadura; torzal; v. enroscar(se); torcer(se); entrelazar.
twinge (tuíny) s. punzada; v. punzar; atormentar, sufrir.
twinkle (tuínkl) v. centellear; rutilar; destellar; parpadear; pestañear; s. titilación; pestañeo; parpadeo; guiño; **in the twinkling of an eye** en un abrir y cerrar de ojos; momento; instante.
twirl (tuerl) v. girar; hacer girar; dar vueltas; s. giro; molinete; vuelta; floreo.
twist (tuíst) v. torcer(se); retorcer(se); trenzar; enrollar; enroscar(se); entretejer; doblar; serpentear; caracolear; s. torsión; torcedura; torzal; contorsión.

— 245 —

twitch (tuítch) v. crisparse; encogerse; contraerse; torcerse convulsivamente (un músculo); temblar (los) párpados; s. temblor; sacudida; contracción nerviosa; tirón.
twitter (tuíter) v. gorjear; temblar; agitarse; s. gorjeo; inquietud; agitación; estremecimiento nervioso.
twofold (túfould) adj. doble; duplicado; adv. al doble.
typewrite (táiprrait) v. escribir a máquina.
typewriter (táipraiter) s. máquina de escribir.
typewriting (táipraiting) s. mecanografía; trabajo de mecanógrafo.
typewritten (táipritn) adj. escrito a máquina.
typhoid (táifoid) s. tifoidea; fiebre tifoidea.
typhus (táifos) s. tifo.
typical (típical) adj. típico.
typist (táipist) s. mecanógrafo; mecanógrafa.
tyrannical (tiránikal) adj. tiránico; tirano.
tyranny (tírani) s. tiranía.
tyrant (táirant) s. tirano.

U

udder (óder) s. ubre; teta.
ugliness (óglines) s. fealdad; deformidad; fiereza; perversidad.
ugly (ógli) adj. feo; deforme; fiero; perverso; de mal genio; desagradable.
ulcer (ólser) s. úlcera.
ulterior (oltírior) adj. ulterior.
ultimate (óltimeit) adj. último; final; esencial; fundamental; —ly últimamente; al fin.
umbrella (ombréla) s. paraguas; sombrilla.
umpire (ómpair) s. árbitro; tercero en discordia; v. arbitrar.
un (on) prefijo equivalente a sin, no, in, des.
unaccustomed (onekóstomd) adj. desacostumbrado; inhabituado; insólito.
unaffected (onefékted) adj. inafectado; natural; franco; sincero.
unalterable (onólterabl) adj. inalterable; inmutable.
unanimity (iunanímity) s. unanimidad.
unanimous (iunánimos) adj. unánime.

unarmed (onármd) adj. desarmado.
unavoidable (onavóidabl) adj. inevitable, ineludible.
unaware (oneuér) adj. desprevenido; inadvertido; incauto; ignorante; adv. inesperadamente; inopinadamente; impensadamente.
unbalanced (onbálanst) adj. desequilibrado; — account cuenta no saldada.
unbearable (onbérabl) adj. inaguantable; insoportable.
unbecoming (onbikóming) adj. impropio; an — dress un vestido que no sienta bien o cae mal.
unbelief (onbilíf) s. incredulidad.
unbelievable (onbilívabl) adj. increíble.
unbeliever (onbilíver) s. descreído; irreligioso, infiel, incrédulo.
unbelieving (onbilíving) adj. descreído; irreligioso, infiel, incrédulo.
unbending (onbénding) adj. inflexible.
unbiased (onbáiest) adj. imparcial, libre de prejuicio.
unbosom (onbúsom) v. revelar, confesar; descubrir (secretos); abrir su pecho a uno; desahogarse; to — oneself desahogarse con alguien.
unbound (onbáund) adj. desencuadernado, suelto, desatado.
unbroken (onbróukn) adj. intacto, entero; indómito; inviolado; no interrumpido; continuo.
unbutton (onbótn) v. desabotonar; desabrochar.
uncanny (onkáni) adj. extraño, raro, misterioso; pavoroso.
unceasing (onsísing) adj. incesante.
uncertain (onsértn) adj. incierto; dudoso; variable, inconstante.
uncertainty (onsérteni) s. incertidumbre, falta; duda, ambigüedad.
unchangeable (onchényebl) adj. inmutable, inalterable, igual.
unchanged (onchényed) adj. inalterado; igual.
uncharitable (onchéritebl) adj. duro; falto de caridad; nada caritativo.
uncle (onkl) s. tío.
unclean (onklín) adj. inmundo, sucio, impuro; desaseado.
uncomfortable (onkómfortabl) adj. incómodo; molesto; penoso, desagradable.

UNCOMMON **UNDERWORLD**

uncommon (onkómon) adj. poco común; poco frecuente, raro, insólito.
uncompromising (onkómpromaising) adj. intransigente; firme.
unconcern (onkonsérn) s. indiferencia.
unconditional (oncondíshonal) adj. incondicional; absoluto, limitado.
uncongenial (onkonyínial) adj. que no congenia, antipático.
unconquerable (oncónkerabl) adj. invencible; insuperable.
unconquered (onkónkerd) adj. no conquistado.
unconscious (onkónshos) adj. inconsciente; privado.
unconsciousness (onkónshosnes) s. inconsciencia; insensibilidad.
uncontrollable (onkontrólabl) adj. ingobernable; indomable.
unconventional (onkonvénshonal) adj. despreocupado; informal; que no ajusta a las reglas establecidas.
uncouth (oncúz) adj. rudo, tosco; grosero; rústico; extraño.
uncover (onkóver) v. destapar; descubrir; revelar; desabrigarse.
unction (ónkshon) s. unción; fervor; **Extreme Unction** Extremaunción.
unctuous (ónkshos) adj. untuoso.
uncultivated (onkóltiveited) adj. inculto; rústico; sin cultura.
uncultured (onkólchurd) adj. inculto; grosero; carente de cultura.
undecided (ondisáided) adj. indeciso.
undeniable (ondenáiabl) adj. innegable; irrefutable; incontrastable.
underbrush (ónderbrosh) s. maleza.
underclothes (ónderclouz) s. pl. ropa interior.
underestimate (onderéstimeit) v. menospreciar; salir corto en un cálculo; apreciar en menos de lo que es justo.
underfed (ónderfed) adj. mal nutrido.
undergo (ondergó) s. sufrir; aguantar; padecer; arrostrar.
undergone (ondergón) p.p. de **to undergo**.
undergraduate (ondergráyueit) s. estudiante del bachillerato; — **course** curso de bachillerato.
underground (óndergraund) adj. subterráneo; s. sótano, subterráneo; adv. bajo tierra; ocultamente.
underhanded (onderjánded) adj. disimulado; clandestino; socarrón.
underline (onderláin) v. subrayar.
underlying (onderláing) adj. fundamental; subyacente.
undermine (ondermáin) v. minar; socavar; zapar.
underneath (onderníz) prep. bajo; debajo de; adv. debajo.
underpay (onderpéi) v. pagar insuficientemente; malpagar; escatimar la paga; s. retribución insuficiente.
undersell (ondersél) v. vender a menos precio que otro.
undershirt (óndershert) s. camiseta.
undersigned (ondersáind) s. firmante; infrascrito; **the —** el infrascrito; el suscrito.
undersized (ondersáisd) adj. de talla menor que mediana.
underskirt (ónderskert) s. enaguas; refajo.
understand (onderstánd) v. entender; ser sabedor; comprender; sobrentender; percibir; alcanzar.
understandable (onderstándabl) adj. comprensible.
understanding (onderstánding) s. comprensión; entendimiento; inteligencia; conocimiento.
understood (onderstúd) pret. y p.p. de **to understand**; adj. entendido; comprensivo; sobrentendido.
understudy (ónderstodi) s. sobresaliente; actor suplente; v. servir de sobresaliente o actor suplente.
undertake (ondertéik) v. emprender; acometer; intentar; tomar a su cargo o por su cuenta.
undertaken (ondertéiken) p.p. de **to undertake**.
undertaker (óndertelker) s. empresario de pompas fúnebres.
undertaking (ondertéiking) s. empresa.
undertook (ondertúk) pret. de **to undertake**.
undertow (óndertou) s. resaca.
underwear (ónderuer) s. ropa interior.
underwent (onderuént) pret. de **to undergo**.
underworld (ónderuerld) s. ham-

— 247 —

pa; barrios bajos; clase criminal; malhechores.
undesirable (ondesáirabl) adj. indeseable; inconveniente.
undid (ondíd) pret. de **to undo**.
undisturbed (ondistérbd) adj. impasible; imperturbable; sereno; tranquilo; intacto.
undo (ondú) v. deshacer; desatar; arruinar; perder; desenredar; **to — one's hair** soltarse el cabello.
undone (ondón) p.p. de **to undo**; sin hacer; sin terminar; **still —** todavía sin hacer; por hacer; **to come —** desatarse.
undoubtedly (ondáutedli) adv. indudablemente; sin duda.
undress (ondrés) v. desvestir(se); desnudar(se).
undue (ondiú) adj. indebido; desmedido; impropio; excesivo; ilícito; no vencido (un documento).
undulate (óndiuleit) v. ondear.
unduly (ondiúli) adv. indebidamente.
undying (ondáing) adj. imperecedero; inmortal, eterno.
unearth (onérz) v. desenterrar.
uneasily (onísili) adv. con ansia; con desasosiego; intranquilamente, con inquietud.
uneasiness (onísines) s. malestar; intranquilidad; desasosiego.
uneasy (onísi) adj. ansioso; desasosegado; intranquilo; inquieto.
uneducated (onédiukeited) adj. mal educado; inculto; indocto; ignorante; carente de instrucción.
unemployed (onemplóid) adj. cesante; desocupado; sin empleo; ocioso; **— funds** fondos inactivos.
unemployment (onemplóiment) s. cesantía; desempleo; desocupación; falta de trabajo.
unending (onénding) adj. interminable; inacabable.
unequal (oníkual) adj. desigual; insuficiente; falto de uniformidad.
uneven (oníven) adj. disparejo; irregular; impar; accidentado; desigual; escabroso; barrancoso.
unevenness (onívenes) s. desigualdad; inconstancia; desnivel; irregularidad, escabrosidad del terreno; falta de regularidad.
unexpected (onekspécted) adj. inesperado; imprevisto; inopinado; **—ly** adv. inesperadamente; de improviso.

unfailing (onféiling) adj. infalible; inagotable; seguro; indefectible; constante.
unfair (onfér) adj. injusto; falso; de mala fe.
unfaithful (onféizful) adj. infiel; desleal; pérfido; traidor.
unfamiliar (onfamiliar) adj. poco común; poco conocido; **to be — with** no tener conocimiento de; no estar al tanto; ignorar.
unfasten (onfásn) v. desatar; desabrochar; aflojar; soltar.
unfavorable (onféivorabl) adj. desfavorable; adverso; contrario.
unfeeling (onfiling) adj. insensible; apático; cruel; duro de corazón.
unfinished (onfínisht) adj. incompleto; sin terminar; sin pulimento; imperfecto.
unfit (onfít) adj. impropio; inadecuado; incompetente; inepto; incapaz; v. inhabilitar; incapacitar.
unfold (onfóuld) v. desarrollar(se); desplegar; revelar; descubrir.
unforeseen (onforsín) adj. imprevisto.
unforgettable (onforguétabl) adj. inolvidable.
unfortunate (onfórchuneit) adj. desafortunado; desventurado; infeliz; desdichado; **—ly** adv. desgraciadamente; desventuradamente.
unfriendly (onfréndli) adj. hostil; adv. hostilmente; poco amistoso.
unfurl (onférl) v. desplegar; desplegar; desdoblar; extender.
unfurnished (onfórnisht) adj. desamueblado.
ungrateful (ongréitful) adj. ingrato; desagradecido.
unhappy (onjápi) adj. infeliz; desgraciado; desdichado.
unharmed (onjármd) adj. ileso; sano y salvo.
unhealthy (onjélzi) adj. enfermizo; malsano; insalubre.
unheard-of (onjérdof) adj. inaudito; singular; desconocido; sin fama.
unhitch (onjítch) v. desenganchar; desunir; desatar.
unhook (onjúk) v. desenganchar; descolgar.
unhurt (onjért) adj. ileso.
uniform (iúniform) adj. uniforme; armonioso; consistente; s. uniforme.

— 248 —

uniformity (iunifórmiti) s. uniformidad; armonía; conformidad.
unify (iúnifai) v. unificar; unir.
unimportant (onimpórtant) adj. insignificante.
union (iúnion) s. unión; confederación; liga; — **leader** jefe de un gremio obrero; **trade** — gremio obrero.
unique (iuník) adj. único, singular.
unison (iúnison) adj. unísono; s. unisonancia; unisón.
unit (iúnit) s. unidad.
unite (iunáit) v. unir(se).
unity (iúniti) s. unidad, unión; concordia; conformidad.
universal (iunivérsal) adj. universal.
universe (iúnivers) s. universo.
university (iunivérsiti) s. universidad.
unjust (onyóst) adj. injusto.
unjustifiable (onyostifáiabl) adj. injustificable; sin excusa.
unkempt (onkémpt) adj. desaseado; despeinado; desgreñado.
unkind (onkáind) adj. adusto; áspero; descortés; cruel.
unknown (onnóun) adj. desconocido; ignoto; incógnito; — **quantity** s. incógnita; **it is** — **se** ignora; no se sabe; se desconoce.
unlawful (onlóful) adj. ilegal.
unless (onlés) conj. a menos que; a no ser que; excepto; sino.
unlike (onláik) adj. diferente; distinto; prep. a diferencia de.
unlikely (onláikli) adj. improbable.
unlimited (onlímited) adj. ilimitado.
unload (onlóud) v. descargar; aligerar.
unlock (onlók) v. abrir una cerradura; soltar; revelar; desapretar (las formas); dar libre acceso.
unlucky (onlóki) adj. desdichado; desgraciado; infortunado; desventurado; funesto, infausto; nefasto; azaroso; aciago; de mal agüero; siniestro.
unmanageable (onméneyebl) adj. inmanejable, ingobernable; indomable; intratable.
unmarried (onmárrid) adj. soltero.
unmerciful (onmérsiful) adj. despiadado; inclemente, riguroso.
unmistakable (onmistéikebl) adj. inequívoco; inerrable, evidente.
unmoved (onmúvd) adj. fijo; inmutable; inmoto, inmóvil; impasible; indiferente; inalterable.
unnatural (onéchural) adj. afectado; contranatural; violento; cruel; monstruo; inhumano.
unnecessary (onéseseri) adj. innecesario; excusado, superfluo.
unnoticed (onóutist) adj. inadvertido; desadvertido.
unoblinging (onobláiyin) adj. poco complaciente; descortés.
unobserved (onobsérvd) adj. inadvertido; sin ser visto.
unobtainable (onobtéinebl) adj. inobtenible, inasequible.
unoccupied (onókiupaid) adj. desocupado; vacío; vacante, libre.
unprecedented (onprésedented) adj. sin precedente; inaudito.
unprepared (ompripérd) adj. desprevenido, desapercibido, no listo.
unpublished (onpóblisht) adj. inédito; secreto, oculto.
unquenchable (onkuénchebl) adj. inapagable, inextinguible.
unquestionable (onkuéschoneibl) adj. indisputable; incuestionable.
unravel (onréivl) v. desenredar; desenmarañar; deshilar, aclarar.
unreal (onríal) adj. irreal; ilusorio, imaginario.
unreasonable (onrísnabl) adj. desrazonable; irracional, inmoderado.
unquestionable (onkuéschonebl) adj. irreconocible; que no puede reconocerse; no conocible, incapaz de reconocerse.
unrefined (onrifáind) adj. no refinado; impuro; en bruto; inculto.
unrest (onrést) s. inquietud; desasosiego.
unroll (onróul) v. desenrollar(se); desenvolver(se); desplegar.
unruly (onrúli) adj. indómito; indócil; ingobernable, irrefrenable.
unsafe (onséif) adj. inseguro.
unsalable (onséilebl) adj. invendible.
unsatisfactory (onsatisfáctori) adj. no satisfactorio; poco satisfactorio, inaceptable.
unseen (onsín) adj. no visto; oculto; invisible.
unselfish (onsélfish) adj. desinteresado; generoso, desprendido.
unselfishness (onsélfishnes) s. desinterés, abnegación; generosidad.
unsettled (onsétld) adj. estable; variable, inconstante; vago, erran-

te, sin residencia fija; deshabitado; — **bills** cuentas no liquidadas; cuentas pendientes; — — **weather** tiempo variable.
unshaken (onshéikn) adj. inmóvil; inmovible; firme.
unsightly (onsáitli) adj. feo, desagradable a la vista.
unskilled (onskíld) adj. inexperto.
unskillful (onskílful) adj. inhábil, desmañado; inexperto, imperito.
unsociable (onsóshebl) adj. insociable, huraño; intratable.
unspeakable (onspíkebl) adj. indecible, inefable; inexplicable.
unstable (onstéibl) adj. inestable, voluble; movedizo, variable.
unsteady (onstédi) adj. inseguro;
unsuccessful (onsoksésful) adj. sin éxito, desafortunado, infructuoso; **to be** — no tener éxito.
unsuitable (onsútabl) adj. impropio; inapropiado; indigno, incongruo; inepto; inconveniente.
unsuspected (onsospékted) adj. insospechado.
untidy (ontáidi) adj. desaliñado; desarreglado, desaseado.
untie (ontái) v. desatar(se); desprender, desenlazar; desligar.
until (ontíl) prep. hasta; conj. hasta que.
untimely (ontáimli) adj. inoportuno; prematuro; intempestivo; adv. inoportunamente.
untiring (ontáiring) adj. incansable.
untold (ontóuld) adj. indecible, innumerable; nunca dicho, no narrado.
untouched (ontócht) adj. intacto; íntegro; inconmovible; inafectable; imposible; **to leave** — dejar intacto; no conmover.
untrained (ontréind) adj. desentrenado; indisciplinado; inexperto; imperito; sin preparación.
untried (ontráid) adj. virgen, no probado; no ensayado; — **law case** causa todavía no vista.
untroubled (ontróbld) adj. quieto; apacible; tranquilo; sosegado.
untrue (ontrú) adj. falso; mendaz; infiel; mentiroso; pérfido.
untruth (ontrúz) s. falsedad, mentira.
unused (oniúst) adj. desusado; desacostumbrado; no habituado a; no hecho a.
unusual (oniúshual) adj. inusitado; insólito; desusado; raro; excepcional; poco frecuente.
unveil (onvéil) v. descubrir; revelar; quitarse el velo.
unwary (onuéri) adj. incauto; imprudente; irreflexivo.
unwashed (onuásht) adj. sucio; puerco; no lavado.
unwelcome (onuélcom) adj. inoportuno; indeseable; mal quisto.
unwholesome (onjóulsom) adj. malsano; insalubre; nocivo; malo; dañino; perjudicial.
unwieldy (onuíldi) adj. pesado; difícil de manejarse; ponderoso; engorroso.
unwilling (onuíling) adj. renuente; reacio; mal dispuesto; **to be** — **to** no querer, no estar dispuesto a; —**ly** adv. de mala gana; sin querer.
unwillingness (onuílingnes) s. renuencia; mala gana; falta de voluntad.
unwise (onuáis) adj. ignorante; imprudente; indiscreto; necio.
unworthy (onuérzi) adj. indigno.
unwrap (onráp) v. desenvolver.
up (op) adj. levantado; erecto; ascendente; terminado; concluido; arriba; hacia arriba; adv. en lo alto; hacia arriba; adv. en lo derecho; hasta; enteramente,completamente — **and down** de arriba abajo; de acá para allá; —**s and downs** altibajos; fluctuaciones; vaivenes; — **to date** hasta la fecha, al día; **it is all** — **now** todo se acabó; — **the river** río arriba; **that is** — **to you** eso es cosa de usted; **prices are** — los precios han subido; **drink it** — bébaselo todo; **to be** — **against it** estar perplejo, no saber qué hacer; **to be** — **on the news** estar enterado de las noticias; **to lay** — **money** acumular dinero; **to be** — **to one's old tricks** hacer de las suyas; **what is** —? ¿qué pasa?; **time is** — expiró el plazo; ha pasado el tiempo fijado.
upbraid (opbréid) v. reconvenir; regañar; reprender.
upheld (opjéld) pret. y p.p. to uphold.
uphill (opjíl) adv. cuesta arriba; adj. trabajoso; ascendente.
uphold (opjóuld) v. sostener; apoyar.
upholster (opjóulster) v. tapizar; rellenar los muebles.

upholstery (opjóulsteri) s. tapicería.
upkeep (opkíp) s. conservación.
upland (ópland) s. altiplanicie; meseta; tierra adentro.
uplift (oplíft) s. elevación; levantamiento; v. edificar, elevar; levantar (el espíritu).
upon (opón) prep. sobre, encima de; en; — **arriving** al llegar.
uprightness (oprráitnes) s. rectitud; integridad; probidad.
uprising (oprráising) s. revuelta; levantamiento; sublevación.
uproar (óprrour) s. tumulto; gritería; alboroto; conmoción; bulla.
uproarious (oprróurios) adj. tumultuoso; bullicioso; ruidoso.
uproot (oprút) v. desenraizar; desarraigar.
upset (opsét) v. trastornar; tumbar; volcar; perturbar; turbar; desordenar; contrariar; pret. y p.p. de to upset; **to become —** sufrir un trastorno, vuelco o turbación; adj. indispuesto; descompuesto; s. vuelco; trastorno; turbación; indisposición.
upshot (ópshot) s. resultado final.
upside (ópsaid) s. parte superior; lo de arriba; — **down** al revés; patas arriba; en desorden.
upstairs (opstérs) adv. arriba, en el piso de arriba; adj. de arriba; s. piso de arriba.
upstart (ópstart) s. advenedizo; principiante presuntuoso.
up-to-date (óptudeit) adj. moderno; al día; al corriente; al tanto.
upturn (óptern) v. volver hacia arriba; s. alza (de precios).
upward (ópuord) adv. arriba; hacia arriba; más; — **of** más de; adj. ascendente; hacia arriba, para arriba.
upwards (ópuords) adv. véase **upward**.
urban (érban) adj. urbano.
urchin (érchin) s. granuja; pilluelo; rapazuelo; **sea —** erizo de mar.
urge (ery) v. urgir, instar; impeler, empujar, forzar; recomendar o solicitar con instancia; apretar, acosar, seguir de cerca.
urgency (éryensi) s. urgencia.
urgent (éryent) adj. urgente.
urinate (iúrineit) v. orinar.
urine (iúrin) s. orina, orines.
urn (ern) s. urna; jarrón.
us (os) pron. nos; nosotros (con preposición).

usage (iúsey) s. usanza; uso; trato, tratamiento; uso constante.
use (iús) s. uso, empleo, utilidad; aprovechamiento; manejo; costumbre, práctica, estilo; **of no —** inútil, inservible; **out of —** inusitado; pasado de moda; **to have no further — for** ya no tener necesidad de; no querer saber más de alguien; **to make — of** servirse de; utilizar; v. usar; emplear; valerse de; servirse de; acostumbrar; soler; — **your judgment** haz lo que te parezca; **to — up** gastar, agotar; consumir; **what is the — of it?** ¿para qué sirve?; ¿qué objeto tiene?; **to be —d to** estar acostumbrado a; **he —d to do it** solía hacerlo, lo hacía.
useful (iúsful) adj. útil.
usefulness (iúsfulnes) s. utilidad.
useless (iúsles) adj. inútil.
uselessness (iúslesnes) s. inutilidad.
usher (ósher) s. acomodador (en un teatro o iglesia); ujier; v. conducir; llevar, introducir, acomodar, anunciar; acompañar.
usual (iúshual) adj. usual; corriente, común; acostumbrado; ordinario; **—ly** adv. usualmente.
usurer (iúshurer) s. usurero.
usurp (iusérp) v. usurpar.
usury (iúsuri) s. usura.
utensil (iuténsl) s. utensilio.
uterus (iúteros) s. útero.
utility (iutíliti) s. servicio.
utilize (iútilais) v. utilizar.
utmost (ótmoust) adj. sumo, extremo, más distante; más posible; último; **do you — haga** usted cuanto pueda; **he did his —** hizo cuanto pudo; **to the —** hasta más no poder.
utter (óter) v. proferir; decir; articular, pronunciar, expresar, publicar; adj. perentorio, terminante.
utterance (óterans) s. declaración; expresión; pronunciación.
uttermost (ótermoust) véase **utmost**.
uvula (iúviula) s. úvula; campanilla; galillo.

V

vacancy (vékensi) s. vacante, empleo vacante; hueco, laguna; vacación, baja; habitación o apartamiento desocupado; vacío.

vacant (vékent) adj. vacante; vacío; vacuo; libre, desembarazado; ocioso.
vacate (vekéit) v. desocupar, dejar vacío; evacuar; dejar o renunciar la posesión de un empleo.
vacation (vekéshon) s. vacación, días feriados; fiesta; asueto.
vaccinate (váccineit) v. vacunar.
vaccination (vaksinéshon) s. vacunación.
vaccine (váksin) s. vacuna.
vacillate (véslet) v. vacilar.
vacuum (vákium) s. vacío; vacuo; — cleaner escoba eléctrica.
vagabond (véguebond) adj. y s. vagabundo, vagamundo, errante.
vagrant (végrant) adj. vago, vagabundo, errante; vagoroso; s. vago.
vague (véig) adj. vago, indefinido.
vain (véin) adj. vano; vanidoso; presuntuoso.
vainglory (véinglori) s. vanagloria.
vale (véil) s. valle; cañada.
valentine (válentain) s. tarjeta o regalo del día de San Valentín (el día de los enamorados); **to my —** a mi querido(a).
valet (válet) s. criado, camarero; paje, asistente.
valiant (váliant) adj. valiente.
valid (válid) adj. válido.
validity (valíditi) s. validez.
valise (valís) s. valija, maleta; saco de viaje; veliz, petaca.
valley (válei) s. valle.
valor (válor) s. valor, ánimo.
valorous (váloros) adj. valeroso, valiente, intrépido, bizarro.
valuable (váliuabl) adj. valioso, costoso, precioso; preciado; **—s** s. pl. objetos de valor, joyas.
valuation (valiuéshon) s. valuación; valoración, avalúo; tasa.
value (váliu) s. valor, precio, mérito; valor intrínseco; valía, monta; justiprecio; valuación; sentido, entidad; importancia; v. avaluar; tasar, apreciar; estimar.
valueless (váliules) adj. sin valor.
valve (valv) s. válvula; valva (de los moluscos); ventalla, lámpara.
van (ven) s. camión (para transportar muebles); mudanza; vanguardia.
vane (véin) s. veleta, aspa (de molino de viento); grímpola.
vanilla (vanila) s. vainilla.
vanish (vánish) v. desvanecerse; desaparecer; disipar.

vanity (vániti) s. vanidad; engreimiento; presunción, alarde.
vanquish (vánkuish) v. vencer.
vantage (vántey) s. ventaja; superioridad; **point of —** lugar estratégico.
vapor (vépor) s. vapor, vaho.
variable (váriabl) adj. y s. variable.
variance (vérians) s. variación, cambio; mudanza, discordia; desavenencia, disensión; **to be at —** no estar de acuerdo.
variation (variéshon) s. variación; cambio, alteración, mudanza.
varied (vérid) adj. variado.
variegated (vérigueited) adj. abigarrado, variado, pintarrajeado.
variety (varáieti) s. variedad.
various (vérios) adj. varios; diferentes, distintos.
varnish (várnish) s. barniz.
vary (véri) s. variar, cambiar.
vase (veis) s. vaso, jarrón.
vassal (vásal) adj. y s. vasallo.
vast (vast) adj. vasto; inmenso; extenso; dilatado; **—ly** adv. vastamente, sumamente; en sumo grado.
vastness (vástnes) s. inmensidad.
vat (vat) s. tina, tanque.
vaudeville (vódevil) s. vodevil; función de variedades; zarzuela.
vault (volt) s. bóveda; tumba; cúpula; cueva, bodega; subterráneo, sibil; cielo, firmamento; **bank —** caja fuerte, depósito; v. abovedar, saltar por encima con garrocha; voltear.
vaunt (vont) v. jactarse; ostentar; alardear; hacer gala; s. jactancia.
veal (vil) s. carne de ternera; **bob —** carne de ternera demasiado tierna; **— cutlet** chuleta de ternera.
veer (vir) v. virar; s. virada.
vegetable (véyetebl) s. vegetal, planta; legumbre; hortalizas, legumbres; **—s** verduras; adj. vegetal de legumbres, de hortalizas; **— garden** hortaliza.
vegetate (véyeteit) v. vegetar.
vegetation (veyetéshon) s. vegetación.
vehemence (víjemens) s. vehemencia.
vehement (víjement) adj. vehemente.
vehicle (víjikl) s. vehículo.
veil (veil) s. velo; v. velar.

vein (vein) s. vena, veta; capa.
veined (véind) adj. veteado; jaspeado; venoso, avetado.
velocity (velóciti) s. velocidad.
velvet (vélvit) s. terciopelo; velludo; adj. aterciopelado.
velvety (vélviti) adj. aterciopelado.
vendor (véndor) s. vendedor; buhonero, vendedor ambulante.
veneer (venír) s. chapa; hoja para chapear; v. chapear; ocultar.
venerable (vénerabl) adj. venerable; almo, sagrado, venerado.
venerate (vénereit) v. venerar.
veneration (veneréshon) s. veneración, respeto, reverencia.
Venezuelan (venesuílan) adj. y s. venezolano.
vengeance (vényens) s. venganza; vindicta; with a — con violencia.
venison (vénesn) s. venado; carne de venado.
venom (vénom) s. veneno, ponzoña.
venomous (vénomos) adj. venenoso; ponzoñoso, dañoso, maligno.
ventilate (véntileit) v. ventilar.
ventilation (ventiléshon) s. ventilación.
ventilator (véntileitor) s. ventilador, aventador, abano.
venturous (vénchuros) adj. aventurado; osado, atrevido.
veranda (veránda) s. galería; terraza; pórtico, veranda.
verb (verb) s. verbo.
verbal (vérbal) adj. verbal.
verbose (verbós) adj. verboso.
verdict (vérdikt) s. veredicto; fallo, decisión, opinión, dictado; sentencia.
verdure (véryur) s. verdura, verdor, fronda, vegetación.
verge (very) s. borde, margen, orilla; veril; círculo; anillo, enlace, esfera; v. to — on rayar, estar al margen de.
verify (vérifai) v. verificar.
verily (vérili) adv. en verdad.
veritable (véritabl) adj. verdadero.
verse (vers) s. verso.
versed (verst) adj. versado, perito; práctico, experto.
version (vérshon) s. versión.
vertical (vértikal) adj. vertical.
very (véri) adv. muy; mucho, sumamente; — much muchísimo; at that — moment en aquel mismísimo instante; it is — cold today hoy hace mucho frío; adj. mismo, mismísimo; idéntico, verdadero, real.
vespers (véspers) s. pl. vísperas.
vessel (vésl) s. vasija; barco; nave, embarcación; blood — vena; arteria; vaso capilar.
vest (vest) s. chaleco; v. conferir; investir; to — with power conferir poder a.
vestibule (véstibiul) s. vestíbulo; zaguán; pórtico; portal; atrio.
vestige (véstiy) s. vestigio.
vestment (véstment) s. vestidura.
veteran (véteran) adj. y s. veterano.
veterinary (véterineri) s. veterinario o albéitar.
veto (víto) s. veto; prohibición; v. poner veto a; negarse a aprobar; vedar; prohibir.
vex (veks) s. vejar; irritar; enfadar; molestar; provocar.
vexation (vekséshon) s. vejación; maltrato; enojo; enfado.
via (váia) prep. por, por la vía de
viaduct (váiadokt) s. viaducto.
vial (váial) s. redoma; botella; vaso; small — ampolleta.
viand (váiand) s. vianda; carne; comida; alimento.
vibrate (váibreit) v. vibrar; arrojar con ímpetu.
vibration (vaibréshon) s. vibración; movimiento trémulo.
vice (váis) s. vicio; maldad habitual; falta; defecto.
vice-president (váispresident) s. vicepresidente.
viceroy (váisroi) s. virrey.
vice versa (váisversa) viceversa.
vicinity (visíniti) s. vecindad; cercanía; proximidad; inmediaciones.
vicious (víshos) adj. vicioso; maligno; enconado; depravado; — dog perro bravo, que muerde.
vicissitude (visísitiud) s. vicisitud; altibaja; mundanza, inestabilidad; peripecia.
victim (víktim) s. víctima.
victor (víktor) s. vencedor.
victorious (viktórios) adj. victorioso; triunfante.
victory (víktori) s. victoria.
victuals (víkchuals) s. pl. vituallas; víveres; provisiones.
vie (vái) v. contender; competir; disputar; emular.
view (viú) s. vista; paisaje; perspectiva; inspección; apariencia; opinión; mira; propósito; in —

— 253 —

of en vista de; with a — to con el propósito (o la mira) de; at one — de una ojeada; de una mirada v. mirar; examinar; inspeccionar.
viewpoint (viúpoint) s. punto de vista.
vigil (víyil) s. vigilia; velada.
vigilance (víyilans) s. vigilancia; desvelo; cuidado.
vigilant (víyilant) adj. vigilante.
vigor (vígor) s. vigor.
vigorous (vígoros) adj. vigoroso.
vile (váil) adj. vil; ruin; bajo.
villa (víla) s. villa; quinta; casa de campo.
village (víley) s. aldea; villa.
villager (víleyer) s. aldeano.
villain (vílen) s. villano; ruin; pícaro; bellaco; malvado.
villainous (vílenos) adj. villano; truhán; malhechor; ruin; vil.
villany (víleni) s. villanía.
vim (vim) s. fuerza; vigor; energía.
vindicate (víndekeit) v. vindicar; vengar; defender, justificar.
vindictive (vindíktiv) adj. vengativo.
vine (vain) s. vid, enredadera.
vinegar (vínegar) s. vinagre.
vineyard (víniard) s. viñedo.
vintage (víntey) s. vendimia; época; edad.
violate (váioleit) v. violar, infringir; quebrantar; forzar.
violation (vaioléshon) s. violación.
violence (váiolens) s. violencia.
violet (váiolet) s. violeta; violado.
violin (vaiolín) s. violín.
violinist (vaiolínist) s. violinista.
viper (váiper) s. víbora.
virgin (véryin) s. y adj. virgen.
virginal (véryinal) adj. virginal.
virtual (vérchual) adj. virtual; —ly adv. virtualmente.
virtue (vérchu) s. virtud.
virtuous (vérchos) adj. virtuoso.
visa (víse) s. visa; v. visar, refrendar.
visé véase visa.
vise (vais) s. tornillo de banco.
visible (vísibl) adj. visible.
vision (víshon) s. visión, vista; sueño; fantasía.
visionary (víshoneri) adj. ilusorio; quimérico, visionario; s. visionario, iluso, soñador.
visit (vísit) v. visitar; s. visita; registro, inspección; to — punishment upon mandar un castigo a, castigar a

visitor (vísitor) s. visitador.
visor (váisor) s. víscra.
vista (vísta) s. vista, paisaje.
vital (váital) adj. vital.
vitality (vaitáliti) s. vitalidad.
vitamin (váitamin) s. vitamina.
vivacious (vaivéshos) adj. vivaz vivaracho; animado, despejado.
vivacity (vaivásiti) s. viveza.
vivid (vívid) adj. vívido, vivo.
vocabulary (vokébiuleri) s. vocabulario, léxico.
vocal (vókal) adj. vocal; oral.
vocation (vokéshon) s. vocación.
vogue (voug) s. boga; moda; in — de moda.
voice (vóis) s. voz, habla; voto; v. expresar; decir; vocear; hacerse eco de; dar el tono.
voiceless (vóisles) adj. mudo; sin voz; — **consonant** consonante muda.
void (vóid) adj. vacío; nulo; inválido; — **of** falto de; s. vacío; v. hacer el vacío; anular; vaciar
volatile (vólatil) adj. volátil.
volcanic (volkánik) adj. volcánico.
volcano (volkéino) s. volcán.
volition (volíshon) s. volición; voluntad.
volley (vóli) s. descarga; andanada; lluvia de piedras, balas, etc.; salva; v. lanzar una descarga de proyectiles; volear una pelota.
volt (volt) s. voltio.
voltage (vóltey) s. voltaje.
volume (vólium) s. volumen; bulto; tomo; suma; cantidad; caudal.
voluminous (volúminos) adj. voluminoso; prolijo; copioso.
voluntary (vólonteri) adj. voluntario; espontáneo.
volunteer (volontír) s. voluntario; espontáneo; adj. de voluntarios; v. ofrecer; contribuir.
voluptuous (volópchos) adj. voluptuoso; lujurioso.
vomit (vómit) s. vómito v. vomitar; deponer.
voracious (voréshos) adj. voraz.
vote (vóut) s. voto; votación; v. votar por.
voter (vóuter) s. elector, votante.
vouch (váuch) v. atestiguar; testificar; — **for** dar fe de; garantizar; responder por; salir fiador de.
voucher (váucher) s. comprobante; justificante; recibo; fiador.

vouchsafe (vauchséif) v. conceder; otorgar; condescender.
vow (váu) s. voto; juramento; promesa solemne; v. hacer voto de; juramentar; prometer.
vowel (váuel) s. y adj. vocal.
voyage (vóley) s. viaje; travesía; v. viajar; navegar.
vulgar (vólgar) adj. soez, ordinario; vulgar; grosero.
vulture (vólchur) s. buitre; aura.

W

wabble (uábl) v. tambalear(se); bambolear(se); vacilar; temblar; s. tambaleo; bamboleo; balanceo.
wad (uad) s. guata; taco; bodoque; pelotilla; bolita; rollo; — **of money** rollo de billetes; dinero; v. atacar un arma de fuego; rellenar; hacer una pelotilla de.
waddle (uádl) v. anadear; contonearse, zarandearse (al andar); s. anadeo; zarandeo.
wade (uéid) v. vadear, chapotear; andar descalzo por la orilla del agua; to — **through a book** leer con dificultad un libro.
wafer (uéifer) s. oblea, hostia (consagrada); barquillo, fulminante; v. pegar o cerrar con oblea.
waft (uáft) v. llevar en vilo; llevar por el aire; s. ráfaga de aire o de olor; movimiento de la mano; señal hecha con bandera.
wag (uág) v. menear, sacudir; mover ligeramente; to — **the tail** menear la cola; s. meneo, coleada.
wage (uéy) v. hacer (guerra); dar (batalla); sostener; empeñar; s. pl. —s paga, jornal, sueldo; salario, soldada; — **earner** jornalero; obrero, trabajador.
wager (uéyer) s. apuesta; **to lay a —** hacer una apuesta; v. apostar.
wagon (uágon) s. carro, carreta; vagón, galera; vehículo, coche.
waist (uéist) s. cintura; talle.
waistcoat (uéiscout) s. chaleco.
wait (uéit) v. esperar, aguardar; servir; s. espera.
waiter (uéiter) s. mozo, camarero; sirviente, criado; mesero.
waiting (uéiting) s. espera; servicio; — **room** sala de espera.

waitress (uéitres) s. camarera, moza; criada, mesera.
waive (uéiv) v. renunciar; repudiar; **to — one's right** renunciar voluntariamente a sus derechos.
wake (uéik) v. despertar(se); resucitar; excitar; velar a un muerto; **to — up** despertar(se); despabilar(se); s. velorio; vela o velación de un muerto; fiesta nocturna o verbena; estela, aguaje.
wakeful (uéikful) adj. desvelado, despierto; vigilante, en vela.
waken (uéiken) v. despertar(se); recordar (a una persona que está dormida); llamar al dormido.
walk (uók) v. andar, caminar, ir a pie; pasear; marchar; obrar, conducirse, comportarse; aparecer (fantasmas, espectros, etc.); liar el petate; ser despedido; andar o pasar de una parte a otra; **to — away** irse, marcharse; **to — back home** volver a casa (a pie); **to — the hospitals** estudiar clínica en los hospitales; **to — down** bajar; **to — in** entrar; **to — the streets** andar por las calles, andorrear; s. paseo, senda, vereda; caminata; modo de andar; paso del caballo; acera; método de vida.
wall (uól) s. pared; muro; muralla; tapia, seto; banca de roca natural; **low mud —** tapia; **to drive to the —** poner entre la espada y la pared; poner en un aprieto.
wallet (uálet) s. cartera.
wallflower (uólflauer) s. alhelí; **to be a — at a dance** comer pavo; planchar el asiento.
wallop (uálop) v. pegar, zurrar; bullir, hervir; s. golpe, tunda.
wallow (uálou) v. revolcarse.
wallpaper (uólpeiper) s. papel tapiz.
walnut (uólnot) s. nuez de nogal; madera de nogal.
waltz (uólts) s. vals; v. valsar, bailar el vals.
wan (uon) adj. pálido, enfermizo; descolorido; lánguido.
wand (uónd) s. varita, vara; varita de virtudes; **magic —** varita mágica.
wander (uánder) v. vagar, errar; rondar, andorrear; corretear; delirar; **my mind —s easly** me distraigo fácilmente.
wanderer (uánderer) s. vago.

— 255 —

wane (uéin) v. menguar; **decaer**; s. mengua, disminución; decadencia; decrecer; **menguante de la luna**.

want (uónt) v. querer, desear; necesitar; haber menester; estar desprovisto de; s. falta, necesidad.

wanting (uónting) adj. falto, deficiente, defectuoso, necesitado; menguado; escaso.

wanton (uánton) adj. desenfrenado, libre; licencioso; protervo; retozón, travieso; extravagante.

war (uor) s. guerra; arte militar; estrategia; lucha; v. guerrear; hacer guerra; to — on guerrear con.

warble (uórbl) v. gorjear; trinar; cantar con quiebros y trinos.

warbler (uórbler) s. cantor; pájaro gorjeador; pájaro cantor.

ward (uord) s. pupilo, menor o huérfano (bajo tutela); sala, división; cuadra del hospital; v. guardar, defender, proteger; to — on resguardarse de; parar (un golpe).

warden (uórdn) s. guardián, alcaide.

wardrobe (uórdrob) s. guardarropa; armario, escaparate; vestuario.

warehouse (uérjaus) s. almacen, depósito; — keeper guardalmacén.

wares (uers) s. pl. artículos; mercancías, mercaderías, efectos.

warfare (uórfer) s. guerra.

warlike (uórlaik) adj. guerrero.

warm (uórm) adj. caliente, cálido; caluroso, ardiente; vivo, activo; cordial, reciente; celoso, conmovido; — **hearted** de buen corazón; — **temper** genio vivo, ardiente; v. calentar(se); caldear; abrigar; acalorar, avivar; encender.

warmth (uórmz) s. calor, cordialidad.

warn (uórn) v. avisar, advertir; caucionar, prevenir, apercibir.

warning (uórning) s. aviso, advertencia; amonestación; escarmiento; admonición, lección; let that be a — to you que te sirva de escarmiento; to take — estar alerta.

warp (uórp) s. urdimbre (de un tejido); torcedura; curvatura; comba; deformación; v. combar(se); deformar (se); torcer (se); desviar(se); alejarse, apartarse del camino recto; urdir (los hilos de un telar).

warrant (uórrant) s. autorización; garantía, justificación; v. autorizar; garantizar; responder por.

warrior (uórrior) s. guerrero.

warship (uórship) s. buque de guerra; acorazado.

wart (uórt) s. verruga.

wary (uéri) adj. cauteloso, cauto, precavido; prudente, avisado; astuto, sagaz.

was (uós) pret. de to be (primera y tercera persona del singular).

wash (uósh) v. lavar(se); bañar, regar; purificar; dar un baño o capa de metal; dar una mano o capa de color; to — **away** deslavarse; hacer desaparecer; **to be —ed away by the waves** ser arrastrado por las olas; s. lavado, lavatorio; colada; loción, agua de tocador; cosmético; batiente del mar; ropa lavada; chapaleo, aluvión.

washable (uóshabl) adj. lavable.

washed-out (uóshd-aut) adj. desteñido; sin fuerzas, agotado.

washer (uósher) s. lavadora, máquina de lavar; disco de cuero o de goma; — **woman** lavandera.

washing (uóshing) s. lavado, ropa sucia o para lavar; loción, lavatorio; — **machine** lavadora.

wasp (uósp) s. avispa.

waste (uéist) v. gastar; desgastar; malgastar, derrochar, prodigar; despilfarrar; obstruir, echar a perder; desperdiciar; disipar; **to — away** gastarse, consumirse, desgastarse; ir a menos, menguar, mermar; disminuirse s. desperdicio; despilfarro, gasto inútil; derroche, disminución, merma; desierto, baldío; — **of time** pérdida de tiempo; — **basket** cesto para papeles y desechos; to go to — gastarse, perderse; desperdiciarse; **to lay —** asolar, arruinar; — **pipe** tubo de desagüe.

wasteful (uéistful) adj. despilfarrado, gastador; manirroto, desperdiciado, ineconómico.

watch (uótch) v. mirar, observar; vigilar; velar, cuidar; hacer centinela o guardia; — **out!** ¡cuidado!; —**ed pot never boils** el que espera desespera; s. reloj de bolsillo; vela, desvelo; centinela, vigía, atalaya; vigilante; — **chain**

— 256 —

cadena de reloj; — glass cristal de reloj; ampolleta de media hora; to keep — over vigilar a.

watchful (uótchful) adj. alerta, vigilante, despierto; desvelado.

watchman (uótchman) s. sereno, vigilante, guardia; salvaguardia.

watchtower (uótchtauer) s. atalaya; mirador.

watchword (uótchuerd) s. contraseña; santo y seña; consigna.

water (uóter) s. agua; v. regar; aguar; abrevar; tomar agua.

watermelon (uótermelon) s. sandía.

waterproof (uóterpruf) adj. y s. impermeable; v. hacer impermeable.

waterspout (uóterspaut) s. surtidor; manga o bomba marina.

waterway (wóteruei) s. vía de agua; río navegable; canal.

watery (uóteri) adj. aguado; ácueo; claro, ralo; insípido, evaporado.

wave (uéiv) v. ondear; ondular; tremolar; hacer señas o señales; agitar; blandir (una espada, blasón, etc.); to — aside apartar, rechazar; beating of the —s embate de las olas; to — good-by hacer una seña o ademán de despedida; shock of a — golpe de mar; sound — onda sonora; s. onda, ola; arrullo; ondulación; movimiento de la mano; ademán.

waver (uéiver) v. oscilar; ondear; tambalear; balancearse; s. vacilación; titubeo.

wavy (uéivi) adj. rizado; ondulado; ondeado; undívago; undoso.

wax (uáks) s. cera; ear — cera de los oídos, cerumen; — candle vela de cera; — paper papel encerado; v. encerar, pulir con cera; crecer; aumentarse, hacerse; ponerse.

way (uéi) s. vía; camino; ruta; senda; conducto, paso; calzada, calle; canal; modo, manera; — in entrada; any — de cualquier modo; de cualquiera manera; como se quiera; — out salida; a long — off muy lejos; a una larga distancia; to go out of the — extraviarse; to make — abrirse camino; abrir paso; by — of por, por vía de; to keep out of the — esconderse, ocultarse; evitar el encontrarse con alguno; — of comparison a modo de comparación; by the — de paso; out of the — fuera del camino; apartado; a un lado; impropio, extraordinario; to have one's — salirse con la suya; use your own — hágalo usted como quiera o hágalo usted a su modo.

waylay (ueiléi) v. estar en acecho (de alguien); insidiar; poner celadas.

wayside (uéisaid) s. borde del camino; adj. junto al camino.

wayward (uéiuerd) adj. voluntarioso; desobediente; descarriado, díscolo; avieso, vacilante.

we (ui) pron. nosotros(as).

weak (uik) adj. débil; flaco; endeble; delicado; frágil; resistente; inseguro — market mercado flojo.

weaken (uíken) v. debilitar(se); desmayar, flaquear; disminuir; desfallecer; perder ánimo.

weakly (uíkli) adv. débilmente; adj. enfermizo, débil; enclenque, canijo.

weakness (uíknes) s. debilidad.

wealth (uélz) s. riqueza; copia, abundancia; fortuna, opulencia.

wealthy (uélzi) adj. rico.

wean (uín) v. destetar; apartar gradualmente (de un hábito).

weapon (uépon) s. arma.

wear (uer) v. llevar; usar; exhibir; gastar, consumir; desgastar, deteriorar; to — away gastar(se); desgastar(se); consumir, decaer; to — down disminuir por el roce; consumir, gastar; to — one's heart on one's sleeve andar con la cara descubierta; llevar el corazón en la mano; as the day wore on a medida que pasaba el día; s. uso, gasto; durabilidad; deterioro; moda; boga; it is for my own — es para mi propio uso.

wearily (wírili) adv. fatigosamente; con pena; con cansancio.

weariness (uírines) s. cansancio; fatiga; lasitud, aburrimiento.

wearing (uéring) adj. cansado; s. uso; desgaste, deterioro; pérdida.

wearisome (uírisom) adj. fatigoso, molesto; pesado, cansado.

weary (uíri) adj. cansado; fatigado; v. cansar(se); fatigar.

weasel (uísl) s. comadreja.

weather (uéder) s. tiempo; fenó-

— 257 —

weave meno o cambio meteorológico (viento, lluvia, nieve, etc.); — beaten desgastado o curtido por la intemperie; how is the — to day? ¿qué tiempo hace hoy? — bureau oficina meteorológica; — bound detenido por el mal tiempo; — vane veleta; — conditions condiciones atmosféricas; v. exponer a la intemperie; orear; airar; secar al aire; doblar, resistir a, sufrir.

weave (uív) v. tejer, entretejer; tramar, trenzar; urdir; trabajar en telar; s. tejido.

weaver (uíver) s. tejedor.

web (ueb) s. tela; membrana (entre los dedos de los pájaros acuáticos); rollo de papel continuo.

wed (ued) v. casar con; unir en matrimonio; contraer matrimonio; p.p. de to wed.

wedded (uéded) p.p. y adj. casado, unido; — to his own opinion aferrado en su opinión, testarudo.

wedding (uéding) s. boda, casamiento, nupcias; unión, enlace; — day día de la boda; — trip viaje de novios; silver — bodas de plata.

wedge (uédy) s. cuña; alzaprima; prisma triangular; entrada; medio de entrar; v. meter cuñas; to be —ed between estar encajado entre.

Wednesday (uédnesdei) s. miércoles.

wee (uí) adj. diminuto, pequeñito, chiquito.

weed (uíd) s. cizaña, mala hierba; tabaco, ropa o gasa de luto; v. desherbar (o desyerbar); escardar; sollar; quitar lo inútil o nocivo; to — out escardar, eliminar.

weedy (uídi) adj. herboso, lleno de malas hierbas; algoso.

week (uík) s. semana; this day —, a — from today de hoy en ocho; —end fin de semana; fiestas del sábado por la tarde; domingo y madrugada del lunes; — day día de trabajo.

weekly (uíkli) adj. semanal; semanario; hebdomario; adv. semanalmente; por semana; s. semanario; periódico o revista semanal.

weep (uíp) v. llorar.

weeping (uíping) adj. llorón; lloroso; — willow sauce llorón; s. llanto; lloro; lágrimas.

weevil (uívl) s. gorgojo.

weigh (uél) v. pesar; ponderar; medir; suspender; levar (anclas); considerar; to — anchor zarpar; levar anclas; to — down exceder en peso; hundirse por su propio peso; sobrepujar; sobrecargar.

weight (uéit) s. peso; pesa (de reloj o medida para pesar); gravedad; paper — pisapapeles; v. cargar; sobrecargar; aumentar el peso; asignar un peso o valor.

weighty (uéiti) adj. grave; ponderoso; de mucho peso; serio.

weird (uírd) adj. extraño; raro; misterioso; sobrenatural; fantástico.

welcome (uélkom) s. bienvenida; buena acogida; parabién; enhorabuena; feliz llegada o arribo; adj. grato, agradable; bienvenido; bien llegado; bien quisto; — home! ¡bienvenido! you are — no hay de qué; de nada (úsase para contestar a thank you); you are — here está usted en su casa; v. dar la bienvenida; recibir con agasajo; acoger o recibir con gusto.

weld (uéld) v. soldar(se).

welfare (uélfer) s. bienestar; bien; felicidad; bienandanza; prosperidad; — labor trabajo o labor social.

well (uél) s. pozo; cisterna; fuente; manantial; ojo de agua; cavidad; vaso o copa de un tintero; caja de bombas, sentina; v. manar; derramar; fluir; brotar; adj. conveniente, grato, satisfactorio; adv. bien, felizmente, convenientemente.

welt (uelt) s. verdugón; roncha.

went (uént) pret. de to go.

wept (uépt) pret. y p.p. de to weep.

were (uér) pret. de to be (para el plural y la segunda persona del singular); if I — you si yo fuera usted; there — había o hubo (pl.); they — gone se habían ido.

west (uést) s. Oeste, Occidente; Poniente; adj. occidental, del oeste; West Indies Antillas; adv. hacia el oeste; al oeste.

western (uéstern) adj. occidental; del oeste.

westerner (uésterner) s. natural del oeste; habitante del oeste.

westward (uéstuord) adv. hacia el oeste; adj. occidental; oeste.

wet (uét) adj. mojado; húmedo; humedecido; lluvioso; — **nurse** nodriza; v. mojar; humedecer; pret. y p.p. de to wet.

wetness (uétnes) s. humedad.

whack (juák) v. pegar; golpear; dar una tunda; s. golpe; golpiza; participación; ganga; prueba.

whale (juéil) s. ballena; v. dedicarse a la pesca de la ballena.

wharf (juórf) s. muelle; embarcadero.

what (juát) pron. qué, qué cosa, el que, la que; — **for?** ¿para qué? adj. que; — **though** aun cuando; — **he said is not true** lo que dijo no es cierto; **take — books you need** tome los libros que necesite; — **with** en parte; tanto; sea; — **if he should come?** ¿y si viniese?

whatever (juatéver) pron. cualquier cosa que; todo lo que; cuanto; sea lo que fuere; — **happens** pase lo que pase; **any person —** una persona cualquiera; **no money —** nada de dinero; — **do you mean?** ¿qué quiere usted decir?

whatsoever véase whatever.

wheat (juít) s. trigo; **cream of —** crema de trigo.

wheel (juíl) s. rueda; disco; rodaja; polea, bicicleta; muela de molino; timón; volante de automóvil; noria; **fly —** polea loca; **spinning —** torno de hilar; **cog —** rueda dentada; **paddle —** rueda de paletas; v. rodar, girar; dar vueltas; acarrear; andar en bicicleta; **to — around** girar sobre los talones.

wheelbarrow (juilbárrou) s. carretilla de mano.

when (juén) adv. y conj. cuando.

whence (juéns) adv. de donde, de que.

whenever (juenéver) adj. y conj. cuando; siempre que; en cualquier momento; cada vez que.

where (juér) adv. donde, dónde; adonde, adónde.

whereabouts (juérabauts) s. paradero; adv. dónde, en qué lugar.

whereas (juéras) conj. considerando; por cuanto; visto que; puesto que; mientras que; pues que; ya que; siendo así que.

whereby (juérbai) adv. por lo cual, con lo cual, por medio del cual, por donde.

wherefore (juérfor) adv. porque; por lo tanto; por eso; por lo cual; por consiguiente.

wherein (juérin) adv. en donde; en lo cual, en que.

whereof (juérof) adv. de lo cual; de que; cuyo; ¿de qué?, de quien.

whereupon (jueropón) adv. después que; así que sucedió esto; entonces; sobre que.

wherever (jueréver) adv. dondequiera que; adondequiera; por dondequiera que.

wherewithal (jueruidól) adv. con que; con lo cual; s. medios, fondos; dinero.

whet (juét) v. afilar; aguzar; estimular; abrir el apetito.

whether (juéder) conj. si; ya sea que; sea que; sea; ora; — **we go or not** sea que vayamos o no; **I doubt —** dudo (de) que.

which (juích) pron. que, el cual, lo cual, quien, cuyo; los cuales, las cuales, los que, las que; el que, la que; adj. interr. ¿qué?; **during — time** tiempo durante el cual; **all of —**, **all —** todo esto, todo lo cual; — **way?** ¿por dónde?; — **do you prefer?** ¿cuál prefiere usted?; **both of —** ambos; los dos.

whichever (juichéver) pron. y adj. (que); — **road you take** cualquier camino que tome usted.

whiff (juíf) s. fumada; bocanada; soplo; repentino hedor u olor; soplo de viento; v. soplar; echar bocanadas.

whilst (juáilst) conj. mientras, mientras que.

whim (juím) s. caprichoso; antojo; genialidad; extravagancia.

whimper (juímper) v. lloriquear; sollozar; plañir; gemir; quejarse; s. lloriqueo gimoteo; quejido.

whimsical (juímsikal) adj. caprichoso.

whine (juáin) s. lamentarse; lloriquear; plañir; quejarse.

whiner (juáiner) s. llorón; persona quejosa o quejumbrosa.

whip (juíp) s. azote; látigo; fuste; fuete; v. azotar; fustigar; zurrar; batir huevos o crema; ven-

WHIPPING   WHY

cer; **to — down** bajar corriendo o volando; **to — out** zafarse; escaparse; **to — up** batir; coger o asir de repente.

whipping (juíping) s. azotaina, flagelación, zurra; tunda.

whir (juír) v. zumbar; girar; s. zumbido; aleteo.

whirl (juírl) v. girar; dar vuelta; arremolinarse; **my head —s** estoy desvanecido; s. giro, vuelta; remolino; rotación; espiral de humo.

whirlpool (juírlpul) s. remolino; vorágine; vórtice.

whirlwind (juírluind) s. torbellino; remolino de viento.

whisk (juísk) v. cepillar; barrer; arrastrar; moverse con velocidad; **to — off** arrebatar; marcharse de prisa; **to — something out of sight** escamotear algo; esconder algo de prisa; **— broom** escobilla; **with a — of the broom** de un escobillazo.

whisker (juísker) s. patillas; bigotes del gato; barba.

whiskey (uíski) s. aguardiente de maíz, centeno; etc.

whisper (juísper) v. cuchichear; murmurar; hablar en secreto o al oído; susurrar; soplar; s. cuchicheo; murmullo; secreto; susurro; **to talk in a —** hablar en secreto; susurrar.

whistle (juísl) s. silbido; silbato; rechifla; pito; **fog — pito** de alarma en tiempo de niebla; v. silbar; chiflar; pitar; **to — for someone** llamar a uno a silbidos.

whit (juít) s. pizca; ápice; brizna.

white (juáit) adj. blanco; albo; pálido; cano; puro; inmaculado; honrado; recto; **— lead** albayalde; **— livered** cobarde; envidioso; **snow —** niveo; ampo de la nieve; **to show the — feather** portarse como un cobarde; s. clara de huevo; esclerótica.

whiten (juáitn) v. blanquear; emblanquecer(se).

whiteness (juáitnes) s. blancura; palidez; pureza; candor.

whitewash (juáituosh) v. blanquear; encalar; dar lechada; cubrir faltas o errores; dejar al contrario zapatero (en el juego).

whither (juíder) adv. a dónde, a qué parte; donde quiera.

whitish (juáitish) adj. blanquecino; blanquizco.

whittle (juítl) v. cortar; mondar; cercenar; aguzar; sacar punta; **to — down** expenses recortar o reducir los gastos; s. cuchillo; faca.

whiz (juís) v. zumbar, silbar; s. zumbido o silbido; **to be a —** ser un águila; ser muy listo.

who (jú) pron. pers. quien, quién; quienes, quiénes; que; el que; la que; **know —'s —** lo conoce al dedillo; **— is it?** ¿quién es? ¿quién toca?

whoever (juéver) pron. quien quiera que; cualquiera que.

whole (jóul) adj. todo; total; entero; íntegro; **the — day** el día entero; **— hearted** sincero, cordial; de todo corazón; s. total; el todo; conjunto; **on the — en general**; en conjunto.

wholesale (jóulseil) s. venta al por mayor; mayoreo; **— dealer** mayorista; adv. al por mayor, en grande; v. vender al por mayor; comerciar al mayoreo.

wholesome (jóulsom) adj. sano, individuo normalmente sano; **—ly** adv. saludablemente.

wholesomeness (jóulsomnes) s. salud; sanidad; salubridad.

wholly (jóuli) adv. cabalmente; enteramente, completamente, íntegramente; totalmente.

whom (jum) pron. per. a quien; a quienes; que; al que; a la que; a los que; al cual; a la cual; a los cuales; **for —** para quien; **— did you see?**, ¿a quién vio usted? **to — it may concern** a quien corresponda; a quien concierna.

whoop (jup) s. grito; alarido; estertor de la tosferina; chillido del búho; v. insultar a gritos; respirar convulsivamente; gritar, vocear; **—ing cough** tos ferina.

whore (jour) s. ramera; prostituta; trotacalles.

whose (jus) pron. cuyo, cuya; cuyos; cuyas; interr. ¿de quién? ¿de quiénes? **— book is this?** ¿de quién es este libro?

why (juai) adv. ¿por qué?; **the reason —** la razón por la cual; **—, of course** sí, por supuesto, claro que sí; **—, I just saw it** pero, si lo acabo de ver; **—, that is not true** pero si eso no es

wick cierto; s. el porque, causa, razón, motivo.

wick (uik) **s.** mecha; pabilo; — o **wich** aldea o pueblo (en voces compuestas v. gr. **Berwick, Greenwich**).

wicked (uíked) adj. malo, perverso; inicuo; malvado; travieso; picaresco; juguetón.

wickedness (uíkednes) s. maldad; malignidad; perversidad; vicio; pecado; iniquidad.

wicker (uíker) s. mimbre; — **chair** silla de mimbre.

wicket (uíket) s. portillo; portezuela; ventanilla.

wide (uáid) adj. ancho, espacioso; vasto; amplio; extenso; remoto; apartado; liberal; lejano; muy abierto; adv. lejos a gran distancia; extensamente; muy; — **awake** bien despierto; — **open** abierto de par en par; **far and — ** por todas partes; **to cut a — swath** hacer alarde u ostentación de; — **of the mark** lejos del blanco.

widely (uáidli) adv. ampliamente; extensamente; muy; mucho.

widen (uáidn) v. ampliar(se); dilatar(se); ensanchar(se).

widespread (uáidspred) adj. muy extenso; generalizado; muy difundido; extendido por todas partes; esparcido ampliamente.

widow (uídou) s. viuda.

widower (uídouer) s. viudo.

width (wiz) s. ancho; anchura.

wield (uíld) v. manejar; esgrimir (la espada o la pluma); ejercer (el poder), gobernar.

wife (uáif) s. esposa.

wig (uig) s. peluca.

wiggle (uígl) v. menear rápidamente.

wigwam (uíguom) s. choza de los indios norteños.

wild (uáild) adj. silvestre; salvaje; montaraz; agreste; indómito; fiero; cimarrón; desierto; alborotado; impetuoso; desenfrenado; loco; insensato; **to talk —** decir disparates o desatinos; s. yermo; desierto; monte.

wildcat (uáildcat) s. gato montés; — **scheme** empresa arriesgada.

wilderness (uíldernes) s. desierto; páramo; yermo; inmensidad.

wildness (uáildnes) s. rusticidad; fiereza; ferocidad; locura.

wile (uáil) s. ardid; fraude; engaño.

wilful, willful (uílful) adj. voluntarioso, caprichudo; testarudo.

will (uil) s. voluntad; albedrío; volición; decisión; intención; legado; testamento; mandato; determinación; v. querer; decidir; ordenar; mandar; legar; v. aux. forma del futuro; **I — go by all means** iré a todo trance; **I — not do it** no lo haré; no quiero hacerlo; **to make one's —** hacer testamento; **he — sit for hours by the fire** se pasa las horas sentado junto a la chimenea; — **power** fuerza de voluntad.

willing (uíling) adj. bien dispuesto; gustoso; complaciente; pronto; voluntario; espontáneo; **—ly** adv. voluntariamente; con gusto; de buena gana; de buena voluntad.

willingness (uílingnes) s. buena voluntad; buena gana; complacencia.

willow (uílou) s. sauce; mimbrera; **weeping —** sauce llorón.

wilt (uilt) v. marchitarse; decaer; ajarse; secarse una planta; desmayar; languidecer.

wily (uáili) adj. astuto, mañonoso.

win (uín) v. ganar; lograr; obtener; conquistar; alcanzar; persuadir; atraer; **to — out** salirse con la suya; triunfar; **to — over** alcanzar o ganarse el favor de.

wince (uíns) v. retroceder; cejar; encogerse (de dolor, susto, etc.); echar pie atrás.

winch (uínch) s. malacate.

wind (uínd) s. viento; aire; resuello; flatulencia; — **instrument** instrumento de viento; **gale of —** temporal; **gust of —** racha, ráfaga de viento.

wind (uáind) v. dar cuerda; serpentear (un camino); devanar; virar; **to — about** enrollarse alrededor de; **to — up** concluir; acabar; finiquitar; **to — out** desenredar; salir de algún enredo o laberinto; **to — up thread** hacer ovillos; s. recodo; vuelta; rodeo.

windbag (uíndbag) s. fuelle; parlanchín; hablador.

windfall (uíndfol) s. golpe de fortuna; ganancia repentina; herencia inesperada

winding (uáinding) adj. sinuoso; tortuoso; que da vueltas; — staircase escalera de caracol; — road camino sinuoso.

windmill (uíndmil) s. molino de viento.

window (uíndou) s. ventana; show — aparador; escaparate; vitrina; — shades oscuros; visillos; cortinillas; persianas; transparentes; — frame bastidor o marco de ventana.

windowpane (uíndopein) s. cristal de ventana; vidriera.

windpipe (uíndpaip) s. tráquea; gaznate.

windshield (wíndshild) s. parabrisa; guardabrisa.

windy (uíndi) adj. airoso; it is — hace aire; sopla el viento.

wine (uáin) s. vino; — cellar bodega.

wing (uing) s. ala; bastidor de escenario; under the — of bajo la tutela de; on the — al vuelo.

winged (uíngued) adj. alado.

wink (uink) s. hacer un guiño; pestañear; parpadear; s. guiño; parpadeo; I did not sleep a — all night no pegué los ojos en toda la noche.

winner (uíner) s. ganador; vencedor; — of a prize agraciado, premiado.

winning (uíning) adj. ganancioso; victorioso, triunfante; que gana; afortunado; —s s. pl. ganancias.

winsome (uínsom) adj. simpático, atractivo; saleroso, retrechero.

winter (uínter) s. invierno; — clothes ropa de invierno; v. invernar; guardar durante el invierno.

wintry (uíntri) adj. invernal, de invierno; helado.

wipe (uáip) v. secar, enjugar; limpiar; frotar, restregar; cepillar; to — away one's tears limpiarse las lágrimas; to — out borrar, cancelar; testar, destruir.

wire (uáir) s. alambre; telegrama; hilo o cuerda metálica; by — por telégrafo; iron -- alambre de hierro; v. poner alambrado; atar o liar con hilo metálico; instalar alambres eléctricos; coger con lazo de alambre; telegrafiar.

wireless (uáirles) adj. inalámbrico; s. telefonía o telegrafía sin hilos; radio, radiotelegrafía; radiograma.

wiry (uáiri) adj. de alambre; como alambre; tieso; tenso, flaco pero fuerte y nervioso; débil (pulso); semejante a un alambre.

wisdom (uísdom) s. sabiduría, saber; sapiencia; juicio, buen criterio; prudencia; cordura.

wisecrack (uáiscrak) s. bufonada, dicho agudo chocarrero; dicharacho.

wish (uish) v. desear; querer, apetecer; anhelar; ansiar; I — it were true! ¡ojalá (que) fuera verdad! s. deseo, anhelo, ansia.

wistful (uístful) adj. anhelante; deseoso, ganoso; ansioso; ávido.

wit (uit) s. agudeza, sal, chiste; ingenio; hombre agudo o de ingenio; v. saber, tener noticia; to be at one's wit's end haber agotado todo su ingenio; the five —s los cinco sentidos; mother — sentido común, talento.

witch (uítch) s. hechicera, bruja.

witchcraft (uítchcraft) s. hechicería.

with (uiz) prep. con; para con; en compañía de; ill — enfermo de; to part — separarse de; smitten — enamorado de.

withdraw (uizdró) v. retirar(se); apartar; separar; quitar; sacar de.

withdrawal (uizdróul) s. retirada.

withdrawn (uizdrón) p.p. de to withdraw.

withdrew (uizdrú) pret. de to withdraw.

wither (uíder) v. marchitar(se); ajar, deslucir; poner mustio.

withheld (uizjéld) pret. y p.p. de to withhold.

withhold (uizjóld) v. retener; detener; impedir; apartar, contener; negar, rehusar.

without (uidáut) prep. sin; falto de, fuera de; — my seeing him sin que yo le viera.

withstand (uizstánd) v. resistir; aguantar; oponer.

withstood (wizstúd) pret. y p.p. de to withstand.

witness (uítnes) s. testigo; testimonio; espectador; atestación; prueba; declarante; v. ver.

witticism (uíticism) s. ocurrencia; agudeza; chiste, gracia.

witty (uíti) adj. agudo, ocurrente,

WIVES   **WORKINGMAN**

gracioso; ingenioso, chistoso; — remark dicho agudo, agudeza.

wives (uáivs) s. pl. de wife.

wizard (uísard) s. genio; hombre de ingenio; mago; hechicero, brujo; adivino; nigromante.

woe (uóu) s. miseria, aflicción; dolor; pena; pesar, calamidad; — is me! ¡miserable de mí!

woke (uóuk) pret. de to wake.

wolf (ulf) (pl. wolves) (ulvs); s. lobo; she — loba.

woman (úman) pl. women (uímen) s. mujer; criada, sirvienta.

womanhood (úmanjud) s. estado de mujer; madurez femenina; integridad femenil.

womankind (úmankind) s. la mujer, las mujeres.

womanly (úmanli) adj. femenil; mujeril; femenino; adv. como una mujer, femenilmente.

womb (um) s. vientre, entrañas; útero, matriz; caverna, seno.

won (uón) pret. y p.p. de to win.

wonder (uónder) s. maravilla; prodigio; admiración; milagro, portento, pasmo; to do —s hacer maravillas; in — maravillado; no — that no es mucho que, no es extraño que; it is a — es un prodigio; v. asombrarse, maravillarse; tener curiosidad por saber.

wonderful (uónderful) adj. maravilloso; admirable; portentoso; pasmoso; —ly adv. admirablemente; maravillosamente; a las mil maravillas.

wondrous (uóndros) adj. maravilloso; extraño, admirable, pasmoso.

wont (uónt) adj. acostumbrado; to be — to soler, acostumbrar; tener costumbre de; s. costumbre.

woo (u) v. cortejar, enamorar; galantear; pretender a una mujer.

wood (ud) s. madera, palo; leña; bosque, selva; monte; — engraving gravado en madera; —shed leñera; cobertizo para leña; — chopper leñador; — screw tornillo para madera.

wooded (úded) adj. arbolado; poblado de árboles; plantado de árboles; arboleda.

wooden (údn) adj. de madera; duro, torpe, sin espíritu.

woodland (údland) s. monte, bosque; arbolado, selva.

woodman (údman) s. leñador, habitante del bosque; guardabosque.

woodpecker (údpeker) s. pájaro carpintero.

woodwork (úduork) s. maderamen; labrado en madera.

woof (uf) s. trama (de un tejido); textura; tejido.

wool (ul) s. lana; adj. de lana, lanar; — combing cargadura; — dress vestido de lana.

woolen (úlen) adj. de lana; lanoso; lanudo — n ill fábrica de tejidos de lana; s. tejido de lana; género o paño de lana.

woolly (úli) adj. lanudo; de lana.

word (uérd) s. palabra, vocablo, voz; habla; dicho, sentencia, apotegma; noticia, mandato, orden; aviso; pass — contraseña; to keep one's — cumplir su palabra; by — of mouth de palabra; v. expresar; redactar.

wordy (uérdi) adj. palabrero, verboso; difuso.

wore (uor) pret. de to wear.

work (uérk) s. trabajo; obra; tarea; faena, empleo; bordado; acto; ocupación, —s taller, fábrica; maquinaria; mecanismo; v. trabajar; operar; bordar; fabricar, elaborar; producir; funcionar; manipular; resolver un problema; surtir efecto; fermentar; to — one's way abrirse paso, camino; to — out acabar alguna cosa a fuerza de trabajo; to — loose soltarse, aflojarse; to — through penetrar, atravesar con dificultad; salir al otro lado; to be all —ed up estar sobreexcitado; it did not — out no dio resultado; the plan —ed well el plan tuvo buen éxito; to set to — emplear, ocupar.

worker (uérker) s. trabajador; obrero; operario.

working (uérking) s. funcionamiento; movimiento, operación; maniobra; juego, función; cálculo (de un problema); explotación, laboreo; explotación (de una mina); — class clase obrera o trabajadora; — model modelo práctico.

workingman (uérkingman) s. trabajador, obrero; jornalero.

— 263 —

workman (uérkman) s. trabajador; obrero, operario; oficial, artífice.
workmanship (uérkmanship) s. hechura; manufacturera; mano de obra.
workshop (uérkshop) s. taller.
world (uérld) s. mundo; the other — el otro mundo; the World War la Guerra Mundial.
worldly (uérdli) adj. mundano, mundanal; carnal, terreno; seglar.
worm (uérm) s. gusano; lombriz; oruga; coco, gorgojo; — eaten comido de gusanos; carcomido; apolillado; silk — gusano de seda; to — a secret out of someone extraerle o sonsacarle un secreto a una persona.
worn (uórn) p.p. de to wear; — out gastado, roto, raído.
worry (uérri) s. inquietud, ansiedad; cuidado; zozobra, mordedura; v. desgarrar; zozobrar; inquietar(se); acosar, vejar; molestar.
worse (uers) adj. peor; más malo, inferior, más enfermo; adv. peor; menos; — and — de mal en peor; — than ever peor que nunca; to be — valer menos; he had the — llevó la peor parte.
worship (uérship) s. adoración, culto, veneración; respeto, tratamiento; v. adorar; reverenciar.
worshiper (uérshiper) s. adorador; the —s los fieles.
worst (uérst) adj. peor; pésimo, malísimo; adv. peor; the — el peor.
worthless (uérzles) adj. sin valor; indigno, inútil; despreciable.
worthy (uérzi) adj. digno, valioso; apreciable; benemérito; acreedor; s. hombre ilustre.
would (ud) imperf. de indic. y de subj. del verbo defect. will: she — come every day solía venir (o venía) todos los días; — that I knew it! ¡quién lo supiera! ¡ojalá que yo lo supiera!; if you — do it si lo hiciera Ud.; expresa a veces deseo; v. aux. del condicional, she said she — go dijo que iría.
wound (und) s. herida; llaga; lesión, ofensa; v. herir, lastimar.
wound (uáund) pret. y p.p. de to wind.
wove (uov) pret. de to weave.
woven (uóvn) p.p. de to weave.

wrangle (rángl) v. altercar, disputar; contender, pelotear; rodear (el ganado) s .riña; pendencia; contienda, disputa; reyerta; camorra.
wrap (rap) v. envolver; enrollar; arrollar; to — up envolver(se); abrigarse; to be —ped up in estar envuelto o enrollado en; s. abrigo, manto; pl. abrigos y mantas de viaje.
wrapper (ráper) s. envoltura; funda; cubierta; sobrepaño, carpeta.
wrapping (ráping) s. envoltura; — paper papel de envolver.
wrath (raz) s. ira, cólera, rabia.
wrathful (rázful) adj. colérico; rabioso; airado; iracundo.
wreath (riz) v. hacer guirnaldas; s. corona; festón; trenza, espiral; —d in smiles sonriente.
wreck (rek) s. ruina; destrucción; naufragio; accidente; buque naufragado, barco perdido; v. arruinar; naufragar; echar a pique; zozobrar; fracasar; to — a train descarrilar un tren.
wrench (rench) v. torcer, retorcer; arrancar, arrebatar; dislocar; desencajar; s. torcedura; torsión; tirón, arranque; monkey — llave inglesa.
wrest (rest) v. arrebatar, arrancar; desvirtuar; pervertir; usurpar.
wrestle (resl) v. luchar a brazo partido; esforzarse, disputar; s. lucha a brazo partido.
wrestler (résler) s. luchador (a brazo partido); atleta.
wretch (retch) s. miserable, infeliz; despreciable; villano.
wretched (rétched) adj. miserable; desdichado; desgraciado; vil; afligido; despreciable, perverso, mezquino; bajo, malísimo; a — piece of work un trabajo pésimo o molísimo.
wriggle (rígl) v. menear(se); retorcer(se); hacer colear, culebrear; to — out of salir de.
wring (ring) v. torcer; retorcer; exprimir; arrancar, estrujar; to — money from someone arrancar dinero a alguien.
wrist (rist) s. muñeca; — watch reloj de pulsera.
writ (rit) s. auto, orden judicial; mandato jurídico; escritura, mandamiento; the Holy Writ la Sagrada Escritura.

write (ráit) v. escribir; **to — down** apuntar, poner por escrito.
writing (ráiting) s. escritura; escrito; letra, manuscrito; forma o estilo literario; composición; artículo, obra; **— desk** escritorio; **— paper** papel de escribir.
written (ritn) p.p. de to write.
wrong (rong) adj. falso; incorrecto; malo, injusto; equivocado; desacertado; erróneo; inexacto; irregular; equivocado; mal hecho; inoportuno; **I took the — glove** cogí un guante en lugar de otro; **to be —** ser malo; no ser justo; **the — side of a fabric** el envés o el revés de un tejido; **to be very —** tener mucha culpa; **the — side of the road** el lado izquierdo o contrario del camino; **that is the — book** ése no es el libro; s. mal, daño; perjuicio, injusticia; culpa, sinrazón; error; extravío; v. perjudicar, agraviar; hacer mal a; ser injusto con alguno.
wrote (rout) pret. de to write.
wrought (rót) pret. y p.p. irr. de **to work** adj. labrado; forjado; **— iron** hierro forjado o batido; **— silver** plata labrada; **— up** to excitado, impelido a.
wrung (rong) pret. y p.p. de to wring.
wry (rai) adj. torcido; doblado; **to make a — face** hacer una mueca.

Y

yacht (iat) s. yate; v. navegar en yate; viajar en yate.
Yankee (iánki) adj. y s. yanqui.
yard (iard) s. yarda (medida de longitud); patio; cercado; corral; terreno (adyacente); navy — arsenal; **ship —** astillero.
yardstick (iárdstik) s. yarda (de medir); medida (metro, vara, etc.); patrón, norma.
yarn (iarn) s. estambre; hilado, hilaza; cuento largo e increíble; andaluza.
yawn (ion) v. bostezar; s. bostezo.
yea (iea) adv. sí; s. sí.
year (llir) s. s. año; pl. años, edad; vejez; **once a —** una vez al año; cada año.
yearly (llírli) adj. anual; adv. anualmente; todos los años, cada año.

yearn (llern) v. anhelar; desear vivamente; suspirar por.
yearning (yérning) s. anhelo.
yeast (llist) s. levadura, fermento.
yell (iel) v. gritar; dar gritos; dar alaridos, vociferar.
yellow (iélou) adj. amarillo; rubio.
yelp (ielp) v. aullar; ladrar; latir; s. aullido; ladrido.
yes (ies) adv. sí, ciertamente.
yesterday (iésterdei) adv. y s. ayer; **day before —** anteayer o antier.
yet (iet) adv. y conj. todavía, aun; sin embargo, no obstante.
yield (llíld) v. ceder, rendir; producir; someterse; dar de sí; condescender; **to — five percent** redituar el cinco por ciento; s. rendimiento; rendición; rédito.
yoke (llóuk) s. yugo; yunta (de bueyes); horcajo, camella; opresión, servidumbre; v. uncir, unir.
yolk (llolk) s. yema (de huevo).
yonder (iónder) adj. aquel; aquella; adv. ahí, allí, allá, acullá; más allá.
yore (ior) s. otro tiempo, antaño; **in days of —** antaño.
you (iu) pron. per. usted, ustedes; vosotros; tú, te, le, la, os, las, los; **to —** a usted, a ustedes, a ti, a vosotros; impers. se, uno.
young (iong) adj. joven, nuevo; mozo; verde; fresco, reciente; **— man** un joven; **— leaves** hojas tiernas; **the — people** la juventud; s. jóvenes; cría; hijuelos de los animales.
youngster (ióngster) s. jovencito; chiquillo; muchacho, mocito.
your (iur) adj. su, sus, de ustedes o de usted; tu, tus; vuestro, vuestra, vuestros (as).
yours (iurs) pron. pos. tuyo(a, os, as); vuestro (a, os, as); suyo (a, os, as) de usted o de ustedes; el suyo, la suya, los suyos; las suyas de usted o de ustedes; **a friend of —** un amigo de usted o de ustedes.
yourself (iursélf) pron. te, se (como reflexivo); **to —** a ti mismo; a usted mismo; **you —** tú mismo; usted mismo; véase herself.
yourselves (iursélvs) pron. os, se (como reflexivo); **to —** a vosotros mismos; a ustedes mismos; **you —** vosotros mismos.
youth (iuz) s. juventud, joven.
youthful (iúzful) adj. joven.
Yuletide (iúletaid) s. Pascua de Navidad.

Z

zeal (sil) s. celo, fervor, ardor; entusiasmo.
zealot (sélot) s. fanático; partidario acérrimo.
zealous (sélos) adj. celoso; fervoroso, ardoroso, entusiasta.
zenith (síniz) s. cenit; apogeo; cumbre.
zephyr (séfer) s. céfiro.
zero (siro) s. cero.
zest (sest) s. gusto, sabor; entusiasmo.
zigzag (sígsag) s. zigzag; adj. y adv. en zigzag; v. zigzaguear; culebrear, serpentear.
zinc (sink) s. cinc.
zipper (síper) s. cierre relámpago; broche corredizo o de corredera.
zodiac (sódiak) s. zodíaco.
zone (sóun) s. zona.
zoo (sú) s. jardín zoológico.
zoological (soolóyikal) adj. zoológico.
zoology (soóloyi) s. zoología.

VOCABULARIO DE TERMINOS COMERCIALES Y FINANCIEROS EN INGLES

A

Abstract Sumario, extracto, resumen.
Acceptance Aceptación, giro aceptado.
Account Cuenta.
Accounting Contabilidad.
Acrued Devengado.
Acid-test ratio Relación entre activo disponible y pasivo corriente.
Acknowledgement of receipt Acuse de recibo.
Advance Anticipo, adelanto, entrega anticipada.
Advantage Ventaja, ganancia, lucro, beneficio.
Adventure Especulación.
Advertisements Pequeños anuncios clasificados, anuncios económicos, anuncios por palabras.
Advertising Anuncio, notificación, publicidad.
Agreed value Valor convenido.
Agreement Convenio, acuerdo.
Air freight Flete aéreo, aerocarga.
Amount Monto, importe, suma, cantidad.
Annuity Anualidad.
Application Solicitud, petición
Appraisal Tasación, valoración.
Approach Acceso, proximidad, introducción.
Assets Activo, haber, propiedades.
At sight A la vista.
Auction Subasta, remate, almoneda.
Audit Auditoría.
Average Promedio, media.

B

Background Antecedentes, fondo, fundamento.
Back-shop Trastienda.
Back to back credit Crédito subsidiario (crédito que garantiza a otro).
Backwardation Retrovardación (prima que se paga por retraso en la entrega de valores comprados).
Bad debt Deuda irrecuperable.
Bailor Fiador.
Balance Saldo, balance.
Balance due Saldo pagadero.
Balance in hand Saldo disponible.
Balance of trade Balanza comercial.
Bank bill Letra bancaria.
Bank draft Giro bancario.
Banking rate Tipo de redescuento.
Bankruptcy Bancarrota, quiebra, insolvencia.
Bargaining Transacción.
Bargain price Precio de ocasión, bagatela, saldo.
Bear Bajista, a la baja.
Bearer Portador.
Best-seller El más vendido.
Bid Postura (en una subasta); oferta.
Bidder Postor.
Bill Cuenta, factura, billete.
Bill of credit Carta de crédito.
Bill of exchange Letra de cambio.
Bill of lading Conocimiento de embarque.
Billing Facturación, cuenta.
Block Bloque, conjunto compacto.
Bluff Engaño, mentira.
Board Consejo de administración, comité de dirección.
Bond Obligación, bono.

Bondholder Obligacionista, tenedor de bonos.
Bookkeping Teneduría de libros, contabilidad.
Boom Auge, expansión, éxito comercial.
Borrower Prestatario.
Bounce Rechazar (un cheque sin fondos).
Bourse Bolsa, mercado monetario.
Brainstorming Búsqueda de ideas, razonamiento en grupo.
Branch Sucursal.
Brand Marca, etiqueta.
Breakeven point Umbral de rentabilidad, punto de equilibrio.
Breakdown Desglose.
Briefing Informe, sumario, instrucciones.
Broker Corredor, agente de bolsa y cambio.
Brokerage Corretaje.
Budget Presupuesto. Estimado de ingresos y egresos.
Building Edificio, edificación, construcción, creación.
Bulkcarrier Granelero, buque para carga a granel.
Bundle Fardo, fardo de chatarra férrica.
Bundling Facturación global.
Buoyant Próspero, en alza.
Burden Carga, obligación, gravamen.
Burst-up Quiebra comercial.
Business Negocio, ocupación.
Business address Dirección comercial.
Business game Juego de empresa, con simulación de situaciones.
Buyer Comprador.
Buyer's market Mercado del comprador (en el que abundan los bienes de consumo y los precios tienden a bajar).
By-pass Derivación, desvío.

C

Calendar days Días corridos.
Call Citación, opción de compra de acciones a bajo precio.
Callable Pagadero a la vista.
Call loan Préstamo pagadero a la demanda.
Call money Préstamo interbancario.
Call rate Tasa de interés aplicable a préstamos a la vista.
Capital budget Presupuesto de gastos de capital.
Capital goods Bienes de capital (dedicados a la producción).
Card Tarjeta, ficha.
Card index Tarjetero, fichero.
Carried interest Interés resultante, interés arrastrado.
Carry Acarreo, arrastre.
Cartel Cartel, unión sectorial de empresas, agrupamiento de empresas para controlar mercados.
Cash Al contado, efectivo.
Cash and carry Establecimiento de comercio al mayoreo.
Cash discount Descuento por pago en efectivo.
Cash flow Flujo de caja, movimiento de tesorería, recursos generados.
Cash in advance Pago adelantado, anticipo.
Cash on delivery Pago contra entrega.
Cash payment Pago al contado.

CASHIER'S CHEK

Cashier's chek Cheque de caja.
Claim Reclamación.
Clearing Compensación, sistema de compensación o pago entre operantes de distintos países. Liquidación de saldos.
Clerk Dependiente, vendedor de mostrador.
Closedown Cierre definitivo.
Closing price Cotización al cierre (en la bolsa de valores).
Cluster Agrupamiento.
Coinsurance Coaseguro.
Collect Por cobrar.
Collection Recaudación (de impuestos); cobranza.
Composite price Precio compuesto.
Computer Ordenador, computadora, computador.
Consulting Consultor.
Consumer Consumidor.
Controller Interventor, controlador.
Cost-efectiveness Rentabilidad.
Countervailing Compensación.
Coverage Cobertura (de un seguro); fondos (de un cheque).
Crack Rotura, estallido, quiebra, bancarrota.
Credit balance Saldo acreedor.
Credit card Tarjeta de crédito.
Credit line Límite de crédito.
Creditor Acreedor.
Credit-worthy Digno de crédito, solvente.
Currency Moneda corriente.
Current rate Tipo actual o corriente.
Customs Aduana.
Customers services Servicio a clientes.

DELINQUENT

Ch

Chain store Tienda perteneciente a una cadena.
Chairman Máxima autoridad en una empresa, presidente.
Chamber of commerce Cámara de comercio.
Change notice Aviso de cambio.
Charge account Cuenta de crédito, cuenta abierta.
Charge off Deudor.
Charges Cargos, débitos.
Charter Alquiler o flete de un barco; concesión.
Check Cheque, reconocimiento, talón.
Checkbook Chequera.
Checking account Cuenta de cheques.
Check-list Lista de comprobación.
Choice Elección, preferencia, selección.

D

Data bank Banco de datos.
Data sheet Ficha, tarjeta de datos.
Daybook Libro diario.
Deal Trato, pacto, convenio.
Dealer Comerciante, agente, concesionario.
Dearth Carestía, escasez.
Debentures Títulos de crédito, obligaciones.
Debit Débito, cargo, adeudo, pasivo.
Debit balance Saldo deudor.
Debtor Deudor.
Deferred payment Pago a plazos.
Delinquent Moroso, atrasado.

DELIVERY

Delivery Entrega.
Demand Pagadero a la vista.
Depot Almacén, bodega.
Developing market Mercado en expansión.
Disbursement Desembolso, gasto, egreso.
Discount Descuento, deducción, rebaja.
Dishonored check Cheque rechazado (por falta de fondos).
Display Expositor, muestra, visualización, exhibición.
Divisional coin Moneda fraccionaria.
Dock Dársena, almacén, muelle, cobertizo.
Dollar bond Bono pagadero en dólares.
Dollar-gold link Enlace dólar-oro.
Domestic trade Comercio interior.
Double entry Partida doble.
Down payment Enganche, pago inicial.
Draft Boceto, borrador.
Draw Girar, librar, expedir.
Drawes Librado (persona a cuya orden se libra un documento).
Dressing Embalaje, envoltura.
Due Vencido, pagadero.
Due bill Pagaré.
Due date Fecha de vencimiento.
Dumping Desplome, venta a bajo costo, venta de un producto a diferentes precios en distintos mercados, rebaja desleal de precios.
Dunning letter Carta de requerimiento o de cobranza.
Duty Impuesto, arancel, derecho de aduana.

FACILITIES

E

Earnest Adelanto, pago a cuenta, prenda, fianza.
Earnings Ingresos, ganancias, utilidades.
Effective date En vigor, vigente.
Encumbrance Gravamen.
Endorsement Endoso.
Engineering Tecnología, ciencia de todo lo mecánico, ingeniería.
Enterprise Empresa.
Entertainment allowance Asignación para gastos de representación.
Entry Asiento, partida, entrada, registro.
Equipment Equipo.
Estate Patrimonio, fortuna, propiedades.
Estimate Estimación, presupuesto.
Exchange Cambio, canje, comisión de cobro.
Exemption Exención.
Expense Gasto, salida, pérdida, detrimento.
Expensive Costoso, caro.
Expert Perito.
Export trade Comercio de exportación.
Extend Prorrogar (un plazo); conceder (crédito).
Extension Prórroga.
External work Trabajo externo.
Extra charge Sobreprecio.

F

Face value Valor nominal.
Facilities Recursos materiales, servicios.

Factoring Sociedad de cobro.
Factory agreement Acuerdo de empresa.
Factory outlet Expendio de fábrica.
Fair play Juego limpio.
Fair trade Práctica comercial en la que el fabricante fija precios mínimos de venta de sus productos.
Fare Tarifa de viaje, pasaje.
Fashion good Artículos de moda.
Faulty Defectuoso.
Fax Medios de producción, equipo, grupo de trabajo. Gráfico teletransmitido.
Feedback Retroalimentación, retroacción, marcha atrás.
Fees Honorarios, derechos.
Ferry-boat Transbordador, barco de transbordo.
Fiat money Moneda fiduciaria o de curso forzoso.
Fifty-fifty A medias, al cincuenta por ciento.
Fine Multa.
Firm name Razón social.
Firm order Pedido en firme.
First cost Costo inicial.
First of exchange Primera de cambio.
Fitting Ajuste.
Fixed charge Gasto fijo.
Fixing Fijación.
Flag Símbolo, marca, indicador.
Flash Destello, boletín informativo breve.
Flash-back Vuelta hacia atrás.
Flat rate Tarifa única.
Folder Carpeta cubierta.
Forecast Pronóstico.
Foreign exchange Cambio de divisas.
Foreman Capataz.

Franchising Franquicia, contrato de colaboración, intermediario.
Free lance Trabajador independiente.
Free sample Muestra gratuita.
Foreign trade Comercio exterior.
Fuel-oil Aceite combustible, aceite pesado.
Full costing Representación y medida de costos totales.
Full set Juego completo de conocimientos de embarque.
Full-time Plena dedicación, dedicación exclusiva, de tiempo completo.
Freight Flete, tarifa de transporte.
Fund Fondo, reserva; subvencionar; consolidar (una deuda).
Funded debt Deuda consolidada.
Furnish Proveer.

G

Gainful Lucrativo, ventajoso.
Gains Ganancias, utilidades, provecho, incremento.
Gain sharing Participación en las ganancias.
Gang Equipo, grupo.
Gang boss Jefe de equipo.
Gap Intervalo, espacio, vacío, diferencia entre demanda global y oferta global.
Garnishment Embargo; retención de sueldo (para pagar una deuda).
Ghetto Judería, barrio marginado dentro de una ciudad.
Gilt-edged shares Acciones de primera clase.
Glamour Encanto, atracción.
Goal Objetivo.
Go-between Agente, corredor, intermediario.

GOLD RESERVE

Gold reserve Reserva de oro, encaje de oro.
Gold standard Patrón oro.
Goods Efectos de comercio, mercancías.
Goodwill Fondo de comercio, activo intangible de una empresa, crédito mercantil, buen nombre, valor extrínseco, plusvalía, valor de la clientela, valor de prestigio.
Grace period Periodo de gracia.
Grade rate Clase de tarifa.
Grant Conceder; concesión, permiso.
Grantee Concesionario, permisionario.
Groceries Víveres.
Grocer's shop Bodega, tienda de comestibles o abarrotes.
Gross Total, bruto, íntegro, sin deducciones.
Gross amount Importe total.
Gross margin Beneficio bruto.
Gross national product Producto nacional bruto.
Gross profit Utilidad bruta.
Gross receipts Ingresos brutos, ganancia total.
Group buying Compras agrupadas.
Growth company Compañía en expansión (la que crece más aceleradamente que la economía en conjunto).
Grubstake Avío, financiamiento.
Guaranteed minimum circulation Tirada mínima garantizada.
Guaranty Caución, garantía.
Guild Gremio, corporación.

HOME MARKET

H

Handicap Desventaja, estorbo, impedimento, sobrecarga. Ventaja impuesta.
Handling time Tiempo de transporte.
Hand-to-mouth buying Compras al día, compras improvisadas.
Hard currency Moneda firme.
Hard goods Bienes de consumo duradero.
Hard money Moneda metálica.
Hard selling times Periodos de contratación de la demanda.
Hardware Material, equipo material, equipo físico.
Headquarters Casa central o matriz, oficinas centrales.
High-grade De buena calidad, de primera clase.
High-life Gran mundo, sociedad elegante.
High rating Alta puntuación.
Hiterland Zona de influencia comercial, entorno.
Hire Alquiler, contratación; alquilar, contratar, emplear (a alguien).
Hit Impacto, éxito.
Hoarding Acaparamiento.
Hobby Afición, pasatiempo.
Holder Tenedor, poseedor, portador.
Holding Sociedad matriz de un grupo de empresas, grupo empresarial.
Holding company Compañía tenedora, sociedad inversionista controladora.
Holdings Valores en cartera, tenencias.
Home delivery Entrega a domicilio.
Home market Mercado interior, mercado nacional.

Home office Oficina o casa matriz.
Home products Productos del país o nacionales.
Home trade Comercio interior.
Honor Aceptar y pagar (un cheque); cumplir (un contrato).
Hot money Capitales fugitivos, dinero desestabilizador.
Hourly earnings Ganancia por hora, ganancia por unidad de tiempo.
Household appliances Aparatos domésticos.
House-to-house canvasser Agente de publicidad a domicilio.
Human engineering Estudio de la adaptación de la máquina al hombre.
Human factor Factor humano.

I

Identification codes Claves de identificación.
Idle money Dinero ocioso, improductivo.
Idle plant Planta parada.
Illiquid Ilíquido, no realizable.
Imbalance Saldo desfavorable, saldo en contra.
Immovables Inmuebles, bienes raíces.
Impasse Punto muerto, compás de espera, atolladero.
Imperishable goods Bienes imperecederos.
Implements Implementos, útiles, herramientas.
Import Importar; mercancía importada.
Import duties Derechos o impuestos de importación.
Import house Casa importadora.
Import permits Permisos de importación.
Improve Aumentar, estar en alza.
Improvements Mejoras.
Inactive account Cuenta inactiva.
In advance Por adelantado.
In cash En efectivo, al contado.
Income Ingreso, utilidad.
Income tax Impuesto sobre la renta.
Incorporation Constitución (de una sociedad).
Increase Aumento, alza.
Indebtedness Endeudamiento; pasivo, obligaciones.
Inmaterial assets Activo intangible.
In process En proceso, en curso de fabricación.
Input Entrada, consumo, gasto, potencia o energía absorbida, importación.
Input-output Entrada y salida.
Inquest Investigación, encuesta.
Inquiries Informaciones, datos, pesquisas, encuestas.
Inquiry Consulta, pregunta, encuesta, cuestionario.
Inquiry docket Ficha de información, cartel de informes.
Inquiry office Oficina de información.
Inside work Trabajo interno.
Installment Abono, pago parcial.
Installment plan Facilidades de pago.
Insufficient funds Falta de fondos (para el pago de un cheque).
Insurance broker Corredor de seguros.
Insurance premium Prima de seguro.
Interest Interés, rédito.

INTERFACE

Interface Contacto, interconexión.
Interim dividend Dividendo provisional.
Intrinsic value Valor intrínseco.
Inventory Inventario.
Investment Inversión, colocación, capital empleado.
Invoice Factura.
Invoice copybook Copiador de facturas.
Invoice price Precio de factura.
Invoicing Facturación.
Issue Emisión.
Issued capital Capital emitido.
Item Artículo, efecto; partida, asiento.
Items in transit Efectos en tránsito.

J

Jacket Envoltura.
Jingles Anuncios en canciones, anuncios cantados.
Job Trabajo, tarea, actividad.
Jobs analysis Análisis del trabajo.
Jobber Pequeño mayorista; especulador.
Job lot Lote de mercancías variadas (para reventa).
Job-time recording clock Reloj marcador, reloj de control.
Joint account Cuenta conjunta o mancomunada.
Joint bank Sociedad bancaria anónima.
Joint company Sociedad en participación o en comandita.
Joint liability Responsabilidad solidaria.
Joint owner Condominio, copropiedad.
Joint property Propiedad indivisa.

LADING

Joint stock Capital social.
Joint-stock company Compañía por acciones, sociedad anónima.
Joint venture Acción conjunta, riesgo compartido.
Journal Diario, libro diario.
Judgment sample Muestra comparativa.
Junior partner Socio menor.

K

Keep down Mantener bajo control (precios, gastos, etcétera).
Key advertising Publicidad cifrada.
Key process Procedimiento clave.
Killing Ganancias repentinas y abundantes.
Kit Equipamiento, equipo.
Kite Cheque sin fondos.
Kitsch Falsedad, pacotilla.
Know-how Conocimiento, saber cómo, técnica de fabricación exclusiva.

L

Label Etiqueta, marca de calidad, marbete, rótulo.
Lability Labilidad, flexibilidad.
Labor o labour Trabajo, labor, mano de obra.
Labor-management cooperation Colaboración obrero-patronal.
Labor relations Relaciones laborales.
Labor union Sindicato.
Laborer Trabajador, obrero, operario, jornalero, bracero.
Lack Falta, carencia.
Lading Cargamento, conocimiento de embarque.

Lag Retardo, demora.
Land agent Corredor de bienes raíces.
Land-jobbing Especulación con inmuebles.
Land tax Impuesto predial.
Lawful money Moneda legal, dinero lícito.
Law merchant Derecho mercantil.
Lease Arrendamiento.
Leasing Arriendo con opción a compra.
Ledger Mayor, libro mayor.
Ledger date Fecha de liquidación.
Legal expenses Gastos legales o jurídicos.
Legal reserve Encaje legal.
Legal tender Moneda corriente o legal.
Lending Prestación.
Letter of advise Carta de aviso, anuncio.
Letter of credit Carta de crédito.
Letter of introduction Carta de presentación.
Liability insurance Seguro contra responsabilidad civil.
Liabilities Deudas, obligaciones, pasivo.
Liable Responsable, obligado.
License Licencia, matrícula, permiso, título.
Licensee Concesionario, permisionario.
Licensing Concesión de licencias y patentes.
Lien Gravamen, hipoteca.
Life insurance Seguro de vida.
Light goods Productos ligeros.
Limited partnership Compañía limitada, sociedad en comandita.
Link Conexión, enlace.

Liquid assets Activo circulante.
Liquidity Liquidez.
List Lista, planilla, catálogo.
List price Precio de lista (sin descuento).
Listed securities Valores bursátiles, valores cotizables.
Literature Catálogos, folletos.
Loan Préstamo, anticipo.
Lobby Grupo de presión, organización para cabildeo.
Lock out Cierre patronal, paro forzoso, huelga de patronos.
Long bill Letra a largo plazo.
Long term Largo plazo.
Loss Pérdida.
Loss leader Artículo de propaganda (que se vende con pérdida para atraer clientela).
Lot Partida, lote.
Low capacity Capacidad baja.
Low price Precio bajo.
Lump-entry Asiento global.
Luxury goods Artículos de lujo.
Luxury tax Impuesto suntuario.

M

Machine costing Contabilización mecánica.
Macroeconomics Macroeconomía.
Made in Hecho en, manufacturado en.
Magazine Almacén, depósito.
Mail order Pedido por correo.
Mailing Envío por correo, publicidad directa o por correo.
Maker Fabricante, artífice, productor.
Mall Centro comercial.

Managed currency Circulación monetaria.

Management Dirección, gerencia, jefatura.

Manager Director, gerente, jefe.

Managing director Director gerente.

Manufacture Fabricación, manufactura.

Manufacturer Fabricante, industrial.

Manufacturing expenses Gastos de fabricación.

Margin Margen, beneficio.

Markdown Reducción de precios, rebaja.

Market Mercado.

Market gap Búsqueda de oportunidades en un mercado.

Marketability Potencial de venta, vendibilidad.

Marketing Mercadotecnia o mercología. Estudio de la situación de los consumidores por niveles de ingresos, motivaciones que influyen en las decisiones de compra, reacciones ante nuevos productos, problemas de comercialización, distribución, etcétera.

Mark up Margen comercial, diferencia de precio, ganancia fija.

Mass produced article Producto fabricado en serie, producto masivo.

Master control Control principal.

Master sample Muestra patrón, prototipo.

Materials in transit Materiales en tránsito.

Materials received Materiales recibidos.

Maturity Vencimiento, cumplimiento.

Maximize Aumentar al máximo.

Maximum capacity Capacidad máxima.

Maximum price Precio máximo.

Memorandum clause Cláusula de exenciones (en un contrato de seguro).

Mercantile paper Documentos negociables.

Merchandise Mercancía.

Merchandise accounting Contabilidad de las mercancías.

Merchandising Comercialización, mercantilización, compraventa.

Merchant Comerciante, negociante.

Merger Fusión, consolidación de empresas.

Message Mensaje, comunicado.

Minimize Reducir al mínimo.

Mint Casa de moneda; acuñar.

Minute Acta, minuta.

Money at call Dinero a muy corto plazo.

Money-exchange office Casa de cambio.

Money making Lucrativo, ganancioso.

Money market Mercado monetario.

Money-order Giro, libranza u orden de pago postal.

Monopoly Monopolio.

Moot Conferencia, debate, discusión.

Mortgage Hipoteca.

Motion Movimiento.

Multiple management Dirección múltiple.

Multiple store Empresa múltiple, empresa con muchas sucursales.

N

National debit Deuda pública.
National income Renta nacional.
Need Necesidad, impulso.
Net Neto, líquido.
Net avails Productos líquidos.
Net balance Saldo neto o líquido.
Net profit Ganancia neta, beneficio líquido.
Net sales Ventas netas.
Net wort Capital contable.
New Noticia, novedad.
Noise Distorsión, interferencia.
Nonassignable Intransferible, no negociable.
Normal selling unit Unidad normal de venta.
Notarial instrument Escritura pública.
Note Pagaré o abonaré, documento, nota.
Note of hand Vale, pagaré.
Notes receivable Efectos por cobrar.
Notice Noticia, información.
Null and void Nulo y sin efecto.
Numbering Numeración, foliación.
Numerical information Datos numéricos.

O

Ocurrence Frecuencia.
Offer Oferta; ofrecer en venta.
Office equipment Equipo de oficina.
Office worker Oficinista.
Offset account Contracuenta o cuenta de compensación.
Off the record Fuera de registro.
On-line En línea.
On-the-job training Capacitación durante el trabajo.
Open-end Sin límite de importe, de cantidad indefinida.
Open market Mercado abierto o libre.
Opening Iniciación de operaciones; inaguración.
Opening price Cotización de apertura (en la bolsa de valores).
Operating expenses Gastos de operación.
Operating profits Utilidades de explotación.
Operations research Investigación operativa.
Option to purchase Opción de compra.
Oral interview Entrevista personal.
Order blank Formulario de pedido.
Order control Control de pedidos.
Order delivery Entrega de pedidos.
Order invoicing Facturación de pedidos.
Order size Volumen de pedidos.
Organization chart Diagrama de organización, organigrama.
Outdoor sign Rótulo exterior.
Outfitter Abastecedor, proveedor.
Outlay Desembolso, salida, expendio.
Outlet Sucursal, agencia, distribuidor.
Outlines Lineamientos.
Output Producción, salida, cantidad de producto elaborado.
Outsider Competidor.
Outstanding Pendiente, por pagar.
Outstanding account Cuenta pendiente.
Outstanding shares Acciones en circulación.

OVERAGE

Overage Mercancías excedentes.
Overall probability Probabilidad total.
Overall study Estudio general.
Overcharge Recargo de precio.
Overdraft Giro en descubierto, sobregiro.
Overdraw Sobregirar, girar en descubierto.
Overdrawn account Cuenta en descubierto.
Overdue Vencido y no pagado, moroso, retrasado.
Overhead Sobrecarga, gastos indirectos, gastos de fábrica.
Overhead cost Gastos generales.
Overissue Emisión excesiva.
Overstock Exceso de existencias.
Overtime Horas extraordinarias.
Overweight Sobrepeso, peso excesivo.
Owe Adeudar, deber.
Own account, for Por cuenta propia.
Own cost and risk Costo y riesgo propio.
Owner Propietario.

P

Pace Ritmo, velocidad.
Package Paquete, empaquetado, lote.
Package deal Estabilización económica.
Packaging Embalaje.
Pallet Plataforma.
Pamphlet Folleto.
Paper money Papel moneda, billete de banco.
Parade Exposición, desfile.
Parcel post Paquete postal, encomienda postal.

POOLED CONCESSION

Parent company Empresa matriz.
Partial payment Pago parcial.
Partnership Sociedad, compañía.
Patent office Oficina de patentes.
Pattern Modelo.
Pawnshop Monte de piedad, casa de empeños.
Payable Pagadero.
Payback Recuperación.
Payment Pago, liquidación.
Performance Rendimiento, realización, cumplimiento, actuación.
Perishable Perecedero.
Personal acquaintances Relaciones personales.
Personalty Bienes muebles.
Petty cash Caja chica, gastos menores de caja.
Petty expenses Gastos menores.
Petty wares Géneros menudos.
Phase Operación.
Physical strain Esfuerzo físico.
Piece work price Precio por pieza, precio unitario.
Place of business Domicilio social, domicilio comercial.
Planned markdowns Rebajas previstas.
Planned sales Ventas previstas.
Planning Planteamiento, programación, planificación.
Plant Equipo, instalación de maquinaria, planta.
Plant-proven Prueba de fábrica.
Pledge card Ficha de garantía.
Polling Votación, elección, escrutinio.
Pool Consorcio, conjunto, mancomunidad de empresas, acuerdo comer-cial entre empresas.
Pooled concession Concesión mancomunada.

Postage Porte de correos.
Poster Cartel, letrero, mural.
Prelevement Descuento, derecho regulador.
Premeditated purchase Compra premeditada.
Premises Local, establecimiento.
Premium Prima.
Prepayment Pago adelantado.
Presold Mercancía vendida de antemano.
Pressing Presión, compulsión.
Price advance Encarecimiento, alza.
Productivity index Indice de productividad.
Product mix Mezcla de productos.
Profit Utilidad, ganancia.
Profit margin Porcentaje de utilidad.
Profit sharing Participación en los beneficios.
Profitability Rentabilidad.
Programming Programación, programa.
Promisory note Pagaré.
Promotion matter Material de promoción.
Prompt payment Pago al contado.
Proof Prueba.
Proof study Estudio de comprobación.
Prorate Prorratear.
Prospect Cliente probable.
Protective tariff Tarifa proteccionista.
Provision market Mercado de abastecimiento.
Public utility Servicio público, utilidad pública.
Purchase order Orden o nota de compra.
Purchasing Compra.

Purchasing power Poder de compra, solvencia.

Q

Qualified acceptance Aceptación condicional.
Qualitative market research Investigación cualitativa del mercado.
Quality control Control de calidad.
Quality standard Norma de calidad.
Quantificable data Datos cuantificativos.
Quantity standard Norma de cantidad o cuantitativa.
Quick assets Activo disponible o realizable; bienes negociables.
Quiet market Mercado en calma o tranquilo.
Quire Mano de papel (24 ó 25 hojas).
Quittance Finiquito, liquidación; compensación.
Quotable Cotizable.
Quota sampling Muestreo por cupos.
Quota-setting Fijación de cupos.
Quotation Cotización.

R

Radio announcement Anuncio radiofónico.
Raid Recorrido, expedición, excursión.
Railway bill Carta de porte.
Raise Reunir, obtener (fondos); aumentar (precios, intereses).
Range Rango, orden, zona.
Ranking Clasificación, rango, ordenamiento.
Rappel Descuento, bonificación por

alto consumo.
Rapport Informe, reseña, relato.
Rate Indice, tipo.
Rate of exchange Tipo de cambio.
Rate of output Rendimiento, índice de rendimiento.
Rating Apreciación, valoración, evaluación.
Ratio Proporción, relación, razón.
Raw material Materia prima.
Reading Indicación, leyenda.
Reading note Anuncio en forma de texto.
Real estate Bienes raíces.
Realtor Corredor de bienes raíces.
Rebate Rebajar, descontar; rebaja, descuento.
Receipts Ingresos, entradas, rentas, recaudos.
Receivables Activo exigible, efectos por cobrar.
Record Marca, registro.
Refund Reembolsar; reembolso.
Reimbursement Reembolso, reintegración.
Rejection Fracaso.
Reliable sample Muestra digna de confianza.
Remainder sale Venta de remanentes o saldos.
Remake Refundición, nueva versión.
Renting Arrendamiento, renta.
Report writing Redacción de informes.
Retail Venta al menudeo.
Retained income Utilidades incorporadas.
Revenue Renta, entrada, ingreso; rentas públicas, ingreso del erario.
Risk capital Capital aventurado o de riesgo.
Roll Rodillo, cilindro.
Rollover Crédito flotante.
Round Ronda.
Route Ruta.
Royalty Derechos de patente o de autor, regalía, tributo.
Running expenses Gastos corrientes.
Ruse Subterfugio.

S

Safety Seguridad.
Salability o salableness Vendibilidad, salida fácil.
Sale Venta.
Sales allowance Rebaja del precio de factura.
Sales approach Enfoque de las ventas, políticas de ventas.
Sales control Fiscalización de ventas.
Sales data Datos sobre las ventas.
Sales engineer Técnico en ventas.
Sales force Equipo de vendedores, fuerza de venta.
Sales index Indice de ventas.
Sales letter Carta de prospección.
Sales performance Rendimiento de ventas.
Sales promotion Promoción de ventas.
Salesman Vendedor.
Sample Muestra.
Sampling Muestreo.
Saturated market Mercado saturado.
Saving Ahorro, economía.
Scanner Escrutador, explorador.
Schedule Cédula, programa.
Scoop Ganancia fácil.
Score Cómputo, tanteo, puntuación.
Scrap Chatarra, desperdicio.

Screening Selección de productos.
Seasonal goods Artículos de temporada.
Second-hand shop Tienda de lance, baratillo.
Securities Valores, obligaciones, títulos.
Seizure Embargo, decomiso.
Selection Surtido.
Self man Autoforjado, autodidacta, hombre hecho por sí mismo.
Seller Vendedor.
Seller's market Mercado del vendedor (en el que escasean los bienes de consumo y los precios tienden a subir).
Selling campaign Campaña de ventas.
Selling floor Piso o lugar de venta.
Selling off Liquidación.
Senior Superior, mayor, experto.
Senior partner Socio principal o más antiguo.
Share Acción; participación.
Shareholder Accionista.
Shifter Enunciación.
Shipping Expedición, envío.
Shopping center Centro comercial.
Short account Cuenta al descubierto.
Short rates Rebaja de precios.
Short-run operational sales Operación de venta a corto plazo.
Shortage Escasez.
Shortfall Déficit.
Show Pequeña exposición, exhibición, demostración.
Showcase Vitrina, vidriera.
Shrinkage Contracción, reducción, depreciación.
Sliding-scale contract Contrato de precio revisable.

Slip Volante, talón, formulario, etiqueta, ficha.
Slogan Consigna, lema, frase publicitaria, publifrase.
Slow assets Activo fijo no realizable.
Slump Periodo de crisis, baja de precios y paralización comercial.
Smog Niebla humosa, holliniebla.
Sole agent Agente exclusivo.
Sole right Derecho exclusivo.
Sophistication Determinación del grado de aceptación.
Speciality salesman Vendedor de especialidades.
Specified account Cuenta detallada.
Speech Discurso, plática, conversación, charla.
Speed Velocidad.
Spending Gasto, desembolso; dispendio.
Spoilage Chatarra, desperdicios.
Spot Al contado, de pago inmediato, disponible, anuncio breve.
Spot market Mercado de productos disponibles o de venta inmediata.
Spray Aerosol, rociador, pulverizador.
Spread Divulgación, propaganda, diferencia entre los precios de oferta y demanda, margen.
Spreader Divulgador, propagador, comprador y vendedor en los mercados, distribuidor.
Spread of risk Diversificación de los riesgos.
Squeeze Falta de productos entregables por contrato.
Staff Equipo asesor de dirección, cuerpo de especialistas, dirección funcional, asesoría.
Staffer Directivo o jefe de personal.
Staffing Cuadro de mandos, plantilla

de personal.
Stage Etapa, paso.
Stale bill of landing Conocimiento de embarque vendido.
Stand Puesto publicitario en un mercado o una feria, quiosco.
Standard Norma, tipo, patrón, regla fija, modelo.
Standardized accounts Cuentas tipificadas.
Standard of life Nivel de vida, tipo de vida.
Standard make Marca corriente, tipo común.
Standard parts Piezas normalizadas.
Standard price Precio regulador.
Standard question Pregunta típica, pregunta clave.
Standard size Tamaño normalizado.
Standard time Hora legal (la de Greenwich), hora oficial, tiempo tipo, tiempo normal.
Stand-by underwriting Compromiso de compra de valores no vendidos.
Standing Posición, reputación, situación, solvencia, crédito.
Standing order Pedido pendiente, orden vigente.
Staple Producto básico o principal, materia prima, emporio comercial, producto de uso general, reconocido y vendible.
Start-up Puesta en marcha, periodo de arranque.
Statement of account Estado de cuenta.
Stationery store Tienda de papelería.
Stationing expenses Gastos de escritorio.
Statistics Estadística.

Steadiness Estabilidad, uniformidad.
Steepening incentive Incentivo progresivo.
Steerage Control, mando, dirección.
Sticker Rótulo, etiqueta engomada.
Stock Existencias, depósito, reserva, mercancías almacenadas, producción diaria, capital comercial, acciones, cantidad, provisión.
Stock exchange Bolsa de valores.
Stock in trade Bienes comerciales.
Stock-jobbing Agiotaje.
Stock-sales ratio Proporción entre existencias y ventas.
Stockholder Accionista.
Stocktaking Inventario de mercancías.
Stop Parada.
Stop work Abandono de trabajo.
Storage Almacenaje, almacenamiento.
Storing Almacenamiento.
Straight bill of landing Conocimiento de embarque intraspasable.
Straight information Información directa.
Straight-line production Producción continua.
Straight rate Tasa constante.
Strain Esfuerzo.
Street hawker or seller or vendor Vendedor ambulante.
Stress Esfuerzo, tensión, compulsión, fatiga, carga.
Strike Huelga, ganga, golpe.
Strikebreaking Esquirol, rompehuelgas.
Striker Huelguista.
String Hilera, cadena.
Stripping Desmontaje, desmonte.
Strong market Mercado firme.

STUB

Stub Talón, matriz.
Stunt Anuncio detonante, noticia "bomba" o extraordinaria.
Style Estilo, tipo, clase, género, especie, moda, modo, uso.
Subaccount Cuenta subsidiaria, subcuenta.
Substandard work Trabajo deficiente.
Supermarket Supermercado.
Supplier Abastecedor, suministrador, distribuidor.
Supply Suministro.
Supply and demand Oferta y demanda.
Surcharge Recargo, sobrecargo, sobreprima.
Surety bond Fianza.
Surrotage Sustituto.
Surtax Sobretasa, impuesto adicional.
Survey Examen, estudio, anteproyecto, peritaje, inspección, reconocimiento, investigación, encuesta, supervisión.
Swap Cambio, trueque.
Sweat Fatiga, trabajo agotador.
Syllabus Sumario, compendio, resumen, extracto, plan de estudios.
Symbolization Simbolización, expresión por medio de símbolos.

T

Tao Etiqueta, marbete, rótulo.
Takeover Adquisición (de una compañía por otra).
Taking Ingresos, recaudación.
Tally Anotación, talón, resguardo.
Tare and tret Tara y merma.
Task Tarea, trabajo, misión, actividad, deber.

TIME OFF

Taskwork Trabajo a destajo, trabajo convencional.
Tax exemption Exención de impuestos.
Tax rate Tasa impositiva.
Tax return Declaración de impuestos.
Taxability Imposición.
Taxable income Ingreso gravable.
Taxpayer Contribuyente.
Team Equipo, grupo de trabajo, medios de producción.
Teamster Camionero.
Technical position Relación de oferta y demanda.
Telephone interview Entrevista telefónica.
Telex Teletipo, télex.
Teller Cajero.
Tellership Contaduría.
Template Molde, modelo, maqueta.
Temporary price list Lista provisional de precios.
Temporary standard Norma provisional.
Term Plazo, vencimiento, término.
Test Prueba, ensayo, examen, experiencia, experimento, criterio.
Thick market Mercado de gran consumo.
Thin market Mercado de poco consumo.
Ticket Etiqueta, billete, tarjeta, ficha.
Tightness Escasez de dinero, tacañería.
Time bargain Negocio a plazos, mercado a término.
Time bill Letra a plazo.
Time clock Reloj registrador.
Time loan Préstamo a plazo.
Time off Hora de cierre.

—283—

Time on Hora de apertura.

Time on delivery Fecha de entrega.

Time-out Retraso.

Time-sharing Simultaneidad, tiempo compartido.

Time taken Tiempo empleado, tiempo real.

Timing Cronometraje, calendario de trabajo.

Tipewriter Máquina de escribir.

Tipping Mecanografiado.

Tonnage production Producción en gran escala.

Top Vértice, punta.

Topnotch Muy bien hecho, de calidad inmejorable, renombrado.

Total work volume Volumen total de trabajo.

Trade Comercio, negocio, gremio, industria, ramo de comercio.

Trade draft Giro comercial.

Trade guild Corporación, gremio, sindicato.

Trade-in Cambio, canje, trueque, entrega a cuenta.

Trade or trading areas Zonas comerciales.

Trade-mark Marca registrada.

Trade price Precio comercial, precio neto.

Trade promotion Fomento al comercio, promoción comercial.

Trader Vendedor, comerciante, mercader, negociante.

Trade union Sindicato.

Trading Registro de patentes, compraventa.

Trading center Centro comercial.

Traffic Tráfico, negocio, circulación, tránsito, movimiento de mercancías.

Trailer Remolque.

Training Adiestramiento, formación, capacitación, aprendizaje.

Transactions Transacciones, negocios, operaciones mercantiles.

Transfer files Ficheros inactivos.

Transfer of personnel Traslado de personal.

Transportation expenses Gastos de transporte.

Traveler's chek Cheque de viajero.

Traveling expenses Gastos de viaje, viáticos.

Traveling salesman Agente viajero.

Treasury Tesorería.

Trend Tendencia, dirección, rumbo.

Trial Ensayo, prueba, comprobación, esfuerzo, intento.

Trial and error Método de tanteos.

Trial period Periodo de prueba.

Trigger Referencia, precio de gatillo.

Trim cost Costos reducidos.

Trim prices Precios reducidos.

Truck Camión, carretón.

True discount Descuento real, descuento externo.

Trust Monopolio, negocios asociados.

Trust mortgage Hipoteca fiduciaria.

Trustee Administrador o fideicomisario de un trust.

Turnoff Rendimiento.

Turnout overall industry Producción industrial total.

Turnover Cifra de negocios, facturación, entradas, ingresos totales, ganancia total, total de ventas, inversión, rotación de mercancías, tonelaje. Rotación de personal.

U

Ullage Merma.

Unbalance Diferencia.
Unbusinesslike Inhábil para los negocios, poco práctico.
Uncollected items Efectos por cobrar.
Uncollectible accounts Cuentas incobrables.
Underwork Trabajo de mala calidad.
Undivided profits Utilidades por distribuir.
Unemployment Desempleo.
Unfair competition Competencia desleal.
Unfavorable balance of trade Balanza comercial desventajosa, saldo desfavorable.
Uniform price policy Política uniforme de precios.
Union Sindicato.
Unit Unidad, elemento unitario.
Unit of currency Unidad monetaria.
Unit price Precio unitario, precio por unidad.
Unit-sales information Información sobre las unidades vendidas.
Unsecured debt Deuda sin caución.
Unsecured trade Negocio no garantizado.
Unsettled Pendiente, por pagar.
Unsound business Negocio improductivo.
Unsound money or currency Moneda inestable.
Up market Mercado ascendente.
Upscale buying Compras a precios escalonados ascendentes.
Upset price Precio de primera oferta, precio mínimo fijado, precio de subasta.
Upward movement Movimiento de alza.

Usance Usanza, plazo, uso, condiciones de pago.
Usance bill Letra a plazo.
Used equipment Planta de segunda mano, equipo usado.
Useful load Carga útil.
User Usuario, consumidor.
User's demand Demanda del consumidor.
Utility Utilidad, empresa de servicio público.

V

Vacant post Puesto o empleo vacante, cargo libre.
Validity Validez.
Valuation Valuación, justiprecio, tasa, avalúo, estimación.
Value date Día de pago, fecha efectiva.
Value in account Valor en cuenta.
Value increase Plusvalía.
Variable burden Gastos generales variables.
Vendee Cesionario, comprador.
Vending machine Máquina de venta automática.
Venture Empresa; negocio arriesgado; especulación.
Venture capital Capital aventurado o de riesgo.
Vocational training Formación profesional.
Void Nulo, cancelado.
Volume production Producción en serie o en masa.
Voluntary chain Asociación cooperativa de empresas comerciales.
Voucher Bono, vale, comprobante, justificante, resguardo.

Voucher chek Cheque con comprobante.
Vouchers payable Bonos pendientes, comprobantes por pagar.]

W

Wad Fajo de billetes.
Wage Salario, remuneración, sueldo, paga, jornal.
Wage floor Salario base, salario mínimo garantizado.
Wage scale Escala de sueldos, escalafón.
Wall sign Rótulo, umbral, cartelera.
Wantage Merma, falta, deficiencia.
Want-slips Artículos necesarios o convenientes.
Warehouse Almacén, depósito, bodega.
Warehouse rent Almacenaje, gastos de depósito.
Wares Mercaderías, mercancías.
Warning Aviso, caución.
Warrant Certificado, opción (para comprar acciones).
Warranty Garantía.
Wash sales Ventas fictícias.
Wastage Despilfarro, desperdicio.
Waste Desecho, subproducto.
Waybill Factura, hoja de ruta, guía de carga, conocimiento de embarque, hoja de marcha, boleta de expedición, carta de porte, guía de campaña.
Weak market Mercado contraído.
Wealth Riqueza, caudal, dineral.
Week about Semanas alternas.
Weighted index Indice exacto, ponderado o verificado.
White paper Documento oficial.

Wholesale Comercio mayorista, venta por mayor, mayoreo.
Wholesaler Comerciante o vendedor mayorista, almacenista.
Widened sales Ventas ampliadas.
Winch Montacargas.
Windfall losses Pérdidas imprevistas.
Winding-up Liquidación de una sociedad.
Window card Cartel de escaparate.
Winnings Utilidades, ganancias.
Withdrawal Retiro de mercancías.
Work Obra, empleo, trabajo, faena, labor, actividad.
Work experience Experiencia laboral.
Working Funcionamiento, operación, maniobra, tiraje.
Working assets Activo realizable.
Working capital Capital circulante; capital de explotación.
Working rule Regla práctica.
Workman Trabajador.
Workmanlike Bien hecho, bien realizado.
Workmanship Hechura, mano de obra, manufactura, pericia.
Works Fábrica, taller, establecimiento, trabajos, obras.
Work study Estudio del trabajo.
World bank Banco mundial.
World industrial standard Norma industrial universal.
World-market price Precio de mercado mundial.
Worth Valor; capital, fortuna, valía.
Wrapping Envoltura, faja, envoltorio.
Wrinkle Estilo, moda.
Write in Intercalar.
Write off Anular, eliminar, suprimir,

saldar, amortizar.
Write out Redactar.
Writer Escritor, autor.
Written agreement Acuerdo por escrito.
Written notice Aviso escrito.

Y

Year book Anuario.
Year-end dividend Dividendo a fin de año o anual.
Yearly income Renta anual.
Yearly range Precios máximos y mínimos del año.
Yield Producción, rendimiento, rique-za, beneficio, rentabilidad.
Yield table Tabla de rendimiento.

Z

Zero proof Prueba a cero.
Zigzag scanning Exploración oscilante.
Zip pan Panorama rápido.
Zoom Desplazamiento en profundidad.

ESTA EDICIÓN SE TERMINÓ DE IMPRIMIR
EL 9 DE JUNIO DE 2005 EN LOS TALLERES DE
TRABAJOS MANUALES ESCOLARES, S. A. DE C. V.
ORIENTE 142 NO. 216, COL. MOCTEZUMA 2A. SECC.
15500, MÉXICO, D.F.